THE OFFICIAL®
PRICE GUIDE TO

W9-CFJ-093

Country

Music

Records

FIRST EDITION

JERRY OSBORNE

HOUSE OF COLLECTIBLES • NEW YORK

Important Notice. All of the information, including valuations, in this book has been compiled from the most reliable sources, and every effort has been made to eliminate errors and questionable data. Nevertheless, the possibility of error, in a work of such immense scope, always exists. The publisher will not be held responsible for losses which may occur in the purchase, sale, or other transaction of items because of information contained herein. Readers who feel they have discovered errors are invited to *write* and inform us, so they may be corrected in subsequent editions. Those seeking further information on the topics covered in this book are advised to refer to the complete line of *Official Price Guides* published by the House of Collectibles.

©1996 by Jerry Osborne
This is a registered trademark of Random House, Inc.

Published by: House of Collectibles
201 East 50th Street
New York, New York 10022

Distributed by Ballantine Books, a division of Random House, Inc., New York, and simultaneously in Canada by Random House of Canada Limited, Toronto.

Cover design by Kristine V. Mills
Cover photo by George Kerrigan

Manufactured in the United States of America

ISBN: 0-676-60004-2

First Edition: April 1996

10 9 8 7 6 5 4 3 2 1

CONTENTS

ACKNOWLEDGMENTS

The single most important element in updating and revising a price and reference guide is reader input. From dealers and collectors scattered throughout the country we receive suggestions, additions and corrections. Every single piece of data we receive is carefully reviewed, with all appropriate and usable information utilized in the next edition of this guide.

As enthusiastically as we encourage your contribution, let us equally encourage that when you write, you will either type or print your name clearly on both the envelope and contents. It's as frustrating for us to receive a mailing of useful information, and not be able to credit the sender, as it probably is for the sender to not see his or her name in the Acknowledgments section.

In compiling this edition, information supplied by the people whose names appear below was of great importance. To these good folks, our deepest gratitude is extended. The amount of data and investment of time, of course, varied, but without each and every one of them this book would have been something less than it is.

Here then, alphabetically listed, are the contributors to this edition:

James M. Ahles	John Boothroyd	George Collange
Kevin O. Allen	Susan K. Bowman	R. Collazo
Ronald R. Allen	Ronald E. Brackney	Michael L. Cooper
Dr. Götz Alsmann	R. Lee Bracy, Jr.	John C. Crawley
Cora Apostal	Rodney Branham	S.C. Cruce
John F. Arnold	Keith Brock	Allen Damron
John G. Auker	William A. Bronk	James C. Davidson
James Aull	Allan E. Brown	Judy Davis
Jerry B.	Ben Brown	Tex Davis
J. Baart	Bob Brown	Chuck Dawson
Paul H. Bader	Denise Brown	Devon Dawson
Sam Babcock	Pat Brown	Ron Day
Tom Ball	D.L. Buchanan Jr.	Karl Michael Deeg
Timothy Bartkus	Mark Burchill	Robert Delbaugh
Carolyn Bass	Robert Burns	Michael Devich
Alfred E. Bavart	Leo J. Callahan	Wolfgang R. Dobrikat
Richard Bell	Jim Carlin	Jim Doidge
Andy Benyo	Tom Carroll	Heather Dominizio
Daniel S. Berkman	R.P. Causey	Lora Duran
Bill Berry	Rich Cherry	Paul Duran
George Biggans	John Chintala	Jean-Marie Ebner
Reimar Binge	Peter Cinquegrana	Judith M. Ebner
Frank Black	Ritchie Clayton	P.W. Elliott
John Blair	Michael H. Coffy	Bruce Elrod
Dale Blount	Stephen Joseph Colfer	Michael S. English

Sue D. Fallin
David N. Ferguson
David Fern
Debbie Fleischer
Sven Forsberg
John Froidl
Jean-Marc Gargiulo
Al Gerber
George Gimarc
Clermont Giroux
Tim Goebel
Paul Goldstein
Robert Grass
Charles T. Gray
Tom Grenfell
Paul Grenyo
Fred J. Griego
Gary Griffin
Don L. Guenther
Lennart Gustavsson
Bill Hall Jr.
Ted Harding
Rita Harris
Walter F. Harwood
Fred Heggeness
Sytze Hempenius
Jim Henry
Brehon Herlihy
Iva Hill
Jerry Hilliard
Susan Cooper Holl
Larry Holloway
Pauline Hubbard
Maurice Hubbs
Scott Hucks
A.L. Hughes
Rich Hughes
Robert Humphrey
Edward Hunt
J. Barry Hutchins
Tom Isenhour
Ray Janosko
Jim's Records
Bill D. Johnson
Ron R. Johnson
Wayne Jones
Jenny Jordan
Jim Kaysinger
John Keller

Randy P. Keller
Colin Kilts
Otto C. Kitsinger II
Butch Klein
Terry Kline
Keith Kolby
Tony Kolodziej
Tracy Kolodziej
Robert Kotabish
Mark Kramer
Prassery Kuch
Volker Kurze
Gladys Lambert
Jerry Landers
Bruce Laytham
Craig A. Lewis
Ed Leonardo
Joe Lindsay
Joe Loglisci
Terry Love
Colleen Lybesma
C. V.d. Maagdenberg
Joseph Madrano
Thomas Markris
Dan Martin
Harold D. Mathews
Ron McBride
Alex McNeil
Lee Mercier
Chris Messner
Bob Michalski
Arlyn Miller
Vincent Miller
Howard Moser
George Mull
Quincy Mumford
Mike Murray
Derek J. Myers
Charles Neu
John Newbert
Randy L. Nix
Jon Noeth
Bob O'Reilly
Linda Ann Osborne
James L. Padrick
Tony Palumbo
Carl Pascarelli
Richard H. Pearce
Victor Pearlin

Carol A. Pearson
Alex Peavey
Marty Pekar
Wesley Peterson
Pete's Recycled Records
Ernest Pfister
Steve Pierce
Gerald E. Pike
Steve Pillow
Mike R. Pitts
Nolan Porterfield
Dennis Price
Chester Prudhomme
Gilbert Quintero
T. Ramsden
Pam Rasmussen
Dennis Remme
David Rezny
Donald L. Riis
H. Allan Roark
Larry Kevin Roberts
Rockin' Randy
Glenn Reberds
George R. Rogers
Peter A. Romano
Arthur Root
Eric Rubin
Lynn Russwurm
Patricia A. Scarmuzzi
Robert Schmidt
Jack W. Scott
Bill Screws
Michael Sharritt
Al Sheppard
Ralph W. Sims
Rick Siebler
Jim Sisco
John Smith
Thomas Stanberry
Jeff Stark
Melvin Steinmetz
Don Stephan
Stephen Sterns
Linda Lou Stone
Kerry Sugden
Michael J. Sweeney
Ed Tataryn
Clinton Taylor
Springfield Bear Tebblorr

Ray Thigpen
George Trabant
Peter D. Trenholm
Justin Tubb
Richard Tucker
Big Al Turner
Dan R. Turpin
Jim Ulmer
Paul Verner
Bill Vernon

August Vrchota
Brian Wall
Jim Weaver
Bud Webster
Richard Weize
Ed Whalen
Joel Whitburn
Danny A. White
Jerry Williams
Jack Wise

W. Watts
Scott Wikle
Pete T. Wilgus
Morgan Wright
Ron Wyly
Jay Yardley
Dave Yerlon
Everett Yocam
Pinhas Zilbergelo
Roy Zinklewicz

Country

Music

Records

INTRODUCTION

For the record, though catalogued as a first edition this guide is really our third country music record price guide. Is is, however, the first country music guide ever to combine all sizes and speeds in a single publication — using the same format as is found in the popular *Official Price Guide to Records*.

Our first C&W book, *55 Years of Recorded Country & Western Music* (1976), included only singles. In 1984, we added *Country Music* to the series, a guide for EPs and LPs. Now, all types of records — singles (45 and 78rpm), extended plays, and long plays — can be found in this one all-purpose guidebook.

Noteworthy too is that *Country Music* did not include various artists C&W compilation albums, several thousand of which appear in this edition.

The complete recorded output of nearly 2,400 of America's all-time top-selling country and western artists make up this edition. Among this varied gathering, you'll find all of the Country Music Hall of Fame legends alongside many long-forgotten artists who managed, perhaps, just one insignificant hit.

Qualifying for inclusion in this edition is anyone who managed to hit the Billboard C&W chart with a vinyl disc — anytime from 1944 to present. Our chart source for this information is Joel Whitburn's [Billboard] *Top Country Singles 1944-1993*.

Since Billboard magazine didn't begin publishing separate country music charts until 1944, country music artists who made the pop charts before 1944 are also included.

Knowing this, the reader will understand why the "first charted" reference for some of country music's pioneers (Roy Acuff, Bob Wills, Carter Family, etc.) indicates "P&R" (Pop & Rock, but signifying only "Pop" in this usage) first, followed by the year they first appeared on the C&W chart.

At the other extreme of the time frame—the 1990s—we have encountered a quandary of a different sort. Which recent releases exist on vinyl?

While many collectors have a "who cares" attitude regarding '90s releases, fanciers of certain performers usually are concerned about which singles and albums are manufactured on vinyl, in addition to compact discs.

Reliable sources report that a great many country singles are still being made on vinyl, primarily for jukebox use. Though true, knowing with certainty which ones are and which are not on vinyl can be impossible.

We have opted to maintain our usual conservative approach, listing *only* those vinyl discs that we have seen or have been told of by our correspondents. We encourage those of you in the trenches of collecting to submit specifics about other recent vinyl releases.

Pricewise, if the most recent year for which we indicate vinyl singles is, say, 1992, it is safe to assume the same price range for singles you might have from 1993 or '94.

Though we do not anticipate an attempt in the future to include every country and western recording ever made in *Country Music Records*, we did at least want the complete recorded output of every artist appearing on Billboard's C&W charts—no matter how brief or insignificant their chart success.

In addition to those charted country artists, *Country Music Records* includes a random assortment of other country music performers. They are likely here because they are somehow consequential to another artist's listings. Their inclusion should not be viewed as a desire on our part to have every *non-charted* C&W artist in history in this guide.

Between the first country and western 78s and digital CDs, *Country Music Records* now fills a long-standing price guide void.

How the Prices Are Determined

Record values shown in *Country Music Records* are averaged using information derived from a number of traditional sources. Most influential in arriving at current values is our established "marked copy" review program. Dozens of the world's most active dealers and collectors receive a copy of the most recent edition in which, throughout the year, they mark changing prices. When it's time to prepare a revised edition, all marked copies are returned to us for analysis and processing.

Besides the annotated copies, we receive hundreds of letters each year, from folks like yourself, suggesting corrections and/or additions to the guide.

Another extremely important source of pricing information are marketplace publications where hobbyists buy, sell, and trade music collectibles. We painstakingly review those periodicals, as well as other industry publications, carefully comparing prices being asked to those shown in our most recent edition. Keep in mind, however, that while *asking* prices are considered, greater weight is given to actual *sales* prices.

If active trading indicates prices in the guide need to be increased or decreased, those changes are made. With our annual publishing schedule, it is never long before the corrected data appear in print.

What makes this step in the pricing process so vital is that nothing more verifiably illustrates the out-of-print record marketplace than everyday sales lists placed by dealers from around the country and around the globe.

Record prices, as with most collectibles, can vary drastically from one area of the country to another. Having reviewers and annotators in every state—as well as in Europe, Asia, and beyond—enables us to present a realistic average of the highest and lowest current trading prices for an identically graded copy of each record.

Other sources of consequential information include: set sales and auction lists in other magazines as well as private sales list mailings, record convention trading, personal visits with collectors and to retail locations around the country, and hundreds of hours on the telephone with key advisors.

Although the record marketplace information in this edition was believed accurate at press time, it is ever subject to market changes. At any time, major bulk discoveries, quantity dumps, sudden increases brought about by an artist's death, overnight stardom that creates a greater demand for earlier material, and other such events and trends can easily affect scarcity and demand. Through diurnal research, keeping track of the day-to-day changes and discoveries taking place in the fascinating world of record collecting is a relatively simple and ongoing procedure.

To ensure the greatest possible accuracy, *Country Music Records* prices are averaged from data culled from all of the aforementioned sources.

How You Can Help

Obviously, we can never get too much input or too many reviewers. We wholeheartedly encourage you to submit whatever information you feel would be useful in building a better record guide. The quantity of data is not a factor—no amount is too little or too much. The extensive list of names always found in the Acknowledgments chapter indicates the development of our advisor team.

When preparing additions for *Country Music Records* please try to list records in generally the same format as is used in the guide: artist's name, label, selection number, title, year of release (if known), and price range. Since our data base is stored alphabetically by artist, there's no need to note the *Country Music Records* page number.

A word of caution here, however. Please *do not* submit any information to us merely because it appears in another record guide. Make certain all info can be verified in some other manner.

There are some fine publications in print, but there are also some really screwy books out there that are liberally laced with mistakes—from generally erroneous information and absurd prices to listing absolutely non-existent recordings. One guide in particular has, over the past few years, progressively *tripled* the value of a record that never did exist; one fabricated long ago as a joke.

Wax Fax

One frequently used method of forwarding data to us is by fax. For your convenience, we have a dedicated fax line: (360) 385-6572. Use this service to quickly and easily transmit additions, corrections, price updates, and suggestions. Be sure to include your name, address, and phone number so we can acknowledge your contribution and, if necessary, contact you.

Whether sending a marked copy of the guide, a letter, or a fax, please type or clearly print your name so we may accurately credit you in the next edition. Send all additions, corrections, and suggestions to:

Jerry Osborne
P.O. Box 255
Port Townsend, WA 98368
FAX: (360) 385-6572

About the Format

Our arrangement of listings is the most logical way to present so much information in a single volume — a format with unlimited potential for expansion.

The structure of *Country Music Records* allows us to include all of the following in one multi-purpose guidebook: 7–inch 45rpm singles, both 33⅓rpm and 45rpm; 78rpm singles; 12–inch singles, both 33 and 45rpm; extended play 33⅓rpm and 45rpm EPs; 78rpm albums, long play 10– and 12–inch LPs; picture sleeves; promotional issues, and more.

Once you locate an artist's section, their records are listed alphabetically by LABEL. Individual listings for each label appear in numerical order. In many instances, listings that are numerical by selection number are also chronological in sequence of release, but there are times when this is not the case. This format is especially helpful when using the guide along with an artist or label discography. Since the year of release is also provided for each listing, the reader knows immediately the pattern being followed by the label at the time.

Once familiar with the format, you'll find it easy and functional. See the "Sample" page for more information. New users should take time to familiarize themselves with the array. Reading all of the introductory pages should answer most reader questions.

The documenting and pricing of so many recordings is made possible by selectively economizing on space; listing individual titles when necessary but not when it's possible to group a number of equally valuable releases together on one line. Again, *any time* it is necessary to have a separate listing on a record in order to clearly and accurately present the information, we will do it. Also, whenever a specific selection number is noted, whether listed as an exception or not, the title will also be given for easy identification.

One facet of our approach of great concern is the artist who had one or more records of a value indicated for a particular label or series, but who also had one release (or more) that is a notable exception. Every effort has been made to separately document such exceptions, however, due to the sheer bulk of information herein, some may be missed. If you know of any, let us know about them.

You will find that the expansion of an artist's section, moving more toward individual rather than grouped listings, will be commonplace in subsequent volumes of this series. With some performers, it is, or perhaps soon will be, necessary to list every single record separately.

The decision to expand a section is partly based on reader input. Many examples of individual pricing in this edition can be directly attributed to a letter or call suggesting the need to do so.

Grading and the Price Range

The pricing shown in this edition represents the price *range* for NEAR-MINT condition copies. The value range allows for the countless variables that affect record pricing. Often, the range will widen as the dollar amount increases, making a $500 to $1,000 range as logical as a $5 to $10 range.

One standardized system of record grading, used and endorsed by *Country Music Records* and buyers and sellers worldwide, is:

MINT: A *mint* item must be absolutely perfect. Nothing less can be honestly described as mint. Even brand new purchases can easily be flawed in some manner and not qualify as mint. To allow for tiny blemishes, the highest grade used in our record guide series is *near-mint*. An absolutely pristine mint, or still sealed, item may carry a slight premium above the near-mint range shown in this guide.

VERY GOOD: Records in *very good* condition should have a minimum of visual or audible imperfections, which should not detract much from your enjoyment of owning them. This grade is halfway between good and near-mint.

GOOD: Practically speaking, the grade of *good* means that the item is good enough to fill a gap in your collection until a better copy becomes available. Good condition merchandise will show definite signs of wear and tear, probably evidencing that no protective care was given the item. Even so, records in good condition should play all the way through without skipping.

Most older records are going to be in something less than near-mint, or "excellent" condition. It is very important to use the near-mint price range in this guide only as a starting point in record appraising. Be honest about actual condition. Apply the same standards to the records you trade or sell as you would want one from whom you were buying to observe. Visual grading may be unreliable. Accurate grading may require playing the record (play-grading).

Use the following formula to determine values on lesser condition copies:

For **VERY GOOD** condition, figure about 50% to 75% of the near-mint price range given in this guide.

With many of the older pieces that cannot be found in near-mint, VG or VG+ may be the highest grade available. This significantly narrows the gap between VG and the near-mint range.

For **GOOD** condition, figure about 15% to 30% of the near-mint price range given in this guide.

The 10 Point Grading System

Quickly gaining in popularity is a grading system based on the often-used 10 point scale. Many feel that grading with the 10 point system allows for a more precise description of records that are in less than mint condition. Instead of vague terms, such as VG++ (is this the same as M- -?), assigning a specific number provides a more accurate classification of condition.

Most of the records you are likely to buy or sell will no doubt be graded somewhere between 5 and 10.

After using this system ourselves for a few years, we are inclined to agree that it is more precise. Customers who have purchased records from us have, without exception, been pleased with this way of grading.

The table below shows how the 10 point system equates with the more established terms:

10: MINT

9: NEAR-MINT

8: Better than VG but below NM

7: VERY GOOD

6: Better than G but below VG

5: GOOD

4: Better than POOR but below G

3: POOR

2: Really trashed

1: It hurts to think about it

The Bottom Line

All the price guides and reporting of previous sales in the world won't change the fundamental fact that true value is nothing more than what one person is willing to accept and what another is prepared to pay. Actual value is based on scarcity and demand. It's always been that way and always will.

A recording — or anything for that matter — can be 50 or 100 years old, but if no one wants it, the actual value will certainly be minimal. Just because something is old does not necessarily make it valuable. Someone has to want it!

On the other hand, a recent release, perhaps just weeks old, can have exceptionally high value if it has already become scarce and is by an artist whose following has created a demand. A record does not have to be old to be valuable.

Record Types Defined

With the inconsistent language used by the record companies in describing an EP or an LP, we've determined that a language guideline of some kind is needed in order to compile a useful record guide.

Some labels call a 10–inch album an "EP" if it has something less than the prescribed number of tracks found on their LPs. Others call an EP a "Little LP." A few companies have even created special names, associated only with their own label, for the basic record formats.

Having carefully analyzed all of this, we have adopted the following classifications of record configurations, which consistently categorize all types, sizes, and speeds in one section or another:

Singles: 78rpm are those that play at 78rpm. Though 78s are almost always 10–inch discs, a few 7–inch 78rpm singles have been made.

Singles: 7–Inch can be either 45rpm or 33$1/3$ (always referred to simply as "33") speed singles. If a 7–inch single has more than one track on either side, *Country Music Records* considers it an EP.

Singles are priced strictly as a disc, with a separate section devoted to picture sleeves (which are often traded separately). If we know that picture sleeves exist for a given artist, a separate grouping will appear for the label, price, and applicable year of release. Should you know of picture sleeves not documented in this edition, please advise us accordingly.

There have been a few 5–inch discs manufactured, but for the sake of keeping singles with singles (and since we don't want to establish a "Singles: 5–inch" category), such curios will be included with the 7–inch singles, with an explanatory note.

EPs: 7–Inch 33/45rpm are 7–inch discs that have more than one track on one or both sides. Even if labeled an "EP" by the manufacturer, if it's pressed on a 10–, or 12–inch disc it's an LP in our book. Unless so noted, all EPs are presumed to be accompanied by their original covers, in a condition about equal to the disc. An appropriate adjustment in value should be made to compensate for any differences in this area. Exceptions, such as EPs with paper sleeves or no sleeve at all, are designated as such when known.

LPs: 10/12–Inch 33rpm is self explanatory. The only possible confusion that might exist here is with 12–inch singles. If it's 10 or 12 inches in diameter, and labeled, priced, and marketed as a 12–inch single (Maxi-Single, etc.), then that's where you'll find it in this guide, regardless of its speed. Often, 12–inch singles will have a 12–inch die-cut cardboard sleeve or jacket; but many have covers that are exactly like LP jackets, with photos of the artist, etc. Unless so noted, all LPs are presumed to be accompanied by their original covers, in a condition about equal to the disc. An appropriate adjustment in value should be made to compensate for any differences in this area.

Other record type headings used such as Picture Sleeves, Promotional Singles, etc., should be clear.

Cross-referencing and Multiple Artists' Recordings

The cross-referencing in *Country Music Records* should provide the easiest possible method of discovering other sections of the book where a particular artist is featured or appears in any capacity.

We've tried to hold to a minimum unexplained cross-references, opting to concentrate more on those cross-references for which the reader can effortlessly understand the rationalization. Minimized is the unnecessary duplication of cross-references. For example, it is not necessary to list every group in which Glen Campbell played, under each and every one of those sections. What we've done is simply indicate "Also see CAMPBELL, Glen" where you will find a complete cross-referencing to all other sections where he appears.

Some artists have several sections, one right after the other, because they were involved in different duets and/or compilation releases. In such instances, the primary artist (whose section begins first) is not cross-referenced after each and every subsequent section, but only after the last section wherein that artist is involved. This, in effect, blocks the beginning and the end of releases pertaining to that performer. If you don't find the listing you're searching for right away, remember to check the sections that follow, as the artist may have been joined by someone else on that recording causing it to appear in a separate section.

Cross-references in bold typeface are charted artists; those in normal typeface did not chart.

Artist headings and resultant cross-referencing appear in two different formats in this guide. For example:

LEWIS, Jerry Lee, Carl Perkins & Johnny Cash

Listings under this type heading are those wherein the artists perform *together*. Often these releases will also include solo tracks by one or all of the performers in addition to those on which they collaborate.

LEWIS, Jerry Lee / Carl Perkins / Johnny Cash

This heading, with names separated by a slash, indicates there are selections on *separate* tracks by each of the named artists, but they do not perform together.

The parameter set for these compilation releases in the body of the book is four different performers or less. Compilations containing five or more individual performers are found in the Various Artists Compilations chapter.

Whenever more than one act is featured on a record, cross-references appear under all of the other artists on the disc, who have a section of their own in this edition, directing the reader to the location of the listing in question. If you're looking up a record with a different artist on each side, and you don't find it under one artist, be sure to try looking for the flip-side artist.

Not all releases containing more than one artist are given separate sections. In some cases it makes more sense to include such records in the primary section for the most important artist. We will rarely create separate sections for multiple artist discs when the other performers on the issue do not have a section of their own in this edition.

To illustrate this point, Bobby Bare recorded with both his wife, Jeannie, and his son, Bobby Bare Jr. Even though Jeannie and Bobby Jr. do not have individual sections in this book (they didn't make the Billboard country music charts), such recordings are still important to collectors of Bobby Bare. For that reason, they are included in his section.

On the other hand, a duet by Brenda Lee and Willie Nelson requires a separate section, since either or both may be of interest to the researcher. Also, both are individually charted artists. There are a few isolated exceptions to this policy, simply because every section in this edition was separately prepared and customized in whatever manner necessary to provide the user with the most usable information.

Promotional Issues

Separate documenting and pricing of promotional issues is, in most cases, unnecessary. Because most of the records issued during the primary four decades covered in this guide were simultaneously pressed for promotional purposes, a separate listing of them would theoretically double the size of an already large book.

Rather, we've chosen to list promotional copies separately when we have the knowledge that an alternate price (either higher or lower) consistently is asked for them. For the most part, promos of everyday releases will fall into the same range—usually toward the high end—given for store stock copies. Some may stretch the range slightly, but not enough to warrant separate pricing. Premiums may be paid for promos that have different (longer, shorter, differently mixed, etc.) versions of tunes, even though the artist may not be particularly hot in the collecting marketplace.

When identified as a "Promotional issue," we are usually describing a record with a special promotional ("Not For Sale," "Dee Jay Copy," etc.) label or sleeve, and not a *designate* promo. Designate promos are identical to commercial releases, except they have been rubber or mechanically stamped, stickered, written on by hand, or in some way altered to accommodate their use for promotional purposes. There are very few designate promos listed in this edition, and those that are (such as in the Elvis Presley section) are clearly identified as such.

Colored Vinyl Pressings

Records known to exist on both black vinyl and colored vinyl (vinyl is the term used regardless of whether it's polystyrene or vinyl) are listed separately since there is usually a value difference. However, some colored vinyl releases were never pressed on black vinyl, and since there is no way to have the record other than on colored vinyl, it may or may not be specifically noted as being on colored vinyl.

Because the true color of some colored vinyl pressings may be a judgment call (is it red or maroon . . . is it dark blue or is it purple?), we're using "colored vinyl" to indicate most pressings that are not standard black vinyl. Exceptions exist when for the sake of exactness — such as when different colors exist and are priced differently — it is necessary to be more specific.

Foreign Releases

For the most part, *Country Music Records* lists only U.S. releases; however, there are some exceptions. A handful of records that were widely distributed in the United States or sold via widespread U.S. advertising, even though manufactured outside the country, are included. Such anomalies would appear only in the more sophisticated sections of the guide.

There are many Canadian releases in *Country Music Records*, with more planned for future editions. The collectors' market for out-of-print Canadian records is mostly a U.S. market. The trading of rare Canadian discs between Canadian collectors is not quite as widespread as those instances that involve a U.S. buyer or seller. Yet it is from Canadian collectors that we receive most of our information on those releases, and we expect to have more listed in future editions.

There are millions of overseas releases that have collector value to fans in those countries as well as to stateside collectors. Unfortunately, the tremendous volume of material and the variances in pricing make it impossible to comprehensively document and price imports.

Bootlegs and Counterfeits

Bootleg and counterfeit records are not priced in this guide, though a few are cited, along with information on how to distinguish them from an original.

For the record, a bootleg recording is one illegally manufactured, usually containing material not previously available in a legitimate form. Often, with the serious collector in mind, a boot will package previously issued tracks that have achieved some degree of value or scarcity. If the material is easily available, legally, then there would be no gain for the bootlegger.

The counterfeit record is one manufactured as close as possible in sound and appearance to the source disc from which it was inspired. Not all counterfeits were created to fool an unsuspecting buyer into thinking he or she was buying an authentic issue, but some were. Many were designated in some way, such as a slight marking or variance, so as not to allow them to be confused with originals. Such a fake record primarily exists to fill a gap in the collector's file until the real thing comes along.

With both bootleg and counterfeit records, the appropriate and deserving recipients of royalties are, of course, denied remuneration for their works.

Since most of the world's valuable records have been counterfeited, it is always a good idea to consult with an expert when there is any doubt. The trained eye can usually spot a fake.

This is not to say *unauthorized* releases are excluded from the book. There are many legitimate releases that are unauthorized by one entity or another; records that are neither bootleg nor counterfeit. Unauthorized does not necessarily mean illegal.

Group Names and Personnel

One problem that we'll never completely solve involves the many instances where groups using the exact same name are lumped together with other groups who are completely different. Whenever known to be different, these groups are given separate sections; however, there are times when we simply do not know.

As often as not, there will have been group members that have come and gone over the years. Reflecting this turnover in our listing of members' names may cause some confusion, when the reader sees more members shown for a group than were known to be in the group at a specific time. We've tried, whenever possible, to list the original line-up first, followed by later members. Also, the lead singer is usually listed first. We welcome additional information on group members from readers. One of the most reliable sources of this data is the LP covers, which often list members. If you can fill in the members' names on any groups where we don't list that information, we'll see that it gets into our next edition.

When group members' names are given, there is a likelihood that not all of the members named appear on *all* of the releases documented. It is also possible that not all of the members named ever recorded with all of the other members shown at the same time.

When names are given for a solo performer, those named are likely noteworthy sidemen and are identified as "Session" members.

Various Artists Compilations

About the only priority used in determining which C&W compilations are included in this edition is that a special effort was made to add as many as possible from the '50s and '60s, especially ones containing the more collectible rock era artists. Otherwise, we mainly focused on those releases that we could easily document and verify. We realize there are many other C&W various artists LPs from the '70s to present; however, very few of this batch command prices greater than $5 to $10. While including them in future editions is planned, you can feel safe for now in assigning that price range to these fairly recent ones.

Crucial to one's appreciation and/or desire of compilation releases is which performers are being featured on them. We are not fond of listing compilation releases without giving you a clue as to whom or what is heard on the disc, though sometimes it could not be helped. We have tried to provide the artist lineup on as many discs as possible. When we lack the complete cast, we provide as many names as possible. Often, just a name or two will offer some insight as to the type of music one might expect on a particular LP.

There are a few various artists records in *Country Music Records* that have no artists shown, but by listing them readers will then know which ones we need help with. We encourage you to compare the data here to their actual records, providing missing artists' names as well as other tidbits of information that can be used to make future editions even more complete. Because of the volume of data received, information we receive may not always appear in the very next edition.

Some other notes about the Various Artists Compilations chapter:

• Many records labeled as soundtracks are really various artists compilations in disguise. We have included quite a few soundtracks of this type, but there are plenty of others out there. See *The Official Price Guide to Movie/TV Soundtracks and Original Cast Albums* for more listings of this type. Most of the ones we didn't squeeze into this edition are of recent vintage and sell for under $10.

• Following each label name, one of the following notations will be found:

(M): MONAURAL.

(S): STEREO. Labeled stereo, but may in truth be either true stereo, electronically reprocessed stereo (i.e. fake stereo), or a combination of both.

(SE): Completely electronically reprocessed stereo.

(ST): Completely true stereo.

(SP): Part electronically reprocessed stereo and part true stereo.

(EP): Extended play, 7–inch 45 or 33rpm.

• Various artists compilations are listed in alphabetical order by title. Those having titles beginning with numerals are at the beginning of the chapter. To keep things somewhat organized, ones having titles beginning with numbers *spelled out* have been converted to numerals and put in numerical order. We chose this system over listing by label because only by having them in order by title is it possible to always find all of the releases in a specific series grouped together. Also, many find it easier to remember titles than label names.

• Compilation releases that contain tracks by folks like Elvis Presley, for example, usually command premium prices. Whenever possible we have listed these artists first so that you may quickly see why one particular album is valued higher than others that are similar.

• Regardless of how many tracks appear on an album by an artist, their name is only listed once.

• At this time, we have chosen not to include vinyl radio shows in this edition. Radio shows are a completely separate pail of worms that we would rather avoid—at least until we have made the rest of the chapter more comprehensive. Same goes for armed forces and public service broadcasting recordings.

• You will find a few listings that are lacking one piece of information or another, such as a name or selection number. Rather than omit these records entirely, we have included them and used question marks in place of the missing numbers or text. Can you help by providing that portion we're missing?

Parenthetical Notes

Some of the information that may be found in parentheses following the artist heading has already been covered. However, other uses of this space include:

• Complete artist and group or artist and band names. Some artists were shown as being with one group on a few releases, solo on some, and with yet another group on other issues. We've tried to present the information the way, or ways, that it is shown on the actual record label.

• Variations of spelling or names for the same artist. With some artists, it's convenient to have everything in one section; however, when it is illogical to combine listings, perhaps because the performer was popular under more than one name (such as Gene Autry and his many pseudonyms), you'll find individual sections for each name. Cross-references will be used to help you locate things easily. Having "Kenneth Rogers" in parentheses is not intended to mean that Kenneth is Kenny's real name. Rather, we're letting you know that on at least one of his records he is credited as Kenneth Rogers instead of Kenny Rogers. We may at times provide real names of artists, but only when we feel they need to be given. While we have no desire to give the real names of everyone who has recorded under a pseudonym, there are times when you do need this information. This is especially true when they have also recorded under their real name or when more than one person has recorded under the same pseudonym. To help sort things out, we will, when known, give you the real name of someone who has recorded under a nom de guerre.

• Names of guest performers who may or may not be credited on the actual label, but who we feel you should know were involved in some of the records listed in that section.

Using This Guide: Some Additional Points

• A few of the more prolific labels with lengthy names are abbreviated in this guide. They are:

     ABC-PAR.....................ABC-Paramount

MFSL............Mobile Fidelity Sound Lab	
RCA......................................RCA Victor	
20TH FOX ....20th Century-Fox	
U.A.....................................United Artists	
W.B...............................Warner Brothers	

To avoid confusion, when an artist has records on the old Memphis Sun label, as well as Shelby Singleton's Nashville-based Sun label, the latter is shown as "SSS/Sun."

• The alphabetization in *Country Music Records* makes finding any artist or label easy, but a few guidelines may speed the process along for you:

• Names that are simply letters (and are not intended to be pronounced as a word) are found at the beginning of the listings under each letter of the alphabet. The same rule applies to acronyms and to initialisms. When known, we'll parenthetically tell you what the abbreviation represents.

• Names are listed in the alphabetical order of the first word. Hyphenated words are looked upon as whole words. Divided names are alphabetically listed as though they were a one-word name.

• The articles "A" or "The" have been dropped from group names in this guide even though they may appear on the records as part of the name.

• With record labels in *Country Music Records*, the listings appear in alphabetical/numerical/chronological order. Selection prefixes are generally not used (they make it more difficult to scan the numbers) unless they are necessary for identification. With some artists (Marty Robbins, Elvis Presley, etc.) it is essential at times because of the many reissues.

• Some sections make use of the label prefixes to sort things out, but most use a number series. If the numbers are duplicated by the label, or if any of a variety of confusing similarities exist, we may resort to the prefixes for clarity.

• Whenever possible, records priced in the $25 to $35 range and up are listed individually with label, selection number, and title.

• Anytime we find that the monaural or the stereo issue of a particular record is in need of a separate listing (because there is a price difference for one that is outside the boundaries of the price range of the other), we will gladly provide same. If there is but one listing, this indicates that we have no reason to believe there is much difference in the two forms. A little application of the known variables will help in this area. For example, if the range is $20-$40 for a 1960 LP and you know that the stereo issue is in true stereo, it's safe to place the mono at the low end of the range ($20-$30) and the stereo at the high end ($30-$40). The calculation may be reversed for late '60s and for most electronically reprocessed issues.

• We believe the year or years of release given in the far-right column to be accurate. If we don't know the correct year, the column is left blank. In some cases the record may have been released in one year and debuted on the nation's music charts the following year. This is common for year-end issues and explains why you may remember a hit as being from 1966, although we list it as a 1965 release.

• When multiple years are indicated, such as "64-66," it means the records described on that line spanned the years 1964 through 1966. They may have had one issue in 1964 and another in 1966, or may have had eight releases during those years. It does *not* mean that we believe the release came out sometime between 1964 and 1966. If the exact year is not known but the decade of release is, then we will provide that ('50s, '60s, '70s, etc.)

• When a selection number series, such as a "4000 series," is shown, it includes numbers 4000 through 4999. If it were meant to indicate only 4000 through 4099, then separate listings would be found for 4100, 4200, etc.

• Goofy as it seems, a few records have been issued with no artist or label given. You will find this on both singles and albums. These items are filed here by title.

• There are hundreds of double albums (two discs in one package) priced in the guide, but they are not necessarily identified as double LPs. They are, nevertheless, included in the price range.

• To conserve space, when the same title is listed as both 45 and 78, we may not list the title in both sections if it requires more than one line. You may therefore find only the label name in the 78 section, whereas the complete number and title will be in the 45 section.

• In most cases, we have no specifics regarding which 78s came on both black and colored plastic. Lacking comments to the contrary, all 78s in *Country Music Records* are presumed to be black plastic.

Guidelines for Pricing Country Music Records Not in This Edition

Since it is impossible for us to include *every* record ever produced, a few guidelines may assist you in evaluating records not found in this edition:

♦ Country Music on 45rpm: Most country music vocal and instrumental 45s from the '50s are available for under $15; many for less than $10. Obvious exceptions are any that border on rockabilly or country rock. Don't take any country record for granted! Play both sides of every disc, as it is always possible you'll discover a great country rocker.

♦ Country music singles from the '60s to present are seldom going to sell for more than $4 to $8.

♦ Country Music on 78rpm: Most of the country 78s should fall into the $10 to $40 range. There are, however, many older 78s with prices well into three figures; some even higher.

♦ Country Music Long Play Albums: From the '50s, 12–inch LPs generally are found for under $30 to $60. Ten–inch LPs may go for $50 to $100. As always, the range will vary widely depending on the following and collectibility of the artist.

♦ Most country LPs from the '60s to present can be found for $10 to $25. Again, there are exceptions.

♦ Country Music Extended Play Albums: Very, very few country music EPs were big sellers, which means nearly all are rare. You may find they are in the same price range as the '50s LPs above; some will bring even more than LPs from the same time period.

In summary, there is no way these few paragraphs can constitute a complete price guide for the millions of country and western records that exist. If such generic generalizations were possible, while guaranteeing unerring accuracy, the entire price guide would be about ten pages. It is the exceptions that make record pricing so complicated and difficult to document. Our goal here is simply to provide a rough idea of the value of C&W recordings that are outside the parameters of this edition.

What to Expect When Selling Your Records to a Dealer

As most know, there is a noteworthy difference between the prices reported in this guide and the prices that one can expect a dealer to pay when buying records for resale. Unless a dealer is buying for a personal collection and without thoughts of resale, he or she is simply not in a position to pay full price. Dealers work on a percentage basis, largely determined by the total dollar investment, quality, and quantity of material offered as well as the general financial condition and inventory of the dealer at the time.

Another very important consideration is the length of time it will take the dealer to recover at least the amount of the original investment. The greater the demand for the stock and the better the condition, the quicker the return and therefore the greater the percentage that can be paid. Our experience has shown that, day-in and day-out, most dealers will pay from 25% to 50% of *guide* prices. And that's assuming they are planning to resell at guide prices. If they traditionally sell below guide, that will be reflected in what they can pay for stock.

If you have records to sell, it would be wise to check with several shops. In doing so you'll begin to get a good idea of the value of your collection to a dealer.

Also, consult the Directory of Buyers and Sellers in this guide for the names of many dealers who not only might be interested in buying, but from whom many collectible records are available for purchase.

Whether you wish to sell the records you have, or add out-of-print discs to your collection, check out *DISCoveries* magazine. Each issue is packed with ads, features, discographies, collecting tips and more. If getting into the record marketplace is important to you — whether for country or other types of music — *DISCoveries* is not just recommended, it is essential. For more information, contact: Trader Publications, P.O. Box 1050, Dubuque, Iowa 52003. A sample issue is available upon request.

Concluding Thoughts

The purpose of this guide is to report as accurately as possible the most recent prices asked and paid for records within the area of its coverage. There are two key words here that deserve emphasis: **guide** and **report**.

We cannot stress enough that this book is only a guide. There always have been and always will be instances of records selling well above and below the prices shown within these pages. These extremes are recognized in the final averaging process; but it's still important to understand that just because we've reported a 30-year-old record as having a $25 to $50 near-mint value, doesn't mean that a collector of that material should be hesitant to pay $75 for it. How badly he or she wants it and how often it's possible to purchase it *at any price* should be the prime factors considered, not the fact that we last reported it at a lower price. Of course, we'd like to know about sales of this sort so that the next edition can reflect the new pricing information.

Our objective is to report and reflect record marketplace activity; not to *establish* prices. For that reason, and if given the choice, we'd prefer to be a bit behind the times rather than ahead. With this guide being regularly revised, it will never be long before the necessary changes are reported within these pages.

We encourage record companies, artist management organizations, talent agencies, publicists, and performers to make certain that we are on the active mailing list for new release information, press releases, bios, publicity photos, and anything pertaining to recordings.

There is an avalanche of helpful information in this guide to aid the collector in determining what is valuable and what may not be worth fooling with, but the wise fan will also keep abreast of current trends and news through the pages of the fanzines and publications devoted to his or her favorite forms of music.

Who are all these people?
Why are they in a Country Music guide?

There are many artists listed in this book that could not, under any stretch of the imagination, be regarded as either country or western. However, since our chosen parameter is to include every artist who made the Billboard Top Country Singles chart, we cannot randomly eliminate folks here and there just because they are not country artists. Besides, there is no extra charge for the additional listings.

Hopefully, readers will now understand why singers like Fats Domino, Petula Clark, Paul McCartney & Wings, Perry Como, Eric Clapton, and many others, are included.

SAMPLE LISTING

(Excerpted from the Hank Thompson section)

Artist's primary heading.

THOMPSON, Hank
(With the Brazos Valley Boys)

May also be shown on some releases as . . .

C&W '48

Singles: 78 rpm
GLOBE (124 "Whoa Sailor") 100-200   46

The chart or charts and year artist first appeared on Billboard. Indicates that Hank Thompson first made the C&W charts in 1948.

Singles: 7–inch
ABC	3-5	75-79
ABC/DOT	3-5	74-77
CAPITOL (1000 thru 3000 series)	5-15	50-58
CAPITOL (4000 & 5000 series)	4-8	58-66
CHURCHILL	3-4	81-83
DOT	3-5	68-74
MCA	3-4	79-80
W.B.	4-6	66-67

Year or years of release.

Picture Sleeves

Type or format of items listed in this section.

CAPITOL (4649 "Lost John") 5-10   61

LPs: 10/12–inch 33rpm

Label names, selection numbers and titles.

CAPITOL (H-418 "Songs of the Brazos
Valley") 60-80   53
(10-inch LP.)

Near-mint price range.

CAPITOL (T-729 "New Recordings") . . . 30-50   55
CAPITOL (T-826 "Hank!") 30-40   57
CAPITOL (T-975 "Dance Ranch") 30-40   58
CAPITOL (H-9111 "Favorites") 50-100   52
(10-inch LP.)

Decade shown when exact year not known.

SEARS (135 "How Many Teardrops Will
It Take") 10-15   60s
WACO (101 "Hank Thompson Sings and Plays
Bob Wills") 30-50

Also see CAGLE, Buddy
Also see POTTER, Curtis

Cross references to other, related, artist's sections.

ABBOTT, Jerry   *C&W '78*
Singles: 7–inch
CHURCHILL.................................. 3-5   78
DALLAS STAR............................. 3-4   82

ABERNATHY, Mack   *C&W '88*
Singles: 7–inch
CMI.. 3-4   88-89

ACE in the HOLE BAND
Singles: 7–inch
D (1310 "I Just Can't Go on Dying Like This").. 20-25   76
D (1313 "The Way I Feel About You") 15-20   78
D (1316 "I Don't Want to Talk It Over Anymore") 15-20   79
Members: George Strait; Mike Daily; Tom Foote; Terry Hale; Bill Mabry.
Also see STRAIT, George

ACUFF, Roy   *P&R '38/C&W '44*
(With the Smoky Mountain Boys; with Crazy Tennesseeans)
Singles: 78rpm
BANNER 10-20
CAPITOL.................................... 4-8   53-55
COLUMBIA 5-10   45-49
CONQUEROR 10-20
DECCA....................................... 4-8   55
MGM 5-10   51
MELOTONE 10-20
OKEH 5-10   40-45
ORIOLE...................................... 10-20
PERFECT 10-20
ROMEO...................................... 10-20
VOCALION................................. 8-12   38-40
Singles: 7–inch
CAPITOL (2385 thru 3209) 5-10   53-55
COLUMBIA (20000 series) 10-20   52
DECCA....................................... 5-10   55
ELEKTRA.................................... 3-5   78
HICKORY (314 thru 362) 3-6   73-75
HICKORY (1073 thru 1664) 4-8   58-72
MGM 10-20   51

EPs: 7–inch 33/45rpm
CAPITOL (617 "Songs of the Smokey Mountains").............................10-15   55
(Price is for any of three volumes.)
COLUMBIA 10-20   51-57
LP: 10/12–inch 33rpm
CAPITOL (617 "Songs of the Smokey Mountains").............................20-40   55
CAPITOL (2276 "The Voice of Country Music")..................................10-20   65
CAPITOL (T-1870 "Country Music Hall of Fame's Roy Acuff") 10-20   63
(Monaural.)
CAPITOL (SM-1870 "Country Music Hall of Fame's Roy Acuff") 5-10   79
(Reprocessed stereo.)
COLUMBIA (9004 "Songs of the Smokey Mountains").............................30-50   50
(10–inch LP.)
COLUMBIA (9010 "Old Time Barn Dance") 30-50   50
(10–inch LP.)
COLUMBIA (CS-1034 "Roy Acuff's Greatest Hits") 8-12   70
COLUMBIA (PC-1034 "Roy Acuff's Greatest Hits") 8-12   70
COLUMBIA (39998 "Roy Acuff") 5-8   85
ELEKTRA.....................................5-10   78-82
CAPITOL (2103 "The Great Roy Acuff") 10-20   64
GOLDEN COUNTRY 5-10
HARMONY.................................8-20   58-70
HICKORY (101 thru 119)...........20-35   61-65
HICKORY (125 thru 162)...........15-30   65-70
HICKORY/MGM..........................8-12   74-75
METRO.......................................10-20   65
MGM (3707 "Favorite Hymns") 30-40   58
MGM (4044 "Hymn Time").........15-25   62
PICKWICK 5-10   70s
PICKWICK/HILLTOP 8-15   65-69
ROUNDER....................................5-8   85
TIME-LIFE....................................5-10   80s
Session: Jordanaires.
Also see JORDANAIRES
Also see LOUVIN, Charlie, & Roy Acuff
Also see NITTY GRITTY DIRT BAND & Roy Acuff
Also see WILLIAMS, Hank / Roy Acuff

ACUFF, Roy, & Kitty Wells
Singles: 78rpm
DECCA 4-6   56

Singles: 7–inch

DECCA...5-10   56
Also see ACUFF, Roy
Also see WELLS, Kitty

ADAMS, Don   *C&W '67*
(With Greenfield Express)
Singles: 7–inch

ATLANTIC.................................. 3-5   73-74
JACK O'DIAMONDS 3-6   67
MUSICOR 4-8   65
Also see YOUNG, Faron

ADAMS, Kay   *C&W '66*
(With the Cliffie Stone Group)
Singles: 7–inch

TOWER... 4-8   65-68

Picture Sleeves

TOWER (445 "Gonna Have a Good
  Time").. 5-10   68

LP: 10/12–inch 33rpm

FRONTLINE............................... 5-10
TOWER...................................... 10-15   66-68
Also see STONE, Cliffie

ADAMS, Kaylee   *C&W '86*
Singles: 7–inch

W.B. 3-4   86

ADEN, Terry   *C&W '81*
Singles: 7–inch

AMI.. 3-4   82
B&B 3-4   81

ADKINS, Wendel   *C&W '77*
Singles: 7–inch

HITSVILLE 3-5   77
MC... 3-5   77

LP: 10/12–inch 33rpm

GILLEY'S (5007 "Live at
  Gilley's") 10-15   83
  (Includes Gilley's club bumper sticker.)
HITSVILLE 5-10   77

AGNES & ORVILLE
Singles: 7–inch

COLUMBIA 4-6   68
Members: Lefty Frizzell; June Stearns.
Also see FRIZZELL, Lefty
Also see STEARNS, June

ALABAMA   *C&W '77*
(Alabama Band)
Singles: 7–inch

GRT... 4-8   77
MDJ.. 3-5   79-80

RCA 3-5   80-93
RCA GOLD STANDARD 3-4   82
SUN (Colored vinyl) 4-8   81

Picture Sleeves

GRT 10-20   77
RCA 3-4   80-90

LPs: 10/12–inch 33rpm

ABC/WATERMARK ("American Country
  Countdown Presents
  Alabama") 8-12   88
  (No selection number used. Promotional
  issue only.)
ALABAMA RECORDS (78 9-01 "The
  Alabama Band")...................200-400   78
PLANTATION (44 "Wild
  Country").................................40-60   81
RCA 5-10   80-90
SONNY 30-50   79
Members: Randy Owen; Jeff Cook; Teddy Gentry; R.
Scott; Mark Herndon.
Also see RICHIE, Lionel, & Alabama
Also see WILD COUNTRY

ALAN, Buddy   *C&W '68*
(With Don Rich & Buckaroos)
Singles: 7–inch

CAPITOL.......................................3-5   68-75
SUN DEVIL (1001 "Ride 'Em
  Cowboy") 4-8   78

LP: 10/12–inch 33rpm

CAPITOL.......................................5-10   70-75
Also see BUCKAROOS
Also see OWENS, Buck, & Buddy Alan

ALBERT, Urel   *C&W '73*
Singles: 7–inch

TOAST..3-5   73

LP: 10/12–inch 33rpm

SPAR (3016 "Saturday Night in
  Nashville")...............................20-30
CINNAMON 20-30

ALEXANDER, Daniele   *C&W '89*
Singles: 7–inch

MERCURY.....................................3-4   89-90

ALEXANDER, Daniele, & Butch Baker   *C&W '90*
Singles: 7–inch

MERCURY.....................................3-4   90
Also see BAKER, Butch

ALEXANDER, Wyvon   *C&W '81*
Singles: 7–inch

GERVASI.....................................3-4   81-84

ALIBI *C&W '87*

Singles: 7–inch
COMSTOCK	3-4	87-88
POLYDOR	3-5	80

LPs: 10/12–inch 33rpm
POLYDOR	5-10	80

ALLANSON, Susie *C&W '77*

Singles: 7–inch
OAK	4-6	77
ELEKTRA/CURB	3-5	79
LIBERTY	3-4	80-82
TNP	3-4	86-87
U.A.	3-4	80
W.B./CURB	3-5	77-78

LP: 10/12–inch 33rpm
ABC	5-10	79
ELEKTRA/CURB	5-8	79
U.A.	5-8	80
W.B./CURB	5-10	78

ALLEN, Deborah *C&W '79*

Singles: 7–inch
CAPITOL	3-5	80-82
GIANT	3-4	92-93
RCA	3-4	80-84

Picture Sleeves
RCA	3-4	83

LPs: 10/12–inch 33rpm
CAPITOL	5-10	80
RCA	5-8	84

Also see MANDRELL, Barbara
Also see REEVES, Jim, & Deborah Allen

ALLEN, Joe *C&W '75*

Singles: 7–inch
W.B.	3-5	75

ALLEN, Judy *C&W '78*

Singles: 7–inch
POLYDOR	3-5	78

LP: 10/12–inch 33rpm
STOP	5-10	70s

ALLEN, Melody *C&W '75*

Singles: 7–inch
MERCURY	3-5	75

ALLEN, Red: see OSBORNE BROTHERS

ALLEN, Rex *C&W '49*

(With the Arizona Wranglers & Jerry Byrd)

Singles: 78rpm
DECCA (Except 30651)	5-10	52-57
DECCA (30651 "Knock Knock, Rattle")	10-20	56
MERCURY	5-10	49-55

Singles: 7–inch
BUENA VISTA	4-8	59
DECCA (Except 28000 thru 30000 series)	3-8	56-72
DECCA (28000 & 29000 series)	5-10	52-56
DECCA (30000 series except 30651)	5-10	56
DECCA (30651 "Knock Knock, Rattle")	15-20	56
JMI	3-5	73
MERCURY	5-10	53-62
WILDCAT	4-6	

Picture Sleeves
MERCURY	5-10	63

EPs: 7–inch 33/45rpm
DECCA	10-20	56
MERCURY	10-20	53-56

LPs: 10/12–inch 33rpm
BUENA VISTA (3307 "Rex Allen Sings 16 Favorites")	40-50	61
COLLECTOR'S CLASSICS	5-10	
CORAL	5-10	73
DECCA (5000 series)	10-15	68-70
(Decca LP numbers in this series preceded by a "7" or a "DL-7" are stereo issues.)		
DECCA (8000 series)	20-30	56-58
DESIGN	10-15	62
DISNEYLAND	6-10	70
HACIENDA (101 "Country Songs I Love")	50-60	
JMI (4003 "Rex Allen Sings")	20-30	
MCA	5-10	
MERCURY (20719 "The Faith of a Man") (Monaural.)	15-25	62
MERCURY (20752 "Rex Allen Sings and Tells Tales") (Monaural.)	15-25	62
MERCURY (60719 "The Faith of a Man") (Stereo.)	20-30	62
MERCURY (60752 "Rex Allen Sings and Tells Tales") (Stereo.)	20-30	62

PICKWICK/HILLTOP 10-15   65
VOCALION.................................. 6-10   70
WING 10-15 64-66

Session: Jud Conlon Singers.
Also see CURTIS, Ken / Rex Allen & Arizona
 Wranglers
Also see PAGE, Patti, & Rex Allen

ALLEN, Rex, Jr.   *C&W '73*
(With Arizona)

Singles: 7–inch

MOON SHINE 3-4 83-85
TNP 3-4   87
W.B. 3-5 73-82

LP: 10/12–inch 33rpm

ACCORD..................................... 5-8   84
OUT OF TOWN........................... 5-8   80s
W.B. 3-5 74-81
SSS 5-10

Session: Rex Allen.

ALLEN, Rex, Jr., & Margo Smith   *C&W '81*

Singles: 7–inch

W.B. 3-4   81

Also see SMITH, Margo

ALLEN, Rex, Jr., & Sons of the Pioneers   *C&W '76*

Singles: 7–inch

W.B. 3-5   76

Session: Rex Allen.
Also see ALLEN, Rex
Also see SONS of the PIONEERS

ALLEN, Rosalie   *C&W '46*
(With the Black River Riders; with Sons of the
Purple Sage; with Tex Fletcher)

Singles: 78rpm

BLUEBIRD 5-10 49-50
GRAND AWARD...................... 12-25 56-57
RCA... 5-10 46-50

LP: 10/12–inch 33rpm

GRAND AWARD (330 "Songs of the Golden
 West") 30-40   56
GRAND AWARD (350
 "Rodeo").................................. 25-35   57
WALDORF (150 "C&W Hits").... 25-45   56

Also see BRITT, Elton, Rosalie Allen & Skytoppers
Also see THREE SUNS, Rosalie Allen & Elton Britt

ALLEY, Jim   *C&W '68*

Singles: 7–inch

AVCO 3-5   75
DOT.. 4-6   68

PEARL (4448 "Dig That Rock &
 Roll") 75-125   50s

ALMOST BROTHERS   *C&W '85*

Singles: 7–inch

MTM...3-4 85-86

Members: Steve Mosto; Mike Ragogna.

ALVIN & CHIPMUNKS: see CHIPMUNKS

AMARILLO   *C&W '80*
(Barry Grant)

Singles: 7–inch

NSD 3-4 80-81

Also see GRANT, Barry

AMAZING RHYTHM ACES   *C&W/P&R/LP '75*

Singles: 7–inch

ABC..3-5 75-79
COLUMBIA 3-4   79
W.B. 3-4   80

LPs: 10/12–inch 33rpm

ABC..10-20 75-78
COLUMBIA 10-15   79
W.B. 8-10   80

Members: Russell Smith; James Brown Jr; Byrd
Burton; Stick Davis; Billy Earhart III; James Hooker;
Butch McDade.
Also see BAMA BAND
Also see SMITH, Russell

AMES, Durelle   *C&W '87*

Singles: 7–inch

ADVANTAGE.................................3-4 87-88

AMIGOS DE MUSICA

Singles: 7–inch

FONTANA......................................4-8 69-70

Also see MEYERS, Augie
Also see SIR DOUGLAS QUINTET

AMY   *C&W '79*

Singles: 7–inch

DECADE.......................................3-5   79
SCORPION...................................3-5   79

ANDERS, Lisa, & Victory Five
(Liz Anderson)

Singles: 7–inch

SENATOR (711 "Old
 Enough") 10-20   60

Also see ANDERSON, Liz

ANDERSON, Bill   *C&W '58*

(With the Po' Folks; with Jordanaires; Whispering Bill Anderson)

Singles: 12–inch 33/45rpm

MCA	4-8	78

Singles: 7–inch

DECCA (30000 series)	5-10	58-59
DECCA (31000 series)	4-8	60-66
DECCA (32000 & 33000 series)	3-6	67-72
MCA	3-4	73-81
SOUTHERN TRACKS	3-4	82-87
SWANEE	3-4	85
TNT	4-6	59

Picture Sleeves

DECCA	4-8	63-69

EPs: 7–inch 33/45rpm

DECCA	5-10	63-65

LPs: 10/12–inch 33rpm

BILL ANDERSON LABEL (11316 "On the Road")	15-25	
(Promotional issue only.)		
CORAL	4-6	73
DECCA (4192 thru 4686)	15-20	62-65
DECCA (4771 thru 5344)	10-15	66-72
(Decca LP numbers in this series preceded by a "7" or a "DL-7" are stereo issues.)		
DECCA (7100 series)	15-20	69
DECCA (7200 series)	10-12	72
EPIC	5-10	82-85
MCA	5-10	73-80
PICKWICK	5-10	70s
SOUTHERN TRACKS	5-10	84
VOCALION	8-12	68-71

Session: Jordanaires.
Also see COE, David Allan, & Bill Anderson
Also see JORDANAIRES
Also see KERR, Anita
Also see WELLS, Kitty / Bill Anderson

ANDERSON, Bill, & Jan Howard   *C&W '66*

Singles: 7–inch

DECCA	3-5	66-71

LP: 10/12–inch 33rpm

DECCA	6-12	68-72

Also see HOWARD, Jan

ANDERSON, Bill, & Mary Lou Turner   *C&W '78*

Singles: 7–inch

MCA	3-5	78

LP: 10/12–inch 33rpm

MCA	5-10	76-77

Also see ANDERSON, Bill
Also see TURNER, Mary Lou

ANDERSON, Ivie   *C&W '44*

Singles: 78rpm

EXCLUSIVE	5-10	44

ANDERSON, John   *C&W '77*

Singles: 7–inch

ACE of HEARTS	4-6	74
MCA	3-4	87
W.B.	3-5	77-87

LPs: 10/12–inch 33rpm

W.B.	5-8	77-87

Session: Waylon Jennings.
Also see HAGGARD, Merle
Also see HARRIS, Emmylou
Also see JENNINGS, Waylon

ANDERSON, Liz   *C&W '66*

Singles: 7–inch

EPIC	3-5	71-73
RCA (8000 & 9000 series)	3-8	64-70
SCORPION	3-5	78

LPs: 10/12–inch 33rpm

CAMDEN	10-15	66
RCA	10-20	67-70
TUDOR	5-8	83

Also see ANDERS, Lisa, & Victory Five
Also see BARE, Bobby, Liz Anderson & Norma Jean

ANDERSON, Liz & Lynn   *C&W '68*

Singles: 7–inch

RCA	3-6	68

Also see ANDERSON, Liz
Also see ANDERSON, Lynn

ANDERSON, Lynn   *C&W '66*

Singles: 7–inch

CBS (165211 "Isn't It Always Love")	25-30	79
(Picture disc. Promotional issue only. 1200 made.)		
CHART	3-5	66-71
COLUMBIA	3-4	70-80
MERCURY	3-4	86-89
PERMIAN	3-4	83
RCA	3-5	68

Picture Sleeves

COLUMBIA	3-6	70-72

EPs: 7–inch 33/45rpm

COLUMBIA	4-8	72
(Promotional only.)		

LPs: 10/12–inch 33rpm

ALBUM GLOBE	5-10	76
CHART	10-20	67-72

COLUMBIA 5-10   70-80

COLUMBIA HOUSE (6033 "Lynn Anderson
   Treasury") 30-40   73
   (Boxed, 5-LP set. Mail order offer.)

COLUMBIA HOUSE (6034 "The Ways to
   Love a Man") 5-10   73

COLUMBIA SPECIAL
   PRODUCTS 5-10   83

ERA 5-8   82

51 WEST 5-8   82

HARMONY 5-10   71-73

MOUNTAIN DEW 5-10

PERMIAN 5-10   83

PICKWICK 5-10

TIME-LIFE 5-10   81

Session: Jordanaires.
Also see ANDERSON, Liz, & Lynn
Also see BRUCE, Ed, & Lynn Anderson
Also see JORDANAIRES
Also see TOMORROW'S WORLD

ANDERSON, Lynn, & Jerry Lane *C&W '67*
Singles: 7–inch

CHART 3-5   67
Also see LANE, Jerry

ANDERSON, Lynn, & Gary Morris *C&W '83*
Singles: 7–inch

PERMIAN 3-4   83
Also see MORRIS, Gary

ANDERSON, Lynn / Ray Price
LP: 10/12–inch 33rpm

COLUMBIA HOUSE (5658 "Heart to
   Heart") 15-25   72
   (Boxed, 4-LP set. Mail order offer.)
Also see PRICE, Ray

ANDERSON, Lynn / Charley Pride
LP: 10/12–inch 33rpm

TELEHOUSE 5-8
Also see ANDERSON, Lynn
Also see PRIDE, Charley

ANDI & BROWN SISTERS *C&W '88*
(Andy & the Brown Sisters)
Singles: 7–inch

DOOR KNOB 3-4   89
KILLER 3-4   88-89

ANDREWS, Sheila *C&W '78*
Singles: 7–inch

OVATION 3-5   78-80

LP: 10/12–inch 33rpm

OVATION 5-8   79

ANDREWS, Sheila, & Joe Sun *C&W '80*
Singles: 7–inch

OVATION 3-5   80
Also see ANDREWS, Sheila
Also see SUN, Joe

ANDREWS SISTERS
P&R '38/C&W '44
Singles: 78rpm

CAPITOL 3-5   56
DECCA 5-10   38-57

Singles: 7–inch

ABC 3-4   74
CAPITOL 4-8   56
DECCA 5-10   50-57
DOT 3-5   64
KAPP 3-6   59
PARAMOUNT 3-4   73-74

Picture Sleeves

DECCA 5-10   57

EPs: 7–inch 33/45rpm

DECCA 5-15   51-58

LPs: 10/12–inch 33rpm

ABC 5-10   74
CAPITOL 5-10   64
DECCA (4000 series) 8-12   67
   (Decca LP numbers in this series preceded
   by a "7" or a "DL-7" are stereo issues.)
DECCA (5000 series) 20-40   49-54
   (10–inch LPs.)
DECCA (8000 series) 15-25   55-58
DOT 6-12   61-67
HAMILTON 5-10   64-65
MCA 8-12   73
PARAMOUNT 5-10   73-74

Members: Patty Andrews; Maxene Andrews; Laverne
Andrews.
Also see ANDREWS, Patty
Also see CROSBY, Bing
Also see FOLEY, Red, & Andrews Sisters
Also see PAUL, Les

ANDREWS SISTERS & Ernest Tubb *C&W '49*
(With the Texas Troubadors)
Singles: 78rpm

DECCA 5-8   49
Also see ANDREWS SISTERS
Also see TUBB, Ernest

ANGELLE, Lisa   *C&W '85*
Singles: 7–inch
EMI 3-4   85

ANITA & So-And-So's   *P&R '62*
(Anita Kerr Singers)
Singles: 7–inch
RCA... 5-8   62
  Also see KERR, Anita

ANTHONY, Rayburn   *C&W '76*
(Ray B. Anthony)
Singles: 7–inch
MEGA.. 4-6   71
MERCURY 3-5   79
POLYDOR....................................... 3-5   76-78
SUN.. 15-25   59-62
  Member: Brad Suggs.

ANTHONY, Rayburn, & Kitty
Wells   *C&W '79*
Singles: 7–inch
MERCURY 3-5   79
  Also see ANTHONY, Rayburn
  Also see WELLS, Kitty

ANTHONY, Vince   *C&W '82*
(With the Country Blue Notes)
Singles: 7–inch
HILTON (0007 "Too Hot to
  Handle") 30-50
MIDNIGHT GOLD 3-4   82
VIKING (1018 "All Over
  Again")..................................... 15-25   60s

ANTON, Susan
Singles: 7–inch
COLUMBIA 3-5   78
SCOTTI BROTHERS................... 3-4   80
Picture Sleeves
COLUMBIA 4-6   78
  Also see KNOBLOCK, Fred, & Susan Anton

ARATA, Tony   *C&W '84*
Singles: 7–inch
NOBLE VISION............................ 3-4   84-85

ARGO, Judy   *C&W '79*
Singles: 7–inch
ASI 3-5   79
MDJ... 3-4   79

ARMSTRONG, Wayne   *C&W '80*
Singles: 7–inch
NSD 3-4   80

ARNOLD, Eddy   *C&W '45*
("The Tennessee Plowboy"; with His
Tennessee Plowboys)
Singles: 78rpm
BLUEBIRD (0527 "Each Minute Seems Like a
  Million Years")........................... 25-50   45
RCA (Except 1800 thru 3100
  series)...................................... 10-20   46-49
RCA (1800 thru 3100 series) 15-30   46-49
Singles: 7–inch
DIAMOND P (1009 "If the Whole World
  Stopped Lovin") 5-10   73
  (Promotional issue only.)
MGM 3-5   73-76
RCA (0001 thru 0476)................ 10-20   50-51
  (Black vinyl. Black & turquoise labels.)
RCA (0001 thru 0476)................ 25-50   50-51
  (Colored vinyl. Price for any in this series on
  colored vinyl.)
RCA (0100 thru 0700 series) 3-5   69-72
  (Orange labels.)
RCA (2000 series) 5-10   62
  (Compact 33 stereo single.)
RCA (3000 thru 6000 series) 10-20   50-57
RCA (7000 series) 5-12   57-62
RCA (8000 & 9000 series)............. 3-8   62-71
RCA (10000 thru 13000 series) 3-5   76-83
RCA GOLD STANDARD 3-8   59-70s
  (With "447" prefix.)
Picture Sleeves
RCA 8-15   56-66
EPs: 7–inch 33/45rpm
RCA (100 series) 10-12   61
  (With "LPC" prefix. Compact 33 Double.)
RCA (280 "Best Wishes") 10-20
  (Promotional issue only.)
RCA (200 thru 900 series) 10-15   52-56
  (With "EPA" prefix.)
RCA (1100 & 1200 series)......... 15-20   55-56
  (With "EPB" prefix.)
RCA (1400 & 1500 series)........... 8-12   57
  (With "EPA" prefix.)
RCA (3000 series) 20-40   52-54
  (With "EPB" prefix.)
RCA (4000 & 5000 series)........... 8-15   57-59
  (With "EPA" prefix.)
LPs: 10/12–inch 33rpm
CAMDEN (Except "ACL1
  series)...................................... 8-18   60-72
CAMDEN ("ACL1" series)............ 5-10   72-76
GREEN VALLEY...........................8-10   76
K-TEL.. 8-10   74
MGM 8-12   74-76

RCA (AHL1, ANL1, APL1, & AYL1
series) 5-10   73-81
RCA (CPL1 series)...................... 8-12   83
RCA (0051 "Greatest Hits")......... 8-12
(Mail order offer.)
RCA (168 "Welcome to My
World") 10-20   75
RCA (209 "Eddy Arnold").......... 15-20   66
(Promotional issue only.)
RCA (1100 thru 2200 series) 20-30   55-60
(Monaural. with "LPM" prefix.)
RCA (2300 thru 2900 series) 12-20   60-64
(Monaural. with "LPM" prefix.)
RCA (3000 series)...................... 45-55   52-54
(10–inch LPs. with "LPM" prefix.)
RCA (3000 series)...................... 8-12   64-68
(12–inch LPs. with "LPM" prefix.)
RCA (1900 thru 3400 series) 15-25   60-65
(Stereo. with "LSP" prefix. "LSP" numbers
below 1900 were reprocessed stereo issues
of '50s LPs. They were issued in the '60s
and are in the $10-$15 range.)
RCA (3500 thru 4800 series) 10-20   66-73
RCA (6000 series)...................... 8-12   70
RCA SPECIAL PRODUCTS (0051 "Eddy
Arnold") 8-12   73
RCA SPECIAL PRODUCTS (346 "Bissell
Presents Sound America")...... 10-15   71
SUNRISE 5-10   79
TIME-LIFE 5-10   81
Also see SOME of CHET'S FRIENDS
Also see PRESLEY, Elvis / Hank Snow / Eddy Arnold /
Jim Reeves

ARNOLD, Rick   *C&W '89*
Singles: 7–inch
LYNN... 3-4   89

ASHLEY, Leon   *C&W '67*
Singles: 7–inch
ASHLEY 4-6   67-69
DOT... 5-8   64
IMPERIAL 6-10   61
LP: 10/12–inch 33rpm
ASHLEY 8-15   69-70
PICKWICK/HILLTOP 10-15   68
RCA.. 10-20   67

ASHLEY, Leon, & Margie
Singleton   *C&W '67*
Singles: 7–inch
ASHLEY 4-6   67-68
LP: 10/12–inch 33rpm
ASHLEY 10-15   69

PICKWICK 5-10   70s
Also see ASHLEY, Leon
Also see SINGLETON, Margie

ASHWORTH, Ernest   *C&W '60*
(Ernie Ashworth)
Singles: 7–inch
DECCA 4-8   60-61
HICKORY....................................... 3-6   62-70
O'BRIEN 3-6
LP: 10/12–inch 33rpm
HICKORY.................................... 10-20   64-68
SEA SHELL 5-8   82
STARDAY 10-20   76

ASLEEP at the Wheel   *C&W '74*
Singles: 7–inch
ARISTA.. 3-4   90-91
CAPITOL.. 3-4   75-79
EPIC (06671 thru 08087)............... 3-4   87-88
EPIC (50000 series)...................... 4-6   74
LPs: 10/12–inch 33rpm
CAPITOL..................................... 10-15   75-79
EPIC (BG-33000 series) 15-25   75
EPIC (EG-33000 series) 10-15
EPIC (KE-33000 series)............. 10-15   74
EPIC (PE-33000 series).............. 5-10
MCA.. 5-10   80-84
U.A.. 15-25   73
Members: Ray Benson; Chris O'Connell; Danny Levin;
Reuben Gosfield. Session: Texas Playboys.
Also see BENSON, Ray
Also see TEXAS PLAYBOYS

ATCHER, Bob   *C&W '46*
(With Bonnie Blue Eyes)
Singles: 78rpm
COLUMBIA 5-10   46-49
TIFFANY 5-10
VOCALION 8-12
EPs: 7–inch 33/45rpm
COLUMBIA 10-20   50s
LP: 10/12–inch 33rpm
COLUMBIA (9006 "Early American Folk
Songs") 30-50   50s
(10–inch LP.)
COLUMBIA (9013 "Songs of the
Saddle") 30-50   50s
(10–inch LP.)
COLUMBIA (2232 "Dean of Cowboy
Singers") 20-30   64
(Monaural.)

COLUMBIA (9032 "Dean of Cowboy
Singers") 15-25   64
(Stereo.)

HARMONY (7313 "Early American Folk
Songs") 15-20   64

ATKINS, Big Ben   *C&W '78*
Singles: 7–inch

GRT................................. 3-6   78

ATKINS, Chet   *C&W '55*
Singles: 78rpm

BLUEBIRD (0072 "I Know When I'm
Blue")..................................... 10-20   50

BULLET (617 "Guitar Blues").. 50-100   46

RCA.. 5-15   47-57

Singles: 7–inch

RCA (0100 thru 0400 series) 12-25   50-51
(Black or turquoise labels.)

RCA (0100 thru 0700 series) 3-5   71-74
(Orange labels.)

RCA (4000 & 5000 series) 10-20   51-55

RCA (6000 & 7000 series) 5-15   55-62

RCA (8000 & 9000 series) 3-8   62-71

RCA (10000 thru 13000 series) 3-5   75-83

Picture Sleeves

RCA.. 5-10   61-67

EPs: 7–inch 33/45rpm

RCA (100 series)......................... 8-12   61
(With "LPC" prefix. Compact 33 Double.)

RCA (500 thru 900 series) 8-15   55-56
(With "EPA" prefix.)

RCA (1100 & 1200 series) 10-20   55-56
(With "EPB" prefix.)

RCA (1300 thru 1500 series) 8-15   56-57
(With "EPA" prefix.)

RCA (3000 series)..................... 15-25   52-54
(With "EPB" prefix.)

RCA (4000 & 5000 series) 5-10   58-60

SESAC (13 "Mr. Atkins, If You
Please")................................... 20-30   59
(Promotional issue only.)

LPs: 10/12–inch 33rpm

CAMDEN...................................... 8-12   61-72

CANDLELITE............................ 10-15

COLUMBIA 5-10   83-85

DOLTON 15-20   67

PICKWICK/CAMDEN.................. 8-10   75

RCA (AHL1, ANL1, APL1, & AYL1
series) 5-10   73-83

RCA (CPL1 series)..................... 8-12   ·77

RCA (1000 series)..................... 25-35   54
(With "LPM" prefix.)

RCA (1100 thru 2200 series, except
1236)...............................15-25   55-60
(With "LPM" prefix.)

RCA (1236 "Stringin' Along with Chet
Atkins").....................................30-40   55
(With "LPM" prefix.)

RCA (2300 thru 2900 series) 10-15   60-64
(With "LPM" prefix.)

RCA (3000 series) 45-55   53
(10–inch LPs. With "LPM" prefix.)

RCA (3000 series) 8-12   64-68
(12–inch LPs. With "LPM" prefix.)

RCA (2000 & 3000 series).........10-15   66-69
(With "LSC" prefix.)

RCA (1900 thru 3500 series) 10-20   60-66
(Stereo. With "LSP" prefix. LSP numbers
below 1900 were reprocessed stereo issues
of '50s LPs. They were issued in the '60s are
in the $10 to $15 range.)

RCA (3500 thru 4800 series) 8-15   68-73

RCA (6000 series) 8-12   70-72

SESAC......................................40-50

TIME-LIFE....................................5-10   81

Also see ATKINS STRING COMPANY
Also see CHARLES, Ray, George Jones, & Chet
Atkins
Also see COUNTRY ALL STARS
Also see COUNTRY HAMS
Also see GIBSON, Don
Also see KERR, Anita
Also see NASHVILLE ALL-STARS
Also see NELSON, Willie
Also see PRESLEY, Elvis
Also see PURE PRAIRIE LEAGUE
Also see REED, Jerry, & Chet Atkins
Also see SNOW, Hank, & Chet Atkins

ATKINS, Chet, & Boston Pops
LP: 10/12–inch 33rpm

RCA 10-20   66-69

ATKINS, Chet, Floyd Cramer & Danny Davis
Singles: 7–inch

RCA 3-5   77

LPs: 10/12–inch 33rpm

RCA 5-8   77

Also see DAVIS, Danny

ATKINS, Chet, Floyd Cramer & Boots Randolph
LPs: 10/12–inch 33rpm

PICKWICK 5-8   71

Also see CRAMER, Floyd
Also see RANDOLPH, Boots

ATKINS, Chet, & Mark Knopfler

LPs: 10/12–inch 33rpm

COLUMBIA 5-8   90
Also see KNOPFLER, Mark

ATKINS, Chet, & Les Paul

Singles: 7–inch

RCA.. 3-4   78

LPs: 10/12–inch 33rpm

RCA.. 5-10   76-80
Also see PAUL, Les

ATKINS, Chet / Faron Young

EPs: 7–inch 33/45rpm

SESAC (48 "No Greater
Love")...................................... 20-30   59
(Promotional issue only.)
Also see YOUNG, Faron

ATKINS, Chet, & Doc Watson

LP: 10/12–inch 33rpm

RCA.. 5-10   80
Also see WATSON, Doc
Also see ATKINS, Chet

ATKINS STRING COMPANY
    C&W '75

Singles: 7–inch

RCA.. 3-4   75

LP: 10/12–inch 33rpm

RCA.. 5-10   75
Members: Chet Atkins; Johnny Gimble; Paul Yandell;
Lisa Silver.
Also see ATKINS, Chet

ATLANTA
    C&W '83

Singles: 7–inch

MCA 3-4   84-85
MDJ.. 3-5   83
SOUTHERN TRACKS 3-4   87-88

Picture Sleeves

MDJ.. 3-4   83

LPs: 10/12–inch 33rpm

MCA 5-10   84
Members: Dick Stevens; Brad Griffis; Tony Ingram;
Allen David; John Holder; Jeff Baker; Al Collay; Bill
Packard.
Also see SPURZZ

ATLANTA JAMES
    C&W '74

(Mack Vickery)

Singles: 7–inch

MCA 3-5   74
Also see VICKERY, Mack

ATLANTA RHYTHM SECTION
    P&R/LP '74/C&W '79

Singles: 7–inch

COLUMBIA 3-4   81
DECCA 3-5   72
MCA 3-4   73
POLYDOR 3-4   74-80

LPs: 10/12–inch 33rpm

COLUMBIA 5-10   81
DECCA 12-20   72
MCA 5-10   77
MFSL (038 "Champagne
Jam")................................... 25-50   79
POLYDOR 5-10   74-80
Members: Ronnie Hammond; Rodney Justo; Robert
Nix; Barry Bailey; James Cobb; Dean Daughtry; Paul
Goddard.

ATLANTA RHYTHM SECTION / Barry Manilow

Singles: 7–inch

WHAT'S IT ALL ABOUT 3-5   79

AUSTIN, Bobby
    C&W '66

Singles: 7–inch

ATLANTIC.................................... 3-5   72-73
CAPITOL...................................... 3-6   67-69
CHALLENGE 10-15   59
TALLY 4-8   66

LP: 10/12–inch 33rpm

CAPITOL................................. 15-20   67-68
DESIGN 8-12   60s
HURRAH..................................5-10
SYNDICATE 5-10
Also see STEWART, Wynn

AUSTIN, Chris
    C&W '88

Singles: 7–inch

W.B. 3-4   88-89
Also see McENTIRE, Reba

AUSTIN, Darlene
    C&W '82

Singles: 7–inch

CBT.. 3-4   86
MAGI.. 3-4   87
MYRTLE 3-4   82-83

LP: 10/12–inch 33rpm

MUSIC MASTERS 6-12   80s

AUSTIN, Kay
    C&W '80

Singles: 7–inch

E.I.O. 3-4   80

AUTRY, Gene   *P&R '33/C&W '44*
(With the Cass County Boys & the Pinafores)
Singles: 78rpm

BRUNSWICK (12936 "There's an Empty Cot in the Bunkhouse Tonight")................ 100-200   30s
(Flip side, #12899, is credited to "Gene Autry & Jimmy Long.")
CHAMPION (16096 "Cowboy Yodel").................................. 100-150   30s
CHAMPION (16119 "Texas Blues")................................. 100-150   30s
CHAMPION (16141 "In the Jailhouse Now, No. 2") 100-150   30s
CHAMPION (16210 "Mean Mama Blues").................................. 100-150   30s
CHAMPION (16228 "Pistol Packin' Mama")................................. 100-150   30s
CHAMPION (16245 "Blue Days") 100-150   30s
CHAMPION (16275 "T.B. Blues").................................. 100-150   30s
CLARION (5025 "Hobo Yodel")..................................... 75-125   30s
CLARION (5026 "No One to Call Me Darling") 75-125   30s
CLARION (5058 "I'll Be Thinking of You Little Girl") 75-125   30s
CLARION (5075 "Cowboy Yodel").................................... 75-125   30s
CLARION (5154 "Dust Pan Blues").................................. 75-125   30s
CLARION (5155 "Waiting for a Train") 75-125   30s
CLARION (5239 "Left My Gal in the Mountains") 75-125   30s
CLARION (5240 "Daddy and Home")..................................... 75-125   30s
CLARION (5243 "Lullaby Yodel")...................................... 75-125   30s
CLARION (5272 "True Blue Bill")... 75-125   30s
CLARION (5308 "A Gangster's Warning") 75-125   30s
CONQUEROR 30-90   30s
COLUMBIA 5-15   45-56
DECCA (5426 "Blue Days") 50-100   30s
DECCA (5464 "In the Shadow of the Pine")...................................... 50-100   30s
DECCA (5488 "Bear Cat Papa Blues")................................... 50-100   30s
DECCA (5501 "My Carolina Sunshine Girl").. 50-100   30s
DECCA (5426 "Blue Days").....50-100   30s
DECCA (5517 "T.B. Blues").....50-100   30s
DECCA (5527 "Yodeling Hobo")..................................50-100   30s
DECCA (5544 "Pistol Packin' Mama") 50-100   30s
DIVA (6030 "Hobo Yodel").......50-100   30s
DIVA (6031 "Waiting for a Train")..................................50-100   30s
DIVA (6032 "Blue Yodel No. 4")....................................50-100   30s
DIVA (6033 "Lullaby Yodel") 50-100   30s
DIVA (6035 "No One to Call Me Darling") 50-100   30s
DIVA (6037 "Frankie and Johnny")..................................50-100   30s
DIVA (6049 "My Rough and Rowdy Ways") 50-100   30s
DIVA (6057 "Cowboy Yodel") ..50-100   30s
HARMONY (1046 "Blue Yodel No. 5").....................................25-50   49
MONTGOMERY WARD (4242 "Bear Cat Papa Blues") 100-200   30s
MONTGOMERY WARD (4243 "My Carolina Sunshine Girl")....................100-200   30s
MONTGOMERY WARD (4243 "Don't Do Me That Way")...........................100-200   30s
MONTGOMERY WARD (4244 "High-Steppin' Mama Blues") 100-200   30s
MONTGOMERY WARD (4245 "Rheumatism Blues") 100-200   30s
MONTGOMERY WARD (4275 "Wildcat Mama") 150-250   30s
MONTGOMERY WARD (4326 "That Ramshackle Shack")............100-200   30s
MONTGOMERY WARD (4333 "I'm Always Dreaming of You") 100-200   30s
MONTGOMERY WARD (4767 "Old Woman and the Cow") 200-300   30s
MONTGOMERY WARD (4767 "Left My Gal in the Mountains")....................100-200   30s
MONTGOMERY WARD (4768 "She Wouldn't Do It")...................................100-200   30s
MONTGOMERY WARD (4768 "She's a Low Down Mama") 150-250   30s
MONTGOMERY WARD (4931 "Pictures of My Mother") 100-200   30s
MONTGOMERY WARD (4932 "Yodeling Hobo")..................................100-200   30s
MONTGOMERY WARD (4933 "In the Shadow of the Pine") 100-200   30s
MONTGOMERY WARD (4975 "In the Jailhouse Now, No. 2") 100-200   30s

MONTGOMERY WARD (4975 "T.B. Blues")................................. 150-250 30s

MONTGOMERY WARD (4976 "True Blue Bill")..................................... 100-200 30s

MONTGOMERY WARD (4977 "Jailhouse Blues").................................. 100-200 30s

MONTGOMERY WARD (4977 "Pistol Packin' Mama")................................... 100-200 30s

MONTGOMERY WARD (4978 "Whisper Your Mother's Name") 150-250 30s

MONTGOMERY WARD (4978 "My Carolina Sunshine Girl").................... 100-200 30s

MONTGOMERY WARD (8016 "Money Ain't No Use Anyway")................ 100-200 30s

MONTGOMERY WARD (8017 "Cowboy Yodel")...................................... 100-200 30s

MONTGOMERY WARD (8017 "Yodeling Hobo")...................................... 100-200 30s

MONTGOMERY WARD (8034 "Train Whistle Blues")................................. 150-250 30s

MONTGOMERY WARD (8034 "Texas Blues")................................. 150-250 30s

Note: Some Montgomery Ward numbers appear to have been used twice, with different titles, and often slightly different pricing. Since this information came from the same source, we are assuming it to be accurate until proven otherwise.)

OKEH.................................... 10-20 40-45

PERFECT 30-60

QRS (1044 "Living in the Mountains")..................... 3500-4500 29

ROMEO (5109 "Silver Haired Daddy of Mine")................................. 300-500 32

ROMEO (5110 "Jailhouse Blues").................................. 300-500 32

VELVET TONE (2338 "True Bill Bill")....................................... 50-100 30s

VELVET TONE (2374 "A Gangster's Warning") 50-100 30s

VELVET TONE (7056 "Hobo Yodel")................................... 50-100 30s

VELVET TONE (7057 "Waiting for a Train") 50-100 30s

VELVET TONE (7058 "Blue Yodel No. 4") 50-100 30s

VELVET TONE (7059 "Lullaby Yodel")................................... 50-100 30s

VELVET TONE (7061 "No One to Call Me Darling") 50-100 30s

VELVET TONE (7063 "Frankie and Johnny")................................ 50-100 30s

VELVET TONE (7075 "My Rough and Rowdy Ways")................................. 50-100 30s

VELVET TONE (7083 "Cowboy Yodel") 50-100 30s

VOCALION 25-50 35-40

Singles: 7–inch

COLUMBIA (06189 "Statue in the Bay") 3-4 86

COLUMBIA (20700 thru 21500 series)..........................5-10 50-56

COLUMBIA (38700 thru 40500 series) 5-10 50-55

COLUMBIA (44000 series) 3-5 68

MISTLETOE.................................3-5 74

REPUBLIC....................................3-8 59-76

Picture Sleeves

COLUMBIA HALL of FAME (33165 "Rudolph the Red-Nosed Reindeer").........4-6 69

REPUBLIC (2002 "Santa's Comin' in a Whirlybird")..............................5-10 59

EPs: 7–inch 33/45rpm

COLUMBIA 40-50 51-56

LPs: 10/12–inch 33rpm

BIRCHMOUNT.............................8-12

BULLDOG....................................5-10

CHALLENGE 25-30 58

COLUMBIA (55 thru 154).........80-100 51-55 (10–inch LPs.)

COLUMBIA (600 series)..........80-100 55

COLUMBIA (1000 series) 8-10 70-82

COLUMBIA (1500 series) 10-20 61

COLUMBIA (2500 series) ....75-100 56 (10–inch LPs.)

COLUMBIA (6020 "Gene Autry Western Classics")...................................40-60 49 (10–inch LP.)

COLUMBIA (6137 "Merry Christmas") ....40-60 50 (10–inch LP.)

COLUMBIA (8000 series) 80-100

COLUMBIA (9001 "Western Classics")...................................40-60 51 (10–inch LP.)

COLUMBIA (9002 "Western Classics, Vol. 2").................................40-60 51 (10–inch LP.)

COLUMBIA (15000 series) 8-10 81

COLUMBIA (37000 series) 5-10 82

DESIGN 8-10

ENCORE......................................6-10 80

GRT 10-15 77

GOLDEN AGE 5-10 77

GRAND PRIX..............................8-10

HALLMARK.................................8-12

HARMONY (7100 thru 7300 series)	20-30	56-65
HARMONY (9500 series)	15-25	59-64
HARMONY (11000 series)	10-15	64-66
HURRAH	5-10	
INTERNATIONAL AWARD	5-10	
MELODY RANCH (101 "Melody Ranch")	30-50	65
MISTLETOE	8-12	74
MURRAY HILL (61072 "The Gene Autry Collection") (Four-LP set.)	45-55	83
MURRAY HILL (897296 "Melody Ranch Radio Show") (Four-LP set.)	45-55	80s
RCA (2600 series)	25-30	62
RADIOLA	5-10	75
REPUBLIC (1900 series)	5-10	
REPUBLIC (6000 series)	5-15	76-78
STARDAY	6-10	78
TIMELESS TREASURES	5-8	83

Sessions: Johnny Bond; Pat Buttram.
Also see BOND, Johnny
Also see CLAYTON, Bob
Also see CLAYTON and Breen
Also see DODDS, Johnny
Also see HANDY, John
Also see HATFIELD, Overton
Also see HILL, Sam
Also see JOHNSON, Gene
Also see LONG, Tom
Also see PARKER, Fess, & Buddy Ebsen / Gene Autry
Also see SMITH, Jimmy

AXTON, Hoyt   *C&W/P&R '74*

(With the Sherwood Singers)

Singles: 7–inch

A&M	3-5	73-76
BRIAR	4-8	61
CAPITOL	3-5	71-72
COLGEMS	3-6	67
COLUMBIA	3-5	69
ELEKTRA	3-4	81
HORIZON	4-6	62-63
JEREMIAH	3-4	79-83
MCA	3-4	77-78
20TH FOX	4-6	66
VEE JAY	4-6	64-65

Picture Sleeves

A&M	3-5	73-74

LPs: 10/12–inch 33rpm

A&M	5-10	73-77
ACCORD	5-10	82
ALLEGIANCE	5-10	84
BRYLEN	5-10	82

CAPITOL	8-10	71
COLUMBIA	8-10	69
EXODUS	10-15	66
HORIZON	15-20	62-63
JEREMIAH	8-10	79-82
LAKE SHORE	5-10	81
MCA	5-10	77-78
SURREY	15-18	65
VEE JAY	10-15	64-65
VEE JAY INT'L (Except 1000 series)	5-10	74-77
VEE JAY INT'L (1000 series)	10-12	74

Session: Linda Ronstadt; Tanya Tucker; Ronee Blakley.
Also see RONSTADT, Linda
Also see TUCKER, Tanya

AXTON, Hoyt, & Chambers Brothers

Singles: 7–inch

HORIZON	4-8	62

LPs: 10/12–inch 33rpm

HORIZON	15-20	63

Also see AXTON, Hoyt

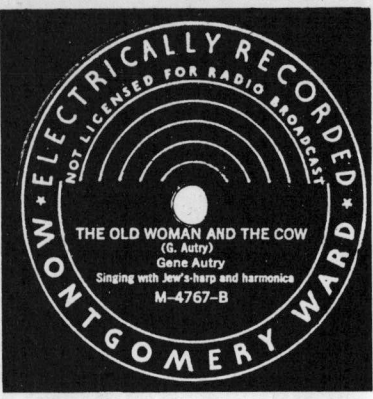

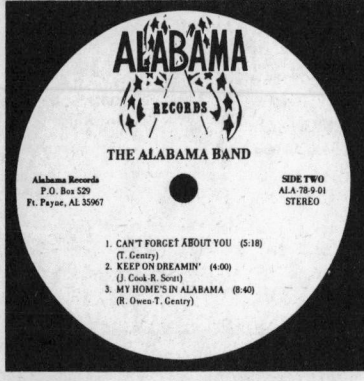

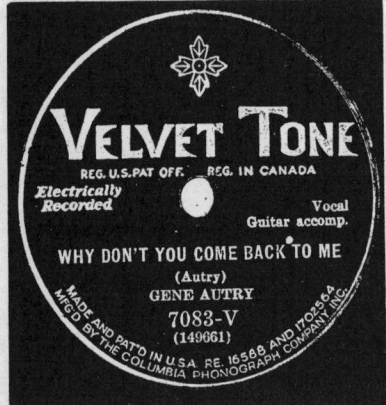

B

BACK PORCH MAJORITY
Singles: 7–inch

EPIC 4-8   64-67

LPs: 10/12–inch 33rpm

EPIC 10-20   65-67

Member: Michael Johnson.
Also see JOHNSON, Michael

BACKROADS   *C&W '83*
Singles: 7–inch

SOUNDWAVES 3-4   83

BACKTRACK   *C&W '85*
(Featuring John Hunt)
Singles: 7–inch

GOLDMINE 3-4   85

BADALE, Andy
Orchestra   *C&W '80*
Singles: 7–inch

GP 3-4   80

BAILES, Eddy   *C&W '76*
(With the Cadillacs with the Accents)
Singles: 7–inch

CIN KAY 3-5   76
RITE (1209 "If This Is Sin") 10-20

BAILEY, Glen   *C&W '82*
Singles: 7–inch

YATAHEY 3-4   82

BAILEY, Johnny   *C&W '83*
Singles: 7–inch

SOUNDWAVES 3-4   83

BAILEY, Judy   *C&W '81*
Singles: 7–inch

COLUMBIA 3-4   81
W.B. 3-4   83
WHITE GOLD 3-4   85
Also see BANDY, Moe, & Judy Bailey

BAILEY, Lynn   *C&W '80*
Singles: 7–inch

FRATERNITY................................. 3-5   75
WARTRACE................................... 3-4   80

BAILEY, Mary   *C&W '81*
Singles: 7–inch

E&R.. 3-4   81

BAILEY, Razzy   *P&R '74/C&W '76*
(Razzie Bailey; Razzy)
Singles: 7–inch

ABC-PAR 4-6   67
B&K 8-12   59
CAPRICORN 3-5   75
ERASTUS 3-5   76
MCA 3-4   84-86
MGM 3-5   74
1-3-4 3-5   69
PEACH... 5-10   66
RCA 3-4   77-84
SOUNDS of AMERICA 3-4   86-89

Picture Sleeves

RCA 3-4   80-81

LPs: 10/12–inch 33rpm

MCA 5-10   85-86
PLANTATION 5-8   81
RCA 5-10   79-84

BAILLIE & BOYS   *C&W '87*
Singles: 7–inch

RCA 3-4   87-91

LP: 10/12–inch 33rpm

RCA 5-8   87-90

Members: Kathie Baillie; Mike Bonagura; Alan
LeBoeuf.

BAKER, Adam   *C&W '85*
Singles: 7–inch

AVISTA... 3-4   86-87
SIGNATURE 3-4   85

BAKER, Butch   *C&W '84*
Singles: 7–inch

MERCURY..................................... 3-4   84-90

Also see ALEXANDER, Daniele, & Butch Baker
Also see TOMORROW'S WORLD

BAKER, Carroll   *C&W '81*
Singles: 7–inch

EXCELSIOR 3-4   81
GAIETY... 4-6   70
RCA 3-5   77
TEMBO 3-4   85

LP: 10/12–inch 33rpm

COLUMBIA 5-10
GAIETY... 10-20   70
RCA 5-10   77
TEE VEE....................................... 5-10   78

BAKER, George   *P&R/LP '70/C&W '76*
(George Baker Selection)
Singles: 7–inch
COLOSSUS	4-6	70
W.B.	3-5	75-76
Picture Sleeves
COLOSSUS	5-8	70
LPs: 10/12–inch 33rpm
COLOSSUS	15-20	70
W.B.	10-15	76

BALL, David   *C&W '88*
Singles: 7–inch
RCA	3-4	88-89

BALL, Marcia   *C&W '78*
Singles: 7–inch
CAPITOL	3-5	78
LP: 10/12–inch 33rpm
CAPITOL	5-8	78

BALLARD, Roger   *C&W '93*
Singles: 7–inch
ATLANTIC	3-4	93

BALLEW, Michael   *C&W '81*
Singles: 7–inch
LIBERTY	3-4	81-82

BAMA BAND   *C&W '82*
Singles: 7–inch
COMPLEAT	3-4	85-87
MERCURY	3-4	88-89
OASIS	3-5	82-83
SOUNDWAVES	3-4	83
LPs: 10/12–inch 33rpm
COMPLEAT	5-10	86

Members: Lamar Morris; Billy Earhart III.
  Also see AMAZING RHYTHM ACES
  Also see MORRIS, Lamar
  Also see WILLIAMS, Hank, Jr.

BANDANA   *C&W '82*
(BANDANNA)
Singles: 7–inch
HAVEN	3-5	76
PARAMOUNT	3-5	73
W.B.	3-4	81-86
LPs: 10/12–inch 33rpm
W.B.	5-10	86

BANDIT BAND   *C&W '87*
Singles: 7–inch
PEGASUS	3-4	87

BANDIT BROTHERS   *C&W '91*
Singles: 7–inch
CURB	3-4	91

BANDY, Charlie   *C&W '84*
Singles: 7–inch
RCI	3-4	84

BANDY, Moe   *C&W '74*
(With Janie Fricke)
Singles: 7–inch
COLUMBIA	3-5	75-85
CURB	3-4	88-89
FOOTPRINT	5-10	74
GRC	3-5	74-75
MCA/CURB	3-4	86-87
LP: 10/12–inch 33rpm
COLUMBIA	5-10	76-85
FANFARE	5-10	
GRC	10-15	74-75
MCA/CURB	5-8	86

Session: Janie Fricke; Jordanaires; Merle Haggard;
Bobby Wood; Johnny Gimble; Laverna Moore; Pig
Robbins; Terry McMillan.
  Also see FRICKE, Janie
  Also see HAGGARD, Merle
  Also see JORDANAIRES
  Also see ROBBINS, Hargus "Pig"

BANDY, Moe, & Becky Hobbs   *C&W '83*
Singles: 7–inch
COLUMBIA	3-4	83

Also see HOBBS, Becky

BANDY, Moe, & Joe Stampley   *C&W '79*
(Moe & Joe)
Singles: 7–inch
COLUMBIA	3-5	79-85
LP: 10/12–inch 33rpm
COLUMBIA	5-10	81-84

Also see BANDY, Moe
  Also see STAMPLEY, Joe

BANNON, R.C.   *C&W '77*
Singles: 7–inch
COLUMBIA	3-5	77-80
RCA	3-4	82

Also see MANDRELL, Louise, & R.C. Bannon

BARBER, Ava   *C&W '77*
Singles: 7–inch
OAK	3-5	81
RANWOOD	3-5	77-78
LP: 10/12–inch 33rpm
RANWOOD	5-10	77-78

BARBER, Debra   *C&W '75*
Singles: 7–inch
RCA.................................. 3-5   73-75
SOUNDS of MEMPHIS................. 3-5   73

BARBER, Glenn   *C&W '64*
Singles: 78rpm
STARDAY (Except 166 & 249) ... 5-10   54-56
STARDAY (166 "Ice Water")..... 10-20   54
STARDAY (249 "Shadow My
   Baby") 15-25   56
Singles: 7–inch
CENTURY 21................................. 3-5   78-79
GROOVY 3-5   77
HICKORY...................................... 3-6   68-74
MMI 3-5   79
SIMS 4-8   64
STARDAY (Except 166, 249 & 600
   series)................................... 8-12   54-56
STARDAY (166 "Ice Water")..... 25-50   54
STARDAY (249 "Shadow My
   Baby") 50-75   56
STARDAY (600 series")................ 4-8   64
SUNBIRD 3-4   80
LP: 10/12–inch 33rpm
BRYLEN.. 5-10   83-84
HICKORY...................................... 8-12   70-72
HICKORY/MGM........................... 5-10   74
TUDOR 5-10   83

BARE, Bobby   *C&W/P&R '62*
(With the All American Boys; with Hillsiders;
with Bobby Bare Jr; Bobby Bare & Family; with
Jeannie Bare)
Singles: 78rpm
CAPITOL..................................... 5-10   57
Singles: 7–inch
CAPITOL..................................... 10-15   57
COLUMBIA 3-5   78-85
EMI AMERICA 3-4   85-86
FRATERNITY................................ 8-15   58-61
MERCURY 3-5   70-72
RCA (Except 8000 & 9000
   series).. 3-5   69-77
RCA (8000 & 9000 series) 4-8   62-68
RICE.. 3-5   73-74
Picture Sleeves
RCA... 5-10   62-65
LPs: 10/12–inch 33rpm
CAMDEN..................................... 8-12   68-73
COLUMBIA 5-10   78-85
MERCURY 10-15   70-72

OVATION.............................5-10   80
PHONORAMA 5-8   82
PICKWICK 5-10   75-80
PICKWICK/HILLTOP 10-15   65
RCA (ANL1 & APL1 series).........8-12   73-77
RCA (AYL1 series).......................5-10   81
RCA (0079 "Singin' in the
   Kitchen") 15-25   74
   (Promotional issue only.)
RCA (LPM-2776 thru
   LPM-3994)................................10-20   63-68
   (Monaural.)
RCA (LSP-2776 thru
   LSP-3994)................................15-25   63-68
   (Stereo.)
RCA (4000 series) 10-15   69-71
   RCA (6000 series) 8-15   73
SEARS 10-15
SUN (136 "Bobby Bare's Greatest
   Hits").......................................15-25   74
U.A. 8-12   75-76

Session: Anita Kerr Singers; Floyd Cramer; Lacy J.
Dalton; Charlie Daniels; Waylon Jennings.
Also see BOWMAN, Don
Also see CASH, Rosanne, & Bobby Bare
Also see CRAMER, Floyd
Also see DALTON, Lacy J.
Also see DANIELS, Charlie
Also see JENNINGS, Waylon
Also see KERR, Anita
Also see ORBISON, Roy / Bobby Bare / Joey Powers
Also see PARSONS, Bill
Also see SOME of CHET'S FRIENDS
Also see TENNESSEE PULLYBONE

BARE, Bobby, Liz Anderson & Norma Jean   *C&W '66*
Singles: 7–inch
RCA 4-6   66
LPs: 10/12–inch 33rpm
BARE TRACKS...........................8-12
RCA 15-20   67

Also see ANDERSON, Liz
Also see NORMA JEAN

BARE, Bobby, & Skeeter Davis   *C&W '65*
(Skeeter Davis & Bobby Bare)
Singles: 7–inch
RCA (8000 & 9000 series).............3-6   65-70
LPs: 10/12–inch 33rpm
RCA 15-20   65-70

Also see DAVIS, Skeeter

BARE, Bobby, / Donna Fargo / Jerry Wallace
LPs: 10/12–inch 33rpm
OUT of TOWN DIST 5-10   82

Also see BARE, Bobby
Also see FARGO, Donna
Also see WALLACE, Jerry

BAREFOOT JERRY
Singles: 7–inch

CAPITOL	13-5	71
MONUMENT	3-5	74-77
W.B.	3-5	73

LP: 10/12–inch 33rpm

CAPITOL	10-15	71
MONUMENT	5-10	74-77
W.B.	8-12	73

Also see McCOY, Charlie

BARLOW, Jack   *C&W '68*
Singles: 7–inch

ANTIQUE	3-5	75
DIAL	4-8	65
DOT	3-6	68-73
GOLDEN RING	4-8	64
SOMA	4-8	62-64

LP: 10/12–inch 33rpm

ANTIQUE	5-10	75
DOT	8-12	69-70

Also see FENSTER, Zoot

BARLOW, Randy   *C&W '74*
Singles: 7–inch

CAPITOL	3-4	74
GAZELLE	3-5	76-83
JAMEX	3-5	
PAID	3-4	80-81
REPUBLIC	3-5	78-84
SOUL, COUNTRY & BLUES	3-6	75

LP: 10/12–inch 33rpm

GAZELLE	6-12	77
PAID	5-10	81
REPUBLIC	5-10	78-79

BARMBY, Shane   *C&W '89*
Singles: 7–inch

MERCURY	3-4	89

Also see TOMORROW'S WORLD

BARNES, Benny   *C&W '56*
Singles: 78rpm

STARDAY	10-20	56-57

Singles: 7–inch

D (1052 "Gold Records in the Snow")	25-50	59
HALL-WAY	4-8	64
MEGA	8-12	72
MERCURY	10-20	58-61
MUSICOR	4-6	65-66

PLAYBOY	4-8	77
STARDAY (200 series)	15-30	56-57
STARDAY (400 series)	10-20	58

LPs: 10/12–inch 33rpm

CRAZY CAJUN	5-10	

Also see JONES, George

BARNES, Kathy   *C&W '75*
(With Larry Barnes)
Singles: 7–inch

MGM	3-5	75
REPUBLIC	3-4	76-78

LPs: 10/12–inch 33rpm

REPUBLIC (Except 5002)	6-12	76-78
REPUBLIC (5002 "Kathy Barnes Sings Gene Autry")	10-20	78

BARNES, Max D.   *C&W '77*
Singles: 7–inch

OVATION	3-4	80-81
POLYDOR	3-5	77-78

LP: 10/12–inch 33rpm

OVATION	6-10	77-80

BARNETT, Bobby   *C&W '60*
Singles: 7–inch

CIN KAY	3-5	78
COLUMBIA	4-6	68-69
HERITAGE	3-5	74
K-ARK	4-6	67
PRESTA	4-6	60s
RAZORBACK	5-10	60
SIMS	4-8	64

LP: 10/12–inch 33rpm

COLUMBIA	8-15	68
HERITAGE	5-10	74
SIMS (118 "At the Crystal Palace")	15-25	64

BARNHILL, Joe   *C&W '89*
(Joe Bob Barnhill)
Singles: 7–inch

UNIVERSAL	3-4	89

LP: 10/12–inch 33rpm

RPA	5-10	

BARNHILL, Leslie   *C&W '78*
Singles: 7–inch

REPUBLIC	3-4	78-79

BASS, Sam D.   *C&W '80*
Singles: 7–inch

3J	3-5	80

Also see McAULIFFE, Leon

BAUER, Kathy   *C&W '83*
Singles: 7–inch
NSD.. 3-4   83

BAUGH, Phil   *C&W '65*
Singles: 7–inch
LONGHORN 4-6   65
LPs: 10/12–inch 33rpm
ERA.. 10-15   69
LONGHORN 20-30   65
TORO...................................... 10-15
  Also see NASHVILLE SUPERPICKERS

BAXTER, BAXTER & BAXTER   *C&W '81*
Singles: 7–inch
A.M.I.. 3-4   83
SUN... 3-5   81
  Members: Duncan Baxter; Mark Baxter; Rick Baxter.

BEAN, Jim   *C&W '88*
Singles: 7–inch
HUB.. 3-4   88

BEACH BUMS
Singles: 7–inch
ARE YOU KIDDING ME?.......... 20-30   66
  Member: Bob Seger.
  Also see SEGER, Bob

BEAR CREEK Featuring Leonda   *C&W '88*
Singles: 7–inch
BEAR CREEK 3-4   88

BEARDS   *C&W '88*
Singles: 7–inch
BEARDO 3-4   88
  Members: Randy Beard; Ron Beard.

BEATTY, Susi   *C&W '89*
Singles: 7–inch
STARWAY 3-4   89

BEAVERS, Clyde   *C&W '60*
Singles: 7–inch
DECCA... 5-10   60
HICKORY...................................... 4-6   66
TEMPWOOD................................. 4-8   63
LPs: 10/12–inch 33rpm
KASH COUNTRY........................ 5-10

BEAVERS, Clyde, & Red Sovine
LPs: 10/12–inch 33rpm
ALSHIRE..................................... 5-10
  Also see BEAVERS, Clyde
  Also see SOVINE, Red

BECKHAM, Bob   *P&R '59/C&W '67*
Singles: 7–inch
DECCA 4-8   59-63
MONUMENT.................................. 3-5   67
SMASH 3-6   65
Picture Sleeves
DECCA 5-10   59
LPs: 10/12–inch 33rpm
DECCA 15-20   59

BECKHAM, Charlie   *C&W '88*
Singles: 7–inch
OAK 3-4   88

BEE, Kathy   *C&W '88*
Singles: 7–inch
LILAC 3-4   88

BEE, Molly   *P&R '53/C&W '74*
Singles: 78rpm
CAPITOL...................................... 3-8   53-58
CORAL... 3-6   55
DOT 3-6   56
Singles: 7–inch
CAPITOL...................................... 5-10   53-58
CORAL... 5-10   55
DOT 5-10   56
GRANITE...................................... 3-5   74-75
LIBERTY....................................... 4-8   63-64
MGM 3-6   65-67
Picture Sleeves
MGM 5-10   65
EPs: 7–inch 33/45rpm
CAPITOL...................................... 5-10   58
LPs: 10/12–inch 33rpm
ACCORD 5-10   82
ALBUM GLOBE 5-10
CAPITOL.................................... 15-25   58
GRANITE...................................... 5-10   74
MGM 10-15   65-67

BEE GEES   *P&R/LP '67/C&W '78*
Singles: 7–inch
ATCO.. 4-10   67-72
ATLANTIC..................................... 3-5
RSO 3-5   73-84
W.B. 3-4   87-89
Picture Sleeves
RSO 3-5   83
W.B. 3-4   87-89

EPs: 7–inch 33/45rpm

ATCO (4523 Horizontal") 15-25   68
(Promotional issue only. Tracks are from *Horizontal*, though shown only as "Atco LP 33-233" on this label.)

ATCO (4535 Odessa") 10-20   69
(Promotional issue only.)

ATCO (37264 "Rare, Precious and Beautiful")................................ 8-15   69
(Promotional issue only.)

RSO (200 "Greatest Hits") 5-10   79
(Promotional issue only.)

LPs: 10/12–inch 33rpm

ATCO (Except TL-ST-142) 12-25 67-72

ATCO (TL-ST-142 "Odessa").... 30-50   69
(Promotional issue only.)

RSO (Except 1).......................... 5-10 73-84

RSO (1 "Words and Music")...... 40-60
(Promotional issue only.)

W.B. 5-10 87-89

Members: Barry Gibb; Maurice Gibb; Robin Gibb; Vince Melouney; Colin Petersen.

BEEFEATERS

Singles: 7–inch

ELEKTRA (45013 "Please Let Me Love You") 50-75   64

Members: David Crosby; Gene Clark; Jim McGuinn. Also see BYRDS

BELEW, Carl   *C&W '59*

Singles: 7–inch

BRUNSWICK 5-10   58

DECCA (Except 30947) 3-8 59-72

DECCA (30947 "Cool Gator Shoes") 20-30   59

4 STAR (1700 series)............... 10-20 58-59

MCA 3-5   74

RCA 4-8 62-68

EPs: 7–inch 33/45rpm

DECCA.. 8-12   60

LP: 10/12–inch 33rpm

BUCKBOARD 5-10

DECCA (4074 "Carl Belew") 20-25   60
(Monaural.)

DECCA (7-4074 "Carl Belew") .. 25-35   60
(Stereo.)

FORUM...................................... 5-10

PICKWICK/HILLTOP 10-20   65

PLANTATION............................. 5-10   81

RCA.. 10-20 64-68

VOCALION................................ 10-15 66-67

WRANGLER 15-25   62

BELEW, Carl, & Betty Jean Robinson   *C&W '71*

Singles: 7–inch

DECCA 3-5   71

LP: 10/12–inch 33rpm

DECCA 8-12   71

Also see BELEW, Carl
Also see ROBINSON, Betty Jean

BELL, Delia   *C&W '83*

Singles: 7–inch

W.B. 3-4   83

LP: 10/12–inch 33rpm

W.B. 5-8   83

BELL, James   *C&W '68*
(James Mullins)

Singles: 7–inch

BELL 4-8 67-68

BELL, Tommy   *C&W '82*

Singles: 7–inch

GOLD SOUND...............................3-4 82-83

ZIL (9001 "Swamp Gal") 50-75

BELL, Vivian   *C&W '77*

Singles: 7–inch

GRT 3-5   77

BELLAMY, David   *P&R '75*

Singles: 7–inch

W.B. 3-5   75

Also see BELLAMY BROTHERS

BELLAMY BROTHERS

   C&W/P&R/LP '76

Singles: 7–inch

CURB..3-4 84-87

CURB/MCA..................................3-4 88-89

ELEKTRA/CURB 3-4   82

MCA 3-4   87

W.B./CURB..................................3-4 76-83

LPs: 10/12–inch 33rpm

ELEKTRA....................................5-10   83

MCA/CURB..................................5-10 84-90

W.B. 8-10 76-83

Members: David Bellamy; Howard Bellamy. Also see BELLAMY, David

BELLAMY BROTHERS & Forester Sisters   *C&W '86*

Singles: 7–inch

CURB..3-4   86

W.B. 3-4   90

Also see BELLAMY BROTHERS
Also see FORESTER SISTERS

BENEDICT, Ernie, & His
Polkateers   *C&W '49*
(With the Kendall Sisters)
Singles: 78rpm

RCA.................................... 4-6   49

LP: 10/12–inch 33rpm
CONTINENTAL......................... 8-10

BENONI, Arne   *C&W '89*
Singles: 7–inch
ROUND ROBIN............................. 3-4   89

BENSON, Matt   *C&W '89*
Singles: 7–inch
STEP ONE.................................. 3-4   89

BENSON, Ray   *C&W '91*
Singles: 7–inch
ARISTA 3-4   91
Also see ASLEEP at the WHEEL

BENTON, Barbi   *C&W '75*
Singles: 7–inch
PLAYBOY 3-5   74-77
Picture Sleeves
PLAYBOY 4-8   74-76
LPs: 10/12–inch 33rpm
PLAYBOY 8-12   74-77
Also see GILLEY, Mickey, & Barbi Benton

BERG, Matraca   *C&W '90*
Singles: 7–inch
RCA... 3-4   90-91

BICKHARDT, Craig   *C&W '84*
Singles: 7–inch
LIBERTY 3-4   84
Also see SCHUYLER, KNOBLOCH & BICKHARDT

BILL & TAFFY
Singles: 7–inch
RCA... 3-6   74
LPs: 10/12–inch 33rpm
RCA... 10-12   73-74
Members: Bill Danoff; Taffy Danoff.
Also see FAT CITY
Also see STARLAND VOCAL BAND

BILLY & BEATERS   *LP '81*
Singles: 7–inch
ALFA 3-4   81
Picture Sleeves
ALFA 3-4   81
LPs: 10/12–inch 33rpm
ALFA 5-10   81
Member: Billy Vera.
Also see VERA, Bill

BILLY & CLIFF
Singles: 7–inch
CHALLENGE (59089 "The Gun, the Gold and
   the Girl")................................... 10-15   60
DORE (534 "Summer's End") 10-15   59
Member: Billy Mize.
Also see MIZE, Billy

BILLY HILL   *C&W '89*
Singles: 7–inch
REPRISE 3-4   89
Member: Dennis Robbins.
Also see ROBBINS, Dennis
Also see TOMORROW'S WORLD

BILLY the KID   *C&W '79*
Singles: 7–inch
CYCLONE....................................... 3-4   79

BIRD, Vicki   *C&W '87*
Singles: 7–inch
AVCO...3-5   74
16TH AVE. 3-4   87-89

BISHOP, Bob   *C&W '68*
(Bobby Bishop; Bobby Sykes)
Singles: 7–inch
ABC...3-5   68
GOLDISC.....................................5-10   61
MALA 5-10   60
WAYSIDE......................................4-8   67
LP: 10/12–inch 33rpm
ABC..8-10   68
Also see ROBBINS, Marty
Also see SYKES, Bobby

BISHOP, Joni   *C&W '87*
Singles: 7–inch
COLUMBIA 3-4   87

BISHOP, Terri   *C&W '78*
Singles: 7–inch
U.A. 3-5   78

BLACK, Bill   *P&R/R&B '59/C&W '75*
(Bill Black's Combo)
Singles: 7–inch
COLUMBIA 3-5   70
ECHO...3-5   72
GUSTO 3-4   83
HI (Except 2000 series) 3-6   67-78
HI (2000 series) 5-10   59-66
LONDON..3-4   84
MEGA 3-5   71-74
MOTOWN 3-4   83

Picture Sleeves

HI.. 5-10   60-62

EPs: 7–inch 33/45rpm

MEGA (192 "Jukebox
 Favorites")................................. 5-10   72
 (Jukebox issue.)

LPs: 10/12–inch 33rpm

COLUMBIA 8-10   69-70
51 WEST..................................... 5-10   84
HI (6000 & 8000 series) 5-10   77-78
HI (12001 thru 12005).............. 15-30   60-62
HI (12006 thru 12041).............. 10-20   62-68
HI (32000 thru 32010).............. 15-30   61-63
HI (32011 thru 32110).............. 10-20   63-77
MEGA.. 5-10   71-74
ZODIAC....................................... 5-10   77

Also see CANNON, Ace
Also see PRESLEY, Elvis

BLACK, Clint   *C&W/LP '89*
Singles: 7–inch

RCA.............................. 3-4   89-92

LPs: 10/12–inch 33rpm

RCA.............................. 5-8   89-90

Also see ROGERS, Roy, & Clint Black

BLACK, Jeanne   *C&W/P&R/R&B '60*
Singles: 7–inch

CAPITOL.......................... 4-8   60-62

LPs: 10/12–inch 33rpm

CAPITOL.......................... 15-20   60

BLACK TIE   *C&W '90*
Singles: 7–inch

BENCH............................. 3-4   90

LPs: 10/12–inch 33rpm

BENCH ("When the Night
 Falls")................................. 20-30   85
 (Selection number not known.)

Members: James Griffin; Billy Swan; Randy Meisner;
T-Bone Burnett; Robb Royer.
Also see SWAN, Billy

BLACKWELL, Karon   *C&W '77*
(Kay-Ron Blackwell)
Singles: 7–inch

BLACKLAND................................. 3-5   76-77

BLACKWOOD, R.W.   *C&W '76*
(With the Blackwood Singers)
Singles: 7–inch

CAPITOL.......................... 3-5   76
SCORPION 3-5   78

LP: 10/12–inch 33rpm

CAPITOL.......................... 5-10   76

BLAIR, Kenny   *C&W '88*
Singles: 7–inch

AWESOME 3-4   88

BLAKER, Clay, & Texas Honky-Tonk Band   *C&W '87*
(With the Texas Honkey-Tonk Band)
Singles: 7–inch

RAIN FOREST................... 3-4   88
TEXAS 3-4   87

BLANCH, Arthur   *C&W '78*
Singles: 7–inch

MC 3-5   78
RIDGETOP 3-5   79

BLANCH, Jewel   *C&W '78*
Singles: 7–inch

RCA 3-5   78-79

BLANCHARD, Jack, & Misty Morgan   *C&W '69*
Singles: 7–inch

EPIC................................. 3-4   73-75
MEGA 3-5   71-73
WAYSIDE 3-5   69-70

LPs: 10/12–inch 33rpm

MEGA 8-12   72
WAYSIDE 10-15   70

BLANTON, Loy   *C&W '85*
Singles: 7–inch

SOUNDWAVES.................. 3-4   85

BLIXSETH, Tim, & Kathy Walker   *C&W '85*
Singles: 7–inch

COMPLEAT 3-4   85

BLOCK, Doug   *C&W '84*
Singles: 7–inch

REVOLVER 3-4   84

Also see DOUGLAS

BLUE, Bobby   *C&W '86*
(Bobby & Blue Jays)
Singles: 7–inch

CANADIAN AMERICAN 5-10   63
HEARTBREAK.................... 5-10   64
HERALD 5-10   64
IMPERIAL 4-8   69-70
LOVE 8-12   59
MUSIC VOICE 5-10   64
NITE................................. 3-4   86

BLUE BOYS   *C&W '67*
Singles: 7–inch
RCA.................................. 5-10   65-68
LP: 10/12–inch 33rpm
RCA.................................. 15-25   65-68
Members: Bud Logan; Leo Jackson; Bunky Keels; Mel Rogers.
Also see LOGAN, Bud, & Wilma Burgess
Also see REEVES, Jim

BLUE RIDGE RANGERS
(John Fogerty)   *C&W/P&R '73*
Singles: 7–inch
FANTASY....................................... 3-5   72-73
LPs: 10/12–inch 33rpm
FANTASY.............................. 10-12   73
Also see FOGERTY, John

BLUESTONE   *C&W '80*
Singles: 7–inch
DIMENSION................................. 3-5   80
SCOTTI BROTHERS.................... 3-4   82
Members: Ray Pennington; Jerry McBee.
Also see PENNINGTON, Ray

BOARDO, Liz   *C&W '87*
Singles: 7–inch
MASTER 3-4   87

BOB & LUCILLE
Singles: 7–inch
DITTO (121 "Eeny Meeny Miney
  Moe")...................................... 50-75   62
DITTO (126 "What's the
  Password")............................... 50-75   62
KING (5631 "Eeny Meeny Miney
  Moe")...................................... 20-30   62
Member: Lucille Starr.
Also see CANADIAN SWEETHEARTS
Also see STARR, Lucille

BOCEPHUS
(Hank Williams Jr.)
Singles: 7–inch
VERVE (10540 "Meter Reader
  Maid")...................................... 20-30   67
Also see WILLIAMS, Hank, Jr.

BOGGUSS, Suzy   *C&W '87*
Singles: 7–inch
CAPITOL....................................... 3-4   87-91
LP: 10/12–inch 33rpm
CAPITOL....................................... 5-8   87-90
Also see TOMORROW'S WORLD

BOLT, Al   *C&W '76*
Singles: 7–inch
CIN KAY....................................... 3-5   76

BOND, Bobby   *C&W '72*
Singles: 7–inch
DANCELAND...............................5-10   61
HICKORY.......................................3-5   72
MGM 3-5   68
PARROT..4-8   66
WAND...4-8   65
W.B. 3-5   69
LP: 10/12–inch 33rpm
ALSHIRE.....................................8-10   69
SOMERSET/STEREO
  FIDELITY 10-20   60s
TIME 15-25   64

BOND, Johnny   *C&W '47*
(With the Red River Valley Boys)
Singles: 78rpm
COLUMBIA (Except 21521).........5-15   45-56
(Columbia 20545 through 20787 were also
  issued on 7–inch 33 singles, any of which
  may be in the $15 to $25 range.)
COLUMBIA (21521 "The Little Rock
  Roll") 8-12   56
Singles: 7–inch
COLUMBIA (Except 21521).......10-20   51-56
COLUMBIA (21521 "The Little Rock
  Roll") 30-45   56
CONQUEROR 10-25
DITTO..5-10   59
GILLETTE.....................................3-4
KING 3-4
LAMB & LION 3-5   74
LONDON.......................................3-5
MGM 3-5   73
OKEH 8-15   41-45
REPUBLIC (2000 series)..............5-10   60
SMASH 4-6   62
STARDAY (618 thru 951) 4-8   63-72
STARDAY (7021 thru 9292) 3-4   72-74
20TH FOX....................................4-8   60
EPs: 7–inch 33/45rpm
COLUMBIA 10-20   58
REPUBLIC..................................10-20   60
STARDAY 10-15   63
LPs: 10/12–inch 33rpm
CMH...5-10   77
CAPITOL.....................................8-12   69
CATTLE 15-20
DANNY 15-20
HARMONY..................................10-20   64-65
LAMB & LION 5-10   74

41

NASHVILLE 5-10   71
SHASTA.................................... 10-15
STARDAY (147 thru 298).......... 20-30   61-64
STARDAY (333 "Ten Little
   Bottles")................................. 15-20   65-66
STARDAY (354 "Famous Hot Rodders I Have
   Known")................................. 25-30   65
STARDAY (368 thru 472).......... 20-30   66-71
STARDAY (900 series) 6-10   74
   Also see AUTRY, Gene
   Also see HANK & FRANK
   Also see TRAVIS, Merle, & Johnny Bond

BOND, Johnny, & Lefty Frizzell
Singles: 78rpm
COLUMBIA 5-10   56-57
Singles: 7–inch
COLUMBIA 10-15   56-57
   Also see BOND, Johnny
   Also see FRIZZELL, Lefty

BONNERS   C&W '88
Singles: 7–inch
OL 3-4   88
   Members: James Bonner; Edith Bonner.

BONNIE & BUDDY   C&W '69
Singles: 7–inch
PARAMOUNT 3-5   69
   Members: Bonnie Guitar; Buddy Killen.
   Also see GUITAR, Bonnie

BONNIE LOU   C&W '53
(Bonnie Lou Kath)
Singles: 78rpm
KING 4-8   53-55
Singles: 7–inch
FRATERNITY.............................. 5-10   58
KING 5-10   53-55
TODD (1073 "Twenty-four Hours of
   Loneliness") 5-10   62
EPs: 7–inch 33/45rpm
KING 10-15   58
LP: 10/12–inch 33rpm
KING (595 "Bonnie Lou
   Sings").................................. 25-50   58
WRAYCO 5-10

BOOKER, Jay   C&W '87
Singles: 7–inch
EMI.. 3-4   87

BOONE, Debby   P&R/C&W/LP '77
Singles: 7–inch
LAMB & LION................................ 3-4   80-84
W.B./CURB 3-4   77-81

Picture Sleeves
W.B./CURB...................................3-4   78
LPs: 10/12–inch 33rpm
LAMB & LION 5-10   80-84
W.B./CURB.................................5-10   77-80
   Also see BOONE, Pat, & Boone Girls

BOONE, Larry   C&W '86
Singles: 7–inch
MERCURY....................................3-4   86-91

BOONE, Pat   P&R/R&B '55/C&W '75
Singles: 78rpm
DOT 10-20   55-58
REPUBLIC 5-10   54
Singles: 7–inch
ABC...3-4   74-75
BUENA VISTA 3-5   73
CAPITOL......................................3-5   70
CHEVROLET/RCA (4988 "June Is Bustin' Out
   All Over")...............................10-15   58
   (Promotional issue for Chevrolet dealers.
   Narration by Bob Lund.)
DOT (200 series) 8-12   59-60
   (Stereo.)
DOT (15000 series) 5-10   55-57
   (Maroon label.)
DOT (15000 & 16000 series, except
   16658)....................................4-8   57-66
   (Black label.)
DOT (16658 "Beach Girl")............5-10   64
   (With Bruce Johnston and Terry Melcher.)
DOT (17000 series) 3-6   66-75
HITSVILLE....................................3-5   76-77
LION...3-4   72
MC 3-4   77
MCA..3-4   84
MGM...3-5   71-73
MELODYLAND 3-5   74-76
ORCHID..3-4   89
REPUBLIC 10-15   54
SRG 3-4   88
TETRAGRAMMATON 3-5   69
W.B. 3-4   80-81
Picture Sleeves
DOT 8-15   57-62
EPs: 7–inch 33/45rpm
DOT 8-12   57-60
LPs: 10/12–inch 33rpm
ABC...5-10   74
BIBLE VOICE..............................5-10   70
CANDLELITE...............................6-10
   (Mail-order offer.)

DOT (3000 series)..................... 20-35   55-56
  (Maroon label.)

DOT (3000 series, except
  3501).. 10-20   57-67
  (Black label. Monaural series.)

DOT (3501 "Pat Boone Sings Guess
  Who") 25-35   63

DOT (9000 "April Love")............ 30-40   57
  (Soundtrack.)

DOT (25000 series, except 25270 &
  25501)...................................... 10-20   58-68
  (Stereo series.)

DOT (25270 "Moonglow") 10-20   60
  (Black vinyl.)

DOT (25270 "Moonglow") 30-50   60
  (Colored vinyl.)

DOT (25501 "Pat Boone Sings Guess
  Who") 25-40   63

FAMOUS TWINSET..................... 5-8   74

HAMILTON............................... 10-12   65

HITSVILLE 8-10   76

LAMB & LION............................ 5-10   73-81

MC.. 5-10   77

MCA 5-10   82

MGM 5-10   73

PARAMOUNT 5-10   74

PICKWICK ,................................. 5-10   79

SUPREME 6-10   70

TETRAGRAMMATON.............. 10-12   69

WORD... 5-10   75-84
  Also see HUSKY, Ferlin / Pat Boone

BOONE, Pat & Shirley
(Pat Boone Family)
Singles: 7–inch

DOT... 4-6   62-64

MGM 3-5   72

MELODYLAND 3-5   75

MOTOWN 3-5   74

W.B. 3-4   79

EPs: 7–inch 33/45rpm

DOT... 5-10   59

LPs: 10/12–inch 33rpm

DOT... 10-20   62

LION... 5-10   72

WORD.. 5-10   71

BOONE, Pat, & Boone Girls
Singles: 7–inch

LION.. 3-4   72
  Also see BOONE, Pat & Shirley

BOOTH, Larry   *C&W '78*
Singles: 7–inch

CREAM 3-5   78

BOOTH, Tony   *C&W '70*
Singles: 7–inch

CAPITOL.................................... 3-5   71-75

MGM 3-5   70

U.A. 3-5   77

LP: 10/12–inch 33rpm

CAPITOL.................................. 10-20   72-74

MGM 10-20   70
  Also see WATSON, Gene

BORCHERS, Bobby   *C&W '76*
Singles: 7–inch

EPIC.. 3-5   78-79

LONGHORN 3-4   87

PLAYBOY 3-5   76-78

LP: 10/12–inch 33rpm

PLAYBOY 8-12   77

BOTTOMS, Dennis   *C&W '85*
Singles: 7–inch

W.B. 3-4   85

BOWES, Margie   *C&W '59*
Singles: 7–inch

DECCA 4-6   63-64

HICKORY.................................... 5-10   59-60

MERCURY................................... 4-8   61-63

LP: 10/12–inch 33rpm

DECCA 15-25   67-69

BOWLING, Roger   *C&W '78*
Singles: 7–inch

LOUISIANA HAYRIDE.................. 3-5   78

MERCURY................................... 3-4   81

NSD 3-4   80

BOWMAN, Billy Bob, with Bearmont Bag & Burlap Company   *C&W '72*
(Biff Collie)
Singles: 7–inch

U.A. 3-5   72

BOWMAN, Don   *C&W '64*
(With "Friends")
Singles: 7–inch

LAGREE 3-5   70s

RCA 4-8   64-69

LP: 10/12–inch 33rpm

LONE STAR................................. 5-10   79

MEGA	6-12	72
RCA	10-20	64-70

Session: Waylon Jennings; Bobby Bare; Willie Nelson.
Also see BARE, Bobby
Also see DAVIS, Skeeter, & Don Bowman
Also see JENNINGS, Waylon
Also see NELSON, Willie
Also see SOME of CHET'S FRIENDS

BOWSER, Donnie   *C&W '89*
(Donnie Bowshier)
Singles: 7–inch

BAMBOO	5-10	61
CHOICE	4-8	
ERA	5-10	60
J.D.	5-10	
RIDGEWOOD	3-4	89
ROME	4-8	
SAGE	10-20	58

Also see BOWSHIER, Little Donnie, & Radio Ranch Boys

BOWSHIER, Little Donnie, & Radio Ranch Boys
Singles: 7–inch

DESS (7002 "Rock & Roll Joys")	150-200	57
DESS (7004 "I Love You Baby")	10-20	57
FRATERNITY (801 "I Love You Baby")	40-60	58
ROBBINS (1001 "I Love You Baby")	75-125	58

Also see BOWSER, Donnie

BOXCAR WILLIE   *C&W '80*
(Lecil T. Martin)
Singles: 7–inch

COLUMN ONE	3-5	80
MAIN STREET	3-4	81-84

LP: 10/12–inch 33rpm

AMERICAN HERITAGE	8-12	70
COLUMN ONE	6-12	76-80
MAIN STREET	5-10	82-84
STAR FLEET	10-15	81
SUFFOLK MARKETING	5-10	80-83

BOY HOWDY   *C&W '92*
Singles: 7–inch

CURB	3-4	92

BOYD, Bill, & Cowboy Ramblers   *C&W '45*
(With Jim Boyd)
Singles: 78rpm

BLUEBIRD	10-15	34-45

RCA	5-10	46

Singles: 7–inch

RCA GOLD STANDARD	5-10	50s

LP: 10/12–inch 33rpm

BLUEBIRD	20-30	
TEXAS ROSE	10-20	

BOYD, Jimmy   *P&R/C&W '52*
(Little Jimmy Boyd)
Singles: 78rpm

COLUMBIA (Except 21571)	4-8	52-56
COLUMBIA (21571 "Rockin' Down the Mississippi")	10-15	56

Singles: 7–inch

CAPITOL	4-8	63
COLUMBIA (152 "I Saw Mommy Kissing Santa Claus")	10-20	52
COLUMBIA (21571 "Rockin' Down the Mississippi")	30-40	56
COLUMBIA (39000 & 40000 series)	10-20	52-56
IMPERIAL	3-6	66-67
MGM (12788 "Cream Puff")	40-50	59
TAKE TEN	4-8	63
VEE JAY	4-8	65

Picture Sleeves

COLUMBIA (152 "I Saw Mommy Kissing Santa Claus")	15-25	52
(With die-cut center hole.)		

EPs: 7–inch 33/45rpm

COLUMBIA (1913 "Jimmy Boyd")	10-15	50s

Also see LAINE, Frankie, & Jimmy Boyd

BOYD, Jimmy, & Rosemary Clooney   *P&R '53*
Singles: 78rpm

COLUMBIA	4-8	53

Singles: 7–inch

COLUMBIA (39000 series)	8-12	53
COLUMBIA (41000 series)	4-8	60

Also see BOYD, Jimmy

BOYD, Mike   *C&W '76*
Singles: 7–inch

BLAST-OFF	3-6	69
CLARIDGE	3-5	76
INERGI	3-5	78
MBI	3-5	77

BOYER TWINS   *C&W '80*
Singles: 7–inch

GUSTO	3-4	78
SABRE	3-4	80-81

Members: Gene Boyer; Dean Boyer.

BRADDOCK, Bobby *C&W '67*
Singles: 7–inch
ELEKTRA..................................... 3-5　79-80
MGM .... 4-6　67-69
LP: 10/12–inch 33rpm
ELEKTRA.................................... 6-12　79-80
RCA.. 5-10　83-84
Also see ROBBINS, Marty

BRADFORD, Keith *C&W '78*
Singles: 7–inch
MU-SOUND .... 3-5　78
SCORPION.................................. 3-5　79

BRADING, Susie *C&W '84*
Singles: 7–inch
RIDDLE....................................... 3-4　84

BRADLEY, Owen *C&W/P&R '49*
(Owen Bradley Quintet)
Singles: 78rpm
CORAL.. 4-8　49-50
DECCA....................................... 5-10　54-57
Singles: 7–inch
CORAL.. 5-10　50
DECCA....................................... 5-15　54-61
EPs: 7–inch 33/45rpm
CORAL.. 10-20　54
DECCA....................................... 10-20　58
LPs: 10/12–inch 33rpm
CORAL.. 20-30　53-55
DECCA....................................... 15-25　58-60
VOCALION.................................. 5-15　60s

BRADSHAW, Carolyn *C&W '53*
Singles: 78rpm
ABBOTT...................................... 4-8　53
Singles: 7–inch
ABBOTT...................................... 5-10　53

BRADSHAW, Terry *C&W/P&R '76*
Singles: 7–inch
BENSON .... 3-4　80
MERCURY .... 3-5　76
Picture Sleeves
BENSON .... 3-4　80
LPs: 10/12–inch 33rpm
BENSON .... 5-10　80
HEARTWARMING .... 5-10　82
MERCURY .... 6-12　76

BRANDON, T.C. *C&W '89*
Singles: 7–inch
BEAR .... 3-4　89

BRANÉ, Sherry *C&W '78*
Singles: 7–inch
E.I.O... 3-4　80
MMI .... 3-4　79
OAK .... 3-5　78
TEJAS... 3-5　80

BRANNON, Kippi *C&W '81*
Singles: 7–inch
MCA.. 3-4　81-82

BREAKFAST BARRY *C&W '79*
(Barry Grant)
Singles: 7–inch
COUNTRYSTOCK......................... 3-5　79
Also see GRANT, Barry

BRENNAN, Walter *P&R '60/C&W '62*
(With Billy Vaughn's Orchestra & Chorus; with Patriots)
Singles: 7–inch
DOT .... 5-10　60
KAPP .... 3-5　71
LIBERTY...................................... 4-8　62-64
RPC .... 8-10　61
Picture Sleeves
DOT .... 10-15　60
LIBERTY...................................... 8-12　62-63
LPs: 10/12–inch 33rpm
DOT .... 20-30　60
EVEREST .... 20-30　60
HAMILTON .... 15-25　65
LIBERTY...................................... 20-30　62
LONDON...................................... 15-20　70
RPC .... 20-30　62
SUNSET .... 8-10　66
U.A. .... 5-10　75

BRENTWOOD *C&W '83*
Singles: 7–inch
HOT SCHATZ.............................. 3-4　83-84

BRESH, Tom *C&W '76*
Singles: 7–inch
ABC.. 3-5　78
ABC/DOT..................................... 3-5　77-78
FARR .... 3-5　76-77
LP: 10/12–inch 33rpm
ABC.. 5-10　78
ABC/DOT..................................... 5-10　77-78

FARR 6-12   76-77

BRESH, Tom, & Lane
Brody   *C&W '82*
Singles: 7–inch

LIBERTY 3-4   82
Also see BRESH, Tom
Also see BRODY, Lane

BRILEY, Jebry Lee   *C&W '79*
Singles: 7–inch

IBC 3-5   79
PAID.. 3-4   82

BRITT, Elton   *C&W '45*
(With the Skytoppers with Zeke Manners Band;
with Renfro Valley Pioneers)
Singles: 78rpm

BLUEBIRD 10-15   40-45
RCA.. 5-10   49-56
VICTOR....................................... 8-12   46-48
Singles: 7–inch
ABC-PAR 5-8   60
RCA (0006 thru 6429)............... 10-20   49-56
RCA (9000 series)........................ 4-6   68-69
EPs: 7–inch 33/45rpm
RCA.. 10-20   55-56
LP: 10/12–inch 33rpm
ABC-PAR (293 thru 521)........... 20-30   59
ABC-PAR (322 thru 521)........... 15-25   60-66
ABC-PAR (744 "16 Great Country
   Performances") 10-15   71
CAMDEN.................................... 10-20   69
CERTRON 8-12   70
KOALA 8-10   79
PREMIER.................................... 5-10   60s
RCA (1288" Yodel Songs") 30-50   56
RCA (2669 "Best of Elton
   Britt").................................... 20-30   63
RCA (3222" Yodel Songs") 50-100   54
   (10–inch LP.)
RCA (4822 "Best of Elton Britt, Vol.
   2")... 5-10   73
SPIN-O-RAMA 8-15   60s
Also see MANNERS, Zeke, & His Band
Also see THREE SUNS, Rosalie Allen & Elton Britt

BRITT, Elton, Rosalie Allen &
Skytoppers   *C&W '50*
(Elton Britt / Rosalie Allen)
Singles: 78rpm
RCA.. 5-10   50
EPs: 7–inch 33/45rpm
RCA.. 15-25   55

LP: 10/12–inch 33rpm
GRAND AWARD (262 "Starring Elton Britt &
   Rosalie Allen") 15-25   66
WALDORF (1206 "Rosalie Allen & Elton
   Britt")..20-30   57
Also see ALLEN, Rosalie
Also see BRITT, Elton

BROCK, Joe   *C&W '76*
Singles: 7–inch
RONNIE.......................................3-5   76

BRODY, Lane   *C&W '82*
Singles: 7–inch
EMI..3-4   84-85
LIBERTY 3-4   82-84
Also see BRESH, Tom, & Lane Brody
Also see LEE, Johnny, & Lane Brody

BROOKS, Garth   *C&W '89*
Singles: 7–inch
CAPITOL.......................................3-4   89-92
LPs: 10/12–inch 33rpm
CAPITOL.......................................5-8   90-92

BROOKS, Karen   *C&W '82*
Singles: 7–inch
W.B. 3-4   82-85
LP: 10/12–inch 33rpm
W.B. 5-8   82-84
Also see CROWELL, Rodney
Also see SHEPPARD, T.G., & Karen Brooks

BROOKS, Karen, & Johnny
Cash   *C&W '85*
Singles: 7–inch
W.B. 3-4   85
Also see BROOKS, Karen
Also see CASH, Johnny

BROOKS, Kix   *C&W '83*
Singles: 7–inch
AVION...3-5   83
CAPITOL.......................................3-4   89
Also see BROOKS & DUNN
Also see TOMORROW'S WORLD

BROOKS & DUNN   *C&W '91*
Singles: 7–inch
ARISTA...3-4   91
Members: Kix Brooks; Ronnie Dunn.
Also see BROOKS, Kix
Also see DUNN, Ronnie

BROOKS BROTHERS   *C&W '85*
(Brooks Brothers Band)
Singles: 7–inch
BUCKBOARD 3-4   85

YATAHEY 3-4   80
Members: Randy Brooks; Bill Brooks.

BROWN, Billy   *C&W '79*
Singles: 7–inch
ACCENT 3-5   75
BERNES 3-4   79

BROWN, Floyd   *C&W '77*
Singles: 7–inch
ABC/DOT 3-5   77
MAGNUM 3-4   83

BROWN, Jim Ed   *C&W '65*
(Jim Edward Brown)
Singles: 7–inch
RCA (Except 8000 & 9000
series) 3-5   69-81
RCA (8000 & 9000 series) 3-8   65-68
LPs: 10/12–inch 33rpm
PICKWICK 5-8   80
RCA (Except 3000 & 4000
series) 5-10   73-81
RCA (3000 & 4000 series) 8-15   66-72
(With "LPM" or "LSP" prefix.)
Session: Mary Cates; Margie Cates.
Also see BROWNS
Also see CATES SISTERS
Also see SOME of CHET'S FRIENDS

BROWN, Jim Ed, & Helen
Cornelius   *C&W '76*
Singles: 7–inch
RCA..................... 3-5   76-81
LP: 10/12–inch 33rpm
RCA..................... 5-10   76-82
Also see BROWN, Jim Edward
Also see CORNELIUS, Helen

BROWN, Jim Edward & Maxine: see BROWNS

BROWN, Jim Edward, Maxine & Bonnie: see BROWNS

BROWN, Josie   *C&W '73*
Singles: 7–inch
RCA..................... 3-5   73-74

BROWN, Marti   *C&W '73*
Singles: 7–inch
ATLANTIC..................... 3-5   73
LPs: 10/12–inch 33rpm
ATLANTIC..................... 8-10   73

BROWN, Max   *C&W '79*
Singles: 7–inch
DOOR KNOB 3-5   79

BROWN, Maxine   *C&W '68*
Singles: 7–inch
CHART..................... 4-6   68
LP: 10/12–inch 33rpm
CHART..................... 10-20   69
Also see BROWNS

BROWN, Roy   *R&B/C&W '48*
(With His Mighty-Mighty Men)
Singles: 78rpm
DELUXE..................... 20-50   47-51
GOLD STAR 15-25   48
IMPERIAL 15-25   57
KING..................... 15-25   52-57
Singles: 7–inch
BLUESWAY 4-8   67
DELUXE (3319 "Bar Room
Blues") 150-200   51
(Black vinyl.)
DELUXE (3319 "Bar Room
Blues") 200-400   51
(Colored vinyl.)
DELUXE (3323 "I've Got the Last Laugh
Now") 75-100   51
(Black vinyl.)
DELUXE (3323 "I've Got the Last Laugh
Now") 150-250   51
(Colored vinyl.)
FRIENDSHIP 5-10
GUSTO 3-4   83
HOME of the BLUES (107 "Man with the
Blues") 15-25   60
HOME of the BLUES (110 "Rockin' All the
Time") 15-25   60
HOME of the BLUES (115 "Sugar
Baby") 15-25   60
HOME of the BLUES (122 "Rock & Roll
Jamboree") 15-25   61
IMPERIAL (5427 "Party Doll")....20-30   57
IMPERIAL (5439 "Let the Four Winds
Blow") 20-30   57
IMPERIAL (5510 "Hip Shakin'
Baby") 20-30   57
KING (4602 "Travelin' Man")......25-50   53
(Black vinyl.)
KING (4602 "Travelin' Man")..100-150   53
(Colored vinyl.)
KING (4609 "Money Can't Buy
Love")..................... 25-50   53
KING (4627 "Gamblin' Man") 25-50   53
KING (4637 "Old Age
Boogie") 25-50   53
KING (4654 "Laughing But
Crying")..................... 25-50   53

KING (4669 "A Fool in Love") ...	25-50	53
KING (4684 "Midnight Lover Man")	25-50	53
KING (4704 "Bootleggin' Baby")	25-50	54
KING (4715 "This Is My Last Goodbye")	25-50	54
KING (4722 "Don't Let It Rain")	25-50	54
KING (4731 "Ain't It a Shame")	25-50	54
KING (4743 "Worried Life Blues")	25-50	54
KING (4761 "Fanny Brown Got Married")	25-50	54
KING (4816 "Letter to Baby")	25-50	55
KING (4834 "She's Gone Too Long")	25-50	55
KING (5000 series)	10-20	56-60
MERCURY	3-5	71
MOBILE FIDELITY	3-5	72
TRU-LOVE	4-6	

EPs: 7–inch 33/45rpm

KING (254 "Roy Brown")	50-100	53

LPs: 10/12–inch 33rpm

BLUESWAY	10-20	68-73
EPIC	10-15	71
INTERMEDIA	5-10	84
KING (956 "24 Hits")	35-45	66
KING (1100 series)	10-15	71
KING (5000 series)	8-10	79

BROWN, T. Graham   *C&W '85*

Singles: 7–inch

CAPITOL	3-4	85-90

Also see TOMORROW'S WORLD
Also see TUCKER, Tanya, & T. Graham Brown

BROWNS   *C&W '54*

(Jim Edward & Maxine Brown; Jim Edward, Maxine & Bonnie Brown; with the Louisiana Hayride Band; Browns featuring Jim Edward Brown)

Singles: 78rpm

FABOR	5-15	54-55
RCA	5-15	56-57

Singles: 7–inch

COLUMBIA	4-8	62
FABOR	10-20	54-55
RCA (6480 thru 7427)	10-15	56-58
RCA (47-7555 "The Three Bells") (Monaural.)	5-10	59
RCA (61-7555 "The Three Bells") (Stereo.)	10-15	59
RCA (47-7614 "Scarlet Ribbons") (Monaural.)	5-10	59
RCA (61-7614 "Scarlet Ribbons") (Stereo.)	10-15	59
RCA (47-7700 "The Old Lamplighter") (Monaural.)	5-10	60
RCA (61-7700 "The Old Lamplighter") (Stereo.)	10-15	60
RCA (47-7755 "Lonely Little Robin") (Monaural.)	5-10	60
RCA (61-7755 "Lonely Little Robin") (Stereo.)	10-15	60
RCA (47-7780 "Wiffenpoof Song") (Monaural.)	5-10	60
RCA (61-7780 "Wiffenpoof Song") (Stereo.)	10-15	60
RCA (47-7820 "Send Me the Pillow You Dream On") (Monaural.)	5-10	60
RCA (61-7820 "Send Me the Pillow You Dream On") (Monaural.)	10-15	60
RCA (7820 "Blue Christmas")	5-10	60
RCA (37-7866 "Angel's Dolly") (Compact 33 single.)	10-15	61
RCA (47-7866 "Angel's Dolly")	4-8	61
RCA (37-7917 "My Baby's Gone") (Compact 33 single.)	10-15	61
RCA (47-7917 "My Baby's Gone")	4-8	61
RCA (37-7969 "Foolish Pride") (Compact 33 single.)	10-15	61
RCA (47-7969 "Foolish Pride")	4-8	61
RCA (37-7997 "Remember Me") (Compact 33 single.)	10-15	62
RCA (47-7997 "Remember Me")	4-8	62
RCA (8066 thru 9364)	4-8	62-67

Picture Sleeves

RCA (7700 "The Old Lamplighter")	10-15	60

RCA (7755 "Lonely Little
Robin") 10-15   60

RCA (7780 "Wiffenpoof
Song") 10-15   60

EPs: 7–inch 33/45rpm

RCA.. 10-20   57-60

LPs: 10/12–inch 33rpm

CAMDEN.................................... 8-12   65-68

CANDLELITE (0422 "Beautiful Country Music
of the Browns")........................ 5-10   80
(Mail order offer.)

MCA/DOT.................................... 5-8   86

RCA (524 "20 of the Best") 5-8   85

RCA (1000 thru 3000 series) 5-10   75-81
(With "ANL1" or "AYL1" prefix.)

RCA (1438 Jim Edward, Maxine & Bonnie
Brown") 35-55   57
(With "LPM" prefix.)

RCA (2000 series).................... 15-30   59-65
(With "LPM" or "LSP" prefix.)

RCA (3000 series).................... 12-20   65-67
(With "LPM" or "LSP" prefix.)

Members: Jim Edward Brown; Maxine Brown; Bonnie
Brown.
Also see BROWN, Jim Ed
Also see BROWN, Maxine

BROWNS / Sam Cooke / Rod Lauren / Neil Sedaka
EPs: 7–inch 33/45rpm

RCA (33-99 "Compact 33
Double") 15-20   60
(With the same four songs on each side,
mono on one side, stereo on the reverse.)

Also see BROWNS

BRUCE, Ed   *C&W '67*
(Edwin Bruce)
Singles: 78rpm

SUN (276 "Rock Boppin'
Baby") 50-100   57

Singles: 7–inch

EPIC.. 3-5   77-78

GOOD BUDDY............................ 3-5   76

MCA 3-4   80-85

MONUMENT 4-6   68-69

RCA (5000 series)...................... 3-4   86

RCA (47-7842 "Flight 303").... 5-10   61
(Monaural.)

RCA (61-7842 "Flight 303")...... 10-20   61
(Stereo.)

RCA (9000 series)...................... 4-8   66-68

RCA (13000 & 14000 series) 3-4   84-86

SUN (276 "Rock Boppin'
Baby") 25-50   57

SUN (292 "Sweet Woman")........20-40   58

U.A. 3-5   73-76

WAND.......................................10-15   63

Promotional Singles

MCA (52109 "Ever Never Lovin'
You")......................................3-5   82
(5-inch disc with LP size hole and label.
Packaged in a special sleeve that unfolds to
make a 1983 calendar.)

LPs: 10/12–inch 33rpm

EPIC.......................................6-10   77-78

MCA 5-10   80-83

MONUMENT...............................10-15   69

RCA (3900 series) 12-20   68

RCA (5000 series).....................5-10   84-85

U.A. 8-10   76

Session: Willie Nelson.
Also see NELSON, Willie

BRUCE, Ed, & Lynn Anderson
Singles: 7–inch

RCA 3-4   86

Also see ANDERSON, Lynn
Also see BRUCE, Ed

BRUSH ARBOR   *C&W '72*
Singles: 7–inch

CAPITOL.....................................3-5   72-73

MONUMENT.................................3-5   75-77

LP: 10/12–inch 33rpm

CAPITOL.....................................8-12   72-73

MONUMENT.................................5-10   75-77

MYRRH.......................................5-10

BRYAN, Billy
(Gene Pitney)
Singles: 7–inch

BLAZE (351 "Going Back to My
Love")....................................20-30   59

Also see PITNEY, Gene

BRYANT, Ronnie   *C&W '89*
Singles: 7–inch

EVERGREEN 3-4   89

BRYCE, Sherry   *C&W '73*
Singles: 7–inch

MGM 3-5   73-77

LP: 10/12–inch 33rpm

MGM 5-10   74-75

Also see TILLIS, Mel, & Sherry Bryce

BUCHANAN, Wes   *C&W '68*
Singles: 7–inch

COLUMBIA 4-6   68

PEP (114 "Give Some Love My
Way") 15-25   58

BUCHANAN BROTHERS   *C&W '46*
Singles: 78rpm
VICTOR.. 5-10   46

BUCK, Gary   *C&W '63*
Singles: 7-inch
CHATEAU 5-10   62
DIMENSION................................... 3-4   82
PETAL... 4-6   63-64
TOWER 4-6   66-67
LP: 10/12-inch 33rpm
PETAL 15-20   64
TOWER.. 10-15   67

BUCKAROOS   *C&W '67*
(Featuring Don Rich)
Singles: 7-inch
CAPITOL.. 4-8   67-69
LP: 10/12-inch 33rpm
CAPITOL (322 "Roll Your
Own") 15-25   69
CAPITOL (440 "Rompin &
Stompin") 15-25   70
CAPITOL (550 "Boot Hill").......... 15-25   70
CAPITOL (767 "The Buckaroos Play the
Hits") 15-25   70
CAPITOL (2436 "The Buck Owens
Songbook") 20-30   66
CAPITOL (2828 "Again")........... 20-30   67
CAPITOL (2973 "Meanwhile, Back at the
Ranch") 15-25   68
Members: Don Rich; Doyle Holly; Tom Brumley; Willie
Cantu.
Also see ALAN, Buddy
Also see HOLLY, Doyle
Also see OWENS, Buck
Also see RICH, Don

BUDDE, Rusty   *C&W '86*
Singles: 7-inch
BPC... 3-4   86

BUDDY ALAN: see ALAN, Buddy

BUFF, Beverly   *C&W '62*
Singles: 7-inch
BETHLEHEM 4-8   62-63
SUR-SPEED 4-8   67

BUFFETT, Jimmy   *C&W '73*
Singles: 7-inch
ABC... 3-5   75-78
ASYLUM 3-4   80
BARNABY 3-5   70-72

DUNHILL... 3-5   73-75
FULL MOON 3-4   80
MCA (Black vinyl)........................... 3-4   79-86
MCA (Colored vinyl)....................... 3-6   85
LPs: 10/12-inch 33rpm
ABC.. 8-10   76-78
BARNABY (6014 "High Cumberland
Jubilee") 50-100   76
BARNABY (30093 "Down to
Earth")...................................... 150-250   70
DUNHILL.. 10-15   73-74
MCA 5-10   79-90
U.A. 8-10   75

BURBANK, Gary, & Band McNally / Tennessee Valley Authority
C&W/P&R '80
Singles: 7-inch
OVATION....................................... 3-5   80

BURBANK STATION   *C&W '88*
Singles: 7-inch
PRAIRIE... 3-4   88-89

BURCH SISTERS   *C&W '88*
Singles: 7-inch
MERCURY...................................... 3-4   88-89
Members: Cindy Burch; Cathy Burch; Charlene Burch.
Also see TOMORROW'S WORLD

BURGESS, Frank   *C&W '88*
Singles: 7-inch
TRUE 3-4   88-89

BURGESS, Wilma   *C&W '65*
Singles: 7-inch
DECCA 3-6   64-70
SHANNON...................................... 3-5   73-75
U.A. 5-8   62
LP: 10/12-inch 33rpm
CORAL... 5-10   73
DECCA 10-20   66-69
Also see LOGAN, Bud, & Wilma Burgess

BURKE, Fiddlin' Frenchie   *C&W '74*
(Fiddlin' Frenchie Bourque & Outlaws;
Frenchie Bruke)
Singles: 7-inch
CHERRY... 3-5   78
DELTA 3-4   81
20TH CENTURY............................. 3-5   74-75
LP: 10/12-inch 33rpm
DELTA 5-10   80-82
20TH CENTURY............................. 6-12   75
Also see BUSH, Johnny

BURNETTE, Billy   *C&W '79*
(With Jawbone)
Singles: 7–inch

A&M	3-5	76
COLUMBIA	3-4	80-81
CURB	3-4	86
POLYDOR	3-5	79
W.B. (7300 series)	4-6	69

LPs: 10/12–inch 33rpm

COLUMBIA	5-10	80-81
ENTRANCE	10-12	72
MCA/CURB	5-10	86
POLYDOR	5-10	79

BURNETTE, Billy, & Christine McVie
Singles: 12–inch 33/45rpm

MCA/CURB (17040 "It Ain't Over")	5-8 ,	85
(Promotional issue only.)		

Also see BURNETTE, Billy

BURNETTE, Billy Joe   *C&W '90*
(Billy Burnette)
Singles: 7–inch

BADGER	3-4	90
DEVILLE (134 "Blue Misery")	8-12	65
GOLD STANDARD	3-5	
GUSTO-STARDAY (167 "Welcome Home Elvis")	4-8	77
GUSTO-STARDAY (9009 "The Colonel and the King")	8-12	78
(Promotional issue only.)		
K-ARK	3-5	70
MAGIC LAMP (613 "Miss Ping Pong")	10-15	65
PD	3-5	
PALOMINO	3-5	
TEDDY BEAR	4-6	77
TELEMEDIA	3-4	81
W.B.	4-8	69

LPs: 10/12–inch 33rpm

GUSTO	10-20	77

Also see BARNETT, Billy

BURNETTE, Dorsey

         P&R '60/C&W '72
Singles: 78rpm

ABBOTT	15-25	56

Singles: 7–inch

ABBOTT (188 "Devil's Queen")	25-35	56
ABBOTT (190 "At a Distance")	25-35	56
CALLIOPE	3-5	77

CAPITOL	3-5	71-74
CEE-JAM (16 "Bertha-Lou")	50-75	57
COLLECTABLES	3-4	81
CONDOR	4-6	70
DOT	8-12	61
ELEKTRA	3-5	79-80
ERA	5-10	60-69
HAPPY TIGER	4-6	70
HICKORY	4-8	67
IMPERIAL (5561 "Try")	10-20	59
IMPERIAL (5597 "Misery")	10-20	59
IMPERIAL (5668 "Your Love")	10-20	60
IMPERIAL (5987 "Circle Rock")	8-10	63
LIBERTY	4-8	69
MC	3-5	77
MEL-O-DY	10-15	64
MELODYLAND	3-5	75-76
MERRI (206 "Lucy Darling")	8-12	60
MOVIE STAR	4-8	
MUSIC FACTORY	4-8	68
REPRISE	5-10	62-63
SMASH	5-10	66
SURF (5019 "Bertha Lou")	150-200	57
U.S. NAVY ("Be a Navy Man")	10-20	60s
(U.S. Navy recruiting promotional issue.)		

Picture Sleeves

ERA (3033 "The River and the Mountain")	15-25	61
REPRISE (246 "Four for Texas")	20-30	63
U.S. NAVY ("Be a Navy Man")	15-25	60s
(U.S. Navy recruiting promotional issue.)		

LPs: 10/12–inch 33rpm

BUCKBOARD (1024 "Dorsey")	8-10	
CALLIOPE	8-10	77
CAPITOL	10-12	72-73
DOT (3456 "Dorsey Burnette Sings")	20-40	63
(Monaural.)		
DOT (25456 "Dorsey Burnette Sings")	25-50	63
(Stereo.)		
ERA (EL-102 "Tall Oak Tree")	40-80	60
(Monaural.)		
ERA (ES-102 "Tall Oak Tree")	100-150	60
(Stereo.)		
ERA (800 series)	15-20	69
GUSTO	5-10	79
TRIP	8-12	74

Also see BURNETTE, Johnny & Dorsey

BURNS, Brent   C&W '78
Singles: 7–inch
PANTHEON DESERT.................. 3-5   78

BURNS, George   P&R/C&W/LP '80
Singles: 7–inch
MERCURY 3-4   80-81
Picture Sleeves
MERCURY 3-4   80
EPs: 7–inch 33/45rpm
COLPIX 5-10   60s
LPs: 10/12–inch 33rpm
BUDDAH 6-10   72
MERCURY 5-10   80
PRIDE 5-10
Also see MARTIN, Dean

BURNS, Hughie   C&W '80
Singles: 7–inch
C-S-I... 3-4   80

BURNS, Jackie   C&W '69
Singles: 7–inch
HONOR BRIGADE....................... 3-6   69
JMI 3-5   72

BURRITO BROTHERS   C&W '81
Singles: 7–inch
CURB 3-4   81-84
EPIC 3-4   81
LPs: 10/12–inch 33rpm
A&M 8-10   80
CURB 5-10   81-82
Members: Pete Battin; Pete Kleinow; Greg Harris; Ed Ponder; Gib Guilbeau; John Beland.
Also see FLYING BURRITO BROTHERS
Also see SWAMPWATER

BUSH, Johnny   C&W '67
(With Bill Freeman & His Texas Plainsmen)
Singles: 7–inch
ALLSTAR (7172 "Your Kind of Love")................................... 50-75   58
DELTA... 3-4   81-82
GUSTO 3-5   78
MILLION 3-6   72
NEW STAR 4-6   60s
RCA.. 3-5   72-74
STOP 4-8   67-71
WHISKEY RIVER.......................... 3-5   79
LP: 10/12–inch 33rpm
BUCKBOARD 5-10
DELTA..................................... 10-15   80-83
MILLION.................................... 15-25   72

PICKWICK 5-10   70s
PICKWICK/HILLTOP 10-15
POWER PAK 5-10   74
RCA 10-15   73
STOP.......................................10-20   68-72
WHISKEY RIVER 15-20
Session: Fiddlin' Frenchie Burke.
Also see BURKE, Fiddlin' Frenchie
Also see NELSON, Willie
Also see PRICE, Ray

BUTLER, Bobby "Sofine"   C&W '76
Singles: 7–inch
IBC...3-5   79
PANTHEON DESERT 3-5   76

BUTLER, Carl   C&W '61
Singles: 78rpm
CAPITOL....................................5-10   51-52
OKEH...4-8   54-55
Singles: 7–inch
CAPITOL....................................8-12   51-52
COLUMBIA 4-8   59-63
OKEH...6-10   54-55
LPs: 10/12–inch 33rpm
COLUMBIA 10-20   63
HARMONY.................................8-15   66-71

BUTLER, Carl & Pearl   C&W '62
Singles: 7–inch
COLUMBIA 4-8   62-69
LPs: 10/12–inch 33rpm
CMH...5-10   80
CHART..3-5   71
COLUMBIA 10-20   64-70
HARMONY.................................8-12   72
PEDACA 5-10
Also see BUTLER, Carl
Also see BUTLER, Pearl

BUTLER, Larry, & Friends
LP: 10/12–inch 33rpm
PICKWICK (3726 "Larry Butler & Friends, Featuring Crystal Gayle & Billy Jo Spears")..............................5-10   77
Also see GAYLE, Crystal
Also see SPEARS, Billy Jo

BUTLER, Pearl
Singles: 7–inch
COLUMBIA 3-5   69
Also see BUTLER, Carl & Pearl

BUZZI, Ruth   C&W '77
Singles: 7–inch
U.A..3-5   77

BYERS, Brenda   C&W '68
Singles: 7–inch
MTA.. 3-6   66-71
LPs: 10/12–inch 33rpm
MTA... 8-12   70

BYRAM, Judy   C&W '87
Singles: 7–inch
F&L.. 3-4   87
REGAL 3-4   88

BYRDS   P&R/LP '65
Singles: 7–inch
ASYLUM 3-5   73
COLUMBIA (1600 series) 4-6   73
COLUMBIA (43271 "Mr. Tambourine
  Man")...................................... 5-10   65
  (Black vinyl.)
COLUMBIA (43271 "Mr. Tambourine
  Man").................................... 50-75   65
  (Colored vinyl. Promotional issue only.)
COLUMBIA (43332 "I'll Feel a Whole Lot
  Better")................................. 5-10   65
  (Black vinyl.)
COLUMBIA (43332 "I'll Feel a Whole Lot
  Better")............................... 50-75   65
  (Colored vinyl. Promotional issue only.)
COLUMBIA (43332 "All I Really Want
  to Do").................................. 5-10   65
  (Black vinyl.)
COLUMBIA (43332 "All I Really Want
  to Do").............................. 50-75   65
  (Colored vinyl. Promotional issue only.)
COLUMBIA (43424 "Turn Turn
  Turn") 5-10   65
  (Black vinyl.)
COLUMBIA (43424 "Turn Turn
  Turn") 50-75   65
  (Colored vinyl. Promotional issue only.)
COLUMBIA (43501 thru 45761).... 4-8   66-72
SCHOLASTIC 5-10   66
Picture Sleeves
COLUMBIA (Except 43271) 12-25   65-71
COLUMBIA (43271 "Mr. Tambourine
  Man")................................. 100-150   65
  (Promotional issue only.)
COLUMBIA (43578 "Eight Miles
  High") 15-25   65
COLUMBIA (44157 "Have You Seen Her
  Face")................................. 15-25   65
EPs: 7–inch 33/45rpm
COLUMBIA (10287 "The
  Byrds") 40-60   66

(Columbia Special Products issue for the
Scholastic Book Services.)
COLUMBIA (116003/4 "Fifth Dimension
  Open-End Interview") 50-75   66
  (Promotional issue only.)
LPs: 10/12–inch 33rpm
ASYLUM 8-10   73
COLUMBIA (2000 series) 20-25   65-67
COLUMBIA (9000 series) 15-25   65-69
COLUMBIA (30000 thru 33000
  series)................................... 8-12   70-75
COLUMBIA (34000 thru 37000
  series)................................... 5-10   75-81
COLUMBIA (46773 "The
  Byrds")................................. 30-40   90
  (Four-LP set. Includes booklet.)
TOGETHER 15-20   69
Promotional LPs
BROADCAST ("Byrds Live")......35-45   81
COLUMBIA (2000 series) 40-50   65-67
  (White label.)
COLUMBIA (9000 series) 35-45   65-69
  (White label.)
COLUMBIA (116003/4 "Fifth Dimension"
  Interview Album)..................100-125   66
MURRAY HILL.............................5-10   87
PAIR...10-12   83
REALM.......................................8-12   76
RHINO 5-10   88

Members: Jim (Roger) McGuinn; Gene Clark; David
Crosby; Chris Hillman; Michael Clarke; Gram Parsons;
Clarence White; Gene Parsons; John York; Skip
Battin. Session: Jay Dee Maness.
  Also see BEEFEATERS
  Also see CROSBY, STILLS & NASH
  Also see DILLARDS
  Also see HILLMAN, Chris
  Also see PACIFIC STEEL CO.

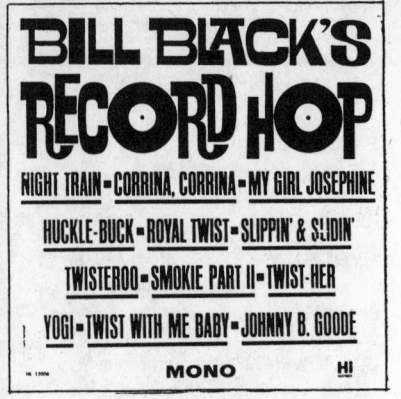

C

C COMPANY Featuring Terry Nelson
C&W '71

Singles: 7–inch
PLANTATION	3-5	71

LP: 10/12–inch 33rpm
PLANTATION	5-10	71

CAGLE, Buddy
C&W '63

Singles: 7–inch
CAPITOL	4-8	63
IMPERIAL	4-6	66-68
MERCURY	4-6	65
U.A.	3-5	70

LP: 10/12–inch 33rpm
IMPERIAL	8-5	66-68

Also see THOMPSON, Hank

CAIN, Hunter
C&W '88

Singles: 7–inch
DISCOVERY	3-4	88-89

CALAMITY JANE
C&W '81

Singles: 7–inch
COLUMBIA	3-4	81-82

LP: 10/12–inch 33rpm
COLUMBIA	5-10	82

Members: Pam Rose; Mary Fiedler; Linda Moore; Mary Ann Kennedy.
Also see ROSE, Pam

CALHOUN, Linda
C&W '79

Singles: 7–inch
GRAPE	3-5	79

CAMERON, Bart
C&W '86

Singles: 7–inch
REVOLVER	3-4	86

CAMP, Colleen
C&W '82

Singles: 7–inch
MOON PICTURES	3-4	82

CAMPBELL, Archie
C&W '60

Singles: 7–inch
ELEKTRA	3-5	76-77
RCA (0147 thru 0766)	3-5	72-73
RCA (7660 thru 9987)	4-8	60-71

STARDAY	4-8	61-64

LP: 10/12–inch 33rpm
ELEKTRA	5-10	76
NASHVILLE	10-15	68
RCA	10-15	66-71
STARDAY (167 "Bedtime Stories for Adults")	20-25	62
STARDAY (223 "The Joker Is Wild")	15-20	63
STARDAY (377 "Grand Ole Opry's Good Humor Man")	10-20	66

Also see SOME of CHET'S FRIENDS

CAMPBELL, Archie, & Lorene Mann
C&W '68

Singles: 7–inch
RCA	4-6	68

LP: 10/12–inch 33rpm
RCA	8-12	68

Also see MANN, Lorene

CAMPBELL, Archie, & Junior Samples

LP: 10/12–inch 33rpm
CHART	10-15	68
MOUNTAIN DEW	5-8	

Also see CAMPBELL, Archie

CAMPBELL, Cecil
C&W '49

(With the Tennessee Ramblers)

Singles: 78rpm
MGM (12118 "Steel Guitar Waltz")	5-10	55
MGM (12245 "Dixieland Rock")	20-40	56
MGM (12482 "Rock & Roll Fever")	50-75	
RCA	5-8	49

Singles: 7–inch
MGM (12118 "Steel Guitar Waltz")	10-15	55
MGM (12245 "Dixieland Rock")	25-50	56
MGM (12482 "Rock & Roll Fever")	75-100	57

LP: 10/12–inch 33rpm
STARDAY (254 "Steel Guitar Jamboree")	30-40	63

CAMPBELL, Glen
P&R '61/C&W '62

(With the Glen-Aires; with Green River Boys; with Bandits)

Singles: 7–inch
ATLANTIC AMERICA	3-4	82-86

CAPEHART............................ 10-20	61	
CAPITOL (2000 & 3000 series) 3-6	68-74	
CAPITOL (4000 series)................ 3-5	75-81	
(Orange or purple labels.)		
CAPITOL (4783 thru 5360) 5-10	61-65	
(Orange/yellow swirl labels.)		
CAPITOL (5441 "Guess I'm		
Dumb")................................. 30-40	65	
(With Brian Wilson.)		
CAPITOL (5504 thru 5939,		
except 5927) 4-8	65-67	
CAPITOL (5927 "My Baby's Gone/Kelli		
Hoedown")................................ 6-12	67	
(Has alternate takes. Promotional issue		
only.)		
CAPITOL STARLINE 3-5		
CENECO (1324 "Dreams for		
Sale") 10-25	59	
CENECO (1356 "You, You,		
You") 10-15	59	
CREST 10-15	61-62	
(Mistakenly shown as "Glen Cambpbell" on		
some Crest labels.)		
EVEREST 3-6	69	
STARDAY 3-6	68	
MCA 3-4	84-89	
MIRAGE 3-4	81	
UNIVERSAL................................... 3-4	89	
W.B. 3-4	80	

Picture Sleeves

CAPITOL (Except 4856 & 5279) ... 3-6	68-74	
CAPITOL (4856 "Long Black		
Limousine") 10-15	62	
CAPITOL (5279 "Summer, Winter, Spring and		
Fall").. 8-12	64	

EPs: 7–inch 33/45rpm

CAPITOL.................................... 5-10	68-71	
(Jukebox issues.)		
CAPITOL/CHEVROLET (55 "The Glen		
Campbell Good Time Hour")..... 5-10	60s	
CAPITOL CREATIVE		
PRODUCTS............................. 5-10	60s	

LPs: 10/12–inch 33rpm

ATLANTIC AMERICA 5-10	82-86	
BUCKBOARD 8-10		
CAPITOL (103 thru 752) 8-15	68-71	
CAPITOL (1810 "Big Bluegrass		
Special")................................. 25-75	62	
(Credits the "Green River Boys Featuring		
Glen Campbell.")		
CAPITOL (1881 thru 2392) 10-20	63-65	
(With "T" or "ST" prefix.)		

CAPITOL (2809 thru 2978).......... 8-15	67-69	
(With "T" or "ST" prefix.)		
CAPITOL (SM-300 series)........... 5-10	82	
CAPITOL (SM-2000 series)......... 5-10	78	
CAPITOL (4000 series) 5-10	73	
CAPITOL (11000 thru 16000		
series).................................... 5-10	72-85	
CAPITOL (80000 series) 5-10		
CAPITOL (94000 series) 8-15	72	
(Capitol Record Club issues.)		
CAPITOL (120000 series) 5-10		
(Capitol Record Club issues.)		
CAPITOL CREATIVE		
PRODUCTS............................. 8-12		
CAPITOL SPECIAL		
PRODUCTS.............................. 5-8	84	
CUSTOM TONE 15-20		
LONGINES (5408 "Gentle on My		
Mind")..................................... 5-10	69	
LONGINES ("Glen Campbell's Golden		
Favorites") 20-30	72	
(Boxed, 6-LP set.)		
PAIR... 5-8	84	
PICKWICK 8-10	64-79	
SEARS.. 8-12		
STARDAY 15-20	68-69	

Session: Jerry Puckett.
Also see FORD, Tennessee Ernie, & Glen Campbell
Also see IN-GROUP
Also see MARTIN, Dean / Glen Campbell
Also see MR. TWELVE STRING
Also see NELSON, Willie
Also see PUCKETT, Jerry
Also see TILLIS, Mel, & Glen Campbell
Also see TUCKER, Tanya, & Glen Campbell

CAMPBELL, Glen, & Rita
Coolidge   *C&W/P&R '80*

Singles: 7–inch

CAPITOL...3-4	80	

Also see COOLIDGE, Rita

CAMPBELL, Glen, & Bobbie
Gentry   *C&W/LP '68*

Singles: 7–inch

CAPITOL...3-5	68-70	

EPs: 7–inch 33/45rpm

CAPITOL...8-10	68	
(Jukebox issue only.)		

LPs: 10/12–inch 33rpm

CAPITOL...8-10	68	

Also see GENTRY, Bobbie

CAMPBELL, Glen / Lettermen / Ella Fitzgerald / Sandler & Young
LPs: 10/12–inch 33rpm
CAPITOL (56 "B.F. Goodrich Presents Christmas 1969") 10-15   69
(Promotional, special products issue.)

CAMPBELL, Glen, & Anne Murray   *C&W/P&R/LP '71*
Singles: 7–inch
CAPITOL.. 3-5   71-72
LPs: 10/12–inch 33rpm
CAPITOL...................................... 5-10   71-80

CAMPBELL, Glen / Anne Murray / Kenny Rogers / Crystal Gayle
LP: 10/12–inch 33rpm
CAPITOL/U.A. (11743-F-19 "Glen/Anne/ Kenny/ Crystal") 300-500   78
(Four framed picture disc set. Promotional issue only.)
Also see GAYLE, Crystal
Also see MURRAY, Anne
Also see ROGERS, Kenny

CAMPBELL, Glen, & Billy Strange
LPs: 10/12–inch 33rpm
SURREY 12-20   65

CAMPBELL, Glen / Texas Opera Company
Singles: 7–inch
W.B./VIVA 3-5   80

CAMPBELL, Glen, & Steve Wariner   *C&W '87*
Singles: 7–inch
MCA 3-4   87
Also see WARINER, Steve

CAMPBELL, Glen / Dionne Warwick / Burt Bacharach
LPs: 10/12–inch 33rpm
CHEVROLET (6658 "On the Move")....................................... 5-10   70
(Chevrolet promotional issue.)
Also see CAMPBELL, Glen

CAMPBELL, Jo Ann

P&R '60/C&W '62
Singles: 78rpm
ELDORADO 25-50   57
POINT 10-20   56

Singles: 7–inch
ABC-PAR 10-20   60-62
(Monaural.)
ABC-PAR (10134 "Kookie Little Paradise") 20-40   60
(Stereo.)
CAMEO..................................5-10   62-63
ELDORADO (504 "Forever Young").....................................15-25   57
GONE 10-20   59
POINT.......................................15-25   56
RORI...4-8

LPs: 10/12–inch 33rpm
ABC-PAR (393 "Twistin' and Listenin'") 40-50   62
(Monaural.)
ABC-PAR (393 "Twistin' and Listenin'") 50-60   62
(Stereo.)
CAMEO (1026 "All the Hits of Jo Ann Campbell") 25-30   62
CORONET (199 "Starring Jo Ann Campbell") 10-20   62
END (306 "I'm Nobody's Baby") 40-60   59

CAMPBELL, Mike   *C&W '81*
Singles: 7–inch
COLUMBIA 3-4   81-84
RSVP 4-6

CAMPBELL, Mike, & Tom Garvin
LPs: 10/12–inch 33rpm
ITI..5-10   84
Also see CAMPBELL, Mike

CAMPBELL, Stacy Dean   *C&W '92*
Singles: 7–inch
COLUMBIA 3-4   92

CANADIAN SWEETHEARTS   *C&W '64*
Singles: 7–inch
A&M 5-10   63
EPIC...4-8   68
SOMA (1156 "No Help Wanted") 30-50   61
LP: 10/12–inch 33rpm
A&M (106 "Introducing the Canadian Sweethearts") 20-30   64
Member: Lucille Starr.
Also see BOB & LUCILLE
Also see STARR, Lucille

CANNON, Ace   *P&R '61*
(Johnny "Ace" Cannon)
Singles: 7–inch
FERNWOOD (135 "Hoe Down Rock")	5-10	63
FERNWOOD (137 "Big Shot")	5-10	64
HI (2000 series)	5-10	61-66
HI (2100 thru 2300 series)	3-8	66-76
LOUIS (2001 "Tuff")	15-25	61
MOTOWN	3-4	82
SANTO	4-8	62

Picture Sleeves
HI	5-10	62-63

EPs: 7–inch 33/45rpm
HI (1133 "In the Spotlight")	5-10	68

(Jukebox issue.)

LPs: 10/12–inch 33rpm
ALLEGIANCE	5-10	84
GUSTO	5-10	80
HI (007 thru 040)	10-20	62-67

(Numbers in this series are preceeded by a "12" for mono or a "32" for stereo issues.)

HI (043 thru 090)	6-10	68-75

(Numbers in this series are preceded by a "32," indicating stereo.)

HI (6000 & 8000 series)	8-10	77-79
MOTOWN	5-10	83

Also see BLACK, Bill
Also see CANNON, Johnny

CANNON, Jimmi   *C&W '81*
Singles: 7–inch
W.B.	3-4	81-82

CANNON, Johnny
("Ace" Cannon)
Singles: 7–inch
FERNWOOD (117 "Big Shot")	15-25	60

Also see CANNON, Ace

CANNONS   *C&W '83*
Singles: 7–inch
COMPLEAT	3-4	83
MERCURY	3-4	86-87

Members: Carla Cannon; Darla Cannon; Larry Cannon.

CANYON   *C&W '88*
Singles: 7–inch
16TH AVENUE	3-4	88-90

CAPITALS   *C&W '80*
Singles: 7–inch
RIDGETOP	3-4	80-81

CAPPS, Hank   *C&W '72*
Singles: 7–inch
CAPITOL	3-5	72

CAPTAIN & TENNILLE   *P&R/LP '75/C&W '78*
Singles: 7–inch
A&M	3-5	75-78
BUTTERSCOTCH CASTLE (001 "The Way I Want to Touch You")	50-75	73
JOYCE (101 "The Way I Want to Touch You")	20-40	74
CASABLANCA	3-5	79-80

Picture Sleeves
A&M	4-6	75-78

LPs: 10/12–inch 33rpm
A&M	8-10	75-79
CASABLANCA	5-10	79

Members: Daryl Dragon; Toni Tennille.

CAPTAIN STUBBY & BUCCANEERS: see STUBBY & BUCCANEERS

CARDWELL, Jack   *C&W '53*
Singles: 78rpm
KING	5-15	53-55

Singles: 7–inch
KING	10-15	53-55
SANDY	8-10	59

CARGILL, Henson   *P&R/C&W '67*
Singles: 7–inch
ARCO	4-6	67
ATLANTIC	3-5	73-74
COPPER MOUNTAIN	3-4	79-80
ELEKTRA	3-5	75
MEGA	3-5	71-73
MONUMENT	4-6	67-70
RUFF	4-6	
TOWER	3-6	68

LPs: 10/12–inch 33rpm
ATLANTIC	6-10	73
BUCKBOARD	5-10	
HARMONY	6-10	72
MEGA	6-10	72
MONUMENT	8-12	68-70

CARLETTE   *C&W '85*
(Carlette Ruff)
Singles: 7–inch
LUV	3-4	85-87
OAK	3-4	85

CARLILE, Tom   *C&W '81*
Singles: 7–inch

DOOR KNOB 3-4 81-83

CARLISLE, Bill   *C&W '48*
(With the Carlisles; Bill Carlisle's Kentucky Boys)
Singles: 78rpm

BLUEBIRD (Except 6478) 10-15
BLUEBIRD (6478 "Rattlin'
  Daddy") 25-40
DECCA................................... 10-20   30s
FEDERAL................................. 5-10
KING ....: 5-10   48
MERCURY 4-8   53
VOCALION (02520 "Rattle Snake
  Daddy") 20-40
VOCALION (02946 "I'm Gonna Kill
  Myself") 20-40

Singles: 7–inch

COLUMBIA 4-8   62
HICKORY.................................... 4-6   65
MERCURY 10-15   53

EPs: 7–inch 33/45rpm

MERCURY 10-20   56

LP: 10/12–inch 33rpm

BRYLEN.................................... 5-10   83
HICKORY................................ 10-20   66
  Also see CARLISLES

CARLISLES   *C&W '46*
(Carlisle Brothers; Carlisle Family)
Singles: 78rpm

DECCA................................... 10-15 40-41
KING 8-12   46
MERCURY 5-10 53-56

Singles: 7–inch

MERCURY 10-20 51-54

EPs: 7–inch 33/45rpm

MERCURY 10-20   55

LP: 10/12–inch 33rpm

GUEST STAR 10-15   60s
KING (643 "Fresh from the
  Country") 15-25   59
MERCURY (20359 "On Stage") 30-40   58
OLD HOMESTEAD 5-8   80s
  Members: Bill Carlisle; Cliff Carlisle.
  Also see CARLISLE, Bill

CARLLILE, Kathy   *C&W '80*
Singles: 7–inch

FRONTLINE................................. 3-5   80

CARLSON, Paulette   *C&W '83*
Singles: 7–inch

RCA ....:.....3-4 83-84
  Also see HIGHWAY 101

CARNES, Kim   *P&R '79/C&W '88*
Singles: 12–inch 33/45rpm

EMI AMERICA 4-6 80-85

Singles: 7–inch

A&M 3-5 75-82
AMOS 3-6 71-72
EMI AMERICA 3-4 79-86
ELEKTRA......................................3-4   84

Picture Sleeves

EMI AMERICA 3-4 80-86

LPs: 10/12–inch 33rpm

A&M (3000 series) 5-10   82
A&M (4000 series) 8-10 75-77
AMOS 12-18   71
EMI AMERICA 5-10 79-86
MCA 5-10   84
MFSL (073 "Mistaken Identity") .20-30   82
  Session: Lyle Lovett.
  Also see COTTON, Gene, & Kim Carnes
  Also see LOVETT, Lyle
  Also see ROGERS, Kenny, & Kim Carnes
  Also see STREISAND, Barbra, & Kim Carnes
  Also see U.S.A. for AFRICA

CARNES, Kim, & Dave Ellington
Singles: 7–inch

AMOS 3-5   72
  Also see CARNES, Kim

CARNES, Rick & Janis   *C&W '82*
Singles: 7–inch

ELEKTRA......................................3-4   82
MCA 3-4   84
W.B. 3-4   83

CARPENTER, Kris   *C&W '81*
Singles: 7–inch

DOOR KNOB.................................3-4   81

CARPENTER, Mary
Chapin   *C&W/LP '89*
Singles: 7–inch

COLUMBIA 3-4 89-92

LPs: 10/12–inch 33rpm

COLUMBIA 5-8 89-90

CARPENTERS   *P&R/LP '70/C&W '78*
Singles: 7–inch

A&M (Except 2735).......................3-6 69-82

A&M (2735) 10-15
(Promotional issue only. Title not known.)

Picture Sleeves

A&M (Except 2735) 3-6   70-81
A&M (2735 "Yesterday Once
More") 10-15
(Promotional issue only. With paper sleeve.)

EPs: 7–inch 33/45rpm

A&M 10-15   72-85

LPs: 10/12–inch 33rpm

A&M (3000 series) 8-15   71-85
A&M (4000 series, except 4205). 8-15   70-83
A&M (4205 "Offering").............. 20-35   69
A&M (4205 "Ticket to Ride") 10-15   71
A&M (5100 series") 5-8   90
A&M (50000 series) 15-25   74-75
(Quadraphonic series.)
A&M (6000 series) 8-12   85
MFP (50431 "Ticket to Ride").... 10-15   70
Members: Karen Carpenter; Richard Carpenter; Tony Peluso.

CARR, Eddie Lee   *C&W '89*

Singles: 7–inch

EVERGREEN................................ 3-4   89

CARR, Kenny   *C&W '88*

Singles: 7–inch

KOTTAGE 3-4   88-89

CARSON, Joe   *C&W '63*

Singles: 7–inch

LIBERTY 4-8   63-64

LP: 10/12–inch 33rpm

LIBERTY 20-30   64

CARSON, Wayne   *C&W '73*

Singles: 7–inch

EMH 3-4   83
ELEKTRA.................................... 3-5   76-77
MONUMENT 3-5   70-73

LP: 10/12–inch 33rpm

MONUMENT 6-10   72

CARTEE, Alan   *C&W '77*

Singles: 7–inch

GROOVY 3-5   77
Also see CARTEE BROTHERS

CARTEE BROTHERS

(Cartees)

Singles: 7–inch

QUALLA 4-8   65
REPRISE 4-8   66

Members: Alan Cartee; Wayne Cartee.
Also see CARTEE, Alan
Also see CARTEE, Wayne

CARTER, Anita   *C&W '51*

Singles: 78rpm

COLUMBIA 4-8   53-54
RCA 4-8   51-56

Singles: 7–inch

CAPITOL.................................... 3-5   71
COLUMBIA 5-10   53-54
JAMIE 4-8   60
MERCURY................................... 4-8   63-64
RCA (0426 thru 0493)............... 10-20   51-53
RCA (6000 series) 8-15   55-56
RCA (8000 & 9000 series)............. 4-8   66-67
U.A. 4-6   68-69

LP: 10/12–inch 33rpm

CAPITOL.................................... 8-10   72
MERCURY................................... 15-25   63-64
Also see CARTER FAMILY
Also see CARTER SISTERS
Also see DARRELL, Johnny, & Anita Carter
Also see JENNINGS, Waylon, & Anita Carter
Also see SNOW, Hank, & Anita Carter

CARTER, Benny, & His
Orchestra   *R&B/C&W '44*

(Featuring Savannah Churchill)

Singles: 78rpm

BLUEBIRD 4-8   41
BRUNSWICK................................ 4-8   46
CAPITOL.................................... 4-8   42-44
COLUMBIA (2898 "Devil's
Holiday")............................... 10-20   33
(Colored plastic.)
DECCA 4-8   40
OKEH 4-8   40
VOCALION 4-8   35-40

CARTER, Carlene   *C&W '79*

(With Rockpile)

Singles: 7–inch

EPIC... 3-4   83
REPRISE 3-4   90-91
W.B. 3-4   78-82

LPs: 10/12–inch 33rpm

EPIC... 5-10   83
W.B. 5-10   78-82
Also see CARTER FAMILY
Also see EDMUNDS, Dave, & Carlene Carter
Also see ORRALL, Robert Ellis
Also see SOUTHERN PACIFIC & Carlene Carter

CARTER, Carlene, & Dave Edmunds

C&W '80

Singles: 7–inch

W.B. 3-4   80
  Also see CARTER, Carlene

CARTER, Fred, Jr.

C&W '67

Singles: 7–inch

MONUMENT 4-6   67

LP: 10/12–inch 33rpm

U.A. 8-12   67
  Also see TWITTY, Conway

CARTER, June

C&W '71

(June Carter Cash)

Singles: 78rpm

COLUMBIA	5-10	55-56
RCA	5-10	50-51

Singles: 7–inch

COLUMBIA (21000 series)	5-10	55-56
COLUMBIA (40700 series)	5-10	56
COLUMBIA (42000 thru 45000 series)	3-5	63-71
LIBERTY	4-8	61-62
RCA (0355 thru 0439)	8-12	50-51

LP: 10/12–inch 33rpm

COLUMBIA 6-10   75
  Also see CARTER FAMILY
  Also see CARTER SISTERS
  Also see CASH, Johnny, & June Carter
  Also see HOMER & JETHRO with June Carter

CARTER, Woody, & Hoedown Boys

C&W '49

Singles: 78rpm

LUCKY	10-15	52
MACY'S	10-15	49

CARTER FAMILY   *P&R '28/C&W '72*

Singles: 78rpm

BANNER	15-25	35
BLUEBIRD	15-25	30s
DECCA	10-20	30s
ELEKTRADISK	25-50	32-33
(Made for sale through Woolworth Stores.)		
MONTEGOMERY WARD	15-25	30s
VICTOR (20000 series)	50-150	28
VICTOR (40000 series)	25-75	28
VOCALION	25-35	

EPs: 7–inch 33/45rpm

ACME	25-50	50s
DECCA	10-20	65

LP: 10/12–inch 33rpm

ACME (1 "All Time Favorites")	100-200	50s
ACME (2 "In Memory of A.P. Carter: Keep on the Sunny Side")	100-200	50s
ANTHOLOGY of COUNTRY MUSIC	10-15	
COLUMBIA ("CL" & "CS" series)	10-20	64-67
DECCA (4404 "The Carter Family")	20-30	63
DECCA (4557 "More Favorites")	20-30	65
LIBERTY	15-25	62
CAMDEN (Except 586)		71-74
CAMDEN (586 "Original and Great Carter Family")	15-20	62
COLUMBIA ("KC" & "PC" series)	5-10	72-80s
HARMONY (7280 "Famous Carter Family")	15-25	61
HARMONY (7300 "Carter Family")	15-25	63
HARMONY (7344 "Home Among the Hills")	15-25	65
HARMONY (7396 "Sacred Songs")	10-15	66
HARMONY (7422 "Country Sounds")	10-20	67
HARMONY (11000 series)	10-15	69-70
J.E.M.F.	10-15	
OLD HOMESTEAD	5-8	
OLD TIME CLASSICS	5-10	
PICKWICK	5-10	75
PINE MOUNTAIN	8-10	
RCA (Except 2772)	5-15	75-78
RCA (2772 "Mid the Green Fields of Virginia")	15-25	63
SUNSET	10-15	67

Members: A.P. Carter; Sara Carter; Maybelle Carter; Anita Carter; June Carter; Helen Carter; Joe Carter; Janette Carter; Carlene Carter. Session: Johnny Cash.
  Also see CARTER, Anita
  Also see CARTER, June
  Also see CARTER SISTERS
  Also see CASH, Johnny, & Carter Family
  Also see HAGGARD, Merle

CARTER SISTERS

(With Mother Maybelle)

Singles: 78rpm

COLUMBIA	5-10	52-53
RCA	5-10	50-51

Singles: 7–inch
COLUMBIA	10-15	52-53
RCA	10-15	50-51

Members: Anita Carter; June Carter; Helen Carter.
Also see CARTER, Anita
Also see CARTER, June
Also see CARTER FAMILY

CARTWRIGHT, Lionel   *C&W '88*
Singles: 7–inch
MCA	3-4	90-92

CARVER, Johnny   *C&W '67*
Singles: 7–inch
ABC	3-5	73-75
ABC/DOT	3-5	75-77
DOT	4-6	66
EQUITY	3-5	80
EPIC	3-5	71-72
IMPERIAL	4-6	67-70
REL	4-8	
TANGLEWOOD	3-4	80
U.A.	3-5	70

LP: 10/12–inch 33rpm
ABC	8-15	74-75
ABC/DOT	8-12	76-77
HARMONY	8-12	73
IMPERIAL	10-15	67-69

Session: Anita Kerr Singers.
Also see KERR, Anita

CASEY, Al   *P&R/R&B '62*
(Al Casey Combo; with the K-C Ettes)
Singles: 78rpm
DOT	20-30	56-57
MCI	10-20	55

Singles: 7–inch
BLUE HORIZON (925 "Cookin")	15-25	62
CHALLENGE	5-10	60
DOT (15524 "A Fool's Blues")	10-20	56
DOT (15563 "Guitar Man")	15-25	57
GREGMARK (5 "Caravan")	5-10	61
(Shown as by Duane Eddy, but actually by Al Casey.)		
HIGHLAND (1002 "Got the Teenage Blues")	25-40	59
HIGHLAND (1004 "Night Beat")	15-25	60
LIBERTY	10-20	58
MCI	15-25	55
RAMCO	8-10	61
STACY (Except 962)	10-15	62-64
STACY (962 "Surfin' Hootenany") (Black vinyl.)	10-15	63
STACY (962 "Surfin' Hootenany") (Colored vinyl.)	25-40	63
U.A. (158 "Stinger")	10-20	59

LPs: 10/12–inch 33rpm
STACY (100 "Surfin' Hootenany") (Black vinyl.)	30-50	63
STACY (100 "Surfin' Hootenany") (Colored vinyl.)	100-125	63

Also see CLARK, Sanford
Also see EDDY, Duane
Also see EXOTIC GUITARS
Also see REYNOLDS, Jody

CASEY, Karen   *C&W '80*
Singles: 7–inch
WESTERN PRIDE	3-5	80

CASH, Johnny   *C&W '55*
(With the Tennessee Two; with Tennessee Three)
Singles: 78rpm
SUN	20-40	55-57

Singles: 7–inch
CACHET	3-5	80
COLUMBIA (Except 41000 thru 43000 series)	3-8	67-85
COLUMBIA (41000 & 42000 series)	10-20	60-62
(With "3" prefix. Compact 33 singles)		
COLUMBIA (41000 & 42000 series)	6-12	58-64
(With "4" prefix.)		
COLUMBIA (43000 series)	4-8	64-66
COLUMBIA BOOK/RECORD LIBRARY ("The Bug That Tried to Crawl Around the World")	4-8	60s
SSS/SUN (Black vinyl)	3-5	69-70
SSS/SUN (Colored vinyl)	5-10	69-70
(Promotional issues only.)		
SCOTTI BROS.	3-4	82
SUN (200 series)	10-20	55-58
SUN (300 series)	8-12	58-62

EPs: 7–inch 33/45rpm
COLUMBIA	15-30	58-69
SUN	15-30	58

Picture Sleeves
COLUMBIA (Except 41000 & 42000 series)	3-5	67-85

COLUMBIA (41000 series) 10-15	58-61
COLUMBIA (42000 series) 5-10	61-64
COLUMBIA (44000 series) 4-6	68
SUN (295 "Guess Things Happen That Way") 10-15	58

LPs: 10/12–inch 33rpm

BLAINE HOUSE........................... 6-12	
(Mail order offer.)	
BUCKBOARD 5-10	
CBS 5-10	82
CACHET 5-10	
COLUMBIA (29 "The World of Johnny Cash") 8-12	70
COLUMBIA (363 "Legends and Love Songs") 10-15	68
(Columbia Record Club issue.)	
COLUMBIA (1200 thru 1799).... 15-30	58-61
(With "CL" prefix. Monaural.)	
COLUMBIA (8100 thru 8599).... 20-40	58-61
(With "CS" prefix. Stereo.)	
COLUMBIA (1800 thru 2650).... 10-20	62-68
(With "CL" prefix. Monaural.)	
COLUMBIA (2004 "The Heart of Johnny Cash") 15-25	60s
(Columbia Star Series.)	
COLUMBIA (8600 thru 9478).... 10-20	62-68
(With "CS" prefix. Stereo.)	
COLUMBIA (9600 thru 9943)...... 8-12	69-70
(With "CS" prefix.)	
COLUMBIA (10000 series) 5-10	73
COLUMBIA (30000 thru 38000 series) 5-15	70-82
COLUMBIA SPECIAL PRODUCTS............................. 5-10	75
COLUMBIA/SUFFOLK............... 8-10	79
DESIGN 5-8	
DORAL...................................... 20-40	
(Promotional mail-order LP from Doral cigarettes.)	
HARMONY................................... 8-12	69
IMPERIAL HOUSE....................... 5-10	
(Mail order offer.)	
LONGINES.................................... 5-8	
(Mail order offer.)	
OUT of TOWN DIST 5-10	82
PICKWICK 5-10	70s
POWER PAK 5-10	
PRIORITY 5-10	81-82
SSS/SUN 5-15	69-84
(Some may be colored vinyl.)	
SHARE....................................... 5-10	
STACK-O-HITS............................. 5-8	

SUN (1220 "Johnny Cash and His Hot and Blue Guitar") 20-40	56
SUN (1235 "Songs That Made Him Famous") 20-40	58
SUN (1240 "Greatest")...............20-30	59
SUN (1245 "Johnny Cash Sings Hank Williams and Other Favorties").....15-25	60
SUN (1255 "Now Here's Johnny Cash")..15-25	61
SUN (1270 "All Aboard the Blue Train") 15-25	63
SUN (1275 "Original Sun Sound of Johnny Cash")..15-25	64
SUN/CAPITOL (90000 series)...15-20	60s
(Record club issues.)	
SUNRISE MEDIA.........................5-10	81
SUNNYVALE 5-8	
TIME-LIFE ("Johnny Cash").......10-15	82
(3 LP set.)	
TRIP...8-10	74
U.A. 10-12	68

Session: George Jones; Marty Robbins; Waylon Jennings.
Also see BROOKS, Karen, & Johnny Cash
Also see DEL RAY, Martin
Also see HARRIS, Emmylou
Also see JONES, George
Also see KILGORE, Merle
Also see RICH, Charlie
Also see ROBBINS, Marty / Johnny Cash / Ray Price
Also see STATLER BROTHERS
Also see STUART, Marty
Also see TUBB, Ernest

CASH, Johnny, & June Carter   *C&W '64*

(Johnny Cash & June Carter Cash)

Singles: 7–inch

COLUMBIA 3-5	67-83

LPs: 10/12–inch 33rpm

COLUMBIA (9500 series) 10-20	64-67
COLUMBIA (32000 series) 5-10	73
HARMONY....................................6-10	72

Also see CARTER, June
Also see JENNINGS, Waylon, Willie Nelson, Johnny Cash, & Kris Kristofferson

CASH, Johnny, & Carter Family   *C&W '63*

(Carter Family with Johnny Cash)

Singles: 7–inch

COLUMBIA 3-8	63-72

CASH, Johnny, Carter Family & Oak Ridge Boys   *C&W '73*
Singles: 7–inch
COLUMBIA 3-5   73
  Also see CARTER FAMILY
  Also see OAK RIDGE BOYS

CASH, Johnny, & Mother Maybelle Carter   *C&W '73*
Singles: 7–inch
COLUMBIA 3-5   73
  Also see CARTER FAMILY

CASH, Johnny, Rosanne Cash & Everly Brothers   *C&W '89*
Singles: 7–inch
MERCURY (872 420-7 "Ballad of a Teenage
  Queen").. 3-4   89
  Also see CASH, Rosanne
  Also see EVERLY BROTHERS

CASH, Johnny / Roy Clark / Linda Ronstadt
LPs: 10/12–inch 33rpm
POINTED STAR (10178 "Concert Behind
  Prison Walls")........................... 10-15   78
  (NAPA special products TV soundtrack.)
  Also see CASH, Rosanne
  Also see CLARK, Roy
  Also see RONSTADT, Linda

CASH, Johnny / Billy Grammer / Wilburn Brothers
LPs: 10/12–inch 33rpm
PICKWICK/HILLTOP 10-15   65
  Also see GRAMMER, Billy

CASH, Johnny, & Levon Helm
Singles: 7–inch
A&M 3-4   80
  Also see HELM, Levon

CASH, Johnny, & Waylon Jennings   *C&W '86*
Singles: 7–inch
COLUMBIA 3-4   78-86
EPIC... 3-4   80
  Also see JENNINGS, Waylon

CASH, Johnny / Jerry Lee Lewis / Jeanie C. Riley
LPs: 10/12–inch 33rpm
PICKWICK 5-10   70s
  Also see RILEY, Jeanie C.

CASH, Johnny, Carl Perkins & Jerry Lee Lewis
LPs: 10/12–inch 33rpm
COLUMBIA 5-10   82
  Also see PERKINS, Carl, Jerry Lee Lewis, Roy Orbison
  & Johnny Cash

CASH, Johnny / Jeanie C. Riley
LP: 10/12–inch 33rpm
LONGINES (5288 "Rock Island
  Line")...5-8
  (Mail order offer.)
  Also see RILEY, Jeanie C.

CASH, Johnny, & Hank Williams Jr.   *C&W '88*
Singles: 7–inch
MERCURY.......................................3-4   88
  Also see WILLIAMS, Hank, Jr.

CASH, Johnny / Tammy Wynette
LPs: 10/12–inch 33rpm
COLUMBIA (5418 "King &
  Queen")....................................10-15
  (Columbia Musical Treasury issue.)
  Also see CASH, Johnny
  Also see WYNETTE, Tammy

CASH, Rosanne   *C&W '80*
Singles: 7–inch
COLUMBIA 3-4   80-90
Picture Sleeves
COLUMBIA 3-4   81
EPs: 7–inch 33/45rpm
COLUMBIA 4-8   85
LPs: 10/12–inch 33rpm
COLUMBIA 5-10   79-90
  Session: Bobby Bare; Rodney Crowell; Emmylou
  Harris; Ricky Skaggs.
  Also see CASH, Johnny, Rosanne Cash & Everly
   Brothers
  Also see CROWELL, Rodney, & Rosanne Cash
  Also see HARRIS, Emmylou
  Also see NITTY GRITTY DIRT BAND, Rosanne Cash
   & John Hiatt
  Also see SKAGGS, Ricky

CASH, Rosanne, & Bobby Bare   *C&W '79*
Singles: 7–inch
COLUMBIA 3-4   79
  Also see BARE, Bobby
  Also see CASH, Rosanne

CASH, Tommy   *C&W '68*
Singles: 7–inch
AUDIOGRAPH	3-4	83
ELEKTRA	3-5	75
EPIC	3-6	68-73
MONUMENT	3-4	77-79
MUSICOR	4-8	65
20TH FOX	3-4	76
U.A.	4-6	66-68

LPs: 10/12–inch 33rpm
ELEKTRA	5-10	75
EPIC	8-12	69-72
MONUMENT	5-10	78
U.A.	10-12	68

CASHMAN & WEST   *P&R/LP '72*
Singles: 7–inch
ABC	3-4	74
DUNHILL	3-5	72-74
LIFESONG	3-5	75

Picture Sleeves
DUNHILL	3-5	72

LPs: 10/12–inch 33rpm
ABC	8-10	74
DUNHILL	8-12	72-74

Members: Terry Cashman; Tommy West.
Also see CROCE, Jim

CASHMAN & WEST / Gordon Jenkins & His Orchestra
LPs: 10/12–inch 33rpm
DUNHILL (SPDJ-17 "Manhattan Tower")	10-15	72
(10–inch LP.)		

CASHMAN, PISTILLI & WEST
Singles: 7–inch
ABC	4-6	68
CAPITOL	3-5	69-71

LPs: 10/12–inch 33rpm
ABC	12-15	68
CAPITOL	10-15	69-71

Members: Terry Cashman; Gene Pistilli; Tommy West.

CASHMAN, PISTILLI & WEST / Steve Karmen
Singles: 7–inch
PONTIAC ("GTO Rock")	10-15	70
(Promotional issue of "1970 Pontiac Theme Music.")		

CASSADY, Linda   *C&W '76*
(With Bobby Spears)
Singles: 7–inch
CIN KAY	3-5	76-78

LP: 10/12–inch 33rpm
AMIGO	5-10	70s
CIN KAY	5-10	77

Also see SPEARS, Bobby

CATES SISTERS   *C&W '76*
(The Cates)
Singles: 7–inch
CAPRICE	3-5	76-78
OVATION	3-5	79-80

LP: 10/12–inch 33rpm
CAPRICE	5-10	77
OVATION	5-10	79

Members: Mary Cates; Margie Cates.
Also see BROWN, Jim Ed

CATO, Connie   *C&W '74*
Singles: 7–inch
CAPITOL	3-5	74-77
MCA	3-4	80

LP: 10/12–inch 33rpm
CAPITOL	5-10	74-77

CAUDELL, Lane   *C&W '87*
Singles: 7–inch
MCA	3-4	78
METROMEDIA	3-5	73
PRIVATE STOCK	3-5	76
16TH AVE.	3-4	87-88

LPs: 10/12–inch 33rpm
MCA	8-10	78-79

CEDAR CREEK   *C&W '81*
Singles: 7–inch
MOON SHINE	3-4	81-83

Members: Dave Holcraft; Garland Craft; Chris Golden.
Also see GOLDENS

CERRITO   *C&W '89*
Singles: 7–inch
SOUNDWAVES	3-4	89

CHAMBERLAIN, David   *C&W '88*
Singles: 7–inch
COUNTRY INT'L	3-4	88

CHAMBERS, Carl   *C&W '81*
Singles: 7–inch
PRAIRIE DUST	3-5	81

CHANCE · C&W '85

Singles: 7–inch

MERCURY 3-4 85-86
Member: Jeff Chance
Also see CHANCE, Jeff

CHANCE, Jeff · C&W '88

Singles: 7–inch

CURB 3-4   88
Also see CHANCE

CHANEY, Hank · C&W '86

Singles: 7–inch

CMI... 3-4   86

CHANTILLY · C&W '82

(Featuring Kim Williams)

Singles: 7–inch

F&L... 3-4 82-84
JAROCO 3-5   82
Members: Kim Williams; Debbie Pierce; P.J. Allman;
Joci Stevens.

CHAPARRAL BROTHERS · C&W '68

Singles: 7–inch

CAPITOL.. 3-6 68-70

LP: 10/12–inch 33rpm

CAPITOL.. 8-12 68-70
Members: John Chaparral; Paul Chaparral.

CHAPARRO, Tommy · C&W '83

Singles: 7–inch

COMPASS 3-4   83

CHAPMAN, Cee Cee · C&W '88

(With Santa Fe)

Singles: 7–inch

CURB 3-4 88-89

CHAPMAN, Gary · C&W '88

Singles: 7–inch

RCA... 3-4   88

CHAPMAN, Marshall · C&W '77

Singles: 7–inch

EPIC... 3-5 76-80

LPs: 10/12–inch 33rpm

EPIC... 8-12 77-79
ROUNDER 5-10   82

CHARLENE · P&R '77/C&W '82

(Charlene Duncan)

Singles: 7–inch

MOTOWN 3-5 76-85
PRODIGAL.. 3-5 76-77

Picture Sleeves

PRODIGAL 3-5   77

LPs: 10/12–inch 33rpm

MOTOWN 5-10 82-85
PRODIGAL 8-10   76

CHARLENE & Stevie Wonder · P&R '82

Singles: 7–inch

MOTOWN 3-4   82

Picture Sleeves

MOTOWN 3-4   82
Also see CHARLENE

CHARLES, Kim · C&W '79

Singles: 7–inch

MCA... 3-5   79

CHARLES, Ray · R&B '51/C&W '82

(With the Raelettes)

Singles: 78rpm

ATLANTIC................................. 10-30 52-58
JAX 15-25   52
ROCKIN' 15-25   53
SWING BEAT 20-30   49
SWING TIME 15-30 50-53

Singles: 7–inch

ABC.. 3-8 66-73
ABC-PAR (Monaural).................. 4-8 60-66
ABC-PAR (Stereo)..................... 10-15 61-62
ABC/TRC 3-6
ATLANTIC (976 "Roll with Me
   Baby") 50-75   52
ATLANTIC (984 "The Sun's Gonna Shine
   Again") 30-60   53
ATLANTIC (999 "Mess
   Around")............................... 30-60   53
ATLANTIC (1000 series) 12-25 53-57
ATLANTIC (2000 series) 5-10 58-68
ATLANTIC (3000 series) 3-5 77-79
BARONET.................................. 4-8   62
COLUMBIA 3-4 82-87
CROSSOVER 3-5 73-78
DUNHILL GOLDIES..................... 3-4   73
HURRAH................................... 8-12
IMPULSE 5-10   61
MAYFAIR (121 "Pony Boy").......... 4-8
   (With "Uncle Stu.")
RCA 3-5   76
ROCKIN' (504 "Walkin' and
   Talkin'") 100-200   53

SITTIN' in WITH (641 "Baby Let Me Hear
You Call My Name").............. 75-150   52
SWING TIME (250 "Baby Let Me Hold Your
Hand").................................. 75-100   51
SWING TIME (274 "Kiss Me
Baby") 75-100   52
SWING TIME (300 "Baby Let Me Hear You
Call My Name").................... 75-100   52
SWING TIME (326 "The Snow Is
Falling") 50-100   53
TANGERINE 3-4   71
TIME.. 3-5   62

Picture Sleeves

ABC.. 3-6   68-70

EPs: 7–inch 33/45rpm

ABC-PAR 10-20   60-62
ATLANTIC................................. 20-30   56-59

LPs: 10/12–inch 33rpm

ABC (Except 590) 10-12   66-73
ABC (590 "A Man and His
Soul") 20-25   67
ABC-PAR (300 series) 15-25   60-61
ABC-PAR (400 & 500 series).... 10-20   62-66
AHED 8-12
(TV mail-order offer.)
ATLANTIC (500 series)............. 10-15   73
ATLANTIC (900 "The Ray Charles Story,
Vols. 1 & 2") 30-40   62
(Combines Atlantic 8063 and 8064.)
ATLANTIC (1259 "The Great Ray
Charles") 45-60   57
ATLANTIC (1279 "Soul
Brothers")............................... 40-50   58
(With Milt Jackson.)
ATLANTIC (1289 "Ray Charles at
Newport") 40-50   58
ATLANTIC (1312 "Genius of Ray
Charles") 30-45   59
ATLANTIC (1360 "Soul
Meeting")................................ 20-35   62
(With Milt Jackson. Number indicates a '61
release, but not actually issued until 1962.)
ATLANTIC (1369 "Genius After
Hours") 20-35   61
ATLANTIC (1500 series)............. 8-10   70
ATLANTIC (3700 series).......... 20-22   82
ATLANTIC (7000 series).......... 12-15   64
ATLANTIC (8006 "Ray
Charles") 45-60   57
(Black label.)
ATLANTIC (8006 "Ray
Charles") 25-35   59
(Red label.)

ATLANTIC (8025 "Yes
Indeed") 30-40   59
(Black label.)
ATLANTIC (8025 "Yes
Indeed") 25-35   60
(Red label.)
ATLANTIC (8029 "What'd I
Say")......................................30-40   59
(Black label.)
ATLANTIC (8029 "What'd I
Say")......................................25-35   60
(Red label.)
ATLANTIC (8039 "Ray Charles
in Person") 30-40   60
(Black label.)
ATLANTIC (8039 "Ray Charles
in Person")............................25-35   60
(Red label.)
ATLANTIC (8052 "The Genius
Sings the Blues") 20-30   61
ATLANTIC (8054 "Dot the
Twist").....................................20-30   61
ATLANTIC (8063 "The Ray Charles Story,
Vol. 1")...................................20-25   62
ATLANTIC (8064 "The Ray Charles Story,
Vol. 2")...................................20-25   62
ATLANTIC (8083 "The Ray Charles Story,
Vol. 3")...................................20-25   63
ATLANTIC (8094 "The Ray Charles Story,
Vol. 4") 20-25   64
ATLANTIC (19000 series) 5-10   77-80
BARONET.................................15-20   62
BLUESWAY 8-10   73
BULLDOG...................................5-10   84
COLUMBIA 5-10   83-86
CORONET 8-10
CROSSOVER...............................8-15   73-76
DESIGN 10-15   62
EVEREST 8-10   70-82
GUEST STAR 10-20   64
HOLLYWOOD (504 "The Original Ray
Charles")............................100-150   59
HOLLYWOOD 505: see CHARLES, Ray /
Charles Brown)
HURRAH.....................................5-10
IMPULSE 20-30   61
INTERMEDIA...............................5-10   84
KING 8-10   77
PALACE......................................5-10
PREMIER....................................8-10
SCEPTER 8-12
STRAND 10-15   60s
TANGERINE.............................10-12   70-73

UPFRONT.....................................8-10   70s
Also see U.S.A. for AFRICA

CHARLES, Ray / Charles Brown
LPs: 10/12–inch 33rpm
HOLLYWOOD (505 "The Fabulous Artistry of
Ray Charles").....................100-150   59
(Brown, barely credited, provides four
tracks.)

CHARLES, Ray / Solomon Burke
LPs: 10/12–inch 33rpm
GRAND PRIX...........................10-20   64

CHARLES, Ray, & Betty Carter
LP '61
Singles: 7–inch
ABC-PAR 5-10   61-62
LPs: 10/12–inch 33rpm
ABC-PAR (ABC-385 "Ray Charles & Betty
Carter")...................................50-75   61
(Monaural.)
ABC-PAR (ABCS-385 "Ray Charles & Betty
Carter")................................75-100   61
(Stereo.)
DCC (2005 "Ray Charles & Betty
Carter")......................................8-12   95

CHARLES, Ray, & Clint Eastwood
C&W '80
Singles: 7–inch
W.B. 3-4   80
Also see EASTWOOD, Clint

CHARLES, Ray, & Mickey Gilley
C&W '85
Singles: 7–inch
COLUMBIA 3-4   85
Also see GILLEY, Mickey

CHARLES, Ray / Ivory Joe Hunter / Jimmy Rushing
LPs: 10/12–inch 33rpm
DESIGN (909 "Three of a
Kind") 15-20   60s
(Black label, silver print.)
DESIGN (909 "Three of a
Kind") 10-15   60s
(Black, red, blue and yellow label.)

CHARLES, Ray, George Jones & Chet Atkins
C&W '83
Singles: 7–inch
COLUMBIA 3-4   83
Also see ATKINS, Chet

Also see JONES, George

CHARLES, Ray, & Cleo Laine
LP '76
LPs: 10/12–inch 33rpm
RCA 10-12   76

CHARLES, Ray & Jimmy Lewis
P&R/R&B '69
Singles: 7–inch
ABC...3-4   69
TANGERINE 3-6   68

CHARLES, Ray / Little Richard / Sam Cooke
LPs: 10/12–inch 33rpm
ALMOR (102 "Soul Blues").........10-20

CHARLES, Ray, & Willie Nelson
C&W '84
Singles: 7–inch
COLUMBIA 3-4   84
Also see NELSON, Willie

CHARLES, Ray / Arbee Stidham / Li'l Son Jackson / James Wayne.
LPs: 10/12–inch 33rpm
MAINSTREAM 8-12   71

CHARLES, Ray, & B.J. Thomas
C&W '84
Singles: 7–inch
COLUMBIA 3-4   85
Also see THOMAS, B.J.

CHARLES, Ray, & Hank Williams Jr.
C&W '85
Singles: 7–inch
COLUMBIA 3-4   85
Also see CHARLES, Ray
Also see WILLIAMS, Hank, Jr.

CHARLESTON EXPRESS with Jesse Wales
C&W '84
Singles: 7–inch
SOUNDWAVES 3-4   84-85

CHARMS
P&R/R&B '54
(Otis Williams & the Charms)
Singles: 78rpm
CHART..15-25   55-56
DELUXE.....................................25-75   54-57
QUALITY/KING..........................40-60   54
(Canadian.)
ROCKIN' 50-75   53

Singles: 7–inch

CHART (608 "Love's Our Inspiration")	15-25	55
CHART (613 "Heart of a Rose")	15-25	56
CHART (623 "I'll Be True")	15-25	56
DELUXE (6000 "Heaven Only Knows")	75-125	53
DELUXE (6014 "Happy Are We")	75-100	53
DELUXE (6034 "Bye-Bye Baby")	75-100	54
DELUXE (6050 "Quiet Please")	50-100	54
DELUXE (6056 "My Baby Dearest Darling")	50-100	54
DELUXE (6062 thru 6098)	15-30	54-56
DELUXE (6100 series) (Monaural)	12-25	57-59
DELUXE (6185 "Tears of Happiness") (Stereo.)	25-45	59
GUSTO	3-4	77
KING	5-10	60-63
OKEH	4-8	65-66
QUALITY/KING (4302 "Hearts of Stone") (Canadian.)	50-100	54
ROCKIN' (516 "Heaven Only Knows")	200-350	53
STOP	5-8	

EPs: 7–inch 33/45rpm

DELUXE (357 "Hits by the Charms")	150-200	55
DELUXE (364 "Hits by the Charms")	150-200	55
DELUXE (385 "Otis Williams and the Charms")	100-200	56
KING (357 "Hits by the Charms")	50-75	58
KING (364 "Hits by the Charms, Vol. 2")	50-75	58
KING (385 "Otis Williams & His Charms")	50-75	58

LPs: 10/12–inch 33rpm

DELUXE (570 "All Their Hits") (With color photo of the group on cover.)	300-400	58
KING (614 "This Is Otis Williams and the Charms")	100-125	59

Members: Otis Williams; Ron Bradley; Don Peark; Joe Renn; Richard Parker.
Also see WILLIAMS, Otis

CHASE, Becky   *C&W '85*
Singles: 7–inch
SPRIT HORSE	3-4	85

CHASE, Carol   *C&W '79*
Singles: 7–inch
CASABLANCA	3-4	79-80
JANUS	3-5	75
MCA	3-4	80

LPs: 10/12–inch 33rpm
CASABLANCA	5-10	80

Also see WEST, Jim

CHASTAIN, Dawn   *C&W '78*
Singles: 7–inch
OAK	3-5	79
PRAIRIE DUST	3-5	78
SRC	3-5	79

CHER   *P&R/LP '65/C&W '79*
(Cher Bono; Cher Allman)
Singles: 12–inch 33/45rpm
CASABLANCA	8-10	79-82

Singles: 7–inch
ATCO	3-6	69-72
ATLANTIC	4-6	69
CASABLANCA	3-5	79
COLUMBIA	3-5	82
GEFFEN	3-4	87-90
IMPERIAL	5-10	64-68
KAPP	3-5	71-72
LIBERTY	3-4	82
MCA	3-5	73-75
U.A.	3-5	71-72
W.B.	3-5	75-77
W.B./SPECTOR	3-5	74

Picture Sleeves
COLUMBIA	3-5	82
GEFFEN	3-4	87-89

LPs: 10/12–inch 33rpm
ATCO	15-20	69
CASABLANCA (Except NBPIX-7133)	8-12	79
CASABLANCA (NBPIX-7133 "Take Me Home") (Picture disc.)	30-40	79
COLUMBIA	5-10	82
GEFFEN	5-10	87-91
IMPERIAL	15-25	65-68
KAPP	12-15	71-72
LIBERTY	5-10	81
MCA	10-15	73-74

SPRINGBOARD	8-10	72
SUNSET	8-10	70
U.A.	8-10	71-75
W.B.	8-15	75-77

Also see CHERILYN / Cherilyn's Group
Also see MASON, Bonnie Jo

CHER & Peter Cetera   *P&R '89*
Singles: 7–inch
GEFFEN	3-4	89

Picture Sleeves
GEFFEN	3-4	89

CHER & NILSSON
Singles: 7–inch
SPECTOR	3-5	75

Members: Cher; Harry Nilsson.
Also see CHER
Also see NILSSON

CHERILYN / Cherilyn's Group
(Cher Bono)
Singles: 7–inch
IMPERIAL (66081 "Dream Baby")	20-30	64

Also see CHER

CHERRY, Don   *P&R '54/C&W '68*
Singles: 78rpm
COLUMBIA	5-10	55-57
DECCA	5-10	50-56

Singles: 7–inch
COLUMBIA	5-10	55-59
DECCA	8-12	50-56
MONUMENT	3-5	65-78
STRAND	4-8	59
VERVE	4-8	62
WARWICK	4-8	60

EPs: 7–inch 33/45rpm
COLUMBIA	8-15	56

LPs: 10/12–inch 33rpm
COLUMBIA	15-25	56
HARMONY	10-15	59
MONUMENT	8-12	66-73

CHESNUT, Jim   *C&W '77*
Singles: 7–inch
ABC/HICKORY	3-5	77-78
LIBERTY	3-4	81
MCA	3-5	79
U.A.	3-4	80

LP: 10/12–inch 33rpm
ABC/HICKORY	6-12	77-78

CHESNUTT, Mark   *C&W/LP '90*
Singles: 7–inch
MCA	3-4	90-91

LPs: 10/12–inch 33rpm
MCA	5-8	90-91

CHET, FLOYD & DANNY: see ATKINS, Chet, Floyd Cramer & Danny Davis

CHICK & HOT RODS   *C&W '61*
Singles: 7–inch
KING	5-10	61

Members: Don Reno; Red Smiley.
Also see RENO & SMILEY

CHILDRESS, Lisa   *C&W '86*
Singles: 7–inch
AMI	3-4	86-87
TRUE	3-4	88-89

CHINNOCK, Bill   *C&W '85*
Singles: 7–inch
ATLANTIC	3-5	78
NORTH COUNTRY	3-5	80
PARADISE	3-4	85
PARAMOUNT	3-5	74

LPs: 10/12–inch 33rpm
ATLANTIC	5-10	78
NORTH COUNTRY	5-10	80
PARAMOUNT	8-10	74

CHIPMUNKS   *P&R/R&B '58*
(Starring Alvin, Theodore, & Simon; Featuring David Seville)
Singles: 7–inch
AMERICAN TELECARD	10-15	64
(Cardboard flexi-disc.)		
DOT	4-6	67
LIBERTY (Except 77000 series)	5-10	58-74
LIBERTY (77000 series)	10-20	59
(Stereo.)		
MISTLETOE	3-5	75
SUNSET	3-6	68
U.A.	3-5	74

Picture Sleeves
LIBERTY	5-10	59-65

EPs: 7–inch 33/45rpm
LIBERTY	10-20	59-64

LPs: 10/12–inch 33rpm
LIBERTY (3132 "Let's All Sing with the Chipmunks")	20-30	59

(Monaural. Black vinyl. Cover shows Chipmunks as animals. If Chipmunks are drawn as cartoon characters, deduct 50%.)

LIBERTY (3132 "Let's All Sing with the Chipmunks")............................ 25-40   59
(Monaural. Colored vinyl. Cover shows Chipmunks as animals. If Chipmunks are drawn as cartoon characters, deduct 50%.)

LIBERTY (3159 "Sing Again with the Chipmunks")............................ 20-30   60
(Monaural. Cover shows Chipmunks as animals. If Chipmunks are drawn as cartoon characters, deduct 50%.)

LIBERTY (3170 "Around the World with the Chipmunks")............................ 20-30   60
(Monaural. Cover shows Chipmunks as animals. If Chipmunks are drawn as cartoon characters, deduct 50%.)

LIBERTY (3200 thru 3400 series)10-20 61-65
(Monaural.)

LIBERTY (7132 "Let's All Sing with the Chipmunks")............................ 20-35   59
(Stereo. Black vinyl. Cover shows Chipmunks as animals. If Chipmunks are drawn as cartoon characters, deduct 50%.)

LIBERTY (7132 "Let's All Sing with the Chipmunks")............................ 25-45   59
(Stereo. Colored vinyl. Cover shows Chipmunks as animals. If Chipmunks are drawn as cartoon characters, deduct 50%.)

LIBERTY (7159 "Sing Again with the Chipmunks")............................ 20-35   60
(Stereo. Cover shows Chipmunks as animals. If Chipmunks are drawn as cartoon characters, deduct 50%.)

LIBERTY (7170 "Around the World with the Chipmunks")............................ 20-35   60
(Stereo. Cover shows Chipmunks as animals. If Chipmunks are drawn as cartoon characters, deduct 50%.)

LIBERTY (7200 thru 7400 series)10-20 61-65
(Stereo.)

LIBERTY (10000 series) 5-10   82
PICKWICK 5-10   80
SUNSET...................................... 8-15 68-69
U.A. 5-10 74-76

CHIPMUNKS   *LP '80/C&W '92*

(Starring Alvin, Theodore, & Simon; Featuring David Seville Jr.)

Singles: 7–inch

EPIC.. 3-4   92
EXCELSIOR.................................. 3-4   80
RCA... 3-4 81-82

Picture Sleeves

EXCELSIOR.................................. 3-4   80
RCA... 3-4   81

LPs: 10/12–inch 33rpm

EXCELSIOR 5-10   80
PICKWICK INT'L........................5-10   80
RCA 5-10 81-82

CHOATES, Harry   *C&W '47*

(Harry Coates)

Singles: 78rpm

ALLIED....................................10-15
GOLD STAR 10-15 46-50
MACY'S....................................10-15
MODERN MOUNTAIN...............10-15   46

LP: 10/12–inch 33rpm

ARHOOLIE 5-10
D (7000 "Jole Blon")...................25-35
D (7000 "Original Cajun Fiddle").....................................10-15
(Repackage of *Jole Blon*.)

CHRIS & LENNY   *C&W '89*

Singles: 7–inch

HAPPY MAN................................. 3-4   89

CHRISTINE, Anne   *C&W '71*

Singles: 7–inch

CME.. 3-8   71

CLANTON, Darrell   *C&W '83*

Singles: 7–inch

AUDIOGRAPH............................... 3-4 83-84
W.B. 3-4 84-85

LP: 10/12–inch 33rpm

AUDIOGRAPH............................... 5-8   83

CLAPTON, Eric   *P&R/LP '70/C&W '78*

Singles: 12–inch 33/45rpm

W.B. (2248 "Forever Man")..........5-10   85
(Promotional issue only.)
W.B. (2683 "Miss You")..............5-10   85
(Promotional issue only.)

Singles: 7–inch

ATCO 4-6 70-71
DUCK.. 3-4 83-86
POLYDOR 3-5 72-73
RSO 3-5 74-82
W.B. 3-4   86

Picture Sleeves

DUCK.. 3-4 85-89
RSO 3-5 80-81
W.B. 3-4   86

LPs: 10/12–inch 33rpm

ATCO (329 "Eric Clapton") 20-30   70

ATCO (803 "History of Eric
Clapton") 20-30   72

DUCK.. 5-10   83-89

MFSL (030 "Slowhand") 25-50   79

MFSL (183 "Bluesbreakers")..... 15-20   87

POLYDOR (Except 835261) 8-15   72-73

POLYDOR (835261
"Crossroads").......................... 30-40   88
(Boxed 6-LP set.)

RSO (Except 035, 1009 &
4801).. 8-20   73-82

RSO (035 "Slowhand").............. 20-25   77
(Colored vinyl. Promotional issue only.)

RSO (1009 "Limited
Backless") 40-50   78
(Colored vinyl. Promotional issue only.)

RSO (4801 "461 Ocean Blvd.")... 8-12   74
(With *Give Me Strength*.)

RSO (4801 "461 Ocean Blvd.")... 5-10   74
(*Give Me Strength* is replaced with *Better
Make It Through the Day*.)

   Also see COOLIDGE, Rita
   Also see CURTIS, Sonny

CLAPTON, Eric, Jeff Beck & Jimmy Page

LPs: 10/12–inch 33rpm

RCA (4624 "Guitar Boogie")...... 10-15   71

CLAPTON, Eric, & Tina Turner

Singles: 7–inch

DUCK... 3-4   87

Picture Sleeves

DUCK... 3-4   87

   Also see CLAPTON, Eric

CLARK, Guy   *C&W '79*

Singles: 7–inch

RCA... 3-5   76

W.B. 3-5   78-83

LP: 10/12–inch 33rpm

RCA... 5-10   75-83

W.B. 5-8   78-83

   Session: Waylon Jennings.
   Also see COE, David Allan
   Also see JENNINGS, Waylon

CLARK, Jay   *C&W '85*

Singles: 7–inch

CONCORDE 3-4   85-86

CLARK, Lucky   *C&W '77*

Singles: 7–inch

POLYDOR...................................... 3-5   76-77

PUMA.. 3-5   76

CLARK, Mickey   *C&W '83*

Singles: 7–inch

EVERGREEN 3-4   87

MONUMENT..................................3-4   83

CLARK, Petula   *P&R '64/C&W '82*
(Pet Clark)

Singles: 78rpm

CORAL..5-15   53-54

KING 5-15   54

MGM 5-15   55

Singles: 7–inch

CORAL..10-20   53-54

DUNHILL..3-5   74

ERIC 3-4   83

IMPERIAL 5-10   59-60

JANUS 3-5   76

KING 10-20   54

LAURIE 4-8   62-63

LONDON..4-8   62

MGM (12000 series) 10-20   55

MGM (14000 series) 3-6   72-74

ROWE/AMI 5-10   66
("Play Me" Sales Stimulator promotional
issue.)

SCOTTI BROTHERS....................3-4   82

W.B. 3-8   64-69

WARWICK 5-10   61

EPs: 7–inch 33/45rpm

W.B. 5-10   65-66
(Jukebox issues only.)

LPs: 10/12–inch 33rpm

GNP 8-10   73

IMPERIAL (9079 "Pet Clark") 20-40   59
(Monaural.)

IMPERIAL (9281 "Uptown").......15-25   65

IMPERIAL (12027 "Pet Clark") ..20-30   65
(Stereo.)

LAURIE (2032 "In Love") 20-25   65
(Monaural.)

LAURIE (S-2032 "In Love").........25-35   65
(Stereo.)

LAURIE (2043 "Petula Clark Sings for
Everybody") 15-20   65
(Monaural.)

LAURIE (2043 "Petula Clark Sings for
Everybody") 20-25   65
(Stereo.)

MGM 8-12   72

PREMIER....................................15-25   64

SUNSET 10-20   66

W.B. 10-20   65-71

CLARK, Roy   *C&W/P&R '63*
(With Buck Trent)

Singles: 78rpm

4 STAR...................................... 15-25	54	

Singles: 7–inch

ABC.. 3-5	74-79	
ABC/DOT 3-5	75-77	
CAPITOL...................................... 4-8	61-66	
CHURCHILL................................. 3-4	82-84	
DOT 3-6	68-74	
4 STAR (1659 "Mysteries of Life")....................................... 25-50	54	
HALLMARK................................... 3-4	89	
MCA 3-4	79-84	
SILVER DOLLAR.......................... 3-4	86	
SONGBIRD................................... 3-4	81	
TOWER.. 3-6	67	

LPs: 10/12–inch 33rpm

ABC.. 5-10	77-79	
ABC/DOT 6-10	74-77	
ABC SPECIAL PRODUCTS (1002 "Roy Clark")..................................... 10-15	78	
(Promotional issue, made for Pringles.)		
CAPITOL (300 series).............. 10-12	69	
CAPITOL (1700 thru 2500 series) 10-25	62-66	
(With "T" or "ST" prefix.)		
CAPITOL (2400 series).............. 5-10	81	
(With "SM" prefix.)		
CAPITOL (11000 series)............. 8-12	74-75	
CAPITOL (12000 thru 16000 series) 5-10	80-81	
CHURCHILL................................. 5-10	82	
DOT.. 8-12	68-74	
GUEST STAR 8-12	60s	
MCA 5-8	79-84	
PICKWICK 5-10	70s	
PICKWICK/HILLTOP 8-15	66	
SONGBIRD................................. 5-10	81	
TOWER...................................... 10-15	67-68	
WORD.. 5-10	75	

Also see CASH, Johnny / Roy Clark / Linda Ronstadt

CLARK, Sanford   *P&R/R&B/C&W '56*
Singles: 78rpm

DOT.. 15-25	56	
MCI (1003 "The Fool") 25-50	55	

Singles: 7–inch

ABC.. 3-4	74	
DOT (15000 series).................. 20-30	56	
(Maroon label.)		

DOT (15000 series, except 15738)...............................10-20	56-58	
(Black label.)		
DOT (15738 "Modern Romance")...........................75-100	58	
JAMIE 10-15	58-60	
LHI 4-8	67-68	
MCI (1003 "The Fool") 50-75	55	
RAMCO...4-8	66	
TREY 5-8	61	
W.B. 4-8	64-65	

Also see CASEY, Al

CLARK, Sanford, & Duane Eddy
Singles: 7–inch

JAMIE (1107 "Sing 'Em Some Blues") 15-25	58	

Also see CLARK, Sanford
Also see EDDY, Duane

CLARK, Steve   *C&W '84*
Singles: 7–inch

MERCURY......................................3-4	84	

CLAYTON, BOB
(Gene Autry)

Singles: 78rpm

BROADWAY (4004 "Dallas County Jail Blues") 25-75	
BROADWAY (4062 "In the Jailhouse Now, No. 2").............................25-75	
BROADWAY (4067 "Jailhouse Blues") 25-75	
BROADWAY (4073 "Silver Haired Daddy of Mine")....................................25-75	
BROADWAY (4093 "Crimes I Didn't Do")...25-75	
BROADWAY (4094 "Back to Old Smokey Mountain")................................25-75	
BROADWAY (4095 "My Carolina Mountain Home")...................................25-75	

Also see AUTRY, Gene
Also see CLAYTON & BREEN

CLAYTON & BREEN
Singles: 78rpm

BROADWAY (4095 "Alone with My Sorrows") 25-75	

Member: Gene Autry.
Also see AUTRY, Gene
Also see CLAYTON, Bob

CLEMENT, Jack   *C&W '78*
Singles: 7–inch

ELEKTRA......................................3-5	78	

RCA	5-10	59
SUN	10-15	58

LP: 10/12–inch 33rpm

ELEKTRA	5-10	78

CLEMENTS, Boots   *C&W '86*

Singles: 7–inch

WEST	3-4	86

CLEMENTS, Vassar   *C&W '80*

Singles: 7–inch

FLYING FISH	3-5	80
SHIKATA	3-4	88

LP: 10/12–inch 33rpm

FLYING FISH	5-10	77-81
MCA	5-10	77-84
MERCURY	6-12	75
MIND BEST	5-8	84
ROUNDER	5-10	80s
RURAL RHYTHM	8-12	

Session: Doug Jernigan; David Bromberg.
Also see JIM & JESSE
Also see MARSHALL TUCKER BAND
Also see MONROE, Bill
Also see NITTY GRITTY DIRT BAND
Also see YOUNG, Faron

CLIFFORD, Buzz   *P&R/C&W/R&B '61*

Singles: 7–inch

BOW ("14 Karet")	20-30	59
(Selection number not known.)		
CAPITOL	4-8	67
COLUMBIA (41876 "Baby Sittin' Boogie")	30-50	60
(With "3" prefix. Compact 33 Single.)		
COLUMBIA (41979 "Simply Because")	30-50	61
(With "3" prefix. Compact 33 Single.)		
COLUMBIA (42019 "I'll Never Forget")	30-50	61
(With "3" prefix. Compact 33 Single.)		
COLUMBIA (42290 "Forever")	30-50	62
(With "3" prefix. Compact 33 Single.)		
COLUMBIA (41774 "Hello Mr. Moonlight")	10-15	60
(With "4" prefix.)		
COLUMBIA (41876 "Baby Sitter Boogie")	20-30	60
(Note slightly different title. With "4" prefix.)		
COLUMBIA (41876 "Baby Sittin' Boogie")	5-10	61
(With "4" prefix.)		
COLUMBIA (41979 "Simply Because")	15-25	61
(With "4" prefix.)		
COLUMBIA (42019 "I'll Never Forget")	15-25	61
(With "4" prefix.)		
COLUMBIA (42177 "Moving Day")	5-10	61
(With "4" prefix.)		
COLUMBIA (42290 "Forever")	15-25	62
(With "4" prefix.)		
DOT	4-6	69-70
ERIC	3-4	83
RCA	4-8	66
ROULETTE	4-8	62-63

Picture Sleeves

COLUMBIA	15-20	61-62

LPs: 10/12–inch 33rpm

COLUMBIA (1616 "Baby Sittin' Boogie")	40-60	61
(Monaural.)		
COLUMBIA (8416 "Baby Sittin' Boogie")	50-75	61
(Monaural.)		
DOT	15-20	69

CLINE, Patsy   *C&W/P&R '57*

Singles: 78rpm

CORAL	10-20	55-56
DECCA (30221 "Walking After Midnight")	50-80	57

Singles: 7–inch

CORAL	15-25	55-56
DECCA (25000 series)	3-8	65-69
DECCA (29963 thru 30846)	8-12	57-59
DECCA (30929 "Gotta Lot of Rhythm in My Soul")	10-15	59
DECCA (31000 series)	4-8	59-64
EVEREST (2000 series)	4-8	62-64
EVEREST (20005 "I Don't Wanta")	10-15	62
4 STAR (11 "Hidin' Out")	5-10	56
4 STAR (1033 "Life's Railway to Heaven")	3-5	78
KAPP	4-8	65
MCA	3-5	73-80
STARDAY (7000 series)	4-8	65
STARDAY (8000 series)	3-5	71

Picture Sleeves

DECCA (Except 30221)	5-10	62-63
DECCA (30221 "Walkin After Midnight")	15-25	62-63

EPs: 7–inch 33/45rpm

CORAL (81159 "Songs by Patsy Cline")	35-50	58
DECCA (Except 2542)	15-25	61-65

DECCA (2542 "Patsy Cline") 35-50	57	
4 STAR ("Patsy Cline") 25-35	57	
(Reissue of *Patsy Cline* [Decca 2542]. Issued with paper sleeve. Number not known. Promotional issue only.)		
PATSY CLINE 25-35	57	

LPs: 10/12–inch 33rpm

ACCORD 5-10	81	
ALBUM GLOBE 5-10	80s	
ALLEGIANCE 5-10	84	
AUDIO FIDELITY (204 "Patsy Cline") .... 10-15 (Picture disc.)	84	
AUDIO FIDELITY (205 "Crazy Dreams") .... 10-15 (Picture disc.)	84	
BREAKAWAY 5-10		
BULLDOG 5-10		
COLUMBIA .... 10-15 (Columbia Musical Treasury issue.)	69	
COUNTRY FIDELITY 5-10	82	
DECCA (176 "Patsy Cline Story") .... 25-40 (Monaural. Includes booklet.)	63	
DECCA (7-176 "Patsy Cline Story") .... 30-45 (Stereo. Includes booklet.)	63	
DECCA (4202 "Showcase") ...... 20-30 (Monaural.)	61	
DECCA (7-4202 "Showcase") ... 25-35 (Stereo.)	61	
DECCA (4282 "Sentimentally Yours") .... 15-25 (Monaural.)	62	
DECCA (4282 "Sentimentally Yours") .... 20-30 (Stereo.)	61	
DECCA (4508 "Portrait") .... 15-25 (Monaural.)	64	
DECCA (7-4508 "Portrait") .... 20-30 (Stereo.)	64	
DECCA (4586 "That's How a Heartache Begins") .... 30-50 (Monaural.)	64	
DECCA (7-4586 "That's How a Heartache Begins") .... 40-60 (Stereo.)	64	
DECCA (4854 "Greatest Hits") .. 10-15 (Monaural.)	67	
DECCA (7-4854 "Greatest Hits") .... 10-15 (Stereo.)	67	
DECCA (8611 "Patsy Cline") 30-50	57	
EVEREST (300 series) 5-10	75	

EVEREST (1200 series) 15-20		62-64
EVEREST (90000 series) 8-12		
51 WEST 5-10		82
H.S.R.D. 8-10		84
LONGINES 8-12		
MCA 5-10		80-89
METRO 10-20		65
MUSIC MASTERS 5-10		
PICCADILLY 5-10		80
PICKWICK 5-12		70s
PICKWICK/HILLTOP 10-12		65-68
ROLLER SKATE 5-10		82
SEARS 10-15		
VOCALION 10-15		65-69

Session: Jordanaires; Anita Kerr Singers.
Also see HAGGARD, Merle / Patsy Cline
Also see JORDANAIRES
Also see KERR, Anita
Also see LEWIS, Jerry Lee / Patsy Cline / Jimmy Clanton / Frankie Ford
Also see PIERCE, Webb / Patsy Cline / T. Texas Tyler
Also see REEVES, Jim, & Patsy Cline
Also see TUBB, Ernest

CLINE, Patsy / Cowboy Copas / Hawkshaw Hawkins
LPs: 10/12–inch 33rpm

STARDAY 15-20		65

Also see HAWKINS, Hawkshaw

CLINE, Patsy / Cowboy Copas / Johnny Horton
LPs: 10/12–inch 33rpm

HILLTOP 10-15		60s

Also see COPAS, Cowboy
Also see HORTON, Johnny

CLINE, Patsy / Hank Locklin / Miller Brothers / Eddie Marvin
EPs: 7–inch 33/45rpm

4 STAR (136 "Hidin' Out") 25-50		56
(Promotional 10–inch, 45rpm. Not issued with cover.)		

Also see LOCKLIN, Hank

CLINE, Patsy / Pete Pike / Jack Bradshaw / Miller Brothers
EPs: 7–inch 33/45rpm

4 STAR (137 "Come On In") 25-50		56
(Promotional 10–inch, 45rpm. Not issued with cover.)		

CLINE, Patsy / T. Texas Tyler / Bill Taylor / Eddie Marvin

EPs: 7-inch 33/45rpm

4 STAR (139 "Dear God") 25-50   56
(Promotional 10-inch, 45rpm. Not issued
with cover.)
   Also see CLINE, Patsy
   Also see TYLER, T. Texas

COCHRAN, Cliff   *C&W '74*

Singles: 7-inch

ENTERPRISE 3-5   74-75
RCA 3-4   79

COCHRAN, Hank   *C&W '62*

Singles: 7-inch

CAPITOL 3-4   78
DOT 3-5   70
ELEKTRA 3-4   80
GAYLORD 4-8   62-63
LIBERTY 4-8   62-63
MONUMENT 3-6   67-68
RCA 4-8   64-66

LPs: 10/12-inch 33rpm

CAPITOL 10-20   78
ELEKTRA 5-10   80
MONUMENT 10-15   68
RCA 10-20   65
   Session: Jack Greene; Merle Haggard; Willie Nelson;
   Jeannie Seely; Rafe Van Hoy
   Also see COCHRAN BROTHERS
   Also see GREENE, Jack
   Also see HAGGARD, Merle
   Also see SEELY, Jeannie

COCHRAN, Hank, & Willie Nelson

Singles: 7-inch

CAPITOL 3-5   78
   Also see COCHRAN, Hank
   Also see NELSON, Willie

COCHRAN BROTHERS

Singles: 78rpm

EKKO (1003 "Two Blue Singing
Stars") 50-100   56
EKKO (1005 "Guilty
Conscience") 50-100   56
EKKO (3001 "Tired and
Sleepy") 75-125   56

Singles: 7-inch

EKKO (1003 "Two Blue Singing
Stars") 75-125   56
EKKO (1005 "Guilty
Conscience") 75-125   56

EKKO (3001 "Tired and
Sleepy") 100-150   56
   Members: Eddie Cochran; Hank Cochran. (Eddie and
   Hank were not really brothers).
   Also see COCHRAN, Hank

CODY, Betty   *C&W '53*

Singles: 78rpm

RCA 4-8   53

Singles: 7-inch

RCA 5-10   53

CODY, Commander: see COMMANDER CODY

COE, David Allan   *C&W '74*

Singles: 7-inch

COLUMBIA 3-5   74-87
PLANTATION 3-5   73
SSS INT'L (Black vinyl) 3-5   71-72
SSS INT'L (Colored vinyl) 5-10   71-72
   (Promotional issues only.)

LPs: 10/12-inch 33rpm

COLUMBIA 5-10   72-86
SSS INT'L (9 "Penitentiary
Blues") 25-40   70
   Session: Lacy J. Dalton; Dianne Sherrill; Eve Shaprio;
   Bill Anderson; George Jones; Dickey Betts; Kris
   Kristofferson; Guy Clark; Larry Jon Wilson; Waylon
   Jennings.
   Also see CLARK, Guy
   Also see DALTON, Lacy J.
   Also see JENNINGS, Waylon
   Also see JONES, George
   Also see JONES, George, & David Allan Coe
   Also see KRISTOFFERSON, Kris
   Also see WILSON, Larry Jon

COE, David Allan, & Bill Anderson

Singles: 7-inch

COLUMBIA 3-5   80
   Also see ANDERSON, Bill

COE, David Allan, & Willie Nelson   *C&W '86*

Singles: 7-inch

COLUMBIA 3-4   86
   Also see COE, David Allan
   Also see NELSON, Willie
   Also see NELSON, Willie / Jerry Lee Lewis / Carl
   Perkins / David Allan Coe

COHN, Marc   *C&W/LP '91*

Singles: 7-inch

ATLANTIC 3-4   91

LPs: 10/12-inch 33rpm

ATLANTIC 5-8   91

COHRON, Phil   *C&W '90*
Singles: 7–inch
AIR 3-4   89-90

COIN, R.C.   *C&W '87*
Singles: 7–inch
BGM 3-4   87

COLDER, Ben   *C&W/P&R '62*
(Sheb Wooley)
Singles: 7–inch
MGM 4-8   62-73
PORTLAND................................. 3-6   78
SCORPION 3-5   79-80
SUNBIRD 3-4   80
TPL... 3-5   87

LPs: 10/12–inch 33rpm
LAKESHORE (621 "Ben Colder & Sheb
  Wooley")................................. 10-20
  (Mail order offer.)
LAKESHORE/GUSTO (110 "Greatest Hits of
  Sheb Wooley & Ben Colder").... 8-12   79
  (Mail order offer.)
MGM (139 "Ben Colder") 8-12   70
MGM (4421 thru 4876).............. 10-20   66-73
MGM (4173 "Spoofing the Big
  Ones") 15-25   63
   Also see WOOLEY, Sheb

COLE, Brenda   *C&W '87*
Singles: 7–inch
MELODY DAWN 3-4   87-88

COLE, Nat "King"   *R&B '42/C&W '44*
(King Cole Trio; Quintet; Quartet)
Singles: 78rpm
AMMOR 15-25   42
ATLAS...................................... 10-20   43-45
CAPITOL (100 thru 700 series)... 5-10   43-49
CAPITOL (800 thru 4600 series).. 4-8   50-58
CAPITOL (15000 series).............. 3-8   47-49
DAVIS & SCHWEGLER............ 20-40   39-40
DECCA..................................... 10-20   42-47
DISC 15-25   42
EXCELSIOR............................. 10-20   42-45
PREMIER................................. 10-20   44
SAVOY..................................... 10-15   46
VARSITY.................................. 15-25   40

Singles: 7–inch
CAPITOL (Except 800 thru 4200
  series) 4-8   61-69
CAPITOL (889 thru 4623) 5-15   50-61
  (Purple label.)

TAMPA (134 "Vom-Vim-
  Veedle") 8-12   57
Picture Sleeves
CAPITOL.................................... 5-10   59-66
TAMPA (134 "Vom-Vim-
  Veedle") 10-20   57
EPs: 7–inch 33/45rpm
CAPITOL................................... 10-20   50-60
DECCA 10-20   56
LPs: 10/12–inch 33rpm
CAMAY... 8-12
CAPITOL (Except 100 thru 2900
  series) 5-15   61-82
CAPITOL (H-156 "Nat 'King' Cole at the
  Piano") 50-100   49
  (10–inch LP.)
CAPITOL (H-177 "Nat 'King' Cole
  Trio") 50-75   49
  (10–inch LP.)
CAPITOL (H-220 "Nat 'King' Cole
  Trio") 50-75   50
  (10–inch LP.)
CAPITOL (H-332 "Penthouse
  Serenade")............................. 50-75   52
  (10–inch LP.)
CAPITOL (H-357
  "Unforgetable") 50-75   52
  (10–inch LP.)
CAPITOL (100 thru 900
  series).............................. 20-35   55-58
  (With "T" or "W" prefix.)
CAPITOL (1000 thru 2900
  series).............................. 10-20   58-68
  (With "T," "ST" or "W" prefix.)
CAPITOL 5-10
  (With "SM" prefix.)
CROWN....................................... 8-12   64
DECCA (8260 "In the
  Beginning") 35-50   56
DYNAMIC HOUSE...................... 5-10   72
MCA 5-10   73
MARK '56................................... 5-10   76
MONARCH ("Nat 'King' Cole").. 75-100   53
  (Colored vinyl.)
PICKWICK 5-10   70s
SCORE (4019 "The King Cole
  Trio") 20-40   58
SPINORAMA 10-15   60s
VSP... 10-15   66

WYNCOTE.............................. 10-15   63

Also see MARTIN, Dean, & Nat "King" Cole

Also see NELSON, Willie / Nat "King" Cole / Johnny Mathis / Shirley Bassey

Also see PRESLEY, Elvis

Also see PRESLEY, Elvis / Frank Sinatra / Nat "King" Cole

COLE, Nat "King" / Phil Flowers
LPs: 10/12–inch 33rpm
EXCELSIOR............................... 5-10

COLE, Nat "King," & Stubby Kaye
Singles: 7–inch
CAPITOL.................................... 3-6   65
Picture Sleeves
CAPITOL.................................... 4-8   65

COLE, Nat "King," & His Trio / George Kingston
LPs: 10/12–inch 33rpm
WYNCOTE................................ 10-15   60s

COLE, Nat "King," & George Shearing
LPs: 10/12–inch 33rpm
CAPITOL.................................... 20-30   61

Also see COLE, Nat "King"

COLE, Patsy   *C&W '89*
Singles: 7–inch
TRA-STAR 3-4   89

COLE, Sami Jo   *C&W/P&R '74*
(Sami Jo & Friends; Sami Jo Cole)
Singles: 7–inch
ELEKTRA 3-4   81
FAME 3-5   71-72
MGM 3-5   74-75
POLYDOR..................................... 3-5   76
LPs: 10/12–inch 33rpm
MGM 5-10   74-75

COLEMAN, Albert   *C&W '82*
(Albert Coleman's Atlanta Pops)
Singles: 7–inch
EPIC.. 3-4   82
LP: 10/12–inch 33rpm
EPIC.. 5-8   83

COLLIE, Mark   *C&W '90*
Singles: 7–inch
MCA 3-4   90-92

COLLIE, Shirley   *C&W '61*
Singles: 7–inch
LIBERTY 5-10   61

Also see NELSON, Willie, & Shirley Collie

Also see SMITH, Warren, & Shirley Collie

COLLINS, Brian   *C&W '71*
Singles: 7–inch
ABC/DOT.....................................3-5   74-77
DOT 3-5   73-74
MEGA 3-5   71-72
PRIMERO 3-4   82-83
RCA 3-5   78-79
LP: 10/12–inch 33rpm
ABC...5-10   77
ABC/DOT.....................................6-12   74
DOT 8-12   73

COLLINS, Dugg   *C&W '77*
Singles: 7–inch
SCR 3-5   77

COLLINS, Gwen
Singles: 7–inch
BRAGG..4-8   65
NEW WORLD 4-8   66

COLLINS, Gwen & Jerry   *C&W '70*
Singles: 7–inch
BRAGG..4-8   65
CAPITOL.......................................3-6   69-70
NEW WORLD 4-6   67

Also see COLLINS, Gwen

COLLINS, Jim   *C&W '85*
Singles: 7–inch
TKM 3-4   86
WHITE GOLD 3-4   85

COLLINS, Judy   *LP '64*
Singles: 7–inch
ELEKTRA (Except 45253 & 45008 thru 45680)..3-5   70-84
ELEKTRA (45253 "Send in the Clowns")...................................3-5   75
ELEKTRA (45008 thru 45680).......4-8   64-69
Picture Sleeves
ELEKTRA (Except "The Hostage")....................................3-5   69-84
ELEKTRA ("The Hostage")............4-8   73
(Promotional issue only.)
LPs: 10/12–inch 33rpm
ELEKTRA (Except 200 & 300 series)....................................10-15   67-84

ELEKTRA (209 "Maid of Constant
Sorrow") 30-40   61

ELEKTRA (222 "Golden Apples of the
Sun") 25-35   62

ELEKTRA (243 "Judy Collins
No. 3") 20-30   63
(Monaural.)

ELEKTRA (7-243 "Judy Collins
No. 3") 25-35   63
(Stereo.)

ELEKTRA (253 "Running for My
Life")... 5-8   80

ELEKTRA (300 series).............. 15-20   65-68
(Monaural.)

ELEKTRA (7-300 series).......... 15-20   65-72
(Stereo.)

ELEKTRA (60001 "Times of Our
Lives") 5-8   82

COLLINS, Judy, & T.G.
Sheppard   *C&W '84*
Singles: 7–inch
ELEKTRA... 3-4   84
Also see COLLINS, Judy
Also see SHEPPARD, T.G.

COLLINS, Tommy   *C&W '54*
(With Wanda Collins)
Singles: 78rpm
CAPITOL................................... 10-20   54-56
Singles: 7–inch
CAPITOL (2000 & 3000 series) 15-25   54-58
CAPITOL (4000 & 5000 series
except 4495) 5-15   58-64
CAPITOL (4495 "Black Cat") 20-30   61
COLUMBIA 5-8   66-68
EPs: 7–inch 33/45rpm
CAPITOL (607 "Tommy
Collins")..................................... 30-50   54
CAPITOL (776 "Words and Music Country
Style")... 25-40   56
(Price is for any of three volumes in this
series.)
CAPITOL (1100 series)............. 10-20   59
LPs: 10/12–inch 33rpm
CAPITOL (776 "Words and Music Country
Style")... 30-50   56
CAPITOL (1125 "Light of the
Lord") 50-60   59
CAPITOL (1196 "This Is Tommy
Collins")..................................... 30-40   59
CAPITOL (1436 "Songs I Love to
Sing") 30-40   61
COLUMBIA 20-35   66-68

GOLDEN COUNTRY.................... 5-8   83
STARDAY 10-15   72
TOWER...................................... 15-25   66-68
VERVE (10565 "I Wanna Thank
You")... 10-15   67
Session: Buck Owens.
Also see OWENS, Buck

COLLINS, Tommy, & Paragons
Singles: 7–inch
WINLEY 10-20   59

COLTER, Jessi   *C&W/P&R '75*
(Mirriam Johnson; Mirriam Eddy)
Singles: 7–inch
CAPITOL...................................... 3-5   75-82
RCA 3-6   69-72
LPs: 10/12–inch 33rpm
CAPITOL.................................... 5-10   75-81
RCA (4333 "A Country Star Is
Born")....................................... 10-20   70
Session: Waylon Jennings; Gary Scruggs.
Also see EDDY, Duane & Mirriam
Also see JENNINGS, Waylon, & Jessi Colter
Also see JOHNSON, Mirriam

COMMANDER CODY   *LP '71/C&W '72*
(With His Lost Planet Airmen)
Singles: 7–inch
ABC... 3-5   75
ARISTA 3-5   77
DOT 3-5   73-74
MCA 3-4   83
PARAMOUNT 3-5   71-74
W.B. 3-5   75
Picture Sleeves
PARAMOUNT 3-5   72-73
LPs: 10/12–inch 33rpm
ARISTA 5-10   77
PARAMOUNT 10-12   71-74
W.B. 8-10   75-76

COMO, Perry   *P&R '43/C&W '76*
**(With Hugo Winterhalter's Orchestra; with
Ramblers; with Ray Charles Singers)**
Singles: 78rpm
BLUEBIRD 5-10   50
RCA 5-10   43-58
Singles: 7–inch
BLUEBIRD 10-20   50
(May also be shown as RCA Victor "Bluebird
Children's Records.")

RCA (237 "Supper Club Favorites").............................. 15-25	49	
(Three disc set.)		
RCA (0071 "Ave Maria") 10-15	49	
(Black vinyl.)		
RCA (0071 "Ave Maria") 15-25	49	
(Colored vinyl.)		
RCA (0100 thru 0900 series) 3-6	69-73	
RCA (VP-2000 series)................. 8-12	59	
(Stereo.)		
RCA (2700 thru 7400 series) 8-20	48-59	
RCA (61-7000 series) 8-12	58-60	
(Stereo.)		
RCA (7500 thru 9700 series) 4-10	59-69	
RCA (10000 thru 13000 series) 3-5	74-83	

Picture Sleeves

RCA (3800 thru 7100 series) 10-20	53-58	
RCA (7200 thru 9700 series) 5-15	58-69	

EPs: 7–inch 33/45rpm

CAMDEN...................................... 5-10	50s	
RCA (Except SPD series) 10-25	52-70	
RCA (SPD-27 "Perry Como").... 40-60	56	
(Boxed 10-EP set. Includes inserts and biography booklet.)		
RCA (SPD-28 "Perry Como Highlighter") 20-30	56	
(Sampler from Kleenex Tissue. Includes picture cover.)		

LPs: 10/12–inch 33rpm

CAMDEN..................................... 5-15	57-74	
RCA (0100 thru 4000 series) 5-15	73-83	
(With "AFL1," "ANL1," "APL1," "AQL1," "AYL1," "CPL1," or "DVL2" prefix.)		
RCA (1004 "Saturday Night with Mr. C")...................................... 20-30	58	
RCA (1007 "Golden Records").. 20-30	58	
RCA (LPM-1085 "So Smooth") . 20-40	55	
RCA (LPM-1172 "I Believe") 20-40	56	
RCA (LPM-1176 "Relaxing with Perry Como").................................... 20-40	56	
RCA (LPM-1177 "Sentimental Date with Perry Como").................................... 20-40	56	
RCA (LPM-1191 "Perry Como Sings Hits from Broadway Shows").................. 20-40	56	
RCA (LPM-1243 Perry Sings Christmas Music")..................................... 20-40	56	
RCA (LPM-1463 We Get Letters")................................. 20-30	57	
RCA (LPM-1800 thru LPM-2900 series) 15-25	58-63	
RCA (LSP-1085 thru LSP-1463) 10-20	62-68	
(Electronic stereo reissues.)		

RCA (LSP-1800 thru LSP-2900 series)..15-30	58-63	
(Stereo.)		
RCA (3013 "TV Favorites").........25-50	52	
(10–inch LP.)		
RCA (3044 "Supper Club Favorites") 25-50	52	
(10–inch LP.)		
RCA (3124 "Broadway") 25-50	53	
(10–inch LP.)		
RCA (3133 "Christmas") 25-50	53	
(10–inch LP.)		
RCA (3188 "I Believe").................25-50	53	
(10–inch LP.)		
RCA (3224 "Golden Records") ..25-50	54	
(10–inch LP.)		
RCA (3300 thru 4500 series) 8-15	64-71	
(With "LPM" or "LSP" prefix.)		
READER'S DIGEST 8-15	75	

COMO, Perry / Ames Brothers / Harry Belafonte / Radio City Music Hall Orchestra

EPs: 7–inch 33/45rpm

RCA (SP-35 "Merry Christmas") 10-20	56	
(Record dealer giveaway. Issued with paper sleeve.)		

COMO, Perry, & Eddie Fisher   *P&R '52*

Singles: 78rpm

RCA 4-8	52	

Singles: 7–inch

RCA 5-10	52	

COMO, Perry, & Fontane Sisters   *P&R '50*

Singles: 78rpm

RCA 4-8	50-51	

Singles: 7–inch

RCA 8-15	50-51	

COMO, Perry, & Betty Hutton   *P&R '50*

Singles: 78rpm

RCA 4-8	50	

Singles: 7–inch

RCA 8-15	50	

COMO, Perry, & Jaye P. Morgan

Singles: 78rpm

RCA 4-8	55	

Singles: 7–inch

RCA... 5-10   55
  Also see COMO, Perry

COMPTON BROTHERS   *C&W '66*
Singles: 7–inch

ABC/DOT 3-5   75
DOT.. 3-6   66-73
LP: 10/12–inch 33rpm
DOT.. 10-15   68-72
  Members: Bill Compton; Harry Compton.

CONCRETE COWBOY BAND   *C&W '81*
Singles: 7–inch

EXCELSIOR................................... 3-4   81
LP: 10/12–inch 33rpm
EXCELSIOR............................... 5-10   81

CONFEDERATE RAILROAD   *C&W '92*
Singles: 7–inch

ATLANTIC..................................... 3-4   92-93
  Members: Danny Shirley; Chris McDaniel.
  Also see SHIRLEY, Danny

CONLEE, John   *C&W '78*
Singles: 7–inch

ABC.. 3-4   78
ABC/DOT....................................... 3-4   76-77
COLUMBIA 3-4   86-87
MCA 3-4   79-85
16TH AVE. 3-4   89-90
LPs: 10/12–inch 33rpm
ABC.. 8-10   78
COLUMBIA 5-10   86-87
MCA 5-10   79-86

CONLEY, Earl Thomas   *C&W '75*
(Earl Conley; ETC Band)
Singles: 7–inch

GRT.. 4-6   75-76
RCA.. 3-4   81-92
SUNBIRD 3-4   80-81
W.B. 3-5   78-79
LP: 10/12–inch 33rpm
RCA.. 5-10   81-84
SUNBIRD 8-15   80
  Also see HARDIN, Gus, & Earl Thomas Conley
  Also see WHITLEY, Keith, & Earl Thomas Conley

CONLEY, Earl Thomas, & Emmylou Harris   *C&W '88*
Singles: 7–inch

RCA 3-4   88
  Also see HARRIS, Emmylou

CONLEY, Earl Thomas, & Anita Pointer   *C&W '86*
Singles: 7–inch

RCA.. 3-4   87
  Also see CONLEY, Earl Thomas
  Also see POINTER, Anita

CONWAY, Dave   *C&W '77*
Singles: 7–inch

TRUE... 3-5   77

COOK, Steven Lee   *C&W '79*
Singles: 7–inch

GRINDER'S SWITCH 3-5   79

COOLEY, Spade, & His Orchestra   *C&W '45*
(With the Buckle Busters; with Tex Williams)
Singles: 78rpm

BLUEBIRD 5-10
COLUMBIA 5-10   46-47
DECCA 4-8   51-55
OKEH.. 5-10   45-46
RCA 5-10   47-48
Singles: 7–inch
DECCA 8-10   51-52
EPs: 7–inch 33/45rpm
DECCA (2225/2226 "Dance-O Rama").................................... 10-20   55
(Price is for either volume.)
RCA (3041 "Roy Rogers Souvenir Album") 20-40   52
LP: 10/12–inch 33rpm
CLUB of SPADE 8-15
COLUMBIA (9007 "Sagebrush Swing").................................... 40-60   50s
(10-inch LP.)
COLUMBIA (37000 series) 5-10
DECCA (5563 "Dance-O-Rama")..................................... 30-50   55
RAYNOTE (RN-5007 "Fidoodlin")............................. 20-30   59
(Monaural.)
RAYNOTE (RS-5007 "Fidoodlin").............................. 30-40   59
(Stereo.)

RCA (3041 "Roy Rogers Souvenir
Album") 40-60   52
(10–inch LP.)

ROULETTE (R-25145
"Fidoodlin")............................. 15-20   61
(Monaural.)

ROULETTE (S-25145
"Fidoodlin")............................. 20-25   61
(Stereo.)

COOLIDGE, Rita   *P&R '69/C&W '73*
Singles: 7–inch
A&M 3-5   71-83
PEPPER.. 4-8   68-69
Picture Sleeves
A&M 3-6   72-83
LPs: 10/12–inch 33rpm
A&M 5-10   71-83
Promotional LPs
A&M ("In-Store Sampler - Rita
Coolidge") 10-15
Also see CAMPBELL, Glen, & Rita Coolidge
Also see CLAPTON, Eric
Also see KRISTOFFERSON, Kris, & Rita Coolidge

COOLIDGE-JONES, Priscilla
(Priscilla)
Singles: 7–inch
CAPRICORN.................................... 3-4   79
YORK... 4-8   67-68
LPs: 10/12–inch 33rpm
A&M 8-12   71
CAPRICORN................................. 5-10   79
SUSSEX....................................... 8-12   70

COOPER, Jerry   *C&W '87*
Singles: 7–inch
BEAR 3-4   87-88

COOPER, Wilma Lee &
Stoney   *C&W '56*
(With the Clinch Mountain Clan; with Carolee &
Clinch Mountain Clan)
Singles: 78rpm
COLUMBIA 4-8   54-55
HICKORY....................................... 4-8   56-57
Singles: 7–inch
COLUMBIA 5-10   54-55
HICKORY....................................... 5-10   56-64
EPs: 7–inch 33/45rpm
COLUMBIA 10-15   59
LP: 10/12–inch 33rpm
COUNTY 5-10
DECCA... 15-20   66

HARMONY................................... 15-25   60-66
HICKORY..................................... 10-20   60-62
POWER PAK 6-10
ROUNDER.................................... 5-10
SKYLIGHT COUNTRY 8-12
STARDAY 8-12   77
Also see WILMA LEE

COPAS, Cowboy   *C&W '46*
(Cowboy "Poppy" Copas; Lloyd Copas; with
Kathy Copas)
Singles: 78rpm
KING 5-15   44-57
Singles: 7–inch
DOT 10-20   57-58
KING (951 thru 1507)................ 10-20   50-55
KING (4865 thru 5270).............. 5-10   55-59
KING (5392 thru 5734).............. 4-8   60-63
STARDAY (476 thru 750) 4-8   60-66
STARDAY (7000 series)................ 3-6   64
STARDAY (8000 series)................ 3-4   71
EPs: 7–inch 33/45rpm
KING 15-25   52-53
STARDAY 10-20   60
LPs: 10/12–inch 33rpm
BUCKBOARD 5-10
GUEST STAR 10-15
KING (553 "All-Time Hits").......... 45-55   57
KING (556 "Favorite Sacred
Songs").................................. 40-50   57
KING (619 thru 835)................... 25-35   59-64
KING (894 thru 1049)................. 8-12   64-69
NASHVILLE 8-12   68-70
PICKWICK/HILLTOP 10-20   66
STARDAY (113 "All Time Country Music
Great") 20-30   60
STARDAY (133 "Inspirational
Songs") 20-30   61
STARDAY (144 "Songs That Made Him
Famous") 20-30   62
STARDAY (157 "Opry Star
Spotlight") 20-30   63
STARDAY (175 "Mr. Country
Music").................................. 20-30   64
STARDAY (200 series)............. 12-25   64-67
STARDAY (300 series)............. 10-20   65-67
STARDAY (400 series)................ 8-12   68-70
TRIO CLUB................................. 5-10   82
Session: Ralph Mooney.
Also see COPAS, Lloyd
Also see MULLICAN, Moon / Cowboy Copas / Red
Sovine

COPAS, Cowboy / Hawkshaw Hawkins

LPs: 10/12–inch 33rpm

KING 12-25 63-66

Also see CLINE, Patsy / Cowboy Copas / Hawkshaw
  Hawkins
Also see COPAS, Cowboy
Also see HAWKINS, Hawkshaw

COPAS, Lloyd

Singles: 7–inch

DOT (15735 "Circle Rock") 60-80   58

Also see COPAS, Cowboy

CORBIN, Ray   *C&W '69*

Singles: 7–inch

COLUMBIA 4-6   69-70
MONUMENT 4-6   67-68
TREND... 5-10   60s

CORBIN & HANNER   *C&W '79*

(Corbin-Hanner Band)

Singles: 7–inch

ALFA 3-5   81-82
LIFESONG 3-5   78-82
MERCURY 3-4   90-92

LPs: 10/12–inch 33rpm

ALFA 5-10   81-82

Members: Bob Corbin; Dave Hanner.

CORNBREAD & JERRY

Singles: 7–inch

LIBERTY 5-10   61

Member: Jerry Smith.
  Also see SMITH, Jerry

CORNELIUS, Helen   *C&W '76*

Singles: 7–inch

AMERI-CAN 3-4   83
CAPITOL.. 3-5   71
COLUMBIA 3-5   73
ELEKTRA....................................... 3-4   81
RCA... 3-5   76-79

Also see BROWN, Jim Ed, & Helen Cornelius

CORNOR, Randy   *C&W '75*

Singles: 7–inch

ABC/DOT 3-5   75-77
CHERRY 3-5   78

LP: 10/12–inch 33rpm

ABC/DOT 6-12   76

COTTON, Gene   *P&R '74/C&W '76*

Singles: 7–inch

ABC..3-5   75-77
ARIOLA AMERICA 3-5   77-79
GENE COTTON ("Child of
  Peace")..4-6   81
  (No actual label name or number. A gift to
  radio stations. With explanatory insert.)
KNOLL 3-4   81-82
MYRRH...3-5   74

LPs: 10/12–inch 33rpm

ABC..8-10   76-77
ACCORD 5-10   83
ARIOLA AMERICA 5-10   78-79
BUDDAH..8-10   74-75
CAPITOL..8-10   71
IMPACT 15-20
KNOLL 5-10   81-82
MYRRH...8-10   73

COTTON, Gene, & Kim Carnes   *P&R '78*

Singles: 7–inch

ARIOLA AMERICA 3-4   78

Also see CARNES, Kim
  Also see COTTON, Gene

COUCH, Orville   *C&W '62*

Singles: 7–inch

CUSTOM 6-10   62
DERBY
MERCURY.....................................5-10   60
MONUMENT..................................4-8   66
VEE JAY 4-8   62-64

LP: 10/12–inch 33rpm

VEE JAY 15-25   64

COULTERS   *C&W '83*

Singles: 7–inch

DOLPHIN.......................................3-4   83
EPIC..3-5   80

COUNT ROCKIN' SYDNEY

(With His Dukes)

Singles: 7–inch

GOLDBAND....................................4-8   65-66

Also see ROCKIN' SYDNEY

COUNTRY ALL STARS

Singles: 78rpm

RCA 5-10   52-56

Singles: 7–inch

RCA.............................. 10-20 52-56

Members: Chet Atkins; Homer & Jethro.
Also see ATKINS, Chet
Also see HOMER & JETHRO

COUNTRY CAVALEERS   *C&W '73*

Singles: 7–inch

COUNTRY SHOWCASE 3-5   76
MGM 3-5   73

Members: James Marvell; Buddy Good.
Also see MARVELL, James

COUNTRY GENTLEMEN   *C&W '65*

Singles: 78rpm

RCA.. 5-8   56

Singles: 7–inch

BRENT (7058 "For You") 15-25   67
RCA (6000 series)...................... 8-12   56
REBEL 4-8   65

EPs: 7–inch 33/45rpm

STARDAY 5-10

LP: 10/12–inch 33rpm

CIMMARON (2001 "Songs of the
Pioneers") 25-35   62
CROWN 10-15   60s
DESIGN 5-10   63
FOLKWAYS (2409 "Country Gentlemen, Vol.
1")... 15-25   60
(Includes booklet.)
FOLKWAYS (2410 "Country Gentlemen, Vol.
2")... 15-25   60
(Includes booklet.)
FOLKWAYS (2411 "Country Gentlemen, Vol.
3")... 15-25   60
(Includes booklet.)
FOLKWAYS (31031 "Going Back to the Blue
Ridge Mountains").................... 10-15
GUSTO 5-10
MERCURY 10-20   63
PICKWICK/HILLTOP 10-15   60s
REBEL 5-10   70s
SUGAR HILL............................... 5-10   83
STARDAY (109 "Traveling Dobro
Blues")..................................... 25-50   59
STARDAY (174 "Bluegrass At Carnegie
Hall") 15-25   62
STARDAY (311 "Songs of the
Pioneers") 15-20   65
VANGUARD (40021 "The Country
Gentlemen")............................. 15-25   73
(Quardophonic.)

VANGUARD (79331 "The Country
Gentlemen")............................. 10-15   73
(Stereo.)
ZAP 10-15

Members: Charlie Waller; Ricky Skaggs.
Also see SKAGGS, Ricky

COUNTRY HAMS

Singles: 7–inch

EMI (3977 "Walking in the Park with
Eloise")....................................10-20   74

Picture Sleeves

EMI (3977 "Walking in the Park with
Eloise")....................................50-60   74

Promotional Singles

EMI (3977 "Walking in the Park with
Eloise")....................................25-35   74

Members: Paul McCartney & Wings; Chet Atkins;
Floyd Cramer.
Also see ATKINS, Chet
Also see CRAMER, Floyd
Also see McCARTNEY, Paul

COWBOY COPAS: see COPAS, Cowboy

COX, Don   *C&W '79*

Singles: 7–inch

ARC 3-5   79

CRADDOCK, Billy "Crash"   *P&R '59/C&W '71*

(Billy Craddock "Crash" Craddock; Billy Graddock)

Singles: 7–inch

ABC..3-5   72-78
ABC/DOT.......................................3-5   75-77
ATLANTIC.......................................3-4   89
CAPITOL...3-5   78-82
CARTWHEEL 3-5   71-72
CEE CEE 3-4   83
CHART..3-6   67-73
COLONIAL......................................10-15   58
COLUMBIA 5-10   59-60
DATE 8-12   58
KING (Except 5912)....................5-10   64-65
KING (5912 "Betty Betty")..........15-25   64
MERCURY.....................................5-10   61-62
SKY CASTLE ("Smacky
Mouth") 20-30
(No selection number used. Shows
Columbia identification numbers,
26671/26672.)

Picture Sleeves

COLUMBIA (41470 "Don't Destroy
Me") 15-25   59

COLUMBIA (41619 "All I Want Is You")	15-25	60

EPs: 7–inch 33/45rpm

ABC	5-10	74
(Jukebox issue only.)		

LPs: 10/12–inch 33rpm

ABC	6-10	72-78
ABC/AT EASE	10-12	78
(Special issue for the Armed Forces.)		
ABC/DOT	8-10	76-77
CAPITOL	5-10	78-83
CARTWHEEL	10-12	71-72
CHART	8-12	73
HARMONY	10-12	73
KING (912 "I'm Tore Up")	45-55	64
PICKWICK	5-10	79
POWER PAK	5-10	75
STARDAY	8-10	
MCA	5-10	82

CRAFT, Paul   *C&W '74*

Singles: 7–inch

RCA	3-5	77-78
TRUTH	3-5	74

CRAMER, Floyd   *P&R '54/C&W '60*

(With the Louisiana Hayride Band; with Keyboard Kick Band)

Singles: 78rpm

ABBOTT	3-5	53-54
MGM	3-5	55-57

Singles: 7–inch

ABBOTT	5-10	53-54
MGM	5-8	55-57
RCA (Except 7000 & 8000 series)	3-5	67-81
RCA (7000 & 8000 series)	4-8	61-66

Picture Sleeves

RCA	6-12	61-63

EPs: 7–inch 33/45rpm

MGM	8-12	57
RCA	5-10	61-63

LPs: 10/12–inch 33rpm

ALSHIRE	8-12	68
CAMDEN	6-12	65-74
MGM (3500 series)	15-20	57
MGM (4200 series)	10-15	64
MGM (4600 series)	8-12	70
RCA (0100 thru 4000 series)	5-10	73-81
(With "AHL1," "ANL1," "APD1," "APL1," or "AYL1" prefix.)		
RCA (2000 thru 4000 series)	10-20	60-73
(With "LPM" or "LSP" prefix.)		

Also see ATKINS, Chet, Floyd Cramer & Danny Davis
Also see ATKINS, Chet, Floyd Cramer & Boots Randolph
Also see BARE, Bobby
Also see COUNTRY HAMS
Also see FRANCIS, Connie
Also see NASHVILLE ALL-STARS
Also see PRESLEY, Elvis
Also see REEVES, Jim
Also see SOME of CHET'S FRIENDS

CRAMER, Floyd / Peter Nero / Frankie Carle

LPs: 10/12–inch 33rpm

RCA	10-15	63

Also see CRAMER, Floyd

CREECH, Alice   *C&W '71*

Singles: 7–inch

TARGET	3-5	71-72

CREED

Singles: 7–inch

ASYLUM	3-4	78

LPs: 10/12–inch 33rpm

ASYLUM	8-10	78

CREEDENCE CLEARWATER REVIVAL   *P&R/LP '68/C&W '81*

Singles: 12–inch 33/45rpm

FANTASY (238 "Creedence Medley")	10-15	85
FANTASY (759 "I Heard It Through the Grapevine")	15-20	76
(Promotional issue only.)		

Singles: 7–inch

FANTASY (Except 2832)	3-6	69-85
FANTASY (2832 "45 Revolutions Per Minute")	40-60	70
LIBERTY	3-5	
SCORPIO (412 "Porterville")	15-25	68

Picture Sleeves

FANTASY (Except 2832)	5-10	69-76
FANTASY (2832 "45 Revolutions Per Minute")	20-25	70

LPs: 10/12–inch 33rpm

BEVERLY ("Willie and the Poor Boys")	75-100	
(Half-speed mastered. Number not known.)		
FANTASY (1 thru 70)	8-15	73-78
FANTASY (4500 series)	5-10	80-85
(Includes reissues of 8382 through 9404.)		
FANTASY (8382 thru 9404)	8-15	68-72
FANTASY (9418 thru 9621)	5-10	72-82
K-TEL	8-12	78

MFSL (037 "Cosmo's Factory")................................. 30-50   79

SWEET THUNDER (13 "Green River") 75-100   75
(Half-speed mastered.)

W.B. SPECIAL PRODUCTS (3514 "Greatest Hits") 10-15   85
(TV mail-order offer.)

Members: John Fogerty; Tom Fogerty; Doug Clifford; Stuart Cook.
Also see FOGERTY, John
Also see FOGERTY, Tom
Also see GOLLIWOGS
Also see SOUTHERN PACIFIC

CREWS, Dwayne   *C&W '90*
Singles: 7-inch
KILLER 3-4   90

CRICKETS
Singles: 7-inch
BARNABY 15-25   72

BRUNSWICK (55124 "Love's Made a Fool of You") 15-25   59

BRUNSWICK (55153 "When You Ask About Love")..................................... 15-25   59

CORAL (62198 "More Than I Can Say") 15-25   60

EPIC (08028 "T-Shirt") 3-4   88

LIBERTY 10-20   61-65
(Black labels.)

LIBERTY 15-25   61-65
(Promotional issues. With cream color or white labels.)

MGM 10-15   73

MUSIC FACTORY 15-20   68

Note: Records by Buddy Holly & Crickets, even if credited only to the Crickets, are listed in the BUDDY HOLLY section.

Promotional Singles
BRUNSWICK (55124 "Love's Made a Fool of You") 20-30   59

BRUNSWICK (55153 "When You Ask About Love")..................................... 20-30   59

CORAL (62198 "More Than I Can Say") 20-30   60

EPIC (08028 "T-Shirt") 3-4   88

EPs: 7-inch 33/45rpm
B.H.M.S. 3-6   78

CORAL (81192 "The Crickets")............................. 75-100   63
(With Buddy Holly on one track, *It's Too Late.*)

LPs: 10/12-inch 33rpm
BARNABY (30268 "Rockin' '50s Rock & Roll") 15-25   70

CORAL (57320 "In Style")..........40-60   60

KOALA..8-10

LIBERTY (3272 "Something Old, Something New, Something Blue, Somethin' Else") 30-40   64
(Monaural.)

LIBERTY (3351 "California Sun")..................................30-40   64
(Monaural.)

LIBERTY (7272 "Something Old, Something New, Something Blue, Somethin' Else") 40-50   64
(Stereo.)

LIBERTY (7351 "California Sun")..................................40-50   64
(Stereo.)

VERTIGO...................................10-20   73

Note: Records by Buddy Holly & Crickets, even if credited only to the Crickets, are listed in the BUDDY HOLLY section.

Members: Sonny Curtis; Jerry Naylor; Glen D. Hardin; Jerry Allison; Joe Mauldin; Earl Sinks; David Box.
Also see CURTIS, Sonny
Also see HOLLY, Buddy
Also see JENNINGS, Waylon
Also see NAYLOR, Jerry
Also see PRESLEY, Elvis

CROCE, Jim   *P&R/LP '72/C&W '74*
Singles: 7-inch
ABC..3-5   72-74

LIFESONG......................................3-5   75-76

Picture Sleeves
ABC..4-6   73

EPs: 7-inch 33/45rpm
ABC...10-12   73
(Jukebox issue only.)

LPs: 10/12-inch 33rpm
ABC...10-12   72-74

BURNS MEDIA (1-2 "The Faces I've Been")......................................40-60   75
(Two-LP set. Promotional issue only.)

CASHWEST.................................8-10   77

COMMAND 12-15   74-75

LIFESONG..............................10-15   75-78

MFSL (079 "You Don't Mess Around with Jim")...............................25-50   82

Session: Maury Muehleisen; Tommy West; Gary Chester; Marty Nelson; Joe Macho; Terry Cashman; Ellie Greenwich; David Spinozza.

CROCE, Jim & Ingrid

(Jim & Ingrid)

Singles: 7–inch

CAPITOL	10-15	69

LPs: 10/12–inch 33rpm

CAPITOL (315 "Croce")	30-35	69
PICKWICK	5-10	70s

Also see CROCE, Jim

CROCKETT, Howard   *C&W '73*

Singles: 78rpm

DOT (15593 "If You'll Let Me")	35-50	57

Singles: 7–inch

DOT (15593 "If You'll Let Me")	35-50	57
DOT (17000 series)	3-5	73
MANCO	5-10	60
MEL-O-DY	10-20	64-65

CROFT, Sandy   *C&W '83*

Singles: 7–inch

ANGELSONG	3-4	83
CAPITOL	3-4	84-85

CROSBY, Bing   *P&R '31/C&W '44*

(With the Andrews Sisters; with Gary Crosby; with Victor Young Orchestra; with Grady Martin & His Slew Foot Five)

Singles: 78rpm

BRUNSWICK	10-20	32-34
DECCA	5-15	34-57
KAPP	3-5	57
VICTOR	10-20	31

Singles: 7–inch

AMOS	3-5	69
CAPITOL	4-6	63
COLUMBIA	4-6	59
CROWLEY'S/CROSBY ("How Lovely Is Christmas")	10-20	
(Promotional issue made for Crowley's Milk Co.)		
DAYBREAK	3-5	71
DECCA (23281 thru 30828)	5-10	51-59
DECCA (31000 series)	4-8	61-65
KAPP	4-6	57
LONDON	3-4	77
MGM	4-6	60
POLYDOR	3-4	78
RCA	4-6	60
REPRISE	4-6	64-67
U.A.	3-5	75
VERVE	4-6	

Picture Sleeves

DECCA	5-10	53-63
DAYBREAK	3-5	71
KAPP	4-8	57

EPs: 7–inch 33/45rpm

BRUNSWICK	5-15	50-55
COLUMBIA	8-12	50-57
DECCA ("Old Masters")	20-30	
(Boxed EP set. No number shown.)		
DECCA (Except 1700)	6-15	50-59
DECCA (1700 "Deluxe Box Set")	75-100	54
(17-EP set.)		
RCA	5-10	57
THREE on ONE (407 "Bing Crosby Sings 2 New Christmas Songs")	5-10	50s
(Though labeled "45 Extended Play," actually has only one song on each side. May not have been issued with cover.)		
VERVE (5022 "Bing Sings While Bregman Swings")	10-15	59
(With envelope/sleeve.)		

LPs: 10/12–inch 33rpm

AMOS	8-10	69
ARGO	10-15	76
BIOGRAPH	5-10	73
BRUNSWICK (54000 series)	15-25	55
BRUNSWICK (58000 series)	25-40	52
(10-inch LPs.)		
CAPITOL (2300 series)	8-12	65
CAPITOL (11000 series)	5-10	77-78
CITADEL	5-10	78
COLUMBIA (43 "Bing in Hollywood")	10-15	67
COLUMBIA (2502 "Der Bingle")	20-30	56
(10-inch LP.)		
COLUMBIA (6027 "Classics")	20-40	49
(10–inch LP.)		
COLUMBIA (6105 "Classics, Vol. 2")	20-40	50
(10–inch LP.)		
COLUMBIA (35000 series)	5-10	78-79
COLUMBIA SPECIAL PRODUCTS	5-8	77
DECCA (154 "Bing")	50-100	54
(Boxed 5-LP set. Includes booklet.)		
DECCA (184 "Best of Bing Crosby")	10-15	65
DECCA (4000 series)	20-50	61-64
DECCA (5000 series)	15-25	49-55
(10–inch LPs.)		
DECCA (6000 series)	25-50	55-56
(10–inch LPs.)		

DECCA (8000 series)............... 15-25 54-59
  (Black label with silver print.)
DECCA (8000 series)................ 8-15 60-72
  (Black label with horizontal rainbow stripe.)
DECCA (8700 series)................ 8-12 64
DECCA (9000 series)........... 10-20 61-62
  (Decca LP numbers in this series preceded
  by a "7" or a "DL-7" are stereo issues.)
DECCA CUSTOM (34461 "Bing
  Crosby").................................. 10-20
  (Promotional issue, made for La-Z-Boy.)
ENCORE..................................... 8-10 68
GOLDEN 10-15 57-59
HARMONY (7000 series)......... 10-15 57
HARMONY (11000 series)......... 5-10 69
LONDON............................... 5-10 77
MCA 5-10 73-82
MGM 10-15 61-64
METRO 5-10 65
P.I.P. 5-10 71
POLYDOR............................ 5-10 77
RCA (500 series)........................ 6-10 72
RCA (1400 thru 2000 series) 10-20 57-59
  (With "LPM" or "LSP" prefix.)
RCA (2000 series)...................... 5-10 77
  (With "CPL1" prefix.)
REPRISE 8-12 64
20TH FOX 5-10 79
U.A. 5-10 76
VERVE/MGM (2030 "Bing Sings While
  Bregman Swings") 25-50 56
VOCALION (3600 series)......... 10-15 57
VOCALION (3700 series)........... 5-10 66
W.B. 10-15 60-62
X... 15-25 54
  Also see ANDREWS SISTERS
  Also see CROSBY, Gary, Phillip, Dennis, Lindsay &
  Bing

CROSBY, Bing & Gary   *P&R '50*
Singles: 78rpm
DECCA.. 3-5 50-51
Singles: 7–inch
DECCA.. 4-8 50-51

CROSBY, Bing, & Louis Armstrong   *P&R '51*
Singles: 78rpm
CAPITOL...................................... 3-5 56
DECCA... 3-5 51
Singles: 7–inch
CAPITOL...................................... 4-8 56
DECCA.. 4-8 51

MGM 3-5 60
LPs: 10/12–inch 33rpm
MGM (100 series) 5-10 70
MGM (3800 series) 10-20 60
SOUNDS RARE...........................5-10 83

CROSBY, Bing, Louis Armstrong, Rosemary Clooney & Hi-Los
Singles: 7–inch
COLUMBIA (6277 "Music to Shave
  By")..5-10 50s
  (Special products flexi-disc from Remington.)
  Also see ARMSTRONG, Louis
  Also see CROSBY, Bing, & Louis Armstrong

CROSBY, Bing, & Fred Astaire
LPs: 10/12–inch 33rpm
U.A...5-8 77

CROSBY, Bing, & Count Basie
LPs: 10/12–inch 33rpm
DAYBREAK 8-12 72

CROSBY, Bing, & Connee Boswell   *P&R '37*
Singles: 78rpm
DECCA 4-8 37-40
LPs: 10/12–inch 33rpm
DECCA 15-25 52

CROSBY, Bing, & Judy Garland   *P&R '45*
Singles: 78rpm
DECCA 5-10 45

CROSBY, Bing, Dick Haymes & Andrews Sisters   *P&R '47*
Singles: 78rpm
DECCA 5-10 47

CROSBY, Bing, & Bob Hope   *P&R '45*
Singles: 78rpm
DECCA 5-10 45
EPs: 7–inch 33/45rpm
CAPITOL CUSTOM (2263 "Vacation Road to
  Minnesota")...............................5-10
  (Issued to promote Minnesota tourism.)

CROSBY, Bing, & Louis Jordan   *P&R '45*
Singles: 78rpm
DECCA 5-10 45
  Also see JORDAN, Louis

CROSBY, Bing, & Grace Kelly / Bing Crosby & Frank Sinatra

(With Johnny Green's Orchestra)   *P&R '56*

Singles: 78rpm

CAPITOL 3-5   56

Singles: 7-inch

CAPITOL 5-10   56

CROSBY, Bing / Grace Kelly / Frank Sinatra / Celeste Holm

Singles: 7-inch

CAPITOL (281 "Interviews for use with Capitol
  Soundtrack LP, *High
  Society*") 50-100   56
  (Promotional issue only.)

CROSBY, Bing, & Peggy Lee

Singles: 78rpm

DECCA 3-5   52

Singles: 7-inch

DECCA 5-10   52

  Also see LEE, Peggy

CROSBY, Bing, & Johnny Mercer   *P&R '38*

Singles: 78rpm

DECCA 5-8   38-40

  Also see MERCER, Johnny, Jo Stafford & Pied Pipers

CROSBY, Bing, & Mills Brothers   *P&R '31*

(With Connee Boswell)

Singles: 78rpm

BRUNSWICK 5-10   31-32

  Also see MILLS BROTHERS

CROSBY, Bing, & Frank Sinatra

Singles: 78rpm

CAPITOL 3-5   56

Singles: 7-inch

CAPITOL 5-10   56

CROSBY, Bing, & Mel Torme   *P&R '46*

(With the Mel-Tones)

Singles: 78rpm

DECCA 4-8   46

CROSBY, Bing, & Orson Welles

LPs: 10/12-inch 33rpm

DECCA (6000 "The Small One, the Happy
  Prince") 10-25   50
  (10-inch LP.)

  Also see CROSBY, Bing

CROSBY, Eddie   *C&W '49*

Singles: 78rpm

DECCA 4-8   49

CROSBY, Rob   *C&W '90*

Singles: 7-inch

ARISTA 3-4   90-92

CROSBY, STILLS & NASH

P&R/LP '69/C&W '82

Singles: 7-inch

ATLANTIC 3-6   69-89

Picture Sleeves

ATLANTIC 3-8   70-89

LPs: 10/12-inch 33rpm

ATLANTIC (Except 8229) 8-10   77-83
ATLANTIC (8229 "Crosby, Stills &
  Nash") 15-20   69
  Members: David Crosby; Stephen Stills; Graham
  Nash.

CROSBY, STILLS, NASH & YOUNG   *P&R/LP '70*

Singles: 7-inch

ATLANTIC 3-5   70

Picture Sleeves

ATLANTIC 3-6   70

EPs: 7-inch 33/45rpm

ATLANTIC 10-15   70
  (Jukebox issue only.)

LPs: 10/12-inch 33rpm

ATLANTIC (165 "Celebration
  Copy") 25-35   70s
  (Promotional issue only.)
ATLANTIC (902 "4-Way
  Street") 12-20   71
  (With photo applied to cover.)
ATLANTIC (7200 "Deja Vu") 15-20   70
  (With photo applied to cover.)
ATLANTIC (7200 "Deja Vu") 8-12
  (With photo printed on cover.)
ATLANTIC (16000 thru 19000
  series) 5-10   74-82
ATLANTIC (8000 series) 5-10   83
MFSL (088 "Deja Vu") 25-50   82

Promotional LPs

  Members: David Crosby; Stephen Stills; Graham
  Nash; Neil Young.
  Also see CROSBY, STILLS & NASH

CROW, Alvin   *C&W '77*

(With the Pleasant Valley Boys; with Tommy Allsup; with Jesse Ashlock)

Singles: 7–inch

POLYDOR	3-5	77-78

LP: 10/12–inch 33rpm

LONGNECK	6-12	76
POLYDOR	5-10	76-77

CROWELL, Rodney   *C&W '78*

Singles: 7–inch

COLUMBIA	3-4	86-90
W.B.	3-4	78-82

LPs: 10/12–inch 33rpm

COLUMBIA	5-8	86-90
W.B.	5-10	78-81

Session: Karen Brooks.
Also see BROOKS, Karen
Also see HARRIS, Emmylou
Also see SHAVER, Billy Joe
Also see STEWART, Gary

CROWELL, Rodney, & Rosanne Cash   *C&W '88*

Singles: 7–inch

COLUMBIA	3-4	88

Also see CASH, Rosanne
Also see CROWELL, Rodney

CROWLEY, J.C.   *C&W '88*

Singles: 7–inch

RCA	3-4	88

CRUM, Simon   *C&W '55*

(Ferlin Husky)

Singles: 78rpm

CAPITOL	5-15	55-57

Singles: 7–inch

ABC	3-5	74
CAPITOL	5-15	55-63

LPs: 10/12–inch 33rpm

CAPITOL (1880 "The Unpredictable Simon Crum")	75-100	63

Also see HUSKY, Ferlin

CUMMINGS, Barbara   *C&W '66*

Singles: 7–inch

LONDON	4-8	66-67

CUMMINGS, Burton

      P&R/LP '76/C&W '79

Singles: 7–inch

ALFA	3-4	81
PORTRAIT	3-5	76-78

Picture Sleeves

ALFA	3-4	81
PORTRAIT	3-5	78

EPs: 7–inch 33/45rpm

PORTRAIT	4-8	77

(Issued with a paper sleeve.)

LPs: 10/12–inch 33rpm

ALFA	5-10	81
PORTRAIT	8-10	76-78

Also see GUESS WHO
Also see ROGERS, Dann

CUMMINGS, Burton / Cheap Trick / Crawler

EPs: 7–inch 33/45rpm

COLUMBIA (1129 "Music for Every Ear")	15-25	77

(Promotional issue only.)

CUNHA, Rick   *P&R/C&W '74*

Singles: 7–inch

COLUMBIA	3-5	75
GRC	3-5	74

LPs: 10/12–inch 33rpm

COLUMBIA	8-10	75
GRC	10-12	74
SIERRA BRIAR	5-10	

Also see JENNINGS, Waylon

CUNNINGHAM, J.C.   *C&W '80*

Singles: 7–inch

SCOTTI BROS.	3-5	80
VIVA	3-4	84

CURLESS, Dick   *C&W '65*

Singles: 7–inch

ALLAGASH (101 "A Tombstone Every Mile")	10-15	65
CAPITOL	3-6	70-73
TOWER	4-8	65-68

LP: 10/12–inch 33rpm

BELMONT	6-10	80
CAPITOL	10-20	70-73
INTERSTATE	8-12	76
PICKWICK/HILLTOP	8-15	70s
TIFFANY (1016 "Songs of the Open Country")	50-75	58
TIFFANY (1028 "Singin' Just for Fun")	50-75	59
TIFFANY (1033 "I Love to Tell a Story")	75-100	60
TOWER	15-25	65-68

CURREY, Diana Sicily   *C&W '89*
Singles: 7–inch
CONDOR 3-4   90

CURTIS, Larry   *C&W '78*
Singles: 7–inch
SCRIMSHAW................................ 3-5   78

CURTIS, Ken
LP: 10/12–inch 33rpm
CAPITOL.................................... 30-40   66
DOT.. 25-35   67
PICKWICK 10-20

CURTIS, Ken / Rex Allen & Arizona Wranglers
Singles: 78rpm
MERCURY/SAV-WAY (6045 "Lemme Outa Here").................................. 100-150   47
(Picture disc. Promotional issue only.)
Also see ALLEN, Rex
Also see CURTIS, Ken
Also see SONS of PIONEERS

CURTIS, Mac   *C&W '68*
Singles: 78rpm
KING 25-75   56-57
Singles: 7–inch
DOT.. 4-8   62
EPIC.. 4-6   68-70
FELSTED (8592 "Come Back Baby") 10-15   60
GRT.. 3-6   70
KING (4927 "If I Had Me a Woman") 50-100   56
(Blue label.)
KING (4927 "If I Had Me a Woman") 100-150   56
(White bio label. Promotional issue only.)
KING (4949 "Grandaddy's Rockin")................................. 100-200   56
KING (4965 "You Ain't Treatin' Me Right") 100-200   56
KING (4995 "That Ain't Nothin' But Right") 100-200   56
KING (5059 "Say So")............... 25-50   57
KING (5107 "What You Want") 40-60   57
KING (5121 "Little Miss Linda")....................................... 40-60   58
SHAH 4-8   64
SHALIMAR.................................... 4-8   63
TOWER... 4-8   67

LP: 10/12–inch 33rpm
EPIC...12-20   68
GRT 10-15   71
ROLLIN' ROCK...........................8-10

CURTIS, Sonny   *C&W '66*
Singles: 7–inch
A&M (1359 "The Lights of L.A.")..20-30   72
CAPITOL.......................................8-12   75-76
DIMENSION...............................8-12   63-64
DOT 10-20   58
ELEKTRA.......................................3-4   79-81
LIBERTY 10-15   64
MERCURY......................................8-12   73
OVATION......................................10-15   70
'STEEM..3-4   85
VIVA..8-10   66-69
LPs: 10/12–inch 33rpm
ELEKTRA......................................8-15   79-81
IMPERIAL (9276 "Beatle Hits") 25-35   64
(Monaural.)
IMPERIAL (12276 "Beatle Hits") 30-40   64
(Stereo.)
VIVA (36012 "1st of Sonny Curtis")......................................20-30   68
VIVA (36021 "The Sonny Curtis Style") 20-30   69
Also see CLAPTON, Eric
Also see CRICKETS
Also see HOLLY, Buddy

D

D&M

Singles: 12–inch 33/45rpm

POLYDOR (054 "On the Shelf").... 5-8   79
Members: Donnie Osmond; Marie Osmond.
Also see OSMOND, Donny & Marie

DAFFAN, Ted   *C&W '44*
(With His Texans)

Singles: 78rpm

COLUMBIA	4-8	46-55
OKEH	4-8	44-45

Singles: 7–inch

COLUMBIA (21400 "Born to
Lose") 8-12   55
Members: George Strange; Chuck Keeshan; Leon
Seago.

DAISY, Pat   *C&W '72*

Singles: 7–inch

RCA 3-5   72-73

DALE, Kenny   *C&W '77*

Singles: 7–inch

BGM	3-4	86
CAPITOL	3-5	77-80
FUNDERBURG	3-4	82
REPUBLIC	3-4	84
SABA	3-4	85

LP: 10/12–inch 33rpm

CAPITOL 6-12   77-81

DALE, Terry   *C&W '82*

Singles: 7–inch

LANEDALE 3-4   82

DALHART, Vernon   *P&R '17*
(With Gladys Rice; with Al Bernard)

Singles: 78rpm

BANNER	15-25	20s
BLACK PATTI	75-125	
BRUNSWICK	10-20	20s
BUDDY	50-100	
CAMEO	15-25	20s
CHAMPION	15-25	20s
CLARION	10-20	
COLUMBIA	5-15	22-30s
DOMINO	15-25	20s
EDISON	20-50	17-20s
EDISON AMBEROL	15-25	20s
GENNETT	15-25	20s
HARMONY	15-25	20s
HERSCHEL	25-50	
HERWIN	25-50	
OKEH	10-20	24
PATH	15-25	20s
PERFECT	15-25	20s
RCA	5-10	49
REGAL	15-25	20s
VICTOR	10-20	21-30s
VOCALION	15-25	20s

Singles: 7–inch

RCA (0016 "Prisoner's Song") ... 15-25   49

LP: 10/12–inch 33rpm

DAVIS UNLIMITED	10-20
GOLDEN OLDEN COUNTRY	8-10
MARK 56	8-10
OLD HOMESTEAD	8-10

DALHART, Vernon, & Carson Robison   *P&R '28*

Singles: 78rpm

VICTOR 10-20   27-28
Also see DALHART, Vernon
Also see ROBISON, Carson

DALICE   *C&W '90*

Singles: 7–inch

COUNTRY PRIDE 3-4   90

DALLAS, Johnny   *C&W '66*

Singles: 7–inch

LITTLE DARLIN' 4-6   66

DALTON, Bob   *C&W '70*

Singles: 7–inch

MEGA 3-5   70

DALTON, Lacy J.   *C&W '79*

Singles: 7–inch

CAPITOL	3-4	90
COLUMBIA	3-5	79-86
UNIVERSAL	3-4	89

LP: 10/12–inch 33rpm

CBS	5-10	
COLUMBIA	6-12	78-83

Also see BARE, Bobby
Also see COE, David Allan
Also see JONES, George, & Lacy J. Dalton

DALTON, Larry, & Dolton Gang   *C&W '81*
Singles: 7–inch
SOUNDWAVES 3-4   81

DANDY   *C&W '79*
(With the Doolittle Band)
Singles: 7–inch
COLUMBIA 3-4   80
W.B. 3-5   79

DANIEL   *C&W '77*
(Daniel Willis)
Singles: 7–inch
LS 3-5   77-78

DANIEL, Cooter   *C&W '80*
Singles: 7–inch
CONNECTION 3-4   80

DANIEL, Davis   *C&W '91*
Singles: 7–inch
MERCURY 3-4   91

DANIEL, Pebble   *C&W '80*
Singles: 7–inch
ELEKTRA 3-4   80

DANIELLE, Tina   *C&W '86*
(With the Laverna Moore Singers; with Carol Lee Singers)
Singles: 7–inch
CHARTA 3-4   86-87

DANIELS, Charlie   *C&W/P&R/LP '73*
(Charlie Daniels Band; with the Jaguars)
Singles: 7–inch
EPIC 3-5   76-86
HANOVER (4541 "Robot Romp") 10-20   59
KAMA SUTRA 3-6   73-76
PAULA (200 series) 5-10   66
PAULA (400 series) 3-5   76
EPs: 7–inch 33/45rpm
KAMA SUTRA (10 "Volunteer Jam") 5-8   74
   (Bonus EP packaged with *Fire on the Mountain* LP.)
LPs: 10/12–inch 33rpm
CAPITOL (11000 series) 8-10   75
CAPITOL (16000 series) 5-10   80
EPIC (Except 273) 5-10   76-91

EPIC (273 "Everything You Always Wanted to Hear") 10-15   77
   (Promotional issue only.)
KAMA SUTRA 10-15   73-76
MFSL (176 "Million Mile Reflections") 15-20   85
   Also see BARE, Bobby
   Also see LEE, Johnny, Michael Martin Murphey, & Charlie Daniels
   Also see TUBB, Ernest

DARIN, Bobby   *P&R/R&B/C&W '58*
(With the Jaybirds; with Rinky Dinks; Bob Darin)
Singles: 78rpm
ATCO 30-50   57-58
DECCA 20-30   56-57
Singles: 7–inch
ATCO ("She's Tanfastic") 25-35
   (Promotional issue only. No selection number used.)
ATCO (6092 "So Mean")............15-25   57
ATCO (6103 "Pretty Betty") 25-35   57
ATCO (6109 "Just in Case You Change Your Mind")...25-35   58
ATCO (6121 "Early in the Morning") 20-30   58
   (This same track was previously issued as by "The Rinky Dinks on Atco and by the Ding Dongs on Brunswick.")
ATCO (6127 "Queen of the Hop")..10-20   58
ATCO (6128 "Mighty Mighty Man") 25-35   58
ATCO (6133 "Plain Jane") 10-20   59
   (Monaural.)
ATCO (SD-45-6133 "Plain Jane")..25-50   59
   (Stereo.)
ATCO (6140 thru 6334) 8-15   59-65
ATLANTIC.......................................4-8   65-67
CAPITOL (2263 "18 Yellow Roses") 20-30   63
   (Promotional issue only.)
CAPITOL...5-8   62-65
DECCA (29883 "Rock Island Line")..20-30   56
DECCA (29922 "Blue Eyed Mermaid") 30-50   56
DECCA (30031 "The Greatest Builder") 20-30   56
DECCA (30225 "Dealer in Dreams")....................................25-40   57
DECCA (30737 "Dealer in Dreams")....................................10-20   59

DIMENSION 3-6	70
DIRECTION 3-6	68-70
MOTOWN 3-5	71-72

Picture Sleeves

ATCO (6133 thru 6206)............. 20-40	59-61
ATCO (6211 "Ave Maria") 75-100	61
ATCO (6214 thru 6221)............. 10-25	62
CAPITOL (2263 "18 Yellow Roses") .... 25-50 (Promotional issue only.)	63
CAPITOL (4837 thru 5443) 10-20	62-65

EPs: 7–inch 33/45rpm

ATCO (115 "This Is Darin") ..... 50-100 (Promotional issue only. Issued with paper sleeve.)	59
ATCO (1001 "For Teenagers Only") .... 50-100 (Promotional issue only. Issued with paper sleeve.)	60
ATCO (4502 "Bobby Darin") 35-45	58
ATCO (4504 "That's All")........... 25-35	59
ATCO (4505 "Queen of the Hop")................................... 30-45	59
ATCO (4508 "This Is Darin")..... 20-30	59
ATCO (4512 "At the Copa") 20-30	60
ATCO (4513 "For Teenagers Only") 30-50	60
CAPITOL (1791 "Look At Me Now") .... 25-50 (Jukebox issue only.)	62
CAPITOL CUSTOM ("Scripto Presents Bobby Darin")....................................... 25-50 (Promotional issue only. Made with two different color paper sleeves, each offered in conjunction with a different pen: One with light blue sleeve came with Scripto Wordmaster ball point pen; one with yellow sleeve came with ink cartridge fountain pen. Picture of Bobby Darin is the same on both sleeves.)	63
CAPITOL CUSTOM/ARTISTIC ("Bobby Darin")....................................... 25-50 (Promotional issue only. Issued with paper sleeve.)	63
DECCA (2676 "Here Them Bells").. 50-75	60

LPs: 10/12–inch 33rpm

ATCO (102 "Bobby Darin") 50-75	58
ATCO (104 "That's All")............. 25-45 (Monaural.)	58
ATCO (SD-104 "That's All") ...... 35-55 (Stereo.)	58
ATCO (115 "This Is Darin") .... 15-25 (Monaural.)	60

ATCO (SD-115 "This Is Darin")..20-30 (Stereo.)	60
ATCO (122 "Darin at the Copa").....................................15-25 (Monaural.)	60
ATCO (SD-122 "Darin at the Copa").....................................20-30 (Stereo.)	60
ATCO (124 "It's You Or No One").....................................15-25 (Monaural.)	63
ATCO (SD-124 "It's You Or No One").....................................20-30 (Stereo.)	63
ATCO (125 "The 25th Day of December")..............................25-35 (Monaural.)	60
ATCO (SD-125 "The 25th Day of December")..............................35-50 (Stereo.)	60
ATCO (126 "Two of a Kind") ......15-25 (Monaural.)	61
ATCO (SD-126 "Two of a Kind") ....20-30 (Stereo.)	61
ATCO (131 "The Bobby Darin Story")...............................35-45 (Monaural. White cover.)	61
ATCO (SD-131 "The Bobby Darin Story")...............................45-55 (Stereo. White cover.)	61
ATCO (131 "The Bobby Darin Story")...............................10-15 (Black cover.)	72
ATCO (134 "Love Swings")........15-25 (Monaural.)	61
ATCO (SD-134 "Love Swings") .20-30 (Stereo.)	61
ATCO (138 "Twist")....................15-25 (Monaural.)	61
ATCO (SD-138 "Twist") ....20-30 (Stereo.)	61
ATCO (140 "Bobby Darin Sings Ray Charles")...................................15-25 (Monaural.)	62
ATCO (SD-140 "Bobby Darin Sings Ray Charles")...................................20-30 (Stereo.)	62
ATCO (146 "Things") ....15-25 (Monaural.)	61
ATCO (SD-146 "Things")...........20-30 (Stereo.)	61
ATCO (167 "Winners")...............15-25 (Monaural)	64
ATCO (SD-167 "Winners").........20-30 (Stereo.)	64

ATCO (1001 "Bobby Darin for Teenagers Only") 100-150   60
(With color foldout photo.)

ATLANTIC 15-25   66-67

BAINBRIDGE 5-10   81

CANDLELITE 15-20   76

CAPITOL 20-25   62-66

CLARION 15-20   64

DIRECTION 12-20   68-70

IMPERIAL HOUSE..................... 12-15   76

MOTOWN (100 series) 5-10   82

MOTOWN (738 "Finally") 150-250   72
(Promotional issue only.)

MOTOWN (753 "Bobby Darin")..................................... 10-20   72

MOTOWN (813 "Darin: 1936-1973").................................. 10-20   74

W.B. (3501 "Original Bobby Darin")..................................... 20-30   76
(Three-LP mail-order offer.)

Session: King Curtis.
Also see DING DONGS
Also see RINKY DINKS

DARRELL, Johnny   *C&W '65*
Singles: 7–inch
CAPRICORN................................. 3-5   74-75

CARTWHEEL................................ 3-5   71-72

GUSTO 3-4   78

MONUMENT 3-5   73

U.A. 4-6   65-70

Picture Sleeves
U.A. 3-6   67

LPs: 10/12–inch 33rpm
CAPRICORN................................. 6-10   75

GUSTO 5-10

SUNSET...................................... 6-10   68-70

U.A. 8-12   66-70

DARRELL, Johnny / George Jones / Willie Nelson
LPs: 10/12–inch 33rpm
SUNSET...................................... 8-12   69

Also see DARRELL, Johnny
Also see JONES, George
Also see NELSON, Willie

DARREN, James   *P&R '59/C&W '78*
(Jimmy Darren)
Singles: 7–inch
ABC.. 3-4   74

BUDDAH 3-5   70

COLPIX (102 "There's No Such Thing")..................................... 5-10   58

COLPIX (113 "Gidget") 5-10   59

COLPIX (119 "Angel Face")......... 5-10   59
(Monaural.)

COLPIX (SCP-119 "Angel Face") 10-20   59
(Stereo.)

COLPIX (128 thru 708) 5-10   59-63

COLPIX (758 "Punch and Judy") 10-20   64

COLPIX (765 "Married Man")....... 5-10   64

ERIC 3-4

KIRSHNER 3-5   71-72

MCA... 3-4

MGM 3-5   73

PRIVATE STOCK 3-5   75-77

RCA 3-5   78

W.B. 4-8   65-68

Picture Sleeves
COLPIX....................................... 8-15   58-61

EPs: 7–inch 33/45rpm
RMR JUNIORS ("James Darren") 10-15
(Promotional issue, with fashion spots.)

LPs: 10/12–inch 33rpm
COLPIX (406 "Album No. 1").....20-30   60

COLPIX (418 "Gidget Goes Hawaiian")...............................20-30   61

COLPIX (424 "For All Sizes").....20-30   62

COLPIX (428 "Love Among the Young")...............................20-30   62

KIRSHNER 10-20   71-72

W.B. 15-20   67

DARREN, James / Shelley Fabares / Paul Petersen   *LP '63*
LPs: 10/12–inch 33rpm
COLPIX (444 "Teenage Triangle")...............................25-35   63

COLPIX (468 "More Teenage Triangle") 25-35   63

DAVE & SUGAR   *C&W '75*
(Dave Rowland & Sugar)
Singles: 7–inch
ELEKTRA....................................3-4   81

RCA 3-5   75-82

LPs: 10/12–inch 33rpm
ELEKTRA....................................5-10   81

RCA 5-10   76-82

Members: Dave Rowland; Vicki Hackeman-Baker;
Jackie Frantz; Sue Powell; Melissa Dean; Jamie Kaye.
Also see POWELL, Sue
Also see PRIDE, Charley
Also see ROWLAND, Dave

DAVID & LEE
Singles: 7–inch
G.S.P. (1 "Sad September")...... 20-30   62
Members: David Gates; Leon Russell.
Also see RUSSELL, Leon

DAVIES, Gail   *C&W '78*
Singles: 7–inch
LIFESONG..................................... 3-5   78-79
MCA 3-4   89
RCA.. 3-4   84-85
W.B. 3-5   79-84
LP: 10/12–inch 33rpm
LIFESONG.................................. 6-12   78
MCA 5-8   89
RCA.. 5-8   85
W.B. 5-10   80-83
Also see WILD CHOIR

DAVIS, Carrie   *C&W '89*
Singles: 7–inch
FOUNTAIN HILLS......................... 3-4   89

DAVIS, Danny   *LP '69/C&W '70*
(With the Nashville Brass; with Arlene Baird; with Titans; with Nashville Strings; Danny Davis Orchestra;)
Singles: 78rpm
BLUE JAY 3-5   54
HICKORY.. 3-5   54
MGM 3-6   51-53
Singles: 7–inch
BLUE JAY 4-8   54
CABOT.. 3-6   59
HICKORY.. 4-8   54
LIBERTY 3-6   59
MGM (11000 series) 5-10   51-53
MGM (13000 series) 3-5   62-65
RCA.. 3-4   69-84
THUNDER....................................... 3-6   59
VERVE... 3-5   61
LPs: 10/12–inch 33rpm
MGM 8-18   61-65
RCA SPECIAL PRODUCTS (0176 "America 200 Years Young").................. 10-15   76
(Special Products issue for the Amana Corp.)
RCA.. 5-10   69-84
Also see ATKINS, Chet, Floyd Cramer & Danny Davis
Also see LOCKLIN, Hank, with Danny Davis & Nashville Brass

DAVIS, Danny, & Byron Lee
Singles: 7–inch
MGM 4-6   64

DAVIS, Danny, Nashville Brass & Dona Mason   *C&W '87*
Singles: 7–inch
JAROCO 3-4   87

DAVIS, Danny, Willie Nelson, & Nashville Brass   *LP '80*
Singles: 7–inch
RCA 3-4   80
LPs: 10/12–inch 33rpm
RCA 5-10   80
Also see DAVIS, Danny
Also see LOCKLIN, Hank
Also see NEWMAN, Jimmy C., Danny Davis & Nashville Brass

DAVIS, Dianne   *C&W '89*
Singles: 7–inch
16TH AVE. 3-4   89

DAVIS, Gene   *C&W '76*
Singles: 7–inch
MAVERICK 3-5   76

DAVIS, Jimmie   *C&W '44*
(With the Jimmie Davis Singers; with Anita Kerr Singers)
Singles: 78rpm
BLUEBIRD.................................25-75   30s
DECCA (1500 thru 6100 series)...............................20-40   35-45
DECCA (20000 & 30000 series)...................................8-15   43-57
Electradisk 100-200   30s
(Made for sale through Woolworth Stores.)
SUNRISE (3128 "Bear Cat Mama from Horner Corners") 100-200   33
SUNRISE (3237 "It's All Coming Home to You")....................................100-200   33
SUNRISE (3267 "I Wonder If She's Blue") 100-200   33
SUNRISE (3400 "There's Evil in Ye Children Gather 'Round")..................100-200   33
SUNRISE (3440 "I Want Her Tailor Made") 100-200   33
VICTOR (23000 series) 75-150   30s
Singles: 7–inch
DECCA (28000 thru 30000 series)..8-20   50-57
DECCA (31000 & 32000 series)....3-8   59-71

EPs: 7–inch 33/45rpm

DECCA	5-15	55-65

LP: 10/12–inch 33rpm

CANAAN	4-8	74-81
CORAL	4-8	73
DECCA	8-20	55-72
MCA	4-10	75
PAULA	6-10	74-75
PLANTATION	6-12	78-81
RIVERSONG	5-8	
VOCALION	5-15	60-69

Also see FOLEY, Red / Jimmie Davis
Also see KERR, Anita

DAVIS, Joey   *C&W '78*
Singles: 7–inch

MRC	3-5	78

DAVIS, Linda   *C&W '88*
Singles: 7–inch

CAPITOL	3-4	90-91
EPIC	3-4	88-89

Also see ROGERS, Kenny

DAVIS, Mac   *C&W/P&R '70*
Singles: 7–inch

CAPITOL	4-8	65
COLUMBIA	3-5	70-78
CASABLANCA	3-4	80-84
JAMIE	5-10	62
MCA	3-4	85-86
VEE JAY	5-10	63

Picture Sleeves

COLUMBIA	3-5	70-75

LPs: 10/12–inch 33rpm

ACCORD	5-10	82
CASABLANCA	5-10	81-85
COLUMBIA	8-10	70-83
MCA	5-10	86
SPRINGBOARD	6-10	
TRIP	8-10	73

DAVIS, Mac / Classics IV
LPs: 10/12–inch 33rpm

VINTAGE	10-15

Also see DAVIS, Mac

DAVIS, Paul   *C&W '60*
Singles: 7–inch

DOKE	5-10	60

DAVIS, Paul   *P&R '70/C&W '75*
(With Susan Collins)
Singles: 7–inch

ARISTA	3-4	81-82
BANG (Except 500 series)	3-5	73-80
BANG (500 series)	4-6	68-72
CAPITOL/CURB	3-4	86
FLASHBACK	3-4	82
SOLID GOLD	3-5	73

LPs: 10/12–inch 33rpm

ARISTA	5-10	81
BANG	10-12	72-82

Also see COLLINS, Sue
Also see OSMOND, Marie, & Paul Davis
Also see TUCKER, Tanya, Paul Davis & Paul Overstreet

DAVIS, Sammy, Jr.   *P&R '54/C&W '82*
(Sammy Davis)
Singles: 7–inch

A.L.B.B. (38032 "The House I Live In")	3-5	
(Promotional issue only.)		
APPLAUSE	3-4	82
DECCA (25500 series)	3-6	62
DECCA (29000 thru 31000 series)	5-10	54-60
DECCA (32000 series)	3-5	69
ECOLOGY	3-4	71
MGM	3-5	71-79
VERVE	4-6	60
REPRISE	3-6	61-71
20TH FOX	3-5	75-76
W.B.	3-4	77

Picture Sleeves

A.L.B.B. (38032 "The House I Live In")	5-10	
(Promotional issue only.)		

EPs: 7–inch 33/45rpm

CAPITOL	5-15	54
DECCA	8-12	54-55

LPs: 10/12–inch 33rpm

DECCA (100 series)	10-20	66
DECCA (4000 series)	10-20	61-65
DECCA (8100 thru 8700 series)	20-30	54-58
DECCA (8900 series)	10-20	59
DECCA (9032 "Mr. Wonderful")	60-70	56
(Soundtrack.)		
HARMONY	5-10	69-71
MCA	5-10	77
MGM	5-10	72-73

MOTOWN 6-10		70
RCA (1086 "Three Penny Opera").................................. 15-25		64
REPRISE 10-20		61-69
20TH FOX (Except 5014)............ 5-10		76
20TH FOX (FXG-5014 "Of Love and Desire") .... 25-30 (Soundtrack. Monaural.)		64
20TH FOX (SXG-5014 "Of Love and Desire") .... 35-40 (Soundtrack. Stereo.)		64
W.B. 5-10		77
U.A. (5187 "Salt and Pepper")... 15-20 (Soundtrack.)		68
VOCALION.................................. 5-10		68

DAVIS, Sammy, Jr., & Laurindo Almeida

LPs: 10/12–inch 33rpm

REPRISE 10-15   67

DAVIS, Sammy, Jr., & Count Basie   *LP '65*

Singles: 7–inch

VERVE.. 3-5   65

LPs: 10/12–inch 33rpm

MGM 6-10   73
VERVE 10-15   65

DAVIS, Sammy, Jr., & Carmen McRae

Singles: 7–inch

DECCA.................................... 5-10   55

EPs: 7–inch 33/45rpm

DECCA.................................... 5-10   59

LPs: 10/12–inch 33rpm

DECCA.................................. 10-20   59

DAVIS, Sammy, Jr., & Buddy Rich

LPs: 10/12–inch 33rpm

REPRISE 10-20   66

DAVIS, Sammy, Jr. / Joya Sherril

LPs: 10/12–inch 33rpm

DESIGN 5-10   60s
  Also see DAVIS, Sammy, Jr.

DAVIS, Skeeter   *C&W '58*

Singles: 7–inch

MERCURY 3-5   76-77
PART TWO 3-4   80
RCA (Except 7000 thru 9600 series) 3-5   69-74

RCA (7000 thru 8300 series).......5-10		58-64
RCA (8400 thru 9600 series).........4-8		64-68

Picture Sleeves

RCA 5-8   63

EPs: 7–inch 33/45rpm

RCA 5-10   63

LPs: 10/12–inch 33rpm

CAMDEN 5-10   65-74
GUSTO 5-10   78
RCA (2000 & 3000 series, except 3790)....................................10-15   60-68
RCA (3790 "Skeeter Davis Sings Buddy Holly") 20-30   67
TUDOR 5-10   84
  Also see BARE, Bobby, & Skeeter Davis
  Also see DAVIS SISTERS
  Also see HAMILTON, George, IV, & Skeeter Davis
  Also see JENNINGS, Waylon
  Also see POSEY, Sandy / Skeeter Davis
  Also see SOME of CHET'S FRIENDS
  Also see WAGONER, Porter, & Skeeter Davis

DAVIS, Skeeter, & Don Bowman   *C&W '68*

Singles: 7–inch

RCA 4-8   68

LP: 10/12–inch 33rpm

RCA 10-15   68
  Also see BOWMAN, Don

DAVIS, Skeeter, & George Hamilton IV   *C&W '70*

Singles: 7–inch

RCA 3-5   70

LPs: 10/12–inch 33rpm

RCA 10-12   70
  Also see HAMILTON, George, IV

DAVIS, Skeeter, & NRBQ

Singles: 7–inch

ROUNDER.....................................3-5   85
  Also see DAVIS, Skeeter
  Also see NRBQ

DAVIS SISTERS   *C&W '53*

Singles: 78rpm

FORTUNE...................................10-20   52
RCA 10-15   53-56

Singles: 7–inch

FORTUNE (174 "Kaw-Liga").......15-25   52
FORTUNE (3000 series) 4-8
RCA (5000 & 6000 series).........10-15   53-56
  Members: Skeeter Davis; Betty J. "Bee Jay" Davis.
  Also see DAVIS, Skeeter

DAVIS SISTERS / Chuck Hatfield & the Treble-Aires
Singles: 7–inch
FORTUNE.................................. 10-15   52
Singles: 7–inch
FORTUNE (175 "Heartbreak
  Ahead") 15-25   52

DAVIS SISTERS / Roy Hall & His Cahutta Mountain Boys
Singles: 78rpm
FORTUNE................................. 10-20   53
Singles: 7–inch
FORTUNE (170 "Jealous
  Love").................................... 20-40   53
Also see DAVIS SISTERS
Also see HALL, Roy

DEAL, Don   *C&W '79*
Singles: 7–inch
CAPITOL...................................... 4-8   63
CHALLENGE 4-8   68
DONJIM 3-5   79
ERA... 10-15   57-58
MGM 4-8   64
SAND 4-6   69

DEAL, Billy   *C&W '90*
Singles: 7–inch
CAPITOL/SBK.............................. 3-4   90-91
LPs: 10/12–inch 33rpm
CAPITOL/SBK.............................. 5-8   91

DEAN, Eddie   *C&W '48*
(With the Frontiersmen; with Cort Johnson)
Singles: 78rpm
CAPITOL...................................... 4-8   51-52
CORAL... 4-8   52
CRYSTAL..................................... 5-10   48
SAGE & SAND.............................. 4-8   54-55
Singles: 7–inch
CAPITOL...................................... 5-10   51-52
CORAL... 5-10   52
SAGE & SAND.............................. 5-10   54-55
LP: 10/12–inch 33rpm
CRICKET 5-10
CROWN 10-20   60s
DESIGN 10-20   60s
SAGE (1 "Greatest
  Westerns") 25-50   56
SAGE (5 "Hi-Country").............. 25-50   57
SAGE (16 "Hillbilly Heaven")..... 20-30   61

SHASTA..8-12   74
SOUND (603 "Greatest
  Westerns") 25-50   56
SUTTON 10-20
TIARA 5-10
WFC..5-10   76
Also see WILLING, Foy, Eddie Dean & His Riders of
the Purple Sage

DEAN, Eddie / Cort Johnson
LP: 10/12–inch 33rpm
TIARA 5-10
Also see DEAN, Eddie

DEAN, Jimmy   *C&W '53*
(Jimmie Dean)
Singles: 78rpm
COLUMBIA 5-10   57
4 STAR 5-10   54
MERCURY.....................................4-8   56
Singles: 7–inch
CASINO 3-5   76
CHURCHILL 3-4   83
COLUMBIA (40000 thru 43000 series,
  except 42175)............................5-10   57-66
COLUMBIA (42175 "Big
  John")......................................10-12   61
(Dean says: "At the bottom of this mine
lies one hell of a man.")
COLUMBIA (42175 "Big Bad
  John").......................................4-8   61
(Dean says: "At the bottom of this mine
lies a big, big man." Note slight title change.)
COLUMBIA (45000 & 46000
  series)......................................3-5   74
4 STAR (1600 series) 10-15   54
4 STAR (1700 series) 5-8   59
KING 4-6   64
MERCURY.....................................5-10   56
RCA 3-6   66-71
Picture Sleeves
COLUMBIA (Except 41025).........5-10   59-66
COLUMBIA (41025 "Little Sandy
  Sleighfoot") 10-20   57
EPs: 7–inch 33/45rpm
COLUMBIA 8-12   57
LPs: 10/12–inch 33rpm
ACCORD 5-10   82
BRYLEN.......................................5-10
CASINO 5-10   76
COLUMBIA (1025 thru 2500
  series).....................................10-25   57-66
(Monaural.)

COLUMBIA (8000 & 9000 series) 10-25   61-68
(Stereo. With "CS" prefix.)

COLUMBIA (9200 series) 5-10
(With "PC" prefix.)

COLUMBIA (10000 series) 6-10   73

COLUMBIA SPECIAL PRODUCTS............................. 5-10

CROWN 10-15   60s

CUSTOM.................................... 5-10

GRT... 5-10   77

GUEST STAR 8-10   60s

HARMONY................................... 8-12   60-69

KING (686 "Favorites of Jimmy Dean")...................................... 25-35   60

LA BREA (8014 "Bummin' Around with Jimmy Dean").................................... 20-30

MERCURY (20319 "Jimmy Dean Sings His Television Favorites").............. 15-25   57

PICKWICK 5-10   70s

PICKWICK/HILLTOP 10-12   65

PREMIER..................................... 5-10

RCA... 8-12   67-71

SPIN-O-RAMA 8-10   60s

WING 8-12   64
   Also see SOME of CHET'S FRIENDS

DEAN, Jimmy / Luke Gordon
LP: 10/12–inch 33rpm

PREMIER.................................... 10-15   60s

SPIN-O-RAMA 10-15   60s

DEAN, Jimmy / Johnny Horton
LPs: 10/12–inch 33rpm

STARDAY 15-20   65
   Also see HORTON, Johnny

DEAN, Jimmy / David Houston / Warner Mack / Autry Inman
LP: 10/12–inch 33rpm

DIPLOMAT.................................. 10-15   60s
   Also see HOUSTON, David
   Also see INMAN, Autry
   Also see MACK, Warner

DEAN, Jimmy / Marvin Rainwater
LPs: 10/12–inch 33rpm

MOUNT VERNON........................ 5-10

PREMIER (9054 "Nashville Showtime")................................ 5-10

DEAN, Jimmy / Marvin Rainwater / Rusty Evans
LPs: 10/12–inch 33rpm

ALMOR 5-10   60s
   Also see RAINWATER, Marvin

DEAN, Jimmy / Stoneman Family
LP: 10/12–inch 33rpm

WYNCOTE...................................5-10   62
   Also see STONEMANS

DEAN, Jimmy, & Dottie West
Singles: 7–inch

RCA 3-5   71

LPs: 10/12–inch 33rpm

RCA 10-20   70
   Also see DEAN, Jimmy
   Also see WEST, Dottie

DEAN, Larry   *C&W '89*
Singles: 7–inch

USA...3-4   89

DEBONAIRES   *C&W '85*
Singles: 7–inch

MTM...3-4   85

DEE, Duane   *C&W '67*
Singles: 7–inch

ABC...3-5   74

CAPITOL...4-6   67-68

CARTWHEEL 3-5   71-72

LP: 10/12–inch 33rpm

CAPITOL..8-12   68

DEE, Gordon   *C&W '84*
Singles: 7–inch

SOUTHERN TRACKS 3-4   84

DEE, Johnny   *P&R '57*
(John D. Loudermilk; Featuring Joe Tanner on Guitar)
Singles: 78rpm

COLONIAL (430 "Sittin' in the Balcony").................................25-50   57

Singles: 7–inch

BULLET 8-12   53

COLONIAL (430 "Sittin' in the Balcony")...................................15-20   57
(Has "45 RPM" on left side of label.)

COLONIAL (430 "Sittin' in the Balcony")...................................10-15   57
(Has "45 RPM" on right side of label.)

COLONIAL (430 "Sittin' in the Balcony")......................................8-12   57

(No "45 RPM" on label. Reads "Dist. by AM-PAR Record Corp.")

COLONIAL (435 "1000 Concrete
  Blocks").................................. 15-20   57
DOT... 5-10   58

Picture Sleeves

COLONIAL (430 "Sittin in the
  Balcony").............................. 30-40   57
  Also see LOUDERMILK, John D.

DEE, Kathy   *C&W '63*

Singles: 7–inch

B-W (619 "If I Never Get to
  Heaven")................................... 4-8   63
U.A. 4-8   63-64

Picture Sleeves

B-W (619 "If I Never Get to
  Heaven") 10-20   63

LP: 10/12–inch 33rpm

B-W 10-20   63
GUEST STAR 10-20   64

DEER, John   *C&W '70*

(John Deer Company)

Singles: 7–inch

ROYAL AMERICAN 3-5   70

DeHAVEN, Penny   *C&W '69*

Singles: 7–inch

IMPERIAL 3-6   69-70
MAIN STREET 3-4   82-84
MERCURY 3-5   73-74
STARCREST 3-5   76
U.A. 3-5   70-72

LP: 10/12–inch 33rpm

MAIN STREET 5-8   84
U.A. 8-12   72
  Also see BOXCAR WILLIE & Penny DeHaven
  Also see REEVES, Del, & Penny DeHaven
  Also see STARR, Penny

DEKLE, Mike   *C&W '84*

Singles: 7–inch

NSD... 3-4   84

DELBERT & GLEN

                                        P&R '72

Singles: 7–inch

CLEAN 3-5   72-73

LPs: 10/12–inch 33rpm

CLEAN (601 "Subject to
  Change")................................ 15-20   72
  Members: Delbert McClinton; Glen Clark.
  Also see McCLINTON, Delbert

DELICATO, Paul   *C&W '75*

Singles: 7–inch

ARTISTS of AMERICA 3-5   75-76

LPs: 10/12–inch 33rpm

A.V.I. 6-10   77-78
ARTISTS of AMERICA 8-10   76

DELMORE BROTHERS   *C&W '46*

(Delmores)

Singles: 78rpm

BLUEBIRD 20-40   30s-41
COLUMBIA (15724 "Alabama
  Lullaby")............................... 25-50   30s
DECCA 10-20   40-48
KING 5-15   43-57

Singles: 7–inch

KING (769 thru 5407)................... 8-18   52-60

EPs: 7–inch 33/45rpm

KING 5-10

LP: 10/12–inch 33rpm

COUNTY 5-10
KING (589 thru 785)................... 15-30   58-62
KING (910 thru 1090)................ 10-20   64-70
OLD HOMESTEAD........................ 5-8
STARDAY 5-10
  Members: Alton Delmore; Rabon Delmore.

DEL RAY, Martin   *C&W '85*

(With Johnny Cash)

Singles: 7–inch

ATLANTIC...................................... 3-4   91
  Also see CASH, Johnny
  Also see MARTIN, Mike

DENNY, Burch   *C&W '89*

Singles: 7–inch

OAK 3-4   89

DENTON, Jack   *C&W '89*

Singles: 7–inch

M.V.P. 3-4   89

DENVER, John   *LP '69*

Singles: 12–inch 33/45rpm

RCA (11189 "Bet on the Blues")..5-10   77
(Promotional issue only.)

Singles: 7–inch

ALLEGIANCE 3-4
CHERRY MOUNTAIN (02 "Flying Or
  Me") 3-5   86
RCA (Except 0067 thru 0955)........3-5   74-86
RCA (0067 thru 0955)................... 4-8   70-74

Promotional Singles

EVA-TONE (106026 "Trees for
America") 3-5   86

RCA (2008 "Rocky Mountain
High") 5-10   72

Picture Sleeves

ALLEGIANCE................................. 3-4

CHERRY MOUNTAIN (02 "Flying Or
Me")... 3-5   86

RCA (Except 2008) 3-5   74-86

RCA (2008 "Rocky Mountain
High") 5-10   72
(Promotional issue only.)

LPs: 10/12–inch 33rpm

HJD (66 "John Denver
Sings")................................... 200-300   66
(Promotional issue only. Less than 300
copies made as Christmas gifts for friends.)

MOS ("Something to sing
About") 50-100   66
(Promotional issue only. No actual label
name is used. Various artists LP with three
Denver tracks not available elsewhere.)

MERCURY (704 "Beginnings")   10-15   72
(With illustration on cover.)

MERCURY (704 "Beginnings") ... 8-10   74
(With mountain scene photo on cover.)

RCA (0101 thru 3449) 5-10   73-80

RCA (0075 "The John Denver Radio
Show").................................... 20-30   74
(Single-sided LP. Promotional issue only.)

RCA (0683 "The Second John Denver Radio
Show").................................... 20-30   74

RCA (4000 series)..................... 10-15   69-72
(Orange labels.)

RCA (4000 & 5000 series) 5-10   81-85
(Black labels.)

RCA (5398 "The John Denver Holiday Radio
Show").................................... 10-20   84
(Promotional issue only.)

WINDSTAR 5-8   90

Also see DENVER, BOISE & JOHNSON
Also see FAT CITY
Also see MITCHELL, Chad, Trio
Also see MURPHEY, Michael

DENVER, John, & Placido Domingo   *P&R '82*

Singles: 7–inch

COLUMBIA 3-4   82

DENVER, John, & Emmylou Harris   *C&W '83*

Singles: 7–inch

RCA.. 3-4   83

Also see HARRIS, Emmylou

DENVER, John, & Muppets   *LP '79*

Singles: 7–inch

RCA 3-4   79

LPs: 10/12–inch 33rpm

RCA 5-10   79-83

DENVER, John, & Olivia Newton-John   *P&R '75*

Singles: 7–inch

RCA 3-5   75

Also see NEWTON-JOHN, Olivia

DENVER, John, & Nitty Gritty Dirt Band   *C&W '89*

Singles: 7–inch

UNIVERSAL.................................. 3-4   89

Also see NITTY GRITTY DIRT BAND

DENVER, John / Diana Ross

Singles: 7–inch

WHAT'S IT ALL ABOUT 4-8   81
(Public service, radio station issue.)

DENVER, John, & Sylvie Vartan

Singles: 7–inch

RCA 3-4   84

DENVER, John / Stevie Wonder

Singles: 7–inch

WHAT'S IT ALL ABOUT 4-8   80
(Public service, radio station issue.)

DENVER, BOISE & JOHNSON

Singles: 7–inch

REPRISE (0695 "Take Me to
Tomorrow") 5-10   68

Member: John Denver; Michael Johnson.
Also see DENVER, John
Also see JOHNSON, Michael

DESERT ROSE BAND   *C&W '87*

Singles: 7–inch

CURB/MCA.................................... 3-4   87-92

LPs: 10/12–inch 33rpm

CURB/MCA.................................... 5-8   87-92

Members: Chris Hillman; Herb Pedersen; John
Jorgenson.
Also see HILLMAN, Chris
Also see PEDERSEN, Herb

DeWITT, Lew   *C&W '85*

Singles: 7–inch

COMPLEAT 3-4   85

Also see STATLER BROTHERS

DEXTER, Al, & Troopers

P&R/R&B '43/C&W '44
Singles: 7–inch

COLUMBIA 4-8	46	
EKKO 4-6	55	
OKEH 5-10	43-44	
VOCALION...................................... 10-20		

Singles: 7–inch
EKKO 5-10	55	

LPs: 10/12–inch 33rpm
AUDIO LAB 8-12		
CAPITOL (1701 "Greatest Hits") 20-30	62	
COLUMBIA (9005 "Songs of the Southwest").............................. 30-40 (10–inch LP.)		
HARMONY.................................. 8-10		
HILLTOP 8-10		

DIAMOND, Neil   *P&R/LP '66/C&W '78*
Singles: 12–inch 33/45rpm
COLUMBIA (1586 "Heartlight") ... 6-10	82	

Singles: 7–inch
BANG (100 series)........................ 3-4 ("Best Hits" reissue series.)		
BANG (500 & 700 series).............. 3-8	66-73	
CAPITOL...................................... 3-4	80-81	
COLUMBIA (02600 thru 06100 series) 3-4	81-86	
COLUMBIA (10000 & 11000 series) 3-5	74-80	
COLUMBIA (33000 series) .... 3-4 ("Hall of Fame" series.)		
COLUMBIA (42809 "Clown Town").................................... 150-200	63	
COLUMBIA (45000 series) 3-5	73-74	
MCA (40000 series) 3-5	73	
MCA (60000 series) 3-4	73	
PHILCO....................................... 10-20 ("Hip-Pocket" flexi-disc.)	66-67	
SOLID ROCK................................. 3-4		
UNI 3-6	68-72	

Promotional Singles
BANG (Except 55075)................. 5-10	66-73	
UNI (55075 "Two-Bit Manchild") 15-20 (Colored vinyl.)	68	
CAPITOL....................................... 3-5	80-81	
COLUMBIA (1115 "Song Sung Blue") 3-6	77	

COLUMBIA (1193 "September Morn")..3-6 (An alternate version.)	79	
COLUMBIA (02600 thru 11000).....3-5	74-86	
COLUMBIA (42809 "Clown Town")..................................100-200	63	
COLUMBIA (45000 series)............4-8	73-74	
MCA..3-5	73	
UNI..5-10	68-72	
WHAT'S IT ALL ABOUT 8-15	70s	

Picture Sleeves
CAPITOL.......................................3-5	80-81	
COLUMBIA 3-6	73-86	
UNI..4-8	68-70	

EPs: 7–inch 33/45rpm
COLUMBIA (32919 "Serenade") 10-20	74	
MCA (34989 "12 Greatest Hits") 10-20	74	
UNI (34818 "Neil Diamond Gold")..10-20	71	
UNI (34871 "Stones").................10-20	71	

Note: all EPs listed were made for jukebox use.

LPs: 10/12–inch 33rpm
BANG (214 "The Feel of Neil Diamond")...............................50-100	66	
BANG (217 "Just For You") 20-40	67	
BANG (219 "Greatest Hits").......20-40	68	
BANG (221 "Shilo")....................40-50	70	
BANG (224 "Do It") 30-40	71	
BANG (227 "Double Gold")........20-35	73	
CAPITOL..5-10	80	
COLUMBIA (30000 series) 8-12	73-86	
COLUMBIA (40000 series) 5-10	86-89	
COLUMBIA (42550 "Jonathan Livingston Seagull") ....15-25 (Half-speed mastered.)	81	
COLUMBIA (45025 "Best Years of Our Lives").....................................5-8	89	
COLUMBIA (46525 "You Don't Bring Me Flowers")................................15-25 (Half-speed mastered.)	80	
COLUMBIA (47628 "On the Way to the Sky") ....15-25 (Half-speed mastered.)	82	
DIRECT-to-DISK........................10-20		
FROG KING (1 "Early Classics").................................25-50 (Includes music and lyrics songbook. Columbia Record Club issue.)	78	
HARMONY (30023 "Chartbusters") ....15-25 (Various artists LP, containing the 1963	70	

Columbia tracks, and the otherwise
unavailable *I've Never Been the Same*.)

MCA	6-15	72-81
MFSL (024 "Hot August Night")	25-50	79
MFSL (071 "Jazz Singer")	20-30	82
UNI (11 Neil Diamond D.J. Sampler")	25-50	71

(Promotional souvenir issue only.)

UNI (1913 "Open-End Interview with Neil Diamond")	25-50	72

(Promotional issue only.)

UNI (73030 "Velvet Gloves and Spit")	20-35	68

(Does not contain *Shilo*.)

UNI (73030 "Velvet Gloves and Spit")	15-25	70

(With *Shilo*.)

UNI (73047 "Brother Love's Traveling Salvation Show")	20-35	69
UNI (73047 "Sweet Caroline/Brother Love's Traveling Salvation Show")	15-25	69
UNI (73071 "Touching You, Touching Me")	15-25	69
UNI (73084 "Gold")	15-25	70
UNI (73092 "Tap Root Manuscript")	15-25	70

(Some 70000 series LPs were reissued in the 90000 series, with the only change being the first digit.)

UNI (93106 "Stones")	15-25	71
UNI (93136 "Moods")	15-25	72
UNI (93501 "Tap Root Manuscript")	15-25	70

(Capitol Record Club issue.)

Also see NEIL & JACK
Also see STREISAND, Barbra, & Neil Diamond

DIAMOND, Neil / Diana Ross & Supremes

LPs: 10/12–inch 33rpm

MCA (734727 "It's Happening")	30-40	72

(One side of LP devoted to each artist.)

Also see DIAMOND, Neil

DIAMOND RIO *C&W/LP '91*

Singles: 7–inch

ARISTA	3-4	91

LPs: 10/12–inch 33rpm

ARISTA	5-8	91

Members: Marty Roe; Dan Truman; Brian Prout; Jim Olander; Dana Williams; Gene Johnson.

DIAMONDS *C&W '87*

Singles: 7–inch

CHURCHILL	3-5	

Member: Bob Duncan.

DIANA *C&W '79*
(Diana Murrell)

Singles: 7–inch

ADAMAS	3-4	82
ELEKTRA	3-5	79
SUNBIRD	3-4	81

DICKENS, Jimmy *C&W '49*
(Little Jimmy Dickens; Jimmie Dickens)

Singles: 78rpm

COLUMBIA	5-10	49-57

Singles: 7–inch

COLUMBIA (10000 series)	3-5	76
COLUMBIA (20000 & 21000 series)	10-20	50-56
COLUMBIA (40000 series)	8-12	56
COLUMBIA (41000 series, except 41173)	8-12	57-60
COLUMBIA (41173 "I Got a Hole in My Pocket")	30-45	57
COLUMBIA (42000 thru 44000 series)	4-8	60-67
DECCA	3-6	67-69
LITTLE GEM	3-5	75
PARTRIDGE	3-4	80
STARDAY	3-5	73
U.A.	3-5	70-72

EPs: 7–inch 33/45rpm

COLUMBIA (Except 2800 series)	15-20	52-57
COLUMBIA (2800 series)	10-15	57-58

LPs: 10/12–inch 33rpm

COLUMBIA (1047 "Raisin' the Dickens")	40-50	57
COLUMBIA (1500 thru 2500 series)	10-20	60-66

(Monaural.)

COLUMBIA (8300 thru 9600 series)	15-25	60-68

(Stereo.)

COLUMBIA (10000 & 11000 series)	6-10	70-73
COLUMBIA (38000 series)	5-10	84
DECCA	10-12	68-69
GUSTO	5-10	
HARMONY (7000 series)	10-15	64-65
HARMONY (9000 series)	20-30	54
HARMONY (11000 series)	8-12	67
QCA	5-10	75

DICKEY, Dan   *C&W '79*
Singles: 7–inch
CHARTWHEEL 3-5   79

DICKINSON, Hal   *C&W '66*
Singles: 7–inch
GRASS... 4-8   66

DIFFIE, Joe   *C&W '90*
Singles: 7–inch
EPIC 3-4   90-92

DILLARD & CLARK
LP: 10/12–inch 33rpm
A&M 10-15   68-69

Members: Doug Dillard; Gene Clark.
Also see BYRDS
Also see DILLARDS

DILLARDS   *P&R '71*
Singles: 7–inch
ANTHEM 3-5   71-72
CAPITOL....................................... 4-6   65
ELEKTRA....................................... 4-8   63-69
POPPY 3-5   74
U.A. 3-5   75
WHITE WHALE.............................. 3-5   70
LPs: 10/12–inch 33rpm
ANTHEM 6-10   72
ELEKTRA (200 series)............... 20-30   63-65
  (Gold label.)
ELEKTRA (7-200 series)........... 20-30   63-65
  (Gold label.)
ELEKTRA (7-200 series)........... 10-15
  (Brown label.)
ELEKTRA (74000 series)............. 8-12   68
FLYING FISH 5-10   77-81
POPPY.. 8-12   73
20TH FOX 8-12   73

Members: Doug Dillard; Rodney Dillard; Dean Webb;
Mitch Jayne; Joe Osborn.
Also see DILLARD & CLARK
Also see NELSON, Rick

DILLINGHAM, Craig   *C&W '83*
Singles: 7–inch
MCA/CURB 3-4   83-86
Also see HINOJOSA, Tish, & Craig Dillingham

DILLON, Dean   *C&W '79*
Singles: 7–inch
ATLANTIC...................................... 3-4   91-92
CAPITOL.. 3-4   88-89
RCA.. 3-5   79-83
Also see STEWART, Gary, & Dean Dillon

DING DONGS
(Bobby Darin)
Singles: 7–inch
BRUNSWICK (55073 "Early in the
  Morning") 100-150   58
(This same track was reissued as by "The
Rinky Dinks and later by "Bobby Darin & the
Rinky Dinks.")
Also see DARIN, Bobby

DIRKSEN, Senator Everett
McKinley   *P&R '66/C&W '67*
Singles: 7–inch
CAPITOL.......................................3-6   66
Picture Sleeves
CAPITOL.......................................4-8   66
LPs: 10/12–inch 33rpm
BELL 5-10   70
CAPITOL.................................10-15   66-67

DIRT BAND: see NITTY GRITTY DIRT BAND

DR. HOOK   *P&R/LP '72/C&W '76*
(With the Medicine Show)
Singles: 7–inch
CAPITOL (4000 series) 3-5   75-80
CAPITOL (8220 "The Stimu") 4-8   75
  (Promotional issue only.)
CASABLANCA................................3-4   80-82
COLUMBIA 3-5   71-74
Picture Sleeves
CAPITOL (4000 series) 3-5   75-80
CAPITOL (8220 "The Stimu") 8-10   75
  (Promotional issue only.)
CASABLANCA................................3-4   82
COLUMBIA 3-5   71-72
LPs: 10/12–inch 33rpm
CAPITOL.......................................8-10   75-81
CASABLANCA..........................5-10   80-82
COLUMBIA (Except 34147).......15-20   72-74
COLUMBIA (34147 "Best of
  Dr. Hook") 5-10   76
Also see SAWYER, Ray

DODDS, Johnny
(Gene Autry)
Singles: 78rpm
OKEH (45317 "Railroad
  Boomer").................................25-75   30s
OKEH (45417 "Frankie and
  Johnny").................................25-75   30s
OKEH (45462 "No One to Call Me
  Darling")..................................25-75   30s

OKEH (45472 "Slu Foot Lou")... 25-75   30s
OKEH (45560 "Cowboy
  Yodel") 25-75   30s
  Also see AUTRY, Gene

DODSON, Darrell   *C&W '77*
    Singles: 7–inch
SCR.. 3-5   77

DOLAN, Madonna   *C&W '88*
    Singles: 7–inch
TRUE 3-4   88

DOLAN, Ramblin' Jimmie   *C&W '51*
    Singles: 78rpm
CAPITOL.................................... 5-10   51-54
    Singles: 7–inch
CAPITOL.................................. 10-20   51-54

DOLLAR, Johnny   *C&W '66*
(Johnny $ Dollar)
    Singles: 7–inch
CHART.. 3-6   68-70
COLUMBIA 4-8   66
D (1011 "Walking Away") 10-20   58
DATE... 4-6   67-68
DOT.. 4-6   67
    LP: 10/12–inch 33rpm
CHART...................................... 10-15   69
DATE... 15-20   67

DOMINO, Fats   *R&B '50/C&W '80*
    Singles: 78rpm
IMPERIAL 10-30   50-57
    Singles: 7–inch
ABC.. 3-5   73
ABC-PAR (455 "I Got a Right to
  Cry")....................................... 10-20   63
  (Stereo Compact 33.)
ABC-PAR (10000 series) 5-10   63-64
BROADMOOR 4-8   67
IMPERIAL (5099 "Korea
  Blues")................................ 200-225   52
IMPERIAL (5167 "You Know I Miss
  You") 150-200   52
IMPERIAL (5180 "Goin'
  Home") 100-150   52
IMPERIAL (5197 "Poor Poor
  Me").................................... 50-100   52
IMPERIAL (5209 "How Long") 50-100   52
  (Black vinyl.)
IMPERIAL (5209 "How
  Long")................................. 150-250   52
  (Colored vinyl.)

IMPERIAL (5220 "Nobody Loves
  Me") 50-100   53
  (Black vinyl.)
IMPERIAL (5220 "Nobody Loves
  Me") 150-250   53
  (Colored vinyl.)
IMPERIAL (5231 "Going to the
  River")..................................50-100   53
  (Black vinyl.)
IMPERIAL (5231 "Going to the
  River")................................150-250   53
  (Colored vinyl.)
IMPERIAL (5240 "Please Don't Leave
  Me") 40-80   53
  (Black vinyl.)
IMPERIAL (5240 "Please Don't Leave
  Me") 150-250   53
  (Colored vinyl.)
IMPERIAL (5251 "You Said You Love
  Me")......................................40-80   53
IMPERIAL (5262 "Something's
  Wrong")................................25-50   53
  (Black vinyl.)
IMPERIAL (5262 "Something's
  Wrong")..............................100-200   53
  (Colored vinyl.)
IMPERIAL (5272 "Little School
  Girl")....................................20-40   54
IMPERIAL (5283 "Baby,
  Please") 20-40   54
IMPERIAL (5301 "You Can Pack Your
  Suitcase")..............................20-40   54
IMPERIAL (5313 "Love Me") 20-40   54
IMPERIAL (5323 "I Know") 20-40   54
IMPERIAL (5340 "Don't You
  Know").................................20-30   55
IMPERIAL (5348 thru 5396).......10-20   55-56
IMPERIAL (5407 "Blueberry
  Hill") 10-15   56
  (Black vinyl.)
IMPERIAL (5407 "Blueberry
  Hill")...................................75-125   56
  (Colored vinyl.)
IMPERIAL (5417 thru 5477).......10-15   56-57
IMPERIAL (5492 "Yes, My
  Darling")................................8-12   58
  (Black vinyl.)
IMPERIAL (5492 "Yes, My
  Darling")..............................75-125   58
  (Colored vinyl.)
IMPERIAL (5515 thru 5980).........5-10   58-63
IMPERIAL (66000 series) 4-6   64
IMPERIAL GOLDEN SERIES........3-5   70s
MERCURY....................................4-8   65

REPRISE 4-6	68-70	
TOOT TOOT (001 "My Toot		
Toot") 3-5	85	
(With Doug Kershaw.)		
U.A. 3-5	74	
W.B. 3-5	80	

Picture Sleeves

IMPERIAL (5428 "I'm Walkin") .. 15-25	57
IMPERIAL (5477 "The Big	
Beat") 15-20	57
IMPERIAL (5606 "I Want to Walk You	
Home") 10-20	59
IMPERIAL (5629 "Be My	
Guest") 10-20	59
MERCURY (72485 "It's Never Too	
Late") 20-30	65

EPs: 7–inch 33/45rpm

ABC-PAR 15-25	64-65
IMPERIAL (Except 127) 25-50	56-57
IMPERIAL (127 "Fats Domino-America's	
Outstanding Piano Stylist") ... 50-100	53
(Red, script logo label.)	
IMPERIAL (127 "Fats Domino-America's	
Outstanding Piano Stylist") 25-50	56
(Maroon label.)	
MERCURY 15-25	65
(Jukebox issues only.)	

LPs: 10/12–inch 33rpm

ABC-PAR 15-20	63-65
CANDLELITE 12-15	76
EVEREST 8-10	74-77
GRAND AWARD 10-15	60s
HARLEM HITPARADE 8-10	75
HARMONY 10-15	'69
IMPERIAL (Except 9004 thru	
9040) 20-40	58-63
IMPERIAL (9004 "Rock 'n	
Rollin") 60-100	56
IMPERIAL (9009 "Fats Domino	
Rock 'n Rollin") 60-100	56
IMPERIAL (9028 "This Is Fats	
Domino") 60-100	57
IMPERIAL (9038 "Here Stands Fats	
Domino") 60-100	57
IMPERIAL (9040 "This Is	
Fats") 60-100	57
LIBERTY 5-10	80-81
MERCURY (21039 "Fats	
Domino '65") 15-20	65
(Monaural.)	
MERCURY (61039 "Fats	
Domino '65") 15-20	65
(Stereo.)	

PICKWICK 8-12	70s	
REPRISE (6304 "Fats Is		
Back") 20-30	68	
REPRISE (6439 "Fats") 300-400	71	
SILVER EAGLE 5-8	86	
SUNSET 12-15	66-71	
TOMATO 10-20	89	
U.A. 8-10	71-80	

DON JUAN   *C&W '88*

Singles: 7–inch

MAXX 3-4	88

Members: Stu Stewart; Ed Allen; Toby Strause.

DONALDSON, Craig   *C&W '76*

Singles: 7–inch

GREAT AMERICAN 3-5	76

DORSEY, Gerry

Singles: 7–inch

HICKORY (1337 "Baby, Turn	
Around") 8-12	65

Also see HUMPERDINCK, Engelbert

DOTTSY   *C&W '75*

Singles: 7–inch

RCA 3-5	75-79
TANGLEWOOD 3-4	81

LP: 10/12–inch 33rpm

RCA 5-10	76-79

Session: Waylon Jennings.

Also see JENNINGS, Waylon

DOUGLAS   *C&W '81*

(Douglas Block)

Singles: 7–inch

DOOR KNOB 3-5	81

Also see BLOCK, Doug

DOUGLAS, Joe   *C&W '79*

Singles: 7–inch

D 3-5	79
FOXY CAJUN 3-5	80-81

DOUGLAS, Steve   *C&W '80*

Singles: 7–inch

DEMON 3-5	80
DORMAN 3-4	89-90

DOUGLAS, Tony   *C&W '63*

(With His Shrimpers)

Singles: 7–inch

COCHISE 3-4	82
D 5-8	61
DOT 3-5	72-73

PAULA	3-6	67-69
20TH CENTURY	3-5	75
VEE JAY	4-8	63

LP: 10/12–inch 33rpm

DOT	8-12	73
PAULA	10-15	67-69
SIMS	15-25	64-66

DOVE, Ronnie   *P&R '64/C&W '72*
(With the Beltones)

Singles: 7–inch

ABC	3-4	74
DECCA (31288 "Party Doll")	8-10	61
DECCA (32000 & 33000 series)	3-5	71-73
DIAMOND (100 & 200 series)	4-6	64-70
DIAMOND (300 series)	3-4	87
ERIC	3-4	70s
HITSVILLE	3-5	76
JALO (1406 "Saddest Song")	15-20	62
MC	3-4	78
MCA	3-4	73
MELODYLAND	3-5	75-76
MOTION	3-4	81
MOON SHINE	3-4	83
SWAN	4-6	63
WRAYCO	3-5	71

Picture Sleeves

DIAMOND	4-8	66

LPs: 10/12–inch 33rpm

CERTRON	10-12	70
DESIGN (186 "Swingin' Teen Sounds")	10-15	64

(Four tracks by Dove; six by Terry Phillips.)

DIAMOND	15-25	65-70
MCA	8-10	72-73
POWER PAK	8-12	75

DOWNEY, Sean   *C&W '81*
(Shawn Downey; Shawn Morton Downey; Morton Downey Jr.)

Singles: 7–inch

BULL DOG	5-10	59
CUB	8-12	58
ESO	3-5	81

DOWNHOMERS   *C&W '49*
(Kenny Roberts & the Downhomers)

Singles: 78rpm

CORAL	4-8	49-50
VOGUE (736 "Who's Gonna Kiss You When I'm Gone")	200-300	46

(Picture disc.)

VOGUE (786 "Boogie Woogie Yodel")	300-500	47

(Picture disc.)

LP: 10/12–inch 33rpm

SOMERSET (22400 "The Downhomers")	15-20	60s

DOWNING, Al   *P&R '63/C&W '78*
(Big Al Downing)

Singles: 7–inch

CARLTON (489 "Miss Lucy")	20-30	58
CHALLENGE (59006 "Down on the Farm")	20-30	58
CHESS (1000 series)	5-10	62
CHESS (2000 series)	3-5	75
COLUMBIA	4-8	64
DOOR KNOB	3-4	89
HOUSE of the FOX	3-5	71
JANUS	3-5	74
KANSOMA	4-8	62
LENOX	4-8	63
POLYDOR	3-5	76
SILVER FOX	3-4	
TEAM	3-4	82-84
V-TONE	5-10	61
VINE ST.	3-4	87
W.B.	3-4	78-80
WHITE ROCK (1111 "Down on the Farm")	50-100	58
WHITE ROCK (1113 "Miss Lucy")	50-100	58

LPs: 10/12–inch 33rpm

TEAM	5-10	83-85

Also see LITTLE ESTHER & Big Al Downing

DOWNS, Laverne   *C&W '60*

Singles: 7–inch

PEACH	5-10	60

DRAKE, Guy   *C&W/P&R '70*
(With Tom Johnson)

Singles: 7–inch

MALLARD	3-5	71
ROYAL AMERICAN	3-5	70
TRIP UNIVERSAL	3-5	70s

LPs: 10/12–inch 33rpm

OVATION	5-10	74
ROYAL AMERICAN	15-20	70
TRIP UNIVERSAL	8-12	70s

DRAPER, Rusty   *C&W/P&R '53*

Singles: 78rpm

MERCURY	5-10	52-57

Singles: 7–inch		
KL	3-5	80
MERCURY	4-8	52-62
MONUMENT	3-5	63-70

EPs: 7–inch 33/45rpm		
MERCURY	10-15	54-56

LPs: 10/12–inch 33rpm		
GOLDEN CREST	5-10	73
HARMONY	5-10	72
MERCURY	10-20	54-62
MONUMENT	8-12	65-75
WING	8-12	63-64

DRAPER, Rusty, & Lola Dee

Singles: 78rpm		
MERCURY	3-6	56

Singles: 7–inch		
MERCURY	5-10	56

Also see DRAPER, Rusty

DRESSER, Lee   *C&W '78*

Singles: 7–inch		
AIR INT'L	3-4	83
CAPITOL	3-5	78

DRIFTING COWBOYS   *C&W '78*

(With Jim Owen)

Singles: 78rpm		
MGM	4-8	53-54

Singles: 7–inch		
MGM	5-10	53-54

LP: 10/12–inch 33rpm		
DELTA	5-10	
STANDING STONE	5-10	80

Members: Jerry Rivers; Bob McNett; H.B. Butrum; Don Helms.
Also see OWEN, Jim
Also see WILLIAMS, Hank

DRIFTWOOD, Jimmy   *C&W '59*

Singles: 7–inch		
CD	8-12	
RCA	5-10	59-60

EPs: 7–inch 33/45rpm		
RCA	10-20	59

LP: 10/12–inch 33rpm		
MONUMENT	10-20	63-76
RCA (1635 "Newly Discovered Early American Folk Songs")	45-65	58
RCA (1994 thru 2443)	20-50	59-62
RACKENSACK	8-12	
RIMROCK	8-12	

DRUMM, Don   *C&W '74*

Singles: 7–inch		
CHART	3-5	74
CHURCHILL	3-5	78

DRUSKY, Roy   *C&W '60*

Singles: 78rpm		
COLUMBIA	5-10	55-56
STARDAY	5-10	55

Singles: 7–inch		
CAPITOL	3-5	74-76
COLUMBIA	8-12	55-56
DECCA	5-10	60-64
MERCURY	3-8	63-73
PLANTATION	3-4	79-80
SCORPION	3-5	77
STARDAY (185 "Such a Fool")	10-15	55

EPs: 7–inch 33/45rpm		
DECCA	4-8	61-63

LPs: 10/12–inch 33rpm		
BUCKBOARD	5-10	
CAPITOL	5-10	76
DECCA	12-20	61-62
HARMONY	10-12	65
MCA	5-8	80s
MERCURY	10-20	64-72
MOUNTAIN DEW	5-10	
PICKWICK	5-10	70s
PICKWICK/HILLTOP	8-12	70s
PLANTATION	5-10	79-80
SCORPION	5-10	76
VOCALION	8-12	70
WING	10-15	64-66

Also see WELLS, Kitty, & Roy Drusky

DRUSKY, Roy, & Priscilla Mitchell   *C&W '67*

Singles: 7–inch		
MERCURY	4-6	65-68

LP: 10/12–inch 33rpm		
MERCURY	8-15	65-68

Also see DRUSKY, Roy
Also see MITCHELL, Priscilla

DUDLEY, Dave   *C&W '61*

(With Charlie Douglas)

Singles: 78rpm		
KING	5-10	55-56

Singles: 7–inch		
COLUMBIA	3-4	78
CURIO	4-8	
GOLDEN RING	4-8	63

GOLDEN WING (3020 "Six Days on the Road") (Black vinyl.)	5-8	63
GOLDEN WING (3020 "Six Days on the Road") (Colored vinyl.)	10-20	63
JUBILEE	5-10	62
KING (4000 series)	8-12	55-56
KING (5000 series)	4-6	63
MERCURY	3-8	63-73
NRC	5-10	59
NEW STAR	4-8	62
RICE	3-5	73-78
STARDAY	5-10	60
SUN (Black vinyl)	3-4	79-80
SUN (Colored vinyl)	4-6	79-80
U.A.	3-5	75-76
VEE (7003 "Maybe I Do")	10-15	61

LPs: 10/12–inch 33rpm

CORONET/PREMIER	8-12	60s
CROWN	8-12	60s
DESIGN	8-12	60s
GOLDEN RING (110 "Six Days on the Road")	25-30	63
HILLTOP	8-12	
MERCURY	10-15	64-73
MOUNTAIN DEW	8-12	69
NASHVILLE	8-12	68
PICKWICK	5-10	70s
PLANTATION	5-10	81
RICE	3-4	78
SPIN-O-RAMA	5-10	60s
SUN	5-10	80
U.A.	8-12	75-76
WING	8-12	68

Also see JAMES, Sonny / Dave Dudley / Sunny Williams

DUDLEY, Dave, & Tom T. Hall
C&W '70
Singles: 7–inch

MERCURY	3-5	70

Also see HALL, Tom T.

DUDLEY, Dave, & Karen O'Donnal
C&W '72
Singles: 7–inch

MERCURY	3-5	72

DUDLEY, Dave / Link Wray
LPs: 10/12–inch 33rpm

GUEST STAR	10-20	63

Also see DUDLEY, Dave

DUFF, Arlie
C&W '53
Singles: 78rpm

DECCA	5-10	56
STARDAY	5-10	53

Singles: 7–inch

DECCA	10-20	56
STARDAY	10-15	53

DUGAN, Jeff
C&W '87
Singles: 7–inch

W.B.	3-4	87-88

DUNCAN, Johnny
C&W '67
Singles: 7–inch

COLUMBIA	3-6	67-81
LEADER (807 "Bring Your Heart")	20-30	60
LEADER (812 "Freddy and His Go-Cart")	10-20	60
LEADER (814 "Raindrops")	10-15	61
PHAROAH	3-4	86

LPs: 10/12–inch 33rpm

COLUMBIA	5-10	69-80
HARMONY	5-10	73
PHAROAH	5-10	86

Session: Janie Fricke.

DUNCAN, Johnny, & Janie Fricke
C&W '77
Singles: 7–inch

COLUMBIA	3-5	77

LP: 10/12–inch 33rpm

COLUMBIA	5-10	80

Also see FRICKE, Janie

DUNCAN, Johnny, & June Stearns
C&W '69
Singles: 7–inch

COLUMBIA	3-5	69

LP: 10/12–inch 33rpm

COLUMBIA	5-10	69

Also see DUNCAN, Johnny
Also see STEARNS, June

DUNCAN, Tommy
C&W '49
(With His Western All Stars)
Singles: 78rpm

CAPITOL	4-8	48-50
CORAL	4-6	53-54

Singles: 7–inch

CAPITOL	8-12	50
CHEYENE	10-15	
CORAL	5-10	53-54

LP: 10/12–inch 33rpm

LONGHORN 5-10   83-84
  Also see WILLS, Bob

DUNN, Holly   *C&W '85*
Singles: 7–inch

MTM... 3-4   85-88
W.B. 3-4   89-91

LP: 10/12–inch 33rpm

MTM... 8-10   80s
  Also see MURPHEY, Michael Martin, & Holly Dunn
  Also see ROGERS, Kenny, & Holly Dunn
  Also see TOMORROW'S WORLD

DUNN, Ronnie   *C&W '83*
Singles: 7–inch

CHURCHILL.................................. 3-5   83-84
  Also see BROOKS & DUNN

DURHAM, Bobby   *C&W '88*
Singles: 7–inch

HIGHTONE 3-4   88

DURRENCE, Sam   *C&W '73*
Singles: 7–inch

RIVER 3-5   73

DYCKE, Jerry   *C&W '80*
Singles: 7–inch

CHURCHILL.................................. 3-4   80-81

E

EME   *C&W '81*
Singles: 7–inch

EPI 3-5   81

E.W.B.   *C&W '81*
Singles: 7–inch

PAID.. 3-5   81

EAGLES   *P&R/LP '72/C&W '75*
Singles: 7–inch

ASYLUM 3-5   72-80
FULL MOON 3-4   81

Picture Sleeves

ASYLUM 3-5   78

LPs: 10/12–inch 33rpm

ASYLUM 8-12   72-82
MFSL (126 "Hotel California") ... 25-35   84

Members: Don Felder; Glenn Frey; Don Henley; Randy Meisner; Timothy B. Schmit; Joe Walsh; Bernie Leadon.
  Also see HENLEY, Don
  Also see LEE, Johnny / Eagles
  Also see LONGBRANCH PENNYWHISTLE
  Also see NEWMAN, Randy
  Also see POCO
  Also see RONSTADT, Linda

EARL, Kenny   *C&W '81*
Singles: 7–inch

KARI... 3-5   81
KIK 3-6   81
  Also see WOLFPACK

EARLE, Steve   *C&W '83*
(With the Dukes)
Singles: 12–inch 33/45rpm

MCA..4-6   86

Singles: 7–inch

EPIC... 3-4   83-85
MCA... 3-4   86-90
UNI..3-4   88

Picture Sleeves

EPIC..3-4   84

EPs: 7–inch 33/45rpm

LSI..5-10   82

LPs: 10/12–inch 33rpm

MCA..5-10   86-90
UNI..5-8   88

EARWOOD, Mundo   *C&W '72*
(Mundo Ray)
Singles: 7–inch

EPIC..3-5   75-76
EXCELSIOR 3-4   81
GMC... 3-5   78-80
GRT 3-5   74
PEGASUS.....................................3-4   89
PRIMERO.....................................3-4   82
ROYAL AMERICAN.......................3-5   72
TRUE 3-5   77

LP: 10/12–inch 33rpm

EXCELSIOR 5-10   81
GMC..5-10   79
TRUE 6-12   77

Session: Larry Gatlin; Tompall Glaser; Chuck Glaser; Jim Glaser; Mel Tillis.
  Also see GATLIN, Larry
  Also see GLASER, Chuck
  Also see GLASER, Jim
  Also see GLASER, Tompall
  Also see TILLIS, Mel

EAST, Lyndel   *C&W '78*

Singles: 7–inch

NSD	3-5	78

EASTON, Sheena

P&R/LP '81/C&W '84

Singles: 12–inch 33/45rpm

EMI AMERICA	4-6	81-86

Singles: 7–inch

EMI AMERICA	3-4	81-86
LIBERTY	3-4	81
MCA	3-4	88-91
RCA	3-4	89

Picture Sleeves

EMI AMERICA	3-6	81-86
RCA	3-4	89

LPs: 10/12–inch 33rpm

EMI AMERICA	5-10	81-86
MCA	5-8	88-91

Also see ROGERS, Kenny, & Sheena Easton

EASTON, Sheena & Prince *P&R '87*

Singles: 7–inch

PAISLEY PARK	3-5	87
W.B.	3-4	89

Picture Sleeves

W.B.	3-5	89

Also see EASTON, Sheena

EASTWOOD, Clint

Singles: 7–inch

CAMEO (240 "Rowdy")	10-20	63
CERTRON	4-6	70
GNP (177 "Get Yourself Another Fool")	15-25	65
GOTHIC (005 "Unknown Girl")	10-20	61
PARAMOUNT	4-8	69
W.B.	3-4	81

Picture Sleeves

CAMEO (240 "Rowdy")	30-50	63
CERTRON	5-8	70
GNP (177 "Get Yourself Another Fool")	50-75	65
GOTHIC (005 "Unknown Girl")	10-20	61

LPs: 10/12–inch 33rpm

CAMEO (1056 "Cowboy Favorites")	75-125	63

Also see CHARLES, Ray, & Clint Eastwood
Also see HAGGARD, Merle, & Clint Eastwood
Also see SHEPPARD, T.G., & Clint Eastwood

EATON, Connie   *C&W '70*

Singles: 7–inch

ABC	3-5	75
CHART	3-5	70-71
DUNHILL	3-5	75
ENTERPRISE	3-5	
MUSIC TOWN	3-5	

LP: 10/12–inch 33rpm

ABC/DOT	6-10	75
CHART	8-12	70-71

EATON, Connie, & Dave Peel   *C&W '70*

Singles: 7–inch

CHART	3-5	70

LP: 10/12–inch 33rpm

CHART	8-12	70

Also see EATON, Connie
Also see PEEL, Dave

EBERLY, Bob, & Sunshine Serenaders   *C&W '49*

Singles: 78rpm

DECCA	5-10	48-49

ECHOES

Singles: 7–inch

DOLTON	5-10	60

Members: Bonnie Guitar; Don Robertson.
Also see GUITAR, Bonnie

EDDY, Duane   *P&R/C&W/R&B '58*

(With the Rebels; with Rebelettes; with His
Rock-a-billies; with His Twangy Guitar)

Singles: 78rpm

FORD (500 "Ramrod")	75-125	57
JAMIE	25-50	58

Singles: 7–inch

BIG TREE	5-10	72
CAPITOL	3-4	87
COLPIX	5-10	65-66
CONGRESS	3-5	70
ELEKTRA	3-5	77
FORD (500 "Ramrod")	75-125	57
(Credited to Duane Eddy, but is by Al Casey.)		
GREGMARK (5 "Caravan")	5-10	61
(Credited to Duane Eddy, but is by Al Casey.)		
JAMIE (73 "Peter Gunn")	25-50	61
(Compact 33 single.)		
JAMIE (1100 series)	8-15	58-61
(Monaural.)		

JAMIE (1100 series).................	15-25	59-60
(Stereo.)		
JAMIE (1200 series)...................	5-10	61-62
RCA......	5-10	61-65
REPRISE	5-15	66-68
UNI.................................	4-6	70

Picture Sleeves

CAPITOL..	3-4	87
COLPIX (788 "House of the Rising Sun")	25-40	66
JAMIE..	15-25	59-61
RCA..	10-15	62-64

EPs: 7–inch 33/45rpm

JAMIE..	20-40	59-60
RCA/WURLITZER DISCOTHEQUE MUSIC	15-25	64

LPs: 10/12–inch 33rpm

CAMDEN......................................	8-15	
CAPITOL......................................	8-10	87
COLPIX (490 "Duane A-Go-Go").................................	25-30	65
COLPIX (494 "Duane Eddy Does Bob Dylan")	25-30	65
JAMIE (Except 3000, 3011 & 3026)................................	15-30	59-63
JAMIE (3000 "Have Twangy Guitar Will Travel")...................................	20-40	58
(White cover.)		
JAMIE (3000 "Have Twangy Guitar Will Travel")...................................	15-30	58
(Red cover.)		
JAMIE (3011 "Songs of Our Heritage").................................	50-75	60
(Colored vinyl.)		
JAMIE (3011 "Songs of Our Heritage").................................	20-30	60
(Gatefold cover. Black vinyl.)		
JAMIE (3011 "Songs of Our Heritage").................................	15-20	61
(Standard cover. Black vinyl.)		
JAMIE (3026 "16 Greatest Hits")	15-20	64
RCA ("LPM"/"LSP" series)	20-30	62-66
RCA ("ANL1" series)	5-10	78
REPRISE	15-20	66-67
SIRE..	10-15	75

Session: Duane Eddy; Al Casey; Corki Casey; Donnie Owens; Plas Johnson; Steve Douglas; Ike Clanton; Mike Bermani; Waylon Jennings; Willie Nelson; Kin Vassy.
  Also see CASEY, Al
  Also see CLARK, Sanford, & Duane Eddy
  Also see FOGERTY, John
  Also see JENNINGS, Waylon
  Also see JIMMY & DUANE

Also see NELSON, Willie
Also see THOMAS, B.J.
Also see VASSY, Kin

EDDY, Duane & Mirriam
Singles: 7–inch

REPRISE (0622 "Guitar on My Mind")...........................10-15		67

Also see EDDY, Duane

EDGE, Kathy *C&W '87*
Singles: 7–inch

NSD 3-4		87

EDWARDS, Bobby *P&R/C&W '61*
Singles: 7–inch

BLUEBONNET...........................5-10		59
CAPITOL....................................4-8		61-63
CHART......................................4-6		68
CREST.....................................5-10		61
MANCO.....................................4-8		62
MUSICOR 4-8		65
POLARIS 3-5		

EDWARDS, Jimmy *C&W '57*
(Jimmie Edwards)
Singles: 78rpm

MERCURY................................10-15		57

Singles: 7–inch

MERCURY................................10-15		57-58
RCA 5-10		59-60

EDWARDS, Jonathan *C&W '88*
Singles: 7–inch

MCA/CURB................................3-4		88-89

EDWARDS, Jonathan & Darlene
(Paul Weston & Jo Stafford)
LPs: 10/12–inch 33rpm

COLUMBIA (1024 "The Piano Artistry of Jonathan & Darlene Edwards") 25-40		57
COLUMBIA (1513 " Jonathan & Darlene Edwards in Paris") 20-30		60
(Monaural.)		
COLUMBIA (8313 " Jonathan & Darlene Edwards in Paris") 25-35		60
(Stereo.)		
CORINTHIAN...............................5-10		
RCA (LPM-2495 "Sing Along with Jonathan & Darlene Edwards")...................15-25		61
(Monaural.)		

RCA (LSP-2495 "Sing Along with Jonathan & Darlene Edwards") 20-30   61
(Stereo.)
Also see STAFFORD, Jo

EDWARDS, Stoney   *C&W '71*
Singles: 7–inch
CAPITOL 3-5   70-76
JMI 3-5   78
MUSIC AMERICA 3-4   80
LP: 10/12–inch 33rpm
BOOT 5-10   83
CAPITOL 10-20   71-76
MUSIC AMERICA 5-10   81

ELLEDGE, Jimmy   *P&R '61/C&W '75*
Singles: 7–inch
4 STAR 3-5   75
HICKORY 3-5   65-67
LITTLE DARLIN' 3-5   68
RCA (Except 8012) 4-8   61-64
RCA (8012 "Can't You See It in My Eyes") 10-20   62
SIMS 3-6   64
Picture Sleeves
RCA 5-10   62-63
LP: 10/12–inch 33rpm
LITTLE DARLIN' 8-10   68

ELLIS, Jimmy
Singles: 7–inch
BOBLO 5-10   77-78
CENTURY CITY (511 "Looking Through the Eyes of Love") 10-15   60s
CHALLENGER 4-6   73
DRADCO 8-12   64
GOLDBAND 5-10   60s
KRISTAL 3-4   85
MCA 3-5   73
SOUTHERN TRACKS 3-4   86-87
SUN 3-6   72-77
TONY LAWRENCE 3-4   83-84
Picture Sleeves
BOBLO (536 "I'm Not Trying to Be Like Elvis") 10-20   78
EPs: 7–inch 33/45rpm
JIMMY ELLIS FAN CLUB ("Merry Christmas") 4-6   81
(No selection number used. Promotional issue only.)
LPs: 10/12–inch 33rpm
BOBLO (829 "By Request, Ellis Sings Elvis") 75-125   77

ROLLER SKATE 8-10   82
Also see LEWIS, Jerry Lee, Carl Perkins & Charlie Rich
Also see ORION

ELLIS, Jimmy / Misty
EPs: 7–inch 33/45rpm
SUN (1136 "D.O.A.") 3-6   77
(Jimmy Ellis is not credited, but is the singer on both tracks on side 2: *That's All Right* and *Blue Moon of Kentucky*. Not issued with a special cover.)
Also see ELLIS, Jimmy

ELLIS, Mike   *C&W '78*
Singles: 7–inch
CIN KAY 3-5   78

ELLWANGER, Sandy   *C&W '89*
Singles: 7–inch
DOOR KNOB 3-4   89

ELMO 'N' PATSY   *C&W '84*
Singles: 7–inch
ELMO 'N' PATSY 3-5   79
EPIC 3-4   84
OINK 3-4   80
SOUNDWAVES 3-4   81
LPs: 10/12–inch 33rpm
OINK 5-10   80
Members: Elmo Shropshire; Patsy Trigg.

ELY, Joe   *C&W '77*
Singles: 7–inch
MCA 3-4   77-81
SOUTHCOAST 3-4   81
LPs: 10/12–inch 33rpm
MCA 5-10   77-81
SOUTHCOAST 5-10   81
Also see SEXTON, Charlie

EMERY, Ralph   *C&W '61*
Singles: 7–inch
LIBERTY 4-8   61-63

ESMERELDY & HER NOVELTY BAND   *C&W '48*
Singles: 78rpm
MUSICRAFT 5-8   48

ETHEL & SHAMELESS HUSSIES   *C&W '88*
Singles: 7–inch
MCA 3-4   88-89
Members: Gayle Zeiler; Valerie Hunt; Becki Fogle.
Also see ZEILER, Gayle

EVANS, Ashley   *C&W '90*
Singles: 7–inch
DOOR KNOB 3-4   89-90

EVANS, Dale
LP: 10/12–inch 33rpm
ALLEGRO (4116)...................... 15-25   50s
  (10-Inch LP.)
CAPITOL.................................... 8-15   67
EVON 5-10
WORD... 5-8
  Also see ROGERS, Roy

EVANS, Paul   *P&R '59/C&W '78*
(With the Curls)
Singles: 7–inch
ATCO 5-10   59-60
BIG TREE 3-5   75
CARLTON 5-10   61-62
CINNAMON INT'L 3-4   80
COLLECTABLES 3-4   80s
COLUMBIA 3-6   68
DECCA....................................... 5-10   58
DOT.. 3-5   73
EPIC... 4-8   64-65
GUARANTEED 5-10   59-60
KAPP.. 4-8   62-63
LAURIE 3-5   71
MERCURY 3-5   74-75
MUSICOR 3-5   77
RCA.. 8-10   57
RANWOOD 3-5   72
SPRING 3-4   78-79
LPs: 10/12–inch 33rpm
CARLTON (129 "Hear Paul Evans in Your
  Home Tonight") 20-30   61
  (Monaural.)
CARLTON (129 "Hear Paul Evans in Your
  Home Tonight") 25-35   61
  (Stereo.)
CARLTON (130 "Folk Songs of Many
  Lands").................................... 15-25   61
  (Monaural.)
CARLTON (130 "Folk Songs of Many
  Lands").................................... 20-30   61
  (Stereo.)
GUARANTEED (1000 "Fabulous
  Teens").................................. 20-40   60
  (Monaural.)
GUARANTEED (1000 "Fabulous
  Teens").................................. 30-40   60
  (Stereo.)

KAPP (1346 "21 Years in a Tennessee
  Jail")......................................15-25   64
  (Monaural.)
KAPP (1475 "Another Town, Another
  Jail")......................................15-25   66
  (Monaural.)
KAPP (3346 "21 Years in a Tennessee
  Jail")......................................20-30   64
  (Stereo.)
KAPP (3475 "Another Town, Another
  Jail")......................................20-30   66

EVANS, Paul & Mimi
Singles: 7–inch
EPIC...4-8   64
  Also see EVANS, Paul

EVANS, Paula   *C&W '77*
Singles: 7–inch
AUTUMN.......................................3-5   77

EVERETTE, Leon   *C&W '77*
Singles: 7–inch
ORLANDO 3-4   79-86
RCA..3-4   80-84
TRUE..5-10   77
LPs: 10/12–inch 33rpm
ORLANDO 5-10   86
RCA 5-10   81-84
TRUE (1002 "Goodbye King of Rock &
  Roll") 15-25   77
  (With 18" x 23" bonus poster of Elvis
  Presley.)
TRUE (1002 "Goodbye King of Rock &
  Roll") 10-15   77
  (Without poster.)

EVERLY, Don   *C&W '76*
Singles: 7–inch
ABC/HICKORY 3-5   75-77
HICKORY/MGM.............................3-5   76
ODE..3-5   70-74
LPs: 10/12–inch 33rpm
ABC/HICKORY 8-10   76-77
ODE 8-12   70-74
  Also see HARRIS, Emmylou
  Also see KIMBERLY, Adrian

EVERLY, Phil   *C&W '80*
Singles: 7–inch
CAPITOL.......................................3-4   83
CURB...3-4   80-81
ELEKTRA.......................................3-4   79
PYE...3-5   73-76

RCA.................................... 3-5   73

LPs: 10/12–inch 33rpm

ELECTRA............................. 5-10   79
PYE................................... 8-10   75-76
RCA................................... 8-10   73

EVERLY BROTHERS

P&R/R&B/C&W '57

Singles: 78rpm

CADENCE......................... 50-100   57-58
COLUMBIA (21496 "The Sun Keeps
  Shining")................................ 50-75   56

Singles: 7–inch

BARNABY.................................. 3-4   70-76
CADENCE............................... 10-15   57-61
  (Silver and maroon, or blue labels)
CADENCE.................................. 5-10   61-62
  (Red label.)
COLUMBIA (21496 "The Sun Keeps
  Shining")............................... 75-100   56
ERIC... 3-4   70s
MERCURY.................................. 3-4   84-86
RCA... 3-6   72-73
W.B. (5151 "Cathy's Clown")....... 8-10   60
  (Monaural.)
W.B. (S-5151 "Cathy's
  Clown")............................. 20-30   60
  (Stereo.)
W.B. (5163 thru 5833)................. 5-10   60-69
W.B. (5857 "Fifi the Flea")......... 15-25   67
  (Credits "Don Everly Brother" on one side,
  and "Phil Everly Brother" on the flip.)
W.B. (5901 thru 7425).................. 4-8   67-70

Promotional Singles

BARNABY.................................. 3-6   70-76
CADENCE............................... 15-25   57-62
  (Black vinyl.)
CADENCE (1348 "All I Have to Do Is
  Dream") 25-50
  (Colored vinyl.)
COLUMBIA (21496 "The Sun Keeps
  Shining")............................ 150-250   56
MERCURY.................................. 3-5   84-86
RCA... 4-8   72-73
W.B. (5151 "Cathy's Clown")..... 35-45   60
  (Colored vinyl.)
W.B. (5163 "So Sad")................ 35-45   60
  (Colored vinyl.)
W.B. (5199 "Ebony Eyes") 35-45   61
  (Colored vinyl.)

Picture Sleeves

CADENCE (1337 "Wake Up Little
  Susie")................................. 50-100   57

CADENCE (1355 "Problems") ...20-40   58
CADENCE (1369 "Till I Kissed
  You")..................................20-40   59
CADENCE (1376 "Let It Be
  Me")....................................20-40   60
W.B. (5151 "Cathy's Clown") 15-25   60
W.B. (5163 "So Sad") 15-20   60
W.B. (5199 "Ebony Eyes").........15-20   61
W.B. (5220 "Temptation") 15-20   61
W.B. (5250 "Crying in the
  Rain").................................10-20   62
W.B. (5273 "That's Old
  Fashioned")..........................10-20   62
W.B. (5297 "Don't Ask Me to Be
  Friends") 10-20   62
MERCURY......................................3-5   84

EPs: 7–inch 33/45rpm

CADENCE (3 "Rockin' with the Everly
  Brothers")............................25-35   61
  (Has single sheet cardboard insert/cover.
  Compact 33.)
CADENCE (4 "Dream with the Everly
  Brothers")............................25-35   61
  (Has single sheet cardboard insert/cover.
  Compact 33.)
CADENCE (104 "The Everly
  Brothers")............................30-50   57
CADENCE (105 "The Everly
  Brothers")............................30-50   57
CADENCE (107 "The Everly
  Brothers")............................30-50   58
CADENCE ("Songs Our Daddy Taught
  Us").................................100-150   58
  (White, typewritten label. No selection
  number shown, only identification numbers
  "K80H-1718/20." Labeled "Cadence Disc
  Jockey Pressing." Promotional issue only.)
CADENCE (108/109/110 "Songs Our Daddy
  Taught Us")............................25-50   58
  (Price is for any of three volumes.)
CADENCE (111 "The Everly
  Brothers")............................25-50   59
CADENCE (118 "The Everly
  Brothers")............................25-35   59
CADENCE (121 "Very Best of The Everly
  Brothers")............................25-35   60
W.B. (1381-1 "Foreverly
  Yours")..................................15-25   60
  (Black vinyl.)
W.B. (1381-1 "Foreverly
  Yours")..................................25-50   60
  (Colored vinyl. Promotional issue only.)
W.B. (1381-2 "Especially for
  You").....................................15-25   60

W.B. (5501 "The Everly Brothers Plus Two Oldies") 15-25   61

LPs: 10/12–inch 33rpm

ARISTA 8-12   84

BARNABY (350 "Original Greatest Hits") 10-15   70

BARNABY (30260 "End of an Era") 10-15   71

BARNABY (4000 series) 6-10   77

BARNABY (6006 "Greatest Hits") 8-12

CADENCE (3003 "The Everly Brothers") 50-100   58

CADENCE (3016 "Songs Our Daddy Taught Us") 40-60   58

CADENCE (3025 "The Everly Brothers' Best") 50-100   59
(Blue cover.)

CADENCE (3040 "The Fabulous Style of the Everly Brothers") 40-60   60

CADENCE (3059 "Folk Songs") 30-50   63

CADENCE (3062 "15 Everly Hits") 30-50   63

CADENCE (25040 "The Fabulous Style of the Everly Brothers") 50-100   60
(Stereo.)

CADENCE (25059 "Folk Songs") 35-55   63
(Stereo.)

CADENCE (25062 "15 Everly Hits") 35-55   63
(Stereo.)

CANDLELITE 10-15   76

HARMONY 10-12   68-70

MERCURY 5-10   84-86

PAIR 8-12   84

PASSPORT 5-10   84-86

RCA 8-12   72

RHINO (214 "All They Had to Do Was Dream") 5-10   85

RHINO (258 "Heartache and Memories") 8-10   85
(Picture disc.)

RONCO 8-10

TIME-LIFE 10-15   86

W.B. (1381 "It's Everly Time") ... 25-40   60

W.B. (1395 "A Date with the Everly Brothers") 30-40   60
(With gatefold cover and eight "wallet pix" cut-out photos.)

W.B. (1395 "A Date with the Everly Brothers") 15-20   61
(With standard cover.)

W.B. (1418 "Songs for Both Sides of an Evening") 25-30   61

W.B. (1430 "Instant Party") 20-30   62

W.B. (1471 "Golden Hits") 20-30   62

W.B. (1483 "Christmas with the Everly Brothers") 20-25   61

W.B. (1513 "Great Country Hits") 20-25   63

W.B. (1554 "Very Best of the Everly Brothers") 15-20   64
(Yellow cover. Green label.)

W.B. (1554 "Very Best of the Everly Brothers") 10-15   70
(Blue cover. Green label.)

W.B. (1554 "Very Best of the Everly Brothers") 8-12   72
(Blue cover. "Skyline" label.)

W.B. (1578 "Rock 'N Soul") 20-25   65

W.B. (1585 "Gone Gone Gone") 20-25   65

W.B. (1605 "Beat and Soul") 15-25   65

W.B. (1620 "In Our Image") 15-25   66

W.B. (1646 "Two Yanks in London") 15-25   66
(With the Hollies.)

W.B. (1676 "The Hit Sound of the Everly Brothers") 15-20   67

W.B. (1708 "Everly Brothers Sing") 15-25   67

W.B. (1752 "Roots") 15-25   68

W.B. (1858 "The Everly Brothers Show") 12-15   70

Promotional LPs

W.B. (134 "The Everly Brothers") 75-100   61
(One sided, 10–inch LP with five tracks from *The Everly Brothers - Both Sides of an Evening* [WB 1418]. Promotional issue only.)

W.B. (135 "Souvenir Sampler")   50-80   61
(Don and Phil discussing *The Everly Brothers - Both Sides of an Evening*. Has an LP discount coupon on sleeve. Promotional issue only.)

W.B. (1381 "It's Everly Time") 50-100   60

W.B. (1395 "A Date with the Everly Brothers") 75-100   60
(With gatefold cover and eight "wallet pix" cut-out photos.)

W.B. (1418 "Both Sides of an Evening") 50-75   61

W.B. (1430 "Instant Party") 50-75   62
W.B. (1471 "Golden Hits")........ 50-75   62
W.B. (1483 "Christmas with the Everly Brothers")................................. 50-75   61
W.B. (1513 "Great Country Hits") 30-60   63
W.B. (1554 "Very Best of the Everly Brothers")............................. 30-60   64
(Yellow cover.)
W.B. (1578 "Rock'N Soul")........ 30-60   65
W.B. (1585 "Gone Gone Gone")................................... 30-60   65
W.B. (1605 "Beat 'N Soul")........ 25-50   65
W.B. (1620 "In Our Image") 25-50   66
W.B. (1646 "Two Yanks in London")............................... 25-50   66
W.B. (1676 "The Hit Sound of the Everly Brothers")................................. 25-50   67
W.B. (1708 "The Everly Brothers Sing") 25-50   67
W.B. (1752 "Roots") 20-40   68
W.B. (1858 "The Everly Brothers Show")................................... 20-30   70

Members: Don Everly; Phil Everly.
Also see CASH, Johnny, Rosanne Cash & Everly Brothers
Also see EVERLY, Don
Also see EVERLY, Phil

EVERLY BROTHERS & Beach Boys
Singles: 7–inch
CAPITOL (44297 "Don't Worry Baby") 3-5   88
Picture Sleeves
CAPITOL (44297 "Don't Worry Baby") 3-5   88

EWING, Skip   *C&W '88*
Singles: 7–inch
MCA 3-4   88-90

EXILE   *P&R '77/C&W '83*
Singles: 7–inch
ARISTA 3-4   89-91
ATCO 3-5   77
COLUMBIA 3-6   69-70
EPIC 3-4   83-88
MCA/CURB 3-4   85-86
W.B./CURB 3-4   78-81
WOODEN NICKEL...................... 3-5   72-73
LPs: 10/12–inch 33rpm
EPIC... 5-10   83-88
MCA/CURB 5-8   85-86
RCA.. 5-10   78

W.B. 5-10   78-81
WOODEN NICKEL 8-10   73
Members: J.P. Pennington; Les Taylor; Sonny LeMaire; Marlon Hargis; Steve Goetzman.
Also see PENNINGTON, J.P.
Also see TAYLOR, Les

EXOTIC GUITARS   *LP '68*
Singles: 7–inch
RANWOOD...................................3-5   68-70
LPs: 10/12–inch 33rpm
RANWOOD...................................5-10   68-70
Member: Al Casey.
Also see CASEY, Al

EXOTIC GUITARS / Platters
LPs: 10/12–inch 33rpm
GUEST STAR 10-15   64
Also see EXOTIC GUITARS

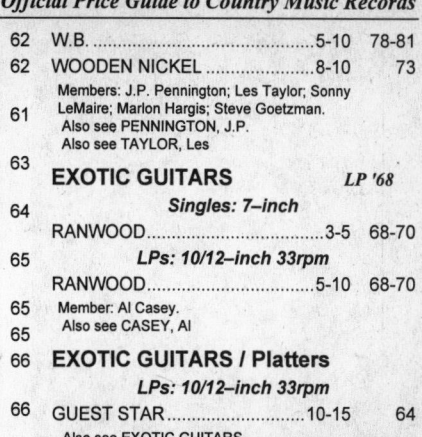

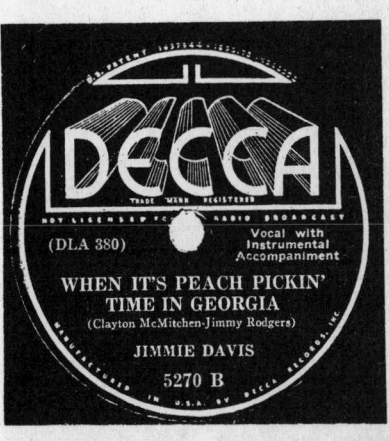

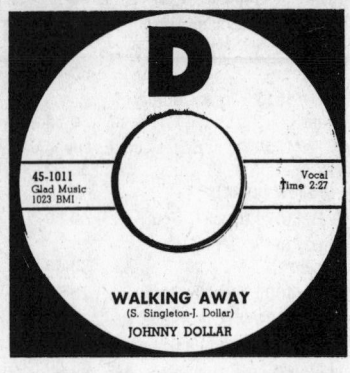

Row 1: Chet Atkins *Finger Style Guitar* ($15–$25); Phil Bough *California Guitar* ($10–$15). **Row 2:** Roy Head and the Traits *Roy Head and the Traits* ($100–$150); Owen Bradley *The Big Guitar* ($15–$25). **Row 3:** Ferlin Husky *Boulevard of Broken Dreams* ($20–$30); Homer & Jethro *Songs My Mother Never Sang* ($15–$30).

Row 1: Leroy Van Dyke *Great Hits of Leroy Van Dyke* ($15–$25); The Browns *Sweet Sounds by the Browns* ($15–$30). **Row 2:** Burl Ives *Burl Ives Sings Pearly Shells and Other Favorites* ($10–$20); George Jones *Walk Through This World With Me* ($10–$20). **Row 3:** Johnny Cash *Greatest Hits, Volume 1* (Promotional issue) ($10–$20); Louvin Brothers *The Louvin Brothers Sing and Play Their Current Hits* ($10–$20).

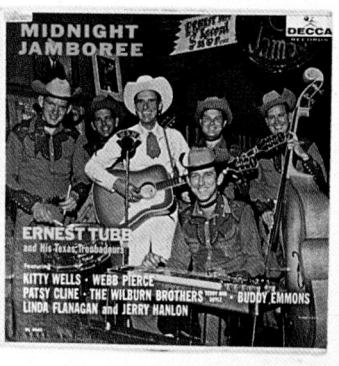

Row 1: Kitty Wells *Burning Memories* ($10–$25); Spade Cooley *Fidoodlin' with Spade Cooley—The King of Western Swing* ($20–$30). **Row 2:** Don Gibson *Oh Lonesome Me* ($20–$30); Mel Tillis *The Great Mel Tillis Sings Walk on By and Other Great Country Hits* ($10–$15). **Row 3:** Floyd Tillman *Floyd Tillman's Country* ($10–$20); Various Artists (Featuring Ernest Tubb) *Midnight Jamboree* ($15–$25).

Row 1: Fred Carter, Jr. *Fred Carter, Jr. Plays Goldsboro* ($8–$12); Speedy West & Jimmy Bryant *2 Guitars Country Style* ($30–$50). **Row 2:** Marty Robbins *More Greatest Hits* ($15–$25); Conway Twitty *Saturday Night with Conway Twitty* (Stereo) ($75–$100). **Row 3:** Jerry Wallace *Just Jerry* ($25–$35); Merle Travis *Strictly Guitar* ($20–$30).

 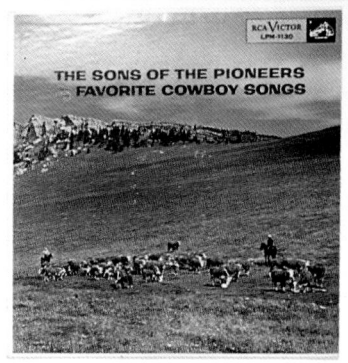

Row 1: Ronnie Milsap *Simply Grand* ($10–$12); Sons of the Pioneers *Favorite Cowboy Songs* ($20–$40). **Row 2:** Waylon Jennings *Waylon Jennings at JD's* ($200–$250); Bobby Bare & Family *Singin' in the Kitchen Radio Show* ($15–$25). **Row 3:** Ernest Tubb *The Legend and the Legacy* ($75–$125); Alabama *Wild Country* ($40–$60).

Row 1: Buck Owens *Best of Buck Owens, Volume 2* ($10–$20); Faron Young *This Is Faron Young* ($20–$25). **Row 2:** Loretta Lynn *Loretta Lynn (Greatest Hits, Volume 2)* ($30–$40); Bobbie Gentry *Ode to Billie Joe: Radio Salute to Bobbie Gentry* ($15–$20). **Row 3:** Johnnie & Jack *The Tennessee Mountain Boys* ($25–$35); George Jones *George Jones (Singing 14 Top Country Song Favorites* ($30–$60).

Row 1: Texas Tyler *The Great Texan* ($25–$40); Susan Raye *Hymns by Susan Raye* ($10–$20). **Row 2:** New Grass Revival *Too Late to Turn Back Now* ($5–$10); Jessie Colter *A Country Star Is Born* ($10–$20). **Row 3:** Bonnie Guitar *Whispering Hope* ($10–$15); Stanley Brothers *Hymns and Sacred Songs* ($15–$30).

Row 1: Homer & Jethro (EP) *This Is a Wife?/16 Tons* ($15–$25); Ferlin Husky (EP) *Wings of a Dove* ($10–$20); Chet Atkins (EP) *Chet Atkins at Home* ($10–$15).   **Row 2:** Johnny Cash *Original Golden Hits, Volume 2* ($8–$12); Lester Flatt & Earl Scruggs *Songs to Cherish* ($10–$15).   **Row 3:** Arthur "Guitar Boogie" Smith *Town and Country Guitar Hits* ($15–$30); B. J. Thomas *B. J. Thomas in Concert* ($5–$10).

FAIRCHILD, Barbara   *C&W '69*
Singles: 7–inch

CAPITOL	3-4	86
COLUMBIA	3-4	69-78
DOWN HOME	3-4	80
KAPP	3-5	68

LPs: 10/12–inch 33rpm

AUDIOGRAPH	5-10	82
COLUMBIA	8-12	70-78
PAID	5-10	81

Session: Jordanaires.
Also see JORDANAIRES
Also see WALKER, Billy, & Barbara Fairchild

FAIRGROUND ATTRACTION

P&R '88/C&W '89
Singles: 7–inch
RCA	3-4	88-89

Picture Sleeves
RCA	3-4	88

LPs: 10/12–inch 33rpm
RCA	5-8	88

Members: Eddi Reader; Mark Nevin.

FALLS, Ruby   *C&W '75*
Singles: 7–inch
50 STATES	3-5	75-80

EPs: 7–inch 33/45rpm
50 STATES	4-6	80

LP: 10/12–inch 33rpm
50 STATES	5-10	80

FAMILY BROWN   *C&W '81*
Singles: 7–inch
OVATION	3-5	81
RCA	3-4	82-86

LP: 10/12–inch 33rpm
RCA	8-10	80s

FARGO, Donna   *C&W/P&R/LP '72*
Singles: 7–inch
ABC	3-4	78
ABC/DOT	3-5	74-77
CHALLENGE (59387 "Daddy")	5-10	68
CHALLENGE (59391 "Wishful Thinking")	5-10	68

CLEVELAND INT'L	3-4	84-91
COLUMBIA	3-4	83
DECCA (33001 "Daddy")	4-6	72
DOT	3-5	72-74
MCA	3-4	81
MERCURY	3-4	86-87
RCA	3-4	82
RAMCO (1982 "You Make Me Feel Like a Woman")	8-12	67
RAMCO (1988 "Whose Been Playing House")	8-12	67
RAMCO (1988 "Whose Been Sleeping on My Bed")	8-12	67
(Note change in title.)		
RAMCO (1991 "Kinda Glad I'm Me")	8-12	67
SONGBIRD	3-4	81
W.B.	3-5	76-81

Picture Sleeves
DOT	3-6	72-74
W.B.	3-5	76-80

LPs: 10/12–inch 33rpm
ABC/DOT	5-10	74-77
DOT	8-12	72-73
MCA	5-8	80s
MERCURY	5-10	86
PICKWICK/HILLTOP	5-10	70s
RCA	5-10	83
SONGBIRD	4-8	81
W.B.	5-10	76-80

Session: Jordanaires.
Also see BARE, Bobby / Donna Fargo / Jerry Wallace
Also see JORDANAIRES

FARGO, Donna, & Billy Joe Royal   *C&W '87*
Singles: 7–inch
MERCURY	3-4	87

Also see FARGO, Donna
Also see ROYAL, Billy Joe

FAT CITY
Singles: 7–inch
PARAMOUNT	3-5	72
PROBE	3-5	69

LPs: 10/12–inch 33rpm
ABC/PROBE	15-20	69
PARAMOUNT	12-15	72

Members: Bill Danoff; Taffy Nivert.
Also see BILL & TAFFY
Also see DENVER, John
Also see STARLAND VOCAL BAND

FAUCETT, Dawnett   *C&W '89*
Singles: 7–inch

STEP ONE	3-4	89

FELICIANO, Jose

P&R/R&B/LP '68/C&W '83
Singles: 7–inch

ALA	3-4	80
MOTOWN	3-4	81-83
PRIVATE STOCK	3-5	76-77
RCA	3-6	64-75

LPs: 10/12–inch 33rpm

CAMDEN	8-10	72
MOTOWN	5-10	81
PRIVATE STOCK	6-10	76-77
RCA	8-15	65-76

FELICIANO, Jose / Petula Clark
EPs: 7–inch 33/45rpm

TK (334 "Mackenna's Gold")	10-20	69

Also see CLARK, Petula

FELICIANO, Jose, & Quincy Jones
LPs: 10/12–inch 33rpm

RCA (4096 "Mackenna's Gold")	15-25	69
(Soundtrack.)		

Also see FELICIANO, Jose

FELL, Terry   *C&W '54*
(With the Fellers)
Singles: 78rpm

RCA	3-8	56
X	3-8	54-55

Singles: 7–inch

RCA	5-10	56
X	5-10	54-55

FELLER, Dick   *C&W '73*
Singles: 7–inch

ASYLUM	3-5	74-75
U.A.	3-4	72-80

LPs: 10/12–inch 33rpm

ASYLUM	6-10	74-75
AUDIOGRAPH ALIVE	5-10	84
U.A.	8-12	73

FELTS, Narvel   *P&R '60/C&W '73*
Singles: 78rpm

MERCURY	10-20	57

Singles: 7–inch

ABC	3-5	78
ABC/DOT	3-5	75-77
ACTION	4-8	70
ARA	4-8	64-65

CELEBRITY CIRCLE	4-8	65
CINNAMON	3-5	73-74
COLLAGE	3-4	79
COMPLEAT	3-4	82-83
CONE	3-4	92
DOT	3-5	75-77
EVERGREEN	3-4	82-91
GMC	3-4	81
GROOVE	4-8	63
HI (2100 series)	4-8	67
HI (2300 series)	3-5	76
HI COUNTRY (8000 series)	4-6	72-73
KARI	3-4	80
LOBO	3-4	82
MCA	3-4	79
MERCURY	10-15	57
PINK	10-15	59-60
RENAY	4-8	62-65
RENEGADE	2-4	91
STARLINE	5-10	62

Picture Sleeves

CONE	3-4	92

LPs: 10/12–inch 33rpm

ABC	5-10	78-79
ABC/DOT	8-10	75-77
CINNAMON	8-10	73-74
MCA	5-8	80s
HI	8-10	76

Also see WOLFPACK

FELTS, Narvel / Red Sovine / Mel Tillis
LPs: 10/12–inch 33rpm

POWER PAK	5-10	77

Also see SOVINE, Red
Also see TILLIS, Mel

FELTS, Narvel, & Sharon Vaughn   *C&W '74*
Singles: 7–inch

CINNAMON	3-5	74

Also see FELTS, Narvel
Also see VAUGHN, Sharon

FENDER, Freddy   *C&W/P&R/LP '75*
(Baldemar Huerta)
Singles: 7–inch

ABC	3-4	76-79
ABC/DOT	4-6	75-77
ARV INT'L	3-5	75
ARGO	10-15	60
DISCOS DOMINANTE	5-10	
DUNCAN	10-20	59

FALCON	5-10	
GRT	4-8	75-76
GOLDBAND	4-8	60s
GOLDIES 45	3-5	74
IDEAL	5-10	
IMPERIAL	8-12	60
MCA	3-4	82
NORCO	5-10	63-65
STARFLITE	3-4	79-80
W.B.	3-4	83

LPs: 10/12-inch 33rpm

ABC	5-10	78-79
ABC/DOT	8-10	75-77
ACCORD	5-10	81
BIRCHMONT	5-10	80s
51 WEST	5-10	79
GRT	8-10	75
PICCADILLY	5-10	81
PICKWICK	5-10	70s
POWER PAK	5-10	75-80s
STARFLITE	5-10	80
SUFFOLK MARKETING	5-10	76

Also see HUERTA, Baldemar
Also see WAYNE, Scotty

FENDER, Freddy, & Tommy McLain
LPs: 10/12-inch 33rpm

CRAZY CAJUN	5-10	78

Also see FENDER, Freddy
Also see McLAIN, Tommy

FENDER, Freddy, & Sir Douglas
LPs: 10/12-inch 33rpm

CRAZY CAJUN	5-10	78

Also see SAHM, Doug

FENDER, Freddy, & Noel Vill
Singles: 7-inch

NORCO (107 "Magic of Love")	4-8	65
SOCK-O (101 "Magic of Love")	10-15	65

Also see FENDER, Freddy

FENDERMEN   *P&R/C&W '60*
Singles: 7-inch

COLLECTABLES	3-4	80s
CUCA (1003 "Mule Skinner Blues")	50-75	60
DAB	4-8	
ERA	3-5	72
ERIC	3-4	70s
KOALA	3-4	
SOMA	8-15	60-61

LPs: 10/12-inch 33rpm

POINT	20-40	
SOMA (1240 "Mule Skinner Blues")	800-1200	60
(Solid black vinyl.)		
SOMA (1240 "Mule Skinner Blues")	1000-1500	60
(Vinyl is clearer and appears colored when held to a light.)		

Members: Phil Humphrey; Jimmy Sundquist; John Howard.

FENSTER, Zoot   *C&W '75*
(Jack Barlow)
Singles: 7-inch

ANTIQUE (23 "Who Wrote That Word")	3-5	70s
ANTIQUE (1408 "Man on Page 602")	5-10	75

Also see BARLOW, Jack

FERRARI, C.W.   *C&W '88*
Singles: 7-inch

SOUTHERN SOUND	3-4	88

FINNEY, Maury   *C&W '76*
Singles: 7-inch

SOUNDWAVES	3-5	75-80

LP: 10/12-inch 33rpm

SOUNDWAVES	5-10	76-78

FIRST EDITION   *P&RLP '68*
Singles: 7-inch

REPRISE	4-8	67-68

LPs: 10/12-inch 33rpm

INTERMEDIA/QUICKSILVER (5056 "The First Edition")	10-15	84
(Picture disc.)		
REPRISE	12-20	67-68

Members: Kenny Rogers; Mike Settle; Thelma Lou Camacho; Terry Williams; Mickey Jones.
Also see NEW CHRISTY MINSTRELS
Also see ROGERS, Kenny, & First Edition

FISCHOFF, George   *C&W '79*
Singles: 7-inch

DRIVE	3-5	79

FISHER, Al, & Lou Marks
LPs: 10/12-inch 33rpm

CAMEO	12-15	64
SWAN (514 "It's a Beatle World")	15-25	64

FITZGERALD, Ella   *P&R '36/C&W '44*
Singles: 78rpm

DECCA (800 thru 3000 series)	10-15	36-41

DECCA (18000 thru 29000 series)	5-10	42-54
VERVE	3-5	54-57

Singles: 7–inch

CAPITOL	3-5	67-68
DECCA (27000 & 28000 series)	10-20	50-53
DECCA (29000 series)	8-15	54-56
DECCA (30000 series except 30405)	5-10	56-67
DECCA (30405 "Goody Goody")	15-25	57
PABLO	3-4	75
PRESTIGE	3-5	69
REPRISE	3-5	69-71
SALLE	4-6	68
VERVE (10000 series)	5-10	56-59
VERVE (10100 thru 10300 series, except 10340)	4-6	60-65
VERVE (10340 "Ringo Beat")	8-12	64

Picture Sleeves

VERVE	5-10	59-60

EPs: 7–inch 33/45rpm

DECCA	15-30	50-58
VERVE	10-25	56-61

LPs: 10/12–inch 33rpm

ATLANTIC	5-10	72
BAINBRIDGE	5-10	81
CAPITOL (2000 series)	8-15	67-68
CAPITOL (11000 series)	5-10	78
CAPITOL (16000 series)	4-6	82
COLUMBIA	5-10	73
CORAL	4-8	73
DECCA (156 "The Best of Ella Fitzgerald")	25-35	58
(Black label with silver print.)		
DECCA (156 "The Best of Ella Fitzgerald")	15-20	65
(Black label with horizontal rainbow band.)		
DECCA (4000 series)	10-20	61-67
DECCA (5084 "Souvenir Album")	75-125	49
(10–inch LP.)		
DECCA (5300 "Gershwin Songs")	75-125	51
(10–inch LP.)		
DECCA (8000 series)	20-40	55-59
EVEREST	5-10	73
MCA	5-10	76-82
MGM	5-10	70
MPS	5-10	72
METRO	10-15	65-66

OLYMPIC	5-10	74
PABLO	5-10	75-83
REPRISE	8-12	69-71
VERVE (29 "Ella Fitzgerald Sings the George & Ira Gershwin Songbook")	30-40	64
(Five-LP reissue of Verve 4029.)		
VERVE (2500 & 2600 series)	5-10	76-82
(Reads "Manufactured By MGM Record Corp.," or mentions either Polydor or Polygram at bottom of label.)		
VERVE (4001 thru 4009)	25-50	56
(Reads "Verve Records, Inc." at bottom of label.)		
VERVE (4010 "Ella Fitzgerald Sings the Duke Ellington Song Book")	75-125	56
(Four-LP set.)		
VERVE (4013 thru 4015)	20-40	57
(Reads "Verve Records, Inc." at bottom of label.)		
VERVE (4019 "Ella Fitzgerald Sings the Irving Berlin Songbook")	20-40	58
VERVE (4020 thru 4028)	20-40	58-59
(Reads "Verve Records, Inc." at bottom of label.)		
VERVE (4029 "Ella Fitzgerald Sings the George & Ira Gershwin Songbook")	40-60	59
(Five-LP set, containing individual LPs 4024 thru 4028.)		
VERVE (4036 thru 4071)	10-20	59-66
VERVE (6000 series)	20-35	57-59
(Reads "Verve Records, Inc." at bottom of label.)		
VERVE (6100 series)	15-20	60
(Reads "Verve Records, Inc." at bottom of label.)		
VERVE (8200 series)	20-30	58
(Reads "Verve Records, Inc." at bottom of label.)		
VERVE (64036 thru 64071)	10-20	59-66
VERVE (67000 & 68000 series)	8-15	67-73
VERVE (2610000 series)	20-30	83
VOCALION	6-10	67

Also see CAMPBELL, Glen / Lettermen / Ella Fitzgerald / Sandler & Young

FITZGERALD, Ella, & Louis Armstrong   *R&B '46*

Singles: 78rpm

DECCA	3-6	53

EPs: 7–inch 33/45rpm

VERVE	15-30	56

LPs: 10/12–inch 33rpm

METRO	5-10	67

VERVE (4003 "Ella & Louis") 40-60   56
VERVE (4006 "Ella & Louis
 Again") 50-100   56
VERVE (4011 "Porgy & Bess") 25-50   57
 (Monaural.)
VERVE (6040 "Porgy & Bess") 40-65   57
 (Stereo.)
VERVE (8811 "Ella & Louis") 5-10   72

FITZGERALD, Ella, & Count
Basie   *LP '63*
LPs: 10/12–inch 33rpm
PABLO 5-10   79
VERVE 15-20   63

FITZGERALD, Ella / Bill Doggett
Singles: 78rpm
DECCA.. 3-5   53
Singles: 7–inch
DECCA....................................... 5-10   53
LPs: 10/12–inch 33rpm
VERVE 10-20   62

FITZGERALD, Ella, & Duke
Ellington
Singles: 7–inch
VERVE 4-6   66
LPs: 10/12–inch 33rpm
VERVE 10-20 65-67

FITZGERALD, Ella / Billie Holiday
LPs: 10/12–inch 33rpm
MCA 5-10   76
VERVE (6022 "At Newport") 40-50   58
 (Stereo.)
VERVE (8234 "At Newport") 30-40   58
 (Monaural.)

FITZGERALD, Ella / Billie Holiday /
Lena Horne
EPs: 7–inch 33/45rpm
COLUMBIA (2531 "Ella, Lena &
 Billie") 25-45   56
LPs: 10/12–inch 33rpm
COLUMBIA (2531 "Ella, Lena &
 Billie") 75-100   56
 (10–inch LP.)

FITZGERALD, Ella, & Ink Spots
Singles: 78rpm
DECCA (18000 series)................. 4-8 44-45
EPs: 7–inch 33/45rpm
DECCA....................................... 5-10   53

FITZGERALD, Ella, & Antonio
Carlos Jobim
LPs: 10/12–inch 33rpm
PABLO 5-10   81

FITZGERALD, Ella, & Louis
Jordan   *R&B '46*
Singles: 78rpm
DECCA (23000 series) 4-8   46
 Also see JORDAN, Louis

FITZGERALD, Ella, & Peggy
Lee   *LP '55*
LPs: 10/12–inch 33rpm
DECCA (8166 "Pete Kelly's
 Blues") 40-60   55

FITZGERALD, Ella, & Mills
Brothers   *P&R '37*
Singles: 78rpm
DECCA 4-8   37
 Also see MILLS BROTHERS

FITZGERALD, Ella, & Oscar
Peterson
LPs: 10/12–inch 33rpm
PABLO 5-10   76
 Also see FITZGERALD, Ella

FIVE RED CAPS   *P&R/R&B/C&W '44*
(5 Red Caps)
Singles: 78rpm
BEACON....................................15-25 43-45
GANNETT...................................15-25 43-45
JOE DAVIS 15-25 43-45
DAVIS 10-20   46
MGM 10-20   48
 Members: Steve Gibson; Jim Springs; Romaine
 Brown; Dave Patillo; Emmett Matthews.
 Also see GIBSON, Steve

FLATT, Lester, & Bill Monroe
LP: 10/12–inch 33rpm
RCA 5-10 74-81
 Also see MONROE, Bill

FLATT, Lester, & Earl
Scruggs   *C&W '52*
(With the Foggy Mountain Boys; Flatt &
Scruggs)
Singles: 78rpm
COLUMBIA 5-15 51-57
MERCURY....................................5-10 49-53
Singles: 7–inch
COLUMBIA (20000 & 21000
 series)...8-15 51-56

125

COLUMBIA (40000 thru 42000 series)	5-10	56-63
COLUMBIA (43000 thru 45000 series)	4-8	64-67
MERCURY	10-15	50-53

Picture Sleeves

COLUMBIA	4-8	62-68
MERCURY	4-6	68

EPs: 7–inch 33/45rpm

COLUMBIA	10-20	57-60

LPs: 10/12–inch 33rpm

CBS	5-10	
COLUMBIA (30 "Flatt & Scruggs")	8-12	75
COLUMBIA (400 series)	10-15	69
COLUMBIA (1000 & 2000 series, except 1019)	10-25	60-68
COLUMBIA (1019 "Foggy Mountain Jamboree")	30-50	57
COLUMBIA (8000 & 9000 series) (With "CS" prefix.)	10-25	60-70
COLUMBIA (8000 & 9000 series) (With "PC" prefix.)	5-10	
COLUMBIA (10000 series)	6-12	73
COLUMBIA (30000 thru 37000 series)	5-12	70-82
COPPER CREEK	5-10	
COUNTY	5-10	
EVEREST	5-10	71-82
51 WEST	5-10	80s
HARMONY	8-15	60-71
MERCURY (20000 series) (Monaural.)	20-40	58-63
MERCURY (60000 series) (Stereo.)	20-30	63
MERCURY (61000 series)	10-15	68
NASHVILLE	8-10	70
PICKWICK/HILLTOP	8-12	68
POWER PAK	5-10	
ROUNDER		
WING	8-12	68

Members: Lester Flatt; Earl Scruggs; Mac Wiseman; Jim Shoemate; Cedric Rainwater.
Also see SCRUGGS, Earl
Also see STUART, Marty

FLATT, Lester, Earl Scruggs & Jim & Jesse
LP: 10/12–inch 33rpm

STARDAY	15-20	66

FLATT, Lester, Earl Scruggs & Bill Monroe
LP: 10/12–inch 33rpm

ROUNDER	5-8	80s

Also see MONROE, Bill

FLATT, Lester, Earl Scruggs, & Doc Watson
LPs: 10/12–inch 33rpm

COLUMBIA	10-15	67

Also see FLATT, Lester, & Earl Scruggs
Also see WATSON, Doc

FLETCHER, Vicky   *C&W '74*
Singles: 7–inch

COLUMBIA	3-5	74
MUSIC ROW	3-5	76

FLORES, Rosie   *C&W '87*
Singles: 7–inch

REPRISE	3-4	87-88

FLYING BURRITO BROTHERS   *LP '69/C&W '80*
Singles: 7–inch

A&M	3-6	69-70
COLUMBIA	3-5	76
REGENCY	3-4	80

LPs: 10/12–inch 33rpm

A&M	10-15	69-76
COLUMBIA	8-10	75-76
REGENCY	5-10	80
SHILO ("Sneaky Pete") (Selection number not known.)	20-30	79

Members: Gram Parsons; Chris Hillman; Bernie Leadon; Al Perkins; Rick Roberts; Mike Clarke; Pete Battin; Pete Kleinow; Greg Harris; Ed Ponder; Gib Guilbeau; John Beland
Also see BURRITO BROTHERS
Also see SHILOH

FLYING MACHINE   *P&R/LP '69*
Singles: 7–inch

CONGRESS	4-8	69-70
JANUS	4-8	69

LPs: 10/12–inch 33rpm

JANUS	10-15	69

Members: Tony Newman; Stuart Coleman; Steve Jones; Paul Wilkinson.
Also see TAYLOR, James

FOGELBERG, Dan   *LP '74/C&W '80*
Singles: 7–inch

COLUMBIA	4-6	73
EPIC	3-5	74-75
FULL MOON/EPIC	3-5	75-82
FULL MOON	3-4	82-87

Picture Sleeves

FULL MOON/EPIC...................... 3-4   80-87

LPs: 10/12–inch 33rpm

COLUMBIA 10-15   72
EPIC.. 8-10   74-78
EPIC/FULL MOON...................... 8-10   75-82
FULL MOON 5-10   82-90

FOGELBERG, Dan, & Tim
Weisberg   *LP '78*
Singles: 7–inch

FULL MOON/EPIC...................... 3-4   78-80

LPs: 10/12–inch 33rpm

FULL MOON/EPIC...................... 5-10   78
Also see FOGELBERG, Dan

FOGERTY, John   *P&R '72/C&W '73*
Promotional Singles: 12–inch 33/45rpm

W.B. (2234 "Old Man Down the
Road").. 5-10   84
W.B. (2267 "Rock & Roll Girls") .. 5-10   85
W.B. (2337 "I Can't Help
Myself")..................................... 5-10   85
W.B. (2362 "Vanz Kant Danz)..... 5-10   85
W.B. (2363 "Vanz Kant Danz-
Edit") 5-10   85
W.B. (2514 "Eye of the Zombie") 5-10   86

Singles: 7–inch

ASYLUM 3-5   75-76
FANTASY..................................... 3-6   73
W.B. 3-4   84-86

Picture Sleeves

W.B. 3-5   84-87

LPs: 10/12–inch 33rpm

ASYLUM (1046 "John Fogerty") . 5-10   75
W.B. (25203 "Centerfield") 10-15   84
  (Last track is mistitled, *Zanz Kant Danz*.)
W.B. (25203 "Centerfield") 5-8   85
  (Last track is *Vanz Kant Danz*.)
W.B. (25449 "Eye of the Zombie") 5-8   85
Also see BLUE RIDGE RANGERS
Also see CREEDENCE CLEARWATER REVIVAL
Also see EDDY, Duane

FOGERTY, Tom   *LP '72*
(With the Blue Velvets)
Singles: 7–inch

FANTASY...................................... 3-5   71-82
ORCHESTRA ("Now You're Not
Mine").................................... 35-50   62
  (Selection number not known.)
ORCHESTRA (1010 "Have You Ever Been
Lonely").................................. 35-50   61

ORCHESTRA (6177 "Come on
Baby")....................................35-50   61
(Despite the higher number, this was the first
Orchestra single.)

Picture Sleeves

FANTASY 3-5   71

LPs: 10/12–inch 33rpm

FANTASY 8-10   72-81
Members: Tom Fogerty; John Fogerty; Doug Clifford;
Stuart Cook.
Also see CREEDENCE CLEARWATER REVIVAL

FOLEY, Betty   *C&W '54*
Singles: 78rpm

DECCA 4-8   54-55

Singles: 7–inch

BANDERA.....................................4-8   59
DECCA 5-10   54-55

FOLEY, Red   *C&W '44*
(With the Cumberland Valley Boys; with His
Log Cabin Quartet; with Betty Foley; with Anita
Kerr Singers; with Grady Martin & His Slew
Foot Five)
Singles: 78rpm

BANNER...................................10-15
DECCA (Except 30067 & 30674).4-10   42-57
DECCA (30067 "Rock 'N
Reelin") 10-20   56
DECCA (30674 "Crazy Little Guitar
Man") 10-20   58
MELOTONE...............................10-15
ORIOLE 10-15

Singles: 7–inch

DECCA (25000 series) 4-8   61-67
DECCA (27000 thru 29000
series)....................................8-15   50-56
DECCA (30000 series, except 30067 &
30674)....................................5-10   56-59
DECCA (30067 "Rock 'N
Reelin") 20-30   56
DECCA (30674 "Crazy Little Guitar
Man") 20-30   58
DECCA (31000 thru 32000
series)....................................4-8   60-67
DECCA (46000 series) 4-6   68
MCA...3-5   73

EPs: 7–inch 33/45rpm

DECCA 10-20   53-59

LPs: 10/12–inch 33rpm

CORAL..5-8   73
COUNTRY MUSIC.......................6-10   76
DECCA (100 series) 15-25   64

DECCA (4000 series, except
4140).. 10-25 61-67

DECCA (4140 "Company's
Comin")..................................... 10-20 61

DECCA (5303 "The Red Foley Souvenir
Album")....................................... 40-60 51
(10–inch LP.)

DECCA (5338 "Lift Up Your
Voice")....................................... 40-60 51
(10–inch LP.)

DECCA (7100 series)................. 15-25 64

DECCA (8294 "The Red Foley Souvenir
Album")....................................... 20-30 56

DECCA (8296 "Beyond the
Sunset").................................... 15-25 56

DECCA (8767 "He Walks with
Thee")....................................... 10-20 58

DECCA (8806 "My Keepsake
Album")...................................... 20-30 58

DECCA (8847 "Let's All Sing with Red
Foley")...................................... 15-25 59

DECCA (8903 "Let's All Sing to
Him").. 10-20 59

DECCA (75000 series)................. 8-12 68-69

DECCA/DICKIES ("Red Foley's Dickies
Souvenir Album").................. 50-100 58
(Special Products issue for the Dickies
company.)

MCA 5-8 80s

PICKWICK/HILLTOP 8-12 66

VOCALION................................... 6-12 65-71
   Also see KERR, Anita
   Also see KNIGHT, Evelyn, & Red Foley
   Also see WELK, Lawrence, & His Orchestra
   Also see WELLS, Kitty, & Red Foley

FOLEY, Red, & Andrews Sisters
Singles: 78rpm

DECCA... 4-8 54
   Also see ANDREWS SISTERS

FOLEY, Red / Jimmie Davis
LP: 10/12–inch 33rpm

GREEN VALLEY.......................... 6-12 76
   Also see DAVIS, Jimmie

FOLEY, Red, & Little Foleys
Singles: 78rpm

DECCA... 4-8 50

Singles: 7–inch

DECCA....................................... 10-15 50

Picture Sleeves

DECCA....................................... 20-30 50
   Members: Red Foley; Shirley Foley, Julie Foley; Jenny
   Foley.
   Also see FOLEY, Red

FOLEY, Red, & Ernest Tubb
EPs: 7–inch 33/45rpm

DECCA 10-20 52-56

LP: 10/12–inch 33rpm

DECCA (8298 "Red & Ernie") 30-50 56

FORD, Joy   *C&W '78*
Singles: 7–inch

COUNTRY INT'L.............................3-5 78-88

FORD, Tennessee Ernie
**(With the Green Valley Singers & Orchestra;
Tennessee Ernie)**   *C&W/P&R '49*
Singles: 78rpm

CAPITOL (1 "Sixteen Tons")........5-10 69
(Promotional "Special Commemorative
Pressing" for Ford's 20th year on Capitol.)

CAPITOL (1200 thru 2900
series)...5-15 50-57

CAPITOL (40000 series) 5-10 49-50

Singles: 7–inch

CAPITOL (1275 thru 2900
series)..5-20 50-54
(Purple labels. Ford's many "Boogie" titles
represent the higher end of this price range.)

CAPITOL (2000 thru 4100
series)...3-5 70-75
(Orange labels.)

CAPITOL (3000 thru 4400
series)...5-10 54-60

CAPITOL (4500 thru 5700
series)...3-6 61-67

Picture Sleeves

CAPITOL.......................................5-15 55-60

EPs: 7–inch 33/45rpm

CAPITOL (Except 413) 5-10 55-61

CAPITOL (413 "Backwoods Boogie and
Blues") 20-30 53

GREEN GIANT (2566 "When Pea-Pickers
Get Together") 10-15
(Mail order offer. Add $3 to $5 if
accompanied by special mailer/sleeve.
Promotional issue made for the Green Giant
Co.)

LPs: 10/12–inch 33rpm

CAPITOL (Except 888) 5-15 56-80

CAPITOL (888 "Ol' Rockin'
Ern")..25-50 57

EVEREST 5-10 70s

LONGINES 5-10

PICKWICK 5-10 70s

READER'S DIGEST (241 "Tennessee Ernie Ford") 20-40
(Boxed, eight-LP set. With booklet.)
Session: Jordanaires.
Also see JORDANAIRES
Also see LAWRENCE, Steve / Tennessee Ernie Ford
Also see LEE, Brenda / Tennessee Ernie Ford
Also see OWENS, Buck / Tennessee Ernie Ford
Also see STARR, Kay, & Tennessee Ernie Ford

FORD, Tennessee Ernie, & Glen Campbell
LPs: 10/12-inch 33rpm
CAPITOL 10-12   75
Also see CAMPBELL, Glen

FORD, Tennessee Ernie, & Joe "Fingers" Carr   *C&W '51*
Singles: 78rpm
CAPITOL 4-8   51
Singles: 7-inch
CAPITOL 5-10   51

FORD, Tennessee Ernie, & Dinning Sisters
Singles: 78rpm
CAPITOL 4-8   50s
Singles: 7-inch
CAPITOL 5-10   50s

FORD, Tennessee Ernie, & Steve Lawrence
LPs: 10/12-inch 33rpm
CAMAY 5-15   60

FORD, Tennessee Ernie, & Andra Willis   *C&W '75*
Singles: 7-inch
CAPITOL 3-5   75
Also see FORD, Tennessee Ernie
Also see WILLIS, Andra

FORESTER SISTERS   *C&W '85*
Singles: 7-inch
W.B. 3-4   84-91
LPs: 10/12-inch 33rpm
W.B. 5-8   85-91
Members: Kathy Forester; Kim Forester; June Forester; Christy Forester.
Also see BELLAMY BROTHERS & Forester Sisters

FORMAN, Peggy   *C&W '77*
Singles: 7-inch
DIMENSION 3-4   80-81
MCA 3-5   77

FORREST, Sylvia   *C&W '89*
Singles: 7-inch
DOOR KNOB 3-4   89

FOSTER, Jerry   *C&W '73*
(With Tennessee Tornado)
Singles: 7-inch
BACK BEAT 5-10   59-61
CINNAMON 3-5   73
HITSVILLE 3-5   76
METROMEDIA 3-5   70
MONUMENT 3-5   78
SPAR 10-15   64
TCF 4-8   66

FOSTER, Lloyd David   *C&W '82*
Singles: 7-inch
COLUMBIA 3-4   84-85
MCA 3-4   82-83

FOSTER & LLOYD   *C&W '87*
Singles: 7-inch
RCA 3-4   87-90
LPs: 10/12-inch 33rpm
RCA 5-10   86-90
Members: Radney Foster; Bill Lloyd.
Also see TOMORROW'S WORLD

FOUR GUYS   *C&W '74*
Singles: 7-inch
COLLAGE 3-5   79
JNB 3-4   82
RCA 3-5   74

FOWLER, Ken   *C&W '86*
Singles: 7-inch
DEJA VU 3-4   86

FOWLER, Wally   *C&W '84*
(With the Tennessee Valley Boys)
Singles: 7-inch
DOVE (100 "A New Star in
   Heaven") 5-10   77
MERCURY 10-15   47
NASHWOOD 3-4   84
SONGS OF FAITH 3-4
EPs: 7-inch 33/45rpm
DECCA 5--10   60
LP: 10/12-inch 33rpm
DECCA 12-20   60
DOVE (1000 "A Tribute to Elvis
   Presley") 15-20   77
KING 20-30   60
NASHWOOD 5-10

PICKWICK 6-12

PICKWICK/HILLTOP 8-12   65

STARDAY 15-25   60-64

VOCALION................................ 10-15   67

Session: J.D. Sumner & Stamps; D.J. Fontana; Charlie
McCoy; Harold Bradley; with Anita Kerr Singers; with
Oak Ridge Quartet.
Also see KERR, Anita
Also see McCOY, Charlie
Also see OAK RIDGE BOYS
Also see PRESLEY, Elvis

FOX, Dolly   *C&W '78*
Singles: 7–inch

ARTIC 3-5   78

FOX, Kent   *C&W '73*
Singles: 7–inch

MCA 3-5   73

MERCANTILE............................... 3-5   77

FOXFIRE   *C&W '79*
Singles: 7–inch

ELEKTRA.. 3-5   80

NSD... 3-5   79

FRADY, Garland   *C&W '73*
Singles: 7–inch

COUNTRYSIDE............................ 3-5   73

GNP 3-5   70s

PAULA 3-5   72

LPs: 10/12–inch 33rpm

COUNTRYSIDE......................... 8-10   73

FRANCIS, Connie

P&R/R&B '58/C&W '60
Singles: 78rpm

MGM 15-35   55-58

Singles: 7–inch

GSF.. 3-5   73

IVANHOE..................................... 3-5   70s

MGM CELEBRITY SCENE (CS6-5 "Connie
Francis")................................. 30-40   66
(Boxed set of five singles with bio insert and
title strips.)

MGM (9 "Rock-a-Bye Your Baby with a Dixie
Melody")................................. 20-30   60
(Stereo.)

MGM (10 "I Almost Lost My
Mind")..................................... 20-30   60
(Stereo.)

MGM (3000 series) 3-5   71

MGM (12015 "Freddy") 25-50   55

MGM (12056 "Oh, Please Make Him
Jealous") 25-50   55

MGM (12122 thru 12555).......... 15-25   55-57

MGM (12588 thru 13116)............5-15   58-63

MGM (13127 thru 14091
except 13550)............................5-10   64-69

MGM (13550 "A Nurse in the U.S. Army
Corp")......................................20-25   66
(Promotional issue only.)

MGM (14500 series) 3-5   81

MGM (50117 "My Happiness") ..20-30   58
(Stereo.)

MGM (50129 "You're Gonna Miss
Me") 20-30   59
(Stereo.)

MGM (50133 "Among My
Souvenirs") 20-30   59
(Stereo.)

POLYDOR 3-4   83

Picture Sleeves

MGM (12000 series except
12738)..5-15   58-61

MGM (12738 "My Happiness") ..10-15   58
(Pink sleeve.)

MGM (12738 "My Happiness") ..15-25   58
(Black and white sleeve.)

MGM (13000 series, except 13505 &
13773)..5-10   61-68

MGM (13505 "Empty Chapel")....10-20   66

MGM (13773 "My Heart Cries for
You")..10-20   67

MGM (14000 series, except 14058 &
14091)..3-6   68-69

MGM (14058 "Gone Like the
Wind")......................................10-20   69

MGM (14091 "Mr. Love") 10-20   69

EPs: 7–inch 33/45

MGM 10-20   58-62

LPs: 10/12–inch 33rpm

LEO..12-15   60s

LION/METRO ("Fun Songs for
Children")................................40-50   60s
(This reissue of MGM 4023 may be on either
Lion or Metro. Selection number not known.)

MGM (100 series) 10-15   70

MGM (E-3686 "Who's Sorry
Now")......................................30-40   58
(Yellow label. Monaural.)

MGM (SE-3686 "Who's Sorry
Now")......................................15-25   60
(Reprocessed stereo.)

MGM (E-3761 "Exciting Connie
Francis") 25-35   58
(Yellow label. Monaural.)

MGM (SE-3761 "Exciting Connie
Francis")..................................30-40   58
(Yellow label. Stereo.)

MGM (E-3776 & E-3969) 20-30 60-61
(Monaural.)
MGM (SE-3776 & SE-3969)...... 20-35 60-61
(Monaural.)
MGM (E-4000 series, except
E-4023) 15-25 62-68
(Monaural.)
MGM (SE-4000 series) 15-30 62-69
(Stereo.)
MGM (E-4023 "Fun Songs for
Children") 50-70 61
MGM (5400 series) 5-10
MGM (10000 series) 8-12 71
MGM (91000 series) 10-15 60s
(Capitol Record Club series.)
MATI-MOR (8002 "Brylcreem Presents Sing
Along with Connie Francis").... 10-20 61
(Promotional issue, made for Brylcreem.)
METRO 10-15 65-66
MGM/SESSIONS 10-12 75
POLYDOR.................................... 5-10 83
Session: Jordanaires; Boots Randolph.
Also see CRAMER, Floyd
Also see JORDANAIRES
Also see RANDOLPH, Boots

FRANCIS, Connie, & Marvin Rainwater
Singles: 78rpm
MGM (12555 "Majesty of Love") 10-20 57
Singles: 7–inch
MGM (12555 "Majesty of Love") 10-20 57
Also see FRANCIS, Connie
Also see RAINWATER, Marvin

FRANCIS, Connie, & Hank Williams Jr.
LPs: 10/12–inch 33rpm
MGM 15-25 64
Also see FRANCIS, Connie
Also see WILLIAMS, Hank, Jr.

FRANKS, Tillman   *C&W '63*
(With the Cedar Grove Three; Tillman Franks
Singers)
Singles: 78rpm
GOTHAM 10-15 51
Singles: 7–inch
GOTHAM (7412 "Hi-Tone
Poppa").................................... 25-35 51
STARDAY 4-8 63-64
LP: 10/12–inch 33rpm
PICKWICK/HILLTOP 8-12 65
Session: Faron Young.
Also see YOUNG, Faron

FRAZIER, Brenda   *C&W '80*
Singles: 7–inch
TYRO..3-5 80

FRAZIER, Dallas   *P&R '66/C&W '67*
Singles: 78rpm
CAPITOL.......................................5-10 54
Singles: 7–inch
CAPITOL (2000 thru 2400 series) .3-6 67-69
CAPITOL (2800 & 2900 series) ...8-12 54
CAPITOL (5500 series) 4-8 65
JAMIE 5-10 59
MERCURY......................................4-6 64
MUSIKRON....................................4-8 61
RCA 3-5 71-73
20TH FOX.....................................3-5 75
LPs: 10/12–inch 33rpm
CAPITOL.....................................10-20 66-67
RCA 8-12 70-71

FRAZIER, Dallas, & Joe "Fingers" Carr
Singles: 78rpm
CAPITOL..3-5 54
Singles: 7–inch
CAPITOL.......................................5-10 54
EPs: 7–inch 33/45rpm
CAPITOL..8-12 54
Also see FRAZIER, Dallas

FREE, Johnny   *C&W '79*
Singles: 7–inch
SABRE..3-5 79

FREEMAN, Ernie   *R&B '56/C&W '58*
(Ernie Freeman Combo)
Singles: 78rpm
CASH..5-10 56
Singles: 7–inch
AVA..4-8 64
CASH..8-12 56
IMPERIAL (Except 5752).............5-10 57-62
IMPERIAL (5752 "Theme from
Igor")...8-12 61
KING 5-10 60
LIBERTY..4-8 62
EPs: 7–inch 33/45rpm
DOOTONE (209 "Jazz Organ") 10-15 56
LPs: 10/12–inch 33rpm
DUNHILL....................................10-15 67
IMPERIAL 15-25 57-62

LIBERTY 10-20 62-63
Members: Ernie Freeman; Irvin Ashby; Joe Comfort; R. Martinez.
 Also see NELSON, Willie

FRICKE, Janie   *C&W '77*
(Janie Frickie)
Singles: 7–inch
COLUMBIA 3-5 77-89
LP: 10/12–inch 33rpm
CBS (99-1535 "On Tour") 50-75 82
(Picture disc. Promotional issue only.)
COLUMBIA 5-10 78-84
Session: Benny Wilson; Larry Gatlin; Steve Gatlin; Ricky Skaggs.
 Also see BANDY, Moe
 Also see DUNCAN, Johnny, & Janie Fricke
 Also see GATLIN, Larry, & Janie Frickie
 Also see HAGGARD, Merle, & Janie Frickie
 Also see MANDRELL, Barbara
 Also see RABBITT, Eddie
 Also see RICH, Charlie, & Janie Fricke
 Also see RUSSELL, Johnny
 Also see SKAGGS, Ricky
 Also see WILSON, Benny

FRIEDMAN, Kinky   *C&W '73*
Singles: 7–inch
ABC.. 3-5 75
EPIC... 3-4 76-85
SOUND FACTORY...................... 3-4 81
SUNRISE 3-4 83
VANGUARD................................. 3-5 73
LPs: 10/12–inch 33rpm
ABC.. 5-10 74
EPIC... 5-10 76
SUNRISE 5-8 83
VANGUARD................................. 5-10 73

FRIZZELL, Allen   *C&W '81*
Singles: 7–inch
EPIC... 3-4 85
SOUND FACTORY...................... 3-5 81

FRIZZELL, David   *C&W '70*
Singles: 7–inch
CAPITOL...................................... 3-5 73-74
CARTWHEEL............................... 3-5 71
COLUMBIA 3-5 70
COMPLEAT 3-4 87
NASHVILLE AMERICA 3-4 86
MCA 3-4 83
RSO 3-5 76
VIVA... 3-4 83-85
W.B. 3-4 81-82
LP: 10/12–inch 33rpm
MCA 5-8 83

VIVA... 5-8 81-84
W.B. 5-10 82-83
 Also see HAGGARD, Merle

FRIZZELL, David, & Shelly West   *C&W '81*
(Frizzell & West)
Singles: 7–inch
VIVA... 3-4 83-85
W.B. 3-4 81-83
LP: 10/12–inch 33rpm
VIVA... 5-8 81-84
W.B. 5-10 81-83
 Also see HAGGARD, Merle

FRIZZELL, Lefty   *C&W '50*
Singles: 78rpm
COLUMBIA 5-15 50-57
Singles: 7–inch
ABC.. 3-5 73-76
COLUMBIA (20000 & 21000 series)................................... 10-20 50-56
COLUMBIA (40000 & 41000 series)................................... 5-15 56-61
COLUMBIA (42000 thru 45000 series, except 42924)................... 3-8 61-72
COLUMBIA (42924 "Saginaw, Michigan")............................ 4-6 64
(Black vinyl.)
COLUMBIA (42924 "Saginaw, Michigan")............................ 10-15 64
(Colored vinyl. Promotional issue only.)
EPs: 7–inch 33/45rpm
COLUMBIA 15-35 51-59
LPs: 10/12–inch 33rpm
ABC.. 8-12 73-77
COLUMBIA (1342 "The One and Only Lefty Frizzell")............... 15-25 59
COLUMBIA (2169 "Saginaw, Michigan")............................ 15-25 64
COLUMBIA (2386 "The Sad Side of Life")............................ 15-25 65
COLUMBIA (2488 "Lefty Frizzell's Greatest Hits")................. 15-25 66
(Monaural.)
COLUMBIA (2772 "Puttin' On").. 15-25 67
COLUMBIA (8969 "Saginaw, Michigan")............................ 15-25 64
COLUMBIA (9019 "Songs of Jimmie Rodgers")....................... 75-100 51
(10–inch LP.)
HARMONY (9021 "Listen to Lefty")................................. 75-100 52
(10–inch LP.)

COLUMBIA (9186 "The Sad Side of
Life")... 20-25   65
COLUMBIA (9288 "Lefty Frizzell's Greatest
Hits") ....: 20-25   66
(Stereo. With "CS" prefix.)
COLUMBIA (9288 "Lefty Frizzell's Greatest
Hits") 5-10
(With "PC" prefix.)
COLUMBIA (9572 "Puttin' On"). 20-25   67
COLUMBIA (10000 series) 5-12   73-83
COLUMBIA (30000 series) 5-12   75-82
HARMONY (7241 "Songs of Jimmie
Rodgers").................................. 15-25   60
HARMONY (11000 series).......... 8-15   66-68
MCA 8-12   82
ROUNDER 5-10   80-83
2X4 (111 "Lefty Frizzell Story") ... 5-10   80
Also see AGNES & ORVILLE
Also see BOND, Johnny, & Lefty Frizzell
Also see PRICE, Ray / Lefty Frizzell / Carl Smith
Also see SMITH, Carl / Lefty Frizzell / Marty Robbins

FRUSHAY, Ray   *C&W '79*
Singles: 7–inch
WESTERN PRIDE 3-4   79-80
LP: 10/12–inch 33rpm
CASINO 6-12   76
WESTERN PRIDE 5-10   79

FUHRMAN, Micki   *C&W '78*
Singles: 7–inch
LOUISIANA HAYRIDE 3-5   77-78
MCA 3-4   79-84
LP: 10/12–inch 33rpm
DAYSPRING 5-10   81
LOUISIANA HAYRIDE 5-10   77-78

FULLER, Jerry   *P&R '59/C&W '79*
Singles: 7–inch
ABC... 3-5   78
BELL 4-6   72
CHALLENGE (59052 "Betty My
Angel") 15-25   59
CHALLENGE (59085 thru
59269)..................................... 10-20   60-65
CHALLENGE (59279 "I Got Carried
Away")...................................... 20-30   65
CHALLENGE (59307 "Don't Look at Me Like
That") 5-10   65
CHALLENGE (59329 "Double
Life").. 15-25   66
COLUMBIA 3-5   70
LIN (5011 "Blue Memories")...... 15-25   58
LIN (5012 "Teenage Love")....... 15-25   58

LIN (5015 "Angel from Above")..15-25   58
LIN (5016 "The Door Is Open")..15-25   58
LIN (5019 "Lipstick & Rouge") ...15-25   59
MCA..3-5   79
LPs: 10/12–inch 33rpm
LIN (100 "Teenage Love") 25-35   60
MCA...5-10   79

FULLER, Jerry, & Diane Maxwell
Singles: 7–inch
CHALLENGE (59074 "Above and
Beyond") 10-15   60

GABRIEL   *C&W '81*
(Gabriel Farago)
Singles: 7–inch
NSD 3-4   81
RODGETOP 3-4   81

GALLIMORE, Byron   *C&W '80*
Singles: 7–inch
LITTLE GIANT 3-5   80

GALLION, Bob   *C&W '58*
Singles: 78rpm
MGM (Except 12195)...................5-15   56-57
MGM (12195 "My Square Dancin'
Mama") 25-50   56
Singles: 7–inch
HICKORY...4-8   60-63
MGM (Except 12195 &
12628") 10-15   55-59
MGM (12195 "My Square Dancin'
Mama") 75-100   56
MGM (12628 "Baby, Love Me") .15-25   58
U.A...4-6   68
LPs: 10/12–inch 33rpm
HICKORY....................................10-20   63
Also see POWELL, Pati, Bob Gallion

GALWAY, James, &
Sylvia   *C&W '83*
Singles: 7–inch
RCA 3-4   83
Also see GALWAY, James
Also see SYLVIA

GARNETT, Gale   *P&R/C&W/LP '64*
Singles: 7–inch
RCA.. 4-8   64-67
Picture Sleeves
RCA.. 4-8   64
LPs: 10/12–inch 33rpm
RCA... 10-15   64-66

GARNETT, Gale, & Gentle Reign
Singles: 7–inch
COLUMBIA 4-6   68
LPs: 10/12–inch 33rpm
COLUMBIA 8-12   68-69
  Also see GARNETT, Gale

GARRETT, Pat   *C&W '77*
Singles: 7–inch
COMPLEAT 3-4   86
GOLD DUST 3-5   80-81
KANSA 3-5   77
MDJ... 3-4   87

GARRISON, Al   *C&W '87*
Singles: 7–inch
MOTION.. 3-4   87

GARRISON, Glen   *C&W '67*
Singles: 7–inch
CREST (1047 "Lovin' Lorene").. 35-50   58
IMPERIAL 4-8   67-68
LODE (106 "Pony Tail Girl") 35-50   59
LPs: 10/12–inch 33rpm
IMPERIAL 10-15   67-68

GARRON, Jess   *C&W '79*
Singles: 7–inch
CHARTA 3-5   79

GATLIN, Larry   *C&W '73*
(With the Gatlin Brothers Band; with Family & Friends; Gatlin Quartet)
Singles: 7–inch
CAPITOL... 3-4   90
COLUMBIA 3-5   79-88
MONUMENT 3-5   73-78
UNIVERSAL.................................... 3-4   89
LPs: 10/12–inch 33rpm
COLUMBIA 5-10   79-86
HITSVILLE 5-10   76
MONUMENT 5-10   74-78
SWORD & SHIELD (9009 "The Old Country
  Church")................................. 25-50   61
  (By the Gatlin Quartet, which included sister
  Donna.)

Members: Larry Gatlin; Steve Gatlin; Rudy Gatlin.
  Also see EARWOOD, Mundo
  Also see NELSON, Willie
  Also see SHEPPARD, T.G.

GATLIN, Larry, & Janie Frickie   *C&W '87*
(With the Gatlin Brothers)
Singles: 7–inch
COLUMBIA 3-4   87
  Also see FRICKE, Janie

GAULT, Lenny   *C&W '78*
Singles: 7–inch
KING COAL 3-5   79
MRC...3-5   78-79

GAYLE, Crystal   *C&W '70*
Singles: 7–inch
COLUMBIA 3-5   79-82
DECCA 4-6   70-72
ELEKTRA..3-4   82
MCA...3-4   77
U.A...3-5   74-80
W.B..3-4   83-90
Picture Sleeves
COLUMBIA 3-5   79-82
U.A...4-8   77
LPs: 10/12–inch 33rpm
COLUMBIA 5-10   79-83
ELEKTRA......................................5-10   82
LIBERTY 5-10   80-82
MCA...5-10   78
MFSL (043 "We Must Believe in
  Magic")......................................20-40   80
U.A. (Except "Somebody Loves You" picture
  disc")..5-10   75-80
U.A. ("Somebody Loves
  You").......................................75-100   78
  (Picture disc. Promotional issue only. One of
  a four-artist, four-LP set.)
W.B..5-10   83-90
  Also see CAMPBELL, Glen / Anne Murray / Kenny
   Rogers / Crystal Gayle
  Also see BUTLER, Larry, & Friends
  Also see RABBITT, Eddie, & Crystal Gayle

GAYLE, Crystal, & Gary Morris   *C&W '88*
Singles: 7–inch
W.B. 3-4   85-88
  Also see MORRIS, Gary

GAYLE, Crystal, & Tom Waits

LPs: 10/12–inch 33rpm

COLUMBIA 5-10   82
   Also see GAYLE, Crystal
   Also see WAITS, Tom

GEEZINSLAW BROTHERS

C&W '66

Singles: 7–inch

CAPITOL............................. 4-6   66-67
COLUMBIA 4-8   63

LP: 10/12–inch 33rpm

CAPITOL.................................. 10-15   66-67
COLUMBIA 15-20   63
LONE STAR................................ 8-12   79

GENTRY, Bobbie

P&R/C&W/R&B/LP '67

Singles: 7–inch

BRUNSWICK 3-5   75
CAPITOL..................................... 3-6   67-76
W.B. 3-5   76-78

Picture Sleeves

CAPITOL..................................... 3-6   67-72
W.B. 3-5   76

LPs: 10/12–inch 33rpm

CAPITOL (Except "SM" series)... 8-15   67-71
CAPITOL ("SM" series)............... 5-10   81
W.B. ("*Ode to Billie Joe:* Radio Salute to
   Bobbie Gentry")........................ 15-20   76
   (Promotional issue only.)
   Also see CAMPBELL, Glen, & Bobbie Gentry
   Also see REYNOLDS, Jody, & Bobbie Gentry

GENTRY, Gary

C&W '81

Singles: 7–inch

ELEKTRA...................................... 3-4   81

**GEORGE & GENE: see JONES, George, &
Gene Pitney**

GEORGE & LOUIS

(George & Louis / Jerry Lee Lewis)
Singles: 7–inch

SUN (301 "Return of Jerry Lee"/"Lewis
   Boogie") 15-20   58
   (*Lewis Boogie* is by Jerry Lee Lewis.)
SUN (301 "Return of Jerry Lee Part
   1"/"Return of Jerry Lee Part 2")10-15   58
   Member: George Klein.
   Also see LEWIS, Jerry Lee

GIBBS, Terri

C&W '80

Singles: 7–inch

HORIZON...................................... 3-4   87

MCA...................................... 3-4   80-83
TEM 3-4   82
W.B. 3-4   85

LPs: 10/12–inch 33rpm

HORIZON 5-8   87
MCA 5-10   81-83
PHONORAMA 5-10   84
W.B. 5-8   85
   Also see MATTEA, Kathy

GIBSON, Don

C&W '56

Singles: 78rpm

COLUMBIA 5-10   52-54
MGM 15-35   55-56
RCA 8-12   51

Singles: 7–inch

ABC/HICKORY 3-5   75-78
COLUMBIA (20000 series)........8-15   52-54
HICKORY.................................3-5   70-72
MCA 3-5   79
MGM (12109 "Run Boy") 15-25   55
MGM (12194 "Sweet Dreams")..15-25   56
MGM (12290 "I Ain't Gonna Waste My
   Time")..................................20-30   56
MGM (12331 "I Believed in
   You").....................................15-25   56
MGM (12393 "I'm Gonna Fool
   Everybody") 20-30   57
MGM (12494 "I Ain't a-Studing You
   Baby") 25-35   57
RCA (0400 series) 10-20   51
RCA (4300 & 4400 series).........10-20   51-52
RCA (7000 series, except 7762)..8-15   58-61
RCA (47-7762 "Legend in My
   Time") 6-10   60
   (Monaural.)
RCA (61-7762 "Legend in My
   Time") 15-20   60
   (Stereo.)
RCA (8000 & 9000 series).............4-8   62-70
W.B./CURB....................................3-4   80

Picture Sleeves

RCA 5-10   63

EPs: 7–inch 33/45rpm

COLUMBIA 15-20   57
RCA 10-20   58-59

LPs: 10/12–inch 33rpm

ABC/HICKORY 6-10   75-78
CAMDEN 10-15   65-74
HARMONY (7300 series) 15-20   65
HARMONY (31000 series) 5-10   72
HICKORY.................................8-12   70-72

HICKORY/MGM 6-10   73-75
LION (70069 "Songs by Don
   Gibson") 25-50   58
MGM 8-12   70
METRO 12-18   65
RCA (1743 thru 2878) 15-30   58-63
   (With "LPM" prefix. Monaural.)
RCA (1743 thru 2878) 20-40   58-63
   (With "LSP" prefix. Stereo.)
RCA (3376 thru 4378) 10-20   63-70
   (With "LPM" or "LSP" prefix.)
   Session: Jordanaires.
   Also see JORDANAIRES
   Also see WEST, Dottie, & Don Gibson

GIBSON, Don, & Sue Thompson   *C&W '71*
   Singles: 7–inch
HICKORY 3-5   71-76
   LPs: 10/12–inch 33rpm
HICKORY 8-12   73
HICKORY/MGM 5-10   75
   Also see GIBSON, Don
   Also see THOMPSON, Sue

GIBSON, Hal   *C&W '89*
   Singles: 7–inch
SUNDIAL 3-4   89

GILL, Vince   *C&W '84*
   Singles: 7–inch
MCA 3-4   89-91
RCA 3-4   84-89
   LPs: 10/12–inch 33rpm
MCA 5-8   90-91
RCA 5-8   84-89
   Also see PURE PRAIRIE LEAGUE
   Also see TOMORROW'S WORLD

GILLETTE, Steve, & Jennifer Warnes   *C&W '80*
   Singles: 7–inch
REGENCY 3-5   80
   LP: 10/12–inch 33rpm
REGENCY 5-10   80

GILLEY, Mickey   *C&W '68*
(With the Urban Cowboy Band)
   Singles: 7–inch
ACT 1 4-8   66
ASYLUM 3-4   80
ASTRO (Except 100 series) 3-5   71-73
ASTRO (100 series) 10-20   63-65
DARYL 4-8   63
DOT (15706 "Call Me Shorty") .. 50-75   58

EPIC 3-4   78-86
ERIC 4-6   64
GOLDBAND 4-8   64
GRT 3-5   70
KHOURY'S (712 "Drive-In
   Movie") 15-20   59
LYNN 10-20   60-61
MINOR (106 "Ooh Wee") 60-80   57
PAULA (Except 400 series) 4-6   66-68
PAULA (400 series) 3-5   74-84
PLAYBOY 3-5   74-77
POTOMAC 10-15   60
PRINCESS 8-12   62
RESCO 3-5   74
REX (1007 "Grapevine") 20-25   58
SABRA 10-15   61
SAN 10-15   63
SUPREME 8-12   62
TCF HALL 4-8   65
   LPs: 10/12–inch 33rpm
ASTRO (Except 101) 8-10   73-78
ASTRO (101 "Lonely Wine") 75-150   64
EPIC 5-10   79-86
PAULA (Except 2000 series) 5-10   81
PAULA (2195 "Down the Line") 20-25   67
PAULA (2224 "Mickey Gilley at His
   Best") 10-12   74
PAULA (2234 "Mickey Gilley") 8-10   78
PLAYBOY 8-12   74-78
   Also see CHARLES, Ray, & Mickey Gilley
   Also see HAGGARD, Merle / Mickey Gilley / Willie
   Knight

GILLEY, Mickey, & Barbi Benton   *C&W '75*
   Singles: 7–inch
PLAYBOY 3-5   75
   Picture Sleeves
PLAYBOY 3-5   75
   Also see BENTON, Barbi

GILLEY, Mickey, & Johnny Lee
   Singles: 7–inch
EPIC 3-4   81
   Also see LEE, Johnny
   Also see NELSON, Willie / Johnny Lee / Mickey Gilley

GILLEY, Mickey, & Charly McClain   *C&W '84*
(Charly McClain & Mickey Gilley)
   Singles: 7–inch
EPIC 3-4   83-84

LP: 10/12–inch 33rpm

EPIC..5-8   84
  Also see GILLEY, Mickey

GILMORE, Jimmie Dale   *C&W '88*
Singles: 7–inch

HIGHTONE.....................................3-4   88-89

GIRLS NEXT DOOR   *C&W '86*
Singles: 7–inch

ATLANTIC......................................3-4   89-90
MTM...3-4   86-88

GLASER, Chuck   *C&W '74*
Singles: 7–inch

MGM 3-5   74
  Also see EARWOOD, Mundo
  Also see TOMPALL & GLASER BROS.

GLASER, Jim   *C&W '68*
(Jim Glaser Singers)
Singles: 7–inch

MCA 3-5   76-86
MGM 3-5   73-75
NOBLE VISION..............................3-4   82-84
RCA...4-6   68-69
LP: 10/12–inch 33rpm

MCA 5-8   86
NOBEL VISION..............................5-8   84
STARDAY (149 "Old Time Christmas
  Singing").................................50-75   60
STARDAY (158 "Just Looking for a
  Home")....................................40-60   61
WYNCOTE (9069 "Country
  Spectacular")..........................10-20   64
  Also see EARWOOD, Mundo
  Also see TOMPALL & GLASER BROS.

GLASER, Tompall   *C&W '73*
(With His Outlaw Band)
Singles: 7–inch

ABC..3-5   77-78
MGM 3-5   73-75
POLYDOR.......................................3-5   76
LPs: 10/12–inch 33rpm

ABC..8-10   77
MGM 8-12   73-76
U.A. 25-35   66
  Also see EARWOOD, Mundo
  Also see TOMPALL & GLASER BROS.

GLENN, Darrell   *C&W/P&R '53*
Singles: 78rpm

DOT...3-6   56
RCA...3-6   54
VALLEY..4-8   53

Singles: 7–inch

COLUMBIA.....................................3-6   66-67
DOT 10-15   56
FASHION...5-10   60
LONGHORN 4-8   65
NRC..8-12   58
POMPEII..3-6   68-69
RCA..5-10   54
ROBBIE 3-6   64
TWINKLE (505 "That's Right") ...30-50
VALLEY...8-12   53
LPs: 10/12–inch 33rpm

NRC (5 "Crying in the Chapel")..15-25   59

GLENN, Howdy   *C&W '77*
Singles: 7–inch

W.B. 3-5   77-78

GODFREY, Ray   *C&W '60*
Singles: 7–inch

ABC...4-8   67
COLUMBIA......................................4-8   67
J&J (001 "The Picture").............10-15   60
PEACH...10-15   62
SAVOY..5-10   62
SIMS 4-8   62-63
SPRING...4-6   70
TOLLIE..5-10   65
YONAH 5-10   61

GOLDEN, Jeff   *C&W '88*
Singles: 7–inch

MGA..3-4   88-89
SOUNDWAVES..............................3-4   89

GOLDEN, William Lee   *C&W '86*
Singles: 7–inch

MCA..3-4   86
  Also see OAK RIDGE BOYS
  Also see TOMORROW'S WORLD

GOLDENS   *C&W '88*
Singles: 7–inch

EPIC..3-4   88
  Members: Chris Golden; Rusty Golden.
  Also see BOYS BAND
  Also see CEDAR CREEK
  Also see TOMORROW'S WORLD

GOLDSBORO, Bobby

P&R '62/C&W '68
Singles: 7–inch

CURB...3-4   80-82
EPIC..3-5   77
LAURIE..5-8   62-63

U.A. (Except 672 thru 980)............ 4-6   66-73
U.A. (672 thru 980)........................ 5-8   63-66
VISTA... 3-5   74

Picture Sleeves

U.A. (Except 710)......................... 4-8   66-74
U.A. (710 "Whenever He Holds
  You") 8-12   64

LPs: 10/12–inch 33rpm

CURB.. 5-10   80-82
DORAL.. 15-25
  (Promotional mail-order issue, from Doral
  cigarettes.)
EPIC.. 8-10   77
K-TEL 5-10
LIBERTY 5-10   81
SUNSET.. 8-12   60s
U.A. 10-20   64-76
  Also see ORBISON, Roy
  Also see REEVES, Del, & Bobby Goldsboro

GOLDSBORO, Bobby / Jimmy Durante
Singles: 7–inch

LIGHT (608 "We Gotta Start
  Lovin") 4-8   71
  Also see GOLDSBORO, Bobby

GOODNIGHT, Gary   *C&W '80*
Singles: 7–inch

DOOR KNOB 5-10   80-82
SOUNDWAVES 3-4   82

LPs: 10/12–inch 33rpm

DOOR KNOB 5-10   81

GOODSON, C.L.   *C&W '75*
Singles: 7–inch

ISLAND 3-5   75

GOODSON, Lloyd   *C&W '76*
Singles: 7–inch

U.A. 3-4   76

GOODSON, Mitch   *C&W '80*
Singles: 7–inch

PARTRIDGE 3-4   80

GOODWIN, Bill   *C&W '63*
Singles: 7–inch

BAND BOX..................................... 4-8   62
VEE JAY 4-8   63

GORDON, Luke   *C&W '58*
Singles: 7–inch

ISLAND 5-10   58
NASHVILLE 4-6

LP: 10/12–inch 33rpm

L&C.. 5-10
MOUNT VERNON 5-10

GORDON, Robert
(With Link Wray)   *P&R/LP '77/C&W '79*
Singles: 12–inch 33/45rpm

PRIVATE STOCK 10-15   78
RCA 8-12   81
  (Promotional issue only.)

Singles: 7–inch

PRIVATE STOCK 4-6   77-78
RCA (Black vinyl) 3-5   79-81
RCA (Colored vinyl) 8-12   79-81
  (Promotional issue only.)

Picture Sleeves

PRIVATE STOCK (45203 "Fire") .5-10   79
RCA (11471 "It's Only Make
  Believe").................................... 5-10   79

LPs: 10/12–inch 33rpm

PRIVATE STOCK 8-10   77-78
RCA (Black vinyl) 5-10   79-82
RCA (Colored vinyl) 20-30   79

Promotional LPs

RCA (3411 "Robert Gordon"/"Live from
  Paradise in Boston") 35-45   79

GORME, Eydie   *P&R '54/C&W '73*
Singles: 78rpm

ABC-PAR....................................... 3-5   55-62

Singles: 7–inch

ABC-PAR....................................... 4-8   55-62
CALENDAR 3-6   67
COLUMBIA 3-8   62-68
  (Black vinyl.)
COLUMBIA (43082 "I Want You to Be My
  Baby")....................................... 5-10   64
  (Colored vinyl.)
CORAL.. 5-10   53-55
GALA 3-5   76
MGM 3-5   71-73
RCA 3-5   69-70
U.A. 3-6   60-76

Picture Sleeves

COLUMBIA 4-8   62-63

LPs: 10/12–inch 33rpm

ABC-PAR...................................... 15-25   57-65
APPLAUSE..................................... 4-6   81
COLUMBIA 10-20   63-73
GALA 5-8   76
HARMONY...................................... 5-10   68-71
MGM 5-10   71

RCA............................... 5-10 68-70
U.A. 10-20 61-62
VOCALION..................................... 8-15 63

GORME, Eydie, & Steve Lawrence
(Steve & Eydie) **P&R '63**
Singles: 78rpm
CORAL.. 5-10 55
Singles: 7–inch
CALENDAR................................. 4-6 68
COLUMBIA 4-8 62-67
CORAL.. 5-10 55
MGM 3-5 72-73
RCA... 3-5 68-69
EPs: 7–inch 33/45rpm
ABC 5-10 60
(Jukebox issues only.)
ADVERTISING COUNCIL (5071 "Celebrity
Spots") 15-30
(Promotional issue, with other artists.)
COLUMBIA 5-10 64-69
(Jukebox issues only.)
CORAL.. 10-15 58
LPs: 10/12–inch 33rpm
ABC 5-10 73-76
ABC/LONGINES ("Romantic
Treasury") 30-45 67
(Six-LP boxed set.)
ABC-PAR 15-25 59-64
CBS... 10-15 63
CALENDAR................................. 8-15 68
COLUMBIA 10-20 63-67
CORAL (57336 "Steve &
Eydie")........................... 15-25 60
ENCORE...................................... 5-8 84
HARMONY.................................. 5-10 64-71
MCA 5-10
MGM 5-10 72-73
MATI-MOR (8003 "It's Us
Again") 10-15
(Promotional issue made for Silvikrin
Shampoo.)
PICKWICK 5-10 70s
RCA... 6-12 69-72
STAGE 2 .... 5-10 78-84
U.A. 10-20 61-62
VOCALION................................. 5-12 67
Also see GORME, Eydie

GOSDIN, Rex *C&W '79*
Singles: 7–inch
GRAPE VINE 3-5 80
MRC... 3-5 79

SUN 3-4 83
Also see GOSDIN BROTHERS

GOSDIN, Rex, & Tommy
Jennings *C&W '80*
Singles: 7–inch
SABRE.. 3-5 80
Also see GOSDIN, Rex
Also see JENNINGS, Tommy

GOSDIN, Vern *C&W '76*
Singles: 7–inch
AMI.. 3-4 82-83
COLUMBIA 3-4 87-91
COMPLEAT 3-4 83-86
ELEKTRA.................................... 3-5 76-79
OVATION..................................... 3-5 81
LP: 10/12–inch 33rpm
AMI.. 5-10 83
COLUMBIA 3-4 87-91
COMPLEAT 5-10 83-84
ELEKTRA.................................... 5-10 76-79
OVATION..................................... 5-8 81
PHONORAMA 5-10 84
Session: Curtis Wright; Janie Fricke; Emmylou Harris;
Roger McGuinn.
Also see FRICKE, Janie
Also see GOSDIN BROTHERS
Also see HARRIS, Emmylou
Also see TUBB, Ernest
Also see WRIGHT, Curtis

GOSDIN BROTHERS *C&W '67*
Singles: 7–inch
BAKERSFIELD INT'L.................... 4-6 67
LP: 10/12–inch 33rpm
CAPITOL.................................... 10-15 68
Members: Vern Gosdin; Rex Gosdin.
Also see GOSDIN, Rex
Also see GOSDIN, Vern

GRADDOCK, Billy: see CRADDOCK, Billy

GRAMMER, Billy

P&R/R&B '58/C&W '59
Singles: 7–inch
DECCA 4-8 61-66
EPIC.. 4-6 66-67
EVEREST 5-8 60
MERCURY................................... 3-6 68-69
MONUMENT (Except 400 series)..3-5 75-76
MONUMENT (400 series)...........5-10 59-63
RICE 4-6 67
STOP 3-5 69
EPs: 7–inch 33/45rpm
DECCA 5-10 64

LPs: 10/12–inch 33rpm		
CLASSIC CHRISTMAS...............	5-10	77
DECCA....................................	10-15	62-64
EPIC.......................................	8-12	67
MONUMENT (4000 "Travelin' On").....................................	15-20	59
(With *Lost in a Small Cafe*.)		
MONUMENT (8039 "Travelin' On").....................................	8-12	66
(*Lost in a Small Cafe* is replaced with *Gotta Travel On*.)		
SKYLITE	5-8	
STONEWAY.............................	5-10	75
VOCALION..............................	6-12	68

Also see CASH, Johnny / Billy Grammer / Wilburn
Brothers
Also see TUBB, Ernest

GRAMMER, Billy / Judy Lynn / Link Wray

LP: 10/12–inch 33rpm

GUEST STAR	10-15	60s

Also see GRAMMER, Billy
Also see JUDY LYNN

GRANT, Al
(Al Cernick)
Singles: 78rpm

KING (15004 thru 15045)..........	10-20	49-50

Also see MITCHELL, Guy

GRANT, Barry   *C&W '79*
Singles: 7–inch

CSI	3-5	79-80

Also see AMARILLO
Also see BREAKFAST BARRY

GRANT, Tom   *C&W '79*
Singles: 7–inch

ELEKTRA....................................	3-4	82
REPUBLIC	3-5	79

Also see SMITH, Margo, & Tom Grant

GRANT, Tom   *R&B '81*
Singles: 7–inch

WMOT......................................	3-5	81

GRAY, Claude   *C&W '60*
(With the Graymen)
Singles: 7–inch

COLUMBIA	4-6	64-66
COUNTRY INT'L...........................	3-4	81-86
D...	5-10	59-60
DECCA....................................	3-6	66-71
GRANNY WHITE	3-5	76-82
MERCURY	4-8	60-64
MILLION....................................	3-5	72-73

LPs: 10/12–inch 33rpm		
DECCA.................................8-12		67-68
MERCURY................................15-25		62
MILLION.................................5-10		72
PICKWICK/HILLTOP 8-12		67

GRAY, Claude, & Norma Jean   *C&W '82*
Singles: 7–inch

GRANNY WHITE...........................3-4		82

Also see GRAY, Claude
Also see NORMA JEAN

GRAY, Dobie   *P&R '63/C&W '86*
Singles: 12–inch 33/45rpm

INFINITY 5-8		79

Singles: 7–inch

ARISTA.......................................3-4		83
CAPITOL (Except 5853) 3-4		86
CAPITOL (5853 "River Deep, Mountain High")...................................5-8		67
CAPRICORN 3-5		76-77
CHARGER 4-8		64-66
COLLECTABLES...........................3-4		81
CORDAK......................................5-10		62-64
DECCA......................................3-5		73
ERIC 3-4		70s
GUSTO 3-4		85
INFINITY......................................3-5		78-79
JAF..4-8		63
MCA..3-4		73-75
REAL FINE 8-12		62
ROBOX......................................3-4		81
STRIPE.....................................8-12		60-61
WHITE WHALE (300 "Rose Garden") 4-8		69
WHITE WHALE (330 "What a Way to Go")..............................100-200		69
WHITE WHALE (342 "Honey, You Can't Take It Back") 25-50		70

LPs: 10/12–inch 33rpm		
CAPITOL....................................5-10		86
CAPRICORN 8-10		76
CHARGER 15-20		65
DECCA......................................8-10		73
INFINITY....................................6-10		79
MCA..8-10		73-74
ROBOX......................................5-10		81
STRIPE.....................................10-12		

GRAY, Jan   *C&W '80*
Singles: 7–inch

CYPRESS....................................3-4		86

JAMEX 3-4   82-84
PAID 3-5   80

GRAY, Mark   *C&W '83*
Singles: 7–inch
COLUMBIA 3-4   83-86

GRAY, Mark, & Bobbi Lace   *C&W '88*
Singles: 7–inch
615 3-4   88
  Also see LACE, Bobbi

GRAY, Mark, & Tammy Wynette   *C&W '85*
Singles: 7–inch
COLUMBIA 3-4   85
615 3-4   88
  Also see GRAY, Mark
  Also see WYNETTE, Tammy

GRAYGHOST   *C&W '89*
Singles: 7–inch
MERCURY 3-4   89
  Also see RAZORBACK

GRAYSON, Jack   *C&W '79*
(With Blackjack; "Blackjack" Jack Grayson; Jack Lebsock)
Singles: 7–inch
AMI 3-4   83-84
CHURCHILL 3-5   79
HITBOUND 3-5   79-80
JOE-WES 3-4   82
KOALA 3-4   80-81
LP: 10/12–inch 33rpm
JOE-WES 5-8   82
  Also see LEBSOCK, Jack

GRAYSON, Kim   *C&W '87*
Singles: 7–inch
SOUNDWAVES 3-4   87-88
Picture Sleeves
SOUNDWAVES 3-4   87

GREAT PLAINS   *C&W '91*
Singles: 7–inch
COLUMBIA 3-4   91
  Members: Michael Young; Russ Pahl; Denny Dadmum-Bixby.
  Also see JOHNSON, Michael

GREEN, Bill   *C&W '76*
Singles: 7–inch
PHONO 3-5   76
NSD 3-5   78

GREEN, Jerry   *C&W '77*
Singles: 7–inch
CONCORDE 3-5   77

GREEN, Lloyd   *C&W '73*
Singles: 7–inch
MONUMENT 3-5   73
OCTOBER 3-5   76
SOUNDWAVES 3-5   77

GREEN RIVER BOYS: see CAMPBELL, Glen

GREENE, Jack   *C&W '65*
(With the Jolly Green Giants)
Singles: 7–inch
DECCA 3-8   65-72
EMH 3-4   83-84
FRONTLINE 3-5   80
MCA 3-5   73-74
LPs: 10/12–inch 33rpm
CORAL 4-8   73
DECCA 8-18 66-71
EMH 5-10   80
51 WEST 5-10   84
FRONTLINE 5-10   80
GUSTO 5-10   83
HILLTOP/PICKWICK 5-10   83
MCA 5-10   73
PICKWICK 5-10   70s
VOCALION 5-10   72
  Also see COCHRAN, Hank

GREENE, Jack, & Jeannie Seely   *C&W '72*
Singles: 7–inch
DECCA 3-5   69-72
LPs: 10/12–inch 33rpm
DECCA 8-12 70-72
GUSTO 5-8
MCA 4-6   73
PINNACLE 5-10   78
RDS 5-10   79
  Also see GREENE, Jack
  Also see SEELY, Jeannie

GREENE, Lorne   *P&R/C&W/LP '64*
Singles: 7–inch
COLUMBIA 3-6   69
GRT 3-5   70-71
RCA 4-8   62-66
Picture Sleeves
RCA 5-10 63-65

LPs: 10/12–inch 33rpm

CAMDEN	5-10	70
MGM	5-10	71
RCA	10-20	63-66

GREENWOOD, Lee   *C&W '81*
(Lee Greenwood Affair)
Singles: 7–inch

DOT	3-6	69
MCA	3-4	81-88
PARAMOUNT	3-5	71

Picture Sleeves

MCA	3-4	83

LPs: 10/12–inch 33rpm

MCA (Except 5305)	5-10	83-88
MCA (5305 "Inside and Out")	10-15	82
(Slightly incorrect title used.)		
MCA (5305 "Inside Out")	5-10	82
(Title corrected.)		

Also see MANDRELL, Barbara, & Lee Greenwood

GREGORY, Terry   *C&W '81*
Singles: 7–inch

HANDSHAKE	3-5	81-82
SCOTTI BROTHERS	3-4	84-85

GRIFF, Ray   *C&W '67*
Singles: 7–inch

ABC/DOT	3-5	75
CAPITOL	3-5	75-77
DOT	3-6	68-74
MGM	4-6	67
RCA	3-4	83-86
ROYAL AMERICAN	3-5	70-72
VISION	3-4	81-82

LP: 10/12–inch 33rpm

ABC/DOT	8-12	74
DOT	8-12	73
BOOT	5-10	79-81
CAPITOL	6-12	76
DOT	8-15	68-73
ROYAL AMERICAN	8-12	72

GRIFFITH, Andy   *P&R '54*
(Deacon Andy Griffith)
Singles: 78rpm

CAPITOL	5-15	53-57

Singles: 7–inch

CAPITOL (2500 series)	4-6	69
CAPITOL (2600 thru 3600 series)	10-20	53-57
CAPITOL (4000 & 5000 series)	4-8	59-63
(Purple or orange/yellow swirl labels.)		

CAPITOL (4000 series)	3-5	76
(Orange labels.)		
COLONIAL ("What It Was—Was Football")	15-25	53
(Number not known.)		
COLUMBIA	5-10	72

EPs: 7–inch 33/45rpm

CAPITOL	20-30	54-61

LPs: 10/12–inch 33rpm

CAPITOL (872 "A Face in the Crowd")	35-50	57
(Soundtrack.)		
CAPITOL (962 "Just for Laughs")	35-45	58
CAPITOL (1100 thru 1600 series)	30-40	59-61
CAPITOL (2000 series)	15-25	64-67
COLUMBIA	5-10	72

GRIFFITH, Glenda   *C&W '78*
Singles: 7–inch

ARIOLA AMERICA	3-5	78

GRIFFITH, Nanci   *C&W '86*
Singles: 7–inch

B.F. DEAL	4-8	77
MCA	3-4	87-91
PHILO	3-5	86

LPs: 10/12–inch 33rpm

MCA	5-8	89-91

GROCE, Larry   *P&R/C&W/LP '76*
Singles: 7–inch

PEACEABLE	3-5	75
W.B.	3-5	75

LPs: 10/12–inch 33rpm

DAYBREAK	8-10	71-72
W.B.	8-10	76

GROOMS, Sherry   *C&W '77*
Singles: 7–inch

ABC (10875 "Night Fall")	15-25	67
PARACHUTE	3-5	78

Also see STEVENS, Even, & Sherry Grooms

GROVES, Edgel   *C&W '81*
Singles: 7–inch

SILVER STAR	3-4	81

GUESS WHO   *P&R '65*
Singles: 7–inch

AMY	10-20	67
FONTANA	10-15	69
HILLTAK	3-5	78-79

QUALITY	10-20	65-68
(Canadian.)		
RCA	3-6	69-76
RCA RECORDING SERVICES (55829 "Two Wheel Freedom")	4-8	
SCEPTER (1295 "Shakin' All Over")	8-12	65
SCEPTER (12000 series)	10-20	65-66

Picture Sleeves

RCA	8-12	70

LPs: 10/12–inch 33rpm

HILLTAK	5-10	79
MGM	12-15	69
PICKWICK	8-10	72
PIP	8-10	71
PRIDE	8-10	73
RCA (Except "AYL1" & LSP-4000 series)	8-12	73-80
RCA ("AYL1" series)	5-10	80
RCA (4141 thru 4830)	12-25	69-72
RCA (1000 "Best of the Guess Who")	10-20	71
(With bonus, black light poster.)		
RCA (1000 "Best of the Guess Who")	8-12	71
(Without poster.)		
SCEPTER	8-10	73
SPRINGBOARD	8-10	72
WAND	12-15	69

Members: Chad Allen; Burton Cummings; Randy Bachman; Domenic Troiano.
Also see CUMMINGS, Burton

GUESS WHO / Discotays
Singles: 7–inch

SCEPTER (1295 "Shakin' All Over")	15-20	65

Also see GUESS WHO

GUITAR, Bonnie   *C&W/P&R '57*
Singles: 78rpm

DOT	10-15	57
FABOR (Except 4018)	5-10	55-56
FABOR (4018 "Dark Moon")	15-25	57
4 STAR	5-10	56

Singles: 7–inch

ABC	3-5	74
CHARTER	4-6	
COLUMBIA	3-5	72
DOLTON	5-10	59
DOT (15000 series)	8-15	57-59
DOT (16000 & 17000 series)	4-6	66-69
FABOR (138 "Ra Ta Ta Ta")	4-8	64

FABOR (4013 "If You See My Love Dancing")	10-20	55
FABOR (4017 "Clinging Vine")	10-20	56
FABOR (4018 "Dark Moon")	20-30	57
4 STAR (1003 "Honey on the Moon")	3-5	80
4 STAR (1006 "I Want to Spend My Life with You")	10-20	56
JERDEN	5-10	63
MCA	3-5	74
PARAMOUNT	3-5	70
PLAYBACK	3-4	89
RCA	10-20	61-62
RADIO	5-10	58

LPs: 10/12–inch 33rpm

CAMDEN	6-12	69
DOT (Except 3069 & 3385)	10-15	59-68
DOT (3069 "Moonlight and Shadows")	15-25	57
DOT (3385 "Dark Moon")	15-20	63
HAMILTON	8-12	65
PARAMOUNT	8-12	70
PICKWICK	6-12	70

Also see BONNIE & BUDDY
Also see ECHOES

GUNN, J.W.   *C&W '82*
Singles: 7–inch

PRIMERO	3-5	82

GURLEY, Randy   *C&W '78*
Singles: 7–inch

ABC	3-5	78
RCA	3-5	79

LP: 10/12–inch 33rpm

ABC	8-10	78

GUTHRIE, Jack   *C&W '45*
Singles: 78rpm

CAPITOL	10-20	45-47

LP: 10/12–inch 33rpm

CAPITOL (2456 "Greatest Songs")	25-35	66

GUY & RALNA   *C&W '75*
Singles: 7–inch

RANWOOD	3-5	75

LP: 10/12–inch 33rpm

BIRCHWOOD	5-10	
RANWOOD	5-10	75

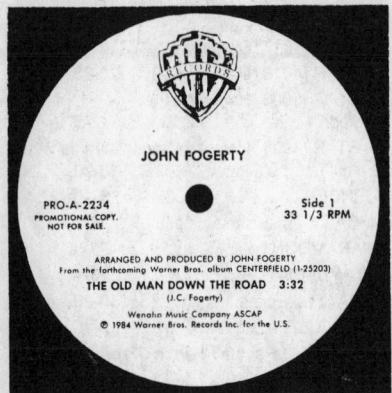

JOHN FOGERTY

PRO-A-2234
PROMOTIONAL COPY.
NOT FOR SALE.

Side 1
33 1/3 RPM

ARRANGED AND PRODUCED BY JOHN FOGERTY
From the forthcoming Warner Bros. album CENTERFIELD (1-25203)

THE OLD MAN DOWN THE ROAD 3:32
(J.C. Fogerty)

Wenaha Music Company ASCAP
℗ 1984 Warner Bros. Records Inc. for the U.S.

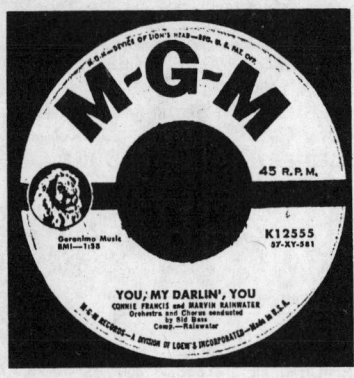

M-G-M

45 R.P.M.

Geronimo Music
BMI—1:58

57-XY-581

K12555

YOU; MY DARLIN', YOU
CONNIE FRANCIS and MARVIN RAINWATER
Orchestra and Chorus conducted
by Sid Bass
Comp.—Rainwater

DUNCAN
RECORDS

45-1000-B

Glad Music
BMI-2:35

HOLY ONE
(Freddie Fender)
FREDDIE FENDER
1000-B

DUNCAN RECORDING CO. • BOX 452 • HARLINGEN, TEXAS

COLUMBIA

NOT
FOR
RESALE

45
RPM

RADIO
STATION
COPY

LEFTY
FRIZZELL

4-42924
JZSP 76394
Pub: Tree Publ. Co.,
Inc. (BMI)

3:00

SAGINAW, MICHIGAN
- D. Wayne

Produced by Don Law and
Frank Jones

℗ 'COLUMBIA' MARCAS REG. PRINTED IN USA

SWORD &
SHIELD

S S

RECORD
CO.

THE GATLIN QUARTET

LMP-9009
Side One

Hi Fidelity
33 1/3 rpm

1. The Old Country Church (Vaughan 3:40) SESAC
2. It's Different Now (Beatty 2:05) SESAC
3. He Hideth My Soul
   (Kirkpatrick 2:47) PD
4. Then I Met The Master
   (Lister 2:35) SESAC
5. Eastern Gate (Doan 2:40) SESAC
6. Crossing Chilly Jordan
   (Bumer 1:35) SESAC

N8OP-2625

HADDOCK, Durwood   *C&W '74*
Singles: 7–inch

CAPRICE	3-5	74
COUNTRY INT'L	3-5	78-79
EAGLE INT'L	3-5	77-80
MONUMENT	3-6	68-69

HAGER, Charley   *C&W '89*
Singles: 7–inch

KILLER	3-4	89

HAGERS   *C&W '69*
Singles: 7–inch

CAPITOL	3-6	69-71
ELEKTRA	3-5	74

LP: 10/12–inch 33rpm

BARNABY	6-12	72
CAPITOL	8-15	70-71
ELEKTRA	6-12	74

Members: Jim Hager; John Hager.

HAGGARD, Marty   *C&W '81*
Singles: 7–inch

DIMENSION	3-5	81
MTM	3-4	86-88

Also see HAGGARD, Merle

HAGGARD, Merle   *C&W '63*
(With the Strangers)
Singles: 7–inch

CAPITOL	3-8	65-77
COLUMBIA	3-4	83
CURB	3-4	90
EPIC	3-4	81-89
MCA	3-5	77-85
MERCURY	3-4	83
TALLY	10-20	63-65

Picture Sleeves

CAPITOL	4-8	67-71
MCA	3-5	77-80

EPs: 7–inch 33/45rpm

CAPITOL	8-15	71

(Jukebox issues only.)

LPs: 10/12–inch 33rpm

ALBUM GLOBE (9005 "Melody Ranch Featuring Merle Haggard & Friends")	40-50	80s
CAPITOL (168 thru 735)	8-15	69-71
(With "T," "ST," "STBB" or "SWBB" prefix.)		
CAPITOL (168 thru 735)	4-8	69-71
(With "SKA0" or "SM" prefix.)		
CAPITOL (796 "Merle Haggard's Strangers and Friends Honky Tonkin'")	20-30	71
CAPITOL (803 "Land of Many Churches")	30-50	71
(With "SWBO" prefix.)		
CAPITOL (835 "Someday We'll Look Back")	8-12	71
CAPITOL (882 "Let Me Tell You About a Song")	8-12	72
CAPITOL (2373 thru 2972)	15-25	65-68
(With "T," "ST" or, in the case of 2951, an "SKAO" prefix.)		
CAPITOL (2702 thru 2972)	5-10	80s
(With "SM" prefix.)		
CAPITOL (11000 thru 16000 series)	5-10	72-82
EPIC	5-10	81-86
MCA	4-8	77-84
MERCURY	5-10	83
PICKWICK/HILLTOP	8-12	60s
RADIANT	5-10	81
RONCO	5-8	
SONGBIRD	5-10	81
SPARTON	30-60	
(Canadian.)		
TEE VEE	5-10	77

Session: Biff Adam; Norm Hamlet; Dennis Hromek; Roy Nichols; Bobby Wayne; Johnny Gimble; Jordanaires; James Burton; Marty Haggard; Ronnie Reno; Bonnie Owens; Carter Family.
Also see ANDERSON, John
Also see BANDY, Moe
Also see COCHRAN, Hank
Also see FRIZZELL, David
Also see HAGGARD, Marty
Also see JORDANAIRES
Also see MADDOX, Rose
Also see NASHVILLE SUPERPICKERS
Also see PAYCHECK & HAGGARD
Also see RENO, Ronnie
Also see TUBB, Ernest
Also see WAYNE, Bobby
Also see WILLS, Bob

HAGGARD, Merle / Patsy Cline
LPs: 10/12–inch 33rpm

OUT of TOWN DIST	5-10	82

Also see CLINE, Patsy

HAGGARD, Merle, & Clint Eastwood
C&W '80

Singles: 7–inch
ELEKTRA.. 3-4 80

Picture Sleeves
ELEKTRA.. 3-4 80
Also see EASTWOOD, Clint

HAGGARD, Merle, & Janie Fricke
C&W '84

Singles: 7–inch
EPIC... 3-4 84
Also see FRICKE, Janie

HAGGARD, Merle / Mickey Gilley / Willie Knight

LPs: 10/12–inch 33rpm
OUT of TOWN DIST 5-10 82
Also see GILLEY, Mickey

HAGGARD, Merle / Sonny James

LPs: 10/12–inch 33rpm
CAPITOL.................................... 10-15 60s
Also see JAMES, Sonny

HAGGARD, Merle, & George Jones
C&W/LP '82

(George Jones & Merle Haggard)

Singles: 7–inch
EPIC (03405 "C.C. Waterback") ... 3-4 82
EPIC (03405 "C.C. Waterback") ... 4-8 82
(Picture disc.)

LPs: 10/12–inch 33rpm
EPIC... 5-10 82
Also see JONES, George

HAGGARD, Merle, & Willie Nelson
C&W/LP '83

(Willie Nelson & Merle Haggard)

Singles: 7–inch
EPIC... 3-4 83-87

LPs: 10/12–inch 33rpm
EPIC... 5-10 83
Also see NELSON, Willie

HAGGARD, Merle, & Bonnie Owens
C&W '64

Singles: 7–inch
TALLY (181 "Just Between the Two of Us") 10-20 64

LP: 10/12–inch 33rpm
CAPITOL (2453 "Just Between the Two of Us") 20-30 66
Also see OWENS, Bonnie

HAGGARD, Merle, & Leona Williams
C&W '78

Singles: 7–inch
CAPITOL.................................... 3-5 78
MERCURY.................................. 3-4 83

LP: 10/12–inch 33rpm
MERCURY.................................. 5-10 83
Also see WILLIAMS, Leona

HALL, Buck
C&W '89

Singles: 7–inch
TRACK....................................... 3-4 89

HALL, Connie
C&W '60

Singles: 7–inch
DECCA 4-8 60-63
MERCURY.................................. 4-8 60

LP: 10/12–inch 33rpm
DECCA 15-25 62
VOCALION 10-20 65
Also see SKINNER, Jimmie

HALL, Rebecca
C&W '85

Singles: 7–inch
CAPITOL.................................... 3-4 85

HALL, Roy

(With His Cohutta Mountain Boys)

Singles: 78rpm
DECCA 15-25 56
FORTUNE.................................. 20-45 49-56
HI-Q 25-35 56

Singles: 7–inch
DECCA (29697 "Whole Lotta Shakin' Goin' On").. 30-40 55
DECCA (29786 "See You Later Alligator") 30-40 56
DECCA (29880 "Blue Suede Shoes").................................... 30-40 56
DECCA (30060 "Three Alley Cats")....................................... 30-40 56
FORTUNE (170 "Going Down That Road")...................................... 35-50 53
FORTUNE (521 "Corrine Corrina")................................... 35-50 56
HI-Q (5045 "Three Alley Cats")..40-60 56
PIERCE (1918 (One Monkey Don't Stop the Show") 75-125 50s
STRATE 8 (1508 "Rockin' the Blues") 20-30 50s
Also see DAVIS SISTERS / Roy Hall

HALL, Sammy   C&W '84

Singles: 7–inch

DREAM 3-4   84

HALL, Tom T.   C&W '67

(With the Storytellers)

Singles: 7–inch

MERCURY (Except 70000
  series) 3-5   77-86
MERCURY (70000 series)............ 3-8   67-77
RCA.. 3-5   77-81

LPs: 10/12–inch 33rpm

K-TEL 5-10   77
MERCURY (500 thru 1100
  series) 5-10   73-77
MERCURY (5000 thru 8000
  series) 5-10   78-84
MERCURY (61000 series).......... 8-15   69-71
MERCURY (80000 series).......... 5-10   83-86
OUT of TOWN DIST 5-10   82
RCA.. 5-10   78-81

Session: Johnny Rodriguez; Gary Sargeants.
Also see DUDLEY, Dave, & Tom T. Hall
Also see PAGE, Patti, & Tom T. Hall
Also see RODRIGUEZ, Johnny
Also see SARGEANTS, Gary

HALL, Tom T., & Earl Scruggs   C&W '82

Singles: 7–inch

COLUMBIA 3-4   82

LPs: 10/12–inch 33rpm

COLUMBIA 5-10   82

Also see FLATT, Lester, & Earl Scruggs
Also see HALL, Tom T.

HALLMAN, Victoria   C&W '87

Singles: 7–inch

EVERGREEN................................ 3-4   87

HALLMARK, Roger, & Thrasher Brothers   C&W '79

Singles: 7–inch

VULCAN....................................... 3-6   79

Also see THRASHER BROTHERS

HAMBLEN, Stuart   C&W '49

Singles: 78rpm

COLUMBIA 4-8   49-57

Singles: 7–inch

BLUEBIRD 5-10   59
COLUMBIA 5-10   50-62
CORAL.. 4-8   59
ELECTRADISK 25-50   30s

(Made for sale through Woolworth Stores.)

KAPP 4-8   66
LAMB & LION 3-5   74
RCA (0500 series) 3-5   71
RCA (5000 & 6000 series)...........5-15   54-56

EPs: 7–inch 33/45rpm

COLUMBIA 5-10   58-59
RCA 5-15   54-60

LPs: 10/12–inch 33rpm

CAMDEN 5-15   59-66
COLUMBIA 5-15   61-62
CORAL.....................................12-25   60
HURRAH 5-10
KAPP 15-20   66
LAMB & LION 5-8   74
RCA 15-30   54-57
SACRED 5-8
VOSS 10-15
WORD 5-8

HAMILTON, George, IV

(With the Country Gentlemen; with Arthur
Smith)   P&R '56/C&W '60

Singles: 78rpm

ABC-PAR 10-20   56-57
COLONIAL (420 "A Rose and a Baby
  Ruth")...................................30-40   56
COLONIAL (451 "Sam") 10-20   56

Singles: 7–inch

ABC...3-5   78
ABC/DOT 3-5   77
ABC-PAR (9000 series).............10-20   56-59
ABC-PAR (10000 series)............5-15   59-65
COLONIAL (420 "A Rose and a Baby
  Ruth")...................................50-75   56
COLONIAL (451 "Sam") 25-35   56
GRT 3-5   76
MCA 3-5   79-80
RCA 3-8   61-74

EPs: 7–inch 33/45rpm

ABC-PAR (220 "On Campus")...15-25   58

LPs: 10/12–inch 33rpm

ABC..8-10   72-77
ABC-PAR (ABC-220 "On
  Campus")................................20-40   58
  (Monaural.)
ABC-PAR (ABCS-220 "On
  Campus")................................25-50   58
  (Stereo.)
ABC-PAR (ABC-251 "Sing Me a Sad
  Song")...................................20-40   58
  (Monaural.)

ABC-PAR (ABCS-251 "Sing Me a Sad Song") 25-50   58
(Stereo.)

ABC-PAR (ABC-461 "Big 15")... 20-30   63
(Monaural.)

ABC-PAR (ABCS-461 "Big 15") 25-35   63
(Stereo.)

CAMDEN 8-10   68-73
GRAND AWARD 5-10
HARMONY 8-10   70
MCA 5-10   80
RCA ("APL1" series) 8-10   74-76
RCA ("LPM" & "LSP" series) 10-20   61-73

Also see ANKA, Paul, George Hamilton IV & Johnny Nash
Also see DAVIS, Skeeter, & George Hamilton IV
Also see SOME of CHET'S FRIENDS

HAMILTON, George, IV / Arthur Smith

LP: 10/12–inch 33rpm

LAMB & LION 5-8   74

Also see HAMILTON, George, IV
Also see SMITH, Arthur

HAMILTON, George, V   *C&W '88*

Singles: 7–inch

MTM 3-4   88

HAMILTON, Penny   *C&W '79*

Singles: 7–inch

DOOR KNOB 3-5   79

HANDY, Cheryl   *C&W '84*

Singles: 7–inch

AUDIOGRAPH 3-4   84
COMPLEAT 3-4   87
RCM 3-4   87

HANDY, John
(Gene Autry)

Singles: 78rpm

BENNETT (7290 "Hobo Bill's Last Ride") 25-75
BENNETT (7310 "Dust Pan Blues") 25-75
RADIEX 25-75

Also see AUTRY, Gene

HANKS, Kamryn   *C&W '89*

Singles: 7–inch

COUNTRY PRIDE 3-4   89

HANSON, Connie, & Friend   *C&W '82*
(With Darrell McCall)

Singles: 7–inch

SOUNDWAVES 3-4   82

Also see McCALL, Darrell

HARDEN, Arlene   *C&W '67*

Singles: 7–inch

CAPITOL 3-5   74-75
COLUMBIA 3-6   67-73
ELEKTRA 3-5   77-78

LPs: 10/12–inch 33rpm

CAPITOL 5-10   75
COLUMBIA 5-12   68-70

Also see ROBBINS, Marty

HARDEN, Arlene, & Bobby   *C&W '68*
(Hardens)

Singles: 7–inch

COLUMBIA 4-6   68

Also see HARDEN, Arlene
Also see HARDEN, Bobby
Also see HARDEN TRIO

HARDEN, Bobby   *C&W '75*

Singles: 7–inch

MEGA 3-5   70-71
U.A. 3-5   75

Picture Sleeves

MEGA 3-5   70

LPs: 10/12–inch 33rpm

STARDAY 6-12   69

Also see HARDEN TRIO

HARDEN, Robbie

Singles: 7–inch

PLANTATION 3-4   70

Also see HARDEN TRIO

HARDEN TRIO   *P&R/C&W/LP '66*

Singles: 7–inch

COLUMBIA 3-4   65-68
PAPA JOE 3-4   72

LPs: 10/12–inch 33rpm

COLUMBIA 10-15   66-68
HARMONY 8-12   70

Members: Arlene Harden; Bobby Harden; Robbie Harden. Session: Karen Wheeler.
Also see HARDEN, Arlene
Also see HARDEN, Bobby
Also see HARDEN, Robbie
Also see WHEELER, Karen

HARDIN, Gus   *C&W '83*
(Carolyn Ann Hardin)
Singles: 7–inch
RCA... 3-4   83-86
LP: 10/12–inch 33rpm
RCA (Except 1-8603)................... 5-10   83-84
RCA (1-8603 "Interview with Gus
   Hardin")..................................... 8-12   83
   (Promotional issue only.)

HARDIN, Gus, & Earl Thomas Conley   *C&W '84*
Singles: 7–inch
RCA... 3-4   84
   Also see CONLEY, Earl Thomas

HARDIN, Gus, & Dave Loggins   *C&W '85*
Singles: 7–inch
RCA... 3-4   85
   Also see HARDIN, Gus
   Also see LOGGINS, Dave

HARDING, Gayle   *C&W '78*
Singles: 7–inch
ROBCHRIS 3-5   78-79

HARDY, Johnny   *C&W '61*
Singles: 7–inch
ACE... 8-12   61
J&J 5-10   61

HARGROVE, Danny   *C&W '78*
Singles: 7–inch
50 STATES 3-5   78

HARGROVE, Linda   *C&W '74*
Singles: 7–inch
CAPITOL....................................... 3-5   75-77
ELEKTRA....................................... 3-5   74
RCA... 3-5   78
LP: 10/12–inch 33rpm
CAPITOL..................................... 5-10   75-77
ELEKTRA..................................... 5-10   73-74

HARLESS, Ogden   *C&W '87*
Singles: 7–inch
DOOR KNOB 3-4   87-88
MSC 3-4   88

HARMS, Joni   *C&W '89*
Singles: 7–inch
UNIVERSAL................................... 3-4   89

HARRELL & SCOTT   *C&W '89*
Singles: 7–inch
ASSOCIATED ARTISTS................3-4   89

HARRINGTON, Carly   *C&W '88*
Singles: 7–inch
OAK 3-4   88

HARRIS, Donna   *C&W '66*
Singles: 7–inch
ABC... 4-6   66

HARRIS, Emmylou   *C&W/P&R '75*
(With Her Hot Band; with Cheryl White & Sharon White)
Singles: 7–inch
JUBILEE 5-10   69-70
REPRISE (Except 1341)................ 3-5   75-77
REPRISE (1341 "Light of the
   Stable")..................................... 4-6   75
W.B. 3-5   77-86
Picture Sleeves
REPRISE 3-5   75-77
WARNER.. 3-4   80-86
LPs: 10/12–inch 33rpm
EMUS..10-20   79
JUBILEE (8031 "Gliding Bird")...60-80   69
MFSL (015 "Quarter Moon in a Ten-Cent
   Town")......................................30-40   78
REPRISE 8-10   75
W.B. 5-10   77-87
   Session: James Burton; Glen D. Hardin; Emory Gordy;
   Ronnie Tutt; Don Williams; Ricky Skaggs; Waylon
   Jennings; Sharon White; Willie Nelson; Johnny Cash.
   Also see ANDERSON, John
   Also see CASH, Johnny
   Also see CASH, Rosanne
   Also see CONLEY, Earl Thomas, & Emmylou Harris
   Also see CRICKETS
   Also see CROWELL, Rodney
   Also see DENVER, John, & Emmylou Harris
   Also see JENNINGS, Waylon
   Also see KENDALLS
   Also see LOUVIN, Charlie, & Emmylou Harris
   Also see MADDOX, Rose
   Also see NELSON, Willie
   Also see ORBISON, Roy, & Emmylou Harris / Craig
   Hundley
   Also see OWENS, Buck, & Emmylou Harris
   Also see PARTON, Dolly
   Also see PARTON, Dolly, Linda Ronstadt, & Emmylou
   Harris
   Also see PEDERSEN, Herb
   Also see PRESLEY, Elvis
   Also see RONSTADT, Linda, & Emmylou Harris
   Also see SHAVER, Billy Joe
   Also see SKAGGS, Ricky
   Also see SOUTHERN PACIFIC
   Also see STEWART, Gary
   Also see TUCKER, Tanya
   Also see WHITES

HARRIS, Emmylou, & Don Williams
C&W '81

Singles: 7–inch

W.B. 3-4   81
Also see WILLIAMS, Don

HARRISON, B.J.
C&W '80

Singles: 7–inch

TELESONIC.................................. 3-5   80

HARRISON, Dixie
C&W '82

Singles: 7–inch

AIR INT'L...................................... 3-4   82

HART, Clay
C&W '69

Singles: 7–inch

METROMEDIA.............................. 3-5   69-70

LP: 10/12–inch 33rpm

METROMEDIA.......................... 6-12   69
RANWOOD 5-10   74-75

HART, Freddie
C&W '59

(With the Heartbeats)

Singles: 78rpm

CAPITOL...................... 5-10   53-55
COLUMBIA (Except 21512)........ 5-15   56-57
COLUMBIA (21512 "Dig Boy
Dig") 15-25   56

Singles: 7–inch

CAPITOL (2500 thru 3000
series) 5-10   53-55
(Purple labels.)
CAPITOL (2600 thru 4600
series) 3-5   70-79
(Orange labels.)
COLUMBIA (Except 21512)........ 5-10   56-63
COLUMBIA (21512 "Dig Boy
Dig") 25-35   56
KAPP....................................... 3-8   65-72
MCA 3-5   73
MONUMENT 4-6   63-64
SUNBIRD 3-4   80-81

Picture Sleeves

KAPP.. 4-6   68
SUNBIRD 3-5   80

LPs: 10/12–inch 33rpm

BRYLEN...................................... 5-10   84
CAPITOL...................................... 5-10   70-79
COLUMBIA (1700 series) 20-25   62
COLUMBIA (13000 series) 10-12   72
CORAL.. 5-8   73
HARMONY................................... 8-12   67-73

KAPP 8-15   65-69
MCA... 8-12   75
PICKWICK 5-10   70s
PICKWICK/HILLTOP 8-12   70s
SUNBIRD..................................... 5-10   80
VOCALION 8-10   72

HART, Freddie / Sammi Smith / Jerry Reed

LPs: 10/12–inch 33rpm

HARMONY..................................6-10   72
Also see HART, Freddie
Also see REED, Jerry
Also see SMITH, Sammi

HART, J.D.
C&W '89

Singles: 7–inch

UNIVERSAL.................................3-4   89

HART, Rod
C&W/P&R '76

Singles: 7–inch

IBC..3-4   80
PHOENIX SUN 3-6   68
PLANTATION 3-5   76-77

LPs: 10/12–inch 33rpm

PLANTATION 5-10   76

HART, Sally June
C&W '75

Singles: 7–inch

BUDDAH.....................................3-5   75

HARTFORD, Chapin
C&W '78

Singles: 7–inch

LS...3-5   78

HARTFORD, John
C&W '67

Singles: 7–inch

AMPEX 3-5   71
FLYING FISH................................3-4   84
RCA 4-8   66-70

LPs: 10/12–inch 33rpm

FLYING FISH...............................5-10   76-84
RCA 8-15   67-70
W.B. 8-12   71-72
Also see DILLARDS & John Hartford

HARTSOOK, Jimmy
C&W '74

Singles: 7–inch

RCA 3-5   74

HARTT, Dolly
C&W '88

Singles: 7–inch

KASS 3-4   88

HARVELL, Nate   C&W '78
Singles: 7–inch
REPUBLIC 3-5   78-79

HATFIELD, Overton
(Gene Autry)
Singles: 78rpm
Columbia (15987 "A Gangster's
  Warning") 50-75   30s
  Also see AUTRY, Gene

HATFIELD, Vince & Diane   C&W '81
Singles: 7–inch
SOUNDWAVES 3-4   81-83

HAUSER, Bruce, & Sawmill Creek
Band   C&W '85
Singles: 7–inch
COWBOY.................................... 3-4   85-86
  Also see SAWMILL CREEK

HAVENS, Bobby, & Country
Company   C&W '78
Singles: 7–inch
CIN KAY.. 3-5   78

HAWK, The
(Jerry Lee Lewis)
Singles: 7–inch
PHILLIPS INT'L (3559 "In the
  Mood")................................... 15-20   60
  Also see LEWIS, Jerry Lee

HAWKINS, Debi   C&W '75
Singles: 7–inch
W.B. 3-5   75-77
  Also see MORRISON, Dorothy

HAWKINS, Erskine P&R '36/C&W '44
Singles: 78rpm
BLUEBIRD 5-15   39-44
BRUNSWICK 5-10   53
DECCA...................................... 5-10   56
CORAL.. 5-10   50-54
KING 5-10   51-52
VICTOR/RCA............................. 5-10   45-52
VOCALION................................ 5-15   36-37
Singles: 7–inch
BRUNSWICK .,............................ 5-10   53
DECCA....................................... 5-10   56
CORAL.. 5-10   52-54
KING (4514 "Steel Guitar Rag") 15-20   52
  (Black vinyl.)

KING (4514 "Steel Guitar Rag").30-40   52
  (Colored vinyl.)
KING (4522 "Down Home
  Jump").................................15-20   52
  (Black vinyl.)
KING (4522 "Down Home
  Jump").................................30-40   52
  (Colored vinyl.)
KING (4574 "New Gin Mill
  Special")..............................15-20   52
KING (4597 "The Way You Look
  Tonight") 15-20   52
EPs: 7–inch 33/45rpm
RCA 10-20   59
LPs: 10/12–inch 33rpm
CORAL.....................................30-50   54
DECCA 20-30   61
IMPERIAL 20-30   62
RCA 25-40   60

HAWKINS, Erskine, & Four Hawks
Singles: 78rpm
KING (4671 "My Baby,
  Please") 25-50   53
KING (4686 "Double Shot") 15-25   53
Singles: 7–inch
KING (4671 "My Baby,
  Please") 50-100   53
KING (4686 "Double Shot") 40-60   53
  Also see HAWKINS, Erskine

HAWKINS, Hawkshaw   C&W '48
Singles: 78rpm
KING 4-8   46-53
RCA 4-8   55-57
Singles: 7–inch
COLUMBIA 4-8   59-62
KING (900 thru 1100 series)........5-10   50-53
KING (5000 series) 4-8   60-64
RCA 5-10   55-59
STARDAY 3-5   71
EPs: 7–inch 33/45rpm
KING 8-12   53
LPs: 10/12–inch 33rpm
CAMDEN 10-15   64-66
GLADWYNNE (2006 "Country & Western
  Cavalcade") 75-100
HARMONY.................................10-15   63
KING (587 "Hawkshaw Hawkins,
  Vol. 1").................................40-60   58
KING (592 "Hawkshaw Hawkins Sings Grand
  Ole Opry Favorites, Vol. 2")
  Vol. 1") 40-60   58

KING (599 "Hawkshaw
Hawkins") 40-60   59

KING (808 "All New Hawkshaw
Hawkins") 20-40   63

KING (858 "Taken From Our Vaults,
Vol. 1") 15-20   63

KING (858 "Taken From Our Vaults,
Vol. 2") 15-20   63

KING (858 "Taken From Our Vaults,
Vol. 3") 15-20   64

KING (1043 "Lonesome
7-7203") 8-12   69

LA BREA (8020 "Hawkshaw
Hawkins") 75-100

NASHVILLE 8-12   69

STARDAY 5-10   77

Also see CLINE, Patsy / Cowboy Copas / Hawkshaw
Hawkins

Also see COPAS, Cowboy / Hawkshaw Hawkins

HAWKS, Mickey   *C&W '89*

(With Moon Mullins & His Night Raiders)
Singles: 7-inch

C-HORSE 3-4   89

HUNCH (347 "Hidi Hidi Hidi").... 10-20   61

PROFILE (4002 "Bip Bop
Boom") 30-50   58

PROFILE (4007 "Hidi Hidi
Hidi") 30-50   59

PROFILE (4010 "Screamin' Mimi
Jeanie") 40-60   59

HAZARD   *C&W '83*
Singles: 7-inch

W.B. 3-4   83

Members: Bernie Faulkner; Wayne Davis; Bruce Dees.

HAZARD, Donna   *C&W '81*
Singles: 7-inch

EXCELSIOR.................................. 3-4 81-82

HEAD, Roy   *P&R/R&B/LP '65/C&W '74*

(With the Traits)
Singles: 7-inch

ABC 3-5 73-79

ABC/DOT 3-5 76-77

AVION 3-4   83

BACK BEAT 4-8 65-67

CHURCHILL................................. 3-4   81

DUNHILL...................................... 3-5   70

ELEKTRA 3-4 79-80

MEGA... 3-5   74

MERCURY 4-6   68

NSD.. 3-4   82

SCEPTER 4-8 65-66

SHANNON 3-5   75

TMI... 3-5 71-73

TNT... 8-10   65

TEXAS CRUDE 3-4   85

LPs: 10/12-inch 33rpm

ABC... 5-10 73-78

CRAZY CAJUN............................. 5-10   77

DUNHILL...................................... 8-12   70

ELEKTRA 5-10 79-80

SCEPTER (532 "Treat Me
Right")................................... 15-25   65
(Monaural.)

SCEPTER (532 "Treat Me
Right")................................... 20-30   65
(Stereo. With an "SS" prefix.)

TMI... 8-10   72

TNT (101 "Roy Head and the
Traits") 100-150   65
(Counterfeits can be identified by their
content. They include *Treat Her Right,* as
well as other later Head tracks on side two.
Originals do not have these.)

TEXAS CRUDE 5-10   85

Also see TRAITS

HEAP, Jimmy   *P&R/C&W '56*

(With the Melody Masters & Perk Williams)
Singles: 78rpm

CAPITOL...................................... 5-15 53-55

Singles: 7-inch

CAPITOL...................................... 10-20 53-55

D 8-10   59

DART 5-10   60

FAME (502 "Little Jewel") 200-250   58

FAME (509 "Night Cap") 8-15   61

FAME (510 "Go Get Em")............ 8-15   61

FAME (511 "Flint Rock").............. 8-15   61

IMPERIAL 4-8   60

HEART of NASHVILLE   *C&W '85*
Singles: 7-inch

COMPLEAT 3-4   85

HEARTLAND   *C&W '88*
Singles: 7-inch

TRA-STAR 3-4 88-89

HEATH, Boyd   *C&W '45*
Singles: 78rpm

BLUEBIRD.................................... 5-10   45

HEAVENER, David *C&W '81*
Singles: 7–inch
BRENT 3-4 81-82

HECKEL, Beverly *C&W '77*
Singles: 7–inch
RCA... 3-5 77-78
 Also see HECKELS
 Also see RUSSELL, Johnny

HECKELS, The *C&W '76*
Singles: 7–inch
RCA... 3-5 76
 Members: Beverly Heckel; Susie Heckel; Denny
 Franks.
 Also see HECKEL, Beverly

HELMS, Bobby *C&W/P&R/R&B '57*
Singles: 78rpm
DECCA.. 5-15 56-57
Singles: 7–inch
BLACK ROSE............................. 3-4 83-84
CAPITOL 3-5 70
CERTRON 3-5 70
COLUMBIA 4-8 64
DECCA (Except 29947) 5-15 57-62
DECCA (29947 "Tennessee Rock and
 Roll") 20-30 56
GUSTO 3-5 74
KAPP... 4-6 65-67
LARRICK...................................... 3-5 75
LITTLE DARLIN'........................... 3-6 67-79
MCA 3-4
MILLION 3-5 72
MISTLETOE 3-5 74
PLAYBACK 3-4
Picture Sleeves
CERTRON 4-6 70
DECCA ("New Singing
 Sensation")............................... 10-20 57
 (Pictures Helms, but no number or title
 shown. With die-cut center hole.)
DECCA (30194 "Fraulein").......... 15-20 57
DECCA (30513 "Jingle Bell
 Rock") 10-15 57
EPs: 7–inch 33/45rpm
DECCA.. 10-20 57-59
LPs: 10/12–inch 33rpm
CERTRON 8-10 70
COLUMBIA 12-15 63
DECCA (8638 "Bobby Helms Sings to My
 Special Angel")......................... 30-40 57
HARMONY................................... 10-12 67

HOLIDAY 5-10 80
KAPP 10-15 66
LITTLE DARLIN' 10-12 68
MCA... 5-10 83
MISTLETOE................................. 5-10 74
VOCALION 10-12 65
 Session: Anita Kerr Singers.
 Also see KERR, Anita

HENDERSON, Brice *C&W '83*
Singles: 7–inch
UNION STATION........................... 3-4 83

HENHOUSE FIVE PLUS
TOO *P&R '77/C&W '77*
Singles: 7–inch
W.B./AHAB 3-5 76-77
 Member: Ray Stevens.
 Also see STEVENS, Ray

HENLEY, Don *P&R/LP '82*
Singles: 12–inch 33/45rpm
GEFFEN 4-6 85
Singles: 7–inch
ASYLUM 3-4 82-83
GEFFEN 3-4 84-89
Picture Sleeves
ASYLUM 3-4 82
GEFFEN 3-4 84-89
LPs: 10/12–inch 33rpm
ASYLUM 5-10 82-83
GEFFEN 5-10 84-89
 Also see EAGLES
 Also see HORNSBY, Bruce
 Also see NICKS, Stevie, & Don Henley
 Also see SHILOH

HENRY, Audie *C&W '85*
Singles: 7–inch
CANYON CREEK 3-4 85

HENSLEY, Tari *C&W '83*
Singles: 7–inch
MERCURY...................................... 3-4 83-86

HERRING, Red *C&W '60*
Singles: 7–inch
COUNTRY JUBILEE.................... 5-10 60

HESTOR, Hoot *C&W '79*
Singles: 7–inch
LITTLE DARLING 3-5 79

HEWITT, Dolph *C&W '49*
Singles: 78rpm
RCA 5-10 49

HICKEY, Sara
"Honeybear"   *C&W '83*
Singles: 7–inch
PCM 3-4   83

HIGGINS, Bertie   *P&R '81/C&W '82*
Singles: 7–inch
CBS ASSOCIATED...................... 3-4   85
KAT FAMILY 3-4   81-82
SOUTHERN TRACKS 3-4   87-89
LPs: 10/12–inch 33rpm
KAT FAMILY 5-10   82

HIGGINS, Bertie, & Roy Orbison
Singles: 7–inch
SOUTHERN TRACKS (2010
   "Leah") 3-4   89
   Also see HIGGINS, Bertie
   Also see ORBISON, Roy

HIGHFILL, George   *C&W '87*
Singles: 7–inch
W.B. 3-4   87

HIGHWAY 101   *C&W '87*
Singles: 7–inch
W.B. 3-4   86-92
LPs: 10/12–inch 33rpm
W.B. 5-10   86-92
   Members: Paulette Carlson; Jack Daniels; Scott
   Moser; Curt Stone; Nikki Nelson.
   Also see CARLSON, Paulette
   Also see TOMORROW'S WORLD

HILKA   *C&W '80*
(Hilka Cornelius)
Singles: 7–inch
IBC 3-5   79-80

HILKA & JEBRY   *C&W '79*
Singles: 7–inch
IBC 3-5   79-80
   Members: Hilka Cornelius; Jebry Briley.
   Also see HILKA

HILL, Goldie   *C&W '53*
(Goldie Hill Smith; The Golden Hillbilly)
Singles: 78rpm
DECCA.. 4-8   52-57
Singles: 7–inch
DECCA.. 5-12   52-59
EPs: 7–inch 33/45rpm
DECCA.. 6-12   55-61
LP: 10/12–inch 33rpm
DECCA.. 10-25   60-62

EPIC.. 10-20   68-69
VOCALION 6-12   67-69
   Also see SOVINE, Red, & Goldie Hill

HILL, Goldie, & Justin
Tubb   *C&W '54*
(Justin Tubb & Goldie Hill)
Singles: 78rpm
DECCA 4-8   54-55
Singles: 7–inch
DECCA 6-12   54-55
   Also see TUBB, Justin

HILL, Sam
(Gene Autry)
Singles: 78rpm
GREYBULL (4281 "My Oklahoma
   Home")...................................25-50
GREYBULL (4310 "No One to Call Me
   Darling")................................25-50
GREYBULL (4314 "Stay Away from My
   Chicken House")......................25-50
VAN DYKE (5001 "Why Don't You Come
   Back Home")...........................25-50
VAN DYKE (7481 "My Oklahoma
   Home")...................................25-50
VAN DYKE (84310 "No One to Call Me
   Darling")..................................25-50
   Also see AUTRY, Gene

HILL, Tiny, & His
Orchestra   *C&W '46*
Singles: 78rpm
MERCURY................................... 5-10   46-54
Singles: 7–inch
MERCURY................................... 5-15   51-54
EPs: 7–inch 33/45rpm
MERCURY................................. 10-15   51-54
LP: 10/12–inch 33rpm
MERCURY (25126 "Tiny Hill") ...20-35   52
(10–inch LP.)

HILL CITY   *C&W '85*
Singles: 7–inch
MOON SHINE............................... 3-4   85

HILLMAN, Chris   *LP '76*
Singles: 7–inch
ASYLUM 3-5   76-77
LPs: 10/12–inch 33rpm
ASYLUM 5-10   76-77

SUGAR HILL.................................. 5-10 82-84

Session: James Burton; Herb Pedersen; Bennie
Leadon; Byron Berline.
Also see BYRDS
Also see DESERT ROSE BAND
Also see FLYING BURRITO BROTHERS
Also see McGUINN, CLARK & HILLMAN
Also see PEDERSEN, Herb
Also see SOUTHER - HILLMAN - FURAY BAND

HILLMAN, Chris, & Roger McGuinn *C&W '89*

Singles: 7–inch

UNIVERSAL................................... 3-4   89

Members: Roger McGuinn; Chris Hillman.
Also see HILLMAN, Chris
Also see McGUINN, Roger

HILTON, Denny *C&W '81*

Singles: 7–inch

OAK... 3-5   81
ROSEBRIDGE 3-4   82-83

HINOJOSA, Tish *C&W '89*

Singles: 7–inch

A&M 3-4   89

HINOJOSA, Tish, & Craig Dillingham *C&W '86*

Singles: 7–inch

MCA/CURB 3-4   86

Also see DILLINGHAM, Craig
Also see HINOJOSA, Tish

HITCHCOCK, Stan *C&W '67*

Singles: 7–inch

CINNAMON.................................. 3-5   73-74
EPIC... 3-6   67-70
GRT.. 3-5   70
MMI 3-5   78-79
RAMBLIN'..................................... 3-4   81

LP: 10/12–inch 33rpm

AUDIOGRAPH ALIVE................. 5-10   82
CINNAMON.................................. 8-12   73
EPIC... 10-15 65-69
GRT.. 8-12   70

HITCHCOCK, Stan, & Sue Richards *C&W '79*

Singles: 7–inch

MMI 3-5   79

Also see HITCHCOCK, Stan
Also see RICHARDS, Sue

HOBBS, Becky *C&W '78*

Singles: 7–inch

EMI AMERICA 3-4   84-85

LIBERTY 3-4   84
MCA 3-5   74
MTM.. 3-4   88
MERCURY.................................... 3-5   78-81
RCA 3-4   89
TATTOO 3-5   76-77

LP: 10/12–inch 33rpm

MCA.. 5-10   74
TATTOO 5-10   76-77

Also see BANDY, Moe, & Becky Hobbs

HOBBS, Bud, & His Trail Herders *C&W '48*

Singles: 78rpm

MGM 4-8   48-49

HOBBS, Lou *C&W '81*

Singles: 7–inch

KIK 3-5   81

HOBBS, Pam *C&W '81*

Singles: 7–inch

50 STATES 3-5   81

HOGSED, Roy *C&W '48*

Singles: 78rpm

CAPITOL...................................... 5-10   48
COAST.. 20-30   47

HOKUM, Suzi Jane *C&W '67*

Singles: 7–inch

LHI 4-6   69

Also see WARNER, Virgil, & Suzi Jane Hokum

HOLDEN, Rebecca *C&W '89*

Singles: 7–inch

TRA-STAR 3-4   89

HOLLADAY, Dave *C&W '86*

Singles: 7–inch

STEP ONE 3-4   86

HOLLIER, Jill *C&W '86*

Singles: 7–inch

W.B. 3-4   86-89

HOLLOWELL, Terri *C&W '78*

Singles: 7–inch

CON BRIO 3-5   78-79

HOLLY, Doyle *C&W '72*

(With the Vanishing Breed)
Singles: 7–inch

BARNABY..................................... 3-5   72-74

LP: 10/12–inch 33rpm		
BARNABY 10-20	73	
PICKWICK 5-10	70s	

HOLM, Johnny   *C&W '77*
Singles: 7–inch
ASI 3-5   77

HOLMES, Monty   *C&W '89*
Singles: 7–inch
ASHLEY 3-4   89

HOLT, Darrell   *C&W '87*
Singles: 7–inch
ANOKA............................... 3-4   87-89

HOMER & JETHRO   *C&W/P&R '49*
Singles: 78rpm
KING 5-15	46-53	
FEDERAL..................................... 8-15	51	
RCA... 5-15	50-58	

Singles: 7–inch
BLUEBIRD 4-8	59	
KING 3-6	63	
RCA (0100 series)..................... 30-50 (Colored vinyl.)	50	
RCA (0100 thru 0468) .... 15-30 (Black vinyl.)	50-51	
RCA (0500 series)......................... 3-5	71	
RCA (4290 thru 7704) 10-20	51-59	
RCA (47-7744 "Sink the Bismarck").................................. 8-12 (Monaural.)	60	
RCA (61-7744 "Sink the Bismarck")............................... 15-25 (Stereo.)	60	
RCA (7790 thru 9922) 4-8	60-70	

Picture Sleeves
RCA (5000 series)........................ 8-12	53	
RCA (8000 series)......................... 3-6	64	

EPs: 7–inch 33/45rpm
AUDIO LAB 10-20	59	
KING 15-25	53-54	
RCA... 15-25	53-57	

LPs: 10/12–inch 33rpm
AUDIO LAB (1513 "Musical Madness").............................. 25-50	58	
CAMDEN................................... 10-20	62-71	
DIPLOMAT 8-12		
GUEST STAR 10-15	63	
KING (639 "They Sure Are Corny").................................. 20-30	59	
KING (800 series) 10-20	63	

KING (1000 series) 8-12	67	
NASHVILLE 8-12	69	
RCA (1412 "Barefoot Ballads") 20-40	57	
RCA (1516 "Worst of Homer & Jethro") 20-40	57	
RCA (LPM-1880 "Life Can Be Miserable")..............................20-30 (Monaural.)	58	
RCA (LSP-1880 "Life Can Be Miserable")..............................25-35 (Stereo.)	58	
RCA (2100 thru 2900 series) .....15-25 (Monaural. With "LPM" prefix.)	60-64	
RCA (2100 thru 2900 series) .....20-30 (Stereo. With "LSP" prefix.)	60-64	
RCA (3112 "Homer & Jethro Fracture Frank Loesser") ....30-60 (10–inch LP.)	53	
RCA (3300 thru 4600 series) 15-30	65-72	

Members: Henry "Homer" Haynes; Kenneth "Jethro" Burns.
Also see COUNTRY ALL STARS

HOMER & JETHRO with June Carter   *C&W '49*
Singles: 78rpm
RCA 5-10   49

Also see CARTER, June

HOMER & JETHRO / Four Lovers
EPs: 7–inch 33/45rpm
RCA (47 "The Four Lovers/Homer & Jethro") 30-50   56
(Promotional only. Not issued with cover.)
Also see HOMER & JETHRO

HOMESTEADERS   *C&W '66*
Singles: 7–inch
LITTLE DARLIN' 4-6   66-68
LP: 10/12–inch 33rpm
HOMESTEADERS......................5-10		
LITTLE DARLIN' 10-15	67	

Members: Frank Evans; Jerry Rivers; Bob Leftridge.

HOOD, Bobby   *C&W '81*
Singles: 7–inch
CHUTE...3-4	78-81	
PLANTATION 3-5	78	

HOOSIER HOT SHOTS   *C&W '44*
(With Sally Foster; with Two Ton Baker)
Singles: 78rpm
BANNER 3-5	30s	
CONQUEROR 3-5	30s	
DECCA 3-5	44-47	

MELOTONE	3-5	30s
ORIOLE	3-5	30s
VOCALION	3-5	30s

LP: 10/12–inch 33rpm

DOT	15-30	64
GOLDEN TONE	10-20	
SPIN-O-RAMA	10-20	60s
SUNBEAM	10-20	75
TOPS	10-20	

Members: Hezzie Trietsch; Nathan Harrison; Gabe Ward; Keith Milheim.

HORN, DeAnne   *C&W '78*

Singles: 7–inch

CHARTWHEEL	3-5	78

HORNSBY, Bruce, & Range   *P&R/C&W/LP '86*

Singles: 7–inch

RCA	3-4	86-90

Picture Sleeves

RCA	3-4	87-88

LPs: 10/12–inch 33rpm

RCA	5-10	86-90

Also see HENLEY, Don

HORTON, Billie Jean   *C&W '61*

Singles: 7–inch

FOX	5-8	61

HORTON, Johnny   *C&W '56*

Singles: 78rpm

ABBOTT	15-25	51-52
COLUMBIA	10-25	56-57
CORMAC	25-50	51
MERCURY	10-20	54-55

Singles: 7–inch

ABBOTT (100 "Candy Jones")	20-30	51
ABBOTT (101 "Happy Millionaire")	20-30	51
ABBOTT (102 "Plaid & Calico")	20-30	51
ABBOTT (103 "Birds and Butterflies")	20-30	51
ABBOTT (104 "Go and Wash")	20-30	51
ABBOTT (105 "Shadows on the Old Bayou")	20-30	51
ABBOTT (106 "Words")	20-30	51
ABBOTT (107 "Long Rocky Road")	20-30	52
ABBOTT (108 "Somebody's Rockin' My Broken Heart")	20-30	52

ABBOTT (109 "Rhythm in My Baby's Walk")	20-30	52
ABBOTT (135 "Plaid & Calico")	15-20	53
CORMAC (1193 "Plaid & Calico")	75-100	51
CORMAC (1197 "Birds and Butterflies")	75-100	51
COLUMBIA (21504 "Honky Tonk Man")	15-25	56
COLUMBIA (21538 "I'm a One Woman Man")	10-20	56
COLUMBIA (40813 "I'm Coming Home")	15-25	57
COLUMBIA (40919 "She Knows Why")	10-15	57
COLUMBIA (40986 "I'll Do It Every Time")	10-15	57
COLUMBIA (41043 "Lover's Rock")	15-25	57
COLUMBIA (41110 "Honky Tonk Hardwood Floor")	30-50	58
COLUMBIA (41210 "All Grown Up")	10-15	58
COLUMBIA (41308 thru 44156)	5-10	58-67
DOT (15996 "Plaid & Calico")	8-12	59
MERCURY (6412 "The Devil Sent Me You")	15-25	52
MERCURY (6418 "The Rest of Your Life")	15-25	52
MERCURY (70014 "I Won't Forget")	15-25	52
MERCURY (70100 "Tennessee Jive")	15-25	53
MERCURY (70156 "S.S. Lureline")	15-25	53
MERCURY (70198 "You You You")	15-25	53
MERCURY (70227 "All for the Love of a Girl")	15-25	53
MERCURY (70325 "Move Down the Line")	15-25	54
MERCURY (70399 "The Door of Your Mansion")	15-25	54
MERCURY (70462 "No True Love")	15-25	54
MERCURY (70636 "Ridin' the Sunshine Special")	15-25	55
MERCURY (70707 "Big Wheels Rollin'")	15-25	55

Picture Sleeves

COLUMBIA (Except 41308)	10-15	59-64

COLUMBIA (41308 "When It's Springtime in Alaska").................................. 15-20   59
(Blue and white sleeve. Promotional only.)
DOT... 10-15   59

EPs: 7–inch 33/45rpm

COLUMBIA (2130 "Honky Tonk Man")...................................... 25-50   57
COLUMBIA (13621/22/23 "The Spectacular Johnny Horton ") 20-40   60
(Price is for either volume.)
COLUMBIA (14781/82/83 "Johnny Horton Makes History")....................... 20-40   60
(Price is for either volume.)
MERCURY (3091 "Requestfully Yours") 25-50   55
SESAC (1201 "Free and Easy Songs") 30-50   59
(Promotional issues only.)

LPs: 10/12–inch 33rpm

BRIAR INT'L (104 "Done Rovin") 100-150
COLUMBIA (CL-1362 "The Spectacular Johnny Horton ") 20-30   60
(Monaural.)
COLUMBIA (CL-1478 "Johnny Horton Makes History") 20-30   60
(Monaural.)
COLUMBIA (CL-1596 "Johnny Horton's Greatest Hits")......................... 20-30   61
(Monaural. Add $10-15 if accompanied by bonus photo.)
COLUMBIA (CL-1721 "Honky Tonk Man")...................................... 20-30   62
(Monaural.)
COLUMBIA (CL-2566 "Johnny Horton on the Louisiana Hayride")................. 20-25   66
(Monaural.)
COLUMBIA (CL-2566 "Johnny Horton on Stage") 10-20   66
(Monaural. Repackage of *Johnny Horton on the Louisiana Hayride*.)
COLUMBIA (CS-8167 "The Spectacular Johnny Horton ") 25-35   60
(Stereo.)
COLUMBIA (CS-8269 "Johnny Horton Makes History") 25-35   60
(Stereo.)
COLUMBIA (CS-8396 "Johnny Horton's Greatest Hits")......................... 25-35   61
(Stereo. Add $10-15 if accompanied by bonus photo.)
COLUMBIA (PC-8396 "Johnny Horton's Greatest Hits")......................... 5-10

COLUMBIA (CS-8779 "Honky Tonk Man") 25-35   62
(Stereo.)
COLUMBIA (CS-9099 "I Can't Forget You").......................:.15-20   65
(Stereo.)
COLUMBIA (CS-9366 "Johnny Horton on the Louisiana Hayride")..................20-25   66
(Stereo.)
COLUMBIA (CS-9366 "Johnny Horton on Stage")......................................10-15   66
(Stereo. Repackage of *Johnny Horton on the Louisiana Hayride*.)
COLUMBIA (CS-9940 "Johnny Horton on the Road")...10-15   69
COLUMBIA (KG-30884 "The World of Johnny Horton")...............................15-20   71
COLUMBIA (CG-30884 "The World of Johnny Horton")...................................10-15
COLUMBIA HOUSE (6418/19 "Johnny Horton, the Legend")................10-15   75
CROWN 10-20   63
CUSTOM 10-15   60s
DOT (3221 "Johnny Horton")......25-40   59
(Monaural.)
DOT (25221 "Johnny Horton")...15-25   66
(Stereo.)
HARMONY (11291 "The Unforgettable Johnny Horton")......................10-15   70
HARMONY (11384 "The Legendary Johnny Horton")...................................10-15   70
HARMONY (30394 "The Battle of New Orleans")...................................10-15   71
JUKE BOX 5-10
MERCURY (20478 "The Fantastic Johnny Horton)....................................25-50   59
PICKWICK/HILLTOP (6060 "All for the Love of a Girl").................................10-15   65
PICKWICK/HILLTOP (6012 "The Voice of Johnny Horton").......................10-15   68
SEARS (110 "Legend of Johnny Horton)....................................10-15   60s
SESAC (1201 "Free and Easy Songs") 100-150   59
(Promotional issue only.)
Also see CLINE, Patsy / Cowboy Copas / Johnny Horton
Also see DEAN, Jimmy / Johnny Horton
Also see PRICE, Ray / Johnny Horton / Carl Smith / George Morgan

HORTON, Johnny / Sonny James

LPs: 10/12–inch 33rpm

CUSTOM 6-12
Also see JAMES, Sonny

HORTON, Johnny / Texas Slim

LP: 10/12–inch 33rpm

CROWN 6-12   60s
  Also see HORTON, Johnny

HORTON, Steven Wayne   *C&W '89*

Singles: 7–inch

CAPITOL 3-4   89

HOSFORD, Larry   *C&W '74*

Singles: 7–inch

SHELTER 3-5   74-76

HOUSE, David   *C&W '82*

Singles: 7–inch

DOOR KNOB 3-4   82

HOUSE, James   *C&W '89*

Singles: 7–inch

MCA 3-4   89-90

HOUSTON, David   *C&W '63*

(With Calvin Crawford; with Sherri Jerrico)
Singles: 78rpm

RCA (6611 "Sugar Sweet") 8-12   56
RCA (6696 "Blue Prelude") 8-12   56
RCA (6927 "One and Only") 15-25   57
RCA (7001 "Teenage Frankie and
  Johnny") 15-25   57

Singles: 7–inch

BLACK ROSE 3-4   82
COLONIAL 3-5   78
COUNTRY INT'L 3-4   80
DERRICK 3-4   79
ELEKTRA 3-5   78-79
EXCELSIOR 3-4   81
EPIC 3-8   63-76
NRC 8-12   59
PHILLIPS INT'L 5-10   61
RCA (6611 "Sugar Sweet") 10-20   56
RCA (6696 "Blue Prelude") 10-20   56
RCA (6927 "One and Only") 30-40   57
RCA (7001 "Teenage Frankie and
  Johnny") 15-25   57
SOUNDWAVES 3-4   83
STARDAY 3-5   77
SUN (400 series) 5-10   66
SUN (1100 series) 3-5   72

Picture Sleeves

EPIC 5-8   66-69

LPs: 10/12–inch 33rpm

CAMDEN 8-12   66

COLUMBIA 6-10   73
DELTA 5-10   82
EPIC 5-15   64-76
EXACT 5-10   80
EXCELSIOR 5-10   81
51 WEST 5-10   84
GUEST STAR 6-12   64
GUSTO 5-10   78
HARMONY 8-12   70-72
STARDAY 6-10   77
  Also see DEAN, Jimmy / David Houston / Warner Mack
    / Autry Inman
  Also see JAMES, Sonny / David Houston
  Also see JERRICO, Sherri
  Also see JONES, George / Buck Owens / David
    Houston / Tommy Hill.

HOUSTON, David, & Barbara Mandrell   *C&W '70*

Singles: 7–inch

EPIC 3-5   70-74

LPs: 10/12–inch 33rpm

EPIC 8-15   72-75
  Also see MANDRELL, Barbara

HOUSTON, David, & Tammy Wynette   *C&W '68*

Singles: 7–inch

EPIC 4-6   67

LPs: 10/12–inch 33rpm

EPIC 8-12   67
51 WEST 5-10   82
  Also see HOUSTON, David
  Also see WYNETTE, Tammy

HOWARD, Chuck   *C&W '80*

Singles: 7–inch

NEW STAR 4-6
W.B. 3-5   80

HOWARD, Eddy   *P&R '40/C&W '47*

Singles: 78rpm

MAJESTIC 4-8   46
MERCURY 3-5   50-57

Singles: 7–inch

MERCURY 5-10   50-61
MISHAWAKA 3-5   72

EPs: 7–inch 33/45rpm

MERCURY 5-10   50-59

LPs: 10/12–inch 33rpm

IMPERIAL 8-15   61
MERCURY 10-20   50-65
WING 5-10   60-63

HOWARD, Harlan

C&W '71

Singles: 7–inch

MONUMENT	4-8	64-65
NUGGET	3-5	71
RCA	4-6	67

LP: 10/12–inch 33rpm

MONUMENT	15-25	65
NUGGET	10-20	71
RCA	15-25	67-68

HOWARD, James Newton

LPs: 10/12–inch 33rpm

KAMA SUTRA	8-10	75
SHEFFIELD	8-10	

HOWARD, Jan

C&W '60

Singles: 7–inch

CHALLENGE	5-10	60
CAPITOL	4-8	63
CON BRIO	3-5	77-78
DECCA	4-6	65-72
GRT	3-5	74

LP: 10/12–inch 33rpm

A.V.I.	5-8	83-84
CAPITOL	15-25	62
CORAL	5-10	73
DECCA	10-20	66-72
FIRST GENERATION	5-10	81
FORUM	10-15	
GRT	6-12	75-76
PHONORAMA	5-8	83
PICKWICK/HILLTOP	6-12	60s
TOWER	15-20	67-68
WRANGLER	10-20	62

Session: Jordaniares.
Also see ANDERSON, Bill, & Jan Howard
Also see JORDANAIRES
Also see STEWART, Wynn, & Jan Howard

HOWARD, Jim

C&W '64

Singles: 7–inch

DEL-MAR	4-6	64

HOWARD, Randy

C&W '83

Singles: 7–inch

ATLANTIC AMERICA	3-4	88
W.B.	3-5	83

HUBBELL, Hal

C&W '78

Singles: 7–inch

50 STATES	3-5	78

HUDSON, Helen

C&W '79

Singles: 7–inch

CYCLONE	3-5	79

HUDSON, Larry G.

C&W '76

Singles: 7–inch

AQUARIAN	3-5	76
LONE STAR	3-5	78-79
MERCURY	3-4	80

HUERTA, Baldemar

(El Bebop Kid)

Singles: 7–inch

FALCON (838 "Encaje De Chantilly [Chantilly Lace]")	15-25	58

Also see FENDER, Freddy

HUGHES, Hollie

C&W '87

Singles: 7–inch

LUV	3-4	87

HUGHES, Joel

C&W '82

Singles: 7–inch

SUNBIRD	3-4	82

HUMMERS

C&W '73

Singles: 7–inch

CAPITOL	3-5	73-74

HUMPERDINCK, Engelbert

(Gerry Dorsey)   *P&R/C&W/LP '67*

Singles: 7–inch

EH (1 "For My Friends")	10-15	
(Promotional issue only.)		
EPIC	3-5	76-83
PARROT	3-6	67-73

Picture Sleeves

PARROT	3-6	67-71

EPs: 7–inch 33/45rpm

PARROT	5-10	67-69
(Jukebox issues.)		

LPs: 10/12–inch 33rpm

EPIC	5-10	76-83
LONDON	5-10	77
PARROT	5-15	67-77
TEE VEE	5-10	
(TV mail order offer.)		

Also see DORSEY, Gerry

HUNLEY, Con

C&W '77

Singles: 7–inch

CAPITOL	3-4	84-86
MCA	3-4	83
PRAIRIE DUST (7600 series)	4-6	77

PRAIRIE DUST (84000 series)..... 3-4   77
W.B. 3-5 78-82

LP: 10/12–inch 33rpm

MCA (5423 "Once You Get the Feel of
It")... 10-15   83
W.B. 5-10 79-82

Session: Porter Wagoner.
Also see WAGONER, Porter

HUNNICUTT, Ed   *C&W '83*
Singles: 7–inch
MCA 3-4 83-84

HUNTER, Tommy   *C&W '67*
Singles: 7–inch
COLUMBIA 4-6   67
RCA.. 4-6   60s

LPs: 10/12–inch 33rpm
COLUMBIA 10-20   60s
HARMONY................................. 10-25   60s
RCA... 10-20   60s

HURLEY, Libby   *C&W '87*
Singles: 7–inch
EPIC... 3-4 87-88

HURT, Charlotte   *C&W '78*
Singles: 7–inch
COMPASS 3-5   78

HURT, Cindy   *C&W '81*
Singles: 7–inch
CHURCHILL................................... 3-4 81-83

HUSKEY, Ferlin: see HUSKY, Ferlin

HUSKEY, Kenni   *C&W '71*
Singles: 7–inch
CAPITOL...................................... 3-5 71-72

HUSKY, Ferlin   *C&W '55*
(With the Hush Puppies; with Hushpuppies;
with Coon Creek Girls; with Bettie Husky;
Ferlin Huskey)
Singles: 78rpm
CAPITOL...................................... 5-15 52-57
Singles: 7–inch
ABC.. 3-5 73-75
ABC/DOT 3-5   75
CAPITOL (2000 thru 3400) 3-6 67-72
  (Orange labels.)
CAPITOL (2300 thru 4300) 5-10 52-60
  (Purple labels.)
CAPITOL (4400 thru 5900) 4-8 60-67
CACHET 3-4   80

FIRST GENERATION.................... 3-5   78
KING 4-8 60-61

EPs: 7–inch 33/45rpm
CAPITOL................................... 10-20 57-60

Picture Sleeves
CAPITOL...................................... 4-8 62-68

LPs: 10/12–inch 33rpm
ABC.. 5-10 73-75
AUDIOGRAPH ALIVE.................. 5-10   82
CAPITOL (718 "Songs of the Home and
Heart)...................................... 20-40   56
CAPITOL (880 "Boulevard of Broken
Dreams").................................. 20-40   57
CAPITOL (1200 thru 2800
series)...................................... 10-20 60-68
  (With "T" or "ST" prefix.)
CAPITOL (1200 thru 2800
series)...................................... 5-10 68-75
  (With "DT" or "SM" prefix.)
FIRST GENERATION.................... 5-10   81
KING (647 "Country Tunes Sung from the
Heart")..................................... 25-35   59
KING (728 "Easy Livin")............. 25-35   60
PHONORAMA 5-8   83
PICKWICK 5-10   70s
PICKWICK/HILLTOP 8-12   65
STARDAY.................................... 5-10   77

Also see CRUM, Simon
Also see OWENS, Buck / Faron Young / Ferlin Husky
Also see PRESTON, Terry
Also see SHEPARD, Jean, & Ferlin Husky
Also see TERRY, Tex
Also see TUBB, Ernest
Also see VINCENT, Gene / Tommy Sands / Sonny
  James / Ferlin Husky

HUSKY, Ferlin / Pat Boone
Singles: 7–inch
U.S.A. 5-10   60
  (Promotional issue only.)
Also see BOONE, Pat

HUSKY, Ferlin / Five Keys
EPs: 7–inch 33/45rpm
CAPITOL (503 "Five Keys/Ferlin
Husky") 60-80   57
Also see HUSKY, Ferlin

HUTCHINS, Loney   *C&W '87*
Singles: 7–inch
ARC 3-4   87

IFIELD, Frank   *P&R '62/C&W '66*
Singles: 7–inch
CAPITOL.. 4-6   63-65
HICKORY...................................... 3-6   66-71
MAM 3-5   71
VEE JAY 5-8   62-63
W.B. 3-5   79
LPs: 10/12–inch 33rpm
CAPITOL...................................... 10-20   63
HICKORY...................................... 8-10   66-68
VEE JAY 10-20   62
Also see BEATLES / Frank Ifield

IGLESIAS, Julio   *LP '83*
Singles: 7–inch
ALAHAMBRA................................. 3-6   72-75
COLUMBIA 3-4   83-89
LPs: 10/12–inch 33rpm
COLUMBIA 5-10   83-90

IGLESIAS, Julio, & Willie Nelson   *C&W/P&R '84*
(Willie Nelson & Julio Iglesias)
Singles: 7–inch
COLUMBIA (Except 04495).......... 3-4   84
COLUMBIA (04495 "As Time Goes By") 8-12   84
Picture Sleeves
COLUMBIA (Except 04495).......... 3-4   84
COLUMBIA (04495 "As Time Goes By") 10-15   84
Also see NELSON, Willie

IGLESIAS, Julio, & Diana Ross   *P&R '84*
Singles: 7–inch
COLUMBIA 3-4   84
Picture Sleeves
COLUMBIA 3-4   84
Also see ROSS, Diana

IGLESIAS, Julio, & Stevie Wonder   *P&R '88*
Singles: 7–inch
COLUMBIA 3-4   88

Picture Sleeves
COLUMBIA 3-4   88
Also see IGLESIAS, Julio

IN-GROUP
LPs: 10/12–inch 33rpm
IN (1002 "Swinging 12 String") ..15-25   64
Members: Glen Campbell; Leon Russell; Earl Palmer.
Also see CAMPBELL, Glen
Also see RUSSELL, Leon

INDIANA   *C&W '87*
Singles: 7–inch
KILLER.. 3-4   87

INGLE, Red, & Natural Seven   *C&W '47*
(With Jo Stafford as "Cinderella G. Stump")
Singles: 78rpm
CAPITOL.. 5-10   47-48
Also see JONES, Spike
Also see STAFFORD, Jo

INGLES, David   *C&W '69*
Singles: 7–inch
CAPITOL.. 3-6   69

INMAN, Autry   *C&W '53*
Singles: 78rpm
DECCA (Except 28629 & 29936)...4-8   53-56
DECCA (28629 "That's All Right") 5-10   56
DECCA (29936 "Be Bop Baby") 5-10   56
Singles: 7–inch
DECCA (Except 28629 & 29936)................................. 5-10   56
DECCA (28629 "That's All Right") 15-25   56
DECCA (29936 "Be Bop Baby") 25-50   56
EPIC.. 4-8   67-69
GLAD 5-10   60
JUBILEE 4-8   65-69
MERCURY..................................... 4-8   62
MILLION... 3-5   72
RCA 5-10   58
RISQUE (103 "Niteclubbin") 5-10   67
RISQUE (105 "The Golf Game").................................... 5-10   67
SIMS 4-8   63-64
U.A. 5-8   60
LPs: 10/12–inch 33rpm
ALSHIRE....................................... 8-12   69
EPIC.. 10-15   68

GUEST STAR 8-12

JUBILEE.................................... 10-20   64-69

MOUNTAIN DEW...................... 15-25   63

SIMS 15-20   64

Also see DEAN, Jimmy / David Houston / Warner Mack / Autry Inman

INMAN, Jerry   *C&W '74*

Singles: 7–inch

CHELSEA 3-5   74

ELEKTRA.................................. 3-5   78-79

LP: 10/12–inch 33rpm

COLUMBIA 10-15   68

ELEKTRA.................................. 5-10   76

IRBY, Jerry   *C&W '48*

(With His Texas Ranchers)

Singles: 78rpm

DAFFAN (106 "Time You Started
Looking") 10-20   56

DAFFAN (108 "Clickety Clack") 20-30   56

MGM 5-8   48

Singles: 7–inch

DAFFAN (106 "Time You Started
Looking") 20-40   56

DAFFAN (108 "Clickety
Clack")..................................... 50-80   56

JER-RAY 10-15

IRBY, Jerry & Jeanne

Singles: 7–inch

JER-RAY (222 "Chantilly
Lace")...................................... 15-25

Also see IRBY, Jerry

IRVING, Lonnie   *C&W '60*

Singles: 7–inch

LONNIE IRVING 10-15   50s

STARDAY 5-10   60

ISAACSON, Peter   *C&W '83*

Singles: 7–inch

UNION STATION......................... 3-4   83-84

IVES, Burl   *P&R '48/C&W '49*

(With the Trinidaddies)

Singles: 78rpm

COLUMBIA 3-8   50-51

DECCA.. 3-8   47-57

Singles: 7–inch

BELL 3-5   70

BIG TREE 3-5   71

BUENA VISTA 4-6   63

COLUMBIA (39000 series) 5-10   50-51

COLUMBIA (44000 series) 3-6   68-69

COLUMBIA (70000 series) 3-6   69

CYCLONE...................................3-5   70

DECCA (25000 series) 4-6   66-69

DECCA (27000 thru 30000
series)......................................5-10   50-59

DECCA (31000 thru 33000
series)......................................3-8   60-73

DISNEYLAND 4-6   64

MCA..3-5   73-74

MONKEY JOE 3-5   78

Picture Sleeves

BUENA VISTA 4-8   63

DECCA 4-8   62

U.A..4-8   62

EPs: 7–inch 33/45rpm

COLUMBIA 5-15   51-55

DECCA 5-15   49-65

LPs: 10/12–inch 33rpm

BELL 5-10   71

CAEDMON..................................4-6   72

COLUMBIA (628 "Wayfaring
Stranger")..............................15-25   55

COLUMBIA (1459 "Return of the Wayfaring
Stranger")..............................10-20   60

COLUMBIA (2570 "Children's
Favorites") 20-35   55
(10–inch LP.)

COLUMBIA (6058 "Wayfaring
Stranger")..............................25-40   50
(10–inch LP.)

COLUMBIA (6109 "Wayfaring Stranger, Vol.
2") 25-40   51
(10–inch LP.)

COLUMBIA (6144 "Wayfaring Stranger, Vol.
3") 25-40   51
(10–inch LP.)

COLUMBIA (9000 series) 8-12   68-69

CORAL.......................................4-8   73

DECCA (100 series) 15-25   61

DECCA (4000 series) 10-20   62-68
(Decca LP numbers in this series preceded
by a "7" or a "DL-7" are stereo issues.)

DECCA (5013 "Ballads and Folk
Songs") 20-40   49
(10–inch LP.)

DECCA (5080 "Ballads and Folk Songs, Vol.
2") 20-40   49
(10–inch LP.)

DECCA (5490 "Women—Songs of the Fair
Sex")....................................20-30   53
(10–inch LPs)

DECCA (8000 series) 10-20   55-59

DISNEYLAND	8-12	63-64
EVEREST	5-10	78
HARMONY	8-15	59-70
MCA	5-10	73-75
PICKWICK	5-10	
SUNSET	5-10	70
UNART	6-12	67
U.A.	10-20	59-62
WORD	5-10	63-66

Session: Anita Kerr Singers.
  Also see KERR, Anita
  Also see MILLS, Hayley, & Burl Ives

IVES, Burl, with Grady Martin & His
Slew Foot Five *C&W '52*

Singles: 78rpm

DECCA	4-8	52

Singles: 7–inch

DECCA	8-12	49

Also see MARTIN, Grady

IVES, Burl, & Hayley Mills
(With Eddie Hodges & Deborah Walley)
Singles: 7–inch

BUENA VISTA (4023 "Summer Magic")	5-8	63
(Alcoa Wrap promotional issue.)		

Picture Sleeves

BUENA VISTA (4023 "Summer Magic")	10-15	63
(Alcoa Wrap promotional issue.)		

IVES, Burl, with Captain Stubby &
Buccaneers *C&W '49*

Singles: 78rpm

DECCA	4-8	49

Also see IVES, Burl
  Also see STUBBY & BUCCANEERS

IVIE, Roger, & Silvercreek *C&W '81*

Singles: 7–inch

CARDINAL	3-4	81

Also see SILVER CREEK

IVORY JACK *C&W '80*

Singles: 7–inch

COUNTRY INT'L	3-4	81
NSD	3-5	80

JACK & TRINK   *C&W '78*
Singles: 7–inch
NSD... 3-5   78
Members: Jack Ruthven; Trink Ruthven.

JACKSON, Alan   *C&W '89*
Singles: 7–inch
ARISTA 3-4   89-92
LPs: 10/12–inch 33rpm
ARISTA 5-8   90-91

JACKSON, Carl   *C&W '84*
Singles: 7–inch
COLUMBIA 3-4   84-86
LP: 10/12–inch 33rpm
CAPITOL...................................... 6-12   73
PRIZE... 5-10
SUGAR HILL............................... 5-10   81

JACKSON, Carl, Marty Stuart & Vicki Cook
LP: 10/12–inch 33rpm
REBEL 5-10   80s
Also see JACKSON, Carl
Also see STUART, Marty

JACKSON, Lolita   *C&W '89*
Singles: 7–inch
OAK... 3-4   89

JACKSON, Nisha   *C&W '87*
Singles: 7–inch
CAPITOL.. 3-4   87

JACKSON, Stonewall   *C&W '58*
Singles: 7–inch
COLUMBIA (Except 41000
   series) 3-8   61-73
COLUMBIA (41000 series) 4-8   58-61
FIRST GENERATION................... 3-4   81
GRT.. 3-5   74
LITTLE DARLIN'............................ 3-5   78-79
MGM 3-5   73
PHONORAMA............................... 3-4   83
Picture Sleeves
COLUMBIA (41393 "Waterloo") .. 8-10   59

EPs: 7–inch 33/45rpm
COLUMBIA 5-10   59
LPs: 10/12–inch 33rpm
AUDIOGRAPH ALIVE....................5-8   82
COLUMBIA (1391 "The Dynamic Stonewall
   Jackson").................................15-25   59
   (Monaural.)
COLUMBIA (1700 thru 2700
   series)....................................10-20   62-67
   (Monaural.)
COLUMBIA (8186 "The Dynamic Stonewall
   Jackson").................................15-30   59
   (Stereo.)
COLUMBIA (8500 thru 9900
   series)......................................8-15   62-70
   (Stereo.)
COLUMBIA (10000 series) 5-8   73
COLUMBIA (30000 series) 5-10   70-72
FIRST GENERATION..................5-10   81
GRT 5-10   75-76
HARMONY....................................8-12   66-74
LITTLE DARLIN' 5-8   79
MYRRH..5-8   76
PHONORAMA 5-8   83
SUNBIRD.......................................5-8   80
Session: Jordanaires.
Also see JORDANAIRES

JACKSON, Wanda   *C&W '56*
(With the Party Timers)
Singles: 78rpm
CAPITOL...................................15-40   56-57
DECCA 10-20   54-55
Singles: 7–inch
ABC..3-5   75
CAPITOL (2000 thru 3000
   series)..3-8   67-72
   (Orange or orange/yellow label.)
CAPITOL (3400 thru 4600
   series)....................................10-25   56-61
   (Purple labels.)
CAPITOL (4700 thru 5900
   series)..4-8   61-67
DECCA (29253 "Right to
   Love")......................................20-40   54
DECCA (29514 "Tears at the Grand Ole
   Op'ry")....................................20-40   55
DECCA (29677 "It's the Same
   World")....................................10-20   55
DECCA (29803 "Wasted") 20-40   55
JIN...3-6
MYRRH..3-4   73-75

Picture Sleeves

CAPITOL	5-10	62-66

EPs: 7–inch 33/45rpm

CAPITOL (1041 "Wanda Jackson")	25-50	58

LPs: 10/12–inch 33rpm

CAPITOL (100 thru 600 series)	15-20	69-71
CAPITOL (1041 "Wanda Jackson")	40-80	58
CAPITOL (1384 "Rockin' with Wanda")	50-100	60
CAPITOL (1511 "There's a Party Goin' On")	40-80	61
(With "T" prefix. Monaural.)		
CAPITOL (1511 "There's a Party Goin' On")	50-100	61
(With "ST" prefix. Stereo.)		
CAPITOL (1596 "Right Or Wrong")	25-50	61
(With "T" prefix. Monaural.)		
CAPITOL (1596 "Right Or Wrong")	30-55	61
(With "ST" prefix. Stereo.)		
CAPITOL (1776 "Wonderful Wanda")	20-30	62
(With "T" prefix. Monaural.)		
CAPITOL (1776 "Wonderful Wanda")	25-35	62
(With "ST" prefix. Stereo.)		
CAPITOL (1911 "Love Me Forever")	20-30	63
(With "T" prefix. Monaural.)		
CAPITOL (1911 "Love Me Forever")	25-35	63
(With "ST" prefix. Stereo.)		
CAPITOL (2030 "Two Sides of Wanda Jackson")	25-35	64
(With "T" prefix. Monaural.)		
CAPITOL (2030 "Two Sides of Wanda Jackson")	30-40	64
(With "ST" prefix. Stereo.)		
CAPITOL (2300 thru 2900 series)	10-20	65-68
CAPITOL (11000 series)	5-8	72-73
DECCA (4224 "Lovin' Country Style")	40-50	62
GUSTO	5-8	80
MYRRH	5-8	73-76
PICKWICK/HILLTOP	8-12	65-68
VARRICK/ROUNDER	5-8	87
VOCALION	8-12	69
WORD	4-8	77

JACKSON, Wanda, & Billy Gray   C&W '54

Singles: 7–inch

DECCA (29140 "You Can't Have My Love")	20-40	54
DECCA (29267 "If You Don't Somebody Else Will")	20-40	54

Also see GRAY, Billy
Also see JACKSON, Wanda

JACOBS, Lori   C&W '80

Singles: 7–inch

NEOSTAT	3-5	80

JACQUES, Rick   C&W '78

Singles: 7–inch

CAPRICE	3-5	78

JAMES, Atlanta: see ATLANTA JAMES

JAMES, Dusty   C&W '79

Singles: 7–inch

SRC	3-5	79

JAMES, George   C&W '79

Singles: 7–inch

JANE	3-5	79

JAMES, Jesseca   C&W '76

(Kathy Twitty)

Singles: 7–inch

MCA	3-5	76-77

Also see TWITTY, Kathy

JAMES, Mary Kay   C&W '74

Singles: 7–inch

AVCO	3-5	75
JMI	3-4	74

JAMES, Sonny   C&W '53

(With the Southern Gentlemen; with Silver; with Tennessee State Prison Band; the Southern Gentleman)

Singles: 78rpm

CAPITOL	5-15	52-57

Singles: 7–inch

CAPITOL (2000 thru 3900)	3-6	67-74
(Orange labels.)		
CAPITOL (2200 thru 3800)	8-15	52-57
(Purple labels.)		
CAPITOL (3900 thru 5900)	4-8	58-67
(Purple or orange/yellow swirl labels.)		
CAPITOL (6000 series)	4-6	60s

CAPITOL CUSTOM ("Salute to
  KRAK")..................................... 15-20   67
(Promotional issue for a Sacramento radio
station.)
COLUMBIA 3-5   72-78
DIMENSION................................... 3-4   81-83
DOT 4-6   62
GROOVE 4-8   61
MONUMENT 3-5   79
NRC 5-8   60
RCA... 4-8   61-62

Picture Sleeves

CAPITOL (Except 4268) 4-10   65-71
CAPITOL (4268 "Who's Next in
  Line).. 6-10   59
COLUMBIA 3-5   72-75
DIMENSION................................... 3-5   80s
NRC (050 "Jenny Lou").............. 10-15   60

EPs: 7–inch 33/45rpm

CAPITOL 8-15   57-58
CAPITOL CREATIVE
  PRODUCTS................................. 5-10   68

LPs: 10/12–inch 33rpm

ABC... 5-8   77
BROOKVILLE 8-12   75
CAMDEN...................................... 8-12   60s
CAPITOL (100 thru 800 series)... 8-12   68-71
CAPITOL (779 "The Southern
  Gentleman").............................. 25-35   57
CAPITOL (867 "Sonny")............. 20-30   57
CAPITOL (988 "Honey") 20-30   58
CAPITOL (1100 series)............... 15-25   59
CAPITOL (2000 thru 2800
  series) 8-15   64-68
CAPITOL (11000 series).............. 5-8   72-75
COLUMBIA 5-10   72-78
CROWN 8-12   60s
DIMENSION................................... 5-8   82
DOT.. 15-20   62
GUEST STAR 10-15   64
HAMILTON................................... 8-12   65
MONUMENT 5-8   79
PICKWICK 5-8   76-78
PICKWICK/HILLTOP 8-12   69
SUNRISE MEDIA......................... 5-10
TEE VEE 8-12   79
TVP 8-12   75
WYNCOTE.................................... 8-12   60s

Also see HAGGARD, Merle / Sonny James
Also see HORTON, Johnny / Sonny James
Also see SUNSHINE RUBY

Also see VINCENT, Gene / Tommy Sands / Sonny
  James / Ferlin Husky
Also see VINCENT, Gene / Frank Sinatra / Sonny
  James / Ron Goodwin

JAMES, Sonny / Dave Dudley / Sunny Williams
LPs: 10/12–inch 33rpm

DIPLOMAT....................................5-10   60s

Also see DUDLEY, Dave

JAMES, Sonny / David Houston
LPs: 10/12–inch 33rpm

PICKWICK/HILLTOP 8-12   67

Also see HOUSTON, David

JAMES, Sonny / Seekers
Singles: 7–inch

CAPITOL (5375 "I'll Keep Holding On"/"I'll
  Never Find Another You")............4-8   65
(These two tracks were unintentionally
pressed back-to-back.)

Also see JAMES, Sonny

JAMES, Tommy
(With the Shondells)

P&R/R&B/LP '66/C&W '80
Singles: 7–inch

ABC...3-5   73
FANTASY 3-4   75-80
MCA..3-5   74
MILLENNIUM.................................3-5   79-81
ROULETTE.....................................4-8   66-73
TWENTY-ONE................................3-4   83

Picture Sleeves

FANTASY 3-5   76
MILLENNIUM.................................3-5   71
ROULETTE....................................5-10   66-67
TWENTY-ONE................................3-4   83

LPs: 10/12–inch 33rpm

FANTASY 8-10   76-80
MILLENNIUM.................................5-8   80
RHINO 8-12   89
ROULETTE...................................10-20   66-72
SCEPTER 8-10   73
SCEPTER/CITATION 5-8   82
TWENTY-ONE................................5-8   83

Members: Tommy James; Mike Vale; Ed Gray; Ron
Rosman; Pete Lucia.
  Also see SHONDELLS

JAMESON, Cody   C&W/P&R '77
Singles: 7–inch

ATCO...3-5   77

JAMIE & JANE

Singles: 7–inch

DECCA (30862 "Strolling")	15-25	59
DECCA (30934 "Faithful Our Love")	15-25	59

Members: Gene Pitney; Ginny Arnell.
Also see PITNEY, Gene

JAN & MALCOLM   *C&W '77*

Singles: 7–inch

PAULA	3-5	77

JANO   *C&W '79*

Singles: 7–inch

SCR	3-5	79

JANSKY, Clifton   *C&W '85*

Singles: 7–inch

AXBAR	3-4	85

JAYE, Jerry   *P&R/LP '67/C&W '75*

Singles: 7–inch

COLUMBIA	3-5	75
CONNIE (101)	10-15	67
(Title not known.)		
HI (2100 series)	4-8	67-68
HI (2300 series)	3-5	76-77
MEGA	3-5	71-74
RAINTREE	3-5	72

LPs: 10/12–inch 33rpm

HI (32000 series)	15-20	67
HI (32100 series)	5-8	76

JEAN, Norma: see NORMA JEAN

JENKINS, Bob   *C&W '82*

Singles: 7–inch

LIBERTY	3-4	82
PICAP	3-4	83

LP: 10/12–inch 33rpm

20TH FOX	6-10	74

JENKINS, Bobby   *C&W '84*

Singles: 7–inch

CONFEDERATE	4-6	
ZONE 7	3-4	83-85

JENKINS, Larry   *C&W '82*

Singles: 7–inch

CAPITOL	3-4	82
MCA	3-4	84

JENNIFER
(Jennifer Warnes)

Singles: 7–inch

PARROT	4-6	67-70

LPs: 10/12–inch 33rpm

PARROT	10-20	68-70

Also see WARNES, Jennifer

JENNINGS, Bob   *C&W '64*

Singles: 7–inch

SIMS	4-8	64

JENNINGS, Tommy   *C&W '75*

Singles: 7–inch

MONUMENT	3-5	78
PARAGON	3-5	75

LPs: 10/12–inch 33rpm

AUDIOGRAPH	5-8	82

Also see GOSDIN, Rex, & Tommy Jennings

JENNINGS, Waylon   *C&W '65*

(With the Waylors; with Kimberlys; with
Crickets; Waylon)

Singles: 7–inch

A&M (739 "Four Strong Winds")	10-15	64
A&M (722 "Rave On")	10-20	63
A&M (753 "The Race Is On")	10-20	64
A&M (762 "The Real House of the Rising Sun")	10-20	65
BAT (121636 "White Lightning")	30-50	62
BAT (121639 "Dream Baby")	25-35	62
BRUNSWICK (55130 "Jole Blon")	100-150	59
(Maroon label. With Buddy Holly & King Curtis.)		
BRUNSWICK (55130 "Jole Blon")	75-100	59
(Yellow label. Promotional issue only.)		
COLUMBIA	3-4	83
EPIC	3-4	91
RCA (Except 8572 thru 9642)	3-6	69-82
RCA (8572 thru 9642)	5-10	65-68
RAMCO	8-12	67
TREND '61 (102 "Another Blue Day")	20-30	61
TREND '63 (106 "The Stage")	50-75	63

Picture Sleeves

RCA	3-5	79-80

LPs: 10/12–inch 33rpm

A&M (4238 "Don't Think Twice")	25-30	69

BAT (1001 "Waylon Jennings at
JD's")................................. 200-300   64
(500 copies were made on Bat, then another
500 were done on Sounds Ltd.)

CAMDEN...................................... 8-15 67-76

EPIC 5-8   90

MCA 5-8

PICKWICK 5-10   75

RCA (AFL-1 series)..................... 5-10   78

RCA (0240 thru 3378)................. 5-10 73-79

RCA (3406 "Greatest Hits")....... 15-20   79
(Picture disc.)

RCA (3493 "What Goes Around Comes
Around")..................................... 5-10   79

RCA (3523 "Folk Country") 15-25   66

RCA (3602 "Music Man") 5-10   80

RCA (3620 "Leavin' Town")....... 20-30   66

RCA (3660 "Waylon Sings Ol'
Harlan")................................... 15-20   67

RCA (3663 "Are You Ready for the
Country")..................................... 5-8   80

RCA (3736 "Nashville Rebel")... 15-25   66
(Soundtrack.)

RCA (3737 "Good Hearted
Woman")..................................... 5-8   80

RCA (3825 "Love of the Common
People") 15-25   67

RCA (3897 "Honky Tonk
Heroes")...................................... 5-8   81

RCA (3918 "Hangin' On").......... 15-20   68

RCA (3942 "This Time")................ 5-8   81

RCA (4023 "Only the
Greatest")................................ 15-20   68

RCA (4072 "Dreaming My
Dreams")..................................... 5-8   81

RCA (4073 "The Ramblin' Man")... 5-8   81

RCA (4085 "Jewels")................. 15-20   68

RCA (4137 "Just to Satisfy
You") 15-20   69

RCA (4163 "Waylon Live") 5-8   81

RCA (4164 "I've Always Been
Crazy").. 5-8   81

RCA (4180 "Country Folk") 15-25   69

RCA (4247 "Black on Black")........ 5-8   82

RCA (4250 "Music Man") 5-8   82

RCA (4260 "Waylon")................ 10-15   70

RCA (4341 "Best of Waylon
Jennings") 8-10   77

RCA (4418 "Singer of Sad
Songs") 10-15   70

RCA (4487 "The Taker/Tulsa") . 10-15   71

RCA (4567 "Cedartown,
Georgia")...................................10-15   71

RCA (4647 "Good Hearted
Woman") 10-15   72

RCA (4673 "It's Only Rock &
Roll") 5-8   83

RCA (4751 "Ladies Love
Outlaws") 10-15   72

RCA (4826 "Waylon & Co.") 5-8   83

RCA (4828 "Best of Waylon
Jennings")...................................5-8   83

RCA (4854 "Lonesome, On'ry and
Mean") 10-15   73

RCA (5473 "Collector's Series") ..5-10   85

SEAGULL 5-8   83

SOUNDS (1001 "Waylon Jennings at
JD's") 200-250   64
(First issued on Bat.)

TIME-LIFE......................................5-8   81

VOCALION 15-20   69

Session: Buddy Holly; King Curtis.
Also see ANDERSON, John
Also see BARE, Bobby
Also see BOWMAN, Don
Also see CASH, Johnny, & Waylon Jennings
Also see CLARK, Guy
Also see COE, David Allan
Also see COLTER, Jessi
Also see CRICKETS
Also see DAVIS, Skeeter
Also see DOTTSY
Also see EDDY, Duane
Also see HARRIS, Emmylou
Also see HOLLY, Buddy
Also see JENNINGS, Tommy
Also see JONES, David Lynn
Also see JONES, George
Also see KIMBERLYS
Also see MANDRELL, Barbara
Also see MONROE, Bill
Also see NELSON, Willie
Also see RABBITT, Jimmy, & Renegade
Also see RODRIGUEZ, Johnny
Also see SCHNEIDER, John
Also see SCRUGGS, Earl
Also see SOME of CHET'S FRIENDS
Also see TUBB, Ernest
Also see U.S.A. for AFRICA
Also see WHITE, Tony Joe
Also see YOUNG, Neil

JENNINGS, Waylon, & Anita Carter
                              C&W '68

Singles: 7–inch

RCA 4-8   68

Also see CARTER, Anita

JENNINGS, Waylon, & Jesse Colter
                                LP '81

(Waylon & Jessi)

Singles: 7–inch

RCA 3-5 69-71

LPs: 10/12–inch 33rpm

RCA (3931 "Leather and Lace").... 5-8   81
   Also see COLTER, Jesse

JENNINGS, Waylon, & Willie Nelson
                     P&R '77

(Waylon & Willie)

Singles: 7–inch

COLUMBIA 3-4   83
MCA 3-4   86
RCA.. 3-5   76-86

LPs: 10/12–inch 33rpm

AURA 5-8   83
COLUMBIA 5-8   83
OUT of TOWN DIST 5-8   80s
RCA (2686 "Waylon & Willie").... 5-10   78
RCA (2686 "Waylon & Willie")... 20-25   78
   (Colored vinyl. Promotional issue only.)
RCA (4455 "Waylon & Willie II").... 5-8   82

JENNINGS, Waylon, Willie Nelson, Jessi Colter, & Tompall Glaser
                     LP '76

LPs: 10/12–inch 33rpm

RCA (1321 "The Outlaws") 5-10   76

JENNINGS, Waylon, Willie Nelson, Johnny Cash, & Kris Kristofferson
                     LP '85

Singles: 7–inch

COLUMBIA 3-4   85-90

LPs: 10/12–inch 33rpm

COLUMBIA 5-8   85-90
   Also see CASH, Johnny
   Also see KRISTOFFERSON, Kris
   Also see NELSON, Willie

JENNINGS, Waylon / Johnny Paycheck

LPs: 10/12–inch 33rpm

OUT of TOWN DIST 5-8   82
   Also see PAYCHECK, Johnny

JENNINGS, Waylon, & Jerry Reed

Singles: 7–inch

RCA... 3-4   83
   Also see REED, Jerry

JENNINGS, Waylon / White Water

Singles: 7–inch

RCA... 3-4   81

JENNINGS, Waylon, & Hank Williams Jr.

Singles: 7–inch

RCA 3-4   83
   Also see JENNINGS, Waylon
   Also see WILLIAMS, Hank, Jr.

JEREMIAH   *C&W '88*

Singles: 7–inch

CHARIOT................................... 3-4   88

JERRICO, Sherri   *C&W '77*

Singles: 7–inch

GUSTO/STARDAY 3-5   77

JIM & JESSE   *C&W '64*

(With the Virginia Boys; with Sweet Mountain Boys)

Singles: 7–inch

CAPITOL................................... 3-5   3-5
EPIC... 3-6   64-70
MSR 3-4   86

LP: 10/12–inch 33rpm

CAPITOL (264 "Twenty Great
   Songs") 20-30   69
CAPITOL (770 "Freight Train") ...20-30   71
CMH.. 8-12   80
EPIC...................................... 15-30   63-75
GATE 10-20   60s
HARMONY 8-12   70
HILLTOP 6-12
MASTERSEAL 10-15
MOUNT VERNON 8-12
OLD DOMINION 10-20
PALACE................................. 10-15
PRIZE 8-12
ULTRA SONIC........................... 8-12
VERNON................................. 8-12
   Also see CLEMENTS, Vassar
   Also see FLATT, Lester, Earl Scruggs & Jim & Jesse

JIM & JESSE & Charlie Louvin
                     C&W '82

Singles: 7–inch

SOUNDWAVES 3-4   82

LP: 10/12–inch 33rpm

SOUNDWAVES 5-10   82
   Also see JIM & JESSE
   Also see LOUVIN, Charlie

JIMMY & DUANE

Singles: 7–inch

EB X. PRESTON (212 "Soda Fountain
   Girl").................................... 100-200   55

Members: Jimmy Delbridge; Duane Eddy.
Also see EDDY, Duane

JIMMY & JOHNNY   *C&W '54*
Singles: 78rpm
CHESS............................... 5-10   54
Singles: 7-inch
CHESS....................................... 10-15   54
Members: Jimmy Fautheree; "Country" Johnny Mathis
Also see MATHIS, Country Johnny

JO, Sami: see SAMI JO

JOE BOB   *C&W '75*
(Joe Bob's Nashville Sound Company)
Singles: 7-inch
CAPITOL............................. 3-5   75
LP: 10/12-inch 33rpm
R.P.A. 5-10   77

JOHN DEER: see DEER, John

JOHNNIE & JACK   *C&W '51*
(With the Tennessee Mountain Boys; with Kitty Wells; Johnny & Jack)
Singles: 78rpm
RCA.. 5-10   51-57
Singles: 7-inch
DECCA.................................... 4-8   62
RCA.................................... 8-15   51-59
EPs: 7-inch 33/45rpm
DECCA.. 8-12   62
RCA.. 10-20   55-57
LP: 10/12-inch 33rpm
ANTHOLOGY of COUNTRY
  MUSIC 8-12
CAMDEN................................. 10-20   63-64
COUNTRY CLASSICS................ 5-10
DECCA (4308 "Smiles and
  Tears") 15-25   62
GOLDEN COUNTRY 5-10
MCA 5-8   80s
RCA (1587 "Tennessee Mountain
  Boys")........................... 25-35   57
RCA (LPM-2017 "Hits").............. 20-30   59
RCA (LSP-2017 "Hits") 30-50   59
RCA (6022 "All the Best")........... 10-20   70
VOCALION.................................. 10-15   68
Members: John Wright; Jack Anglin.
Also see WELLS, Kitty
Also see WRIGHT, Johnny

JOHNS, Sammy   *C&W/P&R '74*
Singles: 7-inch
ELEKTRA....................................... 3-4   81
GRC 3-5   73-75

MCA.................................... 3-4   88
REAL WORLD 3-5   80
W.B./CURB............................. 3-5   76
LPs: 10/12-inch 33rpm
GRC...................................... 8-10   73
W.B. 5-10   77

JOHNS, Sarah   *C&W '75*
Singles: 7-inch
RCA 3-5   75-76

JOHNS, Tricia   *C&W '77*
Singles: 7-inch
ELEKTRA............................. 3-4   80-81
W.B. 3-5   77

JOHNSON, Buddy   *R&B '43/C&W '44*
(Buddy Johnson & His Orchestra)
Singles: 78rpm
ATLANTIC................................... 4-6   53
COLUMBIA 4-8   48
DECCA 4-8   42-54
MERCURY 4-6   53-56
RCA 4-6   56
Singles: 7-inch
ATLANTIC................................... 5-10   53
DECCA (24996 "You Got to Walk That Chalk
  Line")................................. 15-25   50
DECCA (28907 "Talkin' About Another Man's
  Wife") 10-20   53
DECCA (29058 "Handful of Stars")10-20   54
MERCURY 5-10   53-56
RCA 5-10   56
ROULETTE................................. 4-8   59
WING 5-10   56
LPs: 10/12-inch 33rpm
FORUM..................................10-15
MERCURY (20072 "Buddy Johnson
  Wails").........................25-35   58
  (Monaural.)
MERCURY (60072 "Buddy Johnson
  Wails").........................35-55   58
  (Stereo.)
MERCURY (20209 "Rock 'N'
  Roll") 30-40   58
MERCURY (20322 "Walkin") 20-30   58
WING (1211 "Rock 'N' Roll")......10-20   63
WING (12005 "Rock 'N' Roll")....35-50   56

JOHNSON, Buddy & Ella   *P&R '60*
Singles: 78rpm
MERCURY...................................4-6   56-57

Singles: 7–inch

MERCURY	5-10	56-61
ROULETTE	4-8	59

LPs: 10/12–inch 33rpm

MERCURY (20347 "Swing Me")	25-35	58
ROULETTE (R-25085 "Go Ahead and Rock & Roll") (Monaural.)	20-30	59
ROULETTE (SR-25085 "Go Ahead and Rock & Roll")	30-40	59

Also see JOHNSON, Buddy

JOHNSON, Gene
(Gene Autry)

Singles: 78rpm

TIMELY TUNES (1550 "High Steppin' Mama Blues")	25-75	
TIMELY TUNES (1551 "Jimmie the Kid")	25-75	
TIMELY TUNES (1552 "Do Right Daddy Blues")	25-75	

Also see AUTRY, Gene

JOHNSON, Lois   *C&W '69*

Singles: 7–inch

COLUMBIA	3-6	69
MGM	3-5	70-73
POLYDOR	3-5	76-78
20TH FOX	3-5	74

LP: 10/12–inch 33rpm

20TH FOX	8-12	74

Also see WILLIAMS, Hank, Jr., & Lois Johnson

JOHNSON, Lois, & Bill Rice   *C&W '77*

Singles: 7–inch

POLYDOR	3-5	77

Also see JOHNSON, Lois
Also see RICE, Bill

JOHNSON, Michael

P&R/R&B/LP '78/C&W '86

Singles: 7–inch

ATCO	3-5	73
EMI AMERICA	3-5	78-80
RCA	3-4	86-88

Picture Sleeves

EMI AMERICA	3-5	78

LPs: 10/12–inch 33rpm

ATCO	8-10	73
EMI AMERICA	5-8	78-82

Session: Michael Young; Russ Pahl; Denny Dadmum-Bixby.

Also see BACK PORCH MAJORITY
Also see DENVER, BOISE & JOHNSON
Also see GREAT PLAINS
Also see MITCHELL TRIO
Also see SYLVIA & Michael Johnson

JOHNSON, Mirriam
(Miriam Johnson)

Singles: 7–inch

JAMIE (1181 "Young and Innocent")	10-15	61

Picture Sleeves

JAMIE (1181 "Young and Innocent")	15-25	61

Also see COLTER, Jessie
Also see EDDY, Duane & Mirriam

JOHNSON, Roland   *C&W '59*

Singles: 7–inch

BRUNSWICK	5-10	59

JOHNSON, Tim   *C&W '87*

Singles: 7–inch

SUNDIAL	3-4	87

JOHNSTON, Day   *C&W '88*

Singles: 7–inch

ROADRUNNER	3-4	88

JOHNSTON, Don

Singles: 78rpm

CHIC (1014 "Whistle Bait")	10-20	57
MERCURY	15-25	56

Singles: 7–inch

CHIC (1014 "Whistle Bait")	10-20	57
MERCURY (70991 "Born to Love One Woman")	35-50	56

JOHNSTON, Inez

Singles: 7–inch

BRUNSWICK	5-10	60-61

JOHNSTON, Jay

Singles: 7–inch

FREEDOM	5-10	59
LIBERTY	5-10	59

JOHNSTON, Tom   *P&R/LP '79*

Singles: 7–inch

W.B.	3-5	79-81

LPs: 10/12–inch 33rpm

W.B.	5-8	79-81

JOHNSTONS   *C&W '87*

Singles: 7–inch

HIDDEN VALLEY	3-4	87

TETRAGRAMMATON	4-6	68-69

LPs: 10/12–inch 33rpm

MERCURY	8-10	72
TETRAGRAMMATON	10-15	69
VANGUARD	8-10	71

JON & LYNN   *C&W '81*

Singles: 7–inch

SOUNDWAVES	3-4	81-82

Members: Jon Hargis; Lynn Hargis.

JONES, Ann   *C&W '49*

Singles: 78rpm

CAPITOL	5-10	49
KING	4-8	51
SIMS	5-10	55

Singles: 7–inch

KING	5-15	51-61
SIMS (101 "Kind of Love I'm Craving")	15-25	55

LP: 10/12–inch 33rpm

AUDIO LAB	20-30

JONES, Anthony Armstrong

C&W '69

Singles: 7–inch

AIR	3-4	86
CHART	3-6	69-70
EPIC	3-5	73

LP: 10/12–inch 33rpm

CHART	8-12	69-70

Also see TWITTY, Conway

JONES, David Lynn   *C&W '87*

Singles: 7–inch

MERCURY	3-4	87-88

Session: Waylon Jennings.
Also see JENNINGS, Waylon

JONES, George   *C&W '55*

(With the Jones Boys; with Sonny Burns; Tina & Daddy)

Singles: 78rpm

DIXIE (#534)	25-50	56

(With Sleepy La Beef. Title not known. 78rpm EP. Not issued with cover.)

DIXIE (#535)	25-50	56

(78rpm EP. Not issued with cover.)

MERCURY	10-25	57
STARDAY	10-25	54-57

Singles: 7–inch

D	4-8	65-66
EPIC	3-5	72-82

MERCURY (71000 & 72000 series)	5-15	57-64
MUSICOR	3-8	65-71
PROMOTIONAL COPIES ("The Race Is On")	20-25	64

(No label name other than "Promotional Copies," is shown on disc.)

RCA	3-5	72-74
STARDAY (Except 100 & 200 series)	4-8	64-71
STARDAY (100 & 200 series)	10-20	54-57

(Black vinyl.)

STARDAY (264 "Just One More")	30-40	56

(Colored vinyl.)

U.A.	4-8	62-67

Picture Sleeves

MERCURY	8-12	62-64
MUSICOR	5-10	65
U.A.	5-10	62-63

EPs: 7–inch 33/45rpm

DIXIE (501 "Why Baby Why")	25-50	56

(Not issued with cover.)

DIXIE (505 "Heartbreak Hotel")	25-50	56

(Not issued with cover.)

DIXIE (516 "Poor Old Me")	25-50	56

(No cover. Has two track by Benny Barnes.)

DIXIE (518 "Stolen Moments")	25-50	56

(Not issued with cover.)

DIXIE (525 "Don't Do This to Me")	15-25	59

(Has one George Jones track. Not issued with cover.)

MERCURY	10-20	61
RECORD of the MONTH (280 "Heartbreak Hotel")	30-40	56

(Colored vinyl.)

STARDAY	8-15	65

(Jukebox issues. May include title strips.)

LPs: 10/12–inch 33rpm

ACCORD	4-6	82
ALBUM GLOBE	5-8	81
ALLEGIANCE	4-8	84
AMBASSADOR	5-8	
AURA	5-8	82
BUCKBOARD	5-8	76
BULLDOG	8-10	
CAMDEN	5-8	72-74
COLUMBIA	5-8	80-83
EPIC	10-30	72-82
EVEREST	5-8	79
51 WEST	5-8	79-82

GUSTO	5-8	78-81
I&M	5-8	82
KOALA	5-8	
K-TEL	5-8	
LIBERTY	5-8	82
MCA	3-4	91-92
MERCURY (8000 series)	5-10	72
MERCURY (20306 "14 Country Favorites")	40-60	58
MERCURY (20462 "Country Church Time")	40-60	59
MERCURY (20477 "White Lightning")	40-60	59
MERCURY (20621 thru 20836) (Monaural.)	20-30	60-63
MERCURY (20906 thru 21048) (Monaural.)	20-30	64-65
MERCURY (60257 thru 60836) (Stereo.)	25-35	60-63
MERCURY (60906 thru 61048) (Stereo.)	15-25	64-65
MOUNTAIN DEW	5-8	
MUSIC DISC	6-10	69
MUSICOR	10-20	65-77
MUSICOR/RCA	10-20	74-75
NASHVILLE	10-20	70-71
PAIR	6-10	70s
PHOENIX 10	5-8	81
PHOENIX 20	5-8	81
PICADILLY	5-8	81
PICKWICK	4-8	80
PICKWICK/HILLTOP	8-12	69
POWER PAK	5-8	75
RCA	10-20	72-75
ROUNDER	5-8	82-84
RUBY	5-8	
SEARS	8-12	
STARDAY (101 "The Grand Ole Opry's New Star")	50-75	58
STARDAY (102 "George Jones")	40-60	59
STARDAY (125 "George Jones: Crown Prince of Country Music")	40-50	60
STARDAY (150 "George Jones Sings His Greatest Hits")	40-50	62
STARDAY (151 "Fabulous Country Music Sound of George Jones")	40-50	62
STARDAY (335 "George Jones")	25-35	65
STARDAY (344 "Long Live King George")	25-35	65
STARDAY (366 "The George Jones Story") (With bonus 8 x 10 color photo.)	25-35	66
STARDAY (366 "The George Jones Story") (Without bonus photo.)	15-25	66
STARDAY (400 series, except 401)	15-20	69
STARDAY (401 "George Jones Song Book and Picture Album") (With 32-page song booklet.)	35-45	67
STARDAY (401 "George Jones Song Book and Picture Album") (Without song booklet.)	15-25	68
STARDAY (3000 series)	5-8	77
STARDAY (90000 series)	8-12	
SUNRISE	5-8	81
TIME-LIFE	5-15	81-82
TRIP	5-8	76
TROLLY CAR	5-8	
UNART	8-12	67-68
U.A. (85 "Superpak")	10-15	71
U.A. (100 series)	5-8	73
U.A. (3000 series) (Monaural.)	10-20	62-67
U.A. (6000 series) (Stereo.)	12-25	62-69
WHITE LIGHTNING	12-18	
WING	8-12	64-68
WING/PICKWICK	4-6	

Session: Jordanaires; Oak Ridge Boys; Waylon Jennings.
Also see CHARLES, Ray, George Jones & Chet Atkins
Also see COE, David Allan
Also see DARRELL, Johnny / George Jones / Willie Nelson
Also see HAGGARD, Merle, & George Jones
Also see JENNINGS, Waylon
Also see JONES, Thumper
Also see JORDANAIRES
Also see OAK RIDGE BOYS
Also see PARTON, Dolly / George Jones
Also see SMITH, Hank
Also see TRAVIS, Randy, & George Jones
Also see TUBB, Ernest
Also see WILLIAMS, Hank, Jr..

JONES, George / Benny Barnes
EPs: 7–inch 33/45rpm

DIXIE (518 "Stolen Moments") (Not issued with cover.)	25-50	56

Also see BARNES, Benny

JONES, George, & Brenda Lee
C&W '84

Singles: 7–inch
EPIC 3-4   84
Also see LEE, Brenda

JONES, George, & Brenda Carter
C&W '68

Singles: 7–inch
MUSICOR 4-6   68

JONES, George, & David Allan Coe
Singles: 7–inch
COLUMBIA 3-4   81
Also see COE, David Allan

JONES, George, & Lacy J. Dalton
C&W '85

Singles: 7–inch
EPIC 3-4   85
Also see DALTON, Lacy J.

JONES, George, & Jeanette Hicks
C&W '57

Singles: 7–inch
STARDAY 5-8   57
Singles: 7–inch
STARDAY 10-20   57

JONES, George, & Shelby Lynne
C&W '88

Singles: 7–inch
EPIC 3-4   88
Also see LYNNE, Shelby

JONES, George, & Melba Montgomery
C&W '63

Singles: 7–inch
CURIO 4-8   60s
MUSICOR 4-8   66-67
U.A. 4-8   63-66
Picture Sleeves
CURIO (7020 "You're in My
  Heart") 8-10   60s
LPs: 10/12–inch 33rpm
BUCKBOARD 5-8   76
GUEST STAR 8-10   60s
LIBERTY 4-6   82
MUSIC DISC 6-10   69
MUSICOR 10-20   66-74
MUSICOR/RCA 10-20   74
U.A. (200 series) 5-8   73

U.A. (3000 series) 10-20   63-66
  (Monaural.)
U.A. (6000 series) 12-25   63-66
  (Stereo.)
Also see MONTGOMERY, Melba

JONES, George / Buck Owens / David Houston / Tommy Hill
LPs: 10/12–inch 33rpm
NASHVILLE 10-15   60s
Also see HOUSTON, David
Also see OWENS, Buck

JONES, George, & Johnny Paycheck
C&W '80

Singles: 7–inch
EPIC 3-5   78-80
LPs: 10/12–inch 33rpm
EPIC 5-8   80
Also see PAYCHECK, Johnny

JONES, George, & Gene Pitney
C&W/LP '65

(George & Gene, with the Jordanaires)
Singles: 7–inch
MUSICOR 4-6   65-66
Picture Sleeves
MUSICOR 4-6   65
LPs: 10/12–inch 33rpm
DESIGN 6-10
INTERNATIONAL AWARD 8-10
MUSIC DISC 10-12   69
MUSICOR (3044 "George Jones & Gene
  Pitney") 15-25   65
  (Front cover shows title as "For the First
  Time! Two Great Stars, George Jones &
  Gene Pitney.")
MUSICOR (3044 "George Jones & Gene
  Pitney") 15-20   65
  (Front cover shows title as "Recorded in
  Nashville, Tennessee, George Jones &
  Gene Pitney.")
MUSICOR (3065 "It's Country Time
  Again") 10-20   65
TS (439 "Country Cousins") 5-10
Session: Jordanaires.
Also see JORDANAIRES
Also see PITNEY, Gene

JONES, George, Gene Pitney, & Melba Montgomery
LPs: 10/12–inch 33rpm
MUSICOR 10-20   66
  (Has duets by these artists, but none where
  all three perform together.)
Also see MONTGOMERY, Melba

JONES, George, & Margie Singleton
C&W '61

Singles: 7–inch

MERCURY 4-8   61-62

Also see SINGLETON, Margie

LPs: 10/12–inch 33rpm

MERCURY (20747 "Duets")...... 15-25   62
(Monaural.)

MERCURY (60747 "Duets")...... 20-30   62
(Stereo.)

WING 10-15   66

JONES, George, & Ernest Tubb

Singles: 7–inch

FIRST GENERATION 3-4   81

JONES, George, & Tammy Wynette
C&W/LP '71

(George, Tammy & Tina)

Singles: 7–inch

EPIC... 3-5   71-80

LPs: 10/12–inch 33rpm

COLUMBIA 5-8   81

EPIC... 8-12   71-81

TEE VEE/CBS.............................. 5-8   79

Also see JONES, George
Also see WYNETTE, Tammy

JONES, Grandpa
C&W '59

Singles: 78rpm

KING 5-10   44-54

RCA... 4-8   52-54

Singles: 7–inch

DECCA... 5-10   59

KING 4-8   60-63

MONUMENT 4-6   62-67

EPs: 7–inch 33/45rpm

DECCA... 5-10   59

KING 5-15   50s

LP: 10/12–inch 33rpm

CMH 5-10   76-81

CORAL... 5-10   73

DECCA (4364 "Evening with Grandpa
Jones")..................................... 15-25   63

HARMONY................................... 6-12   72

KING (554 "Greatest Hits") 25-35   58

KING (625 "Strictly Country
Tunes")..................................... 30-50   59

KING (809 "Rollin' Along")......... 15-25   63

KING (822 thru 1042)................. 15-25   63-69

MONUMENT 10-20   62-74

POWER PAK 5-10   80s

SKYLITE 5-8   76-82

VOCALION 8-12   70

JONES, Grandpa / Minnie Pearl

LP: 10/12–inch 33rpm

CAMDEN 5-10   74

Also see JONES, Grandpa
Also see MINNIE PEARL

JONES, Harrison
C&W '74

Singles: 7–inch

GRT 3-5   74

JONES, Mickey
C&W '79

Singles: 7–inch

BAYSHORE...................................3-5   79

STOP HUNGER.............................3-4   89

JONES, Thumper

(George Jones)

Singles: 78rpm

STARDAY (240 "Rock-It")..........50-75   56

Singles: 7–inch

STARDAY (240 "Rock-It")........75-100   56

EPs: 7–inch 33/45rpm

DIXIE (502 "Thumper Jones")....20-30   58
(Contains three Jones tracks. Not issued
with cover.)

LPs: 10/12–inch 33rpm

TEENAGE HEAVEN 8-12

Also see JONES, George

JONES, Tom

P&R/R&B/LP '65/C&W '76

Singles: 7–inch

EPIC...3-5   76-80

LONDON.......................................3-5   77

MCA...3-5   79

MERCURY.....................................3-4   81-85

PARROT.......................................3-8   65-75

SYMBOL.......................................4-8   65

TOWER...4-8   65

Picture Sleeves

PARROT (9737 thru 9801) 4-8   65

PARROT (40000 series)...............3-6   69-71

LPs: 10/12–inch 33rpm

EPIC...8-12   70-76

LONDON.......................................5-8   77

MERCURY.....................................5-8   81-85

PARROT.....................................10-20   65-74

JONES, Tom / Freddie & Dreamers / Johnny Rivers

LPs: 10/12–inch 33rpm

TOWER (5007 "Three at the
Top") 15-20   65
   Also see JONES, Tom
   Also see RIVERS, Johnny

JORDAN, Jill   *C&W '88*

Singles: 7–inch

MAXX 3-4   88

JORDAN, Louis   *R&B '42/C&W '44*

(Louis Jordan's Elk Rendezvous Band; with
His Tympani 5)

Singles: 78rpm

DECCA (7500 thru 8600 series) . 5-15   38-43
DECCA (18000 thru 30000
series) 5-10   44-50
VIK 5-10   56

Singles: 7–inch

ALADDIN (3223 "Whiskey Do Your
Stuff") 20-30   54
ALADDIN (3227 "Ooo-Wee") 20-30   54
ALADDIN (3242 "A Dollar
Down") 25-35   54
ALADDIN (3246 "Messy
Bessie") 20-30   54
ALADDIN (3249 "Louis'
Blues") 20-30   54
ALADDIN (3264 "Put Some Money in the
Pot") 20-30   54
ALADDIN (3270 "Fat Back and Corn
Liquor") 20-30   54
ALADDIN (3279 "Gal, You Need a
Whippin") 20-30   54
DECCA (20000 thru 30000
series) 15-25   50-54
LOU-WA 5-10   60
MERCURY 10-20   56-58
PZAZZ 4-6   68
TANGERINE 4-8   62-66
VIK 8-12   56
WARWICK 5-10   60-61
X... 8-12   55

EPs: 7–inch 33/45rpm

DECCA 15-25   56
MERCURY 15-25   57

LPs: 10/12–inch 33rpm

CLASSICAL JAZZ 5-8   82
DECCA (5035 "Greatest Hits").. 10-20   68
DECCA (8551 "Let the Good Times
Roll") 30-40   56

MCA 5-8   75-80
MERCURY (20242 "Somebody Up There
Digs Me") 25-30   57
MERCURY (20331 "Man, We're
Wailin") 25-30   58
SCORE (4007 "Go Blow Your
Horn") 65-85   57
TANGERINE 12-15   64
TRIP 8-10   75
WING 15-20   63
   Also see CROSBY, Bing, & Louis Jordan
   Also see FITZGERALD, Ella, & Louis Jordan

JORDANAIRES

Singles: 78rpm

CAPITOL 3-5   54-57
DECCA 3-5   52-54
RCA 3-5   51-53
X.. 3-5   54

Singles: 7–inch

CAPITOL 5-10   54-60
COLUMBIA (Except 43283) 4-8   64-66
   (Columbia 43283, *Malibu Run*, is by another
   group of Jordanaires—listed in a separate
   section that follows.)
DECCA 5-10   52-54
SESAC 4-6   50s
STOP 3-5   69
RCA 5-10   51-53
X... 5-10   54

EPs: 7–inch 33/45rpm

CAPITOL 5-10   55-59
RCA (3081 "Beautiful City") 15-25   53

LPs: 10/12–inch 33rpm

CAPITOL 5-15   58-62
CLASSIC 10-15   78
COLUMBIA 5-15   64-66
DECCA 10-15   57
100% MUSIC 8-10   86
RCA (3081 "Beautiful City") 20-30   53
   (10–inch LP.)
STEP ONE (0029 "Elvis' Favorite
Spirituals") 8-10   90
SESAC 20-30
STEP ONE 5-8   87
STOP 5-10

177

VOCALION.................................... 4-8   69

Members: Gordon Stoker; Neal Matthews; Hoyt
Hawkins; Hugh Jarrett; Ray Walker; Louis Nunley;
Duane West.
  Also see ACUFF, Roy
  Also see ANDERSON, Bill
  Also see ANDERSON, Lynn
  Also see BANDY, Moe
  Also see CLINE, Patsy
  Also see FAIRCHLILD, Barbara
  Also see FARGO, Donna
  Also see FORD, Tennessee Ernie
  Also see FRANCIS, Connie
  Also see GIBSON, Don
  Also see HAGGARD, Merle
  Also see HOWARD, Jan
  Also see JACKSON, Stonewall
  Also see JONES, George
  Also see JONES, George, & Gene Pitney
  Also see LEE, Brenda
  Also see LOCKLIN, Hank
  Also see LYNN, Loretta
  Also see MACK, Warner
  Also see McDOWELL, Ronnie
  Also see MIZE, Billy
  Also see NELSON, Rick
  Also see PARTON, Dolly
  Also see PAYCHECK, Johnny
  Also see PRESLEY, Elvis
  Also see REEVES, Jim
  Also see RICH, Charlie
  Also see ROBBINS, Marty
  Also see RUSSELL, Johnny
  Also see SNOW, Hank
  Also see TUBB, Ernest
  Also see WEST, Dottie
  Also see YOUNG, Faron

JORDANAIRES

Singles: 7–inch

COLUMBIA (43283 "Malibu
Run").. 10-15   65
(Listed primarily to distinguish this group
from the preceding Jordanaires, as both
groups had releases on Columbia.)

JOY, Homer   *C&W '74*
Singles: 7–inch
CAPITOL................................ 3-5   74

JOYCE, Brenda   *C&W '79*
Singles: 7–inch
MERCURY.................................. 4-8   65
WESTERN PACIFIC

JUDDS   *C&W '83*
Singles: 7–inch
CURB/RCA 3-4   90-91
RCA... 3-5   83-88
RCA/CURB 3-4   89-89
Promotional Singles
RCA... 5-10   83-88
(Black vinyl.)

RCA (13673 "Had a Dream").....15-20   83
(Colored vinyl.)
RCA (13923 "Why Not Me").......10-20   84
(Colored vinyl.)
RCA (13673 "Had a Dream").....15-20   83
(Colored vinyl.)
LPs: 10/12–inch 33rpm
RCA 5-8   83-88
RCA/CURB 5-8   89-89
Members: Naomi Judd; Wynonna Judd.

JUDY LYNN   *C&W '62*
(Judy Lynn Voiten)
Singles: 7–inch
AMARET....................................3-5   71-73
COLUMBIA 3-6   69
MUSICOR..................................4-6   66-67
U.A. 4-8   62-66
W.B./CURB 3-5   75
LP: 10/12–inch 33rpm
AMARET...................................5-10   71-73
COLUMBIA 8-12   69
MUSICOR................................10-15   66-67
U.A. 10-20   62-66
UNART......................................10-15   67
Also see GRAMMER, Billy / Judy Lynn / Link Wray

JURGENS, Dick, & His Orchestra   *C&W '47*
Singles: 78rpm
COLUMBIA 4-6   47

JUSTIS, Bill   *P&R/R&B/C&W '57*
(With the Jury; Bill Justis Orchestra; with
Roger Fakes & Spinners)
Singles: 78rpm
PHILLIPS INT'L...........................15-30   57
Singles: 7–inch
BELL 3-5   70
MONUMENT................................3-5   76
PHILLIPS INT'L...........................8-15   57-59
PLAY ME 8-12   59
MCA...3-5   77
MONUMENT................................4-8   66
NRC...4-8   60
SMASH 4-8   63-65
Picture Sleeves
SMASH 5-10   63
LPs: 10/12–inch 33rpm
HARMONY.................................8-10   72
PHILLIPS INT'L (1950 "Cloud
9") 25-30   57
SMASH 15-20   62-66

SUN.. 8-10   69
WING 10-20   65

JUSTIS, Bill / Jerry Reed
EPs: 7–inch 33/45rpm
MCA (1961 "Music from *Smokey and the Bandit*") 10-15   77
(Promotional issue only.)
Also see JUSTIS, Bill
Also see REED, Jerry

K

KALIN TWINS   *P&R/C&W/R&B '58*
Singles: 78rpm
DECCA....................................... 20-40   58
Singles: 7–inch
AMY 4-8   66
DECCA....................................... 8-10   58-62
Picture Sleeves
DECCA (30977 "Why Don't You Believe Me").. 10-15   59
EPs: 7–inch 33/45rpm
DECCA (2623 "Kalin Twins") 25-50   58
DECCA (2641 "Forget Me Not").. 25-50   59
LPs: 10/12–inch 33rpm
DECCA (8812 "Kalin Twins") 50-75   58
VOCALION (73771 "Kalin Twins") 30-40   66
Members: Hal Kalin; Herb Kalin.
Also see LEE, Brenda / Bill Haley & Comets / Kalin Twins / Four Aces

KANDY, Jim   *C&W '65*
Singles: 7–inch
K-ARK 4-8   65

KANE, Kieran   *C&W '81*
Singles: 7–inch
ELEKTRA..................................... 3-5   81-82
W.B. 3-4   83-84
Also see O'KANES

KANTNER, Hillary   *C&W '84*
Singles: 7–inch
RCA.. 3-4   84-85

KAY, Melissa   *C&W '88*
Singles: 7–inch
REED (Black vinyl)........................3-4   88-89
REED (1119 "After Lovin' You").....4-6   88
(Colored vinyl.)

KAYE, Angela   *C&W '81*
Singles: 7–inch
YATAHEY 3-4   81

KAYE, Barry   *C&W '78*
Singles: 7–inch
MCA..3-5   78

KAYE, Debbie Lori   *C&W '68*
Singles: 7–inch
COLUMBIA 4-8   65-68
Picture Sleeves
COLUMBIA 4-8   65

KAYE, Lois   *C&W '79*
Singles: 7–inch
OVATION.....................................3-5   79
LP: 10/12–inch 33rpm
OVATION.....................................5-10   79

KAYE, Sandra   *C&W '78*
Singles: 7–inch
DOOR KNOB...............................3-5   78-79

KEARNEY, Ramsey   *C&W '85*
Singles: 7–inch
CHALLENGE 4-6   66
DARGON 3-4   84
HICKORY......................................4-6   62-64
JUBAL...3-5   72-73
NASHCO.......................................3-4   85
SAFARI 3-5   74-90
SPOTLIGHT...................................3-4   81-88
Picture Sleeves
SAFARI 3-4   90
LPs: 10/12–inch 33rpm
NASHCO.......................................8-10   85
SAFARI 10-20   90

KELLEY, John   *C&W '82*
Singles: 7–inch
COMSTAR 3-4   82

KELLUM, Murry   *P&R '63/C&W '71*
Singles: 7–inch
CINNAMON 3-5   73-74
EPIC...3-5   71-72

MUSIC MILL	3-5	76
PLANTATION	3-5	78
RANWOOD	3-5	76

LPs: 10/12–inch 33rpm

PLANTATION	5-8	78

KELLUM, Murry, & Alton Lott
Singles: 7–inch

K&M	3-5	61

KELLUM, Murry / Glenn Sutton
Singles: 7–inch

ABC	3-5	73
M.O.C. (Except 658)	10-15	63-64
M.O.C. (658 "I Dreamed I Was a Beatle")	12-18	64

Also see KELLUM, Murry
Also see SUTTON, Glenn

KELLY, Irene   *C&W '89*
Singles: 7–inch

MCA	3-4	89

KELLY, Jerri   *C&W '80*
Singles: 7–inch

CARRERE	3-4	82
LITTLE GIANT	3-4	80-81

Also see MITCHELL, Price, & Jerri Kelly

KELLY, Karen   *C&W '70*
Singles: 7–inch

CAPITOL	3-5	70
SOUND STAGE 7	4-8	64-65

KEMP, Dave   *C&W '83*
Singles: 7–inch

SOUNDWAVES	3-4	83

KEMP, Wayne   *C&W '69*
Singles: 7–inch

DECCA	3-6	69-72
DOOR KNOB	3-4	83-86
MCA	3-5	73-74
MERCURY	3-4	80-82
U.A.	3-5	76-77

LP: 10/12–inch 33rpm

DECCA	5-10	71
MCA	5-10	73

KEMP, Wayne, & Bobby G. Rice   *C&W '86*
Singles: 7–inch

DOOR KNOB	3-4	86

Also see KEMP, Wayne
Also see RICE, Bobby G.

KENDALLS   *C&W '70*
(Featuring Jeannie Kendall)
Singles: 7–inch

DOT	3-5	72-73
EPIC	3-4	89
MCA/CURB	3-4	86
MERCURY	3-4	81-85
OVATION	3-5	77-80
STEP ONE	3-4	87-88
STOP	3-6	70
U.A.	3-5	75-76
VARSITY	10-15	69

LPs: 10/12–inch 33rpm

DOT	8-12	72
GUSTO	5-8	78
MCA/CURB	5-8	86
MERCURY	5-8	81-85
OVATION	5-10	76-80
STOP	10-15	70
PICKWICK	5-8	79
POWER PAK	5-8	74

Members: Jeannie Kendall; Royce Kendall.
Also see HARRIS, Emmylou
Also see KENDALL, Jeannie

KENNARD & JOHN   *C&W '89*
Singles: 7–inch

CURB	3-4	89

Members: Philip Kennard; Ron John.

KENNEDY, Gene   *C&W '86*
Singles: 7–inch

SOCIETY	3-4	86

KENNEDY, Gene, & Karen Jeglum   *C&W '81*
Singles: 7–inch

DOOR KNOB	3-4	81-83

Also see KENNEDY, Gene

KENNEDY, Larry Wayne   *C&W '85*
Singles: 7–inch

JERE	3-4	85

KENNEDY, Mike   *P&R '72*
Singles: 7–inch

ABC	3-5	72

LPs: 10/12–inch 33rpm

ABC	8-10	72

Also see LOS BRAVOS

KENNEDY, Ray   *C&W '90*
Singles: 7–inch

ATLANTIC	3-4	90-91

KENNY O.   *C&W '81*

Singles: 7–inch

RHINESTONE.............................. 3-4   81

KENT, George   *C&W '69*

(With Diana Duke)

Singles: 7–inch

MERCURY 3-6   69-70
SHANNON 3-5   74-76
SOUNDWAVES 3-5

LPs: 10/12–inch 33rpm

SHANNON 10-20   75

KENTUCKY HEADHUNTERS

C&W/LP '89

Singles: 7–inch

MERCURY 3-4   89-91

LPs: 10/12–inch 33rpm

MERCURY 5-8   89-91

Members: Fred Young; Richard Young; Greg Martin; Ricky Lee Phelps; Doug Phelps; Mark Orr; Anthony Kenny.

KENYON, Joe   *C&W '87*

Singles: 7–inch

MERCURY 3-4   87

Members: Jerry Kennedy; David Briggs.
Also see BRIGGS, David
Also see KENNEDY, Jerry

KERR, Anita   *LP '69*

(Anita Kerr Singers; Quartette)

Singles: 78rpm

DECCA... 3-6   51-57

Singles: 7–inch

AMPEX... 3-5   71
DECCA (27000 thru 30000
   series) 5-10   51-60
DECCA (31000 thru 33000
   series) 3-6   60-72
DOT... 3-5   69-70
RCA... 3-8   63-75
W.B.. 3-6   66-68

EPs: 7–inch 33/45rpm

SESAC...................................... 10-15
(Also has tracks by Buddy Hacket, Elliot Lawrence, and Bill Snyder.)

LPs: 10/12–inch 33rpm

AMPEX... 5-8   71
BAINBRIDGE 4-6   81
CAMDEN....................................... 5-10   68
CENTURY 4-8   79
DECCA... 8-15   60-69

DOT 5-10   69-70
RCA 8-15   62-77
VOCALION 5-10   70
W.B. 8-12   66
WORD..4-8   75-77

Also see ANDERSON, Bill
Also see ANITA & So-And-So's
Also see ATKINS, Chet
Also see BARE, Bobby
Also see CARVER, Johnny
Also see CLINE, Patsy
Also see DAVIS, Jimmie
Also see FOLEY, Red
Also see HELMS, Bobby
Also see IVES, Burl
Also see LEE, Brenda
Also see LITTLE DIPPERS
Also see MULLICAN, Moon
Also see NELSON, Willie
Also see PRESLEY, Elvis
Also see REEVES, Jim
Also see RICH, Charlie
Also see WILBURN BROTHERS
Also see WILLIAMS, Lawton
Also see YOUNG, Faron

KERSHAW, Doug   *C&W '69*

Singles: 7–inch

BGM...3-4   88-89
SCOTTI BROS...............................3-4   81
W.B. 3-6   69-78

LP: 10/12–inch 33rpm

BGM...5-8   89
CBS..5-8   79
HICKORY......................................6-12   72
SCOTTI BROS...............................5-8   81
W.B. 6-12   69-78

Also see RUSTY & DOUG

KERSHAW, Doug, & Hank Williams Jr.   *C&W '88*

Singles: 7–inch

BGM...3-4   88

Also see KERSHAW, Doug
Also see WILLIAMS, Hank, Jr.

KERSHAW, Sammy   *C&W '91*

Singles: 7–inch

MERCURY......................................3-4   91-92

KEVIN & AUGIE

Singles: 7–inch

KEVIN KAT 3-4   90

Members: Kevin Kosub; Augie Meyers.

KEVIN & BLACKTEARS

(Kevin Kosub; Kevin Y Los Blacktears
featuring Augie Meyers; Kevin & Augie with
the Blacktears)

Singles: 7–inch

KEVIN KAT 3-4 85-88

Picture Sleeves

KEVIN KAT 3-4 85

LPs: 10/12–inch 33rpm

KEVIN KAT 5-10 87-88

Also see KEVIN & AUGIE
Also see MEYERS, Augie

KILGORE, Merle   *C&W '60*

(With "Friends")

Singles: 7–inch

COLUMBIA 4-6 67
D.. 8-12 59
ELEKTRA....................................... 3-4 81-82
EPIC.. 4-6 65-67
IMPERIAL (5300 series) 15-25 56
IMPERIAL (5409 "Ernie") 35-55 56
IMPERIAL (5500 series) 10-15 58-59
IMPERIAL (8200 series) 10-20 54-55
IMPERIAL (8300 "Everybody Needs
a Little Lovin") 30-40 56
MGM 4-8 63-64
MERCURY 5-8 61-62
STARDAY (400 thru 600 series) . 6-12 59-61
STARDAY (900 series) 3-5 72
W.B. 3-5 74-85

Picture Sleeves

EPIC.. 8-12 65

LPs: 10/12–inch 33rpm

PICKWICK 10-20 70s
STARDAY (251 "There's Gold in Them Thar
Hills")...................................... 20-30 63
STARDAY (400 series) 6-10 73
WING 10-20 66

Session: Johnny Cash; Hank Williams Jr.

KIMBERLY SPRINGS   *C&W '84*

Singles: 7–inch

CAPITOL....................................... 3-4 84

KIMBERLYS   *P&R '71*

Singles: 7–inch

CANADIAN AMERICAN............... 4-8 62-63
COLUMBIA 4-8 65-66
HAPPY TIGER 3-5 70-71
RCA... 3-5 69

LPs: 10/12–inch 33rpm

HAPPY TIGER 8-12 70

Also see JENNINGS, Waylon

KING, Claude   *C&W/P&R '61*

Singles: 7–inch

CINNAMON 3-5 74
COLUMBIA 3-8 61-71
DEE JAY (1248 "Run Baby,
Run").......................................30-50 57
TRUE...3-5 77-80

Picture Sleeves

COLUMBIA 4-8 61-69

LPs: 10/12–inch 33rpm

COLUMBIA 10-20 62-70
GUSTO 5-8 80
HARMONY......................................8-12 68
TRUE...8-10 77

Also see YOUNG, Faron / Carl Perkins / Claude King

KING, Don   *C&W '76*

Singles: 7–inch

BENCH MARK.................................3-4 86
CON BRIO 3-5 76-79
EPIC...3-4 80-82
615...3-4 88

LP: 10/12–inch 33rpm

CON BRIO 5-10 77-78
EPIC...5-8 80-81

KING, Donny   *C&W '75*

Singles: 7–inch

W.B. 3-5 75-76

KING, Pee Wee   *C&W/P&R '48*

(With Redd Stewart; with His Golden West
Cowboys)

Singles: 78rpm

BLUEBIRD......................................5-10 49
RCA 4-8 50-55

Singles: 7–inch

BRIAR...4-8 61
JARO 5-10 60
CUCA..4-8 64-66
LANDA..4-8 61
RCA 10-15 50-55
STARDAY.......................................4-6 64-71
TODD..8-12 59

EPs: 7–inch 33/45rpm

RCA (797 "Swing West") 15-30 56
RCA (3028 "Country
Classics")...............................15-30 53
RCA (3071 "Western Hits")......15-30 53
RCA (3109 "Country Classics,
Vol. 2") 15-30 53

RCA (3280 "Swing West")	15-30	56

LPs: 10/12–inch 33rpm

BRIAR (102 "Golden Olde-Tyme Dances")	50-70	62
CAMDEN	8-15	65-71
CUCA	20-40	64
DETOUR	5-10	
LONGHORN	5-10	
NASHVILLE	10-20	
RCA (1237 "Swing West")	40-60	56
RCA (2464 "Swing West")	5-8	77
RCA (3071 "Western Hits") (10–inch LP.)	25-50	53
RCA (3109 "Country Classics") (10–inch LP.)	50-75	53
STARDAY (200 series)	10-20	64
STARDAY (900 series)	8-10	75-76

KING, Sherri   *C&W '76*

Singles: 7–inch

U.A.	3-5	76

KING, Sherry

Singles: 7–inch

MCM	3-5	77

KING COLE TRIO: see COLE, Nat "King"

KING EDWARD IV & KNIGHTS   *C&W '77*

Singles: 7–inch

SOUNDWAVES	3-5	77-81

KING FAMILY   *LP '65*

Singles: 7–inch

W.B.	3-5	65-66

LPs: 10/12–inch 33rpm

CAPITOL	5-15	65
W.B.	5-15	65

Also see KING SISTERS

KING SISTERS   *C&W '46*

(With Alvino Rey & His Orchestra; with Horace Heidt & His Orchestra)

Singles: 78rpm

ALLIED	4-6	54
BLUEBIRD	4-8	39-44
BRUNSWICK	4-8	37-38
CAPITOL	4-6	47
JUBILEE	4-6	55
MERCURY	4-8	50
RCA VICTOR	4-8	
VICTOR	4-8	44-46

Singles: 7–inch

CAPITOL	5-10	57-59
JUBILEE	5-10	55

LPs: 10/12–inch 33rpm

AJAZZ	5-8	80s
CAMDEN	8-15	66
CAPITOL (T-808 thru T-1333) (Monaural.)	15-25	57-60
CAPITOL (ST-1205 "Warm and Wonderful")	20-30	59
CAPITOL (2397 "TV's Wonderful King Sisters")	10-15	66
CAPITOL CUSTOM	8-12	70
HINDSIGHT	5-8	81-83
JOYCE	5-10	80s
SPIN-O-RAMA	8-15	66-67
W.B.	8-15	66

Members: Luise King; Donna King; Alyce King; Yvonne King; Marilyn King
Also see KING FAMILY

KINGSTON, Larry   *C&W '74*

Singles: 7–inch

JMI	4-6	74
W.B.	3-5	75

KIRBY, Dave   *C&W '69*

Singles: 7–inch

DIMENSION	3-4	81
MONUMENT	3-6	69

LP: 10/12–inch 33rpm

DOT	6-10	74

KIRK, Eddie   *C&W '48*

(With Tex Ritter)

Singles: 78rpm

CAPITOL	5-10	48-49

Also see RITTER, Tex

KIRK, Red   *C&W '49*

Singles: 78rpm

MERCURY	5-8	49-50

Session: Jerry Byrd.
Also see BYRD, Jerry

KNIGHT, Evelyn, & Red Foley   *C&W '51*

Singles: 78rpm

DECCA	4-8	51

Singles: 7–inch

DECCA	5-10	51

Also see FOLEY, Red

KNOBLOCK, Fred   *C&W/P&R/LP '80*
Singles: 7–inch
SCOTTI BROS.............................. 3-4   80-82
LPs: 10/12–inch 33rpm
SCOTTI BROS.............................. 5-8   80-82

KNOBLOCK, Fred, & Susan Anton   *C&W/P&R '80*
Singles: 7–inch
SCOTTI BROS............................. 3-5   80
Also see KNOBLOCK, Fred

KNOPFLER, Mark
Singles: 7–inch
W.B. 3-4   83
LPs: 10/12–inch 33rpm
W.B. 5-8   83
Also see ATKINS, Chet, & Mark Knopfler

KNOTT SISTERS: see SHADES / Knott Sisters

KNOTTS, Bobby
Singles: 7–inch
GEE CLEF (77 "Too Young").... 25-35   61

KNOWBODY ELSE
Singles: 7–inch
FLIP.. 8-12   69
HIP 10-20   69
LPs: 10/12–inch 33rpm
HIP (7003 "Knowbody Else") 20-30   69
Member: James Mangrum.

KNOX, Buddy   *P&R/R&B '57/C&W '68*
(With the Rhythm Orchids)
Singles: 78rpm
ROULETTE............................... 15-40   57
Singles: 7–inch
ABC 3-5   73
LIBERTY 5-10   60-64
REPRISE 4-8   65-66
ROULETTE (4002 "Party Doll") 20-30   57
(With roulette wheel circling label.)
ROULETTE (4002 "Party Doll") 15-20   57
(With roulette wheel on top half of label.)
ROULETTE (4002 "Party Doll") 10-15   58
(No roulette wheel on label.)
ROULETTE (4009 "Rock Your Little Baby to Sleep") 20-30   57
(With roulette wheel circling label.)

ROULETTE (4009 "Rock Your Little Baby to Sleep") 25-20   57
(With roulette wheel on top half of label.)
ROULETTE (4009 "Rock Your Little Baby to Sleep") 10-15   58
(No roulette wheel on label.)
ROULETTE (4018 thru 4262) 8-15   57-60
RUFF 4-8   65
U.A. 4-8   68-71
Picture Sleeves
LIBERTY (55305 "Ling Ting Tong") 10-20   61
EPs: 7–inch 33/45rpm
ROULETTE (301 "Buddy Knox") 50-75   57
LPs: 10/12–inch 33rpm
ACCORD 5-8   82-83
LIBERTY (3251 "Golden Hits") ..20-30   62
(Monaural.)
LIBERTY (7251 "Golden Hits") ..25-35   62
(Stereo.)
ROULETTE (25003 "Buddy Knox") 75-100   57
U.A. 10-15   69

KNOX, Buddy / Jimmy Bowen   *P&R/R&B '57*
(With the Rhythm Orchids)
Singles: 78rpm
ROULETTE..............................20-40   57
TRIPLE-D (797 "Party Doll"/"I'm Stickin' with You") 50-100   57
Singles: 7–inch
ROULETTE (4001 "My Baby's Gone"/"I'm Stickin' with You") 30-50   57
TRIPLE-D (797 "Party Doll"/"I'm Stickin' with You") 300-400   57
LPs: 10/12–inch 33rpm
MURRAY HILL..............................5-8   80s
ROULETTE (25048 "Buddy Knox & Jimmy Bowen") 75-125   58
Also see BOWEN, Jimmy
Also see KNOX, Buddy

KRAMER, Rex   *C&W '76*
Singles: 7–inch
COLUMBIA 3-5   76

KRISTOFFERSON, Kris   *P&R/LP '71*
Singles: 7–inch
A&M 3-4   73
COLUMBIA 3-5   77-81
EPIC...4-8   67
MONUMENT 3-5   70-81

Picture Sleeves

A&M 3-4   73

EPs: 7–inch 33/45rpm

MONUMENT (532
"Kristofferson") 5-10   71
(Promotional issue only.)

LPs: 10/12–inch 33rpm

COLUMBIA 5-8   77-81

MONUMENT 8-12   70-76

Session: Larry Gatlin; Rita Coolidge.
Also see COE, David Allan
Also see JENNINGS, Waylon, Willie Nelson, Johnny
Cash, & Kris Kristofferson
Also see NELSON, Willie, & Kris Kristofferson

KRISTOFFERSON, Kris, & Rita Coolidge   *C&W '73*

Singles: 7–inch

A&M 3-5   73-74

MONUMENT 3-5   74-75

Picture Sleeves

A&M 3-5   73

LPs: 10/12–inch 33rpm

A&M (Except PR-4690) 8-12   73-79

A&M (PR-4690 "Natural Act") ... 10-15   79
(Picture disc, numbered edition. Promotional
issue only.)

MONUMENT 8-12   74

Also see COOLIDGE, Rita

KRISTOFFERSON, Kris, Willie Nelson, Dolly Parton, & Brenda Lee

LPs: 10/12–inch 33rpm

Monument 8-12   82

Also see KRISTOFFERSON, Kris
Also see NELSON, Willie
Also see PARTON, Dolly

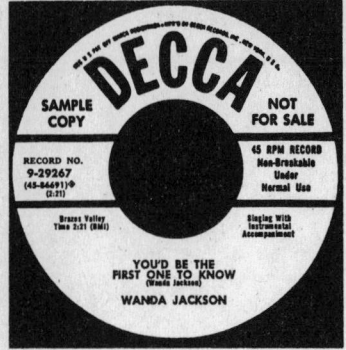

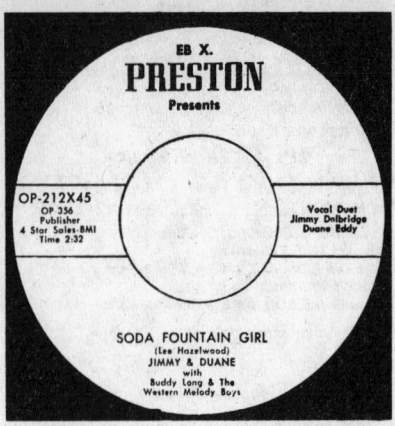

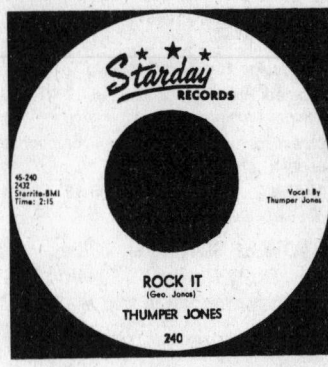

LA BEEF, Sleepy
C&W '68

(Tommy LaBeef)

Singles: 78rpm

MERCURY (71112 "I'm
Through") 50-100   57
MERCURY (71179 "All the
Time") 50-100   57
STARDAY (292 "I'm
Through") 50-100   57

Singles: 7–inch

COLUMBIA 4-8   65-68
CRESCENT (102 "Turn Me
Loose") 100-200
MERCURY (71112 "I'm
Through") 50-100   57
MERCURY (71179 "All the
Time") 50-100   57
PLANTATION (Except 55) 5-10   70-71
PLANTATION (55 "Too Much Monkey
Business") 15-25   70
STARDAY (292 "I'm
Through") 50-100   57
(Issued the same month on both Mercury
and Starday.)
SUN 3-6   68-78

LPs: 10/12–inch 33rpm

BARON 10-12   79
ROUNDER 5-8   81
SUN 8-10   74-78

LACE, Bobbi
C&W '86

Singles: 7–inch

GBS 3-4   86
615 3-4   87-89
Also see GRAY, Mark, & Bobbi Lace

LA COSTA
C&W '74

(La Costa Tucker)

Singles: 7–inch

CAPITOL 3-5   74-80
ELEKTRA 3-4   82

LP: 10/12–inch 33rpm

CAPITOL 5-10   74-77

LaFLEUR, Don
C&W '88

Singles: 7–inch

WORTH 3-4   88

LAMASTER, Don
C&W '89

Singles: 7–inch

K-ARK 3-4   89

LANCE, Linda K.
C&W '69

(With the Gary Paxon Singers)

Singles: 7–inch

ABC 4-6   67
GAR-PAX 3-5   76
ROYAL AMERICAN 3-6   69-71
TRIUNE 3-5   73
WAYSIDE 3-5   70s

LP: 10/12–inch 33rpm

ROYAL AMERICAN 8-12   69
Also see PETERS, Jimmy, & Linda K. Lance

LANDERS, Dave
C&W '49

Singles: 78rpm

MGM 4-8   49

LANDERS, Rich
C&W '81

Singles: 7–inch

AMI 3-4   81-83
OVATION 3-5   81

LANE, Cristy
C&W '77

Singles: 7–inch

LS (100 series) 3-5   77-78
LS (1000 series) 3-4   87
LIBERTY 3-5   81-83
U.A. 3-5   79-80

LP: 10/12–inch 33rpm

LS 5-10   77-83
LIBERTY 5-8   80-83
U.A. 5-10   79-80

LANE, Jerry
C&W '74

(Jerry "Max" Lane)

Singles: 7–inch

ABC 3-5   74-75
CHART 3-5   70
STOCKYARD 3-4   83

LP: 10/12–inch 33rpm

CHART 6-12   70
Also see ANDERSON, Lynn, & Jerry Lane

LANE, Red
C&W '71

Singles: 7–inch

RCA 3-5   71-72

LP: 10/12–inch 33rpm			
RCA	6-12	71	

LANE, Terri   *C&W '73*
(With Nall)
Singles: 7–inch
MONUMENT 3-5   73

LANE, Trinity: see TRINITY LANE

LANE BROTHERS   *P&R '57/C&W '81*
Singles: 78rpm
RCA 5-10   57
Singles: 7–inch
FXL 3-4   81
LEADER 5-8   60
RCA 5-10   57-58

Members: Pete Lane; Arthur Lane; Frank Lane.

LANE BROTHERS / Julius La Rosa
EPs: 7–inch 33/45rpm
RCA 5-10   57
  (Promotional issue only.)
  Also see LANE BROTHERS

LANG, K.D.   *C&W/LP '88*
(k.d. lang & the Reclines)
Singles: 7–inch
SIRE 3-4   88-91
LPs: 10/12–inch 33rpm
SIRE 5-8   88-90
  Also see ORBISON, Roy, & K.D. Lang

LANG, Kelly   *C&W '82*
Singles: 7–inch
SOUNDWAVES 3-4   82

LANSDOWNE, Jerry   *C&W '89*
Singles: 7–inch
STEP ONE 3-4   89

LaPOINTE, Perry   *C&W '86*
Singles: 7–inch
DOOR KNOB 3-4   86-89
  Also see RICE, Bobby G., & Perry LaPointe

LARGE, Billy   *C&W '66*
Singles: 7–inch
COLUMBIA 4-6   66-67
Picture Sleeves
COLUMBIA 4-8   66

LARRATT, Iris   *C&W '79*
Singles: 7–inch
INFINITY 3-5   79

LPs: 10/12–inch 33rpm			
INFINITY	8-10	79	
RCA	8-10		

LARSON, Nicolette
P&R/LP '78/C&W '85
Singles: 7–inch
MCA 3-4   85-86
W.B. 3-5   78-82
LPs: 10/12–inch 33rpm
MCA 5-8   86
W.B. 5-8   78-82
  Session: Steve Wariner.
  Also see NITTY GRITTY DIRT BAND
  Also see WARINER, Steve

LATHAM, Buddy   *C&W '88*
Singles: 7–inch
PRAIRIE DUST 3-4   88

LAUDERDALE, Jim   *C&W '88*
Singles: 7–inch
EPIC 3-4   88

LAWRENCE, Tracy   *C&W '91*
Singles: 7–inch
ATLANTIC 3-4   91

LAWRENCE, Vicki   *P&R/C&W/LP '73*
Singles: 7–inch
BELL 3-5   73-74
ELF 4-6   69
FLASHBACK 3-5   74
PRIVATE STOCK 3-5   75-76
U.A. 3-5   71
LPs: 10/12–inch 33rpm
BELL 8-12   73
WINDMILL 5-10   79

LAWSON, Janet   *C&W '70*
Singles: 7–inch
U.A. 3-5   70

LAY, Rodney   *C&W '81*
(With Wild West)
Singles: 7–inch
CHAN 10-15
CHURCHILL 3-4   82-83
EVERGREEN 3-5   86
SUN 3-5   79-81
LPs: 10/12–inch 33rpm
CHURCHILL 5-8   82
SUN 8-10   79-81

LEAPY LEE   *C&W/P&R '68*
Singles: 7–inch
CADET	4-6	69
DECCA	4-8	68-71
MAM	3-5	72
MCA	3-5	75

Picture Sleeves
MCA	3-5	75

LPs: 10/12–inch 33rpm
DECCA	10-20	68-70

LEATHERWOOD, Bill   *C&W '60*
Singles: 7–inch
COUNTRY JUBILEE	5-8	60

LEATHERWOOD, Patti   *C&W '76*
Singles: 7–inch
EPIC	3-5	76-77

LeBEAU, Tim   *C&W '88*
Singles: 7–inch
ROSE HILL	3-4	88

LEBSOCK, Jack   *C&W '73*
Singles: 7–inch
CAPITOL	3-5	73-74

Also see GRAYSON, Jack

LEDFORD, Susan   *C&W '89*
Singles: 7–inch
PROJECT ONE	3-4	89

LeDOUX, Chris   *C&W '79*
Singles: 7–inch
LUCKY MAN	3-5	73-80

LP: 10/12–inch 33rpm
LUCKY MAN	5-12	73-80

LEE: see MARENO, Lee

LEE, Brenda   *P&R/C&W '57*
(With the Jordanaires; with Holladays)
Singles: 78rpm
DECCA	20-40	56-58

Singles: 7–inch
DECCA (30050 "Jambalaya")	20-30	56
DECCA (30107 "Christy Christmas")	15-25	56
DECCA (30198 "One Step at a Time")	15-20	57
DECCA (30333 "Dynamite")	15-20	57
DECCA (30411 "One Teenager to Another")	10-20	57
DECCA (30535 "Rock-A-Bye Baby Blues")	10-20	57
DECCA (30673 "Ring-A My Phone")	20-30	58
DECCA (30776 "Rockin' Around the Christmas Tree")	10-15	58
DECCA (30806 "Bill Bailey")	10-15	59
DECCA (30967 "Sweet Nothin's")	8-12	59

(Price range of 30050 through 30967 is for black, pink or green label originals. Pink and green were promotional only. Decca multi-color labels in that series are $4 to $8 reissues.)

DECCA (31093 thru 32330)	5-10	60-68
DECCA (32428 thru 32975)	4-6	69-72
DECCA (34330 "Interview")	10-20	72

(Promotional issue only.)

DECCA (88215 "I'm Gonna Lasso Santa Claus")	20-30	56

(Decca "Children's Series.")

ELEKTRA	3-5	78
MCA	3-5	73-86

Picture Sleeves
W.B.	3-4	91
DECCA (30776 "Rockin' Around the Christmas Tree")	15-25	59
DECCA (30967 "Sweet Nothin's")	25-35	59
DECCA (31093 thru 32428)	5-15	60-69
DECCA (34000 series)	5-10	62

(Compact 33 stereo.)

DECCA (88215 "I'm Gonna Lasso Santa Claus")	30-40	56

(For either 45 or 78rpm single sleeve.)

EPs: 7–inch 33/45rpm
DECCA	10-20	60-65

LPs: 10/12–inch 33rpm
CORAL	5-10	73
DECCA (4039 thru 4104)	20-35	60-61

(Monaural.)

DECCA (4176 thru 4755)	15-30	61-66

(Monaural.)

DECCA (4757 "10 Golden Years")	15-25	66

(Gatefold cover. Monaural.)

DECCA (4757 "10 Golden Years")	10-15	60s

(Standard cover. Monaural.)

DECCA (4825 thru 4955)	10-20	66-68

(Monaural.)

DECCA (8873 "Grandma, What Great Songs You Sang")	30-40	59

(Monaural.)

DECCA (74039 thru 74104)...... 25-40   60-61
(Stereo.)

DECCA (74176 thru 74755)...... 20-35   61-66
(Stereo.)

DECCA (74757 "10 Golden
Years")..................................... 20-30   66
(Gatefold cover. Stereo.)

DECCA (74757 "10 Golden
Years")..................................... 10-15   60s
(Standard cover. Stereo.)

DECCA (74825 thru 75232)...... 10-20   66-70
(Stereo.)

DECCA (78873 "Grandma, What Great Songs
You Sang").............................. 35-45   59
(Stereo.)

MCA (Except 700 series)............ 8-10   73-86

MCA (700 series)......................... 5-8

PICKWICK..................................... 5-10   70s

TEE-VEE....................................... 5-10   78

VOCALION................................... 10-12   67-70

WARWICK (5083 "Little Miss
Dynamite")................................. 5-10   80
(TV mail order offer.)

Session: Anita Kerr; Bob Moore; Boots Randolph;
Jordanaires; James "Buzz" Cason.
Also see JORDANAIRES
Also see KERR, Anita
Also see KRISTOFFERSON, Kris, Willie Nelson, Dolly
Parton, & Brenda Lee
Also see MOORE, Bob
Also see NELSON, Willie, & Brenda Lee
Also see RANDOLPH, Boots

LEE, Brenda / Carl Dobkins, Jr.
EPs: 7–inch 33/45rpm
DECCA (38169 "Datesetters,
U.S.A.")...................................... 15-25   60
(Celanese Special Products issue.)
Also see DOBKINS, Carl, Jr.

LEE, Brenda / Bill Haley & Comets / Kalin Twins / Four Aces
EPs: 7–inch 33/45rpm
DECCA (7-2661 "Top Teen
Hits").. 15-25   59
(Stereo.)
Also see HALEY, Bill
Also see KALIN TWINS

LEE, Brenda / Tennessee Ernie Ford
LPs: 10/12–inch 33rpm
DECCA (9226 "Brenda Lee/Tennessee Ernie
Ford Show for Christmas
Seals")..................................... 20-30
(Promotional issue only.)
Also see FORD, Tennessee Ernie

LEE, Brenda, & Pete Fountain
LP '68
Singles: 7–inch
DECCA...4-6   68
EPs: 7–inch 33/45rpm
DECCA (734528 "Brenda and
Pete")......................................5-10   68
(Jukebox issue.)
LPs: 10/12–inch 33rpm
DECCA...10-15   68

LEE, Brenda, & Oak Ridge Boys
Singles: 7–inch
MCA..3-5   82
Also see OAK RIDGE BOYS

LEE, Chandy
C&W '79
Singles: 7–inch
ODC..3-5   79

LEE, Dickey   *P&R/R&B/LP '62/C&W '71*
(With the Collegiates; Dickie Lee)
Singles: 78rpm
SUN (280 "Good Lovin").............15-25   57
SUN (297 "Dreamy Nights").......20-30   57
TAMPA (131 "Dream Boy")........15-25   57
Singles: 7–inch
ABC...3-5   73
ATCO...4-8   68
DIAMOND...4-8   69
DICKIE LEE STORY..................15-20   77
(No label name or number used.
Promotional issue only.)
DOT...10-15   60
ERIC..3-5   70s
HALL...5-10   64
MERCURY..3-5   79-82
OLDIES 45.......................................4-6   65
RCA...3-5   70-78
RENDEZVOUS (188 "Stay True
Baby").......................................15-25   62
SMASH..4-8   62-64
SUN (280 "Good Lovin").............15-25   57
SUN (297 "Dreamy Nights").......20-30   57
TCF..4-8   65
TCF HALL...4-8   64-65
TAMPA (131 "Dream Boy")........15-25   57
TRACIE..4-8   67
LPs: 10/12–inch 33rpm
PICKWICK......................................5-10   70s
RCA...6-12   71-76
MERCURY.......................................5-8   79-80

SMASH 20-25   62
TCF HALL 15-20   65

LEE, Dickey, & Kathy Burdick
C&W '81
Singles: 7–inch
MERCURY 3-4   81-82
  Also see LEE, Dickey

LEE, Don
C&W '82
Singles: 7–inch
CRESCENT 3-4   82

LEE, Harold
C&W '68
Singles: 7–inch
CARTWHEEL................................. 3-5   71
COLUMBIA 4-6   68
ESTA (293 "Blond Headed
  Woman") 100-200   58

LEE, Johnny
C&W '75
Singles: 7–inch
ABC/DOT 3-5   75
ASTRO... 3-5   80
ASYLUM 3-5   80-82
CURB... 3-4   89
EPIC... 3-5   81
FULL MOON/W.B. 3-4   80-86
GRT.. 3-5   76-78
Picture Sleeves
ASYLUM 3-5   80
LPs: 10/12–inch 33rpm
ACCORD.. 5-8   83
ASYLUM 5-10   80-81
FULL MOON/W.B. 5-8   80-86
GRT.. 8-10   77
JMS.. 8-12
PLANTATION............................... 5-10   81
Session: Deborah Allen; Michael Murphey;
  Charlie Daniels.
  Also see ALLEN, Deborah
  Also see DANIELS, Charlie
  Also see GILLEY, Mickey, & Johnny Lee
  Also see MURPHEY, Michael
  Also see NELSON, Willie / Johnny Lee / Mickey Gilley

LEE, Johnny, & Lane Brody
C&W '84
Singles: 7–inch
W.B. 3-4   84-86

LEE, Johnny / Eagles
Singles: 7–inch
ASYLUM 3-5   80-81

Picture Sleeves
ASYLUM 3-5   80
  Also see EAGLES

LEE, Johnny, Michael Martin Murphey, & Charlie Daniels
C&W '82
(Johnny Lee & Friends)
Singles: 7–inch
FULL MOON...................................3-4   82
  Also see DANIELS, Charlie
  Also see LEE, Johnny
  Also see MURPHEY, Michael

LEE, Joni
C&W '75
Singles: 7–inch
MCA...3-5   75-78
LP: 10/12–inch 33rpm
MCA...5-10   76
  Also see TWITTY, Conway

LEE, Leapy: see LEAPY LEE

LEE, Robin
C&W '83
Singles: 7–inch
ATLANTIC.......................................3-4   90-91
ATLANTIC AMERICA 3-4   88
EVERGREEN 3-5   83-86

LEE, Robin, & Lobo
C&W '85
Singles: 7–inch
EVERGREEN 3-4   85
  Also see LEE, Robin
  Also see LOBO

LEE, T.L., & Kathy Walker
C&W '87
Singles: 7–inch
COMPLEAT 3-4   87

LEE, Vicki
C&W '86
Singles: 7–inch
SUNSHINE 3-4   86

LEE, Wilma: see WILMA LEE

LeGARDES
C&W '78
(LeGarde Twins)
Singles: 7–inch
BEAR 3-4   88
4 STAR 3-5   79
INVITATION....................................3-5   80
RAINDROP 3-5   78
LPs: 10/12–inch 33rpm
CAPITOL...10-20
KOALA...8-10
PLATINUM PLATT.......................8-10

LEHR, Zella   *C&W '77*
(Zella)
Singles: 7–inch
COLUMBIA	3-4	81-83
COMPLEAT	3-4	84-85
RCA	3-5	77-80

LP: 10/12–inch 33rpm
COLUMBIA	5-10	82

LEIGH, Bonnie   *C&W '86*
Singles: 7–inch
R.C.P.	3-4	86-87

LEIGH, Richard   *C&W '83*
Singles: 7–inch
CAPITOL	3-4	83
U.A.	3-4	80

LP: 10/12–inch 33rpm
U.A.	5-10	80

LEIGH, Shannon   *C&W '82*
Singles: 7–inch
AMI	3-4	82

LEMMON, Dave   *C&W '83*
Singles: 7–inch
SCP	3-4	83

LESTER, Chester   *C&W '79*
Singles: 7–inch
CON BRIO	3-5	79

LEWIS, Bobby   *C&W '66*
Singles: 7–inch
ACE of HEARTS	3-5	73-75
CAPRICORN	3-5	79
GRT	3-5	74
HME	3-4	85
RPA	3-5	76-77
SABER	3-6	
U.A.	4-8	66-71

LP: 10/12–inch 33rpm
ACE of HEARTS	6-12	73
ALBUM GLOBE	5-8	80s
RPA	6-12	77
U.A.	10-20	66-70

LEWIS, Hugh X.   *C&W '64*
Singles: 7–inch
COLUMBIA	3-6	70
GRT	3-6	70
KAPP	4-6	64-69
LITTLE DARLIN'.	3-5	78-79

LP: 10/12–inch 33rpm
GUINESS	5-10	77
KAPP	10-20	66-68

LEWIS, J.D.   *C&W/R&B '89*
Singles: 7–inch
SING ME	3-4	89

LEWIS, Jerry Lee   *P&R/C&W/R&B '57*
(With His Pumping Piano)
Singles: 78rpm
SUN	25-75	56-58

Singles: 7–inch
AMERICA SMASH	3-5	86
BUDDAH	3-6	71
ELEKTRA	3-5	79-82
MCA	3-5	82-83
MERCURY	3-6	70-82
SCR (386 "Get Out Your Big Roll, Daddy") (Colored vinyl.)	3-5	85
SSS/SUN (Includes numbers below 100 and over 1000.)	3-5	69-84
SMASH (1857 thru 2122)	5-10	63-67
SMASH (2146 thru 2257)	4-8	68-70
SUN (169/213 "Whole Lotta Shakin' Going On"/"Great Balls of Fire") (Colored vinyl. Promotional issue only.)	5-10	94
SUN (259 "Crazy Arms")	20-30	56
SUN (267 thru 296)	15-25	56-58
SUN (300 series)	10-20	58-65

Picture Sleeves
SUN (281 "Great Balls of Fire")	25-50	57
SUN (296 "High School Confidential")	25-50	57

EPs: 7–inch 33/45rpm
MERCURY (6 "Special Radio Cuts from *Would You Take Another Chance on Me*") (Promotional issues only.)	15-25	71
MERCURY (14 "Special Radio Cuts from *The Killer Rocks On*") (Promotional issues only.)	15-25	72
SCR	10-15	86
SSS/SUN (108 "Golden Cream of the Country") (Jukebox issue only.)	15-25	69
SSS/SUN (114 "A Taste of Country") (Jukebox issue only.)	15-25	69
SMASH (2 "Jerry Lee Lewis")	20-25	64

SMASH (28 "Open-End
  Interview") 30-40   64
  (Promotional issue only.)

SUN (107 "Great Ball of
  Fire") 75-100   57
  (Issued with a paper sleeve.)

SUN (108 "Jerry Lee Lewis") 50-75   57

SUN (109 "Jerry Lee Lewis") 50-75   58

SUN (110 "High School
  Confidential") 50-75   58

LPs: 10/12–inch 33rpm

ACCORD 5-8   81-82

AURA 5-8   82

BUCKBOARD 8-10   75

ELEKTRA 5-10   79-82

EVEREST 8-12   75

HILLTOP 10-12   72

KOALA 5-10   79

MCA 5-8   82-84

MERCURY (SRM1 series) 8-15   72-78

MERCURY (SRM2-803
  "Session") 15-20   73

MERCURY (3 "Southern
  Roots") 20-35   73

MERCURY (61318 "In Loving
  Memories") 30-40   71

MERCURY (61323 "There Must Be More to
  Love Than This") 8-12   71

MERCURY (61343 "Touching
  Home") 15-20   71
  (Cover is mostly an artist's drawing with a
  small photo of Lewis on the right side.)

MERCURY (61343 "Touching
  Home") 12-15   71
  (Cover pictures Lewis standing in front of a
  brick wall.)

MERCURY (61346 "Would You Take Another
  Chance on Me") 8-12   71

MERCURY (61366 "Who's Gonna Play This
  Old Piano") 8-12   72

OUT of TOWN DIST 5-8   82

PICKWICK 10-12   70-74

POLYDOR (839516 "Great Ball of
  Fire") 5-8   89
  (Includes tracks by other artists.)

POLYSTAR 8-10

POWER PAK 8-10   74

RHINO 8-10   83

SCR 5-10   85

SSS/SUN 5-10   69-84

SEARS 10-15

SMASH (690 "Jerry Lee Lewis Radio
  Special") 40-50   73
  (Promotional issue only.)

SMASH (7001 "Golden Rock
  Hits") 5-8   82

SMASH (27040 "Golden Hits of Jerry Lee
  Lewis") 20-25   64
  (Monaural.)

SMASH (27056 "Greatest Live Show on
  Earth") 15-20   64
  (Monaural.)

SMASH (27063 "Return of
  Rock") 20-25   65
  (Monaural.)

SMASH (27071 "Country Songs for City
  Folks") 15-20   65
  (Monaural.)

SMASH (27079 "Memphis
  Beat") 20-25   65
  (Monaural.)

SMASH (27086 "By Request") ... 15-20   66
  (Monaural.)

SMASH (27097 "Soul My
  Way") 20-25   67
  (Monaural.)

SMASH (67040 "Golden Hits of Jerry Lee
  Lewis") 20-25   64
  (Stereo.)

SMASH (67040 "Golden Rock Hits of Jerry
  Lee Lewis") 15-20   60s
  (Reissue.)

SMASH (67056 "Greatest Live Show on
  Earth") 20-25   64
  (Stereo.)

SMASH (67063 "Return of
  Rock") 25-30   65
  (Stereo.)

SMASH (67071 "Country Songs for City
  Folks") 20-25   65
  (Stereo.)

SMASH (67071 "All Country") 10-15   69
  (Stereo. Reissue.)

SMASH (67079 "Memphis
  Beat") 25-30   65
  (Stereo.)

SMASH (67086 "By Request") ... 20-25   66
  (Stereo.)

SMASH (67097 "Soul My
  Way") 25-30   67
  (Stereo.)

SMASH (67104 thru 67131) 8-15   68-70

SUN (1230 "Jerry Lee
  Lewis") 75-125   58

SUN (1265 "Jerry Lee's
  Greatest") 75-125   62

SUNNYVALE 8-10   77

TRIP 8-10   74

WING (125 "The Legend of Jerry Lee
   Lewis") 20-30   69

WING (12000 series) 12-15   66-67
   (Monaural.)

WING (16000 series) 15-20   66-67
   (Stereo.)
   Also see GEORGE & LOUIS
   Also see HAWK, The
   Also see McDOWELL, Ronnie, & Jerry Lee Lewis
   Also see MEYERS, Augie
   Also see NELSON, Willie / Jerry Lee Lewis / Carl
   Perkins / David Allan Coe

LEWIS, Jerry Lee / Curly Bridges / Frank Motley
LPs: 10/12–inch 33rpm
DESIGN 10-15   63

LEWIS, Jerry Lee / Johnny Cash
LPs: 10/12–inch 33rpm
SSS/SUN 8-10   71
   Also see CASH, Johnny
   Also see CASH, Johnny / Jerry Lee Lewis / Jeanie C.
   Riley
   Also see PERKINS, Carl, Jerry Lee Lewis, Roy Orbison
   & Johnny Cash

LEWIS, Jerry Lee / Patsy Cline / Jimmy Clanton / Frankie Ford
EPs: 7–inch 33/45rpm
MEMORY LANE............................. 3-5   92
   (Promotional issue only. Not issued with
   cover.)
   Also see CLINE, Patsy

LEWIS, Jerry Lee, & Friends   *C&W '79*
Singles: 7–inch
SSS/SUN (1139 "Save the Last Dance for
   Me")... 3-6   80
LPs: 10/12–inch 33rpm
SSS/SUN (1011 "Duets") 8-10   78
   Members: Jerry Lee Lewis; Jimmy Ellis; Charlie Rich.
   Also see ORION
   Also see RICH, Charlie

LEWIS, Jerry Lee & Linda Gail   *C&W '69*
Singles: 7–inch
SMASH 3-6   69-70

SUN... 5-10   63
LPs: 10/12–inch 33rpm
SMASH 15-25   69

LEWIS, Jerry Lee / Roger Miller / Roy Orbison
LPs: 10/12–inch 33rpm
PICKWICK 8-10   70s
   Also see MILLER, Roger
   Also see ORBISON, Roy

LEWIS, Jerry Lee, Carl Perkins & Charlie Rich
LPs: 10/12–inch 33rpm
SSS/SUN (1018 "Trio +").............8-10   78
   (With Jimmy Ellis.)
   Also see ELLIS, Jimmy
   Also see LEWIS, Jerry Lee, & Friends
   Also see PERKINS, Carl

LEWIS, Jerry Lee / Charlie Rich / Johnny Cash
LPs: 10/12–inch 33rpm
POWER PAK 8-10   80s
   Also see CASH, Johnny, Carl Perkins & Jerry Lee
   Lewis
   Also see LEWIS, Jerry Lee

LEWIS, Linda Gail   *C&W '72*
Singles: 7–inch
MERCURY.......................................3-5   72

SMASH 4-8   69
LP: 10/12–inch 33rpm
SMASH 10-20   69
   Also see LEWIS, Jerry Lee & Linda Gail

LEWIS, Margaret   *C&W '68*
Singles: 7–inch
CAPITOL...5-10   64-65

RAM (1549 "No No Never") 15-25

SSS INT'L 4-6   68

LEWIS, Melissa   *C&W '80*
Singles: 7–inch
DOOR KNOB 3-5   80

LEWIS, Ross   *C&W '88*
Singles: 7–inch
WOLF DOG 3-4   88-89

LEWIS, Texas Jim, & His Lone Star Cowboys   *C&W '44*
Singles: 78rpm
DECCA 5-8   44

VOCALION 5-10   37

LIBBY, Brenda   *C&W '83*
Singles: 7–inch
COMSTOCK 3-4   83

LIGHTFOOT, Gordon

(Gord Lightfoot)   *LP '69/C&W '74*

Singles: 7–inch

ABC-PAR	10-20	62
CHATEAU	5-10	65
REPRISE	3-5	70-77
U.A.	3-8	65-69
W.B. (Except 5621)	3-5	78-86
W.B. (5621 "For Lovin' Me")	5-10	65

Picture Sleeves

U.A. (50152 "The Way I Feel")	5-10	67
W.B.	3-4	86

LPs: 10/12–inch 33rpm

AME ("Early Lightfoot")	75-100	
(Number not known.)		
K-TEL	5-8	
LIBERTY	5-8	80
MFSL (018 "Sundown")	25-50	78
PICKWICK	5-8	79
REPRISE (Except 93228)	5-12	70-76
REPRISE (93228 "Sit Down Young Stranger")	10-20	70
U.A. (Except 3400 & 6400 series)	5-10	69-74
U.A. (3400 series)	10-15	66-69
(Monaural.)		
U.A. (6400 series)	10-20	66-69
(Stereo.)		
W.B.	5-8	78-86

LINCOLN COUNTY   *C&W '81*

Singles: 7–inch

SOUNDWAVES	3-5	81

LINDSEY, Bennie   *C&W '76*

Singles: 7–inch

PHONO	3-5	76

LINDSEY, Judy   *C&W '89*

Singles: 7–inch

GYPSEY	3-4	89

LINDSEY, LaWanda   *C&W '69*

Singles: 7–inch

CAPITOL	3-5	73-74
CHART	3-6	69-72
MERCURY	3-5	77-78

LP: 10/12–inch 33rpm

CAPITOL	5-10	74
CHART	6-12	69-71

LINDSEY, LaWanda, & Kenny Vernon   *C&W '71*

Singles: 7–inch

CHART	3-6	71

LP: 10/12–inch 33rpm

CHART	6-12	70

Also see LINDSEY, LaWanda
Also see VERNON, Kenny

LINTON, Sherwin   *C&W '77*

(With the Cotton Kings)

Singles: 7–inch

BLACK GOLD	3-6	68-72
BREAKER	3-4	86
HICKORY	3-5	69
NEW WORLD	4-6	67
SOMA (1405 "Remember Me")	8-12	63
SOUNDWAVES	3-5	77-83

Picture Sleeves

BREAKER (3902 "Santa Got a DWI")	3-5	86

LP: 10/12–inch 33rpm

BLACK GOLD	8-12	72

LIPTON, Holly   *C&W '89*

Singles: 7–inch

EVERGREEN	3-4	89

LITTLE, Peggy   *C&W '69*

Singles: 7–inch

DOT	3-6	69-71
EPIC	3-5	73

LPs: 10/12–inch 33rpm

DOT	10-15	70

LITTLE DIPPERS   *P&R '60*

(Anita Kerr Singers)

Singles: 7–inch

DOT	4-6	64
UNIVERSITY	5-8	59-60

Also see KERR, Anita

LITTLE DOUG

(Doug Sahm)

Singles: 78rpm

SARG	15-25	55

Singles: 7–inch

SARG (113 "A Real American Joe")	30-50	55

Also see SAHM, Doug

LITTLE ESTHER   *R&B '50*

(Esther Phillips; Little Esther Phillips; with
Earle Warren Orchestra; with Johnny Otis
Orchestra)

Singles: 78rpm

DECCA	15-25	54
FEDERAL	15-25	51
SAVOY	8-15	56

Singles: 7–inch

ATLANTIC	5-15	64-67
DECCA (28804 "Talkin' All Out of My Head")	20-30	54
DECCA (48305 "Stop Cryin")	25-35	54
DECCA (48314 "He's a No Good Man")	40-60	54
FEDERAL (12023 "I'm a Bad Girl")	25-50	51
FEDERAL (12042 "Crying and Sighing")	25-50	51
FEDERAL (12055 "Crying Blues")	25-50	52
FEDERAL (12063 "Summertime")	25-50	52
FEDERAL (12065 "Better Beware")	25-50	52
FEDERAL (12078 "Aged and Mellow")	25-50	52
FEDERAL (12090 "Ramblin' Blues")	25-50	52
FEDERAL (12126 "Hound Dog")	25-50	53
FEDERAL (12142 "Cherry Wine")	25-50	53
GUSTO	3-5	
KUDU	3-5	72-76
LENOX	5-10	62-63
MERCURY	3-5	77-79
ROULETTE	3-6	69
SAVOY (1100 series)	10-20	56
SAVOY (1500 series)	5-15	58-59
WARWICK	5-8	60-61
WINNING	3-5	83

LPs: 10/12–inch 33rpm

ATLANTIC (1500 & 1600 series)	8-12	70-76
ATLANTIC (8100 series)	15-30	65-66
KING (622 "Memory Lane")	800-1200	59
KUDU	8-12	72-76
LENOX (227 "Release Me")	30-50	62
MERCURY	5-10	78-81
YORKSHIRE	8-12	

LITTLE ESTHER & Dominoes

(With the Earle Warren Orchestra)

Singles: 78rpm

FEDERAL	100-150	51

Singles: 7–inch

FEDERAL (12036 "Heart to Heart")	250-350	51

Also see LITTLE ESTHER with the Earle Warren
Orchestra (With the Dominoes)

LITTLE ESTHER & Big Al Downing

Singles: 7–inch

LENOX	5-10	63

Also see DOWNING, Al

LITTLE ESTHER & Junior with the Johnny Otis Orchestra / Johnny Otis Orchestra with the Vocaleers

Singles: 78rpm

SAVOY (824 "Get Together Blues")	20-30	51

LITTLE ESTHER & Little Willie Littlefield

Singles: 78rpm

FEDERAL	15-25	52

Singles: 7–inch

FEDERAL (12108 "Last Laugh Blues")	25-50	52
FEDERAL (12115 "Turn the Lamps Down Low")	25-50	52

LITTLE ESTHER & Clyde McPhatter

Singles: 7–inch

FEDERAL (12344 "Heart to Heart")	15-25	58

LITTLE ESTHER & Bobby Nunn

Singles: 78rpm

FEDERAL	50-100	52-53

Singles: 7–inch

FEDERAL (12100 "Saturday Night Daddy")	150-250	52
FEDERAL (12122 "You Took My Love Too Fast")	150-250	53

LITTLE ESTHER & Mel Walker

(With the Johnny Otis Orchestra)

Singles: 78rpm

FEDERAL	15-25	52
SAVOY	15-25	50

Singles: 7–inch

FEDERAL (12055 "Ring-A-Ding Doo")	35-50	52

SAVOY (735 "Mistrustin'
Blues")...................................... 35-50   50

SAVOY (759 "Deceivin'
Blues")...................................... 35-50   50

LITTLE ESTHER with the Earle Warren Orchestra

(With the Dominoes)

Singles: 78rpm

FEDERAL (12016 "The Deacon Moves
In").. 150-250   51

FEDERAL (12036 "Heart").... 100-200   51

Singles: 7–inch

FEDERAL (12016 "The Deacon Moves
In").. 300-400   51

FEDERAL (12036 "Heart").... 250-350   51

Also see LITTLE ESTHER & DOMINOES

LITTLE PIA

(Pia Zadora)

Singles: 7–inch

LAP INT'L (1002 "Bye Bye
Boy") 20-30

(May have been a promo issue only.)

Also see ZADORA, Pia

LLOYD, Mick, & Jerri Kelly   *C&W '81*

Singles: 7–inch

LITTLE GIANT 3-4   81

LOBO   *P&R/LP '71/C&W '81*

(Roland Kent Lavole)

Singles: 7–inch

BIG TREE 3-6   71-75

ELEKTRA....................................... 3-5   80

EVERGREEN................................. 3-4   85

FLASHBACK.................................. 3-5   73

LOBO 3-5   81-82

MCA 3-4   79

MARIANNE 3-5   77

PHILIPS 3-5

W.B. 3-5   76-78

LPs: 10/12–inch 33rpm

BIG TREE 10-15   71-75

CALUMET.................................... 10-15   73

MCA 5-10   79

Also see LEE, Robin, & Lobo
Also see STAFFORD, Jim
Also see WOLFPACK

LOCKLIN, Hank   *C&W '49*

Singles: 78rpm

DECCA... 5-10   52

4 STAR 5-10   49-54

RCA 5-10   55-57

Singles: 7–inch

COUNTRY ARTISTS.....................3-4   83

DECCA (29000 series) 10-15   52

4 STAR (1500 & 1600 series)....10-15   52-54

KING (5000 series) 5-8   59

MGM 3-5   74

PLANTATION 3-5   76-77

RCA (0030 thru 0900 series).........3-5   72-74

RCA (6100 thru 7600 series).......8-15   55-59

RCA (7700 thru 9900 series).........4-8   60-71

EPs: 7–inch 33/45rpm

RCA 8-15   58-61

LPs: 10/12–inch 33rpm

ARCADE..5-8

CAMDEN 8-15   62-74

DESIGN 10-15   62

INTERNATIONAL AWARD..........8-12   60s

KING (600 & 700 series)............15-25   61

MGM 5-10   75

METRO..10-15   65

PICKWICK/HILLTOP 8-15   65-68

PLANTATION 5-8   77-81

RCA (Except 1673 series) 10-20   62-71

RCA (1673 "Foreign Love") 15-25   58

SEARS...8-12   60s

STEREO SPECTRUM..................5-10   60s

WRANGLER 10-15   62

Session: Jordanaires.
Also see CLINE, Patsy / Hank Locklin / Miller Brothers /
Eddie Marvin
Also see JORDANAIRES
Also see SNOW, Hank / Hank Locklin / Porter Wagoner
Also see SOME of CHET'S FRIENDS

LOCKLIN, Hank, with Danny Davis & Nashville Brass   *C&W '70*

Singles: 7–inch

RCA 3-6   69-70

LPs: 10/12–inch 33rpm

RCA 8-10   70

Also see DAVIS, Danny
Also see LOCKLIN, Hank

LOFTIS, Bobby Wayne   *C&W '76*

Singles: 7–inch

CHARTA 3-5   76-79

LOGAN, Bud, & Wilma Burgess   *C&W '73*

Singles: 7–inch

SHANNON....................................3-5   73-74

LP: 10/12–inch 33rpm

SHANNON 10-15   74
Also see BLUE BOYS
Also see BURGESS, Wilma

LOGAN, Josh   *C&W '88*
Singles: 7–inch

CURB 3-4   88-89

LOGGINS & MESSINA

P&R/LP '72/C&W '75
Singles: 7–inch

COLUMBIA 3-5   72-76
LOS ANGELES KINGS COLUMBIA (10444 "Angry Eyes") 3-5   76
(Promotional issue for "Columbia/Kings Record Night" at the L.A. Forum.)

Picture Sleeves

LOS ANGELES KINGS COLUMBIA (10444 "Angry Eyes") 3-5   76
(Promotional issue for "Columbia/Kings Record Night" at the L.A. Forum.)

LPs: 10/12–inch 33rpm

COLUMBIA (30000 series) 8-10   72-82
COLUMBIA (44000 series) 10-15   82
(Half-speed mastered.)
DIRECT-DISK (16606 "Full Sail") 15-25   82
(Half-speed mastered.)
Members: Kenny Loggins; Jim Messina.

LOGGINS & MESSINA / David Bromberg

LPs: 10/12–inch 33rpm

COLUMBIA 8-15   72
(Promotional only.)
Also see LOGGINS & MESSINA

LONESOME STRANGER   *C&W '89*
Singles: 7–inch

HIGHTONE 3-4   89

LONG, Shorty   *C&W '48*
(With the Santa Fe Rangers; with Searchers)
Singles: 78rpm

DECCA.. 4-8   48
DOLLO 10-20

LONG, Tom
(Gene Autry)

Singles: 78rpm

Sunrise (33070 "I'll Be Thinking Of You Little Girl") 25-75
Also see AUTRY, Gene

LONGBRANCH PENNYWHISTLE
Singles: 7–inch

AMOS 5-10   69

LPs: 10/12–inch 33rpm

AMOS (7007 "Longbranch Pennywhistle") 25-40   69
Members: John David Souther; Glen Frey; James Burton; Ry Cooder.
Also see EAGLES
Also see SOUTHER, J. D.

LONZO & OSCAR   *C&W '48*
(With the Winston County Pea Pickers)
Singles: 78rpm

DECCA 4-8   53-54
DOT 4-8   54
RCA 5-10   48

Singles: 7–inch

DECCA 5-10   53-54
DOT 5-10   54
GRC 3-5   74
NUGGET..4-6   62-64
STARDAY 4-8   60-61

LP: 10/12–inch 33rpm

BRYLEN...5-10   82
COLUMBIA 10-20   68
DECCA 15-25   63
GRC 6-12   75
NUGGET.......................................6-12
PICKWICK/HILLTOP 10-20   65
STARDAY (119 "America's Greatest Country Comedians") 35-45   60
STARDAY (244 "Country Music Time") 25-35   63
Members: Rollin Sullivan; Ken Marvin; John Sullivan; David Hooten.

LORD, Bobby   *C&W '56*
Singles: 78rpm

COLUMBIA (21000 series, except 21339 & 21539).......................................5-10   55-56
COLUMBIA (21339 "No More, No More") 10-15   55
COLUMBIA (21539 "Everybody's Rockin' But Me") 10-20   56
COLUMBIA (40000 series) 5-10   56-57

Singles: 7–inch

COLUMBIA (21000 series, except 21339 & 21539).......................................8-15   55-56
COLUMBIA (21339 "No More, No More") 25-50   55
COLUMBIA (21539 "Everybody's Rockin' But Me") 40-60   56
COLUMBIA (40000 series) 5-15   56-61

DECCA	3-5	68-71
HICKORY	4-6	61-64

LPs: 10/12–inch 33rpm

DECCA	8-10	70
HARMONY	10-20	64
HICKORY	10-12	65

LORD, Mike *C&W '87*
Singles: 7–inch

NSD	3-4	87

LORETTA LYNN: see LYNN, Loretta

LORIE ANN *C&W '88*
Singles: 7–inch

SING ME	3-4	88-89

LORRIO, Myrna
LPs: 10/12–inch 33rpm

HARMONY	20-40

LORRIE, Myrna, & Buddy DeVal *C&W '55*
Singles: 78rpm

ABBOTT	4-8	55

Singles: 7–inch

ABBOTT	5-10	55

LOS LOBOS *LP '84/C&W '87*
Singles: 12–inch 33/45rpm

SLASH	5-8	86

(Promotional issue only.)

Singles: 7–inch

LOS LOBOS	5-10	81
SLASH	3-4	83-90

Picture Sleeves

SLASH	3-4	85-87

LPs: 10/12–inch 33rpm

SLASH	5-8	83-90

Member: David Hidalgo.

LOU, Bonnie: see BONNIE LOU

LOUDERMILK, John D.
P&R '61/C&W '63
Singles: 7–inch

COLUMBIA	5-10	58-60
MUSIC IS MEDICINE	3-5	78-79
RCA	4-8	61-69
W.B.	3-5	71

Picture Sleeves

COLUMBIA (41165 "Yearbook")	10-20	58

RCA (8101 "Road Hog")	5-10	62

LPs: 10/12–inch 33rpm

MUSIC IS MEDICINE	10-20	78
RCA	15-30	61-69
W.B.	8-12	71

Also see DEE, Johnny
Also see SNEEZER, Ebe, & Epidemics
Also see SOME of CHET'S FRIENDS

LOUVIN, Charlie *C&W '64*
Singles: 7–inch

CAPITOL	3-8	64-72
U.A.	3-5	74

LP: 10/12–inch 33rpm

AUDIOGRAPH ALIVE	5-10	82
CAPITOL	8-20	65-72
FIRST GENERATION	5-10	81
LITTLE DARLIN'	8-12	
MUSIC BOX	10-20	
PHONORAMA	5-8	82
PICKWICK	5-8	70s
THUNDERBIRD	5-8	
U.A.	6-12	74

Also see JIM & JESSE & Charlie Louvin
Also see LOUVIN BROTHERS

LOUVIN, Charlie, & Roy Acuff *C&W '89*
Singles: 7–inch

HAL KAT	3-4	89

Also see ACUFF, Roy

LOUVIN, Charlie, & Emmylou Harris *C&W '79*
Singles: 7–inch

LITTLE DARLIN'	3-5	79

Also see HARRIS, Emmylou

LOUVIN, Charlie, & Melba Montgomery *C&W '70*
Singles: 7–inch

CAPITOL	3-5	70-73

LP: 10/12–inch 33rpm

CAPITOL	10-20	71-75

Also see MONTGOMERY, Melba

LOUVIN, Ira *C&W '65*
Singles: 7–inch

CAPITOL	4-8	65

LP: 10/12–inch 33rpm

CAPITOL (2413 "Unforgettable")	25-35	65

Also see LOUVIN BROTHERS

LOUVIN BROTHERS   *C&W '55*

CAPITOL	5-10	55-57
MGM	8-12	52

Singles: 7–inch

CAPITOL	5-15	55-63
MGM	10-20	52

EPs: 7–inch 33/45rpm

CAPITOL	10-20	55-60

LP: 10/12–inch 33rpm

ACM	5-10	
CMF	5-10	
CAPITOL (T-769 "Tragic Songs of Life") (Monaural.)	50-100	56
CAPITOL (DT-769 "Tragic Songs of Life") (Reprocessed stereo.)	25-50	68
CAPITOL (910 "Ira & Charlie")	30-40	58
CAPITOL (T-1061 "Family Who Prays") (Monaural.)	20-40	58
CAPITOL (DT-1061 "Family Who Prays") (Reprocessed stereo.)	10-15	68
CAPITOL (SM-1061 "Family Who Prays") (Reprocessed stereo.)	5-10	
CAPITOL (1106 "Country Love Ballads")	30-40	59
CAPITOL (1449 "Tribute to the Delmore Brothers")	50-75	60
CAPITOL (1547 "Encore")	30-40	61
CAPITOL (1616 "Country Christmas")	20-40	61
CAPITOL (1721 "Weapon of Prayer")	10-20	73
CAPITOL (11000 series)	10-20	62
CAPITOL (1834 "Keep Your Eyes on Jesus")	15-25	63
CAPITOL (2091 "Current Hits")	20-40	64
CAPITOL (2331 "Thank God for My Christian Home")	20-40	65
CAPITOL (2827 "The Great Roy Acuff Songs")	20-30	67
COUNTRY CLASSICS	5-10	
GOLDEN COUNTRY	5-10	
GUSTO	5-10	
MGM (3426 "Louvin Brothers")	75-150	57
METRO (598 "The Louvin Brothers")	20-40	67
PICKWICK/HILLTOP	10-15	66-67

ROUNDER	5-10	79-80s
TOWER (5038 "Two Different Worlds")	20-40	66
TOWER (5122 "Country Heart & Soul")	20-40	68

Members: Charlie Louvin; Ira Louvin
Also see LOUVIN, Charlie
Also see LOUVIN, Ira

LOVELESS, Patty   *C&W '85*

Singles: 7–inch

MCA	3-4	85-92

Also see WHITLEY, Keith

LOVETT, Lyle   *C&W '86*

(With His Large Band)

Singles: 7–inch

CURB/MCA	3-4	86-89

LPs: 10/12–inch 33rpm

CURB/MCA	5-10	86-89

Also see CARNES, Kim

LOWE, Jim   *P&R '53/C&W '57*

Singles: 78rpm

DOT	5-15	55-57
MERCURY	4-8	53-54

Singles: 7–inch

BUDDAH	4-6	68
DECCA	4-8	60-61
DOT (15300 thru 16200 series)	5-10	55-60
DOT (16600 series)	4-8	64
MERCURY	5-10	53-54
20TH FOX	4-8	63
U.A.	4-6	67

EPs: 7–inch 33/45rpm

DOT	10-20	57
MERCURY	10-20	57

LPs: 10/12–inch 33rpm

DOT (3051 "The Green Door")	25-35	57
DOT (3114 "Wicked Women")	25-35	58
DOT (3681 "The Green Door") (Monaural.)	10-20	66
DOT (25681 "The Green Door") (Stereo.)	10-20	66
KATS KARAVAN (100 "Old Favorites")	50-100	50s
MERCURY (20246 "Door of Fame")	25-35	57

LOWES, The   *C&W '86*

Singles: 7–inch

API	3-4	86-87
SOUNDWAVES	3-4	86

LOWRY, Ron   *C&W '70*
Singles: 7–inch
REPUBLIC 3-5   70
LP: 10/12–inch 33rpm
REPUBLIC 8-12   70

LUCAS, Tammy   *C&W '89*
Singles: 7–inch
SOUNDS of AMERICA 3-4   89

LUKE the Drifter: see WILLIAMS, Hank

LUKE the Drifter Jr.: see WILLIAMS, Hank, Jr.

LUMAN, Bob   *C&W/P&R/R&B '60*
Singles: 78rpm
IMPERIAL 20-50   57
Singles: 7–inch
CAPITOL..................................... 10-20   58
EPIC... 3-5   68-77
HICKORY (1200 series)............... 4-8   63-64
HICKORY (1300 thru 1500 series) 3-5   65-70
IMPERIAL (5705 "Red Cadillac and a Black Mustache")............................. 10-20   60
   (Black label. Reissue of 8311.)
IMPERIAL (8311 "Red Cadillac and a Black Mustache")............................. 35-55   57
   (Maroon label.)
IMPERIAL (8313 "Red Hot") 40-60   57
   (Maroon label.)
IMPERIAL (8313 "Red Hot") 30-40   59
   (Black label.)
IMPERIAL (8315 "Make Up Your Mind Baby") 20-30   57
   (Maroon label.)
IMPERIAL (8315 "Make Up Your Mind Baby") 10-15   59
   (Black label.)
POLYDOR..................................... 3-5   77-78
W.B. 5-15   59-62
Picture Sleeves
W.B. 15-25   60-62
EPs: 7–inch 33/45rpm
HICKORY (124-006 "Selections from Livin' Lovin' Sounds") 10-20   65
   (Promotional "Six-Pac" issue only.)
ROLLIN' ROCK (34 "Bob Luman")... 5-8   80s
W.B. (1396 "Let's Think About Livin") 50-75   60
W.B. (5506 "Bob Luman") 50-75   60
   (Promotional issue only.)

LPs: 10/12–inch 33rpm
EPIC..8-15   68-77
HARMONY...................................10-15   72
HICKORY (124 "Livin' Lovin' Sounds")....................................15-25   65
HICKORY (4000 series) 8-12   74
POLYDOR 8-12   78
W.B. (W-1396 "Let's Think About Livin")......................................30-40   60
   (Monaural.)
W.B. (WS-1396 "Let's Think About Livin")......................................40-60   60
   (Stereo.)

LUMAN, Bob, & Sue Thompson
Singles: 7–inch
HICKORY...4-8   63
Also see LUMAN, Bob
Also see THOMPSON, Sue

LUNSFORD, Mike   *C&W '75*
Singles: 7–inch
EVERGREEN 3-4   88
GUSTO 3-5   75-80
STARDAY.......................................3-5   75-78
LP: 10/12–inch 33rpm
STARDAY.....................................6-12   75-77

LYERLY, Bill   *C&W '81*
Singles: 7–inch
RCA 3-5   81

LYNDELL, Liz   *C&W '80*
Singles: 7–inch
KOALA..3-4   80-81

LYNDEN, Tracy   *C&W '85*
Singles: 7–inch
RCA 3-4   85

LYNN, Judy: see JUDY LYNN

LYNN, Loretta   *C&W '60*
(With the Coal Miners)
Singles: 7–inch
DECCA (31384 thru 31966).........5-10   62-66
DECCA (32045 thru 32851)...........4-8   66-71
DECCA (32900 "Here in Topeka") 10-15   71
DECCA (32900 "One's on the Way") 3-6   71
DECCA (32974 thru 33039)...........3-6   72
MCA 3-5   73-86
ZERO (107 "I'm a Honky Tonk Girl")...50-75   60

ZERO (110 "New Rainbow") ... 60-100   61

ZERO (112 "The Darkest Day") 60-100   61

Picture Sleeves

DECCA (31000 series)................ 8-12   66

DECCA (32000 series).................. 4-6   70

MCA 3-5   78

EPs: 7–inch 33/45rpm

DECCA.................................... 10-20   64-65

LPs: 10/12–inch 33rpm

CORAL 5-8   73

COUNTRY MUSIC MAGAZINE 15-20   76
(Mail-order LP sold by *Country Music* magazine.)

DECCA (DL-4457 "Loretta Lynn Sings").................................... 40-60   63
(Monaural.)

DECCA (DL7-4457 "Loretta Lynn Sings").................................... 45-65   63
(Stereo.)

DECCA (DL-4541 "Before I'm Over You") 30-40   65
(Monaural.)

DECCA (DL7-4541 "Before I'm Over You") 35-45   65
(Stereo.)

DECCA (DL-4620 "Songs from My Heart")..................................... 30-40   65
(Monaural.).

DECCA (DL7-4620 "Songs from My Heart")..................................... 35-45   65
(Stereo.)

DECCA (DL-4665 "Blue Kentucky Girl")... 15-25   65
(Monaural.)

DECCA (DL7-4665 "Blue Kentucky Girl")... 20-30   65
(Stereo.)

DECCA (DL-4655 "Hymns")...... 15-25   65
(Monaural.)

DECCA (DL7-4655 "Hymns").... 20-30   65
(Stereo.)

DECCA (DL-4744 "I Like 'Em Country")................................. 15-25   66
(Monaural.)

DECCA (DL-4744 "I Like 'Em Country")................................. 15-25   66
(Monaural.)

DECCA (DL7-4744 "I Like 'Em Country")................................. 15-25   66
(Stereo.)

DECCA (DL7-4783 "You Ain't Woman Enough").................................. 15-25   66
(Monaural.)

DECCA (DL7-4783 "You Ain't Woman Enough").................................. 15-25   66
(Stereo.)

DECCA (DL7-4817 "A Country Christmas").............................. 15-25   66
(Monaural.)

DECCA (DL7-4817 "A Country Christmas").............................. 15-25   66
(Stereo.)

DECCA (DL-4842 "Don't Come Home a Drinkin")................................ 15-25   67
(Monaural.)

DECCA (DL7-4842 "Don't Come Home a Drinkin")................................ 15-25   67
(Stereo.)

DECCA (DL-4928 "Who Says God Is Dead")................................ 15-25   67
(Monaural.)

DECCA (DL7-4928 "Who Says God Is Dead")................................ 15-25   67
(Stereo.)

DECCA (DL-4930 "Singin' with Feeling").................................. 15-25   67
(Monaural.)

DECCA (DL7-4930 "Singin' with Feeling").................................. 15-25   67
(Stereo.)

DECCA (DL-4997 "Fist City")..... 15-25   68
(Monaural.)

DECCA (DL7-4997 "Fist City")... 10-20   68
(Stereo.)

DECCA (75000 "Greatest Hits").................................... 12-25   68

DECCA (75113 "Woman of the World/To Make a Man")........................... 25-35   69

DECCA (75198 "Loretta Lynn Writes 'Em and Sings 'Em")............................. 12-25   70

DECCA (75163 "Wings Upon Your Horns")................................... 12-25   70

DECCA (75253 "Coal Miner's Daughter")............................... 10-20   71

DECCA (75282 "I Want to Be Free")..................................... 12-25   71

DECCA (75310 "You're Looking At Country")................................. 12-25   71

DECCA (75334 "One's on the Way")...................................... 12-25   72

DECCA (75351 "God Bless America Again") 12-25   72

DECCA (75381 "Here I Am Again") 12-25   72

DECCA (75084 "Your Squaw Is on the Warpath") 25-35   69
(Has *Barney*.)

DECCA (75084 "Your Squaw Is on the Warpath") 15-20   69
(Without *Barney*.)

L.L. 20-25   76

MCA 5-10   73-86

TEE VEE 8-12   78

TROLLEY CAR 8-10   81

VOCALION 8-15   68-72

Promotional LPs

MCA (1934 "Loretta Lynn's Greatest Hits") 30-40   74
(Cover shows title as simply *Loretta Lynn*.)

MCA (35013 "Allis-Chalmers Presents Loretta Lynn") 30-40   78

MCA (35018 "Crisco Presents Loretta Lynn's Country Classics") 30-40   79

Session: Bob Hempker; Chuck Flynn; Ken Riley; Dave Thornhill; Gene Dunlap; Don Ballenger; Jordanaires.
Also see PIERCE, Webb / Loretta Lynn
Also see STARR, Kenny
Also see TUBB, Ernest, & Loretta Lynn
Also see TWITTY, Conway, & Loretta Lynn
Also see WEBB, Jay Lee
Also see WILBURN BROTHERS

LYNN, Loretta / Beatles

Singles: 7–inch

VEE JAY (581 "Please Please Me"/"Before I'm Over You") 50-100   64
(This pairing is the result of a production error.)

LYNN, Loretta, & Conway Twitty   *C&W/P&R '71*

Singles: 7–inch

CRLX (7211281"Seasons Greetings") 50-100   80s
(Picture disc. Promotional issue only.)

DECCA 4-6   71-72

MCA 3-5   73-81

LPs: 10/12–inch 33rpm

DECCA 8-15   71-72

MCA 5-10   73-84

TVP 8-12   76

Also see LYNN, Loretta
Also see TWITTY, Conway

LYNN, Loretta / Beatles

Singles: 7–inch

VEE JAY (581 "Before I'm Over You"/"Please Please Me") 50-100   64
(This pairing is the result of a production error.)

LYNN, Loretta / Tammy Wynette

LPs: 10/12–inch 33rpm

RADIANT 5-8   81

Also see LYNN, Loretta
Also see WYNETTE, Tammy

LYNN, Rebecca   *C&W '78*

Singles: 7–inch

SCORPION 3-5   78-79

SUNBIRD 3-5   80

LYNN, Trisha   *C&W '88*
(Trish Lynn)

Singles: 7–inch

OAK 3-4   88-89

LYNNE, Shelby   *C&W '89*

Singles: 7–inch

EPIC 3-4   89-91

Also see JONES, George, & Shelby Lynne
Also see TOMORROW'S WORLD

LYNNE, Shelby, & Les Taylor   *C&W '89*

Singles: 7–inch

EPIC 3-4   91

Also see LYNNE, Shelby
Also see TAYLOR, Les

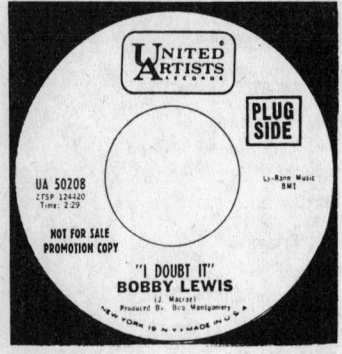

MAC, Jimmy   *C&W '84*
Singles: 7–inch
AV 3-4   84

MacGREGOR, Byron   *P&R/C&W '74*
Singles: 7–inch
CAPITOL.................................... 3-5   75
WESTBOUND............................. 3-5   74
LPs: 10/12–inch 33rpm
WESTBOUND............................. 5-10   74

MacGREGOR, Mary
P&R '76/C&W '77
Singles: 7–inch
ARIOLA.. 3-5   78
ARIOLA AMERICA...................... 3-5   76-77
RSO 3-5   79-80
LPs: 10/12–inch 33rpm
ARIOLA AMERICA...................... 8-10   77

MacGREGOR, Mary / Bobby Vee / Mike Love / Association
LPs: 10/12–inch 33rpm
HITBOUND (1005 "New
  Memories")................................ 10-15   83
   Also see MacGREGOR, Mary

MACK, Bobby   *C&W '73*
Singles: 7–inch
ACE of HEARTS 3-5   73
B-MAC... 10-15
TEMPUS 10-15   59

MACK, Gary   *C&W '76*
Singles: 7–inch
GRAND PRIZE.............................. 3-4   83
SOUNDWAVES 3-5   76

MACK, Warner   *C&W/P&R '57*
Singles: 78rpm
DECCA...................................... 5-15   57
Singles: 7–inch
COLUMBIA HISTORIC
  EDITION 8-10
DECCA (30301 thru 31684)........ 5-15   57-64

DECCA (31774 thru 33045)...........3-6   65-73
KAPP 5-10   61-62
LOST GOLD 3-5   93
MCA 3-5   73-76
PAGEBOY 3-5   77-81
SCARLET 5-10   60
TOP RANK.................................5-10   60
EPs: 7–inch 33/45rpm
DECCA 5-10   65
LPs: 10/12–inch 33rpm
CORAL.......................................5-10   73
DECCA 8-18   65-70
KAPP 12-25   61-66
PAGEBOY 5-10
SAPPHIRE...................................5-10
  Session: Jordanaires.
  Also see DEAN, Jimmy / David Houston / Warner Mack
  / Autry Inman
  Also see JORDANAIRES

MACKEY, Bobby   *C&W '82*
Singles: 7–inch
MOON SHINE................................ 3-4   82

MADDOX, Rose   *C&W '59*
Singles: 7–inch
CAPITOL....................................5-10   58-63
UNI...3-6   67
EPs: 7–inch 33/45rpm
CAPITOL...................................10-20   58-60
COLUMBIA 10-20   58
LP: 10/12–inch 33rpm
CAPITOL (T-1312 "The One
  Rose")....................................25-35   60
  (Monaural.)
CAPITOL (ST-1312 "The One
  Rose")....................................30-40   60
  (Stereo.)
CAPITOL (ST-1437 "Glory Bound
  Train") 30-40   60
  (Stereo.)
CAPITOL (ST-1437 "Glory Bound
  Train") 35-55   60
  (Stereo.)
CAPITOL (T-1548 "Big Bouquet of
  Roses")...................................30-40   60
  (Monaural.)
CAPITOL (ST-1548 "Big Bouquet of
  Roses")...................................35-45   60
  (Stereo.)
CAPITOL (T-1799 "Rose Maddox Sings
  Bluegrass") 30-40   62
  (Monaural.)

CAPITOL (ST-1799 "Rose Maddox Sings
  Bluegrass")................................. 35-45   62
  (Stereo.)

CAPITOL (T-1993 "Alone with
  You") 15-25   63
  (Monaural.)

CAPITOL (ST-1993 "Alone with
  You") 20-30   63
  (Stereo.)

COLUMBIA (1159 "Precious
  Memories")................................ 40-50   58

HARMONY................................ 10-20   64

PICKWICK/HILLTOP 10-15   60s

STARDAY 10-20   70

VARRICK 6-12   83

  Session: Emmylou Harris; Bill Monroe; Vern Williams;
  Merle Haggard and the Strangers.
  Also see HAGGARD, Merle
  Also see HARRIS, Emmylou
  Also see MONROE, Bill
  Also see OWENS, Buck, & Rose Maddox

MAGGARD, Cledus   *C&W/P&R '75*

(With the Citizen's Band)

Singles: 7–inch

MERCURY 3-5   75-79

LPs: 10/12–inch 33rpm

MERCURY 6-12   76

MAGIC ORGAN   *LP '72*

(Jerry Smith)

Singles: 7–inch

RANWOOD 3-5   72-77

LPs: 10/12–inch 33rpm

RANWOOD 4-8   72-83

SUNNYVALE 4-6   79

  Also see SMITH, Jerry

MAINES BROTHERS
BAND   *C&W '83*

Singles: 7–inch

MERCURY...................................... 3-4   83-86

  Members: Lloyd Maines; Donnie Maines; Kenny
  Maines; Steve Maines; Jerry Brownlow; Gary Banks;
  Richard Bowden.

MALCHAK, Tim   *C&W '86*

Singles: 7–inch

ALPINE 3-4   86-88

UNIVERSAL................................... 3-4   89

MALCHAK & RUCKER   *C&W '84*

Singles: 7–inch

ALPINE 3-4   85-86

REVOLVER.................................... 3-4   84-85

  Members: Tim Malchak; Dwight Rucker.
  Also see MALCHAK, Tim

MALENA, Don   *C&W '87*

Singles: 7–inch

MAXIMA...3-4   87-88

MANDRELL, Barbara   *C&W '69*

Singles: 7–inch

ABC...3-5   78-79

ABC/DOT.......................................3-6   75-78

COLUMBIA 4-8   69-75

EMI...3-4   87-88

KFC (003 "Sweet Weekend
  Encounter")................................8-12   79
  (Coincides with "National Winners Kentucky
  Fried Chicken Song Writing Contest."
  Promotional issue only.)

MCA (Black vinyl)..........................3-5   79-86

MCA (52737 "Fast Lanes and Country
  Roads")....................................15-20   85
  (Colored vinyl. Promotional issue only.)

MCA (52802 "When You Get to the
  Heart").....................................15-20   86
  (Colored vinyl. Promotional issue only.)

MOSRITE.....................................10-15   66

Picture Sleeves

MCA...3-5   79-85

LPs: 10/12–inch 33rpm

ABC...8-10   78-79

ABC/DOT.......................................8-12   76-77

COLUMBIA 6-15   71-81

COLUMBIA SPECIAL
  PRODUCTS.................................5-8   82

EMI...5-8   88

MCA...5-10   79-86

SONGBIRD.....................................5-8   82

TIME-LIFE......................................5-8   81

  Session: Deborah Allen; Janie Fricke; Waylon
  Jennings; Charlie McCoy; Randy Wright.
  Also see ALLEN, Deborah
  Also see FRICKE, Janie
  Also see HOUSTON, David, & Barbara Mandrell
  Also see JENNINGS, Waylon
  Also see McCOY, Charlie
  Also see WRIGHT, Randy

MANDRELL, Barbara, & Lee
Greenwood   *C&W/LP '84*

Singles: 7–inch

MCA...3-4   84

LPs: 10/12–inch 33rpm

MCA...5-8   84

  Also see GREENWOOD, Lee

MANDRELL, Barbara, & Oak Ridge Boys
C&W '86

Singles: 7–inch
MCA 3-4   86
Also see MANDRELL, Barbara
Also see OAK RIDGE BOYS

MANDRELL, Louise
C&W '78

Singles: 7–inch
EPIC 3-5   78-80
RCA 3-4   82-88

LP: 10/12–inch 33rpm
RCA 5-10   83-88

MANDRELL, Louise, & R.C. Bannon
C&W '79

Singles: 7–inch
EPIC 3-5   79-82

LP: 10/12–inch 33rpm
EPIC 5-10   79-80
RCA 5-10   82-83
Also see BANNON, R.C.

MANDRELL, Louise, & Eric Carmen
C&W '88

Singles: 7–inch
RCA 3-4   88
Also see MANDRELL, Louise

MANN, Carl
P&R/R&B '59/C&W '76

Singles: 7–inch
ABC/DOT 3-5   76
JAXON (502 "Gonna Rock and Roll
  Tonight") 200-300   57
PHILLIPS INT'L 10-20   59-61
SUN 3-5   70s

LPs: 10/12–inch 33rpm
GRT/SUNNYVALE 6-10   77
PHILLIPS INT'L (1960 "Like
  Mann") 400-500   60

MANN, Lorene
C&W '67

Singles: 7–inch
RCA 4-8   67-69

LP: 10/12–inch 33rpm
RCA 10-15   69
Also see CAMPBELL, Archie, & Lorene Mann
Also see TUBB, Justin, & Lorene Mann

MANNERS, Zeke, & His Band
(With the Singing Lariateers)   C&W '46

Singles: 78rpm
VICTOR 4-8   46
Also see BRITT, Elton

MANNING, Linda
C&W '68

Singles: 7–inch
BULLETIN 4-8   61
DOKE 5-10   60
GAYLORD 4-8   62
MERCURY 4-6   68
RICE 4-8   64-67

MANNING, Rhonda
C&W '87

Singles: 7–inch
RAM 3-4   88
SOUNDWAVES 3-4   87

MANTELLI, Steve
C&W '82

Singles: 7–inch
PICAP 3-4   82-83

MARCIA LYNN
C&W '87
(Marcia Lynn Dickinson)

Singles: 7–inch
EVERGREEN 3-4   87
SOUNDWAVES 3-4   87

MARCY BROTHERS
C&W '88

Singles: 7–inch
ATLANTIC 3-4   91
W.B. 3-4   88-90
Members: Kris Marcy; Kevin Marcy.

MARGO & NORRO: see SMITH, Margo, & Norro Wilson

MARIPAT
C&W '89
(Maripat Davis)

Singles: 7–inch
OAK 3-4   89

MARNEY, Ben
C&W '81

Singles: 7–inch
SOUTHERN BISCUIT 3-4   81

MARR, Leah
C&W '88

Singles: 7–inch
OAK 3-4   88-89

MARRIOTT, John
C&W '89

Singles: 7–inch
PHOENIX 3-4   89

MARSHALL, Roger
C&W '88

Singles: 7–inch
AVM 3-4   88
MASTER 3-4   88

MARSHALL TUCKER BAND
LP '73/C&W '76

Singles: 7–inch

CAPRICORN	3-5	73-78
MERCURY	3-4	87-88
W.B.	3-5	79-83

Picture Sleeves

W.B.	3-5	79

LPs: 10/12–inch 33rpm

CAPRICORN	8-12	73-78
MERCURY	5-10	87
W.B.	5-10	79-83

Members: Doug Gray; Tom Caldwell; Troy Caldwell; Franklin Wilkie; Jack Eubanks; Paul Riddle.
Also see CLEMENTS, Vassar

MARTEL, Marty
C&W '79

Singles: 7–inch

RIDGETOP	3-5	79

MARTELL, Linda
C&W '69
(With the Anglos)

Singles: 7–inch

FIRE (512 "Little Tear")	10-15	62
PLANTATION	3-6	69-70

LP: 10/12–inch 33rpm

PLANTATION	6-12	70

MARTIN, Benny
C&W '63

Singles: 7–inch

ASTRO (109 "Darling Goodbye")	100-150	60
STARDAY	5-10	63
GULF REEF	10-15	62

LP: 10/12–inch 33rpm

CMH	8-10
FLYING FISH	8-10
MARATHON	8-10
(Canadian.)	
WING	8-10

Also see RENO, Don, & Benny Martin

MARTIN, Benny, & Bobby Sykes

LP: 10/12–inch 33rpm

PICKWICK/HILLTOP	10-15	65

Also see MARTIN, Benny
Also see SYKES, Bobby

MARTIN, Betty
C&W '78

Singles: 7–inch

DOOR KNOB	3-5	78

MARTIN, Bobbi
P&R '64/C&W '66

Singles: 7–inch

BUDDAH	3-5	71-72
CORAL	4-8	61-67
GREEN MENU	3-5	75
MGM	3-5	73
MAYPOLE	5-10	60
U.A.	4-6	68-70

Picture Sleeves

CORAL	4-8	65

EPs: 7–inch 33/45rpm

CORAL	5-10	65

LPs: 10/12–inch 33rpm

BUDDAH	5-10	71
CORAL	10-20	65
SUNSET	5-10	71
U.A.	8-12	68-70
VOCALION	5-10	70

MARTIN, Dean
P&R '49/C&W '83

Singles: 78rpm

APOLLO (1088 "Oh Marie")	50-75	47
APOLLO (1116 "Santa Lucia")	50-75	48
CAPITOL (545 thru 2001)	15-25	49-52
CAPITOL (2037 "Hey, Brother, Pour the Wine")	20-30	54
(Seven–inch 78rpm. Promotional issue only.)		
CAPITOL (2071 thru 3841)	10-20	52-57
CAPITOL (15000 series)	20-40	48-49
DIAMOND (2035 "Which Way Did My Heart Go")	50-75	46
DIAMOND (2036 "I Got the Sun in the Morning")	50-75	46
EMBASSY (124 "One Foot in Heaven")	300-400	49

Singles: 7–inch

CAPITOL (401 "Dean Martin Sings")	75-100	53
(Four–disc boxed set.)		
CAPITOL (247 "Silver Bells")	10-15	66
(Promotional issue only.)		
CAPITOL (691 thru 981)	15-25	49-50
CAPITOL (987 "Sleep Warm")	50-100	59
(Promotional issue only.)		
CAPITOL (1002 thru 1458)	10-20	50-51
CAPITOL (1609 "I Met a Girl")	50-100	60
(Promotional issue only.)		
CAPITOL (1703 thru 3238)	10-15	51-55
CAPITOL (3295 thru 4570)	8-12	55-61
CAPITOL (6000 series)	4-6	64

CAPITOL (44153 "That's
Amore") 3-4   88

MCA (52662 "L.A. Is My
Home") 15-25   85

REPRISE (190 thru 193) 4-8   64
(Compact 33 singles. Promotional issues
only.)

REPRISE (200 "Sophia") 150-200   65
(Promotional issue only.)

REPRISE (0252 thru 1178) 3-6   64-73

REPRISE (20,000 series) 4-8   62-63

REPRISE (40,000 series) 10-15   62
(Stereo 33 singles.)

TEXAS DESERT CIRCUS WEEK (2160 "It's
1200 Miles from Texas to Palm
Springs") 50-100   58
(Single-sided promotional disc. Made
especially for play in Palm Springs,
promoting a circus. Incorrect title is shown
on label—should read *It's 1200 Miles from
Palm Springs to Texas.*)

W.B. (29584 "My First Country
Song") 3-4   83
(With Conway Twitty.)

W.B. (29480 "Drinking
Champagne") 3-4   83

Picture Sleeves

CAPITOL (987 "Sleep
Warm") 100-200   59

CAPITOL (1609 "I Met a
Girl") 50-100   60
(Promotional issue only. Sleeve reads:
"From the Soundtrack of the Motion Picture
Bells are Ringing.")

CAPITOL (4028 "Volare") 15-25   58

CAPITOL (4222 "On an Evening in
Roma") 15-25   59

REPRISE (20,116 "Who's Got the
Action") 15-20   62

EPs: 7–inch 33/45rpm

CAPITOL (EAP-401 "Dean Martin
Sings") 25-50   53
(Price is for either of two volumes.)

CAPITOL (EBF-401 "Dean Martin
Sings") 75-125   53
(Double EP boxed set.)

CAPITOL (481 "Sunny Italy") 25-50   53

CAPITOL (576 "Swingin' Down
Yonder") 20-40   59
(Price is for any of three volumes.)

CAPITOL (701 "Memories Are Made of
This") 25-50   55

CAPITOL (702 "Artists &
Models") 25-50   55

CAPITOL (806 "Hollywood Or
Bust") 25-50   57

CAPITOL (840 "Ten Thousand
Bedrooms") 25-50   57

CAPITOL (849 "Pretty Baby") 20-40   58
(Price is for any of three volumes.)

CAPITOL (939 "Return to Me") 20-40   58

CAPITOL (1027 "Volare") 20-40   58

CAPITOL (1285 "Winter
Romance") 20-40   59
(Price is for any of three volumes.)

CAPITOL (1580 "Dean
Martin") 20-30   61
(Compact Double 33.)

CAPITOL (EAP-1659 "Dino - Italian Love
Songs") 15-25   61

CAPITOL (SU-1659 "Dino - Italian Love
Songs") 15-25   61
(Jukebox issue.)

CAPITOL (DU-2601 "The Best of Dean
Martin") 15-25   61
(Jukebox issue.)

CAPITOL (9123 "Dean
Martin") 25-50   54

18 TOP HITS (27 "Dean
Martin") 20-40   54-55
(Price is for either 45 and 78rpm EPs.)

LLOYDS (705 "Dean Martin") 25-50   54
(Mail-order offer.)

REPRISE 10-20   62-73
(Jukebox 33 compact issues.)

LPs: 10/12–inch 33rpm

CAPITOL (100 series) 8-15   69

CAPITOL (300 series) 8-15   69

CAPITOL (H-401 "Dean Martin
Sings") 50-100   53
(10–inch LP.)

CAPITOL (T-401 "Dean Martin
Sings") 25-50   55
(Red cover.)

CAPITOL (TT-401 "Dean Martin
Sings") 10-20   59
(Pink cover.)

CAPITOL (523 "Return to Me"/"You're
Nobody Till Somebody Loves
You") 8-12   70

CAPITOL (576 "Swingin' Down
Yonder") 30-40   55

CAPITOL (849 thru 2601) 15-30   57-66
(With "T" or "ST" prefix.)

CAPITOL (849 thru 2601) 8-15   63-65
(With "DT" prefix.)

CAPITOL (2815 "Dean Martin Deluxe
Set") 15-25   67
(Three-LP boxed set.)

CAPITOL (2941 "Favorites") 8-12   68

COSMIC (450 "Dean Martin") ... 15-20

LONGINES (5234 "Memories Are Made of
This") 25-50   73
(Five-LP boxed set. Includes booklet.)

LONGINES (5235 "That's
Amore") 8-15   73

PAIR 6-10   83

PICKWICK 6-12   70s

REPRISE 8-18   63-78

S.M.I. 10-20

SEARS 15-25   60s

TALKING BOOK (58007 "Look: December 26,
1967") 15-25   67
(Reading of a Dean interview/story in *Look*.
Produced by the American Foundation for
the Blind. Plays at 16 rpm.)

TEE VEE 10-20   78

TOWER (5006 "The Lush
Years") 20-30   65

TOWER (5018 "Relaxin") 20-30   66

TOWER (5036 "Happy in
Love") 20-30   66

TOWER (5059 "Like Never
Before") 20-30   67

WALDORF (27 "Dean Martin
Sings") 50-75   53
(10-inch LP.)

W.B. 5-8   83

Promotional LPs

("Dean Martin Testimonial
Dinner") 200-250   59
(Presented by the Friars Club, and sold as a
"Collectors Item" for $25 at the dinner. Three
LPs in triple pocket jacket. No label name
nor selection number used. With guest
appearances by Jimmy Durante, Joey
Bishop, Tony Martin, George Burns, Dinah
Shore, Mort Sahl, Judy Garland; Sammy
Cahn, Danny Thomas, Sammy Davis Jr.,
Bob Hope, Frank Sinatra and others.)

REPRISE (246 Dean Martin Radio
Sampler") 35-50   66

Also see BURNS, George
Also see TWITTY, Conway

MARTIN, Dean / Glen Campbell
LPs: 10/12-inch 33rpm

ZENITH/CAPITOL 10-20   72
(Issued with paper cover. Special products.)

Also see CAMPBELL, Glen

MARTIN, Dean / Jeff Clark / Arlene James
EPs: 45/78rpm

POPULAR (1035 "Oh Marie") 10-15   54
(78 rpm. Not issued with special cover.)

VICTORY (1031 "Walking My Baby Back
Home") 10-15   54
(78 rpm. Not issued with special cover.)

POPULAR (1035 "Oh Marie") 10-20   54
(45 rpm. Not issued with special cover.)

VICTORY (1031 "Walking My Baby Back
Home") 20-40   54
(45 rpm. Colored vinyl. Not issued with
special cover.)

MARTIN, Dean, & Nat "King" Cole
Singles: 78rpm

CAPITOL 4-6   54

Singles: 7-inch

CAPITOL 5-10   54

Also see COLE, Nat "King"

MARTIN, Dean / Bob Eberly / Gordon MacRae
LPs: 10/12-inch 33rpm

BRIGADE (131 "Dino, Gordon & Bob
Sing") 15-25   50s

MARTIN, Dean / Jane Froman
Singles: 78rpm

CAPITOL 4-6   53

Singles: 7-inch

CAPITOL (20030 "Who's Your Little Who
Zis") 8-15   53
(Promotional issue only.)

MARTIN, Dean / Jackie Gleason
LPs: 10/12-inch 33rpm

CAPITOL SPECIAL MARKETS ... 8-10

MARTIN, Dean / Rock Hudson
Singles: 7-inch

NATIONAL FEATURES (2785
"Showdown") 20-30   73
(Interviews with *Showdown* film stars.
Promotional issue only. Includes script.)

MARTIN, Dean / Red Ingle & Natural Seven
Singles: 78rpm

CAPITOL (726 "Vieni Su") 8-15   49
(Promotional issue only.)

MARTIN, Dean, & Peggy Lee
Singles: 78rpm
CAPITOL (15349 "You Was") ... 15-25   49

MARTIN, Dean, & Jerry Lewis
         P&R '48
Singles: 78rpm
CAPITOL (15000 series) 5-10   48
NATIONAL MASK & PUPPET CORP.
("Puppet Show") 10-20   50s
(Promotional issue only.)
EPs: 7–inch 33/45rpm
CAPITOL (533 "Living It
Up") 100-150   54
CAPITOL (752 "Pardners") ... 100-150   56
LPs: 10/12–inch 33rpm
MEMORABILIA (714 "Dean Martin & Jerry
Lewis - First Show") 10-15   74
RADIOLA (1102 "Dean Martin & Jerry Lewis
on the Radio") 10-15

MARTIN, Dean / Nicolini Lucchesi
LPs: 10/12–inch 33rpm
AUDITION (5936 "Dean Martin Sings,
Niccolini Lucchesi Plays") 25-50   56

MARTIN, Dean / Johnny Mathis / St. James Pop Orchestra
EPs: 7–inch 33/45rpm
JIMMY McHUGH (400 "Music by Jimmy
McHugh") 10-15   81
(Promotional issue only.)

MARTIN, Dean, & Ricky Nelson
Singles: 7–inch
W.B. (2262 "My Rifle, My Pony and
Me") 400-500   59
(Promotional issue only.)
Also see NELSON, Rick

MARTIN, Dean, & Nuggets
Singles: 78rpm
CAPITOL 4-8   55
Singles: 7–inch
CAPITOL 5-10   55

MARTIN, Dean, & Helen O'Connell
Singles: 78rpm
CAPITOL 4-6   51
Singles: 7–inch
CAPITOL 5-10   51

MARTIN, Dean / Patti Page
LPs: 10/12–inch 33rpm
DECCA (79224 "Christmas Seals for
1962") 30-40   62
(Public service program for TB. Dean's show
on one side, Patti's on flip.)
DECCA (79235 "Christmas Seals for
1962") 20-30   62
(Public service program for TB. Dean's and
Patti's shows on one side, flip has Si Zenter
and Vaughn Monroe.)
Also see PAGE, Patti

MARTIN, Dean, & Line Renaud
Singles: 78rpm
CAPITOL 4-6   55
Singles: 7–inch
CAPITOL 5-10   55

MARTIN, Dean / Nelson Riddle
EPs: 7–inch 33/45rpm
CAPITOL (1063 "Rio
Bravo") 250-350   59
(Promotional only. Has special paper
sleeve.)

MARTIN, Dean, & Margaret Whiting
Singles: 78rpm
CAPITOL 4-6   50
Singles: 7–inch
CAPITOL 5-10   50
Also see MARTIN, Dean

MARTIN, Gypsy
         C&W '81
Singles: 7–inch
OMNI 3-4   81

MARTIN, J.D.
         C&W '86
Singles: 7–inch
CAPITOL 3-4   86

MARTIN, Janis
         P&R '56
Singles: 78rpm
RCA (Except 6652) 10-20   56-57
RCA (6652 "My Boy Elvis") 15-25   56
Singles: 7–inch
BIG DUTCH 3-5   77
PALETTE 5-10   61
RCA (6400 & 6500 series) 15-25   56
RCA (6652 "My Boy Elvis") 25-35   56
RCA (6700 thru 7300 series) 10-20   56-58
EPs: 7–inch 33/45rpm
RCA (4093 "Just Squeeze
Me") 75-100   58

MARTIN, Janis / Hank Snow

EPs: 7–inch 33/45rpm

RCA (76 "Love Me to Pieces").. 15-25   56
(Promotional issue only.)
Also see MARTIN, Janis
Also see SNOW, Hank

MARTIN, Jerry   *C&W '91*

Singles: 7–inch

DESERT STORM.......................... 3-5   91

MARTIN, Jimmy   *C&W '58*

(With the Sunny Mountain Boys; with J.D. Crowe)

Singles: 7–inch

DECCA (Except 30703) 3-8   59-72
DECCA (30703 "Rock Hearts"). 10-15   58

EPs: 7–inch 33/45rpm

DECCA....................................... 5-15   59-64

LPs: 10/12–inch 33rpm

ANTHOLOGY of COUNTRY
   MUSIC 10-20
DECCA..................................... 10-30   60-72
GUSTO 5-10
MCA 5-10   72-81
Also see MONROE, Bill
Also see NITTY GRITTY DIRT BAND & Jimmy Martin
Also see OSBORNE BROTHERS

MARTIN, Joey   *C&W '78*

Singles: 7–inch

NICKELODEON 3-5   78

MARTIN, Mike   *C&W '85*

Singles: 7–inch

COMPLEAT 3-4   85
Also see DELRAY, Martin

MARTINDALE, Wink   *P&R/C&W '59*

Singles: 7–inch

ABC/DOT 3-5   76
DOT.. 5-10   58-66
RANWOOD................................... 3-5   73

Picture Sleeves

DOT... 10-20   59-60

LPs: 10/12–inch 33rpm

DOT... 15-25   59-66
HAMILTON................................. 10-20   64

MARTINDALE, Wink, & Robin Ward

Singles: 7–inch

DOT.. 4-8   63-64

LPs: 10/12–inch 33rpm

DOT... 15-25   64
Also see MARTINDALE, Wink

MARTINE, Layng   *P&R '71/C&W '76*

(Layng Martine Jr.)

Singles: 7–inch

BARNABY.....................................3-5   71
DATE 5-10   66
GENERAL INT'L 4-8   66
PLAYBOY 3-5   76

MARTINO, Al   *P&R '52/C&W '69*

Singles: 78rpm

BBS...5-10   52
CAPITOL.....................................3-5   52-57

Singles: 7–inch

BBS (101 "Here in My Heart")....10-15   52
   (Black vinyl.)
BBS (101 "Here in My Heart")....15-25   52
   (Colored vinyl.)
CAPITOL (Except F-2122 thru
   F-4593) 3-8   62-81
CAPITOL (F-2122 thru F-4593) ...5-15   52-61
JUBILEE (6000 series) 10-15   53
   (Colored vinyl.)
MAZE (7025 "There's No
   Tomorrow") 5-10   62
20TH FOX...................................5-10   59-64

Picture Sleeves

CAPITOL.....................................5-10   63-66
MAZE (7025 "There's No
   Tomorrow") 8-12   62

LPs: 10/12–inch 33rpm

CAPITOL.....................................5-20   62-80
GUEST STAR..............................5-10   64
MOVIETONE 5-10   67
SPRINGBOARD 5-8   78
20TH FOX.................................10-20   59-65

MARVELL, James   *C&W '81*

Singles: 7–inch

CAVALEER...................................3-4   81
Also see COUNTRY CAVALEERS
Also see MERCY

MASON, Bonnie Jo

(Cher)

Singles: 7–inch

ANNETTE (1000 "Ringo, I Love
   You")...................................500-1000   64
Also see CHER

MASON, Sandy   *C&W '67*

Singles: 7–inch

HICKORY......................................4-6   67
JMI 4-6

MGM	4-8	65-66
ROULETTE	4-8	63

MASON DIXON *C&W '83*
Singles: 7–inch

CAPITOL	3-4	88-89
PREMIER	3-4	86-87
TEXAS	3-5	83-86

Members: Frank Gilligan; Jerry Dengler; Rick Henderson.

MASSEY, Wayne *P&R '80/C&W '81*
Singles: 7–inch

MCA	3-4	83
MERCURY	3-4	89
POLYDOR	3-5	80

Also see McLAIN, Charly, & Wayne Massey

MASTERS, A.J. *C&W '85*
Singles: 7–inch

BERMUDA DUNES	3-4	85-87

MATA, Billy *C&W '88*
Singles: 7–inch

BGM	3-4	88

MATHIS, Country Johnny *C&W '63*
Singles: 7–inch

D	5-10	59-60
LITTLE DARLIN'	4-6	66
U.A.	4-8	61-65

LP: 10/12–inch 33rpm

HILLTOP	15-25	65
LITTLE DARLIN'	10-20	67-70
PICKWICK	6-12	70s

Also see JIMMY & JOHNNY

MATHIS, Joel *C&W '74*
Singles: 7–inch

CHART	3-5	74
SOUNDWAVES	3-5	78

MATTEA, Kathy *C&W '83*
(With Tim O'Brien)
Singles: 7–inch

MERCURY	3-4	83-92

LPs: 10/12–inch 33rpm

MERCURY	5-8	83-92

Also see GIBBS, Terri

MAY, Ralph *C&W '81*
(With the Ohio River Band)
Singles: 7–inch

AMI	3-4	82
EVERGREEN	3-4	87

PRIMERO	3-4	82
SOUNDWAVES	3-5	81

McAULIFFE, Leon *C&W '49*
(With His Western Swing Band: with His Cimmaron Boys; Leon McAuliffe)
Singles: 78rpm

COLUMBIA	5-10	49

Singles: 7–inch

CAPITOL	4-8	64-65
CIMARRON	5-10	59-62

EPs: 7–inch 33/45rpm

CAPITOL	8-12	60s
DOT	8-12	58

LP: 10/12–inch 33rpm

ABC-PAR (ABC-394 "Cozy Inn") (Monaural.)	25-35	61
ABC-PAR (ABCS-394 "Cozy Inn") (Stereo.)	35-45	61
CAPITOL (2016 "Dancin'est Band Around")	20-30	64
CAPITOL (2148 "Everybody Dance, Everybody Swing")	20-30	64
CIMARRON (2002 "Swingin' Western Strings")	35-55	60
COLUMBIA	5-8	84
DELTA	5-10	82
DOT (3139 "Take Off")	25-50	58
DOT (3689 "Golden Country Hits")	15-20	66
PINE MOUNTAIN	6-12	
SESAC (225 "Just a Minute")	50-75	
SESAC (1601 "Points West")	50-75	59
STARDAY (171 "Mister Western Swing")	20-40	62
STARDAY (280 "Swinging West")	20-40	
STARDAY (309 "Swingin' Western Strings")	20-40	64
STONEWAY	10-20	

Member: Sam D. Bass.
Also see BASS, Sam D.
Also see WILLS, Bob

McBEE, Jerry *C&W '80*
Singles: 7–inch

DIMENSION	3-5	80

McBRIDE, Dale *C&W '71*
Singles: 7–inch

CON BRIO	3-5	76-79
FAME	10-15	59

213

REPRISE	4-8	64
TEAR DROP	5-10	64
THUNDERBIRD	4-6	71

LPs: 10/12–inch 33rpm

CON BRIO	8-10	77

McBRIDE & the RIDE   *LP '91*

Singles: 7–inch

MCA	3-4	91-92

LPs: 10/12–inch 33rpm

MCA	5-8	91-92

Members: Terry McBride; Billy Thomas; Ray Herndon; Kenny Vaughn; Keith Edwards.

McCALL, C.W.   *C&W/P&R '74*

Singles: 7–inch

MGM	3-5	74-75
POLYDOR	3-5	76-79

LPs: 10/12–inch 33rpm

MGM	5-10	75
POLYDOR	5-8	76-79

McCALL, Darrell   *C&W '63*

(With the Milestones)

Singles: 7–inch

ATLANTIC	3-4	74
CAPITOL	4-8	61
COLUMBIA	3-5	76-78
INDIGO	3-4	84
PHILIPS	4-8	61-63
RCA	3-5	80
WAYSIDE	3-6	68-70

LP: 10/12–inch 33rpm

COLUMBIA	10-15	77
WAYSIDE	10-15	70

Also see POTTER, Curtis, & Darrell McCall
Also see HANSON, Connie, & Friend

McCALL, Darrell, & Willie Nelson   *C&W '77*

Singles: 7–inch

COLUMBIA	3-5	77

Also see NELSON, Willie

McCARTERS   *C&W '88*

(Jennifer McCarter & the McCarters)

Singles: 7–inch

W.B.	3-4	88-90

Members: Jennifer McCarter; Lisa McCarter; Teresa McCarter.

McCARTNEY, Paul   *LP '70/C&W '74*

(Wings; with Wings; with Linda McCartney)

Singles: 12–inch 33/45rpm

CAPITOL (15212 "Spies Like Us")	5-8	85
CAPITOL (15235 "Press")	4-8	86
COLUMBIA (03019 "Take It Away")	5-10	82
COLUMBIA (05077 "No More Lonely Nights")	5-8	84
("Playout version.")		
COLUMBIA (05077 "No More Lonely Nights")	10-15	84
("Special Dance Mix.")		
COLUMBIA (10940 "Goodnight Tonight")	10-20	79
COLUMBIA (39927 "No More Lonely Nights")	8-12	84
(Picture disc.)		
PROFILE (7147 "Let It Be")	5-8	87

Promotional 12–inch Singles

CAPITOL (8574 "Maybe I'm Amazed")	75-125	77
CAPITOL (9556 "Spies Like Us")	20-25	85
CAPITOL (9763 "Press")	10-15	86
CAPITOL (9797 "Angry")	10-15	86
COLUMBIA (775 "Coming Up")	50-60	80
(Red label.)		
COLUMBIA (775 "Coming Up")	45-55	80
(White label.)		
COLUMBIA (1940 "No More Lonely Nights")	10-15	84
("Ballad" version.)		
COLUMBIA (1990 "No More Lonely Nights")	10-15	84
("Special Dance Mix.")		
COLUMBIA (05077 "No More Lonely Nights")	10-15	84
("Ballad version.")		
COLUMBIA (10940 "Goodnight Tonight")	10-20	79
PROFILE (7147 "Let It Be")	10-15	87

Singles: 7–inch

APPLE (1829 "Another Day")	4-6	71
APPLE (1837 "Uncle Albert Admiral Halsey")	4-6	71
APPLE (1847 "Give Ireland Back to the Irish")	4-6	72
APPLE (1851 "Mary Had a Little Lamb")	4-6	72

APPLE (1857 "Hi Hi Hi")................ 4-6   72
APPLE (1861 "My Love") 4-6   73
APPLE (1863 "Live and Let Die").. 4-6   73
APPLE (1869 "Helen Wheels") 4-6   73
APPLE (1871 "Jet"/"Mamunia")... 5-10   74
APPLE (1871 "Jet"/"Let Me Roll
   It")... 4-6   74
APPLE (1873 "Band on the
   Run")... 4-6   74
APPLE (1875 "Junior's Farm")...... 4-6   74
CAPITOL (1829 "Another Day").... 3-4   80s
CAPITOL (1837 "Uncle Albert Admiral
   Halsey")... 3-4   80s
CAPITOL (1847 "Give Ireland Back to the
   Irish")... 3-4   80s
CAPITOL (1851 "Mary Had a Little
   Lamb").. 3-4   80s
CAPITOL (1857 "Hi Hi Hi")............ 3-4   80s
CAPITOL (1861 "My Love") 3-4   80s
CAPITOL (1863 "Live and Let
   Die")... 3-4   80s
CAPITOL (1869 "Helen Wheels") . 3-4   80s
CAPITOL (1871 "Jet").................... 3-4   80s
CAPITOL (1873 "Band on the
   Run")... 3-4   80s
CAPITOL (1875 "Junior's Farm").. 3-4   80s
CAPITOL (4091 "Listen to What the Man
   Said")... 3-5   75
CAPITOL (4145 "Letting Go") 3-5   75
CAPITOL (4175 "Venus and Mars Rock
   Show").. 3-5   75
CAPITOL (4256 "Silly Love
   Songs") 3-5   76
   (Capitol custom label.)
CAPITOL (4256 "Silly Love
   Songs") 3-4   80s
   (Black label.)
CAPITOL (4293 "Let 'Em In")........ 3-5   76
   (Capitol custom label.)
CAPITOL (4293 "Let 'Em In")........ 3-4   80s
   (Black label.)
CAPITOL (4385 Maybe I'm
   Amazed") 3-5   77
CAPITOL (4504 "Mull of
   Kintyre") 3-5   77
CAPITOL (4559 "With a Little
   Luck")... 3-5   78
CAPITOL (4594 "I've Had
   Enough") 3-5   78
CAPITOL (4625 "London Town").. 3-5   78
CAPITOL (5537 "Spies Like Us").. 3-4   85
CAPITOL (5597 "Press").............. 3-4   86
CAPITOL (5636 "Stranglehold").... 3-4   86

CAPITOL (17318 "Off the
   Ground") 40-50   94
   (Intended to be red vinyl but issued on black
   vinyl by mistake. Reportedly 800 made. 30th
   Anniversary jukebox issue.)
CAPITOL (17319 "Biker Like an
   Icon")..40-50   94
   (Intended to be red vinyl but issued on black
   vinyl by mistake. Reportedly 800 made. 30th
   Anniversary jukebox issue.)
COLUMBIA (02171 "Silly Love
   Songs") 3-4   81
COLUMBIA (03018 "Take It
   Away")..3-4   82
COLUMBIA (03235 "Tug of
   War")..3-4   82
COLUMBIA (04296 "So Bad") 3-4   83
COLUMBIA (04581 "No More Lonely
   Nights")...3-4   84
COLUMBIA (10939 "Goodnight
   Tonight") 3-4   79
COLUMBIA (11020 "Getting
   Closer")...3-4   79
COLUMBIA (11070 "Arrow Through
   Me")...3-4   79
COLUMBIA (11162 "Wonderful
   Christmastime") 3-4   79
COLUMBIA (11263 "Coming
   Up")..3-4   80
   (Listed here as a single even though there
   are two tracks on the B-side.)
COLUMBIA (11335 "Waterfalls") ...3-4   80
COLUMBIA (33405 "Goodnight
   Tonight") 3-4   80
COLUMBIA (33409 "My Love")......3-4   80
COLUMBIA (33408 "Uncle Albert Admiral
   Halsey") 3-4   80
COLUMBIA (33409 "Band on the
   Run")..3-4   80
PROFILE (5147 "Let It Be") 3-4   87

Picture Sleeves

APPLE (1847 "Give Ireland Back to the
   Irish").......................................10-20   72
APPLE (1851 "Mary Had a Little
   Lamb") 20-30   72
   ("Little Woman Love" printed under photo, on
   reverse side of sleeve.)
APPLE (1851 "Mary Had a Little
   Lamb") 10-15   72
   ("Little Woman Love" not printed under
   photo, on reverse side of sleeve.)
CAPITOL (4091 "Listen to What the Man
   Said") 4-8   75

CAPITOL (4504 "Mull of Kintyre") 8-12 77

CAPITOL (5537 "Spies Like Us").. 3-5 85

CAPITOL (5597 "Press").............. 3-5 86

CAPITOL (5636 "Stranglehold").... 3-5 86

COLUMBIA (03018 "Take It Away").................................. 5-10 82
(Reads "Not for Sale" on back side. Promotional issue only.)

COLUMBIA (03018 "Take It Away") 3-5 82

COLUMBIA (04296 "So Bad")....... 3-5 83

COLUMBIA (04296 "So Bad")..... 5-10 83
(Reads "Not for Sale" on back side. Promotional issue only.)

COLUMBIA (04581 "No More Lonely Nights") 5-10 84

COLUMBIA (11020 "Getting Closer") 20-30 79

COLUMBIA (11162 "Wonderful Christmastime")........................... 4-6 79

COLUMBIA (11263 "Coming Up").. 4-6 80

COLUMBIA (11335 "Waterfalls") 15-20 80

PROFILE (5147 "Let It Be") 3-5 87

Promotional Singles

APPLE (1829 "Another Day").... 35-45 71

APPLE (1837 "Uncle Albert Admiral Halsey")...................................... 15-25 71

APPLE (1851 "Mary Had a Little Lamb").................................... 50-100 72

APPLE (1857 "Hi Hi Hi")............ 10-15 72

APPLE (1861 "My Love") 50-75 73

APPLE (1863 "Live and Let Die") 10-20 73

APPLE (1871 "Jet").................. 20-30 74

APPLE (1873 "Band on the Run").. 25-35 74

APPLE (1875 "Junior's Farm") .. 25-35 74

APPLE (1875 "Sally G") 25-35 74

APPLE (6786 "Helen Wheels") . 25-35 73

APPLE (6787 "Country Dreamer")............................... 50-100 73

CAPITOL (4145 "Letting Go") ... 15-20 75

CAPITOL (4175 "Venus and Mars Rock Show")..................................... 15-20 75

CAPITOL (4256 "Silly Love Songs.") 10-20 76

CAPITOL (4293 "Let 'Em In")...... 8-12 76

CAPITOL (4594 "I've Had Enough") 10-15 78

(Add $3-$5 if accompanied by special promotional flyer.)

CAPITOL (4625 "London Town").....................................10-15 78

CAPITOL (5537 "Spies Like Us")...............................5-10 85

CAPITOL (5597 "Press") 5-10 86

CAPITOL (5636 "Stranglehold") ..5-10 86

CAPITOL (8138 "Listen to What the Man Said") 10-15 75

CAPITOL (8570/1 "Maybe I'm Amazed") 10-15 77

CAPITOL (8746/7 "Mull of Kintyre") 10-15 77

CAPITOL (8812 "With a Little Luck")...................................10-15 78

COLUMBIA (1204 "Coming Up").....................................5-10 80
(Single-sided disc.)

COLUMBIA (03018 "Take It Away")...................................4-6 82

COLUMBIA (03235 "Tug of War").....................................8-10 82

COLUMBIA (04296 "So Bad") 5-8 83

COLUMBIA (04581 "No More Lonely Nights")..................................5-8 84

COLUMBIA (10939 "Goodnight Tonight") 5-8 79

COLUMBIA (11020 "Getting Closer") 10-12 79

COLUMBIA (11070 "Arrow Through Me").........................10-12 79

COLUMBIA (11162 "Wonderful Christmastime") 10-12 79

COLUMBIA (11263 "Coming Up")...................................8-10 80

COLUMBIA (11335 "Waterfalls") 8-10 80

CREATIVE RADIO (PM-1 "Inside Paul McCartney")............................15-20
(Radio show demo. Flip is *The Beatle Invasion*.)

MIRAMAX (4202 "Rock Show") 150-175 75
(Contains three radio spots. Issued to radio stations only.)

PROFILE (5147 "Let It Be") 5-10 87

LPs: 10/12–inch 33rpm

APPLE (3363 "McCartney").......15-20 70
(Label shows Paul's full name beneath LP title.)

APPLE (3363 "McCartney").......10-15 70
(Label doesn't show Paul's name beneath LP title.)

APPLE (3375 "Ram") 10-15   71
APPLE (3386 "Wild Life") 10-15   71
APPLE (3409 "Red Rose
   Speedway") 10-15   73
APPLE (3415 "Band on the
   Run") 10-15   73
   (Price includes bonus poster.)
CAPITOL (3363 "McCartney") 8-10
CAPITOL (3375 "Ram") 8-10
CAPITOL (3386 "Wildlife") 8-10
CAPITOL (3409 "Red Rose
   Speedway") 8-10
CAPITOL (3415 "Band on the
   Run") 8-10
   (Price includes bonus poster.)
CAPITOL (11525 "Wings at the Speed of
   Sound") ....: 8-10   76
CAPITOL (11593 "Wings Over
   America") 12-15   76
CAPITOL (11905 "Greatest
   Hits") 5-10   78
   (Price includes bonus poster.)
CAPITOL (11419 "Venus &
   Mars") ....: 10-15   75
   (Price includes bonus posters and stickers.)
CAPITOL (11777 "London
   Town") 10-15   78
   (Price includes bonus poster.)
CAPITOL (11901 "Band on the
   Run") 20-30   78
   (Picture disc.)
CAPITOL (12475 "Press to
   Play") 8-10   87
CAPITOL (48287 "All the
   Best!") 10-15   87
CAPITOL (91653 "Flowers in the
   Dirt") 5-8   89
CAPITOL (94778 "Tripping the Live
   Fantastic") 10-12   90
CAPITOL (95379 "Tripping the Live Fantastic:
   Highlights") 5-10   90
COLUMBIA (36057 "Back to the
   Egg") 5-10   79
COLUMBIA (36478
   "McCartney") 5-10   80
COLUMBIA (36479 "Ram") 5-10   80
COLUMBIA (36480 "Wild Life") ... 5-10   80
COLUMBIA (36481 "Red Rose
   Speedway") 5-10   80
COLUMBIA (36482 "Band on the
   Run") 5-10   80
COLUMBIA (36511
   "McCartney II") 15-20   80
   (Issued with bonus single [1204] *Coming Up*,

which represents $4 to $8 of the price
range.)
COLUMBIA (36801 "Venus &
   Mars") 5-8   80
   (Price includes bonus posters.)
COLUMBIA (36987 "The McCartney
   Interview") 8-10   80
COLUMBIA (37409 "Wings at the Speed of
   Sound") 5-8   81
COLUMBIA (37462 "Tug of
   War") 5-8   82
   (With Stevie Wonder on *Ebony and Ivory*)
COLUMBIA (39149 "Pipes of
   Peace") 5-8   83
   (With Michael Jackson on *Say Say Say*)
COLUMBIA (39613 "Give My Regards to
   Broad Street") 5-8   84
COLUMBIA (46482 "Band on the
   Run") 10-15   80
   (Half-speed mastered.)
LIBERTY (50100 Live and Let
   Die") 5-8   84
   (With McCartney on title track only.)
LONDON (76007 "Family
   Way") 50-60   67
   (Soundtrack. Monaural.)
LONDON (82007 "Family
   Way") 60-70   67
   (Soundtrack. Stereo.)
U.A. (100 "Live and Let Die") 15-20   73
   (Copies with cut corners are valued at about
   one-half of the above price range.
   McCartney is heard on title track only.)

Promotional LPs

APPLE (3375 "Ram") 80-100   71
   (Monaural.)
APPLE (6210 "Brung to Ewe
   By") 175-200   71
COLUMBIA (821 "The McCartney
   Interview") 40-50   80
COLUMBIA (36057 "Back to the
   Egg") 15-20   79
COLUMBIA (36511
   "McCartney II") 15-20   80
W.B. ("The Family Way") 150-200   67
   (10-inch LP. Ad spots for radio stations.)
   Also see COUNTRY HAMS
   Also see PERKINS, Carl

McCARTNEY, Paul, & Michael Jackson   *P&R/R&B '82*
Singles: 12-inch 33/45rpm
COLUMBIA (1758 "Say Say
   Say") 10-15   83

COLUMBIA (04169 "Say Say
Say") 5-8   83
Promotional 12–inch Singles
COLUMBIA (04169 "Say Say
Say") 12-18   83
Singles: 7–inch
COLUMBIA (04168 "Say Say
Say") 3-4   83
EPIC (03288 "The Girl Is Mine") ... 3-4   82
EPIC (03372 "The Girl Is Mine") ... 5-8   82
(Single-sided pressing with small, LP size,
hole.)
Picture Sleeves
COLUMBIA (04168 "Say Say
Say") 3-4   83
Promotional Picture Sleeves
COLUMBIA (04168 "Say Say
Say") 5-8   83
EPIC (03288 "The Girl Is Mine") ... 5-8   82
Promotional Singles
COLUMBIA (04168 "Say Say
Say") 5-8   83
EPIC (03288 "The Girl Is Mine") ... 5-8   82
(Label shows identification number as
169138.)
EPIC (03288 "The Girl Is
Mine") 10-15   82
(Label shows identification number as
169202. Also reads "New Edited Version.")

McCARTNEY, Paul / Rochestra / Who / Rockpile
Singles: 12–inch 33/45rpm
ATLANTIC (388 "Every Night") . 60-80   81
(Promotional issue only.)

McCARTNEY, Paul, & Stevie Wonder   *P&R/R&B '82*
Singles: 12–inch 33/45rpm
COLUMBIA (02878 "Ebony &
Ivory") 5-8   82
Promotional 12–inch Singles
COLUMBIA (1444
"McCartney") 25-30   82
Singles: 7–inch
COLUMBIA (02860 "Ebony &
Ivory") 3-4   82
Promotional Singles
COLUMBIA (02860 "Ebony &
Ivory") 8-12   82
Picture Sleeves
COLUMBIA (02860 "Ebony &
Ivory") 3-4   82

Promotional Picture Sleeves
COLUMBIA (02860 "Ebony &
Ivory") 5-10   82
Also see McCARTNEY, Paul

McCLAIN, Charly   *C&W '76*
Singles: 7–inch
EPIC 3-5 76-88
MERCURY 3-4 88-89
LP: 10/12–inch 33rpm
EPIC 5-10 77-88
MERCURY 5-8   88
Also see GILLEY, Mickey, & Charly McClain
Also see RODRIGUEZ, Johnny, & Charly McClain

McLAIN, Charly, & Wayne Massey   *C&W '86*
Singles: 7–inch
EPIC 3-4   86
Also see MASSEY, Wayne
Also see McCLAIN, Charly

McCLINTON, Delbert   *LP '79*
Singles: 7–inch
ABC 3-5 75-77
BOBILL 5-10   67
BROWNFIELD 8-12   65
CAPITOL 3-5 80-81
CAPRICORN 3-5   78
LPs: 10/12–inch 33rpm
ABC 5-10 75-77
ACCORD 5-8   81
CAPITOL 5-8 80-81
CAPRICORN 5-8 78-79
INTERMEDIA 5-8   84
MCA 5-8   81
POLYDOR 10-15   79
Also see DELBERT & GLEN

McCLINTON, O.B.   *C&W '72*
(With Peggy Jo Adams)
Singles: 7–inch
ENTERPRISE 3-5 72-75
EPIC 3-5 78-87
MERCURY 3-5   76
MOON SHINE 3-4   84
SUNBIRD 3-5   80
LPs: 10/12–inch 33rpm
ENTERPRISE 8-10 72-74

McCORD, Cali   *C&W '87*
Singles: 7–inch
GAZELLE 3-4 87-88

McCORISON, Dan   C&W '77

Singles: 7–inch

MCA 3-5   77

LP: 10/12–inch 33rpm

MCA 5-10   77

McCOY, Charlie   P&R '61/C&W '72

Singles: 7–inch

CADENCE.................................... 4-8   61-62
MONUMENT 3-6   68-83

LPs: 10/12–inch 33rpm

EPIC... 5-8   82
MONUMENT 5-10   69-78

Session: Barefoot Jerry.
 Also see BAREFOOT JERRY
 Also see FOWLER, Wally
 Also see LEE, Bobby
 Also see MANDRELL, Barbara
 Also see McDOWELL, Ronnie
 Also see NASHVILLE SUPERPICKERS
 Also see TUBB, Ernest

McCOY, Charlie, & Laney
Smallwood   C&W '81

(Charlie McCoy & Laney Hicks)

Singles: 7–inch

MONUMENT 3-5   74

Also see McCOY, Charlie
 Also see SMALLWOOD, Laney

McCOY, Neal   C&W '88

(Neal McGoy)

Singles: 7–inch

ATLANTIC...................................... 3-4   90-91
16TH AVE. 3-4   88

McCULLA, Paula   C&W '88

Singles: 7–inch

RIVERMARK.................................. 3-4   88

McCULLOUGH, Gary   C&W '87

Singles: 7–inch

SOUNDWAVES 3-4   87

McDANIEL, Mel   C&W '76

(With Oklahoma Wind; Mel McDaniels)

Singles: 7–inch

CAPITOL....................................... 3-4   76-89

LP: 10/12–inch 33rpm

CAPITOL............... 5-8   78-84

McDONALD, Skeets   C&W '52

Singles: 78rpm

CAPITOL (Except 3461) 4-8   51-57
CAPITOL (3461 "You Oughta See Grandma
 Rock") 10-20   56

FORTUNE................................. 10-15   50

Singles: 7–inch

CAPITOL (Except 3461) 5-15   51-59
CAPITOL (3461 "You Oughta See Grandma
 Rock")..................................50-75   56
COLUMBIA 3-8   60-67

EPs: 7–inch 33/45rpm

CAPITOL................................15-25   54-58

LPs: 10/12–inch 33rpm

CAPITOL (1040 "Goin' Steady with the
 Blues") 50-75   58
COLUMBIA 15-25   64
FORTUNE................................10-20   69
HILLYBILLY HEAVEN 5-10
SEARS (116 "Skeets")...............30-40   60s

McDOWELL, Ronnie   P&R/C&W '77

Singles: 7–inch

EPIC..3-5   79-85
GRT 3-5   77
MCA/CURB...............................3-4   86
SCORPION (Except 0533) 3-6   77-79
SCORPION (0533 "Only the
 Lonely")................................4-8   77

LPs: 10/12–inch 33rpm

DICK CLARK (79 "Elvis").............8-12   79
 (TV soundtrack.)
EPIC..5-10   79-85
MCA/CURB...............................5-8   86
SCORPION (0010 "Live at the
 Fox")....................................10-15   78
SCORPION (8021 "The King Is
 Gone")..................................10-20   77
 (Includes copy of front page of newspaper
 with news that the king is gone.)
SCORPION (8028 "I Love You, I Love You, I
 Love You") 10-15   78
STRAWBERRY...........................8-10   70s

Session: Jordanaires; Conway Twitty; Kathy
 Westmoreland; Charlie McCoy; David Briggs; Chip
 Young; Dale Sellers; Bobby Ogden; Mike Leech.
 Also see McCOY, Charlie
 Also see JORDANAIRES
 Also see TWITTY, Conway

McDOWELL, Ronnie, & Jerry Lee
Lewis   C&W '89

Singles: 7–inch

CURB.......................................3-5   88

Also see LEWIS, Jerry Lee
 Also see McDOWELL, Ronnie

McENTIRE, Pake
C&W '86
Singles: 7–inch
RCA.. 3-4   86-88
  Also see McENTIRE, Reba

McENTIRE, Reba
C&W '76
Singles: 7–inch
MCA 3-5   84-90
MERCURY 5-15   76-83

LPs: 10/12–inch 33rpm
MCA 5-8   84-90
MERCURY (1177 "Reba
  McEntire") 50-100   77
MERCURY (4047 "Unlimited") .. 15-25   82
MERCURY (5002 "Reba
  McEntire") 25-50   77
MERCURY (5017 "Out of a
  Dream")................................... 25-50   79
MERCURY (5029 "Feel the
  Fire") 20-30   80
MERCURY (6003 "Heart to
  Heart")..................................... 20-30   81
MERCURY (57062 thru
  76157)..................................... 10-15   81-82
MERCURY (812781 "Behind the
  Scene") 10-15   83
  Session: Chris Austin; Pake McEntire.
  Also see AUSTIN, Chris
  Also see McENTIRE, Pake
  Also see WARD, Jacky, & Reba McEntire
  Also see WHITLEY, Keith

McEUEN, John
C&W '85
Singles: 7–inch
W.B. 3-4   85

McGILL, Tony
C&W '87
Singles: 7–inch
KILLER... 3-4   87

McGOVERN, Maureen

P&R/LP '73/C&W '79
Singles: 7–inch
CASABLANCA 3-5   70s
EPIC 3-5   78
MAIDEN VOYAGE 3-5   70s
20TH FOX...................................... 3-5   73-75
W.B. 3-5   79-80
WOODEN NICKEL........................ 3-5   73

LPs: 10/12–inch 33rpm
20TH FOX...................................... 8-12   73-75
W.B. 5-10   79

McGUIRE, Doug
C&W '80
Singles: 7–inch
MULTI-MEDIA.................................3-5   80

McKUHEN, Lanier
C&W '87
Singles: 7–inch
SOUNDWAVES 3-4   87

McLEAN, Don
P&R/LP '71/C&W '81
Singles: 7–inch
ARISTA..3-5   78
CAPITOL..3-4   87-88
EMI AMERICA (Except 9100)........3-4   87
EMI AMERICA (9100 "American
  Pie")...4-8   92
  (Full length [8:30] version.)
LIBERTY 3-5
MEDIARTS 3-6   70
MILLENNIUM...................................3-5   81-83
RCA 3-4   83
U.A. 3-5   71-75

Picture Sleeves
U.A. 3-5   71-73

LPs: 10/12–inch 33rpm
ARISTA (4149 "Prime Time").......5-10   77
  (Black vinyl.)
ARISTA (4149 "Prime Time").....10-15   77
  (Colored vinyl. Promotional issue only.)
CASABLANCA.............................8-10   79
LIBERTY 5-8   82-83
MEDIARTS (41-4 "Tapestry") 8-12   70
MILLENNIUM.................................5-8   81
U.A. 10-12   71-74

Promotional LPs
RCA ("Special Radio Series")....10-15   81

McMILLAN, Jimmy
C&W '80
Singles: 7–inch
BLUM..3-5   80-81

McMILLAN, Terry
C&W '82
Singles: 7–inch
RCA 3-4   82

McPHERSON, Wyley
C&W '82
Singles: 7–inch
I.E. 3-4   82

McQUAIG, Scott
C&W '89
Singles: 7–inch
UNIVERSAL....................................3-4   89

McVICKER, Dana   *C&W '87*
Singles: 7–inch

CAPITOL	3-4	88
EMI AMERICA	3-4	87

MEADE, Donna   *C&W '88*
Singles: 7–inch

MERCURY	3-4	88-89

MEDLEY, Bill

P&R/R&B/LP '68/C&W '79
Singles: 7–inch

A&M	3-5	71-73
CURB	3-5	89
LIBERTY	3-5	81
MGM	4-8	68
PARAMOUNT	3-5	71
PLANET	3-4	82-83
RCA	3-4	83-85
REPRISE	4-8	65
U.A.	3-5	78-80
VERVE	4-8	67

LPs: 10/12–inch 33rpm

A&M	8-12	71-73
LIBERTY	5-10	81
MCA/CURB	5-10	88
MGM	10-20	68-70
PLANET	8-10	82
RCA	5-8	83-85
U.A.	8-10	78-80

Also see SONNY & CHER / Bill Medley / Lettermen / Blendells

MEDLEY, Bill, & Jennifer Warnes   *P&R '87*
Singles: 7–inch

RCA	3-4	87

Picture Sleeves

RCA	3-4	87

Also see MEDLEY, Bill
Also see WARNES, Jennifer

MELLENCAMP, John Cougar   *P&R/LP '79/C&W '89*
(John Cougar; Johnny Cougar; John Mellencamp)
Singles: 7–inch

MERCURY	3-4	87-90
RIVA (Except 211)	3-5	79-85
RIVA (211 "Hand to Hold on To")	3-4	82
RIVA (211 "Hand to Hold on To") (Picture disc.)	10-15	82

Picture Sleeves

MERCURY	3-4	87-90
RIVA	4-8	79-86

EPs: 7–inch 33/45rpm

GULCHER ("U.S. Male")	50-75	75

LPs: 10/12–inch 33rpm

MCA (2225 "Chestnut Street Incident")	15-20	77
MAIN MAN ("Chestnut Street Incident")	30-40	76
MAIN MAN (601 "Kid Inside")	5-10	83
MAIN MAN (4001 "Kid Inside") (Picture disc.)	40-60	83
MERCURY (Except 349)	5-8	87-90
MERCURY (349 "Let It All Hang") (Interview LP. Promotional issue only.)	25-35	87
RIVA	5-10	79-85

Members: John Cougar Mellencamp; Larry Crane; David Parman; Terrence Sala; Wayne Hall; Tom Wince; Michael Wanchic; Doc Rosser; Ken Aronoff; George Perry; Toby Myers; John Cascalle.

MEMPHIS   *C&W '84*
Singles: 7–inch

MPI	3-4	84

Member: Woody Wright.

MENSY, Tim   *C&W '89*
Singles: 7–inch

COLUMBIA	3-4	89-90

MERCER, Johnny, Jo Stafford & Pied Pipers
Singles: 78rpm

CAPITOL	4-8	45

Also see PIED PIPERS
Also see STAFFORD, Jo

MERCY   *P&R/LP '69*
Singles: 7–inch

SUNDI	4-8	69
W.B.	4-8	69

LPs: 10/12–inch 33rpm

SUNDI	15-20	69
W.B.	10-15	69

Members: James Marvell; Buddy Good.
Also see COUNTRY CAVALEERS
Also see MARVELL, James

MEREDITH, Buddy   *C&W '62*
Singles: 7–inch

NASHVILLE	4-8	62

LP: 10/12–inch 33rpm

DAVIS UNLIMITED	6-12	
STARDAY	15-25	63

MERRILL & JESSICA $\quad$ *C&W '87*
Singles: 7–inch
EMI AMERICA .... 3-4 $\quad$ 87
Members: Merrill Osmond; Jessica Boucher.
 Also see OSMONDS

MESSNER, Bud, & His Sky Line Boys $\quad$ *C&W '50*
Singles: 78rpm
ABBEY .... 10-20 $\quad$ 50

MEYERS, Augie $\quad$ *C&W '88*
(Augie)
Singles: 7–inch
ATLANTIC AMERICA .... 3-4 $\quad$ 88
AXBAR .... 3-4 $\quad$ 83
PARAMOUNT .... 3-6 $\quad$ 73
TEXAS RE-CORD CO .... 3-5 $\quad$ 75-79
SUPER BEET (Except 102).......... 3-4 $\quad$ 87
SUPER BEET (102 "Velma from Selma") .... 5-10 $\quad$ 87
SUPER BEET (102 "Mathilda")..... 3-4 $\quad$ 87
 (Both of above are numbered 102.)
Selma.)
VOL... 4-8 $\quad$ 68
LPs: 10/12–inch 33rpm
ATLANTIC AMERICA .... 5-8 $\quad$ 88
PARAMOUNT .... 15-20 $\quad$ 73
POLYDOR.................................. 10-20 $\quad$ 71
SUPER BEET .... 5-8 $\quad$ 87
TEXAS RE-CORD CO .... 10-15 $\quad$ 75-77
Also see AMIGOS DE MUSICA
Also see KEVIN & AUGIE
Also see KEVIN & BLACKTEARS
Also see LEWIS, Jerry Lee
Also see NELSON, Willie
Also see RAT RACE KID
Also see VINCENT, Gene

MEYERS, Michael $\quad$ *C&W '82*
Singles: 7–inch
MBP .... 3-4 $\quad$ 82

MIDDLETON, Eddie $\quad$ *C&W '77*
Singles: 7–inch
EPIC.. 3-5 $\quad$ 77
LP: 10/12–inch 33rpm
EPIC.. 6-12 $\quad$ 77

MILES, Dick $\quad$ *C&W '68*
Singles: 7–inch
CAPITOL.. 4-6 $\quad$ 68
LP: 10/12–inch 33rpm
CAPITOL..................................... 10-15 $\quad$ 68

MILLER, Carl $\quad$ *C&W '83*
Singles: 7–inch
COUNTRY BACH .... 3-4 $\quad$ 83

MILLER, Ellen Lee $\quad$ *C&W '89*
Singles: 7–inch
GOLDEN TRUMPET .... 3-4 $\quad$ 89

MILLER, Frankie $\quad$ *C&W '59*
Singles: 78rpm
COLUMBIA .... 3-6 $\quad$ 54-56
Singles: 7–inch
COLUMBIA .... 5-15 $\quad$ 54-56
STARDAY .... 5-10 $\quad$ 59-67
EPs: 7–inch 33/45rpm
STARDAY .... 8-12 $\quad$ 60
LPs: 10/12–inch 33rpm
AUDIO LAB (1562 "Fine Country Singing") .... 40-50 $\quad$ 63
STARDAY (134 "Country Music's New Star").. 40-50 $\quad$ 61
STARDAY (199 "Country Style") .... 40-50 $\quad$ 62
STARDAY (338 "Blackland Farmer")................................... 40-50 $\quad$ 65

MILLER, Jody $\quad$ *P&R '64/C&W '65*
Singles: 7–inch
CAPITOL.. 4-8 $\quad$ 63-70
EPIC.. 3-5 $\quad$ 70-79
Picture Sleeves
CAPITOL...................................... 5-10 $\quad$ 65
LPs: 10/12–inch 33rpm
CAPITOL (1913 "Wednesday's Child Is Full of Woe")................................ 15-25 $\quad$ 63
CAPITOL (2349 thru 2996)........ 10-20 $\quad$ 65-69
CAPITOL (11000 series) .... 5-10 $\quad$ 73
EPIC.. 5-10 $\quad$ 70-77
PICKWICK/HILLTOP .... 10-15 $\quad$ 66
SEARS.. 8-12

MILLER, Jody, & Johnny Paycheck $\quad$ *C&W '72*
EPIC.. 3-5 $\quad$ 72
Also see MILLER, Jody
Also see PAYCHECK, Johnny

MILLER, Mary K. $\quad$ *C&W '77*
(Mary Miller)
Singles: 7–inch
INERGI... 3-5 $\quad$ 77-80
RCA .... 3-5 $\quad$ 79

LP: 10/12–inch 33rpm

INERGI 5-10   78

MILLER, Ned   *C&W/P&R '62*
Singles: 78rpm
DOT (Except 15601) 8-12   57
DOT (15601 "From a Jack to a King") 15-25   57

Singles: 7–inch
CAPITOL (2000 series)................ 3-6   68
CAPITOL (4600 series)................ 5-8   61
CAPITOL (5400 thru 5800 series) 3-8   65-67
DOT (Except 15601) 8-12   57
DOT (15601 "From a Jack to a King") 15-25   57
FABOR 4-8   62-65
JACKPOT...................................... 8-12   59
REPUBLIC 4-6   69-70

LPs: 10/12–inch 33rpm
CAPITOL 10-15   65-67
FABOR (1001 "From a Jack to a King") 15-25   63 (Black vinyl.)
FABOR (1001 "From a Jack to a King") 50-75   63 (Colored vinyl.)
PLANTATION................................ 5-8   81
REPUBLIC 8-10   70

MILLER, Roger   *C&W '60*
Singles: 7–inch
BUENA VISTA 3-5   70
COLUMBIA 3-5   73-74
DECCA 5-10   59
ELEKTRA...................................... 3-4   81
MCA 3-4   85-86
MERCURY 3-5   70-72
MUSICOR (1102 "You're Forgettin' Me").. 4-8   65
RCA (7000 series)...................... 8-15   60-63
RCA (8000 series)...................... 4-6   62-65
SMASH 3-8   64-76
STARDAY (356 "You're Forgettin' Me") 10-15   58
STARDAY (718 "Playboy") 4-8   65
STARDAY (7029 "Under Your Spell Again") 4-8   65
20TH CENTURY............................ 3-5   79
WINDSONG................................... 3-5   77

Picture Sleeves
BUENA VISTA 4-6   70

SMASH 5-10   64-68
LPs: 10/12–inch 33rpm
CAMDEN 8-10   64-65
COLUMBIA 5-10   73
EVEREST 5-8   75
HILLTOP......................................8-12   60s
MCA 5-8   86
MERCURY....................................5-10   72
NASHVILLE 8-12
PICKWICK 5-10   70s
SMASH (Except 7000 series) 10-20   64-70
SMASH (7000 series) 5-8   82
STARDAY 10-20   65
20TH FOX.....................................5-8   79
WINDSONG....................................5-8   77
WING 6-12   69

Also see LEWIS, Jerry Lee / Roger Miller / Roy Orbison
Also see NELSON, Willie, & Roger Miller
Also see TUBB, Justin / Roger Miller
Also see YOUNG, Donny, & Roger Miller

MILLER, Roger, & Willie Nelson   *C&W '82*
(With Ray Price)
Singles: 7–inch
COLUMBIA 3-5   82
LPs: 10/12–inch 33rpm
COLUMBIA 5-8   82

Also see MILLER, Roger
Also see NELSON, Willie
Also see PRICE, Ray

MILLINDER, Lucky, & His Orchestra   *P&R/R&B '42/C&W '44*
Singles: 78rpm
DECCA 5-15   41-48
KING 10-30   51-57
RCA 10-20   49-51

Singles: 7–inch
KING (4449 "Chew Tobacco Rag").......................................25-45   51
KING (4453 "I'm Waiting for You").......................................25-45   51
KING (4476 "The Grape Vine")..25-45   51
KING (4496 "The Right Kind of Lovin'") 25-45   51 (Black vinyl.)
KING (4496 "The Right Kind of Lovin'") 50-100   51 (Colored vinyl.)
KING (4545 "When I Have You")......................................50-75   52
KING (4571 "Please Be Careful")...................................50-75   52

KING (4803 "Goody Good
Love")...................................... 15-25 55
KING (5200 series) 5-10 59
RCA (0054 "D Natural Blues") .. 30-50 51
(Colored vinyl.)
TODD... 5-10 59
WARWICK 5-10 60

EPs: 7–inch 33/45rpm

KING (268 "Lucky Millinder")..... 25-50 54
KING (336 "Lucky Millinder,
Vol. 2") 25-50 54

MILLINDER, Lucky, & Admirals
Singles: 78rpm

KING 25-35 55

Singles: 7–inch

KING (4792 "It's a Sad Sad
Feeling").................................. 40-60 55

Also see MILLINDER, Lucky

MILLS, Frank   *P&R '72/C&W '79*
Singles: 7–inch

POLYDOR...................................... 3-4 78-79
SUNFLOWER 3-4 72

LPs: 10/12–inch 33rpm

CAPITOL.. 5-8 85
POLYDOR....................................... 5-8 79

MILLS BROTHERS   *P&R '31/C&W '70*
Singles: 78rpm

BANNER 5-10 34
BRUNSWICK 5-10 31-47
CONQUEROR 5-10
DECCA (100 thru 4300 series) ... 5-10 34-42
DECCA (11000 thru 24000
series) 5-10 42-57

Singles: 7–inch

ABC 3-5 74
DECCA... 5-15 50-61
DOT (15000 series).................... 4-8 58-59
DOT (17000 series)..................... 3-6 68-69
MCA 3-5 73-74
PARAMOUNT 3-5 71-72
RANWOOD 3-5 73-76

EPs: 7–inch 33/45rpm

DECCA 5-15 50-63
DOT.. 5-10 58-59

LPs: 10/12–inch 33rpm

ABC 5-8 74
DECCA (100 series)................. 10-15 66
DECCA (4000 series)............... 10-20 61-67

DECCA (5000 series) 20-40 49-55
(10–inch LPs.)
DECCA (7000 series) 20-30 55
DECCA (8000 series) 15-30 55-59
DECCA (75000 series) 5-10 70
DOT 5-15 58-70
EVEREST 5-10 75-77
GNP 5-8 73
MCA.. 5-10 73
PARAMOUNT 5-10 72-74
PICKWICK 5-10 70s
RANWOOD..................................... 5-10 74-81
SONGBIRD.................................... 6-12 74
VOCALION 5-10 66-69

Members: Herb Mills; Harry Mills; Donald Mills; John Mills.
Also see CROSBY, Bing, & Mills Brothers
Also see FITZGERALD, Ella, & Mills Brothers

MILLS BROTHERS, & Louis Armstrong   *P&R '37*
Singles: 7–inch

DECCA 4-6 61

MILLS BROTHERS, & Count Basie
LPs: 10/12–inch 33rpm

ABC... 5-8 74
DOT...8-12 68

Also see MILLS BROTHERS

MILSAP, Ronnie   *R&B '65/C&W '73*
Singles: 7–inch

BOBLO..3-5 77
CHIPS 4-6 70
FESTIVAL 3-5 77
RCA (Black vinyl).........................3-5 74-92
RCA (Colored vinyl) 5-10 74-89
(Promotional only.)
SCEPTER.......................................4-8 65-69
W.B. (5405 "It Went to Your
Head")...................................... 5-10 63
W.B. (8000 series) 3-5 75-76

Picture Sleeves

RCA 3-5 79-85

LPs: 10/12–inch 33rpm

BUCKBOARD 8-10 76
CRAZY CAJUN 8-10 75
51 WEST.......................................5-8 80s
HSRD...8-10 82
PICKWICK 5-10 75
RCA 5-10 74-92
TIME-LIFE.................................. 5-10 81
TRIP...8-10 76

W.B. 8-10 71-75
Also see PRESLEY, Elvis

MILSAP, Ronnie, & Mike Reid   *C&W '88*
Singles: 7–inch
RCA.. 3-4   88
Also see REID, Mike

MILSAP, Ronnie, & Kenny Rogers   *C&W '87*
Singles: 7–inch
RCA.. 3-4   87
Also see MILSAP, Ronnie
Also see ROGERS, Kenny

MINNIE PEARL   *C&W '66*
Singles: 78rpm
RCA... 5-10   54-56
Singles: 7–inch
RCA...................................... 8-15   54-56
STARDAY 4-6   66
LP: 10/12–inch 33rpm
NASHVILLE 10-15   60s
PICKWICK/HILLTOP 10-15   60s
STARDAY (224 thru 397).......... 15-25   63-66
SUNSET..................................... 10-15   67
Also see JONES, Grandpa / Minnie Pearl
Also see STEVENS, Ray

MR. TWELVE STRING
(Glen Campbell)
Singles: 7–inch
WORLD PACIFIC........................... 5-8   65
Also see CAMPBELL, Glen

MINTER, Pat   *C&W '89*
Singles: 7–inch
KILLER.. 3-4   89
SHOWCASE 4-8   79

MITCHELL, Chad
Singles: 7–inch
AMY 3-6   68-69
W.B. 4-8   66-67
LPs: 10/12–inch 33rpm
BELL 10-15   69
W.B. 10-20   66-67

MITCHELL, Chad, Trio   *P&R/LP '62*
Singles: 7–inch
COLPIX...................................... 5-10   59-61
KAPP... 5-8   61-63
MAY 4-8   62
MERCURY.................................... 4-8   63-64

Picture Sleeves
KAPP 10-15   61
MERCURY....................................8-12   63-65
LPs: 10/12–inch 33rpm
COLPIX....................................20-30   60
KAPP 15-25   61-64
MERCURY 15-20   63-64
Members: Chad Mitchell; Joe Frazier; Mike Kobluk;
Jim [Roger] McGuinn.
Also see MITCHELL, Chad
Also see MITCHELL TRIO

MITCHELL, Chad, Trio, & Gatemen
LPs: 10/12–inch 33rpm
COLPIX......................................20-25   64
Also see MITCHELL, Chad, Trio

MITCHELL, Charles, & His Orchestra   *C&W '44*
Singles: 78rpm
BLUEBIRD 4-8   44

MITCHELL, Charlie   *C&W '88*
Singles: 7–inch
SOUNDWAVES............................3-4   88

MITCHELL, Guy   *P&R '50*
(Al Cernick)
Singles: 78rpm
COLUMBIA 5-15   50-57
KING (15125 "Cabaret") 10-15   51
Singles: 7–inch
CHALICE (711 "My Angel"/"Bit of
  Love")....................................15-25   63
CHALICE (711 "My Angel"/"Mr.
  Hobo").................................15-25   63
  (Note different flip.)
CHALICE (712 "Take Your
  Time") 15-25   63
CHALICE (713 "Your
  Imagination")............................15-25   63
COLLECTABLES.........................3-4   80s
COLUMBIA 8-20   50-61
ERIC 3-4   83
GMI 4-6   74
JOY...4-8   62-63
KING (15125 "Cabaret") 20-30   51
  (Previously issued as by Al Grant, Al
  Cernick's pseudonym before using Guy
  Mitchell.)
REPRISE 4-6   66
STARDAY 4-6   67-69

Picture Sleeves

COLUMBIA (40769 "Singing the
Blues").................................. 15-20   56

COLUMBIA (40820 "Knee Deep in the
Blues").................................. 15-20   57

COLUMBIA (40877 "Rock-A-
Billy")................................... 10-20   57

COLUMBIA (41476 "Heartaches By the
Number")............................... 10-15   60

COLUMBIA (41853 "Sunshine
Guitar")................................. 10-15   60

COLUMBIA (42231 "Soft
Rain")................................... 10-15   61

EPs: 7–inch 33/45rpm

COLUMBIA 10-15   54-57

LPs: 10/12–inch 33rpm

COLUMBIA (1211 "Guy in
Love")................................... 15-25   58
(Monaural.)

COLUMBIA (1226 "Greatest
Hits") 15-25   59

COLUMBIA (1552 "Sunshine
Guitar")................................. 15-25   60
(Monaural.)

COLUMBIA (6231 "Open
Spaces")................................ 25-50   53
(10-inch LP.)

COLUMBIA (8011 "Guy in
Love")................................... 20-30   58
(Stereo.)

COLUMBIA (8352 "Sunshine
Guitar")................................. 20-30   60
(Stereo.)

KING (644 "Sincerely
Yours") 150-250   59
(Mitchell pictured but not identified on cover.
Includes tracks recorded as Al Grant.)

NASHVILLE 5-10   70

STARDAY 10-15   68-69

Also see CAVALLARO, Carmen, Featuring Al Cernick
Also see CLOONEY, Rosemary, & Guy Mitchell
Also see GRANT, Al

MITCHELL, Guy, & Mindy Carson

Singles: 78rpm

COLUMBIA 5-10   52-53

Singles: 7–inch

COLUMBIA 8-12   52-53

MITCHELL, Guy / Eileen Rodgers

EPs: 7–inch 33/45rpm

COLUMBIA 10-15   56

Also see MITCHELL, Guy

MITCHELL, Marty   *C&W '74*

Singles: 7–inch

ATLANTIC.................................3-5   74

HITSVILLE.................................3-5   76

MC 3-5   78

LP: 10/12–inch 33rpm

MC 5-10   78

MITCHELL, Price   *C&W '75*
(With Rene Sloane)

Singles: 7–inch

GRT 3-5   75-76

SUNBIRD..................................3-5   80

MITCHELL, Price, & Jerri Kelly   *C&W '75*

Singles: 7–inch

GRT 3-5   75

LP: 10/12–inch 33rpm

GRT 5-10   76

Also see KELLY, Jerri
Also see MITCHELL, Price

MITCHELL, Priscilla   *C&W '65*

Singles: 7–inch

MERCURY.................................4-6   67-68

Also see DRUSKY, Roy, & Priscilla Mitchell

MITCHELL TRIO   *LP '64*

Singles: 7–inch

MERCURY.................................4-8   65-66

REPRISE 4-8   67

Picture Sleeves

MERCURY.................................5-10   63-66

LPs: 10/12–inch 33rpm

MERCURY (20944 "Slightly Irreverent Mitchell
Trio") 15-20   64
(Monaural.)

MERCURY (20992 "Typical American
Boys") 15-20   65
(Monaural.)

MERCURY (21049 "That's the Way It's
Gonna Be") 15-20   65
(Monaural.)

MERCURY (21067 "Violets of
Dawn") 15-20   65
(Monaural.)

MERCURY (60944 "Slightly Irreverent Mitchell
Trio") 20-25   64
(Stereo.)

MERCURY (60992 "Typical American
Boys") 20-25   65

MERCURY (61049 "That's the Way It's Gonna Be") 20-25   65
(Stereo.)

MERCURY (21067 "Violets of Dawn") 20-25   65
(Stereo.)

REPRISE (6354 "Alive")............ 15-20   67

Members: Chad Mitchell; Joe Frazier; Mike Kobluk; John Denver; David Boise; Michael Johnson.
Also see DENVER, John
Also see JOHNSON, Michael
Also see MITCHELL, Chad, Trio

MITCHUM, Robert   *P&R '58/C&W '67*
(With the Calypso Band)
Singles: 78rpm
CAPITOL...................................... 5-15   57-58

Singles: 7–inch
CAPITOL (Except 3986) 5-10   57
CAPITOL (3986 "The Ballad of Thunder Road")...................................... 8-12   58
(Purple label.)
CAPITOL (3986 "The Ballad of Thunder Road").. 4-8   62
(Orange/yellow label.)
MONUMENT 4-6   67

EPs: 7–inch 33/45rpm
CAPITOL (853 "Calypso Is Like So")... 15-25   57
(Price is for any of three volumes.)

LPs: 10/12–inch 33rpm
CAPITOL (853 "Calypso Is Like So") 25-50   57
MONUMENT (8086 "That Man")................................... 15-20   67
(Monaural.)
MONUMENT (18086 "That Man")................................... 20-25   67
(Stereo.)

MIZE, Billy   *C&W '66*
Singles: 7–inch
COLUMBIA 4-6   66-68
IMPERIAL 4-6   69-70
U.A. 3-5   70-74
ZODIAC... 3-5   76-77

LP: 10/12–inch 33rpm
IMPERIAL 10-15   69
U.A. 8-12   71
ZODIAC....................................... 5-10   76

Session: Jordanaires.
Also see BILLY & CLIFF
Also see JORDANAIRES

MOE & JOE: see STAMPLEY, Joe

MOEBAKKEN, Dick   *C&W '78*
Singles: 7–inch
ASI 3-5   78

MOFFATT, Hugh   *C&W '78*
Singles: 7–inch
MERCURY..................................... 3-5   78

MOFFATT, Katy   *C&W '76*
Singles: 7–inch
COLUMBIA 3-5   76
PERMIAN...................................... 3-4   83-84

LP: 10/12–inch 33rpm
COLUMBIA 5-10   76-78

Also see MURPHEY, Michael, & Katy Moffatt

MOLLY & HEYMAKERS   *C&W '90*
Singles: 7–inch
REPRISE 3-4   90-91

Members: Molly Sheer; Andy Dee; Jeff Nelson; "Solid" Joe Lindzius.

MONDAY, Carla   *C&W '87*
Singles: 7–inch
MCM 3-4   87

MONROE, Bill   *C&W '46*
(With His Blue Grass Boys; Monroe Brothers: Charles & Bill)
Singles: 78rpm
BLUEBIRD................................. 15-30   '30s
COLUMBIA 10-20   45-49
DECCA 10-15   50-57

Singles: 7–inch
DECCA (20000 series) 12-25   52-56
DECCA (30000 series) 5-15   56-64
DECCA (40000 series) 20-30   52

EPs: 7–inch 33/45rpm
COLUMBIA 10-15   52-57
DECCA 5-15   56-65

LP: 10/12–inch 33rpm
ALBUM GLOBE 5-10   80s
CAMDEN 5-12   62-64
CORAL.. 5-8   80s
COUNTY....................................... 5-10
DECCA (Except 8731)............... 10-25   60-71
DECCA (8731 "Knee Deep in Bluegrass") 15-25   58
HARMONY................................. 10-20   61-69
MCA... 5-12   73-84

VOCALION .... 8-15　64-70

Members: Bill Monroe; Birch Monroe; Charles Monroe; Lester Flatt; Earl Scruggs; Chubby Wise; Cedric Rainwater; L.E. White. Session: Waylon Jennings.
　Also see CLEMENTS, Vassar
　Also see FLATT, Lester, & Bill Monroe
　Also see FLATT, Lester, Earl Scruggs & Bill Monroe
　Also see JENNINGS, Waylon
　Also see MARTIN, Jimmy
　Also see MADDOX, Rose, & Bill Monroe
　Also see WHITE, L.E., & Lola Jean Dillon

MONROE, Vaughn　*P&R '40/C&W '49*
Singles: 78rpm
BLUEBIRD .... 5-10　40-42
RCA.. 3-8　47-58
VICTOR.. 4-8　42-47
Singles: 7–inch
DOT.. 3-6　62-63
JUBILEE .... 4-6　61
MGM .... 4-6　60
RCA.. 5-8　50-59
ROD .... 3-5　68
U.A. .... 4-6　60
Picture Sleeves
RCA.. 10-15　57
EPs: 7–inch 33/45rpm
CAMDEN..................................... 5-10　56
RCA... 5-10　50-56
LPs: 10/12–inch 33rpm
CAMDEN.................................... 15-25　56
DOT.. 10-20　62-64
HAMILTON................................. 10-20　65
KAPP.. 10-20　65
RCA (11 thru 3066) .... 20-40　50-53
　(10–inch LPs.)
RCA (1400 thru 1700 series) .... 15-25　56-58
　(12–inch LPs.)
RCA (1100 series)...................... 5-10　75
RCA (3800 series).................... 10-15　67
RCA (6000 series)...................... 5-10　72
　Also see MARTIN, Dean / Patti Page
　Also see PRESLEY, Elvis / Vaughn Monroe / Gogi Grant / Robert Shaw

MONTANA　*C&W '81*
Singles: 7–inch
WATERHOUSE .... 3-5　81

MONTANA, Billy, & Long Shots　*C&W '87*
Singles: 7–inch
W.B. .... 3-4　87-88

MONTANA SKYLINE　*C&W '81*
Singles: 7–inch
SNOW..3-5　81

MONTGOMERY, Melba　*C&W '63*
Singles: 7–inch
CAPITOL....................................... 3-5　69-76
COMPASS .... 3-4　86
ELEKTRA...................................... 3-5　73-75
KARI... 3-5　80
MUSICOR .... 3-6　66-69
U.A. (500 thru 900 series)............. 4-8　63-66
U.A. (1000 & 1100 series)............. 3-5　77
Picture Sleeves
MUSICOR .... 4-8　66
LPs: 10/12–inch 33rpm
CAPITOL.....................................8-12　69-75
ELEKTRA....................................5-10　73-75
MUSICOR .... 10-20　66-68
UNART...8-12　67
U.A. (Except 600 series)............ 10-20　64
U.A. (600 series).........................5-10　78
　Also see JONES, George, Gene Pitney & Melba Montgomery
　Also see JONES, George, & Melba Montgomery
　Also see LOUVIN, Charlie, & Melba Montgomery
　Also see PITNEY, Gene, & Melba Montgomery
　Also see WEST, Dottie / Melba Montgomery

MONTGOMERY, Nancy　*C&W '81*
Singles: 7–inch
OVATION......................................3-4　81

MOODY, Clyde　*C&W '48*
(With Tommy Scott)
Singles: 78rpm
DECCA (28785 "What a Life") ...10-15　53
KING ....10-15　48-50
Singles: 7–inch
DECCA (28785 "What a Life") ...15-25　53
LP: 10/12–inch 33rpm
KING (891 "Best of Clyde Moody").................................50-75　64
OLD HOMESTEAD......................5-10
STARDAY ....20-30　78

MOORE, Bob　*P&R/R&B/LP '61*
Singles: 7–inch
HICKORY.......................................4-6　65-68
MONUMENT...................................4-8　59-64
Picture Sleeves
MONUMENT...................................4-8　62-63

LPs: 10/12–inch 33rpm

HICKORY	10-15	66
MONUMENT	10-20	61-67

Also see LEE, Brenda
Also see NASHVILLE ALL-STARS
Also see NELSON, Willie
Also see PRESLEY, Elvis

MOORE, Beth   *C&W '71*
Singles: 7–inch

CAPITOL	3-5	71

MOORE, Jim, & Sidewinder   *C&W '88*
Singles: 7–inch

WILLOW WIND	3-4	88

MOORE, Lattie   *C&W '61*
Singles: 78rpm

KING	10-20	56
SPEED (101 "Juke Joint Johnny")	50-100	52

Singles: 7–inch

ARC (8005 "Juke Joint Johnny")	100-200	57
KING (4955 "Lonesome Man Blues")	25-35	56
KING (5370 "Cajun Doll")	20-30	60
KING (5413 "Drunk Again")	5-10	61
SPEED (101 "Juke Joint Johnny")	300-400	52
STARDAY	10-20	58-59

LPs: 10/12–inch 33rpm

AUDIO LAB (1555 "Best of Lattie Moore")	30-40	60
AUDIO LAB (1573 "Country Side")	25-35	62
DERBYTOWN (102 "Lattie Moore")	10-20	60s

MORGAN, Al   *C&W '49*
Singles: 78rpm

LONDON	4-8	49
UNIVERSAL	6-12	49

MORGAN, Billie   *C&W '59*
Singles: 7–inch

STARDAY	5-10	59

MORGAN, George   *C&W '49*
(With Little Roy Wiggins)
Singles: 78rpm

COLUMBIA	5-10	52-57

Singles: 7–inch

COLUMBIA	5-15	52-65

DECCA	3-5	71-73
4 STAR	3-5	75-79
MCA	3-5	73-74
STARDAY	4-8	67-68
STOP	3-6	69-70

EPs: 7–inch 33/45rpm

COLUMBIA	5-15	52-58

LP: 10/12–inch 33rpm

COLUMBIA (Except 1044)	15-30	61-75
COLUMBIA (1044 "Morgan, By George")	30-40	57
4 STAR	6-12	75-77
HARMONY	8-15	67-69
MCA	5-10	74
NASHVILLE	6-12	69-71
POWER PAK	5-10	74
STARDAY (400 series)	10-20	67-69
STARDAY (900 series)	5-10	74
STOP	8-12	69

Also see MORGAN, Lorrie & George

MORGAN, George, & Marion Worth
LP: 10/12–inch 33rpm

COLUMBIA	20-30	64

Also see MORGAN, George
Also see WORTH, Marion

MORGAN, Jane   *P&R/LP '57/C&W '70*
(With the Troubadors)
Singles: 78rpm

KAPP	3-8	54-57

Singles: 7–inch

ABC	4-6	67-68
EPIC	4-6	65-68
COLPIX	4-8	63-65
KAPP	5-10	54-62
RCA	3-6	69-70

EPs: 7–inch 33/45rpm

KAPP	5-10	55-59

Picture Sleeves

COLPIX	5-10	63
ELEKTRA	3-4	82
EPIC	4-8	65
KAPP	5-12	57-59

LPs: 10/12–inch 33rpm

ABC	5-10	68
COLPIX	10-20	63-66
EPIC	10-15	65-67
KAPP	10-20	56-63
MCA	5-10	73
RCA (Except 1160)	8-12	69-70

RCA (1160 "Marry Me, Marry
Me")... 10-15   69
(Soundtrack.)
HARMONY..................................... 5-8   70
Also see WILLIAMS, Roger, & Jane Morgan

MORGAN, Lorrie   *C&W '79*
Singles: 7–inch
ABC/HICKORY 3-6   79
MCA 3-5   79
RCA.. 3-4   88-91
LPs: 10/12–inch 33rpm
RCA.. 5-8   88-90
Also see WHITLEY, Keith, & Lorrie Morgan

MORGAN, Lorrie &
George   *C&W '79*
Singles: 7–inch
4 STAR... 3-5   79
Also see MORGAN, George
Also see MORGAN, Lorrie

MORI, Miki   *C&W '79*
(Mickie Mori)
Singles: 7–inch
NSD.. 3-5   80
OAK.. 3-5   79-80
RED FEATHER.............................. 3-5   79
STARCOM 3-5   80-81

MORRIS, Bob   *C&W '67*
Singles: 7–inch
TOWER.. 4-6   67

MORRIS, Gary   *C&W '80*
Singles: 7–inch
UNIVERSAL.................................. 3-4   89
W.B. 3-5   80-88
LPs: 10/12–inch 33rpm
W.B. 5-8   82-88
Also see ANDERSON, Lynn, & Gary Morris
Also see GAYLE, Crystal, & Gary Morris

MORRIS, Lamar   *C&W '66*
Singles: 7–inch
MGM 4-6   66-73
Also see BAMA BAND
Also see WILLIAMS, Hank, Jr.
Also see YOUNG, Faron

MORTON, Ann J.   *C&W '76*
Singles: 7–inch
PRAIRIE....................................... 3-5   76-81

MOSBY, Johnny & Jonie   *C&W '63*
Singles: 7–inch
CAPITOL..3-6   67-73
CHALLENGE 5-10   60
COLUMBIA 4-8   62-66
STARDAY.......................................4-6   65
TOPPA...5-8   61
Picture Sleeves
CAPITOL..3-5   70
LPs: 10/12–inch 33rpm
CAPITOL..8-12   68-71
COLUMBIA 10-15   65
HARMONY....................................5-10   70

MOSBY, Jonie   *C&W '73*
Singles: 7–inch
CAPITOL..3-5   72-73
Also see MOSBY, Johnny & Jonie

MULLEN, Bruce   *C&W '74*
Singles: 7–inch
CHART..3-5   74

MULLICAN, Moon   *C&W/P&R '47*
(With the Showboys)
Singles: 78rpm
KING 15-25   46-56
Singles: 7–inch
KING (830 "I'll Sail My Ship
Alone") 25-40   49
KING (1000 series) 20-35   52-54
KING (4000 series) 15-25   55-56
KING (5000 series) 8-15   59-60
STARDAY 5-10   60-61
EPs: 7–inch 33/45rpm
KING (214 "King of the Hillbilly Piano
Players") 20-30   50s
KING (227 "Piano Solos")..........15-25   50s
KING (314 "Moon Mullican") 15-25   50s
STARDAY (154 "Moon
Mullican") 20-30   60
LPs: 10/12–inch 33rpm
CORAL (57235 "Moon Over
Mullican") 150-250   58
KAPP 15-20   69
KING (555 "All-Time Greatest
Hits") 50-100   57
KING (628 "16 Favorite
Tunes") 50-75   59
KING (681 "Many Moods").........50-75   60
KING (937 "24 Favorite
Tunes") 40-60   65

NASHVILLE	10-20	70
PHONORAMA	5-8	83
PICKWICK/HILLTOP	10-15	66
STARDAY	10-20	67
STERLING (601 "I'll Sail My Ship Alone")	50-75	50s
WESTERN	5-8	

Also see KERR, Anita

MULLICAN, Moon / Cowboy Copas / Red Sovine
LP: 10/12–inch 33rpm

| DIPLOMAT | 5-10 | 60s |

MULLICAN, Moon / Cotton Thompson
Singles: 78rpm

| KING | 10-20 | 48 |

Also see MULLICAN, Moon

MULLINS, Dee   *C&W '68*
Singles: 7–inch

MEL-O-DY	10-15	64
PLANTATION	3-5	69-71
SSS INT'L	3-6	68
TRIUNE	3-5	73

LP: 10/12–inch 33rpm

| PLANTATION | 8-12 | 69 |

MUNDY, Jim   *C&W '73*
(With Terri Melton)
Singles: 7–inch

ABC	3-5	73-75
ABC/DOT	3-5	76
HILL COUNTRY	3-5	77

MUNDY, Marilyn   *C&W '89*
Singles: 7–inch

| DOOR KNOB | 3-4 | 89-90 |

MURPHEY, Mark   *C&W '89*
Singles: 7–inch

| TRAVELER ENTERPRISES | 3-4 | 89 |

MURPHEY, Michael
(Michael Martin Murphey; with Ryan Murphey)   *P&R/LP '72/C&W '76*
Singles: 7–inch

A&M	3-5	72
CAPITOL	3-5	74
EMI AMERICA	3-4	84-85
EPIC	3-5	74-79
LIBERTY	3-4	82-84
W.B.	3-4	86-91

Picture Sleeves

| A&M | 3-5 | 72 |
| EPIC | 3-5 | 74 |

LPs: 10/12–inch 33rpm

A&M	8-10	72-73
EMI AMERICA	5-8	84-85
EPIC	8-12	74-78
LIBERTY	5-8	82-83
W.B.	5-8	86-91

Also see DENVER, John
Also see LEE, Johnny, Michael Martin Murphey, & Charlie Daniels
Also see TRINITY RIVER BOYS

MURPHEY, Michael Martin, & Holly Dunn   *C&W '87*
Singles: 7–inch

| W.B. | 3-4 | 87 |

Also see DUNN, Holly

MURPHEY, Michael, & Katy Moffatt   *C&W '81*
Singles: 7–inch

| EPIC | 3-5 | 81 |

Also see MOFFATT, Katy
Also see MURPHEY, Michael

MURPHY, Jimmy   *C&W '86*
Singles: 78rpm

| COLUMBIA | 25-50 | 56 |
| RCA | 10-20 | 51-52 |

Singles: 7–inch

ARK	8-12	63
COLUMBIA (21486 "Here Kitty Kitty")	100-150	56
COLUMBIA (21534 "16 Tons Rock & Roll")	100-150	56
COLUMBIA (21569 "Baboon Boogie")	100-150	56
ENCORE	3-4	86-87
RCA	20-40	51-52
REM (340 "Half a Loaf")	10-20	
SUGAR HILL	3-6	78

LPs: 10/12–inch 33rpm

| SUGAR HILL | 5-10 | 78 |

MURPHY, Vern   *C&W '73*
Singles: 7–inch

| SUNSET | 3-5 | 73 |

MURRAY, Anne   *C&W/P&R/LP '70*
(With Doug Mallory)
Singles: 7–inch

| ARC | 5-10 | 69 |

(Canadian.)

CAPITOL.......................... 3-5   70-86
Picture Sleeves
CAPITOL.......................... 3-4   79-86
LPs: 10/12–inch 33rpm
ARC (782 "What About Me")..... 10-20   69
(Canadian.)
AURA 5-8   83
CAPITOL (Except "Let's Keep It That Way"
picture disc).............................. 5-10   70-87
CAPITOL ("Let's Keep It That
Way")....................................... 50-75   78
(Picture disc. Promotional issue only. One of
a four-artist, four-LP set.)
PICKWICK (3350 "What About
Me")................................. 5-10   70s
<small>Also see CAMPBELL, Glen, & Anne Murray
Also see CAMPBELL, Glen / Anne Murray / Kenny
Rogers / Crystal Gayle</small>

MURRAY, Anne, & Dave
Loggins   *C&W '84*
Singles: 7–inch
CAPITOL....................................... 3-4   84
<small>Also see LOGGINS, Dave</small>

MURRAY, Anne, & Kenny
Rogers   *C&W '89*
Singles: 7–inch
CAPITOL....................................... 3-4   89
<small>Also see MURRAY, Anne
Also see ROGERS, Kenny</small>

MUSIC ROW   *C&W '81*
Singles: 7–inch
DEBUT 3-5   81

MYERS, Frank   *C&W '74*
Singles: 7–inch
CAPRICE 3-5   74

NAIL, Linda
C&W '78

Singles: 7–inch

GRAND PRIX.................................. 3-4   83
RIDGETOP 3-5   78-79
  Also see WHITE, Danny, & Linda Nail

NAILL, Jerry
C&W '80

Singles: 7–inch

EL DORADO 3-5   80

NASH, Bill
C&W '81

Singles: 7–inch

LIBERTY 3-4 81-82

NASH, Linda
C&W '73

Singles: 7–inch

ACE of HEARTS 3-5   73

NASHVILLE ALL-STARS
LPs: 10/12–inch 33rpm

RCA (0126 "That Happy Nashville
  Sound") 8-12   67
RCA (LPM-2302 "After the Riot at
  Newport") 20-30   60
  (Monaural.)
RCA (LSP-2302 "After the Riot at
  Newport") 25-35   60
  (Stereo.)

  Members: Chet Atkins; Boots Randolph; Hank
  Garland; Bob Moore; Floyd Cramer; Buddy Harman;
  Gary Burton; Brenton Banks.
  Also see ATKINS, Chet
  Also see CRAMER, Floyd
  Also see MOORE, Bob
  Also see RANDOLPH, Boots

NASHVILLE BRASS: see DAVIS, Danny

NASHVILLE NIGHTSHIFT
C&W '85

Singles: 7–inch

NCA... 3-5   85

NASHVILLE SUPERPICKERS
C&W '81

Singles: 7–inch

SOUND FACTORY 3-5   81

  Members: Charlie McCoy; Johnny Gimble; Phil Baugh;
  Hargus "Pig" Robbins; Buddy Emmons; Buddy
  Harman; Henry Strzelecki.
  Also see BAUGH, Phil

Also see HAGGARD, Merle
Also see McCOY, Charlie
Also see PRICE, Ray

NAYLOR, Jerry
P&R '70/C&W '75

Singles: 7–inch

COLUMBIA 3-6 68-71
HITSVILLE 3-5   76
MC/CURB 3-5   78
MGM 3-6 71-72
MELODYLAND 3-5 74-75
OAK 3-5   80
PACIFIC CHALLENGER 3-5   82
SKLYA 10-15 61-62
SMASH 5-10   65
TOWER.......................................5-15 65-68
W.B./CURB 3-5   79
WEST..3-4   86
  Session: Davie Allan.
  Also see CRICKETS

NAYLOR, Jerry, & Kelli Warren
C&W '79

Singles: 7–inch

JEREMIAH....................................3-5   79
  Also see NAYLOR, Jerry
  Also see WARREN, Kelly

NEEL, Joanna
C&W '71

(Jo Anna Neel)

Singles: 7–inch

DECCA 3-5 71-72

NEELY, Sam
P&R/LP '72/C&W '74

Singles: 7–inch

A&M 3-5 74-75
CAPITOL.......................................3-5 72-73
ELEKTRA......................................3-5   77
MCA 3-4 83-84

LPs: 10/12–inch 33rpm

A&M 8-10   74
CAPITOL......................................8-12 72-73

NEIL & JACK

Singles: 7–inch

DUEL (508 "You Are My Love at
  Last")..................................100-200   62
DUEL (517 "I'm Afraid") 100-200   62
  Members: Neil Diamond; Jack Parker.
  Also see DIAMOND, Neil

NELSON, Bonnie
C&W '86

Singles: 7–inch

DOOR KNOB..................................3-4 86-87

NELSON, Rick

(With Stone Canyon Band; with Jordanaires; Ricky Nelson)   *P&R/R&B/LP '57/C&W '58*

Singles: 12–inch 33/45rpm

CAPITOL	5-10	82

Singles: 78rpm

IMPERIAL	30-100	57-58
VERVE	50-100	57

Singles: 7–inch

DECCA	4-8	63-72
CAPITOL	3-5	82
EPIC	3-5	77-86
IMPERIAL (5463 "Be-Bop Baby") (Maroon label.)	30-40	57
IMPERIAL (5463 "Be-Bop Baby") (Black label.)	10-20	58
IMPERIAL (5483 "Stood Up") (Maroon label.)	25-35	57
IMPERIAL (5483 "Stood Up") (Black label.)	10-20	58
IMPERIAL (5503 "Believe What You Say")	15-25	58
IMPERIAL (5528 "Poor Little Fool")	15-25	58
IMPERIAL (5545 "Lonesome Town") (Black vinyl.)	15-25	58
IMPERIAL (5545 "Lonesome Town") (Colored vinyl.)	150-200	58
IMPERIAL (5565 "It's Late")	15-25	59
IMPERIAL (5595 "Just a Little Too Much")	10-20	59
IMPERIAL (5614 "Mighty Good")	10-20	59
IMPERIAL (5663 "Young Emotions")	10-20	60
IMPERIAL (5685 "I'm Not Afraid")	10-20	60
IMPERIAL (5707 "You Are the Only One")	10-20	60
IMPERIAL (5741 "Travelin' Man") (Black vinyl.)	10-15	61
IMPERIAL (5741 "Travelin' Man") (Colored vinyl. Promotional issue only.)	150-200	61
IMPERIAL (5770 thru 5935)	10-15	61-63
IMPERIAL (5958 "Long Vacation") (Black vinyl.)	8-12	63
IMPERIAL (5958 "Long Vacation") (Colored vinyl.)	50-100	63
IMPERIAL (5985 "Time after Time")	10-12	63
IMPERIAL (66000 series)	8-15	63-64
LIBERTY	3-4	80s
MCA	3-5	73-75
VERVE (10047 "A Teenager's Romance")	25-35	57
VERVE (10070 "You're My One and Only Love") (Flip is by Barney Kessell.)	25-35	57

Picture Sleeves

DECCA	8-18	63-70
EPIC	3-5	86
IMPERIAL (5483 "Stood Up")	20-30	57
IMPERIAL (5503 "Believe What You Say")	20-30	58
IMPERIAL (5545 "Lonesome Town")	15-25	58
IMPERIAL (5565 "It's Late")	15-25	59
IMPERIAL (5595 "Just a Little Too Much")	15-25	59
IMPERIAL (5614 "Mighty Good")	15-25	59
IMPERIAL (5663 "Young Emotions")	15-20	60
IMPERIAL (5685 "I'm Not Afraid")	15-20	60
IMPERIAL (5707 "You Are the Only One")	15-20	60
IMPERIAL (5741 "Travelin' Man")	10-20	61
IMPERIAL (5770 thru 5935)	10-20	61-63
MCA	3-5	86

EPs: 7–inch 33/45rpm

DECCA (2760 "One Boy Too Late")	25-50	63
DECCA (4419 "For Your Sweet Love") (Jukebox issue.)	25-50	63
DECCA (4460 "Best Always") (Jukebox issue.)	25-50	65
IMPERIAL (153/154/155 "Ricky") (Price is for any of three volumes.)	35-55	58
IMPERIAL (157/158 "Ricky Nelson") (Price is for either of two volumes.)	35-55	58
IMPERIAL (159/160/161 "Ricky Sings Again") (Price is for any of three volumes.)	35-55	58

IMPERIAL (162/163/164 "Songs by
Ricky")................................. 35-55   59
(Price is for any of three volumes.)

IMPERIAL (165 "Ricky Sings
Spirituals")............................. 50-75   60

VERVE (5048 "Ricky") 75-100   57
(Has one track by Barney Kessell.)

LPs: 10/12–inch 33rpm

CAPITOL..................................... 5-8   81

DECCA (DL-4419 "For Your Sweet
Love")..................................... 25-50   63
(Monaural.)

DECCA (DL7-4419 "For Your Sweet
Love")..................................... 25-50   63
(Stereo.)

DECCA (DL-4479 "For You") 25-50   63
(Monaural.)

DECCA (DL7-4479 "For You").. 25-50   63
(Stereo.)

DECCA (DL-4559 "The Very Thought of
You")...................................... 25-50   64
(Monaural.)

DECCA (DL7-4559 "The Very Thought of
You")...................................... 25-50   64
(Stereo.)

DECCA (DL-4608 "Spotlight on
Rick")...................................... 25-50   64
(Monaural.)

DECCA (DL7-4608 "Spotlight on
Rick")...................................... 25-50   64
(Stereo.)

DECCA (DL-4660 "Best
Always") 25-50   65
(Monaural.)

DECCA (DL7-4660 "Best
Always") 25-50   65
(Stereo.)

DECCA (DL-4678 "Love and
Kisses") 25-50   65
(Monaural.)

DECCA (DL7-4678 "Love and
Kisses") 25-50   65
(Stereo.)

DECCA (DL-4779 "Bright Lights and Country
Music") 25-50   66
(Monaural.)

DECCA (DL7-4779 "Bright Lights and Country
Music") 25-50   66
(Stereo.)

DECCA (DL-4827 "Country
Fever") 25-50   67
(Monaural.)

DECCA (DL7-4827 "Country
Fever") 25-50   67
(Stereo.)

DECCA (DL-4944 "Another Side of
Rick")...................................... 25-50   67
(Monaural.)

DECCA (DL7-4944 "Another Side of
Rick") 25-50   67
(Stereo.)

DECCA (75014 "Perspective")... 15-25   68

DECCA (75162 "In Concert")..... 15-25   70

DECCA (75236 "Rick Sings
Nelson") 15-25   70

DECCA (75297 "Rudy the
Fifth") 15-25   71

DECCA (75391 "Garden
Party") 15-25   72

EPIC... 8-15   77-86

EPIC/NU-DISK.......................... 10-15   81

IMPERIAL (9048 "Ricky") 50-80   57
("Imperial" across top of label.)

IMPERIAL (9048 "Ricky") 15-25   64
("IR-Imperial" logo on left.)

IMPERIAL (9050 "Ricky
Nelson")..................................45-65   58
("Imperial" across top of label.)

IMPERIAL (9050 "Ricky
Nelson").................................. 15-25   64
("IR-Imperial" logo on left.)

IMPERIAL (9061 "Ricky Sings
Again")....................................25-50   59
(Monaural.)

IMPERIAL (9082 "Songs by
Ricky") 25-50   59
(Monaural.)

IMPERIAL (9122 "More Songs
by Ricky")................................25-50   60
(Monaural.)

IMPERIAL (9152 "Rick Is 21") ...20-40   61
(Monaural.)

IMPERIAL (9167 "Album
Seven")...................................20-40   62
(Monaural.)

IMPERIAL (9218 "Best
Sellers") 20-40   63
(Monaural.)

IMPERIAL (9223 "It's Up to
You")......................................20-40   63
(Monaural.)

IMPERIAL (9232 "Million Sellers by Rick
Nelson") 20-40   63
(Monaural.)

IMPERIAL (9244 "Long
Vacation") 20-40   63
(Monaural.)

IMPERIAL (9251 "Rick Nelson Sings for You") 20-40   63
(Monaural.)

IMPERIAL (12059 "More Songs by Ricky") 40-60   60
(Stereo. Black vinyl.)

IMPERIAL (12059 "More Songs by Ricky") 300-400   60
(Stereo. Colored vinyl.)

IMPERIAL (12090 "Ricky Sings Again") 20-30   64
(Stereo.)

IMPERIAL (12071 "Rick Is 21") 20-40   61
(Stereo.)

IMPERIAL (12082 "Album Seven") 20-40   62
(Stereo.)

IMPERIAL (12218 "Best Sellers") 20-40   63
(Stereo.)

IMPERIAL (12223 "It's Up to You") 20-40   63
(Stereo.)

IMPERIAL (12232 "Million Sellers by Rick Nelson") 20-40   64
(Stereo.)

IMPERIAL (12244 "A Long Vacation") 20-40   63
(Stereo.)

IMPERIAL (12251 "Rick Nelson Sings for You") 20-40   64
(Stereo.)

LIBERTY 5-10   81-83

MCA (Except 1517) 10-15   73-74

MCA (1517 "The Decca Years") 5-10   82

MCA/SILVER EAGLE 5-10   86

MGM (4256 "Teen Time") 15-25   65
(Reissue of Verve 2083.)

RHINO 5-8   85

SESSIONS (1003 "Ricky Nelson Story") 15-25   79
(Three-LP mail-order offer.)

SUNSET 10-20   66-68

TIME-LIFE 10-15   86

U.A. (330 "Very Best of Rick Nelson") 10-15   75

U.A. (1004 "Ricky") 5-10   80

U.A. (9960 "Legendary Masters") 15-25   71

VERVE (2083 "Teen Time") .. 150-200   57
(Also includes tracks by: Randy Sparks;

Gary Williams; Jeff Allen; Rock Murphy; Barney Kessel; and Johnny Rivers.)
Session: James Burton; Joe Osborn; Jordanaires; Randy Meisner; Al Kemp; Steve Duncan.
Also see DILLARDS
Also see JORDANAIRES
Also see MARTIN, Dean, & Ricky Nelson
Also see RIVERS, Johnny / Ricky Nelson / Randy Sparks

NELSON, Rick, & Jack Lemmon
Singles: 7-inch

THEATRE PROMOTION RECORD (760 "Do You Know What It Means to Miss New Orleans") 150-200   60
(Promotional issue, for theatre play only.)

NELSON, Rick / Joannie Sommers / Dona Jean Young
LPs: 10/12-inch 33rpm

DECCA (DL-4836 "On the Flip Side") 20-30   66
(Monaural.)

DECCA (DL7-4836 "On the Flip Side") 25-35   66
(Stereo.)
Also see NELSON, Rick

NELSON, Willie   *C&W '62*
(Willy Nelson)

Singles: 78rpm

SARG (260 "A Storm Has Just Begun") 100-200   55

Singles: 7-inch

AMERICAN GOLD 3-5   76

ATLANTIC 3-5   73-75

BETTY 10-15   64

BELLAIRE (107 "Night Life") 15-25   63
(Black vinyl.)

BELLAIRE (107 "Night Life") 40-50   63
(Colored vinyl.)

BELLAIRE (5000 series) 3-5   76

CAPITOL 3-5   78

COLUMBIA 3-5   75-91

D (1084 "Man With the Blues") .. 15-25   59

D (1131 "What a Way to Live") .. 15-25   60

DOUBLE BARREL 4-8

LIBERTY (55155 "No Dough") ... 15-25   58

LIBERTY (55386 "Mr. Record Man") 10-15   61

LIBERTY (55439 thru 55638) 5-10   62-64

LIBERTY (56000 series) 4-6   69

LONE STAR 3-5   78

MONUMENT (800 series) 4-6   64

RCA (0100 thru 0800 series) 3-5   69-72

RCA (8500 thru 9900 series)	4-8	65-71
RCA (10000 thru 12000 series)	3-5	75-81
SARG (260 "A Storm Has Just Begun")	200-300	55
SONGBIRD	3-5	80
U.A. (641 "Night Life")	5-10	63
U.A. (700 thru 1200 series)	3-5	76-78
WILLIE NELSON (628 "No Place for Me")...................................	150-250	57
(Reportedly 3,000 made.)		

Picture Sleeves

COLUMBIA	3-5	84
RCA (12000 series)........................	3-5	81

LPs: 10/12–inch 33rpm

ACCORD.....................................	5-8	82-83
ALLEGIANCE................................	5-8	83
ATLANTIC	8-12	73-76
AUDIO FIDELITY (213 "Willie Nelson")	10-15	
(Picture disc.)		
AURA	5-8	82-83
BACK-TRAC	5-8	
CBS (Except PAL-35305)	5-8	78-83
CBS (PAL-35305 "Stardust")	25-45	78
CAMDEN.....................................	8-12	70-74
CASINO	8-10	84
COLUMBIA (30000 series, except 38250 and picture discs)...........................	5-15	75-91
COLUMBIA (38250 "Willie Nelson")...................................	100-150	83
(Ten-LP boxed set. Includes bonus picture disc, which is priced separately below.)		
COLUMBIA (38250 [38258/59] "Always on My Mind")......................................	50-75	83
(Picture disc. Boxed set bonus issue.)		
COLUMBIA (35305 "Stardust")	25-35	78
(Picture disc.)		
COLUMBIA (39943 "Always on My Mind")....................................	10-20	83
(Picture disc.)		
COLUMBIA (40000 series, except "HC," half-speed mastered series)	5-10	85-90
COLUMBIA (HC-40000 series)	20-35	82-83
(Half-speed mastered.)		
DELTA...	5-8	82
EXACT	5-8	83
HBO (171010 "Willie Nelson and Family")	15-25	83
(Picture disc. Promotional issue only.)		
H.S.R.D.	8-10	84
HEARTLAND	10-15	87
HOT SCHATZ	5-10	84

LIBERTY (3239 "And Then I Wrote").......................................	25-35	62
(Monaural.)		
LIBERTY (7239 "And Then I Wrote")..	30-40	62
(Stereo.)		
LIBERTY (10000 series)..............	5-10	80s
LONE STAR................................	8-12	78
MCA...	5-10	80
MASTERS....................................	5-10	
OUT of TOWN DIST.	5-10	
PICKWICK	5-10	74-76
PICKWICK/CAMDEN...................	5-10	70s
PLANTATION	5-10	82
POTOMAC...................................	10-15	82
PREMORE...................................	5-10	
RCA (1100 thru 3200 series)	5-10	75-79
RCA (LPM-3400 thru LPM-3900 series).......................................	10-20	65-68
(Monaural.)		
RCA (LSP-3400 thru LSP-4700 series).......................................	10-25	65-72
(Stereo.)		
RCA (3600 thru 4800 series)..........	4-8	80-83
(With "AYL1" prefix.)		
RCA/CANDELITE	8-10	80
SHOTGUN	10-20	77
SOLID GOLD................................	5-10	
SONGBIRD	5-10	80
SUNSET	10-20	66
TAKOMA......................................	5-8	83
TIME-LIFE (16000 series)	15-25	83
(Three-LP set.)		
U.A.	8-12	73-78

Session: Paul Buskirk; Herb Remington; Bob White; Clyde Brewer; Dick Shannon; Pete Wade; Ray Edenton; Jimmy Day; Hargus "Pig" Robbins; Bob Moore; Willie Ackerman; Billy Strange; Glen Campbell; Leon Russell; Red Callender; Muddy Berry; Harold Bradley; David Briggs; Anita Kerr Singers; Ernie Freeman; Cal Smith; Jerry Reed; Buddy Emmons; Velma Smith; Johnny Bush; Chet Atkins; Bill Pursell; Roy Huskey; Buddy Harman; Buddy Spicher; Doug Sahm; Larry Gatlin.
  Also see ATKINS, Chet
  Also see BOWMAN, Don
  Also see BRUCE, Ed
  Also see BUSH, Johnny
  Also see BUSKIRK, Paul, & His Little Men
  Also see CAMPBELL, Glen
  Also see CHARLES, Ray, & Willie Nelson
  Also see COCHRAN, Hank, & Willie Nelson
  Also see COE, David Allan, & Willie Nelson
  Also see DARRELL, Johnny / George Jones / Willie Nelson
  Also see DAVIS, Danny, Willie Nelson, & Nashville Brass
  Also see EDDY, Duane
  Also see FREEMAN, Ernie

Also see GATLIN, Larry
Also see HAGGARD, Merle, & Willie Nelson
Also see HARRIS, Emmylou
Also see IGLESIAS, Julio, & Willie Nelson
Also see JENNINGS, Waylon, & Willie Nelson
Also see KERR, Anita
Also see KRISTOFFERSON, Kris, Willie Nelson, Dolly Parton, & Brenda Lee
Also see LEE, Brenda, & Willie Nelson
Also see McCALL, Darrell, & Willie Nelson
Also see MILLER, Roger, & Willie Nelson
Also see MOORE, Bob
Also see MYERS, Augie
Also see PARTON, Dolly, & Willie Nelson
Also see PLACE, Mary Kay, & Willie Nelson
Also see PRICE, Ray, & Willie Nelson
Also see PURSELL, Bill
Also see ROSE, Pam, & Willie Nelson
Also see REED, Jerry
Also see SAHM, Doug
Also see SHAVER, Billy Joe
Also see SMITH, Cal
Also see SMITH, Sammi
Also see SOME of CHET'S FRIENDS
Also see TUBB, Ernest

NELSON, Willie / Nat "King" Cole / Johnny Mathis / Shirley Bassey

EPs: 7–inch 33/45rpm

JIMMY McHUGH (300 "Three Guys and a Gal")..8-12   81
(Promotional issue only. Includes Jimmy McHugh bio insert)
Also see COLE, Nat "King"

NELSON, Willie, & Shirley Collie   C&W '62

Singles: 7–inch

LIBERTY 5-10   62

NELSON, Willie, & Kris Kristofferson   C&W/LP '84

LPs: 10/12–inch 33rpm

COLUMBIA 5-8   84
Also see KRISTOFFERSON, Kris

NELSON, Willie, & Brenda Lee   C&W '83

Singles: 7–inch

MONUMENT 3-5   83
Also see LEE, Brenda

NELSON, Willie, & Johnny Lee

LPs: 10/12–inch 33rpm

QUICKSILVER 5-8   84

NELSON, Willie / Johnny Lee / Mickey Gilley

LPs: 10/12–inch 33rpm

PLANTATION............................... 5-8   82
Also see GILLEY, Mickey
Also see LEE, Johnny

NELSON, Willie / Jerry Lee Lewis / Carl Perkins / David Allan Coe

LPs: 10/12–inch 33rpm

PLANTATION 5-10   75
Also see COE, David Allan
Also see LEWIS, Jerry Lee
Also see PERKINS, Carl

NELSON, Willie & Tracy   C&W '74

Singles: 7–inch

ATLANTIC......................................3-5   74
Also see NELSON, Tracy

NELSON, Willie, & Webb Pierce   C&W '82

Singles: 7–inch

COLUMBIA 3-4   82

LPs: 10/12–inch 33rpm

COLUMBIA 5-8   82
Also see PIERCE, Webb

NELSON, Willie, & Ray Price   C&W/LP '80

Singles: 7–inch

COLUMBIA 3-4   80

LPs: 10/12–inch 33rpm

COLUMBIA 5-8   80
Also see PRICE, Ray

NELSON, Willie, & Leon Russell   C&W '79

Singles: 7–inch

COLUMBIA 3-5   79

LPs: 10/12–inch 33rpm

COLUMBIA 5-10   79
Also see RUSSELL, Leon

NELSON, Willie, & Hank Wilson   C&W '84

Singles: 7–inch

PARADISE......................................3-4   84
Also see WILSON, Hank

NELSON, Willie / Faron Young

LPs: 10/12–inch 33rpm

COLUMBIA 5-10
ROMULUS....................................5-10
Also see NELSON, Willie
Also see YOUNG, Faron

NESBITT, Jim   C&W '61
(The "Lasses Sopper")

Singles: 7–inch

ACE..8-12   61
CHART...3-6   64-70
COUNTRY JUBILEE....................8-12   61

DOT	5-10	61-63
RALLY	4-8	62
RUSH	5-10	62
SCORPIO	3-5	75
SMASH	4-8	62

LP: 10/12–inch 33rpm

CHART	8-15	64-71
SCORPION	6-10	76

NESMITH, Michael   *P&R/LP '70*

(With the First National Band; with Second National Band)

Singles: 7–inch

EDAN (1001 "Just a Little Love")	50-75	65
ISLAND	5-8	77
OMNIBUS	15-25	63
PACIFIC ARTS	8-10	75-79
RCA	10-20	70-75

Picture Sleeves

RCA (0453 "Nevada Fighter")	15-25	71

LPs: 10/12–inch 33rpm

PACIFIC ARTS ("Conversation with Michael Nesmith: Music Radio Special")	25-35	78
(Promotional issue only.)		
PACIFIC ARTS (101 "The Prison")	25-50	78
(Boxed edition. With booklet.)		
PACIFIC ARTS (101 "The Prison")	10-20	78
(Standard LP. With booklet.)		
PACIFIC ARTS (106 thru 130)	10-20	78-79
RCA	20-30	70-75
RHINO	8-10	89

Also see TRINITY RIVER BOYS
Also see WICHITA TRAIN WHISTLE

NETTLES, Bill, & Dixie Blue Boys   *C&W '49*

Singles: 78rpm

BRUNSWICK	5-10	37
BULLET	8-12	
MERCURY	5-10	49
VOCALION	10-15	

NEW GRASS REVIVAL   *C&W '86*

Singles: 7–inch

CAPITOL	3-4	87-89
EMI AMERICA	3-4	86

LP: 10/12–inch 33rpm

FLYING FISH	5-10	80s
STARDAY	5-10	73

Members: John Cowan; Sam Bush; Bela Fleck.

NEWBURY, Mickey

P&R/LP '71/C&W '73

Singles: 7–inch

ABC/HICKORY	3-5	77-79
AIRBORNE	3-4	88
ELEKTRA	3-5	71-73
HICKORY (1312 thru 1463)	4-8	65-67
HICKORY (1600 series)	3-4	80
MCA	3-5	79
MERCURY	3-6	69-70
RCA	3-6	68-70

Picture Sleeves

RCA	3-6	68

LPs: 10/12–inch 33rpm

ABC/HICKORY	5-10	77-79
MCA	5-8	79
ELEKTRA	8-10	71-75
MERCURY (4024 "After All These Years")	5-8	81
MERCURY (61236 "Looks Like Rain")	10-12	69
RCA	8-12	68-72

NEWMAN, Jimmy   *C&W '54*

(Jimmy C. Newman; with Cajun Country)

Singles: 78rpm

DOT	5-15	54-57

Singles: 7–inch

DECCA	3-8	60-71
DOT (Except 15766)	5-15	54-57
DOT (15766 "Carry On")	50-75	58
MGM	5-10	58-60
MONUMENT	3-5	72
PLANTATION	3-5	76-80
SHANNON	3-5	73

EPs: 7–inch 33/45rpm

DECCA	5-10	64

LPs: 10/12–inch 33rpm

CROWN	8-12	60s
DECCA	10-25	62-70
DELTA	5-8	82
DOT	12-25	66
LA LOUISANNE	5-8	
MGM	15-30	59-62
PICKWICK/HILLTOP	8-12	
PLANTATION	5-10	77-81
SWALLOW	5-8	

NEWMAN, Jimmy C., Danny Davis & Nashville Brass

Singles: 7–inch

RCA.. 3-4   80

Also see DAVIS, Danny
Also see NEWMAN, Jimmy C.

NEWMAN, Randy   *LP '71/C&W '78*

Singles: 78rpm

REPRISE (0284 "I Think It's Gonna Rain Today").................................... 8-10   78
(Promotional issue only.)

Singles: 7–inch

CHELSEA 3-5   74
DOT.. 4-8   62
REPRISE (Except 0771).............. 3-6   68-88
REPRISE (0771 "Last Night I Had a Dream")................................... 10-20   68
W.B. 3-5   77-85

Picture Sleeves

REPRISE 3-4   88
W.B. 3-5   78

LPs: 10/12–inch 33rpm

EPIC (147 "Peyton Place")........ 20-30   65
(TV Soundtrack.)
REPRISE (Except 6286)............. 5-10   70-88
REPRISE (6286 "Randy Newman") 15-20   68
(Cover pictures Randy in sweater and coat.)
REPRISE (6286 "Randy Newman") 10-15   68
(Cover picture is a close-up of Randy.)
W.B. 5-10   77-85

Also see EAGLES
Also see RONSTADT, Linda
Also see SEGER, Bob

NEWMAN, Randy, & Paul Simon / Randy Newman   *P&R '83*

Singles: 7–inch

W.B. 3-5   83

Picture Sleeves

W.B. 3-5   83

Also see NEWMAN, Randy
Also see SIMON, Paul

NEWMAN, Terri Sue   *C&W '79*

Singles: 7–inch

TEXAS SOUL.............................. 3-5   79

NEWTON, Juice   *P&R '78/C&W '79*

Singles: 7–inch

CAPITOL...................................... 3-5   78-84
RCA.. 3-4   84-89

Picture Sleeves

CAPITOL.................................. 3-5   81-83
RCA 3-4   84

LPs: 10/12–inch 33rpm

CAPITOL.................................. 5-10   77-84
RCA 5-8   84-87

Also see RABBITT, Eddie, & Juice Newton

NEWTON, Juice, & Silver Spur   *C&W '76*

Singles: 7–inch

CAPITOL...................................... 3-5   77
RCA 3-5   75-76

LPs: 10/12–inch 33rpm

CAPITOL (11000 series) 8-10   77
CAPITOL (16000 series) 5-8   81
RCA (1000 series) 8-12   75
RCA (4000 series) 5-8   81

Also see NEWTON, Juice

NEWTON, Wayne

P&R/LP '63/C&W '72

Singles: 7–inch

ARIES II 3-5   79-80
CAPITOL (Except 5338)............... 4-8   63-71
CAPITOL (5338 "Comin' on Too Strong")................................... 10-20   64
(With Bruce Johnston & Terry Melcher.)
CHALLENGE 4-8   64
CHELSEA 3-5   72-76
GEORGE (7777 "Little White Cloud That Cried")................................... 10-15   62
MGM...3-6   68
20TH FOX.................................... 3-5   78
W.B. 3-5   70-77

Picture Sleeves

CAPITOL...................................... 4-8   65-66

LPs: 10/12–inch 33rpm

AIRES II 5-8   79-80
CAMDEN 5-10   74
CAPITOL (573 "Wayne Newton").................................. 15-25   70
(Three-LP set.)
CAPITOL (T-1973 thru T-2797).................................... 10-20   63-67
(Monaural.)
CAPITOL (ST-1973 thru ST-2797)................................... 15-25   63-67
(Stereo.)
CAPITOL (SM-2300 series)...........5-8   75
CAPITOL (SPC-3400 series).........5-8
CAPITOL (11000 series) 5-8   79

CAPITOL (16000 series)............... 5-8	80	
CHELSEA 10-15	72-75	
MGM 6-12	68	
MUSICOR 5-8	79	
20TH FOX 5-8	78	

NEWTON, Wayne, & Tammy Wynette   *C&W '89*

Singles: 7–inch

CURB.. 3-4	89	

Also see NEWTON, Wayne
Also see WYNETTE, Tammy

NEWTON, Wood   *C&W '78*

Singles: 7–inch

ELEKTRA....................................... 3-5   78-79

NEWTON BROTHERS

(Featuring Wayne)

Singles: 7–inch

CAPITOL (4236 "The Real Thing")...................................... 60-80	59	
GEORGE (7778 "Little Jukebox") 15-20	61	
GEORGE (7780 "I Stil ILove You") 10-15	61	
LAMA (7794 "I Was Born When You Kissed Me").. 25-50	63	

Members: Wayne Newton; Jerry Newton.
Also see NEWTON RASCALS

NEWTON RASCALS

Singles: 7–inch

RANGER (401 "If the Easter Bunny Knew the Fun He'd Have on Xmas) 15-25   58
(Issued with a paper insert picturing 12-year-old Wayne and 14-year-old Jerry as "The Rascals in Rhythm." Value of insert is about the same as for disc.)

Members: Wayne Newton; Jerry Newton.
Also see NEWTON, Wayne
Also see NEWTON BROTHERS

NEWTON-JOHN, Olivia

P&R/LP '71/C&W '73

Singles: 12–inch 33/45rpm

MCA (Except 1150)....................... 4-6	81-84	
MCA (1150 "Twist of Fate")......... 5-10	83	

(Promotional issue only.)

Singles: 7–inch

GEFFEN.. 3-4	89	
KIRSHNER (5005 "Goin' Back")....................................... 10-15	70	
MCA (Except 40043)..................... 3-5	73-88	

MCA (40043 "Take Me Home Country Roads").............................5-10	73	
RSO 3-5	78	
UNI (55281 "If Not for You").........5-10	71	
UNI (55304 "Banks of the Ohio) ...4-8	71	
UNI (55317 "What Is Life")............4-8	72	
UNI (55348 "Just a Little Too Much").......................................8-12	72	

Promotional Singles

MCA (1810 "Deeper Than the Night")...................................25-30	79	

(Picture disc. Promotional issue only.)

WHAT'S IT ALL ABOUT 25-50   74

Picture Sleeves

MCA (Except 40418)......................3-5	75-88	
MCA (40418 "Please Mr. Please") 6-10	75	

EPs: 7–inch 33/45rpm

MCA...12-15   73
(Promotional issues only.)

LPs: 10/12–inch 33rpm

GEFFEN...5-8	89	
MCA (389 "Let Me Be There") ...10-12	73	
MCA (411 "If You Love Me, Let Me Know") 12-15	74	

(With *I Love You, I Honestly Love You.* Note longer title.)

MCA (411 "If You Love Me, Let Me Know") 8-10	74	

(With *I Honestly Love You.* Note shorter title.)

MCA (2000 & 3000 series)...........8-10	75-78	
MCA (5000 & 6000 series).............5-8	80-83	
MCA (37000 series)........................5-8	80-83	
MFSL 25-50	80	
UNI (73117 "If Not for You").......50-75	71	

(Cover depicts a field scene.)

UNI (73117 "If Not for You").......20-30	71	

(Field scene removed from cover.)

Also see DENVER, John, & Olivia Newton-John
Also see FOSTER, David, & Olivia Newton-John
Also see TOMORROW

NEWTON-JOHN, Olivia, & Electric Light Orchestra   *P&R/LP '80*

Singles: 7–inch

MCA (41285 "Xanadu")...................3-5   80

Picture Sleeves

MCA (41285 "Xanadu")...................3-5   80

LPs: 10/12–inch 33rpm

MCA (6100 "Xanadu")...................8-10	80	
MCA (10384 "Xanadu")........750-1000	80	

(Picture disc. Promotional issue only. Also

has Cliff Richard, Gene Kelly, and the Tubes.)

NEWTON-JOHN, Olivia, & Andy Gibb
P&R '80

Singles: 12–inch 33/45rpm

POLYDOR (104 "Rest Your Love on Me")... 10-15   79

Singles: 7–inch

RSO 3-5   80
Also see GIBB, Andy

NEWTON-JOHN, Olivia, & Cliff Richard
P&R '80

Singles: 7–inch

MCA 3-5   80

Picture Sleeves

MCA 3-5   80

NEWTON-JOHN, Olivia, & John Travolta
P&R '78

Singles: 7–inch

RSO 3-5   78

Picture Sleeves

RSO 3-5   78
Also see NEWTON-JOHN, Olivia

NEYMAN, June
C&W '78

Singles: 7–inch

STARSHIP 3-5   78-79

NICKS, Stevie
LP '81/C&W '82

Singles: 12–inch 33/45rpm

MODERN 4-8   81-86

Singles: 7–inch

MODERN 3-5   81-89

Picture Sleeves

MODERN 3-5   82-89

LPs: 10/12–inch 33rpm

MFSL (121 "Bella Donna") 20-30   84
MODERN 5-10   81-89

NICKS, Stevie, & Don Henley
P&R '81

Singles: 7–inch

MODERN 3-5   81

NICKS, Stevie, & Tom Petty & Heartbreakers
P&R '81

Singles: 7–inch

MODERN 3-5   81-86

NICKS, Stevie, & Sandy Stewart

Singles: 7–inch

MODERN 3-4   83

NIELSEN, Shaun
C&W '80
(Sherrill Nielsen)

Singles: 7–inch

AUDIOGRAPH................................ 3-5   70s
ADONDA.. 3-5   80
RCA 3-5   78
SCORPION.................................... 3-5   77

LPs: 10/12–inch 33rpm

AUDIOGRAPH................................ 5-10
MCA 5-10   81
Also see PRESLEY, Elvis

NEILSEN WHITE BAND
C&W '86

Singles: 7–inch

VISION.. 3-4   86-87
Members: Gary Nielsen; Jack White; Tom Eckhoff.
Also see DILLMAN BAND

NIGHTSTREETS
C&W '80
(Streets)

Singles: 7–inch

EPIC.. 3-5   80-81
Also see STREETS

NILLES, Lynn
C&W '77

Singles: 7–inch

GRT 3-5   77

NITTY GRITTY DIRT BAND
(Dirt Band)   *P&R/LP '67/C&W '75*

Singles: 78rpm

LIBERTY (2889 "Mr. Bojangles").................................. 20-30   70
(Promotional issue only.)
U.A. (69 "All the Good Times") ..20-30   71
(Promotional issue only. Includes script and booklet.)

Singles: 7–inch

LIBERTY (1000 series).................. 3-5   81-84
LIBERTY (50000 series)................ 4-8   67-70
U.A. 3-5   71-80
W.B. 3-4   84-86

Picture Sleeves

LIBERTY (1000 series).................. 3-5   81-84
LIBERTY (50000 series).............. 8-12   67
U.A. 3-5   71-80

EPs: 7–inch 33/45rpm

LIBERTY (37 "Special Radio Interview")................................ 10-15   70
(Promotional issue only. Has paper cover.)

U.A. (69 "All the Good Times").. 20-30 71
(Promotional issue only. Includes script and booklet.)

LPs: 10/12–inch 33rpm

LIBERTY (1100 series) 5-10 81
LIBERTY (3501 "Nitty Gritty Dirt Band") 15-20 67
(Monaural.)
LIBERTY (7501 "Nitty Gritty Dirt Band") 15-25 67
(Stereo.)
LIBERTY (7501 thru 7611)........ 10-20 67-69
LIBERTY (7642 "Uncle Charlie") 100-125 70
(Gatefold promotional edition. Includes two bonus singles, photos and booklet.)
LIBERTY (LST-7642 "Uncle Charlie") 10-20 70
LIBERTY (LATO-7642 "Uncle Charlie") 5-8
LIBERTY (51146 "Let's Go") 5-8 83
U.A. (117 "Interview") 15-25 75
(Promotional issue only.)
U.A. (UA-LA184 "Stars and Stripes Forever") 10-20 74
U.A. (LWB-184 "Stars and Stripes Forever") 8-10
U.A. (469 "Dream") 8-12 75
U.A. (469 "Dream - Programmers Guide") 15-25 75
(Promotional issue only.)
U.A. (UA-LA670 "Dirt, Silver and Gold") 15-20 76
U.A. (LKCL-670 "Dirt, Silver and Gold") 10-12
U.A.(854 thru 1042) 5-10 78-80
U.A. (5500 series) 8-12 71
U.A. (9801 "Will the Circle Be Unbroken") 30-40 72
(Three-LP set.)
UNIVERSAL (12500 "Will the Circle Be Unbroken, Vol. 2")................... 10-15 89
W.B. 5-10 84-86

Session: Nicolette Larson.
Also see CLEMENTS, Vassar
Also see DENVER, John, & Nitty Gritty Dirt Band
Also see LARSON, Nicolette
Also see SKAGGS, Ricky

NITTY GRITTY DIRT BAND & Roy Acuff   *C&W '71*

Singles: 7–inch

U.A. 3-5 71
Also see ACUFF, Roy

NITTY GRITTY DIRT BAND, Rosanne Cash & John Hiatt   *C&W '90*

Singles: 7–inch

MCA...3-4 90
Also see CASH, Rosanne

NITTY GRITTY DIRT BAND & Jimmy Martin   *C&W '73*

Singles: 7–inch

U.A. 3-5 73
Also see MARTIN, Jimmy

NITTY GRITTY DIRT BAND & Linda Ronstadt

Singles: 7–inch

U.A. 3-5 79
Also see NITTY GRITTY DIRT BAND
Also see RONSTADT, Linda

NIX, Tom   *C&W '81*

Singles: 7–inch

RMA...3-4 80-81

NIXON, Nick   *C&W '74*

Singles: 7–inch

MCA...3-5 79
MERCURY....................................3-5 74-78

LP: 10/12–inch 33rpm

MERCURY....................................5-10 77
Session: Randy Wright.
Also see WRIGHT, Randy

NOACK, Eddie   *C&W '58*

Singles: 78rpm

MERCURY....................................10-20 55
STARDAY.....................................10-25 54-57
TNT..15-25 54

Singles: 7–inch

ALLSTAR......................................3-4
D (1019 "Have Blues, Will Travel") 10-20 58
D (1037 "Walk 'Em Off")............30-50 59
D (1060 "A Thinking Man's Woman")..................................10-20 59
D (1094 "Relief Is Just a Swallow Away') 10-20 59
D (1100 series) 5-10 59-61
D (1200 series) 3-8 61-72
K-ARK...4-6 69
MERCURY....................................15-25 55
STARDAY.....................................15-25 54-57
TNT (110 "Too Hot to Handle")..20-30 54

TNT (1010 "Too Hot to
  Handle") 20-30   54
WIDE WORLD 3-5   70
LPs: 10/12–inch 33rpm
WIDE WORLD 10-20   70

NOBLE, Nick   *P&R '55*
Singles: 78rpm
MERCURY 5-15   56-57
WING 5-10   55-56
Singles: 7–inch
CAPITOL.. 3-5   73
CHESS.. 4-8   63-64
CHURCHILL................................. 3-5   77-80
CORAL.. 4-8   59-66
DATE... 4-6   67-68
EPIC 3-5   77
FRATERNITY............................. 5-10   58
LIBERTY 4-8   62-63
MERCURY 8-15   56-57
TMS.. 3-5   79
20TH FOX 4-8   65
WING 8-15   55-56
LPs: 10/12–inch 33rpm
COLUMBIA 8-12   69
LIBERTY 10-15   63
WING 15-25   60

NOBLE, Nick, & Lew
Douglass   *C&W '79*
Singles: 7–inch
TMS.. 3-5   79
Also see NOBLE, Nick

NOEL   *C&W '82*
(Noel Haughey)
Singles: 7–inch
DEEP SOUTH................................ 3-4   82
MADD CASH................................. 3-4   85

NOEL   *P&R '87*
(Noel Pagan)
Singles: 7–inch
4TH & BROADWAY 3-4   87-88
VIRGIN... 3-4   '79
Picture Sleeves
4TH & BROADWAY 3-4   87-88
VIRGIN... 3-4   79
LPs: 10/12–inch 33rpm
4TH & BROADWAY 5-8   88

NORMA JEAN   *C&W '64*
(Norma Jean Beasler-Taylor)
Singles: 7–inch
COLUMBIA 5-10   58-62
RCA 4-8   63-72
RIVERSIDE...................................4-8   63
LPs: 10/12–inch 33rpm
CAMDEN 8-15   68-71
HARMONY.................................10-15   66
RCA (2961 thru 3977)................20-30   64-67
RCA (4060 thru 4695)................12-25   68-72
Also see BARE, Bobby, Liz Anderson & Norma Jean
Also see GRAY, Claude, & Norma Jean
Also see SOME of CHET'S FRIENDS
Also see WAGONER, Porter

NORMAN, Jim   *C&W '78*
Singles: 7–inch
REPUBLIC....................................3-5   78

NUNLEY, BILL   *C&W '88*
(Country Bill Nunley)
Singles: 7–inch
CANNERY 3-4   88

NUNN, Earl, & His Alabama
Ramblers   *C&W '49*
(With Billy Lee)
Singles: 78rpm
SPECIALTY 5-10   49

NUTTER, Mayf   *C&W '70*
Singles: 7–inch
CAPITOL.......................................3-5   71-73
GNP 3-5   76-77
REPRISE 3-5   70
LP: 10/12–inch 33rpm
CAPITOL.......................................6-12   73
CRESCENDO...............................5-10   77

OAK RIDGE BOYS   *C&W '76*
(Oak Ridge Quartet; Oaks)
Singles: 7–inch
ABC..3-5   78-79
ABC/DOT.......................................3-5   77
CADENCE 6-12   59
COLUMBIA 3-5   73-79

HEARTWARMING	3-5	71
IMPACT	3-5	71
MCA	3-5	79-90
RCA	3-4	90-91
W.B.	3-8	63

LPs: 10/12-inch 33rpm

ABC	5-10	78-79
ABC/DOT	8-10	77
ACCORD	5-10	81-82
CADENCE (3019 "The Oak Ridge Quartet")	35-55	58
CANAAN	8-15	66
COLUMBIA	5-10	74-83
EXACT	5-10	83
51 WEST	5-8	
HEARTWARMING	5-8	71-74
INTERMEDIA	5-8	
MCA	5-10	80-86
NASHVILLE	8-10	70
OUT of TOWN DIST.	5-10	82
PHONORAMA	5-8	83
PICKWICK	5-8	70s
POWER PAK	5-10	70s
PRIORITY	5-10	82
SKYLITE	10-20	64-66
STARDAY	10-20	65
U.A.	10-20	66
VISTA	5-8	
W.B.	10-20	63

Members: William Lee Golden; Duane Allen; Rich Sterban; Joe Bonsall; Steve Sanders; Willie Wynn.
Also see BONSALL, Joe
Also see CASH, Johnny, Carter Family & Oak Ridge Boys
Also see GOLDEN, William Lee
Also see JONES, George
Also see LEE, Brenda, & Oak Ridge Boys
Also see MANDRELL, Barbara, & Oak Ridge Boys
Also see STEVENS, Even
Also see SWEETWATER
Also see TENNESSEANS

O'DAY, Tommy   *C&W '78*
Singles: 7-inch

NU-TRAYL	3-5	78-79

O'DELL, Doye   *C&W '48*
(With the Cass County Boys)
Singles: 78rpm

EXCLUSIVE	5-10	48

LP: 10/12-inch 33rpm

CROWN	10-20	60s
ERA (20004 "Doye O'Dell") (Colored vinyl.)	20-30	60s
LONGHORN	5-10	83

SAGE	10-20	
SUNSET	6-12	

O'DELL, Kenny   *P&R '67*
Singles: 7-inch

ABC	3-5	73
CAPRICORN	3-5	73-79
KAPP	3-5	72
MAR-KAY	5-10	65
VEGAS	4-8	67-68
WHITE WHALE	4-6	69

LPs: 10/12-inch 33rpm

CAPRICORN	5-10	74-78
VEGAS	15-25	68

ODESSA   *C&W '89*
Singles: 7-inch

SING ME	3-4	89

ODOM, Donna   *C&W '68*
Singles: 7-inch

DECCA	3-6	68

O'DOSKI, Gail   *C&W '87*
Singles: 7-inch

DOOR KNOB	3-4	87-88

O'GWYNN, James   *C&W '58*
Singles: 7-inch

D	10-15	58
MERCURY	6-12	59-62

LP: 10/12-inch 33rpm

MERCURY	20-30	62
PLANTATION	5-10	76-78
WING	10-20	64

O'KANES   *C&W '86*
Singles: 7-inch

COLUMBIA	3-4	86-88

Members: Jamie O'Hara; Kieran Kane.
Also see KANE, Kieran

O'KEEFE, Danny   *P&R/C&W/LP '72*
Singles: 7-inch

ATLANTIC	3-5	75
JERDEN	4-8	66
SIGNPOST	3-5	72
W.B.	3-5	77-78

Picture Sleeves

W.B.	3-5	77-78

LPs: 10/12-inch 33rpm

ATLANTIC	8-12	73-75
COTILLION	10-15	70

FIRST AMERICAN 8-10   70s

PANORAMA (105 "Introducing Danny
O'Keefe") 20-30   66

SIGNPOST 10-12   72

W.B. 5-10   77-79

OLD and in the WAY   *LP '75*

LPs: 10/12–inch 33rpm

ROUND (103 "Old and in the
Way") 20-25   75

SUGAR HILL 5-8   85

Members: Peter Rowan; Jerry Garcia; Vassar
Clements; David Grisman.

OLD and in the WAY / Keith & Donna / Robert Hunter / Phil Lesh & Ned Lagin

Singles: 7–inch

ROUND (02 & 03 "Sampler for Dead
Heads") 40-60   75
(Promotional, fan club two-disc set. Price
also includes a letter from Anton Round, a
letter about members of the Grateful Dead,
several miniature LP covers, and a mailer
advertising posters.)

ROUND (02 & 03 "Sampler for Dead
Heads") 20-30   75
(Price is for both discs, without inserts.
Divide in half for either one of the two
records.)
Also see OLD and in the WAY

O'NEAL, Austin   *C&W '83*

Singles: 7–inch

PROJECT ONE............................. 3-4   83

O'NEAL, Coleman   *C&W '63*

Singles: 7–inch

CHANCELLOR.............................. 4-8   62-63

ORBISON, Roy   *P&R '56/C&W '87*

(With the Teen Kings; with Candy Men; with
Roses; with Friends)

Singles: 78rpm

QUALITY 20-40   56

SUN.. 40-80   56-57

Singles: 12–inch 33/45rpm

VIRGIN (2667 "She's a Mystery to
Me").. 10-15   89
(Includes cover.)

Singles: 7–inch

ASYLUM 3-5   78-79

COLLECTABLES 3-4   85

MGM 4-8   65-73

MGM CELEBRITY SCENE (CSN9-5 "Roy
Orbison").................................... 50-75   66
(Boxed set of five singles with bio insert and
jukebox title strips.)

MERCURY..................................... 4-8   74

MONUMENT (409 "Paper
Boy") 20-30   59

MONUMENT (412 "Uptown") 15-20   59

MONUMENT (421 thru 467) 8-12   60-62

MONUMENT (800 & 900
series)... 5-10   63-66

MONUMENT (500 series)............. 4-8   63

MONUMENT (8600 series)........... 3-5   76

MONUMENT (8900 series)........... 3-5   72

MONUMENT (45000 series)......... 3-5   76-77

QUALITY (1499 "Ooby
Dooby").................................... 50-100   56

QUALITY (1559
"Rockhouse") 50-100   56

RCA (7381 "Sweet and
Innocent")................................. 20-30   58

RCA (7447 "Jolie") 20-30   59

SSS/SUN 3-5   70s

SUN (242 "Ooby Dooby") 20-30   56

SUN (251 "Rockhouse") 20-30   56

SUN (265 "Sweet and Easy to
Love")....................................... 20-30   56

SUN (284 "Chicken Hearted")....20-30   58

SUN (353 "Sweet and Easy to
Love")... 8-10   61
(Yellow label.)

SUN (353 "Sweet and Easy to
Love")....................................... 10-15   61
(White label. Promotional issue only.)

VIRGIN.. 3-5   87-89

Picture Sleeves

MGM 8-12   65-67

MONUMENT (400 series)........... 10-20   60-62

MONUMENT (800 series)........... 10-15   63-64

VIRGIN.. 3-5   89

EPs: 7–inch 33/45rpm

MGM (4379 "Classic Roy
Orbison")................................... 30-50   66
(Jukebox issue only.)

MONUMENT (2 "Crying") 20-30   62
(Compact 33, "Special Promotional Six-Pac."
Not issued with special cover.)

MONUMENT (3 "Roy
Orbison")................................... 20-30   62
(Compact 33, "Special Promotional Six-Pac."
Not issued with special cover.)

STARS INC. (101 "Roy Orbison and the Teen
Kings") 300-400   59

(Promotional issue, distributed to fan club members.)

LPs: 10/12–inch 33rpm

ACCORD	5-8	81
ASYLUM	5-8	78-79
BUCKBOARD	8-10	
CANDLELITE MUSIC	10-15	70s
DESIGN	10-15	60s
MGM (E-4308 thru E-4514)	15-25	65-67
(Monaural.)		
MGM (SE-4308 thru SE-4514)	20-30	65-67
(Stereo.)		
MGM (4636 thru 4934)	10-20	69-73
MGM/CAPITOL (90454 "There Is Only One Roy Orbison")	10-20	65
(Label reads "Mfd. by Capitol Records." Record club issue.)		
MERCURY	8-12	75
MONUMENT (4002 "Lonely and Blue")	75-125	61
(Monaural.)		
MONUMENT (4007 "Crying")	20-40	62
(Monaural.)		
MONUMENT (4009 "Greatest Hits")	20-40	62
(Monaural.)		
MONUMENT (6600 series)	8-10	
MONUMENT (7600 "Regeneration")	8-10	76
MONUMENT (8000 "Greatest Hits")	15-25	63
(Monaural.)		
MONUMENT (8003 "In Dreams")	20-30	63
(Monaural.)		
MONUMENT (8024 "More Greatest Hits")	15-25	64
(Monaural.)		
MONUMENT (8035 "Orbisongs")	15-25	65
(Monaural.)		
MONUMENT (8023 "Early Orbison")	15-25	64
MONUMENT (8045 "Very Best")	20-30	66
(Blue cover.)		
MONUMENT (8045 "Very Best")	15-20	66
(Purple cover.)		
MONUMENT (14002 "Lonely and Blue")	100-200	61
(Stereo.)		
MONUMENT (14007 "Crying")	25-50	62
(Stereo.)		
MONUMENT (14009 "Greatest Hits")	25-50	62
(Stereo.)		
MONUMENT (18000 "Greatest Hits")	20-35	63
(Stereo.)		
MONUMENT (18003 "In Dreams")	20-35	63
(Stereo.)		
MONUMENT (18024 "More Greatest Hits")	20-30	64
(Stereo.)		
MONUMENT (18023 "Early Orbison")	20-30	64
MONUMENT (18035 "Orbisongs")	20-30	65
(Stereo.)		
MONUMENT (18045 "Very Best")	25-35	66
(Blue cover.)		
MONUMENT (18045 "Very Best")	20-30	66
(Purple cover.)		
MONUMENT (31484 "All-Time Greatest Hits")	8-12	82
MONUMENT (38384 "All-Time Greatest Hits")	6-10	82
RHINO	5-8	88
SPECTRUM	15-20	60s
SSS/SUN	5-10	69
SUN (1260 "Rock House")	125-225	61
SUNNYVALE	8-10	77
TIME-LIFE	10-15	86
TRIP	8-10	74
VIRGIN	6-12	87-89

Session: Bobby Goldsboro; Bruce Springsteen.
Also see GOLDSBORO, Bobby
Also see HIGGINS, Bertie, & Roy Orbison
Also see LEWIS, Jerry Lee / Roger Miller / Roy Orbison
Also see PERKINS, Carl, Jerry Lee Lewis, Roy Orbison
& Johnny Cash
Also see TEEN KINGS

ORBISON, Roy / Bobby Bare / Joey Powers

LPs: 10/12–inch 33rpm

CAMDEN	15-25	64

Also see BARE, Bobby

ORBISON, Roy / Lesley Gore / Drifters / Los Bravos

EPs: 7–inch 33/45rpm

SWINGERS for COKE	50-75	66

(Promotional issue only. Each artist sings a song about Coca Cola. Has paper cover.)

ORBISON, Roy, & Emmylou Harris / Craig Hundley   *C&W/P&R '80*
Singles: 7–inch
W.B. 3-5   80
    Also see HARRIS, Emmylou

ORBISON, Roy / Jan & Dean / 4 Seasons / Shirelles
EPs: 7–inch 33/45rpm
COKE ("Let's Swing the Jingle for
    Coca-Cola") 40-60   65
    (Coca-Cola radio spots. Issued to radio
    stations only.)

ORBISON, Roy, & K.D. Lang   *C&W '87*
Singles: 7–inch
VIRGIN 3-4   87
    Also see LANG, K.D.
    Also see ORBISON, Roy

ORDGE, Jimmy Arthur   *C&W '81*
Singles: 7–inch
DORE 3-4   81

ORENDER, DeWayne   *C&W '76*
Singles: 7–inch
NU-TRAYL 3-5   78
RCA 3-5   76-77
VOLUNTEER 3-5   78

ORIGINAL TEXAS PLAYBOYS: see TEXAS PLAYBOYS

ORION   *C&W '79*
(Jimmy Ellis)
Singles: 7–inch
KRISTAL 3-5   85
ORCHID 3-5   89
SUN 3-6   79-84
    (Most are colored vinyl)
Promotional Singles
SUN (1142 "Ebony Eyes"/
    "Honey") 8-12   79
    (With unprinted white label. Includes flyer
    explaining blank label idea.)
EPs: 7–inch 33/45rpm
ORION ("Merry Christmas") 8-12   80s
    (Fan club issue.)
SUN (1152 "A Stranger in My
    Place") 15-25   80
    (Promotional issue only. Price includes
    explanatory flyer. Not issued with cover.)

LPs: 10/12–inch 33rpm
ARON 5-10   89
    (Canadian.)
SUFFOLK MARKETING 10-15   81
    (TV mail-order LP.)
SUN (Except 1012) 5-10   79-81
SUN (1012 "Orion Reborn") 15-20   78
    (White cover. Often referred to as with the
    "Coffin Cover.")
SUN (1012 "Orion Reborn") 5-10   78
    (Blue cover.)
    Also see ELLIS, Jimmy
    Also see LEWIS, Jerry Lee, & Friends

ORLEANS   *P&R/LP '75/C&W '86*
Singles: 7–inch
ABC 3-5   73
ASYLUM 3-5   75-77
INFINITY 3-5   79
MCA 3-4   86
LPs: 10/12–inch 33rpm
ABC 10-12   73-78
ASYLUM 8-10   75-76
INFINITY 5-10   79
RADIO 5-8   82
    Member: John Hall.

ORTEGA, Gilbert   *C&W '78*
Singles: 7–inch
LRJ 3-5   78
ORTEGA 3-5   78

ORVILLE & IVY   *C&W '67*
Singles: 7–inch
IMPERIAL 4-6   67
    Members: W.W. "Speedy" West; Jimmy Bryant.

OSBORNE, Jimmie   *C&W '48*
Singles: 78rpm
KING 5-10   48-55
Singles: 7–inch
KING 10-20   52-55
EPs: 7–inch 33/45rpm
AUDIO LAB (3 "Jimmie
    Osborne") 10-15   59
LP: 10/12–inch 33rpm
AUDIO LAB (1527 "Songs He
    Wrote") 25-35   59
KING 15-25   61-65

OSBORNE BROTHERS   *C&W '58*
(With Red Allen)
Singles: 7–inch
CMH 3-5   80

DECCA	3-8	63-72
MCA	3-5	73-75
MGM (100 series)	3-5	64
MGM (12000 & 13000 series)	4-10	59-63

EPs: 7–inch 33/45rpm

MGM	10-15	59

LPs: 10/12–inch 33rpm

CMH	5-10	76-82
CORAL	5-10	73
DECCA	10-20	65-72
MCA	5-10	73-75
MGM (100 series)	5-10	70
MGM (3700 series)	25-35	59
MGM (4000 series)	15-25	62-63
PICKWICK	5-10	70s
ROUNDER	5-8	80s
SUGAR HILL	5-8	84

Members: Bobby Osborne; Sonny Osborne; Benny Birchfield. Session: Ronnie Reno; Jimmy Martin.
Also see MARTIN, Jimmy
Also see RENO, Ronnie

OSBORNE BROTHERS & Mac Wiseman   *C&W '79*

(With Red Allen)

Singles: 7–inch

CMH	3-5	79

Also see OSBORNE BROTHERS
Also see WISEMAN, Mac

O'SHEA, Cathy   *C&W '78*

Singles: 7–inch

MCA	3-5	78

O'SHEA, Shad   *C&W '76*

(With the 18 Wheelers)

Singles: 7–inch

NORMAN	4-8	63
PRIVATE STOCK	3-5	76
SOUND STAGE 7	4-8	64-65

OSLIN, K.T.   *C&W '81*

(Kay T. Oslin)

Singles: 7–inch

ELEKTRA	5-10	81
RCA	3-4	86-91

LPs: 10/12–inch 33rpm

RCA	5-8	87-91

OSMOND, Donny   *P&R/LP '71*

Singles: 7–inch

CAPITOL	3-4	89
MGM	3-5	71-75
POLYDOR	3-5	76-78

Picture Sleeves

CAPITOL	3-4	89
MGM	3-5	71-75

LPs: 10/12–inch 33rpm

CAPITOL	5-8	89-90
MGM	8-10	71-74
POLYDOR	5-10	76-77

Also see OSMONDS

OSMOND, Donny & Marie

P&R/C&W/LP '74

Singles: 7–inch

MGM	3-5	74-75
POLYDOR	3-5	76-78

LPs: 10/12–inch 33rpm

MGM	8-10	74-75
POLYDOR	5-10	76-78

Also see D&M
Also see OSMOND, Donny
Also see OSMOND, Marie

OSMOND, Marie   *C&W/P&R/LP '73*

(Marie)

Singles: 7–inch

CURB	3-4	90
CURB/CAPITOL	3-5	85-89
ELEKTRA/CURB	3-5	82-84
MGM	3-5	73-75
POLYDOR	3-5	76-78
RCA/CURB	3-5	84

Picture Sleeves

MGM	3-5	73-75
POLYDOR	3-5	77
RCA	3-5	84

LPs: 10/12–inch 33rpm

CURB/CAPITOL	5-8	85-88
MGM	8-12	73-75
POLYDOR	5-8	77

Also see OSMOND, Donny & Marie
Also see OSMONDS

OSMOND, Marie, & Paul Davis   *C&W '86*

Singles: 7–inch

CAPITOL	3-4	86-88

Also see DAVIS, Paul

OSMOND, Marie, & Osmond Brothers

LPs: 10/12–inch 33rpm

UNITED (12924 "Our Best to You") 5-10 85
(Special products promotional issue, made for Case International.)

Also see OSMONDS

OSMOND, Marie, & Dan Seals
C&W '85

Singles: 7–inch

CURB/CAPITOL	3-4	85

Also see OSMOND, Marie
Also see SEALS, Dan

OSMONDS
P&R/R&B/LP '71/C&W '82

(Osmond Brothers)

Singles: 7–inch

BARNABY	4-6	68-69
CURB/E.M.I.	3-4	85-86
EMI AMERICA	3-4	85-86
ELEKTRA/CURB	3-5	82-83
MGM (13126 thru 14159)	4-6	63-70
MGM (14193 thru 14831)	3-5	70-75
MERCURY	3-5	79
POLYDOR	3-5	76-77
UNI (55015 "I Can't Stop")	4-8	67
UNI (55276 "I Can't Stop")	3-5	71
W.B./CURB	3-5	83-85

Picture Sleeves

MGM	3-5	73-74

LPs: 10/12–inch 33rpm

EMI AMERICA	5-8	86
ELEKTRA	5-10	82
MGM (7 "Preview—the Osmond Brothers") (Promotional issue only.)	15-20	70s
MGM (4100 & 4200 series)	15-25	63-65
MGM (4724 thru 5012)	8-12	70-75
MERCURY	5-10	79
METRO	10-20	65
POLYDOR	5-10	76-77
W.B./CURB	5-8	83-85

Members: Donny Osmond; Alan Osmond; Merrill Osmond; Wayne Osmond; Jimmy Osmond; Marie Osmond.
Also see CURB, Mike
Also see MERRILL & JESSICA
Also see OSMOND, Donny
Also see OSMOND, Jimmy
Also see OSMOND, Marie

OSMONDS, Steve Lawrence & Eydie Gorme
P&R '72

Singles: 7–inch

MGM	3-5	72

Also see LAWRENCE, Steve, & Eydie Gorme
Also see OSMONDS

OTT, Paul
C&W '79

Singles: 7–inch

ELEKTRA	3-5	79

MONUMENT	3-5	75
SHOW BIZ	3-5	72
THUNDER INT'L (1022 "Kitty Kat")	50-75	60

OVERSTREET, Paul
C&W '82

Singles: 7–inch

MTM	3-4	88
RCA	3-4	82-91

LPs: 10/12–inch 33rpm

BMG	5-8	91

Also see TUCKER, Tanya, Paul Davis & Paul Overstreet

OVERSTREET, Tommy
C&W '69

(With the Nashville Express)

Singles: 7–inch

ABC	3-5	78-79
ABC/DOT	3-5	74-78
AMI	3-4	83
DOT	3-6	69-74
ELEKTRA	3-5	79-80
GERVASI	3-4	84
SILVER DOLLAR	3-4	86
TINA	3-5	79

LP: 10/12–inch 33rpm

ABC	5-10	78
ABC/DOT	6-12	75-77
AUDIOGRAPH ALIVE	5-8	82
CMH	5-10	80
DEJA VU	5-8	84
DOT	8-15	71-74
ELEKTRA	5-10	79-80
MCA	5-8	80s
PINNACLE	5-10	78

OWEN, Jim
C&W '78

(With the Drifting Cowboys)

Singles: 7–inch

EPIC	3-5	78
SUN	3-4	80-82

LP: 10/12–inch 33rpm

EPIC (34852 "A Song for Us All") (With Hank Williams poster.)	10-15	77
EPIC (34852 "A Song for Us All") (Without Hank Williams poster.)	8-10	77
EVET	10-15	
GOLD	10-15	
SUN	10-15	82

Also see see DRIFTING COWBOYS

OWEN BROTHERS *C&W '82*
Singles: 7–inch
AUDIOGRAPH 3-4 82-83

OWENS, A.L. "Doodle" *C&W '78*
Singles: 7–inch
RAINDROP 3-5 78

OWENS, Bonnie *C&W '63*
(With the Strangers)
Singles: 7–inch
CAPITOL...................................... 4-6 65-69
TALLY 5-10 63-64
LP: 10/12–inch 33rpm
CAPITOL (195 thru 557) 10-20 69-70
CAPITOL (2403 thru 2861 .... 15-30 65-68
Also see HAGGARD, Merle, & Bonnie Owens

OWENS, Buck *C&W '59*
(With the Buckaroos)
Singles: 78rpm
CAPITOL.................................... 25-50 57
Singles: 7–inch
CAPITOL (2000 thru 4000
  series) 3-5 67-75
  (Orange label.)
CAPITOL (3824 "Come Back") . 10-15 57
  (Purple label.)
CAPITOL (3957 "Sweet
  Thing") 10-15 58
  (Purple label.)
CAPITOL (4000 series).............. 5-10 59-63
  (Purple or orange/yellow label.)
CAPITOL (5000 series)................. 3-6 63-67
CHESTERFIELD (44223 "Leavin' Dirty
  Tracks")................................... 10-20 60s
HILLTOP (6027 "Hot Dog") 25-50 60s
NEW STAR (6418 "Hot
  Dog") 100-150 50s
PEP (105 "Down on the Corner of
  Love")....................................... 20-30 56
PEP (106 "Right After the
  Dance") 20-30 56
PEP (109 "There Goes My
  Love")....................................... 20-30 57
STARDAY (588 "Down on the Corner of
  Love")... 5-10 61
STARDAY (5000 series) 4-6 64
W.B. (Except 8316) 3-5 76-80
W.B. (8316 "World Famous Holiday
  Inn")... 5-10 77

W.B. (8316 "World Famous Paradise
  Inn") 3-5 77
  (Note title change.)
Picture Sleeves
CAPITOL....................................10-20 66-69
EPs: 7–inch 33/45rpm
CAPITOL....................................10-25 61-65
LPs: 10/12–inch 33rpm
BUCKBOARD 5-10
CAPITOL (131 thru 550
  series).....................................10-20 69-70
CAPITOL (574 "Buck
  Owens").....................................20-30 70
  (Three-LP set.)
CAPITOL (628 thru 860)............10-15 70-72
CAPITOL (T-1482 thru
  T-1989)......................................30-40 61-63
  (Monaural.)
CAPITOL (ST-1482 thru
  ST-1989)....................................35-50 61-63
  (Stereo.)
CAPITOL (DT-1400 series) 10-20 69
CAPITOL (2100 thru 2700
  series).....................................12-25 64-67
CAPITOL (2800 thru 2900
  series).....................................10-20 68
CAPITOL (2980 "Buck Owens Minute
  Masters") 30-40 66
  (Promotional issue only.)
CAPITOL (11000 series) 5-8 72-78
COUNTRY FIDELITY ....?? 83
GUEST STAR..............................8-12 60s
HALL of MUSIC 8-12
LA BREA (8017 "Buck
  Owens")...............................100-200 61
OUT of TOWN DIST 5-8 82
PICKWICK/HILLTOP 5-10 78
SPRINGBOARD 5-10
STARDAY (172 "Fabulous Country Music
  Sound of Buck Owens").........15-25 62
STARDAY (300 series)..............15-20 64-65
STARDAY (400 series)..............10-15 75
STARPAK 5-8 79
SUNRISE MEDIA...........................?? 81
TIME-LIFE....................................5-10 82
TRIP..5-8 76
W.B. 5-10 76-77
Also see COLLINS, Tommy
Also see JONES, Corky
Also see JONES, George / Buck Owens / David
  Houston / Tommy Hill.
Also see WEBBER, Rollie
Also see YOAKAM, Dwight, & Buck Owens

OWENS, Buck, & Buddy Alan

(Buck & Buddy; with the
Buckaroos)   *C&W '68*

Singles: 7–inch

CAPITOL..................................... 4-6   68
  Also see ALAN, Buddy

OWENS, Buck / Tennessee Ernie Ford

LP: 10/12–inch 33rpm

CAPITOL (6720 "Music Hall") 8-12
  Also see FORD, Tennessee Ernie

OWENS, Buck, & Emmylou Harris

Singles: 7–inch

W.B. 3-4   79
  Also see HARRIS, Emmylou

OWENS, Buck, & Rose Maddox   *C&W '63*

Singles: 7–inch

CAPITOL.................................... 5-8   63
  Also see MADDOX, Rose

OWENS, Buck, & Susan Raye   *C&W/LP '70*

Singles: 7–inch

CAPITOL.................................. 3-5   70-73

LPs: 10/12–inch 33rpm

CAPITOL.................................... 5-10   70-73
  Also see RAYE, Susan

OWENS, Buck, & Ringo Starr   *C&W '89*

Singles: 7–inch

CAPITOL.................................... 3-5   89
  Also see STARR, Ringo

OWENS, Buck / Faron Young / Ferlin Husky

LPs: 10/12–inch 33rpm

PICKWICK/HILLTOP 8-12   65
  Also see HUSKY, Ferlin
  Also see OWENS, Buck
  Also see YOUNG, Faron

OWENS, Marie   *C&W '74*

Singles: 7–inch

4 STAR................................... 3-5   75
MCA 3-5   74
MMI 3-5   77
SING ME 3-5   77

OXFORD, Vernon   *C&W '75*

Singles: 7–inch

RCA... 3-6   67-77

LP: 10/12–inch 33rpm

RCA (3704 "Woman, Let Me Sing You a
  Song")....................................20-30   67
RICH-R-TONE 10-20   60s
ROUNDER...............................10-15   78-80s
RUTA BAGA 10-15

OZARK MOUNTAIN DAREDEVILS   *P&R/LP '74/C&W '76*

Singles: 7–inch

A&M 3-5   74-78
COLUMBIA 3-5   80

Picture Sleeves

A&M 3-5   75-76

LPs: 10/12–inch 33rpm

A&M 8-12   73-78
COLUMBIA 5-10   80

P

PACIFIC STEEL CO.   *C&W '80*
(Featuring Jay Dee Maness)
Singles: 7–inch
PACIFIC ARTS 3-5   80
LPs: 10/12–inch 33rpm
PACIFIC ARTS 5-10   79

PACK, Bob   *C&W '88*
Singles: 7–inch
OAK... 3-4   88

PACK, Ray   *C&W '89*
Singles: 7–inch
HAPPY MAN 3-4   89

PAGE, Patti
(With Al Clauser & the Oklahomans)
Singles: 78rpm
OKLA (66 "My Sweet Papa") 5-10   40s
(Listed primarily to distinguish this singer from the following Patti Page.)

PAGE, Patti   *P&R '48/C&W '49*
Singles: 78rpm
MERCURY (A-95 thru A-1025) ... 5-15   50-52
(Boxed set of singles.)
MERCURY (505 "Confess")........ 5-10   50
MERCURY (5061 thru 5899) 5-10   47-52
MERCURY (70025 thru 71101) .. 5-10   52-57
MERCURY (71177 thru 71331).................................... 10-20   57-58
PLAYCRAFT 5-10   53-55
Singles: 7–inch
AVCO 3-5   74-75
COLUMBIA 4-6   62-70
EPIC.. 3-5   73-74
LANGWORTH............................ 10-20   49
(Eight-inch, 33rpm transcriptions.)
MERCURY (A-95 thru A-1025) . 10-20   50-52
(Boxed set of singles.)
MERCURY (505 "Confess")...... 10-15   50
MERCURY (5344 thru 5899) 10-15   50-52
MERCURY (7000 series)........... 5-15   61
(Compact 33 stereo.)
MERCURY (10000 series).......... 5-10   58-60
(Stereo.)

MERCURY (30000 series)........... 5-10   58
MERCURY (70025 thru 72123) ...5-15   52-62
MERCURY (73000 series)............. 3-5   70-72
PLANTATION 3-5   81-83
(Black vinyl.)
PLANTATION 4-8   81-83
(Colored vinyl.)
PLAYCRAFT 5-10   53-55
Picture Sleeves
MERCURY................................... 10-20   54-63
EPs: 7–inch 33/45rpm
MERCURY.................................... 8-18   52-61
PLAYCRAFT................................. 5-10   59
LPs: 10/12–inch 33rpm
ACCORD 5-10   82
AHED.. 5-8   76
BRYLEN.. 5-8   82
CANDLELITE.............................. 8-12   73
COLUMBIA (Except "CL" & "CS" series)...................................... 8-15   70-77
COLUMBIA (CL-2049 thru CL-2761)............................... 10-20   63-68
(Monaural.)
COLUMBIA (CS-8849 thru CS-9999) 15-25   63-69
(Stereo.)
EMARCY (2-100 "The East Side The West Side")...................... 50-80   58
(Two LPs.)
EMARCY (36074 "In the Land of Hi Fi").............................. 40-60   56
(No Mercury logo on cover or label.)
EMARCY (36074 "In the Land of Hi Fi").............................. 30-40   58
(Mercury logo on cover and label.)
EMARCY (80000 "In the Land of Hi Fi").............................. 35-45   58
(Stereo.)
EMARCY (36116 "West Side") ..20-30   58
(Monaural.)
EMARCY (36136 "East Side") ...20-30   58
(Monaural.)
EMARCY (60113 "East Side") ...20-30   59
(Stereo.)
EMARCY (60114 "West Side") ..20-30   59
(Stereo.)
EVEREST 5-8   83
EXACT.. 5-8   80
51 WEST.. 5-8   79
GOOD MUSIC 5-8   85
HARMONY.................................... 5-10   69-70
HARTLAND..................................... 5-8   86
HINDSIGHT 5-8   86

IMPACT..........................5-8   79
MERCURY (100 series)...........8-12   69
MERCURY (20076 thru
   20226)..............................20-40   55-56
MERCURY (20318 thru
   20952)..............................15-30   57-64
   (Monaural.)
MERCURY (25059 thru
   25210)..............................20-40   50-54
   (10-inch LPs.)
MERCURY (60049 thru
   60011)..............................20-40   57-58
   (Stereo.)
MERCURY (60025 thru
   60952)..............................20-35   58-64
   (Stereo.)
MERCURY (61344 "I'd Rather Be
   Sorry")..............................10-20   71
PAIR..................................5-8   87
PICKWICK 5-8   72
PILLSBURY (001 "Big
   Records")........................15-25   57
   (Special products issue made for Pillsbury.)
PLANTATION.......................5-10   81-82
PLAYCRAFT (1300 "Patti
   Page")............................15-25   58
SUFFOLK.............................5-8   88
WING (2-100 series)............5-12   72
WING (12121 thru 12174).........10-20   58-59
   (Monaural.)
WING (12250 thru 12295)...........5-12   65
   (Monaural.)
WING (16000 series) 5-15   61-68
   (Stereo.)
   Also see MARTIN, Dean / Patti Page

PAGE, Patti, & Rex Allen
Singles: 78rpm
MERCURY 5-10   50
EPs: 7-inch 33/45rpm
MERCURY 5-15   53
   Also see ALLEN, Rex

PAGE, Patti, & Vic Damone
Singles: 78rpm
MERCURY 5-10   48

PAGE, Patti, & Rusty Draper
EPs: 7-inch 33/45rpm
MERCURY 5-15   53
PLAYCRAFT...............................5-10   59
   Also see DRAPER, Rusty

PAGE, Patti, & Tom T. Hall
      C&W '72
Singles: 7-inch
MERCURY.....................................3-5   72
   Also see HALL, Tom T.
   Also see PAGE, Patti

PAPA JOE'S MUSIC BOX   *C&W '69*
Singles: 7-inch
ABC...3-6   69
   Member: Jerry Smith.
   Also see SMITH, Jerry

PARIS, Jack   *C&W '76*
Singles: 7-inch
50 STATES 3-5   77-78
2-J..3-5   76

PARKER, Billy   *C&W '76*
(With "Friend"; with "Friends")
Singles: 7-inch
CANYON CREEK 3-4   88-89
OAK 3-4   81
SUNSHINE COUNTRY.................3-5   76-79
SOUNDWAVES...........................3-4   81-83
LP: 10/12-inch 33rpm
RCA 8-15
SOUNDWAVES.........................10-20   82
SUNSHINE COUNTRY.................5-10   76-77

PARKER, Billy, & Cal Smith
      C&W '82
Singles: 7-inch
SOUNDWAVES...........................3-4   82
   Also see PARKER, Billy
   Also see SMITH, Cal

PARKER, Fess   *P&R '55*
(With Buddy Ebsen)
Singles: 78rpm
COLUMBIA 4-8   55
DISNEYLAND..............................5-10   57
Singles: 7-inch
BUENA VISTA 4-8   63
CASCADE...................................5-10   59
COLUMBIA 8-12   55
DISNEYLAND..............................5-10   57
GUSTO.......................................4-8   63
RCA 4-8   64-69
Picture Sleeves
BUENA VISTA 5-10   63
DISNEYLAND............................10-20   57
RCA 4-8   64

EPs: 7–inch 33/45rpm

COLUMBIA (2031 "Indian
Fighter") 20-25   55
COLUMBIA (2032 "Davy Crockett Goes to
Congress") 20-25   55
COLUMBIA (2033 "At the
Alamo") 20-25   55

LPs: 10/12–inch 33rpm

COLUMBIA (666 "Davy
Crockett") 50-75   55
DISNEYLAND (1200 series) 10-20   64-65
DISNEYLAND (1300 series) 5-10   70
DISNEYLAND (1900 series) 10-20   63
DISNEYLAND (3007 "Yarns and
Songs") 25-35   55
DISNEYLAND (3900 series) 10-20   64
HARMONY 10-20   60
RCA 10-20   64

PARKER, Fess, & Buddy Ebsen / Gene Autry

Singles: 7–inch

COLUMBIA\CHRYSLER (3 "Story of Davy
Crockett") 5-10   55
(Promotional issue, made by Columbia for
Chrysler. Plays at 16rpm.)

Picture Sleeves

COLUMBIA\CHRYSLER (3 "Story of Davy
Crockett") 10-15   55
(Promotional issue, made by Columbia for
Chrysler.)
Also see AUTRY, Gene
Also see PARKER, Fess

PARKER, Gary Dale   C&W '90

Singles: 7–inch

615 3-4   90

PARKER, Lori   C&W '76

Singles: 7–inch

CON BRIO 3-5   76-77
CORAL 5-10   60-61

Picture Sleeves

CORAL 8-15   60

PARKS, Michael   LP '69/C&W '70

Singles: 7–inch

MGM 3-5   70

LPs: 10/12–inch 33rpm

MGM 10-15   69-70
VERVE 8-12   71

PARKS, P.J.   C&W '81

Singles: 7–inch

KIK 3-5   81

PARNELL, Lee Roy   C&W '90

Singles: 7–inch

ARISTA 3-4   90-91

LP: 10/12–inch 33rpm

ARISTA 5-8   90

PARSONS, Bill   P&R '58

(Bobby Bare)

Singles: 7–inch

ABC 3-5   73
COLLECTABLES 3-4   80s
FRATERNITY (835 "The All American
Boy") 10-15   58
Also see BARE, Bobby

PARSONS, Bill

Singles: 7–inch

FRATERNITY (838 "Educated Rock &
Roll") 8-12   59
STARDAY (526 "Hot Rod
Volkswagen") 25-35   60
STARDAY (544 "A-Waitin") 5-10   61

PARSONS, Rob   C&W '82

Singles: 7–inch

MCA 3-4   82

PARTON, Dolly   C&W '67

Singles: 12–inch 33/45rpm

RCA (Black vinyl) 4-8   78-83
RCA (Colored vinyl) 8-12   78

Singles: 7–inch

GOLDBAND (1086 "Puppy
Love") 20-40   59
MERCURY (71982 "It's Sure Gonna
Hurt") 15-25   62
MONUMENT (800 thru 1000
series) 5-10   65-68
RCA (0132 thru 0950) 3-6   69-76
RCA (5000 series) 3-4   86
RCA (9500 thru 9900 series) 4-6   68-71
RCA (10031 thru 11240) 3-5   74-78
RCA (11296 "Heartbreaker") 5-10   78
(Label mistakenly reads: "From the *Sure
Thing* album.)
RCA (11296 "Heartbreaker") 3-5   78
(Label reads: "From the *Heartbreaker*
album.)
RCA (11420 thru 14297) 3-5   78-86

RCA GOLD STANDARD.............. 3-4   80

Promotional Singles

RCA (Colored vinyl) 4-8   77-85

Picture Sleeves

RCA.. 3-8   69-85

LPs: 10/12–inch 33rpm

ALSHIRE...................................... 8-12   69-71

CAMDEN...................................... 5-10   72-78

COLUMBIA 5-8   87

MONUMENT (7600 series)......... 5-10   78

MONUMENT (8085 "Hello, I'm
  Dolly")....................................... 15-20   67

MONUMENT (18000 series)..... 12-20   67

MONUMENT (18100 series)....... 8-15   70

MONUMENT (31000 series)....... 8-15   72

MONUMENT (33000 series)....... 8-10   75

PAIR... 8-10   82

PICKWICK/CAMDEN.................. 5-10   76

RCA (0033 thru 5000 series) 5-12   73-87
  (With "AFL1," "AHL1," "APD1," "APL1," or
  "AYL1" prefix.)

RCA (2314 "Personal Music
  Dialogue") 10-20   77
  (Interview. Promotional issue only.)

RCA (CPL1-3413 "Great Balls of
  Fire") 15-20   79
  (Picture disc.)

RCA (LPM-3949 "Just Because I'm a
  Woman") 15-25   68
  (Monaural.)

RCA (LSP-3949 "Just Because I'm a
  Woman") 15-20   68
  (Stereo.)

RCA (LSP-4188 "My Blue Ridge Mountain
  Boy") 15-20   69

RCA (LSP-4099 "In the Good Old
  Days") 15-20   69

RCA (LSP-4288 "Fairest of Them
  All")... 10-20   70

RCA (LSP-4387 "A Real Live
  Dolly")...................................... 20-30   70

RCA (LSP-4398 "Golden Streets of
  Glory") 30-50   71

RCA (4422 "Greatest Hits")....... 25-50   82
  (Without *Islands in the Stream*)

RCA (4422 "Greatest Hits")........... 5-8   82
  (With *Islands in the Stream*.)

RCA (LSP-4449 "Best of Dolly
  Parton") 10-20   70

RCA (LSP-4507 "Joshua") 10-20   71

RCA (LSP-4603 "Coat of Many
  Colors") 10-20   71

RCA (LSP-4686 "Touch Your
  Woman").................................. 10-20   72

RCA (LSP-4752 "Dolly Parton Sings [Porter
  Wagoner]")............................... 10-20   72

RCA ("HBO Presents Dolly") 15-25   83
  (Picture disc. Promotional issue only.)

SOMERSET.............................. 10-20   63-68

STEREO-FIDELITY 10-20   63-68

TIME-LIFE.................................... 5-8   81

Session: Jordanaires; Ricky Skaggs; Porter Wagoner.
Also see HARRIS, Emmylou
Also see JORDANAIRES
Also see KRISTOFFERSON, Kris, Willie Nelson, Dolly
  Parton, & Brenda Lee
Also see PHILLIPS, Bill
Also see ROGERS, Kenny, & Dolly Parton
Also see SKAGGS, Ricky
Also see WAGONER, Porter, & Dolly Parton

PARTON, Dolly / George Jones

LPs: 10/12–inch 33rpm

STARDAY (429 "Dolly Parton and George
  Jones")....................................30-40   68
Also see JONES, George

PARTON, Dolly, & Ricky Van Shelton   *C&W '91*

Singles: 7–inch

COLUMBIA 3-4   91
Also see VAN SHELTON, Ricky

PARTON, Dolly, & Willie Nelson   *C&W '82*

Singles: 7–inch

MONUMENT...................................3-4   82
Also see NELSON, Willie

PARTON, Dolly, Linda Ronstadt, & Emmylou Harris   *LP '87*

LPs: 10/12–inch 33rpm

W.B... 5-8   87
Also see HARRIS, Emmylou
Also see RONSTADT, Linda

PARTON, Dolly, & Ricky Van Shelton   *C&W '91*

Singles: 7–inch

RCA 3-4   91
Also see SHELTON, Ricky Van

PARTON, Dolly / Kitty Wells

LPs: 10/12–inch 33rpm

EXACT...5-8   260
Also see PARTON, Dolly
Also see WELLS, Kitty

PARTON, Randy   *C&W '81*
Singles: 7–inch
RCA................................... 3-4   81-83

PARTON, Stella   *C&W '75*
Singles: 7–inch
AIRBORNE 3-4   89
COUNTRY SOUL......................... 4-6   75
ELEKTRA................................. 3-5   77-79
LUV 3-4   87
SOUL, COUNTRY & BLUES 3-5   75
TOWN HOUSE 3-4   82
LP: 10/12–inch 33rpm
ACCORD.................................... 5-8   82
COUNTRY SOUL........................ 10-15   75
ELEKTRA................................... 5-10   77-79
TOWN HOUSE 5-8   82
Also see TAYLOR, Carmol, & Stella Parton

PASTELL, James   *C&W '77*
Singles: 7–inch
PAULA 3-5   77

PAUL, Buddy   *C&W '60*
Singles: 7–inch
MURCO.. 5-8   60

PAUL, Joyce   *C&W '68*
Singles: 7–inch
DOT.. 4-8   61
IMPERIAL 4-8   64
U.A. 4-6   68

PAUL, Les   *P&R '48*
(Les Paul Trio)
Singles: 78rpm
CAPITOL...................................... 5-10   50-53
DECCA.. 5-10   54
Singles: 7–inch
CAPITOL...................................... 5-15   50-53
DECCA.. 5-15   54
EPs: 7–inch 33/45rpm
DECCA.. 10-20   50-53
LPs: 10/12–inch 33rpm
CAPITOL (200 series)................. 5-10   77
CAPITOL (16000 series).............. 5-8
DECCA (5018 "Hawaiian
   Paradise") 50-100   49
   (10–inch LP.)
DECCA (5376 "Galloping
   Guitars")................................ 50-75   52
   (10–inch LP.)
DECCA (8589 "More of Les").... 30-50   57

GLENDALE.................................... 5-8   78
LONDON...................................... 6-12   68-79
VOCALION 6-12   68
Also see ANDREWS SISTERS
Also see ATKINS, Chet, & Les Paul

PAUL, Les, & Mary Ford   *P&R '50*
(Mary Ford with Les Paul; Mary Ford)
Singles: 78rpm
CAPITOL.................................... 5-15   50-57
Singles: 7–inch
CALENDAR 3-5
CAPITOL.................................... 5-15   50-57
COLUMBIA 4-10   58-64
Picture Sleeves
COLUMBIA 4-8   58-64
EPs: 7–inch 33/45rpm
CAPITOL.................................... 10-20   50-57
LPs: 10/12–inch 33rpm
CAPITOL (SM-200 series)............. 5-8   78
CAPITOL (H-226 thru H-577) 25-50   50-55
   (10–inch LPs.)
CAPITOL (T-226 thru T-802).....20-40   55-57
CAPITOL (T-1400 & T-1500
   series)...................................15-25   60-61
   (Monaural.)
CAPITOL (ST-1400 & ST-1500
   series)...................................20-30   60-61
   (Stereo.)
CAPITOL (11000 series) 5-10   74
COLUMBIA 10-20   61-63
HARMONY................................... 8-12   61-65
Also see PAUL, Les

PAXTON, Gary   *C&W '76*
(With the Road Runners; with Nashville
Mavericks; Gary S. Paxton)
Singles: 7–inch
BAKERSFIELD CENTENNIAL 3-5
CAPITOL......................................4-8   65-67
FELSTED......................................5-10   63
GARPAX.......................................5-10   63-64
LIBERTY 5-10   62-63
LONDON.......................................4-8   64
LUTE...5-10   60
MGM...3-5   71
RCA 3-5   73-76
LPs: 10/12–inch 33rpm
GASLIGHT....................................10-15
NEW PAX 5-10   76-80
PARAGON 5-10   79
PAX...5-10   78-79

257

PAYCHECK, Johnny   *C&W '65*
(With Charnissa)

Singles: 7–inch

ABC	3-5	74
AMI	3-5	84-85
CENTRON	4-6	70
CUTLASS	3-5	72
DAMASCUS	3-4	89
DESPERADO	3-4	88
EPIC	3-5	71-82
HILLTOP	8-15	64-66
LITTLE DARLIN' (008 thru 0072)	5-10	66-69
LITTLE DARLIN' (7000 series)	3-5	78-79
MERCURY	3-5	86-87

LPs: 10/12–inch 33rpm

ACCORD	5-10	82
ALLEGIANCE	5-10	83
CENTRON	8-15	70
COUNTRY FIDELITY	5-8	83
EPIC	5-10	71-83
EXCELSIOR	5-8	80
GUSTO	5-10	83
IMPERIAL	5-10	80
LAKESHORE	5-8	
LITTLE DARLIN' (0571 thru 0792)	5-10	79-80
LITTLE DARLIN' (4001 "Johnny Paycheck at Carnegie Hall") (Monaural.)	20-30	66
LITTLE DARLIN' (4001 "Johnny Paycheck in Concert") (Repackage of *At Carnegie Hall.* Monaural.)	10-15	66
LITTLE DARLIN' (8001 "Johnny Paycheck at Carnegie Hall") (Stereo.)	20-30	66
LITTLE DARLIN' (8001 "Johnny Paycheck in Concert") (Repackage of *At Carnegie Hall.* Stereo.)	15-20	66
LITTLE DARLIN' (4003 thru 4006) (Monaural.)	10-20	66-67
LITTLE DARLIN' (8003 thru 8023) (Stereo.)	10-20	66-69
LITTLE DARLIN' (10000 series)	8-12	79
MERCURY	5-8	86
PICKWICK/HILLTOP	5-10	72
POWER PAK	5-8	

Session: Jordanaires.
Also see HAGGARD, Merle, & Johnny Paycheck
Also see JENNINGS, Waylon / Johnny Paycheck
Also see JONES, George, & Johnny Paycheck
Also see JORDANAIRES
Also see MILLER, Jody, & Johnny Paycheck
Also see TUBB, Ernest
Also see YOUNG, Donny

PAYCHECK & HAGGARD   *C&W '81*

Singles: 7–inch

EPIC	3-4	81

Members: Johnny Paycheck; Merle Haggard.
Also see HAGGARD, Merle
Also see PAYCHECK, Johnny

PAYNE, Dennis   *C&W '88*

Singles: 7–inch

TRUE	3-4	88

PAYNE, Jimmy   *C&W '69*

Singles: 7–inch

EPIC	4-6	66-69
VEE JAY	4-8	63

LPs: 10/12–inch 33rpm

EPIC	10-20	68

PAYNE, Jody, & Willie Nelson Family Band   *C&W '81*

Singles: 7–inch

KARI	3-5	81

Also see NELSON, Willie

PAYNE, Leon   *C&W '49*

Singles: 78rpm

CAPITOL	5-10	49
DECCA	5-10	54
STARDAY	5-10	55-56

Singles: 7–inch

DECCA	10-20	54
STARDAY	10-20	55-56

LP: 10/12–inch 33rpm

STARDAY (231 "Living Legend of Country Music")	25-50	63
STARDAY (236 "Americana")	20-40	63

Also see ROGERS, Rock

PEARCE, Kevin   *C&W '84*

Singles: 7–inch

EVERGREEN	3-4	87-88
ORLANDO	3-4	84-86

PEARL, Minnie: see MINNIE PEARL

PEDERSEN, Herb   *C&W '77*

Singles: 7–inch

EPIC	3-5	76-77

LP: 10/12–inch 33rpm

EPIC (34933 "Sandman")............ 5-10   77

Also see DESERT ROSE BAND
Also see HARRIS, Emmylou
Also see HILLMAN, Chris

PEEK, Everett   *C&W '77*

Singles: 7–inch

COMMERCIAL............................. 3-5   77

PEEL, Dave   *C&W '69*

Singles: 7–inch

CHART.. 3-5   69-71

LP: 10/12–inch 33rpm

CHART.. 6-12   71

Also see EATON, Connie, & Dave Peel

PEGGY SUE   *C&W '69*

Singles: 7–inch

DECCA.. 3-6   69-71
DOOR KNOB 3-5   77-80

LP: 10/12–inch 33rpm

DECCA.. 8-12   69-70
DOOR KNOB 5-10   77

PEGGY SUE & Sonny Wright   *C&W '79*

Singles: 7–inch

DOOR KNOB 3-5   79

LP: 10/12–inch 33rpm

COUNTRY INT'L........................... 5-10   83

Also see PEGGY SUE
Also see WRIGHT, Sonny

PENN, Bobby   *C&W '71*

Singles: 7–inch

50 STATES 3-5   71-76

LP: 10/12–inch 33rpm

50 STATES 5-10   70s

PENNINGTON, J.P.   *C&W '91*

Singles: 7–inch

MCA 3-4   91

Also see EXILE

PENNINGTON, Ray   *C&W '66*

Singles: 7–inch

CAPITOL.. 4-8   66-68
KING 5-10   63
LEE (502 "Boogie Woogie Country
   Girl") 50-75   56
LEE (504 "My Steady Baby") 50-75   58
MONUMENT 3-6   69-71
RUBY (290 "Fancy Free")......... 30-50   57

LPs: 10/12–inch 33rpm

MONUMENT...............................10-15   69-71

Also see BLUESTONE
Also see SWING SHIFT BAND

PENNY, Hank   *C&W '46*

Singles: 78rpm

DECCA 5-10   55
KING 5-10   46-52
RCA 5-10   50-53

Singles: 7–inch

DECCA 10-15   55
KING 10-20   52
RCA 10-20   50-53

LP: 10/12–inch 33rpm

AUDIO LAB (1508 "Hank
   Penny") 20-40   58
RAMBLER......................................8-12

Session: Noel Boggs; Boudleaux Bryant; Sheldon
Bennett; Eddie Duncan.
Also see THOMPSON, Sue

PENNY, Joe   *C&W '64*

Singles: 7–inch

DEL MAR 5-10   65
FEDERAL (12322 "Bip a Little, Bop a
   Lot") 100-200   58
SIMS 10-15   64

PEPPER, Brenda   *C&W '75*

Singles: 7–inch

PLAYBOY 3-5   75

PEREZ, Tony   *C&W '89*

Singles: 7–inch

REPRISE 3-4   89

PERKINS, Carl   *C&W/P&R/R&B '56*

(With the C.P. Express)

Singles: 78rpm

FLIP (501 "Movie Magg").......200-300   55
SUN (224 "Gone Gone
   Gone")...................................50-100   56
SUN (234 thru 287)....................25-75   56-57

Singles: 7–inch

AMERICA/SMASH........................3-5   86-87
BANTAM 4-6
COLUMBIA (3-41000 & 3-42000
   series) 20-40   60-62
   (Compact 33 Singles.)
COLUMBIA (4-41000 thru 4-43000
   series) 10-20   58-64
COLUMBIA (4-44000 & 4-45000
   series).......................................5-10   64-72

DECCA	5-10	63-64
DOLLIE	5-10	67
FLIP (501 "Movie Magg")	300-400	55
JET	3-5	79
MERCURY	4-6	73-77
MUSIC MILL	4-6	76
SSS/SUN	3-5	70s
SUN (224 "Gone Gone Gone")	75-125	56
SUN (234 "Blue Suede Shoes")	15-25	56
SUN (243 "Boppin' the Blues")	20-30	56
SUN (249 "Dixie Fried")	30-40	56
SUN (261 "Matchbox")	25-35	57
SUN (274 "Forever Yours")	25-35	57
SUN (287 "Glad All Over")	25-35	57

(Counterfeits exist of most early Sun releases.)

Picture Sleeves

COLUMBIA (41131 "Pink Pedal Pushers")	25-45	58
COLUMBIA (42405 "Hollywood City")	20-30	62
COLUMBIA (42514 "Hambone")	40-60	62

EPs: 7–inch 33/45rpm

COLUMBIA (12341 "Whole Lotta Shakin")	200-300	58
SUN (115 "Blue Suede Shoes")	100-200	58

LPs: 10/12–inch 33rpm

ACCORD	5-10	82
ALBUM GLOBE	8-12	
ALLEGIANCE	5-10	84
COLUMBIA (1234 "Whole Lotta Shakin")	100-200	58

(Red label.)

COLUMBIA (1234 "Whole Lotta Shakin")	150-250	58

(White label. Promotional issue only.)

COLUMBIA (9833 "Greatest Hits")	10-20	69
COLUMBIA (10117 "Greatest Hits")	8-10	74
DESIGN	10-15	60s
DOLLIE	10-20	67
GRT/SUNNYVALE	8-12	77
HARMONY	8-12	72
JET	8-10	78
KOALA	5-10	80
MERCURY	8-12	73
PICKWICK/HILLTOP	5-10	

ROUNDER	5-10	89
SSS/SUN	5-10	69-84
SUEDE	8-10	81
SUN (1225 "Dance Album")	500-750	57
SUN (1225 "Teen Beat")	200-250	61

(Repackage of *Dance Album*.)

TRIP	8-10	74
UNIVERSAL	5-10	89
TRIP	8-12	74

Also see McCARTNEY, Paul
Also see NELSON, Willie / Jerry Lee Lewis / Carl Perkins / David Allan Coe
Also see STATLER BROTHERS
Also see YOUNG, Faron / Carl Perkins / Claude King

PERKINS, Carl / Sonny Burgess
LPs: 10/12–inch 33rpm

SSS/SUN	5-10

Also see BURGESS, Sonny

PERKINS, Carl, Jerry Lee Lewis, Roy Orbison & Johnny Cash
LP '86

LPs: 10/12–inch 33rpm

AMERICA ("Class of '55")	20-30	86

(Mail-order edition. Has souvenir booklet and audio cassette with interviews of the singers.)

AMERICA/SMASH (830002 "Class of '55")	5-10	86
AMERICA/SMASH (830002 "Class of '55")	30-40	86

(Picture disc. Promotional issue only.)

Also see CASH, Johnny, Carl Perkins & Jerry Lee Lewis
Also see LEWIS, Jerry Lee, Carl Perkins & Charlie Rich
Also see ORBISON, Roy

PERKINS, Carl, & NRBQ
Singles: 7–inch

COLUMBIA	3-5	70

LPs: 10/12–inch 33rpm

COLUMBIA	10-15	70

Also see NRBQ
Also see PERKINS, Carl

PERKINS, Dal
C&W '68
Singles: 7–inch

COLUMBIA	4-6	68
VIV (102 "Shy")	10-20	57

PERRY, Brenda Kaye
C&W '78
Singles: 7–inch

MRC	3-5	77-79

Also see WALKER, Billy, & Brenda Kaye Perry

PETERS, Ben   *C&W '69*
Singles: 7–inch
CAPITOL	3-5	73
LIBERTY	3-6	69

PETERS, Debbie   *C&W '80*
Singles: 7–inch
OAK	3-5	80

PETERS, Doug   *C&W '88*
Singles: 7–inch
COMSTOCK	3-4	88

PETERS, Jimmy   *C&W '77*
Singles: 7–inch
MERCURY	3-5	77-78
SUNBIRD	3-5	80

PETERS, Jimmy, & Linda K. Lance   *C&W '79*
(Jimmie Peters & Linda K. Lance)
Singles: 7–inch
VISTA	3-5	79

Also see LANCE, Linda K.
Also see PETERS, Jimmy

PETERS & LEE   *C&W '74*
Singles: 7–inch
PHILIPS	3-6	65-74

LPs: 10/12–inch 33rpm
PHILIPS	8-12	65-66

Members: Lennie Peters; Dianne Lee.

PETERSON, Colleen   *C&W '76*
Singles: 7–inch
CAPITOL	3-5	76

LP: 10/12–inch 33rpm
CAPITOL	5-10	76-78

PFEIFER, Diane   *C&W '80*
Singles: 7–inch
CAPITOL	3-4	80-82

LP: 10/12–inch 33rpm
CAPITOL	5-10	80

PHILLIPS, Bill   *C&W '64*
(With Dolly Parton)
Singles: 7–inch
DECCA (Except 31901)	3-8	64-71
DECCA (31901 "Put It Off Until Tomorrow")	8-10	66
SOUNDWAVES	3-5	78-79
U.A.	3-5	72-73

LP: 10/12–inch 33rpm
DECCA (Except 4792)	15-25	67-70
DECCA (DL-4792 "Put It Off Until Tomorrow") (Monaural.)	15-20	66
DECCA (DL7-4792 "Put It Off Until Tomorrow") (Stereo.)	20-25	66
HARMONY	12-18	64
GUINNESS	5-10	
SEA SHELL	8-10	

Also see PARTON, Dolly
Also see TILLIS, Mel, & Bill Phillips

PHILLIPS, Charlie   *C&W '62*
Singles: 7–inch
COLUMBIA	4-8	62-63
CORAL (61970 "Be My Bride")	10-20	58

Also see HOLLY, Buddy

PHILLIPS, John   *P&R/C&W/LP '70*
Singles: 7–inch
ATCO	3-5	74
COLUMBIA	3-5	73
DUNHILL	3-5	70

LPs: 10/12–inch 33rpm
DUNHILL	10-15	70

Also see MAMAS & PAPAS

PHILLIPS, Stu   *C&W '66*
Singles: 7–inch
PARAGON	3-5	76
RCA	3-5	66-68

LP: 10/12–inch 33rpm
BANFF	15-30	
PARAGON	5-10	76
RCA	15-30	66-68
RODEO	30-50	

PIED PIPERS   *P&R '44*
(With Paul Weston's Orchestra)
Singles: 78rpm
CAPITOL	5-10	44-51
RCA	4-8	48

Singles: 7–inch
CAPITOL	8-12	49-51
RCA	5-10	48

EPs: 7–inch 33/45rpm
CAPITOL	10-20	50

LPs: 10/12–inch 33rpm

CAPITOL (H-212 "Harvest Moon")	30-45	50
(10–inch LP.)		

Members: Jo Stafford; Chuck Lowry; Hal Hopper; Clark Yocum; June Hutton; Sue Allen.
Also see MERCER, Johnny, Jo Stafford & Pied Pipers
Also see STAFFORD, Jo

PIERCE, Webb   *C&W '52*

Singles: 78rpm

DECCA	5-15	51-52
4 STAR	5-15	51-52

Singles: 7–inch

DECCA (28000 thru 30000 series)	10-20	52-59
DECCA (31000 thru 33000 series)	4-10	59-73
DECCA (46000 series)	8-12	51-52
4 STAR	10-15	51-52
KING	5-10	60
MCA	3-5	73-74
PLANTATION	3-5	75-77
SOUNDWAVES	3-4	83

EPs: 7–inch 33/45rpm

DECCA	10-20	53-65

LPs: 10/12–inch 33rpm

BULLDOG	5-10	
CASTLE	5-10	
CORAL	5-10	73
DECCA (181 "Webb Pierce Story")	15-25	64
(Includes booklet.)		
DECCA (DL-4015 "Webb with a Beat")	15-25	60
(Monaural.)		
DECCA (DL7-4015 "Webb with a Beat")	20-30	60
(Stereo.)		
DECCA (DL-4079 thru 4964)	10-25	60-67
DECCA (DL7-4079 thru 4964)	15-30	60-67
DECCA (5536 "Wondering Boy")	40-60	53
(10–inch LP.)		
DECCA (8129 "Webb Pierce")	20-40	55
DECCA (8295 "Wondering Boy")	20-40	56
DECCA (8728 "Just Imagination")	20-40	57
DECCA (DL-8889 "Bound for the Kingdom")	20-40	59
(Monaural.)		
DECCA (DL7-8889 "Bound for the Kingdom")	25-50	59
(Stereo.)		
DECCA (DL-8899 "Webb!")	20-30	59
(Monaural.)		
DECCA (DL7-8899 "Webb!")	25-35	59
(Stereo.)		
DECCA (74000 & 75000 series)	8-12	68-73
ERA	8-10	77
KING (648 "The One and Only Webb Pierce")	20-40	59
KOALA	5-8	80
MCA	5-12	73-78
MUSIC MASTERS	5-10	
PICCADILLY	5-8	80
PICKWICK/HILLTOP	10-15	65
PLANTATION	5-8	76-77
SEARS	8-12	60s
SKYLITE	5-8	77
VOCALION	5-15	66-70

Also see NELSON, Willie, & Webb Pierce
Also see SOVINE, Red, & Webb Pierce
Also see WELLS, Kitty, & Webb Pierce

PIERCE, Webb / Patsy Cline / T. Texas Tyler

LP: 10/12–inch 33rpm

DESIGN (901 "Three of a Kind")	8-12	63

Also see CLINE, Patsy
Also see TYLER, T. Texas

PIERCE, Webb / Loretta Lynn

LPs: 10/12–inch 33rpm

PHILCO/MCA	15-25	69

Also see LYNN, Loretta

PIERCE, Webb / Wynn Stewart

LPs: 10/12–inch 33rpm

DESIGN	8-12	62

Also see STEWART, Wynn

PIERCE, Webb, & Mel Tillis   *C&W '63*

Singles: 7–inch

DECCA	4-6	62

Also see TILLIS, Mel

262

PIERCE, Webb, & Wilburn Brothers   *C&W '54*

Singles: 78rpm

DECCA	5-10	54

Singles: 7–inch

DECCA.. 10-15   54

Also see PIERCE, Webb
Also see WILBURN BROTHERS

PILLOW, Ray   *C&W '65*
Singles: 7–inch

ABC... 4-6   68
ABC/DOT 3-5   74-75
CAPITOL...................................... 4-8   65-67
FIRST GENERATION 3-4   81
HILLTOP 3-5   78
MCA... 3-5   79
MEGA... 3-5   72-74
PLANTATION............................... 3-6   69
LP: 10/12–inch 33rpm

ABC... 8-12   69
ABC/DOT 6-12   74
ALLIGEANCE............................... 5-8   84
AUDIOGRAPH ALIVE................... 5-8   82
CAPITOL...................................... 10-20 65-67
FIRST GENERATION 5-10   81
MEGA... 6-10   72
PICKWICK/HILLTOP 8-10   70s
PLANTATION............................... 5-10   70

Also see SHEPARD, Jean, & Ray Pillow

PINETOPPERS   *C&W '50*
(With the Bever Valley Sweethearts)
Singles: 78rpm

CORAL.. 4-6   50-54
DECCA.. 3-5   54-56
Singles: 7–inch

CORAL.. 8-12   50-54
DECCA.. 5-10   54-56
PEER SOUTHERN 4-6   67
EPs: 7–inch 33/45rpm

CORAL.. 5-10   50-56
LPs: 10/12–inch 33rpm

CORAL.. 10-20 50-56

Members: Roy Horton; Vaughn Horton. Ray Smith;
Trudy Martin; Gloria Martin; John Bowers; Rusty
Keefer.

PINKARD & BOWDEN   *C&W '84*
Singles: 7–inch

W.B. 3-4   84-89

Members: Sandy Pinkard; Richard Bowden.
Also see SHILOH

PIRATES of the
MISSISSIPPI   *C&W '90*
Singles: 7–inch

CAPITOL...................................... 3-4   90-91

LPs: 10/12–inch 33rpm

CAPITOL....................................... 5-8   91

Members: Bill McCorvey; Rich Alves; Pat Severs;
Dean Townson; Jimmy Lowe.

PITNEY, Gene   *P&R '61*
Singles: 7–inch

COLLECTABLES...........................3-4   80s
EPIC...3-5   77
ERIC 3-4   70s
FESTIVAL (25002 "Please Come Back
  Baby")......................................15-20   61
MUSICOR (1000 series).............5-10   60-65
MUSICOR (1100 thru 1400 series)4-8   65-72
Picture Sleeves

MUSICOR (1000 series).............5-10   60-65
MUSICOR (1100 thru 1400
  series)......................................5-15   66-69
EPs: 7–inch 33/45rpm

MUSICOR (500 "Looking Through the Eyes of
  Love")......................................15-20   65
(Issued without cover. Promotional issue
only.)

LPs: 10/12–inch 33rpm

COLUMBIA HOUSE 10-15   75
(Columbia Record Club issue.)
EVEREST 5-8   81
KOALA 5-10   79
MUSIC DISC................................10-15   69
MUSICOR (1000 series).............8-10
MUSICOR (2001 thru 2008) 20-35   62-64
(Monaural.)
MUSICOR (2015 thru 2134) 15-25   64-67
(Monaural.)
MUSICOR (3001 thru 3008) 20-40   62-64
(Stereo.)
MUSICOR (3015 thru 3134) 15-25   64-67
(Stereo.)
MUSICOR (3148 thru 3193) 10-20   67-71
MUSICOR (3200 series).............8-12   71-73
MUSICOR (5025 "This Is Gene
  Pitney") 15-25   68
(Columbia Record Club issue.)
MUSICOR (5600 series).............8-10   78
PHOENIX 20................................6-12
RHINO 5-8   85
SPRINGBOARD 5-10   76
TRIP...5-10   76
51 WEST......................................5-10   79

Also see BRYAN, Billy
Also see JAMIE & JANE
Also see JONES, George, & Gene Pitney

PITNEY, Gene, & Melba Montgomery
C&W '66

Singles: 7–inch

MUSICOR 4-8   65

LPs: 10/12–inch 33rpm

BUCKBOARD 8-10   76

MUSICOR 15-20   66

Also see MONTGOMERY, Melba

PITNEY, Gene / Newcastle Trio

LPs: 10/12–inch 33rpm

DESIGN 8-12   60s

PITNEY, Gene / Tommy Roe / Bobby Rydell

INT'L AWARD 10-15   60s

Also see PITNEY, Gene

PLACE, Mary Kay
C&W/P&R '76

(Mary Kay Place as Loretta Haggers)

Singles: 7–inch

COLUMBIA 3-5   76-78

LPs: 10/12–inch 33rpm

COLUMBIA 5-10   76-77

Session: Willie Nelson.

PLACE, Mary Kay, & Willie Nelson
C&W '77

Singles: 7–inch

COLUMBIA 3-5   77

Also see NELSON, Willie
Also see PLACE, Mary Kay

PLOWMAN, Linda
C&W '71

Singles: 7–inch

COLUMBIA 3-5   73

JANUS 3-5   71

POACHER
C&W '78

Singles: 7–inch

REPUBLIC 3-5   78

Member: Tim Flaherty.

POCO
LP '69/C&W '79

Singles: 7–inch

ABC.. 3-5   75-79

ATLANTIC..................................... 3-4   82-84

EPIC... 3-6   69-75

MCA 3-5   79-82

RCA... 3-4   89

Picture Sleeves

EPIC 3-6   70-72

MCA 3-5   80

RCA... 3-4   89

LPs: 10/12–inch 33rpm

ABC.................................8-12   75-78

ATLANTIC................................5-8   82-84

EPIC (26460 "Pickin' Up the Pieces").....................................10-15   69

EPIC (26522 "Poco") 10-15   70

EPIC (30209 "Deliverin").............8-12   71

EPIC (EQ-30209 "Deliverin") 15-25   71 (Quadrophonic.)

EPIC (30753 "From the Inside")...5-10   71

EPIC (31601 "A Good Feelin' to Know") 5-10   72

EPIC (32354 "Crazy Eyes") 5-10   73

EPIC (EQ-32354 "Crazy Eyes") 10-15   73 (Quadrophonic.)

EPIC (32895 "Seven") 5-10   74

EPIC (33192 "Cantamos") 5-10   74 (Quadrophonic.)

EPIC (PEQ-33192 "Cantamos") 10-15   74

EPIC (33537 thru 36210).............5-10   75-81

MCA...5-10   80-82

MFSL (020 "Legend") 25-50   78

RCA 5-8   89

Members: Richie Furay; Jim Messina; Rusty Young; Timothy Schmit; Paul Cotton.
Also see EAGLES

POINTER, Anita
R&B '87

Singles: 7–inch

RCA 3-4   87-88

Also see CONLEY, Earl Thomas, & Anita Pointer
Also see POINTER SISTERS

POINTER, Bonnie
P&R/R&B/LP '78

Singles: 12–inch 33/45rpm

MOTOWN 4-8   78-81

PRIVATE I.....................................4-6   84-85

Singles: 7–inch

MOTOWN (Except 1451)...............3-5   78-81

MOTOWN (1451 "Free Me from My Freedom")......................................3-4   78 (Black vinyl.)

MOTOWN (1451 "Free Me from My Freedom")......................................4-8   78 (Colored vinyl.)

PRIVATE I.....................................3-4   84-85

Picture Sleeves

MOTOWN (1451 "Free Me from My Freedom")......................................3-5   78

LPs: 10/12–inch 33rpm

MOTOWN 5-10   78-79

PRIVATE I...................................5-8   84

Also see POINTER SISTERS

POINTER, June   R&B '83

Singles: 12–inch 33/45rpm

PLANET	4-6	83-84

Singles: 7–inch

PLANET	3-4	83-84

LPs: 10/12–inch 33rpm

PLANET	5-8	83

POINTER SISTERS

P&R/R&B/LP '73/C&W '74

Singles: 12–inch 33/45rpm

PLANET	4-8	78-85
RCA	4-6	85-86

Singles: 7–inch

ABC	3-6	75-78
ATLANTIC (2845 "Don't Try to Take the Fifth")	10-20	72
ATLANTIC (2893 "Destination, No More Heartaches")	10-20	72
BLUE THUMB	3-6	73-78
MCA	3-4	87
PLANET	3-5	78-85
RCA	3-4	85-88

Picture Sleeves

MCA	3-4	87
PLANET	3-5	78-85
RCA	3-4	85-86

LPs: 10/12–inch 33rpm

BLUE THUMB	8-12	73-77
MCA	5-10	81
PLANET	5-10	78-84
RCA	5-8	85-88

Members: Bonnie Pointer; Anita Pointer; Ruth Pointer; June Pointer.
  Also see POINTER, Anita, & Earl Thomas Conley
  Also see POINTER, Bonnie
  Also see POINTER, June

POLLARD, Chuck   C&W '78

Singles: 7–inch

MCA	3-5	78

POMSL, Pat   C&W '79

Singles: 7–inch

ASI	3-5	79

POOLE, Cheryl   C&W '68

Singles: 7–inch

PAULA	4-6	68-70

POSEY, Sandy   P&R/LP '66/C&W '71

Singles: 7–inch

AUDIOGRAPH	3-4	83

COLUMBIA	3-5	71-73
MGM	4-6	66-67
MONUMENT	3-5	76
POLYDOR	3-4	83
W.B.	3-5	76-79

Picture Sleeves

MGM	4-8	66-67

LPs: 10/12–inch 33rpm

COLUMBIA	5-10	72
51 WEST	5-8	83
GUSTO	5-8	80s
MGM	8-15	66-70

POSEY, Sandy / Skeeter Davis

LPs: 10/12–inch 33rpm

GUSTO	5-8	

Also see DAVIS, Skeeter
Also see POSEY, Sandy

POTTER, Curtis

Singles: 7–inch

DOT	3-5	71
FOX (409 "Real Glad Daddy")	150-250	58
HILLSIDE	3-5	80
WINSTON	10-15	59

LP: 10/12–inch 33rpm

DOT	10-20	71
HILLSIDE	5-10	80

Also see THOMPSON, Hank

POTTER, Curtis, & Darrell McCall   C&W '80

(With "Friend")

Singles: 7–inch

HILLSIDE	3-5	80

Also see McCALL, Darrell
Also see POTTER, Curtis
Also see SANDERS, Ray / Curtis Potter / Darrell McCall

POWELL, Pati, & Bob Gallion   C&W '73

Singles: 7–inch

METRO COUNTRY	3-5	73

Also see GALLION, Bob

POWELL, Sandy

Singles: 7–inch

HERALD (557 "Bon Bon")	60-80	61
SINGULAR (714 "My Jimmie")	10-20	58

Also see STREET, Mel, & Sandy Powell

POWELL, Sue   *C&W '81*

Singles: 7–inch

RCA.. 3-4   81
   Also see DAVE & SUGAR

POZO - SECO SINGERS   *P&R/LP '66*

**(Susan Taylor & the Pozo Seco Singers; Pozo
Seco; Pozo-Seco Singers Featuring Don
Williams)**

Singles: 7–inch

CERTRON 3-5   70
COLUMBIA 4-8   65-70
EDMARK................................... 10-20   65

LPs: 10/12–inch 33rpm

CERTRON 10-15   70
COLUMBIA 10-20   66-68
EXCELSIOR................................ 5-10   80
   Members: Don Williams; Susan Taylor; Lofton Kline.
   Also see WILLIAMS, Don

PRADO, Perez, & His Orchestra   *P&R '53/C&W '58*

Singles: 78rpm

RCA.. 4-6   50-58

Singles: 7–inch

RCA.. 5-15   50-64
U.A. 3-6   64

Picture Sleeves

RCA.. 8-10   59

EPs: 7–inch 33/45rpm

BELL (2 "Perez Prado") 5-10
RCA.. 8-15   54-61

LPs: 10/12–inch 33rpm

CAMDEN.................................. 10-15   60
RCA.. 5-10   76
  (With "ANL1" prefix.)
RCA.. 10-30   54-72
  (With "LPM," "LSP" or "VPS" prefix.)
SPIN-O-RAMA 8-12   62
SPRINGBOARD........................... 5-10   77
U.A. 10-15   65-68
   Also see CLOONEY, Rosemary, & Perez Prado
   Also see HIRT, Al / Henry Mancini / Perez Prado

PRESLEY, Elvis   *C&W '55*

**(With Scotty & Bill; with Jordanaires; with
Imperials; with J.D. Sumner & Stamps; with
Mello Men; with Amigos; with Jubilee Four &
Carol Lombard Trio)**

Singles: 78rpm

(Commercial and Promotional)

RCA (6357 "Mystery Train").. 100-150   55
RCA (6380 "That's All Right") 100-150   55

RCA (6381 "Good Rockin'
  Tonight") 100-150   55
RCA (6382 "Milkcow Blues
  Boogie") 100-150   55
RCA (6383 "Baby, Let's Play
  House") 100-150   55
RCA (6420 "Heartbreak
  Hotel") 75-100   56
  (Black label.)
RCA (6420 "Heartbreak
  Hotel") 400-500   56
  (White label. Promotional issue only.
  Opinions vary as to authenticity.)
RCA (6540 "I Want You, I Need You, I Love
  You").......................................75-100   56
  (Black label.)
RCA (6540 "I Want You, I Need You, I Love
  You").....................................400-500   56
  (White label. Promotional issue only.
  Opinions vary as to authenticity.)
RCA (6604 "Don't Be Cruel") ...75-100   56
  (Black label.)
RCA (6604 "Don't Be
  Cruel").................................400-500   56
  (White label. Promotional issue only.
  Opinions vary as to authenticity.)
RCA (6636 "Blue Suede
  Shoes") 75-100   56
  (Black label.)
RCA (6637 "I Got a Woman") ..75-100   56
  (Black label.)
RCA (6638 "I'm Gonna Sit Right Down and
  Cry").......................................75-100   56
  (Black label.)
RCA (6639 "Tryin' to Get to
  You").......................................75-100   56
  (Black label.)
RCA (6640 "Blue Moon") 75-100   56
  (Black label.)
RCA (6641 "Money Honey") 75-100   56
  (Black label.)
RCA (6642 "Lawdy Miss
  Clawdy")..................................75-100   56
  (Black label.)
RCA (6643 "Love Me
  Tender")..................................75-100   56
  (Black label.)
RCA (6643 "Love Me
  Tender").................................400-500   56
  (White label. Promotional issue only.   266
  Opinions vary as to authenticity.)
RCA (6800 "Too Much") 75-100   57
  (Black label.)

RCA (6800 "Too Much")........ 400-500   57
(White label. Promotional issue only.
Opinions vary as to authenticity.)

RCA (6870 "All Shook Up")..... 75-100   57
(Black label.)

RCA (6870 "All Shook Up")... 400-500   57
(White label. Promotional issue only.
Opinions vary as to authenticity.)

RCA (7000 "Teddy Bear")....... 75-100   57
(Black label.)

RCA (7000 "Teddy Bear")..... 400-500   57
(White label. Promotional issue only.
Opinions vary as to authenticity.)

RCA (7035 "Jailhouse Rock") . 75-100   57
(Black label.)

RCA (7035 "Jailhouse
Rock") 400-500   57
(White label. Promotional issue only.
Opinions vary as to authenticity.)

RCA (7150 "Don't") 75-100   58

RCA (7240 "Wear My Ring Around Your
Neck") 75-100   58

RCA (7280 "Hard Headed
Woman") 75-125   58

RCA (7410 "One Night") 400-500   58

ROYAL ("Elvis Presley
Show")................................. 150-250   56
(Single-sided disc, issued to radio stations to
promote Elvis in concert. Includes an
excerpt of *Heartbreak Hotel*.)

SUN (209 "That's All
Right") 600-1200   54

SUN (210 "Good Rockin'
Tonight").......................... 500-1000   54

SUN (215 "Milkcow Blues
Boogie") 600-1200   55

SUN (217 "Baby Let's Play
House") 500-1000   55

SUN (223 "Mystery Train").... 500-900   55

Notes: All Elvis RCA and Sun 78s were
simultaneously issued on 45rpm singles. For
78rpm plastic soundsheets and flexi-discs,
see a separate section that follows. RCA
and Sun 78s can be found with many label
variations. Sun promotional singles were
marked with the word "sample" rubber
stamped on the label. White label
promotional 78s are listed; however, their
authenticity has been seriously challenged.

Singles: 7–inch
(Commercial)

COLLECTABLES (Black vinyl)...... 3-5   86-87

COLLECTABLES (Gold vinyl)....... 3-5   92

RCA (0088 "Raised on Rock") 4-6   73

RCA (0130 "How Great Thou
Art")..15-20   69

RCA (0196 "Take Good Care of
Her")...4-6   74

RCA (0280 "If You Talk in Your
Sleep")......................................8-12   74
(Has title on one line.)

RCA (0280 "If You Talk in Your
Sleep") 4-6   74
(Two lines are used for title.)

RCA (0572 "Merry Christmas
Baby") 12-15   71

RCA (0619 "Until It's Time for You to
Go")..4-6   72

RCA (0651 "He Touched
Me") 100-150   72
(Has the *He Touched Me* side pressed at
about 35rpm instead of 45. These
copies—the result of a production
error—were commercial issues. Flip, *Bosom
of Abraham,* plays at 45rpm.)

RCA (0651 "He Touched Me").......4-6   72

RCA (0672 "An American
Trilogy")...................................15-20   72

RCA (0769 "Burning Love") 4-6   72
(Orange label.)

RCA (0769 "Burning Love") ...100-125   72
(Gray label.)

RCA (0815 "Separate Ways").......4-6   71

RCA (0910 "Fool") 4-6   73

RCA (1017 "It's Only Love")...........4-6   71

RCA (2458 "My Boy"/"Loving
Arms")...................................500-750   74
(Produced in the U.S. for European
distribution.)

RCA (6357 "Mystery Train").......30-40   55

RCA (6380 "That's All Right") 30-40   55

RCA (6381 "Good Rockin'
Tonight") 30-40   55

RCA (6382 "Milkcow Blues
Boogie") 30-40   55

RCA (6383 "Baby Let's Play
House")....................................30-40   55

RCA (6420 "Heartbreak
Hotel")......................................20-30   56

RCA (6540 "I Want You, I Need You, I Love
You")..20-30   56

RCA (6604 "Don't Be Cruel") 20-30   56

RCA (6636 "Blue Suede
Shoes").....................................30-40   56

RCA (6637 "I Got a Woman") ...30-40   56

RCA (6638 "I'm Gonna Sit
Right Down and Cry").............:.30-40   56

RCA (6639 "Tryin' to Get to You") .... 30-40 | 56
RCA (6640 "Blue Moon") .... 30-40 | 56
RCA (6641 "Money Honey") ..... 30-40 | 56
RCA (6642 "Lawdy Miss Clawdy") .... 30-40 | 56
(Dog is pictured on label.)
RCA (6642 "Lawdy Miss Clawdy") .... 150-200 | 56
(Dog is not shown on label.)
RCA (6643 "Love Me Tender") . 20-30 | 56
RCA (6800 "Too Much") .... 20-30 | 57
(Dog is pictured on label.)
RCA (6800 "Too Much") .... 200-300 · | 57
(Dog is not shown on label.)
RCA (6870 "All Shook Up") .... 20-30 | 57
RCA (7000 "Teddy Bear") .... 20-30 | 57
RCA (7035 "Jailhouse Rock") ... 20-30 | 57
(Black label, black vinyl.)
RCA (7035 "Jailhouse Rock") .... 750-1000 | 57
(Gold label, gold vinyl.)
Note: All RCA singles from 6357 through 7035 can be found on various black labels, both with or without a horizontal silver line.
RCA (7150 "Don't") .... 12-15 | 58
RCA (7240 "Wear My Ring Around Your Neck") .... 12-15 | 58
RCA (7280 "Hard Headed Woman") .... 12-15 | 58
RCA (7410 "One Night") .... 12-15 | 58
RCA (7506 "I Need Your Love Tonight") .... 12-15 | 59
RCA (7600 "A Big Hunk O' Love") .... 12-15 | 59
RCA (47-7740 "Stuck on You") ... 8-10 | 60
RCA (61-7740 "Stuck on You") .... 350-450 | 60
(Living Stereo.)
RCA (47-7777 "It's Now Or Never") .... 500-750 | 60
(Pressed without the piano track.)
RCA (47-7777 "It's Now Or Never") .... 8-10 | 60
RCA (61-7777 "It's Now Or Never") .... 400-600 | 60
(Living Stereo.)
RCA (47-7810 "Are You Lonesome To-night") .... 8-10 | 60
RCA (61-7810 "Are You Lonesome To-night") .... 400-600 | 60
(Living Stereo.)
RCA (37-7850 "Surrender") .. 450-550 | 61
(Compact 33 Single.)

RCA (47-7850 "Surrender") .... 8-10 | 61
RCA (61-7850 "Surrender") ... 600-800 | 61
(Living Stereo.)
RCA (68-7850 "Surrender") .... 1000-1500 | 61
(Stereo Compact 33 Single.)
RCA (37-7880 "I Feel So Bad") .... 800-1200 | 61
(Compact 33 Single.)
RCA (47-7880 "I Feel So Bad") ... 8-10 | 61
RCA (37-7908 "His Latest Flame") .... 1500-2500 | 61
(Compact 33 Single.)
RCA (47-7908 "His Latest Flame") .... 8-10 | 61
RCA (37-7968 "Can't Help Falling in Love") .... 3000-4000 | 61
(Compact 33 Single.)
RCA (47-7968 "Can't Help Falling in Love") .... 8-10 | 61
RCA (37-7992 "Good Luck Charm") .... 4000-5000 | 62
(Compact 33 Single.)
RCA (47-7992 "Good Luck Charm") .... 8-10 · | 62
RCA (8041 "She's Not You") .... 8-10 | 62
RCA (8100 "Return to Sender") ... 8-10 | 62
RCA (8134 "One Broken Heart for Sale") .... 8-10 | 63
RCA (8188 "Devil in Disguise") .... 75-100 | 63
(Flip side title is incorrectly shown as *Please Don't Drag That String ALONG.*)
RCA (8188 "Devil in Disguise") .... 6-10 | 63
(Flip side title correctly shown as *Please Don't Drag That String AROUND.*)
RCA (8243 "Bossa Nova Baby") .... 6-10 | 63
RCA (8307 "Kissin' Cousins") ...... 6-10 | 64
RCA (8360 "Viva Las Vegas") ..... 6-10 | 64
RCA (8400 "Such a Night") .... 6-10 | 64
RCA (8440 "Ask Me") .... 6-10 | 64
RCA (8500 "Do the Clam") .... 6-10 | 65
RCA (8585 "Easy Question") .... 6-10 | 65
RCA (8657 "I'm Yours") .... 6-10 | 65
RCA (8740 "Tell Me Why") .... 6-10 | 65
RCA (8780 "Frankie and Johnny") .... 6-10 | 66
RCA (8870 "Love Letters") .... 6-10 | 66
RCA (8941 "Spinout") .... 6-10 | 66
RCA (8950 "If Everyday Was Like Christmas") .... 6-10 | 66

RCA (9056 "Indescribably
Blue") 6-10   67
RCA (9115 "Long Legged Girl") .. 6-10   67
RCA (9287 "There's Always
Me")... 6-10   67
RCA (9341 "Big Boss Man") 6-10   67
RCA (9425 "Guitar Man")............ 6-10   68
RCA (9465 "U.S. Male").............. 6-10   68
RCA (9547 "Your Time
Hasn't Come Yet Baby") 6-10   68
RCA (9600 "You'll Never Walk
Alone") 6-10   68
RCA (9610 "Almost in Love") 6-10   68

Note: Commercial issues of all RCA singles
from 6357 through 9600 are on black labels.

RCA (9670 "If I Can Dream") 4-6   68
RCA (9731 "Memories")................ 4-6   69
RCA (9741 "In the Ghetto")........... 4-6   69
RCA (9747 "Clean Up
Your Own Back Yard")................ 4-6   69
RCA (9764 "Suspicious Minds").... 4-6   69
RCA (9768 "Don't Cry Daddy") 4-6   69
RCA (9791 "Kentucky Rain") 4-6   70
RCA (9835 "The Wonder of
You") 4-6   70
RCA (9873 "I've Lost You")........... 4-6   70
RCA (9916 "You Don't Have to Say You Love
Me")... 4-6   70
RCA (9960 "I Really Don't Want to
Know").. 4-6   70
RCA (9980 "Rags to Riches") 4-6   71
RCA (9985 "Life").......................... 4-6   71
RCA (9998 "I'm Leavin") 4-6   71

Note: RCA numbers in the 10000 to 14000
series with a "GB" prefix are Gold Standards
and are listed in a separate Gold Standard
Singles section.

RCA (10074 "Promised Land") 4-6   74
(Orange label.)
RCA (10074 "Promised Land") . 20-30   74
(Gray label.)
RCA (10191 "My Boy").................. 4-6   75
(Orange label.)
RCA (10191 "My Boy")................ 8-12   75
(Tan or brown label.)
RCA (10278 "T-r-o-u-b-l-e") 4-6   75
(Orange label.)
RCA (10278 "T-r-o-u-b-l-e") 8-10   75
(Tan label.)
RCA (10278 "T-r-o-u-b-l-e") 75-100   75
(Gray label.)

RCA (10401 "Bringing It
Back") 150-200   75
(Orange label.)
RCA (10401 "Bringing It Back") 4-6   75
(Tan label.)
RCA (10601 "For the Heart") 4-6   76
(Tan label.)
RCA (10601 "For the Heart") ...90-100   76
(Black label.)
RCA (10857 "Moody Blue") 3-5   76
(Black vinyl. Colored vinyl 45s of *Moody
Blue*, were experimental and are listed in the
Promotional Singles section that follows.)
RCA (10998 "Way Down") 3-5   77
RCA (11099 thru 11113)................3-4   77
(Discs in this series were originally
packaged in either 11301 and/or 11340, both
of which are boxed sets of singles with
sleeves.)
RCA (11165 "My Way") 3-5   77
(Flip side shown as *America*.)
RCA (11165 "My Way") 15-20   77
(Fith flip side shown as *America the
Beautiful*.)
RCA (11212 " Unchained
Melody")......................................3-5   78
RCA (11301 "15 Golden
Records")................................45-55   77
(Boxed set of 15 Elvis singles with picture
sleeves.)
RCA (11320 "Teddy Bear")............3-5   78
RCA (11340 "20 Golden Hits")...65-75   77
(Boxed set of 10 Elvis singles with picture
sleeves.)
RCA (11533 "Are You Sincere") ...3-5   79
RCA (11679 "I Got a Feelin' in My
Body")......................................12-18   79
(With production and backing credits shown
on label.)
RCA (11679 ("I Got a Feelin' in My
Body")..3-5   79
(With backing credits removed, leaving only
production credits.)
RCA (12158 "Guitar Man")............3-5   81
RCA (12205 "Lovin' Arms")............3-5   81
RCA (13058 "You'll Never Walk
Alone") 3-5   82
RCA (13351 "The Elvis Medley") .'.3-5   82
RCA (13500 "I Was the One") 3-5   83
RCA (13547 "Little Sister").............3-5   83
RCA (13875 "Baby, Let's Play
House")....................................30-40   84
(Colored vinyl.)

RCA (13885 thru 13890) 3-4   84
(Discs in this series were originally
packaged in 13897, *Golden Singles, Vol. I.*
May include jukebox title strips.)

RCA (13891 thru 13896) 3-4   84
(Discs in this series were originally
packaged in 13898, *Golden Singles, Vol. II.*
May include jukebox title strips.)

RCA (13897 "Golden Singles,
Vol. I") 15-25   84
(Package of six colored vinyl singles with
sleeves.)

RCA (13898 "Golden Singles,
Vol. II") 15-25   84
(Package of six colored vinyl singles with
sleeves.)

RCA (13929 "Blue Suede
Shoes") 10-15   84
(Colored vinyl. Incorrectly shows *Blue Suede
Shoes* as stereo and *Promised Land* as
mono.)

RCA (13929 "Blue Suede
Shoes") 8-12   84
(Colored vinyl. Correctly shows *Blue Suede
Shoes* as mono and *Promised Land* as
stereo.)

RCA (14090 "Always on My
Mind") 8-12   85
(Colored vinyl.)

RCA (14237 "Merry Christmas
Baby") 10-15   85
(Black vinyl.)

RCA (14237 "Merry Christmas
Baby") 10-15   85
(Colored vinyl.)

RCA (62402 "Don't Be Cruel") .. 10-15   92
(Colored vinyl.)

RCA (62403 "Blue Christmas") . 10-15   92
(Colored vinyl.)

RCA (62449 "Heartbreak
Hotel") 10-15   92
(Colored vinyl.)

Note: RCA numbers in the 10000-14000
series with a "GB" prefix are Gold Standard
Series and are listed in a separate Gold
Standard Singles section. Regular series
issues are in the preceding section.

SUN (209 "That's All Right") .. 500-750   54

SUN (210 "Good Rockin'
Tonight") 500-750   54

SUN (215 "Milkcow Blue
Boogie") 750-1000   55

SUN (217 "Baby Let's Play
House") 500-750   55

SUN (223 "Mystery Train") 450-550   55

TRIBUTE (501 "A Tribute to Elvis
Presley") 50-100   56
(Has Elvis plus guest appearances by
Edward R. Murrow, Steve Allen, Ed Sullivan,
Danny Kaye, Jimmy Durante, Gabriel
Heater, Sid Ceaser, Liberace, Mantovani,
Jack Benny, Gene Vincent, Gloria DeHaven,
Nat King Cole, Nelson Eddy, and Jane
Russell.)

Note: Plastic soundsheets or flexi-discs are
listed in a separate section that follows.

Picture Sleeves
(Commercial and Promotional)

LAUREL (41 623 "Treat Me
Nice") 5000-7500   57
(Pictures Elvis but credits Vince Everett.
Black and white sleeve made as a prop for
the *Jailhouse Rock* film. The printed sheets
have no reverse side, but are applied to a
randomly selected EP. No Laurel records of
this title exist. Unlike 41 624 and 41 625,
there is no question about the authenticity of
this sleeve.)

LAUREL (41 624 "Jailhouse
Rock") 75-100   57

LAUREL (41 625 "Young and
Beautiful") 75-100   57
(Above two picture Elvis but credit Vince
Everett. Black-and-white, cardboard, EP-like
cover. May have been made as a film prop.
While many researchers question the
authenticity—and therefore the date of
production—of these, these prices have
been paid. No Laurel records of these titles
exist.).

PECA ("Could I Fall in
Love") 4000-6000   66
(Pictures Elvis but credits Guy Lambert with
George and His G-Men. A full color sleeve
made as a prop for the *Double Trouble* film.
No Peca records of this title exist.)

RCA (76 "Don't"/"Wear My Ring Around Your
Neck") 1000-1500   60
(Promotional issue only.)

RCA (0088 "Raised on Rock") 8-12   73

RCA (118 "King of the
Whole Wide World") 150-200   62
(Promotional issue only.)

RCA (0130 "How Great Thou
Art") 100-150   69

RCA (162 "How Great Thou   270
Art") 150-200   67
(Promotional issue only.)

RCA (0196 " Take Good Care of
Her") 8-12   74

RCA (0280 "If You Talk in Your
Sleep") 8-12   74

RCA (0572 "Merry Christmas
Baby") 20-30   71

RCA (0619 "Until It's Time for You to
Go")... 8-12   71

RCA (0651 "He Touched Me").. 50-75   71

RCA (0672 "An American
Trilogy")................................. 15-25   72

RCA (0769 "Burning Love") 8-12   72

RCA (0815 "Separate Ways")..... 8-12   71

RCA (0910 "Fool")....................... 8-12   73

RCA (1017 "It's Only Love")........ 8-12   71

RCA (6357 "I Want You, I Need You, I Love
You") 1000-2000   55
(Cartoon "This Is His Life" series. Promo
only.)

RCA (6604 "Don't Be Cruel") 65-75   56
(Shows *Don't Be Cruel* c/w *Hound Dog*.)

RCA (6604 "Hound Dog") 55-65   56
(Shows *Hound Dog* c/w *Don't Be Cruel*.)

RCA (6643 "Love Me
Tender") 100-150   56
(Black and white sleeve.)

RCA (6643 "Love Me Tender") . 60-75   56
(Black and green sleeve.)

RCA (6643 "Love Me Tender") . 35-45   56
(Black and dark pink sleeve.)

RCA (6643 "Love Me Tender") . 30-40   56
(Black and light pink sleeve.)

RCA (6800 "Too Much")............ 50-75   57

RCA (6870 "All Shook Up")....... 50-75   57

RCA (7000 "Teddy Bear") 40-60   57

RCA (7035 "Jailhouse Rock") ... 40-60   57
(Sleeve only.)

RCA/MGM "Jailhouse
Rock") 750-1000   57
(MGM *Jailhouse Rock* film preview invitation
ticket. A promotional item for the media, the
ticket came wrapped around a commercial
single and sleeve. Deduct about 50% if ticket
stub is detached.)

RCA (7150 "Don't") 40-50   58

RCA (7240 "Wear My Ring Around Your
Neck") 40-50   58

RCA (7280 "Hard Headed
Woman") 35-45   58

RCA (7410 "One Night") 35-45   58

RCA (7506 "I Need Your Love
Tonight")............................. 300-500   59
(Has advertising for the *Elvis Sails* EP on
reverse.)

RCA (7506 "I Need Your Love
Tonight")................................. 25-35   59

(Has a listing of Elvis EPs and 45s on
reverse.)

RCA (7600 "A Big Hunk O'
Love").....................................25-35   59

RCA (7740 "Stuck on You").......15-25   60

RCA (7777 "It's Now Or
Never").....................................15-25   60

RCA (7810 "Are You Lonesome
To-night").................................15-25   60

RCA (37-7850 "Surrender") ...600-750   61
(Compact 33 Single sleeve. Copies without
some ring wear are very scarce.)

RCA (47-7850 "Surrender") 15-20   61

RCA (37-7880 "I Feel So
Bad")...................................800-1200   61
(Compact 33 Single sleeve.)

RCA (47-7880 "I Feel So Bad") .15-25   61

RCA (37-7908 "His Latest
Flame") 1800-2200   61
(Compact 33 Single sleeve.)

RCA (47-7908 "His Latest
Flame") 15-25   61

RCA (37-7968 "Can't Help Falling in
Love")................................3000-4000   61
(Compact 33 Single sleeve.)

RCA (47-7968 "Can't Help Falling in
Love").......................................15-20   61

RCA (37-7992 "Good Luck
Charm")..............................4000-5000   62
(Compact 33 Single sleeve.)

RCA (47-7992 "Good Luck
Charm").....................................15-20   62

RCA (8041 "She's Not You")......15-20   62

RCA (8100 "Return to Sender") .15-20   62

RCA (8134 "One Broken Heart for
Sale") 15-20   63

RCA (8188 "Devil in Disguise")..15-20   63

RCA (8243 "Bossa Nova
Baby")......................................15-20   63

RCA (8307 "Kissin' Cousins") 15-20   64

RCA (8360 "Viva Las Vegas") ...15-20   64

RCA (8400 "Such a Night")........15-20   64

RCA (8440 "Ask Me") 15-20   64

RCA (8500 "Do the Clam") 15-20   65

RCA (8585 "Easy Question").....15-20   65

RCA (8657 "I'm Yours") 15-20   65

RCA (8740 "Tell Me Why") 15-20   65

RCA (8780 "Frankie and
Johnny").................................15-20   66

RCA (8870 "Love Letters").........15-20   66

RCA (8941 "Spinout") 15-20   66

RCA (8950 "If Everyday Was Like
Christmas") 15-20   66

RCA (9056 "Indescribably
Blue") 15-20   67

RCA (9115 "Long Legged
Girl") 15-20   67

RCA (9287 "There's Always
Me") 15-20   67

RCA (9341 "Big Boss Man") 15-20   67

RCA (9425 "Guitar Man") 10-20   68

RCA (9465 "U.S. Male") 10-20   68

RCA (9547 "Your Time Hasn't Come Yet
Baby") 10-20   68

RCA (9600 "You'll Never Walk
Alone") 50-75   68

RCA (9610 "Almost in Love") 10-15   68

RCA (9670 "If I Can Dream") 10-15   68

RCA (9731 "Memories") 10-15   69

RCA (9741 "In the Ghetto") 10-15   69

RCA (9747 "Clean Up Your Own Back
Yard") 10-15   69

RCA (9764 "Suspicious Minds").. 8-12   69

RCA (9768 "Don't Cry Daddy") ... 8-12   69

RCA (9791 "Kentucky Rain") 8-12   70

RCA (9835 "The Wonder of
You") 8-12   70

RCA (9873 "I've Lost You") 8-12   70

RCA (9916 "You Don't Have to Say You Love
Me") 8-12   70

RCA (9960 "I Really Don't Want to
Know") 8-12   70

RCA (9980 "Where Did They Go
Lord") 8-15   71

RCA (9985 "Life") 20-30   71

RCA (9998 "I'm Leavin") 8-15   71

RCA (10074 "Promised Land") ... 8-10   74

RCA (10191 "My Boy") 8-10   75

RCA (10278 "T-r-o-u-b-l-e") 8-10   75

RCA (10401 "Bringing It Back") .. 8-12   75

RCA (10601 "For the Heart") 8-10   76

RCA (10857 "Moody Blue") 6-10   76

RCA (10998 "Way Down") 6-10   77

RCA (11099 thru 11113) 3-4   77
(Sleeves in this series were originally
packaged in either RCA 11301 and/or
11340, both boxed sets of singles with
sleeves.)

RCA (11165 "My Way") 6-10   77
(Flip side title shown as *America*.)

RCA (11165 "My Way") 15-25   77
(Flip side title shown as *America the
Beautiful*)

RCA (11212 "Softly, As I Leave
You") 5-10   78

RCA (11320 "Teddy Bear") 5-10   78

RCA (11533 "Are You
Sincere") 5-10   79

RCA (11679 "I Got a Feelin'
in My Body") 5-10   79

RCA (12158 "Guitar Man") 5-10   81

RCA (13058 "You'll Never Walk
Alone") 5-10   82

RCA (13302 "The Impossible
Dream") 75-100   82
(Promotional issue only.)

RCA (13351 "The Elvis
Medley") 5-10   82

RCA (13500 "I Was the One") 5-10   83

RCA (13547 "Little Sister") 5-10   83

RCA (13875 "Baby, Let's Play
House") 20-40   84

RCA (13885 thru 13896) 3-4   84
(Sleeves in this series were originally
packaged in RCA 13897 and 13898, *Golden
Singles*.)

RCA (13929 "Blue Suede
Shoes") 5-10   84

RCA (14090 "Always on My
Mind") 5-10   85

RCA (14237 "Merry Christmas
Baby") 8-12   85

Notes:There may be slight price differences
between "Coming Soon" and "Ask For"
variations, with "Ask For" sleeves rarer
overall. Likewise for variations in colors and
paper stock used. Often, the difference is
simply which one is needed to complete a
run. Regardless, sleeve variations within the
price range given do not require separate
listings. If the value varies beyond the given
range, a separate listing will be added.
Sleeves for the RCA "447" Gold Standard
Series are listed in a separate section
following the Gold Standard Singles. A slight
premium—perhaps $3 to $5—may be placed
on RCA's "Living Stereo" paper sleeves.
These were used for many different RCA
stereo singles and were not exclusively an
Elvis item.

*Gold Standard Singles
with "447" prefix*
(Commercial)

RCA (0600 thru 0639) 10-20   59-64
(Black label, dog on top.)   272

RCA (0600 thru 0639) 8-10   65-66
(Black label, dog on side.)

RCA (0600 thru 0639) 20-30   68-69
(Orange label.)

RCA (0600 thru 0639) 5-8   70-74
(Red label.)

RCA (0600 thru 0639) 4-5   77
(Black label, dog near top.)

RCA (0640 thru 0642) 20-25   64
(Black label, dog on top.)

RCA (0640 thru 0642) 8-10   65-66
(Black label, dog on side.)

RCA (0640 thru 0642) 20-30   68-69
(Orange label.)

RCA (0640 thru 0642) 5-8   70-74
(Red label.)

RCA (0643 "Crying in the
Chapel") 6-10   65
(Black label, dog on side.)

RCA (0643 "Crying in the
Chapel") 5-8   70s
(Red label.)

RCA (0643 "Crying in the
Chapel") 4-5   77
(Black label, dog near top.)

RCA (0644 thru 0646) 25-35   65
(Black label, dog on top.)

RCA (0644 thru 0646) 8-10   65
(Black label, dog on side.)

RCA (0644 thru 0646) 20-30   68-69
(Orange label.)

RCA (0644 thru 0646) 5-8   70-74
(Red label.)

RCA (0644 thru 0646) 4-5   77
(Black label, dog near top.)

RCA (0647 thru 0650) 8-10   65
(Black label, dog on side.)

RCA (0647 thru 0650) 5-8   70-74
(Red label.)

RCA (0647 thru 0650) 4-5   77
(Black label, dog near top.)

RCA (0651 & 0652) 10-15   66
(Black label, dog on side.)

RCA (0651 & 0652) 5-8   70s
(Red label.)

RCA (0653 thru 0658) 8-10   66-68
(Black label, dog on side.)

RCA (0653 thru 0658) 5-8   70-74
(Red label.)

RCA (0653 thru 0658) 4-5   77
(Black label, dog near top.)

RCA (0659 "Indescribably
Blue") 10-15   70
(Red label.)

RCA (0660 "Long Legged
Girl") 35-45   70
(Red label.)

RCA (0661 "Judy") 10-20   70
(Red label.)

RCA (0662 "Big Boss Man") 8-12   70
(Red label.)

RCA (0663 thru 0685) 5-8   70-73
(Red label.)

RCA (0663 thru 0685) 3-5   77
(Black label, dog near top.)

RCA (0720 "Blue Christmas") 10-15   64
(Black label, dog on top.)

Gold Standard Singles
with "GB" prefix
(Commercial)

RCA (10156 thru 10489) 5-8   75-76
(Red label.)

RCA (10156 thru 10489) 4-5   77
(Black label, dog near top.)

RCA (11326 thru 13275) 4-5   77
(Black label, dog near top.)

Gold Standard *promotional* singles are in numerical sequence in the section for Promotional Singles.

Gold Standard
Picture Sleeves

RCA (0601 "That's All Right") 100-200   64

RCA (0602 "Good Rockin'
Tonight") 100-200   64

RCA (0605 "Heartbreak
Hotel") 100-200   64

RCA (0608 "Don't Be
Cruel") 100-200   64

RCA (0618 "All Shook Up") 100-200   64

RCA (0639 "Kiss Me Quick") 20-25   64

RCA (0643 "Crying in the
Chapel") 15-20   65

RCA (0647 "Blue Christmas") 20-25   65
(Pictures Elvis on a Christmas card among wrapped gifts.)

RCA (0647 "Blue Christmas") 8-10   77
(Pictures Elvis in a circle among colored ornaments.)

RCA (0650 "Puppet on a
String") 20-25   65

RCA (0651 "Joshua Fit the
Battle") 50-75   66

RCA (0652 "Milky White Way") .. 50-75   66

RCA (0651 & 0652 "Special Easter
Programming Kit") 750-1000   66
(Picture sleeve-mailer. Contained both 1966 Easter singles, *Joshua Fit the Battle* and *Milky White Way* in their sleeves and an Easter greeting card from Elvis. Price is for the complete kit.)

RCA (0651 & 0652 "Special Easter
Programming Kit")............... 750-850   66
(Picture sleeve-mailer only.)

RCA (0720 "Blue Christmas") ... 30-35   64

Promotional Singles

CREATIVE RADIO ("Elvis 10th Anniversary"/
"The Elvis Hour").................... 15-20   87
(Demonstration disc, promoting the
syndicated 10th anniversary radio special.)

CREATIVE RADIO ("Memories of Elvis"/ "The
Elvis Hour") 15-20   87
(Demonstration disc, promoting the
syndicated 10th anniversary radio special.)
For *Elvis 50th Birthday Special,* see
PRESLEY, Elvis / Buddy Holly.
For *The Elvis Hour,* see PRESLEY, Elvis /
Gary Owens.

CREATIVE RADIO ("Nearer My God to
Thee") 5-10   89
(Promotional souvenir only. Issued as a
bonus single with the LP, *Between Takes
with Elvis.*)

CREATIVE RADIO ("Mystery
Train") 5-10   92
(Single-sided demonstration disc, taken from
the syndicated 15th anniversary radio
special.)

PARAMOUNT PICTURES ("Easy Come,
Easy Go")............................ 200-400   67
(Issued only to select theatres, designed for
lobby play.)

PARAMOUNT PICTURES (1800 "Blue
Hawaii")................................ 300-500   61
(Single-sided pressing. Issued only to select
theatres, designed for lobby play. Has
excerpts of songs from the film.)

PARAMOUNT PICTURES (2017 "Girls! Girls!
Girls!") 500-750   64
(Issued only to select theatres, designed for
lobby play.)

PARAMOUNT PICTURES (2413
"Roustabout").................. 2000-4000   64
(Issued only to select theatres, designed for
lobby play. Track is an alternate take.)

RCA (15 "Old Shep")............. 600-800   56

RCA (76 "Don't"/"Wear My Ring Around Your
Neck") 600-800   60
(Issued with special sleeve, listed in the
Picture Sleeves section.)

RCA (0088 "Raised on Rock") 8-10   73
(Yellow label.)

RCA (118 "King of the Whole Wide
World") 175-225   62
(Issued with a special sleeve, which is listed
in the Picture Sleeves section. Includes dee
jay insert.)

RCA (0130 "How Great Thou
Art")...35-50   69
(Yellow label.)

RCA (139 "Roustabout")........200-250   64

RCA (162 "How Great Thou
Art").....................................150-200   67
(Issued with a special sleeve, listed in the
Picture Sleeves section.)

RCA (0196 "Take Good Care of
Her")...8-10   74
(Yellow label.)

RCA (0280 "If You Talk in Your
Sleep") 8-10   74
(Yellow label.)

RCA (0517 "Little Sister").......100-125   83
(12–inch single.)

RCA (0572 "Merry Christmas
Baby") 12-15   71
(Yellow label.)

RCA (0601 "That's All Right") ..50-100   64
(White label.)

RCA (0602 "Good Rockin'
Tonight") 50-100   64
(White label.)

RCA (0605 "Heartbreak
Hotel")...................................50-100   64
(White label.)

RCA (0608 "Don't Be Cruel") ...50-100   64
(White label.)

RCA (0618 "All Shook Up")......50-100   64
(White label.)

RCA (0619 "Until It's Time for You to
Go")..10-12   72
(Yellow label.)

RCA (0639 "Kiss Me Quick") 20-25   64
(White label.)

RCA (0643 "Crying in the
Chapel")..................................15-20   65
(White label.)

RCA (0647 "Blue Christmas")....25-30   65
(White label.)

RCA (0650 "Puppet on a
String")...................................25-30   65
(White label.)

RCA (0651 "Joshua Fit the
Battle") 50-100   66
(White label.)

RCA (0652 "Milky White
Way") 50-100   66
(White label. See Gold Standard Picture   274
Sleeves section for special mailing
sleeve used with 0651 & 0652.)

RCA (0651 "He Touched Me")...50-75   72
(Yellow label.)

RCA (0672 "An American Trilogy")................................... 12-15   72
(Yellow label.)

RCA (0720 "Blue Christmas") ... 25-30   64
(White label.)

RCA (0769 "Burning Love") 8-10   72
(Yellow label.)

RCA (0808 "Blue Christmas") 1500-2000   57

RCA (0815 "Separate Ways") 8-10   72
(Yellow label.)

RCA (0910 "Fool")....................... 8-10   73
(Yellow label.)

RCA (6357 "Mystery Train").. 200-300   55
(White "Record Prevue" label.)

RCA (8360 "Viva Las Vegas")... 20-25   64
(White label.)

RCA (8400 "Such a Night") 4000-5000   64
(White label.)

RCA (8440 "Ask Me")................ 20-30   64
(White label.)

RCA (8500 "Do the Clam")........ 20-25   65
(White label.)

RCA (8585 "It Feels So Right") . 20-25   65
(White label.)

RCA (8657 "I'm Yours").............. 20-25   65
(White label.)

RCA (8740 "Tell Me Why")........ 20-25   65
(White label.)

RCA (8780 "Frankie & Johnny")................................. 20-25   66
(White label.)

RCA (8870 "Love Letters")........ 20-25   66
(White label.)

RCA (8941 "Spinout")................ 20-25   66
(White label.)

RCA (8950 "If Everyday Was Like Christmas") 20-35   66
(White label.)

RCA (9056 "Indescribably Blue") 20-25   67
(White label.)

RCA (9115 "Long Legged Girl").. 20-25   67
(White label.)

RCA (9287 "There's Always Me").. 20-25   67
(White label.)

RCA (9341 "Big Boss Man") 20-25   67
(White label.)

RCA (9425 "Guitar Man").......... 15-20   68
(Yellow label.)

RCA (9465 "U.S. Male").............15-20   68
(Yellow label.)

RCA (9547 "Your Time Hasn't Come Yet Baby").......................................15-20   68
(Yellow label.)

RCA (9600 "You'll Never Walk Alone") 15-20   68
(Yellow label.)

RCA (9610 "Almost in Love").....10-15   68
(Yellow label.)

RCA (9670 "If I Can Dream").....10-15   68
(Yellow label.)

RCA (9731 "Memories")..............10-15   69
(Yellow label.)

RCA (9741 "In the Ghetto")........10-15   69
(Yellow label.)

RCA (9747 "Clean Up Your Own Back Yard").. 10-15   69
(Yellow label.)

RCA (9764 "Suspicious Minds")......................................10-15   69
(Yellow label.)

RCA (9768 "Don't Cry Daddy")..10-15   69
(Yellow label.)

RCA (9791 "Kentucky Rain") 10-15   70
(Yellow label.)

RCA (9835 "The Wonder of You")..10-15   70
(Yellow label.)

RCA (9873 "I've Lost You")........10-15   70
(Yellow label.)

RCA (9916 "You Don't Have to Say You Love Me") 10-15   70
(Yellow label.)

RCA (9960 "I Really Don't Want to Know") 10-15   70
(Yellow label.)

RCA (9980 "Where Did They Go Lord")..10-15   71
(Yellow label.)

RCA (9985 "Life").......................10-15   71
(Yellow label.)

RCA (9998 "I'm Leavin") 10-15   71
(Yellow label.)

RCA (10074 "Promised Land") 8-10   74
(Yellow label.)

RCA (10191 "My Boy") 8-10   75
(Yellow label.)

RCA (10278 "T-r-o-u-b-l-e")........8-10   75
(Yellow label.)

RCA (10401 "Bringing It Back") ...8-10   75
(Yellow label.)

RCA (10601 "Hurt")......................8-10   76
(Yellow label.)

RCA (10857 "Moody Blue")......... 6-10   76
(Yellow label. Black vinyl.)

RCA (10857 "Moody
Blue") 900-1000   76
(Experimental colored vinyl pressings. Not
intended for distribution.)

RCA (10951 "Let Me Be
There") 100-125   77

RCA (10998 "Way Down") 125-150   77
(White label.)

RCA (10998 "Way Down") 6-10   77
(Yellow label.)

RCA (11165 "My Way")............... 6-10   77
(Yellow label.)

RCA (11212 "Unchained
Melody")................................... 6-10   78
(Yellow label.)

RCA (11320 "Teddy Bear") 6-10   78
(Yellow label.)

RCA (11533 "Are You
Sincere") 6-10   79
(Yellow label.)

RCA (11679 "I Got a Feelin' in My
Body") 6-10   79
(Yellow label.)

RCA (12158 "Guitar Man").......... 6-10   81
(Yellow label. Black vinyl.)

RCA (12158 "Guitar Man").... 200-300   81
(Yellow label. Colored vinyl.)

RCA (12205 "Lovin' Arms").......... 6-10   81
(Yellow label. Black vinyl.)

RCA (12205 "Lovin' Arms")... 200-300   81
(Yellow label. Colored vinyl.)

RCA (13058 "You'll Never Walk
Alone") 6-10   82
(Yellow label.)

RCA (13302 "The Impossible
Dream")................................ 75-100   82

RCA (13351 "Elvis Medley") 6-10   82
(Yellow label. Black vinyl.)

RCA (13351 "Elvis Medley") . 200-300   82
(Gold label. Colored vinyl.)

RCA (13500 "I Was the One")..... 6-10   83
(Yellow label. Black vinyl.)

RCA (13500 "I Was the
One")................................... 200-300   83
(Yellow label. Colored vinyl.)

RCA (13547 "Little Sister").......... 6-10   83
(Yellow label. Black vinyl.)

RCA (13547 "Little Sister").... 200-300   83
(Blue label. Colored vinyl.)

RCA (13875 "Baby, Let's Play
House") 150-250   84
(Gold label. Colored vinyl.)

RCA (13929 "Blue Suede
Shoes) 6-10   84
(Gold label. Colored vinyl.)

RCA (14090 "Always on My
Mind")..6-10   85
(Gold label. Colored vinyl.)

RCA (14237 "Merry Christmas
Baby") 6-10   85

Note: Elvis 50th Anniversary singles—RCA
13875 through 14237—used the same gold
label for both commercial and promotional
issues. Promo singles have "Not For Sale"
printed on the label.

RCA (4-834-115 "I'll Be
Back") 4000-6000   66
(White label. Single-sided disc. Reads "For
Special Academy Consideration Only." Made
for submission to the Academy of Motion
Picture Arts and Sciences.)

ROYAL CARIBBEAN CRUISE LINES (12690
"Follow That Dream - Take 2") 10-20   90
(Souvenir disc for Elvis cruise passengers.)

UNITED STATES AIR FORCE (125 "It's Now
Or Never"): see PRESLEY, Elvis / Jaye P.
Morgan.

UNITED STATES AIR FORCE (159
"Surrender"): see PRESLEY, Elvis /
Lawrence Welk.

WHAT'S IT ALL ABOUT (78 "Life"): see
PRESLEY, Elvis / Helen Reddy

WHAT'S IT ALL ABOUT (1840 "Elvis
Presley") 70-75   80

WHAT'S IT ALL ABOUT (3025 "Elvis
Presley") 50-60   82

Note: Plastic soundsheets and flexi-discs are
listed in a separate section that follows.
Promotional 78s are included with Singles:
78rpm, at the beginning of the Presley
section.

Plastic Soundsheets/Flexi-discs

EVA-TONE (38713 "Elvis Speaks! The Truth
About Me")................................30-40
(Eva-Tone number is not on label but is
etched in the trail-off.)

EVA-TONE (52578 "The King Is Dead Long
Live the King")........................90-100   78

EVA-TONE (831942 "50,000,000 Elvis Fans
Weren't Wrong!") 5-10   83

EVA-TONE (726771 "The Elvis Presley
Story")...5-10   276

EVA-TONE (1037710 "Elvis
Live")......................................30-40   78
(Price for magazine, titled *Collector's
Issue,* with bound-in soundsheet.)

EVA-TONE (1037710 "Elvis
Live")....................................... 15-20   78
(Price for soundsheet only.)

EVA-TONE (1227785 "Thompson Vocal
Eliminator").............................. 15-20   78
(Has segments of songs by three artists
including Elvis.)

EVA-TONE (10287733 "Elvis: Six Hour
Special")................................... 15-20   77

EVA-TONE/RCA ("Love Me
Tender").................................... 25-35   74
(Price for April 1974 issue of *Teen Magazine*
with bound-in soundsheet.)

EVA-TONE/RCA ("Love Me
Tender").................................... 15-25   74
(Price for soundsheet only.)

LYNCHBURG AUDIO ("The Truth About
Me")...................................... 125-150   56
(Lynchburg Audio number is not on label but
is etched in the trail-off.)

RAINBO ("Elvis Speaks, in
Person")............................. 300-325   56
(Price for magazine, *Elvis Answers Back,*
with 78rpm flexi-disc still attached to front
cover.)

RAINBO ("Elvis Speaks, in
Person")............................. 100-125   56
(Price for flexi-disc only.)

RAINBO ("The Truth About
Me")..................................... 300-325   56
(Price for magazine, *Elvis Answers Back,*
with 78rpm paper flexi-disc still attached to
front cover.)

RAINBO ("The Truth About
Me")..................................... 100-125   56
(Price for flexi-disc only.)

Note: All soundsheets and flexi-discs were
used for some type of promotional purpose.

EPs: 7–inch 33/45rpm
(Commercial and Promotional)

RCA (22 "Elvis Presley") ... 1000-1500   56
(May have "Elvis" in either light or dark pink
letters on front cover. Two-EP bonus
promotional item. Discs are numbered 9121
& 9122.)

RCA (23 "Elvis Presley") ... 3500-5000   56
(Three-EP bonus promotional item. Includes
"How to Use and Enjoy Your RCA Victor
Elvis Presley Autograph Automatic 45
Victrola Portable Phonograph," which
represents $75 to $100 of the value. Discs
are numbered 9123, 9124 & 9125.)

RCA (128 "Elvis by Request")... 60-80   61

RCA (747 "Elvis Presley") 200-250   56
(Black label, without dog.)

RCA (747 "Elvis Presley").......75-100   56
(Black label, dog on top. Has song title strip
across the top of front cover.)

RCA (747 "Elvis Presley")..........50-70   65
(Black label, dog on side.)

RCA (747 "Elvis Presley")......100-200   69
(Orange label.)

RCA (747 "Blue Suede
Shoes")...............................600-750   56
(Temporary paper sleeve for 1956 issue of
EPA-747. Price is for sleeve only.)

RCA (821 "Heartbreak
Hotel")................................200-250   56
(Black label, without dog.)

RCA (821 "Heartbreak
Hotel")................................75-100   56
(Black label, dog on top. Has song title strip
across the top of front cover.)

RCA (821 "Heartbeak Hotel") ...50-70   65
(Black label, dog on side.)

RCA (821 "Heartbreak
Hotel")................................100-200   69
(Orange label.)

RCA (830 "Elvis Presley").......75-100   56
(Black label, dog on top. Has song title strip
across the top of front cover.)

RCA (830 "Elvis Presley")......200-250   56
(Black label, without dog.)

RCA (830 "Elvis Presley")..........50-70   65
(Black label, dog on side.)

RCA (830 "Elvis Presley")......100-200   69
(Orange label.)

RCA (940 "The Real Elvis") 75-100   56
(Black label, dog on top. Has song title strip
across the top of front cover.)

RCA (940 "The Real Elvis") ...200-250   56
(Black label, without dog. Reissued as Gold
Standard 5120.)

RCA (965 "Any Way You Want
Me") 75-100   56
(Black label, dog on top. Has song title strip
across the top of front cover.)

RCA (965 "Any Way You Want
Me") 200-250   56
(Black label, without dog.)

RCA (965 "Any Way You Want
Me") 50-70   65
(Black label, dog on side.)

RCA (965 "Any Way You Want
Me") 100-200   69
(Orange label.)

RCA (992 "Elvis, Vol. 1")..........75-100   56
(Black label, dog on top. Has song title strip
across the top of front cover.)

RCA (992 "Elvis, Vol. 1")....... 200-250   56
(Black label, without dog.)

RCA (992 "Elvis, Vol. 1").......... 50-70   65
(Black label, dog on side.)

RCA (992 "Elvis, Vol. 1")....... 100-200   69
(Orange label.)

RCA (993 "Elvis, Vol. 2")......... 75-100   56
(Black label, dog on top. Has song title strip across the top of front cover.)

RCA (993 "Elvis, Vol. 2")....... 200-250   56
(Black label, without dog.)

RCA (993 "Elvis, Vol. 2").......... 50-70   65
(Black label, dog on side.)

RCA (993 "Elvis, Vol. 2")....... 100-200   69
(Orange label.)

RCA (994 "Strictly Elvis") 75-100   56
(Black label, dog on top. Has song title strip across the top of front cover.)

RCA (994 "Strictly Elvis") 200-250   56
(Black label, without dog.)

RCA (994 "Strictly Elvis") 50-70   65
(Black label, dog on side.)

RCA (994 "Strictly Elvis") 100-200   69
(Orange label.)

RCA (1254 "Elvis Presley") ... 500-600   56
(Black label, without dog. Two EP set.)

RCA (1254 "Elvis Presley") ... 300-400   56
(Black label, dog on top. Two EP set.)

RCA (1254 "Most Talked-About New Personality")..................... 2500-3500   56
(Two EPs, also numbered 0793 & 0794, in a single pocket paper sleeve. Promotional issue only. Includes a copy of *Dee-Jay Digest,* which represents $50 to $75 of the value.)

RCA (1254 "Most Talked-About New Personality")........................ 500-750   56
(Price for the two EPs without the sleeve. Either disc would be worth about half the amount shown for both. Discs, numbered 0793 & 0794, are untitled. Promotional issue only.)

RCA (1-1515 "Loving You, Vol. 1") 75-100   57
(Black label, dog on top. Has song title strip across the top of front cover.)

RCA (1-1515 "Loving You, Vol. 1") 50-70   65
(Black label, dog on side.)

RCA (1-1515 "Loving You, Vol. 1") 100-200   69
(Orange label.)

RCA (2-1515 "Loving You, Vol. 2") 75-100   57

(Black label, dog on top. Has song title strip across the top of front cover.)

RCA (2-1515 "Loving You, Vol. 2") 50-70   65
(Black label, dog on side.)

RCA (2-1515 "Loving You, Vol. 2") 100-200   69
(Orange label.)

RCA (2006 "Aloha from Hawaii")....................................60-75   74
(Includes sheet of 10 title strips. Made for jukebox operators only.)

RCA (4006 "Love Me Tender")................................200-250   56
(Black label, without dog. Has song title strip across the top of front cover.)

RCA (4006 "Love Me Tender")..................................75-100   56
(Black label, dog on top. Has song title strip across the top of front cover.)

RCA (4006 "Love Me Tender") ..50-70   65
(Black label, dog on side.)

RCA (4006 "Love Me Tender")................................100-200   69
(Orange label.)

RCA (4041 "Just for You") 200-250   57
(Black label, without dog. Has EP title strip across the top of front cover.)

RCA (4041 "Just for You") 75-100   57
(Black label, dog on top. Has EP title strip across the top of front cover.)

RCA (4041 "Just for You") 50-70   65
(Black label, dog on side.)

RCA (4041 "Just for You") 100-200   69
(Orange label.)

RCA (4054 "Peace in the Valley")....................................75-100   57
(Black label, dog on top. Has EP title strip across the top of front cover. Reissued as Gold Standard 5121.)

RCA (4108 "Elvis Sings Christmas Songs") 75-100   57
(Black label, dog on top. Has EP title strip across the top of front cover.)

RCA (4108 "Elvis Sings Christmas Songs") 50-70   65
(Black label, dog on side.)

RCA (4108 "Elvis Sings Christmas Songs") 100-200   69
(Orange label.)

RCA (4114 "Jailhouse Rock")....65-85   57
(Black label, dog on top.)

RCA (4114 "Jailhouse Rock")....50-70   65
(Black label, dog on side.)

RCA (4114 "Jailhouse Rock") 100-200   69
(Orange label.)

RCA (4319 "King Creole") 75-100   58
(Reissued as Gold Standard 5122.)

RCA (4321 "King Creole, Vol. 2") 65-85   58
(Black label, dog on top.)

RCA (4321 "King Creole, Vol. 2") 50-70   65
(Black label, dog on side.)

RCA (4321 "King Creole, Vol. 2") 100-200   69
(Orange label.)

RCA (4325 "Elvis Sails") 75-100   58
(Reissued as Gold Standard 5157.)

RCA (4340 "Christmas with Elvis") 75-100   58
(Black label, dog on top.)

RCA (4340 "Christmas with Elvis") 50-70   65
(Black label, dog on side.)

RCA (4340 "Christmas with Elvis") 100-200   69
(Orange label.)

RCA (4368 "Follow That Dream") 70-90   62
(Black label, dog on top. Playing times are incorrectly listed for three of the four tracks: *Follow That Dream* shown as 1:35, should be 1:38; *Angel* shown as 2:35, should be 2:40; and *I'm Not the Marrying Kind* shown as 1:49, should be 2:00.)

RCA (4368 "Follow That Dream") 50-70   62
(Black label, dog on top. All playing times are correctly shown.)

RCA (4368 "Follow That Dream") 75-100   62
(Promotional issue only. Marked "Not For Sale.")

RCA (4368 "Follow That Dream") 120-160   62
(Special paper sleeve, issued to radio stations and jukebox operators. Promotional issue only. Price is for sleeve only.)

RCA (4368 "Follow That Dream") 50-70   65
(Black label, dog on side.)

RCA (4368 "Follow That Dream") 100-200   69
(Orange label.)

RCA (4371 "Kid Galahad") 60-80   62
(Black label, dog on top.)

RCA (4371 "Kid Galahad") 50-70   65
(Black label, dog on side.)

RCA (4371 "Kid Galahad") 100-200   69
(Orange label.)

RCA (4382 "Viva Las Vegas") ... 65-85   64
(Black label, dog on top.)

RCA (4382 "Viva Las Vegas") ... 50-70   65
(Black label, dog on side.)

RCA (4382 "Viva Las Vegas") 100-200   69
(Orange label.)

RCA (4383 "Tickle Me") 50-70   65
(Black label, dog on side.)

RCA (4383 "Tickle Me") 100-200   69
(Orange label.)

RCA (4387 "Easy Come, Easy Go") 50-70   67
(Black label, dog on side.)

RCA (4387 "Easy Come, Easy Go") 100-150   67
(White label. Promotional Issue Only.)

RCA (5088 "A Touch of Gold, Vol. I") 450-550   59
(Maroon label.)

RCA (5088 "A Touch of Gold, Vol. I") 75-100   59
(Black label, dog on top. Add $15 to $25 if accompanied by "I am a loyal Elvis fan" insert card.)

RCA (5088 "A Touch of Gold, Vol. I") 50-70   65
(Black label, dog on side.)

RCA (5088 "A Touch of Gold, Vol. I") 100-200   69
(Orange label.)

RCA (5101 "A Touch of Gold, Vol. II") 450-550   59
(Maroon label.)

RCA (5101 "A Touch of Gold, Vol. II") 75-100   59
(Black label, dog on top. Add $15 to $25 if accompanied by "I am a loyal Elvis fan" insert card.)

RCA (5101 "A Touch of Gold, Vol. II") 50-70   65
(Black label, dog on side.)

RCA (5101 "A Touch of Gold, Vol. II") 100-200   69
(Orange label.)

RCA (5120 "The Real Elvis") 500-750   59
(Maroon label. Reissue of 940.)

RCA (5120 "The Real Elvis") 55-75   59
(Black label, dog on top.)

RCA (5120 "The Real Elvis") 50-70   65
(Black label, dog on side.)

RCA (5120 "The Real
Elvis")................................. 100-200   69
(Orange label.)

RCA (5121 "Peace in the
Valley")................................ 500-750   59
(Maroon label. Reissue of 4054.)

RCA (5121 "Peace in the
Valley")................................. 60-80   59
(Black label, dog on top.)

RCA (5121 "Peace in the
Valley")................................. 50-70   65
(Black label, dog on side.)

RCA (5121 "Peace in the
Valley").............................. 100-200   69
(Orange label.)

RCA (5122 "King
Creole")......................... 1500-2500   59
(Maroon label. Reissue of 4319. Though we
have been told of the existence of this item
by one collector, it remains one of very, very
few U.S. Elvis collectibles that we have not
personally confirmed. Price estimate is
based on offers, as we know of no sales.)

RCA (5122 "King Creole")......... 60-80   59
(Black label, dog on top.)

RCA (5122 "King Creole")......... 50-70   65
(Black label, dog on side.)

RCA (5122 "King Creole")..... 100-200   69
(Orange label.)

RCA (5141 "A Touch of Gold,
Vol. 3") 425-500   60
(Maroon label.)

RCA (5141 "A Touch of Gold,
Vol. 3") 75-100   60
(Black label, dog on top.)

RCA (5141 "A Touch of Gold,
Vol. 3") 50-70   65
(Black label, dog on side.)

RCA (5141 "A Touch of Gold,
Vol. 3") 100-200   69
(Orange label.)

RCA (5157 "Elvis Sails") 50-70   65
(Black label, dog on top. Reissue of 4325.)

RCA (5157 "Elvis Sails") 50-70   65
(Black label, dog on side.)

RCA (5157 "Elvis Sails") 100-200   69
(Orange label.)

RCA (8705 "TV Guide Presents
Elvis") 1000-1500   56
(Price for disc only. Insert sheets are priced
separately below. No sleeve or special cover
exists for this disc. Promotional issue only.)

RCA (8705 "TV Guide Presents
Elvis")...................................50-100   56
(Price for "Elvis Exclusively" gray insert.)

RCA (8705 "TV Guide Presents
Elvis")...................................100-200   56
(Price for *Elvis Exclusively* pink insert, with
suggested continuity.)

RCA (9089 "SPD-15 Elvis
EP")......................................400-500   56
(Black label. Just the Elvis disc from SPD-
15.)

RCA (9089 "SPD-15 Elvis
EP")......................................400-500   56
(Gray label. The Elvis disc from SPD-15.
Gray label pressings were for jukebox
operators.)

RCA (9113 "SPD-19 Elvis
EP")......................................300-400   56
(The Elvis disc from SPD-19, *The Sound of
Leadership*.)

RCA (9141 "SPD-26 Elvis
EP")......................................200-250   56
(Black label. The Elvis disc from SPD-15,
Great Country/Western Hits.)

Note: Unless listed and priced separately, all
EP values include both disc and cover with
approximately half of the total attached to
each. Some of the rarer pieces that are often
traded individually (disc or sleeve), as well
as those sleeves that have an exceptionally
higher value than their disc, are listed
separately in this section. All EPs in the
5000 series are Gold Standard Series issues
although none are identified as such on the
labels, only on the covers. Remember, if you
don't find the EP in this section it may
contain two, three or four artists, and will be
listed following the Presley LP section.

LPs: 10/12–inch 33rpm
(Commercial and Promotional)

ABC RADIO (1003 "Elvis
Memories").........................475-575   78
(Three-LP boxed set. Add $25 to $50 if
accompanied by a 16-page programmer's
booklet and four pages of additional
information. Issued only to radio stations.
Add $40 to $50 if accompanied by a 7–inch
reel tape, with spots and promotional
announcements. Highlights of this program
were issued on Michelob 810.)

ASSOCIATED BROADCASTERS (1001
"Legend of a King")..............125-150   280
                                                            80
(White label. Advance pressing.)

ASSOCIATED BROADCASTERS (1001
"Legend of a King")..................25-30   80
(Picture disc. First pressings are

numbered from 3000 through 6000. Number appears under "Side One" on the disc itself. Cover is standard, die-cut, picture disc cover. Has several spelling errors on back cover, including "idle" for idol and "Jordinaires" instead of Jordanaires.)

ASSOCIATED BROADCASTERS (1001 "Legend of a King") 20-25   80
(Picture disc. Second pressings are numbered from 6001 through 9000. Most of the spelling errors were corrected on this cover.)

ASSOCIATED BROADCASTERS (1001 "Legend of a King") 15-20   80
(Picture disc. Third pressings are numbered from 00001 through 02999 and 09001 through 15000. Cover errors have all been corrected.)

ASSOCIATED BROADCASTERS (1001 "Legend of a King") 10-12   84
(Picture disc. Fourth pressings are also numbered from 3000 through 6000, but were packaged in a clear plastic sleeve instead of a conventional cover.)

ASSOCIATED BROADCASTERS (1001 "Legend of a King") 8-10   85
(Picture disc. Discs are not numbered. Packaged in a plastic sleeve.)

ASSOCIATED BROADCASTERS ("Legend of a King") 200-250   85
(Three hour, three-LP set. Not boxed. Price includes six pages of cue sheets. Available to radio stations only.)

ASSOCIATED BROADCASTERS ("Legend of a King") 300-350   85
(Same as above, but packaged in a specially printed box.)

ASSOCIATED BROADCASTERS ("Legend of a King") 300-350   86
(Three-LP boxed set, same as above except time on segment 1-B is increased from 14:25 to 15:15 in order to include a Johnny Bernero interview.)

ASSOCIATED PRESS (1977 "The World in Sound") 80-100   78
(News highlights of 1977, including coverage of Elvis' death.)

BOXCAR ("Having Fun with Elvis on Stage") 100-125   74
(No selection number used. Sold in conjunction with Elvis' concert appearances. Reissued as RCA CPM1-0818.)

CAEDMON (1572 "On the Record") 60-80   78
(Various news items and artists featured.)

CAMDEN (2304 "Flaming Star") 15-20   69
(First issued as RCA PRS-279, reissued in 1975 as Pickwick 2304.)

CAMDEN (2408 "Let's Be Friends") 15-20   70
(Reissued in 1975 as Pickwick 2408.)

CAMDEN (2428 "Elvis' Christmas Album") 15-20   70
(Eight songs on this LP were first issued on RCA LOC-1035. Reissued in 1975 as Pickwick 2428.)

CAMDEN (2440 "Almost in Love") 25-30   70
(With *Stay Away Joe.*)

CAMDEN (2440 "Almost in Love") 15-20   73
(*Stay Away* replaces *Stay Away Joe.* Reissued in 1975 as Pickwick 2440.)

CAMDEN (2472 "You'll Never Walk Alone") 15-20   71
(Reissued in 1975 as Pickwick 2472.)

CAMDEN (2518 "C'mon Everybody") 15-20   71
(Reissued in 1975 as Pickwick 2518.)

CAMDEN (2533 "I Got Lucky") .. 15-20   71
(Reissued in 1975 as Pickwick 2533.)

CAMDEN (2567 "Elvis Sings Hits from His Movies") 15-20   72
(Reissued in 1975 as Pickwick 2567.)

CAMDEN (2595 "Burning Love") 20-30   72
(Add $25 to $35 if accompanied by the bonus 8" x10" Elvis photo. Reissued in 1975 as Pickwick 2595.)

CAMDEN (2611 "Separate Ways") 15-20   73
(Reissued in 1975 as Pickwick 2611.)

CREATIVE RADIO ("Elvis Remembered") 100-125   78
(Three-LP set. Price includes six insert pages. Advance copies of this set, which was not issued with a special cover or package, were with plain white, handwritten, labels. These copies may be valued at $150 to $250. Promotional issue only.)

CREATIVE RADIO ("Elvis, the Country Side") 75-85   84
(Two-LP set. Promotional issue only.)

CREATIVE RADIO ("Elvis 50th Anniversary") 250-275   85
(Six-LP set. Price includes seven pages of programming instructions and cues. Packaged in a plain, unprinted box. Promotional issue only.)

CREATIVE RADIO ("Elvis 10th
Anniversary")...................... 150-175   87
(Six-LP set. Price includes eight pages of
programming instructions and cues.
Packaged in a custom printed box.
Promotional issue only.)

CREATIVE RADIO ("Christmas with
Elvis")...................................... 25-30   87
(Promotional issue only. Not issued with
special cover.)

CREATIVE RADIO ("Birthday Tribute
To Elvis").................................. 25-30   88
(Promotional issue only. Not issued with
special cover.)

CREATIVE RADIO ("The Elvis
Hour")...................................... 10-12   86-88
(Price is for any of the weekly discs in this
series. The first 52 discs in the series have
been selling as a set for $450 to $475.
Promotional issues only.)

CREATIVE RADIO ("Demo of 10 Creative
Radio Programs").................... 25-30   90s
(Includes segments of *The Elvis Hour, 10th
Anniversary Special* and *Memories of Elvis*,
along with portions of other shows by other
artists. Promotional issue only.)

CREATIVE RADIO (E1 "Elvis Exclusive
Interview") 175-200   88
(Price for *complete* 1956 Little Rock concert
copies. Only the first 100 copies were
pressed with the full concert. The only way
to visually identify these is to check the disc.
On the full concert pressings, the grooves
take up nearly the entire disc.)

CREATIVE RADIO (E1 "Elvis Exclusive
Interview") 20-30   88
(Has edited concert songs. On this pressing
the grooves occupy only about two-thirds of
the disc.)

CREATIVE RADIO ("Between Takes with
Elvis") 150-250   89
(Three-LP set. Promotional issue only.
Though not packaged inside covers—shrink
wrapped at the factory—each LP set came
with the bonus single, *Nearer My God to
Thee/You Gave Me a Molehill*.)

Note: On any of the above listings, Creative
Radio may be shown as Creative Radio
Shows or Creative Radio Network.)

DRAKE-CHENAULT ("Elvis: a Three Hour
Special")............................... 300-350   77
(Three-LP boxed set. Includes three pages
of cue sheets.)

EARTH NEWS ("August 29,
1977").................................... 325-375   77

(Promotional issue only. Price includes one-
page letter.)

ELEKTRA (60107 "Diner").........10-20   82
(Soundtrack.)

FRANKLIN MINT (4 "The Official Grammy
Award Winners").................150-200   85
(Boxed set of four colored vinyl discs. One in
a series of 14 boxed sets, but only this one
(titled *The Great Singers*) has Elvis. Includes
booklet.)

GOLDEN EDITIONS LIMITED (1 "The First
Year")..8-15   79
(Print in upper corners on front cover is in
white. Label is black. Add $5 to $8 if
accompanied by a 12-page booklet and one-
page copy of the 1954 Elvis/Scotty Moore
contract.)

GOLDEN EDITIONS LIMITED (101 "The First
Year").....................................15-25   79
(Print in upper corners on front cover is in
gold. Label is white. Add $5 to $8 if
accompanied by a 12-page booklet and one-
page copy of the 1954 Elvis/Scotty Moore
contract. Most of the material on this LP was
previously issued on HALW 00001.)

GREAT NORTHWEST (4005 "The Elvis
Tapes") 10-15   77
(These interviews were repackaged on
Starday 995.)

GREAT NORTHWEST (4006 "The King
Speaks") 8-10   77
(This press conference was first issued as
Green Valley 2001.)

GREEN VALLEY (2001 "Elvis 1961 Press
Conference")...........................30-50   77
(Cover is thin, soft stock and does not have
black bar on spine. Label does not show
selection number.)

GREEN VALLEY (2001 "Elvis 1961 Press
Conference")...........................12-15   77
(Cover is standard stock and has black bar
on spine. Label has the selection number.
Repackaged as one half of Green Valley
2001/2003. It was later repackaged as Great
Northwest 4006.)

GREEN VALLEY (2001/2003 "Elvis Speaks to
You").......................................25-30   78
(GV-2001 was first issued as a single LP.)

HALW (00001 "The First
Years")....................................25-30   78
(Repackaged in 1979 on Golden Editions
1.)   282

INTERNATIONAL HOTEL PRESENTS
ELVIS 1969......................1000-1500   69
(Custom gift box prepared by Col. Parker
and RCA for International Hotel guests.

Originally contained: RCA LPM-4088 & LSP-4155, three 8" x 10" Elvis photos, RCA Elvis catalog, calendar and a nine-page letter. Price is for complete set but box itself represents 90-95% of value.)

INTERNATIONAL HOTEL PRESENTS ELVIS 1970 1000-1500   70
(Custom gift box prepared by Col. Parker and RCA for International Hotel guests. Originally contained: RCA LSP-6020 & 45-9791, one 8" x 10" Elvis photo, photo album, RCA Elvis catalog, calendar, menu and letter. Price is for complete set but box itself represents 90-95% of value.)

K-TEL (9900 "Elvis Love Songs") 15-20   81

LOUISIANA HAYRIDE (3061 "The Beginning Years") 300-400   84
(White label advance pressing from RCA, Indianapolis, where this LP was manufactured.)

LOUISIANA HAYRIDE (3061 "The Beginning Years") 15-25   84
(Price includes 20-page *D.J. Fontana Remembers Elvis* booklet, a four sheet copy of Elvis' Hayride contract and a 10" x 10" *Presleyana, Second Edition* flyer, all of which represent about $5 to $10 of the value. Selections from this LP are also on the Music Works 3601 & 3602.)

LOUISIANA HAYRIDE (8454 "The Louisiana Hayride") 550-650   76
(Yellow label. A program of various artists including Elvis. Issued to radio stations only.)

LOUISIANA HAYRIDE (8454 "The Louisiana Hayride") 300-325   81
(Gold label. A program of various artists including Elvis.)

MFSL (059 "From Elvis in Memphis") 30-50   82
(First issued as RCA LSP-4155.)

MARVENCO (101 "1954-1955, The Beginning") 10-15   88
(Has material perviously issued on Golden Editions 101.)

MEDIA ENTERTAINMENT ("The King's Gold") 50-75   85
(Three reel-to-reel tapes, issued only to radio stations. Price includes cue sheets. Not known to exist on disc.)

MICHELOB (810 "Highlights of Elvis Memories") 175-200   78
(A Michelob in-house promotional issue only.)
Elvis Memories was first issued on ABC Radio 1003.

MUSIC WORKS (3601 "The First Live Recordings") 8-10   84
(This material was first issued on Louisiana Hayride 3061.)

MUSIC WORKS (3602 "Hillbilly Cat") 8-10   84
(This material was first issued on Louisiana Hayride 3061.)

OAK (1003 "Vintage 1955") 70-100   91

PAIR (1010 "Double Dynamite") 20-25   82
(First issued as Pickwick 5001.)

PAIR (1037 "Remembering Elvis") 20-25   83

PICKWICK (2304 "Flaming Star") 8-10   75
(First issued as RCA PRS-279.)

PICKWICK (2408 "Let's Be Friends" Black Vinyl) 8-10   75
(First issued as Camden 2408.)

PICKWICK (2408 "Let's Be Friends" Colored Vinyl) 500-600   70s
(Experimental pressing only. There is no colored vinyl commercial or promotional edition of this issue.)

PICKWICK (2428 "Elvis' Christmas Album") 8-10   75
(First issued as Camden 2428.)

PICKWICK (2428 "Elvis' Christmas Album") 15-25   86
(Has RCA Special Products on label and cover.)

PICKWICK (2440 "Almost in Love") 8-10   75
(First issued as Camden 2440.)

PICKWICK (2472 "You'll Never Walk Alone") 8-10   75
(First issued as Camden 2472.)

PICKWICK (2518 "C'mon Everybody") 8-10   75
(First issued as Camden 2518.)

PICKWICK (2533 "I Got Lucky") 8-10   75
(First issued as Camden 2533.)

PICKWICK (2567 "Elvis Sings Hits from His Movies") 8-10   75
(First issued as Camden 2567.)

PICKWICK (2595 "Burning Love") 8-10   75
(First issued as Camden 2595.)

PICKWICK (2611 "Separate Ways") 8-10   75
(First issued as Camden 2611.)

PICKWICK (5001 "Double
Dynamite") 25-30   75
(Repackaged in 1982 as Pair 1010.)

PICKWICK (7007 "Frankie and
Johnny")................................... 10-15   75
(First issued as RCA 3553.)

PICKWICK (7064 "Mahalo from
Elvis")...................................... 15-20   78

PREMORE (589 "Early Elvis") 5-10   89
(Mail-order album from the Solo Cup
Company.)

RCA (EPC-1 "Special Christmas Program"
Reel Tape) 300-325   67
(Price includes programming inserts, which
represent $25-35 of the value. Never issued
commercially on disc, all 10–inch red vinyl
LPs of this material are bootlegs.)

RCA (TB-1 "Collectors
Edition")............................... 100-150   76
(Five-LP boxed set.)

RCA (010 "Elvis! His Greatest
Hits") 400-450   79
(White box edition. Eight-LP boxed set, sold
mail-order by *Reader's Digest.*)

RCA (010 "His Greatest Hits") .. 40-60   83
(Yellow box edition. Seven-LP boxed set,
sold mail-order by *Reader's Digest.* See
RCA 181 for the bonus LP offered with this
set.)

RCA RBA-040: see READER'S DIGEST 040

RCA (0056 "Elvis").................... 40-50   73
(Mustard color label. Cover shows
"Brookville Records" in upper right. A mail-
order LP offer.)

RCA (0056 "Elvis").................... 20-25   73
(Blue label. Cover doesn't show "Brookville
Records." Mail-order LP offer. Repackaged
in 1978 and titled *Elvis Commemorative
Album.*)

RCA (0056 "Elvis Commemorative
Album") 75-80   78
(Price includes a "Registered Certificate of
Ownership." A mail-order LP offer. First titled
Elvis, using the same selection number.)

RCA (072 "Great Hits of
1956-57") 10-20   87
(Offered as a bonus LP from *Reader's
Digest,* with the purchase of one of their non-
Elvis boxed sets.)

RCA (0168 "Elvis in
Hollywood").............................. 35-45   76
(Add $10 to $15 is accompanied by a 20-
page photo booklet.)

RCA (181 "Elvis Sings Inspirational
Favorites").............................. 15-20   83
(Special Products, Reader's Digest mail-

order bonus LP for buyers of the 1983
edition of RCA 010. Price includes 24-page
Reader's Digest Music catalog.)

RCA (191 "Elvis, the Legend Lives
On")..40-45   86
(Seven-LP boxed set, sold mail-order by
Reader's Digest. Includes booklet.)

RCA (242 "Elvis Sings Country
Favorites") 20-30   84
(Bonus LP from Reader's Digest, given with
the purchase of their seven-disc boxed set,
The Great Country Entertainers, which has
no Elvis tracks.)

RCA (0263 "Elvis Presley
Story")......................................30-40   77
(Special Products five-LP boxed set. A
Candelite Music mail-order offer.)

RCA (0264 "Songs of
Inspiration").............................10-15   77
(Special Products issue. A Candelite Music
mail-order bonus LP for buyers of RCA
0263.)

RCA (279 "Singer Presents
Elvis")......................................70-80   68
(Reissued in 1969 as Camden 2304 and in
1975 as Pickwick 2304.)

RCA (0283 "Elvis, Including
Fool") 50-60   73

RCA (0341 "Legendary Performer,
Vol. 1")....................................20-25   74
(With die-cut cover. Add $5 to $10 if
accompanied by *The Early Years* booklet.)

RCA (0341 "Legendary Performer,
Vol. 1") 5-10   83
(With standard cover—not die-cut.)

RCA (0341 "Legendary Performer,
Vol. 1") 800-1000   78
(Picture discs of the 0341 material but with
pictures from any of about six different LP
covers pressed on the disc. RCA in-house,
experimental items.)

RCA (0347 "Memories of
Elvis")......................................35-45   78
(Special Products five-LP boxed set. A
Candelite Music mail-order offer. Add $8 to
$10 if accompanied by a 16-page booklet
and an Elvis print. Not all sets were issued
with the print and booklet.)

RCA (0348 "Greatest Show on
Earth")....................................10-12   78
(Special Products issue. A Candelite   284
Music mail-order bonus LP for buyers of
RCA 0347.)

RCA (0388 "Raised on Rock")...15-20   73
(Orange label.)

RCA (0388 "Raised on Rock") 8-10   77
(Black label.)

RCA (0401 RCA Radio Victrola Division
Spots") 800-1200   56
(Single-sided disc with four 50-second radio
commercials for RCA's Victrolas, as well as
for the SPD-22 and SPD-23 EPs that were
offered as a bonus. Elvis is the announcer
on all of the spots, which include excerpts of
some of his songs. Issued only to radio
stations scheduling the spots.)

RCA (0412 "The Legendary
Recordings") 30-40   79
(Special Products six-LP boxed set. A
Candelite Music mail-order offer.)

RCA (0413 "Greatest Moments in
Music") 10-15   80
(Special Products issue. A Candelite Music
mail-order bonus LP for buyers of RCA
0412.)

RCA (0437 "Rock 'N Roll
Forever") 10-15   81
(Candelite Music mail-order LP offer.)

RCA (461 "Special Palm Sunday
Programming") 500-600   67
(Add $75 to $100 if accompanied by a
programming packet. Promotional issue
only.)

RCA (0461 "The Legendary
Magic") 10-15   80
(Candelite Music mail-order LP offer.)

RCA (CPL1-0475 "Good
Times") 15-20   74

VICTOR (AFL1-0475 "Good
Times") 8-10   77

RCA (571 " Elvis As Recorded at Madison
Square Garden") 250-300   72
(Two-LP, double pocket issue. Promotional
issue only. Commercially issued as RCA
LSP-4776.)

RCA (APD1-0606 "On Stage in
Memphis") 120-130   74
(Quadradisc. Orange label.)

RCA (CPL1-0606 "On Stage in
Memphis") 15-18   74
(Orange label.)

RCA (DJL1-0606 "On Stage in
Memphis") 250-275   74
(Banded edition. Promotional issue only.)

RCA (CPL1-0606 "On Stage in
Memphis") 10-15   76
(Tan label.)

RCA (CPL1-0606 "On Stage in
Memphis") 8-10   77
(Black label.)

RCA (AFL1-0606 "On Stage in
Memphis") 8-10   77

RCA (0632 "The Elvis Presley
Collection") 50-60   84
(Special Products three-LP boxed set,
produced for Candlelite Music. Includes
booklet. A mail-order LP offer.)

RCA (DPL1-0647 "Elvis
Country") 30-40   84
(Special Products issue for ERA Records.)

RCA (DPK1-0679 "Savage Young
Elvis") 5-10   84
(Cassette tape of a package that was never
available on LP. Price is for tape still
attached to 12" x 12" photo card.)

RCA (0704 "Elvis, HBO
Special") 25-35   84
(Includes color poster. Special Products
issue for HBO cable TV subscribers. This
material was first issued as RCA LPM-4088.)

RCA (0710 "50 Years-50 Hits")..20-25   85
(Three-LP set. Offered by TV mail-order and
through the RCA Record Club.)

RCA (0728 "Elvis, His Songs of Faith and
Inspiration")............................15-20   86
(Two LP, mail-order offer.)

RCA (CPM1-0818 "Having Fun with Elvis on
Stage") 15-20   74
(Orange label.)

RCA (CPM1-0818 "Having Fun with Elvis on
Stage")....................................10-15   76
(Tan label.)

RCA (AFM1-0818 "Having Fun with Elvis on
Stage")......................................8-10   77
(First issued on Boxcar without a selection
number.)

RCA (0835 "Elvis Presley Interview
Record")................................75-100   84
(Promotional issue only.)

RCA (APL1-0873 "Promised
Land") 20-25   75
(Orange label.)

RCA (APL1-0873 "Promised
Land") 10-15   76
(Tan label.)

RCA (AFL1-0873 "Promised
Land") 8-10   77

RCA (APD1-0873 "Promised
Land") 100-125   75
(Quadradisc. Orange label.)

RCA (APD1-0873 "Promised
Land") 40-50   77
(Quadradisc. Black label.)

RCA (ANL1-0971 "Pure Gold")..15-18   75
(Orange label.)

RCA (ANL1-0971 "Pure Gold") . 10-15   76
(Yellow label.)

RCA (ANL1-0971 "Pure Gold") ... 8-10   77
(Black label.)
Reissued in 1980 as AYL1-3732.

RCA (1001 "The Sun
Collection").............................. 20-25   75
(Label does not have "Starcall" on it. Back
cover pictures other LPs.)

RCA (1001 "The Sun
Collection").............................. 15-20   75
(Label has "Starcall" on it. Back cover with
liner notes. This English import was
distributed throughout the U.S. It was
repackaged in 1976 as RCA 1675.)

RCA (LOC-1035 "Elvis' Christmas
Album") 10000-20000   57
(Experimental, one-of-a-kind pressing.)

RCA (LOC-1035 "Elvis' Christmas
Album") 500-550   57
(Black vinyl. With gold foil, gift-giving
sticker.)

RCA (LOC-1035 "Elvis' Christmas
Album") 375-475   57
(Black vinyl. Without gold foil, gift-giving
sticker. Repackaged in 1958 as RCA 1951,
in 1970 as Camden 2428 and in 1985 as
RCA 5486. May be found with either gold or
silver print on the spine.)

RCA (APL1-1039 "Today")........ 20-25   75
(Orange label.)

RCA (APL1-1039 "Today")........ 10-15   76
(Tan label.)

RCA (AFL1-1039 "Today").......... 8-10   77

RCA (APD1-1039 "Today") ... 100-125   75
(Quadradisc. Orange label.)

RCA (APD1-1039 "Today")....... 40-50   77
(Quadradisc. Black label.)

RCA (LPM-1254 "Elvis
Presley")............................ 100-125   56
(Monaural. Black label, "Long Play" at
bottom. Cover has selection number in
upper right corner.)

· RCA (LPM-1254 "Elvis
Presley").................................. 50-75   63
(Black label, "Mono" at bottom. Cover has
selection number on left.)

RCA (LPM-1254 "Elvis
Presley").................................. 25-50   64
(Black label, "Monaural" at bottom. Cover
has selection number on left.)

RCA (LSP-1254e "Elvis
Presley")............................. 150-200   62
(Stereo. Black label, all print on label is
silver.)

RCA (LSP-1254e "Elvis
Presley") 25-50   64
(Black label, RCA logo is white, other label
print is silver.)

RCA (LSP-1254e "Elvis
Presley") 20-30   68
(Orange label.)

RCA (LSP-1254e "Elvis
Presley") 10-20   76
(Tan label.)

RCA (AFL1-1254e "Elvis
Presley") 8-15   77
(Digitally remastered in 1984 on RCA 5198.)

RCA (ANL1-1319 "His Hand in
Mine")......................................10-15   76
(First issued as LPM/LSP-2328.)

RCA (1349 "Legendary Performer,
Vol. 2") 50-65   76
(Does not have the false starts and outtakes
on *Such a Night* and *Cane and a High
Starched Collar*. Mistakenly has only the
complete take of both songs. Add $5 to $10
if accompanied by *The Early Years
Continued* booklet.)

RCA (1349 "Legendary Performer,
Vol. 2") 20-25   76
(With die-cut cover. Add $5 to $10 if
accompanied by *The Early Years Continued*
booklet.)

RCA (1349 "Legendary Performer,
Vol. 2") 5-10   83
(With standard cover—not die-cut.)

RCA (LPM-1382 "Elvis") 750-1000   56
(Monaural. Black label, "Long Play" at
bottom. Cover has selection number in
upper right corner. Has an otherwise
unreleased [on vinyl] alternate take of *Old
Shep*. These usually have either a "15S,"
"17S" or "19S" following the identification
number stamped in the vinyl trail-off.)

RCA (LPM-1382 "Elvis") 200-250   56
(Black label, selections numbered as "Band
1" through "Band 6.")

RCA (LPM-1382 "Elvis") 100-125   56
(Black label, "Long Play" at bottom. Cover
has selection number in upper right corner.)

RCA (LPM-1382 "Elvis") 45-55   63
(Black label, "Mono" at bottom. Cover has
selection number on left.)

RCA (LPM-1382 "Elvis") 25-30   64
(Black label, "Monaural" at bottom.   286
Cover has selection number on left.)

RCA (LSP-1382e "Elvis")...........75-85   62
(Stereo. Black label, all print on label is
silver.)

RCA (LSP-1382e "Elvis") 25-30   64
(Black label, RCA logo is white, other print
on label is silver.)

RCA (LSP-1382e "Elvis") 10-20   68
(Orange label.)

RCA (LSP-1382e "Elvis") 10-15   76
(Tan label.)

RCA (AFL1-1382e "Elvis") 8-10   77
(Digitally remastered in 1984 on RCA 5199.)

RCA (APL1-1506 "From Elvis Presley
Boulevard") 12-15   76

RCA (AFL1-1506 "From Elvis Presley
Boulevard") 8-10   77

RCA (LPM-1515 "Loving You")100-125   57
(Monaural. Black label, "Long Play" at
bottom. Cover has selection number in
upper right corner.)

RCA (LPM-1515 "Loving You") . 45-55   63
(Black label, "Mono" at bottom. Cover has
selection number on left.)

RCA (LPM-1515 "Loving
You") 4000-5000
(Picture disc, but with the cover of a
European *G.I. Blues* album being the picture
imbeded in the vinyl. Experimental
disc—only one copy made. Has just five
Loving You tracks, the others being
randomly selected instrumentals)

RCA (LPM-1515 "Loving You"). 25-30   64
(Black label, "Monaural" at bottom. Cover
has selection number on left.)

RCA (LSP-1515e "Loving
You") 75-85   62
(Stereo. Black label, all print on label is
silver.)

RCA (LSP-1515e "Loving
You") 25-30   64
(Black label, RCA logo is white, other label
print is silver.)

RCA (LSP-1515e "Loving
You") 10-20   68
(Orange label.)

RCA (LSP-1515e "Loving
You") 10-15   76
(Tan label.)

RCA (AFL1-1515e "Loving
You") 5-10   77

RCA (APM1-1675 "The Sun
Sessions") 12-15   76

RCA (AFM1-1675 "The Sun
Sessions") 8-10   77
(First issued as RCA HY-1001 and was
reissued in 1981 as RCA AYM1-3893.)

RCA (LPM-1707 "Elvis' Golden
Records") 100-125   58

(Monaural. Black label, "Long Play" at
bottom. Cover has selection number in
upper right corner and LP title in light blue
letters.)

RCA (LPM-1707 "Elvis' Golden
Records") 45-55   63
(Black label, "Mono" at bottom. Cover has
selection number on left and LP title in white
letters.)

RCA (LPM-1707 "Elvis' Golden
Records") 25-30   64
(Black label, "Monaural" at bottom. Cover
has selection number on left.)

RCA (LSP-1707e "Elvis' Golden
Records") 75-85   62
(Stereo. Black label, all print on label is
silver.)

RCA (LSP-1707e "Elvis' Golden
Records") 25-30   64
(Black label, RCA logo is white, other label
print is silver.)

RCA (LSP-1707e "Elvis' Golden
Records") 10-20   68
(Orange label.)

RCA (LSP-1707e "Elvis' Golden
Records") 10-15   76
(Tan label.)

RCA (AFL1-1707e "Elvis' Golden
Records") 8-10   77

RCA (AQL1-1707e "Elvis' Golden
Records") 5-10   79
(Digitally remastered in 1984 on RCA 5196.)

RCA (LPM-1884 "King
Creole") 100-125   58
(Monaural. Black label, "Long Play" at
bottom. Cover has selection number in
upper right corner. Add $75-100 if
accompanied by an 8" x 10" black and white
bonus photo of Elvis in uniform.)

RCA (LPM-1884 "King
Creole") 45-55   63
(Black label, "Mono" at bottom. Cover has
selection number on left.)

RCA (LPM-1884 "King
Creole") 25-30   64
(Black label, "Monaural" at bottom. Cover
has selection number on left.)

RCA (LSP-1884e "King
Creole") 75-85   62
(Stereo. Black label, all print on label is
silver.)

RCA (LSP-1884e "King
Creole") 25-30   62
(Black label, RCA logo is white, other label
print is silver.)

RCA (LSP-1884e "King
Creole") 10-20   68
(Orange label.)

RCA (LSP-1884e "King
Creole") 10-15   76
(Tan label.)

RCA (AFL1-1884e "King
Creole") 8-10   77
(Reissued in 1980 as RCA AYL1-3733.)

RCA (ANL1-1936 "Wonderful World of
Christmas") 5-10   77
(First issued as RCA LSP-4579.)

RCA (LPM-1951 "Elvis' Christmas
Album") 90-100   58
(Monaural. Black label, "Long Play" at
bottom. Cover has selection number in
upper right corner.)

RCA (LPM-1951 "Elvis' Christmas
Album") 45-55   63
(Black label, "Mono" at bottom. Cover has
selection number on left.)

RCA (LPM-1951 "Elvis' Christmas
Album") 25-30   64
(Black label, "Monaural" at bottom. Cover
has selection number on left.)

RCA (LSP-1951e "Elvis' Christmas
Album") 25-30   64
(Stereo. Black label, RCA logo is white,
other label print is silver.)

RCA (LSP-1951e "Elvis' Christmas
Album") 20-25   68
(Orange label. Repackage of RCA LOC-
1035. It was repackaged in 1970 as Camden
2428 and again in 1985 as RCA AFM1-
5486.)

RCA (1981 "Felton Jarvis Talks About
Elvis") 200-250   81
(Price includes three script sheets. Add $25
to $50 if accompanied by silver and black
Guitar Man engraved Elvis belt buckle.)

RCA (LPM-1990 "For LP Fans
Only") 100-125   59
(Monaural. Black label, "Long Play" at
bottom. Cover has selection number in
upper right corner.)

RCA (LPM-1990 "For LP Fans
Only") 45-55   63
(Black label, "Mono" at bottom. Cover has
selection number on left.)

RCA (LPM-1990 "For LP Fans
Only") 200-225   65
(Black label, "Monaural" at bottom. Cover
has same Elvis photo on front and back.)

RCA (LPM-1990 "For LP Fans
Only") 25-30   65

(Black label, "Monaural" at bottom. Cover
has selection number on left.)

RCA (LSP-1990 "For LP Fans
Only") 200-225   65
(Black label. Cover has same Elvis photo on
front and back.)

RCA (LSP-1990e "For LP Fans
Only") 25-30   65
(Stereo. Black label, RCA logo is white,
other label print is silver.)

RCA (LSP-1990e "For LP Fans
Only") 10-20   68
(Orange label.)

RCA (LSP-1990e "For LP Fans
Only") 10-15   76
(Tan label.)

RCA (AFL1-1990e "For LP Fans
Only") 8-10   77

RCA (LPM-2011 "A Date with
Elvis") 400-600   59
(Monaural. Black label, "Long Play" at
bottom. Has gatefold cover and 1960
calendar. With "New Golden Age of Sound"
wrap-around banner.)

RCA (LPM-2011 "A Date with
Elvis") 150-175   59
(Black label, "Long Play" at bottom. Has
gatefold cover and 1960 calendar, but *does
not* have "New Golden Age of Sound"
banner.)

RCA (LPM-2011 "A Date with
Elvis") 45-55   65
(Black label, "Mono" at bottom. Cover has
selection number on left.)

RCA (LPM-2011 "A Date with
Elvis") 25-30   65
(Black label, "Monaural" at bottom. Cover
has selection number on left.)

RCA (LSP-2011e "A Date with
Elvis") 25-30   65
(Stereo. Black label, RCA logo is white,
other label print is silver.)

RCA (LSP-2011e "A Date with
Elvis") 10-20   68
(Orange label.)

RCA (LSP-2011e "A Date with
Elvis") 10-15   76
(Tan label.)

RCA (AFL1-2011e "A Date with
Elvis") 8-10   77

RCA (LPM-2075 "Elvis' Golden Records,   288
Vol. 2") 100-125   59
(Monaural. Black label, "Long Play" at
bottom. Cover has selection number in
upper right corner.)

RCA (LPM-2075 "Elvis' Golden Records, Vol. 2").. 45-55   63
(Black label, "Mono" at bottom. Cover has selection number on left.)

RCA (LPM-2075 "Elvis' Golden Records, Vol. 2").. 25-30   64
(Black label, "Monaural" at bottom. Cover has selection number on left.)

RCA (LSP-2075e "Elvis' Golden Records, Vol. 2").. 75-85   62
(Stereo. Black label, all print on label is silver.)

RCA (LSP-2075e "Elvis' Golden Records, Vol. 2").. 25-30   64
(Black label, RCA logo is white, other label print is silver.)

RCA (LSP-2075e "Elvis' Golden Records, Vol. 2").. 10-20   68
(Orange label.)

RCA (LSP-2075e "Elvis' Golden Records, Vol. 2").. 10-15   76
(Tan label.)

RCA (AFL1-2075e "Elvis' Golden Records, Vol. 2") 8-10   77
(May also be shown as *50,000,000 Elvis Presley Fans Can't Be Wrong*. Digitally remastered in 1984 on RCA 5197.)

RCA (2227 "Great Performances") 10-20   90

RCA (LPM-2231 "Elvis Is Back")................................... 100-150   60
(Monaural. Black label, "Long Play" at bottom. No song titles printed on cover. May have a yellow sticker on cover showing song titles.)

RCA (LPM-2231 "Elvis Is Back")..................................... 45-55   63
(Black label, "Mono" at bottom. Cover has selection number on left.)

RCA (LPM-2231 "Elvis Is Back")..................................... 25-30   64
(Black label, "Monaural" at bottom. Cover has selection number on left.)

RCA (LSP-2231 "Elvis Is Back")................................... 120-160   60
(Stereo. Black label, "Living Stereo" at bottom. No song titles printed on cover. May have a yellow sticker on cover showing song titles.)

RCA (LSP-2231 "Elvis Is Back")..................................... 25-30   64
(Black label, RCA logo is white, other label print is silver.)

RCA (LSP-2231 "Elvis Is Back")..................................... 10-20   68
(Orange label.)

RCA (LSP-2231 "Elvis Is Back") 10-15   76
(Tan label.)

RCA (AFL1-2231 "Elvis Is Back")..........................8-10   77

RCA (LPM-2256 "G.I. Blues") 100-125   60
(Monaural. Black label, "Long Play" at bottom. Add $15 to $25 if accompanied by "Elvis Is Back" inner sleeve. Add $100 to $150 if cover has a heart-shaped announcement for *Wooden Heart*.)

RCA (LPM-2256 "G.I. Blues")....45-55   63
(Black label, "Mono" at bottom.)

RCA (LPM-2256 "G.I. Blues")....25-30   64
(Black label, "Monaural" at bottom.)

RCA (LSP-2256 "G.I. Blues") 100-125   60
(Stereo. Black label, "Living Stereo" at bottom. Add $15 to $25 if accompanied by "Elvis Is Back" inner sleeve. Add $100 to $150 if cover has a heart-shaped announcement for *Wooden Heart*.)

RCA (LSP-2256 "G.I. Blues").....25-30   64
(Black label, RCA logo is white, other label print is silver.)

RCA (LSP-2256 "G.I. Blues").....10-20   68
(Orange label.)

RCA (LSP-2256 "G.I. Blues").....10-15   76
(Tan label.)

RCA (AFL1-2256 "G.I. Blues").....8-10   77
(Reissued in 1980 as RCA AYL1-3735.)

Note: For *G.I. Blues* picture disc, see *Loving You* (RCA LPM-1515).

RCA (APL1-2274 "Welcome to My World")......................................10-15   77

RCA (AFL1-2274 "Welcome to My World")..8-10   77

RCA (AQL1-2274 "Welcome to My World")..5-10   79

RCA (LPM-2328 "His Hand in Mine")....................................75-100   60
(Monaural. Black label, "Long Play" at bottom.)

RCA (LPM-2328 "His Hand in Mine").....................................40-50   63
(Black label, "Mono" at bottom.)

RCA (LPM-2328 "His Hand in Mine").....................................25-30   64
(Black label, "Monaural" at bottom.)

RCA (LSP-2328 "His Hand in Mine")..................................100-125   60
(Stereo. Black label, "Living Stereo" at bottom.)

RCA (LSP-2328 "His Hand in
Mine")..................................... 25-30   64
(Black label, RCA logo is white, other label
print is silver.)

RCA (LSP-2328 "His Hand in
Mine")..................................... 10-20   68
(Orange label.)

RCA (LSP-2328 "His Hand in
Mine")..................................... 10-15   76
(Tan label.)
(Repackaged in 1976 as RCA ANL1-1319
and in 1981 as RCA AYM1-3935.)

RCA (2347 "Elvis-Greatest Hits,
Vol. One")............................... 10-15   81
(Has embossed letters on front cover.)

RCA (2347 "Elvis-Greatest Hits,
Vol. One")............................... 5-10   83
(Standard cover print—not embossed.)

RCA (LPM-2370 "Something for
Everybody").......................... 75-100   61
(Monaural. Black label, "Long Play" at
bottom. Back cover promotes Compact 33s.)

RCA (LPM-2370 "Something for
Everybody")............................ 40-50   63
(Black label, "Mono" at bottom.)

RCA (LPM-2370 "Something for
Everybody")............................ 25-30   64
(Black label, "Monaural" at bottom.)

RCA (LSP-2370 "Something for
Everybody")......................... 125-150   61
(Stereo. Black label, "Living Stereo" at
bottom. Back cover promotes Compact 33s.)

RCA (LSP-2370 "Something for
Everybody")............................ 25-30   64
(Black label, RCA logo is white, other label
print is silver.)

RCA (LSP-2370 "Something for
Everybody")............................ 10-20   68
(Orange label.)

RCA (LSP-2370 "Something for
Everybody")............................ 10-15   76
(Tan label.)

RCA (AFL1-2370 "Something for
Everybody")............................ 8-10   77
(Reissued in 1981 as RCA AYM1-4116.)

RCA (LPM-2426 "Blue
Hawaii")................................... 75-90   61
(Monaural. Black label, "Long Play" at
bottom.)

RCA (LPM-2426 "Blue
Hawaii")................................... 40-50   63
(Black label, "Mono" at bottom.)

RCA (LPM-2426 "Blue
Hawaii")................................... 25-30   64
(Black label, "Monaural" at bottom.)

RCA (LSP-2426 "Blue
Hawaii")..................................90-100   61
(Stereo. Black label, "Living Stereo" at
bottom.)

RCA (LSP-2426 "Blue
Hawaii")..................................25-30   64
(Black label, RCA logo is white, other label
print is silver.)

RCA (LSP-2426 "Blue Hawaii") .10-20   68
(Orange label.)

RCA (LSP-2426 "Blue Hawaii") .10-15   76
(Tan label.)

RCA (AFL1-2426 "Blue
Hawaii")...................................8-10   77
(Reissued in 1981 as RCA AYL1-3683.)

RCA (AFL1-2428 "Moody
Blue") 1000-1200   77
(Colored vinyl—any color *other than blue or
black*. Experimental production discs for
RCA in-house use only.)

RCA (AFL1-2428 "Moody
Blue") 10-12   77
(Blue vinyl.)

RCA (AFL1-2428 "Moody
Blue") 125-150   77
(Black vinyl.)

RCA (AQL1-2428 "Moody
Blue") 8-10   79

RCA (LPM-2523 "Pot Luck")......75-90   62
(Monaural. Black label, "Long Play" at
bottom.)

RCA (LPM-2523 "Pot Luck")......40-50   63
(Black label, "Mono" at bottom.)

RCA (LPM-2523 "Pot Luck")......25-30   64
(Black label, "Monaural" at bottom.)

RCA (LSP-2523 "Pot Luck") 90-100   62
(Stereo. Black label, "Living Stereo" at
bottom.)

RCA (LSP-2523 "Pot Luck") 25-30   64
(Black label, RCA logo is white, other label
print is silver.)

RCA (LSP-2523 "Pot Luck") 10-20   68
(Orange label.)

RCA (LSP-2523 "Pot Luck") 10-15   76
(Tan label.)

RCA (AFL1-2523 "Pot Luck").......8-10   77

RCA (APL1-2558 "Harum
Scarum")...................................8-10   77
(First issued as RCA LPM/LSP-3468.
Reissued in 1980 as RCA AYL1-3734.)

RCA (APL1-2560 "Spinout") 8-10   77
(First issued as RCA LPM/LSP-3702.
Reissued in 1980 as RCA AYL1-3684.)

RCA (APL1-2564 "Double
Trouble") 8-10   77
(First issued as RCA LPM/LSP-3787.)

RCA (APL1-2565 "Clambake") ... 8-10   77
(First issued as RCA LPM/LSP-3893.)

RCA (APL1-2568 "It Happened at the
World's Fair") 8-10   77
(First issued as RCA LPM/LSP-2697.)

RCA (APL2-2587 "Elvis in
Concert") 15-20   77

RCA (CPL2-2587 "Elvis in
Concert") 12-15   82

RCA (LPM-2621 "Girls! Girls!
Girls!") 75-90   62
(Monaural. Black label, "Long Play" at
bottom.)

RCA (LPM-2621 "Girls! Girls!
Girls!") 40-50   63
(Black label, "Mono" at bottom.)

RCA (LPM-2621 "Girls! Girls!
Girls!") 25-30   64
(Black label, "Monaural" at bottom.)

RCA (LSP-2621 "Girls! Girls!
Girls!") 90-100   62
(Stereo. Black label, "Living Stereo" at
bottom.)

RCA (LSP-2621 "Girls! Girls!
Girls!") 25-30   64
(Black label, RCA logo is white, other label
print is silver.)

RCA (LSP-2621 "Girls! Girls!
Girls!") 10-20   68
(Orange label.)

RCA (LSP-2621 "Girls! Girls!
Girls!") 10-15   76
(Tan label.)

RCA (AFL1-2621 "Girls! Girls!
Girls!") 8-10   77

RCA (CPD2-2642 "Aloha from
Hawaii") 15-20   75
(Orange label.)

RCA (CPD2-2642 "Aloha from
Hawaii") 10-12   77
(Black label. First issued as RCA VPSX-
6089.)

RCA (LPM-2697 "It Happened at the World's
Fair") 75-90   63
(Monaural. Black label, "Long Play" at
bottom. Add $100 to $125 if accompanied by
an 8" x 10" bonus color photo.)

RCA (LPM-2697 "It Happened at the World's
Fair") 40-50   63
(Black label, "Mono" at bottom.)

RCA (LPM-2697 "It Happened at the World's
Fair") 25-30   64
(Black label, "Monaural" at bottom.)

RCA (LSP-2697 "It Happened at the World's
Fair") 90-110   63
(Stereo. Black label, "Living Stereo" at
bottom. Add $100 to $125 if accompanied by
an 8" x 10" bonus color photo.)

RCA (LSP-2697 "It Happened at the World's
Fair") 25-30   64
(Black label, RCA logo is white, other label
print is silver. Reissued in 1977 as RCA
APL1-2568.)

RCA (LPM-2756 "Fun in
Acapulco")................................60-70   63
(Monaural. Black label, "Mono" at bottom.)

RCA (LPM-2756 "Fun in
Acapulco")................................25-30   64
(Black label, "Monaural" at bottom.)

RCA (LSP-2756 "Fun in
Acapulco")................................60-70   63
(Stereo. Black label, all print on label is
silver.)

RCA (LSP-2756 "Fun in
Acapulco")................................25-30   64
(Black label, RCA logo is white, other label
print is silver.)

RCA (LSP-2756 "Fun in
Acapulco")................................10-20   68
(Orange label.)

RCA (LSP-2756 "Fun in
Acapulco")................................10-15   76
(Tan label.)

RCA (AFL1-2756 "Fun in
Acapulco")................................8-10   77

RCA (LPM-2765 "Elvis' Golden Records, Vol.
3") 90-100   63
(Monaural. Black label, "Mono" at bottom.)

RCA (LPM-2765 "Elvis' Golden Records, Vol.
3") 25-30   64
(Black label, "Monaural" at bottom.)

RCA (LSP-2765 "Elvis' Golden Records, Vol.
3") 90-100   63
(Stereo. Black label, all print on label is
silver.)

RCA (LSP-2765 "Elvis' Golden Records, Vol.
3") 25-30   64
(Black label, RCA logo is white, other label
print is silver.)

RCA (LSP-2765 "Elvis' Golden Records, Vol.
3") 10-20   68
(Orange label.)

RCA (LSP-2765 "Elvis' Golden Records, Vol.
3") 10-15   76
(Tan label.)

RCA (AFL1-2765 "Elvis' Golden Records, Vol.
3")... 8-10   77

RCA (AFL1-2772 "He Walks Beside
Me")... 8-10   77

RCA (LPM-2894 "Kissin'
Cousins")............................. 100-200   64
(Monaural. Black label, "Mono" at bottom.
Does not picture film cast in lower right
corner photo on cover.)

RCA (LPM-2894 "Kissin'
Cousins").................................. 60-70   64
(Black label, "Mono" at bottom. Pictures film
cast in lower right corner photo on cover.)

RCA (LPM-2894 "Kissin'
Cousins").............................. 25-30   64
(Black label, "Monaural" at bottom.)

RCA (LSP-2894 "Kissin'
Cousins")............................. 100-150   64
(Stereo. Black label, all print on label is
silver. *Does not* picture film cast in lower
right corner photo on cover.)

RCA (LSP-2894 "Kissin'
Cousins").................................. 60-70   64
(Black label, all print on label is silver.
Pictures film cast in lower right corner photo
on cover.)

RCA (LSP-2894 "Kissin'
Cousins")................................. 25-30   64
(Black label, RCA logo is white, other label
print is silver.)

RCA (LSP-2894 "Kissin'
Cousins")................................. 10-20   68
(Orange label.)

RCA (LSP-2894 "Kissin'
Cousins")................................. 10-15   76
(Tan label.)

RCA (LSP-2894 "Kissin'
Cousins").................../.... 1000-1200   77
(Blue vinyl. Experimental pressing only.)

RCA (AFL1-2894 "Kissin'
Cousins")................................. 8-10   77
(Reissued in 1981 as RCA AYM1-4115.)

RCA (CPL1-2901 "Elvis Sings for
Children") 8-10   78
(Includes "Special Memories" greeting card.)

RCA (LPM-2999 "Roustabout"). 60-70   64
(Monaural. Black label, "Mono" at bottom.)

RCA (LPM-2999 "Roustabout"). 25-30   65
(Black label, "Monaural" at bottom.)

RCA (LSP-2999
"Roustabout")...................... 500-600   64
(Stereo. Black label. All print on
label—including RCA logo—is silver.)

RCA (LSP-2999 "Roustabout") . 25-30   64
(Black label, RCA logo is white, other label
print is silver.)

RCA (LSP-2999 "Roustabout")..10-20   68
(Orange label.)

RCA (LSP-2999 "Roustabout")..10-15   76
(Tan label.)

RCA (AFL1-2999 "Roustabout")..8-10   77

RCA (3078 "Legendary Performer,
Vol. 3") 15-20   78
(Picture disc. Add $5 to $10 if accompanied
by *Yesterdays* booklet. May be found with
the actual disc pressed on either blue or
black vinyl. Also issued on standard black
vinyl as 3082.)

RCA (3082 "Legendary Performer,
Vol. 3") 8-12   78
(Add $5 to $10 if accompanied by
Yesterdays booklet. Also issued on a picture
disc, as RCA 3078.)

RCA (3279 "Our Memories of
Elvis")...8-10   79

RCA (LPM-3338 "Girl Happy")...40-50   65
(Monaural.)

RCA (LSP-3338 "Girl Happy") ...40-50   65
(Stereo. Black label.)

RCA (LSP-3338 "Girl Happy") ...10-20   68
(Orange label.)

RCA (LSP-3338 "Girl Happy") ...10-15   76
(Tan label.)

RCA (AFL1-3338 "Girl Happy")....8-10   77

RCA (3448 "Our Memories of Elvis
Vol. 2") 8-10   79
(A sampling of these tracks is on RCA 3455,
Pure Elvis.)

RCA (LPM-3450 "Elvis for
Everyone")...............................40-50   65
(Monaural.)

RCA (LSP-3450 "Elvis for
Everyone")...............................40-50   65
(Stereo. Black label.)

RCA (LSP-3450 "Elvis for
Everyone")...............................10-20   68
(Orange label.)

RCA (LSP-3450 "Elvis for
Everyone")...............................10-15   76
(Tan label.)

RCA (AFL1-3450 "Elvis for
Everyone")................................8-10   77
Reissued in 1982 as RCA AYL1-4232.

RCA (3455 "Pure Elvis") 275-325   79
(Cover reads "Pure Elvis," but label shows
"Our Memories of Elvis - Vol. 2."   292
Promotional issue only.)

RCA (LPM-3468 "Harum
Scarum")....................................35-50   65
(Monaural. Add $60 to $85 if
accompanied by bonus 12" x 12" photo.)

RCA (LSP-3468 "Harum
Scarum") 35-50   65
(Stereo. Add $60 to $85 if accompanied by
bonus 12" x 12" photo. Reissued in 1977 as
RCA APL1-2558 and in 1980 as RCA AYL1-
3734.)

RCA (LPM-3553 "Frankie and
Johnny") 35-50   66
(Monaural. Add $60 to $85 if accompanied
by bonus 12" x 12" print.)

RCA (LSP-3553 "Frankie and
Johnny") 35-50   66
(Stereo. Add $60 to $85 if accompanied by
bonus 12" x 12" print. Reissued in 1977 as
RCA APL1-2559. A repackage appeared in
1976 on Pickwick 7007.)

RCA (LPM-3643 "Paradise Hawaiian
Style") 35-45   66
(Monaural.)

RCA (LSP-3643 "Paradise Hawaiian
Style") 35-45   66
(Stereo. Black label.)

RCA (LSP-3643 "Paradise Hawaiian
Style") 10-20   68
(Orange label.)

RCA (LSP-3643 "Paradise Hawaiian
Style") 10-15   76
(Tan label.)

RCA (AFL1-3643 "Paradise Hawaiian
Style") 8-10   77

RCA (AYL1-3683 "Blue
Hawaii") 5-10   80
(First issued as RCA LPM/LSP-2426.)

RCA (AYL1-3684 "Spinout") 5-10   80
(First issued as RCA LPM/LSP-3702,
reissued in 1977 as RCA APL1-2560.)

RCA (CPL8-3699 "Elvis Aron
Presley") 80-100   80
(Eight-LP boxed set. Add $5 to $10 if
accompanied by 20-page booklet.)

RCA (CPL8-3699 "Elvis Aron
Presley") 450-500   80
(REVIEWER SERIES edition. Silver sticker
on back also identifies the Reviewer Series
copy as "NS-3699." Add $5 to $10 if
accompanied by 20-page booklet.)

RCA (CPK8-3699 "Elvis Aron
Presley") 80-100   80
(Four-cassette boxed set. Add $10 to $20 if
accompanied by 20-page booklet and eight
12" x 12" Elvis photos.)

RCA (CPS8-3699 "Elvis Aron
Presley") 100-125   80
(Four 8-track boxed set. Add $10 to $20 if
accompanied by 20-page booklet and eight
12" x 12" Elvis photos. *Excerpts* of songs in

this set appeared on RCA 3729. *Selections*
from this LP are on RCA 3781.)

RCA (LPM-3702 "Spinout") 35-50   66
(Monaural. Add $60 to $85 if accompanied
by bonus 12" x 12" photo.)

RCA (LSP-3702 "Spinout") 35-50   66
(Stereo. Add $60 to $85 if accompanied by
bonus 12" x 12" photo. Reissued in 1977 as
APL1-2560.)

RCA (3729 "Elvis Aron Presley
Excerpts") 100-125   80
(Has 37 excerpts from RCA 3699.
Promotional issue only.)

RCA (AYL1-3732 "Pure Gold") 5-10   80
(First issued as RCA ANL1-0971.)

RCA (AYL1-3733 "King
Creole") 5-10   80
(First issued as RCA LSP-1884.)

RCA (AYL1-3734 "Harum
Scarum") 5-10   80
(First issued as RCA LPM/LSP-3468.)

RCA (AYL1-3735 "G.I. Blues") 5-10   80
(First issued as RCA LPM/LSP-2256.)

RCA (LPM-3758 "How Great Thou
Art") 40-50   67
(Monaural.)

RCA (LSP-3758 "How Great Thou
Art") 35-45   67
(Stereo. Black label.)

RCA (LSP-3758 "How Great Thou
Art") 10-20   68
(Orange label.)

RCA (LSP-3758 "How Great Thou
Art") 10-15   76
(Tan label.)

RCA (AFL1-3758 "How Great Thou
Art") 8-10   77

RCA (3781 "Elvis Aron Presley
Selections") 100-125   80
(Has 12 selections from RCA 3699.
Promotional issue only.)

RCA (LPM-3787 "Double
Trouble") 40-50   67
(Monaural. Front cover reads "Special
Bonus Full Color Photo." Add $25 to $35 if
accompanied by bonus 7" x 9" photo.)

RCA (LPM-3787 "Double
Trouble") 30-40   68
("Special Bonus Full Color Photo" is
replaced by "Trouble Double.")

RCA (LSP-3787 "Double
Trouble") 40-50   67
(Stereo. Front cover reads "Special Bonus
Full Color Photo." Add $25 to $35 if

accompanied by bonus 7" x 9" photo. Black label.)

RCA (LSP-3787 "Double Trouble") 30-40   68
("Special Bonus Full Color Photo" is replaced by "Trouble Double.")

RCA (LSP-3787 "Double Trouble") 10-20   68
(Orange label.)

RCA (LSP-3787 "Double Trouble") 10-15   76
(Tan label.)
(Reissued in 1977 as RCA APL1-2564.)

RCA (AYL1-3892 "Elvis in Person") 5-10   81
(First issued as RCA LSP-4428.)

RCA (LPM-3893 "Clambake") 175-200   67
(Monaural. Add $30 to $50 if accompanied by bonus 12" x 12" photo. Reissued in 1977 as RCA APL1-2565.)

RCA (LSP-3893 "Clambake") ... 30-50   67
(Stereo. Add $30 to $50 if accompanied by bonus 12" x 12" photo. Reissued in 1977 as RCA APL1-2565.)

RCA (AYM1-3893 "Sun Sessions") 5-10   81
(First issued as RCA APM1-1675.)

RCA (AYM1-3894 "Elvis TV Special") 5-10   81
(First issued RCA LPM-4088.)

RCA (3917 "Guitar Man") 8-12   81
(Includes a "This Is Elvis" flyer. Producer Felton Jarvis talks about Elvis as well as the making of this LP [RCA 1981].)

RCA (LPM-3921 "Elvis' Gold Records, Vol. 4") 1000-2000   68
(Monaural.)

RCA (LSP-3921 "Elvis' Gold Records, Vol. 4") 60-90   68
(Stereo. Black label.)

RCA (LSP-3921 "Elvis' Gold Records, Vol. 4") 10-20   68
(Orange label.)

RCA (LSP-3921 "Elvis' Gold Records, Vol. 4") 10-15   76
(Tan label.)

RCA (AFL1-3921 "Elvis' Gold Records, Vol. 4") 8-10   77

RCA (AYM1-3935 "His Hand in Mine") 5-10   81
(First issued as RCA LPM/LSP-2328.)

RCA (AYL1-3956 "That's The Way It Is") 5-10   81
First issued as RCA LSP-4460.

RCA (LPM-3989 "Speedway") 1000-2000   68
(Monaural. Add $25 to $50 if accompanied by bonus 8" x 10" photo.)

RCA (LSP-3989 "Speedway") 35-45   68
(Stereo. Black label. Add $25 to $50 if accompanied by bonus 8" x 10" photo.)

RCA (LSP-3989 "Speedway") 10-20   68
(Orange label.)

RCA (LSP-3989 "Speedway") 10-15   76
(Tan label.)

RCA (AFL1-3989 "Speedway") 8-10   77

RCA (4031 "This Is Elvis") 10-15   80

RCA (LPM-4088 "Elvis TV Special") 15-20   68
(Orange label. Rigid disc.)

RCA (LPM-4088 "Elvis TV Special") 10-15   72
(Orange label. Flexible disc.)

RCA (LPM-4088 "Elvis TV Special") 10-15   76
(Tan label.)

RCA (AFM1-4088 "Elvis TV Special") 8-10   77
(Reissued in 1981 as RCA AYM1-3894. Repackaged for HBO as RCA 0704.)

RCA (AYL1-4114 "That's The Way It Is") 5-10   81
(First issued as RCA LSP-4445.)

RCA (AYM1-4115 "Kissin' Cousins") 5-10   81
(First issued as RCA LPM/LSP-2894.)

RCA (AYM1-4116 "Something for Everybody") 5-10   81
(First issued as RCA LPM/LSP-2370.)

RCA (LSP-4155 "From Elvis in Memphis") 20-25   69
(Orange label. Rigid disc. Add $30 to $40 if accompanied by 8" x 10" Elvis photo.)

RCA (LSP-4155 "From Elvis in Memphis") 10-15   72
(Orange label. Flexible disc.)

RCA (LSP-4155 "From Elvis in Memphis") 10-15   69
(Tan label.)

RCA (AFL1-4155 "From Elvis in Memphis") 8-10   77
(A half-speed mastered issue of this LP was released in 1982 as MFSL 059.)

RCA (AYL1-4232 "Elvis for Everyone") 5-10   82   294
(First issued as RCA LPM/LSP-3450.)

RCA (LSP-4362 "On Stage") 15-20   70
(Orange label. Rigid disc.)

RCA (LSP-4362 "On Stage") 10-15   72
(Orange label. Flexible disc.)

RCA (LSP-4362 "On Stage") 10-15   76
(Tan label.)

RCA (AFL1-4362 "On Stage")... 10-12   77

RCA (AQL1-4362 "On Stage") 5-10   83

RCA (4395 "Memories of
Christmas") 8-10   82

RCA (LSP-4428 "Elvis in
Person")................................... 15-20   70
(Orange label.)

RCA (LSP-4428 "Elvis in
Person")................................... 10-15   76
(Tan label.)

RCA (AFL1-4428 "Elvis in
Person") 8-10   77
(First released as half of RCA LSP-6020,
then reissued in 1981 as RCA AYL1-3892.)

RCA (LSP-4429 "Elvis Back in
Memphis")................................ 15-20   70
(Orange label.)

RCA (LSP-4429 "Elvis Back in
Memphis")................................ 10-15   76
(Tan label.)

RCA (AFL1-4429 "Elvis Back in
Memphis")................................. 8-10   77
(First issued as half of RCA LSP-6020.)

RCA (LSP-4445 "That's the Way It
Is").. 15-20   70
(Orange label.)

RCA (LSP-4445 "That's the Way It
Is").. 10-15   76
(Tan label.)

RCA (LSP-4445 "That's the Way It
Is").. 8-10   77
(Black label.)

RCA (AFL1-4445 "That's the Way It
Is")... 8-10   77
(Reissued in 1981 as RCA AYL1-4114.)

RCA (LSP-4460 "Elvis
Country").................................. 15-20   71
(Orange label. Add $10 to $15 if
accompanied by 7" x 9" Elvis photo.)

RCA (LSP-4460 "Elvis
Country").................................. 10-15   76
(Tan label.)

RCA (AFL1-4460 "Elvis
Country").................................... 8-10   77
(Reissued in 1981 as RCA AYL1-3956.)

RCA (LSP-4530 "Love
Letters")................................... 35-45   71
(Orange label. Full title, *Love Letters From
Elvis*, on TWO lines on front cover.)

RCA (LSP-4530 "Love
Letters").................................. 20-35   71

(Orange label. Full title, *Love Letters From
Elvis*, on THREE lines on front cover.)

RCA (LSP-4530 "Love
Letters") 10-15   76
(Tan label.)

RCA (AFL1-4530 "Love
Letters") 8-10   77
(Reissued in 1981 as RCA AYL1-3956.)

RCA (AHL1-4530 "Elvis
Medley").....................................8-10   82

RCA (LSP-4579 "Wonderful World of
Christmas")..............................20-25   71
(Orange label. Add $4 to $8 if accompanied
by a 5" x 7" Elvis postcard. Reissued in 1977
as RCA ANL1-1936.)

RCA (LSP-4671 "Elvis Now").....50-60   72
(Has white titles/times sticker on front cover.
Promotional issue only.)

RCA (LSP-4671 "Elvis Now").....15-18   72
(Orange label.)

RCA (LSP-4671 "Elvis Now").....10-15   76
(Tan label.)

RCA (AFL1-4671 "Elvis Now").....8-10   77

RCA (LSP-4690 "He Touched
Me")...50-60   72
(Has white titles/times sticker on front cover.
Promotional issue only.)

RCA (LSP-4690 "He Touched
Me") 15-18   72
(Orange label.)

RCA (LSP-4690 "He Touched
Me")...10-15   76
(Tan label.)

RCA (AFL1-4690 "He Touched
Me") 8-10   77

RCA (4678 "I Was the One") 8-10   83

RCA (LSP-4776 " Elvis As Recorded at
Madison Square Garden") 50-60   72
(Orange label. Has white programming
stickers applied to front cover. Promotional
issue only. For double disc promotional, see
RCA 571.)

RCA (LSP-4776 " Elvis As Recorded at
Madison Square Garden") 15-20   72
(Orange label.)

RCA (LSP-4776 " Elvis As Recorded at
Madison Square Garden") 10-15   76
(Tan label.)

RCA (AQL1-4776 " Elvis As Recorded at
Madison Square Garden") 8-10   77

RCA (4809 "A Country Christmas,
Vol. 2") 8-10   83

RCA (4848 "Legendary Performer,
Vol. 4") 8-10   83

(Price includes a 12-page *Memories of the King* booklet.)

RCA (4941 "Elvis' Gold Records, Vol. 5") 5-10   84

RCA (5172 "Golden Celebration") 40-50   84
(Six-LP boxed set. Price includes custom inner sleeves and an envelope containing an 8" x 10" Elvis photo and a 50th Anniversary flyer.)

RCA (5172 "Golden Celebration") 15-20   84
(Special "Advance Cassette" boxed set sampler.)

RCA (5182 "Rocker") 5-10   84

RCA (5196 "Elvis' Golden Records") 5-10   84
(Digitally remastered, quality mono pressing. Price includes gold "The Definitive Rock Classic" banner. First issued as RCA LPM-1707.)

RCA (5197 "Elvis' Gold Records, Vol. 2") 5-10   84
(Digitally remastered, quality mono pressing. Price includes gold "The Definitive Rock Classic" banner. First issued as RCA LPM-2075.)

RCA (5198 "Elvis Presley") 5-10   84
(Digitally remastered, quality mono pressing. Price includes gold "The Definitive Rock Classic" banner. First issued as RCA LPM-1254.)

RCA (5199 "Elvis") 5-10   84
(Digitally remastered, quality mono pressing. Price includes gold "The Definitive Rock Classic" banner. First issued as RCA LPM-1382.)

RCA (5353 "Valentine Gift for You") 8-10   85
(Colored vinyl.)

RCA (5353 "Valentine Gift for You") 5-10   85
(Black vinyl.)

RCA (5418 "Reconsider Baby") .. 5-10   85

RCA (5430 "Always on My Mind") 5-10   85

RCA (5486 "Elvis' Christmas Album") 5-10   85
(Colored vinyl.)

RCA (5486 "Elvis' Christmas Album") 20-40   85
(Black vinyl. Thus far, all black vinyl copies discovered were packaged with stickers reading "pressed on green vinyl.")

RCA (5600 "Return of the Rocker") 5-10   86

RCA (5697 "Special Christmas Programming")................... 800-1000   67
(Promotional issue only.)

RCA (LSP-6020 "From Memphis to Vegas") 30-40   69
(Orange label. Incorrectly shows writers of *Words* as Tommy Boyce & Bobby Hart. Also shows writer of *Suspicious Minds* as Frances Zambon. Add $20 to $40 if accompanied by two 8" x 10" black and white Elvis photos.)

RCA (LSP-6020 "From Memphis to Vegas") 20-30   69
(Orange label. Correctly shows writers of *Words* as Barry, Robin & Maurice Gibb, and writer of *Suspicious Minds* as Mark James. Add $20 to $40 if accompanied by two 8" x 10" Elvis photos.)

RCA (LSP-6020 "From Memphis to Vegas") 15-20   76
(Tan label.)

RCA (LSP-6020 "From Memphis to Vegas") 10-15   77
(Black label. Each of the two LPs in this set was reissued individually, *Elvis in Person at the International Hotel* as LSP-4428 and *Elvis Back in Memphis* as LSP-4429, both in 1970.)

RCA (VPSX-6089 "Aloha from Hawaii")........................... 2000-2500   73
(Has "Chicken of the Sea" sticker on cover. Quadradisc and contents stickers also are on cover. Includes programming insert card. Promotional in-house issue by the Van Camps Company.)

RCA (VPSX-6089 "Aloha from Hawaii")............................... 500-750   73
(Has white titles/times sticker on front cover. Promotional issue only.)

RCA (VPSX-6089 "Aloha from Hawaii")................................. 75-100   73
(Has Quadradisc and contents stickers on cover. Red/orange label.)

RCA (VPSX-6089 "Aloha from Hawaii")................................... 25-30   74
(Has Quadradisc/RCA logo in lower right corner of front cover. Titles are printed on back cover. Orange label.)

RCA (VPSX-6089 "Aloha from Hawaii")................................... 25-30   76
(Tan label. Issued through the RCA Record Club as RCA 213736 and later (1977) as RCA CPD2-2642.)   296

RCA (6221 "Memphis Record") . 10-15   87
(Includes a bonus color 15" x 22" poster and *Elvis Talks* LP flyer.)

RCA (6313 "Elvis Talks!") 10-15   87
(Mail-order LP offer.)

RCA (6382 "Number One Hits").. 8-10   87
(Includes a bonus color 15" x 22" poster and
Elvis Talks LP flyer.)

RCA (6383 "Top Ten Hits") 10-12   87
(Includes a bonus color 15" x 22" poster and
Elvis Talks LP flyer.)

RCA (LPM-6401 "Worldwide 50 Gold Hits,
Vol. 1") 60-75   70
(Orange label. Four-LP boxed set. Add $30
to $40 if accompanied by a 16-page Elvis
photo booklet.)

RCA (LPM-6401 "Worldwide 50 Gold Hits,
Vol. 1") 30-40   76
(Tan label.)

RCA (LPM-6401 "Worldwide 50 Gold Hits,
Vol. 1") 20-25   77
(Black label. Two of the LPs in this set were
repackaged for the RCA Record Club in
1974 as RCA 213690. The other two came
out in 1978 as RCA 214657.)

RCA (LPM-6402 "Worldwide 50 Gold Hits,
Vol. 2") 60-75   71
(Orange label. Four-LP boxed set. Add $25
to $50 if accompanied by an Elvis print, and
an envelope with piece of material.)

RCA (LPM-6402 "Worldwide 50 Gold Hits,
Vol. 2") 30-40   76
(Tan label. With bonus items shown as
included.)

RCA (LPM-6402 "Worldwide 50 Gold Hits,
Vol. 2") 25-35   76
(Tan label. No bonus items shown as being
included.)

RCA (LPM-6402 "Worldwide 50 Gold Hits,
Vol. 2") 20-25   77
(Black label. Two of the LPs in this set were
repackaged for the RCA Record Club in
1978 as RCA 214567.)

RCA (6414 "The Complete Sun
Sessions") 10-15   87
(Includes a bonus color 15" x 22" poster and
Elvis Talks LP flyer.)

RCA (6738 "Essential Elvis") 5-10   88

RCA (6985 "The Alternate
Aloha") 5-10   88

RCA (7031 "Elvis Forever") 25-35   74
(TV mail-order offer.)

RCA (7065 "Canadian
Tribute") 10-12   78
(Price includes photo inner-sleeve. Canadian
issues of this LP had the same number but
are clearly marked on back cover as
Canadian.)

RCA (8468 "Elvis in Nashville")... 5-10   88

RCA (9586 "Elvis Gospel") 5-10   89

RCA (9589 "Stereo '57, Essential Elvis,
Vol. 2") 5-10   89

RCA (213690 "Worldwide Gold Award Hits,
Parts 1&2") 75-100   74
(Orange label. RCA Record Club issue only.)

RCA (213690 "Worldwide Gold Award Hits,
Parts 1&2") 25-30   76
(Tan label. RCA Record Club issue only.)

RCA (213690 "Worldwide Gold Award Hits,
Parts 1&2") 12-15   77
(Black label. RCA Record Club issue only.
The two discs in this set were first issued as
half of RCA LPM-6401.)

RCA (213736 "Aloha from
Hawaii") 45-55   73
(Orange label.)

RCA (213736 "Aloha from
Hawaii") 18-20   76
(Tan label.)

RCA (214657 "Worldwide Gold Award Hits,
Parts 3&4") 12-15   78
(RCA Record Club issue only. The two discs
in this set were first issued as half of RCA
LPM-6401.)

RCA (233299 "Country
Classics") 20-25   80
(RCA Record Club issue only.)

RCA (234340 "From Elvis with
Love") 20-25   78
(RCA Record Club issue only.)

RCA (244047 "Legendary Concert
Performances") 20-25   78
(RCA Record Club issue only.)

RCA (244069 "Country
Memories") 20-25   78
(RCA Record Club issue only.)

SILHOUETTE (10001/10002 "Personally
Elvis") 20-25   79

STARDAY (995 "Interviews with
Elvis") 30-50   78
(Previously issued on Great Northwest
4005.)

SUN (1001 "The Sun Years") 75-80   77
(Light yellow label, "Memphis" at bottom.
Light yellow cover with light brown printing.)

SUN (1001 "The Sun Years") 15-20   77
(Darker yellow label, four target circles. Dark
yellow cover with dark brown printing.)

SUN (1001 "The Sun Years") 20-25   77
(White cover with brown printing.)

TM ("The Presley Years") 100-200   81
(12-LP boxed syndicated radio show.
Includes script and cue sheets.)

TIME-LIFE (106 "Elvis Presley:
1954-1961") 15-20   86
(Three-LP boxed set, part of the *Rock 'N'
Roll Era* series of sets available from Time-
Life by mail-order. Includes brochure.)

UNITED STATIONS ("Elvis Presley Birthday
Tribute") 125-150   89
(Four hour radio show. Includes four pages
of cue sheets. Promotional issue only.)

WATERMARK ("The Elvis Presley Story,
1975")................................. 800-900   75
(13-LP set. White label, pink letters. Includes
a 48-page operations manual. Promotional
issue only. Not issued with a special cover
or package.)

WATERMARK ("The Elvis Presley Story,
1977")................................. 700-800   77
(13-LP set. White label, pink letters. Includes
a 48-page operations manual, which
represents about $100 of the value.
Promotional issue only. Not issued with a
special cover or package.)

WESTWOOD ONE ("A Golden
Celebration") 200-250   84
(Three-LP boxed set. Price includes
instructions and cue sheets, which represent
$5-10 of the value. Issued to radio stations
only.)

WORLD of ELVIS PRESLEY .. 50-100   83
(One hour weekly radio show, numbered as
program 1 through program 30. The show
ceased operation after 30 programs. Each
disc was accompanied by a single cue
sheet. Price is for any one of the discs,
although program #3 is by far the rarest of
them all.)

Session: Chet Atkins; Bill Black; Hal Blaine; Blossoms;
David Briggs; James Burton; Floyd Cramer; Glen
Hardin; Jordanaires; Jerry Kennedy; Anita Kerr; Ronnie
Milsap; Bob Moore; Scotty Moore; Larry Muhoberac;
Shaun Neilsen; Boots Randolph; Jerry Reed; J.D.
Sumner & Stamps; Sweet Inspirations; Kathy
Westmoreland; John Wilkinson; Bobby Wood.
 Also see ATKINS, Chet
 Also see BLACK, Bill
 Also see COLE, Nat "King"
 Also see CRAMER, Floyd
 Also see CRICKETS
 Also see FOWLER, Wally
 Also see HARRIS, Emmylou
 Also see JORDANAIRES
 Also see KERR, Anita
 Also see MILSAP, Ronnie
 Also see MOORE, Bob
 Also see NIELSEN, Shaun
 Also see RANDOLPH, Boots
 Also see REED, Jerry
 Also see VINCENT, Gene
 Also see WOOD, Bobby
• Prefix letters or numbers are used on some
LP listings in order to more quickly identify
the variations available.

• A few items that have no label name are
listed by title, such as the International Hotel
boxed sets.

• Beginning in 1961, many Elvis LPs had a
separate sticker, promoting such things as
certain songs or bonus photos. When not
listed separately in this edition, a premium of
10%-20% could be placed on LPs with these
original stickers.

• LPs with a sticker applied over the selection
number, showing a new number, are valued
approximately the same as those without the
sticker.

• Some albums were pressed with the "Dog
Near Top" label using the older LSP prefix,
prior to being switched to the AFL1 series.
These are not listed separately since there
seems to be no consequential price
difference between the two.

• If you don't find a record in the preceding
sections, it may contain two, three or four
artists, and is listed in a section that follows.

• As imposing as our Presley section here
may seem, it is but a drop in the bucket. For
a far more in-depth study of Elvis Presley
collectibles—including records, compact
discs and memorabilia—get Jerry Osborne's
*Official Price Guide to Elvis Presley Records
and Memorabilia.*

PRESLEY, Elvis / Beatles
Singles: 7–inch
OSBORNE ENTERPRISES ("The 1967 Elvis
Medley")......................................4-8   88
(Flip side is titled *The #1 Hits Medley, 1956-
69.* Includes insert. 1000 made.)

OSBORNE ENTERPRISES ("The 1967 Elvis
Medley")....................................8-12   89
(Flip side is titled *The #1 Hits Medley, 1956-
70.* 100 made.)

LPs: 10/12–inch 33rpm
UNITED DISTRIBUTORS (2382 "Lightning
Strikes Twice").........................25-50   81
(Promotional issue only. Has five songs by
each artist.)

PRESLEY, Elvis / Martha Carson / Lou Monte / Herb Jeffries
EPs: 7–inch 33/45rpm
RCA (2 "Dealer's Prevue")...900-1200   57
(Issued with paper envelope/sleeve.   298
Promotional issue only.)

PRESLEY, Elvis / Jean Chapel
EPs: 7–inch 33/45rpm

RCA (7 "Love Me Tender") ... 150-200   56
(Not issued with a special sleeve or cover.
Promotional issue only.)

PRESLEY, Elvis / Buddy Holly
Singles: 7–inch

CREATIVE RADIO ("Elvis 50th Birthday
Special").................................. 10-20   85
(Demonstration disc. A promotional issue.)
Also see HOLLY, Buddy

PRESLEY, Elvis / Fear
LPs: 10/12–inch 33rpm

DISCONET (309 "The Original Elvis Presley
Medley"/"Fear Medley") 25-50   80
(Promotional issue only.)

PRESLEY, Elvis / David Keith
Singles: 7–inch

RCA (8760 "Heartbreak
Hotel") 50-100   88
(White label. Promotional issue only.)

RCA (8760 "Heartbreak Hotel") 4-5   88
(Red label. Printing on both sides of label.)

RCA (8760 "Heartbreak Hotel") 4-8   88
(Red label. Printing on Elvis side only.)

RCA (8760 "Heartbreak Hotel") 4-8   88
(Red label. Printing on David Keith side
only.)

Picture Sleeves

RCA (8760 "Heartbreak
Hotel") 50-100
(Pictures, but doesn't identify, RCA's Butch
Waugh. Promotional issue only.)

RCA (8760 "Heartbreak Hotel") 4-8   88
(Pictures Elvis and others in a Cadillac.)

PRESLEY, Elvis / Vaughn Monroe / Gogi Grant / Robert Shaw
EPs: 7–inch 33/45rpm

RCA (3736 "Pop Transcribed 30 Sec.
Spot") 500-600   58
(Not issued with a special sleeve or cover.
Promotional issue only.)
Also see MONROE, Vaughn

PRESLEY, Elvis / Jaye P. Morgan
Singles: 7–inch

UNITED STATES AIR FORCE (125 "It's Now
Or Never") 300-400   61
(Add $30 TO $50 if accompanied by printed,
cardboard mailing box. Issued only to radio
stations.)

EPs: 7–inch 33/45rpm

RCA (992 & 689 "Elvis/Jaye P.
Morgan") 6000-9000   56
(Two-EP set, with 992 by Presley and 689
by Jaye P. Morgan coupled together in a
promotional double-pocket package. Since
the discs were standard pressings, at least
95% of the value here is represented by the
custom EP cover.)

PRESLEY, Elvis / Gary Owens
Singles: 7–inch

CREATIVE RADIO ("Elvis
Hour")................................... 20-30   86
(Demonstration disc. A promotional issue.)

PRESLEY, Elvis / Helen Reddy
Singles: 7–inch

WHAT'S IT ALL ABOUT (78
"Life") 45-55   77
(Issued only to radio stations.)
Also see REDDY, Helen

PRESLEY, Elvis / Dinah Shore
EPs: 7–inch 33/45rpm

RCA (56 "Too Much") 150-200   57
(Not issued with a special sleeve or cover.
Promotional issue only.)

PRESLEY, Elvis / Frank Sinatra / Nat King Cole
EPs: 7–inch 33/45rpm

CREATIVE RADIO ("Elvis
Remembered")....................... 40-45   79
(Promotional demonstration disc.)
Also see COLE, Nat "King"

PRESLEY, Elvis / Hank Snow / Eddy Arnold / Jim Reeves
EPs: 7–inch 33/45rpm

RCA (12 "Old Shep") 2000-2500   56
(Issued with a paper, "WOHO Featuring
RCA Victor" sleeve. Deduct $1,300 to
$1,700 if sleeve is missing. Promotional
only.)
Also see ARNOLD, Eddy
Also see REEVES, Jim
Also see SNOW, Hank

PRESLEY, Elvis / Lawrence Welk
Singles: 7–inch

UNITED STATES AIR FORCE (159
"Surrender") 300-400   61
(Add $30 to $50 if accompanied by printed,
cardboard mailing box. Issued only to radio
stations.)
Also see WELK, Lawrence

PRESLEY, Elvis / Hank Williams
LPs: 10/12–inch 33rpm
SUNRISE MEDIA (3011 "History of Country Music") 10-20   81
(Has four songs by each artist.)
Also see PRESLEY, Elvis
Also see WILLIAMS, Hank

PRESLEY, Elvis
(Michael Conley)
Singles: 7–inch
ELVIS CLASSIC (5478 "Tell Me Pretty Baby") 4-8   78
(Despite being labeled as a 1954 recording by Elvis Presley, this track is simply a 1978 recording by Michael Conley, performing in an Elvis style. It is listed separately to eliminate confusion.)
Picture Sleeves
ELVIS CLASSIC (5478 "Tell Me Pretty Baby") 8-10   78
(Sleeve pictures an artist's sketch of Elvis Presley.)

PRESTON, Eddie   C&W '89
Singles: 7–inch
PLATINUM 3-4   89

PRESTON, Terry
(Ferlin Husky)
Singles: 78rpm
CAPITOL...................................... 8-15   52-53
FOUR STAR (1438 "Heart of Stone") 15-25   49
FOUR STAR (1464 "Say When") 15-25   49
FOUR STAR (1516 "Guilty Feeling").................................. 15-25   49
FOUR STAR (1518 "The Sabbath") 15-25   49
FOUR STAR (1542 "Irma") 15-25   50
FOUR STAR (1566 "Wise Guy") 15-25   50
FOUR STAR (1571 "Jezebel").. 15-25   50
FOUR STAR (1572 "Crying Heart Blues").................................. 15-25   50
FOUR STAR (1573 "Deadly Weapon") 15-25   50
Singles: 7–inch
CAPITOL...................................... 10-20   52-53
Also see HUSKY, Ferlin

PRICE, Chuck   C&W '74
Singles: 7–inch
PLAYBOY 3-5   74-77

PRICE, David   C&W '64
Singles: 7–inch
EPIC..4-8   62
GAYLORD 4-8   63
RICE 3-8   64-77
ROULETTE....................................4-8   65-66
Also see STEGALL, Red

PRICE, Denise   C&W '82
Singles: 7–inch
DIMENSION..................................3-4   82

PRICE, Kenny   C&W '66
Singles: 7–inch
BOONE..4-8   66-69
DIMENSION..................................3-4   80
MRC...3-5   77-79
RCA 3-6   69-76
LP: 10/12–inch 33rpm
BOONE..10-20   67
DIMENSION..................................5-10   80
PHONORAMA 5-8   82
RCA 10-15   69-71

PRICE, Ray   C&W '52
(With the Cherokee Cowboys)
Singles: 78rpm
BULLET (701 "Jealous Lies") ..75-125   52
COLUMBIA 5-15   52-57
Singles: 7–inch
ABC..3-5   75
ABC/DOT......................................3-5   75-77
COLUMBIA (10000 series) 3-4   74-77
COLUMBIA (20000 & 21000 series)...................................10-20   52-56
COLUMBIA (40000 thru 43000 series)....................................5-15   57-66
COLUMBIA (44000 thru 45000 series)....................................3-6   67-73
GOLDIES 45 3-4
DIMENSION..................................3-4   81-82
MONUMENT...................................3-5   78-79
MYRRH..3-4   74-75
STEP ONE....................................3-4   85-86
W.B. 3-4   82-83
WORD...3-4   78
Picture Sleeves
COLUMBIA 3-5   300
67
EPs: 7–inch 33/45rpm
COLUMBIA (1700 thru 2800 series)....................................15-25   53-57
COLUMBIA (8556 "Ray Price") 10-20   50s

COLUMBIA (10000 thru 14000
    series) 10-20   57-60
    (White label. Promotional issue only.)

LPs: 10/12–inch 33rpm

ABC/DOT 6-12   75-77
ARTCO.. 20-40
    (Titel and selection number not known.)
CBS.. 5-10
COLUMBIA (28 "The World of Ray
    Price") 8-12   70
COLUMBIA (157 "The Same Old
    Me").. 10-15   66
    (Record club exclusive.)
COLUMBIA (1015 "Heart
    Songs") 30-40   57
COLUMBIA (1148 "Talk to Your
    Heart").. 25-35   58
COLUMBIA (1400 thru 2600
    series) 10-25   60-67
    (Monaural)
COLUMBIA (8200 thru 9400
    series) 15-30   60-67
    (Stereo)
COLUMBIA (9700 thru 9900
    series) 8-12   68-70
COLUMBIA (10000 series) 5-10   73-79
COLUMBIA (30000 thru 37000
    series) 5-10   70-81
COLUMBIA SPECIAL
    PRODUCTS................................. 5-10
COLUMBIA STAR SERIES......... 5-10
DIMENSION.................................... 5-8   81
51 WEST... 5-8   84
HARMONY.................................. 8-15   66-71
MONUMENT.................................. 5-10   79
MYRRH 5-8   74
PAIR... 8-10   82
RADIANT 5-8   81
SEASHELL..................................... 5-10
STEP ONE 5-10   86
SUNRISE MEDIA........................... 5-8   81
VIVA 5-10
W.B. 5-8   83
WORD.. 5-8   77

Session:Johnny Bush; Willie Nelson; Johnny Gimble.
    Also see ANDERSON, Lynn / Ray Price
    Also see BUSH, Johnny
    Also see MILLER, Roger, & Willie Nelson
    Also see NASHVILLE SUPERPICKERS
    Also see NELSON, Willie, & Ray Price
    Also see ROBBINS, Marty / Johnny Cash / Ray Price

PRICE, Ray / Lefty Frizzell / Carl Smith

LPs: 10/12–inch 33rpm

COLUMBIA (1257 "Greatest Western
    Hits")..20-30   59
    (Monaural.)
COLUMBIA (8776 "Greatest Western
    Hits")..15-25   63
    (Stereo.)
    Also see FRIZZELL, Lefty
    Also see SMITH, Carl

PRICE, Ray / Johnny Horton / Carl Smith / George Morgan

EPs: 7–inch 33/45rpm

COLUMBIA (2157 "4 Big Hits")..20-25   60
    Also see HORTON, Johnny
    Also see SMITH, Carl

PRICE, Toni   C&W '86

Singles: 7–inch

LUV...3-4   86
MASTER..3-4   86
PRAIRIE DUST..............................3-4   87

PRIDE, Charley   C&W '66

**(With the Pridesmen; with Henry Mancini;
Country Charley Pride)**

Singles: 7–inch

RCA (0073 thru 0942 series).........4-8   69-73
RCA (8700 & 8800 series)............5-10   66
RCA (9000 thru 9996)...................4-8   66-71
RCA (10030 thru 11655).................3-6   74-79
RCA 11736 "Dallas Cowboys")......3-5   79
    (Black label.)
RCA 11736 "Dallas Cowboys")....8-12   79
    (Gray and blue label. Special Dallas
    Cowboys Edition.)
RCA (11751 thru 14296)................3-5   79-86
RCA GOLD STANDARD 3-5
16TH AVE. 3-4   87-89

Picture Sleeves

RCA 4-6   71-74

EPs: 7–inch 33/45rpm

RCA 5-10   60s
    (Jukebox issues.)

LPs: 10/12–inch 33rpm

CAMDEN 5-10   72
RCA (Except LPM/LSP 3700 thru 4800
    series)..5-10   74-86
RCA (3700 thru 4800 series) 10-20   66-73
    (With "LPM" or "LSP" prefix.)
RCA SPECIAL PRODUCTS (0208 "Charley's
    Favorites") 8-12

READER'S DIGEST/RCA ("Charley
Pride") 30-40
(Boxed 6-LP set with booklet. Mail order
offer.)
TELEHOUSE 5-10
Also see ANDERSON, Lynn / Charley Pride
Also see DAVE & SUGAR
Also see MANCINI, Henry
Also see TEXAS VOCAL COMPANY

PROCTOR, Paul *C&W '86*

Singles: 7–inch

AURORA	3-4	86-87
19TH AVE.	3-4	87-88

PROPHET, Ronnie *C&W '75*

Singles: 7–inch

RCA	3-5	75-77

LP: 10/12–inch 33rpm

ART	10-20	
AUDIOGRAPH ALIVE	5-8	82
GLOBE	10-20	
PROPHET	10-20	
RCA	5-10	76
TEE VEE	5-10	
(Mail order offer.)		
TRANS WORLD	10-20	
VERA CRUZ	8-10	

PRUETT, Jeanne *C&W '71*

(Jean Pruett)

Singles: 7–inch

AUDIOGRAPH	3-4	83
DECCA	3-6	68-72
IBC	3-5	79-80
MCA	3-5	73-77
MSR	3-4	87
MERCURY	3-5	78
PAID	3-4	81
RCA	4-6	63-64

LPs: 10/12–inch 33rpm

ALLEGIANCE	5-8	84
AUDIOGRAPH	5-8	83
DECCA	8-12	72
IBC	5-10	79
MCA	5-10	73-75
OUT of TOWN DIST	5-10	82

PRUETT, Jeanne, & Marty Robbins *C&W '83*

Singles: 7–inch

AUDIOGRAPH	3-4	83

Also see PRUETT, Jeanne
Also see ROBBINS, Marty

PRUITT, Lewis *C&W '59*

Singles: 7–inch

DECCA (Except 31201)	5-10	60
DECCA (31201 "Crazy Bullfrog")	50-75	61
GREAT	4-8	68
MUSIC TOWN	3-6	69
PEACH (703 "Pretty Baby")	50-75	59
PEACH (710 "This Little Girl")	50-75	59
PEACH (725 "Timbrook")	10-15	59
VEE JAY	5-10	63-64

Also see SMITH, Carl

PRYOR, Cactus, & His Pricklypears *C&W '50*

Singles: 78rpm

FOUR STAR	5-8	50

PRYSOCK, Arthur *R&B '52/C&W '79*

Singles: 78rpm

DECCA	4-8	52-54
MERCURY	4-8	54-55

Singles: 7–inch

BETHLEHEM	3-5	72
DECCA (25000 series)	4-8	65
DECCA (27000 thru 29000 series)	5-10	52-54
DECCA (31000 series)	4-8	64-65
GUSTO	3-5	79
KING	3-6	69-71
MCA	3-5	78
MGM	3-5	70
MERCURY	5-10	54-55
OLD TOWN (100 series)	3-5	73-76
OLD TOWN (1000 series)	4-8	59-60
(Light blue label.)		
OLD TOWN (1000 series)	3-5	76-77
(Dark blue or black label.)		
OLD TOWN (1100 series)	4-6	61-66
VERVE	3-6	66-69

LPs: 10/12–inch 33rpm

DECCA	15-20	64-65
KING	8-12	69-71
MCA	5-10	78
OLD TOWN (100 series)	20-30	60-62
OLD TOWN (2000 series)	15-25	62-65
OLD TOWN (12000 series)	5-10	73-77
POLYDOR	5-10	77
VERVE	10-20	66-69

Also see ECKSTINE, Billy / Arthur Prysock
Also see JOHNSON, Buddy

PRYSOCK, Arthur, & Count Basie
LP '66
Singles: 7–inch
VERVE..........................3-6   66
LPs: 10/12–inch 33rpm
VERVE........................15-20   66

PRYSOCK, Arthur / Leroy Bivins
LPs: 10/12–inch 33rpm
GUEST STAR.........................5-10   64
Also see PRYSOCK, Arthur

PUCKETT, Jerry
C&W '83
Singles: 7–inch
ATLANTIC AMERICA..................3-4   83
Also see CAMPBELL, Glen

PULLINS, Leroy
C&W/P&R '66
Singles: 7–inch
KAPP...........................4-8   66
LPs: 10/12–inch 33rpm
KAPP (3488 "I'm a Nut")..........20-30   66
KAPP (3557 "Funny Bones and Hearts")..................15-25   68

PUMP BOYS & DINETTES
C&W 83
Singles: 7–inch
CBS.............................3-4   83

PURE PRAIRIE LEAGUE
P&R/LP '75/C&W '76
Singles: 7–inch
RCA................................3-5 72-79
CASABLANCA...........................3-5 80-81
EPIC...............................3-5   77
LPs: 10/12–inch 33rpm
CASABLANCA...........................5-10 80-81
RCA................................6-12 72-80
Members/Session: John Call; George Powell; Billy Hinds; David Sanborn; Mick Ronson; Michael O'Connor; Johnny Gimble; Don Felder; Vince Gill; Chet Atkins; Larry Goshorn.
Also see ATKINS, Chet
Also see GILL, Vince

PUTMAN, Curly
C&W '60
Singles: 7–inch
ABC................................4-6   67
CHEROKEE..............................5-10   60
LPs: 10/12–inch 33rpm
ABC.........................10-20   67

PYLE, Chuck
C&W '85
Singles: 7–inch
URBAN SOUND..........................3-4 85-86.

QUIST, Jack
C&W '82
Singles: 7–inch
GRUDGE......................................3-4   89
MEMORY MACHINE....................3-4   82

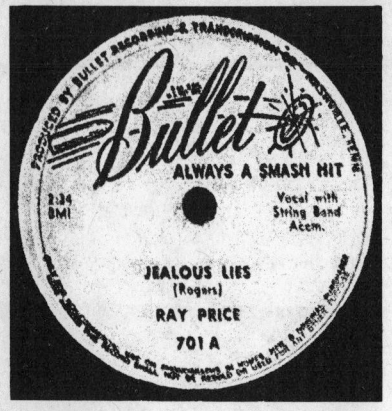

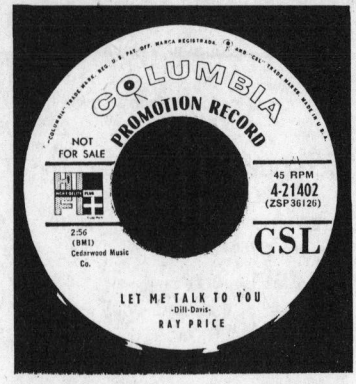

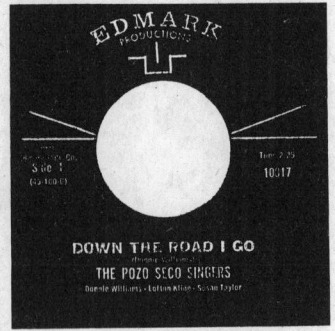

RABBITT, Eddie   *C&W '74*
Singles: 7–inch

DATE.. 4-8   68
ELEKTRA (Except 378) 3-5   74-83
ELEKTRA (378 "Song of
Ireland")...................................... 5-10   78
(Colored vinyl—green of course. With green
insert. Promotional issue only.)
RCA... 3-4   85-89
20TH FOX 5-10   64
UNIVERSAL.................................. 3-4   89
W.B. 3-5   83-85

Picture Sleeves

ELEKTRA...................................... 3-5   81

LPs: 10/12–inch 33rpm

ELEKTRA..................................... 5-10   75-82
RCA.. 5-8   86
W.B. 5-8   84-85
Also see FRICKE, Janie

RABBITT, Eddie, & Crystal
Gayle   *C&W/P&R '82*
Singles: 7–inch

ELEKTRA....................................... 3-5   82
Also see GAYLE, Crystal

RABBITT, Eddie, & Juice
Newton   *C&W '86*
Singles: 7–inch

RCA.. 3-4   86
Also see NEWTON, Juice
Also see RABBITT, Eddie

RABBITT, Jimmy, &
Renegade   *C&W '76*
Singles: 7–inch

CAPITOL....................................... 3-5   76

LP: 10/12–inch 33rpm

CAPITOL...................................... 5-10   76
Session: Waylon Jennings.
Also see JENNINGS, Waylon

RAE, Lana   *C&W '72*
Singles: 7–inch

DECCA.. 3-5   72

RAINES, Leon   *C&W '83*
Singles: 7–inch

AMERICAN SPOTLIGHT............... 3-4   83-84
ATLANTIC AMERICA 3-4   84-85
SOUTHERN TRACKS 3-4   87

RAINFORD, Tina   *C&W '77*
Singles: 7–inch

EPIC... 3-5   77

LP: 10/12–inch 33rpm

EPIC... 5-10   77

RAINSFORD, Willie   *C&W '77*
Singles: 7–inch

LOUISIANA HAYRIDE................... 3-5   77

RAINWATER, Jack   *C&W '77*
Singles: 7–inch

LAURIE... 3-5   77

RAINWATER, Marvin   *C&W/P&R '57*
Singles: 78rpm

CORAL.. 5-10   56
MGM (Except 12240 & 12370) 5-15   55-57
MGM (12240 "Hot and Cold") 10-15   56
MGM (12370 "Get off the
Stool") 10-15   56

Singles: 7–inch

BRAVE... 4-6   63-67
CORAL... 8-12   56
HILLTOP.. 5-10   70s
MGM (12000 & 12100 series).... 10-20   55
MGM (12240 "Hot and Cold") 30-40   56
MGM (12313 "Why Did You Have to Go and
Love Me")................................... 10-20   56
MGM (12370 "Get off the
Stool") 30-40   56
MGM (12412 thru 12938)............. 5-10   57-60
NU TRAYL 3-5   76
U.A. 4-6   65-66
W.B. 3-5   69-70
WARWICK 5-10   61

EPs: 7–inch 33/45rpm

MGM (1464/1465/1466 "Songs by Marvin
Rainwater") 15-25   57
(Price is for any of three volumes.)

LPs: 10/12–inch 33rpm

CROWN 5-10   60s
GUEST STAR............................... 5-10
MARK IV 8-12
MGM (3534 "Songs by Marvin
Rainwater") 50-100   57

MGM (3721 "With a Heart With a
Beat") 50-100   58
MGM (4046 "Gonna Find Me a
Bluebird") 50-100   62
MOUNT VERNON....................... 8-10
SPINORAMA............................... 8-10   60s
   Also see DEAN, Jimmy / Marvin Rainwater
   Also see FRANCIS, Connie, & Marvin Rainwater

RAITT, Bonnie   *LP '72/C&W '80*
Singles: 7–inch
CAPITOL.. 3-4   89-91
W.B. 3-4   72-86
Picture Sleeves
W.B. 3-4   79
LPs: 10/12–inch 33rpm
CAPITOL.. 5-8   89-91
W.B. 6-12   71-86
   Also see MULDAUR, Geoff, & Bonnie Raitt

RAITT, Bonnie / Gilley's "Urban Cowboy" Band
Singles: 7–inch
FULL MOON/ASYLUM 3-5   80
Picture Sleeves
FULL MOON/ASYLUM 3-5   80
   Also see RAITT, Bonnie

RAKES, Pal   *C&W '77*
(With the Prophets)
Singles: 7–inch
ATLANTIC...................................... 3-4   89
ATLANTIC AMERICA 3-4   88
VERVE 4-8   68
W.B. 3-5   77-79
   Also see PAL & PROPHETS

RAMBLING ROGUE   *C&W '45*
(Fred Rose)
Singles: 78rpm
BRUNSWICK 10-20   20s
OKEH 5-10   45

RANDOLPH, Boots   *P&R/R&B/LP '63*
(Homer Randolph)
Singles: 7–inch
MONUMENT 3-5   61-83
PALO ALTO 3-4
RCA.. 4-8   59-61
Picture Sleeves
MONUMENT 5-10   64

EPs: 7–inch 33/45rpm
MONUMENT (361 "Boots &
Stockings")..................................5-10   69
(Promotional issue only.)
LPs: 10/12–inch 33rpm
CAMDEN 10-20   64
GUEST STAR..............................5-10   64
MONUMENT (Except 8000 & 18000
series)..6-12   71-82
MONUMENT (8000 & 18000
series)......................................10-20   63-71
PALO ALTO 5-8
RCA (LPM-2165 "Yakety Sax") 15-25   60
(Monaural.)
RCA (LSP-2165 "Yakety Sax") ..25-35   60
(Stereo.)
TEXIZE (1 "Nashville Sound") ...10-15   68
(Promotional issue only.)
   Also see ATKINS, Chet, Floyd Cramer & Boots
    Randolph
   Also see FRANCIS, Connie
   Also see HALEY, Bill / Boots Randolph
   Also see LEE, Brenda
   Also see NASHVILLE ALL-STARS
   Also see PRESLEY, Elvis
   Also see RANDOLPH, Randy
   Also see TILLOTSON, Johnny

RANDOLPH, Boots, & Al Hirt
Singles: 7–inch
MONUMENT..................................3-5   75

RANDOLPH, Randy
(Homer Randolph)
Singles: 7–inch
RCA 5-10   58-59
   Also see RANDOLPH, Boots

RANEY, Wayne   *C&W '45*
Singles: 78rpm
KING 8-12   48-51
Singles: 7–inch
KING 8-15   51
LP: 10/12–inch 33rpm
KING 20-30
NASHVILLE 10-15
RIMROCK 5-10
STARDAY 15-20

RAT RACE KID
Singles: 7–inch
KEVIN KAT 3-5   80-82
TEXAS RE-CORD 3-5   80-81
LPs: 10/12–inch 33rpm
KEVIN KAT 5-10   82
   Also see MEYERS, Augie

RATTLESNAKE ANNIE   *C&W '87*
Singles: 7–inch
COLUMBIA 3-4   87-88
LPs: 10/12–inch 33rpm
COLUMBIA 5-8   87

RAUSCH, Leon   *C&W '76*
Singles: 7–inch
DERRICK...................................... 3-5   76-79
SOUTHLAND (Black vinyl)............ 3-4   84
SOUTHLAND (Colored vinyl)........ 3-5   84
LP: 10/12–inch 33rpm
DERRICK...................................... 5-10   76
DISCUS.. 10-20
SOUTHLAND (Black vinyl)............ 5-8   84
SOUTHLAND (Colored vinyl)...... 8-10   84
Also see ORIGINAL TEXAS PLAYBOYS

RAVEN, Eddy   *C&W '74*
(Eddie Raven)
Singles: 7–inch
ABC.. 3-5   74-75
ABC/DOT 3-5   75-76
CAPITOL....................................... 3-4   89-90
COSMOS 8-12   62
DIMENSION.................................. 3-5   79-81
ELEKTRA...................................... 3-4   81-82
LA LOUISIANNE (77
  "Pictures") 10-20
MONUMENT.................................. 3-5   78
RCA.. 3-4   84-88
UNIVERSAL................................... 3-4   89
LP: 10/12–inch 33rpm
ABC/DOT 5-10   75-76
DIMENSION.................................. 5-8   80
ELEKTRA...................................... 5-8   81
LA LOUISIANNE 10-15
RCA.. 5-8   84-88

RAY, Mundo: see EARWOOD, Mundo

RAYE, Colin   *C&W/LP '91*
Singles: 7–inch
EPIC.. 3-4   91-92
LP: 10/12–inch 33rpm
EPIC.. 5-8   91
Also see WRAYS

RAYE, Susan   *C&W/LP '70*
Singles: 7–inch
CAPITOL....................................... 3-6   69-76
U.A. 3-5   76-77
WESTEXAS 3-4   85-86

Picture Sleeves
CAPITOL..3-5   71
LPs: 10/12–inch 33rpm
CAPITOL......................................10-20   70-76
U.A. 5-10   77
Also see OWENS, Buck, & Susan Raye

RAZORBACK   *C&W '87*
Singles: 7–inch
COMPLEAT 3-4   87
ICR...3-4   87
MERCURY......................................3-4   88
Also see GRAYGHOST

REAGAN, Joe
LP: 10/12–inch 33rpm
WYNCOTE (9047 "Tribute to Jim
  Reeves") 8-12   63

RECORD, Donnie   *C&W '83*
Singles: 7–inch
BRIARROSE...................................3-4   83

RED, WHITE & BLUE (GRASS)   *C&W '73*
Singles: 7–inch
GRC...3-5   73
Members: Grant Boatwright; Ginger Boatwright.

RED WILLOW BAND   *C&W '79*
Singles: 7–inch
LOST..3-5   79

REDDY, Helen   *P&R/LP '71/C&W '77*
Singles: 12–inch 33/45rpm
CAPITOL..4-6   79
Singles: 7–inch
CAPITOL..3-5   71-81
FONTANA......................................3-6   68
MCA...3-5   81-83
LPs: 10/12–inch 33rpm
CAPITOL..5-10   71-81
MCA...5-8   81-83
Also see PRESLEY, Elvis / Helen Reddy

REDMOND, Robb   *C&W '77*
Singles: 7–inch
NBC 3-5   77

REECE, Ben   *C&W '75*
Singles: 7–inch
POLYDOR 3-5   76
20TH CENTURY............................3-5   75-76

REED, Bobby

C&W '83

Singles: 7–inch

CBO 3-4   83

REED, Jerry

P&R '62/C&W '67

(With the Hully Girlies; with Seidina; with Friends)

Singles: 78rpm

CAPITOL..................................... 5-15   55-56

Singles: 7–inch

CAPITOL..................................... 10-20   55-56
COLUMBIA 5-10   61-63
NRC 5-10   59
RCA (Except 8500 thru 9700)....... 3-5   69-85
RCA (8500 thru 9700) 4-8   65-69

Picture Sleeves

COLUMBIA 8-10   61
RCA... 3-4   72-85

LPs: 10/12–inch 33rpm

CAMDEN..................................... 5-10   72-74
HARMONY................................... 8-12   71
PICKWICK/HILLTOP 5-10
RCA (Except "LPM" & "LSP" series) 5-10   73-83
RCA ("LPM" & "LSP" series)....... 8-18   67-73

    Also see HART, Freddie / Sammi Smith / Jerry Reed
    Also see JENNINGS, Waylon, & Jerry Reed
    Also see JUSTIS, Bill / Jerry Reed
    Also see NELSON, Willie
    Also see PRESLEY, Elvis
    Also see SOME of CHET'S FRIENDS

REED, Jerry, & Chet Atkins

LPs: 10/12–inch 33rpm

RCA... 10-20   72

    Also see ATKINS, Chet
    Also see REED, Jerry

REEVES, Del

C&W '61

(With the Goodtime Charlies)

Singles: 7–inch

CHART... 3-5   70
COLUMBIA 4-6   64
DECCA... 4-8   61-62
KOALA 3-5   80-82
LAS VEGAS 10-15   59
PEACH.. 10-15   60
PLAYBACK 3-4   86
REPRISE 4-8   63
U.A. 3-6   66-78

Picture Sleeves

KOALA 3-4   80
U.A. 3-6   67

LPs: 10/12–inch 33rpm

KOALA 5-8   79-80
STARDAY 5-8
SUNSET 5-10   69-70
U.A. (200 thru 600 series)............ 5-10   73-76
U.A. (3000 & 6000 series).......... 10-20   65-71

REEVES, Del, & Penny DeHaven

C&W '72

Singles: 7–inch

U.A. 3-5   72

    Also see DeHAVEN, Penny

REEVES, Del, & Bobby Goldsboro

C&W '68

Singles: 7–inch

U.A. 3-6   65-71

LPs: 10/12–inch 33rpm

U.A. 10-20   68

    Also see GOLDSBORO, Bobby

REEVES, Del / Red Sovine

LPs: 10/12–inch 33rpm

EXACT 5-8   80

    Also see SOVINE, Red

REEVES, Del, & Billie Jo Spears

C&W '76

Singles: 7–inch

U.A. 3-5   76

LPs: 10/12–inch 33rpm

LIBERTY...................................... 5-8   82
U.A. 5-10   76

    Also see REEVES, Del
    Also see SPEARS, Billie Jo

REEVES, Jim

C&W '53

(With His Circle O Ranch Boys)

Singles: 78rpm

ABBOTT (Black plastic) 15-25   53-55
ABBOTT (Colored plastic) 25-50   53-55
MACY'S (115 "Teardrops of Regret").................................. 150-250   50
MACY'S (132 "I've Never Been So Blue") 150-250   51
RCA 10-20   55-57

Singles: 7–inch

ABBOTT (100 series, except 116)...................................... 10-25   53-55
(Black vinyl.)
ABBOTT (115 "Wagon Load of Love")................................... 15-25   53
(Black vinyl.)

ABBOTT (115 "Wagon Load of
Love")....................................... 35-50   53
(Colored vinyl.)

ABBOTT (116 "Mexican Joe")... 15-25   53
(Black vinyl.)

ABBOTT (116 "Mexican Joe")... 35-50   53
(Colored vinyl.)

ABBOTT (137 "Butterfly Love"). 15-25   53
(Black vinyl.)

ABBOTT (137 "Butterfly Love"). 35-50   53
(Colored vinyl.)

ABBOTT (143 "El Rancho Del
Rio") 15-25   53
(Black vinyl.)

ABBOTT (143 "El Rancho Del
Rio") 35-50   53
(Colored vinyl.)

ABBOTT (148 "Bimbo")............. 15-25   53
(Black vinyl.)

ABBOTT (148 "Bimbo")............. 35-50   53
(Colored vinyl.)

ABBOTT (160 thru 186) 10-20   54-55

ABBOTT (3000 series)............. 10-20   55

ABBOTT (4000 series)................ 4-8

RCA (0135 thru 0963) 3-8   69-74

RCA (6200 thru 7557) 10-20   55-59

RCA (7643 "He'll Have to Go").... 5-10   59

RCA (7643 "He'll Have to
Go")..................................... 150-250   59
(Single-sided. Promotional issue only.)

RCA (7756 thru 9969) 4-10   60-71

RCA (10133 thru 13693) 3-6   75-84

Picture Sleeves

RCA (Except 8252) 8-15   60-65

RCA (8252 "Señor Santa
Claus") 15-20   63

EPs: 7–inch 33/45rpm

RCA (Except 1256) 25-50   56-61

RCA (1256 "Singing Down the
Lane").................................... 50-100   56
(Double EP set.)

LPs: 10/12–inch 33rpm

ABBOTT (5001 "Jim Reeves
Sings").............................. 1000-1500   56

CMF (008 "Live at the Opry")...... 5-10

CAMDEN (Except 583 thru 686) . 5-15   64-73

CAMDEN (583 thru 686) 10-20   60-63

CANDLELIGHT ("Jim
Reeves") 15-25   83
(Boxed 5-LP set.)

GUEST STAR 10-15   64

HISTORY of COUNTRY
MUSIC 6-10   72

PAIR...6-12   82

PICKWICK 5-10   72

PICKWICK/HILLTOP 5-10   74

RCA (0039 thru 5044)..................5-10   73-84
(With "AHL," "ANL," "APL," "AYL" or "CPL"
prefix.)

RCA (0126 "The Jim Reeves
Collection")................................10-15
(Special Products issue, two-LPs.)

RCA (0246 "Take My Hand, Precious
Lord") 10-15
(Special Products issue, two-LPs.)

RCA (0587 "Golden
Collection")................................30-35
(Special Products issue, five-LP set.)

RCA (LPM-1256 "Singing Down the
Lane") 100-200   56

RCA (LPM-1410 "Bimbo")..........40-60   57

RCA (LPM-1576 "Jim
Reeves") 30-50   57

RCA (LPM-1685 "Girls I Have
Known") 25-50   58

RCA (LPM-1950 "God Be with
You")..20-40   58
(Monaural.)

RCA (LSP-1950 "God Be with
You")..20-40   58
(Stereo.)

RCA (LPM-2001 thru
LPM-2339)...............................15-25   59-61
(Monaural.)

RCA (LSP-2001 thru
LSP-2339)................................20-30   59-61
(Stereo.)

RCA (LPM-2487 thru
LPM-3903)...............................10-20   62-67

RCA (LSP-2487 thru
LSP-3903)................................10-25   62-67

RCA (LPM-3987 "A Touch of
Sadness") 25-35   68
(Monaural.)

RCA (LSP-3987 "A Touch of
Sadness") 10-15   68
(Stereo.)

RCA (LSP-4062 thru
LSP-4749)..................................8-15   68-72

RADIANT 5-10

READER'S DIGEST/RCA (210 "Unforgettable
Jim Reeves") 25-35   76
(Boxed 6-LP set.)

TAMPA/RCA SPECIAL PRODUCTS (0126
"Jim Reeves") 8-10   75

Also see BLUE BOYS
Also see CRAMER, Floyd
Also see JORDANAIRES

Also see KERR, Anita
Also see PRESLEY, Elvis / Hank Snow / Eddy Arnold /
Hank Snow
Also see WRIGHT, Ginny

REEVES, Jim, & Deborah Allen   *C&W '79*

Singles: 7–inch

RCA...3-5 79-80
Also see ALLEN, Deborah

REEVES, Jim, & Patsy Cline   *C&W '81*

(Patsy Cline & Jim Reeves)
Singles: 7–inch

MCA 3-5   82
RCA..3-5   81
LPs: 10/12–inch 33rpm

MCA 5-10   82
RCA..5-10   81
Also see CLINE, Patsy

REEVES, Jim / Alvadean Coker

Singles: 78rpm

ABBOTT 10-20   54
Singles: 7–inch

ABBOTT 15-25   54
Also see COKER, Al

REEVES, Jim / Hugi & Lugi Chorus

Singles: 7–inch

U.S.A.F. (89 "In a Mansion Stands My
Love")......................................20-30   60s
(Promotional issue only.)

REEVES, Jim, & Dottie West

Singles: 7–inch

RCA..4-6   64
Also see REEVES, Jim
Also see WEST, Dottie

REEVES, Jimmy, Jr.

LPs: 10/12–inch 33rpm

CHECKER....................................8-10   71

REEVES, John Rex   *C&W '81*

Singles: 7–inch

SOC-A-GEE 3-5   81

REGAN, Bob, & Lucille Starr   *C&W '70*

Singles: 7–inch

DOT...3-5   69
Also see BOB & LUCILLE
Also see CANADIAN SWEETHEARTS

REID, Mike   *C&W '90*

Singles: 7–inch

COLUMBIA 3-4   90
Also see MILSAP, Ronnie, & Mike Reid

REMINGTON, Rita   *C&W '73*

(With the Smokey Valley Symphony)
Singles: 12–inch 33/45rpm

PLANTATION (171 "To Each His
Own")..4-8   78
(Promotional issue only.)
Singles: 7–inch

PLANTATION 3-5   73-82
LP: 10/12–inch 33rpm

PICKWICK 5-10   80
PLANTATION 5-10   77-78

REMINGTONS   *C&W '91*

Singles: 7–inch

BNA...3-4   91-92
Members: James Griffin; Rick Yancey; Richard
Mainegra.
Also see CYMARRON
Also see GRIFFIN, James

RENO, Don

(With His Tennessee Cut-Ups; with Don Wayne Reno)
LP: 10/12–inch 33rpm

CMH...5-10   78-79
DOT (3617 ""Mr. Five Strings")..15-20   65
(Monaural.)
DOT (25617 ""Mr. Five
Strings") 20-25   65
(Stereo.)
KING (1065 "Fastest Five Strings
Alive")..10-15   69
MONUMENT.............................10-20   66
SARDIS...5-10
WANGO 8-12   76

RENO, Don, & Benny Martin   *C&W '66*

(With the Tennessee Cut-Ups)
Singles: 7–inch

MONUMENT..................................4-6   65
LP: 10/12–inch 33rpm

CABIN CREEK..............................5-8
Also see MARTIN, Benny
Also see RENO, Don

RENO, Jack   *C&W '67*

Singles: 7–inch

DOT 3-6   68-70
JAB 4-6   67-68

TARGET................................... 3-5 71-72
U.A. 3-5 73-74

LP: 10/12–inch 33rpm

ATCO 10-15   68
DERBYTOWN............................ 5-10   78
DOT... 10-15 68-69
TARGET.................................... 8-12   72

RENO, Mike, & Ann
Wilson   *P&R '84*

Singles: 7–inch

COLUMBIA 3-4   84

Picture Sleeves

COLUMBIA 3-4   84

RENO, Ronnie   *C&W '83*

Singles: 7–inch

EMH 3-4   83

LP: 10/12–inch 33rpm

MCA... 5-10   75

Also see HAGGARD, Merle
Also see OSBORNE BROTHERS
Also see RENO BROTHERS

RENO & SMILEY   *C&W '61*

Singles: 78rpm

KING 5-10 52-57

Singles: 7–inch

KING (Except 1235 thru 5169)...... 4-8 59-62
KING (1235 thru 5169)................ 5-15 53-58

EPs: 7–inch 33/45rpm

KING 5-10 58-62

LP: 10/12–inch 33rpm

ATTEIRAM.................................. 5-10
DOT.. 10-20   63
GUSTO 5-8
KING (550 thru 693).................. 20-30 58-59
KING (701 thru 1091)................ 10-25 61-70
NASHVILLE 10-15   69
STARDAY 5-10 73-75
STARDAY/KING 5-10

Members: Don Reno; Red Smiley.
Also see CHICK & HOT RODS

RENO BROTHERS   *C&W '88*

Singles: 7–inch

STEP ONE 3-4 88-89

Members: Ronnie Reno; Dale Reno; Don Reno.
Also see RENO, Ronnie

RESTLESS HEART   *C&W '85*

Singles: 7–inch

RCA.. 3-4 85-91

LPs: 10/12–inch 33rpm

RCA 5-8 85-91

REX, Tim, & Oklahoma   *C&W '80*

Singles: 7–inch

DEE JAY 3-5 80-81

REY, Ernest   *C&W '79*

Singles: 7–inch

MCA...3-5   79

REYNOLDS, Allen   *C&W '78*

Singles: 7–inch

CAMEO...4-8   64
HALL WAY......................................4-8   62
RCA 4-8 61-63
TRIPLE I 3-5   78

REYNOLDS, Burt   *C&W/P&R '80*

Singles: 7–inch

MCA...3-5   80
MERCURY......................................3-5 73-74

Picture Sleeves

MCA...3-5   80

LPs: 10/12–inch 33rpm

MERCURY.....................................8-12   73

RHOADS, Randy   *C&W '90*

Singles: 7–inch

BLUE RIDGE 3-4   90

RICE, Bill   *C&W '71*
(Billy Rice)

Singles: 7–inch

CAPITOL...3-5   71
DOT 4-8   61
EPIC...3-5   72
FERNWOOD............................... 10-15   60
ONDA...5-10   59
POLYDOR 3-5 77-78

Also see JOHNSON, Lois, & Bill Rice

RICE, Bobby G.   *C&W '70*

Singles: 7–inch

CHARTA...3-5   81
DOOR KNOB....................................3-4 85-88
GRT 3-5 74-77
MERTOMEDIA.................................3-5 72-73
REPUBLIC.......................................3-5 78-79
ROYAL AMERICAN.........................3-5 70-72
SUNBIRD...3-5 80-81
SUNSET 3-5   79

LP: 10/12–inch 33rpm

AUDIOGRAPH ALIVE	5-8	82
GRT	6-12	74-76
METROMEDIA	6-12	73
ROYAL AMERICAN	6-12	72
SUNBIRD	5-10	80

Also see KEMP, Wayne, & Bobby G. Rice

RICE, Bobby G., & Perry LaPointe   *C&W '88*

Singles: 7–inch

DOOR KNOB	3-4	88

Also see LaPOINTE, Perry
Also see RICE, Bobby G.

RICH, Charlie   *P&R '60/C&W '68*

Singles: 7–inch

ARISTA	3-5	80
COLUMBIA	3-4	82
EPIC	3-5	70-81
ELEKTRA	3-5	78-81
GROOVE	4-8	63-64
HI	4-8	66-67
MERCURY	3-5	73-74
PHILLIPS INT'L	10-20	59-63
RCA (Except 8000 series)	3-5	74-77
RCA (8000 series)	4-8	64-65
SSS/SUN	3-5	70s
SMASH	4-8	65-66
U.A.	3-5	78-80

Picture Sleeves

GROOVE (0020 "She Loved Everybody But Me")	10-20	63
EPIC (AE7-1065)	3-6	73

(Promotional bonus only. Title not known.)

EPs: 7–inch 33/45rpm

EPIC (1099 "Silver Linings")	8-12	76

(Promotional issue only.)

LPs: 10/12–inch 33rpm

BUCKBOARD	8-10	70s
CAMDEN	8-10	70-74
CELEBRITY INT'L	5-8	91
EPIC (Except 139)	6-12	68-78
EPIC (139 "Everything You Wanted to Hear by Charlie Rich")	15-20	76

(Promotional issue only.)

ELEKTRA	5-10	80
51 WEST	5-10	
GROOVE (G-1000 "Charlie Rich")	15-25	64

(Monaural.)

GROOVE (GS-1000 "Charlie Rich")	20-30	64

(Stereo.)

HARMONY	8-10	73
HI (Except 32037)	8-10	74-77
HI (32037 "Charlie Rich")	15-25	67
HILLTOP	8-10	70s
MERCURY	10-15	74
PHILLIPS INT'L (1970 "Lonely Weekends")	400-600	60
PHONORAMA	5-8	83
PICKWICK	5-10	70s
POWER PAK	8-10	74-75
RCA (Except 3000 series)	8-10	73-77
RCA (3000 series)	15-25	65-66
SSS/SUN	5-10	69-79
SMASH	15-25	65-66
SUNNYVALE	5-10	77
TIME-LIFE	5-10	81
TRIP	8-10	74
U.A.	5-10	78-79
WING	10-15	69

Session: Jordanaires; David Wills; Anita Kerr Singers.
Also see CASH, Johnny
Also see JORDANAIRES
Also see KERR, Anita
Also see LEWIS, Jerry Lee, Carl Perkins & Charlie Rich
Also see SHERIDAN, Bobby
Also see TUBB, Ernest
Also see WILLS, David

RICH, Charlie, & Janie Fricke   *C&W '78*

Singles: 7–inch

EPIC	3-5	78

Also see FRICKE, Janie
Also see RICH, Charlie

RICH, Don

LP: 10/12–inch 33rpm

CAPITOL (643 "That Fiddlin' Man")	15-25	71

Also see BUCKAROOS

RICHARDS, Earl   *C&W '69*

Singles: 7–inch

ACE of HEARTS	3-5	73-75
U.A.	3-6	69-70

RICHARDS, Sue   *C&W '71*

Singles: 7–inch

ABC/DOT	3-5	75-76
DOT	3-5	73-74
EPIC	3-5	71-78

LP: 10/12–inch 33rpm

ABC/DOT 5-10   74-76

Also see HITCHCOCK, Stan, & Sue Richards

RICHIE, Lionel

P&R/R&B/LP '82/C&W '84

Singles: 12–inch 33/45rpm

MOTOWN 4-8   83-86

Singles: 7–inch

MOTOWN 3-4   82-87

Picture Sleeves

MOTOWN 3-4   83-87

LPs: 10/12–inch 33rpm

MOTOWN 5-8   82-86

Also see U.S.A. for AFRICA

RICHIE, Lionel, & Alabama   *C&W '86*

Singles: 12–inch 33/45rpm

MOTOWN (195 "Special Motown Service to Country Radio")........................ 8-12   86
(Promotional issue only.)

Singles: 7–inch

MOTOWN 3-4   86

Also see ALABAMA
Also see RICHIE, Lionel

RICKS, Steve   *C&W '86*

Singles: 7–inch

SOUTHWIND 3-4   86

RIDDELL, Allan   *C&W '60*

Singles: 7–inch

PLAID... 5-10   60

RIDE the RIVER   *C&W '87*

Singles: 7–inch

ADVANTAGE 3-4   87-88

RILEY, Jeannie C.   *C&W/P&R/LP '68*

(With the Red River Symphony)

Singles: 7–inch

CAPITOL...	3-6	69
CROSS COUNTRY.......................	3-4	79
GARPAX	3-4	80
GOD'S COUNTRY	3-5	75
MCA	3-4	82
MGM	3-5	71-74
MERCURY	3-5	74
PLANTATION (Black vinyl)	3-4	68-72
PLANTATION (Colored vinyl)	4-8	68-72
W.B.	3-5	76

Picture Sleeves

PLANTATION 4-8   68-72

EPs: 7–inch 33/45rpm

PLANTATION 5-10   68

LPs: 10/12–inch 33rpm

ALBUM GLOBE	5-8	80s
CAPITOL......................................	8-12	69
CROSS COUNTRY	5-10	79
HSRD/PLEASANT SOUNDS.........	5-8	82
HEARTWARMING	4-8	79
LITTLE DARLIN'	10-15	68
MGM	10-15	72-74
OUT of TOWN DIST	5-8	82
PICKWICK	5-10	70s
PLANTATION	5-12	68-82
POWER PAK	5-8	80s
SONGBIRD..................................	4-8	81-83
TRIP...	8-12	74

Also see CASH, Johnny / Jerry Lee Lewis / Jeanie C. Riley
Also see CASH, Johnny / Jeanie C. Riley

RILEY, Larry   *C&W '81*

Singles: 7–inch

F&L 3-4   81

RINKY DINKS   *P&R/R&B '58*

(Featuring Bobby Darin)

Singles: 7–inch

ATCO (6121 "Early in the Morning") 25-50   58
(Previously issued as by the Ding Dongs. Later issued as by "Bobby Darin & the Rinky Dinks.")

Also see DARIN, Bobby

RISHARD, Rod   *C&W '83*

Singles: 7–inch

SOUNDWAVES............................3-4   83-84

RISHERS, Rod   *C&W '83*

Singles: 7–inch

SOUNDWAVES............................3-4   83-84

RITTER, Tex   *C&W/P&R '44*

(With the Texans; with Plainsmen)

Singles: 78rpm

CAPITOL......................................	5-10	44-57
CHAMPION..................................	10-20	30s
CONQUEROR	10-20	30s
DECCA	5-10	30s-41

U.A. ("High Noon Ballad—Do Not Forsake Me") 20-40   52
(Single-sided disc. Promotional issue only.)

Singles: 7–inch

CAPITOL (1100 thru 3900 series) 5-10	50-58
(Purple labels.)	
CAPITOL (2000 thru 4000 series) 3-6	68-76
(Orange labels.)	
CAPITOL (4000 thru 5900 series) 4-8	58-67
CAPITOL (10485 "High Noon"). 15-25	52
(Single-sided disc. Promotional issue only.)	

Picture Sleeves

CAPITOL 4-8	68

EPs: 7–inch 33/45rpm

CAPITOL (Except 431) 10-20	59-60
CAPITOL (431 "Tex Ritter Sings") 20-40	53

LPs: 10/12–inch 33rpm

ALBUM GLOBE 5-8	80s
BUCKBOARD 5-8	80s
CAPITOL (213 thru 467) 8-12	69-71
CAPITOL (971 "Songs from the Western Screen") 25-40	58
CAPITOL (1100 "Psalms") 20-30	59
CAPITOL (T-1292 "Blood on the Saddle") 15-25	60
(Monaural.)	
CAPITOL (ST-1292 "Blood on the Saddle") 15-30	60
(Stereo.)	
CAPITOL (SM-1292 "Blood on the Saddle") 5-10	78
CAPITOL (1623 thru 2800) 10-20	61-68
CAPITOL (W-1562 "The Lincoln Hymns") 25-30	61
(Monaural.)	
CAPITOL (SW-1562 "The Lincoln Hymns") 30-35	61
(Stereo.)	
CAPITOL (4004 "Cowboy Favorites") 50-75	53
(10–inch LP.)	
CORONET 8-12	60s
HILLTOP 10-15	60s
LA BREA (8036 "Jamboree") 30-40	62
PICKWICK/HILLTOP 6-12	66-68
PREMIER 5-10	
SHASTA 8-12	60s
SPIN-O-RAMA 8-12	60s
Session: Rio Grande River Boys.	

RITTER, Tex, & Stan Kenton

LPs: 10/12–inch 33rpm

CAPITOL (T-1757 "Stan Kenton & Tex Ritter") 40-60	62
(Monaural.)	
CAPITOL (ST-1757 "Stan Kenton & Tex Ritter") 50-75	62
(Stereo.)	
Also see RITTER, Tex	

RIVERS, Eddie *C&W '77*

(With the Carol Lee Singers)

Singles: 7–inch

CHARTA 3-5	77-89

RIVERS, Jack *C&W '48*

Singles: 78rpm

CAPITOL 4-8	48

RIVERS, Johnny *P&R/LP '64/C&W '74*

(Johnny Ramistella)

Singles: 7–inch

ATLANTIC 3-5	74
BIG TREE 3-5	77-78
CAPITOL 4-8	62-64
CHANCELLOR 8-12	61-62
CORAL 5-10	64
CUB (9047 "Everyday") 10-20	59
CUB (9058 "Answer Me, My Love") 10-15	60
DEE DEE 10-15	59
EPIC 3-5	75-76
ERA 5-10	61
GONE (5026 "Baby Come Back") 20-30	58
GUYDEN (2003 "Hole in the Ground") 10-15	58
GUYDEN (2110 "Hole in the Ground") 4-8	64
IMPERIAL 4-8	64-70
MGM 5-8	64
RSO 3-5	80
RIVERAIRE (1001 "Don't Bug Me Baby") 10-20	59
ROULETTE (4565 "Baby Come Back") 8-12	64
ROWE/AMI 5-10	66
("Play Me" Sales Stimulator promotional issue.)	
SOUL CITY (Except 008) 3-5	76-77
SOUL CITY (008 "Slow Dancing") 4-8	77
U.A. (Except 700 series) 3-5	71-73

U.A. (700 series) 4-8   64
Picture Sleeves
IMPERIAL 5-10   64-69
U.A. 3-5   71
LPs: 10/12–inch 33rpm
ATLANTIC................................... 8-10   74
BIG TREE 8-10   77
CAPITOL (T-2161 "Sensational Johnny
Rivers") 35-50   64
(Monaural.)
CAPITOL (ST-2161 "Sensational Johnny
Rivers") 50-75   64
(Stereo.)
CUSTOM.................................... 8-12   60s
EPIC 8-10   75
GUEST STAR 10-15   64
IMPERIAL 10-20   64-70
KOALA 5-10   79
LIBERTY 5-8   82
MCA 5-8   85
PICKWICK 8-10   70s
PRIORITY 5-8   83
RSO 5-10   80
SEARS (417 "Mr. Teenage")..... 20-30   60s
(Special Products issue for Sears stores)
SOUL CITY 8-10   77
SUNSET..................................... 8-12   67-69
U.A. (Except UAL, UAS
& UXS series) 5-10   73-75
U.A. (UAL-3386 "Go Johnny
Go").. 20-25   64
(Monaural.)
U.A. (UAS-6386 "Go Johnny
Go").. 20-30   64
(Stereo.)
U.A. (UAS-5532
"Homegrown")......................... 10-15   71
U.A. (UAS-5650 "L.A.
Reggae")................................ 10-15   72
U.A. (UXS-93 "Johnny Rivers"). 12-15   72
UNART...................................... 10-20   67
Also see JONES, Tom / Freddie & Dreamers / Johnny Rivers
Also see RAMISTELLA, Johnny

RIVERS, Johnny / Steve Alaimo
LPs: 10/12–inch 33rpm
CUSTOM...................................... 8-12   60s
Also see ALAIMO, Steve

RIVERS, Johnny / Jerry Cole
LPs: 10/12–inch 33rpm
CROWN 10-20   64

RIVERS, Johnny / 4 Seasons / Jerry Butler / Jimmy Soul
LPs: 10/12–inch 33rpm
GLADWYNNE (2004 "Shindig Hullabaloo
Spectacular") 10-20   65

RIVERS, Johnny / Trini Lopez
LPs: 10/12–inch 33rpm
CUSTOM 8-12   60s

RIVERS, Johnny / Rascals / Buggs / Four Seasons
LPs: 10/12–inch 33rpm
CORONET (283 "The Young
Rascals") 15-25   66

RIVERS, Johnny / Ricky Nelson / Randy Sparks
LPs: 10/12–inch 33rpm
MGM (E-4256 "Johnny Rivers, Ricky Nelson,
Randy Sparks")......................... 20-25   64
(Monaural.)
MGM (SE-4256 "Johnny Rivers, Ricky
Nelson, Randy Sparks") 20-30   64
(Stereo.)
Also see NELSON, Ricky
Also see RIVERS, Johnny

RIVERS, Johnny / Tremonts / Luke Gordon / Charlie Francis
LPs: 10/12–inch 33rpm
CORONET (246 "Swingin'
Shindig") 10-20   64
PREMIER (P-9037 "Swingin'
Shindig") 10-20   64
(Monaural.)
PREMIER (PS-9037 "Swingin'
Shindig") 15-25   64
(Stereo.)
Also see RIVERS, Johnny

ROBBINS, Dennis   *C&W '87*
Singles: 7–inch
MCA...3-4   87
Also see BILLY HILL

ROBBINS, Hargus "Pig"   *C&W '79*
Singles: 7–inch
ELEKTRA......................................3-5   79
Also see BANDY, Moe
Also see LEE, Bobby
Also see NASHVILLE SUPERPICKERS

ROBBINS, Jenny   *C&W '78*
Singles: 7–inch
EL DORADO.................................3-5   78

ROBBINS, Marty   *C&W '52*
(With Ray Conniff; with Lee Emerson)

Singles: 78rpm

COLUMBIA (20965 thru 21324)	15-25	52-54
COLUMBIA (21351 thru 21545)	20-30	54
COLUMBIA (21352 thru 21414)	10-20	54-55
COLUMBIA (40000 thru 41000 series)	20-50	56-58

Singles: 7–inch

COLUMBIA (02000 & 03000 series)	3-4	81-83
COLUMBIA (10305 thru 11425)	3-5	76-81
COLUMBIA (20965 thru 21324)	20-30	52-54
COLUMBIA (21351 "That's All Right")	30-50	54
COLUMBIA (21352 thru 21414)	15-25	54-55
COLUMBIA (21446 "Maybellene")	30-50	55
COLUMBIA (21461 "Pretty Mama")	30-50	55
COLUMBIA (21477 "Tennessee Toddy")	30-50	56
COLUMBIA (21508 "Singing the Blues")	15-25	56
COLUMBIA (21545 "Singing the Blues")	10-20	56
COLUMBIA (30589 "Big Iron") (Compact 33 stereo.)	20-40	60
COLUMBIA (31749 "Little Rich Girl") (Compact 33 stereo.)	20-40	62
COLUMBIA (31751 "Kinda Halfway Feel") (Compact 33 stereo.)	20-40	62
COLUMBIA (33013 "El Paso") (Compact 33 stereo.)	20-40	61
COLUMBIA (40679 "Long Tall Sally")	30-50	56
COLUMBIA (40706 "Respectfully Miss Brooks")	30-50	56
COLUMBIA (40815 thru 41408)	8-15	57-59
COLUMBIA (41511 thru 43770)	4-8	59-66
COLUMBIA (43845 thru 45775)	3-6	67-73
DECCA	4-6	72
MCA	3-5	73-75

Picture Sleeves

COLUMBIA (40815 thru 41408)	10-30	57-59

COLUMBIA (41511 thru 43770)	5-15	59-66

EPs: 7–inch 33/45rpm

COLUMBIA (1785 "Marty Robbins")	20-40	56
COLUMBIA (2116 "Singing the Blues")	20-40	56
COLUMBIA (2134 "A White Sport Coat")	20-30	57
COLUMBIA (2153 "Marty Robbins")	15-25	56
COLUMBIA (2808 "Marty Robbins")	20-30	57
COLUMBIA (2814 "Marty Robbins")	10-20	58
COLUMBIA (9761/9762/9763 "The Song of Robbins") (Price is for any of three volumes.)	10-20	57
COLUMBIA (10000 thru 14000 series)	10-20	57-60

LPs: 10/12–inch 33rpm

ARTCO (110 "Best of Marty Robbins") (Covers shows 110 but label has 644.)	40-50	73
CANDLELITE	8-12	77
CBS (19738 "Cause I Love You")	5-10	84
COLUMBIA (15 "Marty's Country")	10-15	69
COLUMBIA (31 "Open-End Columbia Artists Interviews") (Promotional issue only.)	35-50	60s
COLUMBIA (32 "Columbia Artists Interviews with Frank Jones") (Includes 42-page booklet. Promotional issue only.)	50-75	
COLUMBIA (237 "Saddle Tramp") (Columbia Record Club issue.)	25-35	66
COLUMBIA (445 "Bend in the River") (Columbia Record Club issue.)	35-45	68
COLUMBIA (890 "Marty Robbins Gold")	8-10	75
COLUMBIA (976 "The Song of Robbins")	25-35	57
COLUMBIA (1087 "Song of the Islands")	25-35	57
COLUMBIA (1189 "Marty Robbins")	25-35	58
COLUMBIA (1256 "Return of the Gunfighter") (Columbia "Country Star" series.)	15-20	69
COLUMBIA (1325 "Marty's Greatest Hits")	15-25	59

COLUMBIA (1349 "Gunfighter Ballads and Trail Songs") 15-25 59

COLUMBIA (1481 "More Gunfighter Ballads and Trail Songs") 15-25 60

COLUMBIA (1599 "Marty's Greatest Hits") 15-20 69
(Columbia "Country Star" series issue.)

COLUMBIA (1635 "More Greatest Hits") 15-25 61

COLUMBIA (1666 "Just a Little Sentimental") 15-25 61

COLUMBIA (1801 "Marty After Midnight") 40-50 62

COLUMBIA (1855 "Portrait of Marty") 25-35 62
(With bonus portrait of Marty.)

COLUMBIA (1855 "Portrait of Marty") 15-25 62
(Without bonus portrait of Marty.)

COLUMBIA (1918 "Devil Woman") 15-20 62

COLUMBIA (2016 "The Heart of Marty Robbins") 80-100 69
(Columbia "Country Star" series issue.)

COLUMBIA (2040 "Hawaii's Calling Me") 20-30 62

COLUMBIA (2072 "Return of the Gunfighter") 15-20 63

COLUMBIA (2167 "Island Woman") 25-35 64

COLUMBIA (2220 "R.F.D.") 25-35 64

COLUMBIA (2304 "Turn the Lights Down Low") 20-40 65

COLUMBIA (2448 "What God Has Done") 15-20 65

COLUMBIA (2527 "The Drifter") 10-20 66

COLUMBIA (2563 "What God Has Done") 15-20 69
(Columbia "Country Star" series issue.)

COLUMBIA (2601 "Rock'n Roll'n Robbins") 500-600 56
(10–inch LP.)

COLUMBIA (2645 "My Kind of Country") 15-20 67

COLUMBIA (2725 "Tonight Carmen") 10-20 67

COLUMBIA (2735 "Christmas with Marty Robbins") 20-30 67

COLUMBIA (2762 "More Gunfighter Ballads and Trail Songs") 15-20 69
(Columbia "Country Star" series issue.)

COLUMBIA (2817 "By The Time I Get to Phoenix") 20-30 68

COLUMBIA (3557 "The Drifter") 15-20 69
(Columbia "Country Star" series issue.)

COLUMBIA (3867 "My Kind of Country") 15-20 69
(Columbia "Country Star" series issue.)

COLUMBIA (5489 "Tonight Carmen") 15-20 69
(Columbia "Country Star" series issue.)

COLUMBIA (5498 "Christmas with Marty Robbins") 15-20 69
(Columbia "Country Star" series issue.)

COLUMBIA (5812 "Marty") 20-40 72
(Five-LP set. Columbia Special Products issue.)

COLUMBIA (6994 "I Walk Alone") 15-20 69
(Columbia "Country Star" series issue.)

COLUMBIA (CS-8158 "Gunfighter Ballads and Trail Songs") 15-25 59

COLUMBIA (PC-8158 "Gunfighter Ballads and Trail Songs") 5-10

COLUMBIA (CS-8272 "More Gunfighter Ballads and Trail Songs") 15-25 60

COLUMBIA (PC-8272 "More Gunfighter Ballads and Trail Songs") 5-10

COLUMBIA (CS-8435 "More Greatest Hits") 15-20 61

COLUMBIA (PC-8435 "More Greatest Hits") 5-10

COLUMBIA (8466 "Just a Little Sentimental") 15-25 61

COLUMBIA (8601 "Marty After Midnight") 25-35 62

COLUMBIA (8655 "Portrait of Marty") 25-35 62
(With bonus portrait of Marty.)

COLUMBIA (8655 "Portrait of Marty") 15-25 62
(Without bonus portrait.)

COLUMBIA (8718 "Devil Woman") 15-20 62

COLUMBIA (8840 "Hawaii's Calling Me") 20-30 62

COLUMBIA (8872 "Return of the Gunfighter") 15-20 63

COLUMBIA (8976 "Island Woman") 35-40 64

COLUMBIA (CS-9020 "R.F.D.") 25-35 64

COLUMBIA (CSRP-9020 "R.F.D.") 8-10
(Columbia Special Products issue.)

COLUMBIA (9104 "Turn the Lights Down Low") 20-40   65

COLUMBIA (CS-9248 "What God Has Done") 15-20   65

COLUMBIA (ACS-9248 "What God Has Done") 5-10
(Columbia Special Products issue.)

COLUMBIA (9327 "The Drifter") 10-20   66

COLUMBIA (9421 "The Song of Robbins") 30-40   67

COLUMBIA (9445 "My Kind of Country") 15-25   67

COLUMBIA (9525 "Tonight Carmen") 10-20   67

COLUMBIA (9535 "Christmas with Marty Robbins") 10-20   67

COLUMBIA (9617 "By the Time I Get to Phoenix") 8-12   68

COLUMBIA (9725 "I Walk Alone") 8-15   68

COLUMBIA (9811 "It's a Sin")... 20-30   69

COLUMBIA (9978 "My Woman, My Woman, My Wife") 8-12   70

COLUMBIA (10022 thru 10579).. 8-10   73-75
(Columbia's Limited Edition series. All Have an "LE" prefix.)

COLUMBIA (10980 "Christmas with Marty Robbins") 15-20   70
(Columbia Special Products issue.)

COLUMBIA (11221 "By the Time I Get to Phoenix") 5-10   80s
(Columbia Special Products issue.)

COLUMBIA (11222 "Marty's Greatest Hits") 5-10   75

COLUMBIA (11311 "By the Time I Get to Phoenix") 5-10   70
(Columbia Special Products issue.)

COLUMBIA (11513 "By the Time I Get to Phoenix") 15-20   71
(Columbia Special Products issue.)

COLUMBIA (12416 "Marty Robbins' Own Favorites") 12-15   74
(Special Products issue for Vaseline Hair Tonic.)

COLUMBIA (13358 "Christmas with Marty Robbins") 5-10   72
(Columbia Special Products issue.)

COLUMBIA (14035 "Legendary Music Man") 8-12   77
(Columbia Special Products issue.)

COLUMBIA (14613 "Best of Marty Robbins") 5-10   78
(Columbia Special Products issue.)

COLUMBIA (15594 "Number One Cowboy") 5-10   81
(Columbia Special Products issue.)

COLUMBIA (15812 "Marty Robbins' Best") 5-10   82
(Columbia Special Products issue.)

COLUMBIA (16561 "Reflections") 5-10   82
(Columbia Special Products issue.)

COLUMBIA (16578 "Classics")..15-20   83
(Three-LP set. Columbia Special Products issue.)

COLUMBIA (16914 "Country Classics").................................5-10   83
(Columbia Special Products issue.)

COLUMBIA (17120 "Sincerely") 5-10   83
(Columbia Special Products issue.)

COLUMBIA (17136 "Forever Yours")...5-10   83
(Columbia Special Products issue.)

COLUMBIA (17137 "That Country Feeling").................................5-10   83
(Columbia Special Products issue.)

COLUMBIA (17138 "Banquet of Songs") 5-10   83
(Columbia Special Products issue.)

COLUMBIA (17159 "The Great Marty Robbins") 5-10   83
(Columbia Special Products issue.)

COLUMBIA (17206 "The Legendary Marty Robbins") 5-10   83
(Columbia Special Products issue.)

COLUMBIA (17209 "Country Cowboy") 5-10   83
(Columbia Special Products issue.)

COLUMBIA (17367 "Song of the Islands").................................5-10   83
(Columbia Special Products issue.)

COLUMBIA (17730 "Great Love Songs") 5-10   80s
(Columbia Special Products issue.)

COLUMBIA (30000 thru 40000 series)................................5-12   70-86

DECCA 8-12   72

GUSTO/COLUMBIA 8-10   81

HARMONY (Except 31258) 8-15   69-72

HARMONY (31258 "Song of the Islands")....................................20-25   72

K-TEL..8-10   77

MCA..6-12   73-74

ORBIT..8-10   84

PICKWICK 5-10   70s

READER'S DIGEST (054 "Greatest Hits") 20-30   83
(Five-LP boxed set.)

SUNRISE MEDIA 5-10   81

TIME-LIFE 5-10   81

WORD 5-10

Session: Ray Conniff Singers; Jordanaires; David Briggs; Bobby Braddock; Grady Martin; Bob Bishop; Bill Pursell; Buddy Spicher; Arlene Harden; Bobby Sykes.
  Also see BISHOP, Bob
  Also see BRADDOCK, Bobby
  Also see HARDEN, Arlene
  Also see JORDANAIRES
  Also see PRUETT, Jeanne, & Marty Robbins
  Also see SMITH, Carl / Lefty Frizzell / Marty Robbins
  Also see TUBB, Ernest

ROBBINS, Marty / Johnny Cash / Ray Price

LPs: 10/12–inch 33rpm

COLUMBIA 8-10   70

  Also see CASH, Johnny
  Also see PRICE, Ray

ROBBINS, Marty Jr: see ROBBINS, Ronny

ROBBINS, Ronny   *C&W '78*

(Marty Robbins Jr.)

Singles: 7–inch

ARTIC 3-5   78-79

COLUMBIA 3-4   84

TRC 3-5   79

LP: 10/12–inch 33rpm

COLUMBIA 10-20   70

THUNDER.................................... 5-10   81

ROBERTS, Kenny, & Downhomers: see DOWNHOMERS

ROBERTS, Pat   *C&W '72*

Singles: 7–inch

DOT 3-5   72-74

ROBERTSON, Jack   *C&W '88*

Singles: 7–inch

SOUNDWAVES 3-4   88

ROBERTSON, Texas Jim   *C&W '46*

(With the Panhandle Punchers)

Singles: 78rpm

RCA... 5-10   46-50

EPs: 7–inch 33/45rpm

CAMDEN.................................... 8-12

LP: 10/12–inch 33rpm

DESIGN 10-20   60s

GRAND PRIX.............................. 10-20   60s

INT'L AWARD 10-20   60s

STRAND (1016 "Texas Jim Robertson [Tales and Songs of the Old West]") ..25-35   61

ROBEY, Loretta   *C&W '77*

Singles: 7–inch

SOUNDWAVES 3-5   77

ROBIC, Ivo   *P&R '59*

Singles: 7–inch

LAURIE 4-8   59-60

PHILIPS 3-6   62

ROBIN & CRUISER   *C&W '87*

Singles: 7–inch

16TH AVE.....................................3-4   87

Members: Robin Gordon; Cruiser Gordon.

ROBINSON, Betty Jean   *C&W '74*

(With the Nashville Grass)

Singles: 7–inch

4 STAR 3-5   75

MCA...3-5   74

LP: 10/12–inch 33rpm

CMH...5-10   81

4 STAR 5-10   78

  Also see BELEW, Carl, & Betty Jean Robinson

ROBINSON, Sharon   *C&W '87*

Singles: 7–inch

NIGHTFALL 3-4   87

ROBISON, Carson   *C&W '45*

(With His Pleasant Valley Boys; with His Old Timers)

Singles: 78rpm

CLARION 5-15   40s

COLUMBIA 5-15   55

MGM 5-15   48

VICTOR 5-15   45

Singles: 7–inch

COLUMBIA 5-10   55

EPs: 7–inch 33/45rpm

MGM 6-12   52-58

RCA 6-12   53

LP: 10/12–inch 33rpm

COLUMBIA (2551 "Square Dance")..................................10-20   55
(10–inch LP.)

COLUMBIA (6029 "Square Dance").................................10-20   49
(10–inch LP.)

GLENDALE..................................8-10

MGM (13 "Call Your Own Square Dances") 10-20   52

(10-inch LP.)

MGM (557 "Square Dances").... 10-20   52
(10-inch LP.)

MGM (3258 "Square
Dances") 10-20   55

MGM (3594 "Life Gets Tee-Jus, Don't
It")... 15-20   58

METRO (504 "Square Dance
Calls")...................................... 10-20   60s

RCA (3030 "Square Dances")... 10-25   53
(10–inch LP.)

Also see DALHART, Vernon, & Carson
Robison

ROCKIN' SIDNEY: see ROCKIN' SYDNEY

ROCKIN' SYDNEY   *LP '85*
(With His All Stars; Rockin' Sidney)
Singles: 7–inch

AVENUE 5-10   60s

EPIC.. 3-5   84-85

JIN.. 8-12   59-63

MAISON DE SOUL (1024 "My Toot
Toot") 3-5   85

LPs: 10/12–inch 33rpm

EPIC... 5-10   85

Member: Sidney Sidiem.
Also see COUNT ROCKIN' SYDNEY

ROCKINHORSE   *C&W '86*
Singles: 7–inch

LONG SHOT 3-4   86

RODGERS, Jesse: see ROGERS, Jesse

RODGERS, Jimmie   *C&W '55*
Singles: 78rpm

BLUEBIRD 40-80   30s

ELECTRADISK (1830 "Moonlight and
Skies")................................. 250-500   32

ELECTRADISK (1966 "Looking for a New
Mama")............................... 200-400   32

ELECTRADISK (1983 "Whisper Your
Mother's Name") 200-400   33

ELECTRADISK (1999 "Whippin' That Old
T.B.") 200-400   33

ELECTRADISK (2008 "Mother, the Queen of
My Heart")........................... 200-400   33

ELECTRADISK (2009 "You and My Old
Guitar")............................... 200-400   33

ELECTRADISK (2042 "Mississippi
Moon")................................ 200-400   33

ELECTRADISK (2060 "Waiting for a
Train") 200-400   33

ELECTRADISK (2109 "In the Jailhouse
Now") 200-400   33

ELECTRADISK (2155 "Jimmie Rodgers' Last
Blue Yodel") 200-400   33

MONTGOMERY WARD 50-100   30s

SUNRISE (3104 "Moonlight and
Skies")................................ 200-300   33

SUNRISE (3131 "Looking for a New
Mama") 200-300   33

SUNRISE (3142 "Whisper Your Mother's
Name")................................ 200-300   33

SUNRISE (3157 "Whippin' That Old
T.B.")................................... 200-300   33

SUNRISE (3167 "Mother, the Queen of My
Heart")................................ 200-300   33

SUNRISE (3168 "Down the Old Road to
Home") 200-300   33

SUNRISE (3169 "Why Should I Be
Lonely")............................... 200-300   33

SUNRISE (3170 "You and My Old
Guitar")............................... 200-300   34

SUNRISE (3171 "Let Me Be Your Side
Track")................................ 200-300   34

SUNRISE (3172 "Blue
Yodel")................................ 200-300   34

SUNRISE (3217 "Mississippi
Moon") 200-300   34

SUNRISE (3244 "Waiting for a
Train") 200-300   34

SUNRISE (3306 "In the Jailhouse
Now") 200-300   34

SUNRISE (3362 "Jimmie Rodgers' Last Blue
Yodel") 200-300   34

SUNRISE (3418 "Lullaby
Yodel") 200-300   34

VICTOR (20864 thru 23574)......25-75   27-30s

VICTOR (23580 thru 24456)....50-100   30s

VICTOR (4000 series) 15-25

VICTOR (5000 & 6000 series).....5-15   49-56

VICTOR (18-6000 "Cowhand's Last
Ride") 1500-2500   33
(Picture disc.)

Note: Many of Jimmie Rodgers' releases in
the early '30s were made by Victor/Bluebird
specifically for sale in department store
chains: Elektradisk (Woolworth's), Sunrise
(W.T. Grant, Kress, McCrory), and
Montgomery Ward, with its own label.

Albums: 78rpm

RCA (244 "Yodelingly
Yours")................................100-150   52
(Includes three 78rpm singles.)

RCA (282 "Yodelingly
Yours, Vol. 2")....................100-150   52
(Includes three 78rpm singles.)

RCA (318 "Yodelingly
Yours, Vol. 3")..................... 100-150   52
(Includes three 78rpm singles.)

RCA (3035 "Yodelingly
Yours, Vol. 4")..................... 100-150   52
(Includes three 78rpm singles.)

Singles: 7–inch
RCA (0017 thru 6408).............. 10-20 49-56

EPs: 7–inch 33/45rpm
RCA (6 "Immortal Performances By Jimmie
Rodgers").............................. 35-50   50

RCA (10 "Jimmie Rodgers,
Vol. 1") 35-50   51

RCA (21 "Jimmie Rodgers Memorial Album,
Vol. 1") 35-50   52

RCA (22 "Jimmie Rodgers Memorial Album,
Vol. 2") 35-50   52

RCA (409 "Jimmie Rodgers Memorial Album,
Vol. 4") 35-50   52

RCA (410 "Jimmie Rodgers Memorial Album,
Vol. 5") 35-50   52

RCA (411 "Jimmie Rodgers Memorial Album,
Vol. 6") 35-50   52

RCA (793 "Never No Mo'
Blues")................................... 25-35   56
(Two EPs)

RCA (1232 "Never No Mo'
Blues")................................... 35-55   55
(Two EPs)

RCA (3073 "Travelin' Blues") .. 50-100   52
(2-EPs)

RCA (5097 "Legendary Jimmie
Rodgers").............................. 20-30   58

LP: 10/12–inch 33rpm
ANTHOLOGY of COUNTRY MUSIC (11
"Unissued Jimmie Rodgers") .. 15-25   83

PICKWICK 6-12   76

RCA (0075 "Legendary Jimmie
Rodgers").............................. 10-20   74
(Mail order offer.)

RCA (LPM-1232 ("Never No Mo'
Blues")................................... 20-30   55

RCA (AHM1--1232 ("Never No Mo'
Blues")................................... 5-10   70s

RCA (LPM-1640 "Train Whistle
Blues")................................... 20-30   57

RCA (AHM1--1640 "Train Whistle
Blues")................................... 5-10   70s

RCA (LPM-2112 "My Rough and Rowdy
Ways")................................... 15-25   60

RCA (ANL1-2112 "My Rough and Rowdy
Ways")................................... 5-10   75

RCA (LPM-2213 "Jimmie the
Kid") 15-25   61

RCA (AHM1-2213 "Jimmie the
Kid") 5-10   70s

RCA (2504 "A Legendary
Performer") 6-12   78

RCA (AHM1-2531 "Country Music Hall of
Fame")...................................5-10   70s

RCA (LPM-2531 "Country Music Hall of
Fame")...................................15-25   62

RCA (LPM-2634 "The Short But Brilliant Life
of Jimmie Rodgers") 15-25   55

RCA (AHM1-2634 "The Short But Brilliant Life
of Jimmie Rodgers") 5-10   70s

RCA (LPM-2865 "My Time Ain't
Long")...................................15-25   64

RCA (AHM1-2865 "My Time Ain't
Long")...................................5-10   70s

RCA (3037 "Jimmie Rodgers Memorial
Album, Vol. 1")......................50-100   52
(10–inch LP.)

RCA (3038 "Jimmie Rodgers Memorial
Album, Vol. 2")......................50-100   52
(10–inch LP.)

RCA (3039 "Jimmie Rodgers Memorial
Album, Vol. 3")......................50-100   52
(10–inch LP.)

RCA (3073 "Travelin' Blues")...50-100   53
(10–inch LP.)

RCA (LPM/LSP-3315 "Best of the Legendary
Jimmie Rodgers") 10-15   65

RCA (AHL1-3315 "Best of the Legendary
Jimmie Rodgers") 5-10   70s

RCA (6091 "This Is Jimmie
Rodgers")..................................8-12   73

RODGERS, Jimmie
(With Michele)   *P&R/C&W/R&B/LP '57*

Singles: 78rpm
ROULETTE................................10-30   57

Singles: 7–inch
A&M 3-6 67-70
ABC...3-5   73
DOT 4-8 62-67
EPIC..3-5 71-72
RCA 3-5 73-75
ROULETTE (Monaural) 5-10 57-61
ROULETTE (SSR-4158 "Ring-a-Ling-
a-Lario")................................10-20   59
(Stereo.)
ROULETTE (SSR-4218
"T.L.C.") 10-20   60
(Stereo.)
ROULETTE (SSR-8001 "Bo
Diddley") 15-25   59
(Stereo.)

ROULETTE (SSR-8007 "Froggy Went
A-Courtin") 10-20   59
(Stereo.)

SCRIMSHAW.............................. 3-5   78

Picture Sleeves

DOT................................. 4-8   62-64

ROULETTE.............................. 10-15   58-61

EPs: 7–inch 33/45rpm

ROULETTE 10-20   57-60

LPs: 10/12–inch 33rpm

A&M 8-15   67-70

DOT................................. 10-20   62-67

FORUM 10-20   60

HAMILTON.......................... 10-20   64-65

RCA................................. 8-12   73-75

ROULETTE (25020 thru
25057) 20-30   57-59

ROULETTE (R-25071 thru
R-25199).............................. 10-20   59-63
(Monaural.)

ROULETTE (SR-25071 thru
SR-25199).............................. 15-25   59-63
(Stereo.)

ROULETTE (42000 series)......... 5-10

SCRIMSHAW.............................. 5-10   78

RODMAN, Judy   *C&W '85*

Singles: 7–inch

MTM 3-4   85-88

RODRIGUEZ, Johnny

C&W '72/P&R '73

Singles: 7–inch

CAPITOL............................. 3-4   87-89

COLUMBIA 3-5   80

EPIC................................. 3-5   79-86

MERCURY 3-6   72-79

Picture Sleeves

MERCURY 3-5   77

LPs: 10/12–inch 33rpm

EPIC................................. 5-10   80-85

K-TEL 5-10   77

MERCURY 5-12   73-79

Session: Waylon Jennings.
Also see HALL, Tom T.
Also see JENNINGS, Waylon
Also see TOMORROW'S WORLD

RODRIGUEZ, Johnny, & Charly McClain   *C&W '79*

Singles: 7–inch

EPIC................................. 3-5   79

Also see McCLAIN, Charly

Also see RODRIGUEZ, Johnny

ROE, Marlys   *C&W '73*

Singles: 7–inch

GRC............................... 3-5   73

ROE, Tommy

(With the Satins; with Flamingos; with Roemans)   *P&R/R&B/LP '62/C&W '73*

Singles: 7–inch

ABC................................. 4-8   66-71

ABC-PAR 5-10   62-66

AERTAUN (1108 "Wendy")........... 5-8   60s

CURB/MCA........................... 3-5   85-86

JUDD (1018 "Caveman")........... 15-25   60

JUDD (1022 "Sheila") 25-45   62

MCA................................. 3-4   70s

MGM/SOUTH.......................... 3-5   72-73

MARK IV (001 "Caveman")........ 25-50   60

MERCURY............................. 3-5   86-87

MONUMENT........................... 3-5   72-77

ROULETTE........................... 3-5   70s

TRUMPET (1401 "Caveman") ...50-75   60

W.B./CURB........................... 3-5   78-80

Picture Sleeves

ABC................................. 4-8   66-70

ABC-PAR (10362 "Susie
Darlin")................................. 8-12   62

LPs: 10/12–inch 33rpm

ABC (594 thru 762).................. 10-15   67-72

ABC-PAR (ABC-423 thru
ABC-574)............................. 20-35   62-66
(Monaural.)

ABC-PAR (ABCS-423 thru
ABCS-575)............................. 25-40   62-66
(Stereo.)

ACCORD 5-10   82

GUSTO 5-10   80s

MCA................................. 5-10   82

MONUMENT............................. 8-12   76-77

ROE, Tommy / Impressions / Fats Domino

LPs: 10/12–inch 33rpm

ABC (ABC-504 "Shindig")..........20-25   65
(Monaural.)

ABC (ABCS-504 "Shindig")........25-30   65
(Stereo.)

ROE, Tommy / Bobby Rydell / Gene Pitney

INT'L AWARD 10-15   60s

Also see PITNEY, Gene

ROE, Tommy / Bobby Rydell / Ray Stevens

LPs: 10/12–inch 33rpm

DESIGN (178 "Young Lovers") 15-25   63
Also see STEVENS, Ray

ROE, Tommy / Al Tornello

LPs: 10/12–inch 33rpm

DIPLOMAT 10-20   60s

ROE, Tommy / Bobby Lee Trammell

LPs: 10/12–inch 33rpm

CROWN 15-20   63
Also see ROE, Tommy

ROGERS, Dann   *P&R '79*

Singles: 7–inch

IA.. 3-5   79
MCA 3-4   87

LPs: 10/12–inch 33rpm

IA.. 8-10   79
Also see CUMMINGS, Burton

ROGERS, David   *C&W '68*

Singles: 7–inch

ATLANTIC..................................... 3-5   73-74
COLUMBIA 3-6   68-72
HAL KAT 3-4   84
KARI 3-5   81
MUSIC MASTER........................... 3-4   82-83
REPUBLIC 3-5   76-79
U.A. 3-5   75

LP: 10/12–inch 33rpm

ATLANTIC (7283 "Farewell to the
   Ryman") 10-20   73
ATLANTIC (7306 "Hey There
   Girl") 8-12   74
COLUMBIA 8-12   70-72
HAL KAT 5-10   84
REPUBLIC 5-10   76

ROGERS, James   *C&W '89*

Singles: 7–inch

SOUNDWAVES 3-4   89

ROGERS, Jesse, & His 49ers

(Jesse Rodgers)   *C&W '49*

Singles: 78rpm

BLUEBIRD 10-25   35-49
COWBOY.................................... 8-10

ROGERS, Kenny   *C&W '75*

(Kenneth Rogers; with Linda Davis)

Singles: 7–inch

CARLTON (454 "That Crazy
   Feeling")................................... 25-50   58
CARLTON (468 "For You
   Alone") 25-50   58
EVA-TONE/READER'S DIGEST ("His
   Greatest Hits") 10-15   83
   (Single-sided, square, cardboard
   soundsheet. Promotional issue only.)
JOLLY ROGER.............................. 3-5   73-75
KEN-LEE (102 "Jole Blon")...... 50-100   50s
LIBERTY 3-4   80-86
MERCURY 5-10   66
RCA 3-4   84-89
REPRISE 3-4   89-91
U.A... 3-5   76-80

Picture Sleeves

LIBERTY 3-4   80-83
RCA 3-4   84-86
U.A. 3-5   79-80

LPs: 10/12–inch 33rpm

BREAKAWAY 5-8   84
JOLLY ROGER (5001
   "Backroads") 150-200   75
   (Picture disc. Promotional issue only.)
LIBERTY (Except SLL-8344)....... 5-10   80-85
LIBERTY (SLL-8344 "HBO Presents Kenny
   Rogers Greatest Hits").......... 10-20   83
   (Picture disc. Promotional issue only.)
MFSL (049 "Greatest Hits") 20-30   80
MASTERS.................................... 5-10
PICKWICK 5-10   79
QSP 5-10   84
RCA 5-8   84-87
REPRISE 5-8   89
U.A. (Except 934)........................ 5-8   76-80
U.A. (934 "The Gambler) 5-10   78
U.A. (934 "The Gambler) 50-75   78
   (Picture disc. Promotional issue only. One of
   a four-artist, four-LP set.)
Also see CAMPBELL, Glen / Anne Murray / Kenny
   Rogers / Crystal Gayle
Also see DAVIS, Linda
Also see DOYLE, Bobby
Also see MILSAP, Ronnie, & Kenny Rogers
Also see MURRAY, Anne, & Kenny Rogers
Also see U.S.A. for AFRICA

ROGERS, Kenny, & Kim Carnes   *C&W/P&R '80*

Singles: 7–inch

U.A. 3-5   80

Picture Sleeves

U.A. 3-5   80

Also see CARNES, Kim

ROGERS, Kenny, Kim Carnes & James Ingram   *C&W/P&R/R&B '84*

Singles: 7–inch

RCA.. 3-4   84

Also see INGRAM, James
Also see ROGERS, Kenny, & Kim Carnes

ROGERS, Kenny, & Holly Dunn   *C&W '90*

Singles: 7–inch

REPRISE 3-4   90

Also see DUNN, Holly

ROGERS, Kenny, & Sheena Easton   *C&W/P&R '83*

Singles: 7–inch

LIBERTY 3-4   83

LPs: 10/12–inch 33rpm

LIBERTY 5-10   84

Also see EASTON, Sheena

ROGERS, Kenny, & Dolly Parton   *P&R '83*

Singles: 7–inch

RCA.. 3-4   83-85
REPRISE 3-4   90

Picture Sleeves

RCA.. 3-4   83

Also see PARTON, Dolly

ROGERS, Kenny, & Nickie Ryder   *C&W '86*

Singles: 7–inch

RCA.. 3-4   86

ROGERS, Kenny, & First Edition   *P&R/C&W/LP '69*

Singles: 7–inch

JOLLY ROGERS........................... 3-5   72-73
REPRISE 4-8   68-72

LPs: 10/12–inch 33rpm

JOLLY ROGERS........................ 8-12   72-73
REPRISE 10-25   69-72

Members: Kenny Rogers; Mike Settle; Terry Williams; Mickey Jones; Kin Vassey; Mary Arnold.
Also see FIRST EDITION

ROGERS, Kenny, & Dottie West   *C&W '78*

Singles: 7–inch

LIBERTY 3-5   81-84

U.A. 3-5   78-79

LPs: 10/12–inch 33rpm

U.A. 5-10   78-80

LPs: 10/12–inch 33rpm

Also see ROGERS, Kenny
Also see WEST, Dottie

ROGERS, Ronnie   *C&W '81*

Singles: 7–inch

EPIC.. 3-4   83
LIFESONG.................................... 3-4   81-82
MTM... 3-4   87-88

ROGERS, Roy   *P&R '38/C&W '46*

(With Dale Evans; with Sons of the Pioneers)

Singles: 78rpm

DECCA 10-20   40-44
GOLDEN....................................... 4-6   50s
RCA 5-15   50-57
VICTOR 8-15   45-48
VOCALION 20-30   38

Singles: 7–inch

CAPITOL...................................... 3-5   70-71
GOLDEN....................................... 5-8   50s
MCA 3-5   80
NEW DISC 8-12   56
RCA (Except 215)...................... 5-15   51-52
RCA (215 "Souvenir Album") 20-40   49
  (Boxed set of three colored vinyl 45s.)
20TH FOX.................................... 3-5   74-75

Picture Sleeves

GOLDEN....................................... 5-8   50s

EPs: 7–inch 33/45rpm

BLUEBIRD................................. 10-20   50s
RCA (Except 3041).................... 12-25   50-57
RCA (3041 "Souvenir Album") ...25-50   52

LPs: 10/12–inch 33rpm

BLUEBIRD................................. 15-25   59
CAMDEN 10-20   60-75
CAPITOL................................... 10-30   62-72
GHOST TOWN 10-20
GOLDEN................................... 15-30   62
NOSTALGIA MERCHANT...........8-10
PICKWICK................................. 5-10   70s
RADIOLA 8-10
RCA (1439 "Sweet Hour of
  Prayer")................................20-30   57
RCA (3041 "Souvenir Album") ...40-60   52
  (10–inch LP.)
RCA (3168 "Hymns of Faith") 30-50   54
  (10–inch LP.)
20TH FOX.................................... 5-10   75

WORD.. 4-8   73-77
  Also see EVANS, Dale
  Also see SONS of the PIONEERS

ROGERS, Roy, & Clint
Black   *C&W '91*
Singles: 7–inch
RCA... 3-4   91
  Also see BLACK, Clint
  Also see ROGERS, Roy

ROGERS, Smokey   *C&W '49*
Singles: 78rpm
CAPITOL...................................... 5-10   49
LP: 10/12–inch 33rpm
SHASTA....................................... 5-10

ROHRS, Donnie   *C&W '78*
Singles: 7–inch
AD-KORP...................................... 3-8   78
PACIFIC CHALLENGER............... 3-5   81
LP: 10/12–inch 33rpm
PACIFIC CHALLENGER............. 5-10   81

ROLAND, Adrian   *C&W '60*
Singles: 7–inch
ALLSTAR 5-10   60

RONE, Roger   *C&W '89*
Singles: 7–inch
TRUE 3-4   89

RONICK, Holly   *C&W '89*
Singles: 7–inch
HAPPY MAN 3-4   89

RONSTADT, Linda   *P&R '68/C&W '74*
(With the Stone Poneys; with Nelson Riddle
Orchestra)
Singles: 7–inch
ASYLUM 3-5   73-85
CAPITOL (2004 "Different
  Drum")...................................... 5-10   67
CAPITOL (2110 "Up to My Neck in High
  Muddy Water") 10-15   68
CAPITOL (2195 "Some of
  Shelly's Blues") 5-10   68
CAPITOL (2438 "Dolphins")........ 5-10   69
CAPITOL (2767 "Lovesick
  Blues").. 4-8   70
CAPITOL (2846 thru 4050) 3-6   70-75
CAPITOL (5838 "All the Beautiful
  Things") 8-12   67
CAPITOL (5910 "Evergreen") 5-10   67
ELEKTRA...................................... 3-5   75-78

SIDEWALK (937 "So Fine") 75-100   66
Picture Sleeves
ASYLUM 3-5   78-82
CAPITOL (2110 "Up to My Neck in High
  Muddy Water").......................... 15-25   68
LPs: 10/12–inch 33rpm
ASYLUM (Except 401 & 60489) ..5-10   73-86
ASYLUM (401 "Living in the
  USA")......................................10-15   78
  (Picture disc.)
ASYLUM (60489 "'Round
  Midnight")................................10-15   86
CAPITOL (208 thru 635)............10-15   69-72
CAPITOL (2000 series) 12-18   68
CAPITOL (11000 series) 8-12   74-77
CAPITOL (16000 series) 5-10   80
ELEKTRA.....................................5-10   80-87
MFSL 15-20   85
PICKWICK 8-10   70s
  Session: Davie Allan; Nelson Riddle.
  Also see AXTON, Hoyt
  Also see CASH, Johnny / Roy Clark / Linda Ronstadt
  Also see EAGLES
  Also see NEWMAN, Randy
  Also see NITTY GRITTY DIRT BAND & Linda Ronstadt
  Also see PARTON, Dolly, Linda Ronstadt, & Emmylou
   Harris
  Also see SHILOH
  Also see STONE PONEYS

RONSTADT, Linda, & Emmylou
Harris
Singles: 7–inch
ASYLUM 3-5   75
  Also see HARRIS, Emmylou

RONSTADT, Linda, & James
Ingram   *P&R '86*
Singles: 7–inch
MCA...3-4   86
Picture Sleeves
MCA...3-4   86

RONSTADT, Linda, & Aaron
Neville   *LP '89*
LPs: 10/12–inch 33rpm
ELEKTRA......................................5-8   89

RONSTADT, Linda, & J.D.
Souther   *C&W '82*
Singles: 7–inch
ASYLUM 3-4   82
  Also see RONSTADT, Linda
  Also see SOUTHER, J.D.

ROOFTOP SINGERS
P&R/C&W/R&B/LP '63
Singles: 7–inch
ATCO 4-6   67
VANGUARD................................... 4-8   62-65
Picture Sleeves
VANGUARD................................ 5-10   63
LPs: 10/12–inch 33rpm
VANGUARD............................... 10-20   63-65
Members: Erik Darling; Lynne Taylor; Bill Svanoe.

ROSE, Pam
C&W '77
Singles: 7–inch
CAPITOL.. 3-5   77
Also see CLAMITY JANE

ROSE, Pam, & Willie Nelson
(Pam Rose with Friend)   *C&W '80*
Singles: 7–inch
EPIC.. 3-5   79-80
Also see NELSON, Willie
Also see ROSE, Pam

ROSE, Richard & Gary
C&W '88
Singles: 7–inch
CAPITOL.. 3-4   88

ROSS, Charlie
P&R '75
Singles: 7–inch
BIG TREE 3-5   75-76
TOWN HOUSE 3-4   82-83

ROSS, Jeris
C&W '72
Singles: 7–inch
ABC.. 3-5   73-75
ABC/DOT 3-5   75
CARTWHEEL................................. 3-5   72
DOOR KNOB 3-5   79-80
GAZELLE 3-5   77
LP: 10/12–inch 33rpm
ABC/DOT 6-10   75

ROVERS
C&W '81
(Irish Rovers)
Singles: 7–inch
EPIC.. 3-5   81
LPs: 10/12–inch 33rpm
CLEVELAND INT'L 5-10   81-82
Also see IRISH ROVERS

ROWE, Stacey
C&W '79
Singles: 7–inch
SABRE... 3-5   79

ROWELL, Ernie
C&W '71
Singles: 7–inch
GRASS 3-5   79-81
PRIZE 3-5   71
REVOLVER 3-4   87

ROWLAND, Dave
C&W '82
Singles: 7–inch
ELEKTRA.. 3-4   82
LP: 10/12–inch 33rpm
ELEKTRA.. 5-10   82
Also see DAVE & SUGAR

ROY, Bobbie
C&W '72
Singles: 7–inch
CAPITOL.. 3-5   72-73
LP: 10/12–inch 33rpm
CAPITOL.. 6-12   72

ROYAL, Billy Joe
P&R/LP '65
Singles: 7–inch
ALL WOOD 5-10   62
ATLANTIC (2300 series) 4-8   66
ATLANTIC (87000 thru 89000
series).. 3-4   85-91
ATLANTIC AMERICA 3-5   85-89
COLUMBIA (43305 "Down in the
Boondocks") 4-8   65
(Black vinyl.)
COLUMBIA (43305 "Down in the
Boondocks") 10-20   65
(Colored vinyl. Promotional issue only.)
COLUMBIA (43390 "I Knew You
When").. 4-8   65
(Black vinyl.)
COLUMBIA (43390 "I Knew You
When")....................................... 10-20   65
(Colored vinyl. Promotional issue only.)
COLUMBIA (43465 thru 45620)..... 4-8   65-72
FAIRLANE 8-12   61-62
KAT FAMILY 3-5   81
MGM/SOUTH.............................. 3-5   73
MERCURY...................................... 3-5   80
PLAYER'S...................................... 5-10   65
PRIVATE STOCK 3-5   78
SCEPTER 3-5   76
TOLLIE... 5-10   64
Picture Sleeves
TOLLIE... 8-12   64
LPs: 10/12–inch 33rpm
ATLANTIC AMERICA 5-10   86-89
BACK-TRAC 5-8   85

BRYLEN 5-10
COLUMBIA (Except 45063) 15-25   65-69
COLUMBIA (45063 "Greatest
  Hits") 5-8   89
51 WEST 5-10   83
KAT FAMILY 5-10   81
MERCURY 5-10   80
  Also see FARGO, Donna, & Billy Joe Royal
  Also see SOUTH, Joe / Billy Joe Royal

RUE, Arnie   *C&W '79*
Singles: 7-inch
NSD 3-5   79

RUSHING, Jim   *C&W '80*
Singles: 7-inch
OVATION 3-5   80

RUSSELL, Bobby   *C&W/P&R '68*
(With the Beagles; with Tennessee Three; with Sadie Russell)
Singles: 7-inch
COLUMBIA 3-5   73-74
D 5-10   60
ELF 4-6   68-69
FELSTED 5-10   59
FILLY-COLT 3-5   78
IMAGE 4-8   61
MONUMENT 4-8   65-66
NATIONAL GENERAL 3-5   70
PRIVATE STOCK 3-5   75
RISING SONS 3-5   67
SPAR 10-15   64
U.A. 3-5   71-72
VISTA 3-6   69
LPs: 10/12-inch 33rpm
BELL 8-12   69
ELF 10-15   68
U.A. 8-10   71

RUSSELL, Clifford   *C&W '83*
Singles: 7-inch
SUGARTREE 3-4   83

RUSSELL, Jimmy   *C&W '76*
Singles: 7-inch
CHARTA 3-5   76

RUSSELL, Johnny   *C&W '71*
Singles: 7-inch
MERCURY 3-5   78-81
POLYDOR 3-5   78
RCA 3-5   71-77

LP: 10/12-inch 33rpm
RCA 10-15   71-77
Session: Jordanaires; Beverly Heckel; Janie Fricke
  Also see FRICKE, Janie
  Also see HECKEL, Beverly
  Also see JORDANAIRES

RUSSELL, Lee
(Leon Russell)
Singles: 7-inch
BATON 10-15   59
ROULETTE 10-20   58
  Also see RUSSELL, Leon

RUSSELL, Leon   *LP '70/C&W '84*
(With the Shelter People; with New Grass Revival)
Singles: 7-inch
A&M (700 series) 4-8   64
A&M (1200 series) 3-5   71
ABC 3-5   78
COLUMBIA 3-5   70s
DOT 4-8   65
MCA 3-4
PARADISE 3-5   76-81
SHELTER 3-5   70-76
Picture Sleeves
PARADISE 3-5   78-84
SHELTER 3-5   74
LPs: 10/12-inch 33rpm
MCA 5-10   79
OLYMPIC 8-12   73
PARADISE 5-10   78-81
SHELTER (1000 & 2000
  series) 10-20   70-75
SHELTER (8000 series,
  except 8917) 10-15   71-73
SHELTER (8917 "Leon Live") 12-20   73
SHELTER (52000 series) 8-10   76
  Also see CLAPTON, Eric
  Also see DAVID & LEE
  Also see IN-GROUP
  Also see NELSON, Willie, & Leon Russell
  Also see RUSSELL, Lee
  Also see WILSON, Hank

RUSSELL, Leon & Mary   *P&R '76*
Singles: 7-inch
PARADISE 3-5   76-77
LPs: 10/12-inch 33rpm
PARADISE 8-10   76-77
  Also see RUSSELL, Leon

RUSTY & DOUG C&W '55
Singles: 78rpm
HICKORY 5-15 55-57
Singles: 7–inch
HICKORY (1000 & 1100 series) 10-20 55-61
LP: 10/12–inch 33rpm
HICKORY (103 "Favorites") 30-50 60

Members: Rusty Kershaw; Doug Kershaw.
Also see KERSHAW, Doug

RUUD, Nancy C&W '80
Singles: 7–inch
C&R 3-4 81
CALICO 3-4 80

RYAN, Charlie C&W/P&R '60
(With the Timberline Riders; with Livingston
Brothers)
Singles: 78rpm
SOUVENIR (101 "Hot Rod
Lincoln") 25-35 55
Singles: 7–inch
4 STAR 5-10 60-63
SOUVENIR (101 "Hot Rod
Lincoln") 40-60 55
Picture Sleeves
4 STAR (1745 "Side Car
Cycle") 10-20 60
LPs: 10/12–inch 33rpm
KING (751 "Hot Rod") 40-60 61

RYAN, Jamie C&W '67
(Jamey Ryan)
Singles: 7–inch
ATLANTIC 3-5 73
COLUMBIA 4-6 67
SHOW BIZ 3-5 69-70

RYAN, Tim C&W '90
Singles: 7–inch
EPIC 3-4 90-91

RYAN, Wesley C&W '81
Singles: 7–inch
NSD 3-4 81

RYLES, John Wesley C&W/P&R '68
(John Wesley Ryles I)
Singles: 7–inch
ABC 3-5 78-79
ABC/DOT 3-5 77
COLUMBIA 4-6 68-70
GRT .... 3-5 . 70
MCA 3-5 79-83

MUSIC MILL 3-5 75-76
PLANTATION 3-5 71-73
PRIMERO 3-5 82-83
RCA 3-5 74
16TH AVE. 3-4 84
W.B. 3-4 87-88
LPs: 10/12–inch 33rpm
ABC 5-10 78
ABC/DOT 8-10 77
COLUMBIA 10-15 69
MCA 5-10 79-83
PLANTATION 5-10 77

S

S-K-O: see SCHUYLER, KNOBLOCH & OVERSTREET

SADLER, Barry   *P&R/C&W/LP '66*
(S/SGT. Barry Sadler)
Singles: 7–inch
GAS	3-5	78
RCA	4-6	66-67

Picture Sleeves
RCA	5-10	66-67

LPs: 10/12–inch 33rpm
RCA	10-20	66-67
VETERAN	8-12	74

SADLER, Sammy   *C&W '89*
Singles: 7–inch
EVERGREEN	3-4	89-90

SAHM, Doug   *LP '73/C&W '76*
(With the Mex Trip; with Texas Tornados)
Singles: 7–inch
ABC/DOT	4-6	76
ATLANTIC	5-10	73
CASABLANCA (0828 "Roll with the Punches")	10-20	75
CHRYSALIS	3-5	81
COBRA (116 "Just a Moment")	40-50	61
CRAZY CAJUN	3-5	74
HARLEM (107 "Why, Why, Why")	20-35	60
HARLEM (108 "Baby, Tell Me") (Black vinyl.)	20-30	60
HARLEM (108 "Baby, Tell Me") (Colored vinyl. Promotional issue only.)	40-60	60
HARLEM (116 "Just a Moment")	40-50	61
PERSONALITY (260 "Baby, What's on Your Mind")	30-50	59
PLAYBOY	3-5	76
RENNER (212 "Big Hat") (Black vinyl.)	20-30	61
RENNER (212 "Big Hat") (Colored vinyl. Promotional issue only.)	50-75	61

RENNER (215 "Baby, What's on Your Mind") (Black vinyl.)	20-30	61
RENNER (215 "Baby, What's on Your Mind") (Colored vinyl. (Promotional issue only.)	50-75	61
RENNER (226 "Just Because")	20-30	62
RENNER (232 "Cry")	20-30	63
RENNER (240 "Lucky Me")	20-30	63
RENNER (247 "Mr. Kool")	20-30	64
SATIN (100 "Crazy Daisy")	30-50	59
SOFT (1031 "Cry")	20-30	65
SWINGIN' (625 "Why, Oh Why")	15-25	60
TEXAS RECORD (108 "Henrietta")	10-20	76
W.B.	3-5	74
WARRIOR (507 "Crazy Daisy")	40-60	58

Picture Sleeves
CHRYSALIS	3-5	81

LPs: 10/12–inch 33rpm
ANTONE'S	5-8	88
ATLANTIC	8-12	73
HARLEM	8-10	79
MERCURY	10-20	73
TAKOMA	5-10	80
W.B.	10-20	74

Also see FENDER, Freddy, & Sir Douglas
Also see LITTLE DOUG
Also see NELSON, Willie
Also see SALDAÑA, Sir Doug
Also see SIR DOUGLAS QUINTET

SAHM, Doug, & Augie Meyers
Singles: 7–inch
TEARDROP	3-4	83

Picture Sleeves
TEARDROP	3-5	83

Also see MEYERS, Augie
Also see SAHM, Doug

ST. JOHN, Tommy   *C&W '83*
Singles: 7–inch
RCA	3-4	83

ST. MARIE, Susan   *C&W '73*
Singles: 7–inch
CINNAMON	3-5	73
PINNACLE	3-5	77

SALDAÑA, Sir Doug
(Doug Sahm)
Singles: 7–inch
KEVIN KAT (116 "Will You Love Me
Mañana)....................................... 3-4   90
Also see SAHM, Doug

SAMONE, Stephany   *C&W '80*
Singles: 7–inch
MDJ.. 3-5   80

SAMPLES, Junior   *C&W '67*
Singles: 7–inch
CHART.. 4-6   67
LP: 10/12–inch 33rpm
CHART...................................... 10-15   67
MOUNTAIN DEW...................... 8-10
PICKWICK (6113
"Moonshining")......................... 5-10   70s
Also see CAMPBELL, Archie, & Junior Samples

SAN FERNANDO VALLEY MUSIC
BAND   *C&W '79*
Singles: 7–inch
C&S... 3-5   79

SANDERS   *C&W '88*
(The Sanders)
Singles: 7–inch
AIRBORNE 3-4   88-89
Members: Dale Sanders; Vicki Sanders.
Also see VICKI DAWN

SANDERS, Ben   *C&W '88*
(The 5th Avenue Country Boy)
Singles: 7–inch
LUV 3-4   88

SANDERS, Curly
(With the Sanitones; Ray Sanders)
Singles: 78rpm
JAMBOREE (590 "Brand New Rock &
Roll") 50-75   56
Singles: 7–inch
CONCEPT (897 "Dynamite") .. 75-100   57
CONCEPT (898 "This Time").... 25-50   57
JAMBOREE (590 "Brand New Rock &
Roll") 75-100   56
Also see SANDERS, Ray

SANDERS, Debbie   *C&W '89*
Singles: 7–inch
K-ARK... 3-4   89

SANDERS, Mack   *C&W '78*
Singles: 7–inch
PILOT... 3-5   78

SANDERS, Ray   *C&W '60*
Singles: 7–inch
GNP 4-6   67-68
HILLSIDE....................................3-4   80
IMPERIAL...................................4-6   69
LIBERTY...................................5-10   60-63
REPUBLIC.................................3-5   77-78
STADIUM...................................4-8   64
TOWER.......................................4-8   65-66
U.A...3-5   70-73
LP: 10/12–inch 33rpm
IMPERIAL.................................10-15   69
REPUBLIC.................................8-10   77
U.A...8-12   72
Also see SANDERS, Curly

SANDERS, Ray / Curtis Potter /
Darrell McCall
LP: 10/12–inch 33rpm
HILLSIDE....................................5-10   80
Also see POTTER, Curtis, & Darrell
McCall

SARAH   *C&W '87*
(Sarah Vogt)
Singles: 7–inch
HUB 3-4   87-88

SARGEANTS, Gary   *C&W '73*
Singles: 7–inch
MERCURY....................................3-5   73-74
Also see HALL, Tom T.

SASKIA & SERGE   *C&W '78*
Singles: 7–inch
ABC/HICKORY 3-5   78

SAULS, Corkey   *C&W '79*
Singles: 7–inch
SAND MOUNTAIN.........................3-5   79

SAVANNAH   *C&W '83*
Singles: 7–inch
MERCURY.....................................3-4   83-84

SAWMILL CREEK BAND   *C&W '81*
Singles: 7–inch
COWBOY......................................3-5   81-83

LP: 10/12–inch 33rpm

COWBOY.............................5-10 82-83

Member: Bruce "Bru Hau" Hauser.

Also see HAUSER, Bruce

SAWYER, Ray   *P&R/C&W '76*
Singles: 7–inch

CAPITOL.............................3-5 76-79

SANDY (1030 "Rockin'

Satellite")...............................20-30 60

SANDY (1037 "I'm Gonna

Leave")...............................10-20 61
LPs: 10/12–inch 33rpm
CAPITOL.............................8-10 76

Also see DR. HOOK

SAWYER BROWN   *C&W '84*
Singles: 7–inch
CAPITOL.............................3-5 84-90
LPs: 10/12–inch 33rpm
CAPITOL.............................5-10 85-90

Members: Mark Miller; Bob Randall; Jim Scholten;

Gregg Hubbard; Joe Smyth.

SAWYER BROWN & "Cat" Joe Bonsall   *C&W '86*
Singles: 7–inch
CAPITOL.............................3-4 86

Also see BONSALL, Joe

Also see SAWYER BROWN

SAYER, Leo   *P&R/LP '75/C&W '78*
Singles: 7–inch
W.B. 3-5 73-84
LPs: 10/12–inch 33rpm
W.B. 6-10 75-84

SCARBURY, Joey   *P&R '71*
Singles: 7–inch
BELL 3-5 71-73

BIG TREE 3-5 73

COLUMBIA 3-5 77-79

ELEKTRA.............................3-5 81

LIONEL 3-5 71

PLAYBOY 3-5 74

RCA.............................3-4 84

REENA.............................4-6 68
Picture Sleeves
ELEKTRA.............................3-5 81
LPs: 10/12–inch 33rpm
ELEKTRA.............................5-10 81

SCHAFFER, Norm   *C&W '88*
Singles: 7–inch
DSP.............................3-4 88

SCHEREE   *C&W '79*
Singles: 7–inch
COMPASS.............................3-5 79

SCHLITZ, Don   *C&W '78*
Singles: 7–inch
CAPITOL.............................3-5 78-79

SCHMUCKER, Paul   *C&W '78*
Singles: 7–inch
STAR-FOX.............................3-5 78-79

SCHNEIDER, John   *C&W/P&R/LP '81*
Singles: 7–inch
MCA.............................3-4 84-87

SCOTTI BROS.............................3-5 81-83
Picture Sleeves
MCA.............................3-4 84-87

SCOTTI BROS.............................3-5 81-83
LPs: 10/12–inch 33rpm
MCA.............................5-8 84-87

SCOTTI BROS.............................5-10 81-83

Session: Waylon Jennings.

Also see JENNINGS, Waylon

SCHNEIDER, John, & Jill Michaels
Singles: 7–inch
SCOTTI BROS.............................3-4 83

Also see MICHAELS, Jill

Also see SCHNEIDER, John

SCHUTT, Dawn   *C&W '89*
Singles: 7–inch
MASTER.............................3-4 89

SCHUYLER, Thom   *C&W '83*
Singles: 7–inch
CAPITOL.............................3-4 83
LPs: 10/12–inch 33rpm
CAPITOL.............................5-8 83

Also see SCHUYLER, KNOBLOCH & OVERSTREET

SCHUYLER, KNOBLOCH & OVERSTREET   *C&W '86*
(S-K-O)
Singles: 7–inch
MTM.............................3-4 86-88

SCHUYLER, KNOBLOCH & BICKHARDT   *C&W '87*
Singles: 7–inch
MTM.............................3-4 86-87

Also see BICKHARDT, Craig

Also see SCHUYLER, Thom

SCOTT, Earl *C&W '62*

Singles: 7–inch

DECCA	4-6	65-68
KAPP	4-8	62
MERCURY	4-8	63-64

SCOTT, Jack *P&R/R&B '58/C&W '74*
(With the Chantones)

Singles: 78rpm

ABC-PAR	50-100	57

Singles: 7–inch

ABC (10843 "Before the Bird Flies")	5-10	66
ABC-PAR (9818 "Baby, She's Gone") (Black label.)	50-75	57
ABC-PAR (9818 "Baby, She's Gone") (White label. Promotional issue only.)	40-60	57
ABC-PAR (9860 "Two Timin' Woman") (Black label.)	50-75	57
ABC-PAR (9860 "Two Timin' Woman") (White label. Promotional issue only.)	40-60	57
CAPITOL	10-20	61-63
CARLTON (Except 519)	10-20	58-59
CARLTON (519 "There Comes a Time") (Monaural.)	10-20	59
CARLTON (ST-519 "There Comes a Time") (Stereo.)	25-35	59
COLLECTABLES	3-4	80s
DOT	3-5	73
ERIC	3-4	70s
GRT	3-5	70
GROOVE (0027 "There's Trouble Brewin")	10-15	63
GROOVE (0031 "I Knew You First")	5-10	64
GROOVE (0037 "Wiggle on Out")	10-15	64
GROOVE (0042 "Thou Shalt Not Steal")	5-10	64
GROOVE (0049 "Flakey John")	10-15	64
GUARANTEED (209 "What Am I Living For")	10-20	60
GUARANTEED (211 "Go Wild Little Sadie")	15-25	60
JUBILEE	5-10	67
RCA	5-10	65

TOP RANK (2028 "What in the World's Come Over You")	10-15	60
TOP RANK (2041 "Burning Bridges") (Monaural.)	10-15	60
TOP RANK (2041 "Burning Bridges") (Stereo.)	25-45	60
TOP RANK (2055 "It Only Happened Yesterday")	8-15	60
TOP RANK (2075 "Patsy")	8-15	60
TOP RANK (2093 "Is There Something on Your Mind")	8-15	60

Picture Sleeves

CAPITOL	15-25	61-62
CARLTON	15-25	58-59
TOP RANK	15-25	60-61

EPs: 7–inch 33/45rpm

CARLTON (1070/1071 "Presenting Jack Scott") (Price is for either volume.)	50-75	58
CARLTON (1072 "Jack Scott Sings")	50-75	59
TOP RANK (1001 "Jack Scott")	50-75	60

LPs: 10/12–inch 33rpm

CAPITOL (2035 "Burning Bridges")	60-80	64
CAPITOL (8-2035 "Burning Bridges") (Capitol Record Club issue.)	60-80	64
CARLTON (LP-107 "Jack Scott") (Monaural.)	100-150	58
CARLTON (STLP-12 107 "Jack Scott") (Stereo.)	150-200	58
CARLTON (LP-122 "What Am I Living For") (Monaural.)	75-125	60
CARLTON (STLP-12 122 "What Am I Living For")	100-150	60
JADE	10-15	
PONIE	8-10	74-77
TOP RANK (348 "The Spirit Moves Me")	75-125	60
TOP RANK (319 "I Remember Hank Williams") (Monaural.)	75-125	60
TOP RANK (619 "I Remember Hank Williams") (Stereo.)	100-150	60

TOP RANK (326 "What in the World's Come
Over You") 75-125   61
(Monaural.)

TOP RANK (626 "What in the World's Come
Over You") 100-150   61
(Stereo.)

SCOTT, Lang   *C&W '84*
Singles: 7-inch
MCA 3-4   84

SCRUGGS, Earl   *C&W '70*
(Earl Scruggs Revue)
Singles: 7-inch
COLUMBIA 3-5   70-83
LPs: 10/12-inch 33rpm
COLUMBIA 5-10   73-83
Session: Waylon Jennings.
Also see FLATT, Lester, & Earl Scruggs
Also see HALL, Tom T., & Earl Scruggs
Also see JENNINGS, Waylon
Also see SKAGGS, Ricky

SEA, Johnny   *C&W '59*
(Johnny Seay)
Singles: 7-inch
CAPITOL.. 4-8   61
COLUMBIA 3-5   67-69
NRC 5-10   59-60
PHILIPS 4-6   64-65
VIKING 3-5   70-71
W.B. 4-6   66-67
Picture Sleeves
COLUMBIA 3-5   68
LPs: 10/12-inch 33rpm
GUEST STAR 8-12   66
PHILIPS 10-15   64-65
PICKWICK/HILLTOP 8-12   65
W.B. 10-20   66

SEAL, Jim   *C&W '80*
Singles: 7-inch
NSD... 3-4   80

SEALS, Dan   *P&R '80*
(England Dan Seals)
Singles: 7-inch
ATLANTIC....................................... 3-5   80-82
CAPITOL.. 3-4   87-90
EMI AMERICA 3-4   84-87
LIBERTY 3-4   83-84
LPs: 10/12-inch 33rpm
ATLANTIC..................................... 5-10   80-82
EMI AMERICA 5-8   84-87

LIBERTY 5-8   83
Also see ENGLAND DAN & John Ford Coley
Also see TOMORROW'S WORLD

SEALS, Dan, & Marie Osmond
Singles: 7-inch
CAPITOL... 3-4   85
Also see OSMOND, Marie
Also see SEALS, Dan

SEALS, Troy   *C&W '73*
Singles: 7-inch
ATLANTIC....................................... 3-5   73-74
CALLA.. 4-8   67
ELEKTRA... 3-4   80
COLUMBIA 3-5   75-77
RISING SONS (715 "Mama, Hold My
Hand")...................................... 15-25   69
LPs: 10/12-inch 33rpm
ATLANTIC..................................... 8-12   73
COLUMBIA 5-10   76
Also see JO ANN & TROY

SEBASTIAN, John   *P&R '69*
Singles: 7-inch
KAMA SUTRA................................ 4-6   68-70
MGM 4-6   68-70
REPRISE 3-5   70-77
Picture Sleeves
KAMA SUTRA................................ 4-8   69
LPs: 10/12-inch 33rpm
KAMA SUTRA.............................. 10-15   70
MGM 10-15   69-70
REPRISE 8-12   70-76

SEELY, Jeannie   *C&W/P&R '66*
Singles: 7-inch
CHALLENGE 4-6   64-65
COLUMBIA 3-5   77-78
DECCA 3-5   69-73
MCA 3-5   73-75
MONUMENT.................................... 3-5   66-68
LPs: 10/12-inch 33rpm
DECCA 6-12   69-70
HARMONY.................................... 5-10   72
MCA... 5-8   73
MONUMENT................................. 6-12   66-77
Also see COCHRAN, Hank
Also see GREENE, Jack, & Jeannie Seely

SEEVERS, Les   *C&W '69*
(With Oaks)
Singles: 7-inch
CHESTNUT 4-6

DECCA	3-6	69
EVENT	5-10	

SEGER, Bob   *P&R '68/C&W '83*

(With the Last Heard; with Silver Bullet Band; Bob Seger System)

Singles: 7–inch

ABKCO	3-6	72-75
CAMEO (438 "East Side Story")	10-20	66
CAMEO (444 "Sock It to Me Santa")	15-25	66
CAMEO (465 "Persecution Smith")	10-20	66
CAMEO (473 "Vagrant Winter")	10-20	66
CAMEO (494 "Heavy Music")	8-12	67
CAPITOL (Except 2000 series)	3-5	71-86
CAPITOL (2000 series)	4-8	68-70
HIDEOUT (1013 "East Side Story")	25-50	66
HIDEOUT (1014 "Persecution Smith")	25-50	66
HIDEOUT (1232 "Heavy Music")	50-100	66
(Single-sided.)		
MCA	3-4	87
PALLADIUM	3-6	71-74
REPRISE	3-6	72

Promotional Singles

CAPITOL (Colored vinyl)	4-8	78
CAPITOL (9878 "Shame on the Moon")	3-6	82
(Edited version [4:22], not the promo that runs 4:55.)		

Picture Sleeves

CAPITOL (Except 4951)	3-6	78-86
CAPITOL (4951 "Horizontal Bop")	30-50	80
MCA	3-4	87

LPs: 10/12–inch 33rpm

CAPITOL (ST-172 "Ramblin' Gamblin' Man")	15-25	69
CAPITOL (SM-172 "Ramblin' Gamblin' Man")	8-10	75
CAPITOL (ST-236 "Noah")	50-70	69
CAPITOL (SKAO-499 "Mongrel")	15-25	70
CAPITOL (SM-499 "Mongrel")	8-10	75
CAPITOL (ST-731 "Brand New Morning")	30-50	71
CAPITOL (8433 "Live Bullet, Consensus Cuts")	20-30	75
(Promotional issue only.)		
CAPITOL (11000 series, except 11557 & 11904)	6-12	75-78
CAPITOL (ST-11557 "Night Moves")	5-10	78
CAPITOL (ST-11557 "Night Moves")	30-40	78
(Picture disc. Promotional issue only.)		
CAPITOL (SW-11904 "Stranger in Town")	5-10	78
CAPITOL (SEAX-11904 "Stranger in Town")	15-20	79
(Picture disc.)		
CAPITOL (12000 series)	6-10	80-86
CAPITOL (16000 series)	5-8	80
INNER VIEW ("Demonstration Record: Bob Seger")	15-25	76
(Promotional issue only.)		
MFSL (034 "Night Moves")	25-50	79
MFSL (127 "Against the Wind")	20-30	85
PALLADIUM (1006 "Smokin' O.P.'s")	15-25	72
PALLADIUM (2126 "Back in '72")	50-75	73
REPRISE	10-15	72-74

Also see BEACH BUMS
Also see NEWMAN, Randy

SEGO BROTHERS & NAOMI   *C&W '64*

Singles: 7–inch

SONGS of FREEDOM	4-6	64

SEINER, Barbara   *C&W '79*

Singles: 7–inch

STARSHIP	3-5	79

SELF, Ted   *C&W '60*

Singles: 7–inch

PLAID	5-10	60
SAVOY	5-10	60

SELLARS, Marilyn   *C&W/P&R '74*

Singles: 7–inch

MEGA	3-5	74-77
ZODIAC	3-5	76-77

LPs: 10/12–inch 33rpm

MEGA	5-10	74-77
ZODIAC	5-10	77

SERRATT, Kenny *C&W '72*
(Kenny Seratt)
Singles: 7–inch
HITSVILLE	3-5	76-77
MDJ	3-4	80-81
MGM	3-5	72-73
MELODYLAND	3-5	75

SESSIONS, Ronnie *C&W '72*
(Little Ronnie Sessions)
Singles: 7–inch
COMPLEAT	3-4	86
MCA	3-5	75-79
MGM	3-5	72-73
MOSRITE	4-8	66
PIKE	10-15	61
REPUBLIC	3-6	69
LP: 10/12–inch 33rpm
MCA	5-10	77

SEXTON, Mark *C&W '79*
Singles: 7–inch
SUN-DE-MAR	3-5	79

SHAFER, Whitey *C&W '80*
Singles: 7–inch
ELEKTRA	3-4	80-81

SHAMBLIN, Michael *C&W '86*
Singles: 7–inch
F&L	3-4	86

SHANE, Michael *C&W '89*
Singles: 7–inch
REGAL	3-4	89

SHANNON, Bonnie *C&W '80*
Singles: 7–inch
DOOR KNOB	3-4	80

SHANNON, Del

P&R/R&B '61/C&W '85
Singles: 7–inch
AMY	4-8	64-65
BERLEE	5-10	63-64
BIG TOP	10-20	61-63
COLLECTABLES	3-4	80s
DUNHILL	4-8	69
ERIC	3-5	70s
ISLAND	3-5	75
LANA	3-6	60s
LIBERTY	5-10	66-68
NETWORK	3-5	81-82
TERRIFIC	3-5	
TWIRL	4-6	60s
W.B.	3-5	85

Picture Sleeves
LIBERTY	8-12	68

LPs: 10/12–inch 33rpm
AMY (8003 "Handy Man") (Monaural.)	30-50	64
AMY (S-8003 "Handy Man") (Stereo.)	40-60	64
AMY (8004 "Del Shannon Sings Hank Williams") (Monaural.)	30-50	65
AMY (S-8004 "Del Shannon Sings Hank Williams") (Stereo.)	40-60	65
AMY (8006 "1,661 Seconds") (Monaural.)	30-50	65
AMY (S-8006 "1,661 Seconds") (Stereo.)	40-60	65
BIG TOP (1303 "Runaway") (Monaural.)	100-200	61
BIG TOP (1303 "Runaway") (Stereo.)	400-600	61
BIG TOP (1308 "Little Town Flirt")	40-60	63
BUG	5-10	85
DOT (3834 "Best of Del Shannon") (Monaural.)	25-45	67
DOT (25834 "Best of Del Shannon") (Stereo.)	25-45	67
LIBERTY	20-30	66-68
NETWORK/ELEKTRA	8-10	81
PHOENIX 20	8-10	80
PICKWICK	8-10	70s
POST	10-15	
SIRE	10-15	75
SUNSET	10-15	70
U.A.	10-15	73

SHANNON, Guy *C&W '73*
Singles: 7–inch
CINNAMON	3-5	73

SHARP, Rosemary *C&W '87*
Singles: 7–inch
CANYON CREEK	3-4	87-88

SHARPE, Sunday *C&W '74*
Singles: 7–inch
PLAYBOY 3-5   76-77
U.A. 3-5   74-76
LP: 10/12–inch 33rpm
U.A. 6-12   74

SHATSWELL, Danny *C&W '78*
Singles: 7–inch
MERCURY 3-5   78

SHAVER, Billy Joe *C&W '73*
Singles: 7–inch
CAPRICORN................................... 3-5   78
COLUMBIA 3-4   82
MONUMENT 3-5   73
LP: 10/12–inch 33rpm
CAPRICORN................................... 5-10   76-77
COLUMBIA 5-10   81-82
MONUMENT 6-12   73-78
Also see CROWELL, Rodney
Also see HARRIS, Emmylou
Also see NELSON, Willie
Also see SKAGGS, Ricky

SHAW, Brian *C&W '73*
Singles: 7–inch
RCA... 3-5   73-74
REPUBLIC 3-5   76-77

SHAW, Ron *C&W '77*
(With the Desert Wind Band)
Singles: 7–inch
PACIFIC CHALLENGER.............. 3-5   77-81

SHAW, Victoria *C&W '84*
Singles: 7–inch
MPB 3-4   84

SHAY, Dorothy *C&W '47*
Singles: 78rpm
COLUMBIA 4-8   47

SHELTON, Ricky Van *C&W '86*
Singles: 7–inch
COLUMBIA 3-4   86-92
LPs: 10/12–inch 33rpm
COLUMBIA 5-8   87-91
Also see PARTON, Dolly, & Ricky Van Shelton

SHELTON, Ricky Van / Billy Joel
Singles: 7–inch
EPIC (74422 "All Shook Up") 3-4   92
Also see SHELTON, Ricky Van

SHENENDOAH *C&W '87*
Singles: 7–inch
COLUMBIA 3-4   87-91

SHEPARD, Jean *C&W/P&R '53*
Singles: 78rpm
CAPITOL.. 4-8   53-57
Singles: 7–inch
CAPITOL.. 5-10   53-61
(Purple labels.)
CAPITOL.. 3-8   61-72
(Orange, orange/yellow, or red labels.)
MERCURY 3-5   72
SCORPION 3-4   78
U.A. 3-5   73-77
EPs: 7–inch 33/45rpm
CAPITOL.. 5-10   56-61
LPs: 10/12–inch 33rpm
CAPITOL (100 thru 800
series).. 10-20   69-71
CAPITOL (700 thru 1200
series).. 15-25   56-59
(With a "T" prefix.)
CAPITOL (1500 thru 2900
series).. 10-15   61-68
CAPITOL (11000 series) 5-10   72-79
FIRST GENERATION.................. 5-10   81
MERCURY 5-10   71
PICKWICK/HILLTOP 5-12   67-68
POWER PAK 5-8   75-80s
U.A. 5-10   73-76
Session: Justin Tubb; Red Sovine.
Also see SOVINE, Red
Also see TUBB, Justin

SHEPARD, Jean, & Ferlin Huskey *C&W/P&R '53*
Singles: 78rpm
CAPITOL.. 3-5   53
Singles: 7–inch
CAPITOL.. 4-8   53
Also see HUSKY, Ferlin

SHEPARD, Jean, & Ray Pillow *C&W '66*
Singles: 7–inch
CAPITOL.. 4-6   66
LP: 10/12–inch 33rpm
CAPITOL.. 10-15   66
Also see PILLOW, Ray
Also see SHEPARD, Jean

SHEPPARD, T.G.   *C&W '74*

Singles: 7–inch

COLUMBIA	3-4	85
HITSVILLE	3-5	76
MELODYLAND	3-5	74-75
W.B.	3-4	77-85

LPs: 10/12–inch 33rpm

COLUMBIA	5-8	85
CURB	5-8	82-84
HITSVILLE	5-10	76
MELODYLAND	8-10	75-76
W.B.	5-8	78-83

Also see COLLINS, Judy, & T.G. Sheppard
Also see EASTWOOD, Clint, & T.G. Sheppard
Also see GATLIN BROTHERS

SHEPPARD, T.G., & Karen Brooks   *C&W '82*

Singles: 7–inch

W.B.	3-4	82

Also see BROOKS, Karen

SHEPPARD, T.G., & Clint EASTWOOD   *C&W/P&R '84*

Singles: 7–inch

W.B.	3-4	84

Also see EASTWOOD, Clint
Also see SHEPPARD, T.G.

SHERLEY, Glen   *C&W '71*

Singles: 7–inch

MEGA	3-5	71

LP: 10/12–inch 33rpm

MEGA	5-10	71

SHIBLEY, Arkie   *C&W '50*

(With His Mountain Dew Boys)

Singles: 78rpm

GILT EDGE (#8)	10-20	50
(Title not known.)		
GILT EDGE (5021 "Hot Rod Race")	50-60	51
GILT EDGE (5036 "Arkie Meets the Judge")	50-60	51
MAE-MAE (#77)	35-50	
(Title not known.)		

Singles: 7–inch

4 STAR (1737 "Pickin' My Guitar")	40-60	59
GILT EDGE (5021 "Hot Rod Race")	50-100	51
GILT EDGE (5036 "Arkie Meets the Judge")	50-100	51

MOUNTAIN DEW (101 "Hot Rod Race")	25-50	50s

(Reissue of Gilt Edge 5021. Exact year of issue not yet known.)

SHILOH

Singles: 7–inch

AMOS	4-8	71

LPs: 10/12–inch 33rpm

AMOS (7015 "Shiloh")	15-25	71
LAMB & LION	5-8	

Members: Al Perkins; Don Henley; Jim Ed Norman; Mike Bowden; Richard Bowden.
Also see FLYING BURRITO BROTHERS
Also see HENLEY, Don
Also see PINKARD & BOWDEN
Also see RONSTADT, Linda

SHINER, Murv   *C&W '49*

(Merv Shiner)

Singles: 78rpm

DECCA	4-8	49-50

Singles: 7–inch

MGM	4-6	67-69

LP: 10/12–inch 33rpm

CERTRON	10-15	60s
LITTLE DARLIN'	10-15	60s

SHIRLEY, Danny   *C&W '84*

Singles: 7–inch

AMOR	3-4	84-88

Also see CONFEDERATE RAILROAD

SHIRLEY, Danny, & Piano Red   *C&W '85*

Singles: 7–inch

AMOR	3-4	84-88

Also see PIANO RED
Also see SHIRLEY, Danny

SHIRLEY & SQUIRRELY

    C&W/P&R '76

Singles: 7–inch

GRT	3-5	76

LPs: 10/12–inch 33rpm

GRT	5-10	76

Also see SHIRLEY, SQUIRRELY & MELVIN

SHIRLEY, SQUIRRELY & MELVIN

Singles: 7–inch

EXCELSIOR	3-4	81

Picture Sleeves

EXCELSIOR	3-5	81

LPs: 10/12–inch 33rpm

EXCELSIOR	5-10	81

Also see SHIRLEY & SQUIRRELY

SHONDELL, Troy   *P&R '61*
(Troy Shondel; Troy Shundell; Gary Shelton)
Singles: 7–inch

AVM	3-4	88
BRITE STAR	3-5	73-74
COLLECTABLES	3-4	80s
COMMERCIAL	3-5	78
DECCA	4-8	64
EVEREST	4-8	62-64
GAYE (2010 "This Time")	20-25	61
GOLDCREAST (161 "This Time")	15-20	61
(Note misspelled label name.)		
GOLDCREST (161 "This Time")	10-15	61
LIBERTY	5-10	61-62
LUCKY	3-5	75
MASTER	10-15	60s
RIC	4-8	65
STAR-FOX	3-5	79
SUNSHINE	3-5	76
TRX	4-8	67-69
TELESONIC	3-5	80-81
3 RIVERS	4-8	60s
WRITERS & ARTISTS (001 "This Time")	25-35	61

LPs: 10/12–inch 33rpm

EVEREST (1206 "Many Sides")	25-35	63
STAR-FOX	5-10	79
SUNSET	10-15	67

Also see SHELTON, Gary

SHONDELLS
(Featuring Tommy James)
Singles: 7–inch

RED FOX (110 "Hanky Panky")	15-25	66
SELSOM (102 "Why Do Fools Fall in Love")	10-20	65
SNAP (101 "Pretty Little Red Bird")	25-45	63
SNAP (102 "Hanky Panky")	50-75	63
(No mention of distribution by Red Fox.)		
SNAP (102 "Hanky Panky")	20-25	65
(Reads: "Distributed by Red Fox Records.")		

Also see JAMES, Tommy

SHOOTERS   *C&W '87*
Singles: 7–inch

EPIC	3-4	87-89

Members: Walter Alridge; Gary Baker. Mike Dillon; Barry Billings; Chalmers Davis.

SHOPPE, The   *C&W '80*
Singles: 7–inch

AMERICAN COUNTRY	3-4	84-85
MTM	3-5	88
NSD	3-4	81
RAINBOW SOUND	3-5	80

SHRUM, Walter, & His Colorado Hillbillies   *C&W '45*
Singles: 78rpm

COAST	5-10	45

SHUNDEL, Troy: see SHONDELL, Troy

SHURFIRE   *C&W '87*
Singles: 7–inch

AIR	3-4	87-88

SHYLO   *C&W '76*
Singles: 7–inch

COLUMBIA	3-5	75-76
MERCURY	3-4	82

LPs: 10/12–inch 33rpm

COLUMBIA	8-10	76-79

SIDE of the ROAD GANG   *C&W '76*
Singles: 7–inch

CAPITOL	3-5	76

LPs: 10/12–inch 33rpm

CAPITOL	8-10	76

SIERRA   *C&W '83*
Singles: 7–inch

AWESOME	3-4	84-85
CARDINAL	3-5	83
MUSICOM	3-5	83

SILVER CITY BAND   *C&W '77*
Singles: 7–inch

COLUMBIA	3-5	77-78

SILVER CREEK   *C&W '81*
Singles: 7–inch

CARDINAL	3-4	81

Also see IVIE, Roger, & Silvercreek

SIMMONS, Gene
(Jumpin' Gene Simmons; Morris Gene Simmons)   *P&R/LP '64/C&W '77*
Singles: 7–inch

AGP	4-8	60s
CHECKER	8-12	60
EPIC	3-5	70
DELTUNE	3-5	77-78

HI	4-8	61-67
HURSHEY	3-5	73
MALA	4-8	68
SANDY	4-8	60s
SUN (299 "Drinkin' Wine")	25-35	58
TUPELO	4-8	60s

LPs: 10/12–inch 33rpm

HI (2018 "Jumpin' Gene Simmons")	20-25	64
(Monaural.)		
HI (32018 "Jumpin' Gene Simmons")	25-30	64
(Stereo.)		

SIMON, Carly   *P&R/LP '71*
Singles: 7–inch

ARISTA	3-4	86-90
COLUMBIA	3-5	73
ELEKTRA	3-5	71-79
EPIC	3-4	85-86
MIRAGE	3-5	82
W.B.	3-5	80-83

Picture Sleeves

ARISTA (Except 9525)	3-5	86-89
ARISTA (9525 "Coming Around Again")	4-8	86
(Pictures Meryl Streep and Jack Nicholson.)		
ARISTA (9525 "Coming Around Again")	3-5	86
(Pictures Carly Simon.)		
ELEKTRA	3-5	75-79
W.B.	3-5	80-83

LPs: 10/12–inch 33rpm

ARISTA	5-8	86-90
ELEKTRA	5-10	71-79
EPIC	5-8	85-86
W.B.	5-10	80-83

Also see SIMON SISTERS

SIMON, Carly, & James Taylor   *P&R '74*
Singles: 7–inch

ELEKTRA	3-5	74-78

Also see SIMON, Carly
Also see TAYLOR, James

SIMON & VERITY   *C&W '85*
Singles: 7–inch

EMI AMERICA	3-4	85

SIMON SISTERS   *P&R '64*
Singles: 7–inch

COLUMBIA (02600 series)	3-4	82

COLUMBIA (45000 series)	3-5	73
KAPP	4-8	64-65

LPs: 10/12–inch 33rpm

COLUMBIA (21525 "Lobster Quadrille")	10-15	69
COLUMBIA (21539 "Simon Sisters Sing for Children")	10-12	73
COLUMBIA (24506 "Lobster Quadrille")	15-20	69
(Special childrens' book edition.)		
COLUMBIA (37000 series)	5-10	82
KAPP	15-25	64
W.B.	5-10	80

Members: Carly Simon; Lucy Simon.
Also see DOOBIE BROTHERS / Kate Taylor & Simon-Taylor Family
Also see SIMON, Carly

SIMPSON, Red   *C&W '66*
Singles: 7–inch

CAPITOL	3-6	66-73
K.E.Y.	3-5	79
W.B.	3-5	76

LP: 10/12–inch 33rpm

CAPITOL	10-15	66-73
51 WEST/SEA SHELL	5-8	82
PICKWICK	5-10	70s

SINGLETON, Margie   *C&W '59*
Singles: 7–inch

ASHLEY	4-8	67-68
MERCURY	4-8	61-64
STARDAY	5-10	59-60
U.A.	4-6	65-66

LP: 10/12–inch 33rpm

ASHLEY	10-15	67
PICKWICK	5-10	68-70s
U.A.	10-15	65

Also see ASHLEY, Leon, & Margie Singleton
Also see JONES, George, & Margie Singleton
Also see YOUNG, Faron, & Margie Singleton

SIR DOUGLAS QUINTET   *P&R '65*
(Sir Douglas Band)
Singles: 7–inch

ATLANTIC	4-8	73
CASABLANCA (0828 "Roll with the Punches")	5-15	75
MERCURY	3-5	71
PACEMAKER (260 "Sugar Bee")	15-20	64
PHILIPS	3-5	70-71
SMASH	4-8	68-70

TRIBE.. 5-10   65
(No Indian on label.)
TRIBE.. 4-8   65-67
(Label pictures Indian.)
Picture Sleeves
PHILIPS 3-5   70-71
LPs: 10/12–inch 33rpm
ACCORD.................................... 5-10   82
ATLANTIC................................. 10-15   73
MERCURY 10-15   72
PHILIPS 15-25   70-71
SMASH 15-25   68-70
TAKOMA.................................... 5-10   80-83
TRIBE (47001 "Best of Sir Douglas
Quintet") 40-60   66

Members: Doug Sahm; Augie Meyers; Jack Barber;
Leon Baetty; John Perez; Frank Morin; Jim Stallings.
Also see AMIGOS DE MUSICA
Also see MEYERS, Augie
Also see SAHM, Doug

SIR DOUGLAS QUINTET /
Cascades
Singles: 7–inch
TRIP 3-5   70s
Also see SIR DOUGLAS QUINTET

SKAGGS, Ricky   *C&W '80*
(With Tony Rice; with Sharon White)
Singles: 7–inch
EPIC.. 3-5   81-90
ROUNDER 3-6   80
SUGAR HILL (3700 series)........... 3-6   80
SUGAR HILL (04000 series)......... 3-5   83-84
LPs: 10/12–inch 33rpm
EPIC.. 5-10   81-86
REBEL (1550 "That's It")........... 10-15   75
ROUNDER 5-10   82
SUGAR HILL................................. 5-10   79-80
WEL DUN..................................... 10-15   78

Also see BOONE CREEK
Also see CASH, Rosanne
Also see COUNTRY GENTLEMEN
Also see FRICKE, Janie
Also see HARRIS, Emmylou
Also see NITTY GRITTY DIRT BAND
Also see PARTON, Dolly
Also see SCRUGGS, Earl
Also see SHAVER, Billy Joe

SKAGGS, Ricky, & Keith Whitley
LPs: 10/12–inch 33rpm
REBEL 10-15   71-72

Also see SKAGGS, Ricky
Also see WHITLEY, Keith

SKINNER, Jimmie   *C&W '49*
(Jimmie Skinner / Jimmie Logsdon)
Singles: 78rpm
CAPITOL.................................4-8   51-54
DECCA 4-8   53-55
MERCURY...............................4-8   57
RADIO ARTIST.........................5-10   49
Singles: 7–inch
CAPITOL.................................5-10   51-54
DECCA 5-10   53-55
MERCURY...............................4-8   57-63
STARDAY................................5-10   58-64
EPs: 7–inch 33/45rpm
MERCURY................................5-10   61
LP: 10/12–inch 33rpm
COUNTRY CORNER ("Jimmie
Skinner") 100-150
(Selection number not known.)
DECCA (4132 "Country
Singer") 35-45   61
MERCURY (20352 "Songs That Make the
Juke Box Play") 30-50   57
MERCURY (20700 "Jimmie Skinner Sings
Jimmie Rodgers") 15-25   62
(Monaural.)
MERCURY (60700 "Jimmie Skinner Sings
Jimmie Rodgers") 25-35   62
(Stereo.)
QCA 5-10   70s
RICH-R-TONE 5-10
STARDAY (240 "Jimmie Skinner, the
Kentucky Colonel") 30-40   63
STARDAY (988 "#1
Bluegrass") 5-10
VETCO.....................................10-15   76
WEL DUN 10-15   78
WING 10-15   64
Also see HALL, Connie

SKIP & LINDA   *C&W '82*
Singles: 7–inch
MDJ..3-4   82
Members: Skip Eaton; Linda Davis.

SLATER, David   *C&W '88*
Singles: 7–inch
CAPITOL.....................................3-4   88-89

SLEDD, Patsy   *C&W '72*
Singles: 7–inch
MEGA 3-5   72-76
SHOWTIME 3-4   87

LP: 10/12–inch 33rpm

MEGA... 10-15   73-74

SLEWFOOT   *C&W '86*
Singles: 7–inch
STEP ONE.................................. 3-4   86

SLIGO STUDIO BAND   *C&W '81*
Singles: 7–inch
GBS... 3-4   81

SLYE, Carrie   *C&W '83*
Singles: 7–inch
FRIDAY... 3-4   83

SMALLWOOD, Laney   *C&W '78*
(Laney Hicks)
Singles: 7–inch
MONUMENT.................................. 3-5   78-83
Also see McCOY, Charlie, & Laney Smallwood

SMILEY, Red: see RENO & SMILEY

SMITH, Andy Lee   *C&W '89*
(With the Jordanaires)
Singles: 7–inch
615 3-4   89
Also see JORDANAIRES

SMITH, Arthur   *C&W/P&R '48*
(Arthur "Guitar Boogie" Smith; with
Crossroads Quartet)
Singles: 78rpm
MGM 5-10   48-57
SUPER DISC (1004 "Guitar
 Boogie") 20-30   48
Singles: 7–inch
MGM (10229 thru 12791)............. 5-15   49-60
STARDAY 4-8   63
EPs: 7–inch 33/45rpm
MGM 10-20   51-56
LPs: 10/12–inch 33rpm
ABC-PAR 15-25   63
DOT.. 10-15   65-66
FOLKWAYS 10-15   64
HAMILTON................................. 10-15   64
MGM (236 "Foolish
 Questions") 25-35   54
 (10–inch LP.)
MGM (533 "Fingers on Fire") 25-35   51
 (10–inch LP.)
MGM (3301 "Specials")............. 25-35   56
MONUMENT.............................. 6-12   70-75
NASHVILLE 8-12   68

STARDAY (186 thru 415) 15-30   62-68
Also see HAMILTON, George, IV / Arthur Smith

SMITH, Arthur, Trio
(With the Dixieliners)
Singles: 78rpm
BLUEBIRD................................ 15-30   30s
MONTGOMERY WARD 25-35   30s
LP: 10/12–inch 33rpm
COUNTY.................................... 5-10   80s
STARDAY (202 "Rare, Old Time Fiddle
 Tunes") 15-25   62
(Listed primarily to distinguish this singer
from the preceding Arthur Smith, who also
had releases on Starday.)

SMITH, Bobby   *C&W '77*
Singles: 7–inch
AUTUMN...................................... 3-5   77
LIBERTY....................................... 3-4   81-82

SMITH, Cal   *C&W '67*
Singles: 7–inch
DECCA 3-5   70-73
KAPP 3-6   66-70
PLAID.. 5-10   60
MCA 3-5   73-79
SOUNDWAVES 3-4   82
STEP ONE.................................... 3-4   86
LPs: 10/12–inch 33rpm
CORAL.. 5-10   73
DECCA 8-12   72
KAPP 10-25   66-70
MCA 5-10   73-77
Also see NELSON, Willie
Also see PARKER, Billy, & Cal Smith
Also see TUBB, Ernest

SMITH, Carl   *C&W '51*
(With the Tunesmiths)
Singles: 78rpm
COLUMBIA 5-10   51-57
Singles: 7–inch
ABC/HICKORY 3-5   76-78
COLUMBIA (20000 & 21000
 series)..................................... 8-15   51-56
COLUMBIA (40823 thru 42858)...4-10   57-63
COLUMBIA (42949 thru 45923).....3-8   64-73
HICKORY..................................... 3-5   74-76
Picture Sleeves
COLUMBIA 5-10   59
EPs: 7–inch 33/45rpm
COLUMBIA (2801 thru 10223).....8-15   57-58

COLUMBIA (10964 "Taste of Country") 5-10   72
(Jukebox issue.)

COLUMBIA (11721) 8-15   58

LPs: 10/12–inch 33rpm

ABC/HICKORY 10-15   77-78

COLUMBIA (31 "Anniversary Album") 8-12   70

COLUMBIA (DS-341 thru DS-517)................................ 5-15
(Record club issues.)

COLUMBIA (900 thru 1100 series) 15-25   57-58

COLUMBIA (1500 thru 2600 series) 10-20   60-69

COLUMBIA (2579 "Carl Smith") 35-50   56
(10–inch LP.)

COLUMBIA (8300 thru 9800 series) 10-20   60-72
(12–inch LPs.)

COLUMBIA (9023 "Sentimental Songs") 30-40   54
(10–inch LP.)

COLUMBIA (9026 "Softly and Tenderly")............................... 30-40   54
(10–inch LP.)

COLUMBIA (10000 series) 5-10   73

COLUMBIA (30000 series) 10-20   70-84

COLUMBIA SPECIAL PRODUCTS (8000 series) 10-15

COUNTRY CLASSICS................ 5-10

GUSTO 5-8   80

HICKORY 5-10   75

HARMONY................................... 5-15   64-72

LAKE SHORE 5-10

Session: Lewis Pruitt.
Also see PRICE, Ray / Lefty Frizzell / Carl Smith
Also see PRICE, Ray / Johnny Horton / Carl Smith / George Morgan
Also see PRUITT, Lewis

SMITH, Carl / Lefty Frizzell / Marty Robbins

LPs: 10/12–inch 33rpm

COLUMBIA (2544 "Carl, Lefty & Marty").................................. 150-250   56
(10–inch LP.)

Also see FRIZZELL, Lefty
Also see ROBBINS, Marty
Also see SMITH, Carl

SMITH, Connie   *C&W '64*

Singles: 7–inch

COLUMBIA 3-5   73-77

EPIC... 3-4   85

MONUMENT................................. 3-5   77-83

RCA 3-8   64-74

Picture Sleeves

RCA 4-6   67

LPs: 10/12–inch 33rpm

CAMDEN 10-15   67-72

COLUMBIA 10-20   73-77

MONUMENT................................. 5-8   77-78

RCA (0100 thru 1200 series) 5-10   73-75

RCA (3300 thru 4800 series) 10-20   65-73

Also see SOME of CHET'S FRIENDS

SMITH, Connie, & Nat Stuckey   *C&W '70*

Singles: 7–inch

RCA 3-5   70

Also see SMITH, Connie
Also see STUCKEY, Nat

SMITH, Darden   *C&W '88*

Singles: 7–inch

EPIC... 3-4   88

SMITH, David   *C&W '79*

Singles: 7–inch

MDJ.. 3-5   79

SMITH, Dennis   *C&W '80*

Singles: 7–inch

ADONDA....................................... 3-4   80

SMITH, Hank

(George Jones; with Nashville Playboys; Hank Smith / Bud Roman & Topppers / "Scat" Benny / Sue Richards / Bob Sandy)

Singles: 78rpm

GILMAR 30-40   50s

EPs: 7–inch 33/45rpm

HOLLYWOOD HIT CLUB (280 "Heartbreak Hotel") 30-50   56

TOPS (280 "Heartbreak Hotel") 30-40   56

Also see JONES, George

SMITH, Jerry   *C&W/P&R/LP '69*

(With His Pianos)

Singles: 7–inch

ABC.. 3-5   69

AD.. 4-8   59-61

CHART... 4-6   67

DECCA 3-5   70-72

RANWOOD.................................. 3-5   73-78

RICE 4-6   67

SOUND STAGE 7......................... 4-8   65

LPs: 10/12–inch 33rpm

ABC	5-10	69
DECCA	5-10	70-72
RANWOOD	5-8	73-75

Also see CORNBREAD & JERRY
Also see MAGIC ORGAN
Also see PAPA JOE'S MUSIC BOX

SMITH, Jimmie

(Gene Autry)
Singles: 78rpm

TIMELY TUNES (1554 "I'm a Truthful Fellow")	25-75
TIMELY TUNES (1555 "I'm Blue and Lonesome")	25-75
TIMELY TUNES (1556 "Bear Cat Mama from Horner Corner")	25-75
TIMELY TUNES (1557 "She's a Hum Dinger")	25-75

Also see AUTRY, Gene

SMITH, Kate   *P&R '27/C&W '48*

(With Guy Lombardo's Orchestra)
Singles: 78rpm

COLUMBIA	3-6	27-46
VICTOR	3-6	38-42
MGM	3-5	48

Singles: 7–inch

ATLANTIC	3-5	74
MGM	3-4	78
RCA	3-5	63-68
TOPS	4-6	60

Picture Sleeves

RCA	4-8	63-64

EPs: 7–inch 33/45rpm

MGM	4-8	52-57
RCA	4-8	59

LPs: 10/12–inch 33rpm

CAMDEN	4-8	70-73
CAPITOL	5-15	54-57
COLUMBIA (6000 series) (10–inch LPs.)	10-20	50
HARMONY	5-12	57
KAPP	5-15	58
LION	5-12	57-60
MGM	5-15	52-66
METRO	5-10	67
RCA	5-15	63-80
RONDO	5-10	60s
TOPS	5-10	

SMITH, Lonnie   *LP '70*
Singles: 7–inch

BLUE NOTE	3-6	69-70
GROOVE MERCHANT	3-5	75
LRC	3-5	78-79

LPs: 10/12–inch 33rpm

BLUE NOTE	8-15	68-70
COLUMBIA	10-15	67
GROOVE MERCHANT	5-10	75-76
KUDU	5-10	71
LRC	5-10	78

SMITH, Lou   *C&W '60*
Singles: 7–inch

KRC	8-12	59-60
SALVO	5-10	61
TOP RANK	5-10	60

SMITH, Margo   *C&W '75*
Singles: 7–inch

AMI	3-4	82
BERMUDA DUNES	3-4	85
MOON SHINE	3-4	83-84
PLAYBACK	3-4	88
20TH CENTURY	3-6	75
W.B.	3-5	76-81

LP: 10/12–inch 33rpm

BERMUDA DUNES	10-15	
CAMERON	5-8	81
20TH CENTURY	6-12	75
W.B.	5-10	75-80

Also see ALLEN, Rex, Jr., & Margo Smith

SMITH, Margo, & Tom Grant   *C&W '85*
Singles: 7–inch

BERMUDA DUNES	3-4	85

Also see GRANT, Tom

SMITH, Margo, & Norro Wilson   *C&W '77*

(Margo & Norro)
Singles: 7–inch

W.B.	3-5	77

Also see SMITH, Margo
Also see WILSON, Norro

SMITH, Rick   *C&W '76*
Singles: 7–inch

CIN KAY	3-5	76

SMITH, Russell   *C&W '84*

Singles: 7–inch

CAPITOL	3-4	84
EPIC	3-4	88-89

LP: 10/12–inch 33rpm

CAPITOL	5-10	82

Also see AMAZING RHYTHM ACES

SMITH, Sammi   *C&W '68*

Singles: 7–inch

COLUMBIA	3-8	67-69
CYCLONE	3-5	79
ELEKTRA	3-5	75-78
MEGA	3-5	70-76
SOUND FACTORY	3-4	80-82
STEP ONE	3-4	86
TRIP	3-4	74
ZODIAC	3-4	76

Picture Sleeves

MEGA	3-5	70

LPs: 10/12–inch 33rpm

BARNABY	5-10	
BUCKBOARD	5-10	70s
CYCLONE	5-8	79
ELEKTRA	5-10	76-78
HARMONY	5-10	71
MEGA	5-10	70-75
PICKWICK	5-10	70s
SOUND FACTORY	3-4	80-82
STEP ONE	3-4	85-86
TRIP	5-8	74
U.A.	5-10	75
ZODIAC	5-8	76

Also see HART, Freddie / Sammi Smith / Jerry Reed
Also see NELSON, Willie
Also see STEVENS, Even, & Sammi Smith

SMITH, Warren   *P&R '57/C&W '60*

Singles: 78rpm

QUALITY	50-100	56
(Canadian.)		
SUN	50-100	56-57

Singles: 7–inch

LIBERTY	4-8	60-64
MERCURY	4-6	68
QUALITY (1558 "Ubangi Stomp")	40-60	56
(Canadian.)		
SUN (239 "Rock 'N' Roll Ruby")	50-100	56
SUN (250 "Ubangi Stomp")	40-60	56
SUN (268 thru 314)	15-25	57-59

SSS/SUN	3-5	80
W.B.	5-10	59

LPs: 10/12–inch 33rpm

LIBERTY (3199 "First Country Collection")	35-45	61
(Monaural.)		
LIBERTY (7199 "First Country Collection")	40-60	61
(Stereo.)		

SMITH, Warren, & Shirley Collie   *C&W '61*

Singles: 7–inch

LIBERTY	5-10	61

Also see COLLIE, Shirley
Also see SMITH, Warren

SNODGRASS, Elmer, & Musical Pioneers   *C&W '60*

Singles: 7–inch

DECCA	4-8	60-61

SNOW, Hank   *C&W '49*

(The Singing Ranger & His Rainbow Ranch Boys; with Kelly Foxton)

Singles: 78rpm

BLUEBIRD	15-30	40s
RCA	5-10	49-57

Singles: 7–inch

RCA (0100 & 0900 series)	3-5	69-74
(Orange labels.)		
RCA (0300 & 0400 series)	8-12	50-51
(Green or gray labels.)		
RCA (4346 thru 7748)	5-10	52-60
RCA (7803 thru 9907)	3-6	61-70
RCA (10000 & 11000 series)	3-5	74-80

Picture Sleeves

RCA	4-8	63

EPs: 7–inch 33/45rpm

RCA (295 thru 1113)	12-25	54-56
RCA (1156 "Old Doc Brown")	35-45	55
RCA (1200 series)	20-30	55
RCA (1400 series)	15-25	57
RCA (3000 series)	30-50	52-54
RCA (4000 series)	15-20	58
RCA (5000 series)	12-25	58-60

LPs: 10/12–inch 33rpm

CAMDEN	8-15	59-74
DETOUR	5-10	83
HANK SNOW SCHOOL of MUSIC (1149/50 "The Guitar")	250-300	58

(Special issue from the Hank Snow School of Music. Includes guitar instruction booklet.)

PICKWICK 5-10 75-76

RCA (0134 "Living Legend") 100-125 78
(RCA Special Products issue.)

RCA (0162 thru 0908) 5-10 73-75

RCA (1004 "I'm Movin' On")...... 15-20 82
(RCA Special Products issue.)

RCA (1052 thru 3511) 5-10 75-79
(With ""AHL1, "ANL1" or APL1" prefix.)

RCA (1113 "Just Keep-A-
Movin") 25-35 55
(With "LPM" prefix.)

RCA (1156 "Old Doc
Brown") 150-175 55

RCA (1233 thru 1861) 25-45 55-58

RCA (2043 thru 4708) 10-25 60-72

RCA (3026 "Country
Classics") 50-75 52
(10–inch LP.)

RCA (3070 "Hank Snow
Sings") 50-75 52
(10–inch LP.)

RCA (3131 "Hank Snow Salutes Jimmie
Rodgers") 50-75 53
(10–inch LP.)

RCA (3192 "Tennessee
Jamboree") 50-75 53
(10–inch LP.)

RCA (3220 "Country Western
Caravan") 50-75 54
(10–inch LP.)

RCA (3267 "Country Guitar") 50-75 53
(10–inch LP.)

RCA (3000 & 3100 series) 40-60 52-54
(10–inch LPs.)

RCA (6014 "This Is My Story").. 20-30 66

RCA SPECIAL PRODUCTS/KRAFT
FOODS 10-20 64-67
(TV mail-order offer.)

RCA SPECIAL PRODUCTS/TEE
VEE 10-15 74-78

READER'S DIGEST (216 "I'm Movin'
On") 125-150
(Six-LP boxed set.)

Session: Jordanaires; Anita Kerr Singers; Jimmy
Snow.
Also see JORDANAIRES
Also see KERR, Anita
Also see MARTIN, Janis / Hank Snow
Also see PRESLEY, Elvis / Hank Snow / Eddy Arnold /
  Hank Snow
Also see SOME of CHET'S FRIENDS

SNOW, Hank, & Chet Atkins
Singles: 78rpm

RCA 4-8 55

Singles: 7–inch

RCA (5900 series) 5-10 55

LPs: 10/12–inch 33rpm

RCA (2952 "Reminiscing") 20-30 64

RCA (4254 "By Special
Request") 20-30 70

Also see ATKINS, Chet

SNOW, Hank, & Anita
Carter   *C&W '51*
(Anita Carter & Hank Snow; with the Rainbow
Ranch Boys)

Singles: 78rpm

RCA 4-8 51-56

Singles: 7–inch

RCA 8-12 51-56

LP: 10/12–inch 33rpm

RCA (2580 "Together Again").... 15-25 62

Also see CARTER, Anita

SNOW, Hank / Hank Locklin / Porter
Wagoner
LPs: 10/12–inch 33rpm

RCA (2723 "Three Country
Gentlemen") 15-25 63

Also see LOCKLIN, Hank
Also see SNOW, Hank
Also see WAGONER, Porter

SNUFF   *C&W '82*
Singles: 7–inch

ELEKTRA 3-4 82

W.B./CURB 3-4 83

Member: Jim Bowling.

SNYDER, Jimmy   *C&W '70*
Singles: 7–inch

E.I.O. 3-4 80

WAYSIDE 3-5 70

SNYDER, Rick   *C&W '88*
Singles: 7–inch

CAPITOL 3-4 88

SOLID GOLD BAND   *C&W '81*
Singles: 7–inch

NSD 3-4 81-82

SOME of CHET'S FRIENDS
C&W '67

Singles: 7–inch

RCA... 4-6   67

Members: Eddy Arnold; Bobby Bare; Don Bowman; Jim Ed Brown; Archie Campbell; Floyd Cramer; Skeeter Davis; Jimmy Dean; George Hamilton IV; Homer & Jethro; Waylon Jennings; Hank Locklin; John D. Loudermilk; Willie Nelson; Norma Jean; Jerry Reed; Connie Smith; Hank Snow; Porter Wagoner; Dottie West.
Also see ARNOLD, Eddy
Also see BARE, Bobby
Also see BOWMAN, Don
Also see BROWN, Jim Ed
Also see CAMPBELL, Archie
Also see CRAMER, Floyd
Also see DAVIS, Skeeter
Also see DEAN, Jimmy
Also see HAMILTON, George, IV
Also see JENNINGS, Waylon
Also see LOCKLIN, Hank
Also see LOUDERMILK, John D.
Also see NELSON, Willie
Also see NORMA JEAN
Also see REED, Jerry
Also see SMITH, Connie
Also see SNOW, Hank
Also see WAGONER, Porter
Also see WEST, Dottie

SONNIER, Joel
C&W '75
(Jo-el Sonnier)

Singles: 7–inch

MERCURY 3-5   75-76
RCA.. 3-4   87-90

LPs: 10/12–inch 33rpm

ROUNDER................................. 5-10   80

SONS of the PIONEERS
P&R '34/C&W '45

Singles: 78rpm

DECCA... 5-10   34-44
RCA.. 4-8   45-56

Singles: 7–inch

BLUEBIRD (105 "Sugarfoot")...... 5-10   58
CORAL... 5-10   54
DECCA (29000 series)............... 5-10   56
RCA (0100 thru 0400 series) 5-10   50-51
  (Black vinyl.)
RCA (0100 thru 0400 series) 10-20   50-51
  (Colored vinyl.)
RCA (2000 thru 6000 series) 5-10   50-56

Picture Sleeves

BLUEBIRD (105 "Sugarfoot").... 10-20   58

EPs: 7–inch 33/45rpm

RCA (103 "Tumbling
  Tumbleweeds") 8-15   61

RCA (168 "Cowboy Classics")...25-40   52
  (Colored vinyl, 3-EP boxed set.)
RCA (400 thru 1400 series) 5-15   55-57
RCA (3000 series) 15-25   52-53
RCA (4000 series) 8-12   58
RCA (5000 series) 5-10   59

LPs: 10/12–inch 33rpm

AMERICAN FOLK MUSIC...........6-12   81
CAMDEN 8-18   58-73
COLUMBIA 5-8   82
GRANITE....................................6-10   76
HARMONY................................10-15   64
J.E.M.F. 8-10
LONG.......................................10-15
MCA 4-8   83
PICKWICK..................................5-10   75
RCA (1092 "Cool Water") 5-10   76
RCA (1130 thru 2957, except
  1431)....................................20-40   55-64
  (With "LPM" or "LSP" prefix.)
RCA (1431 "How Great Thou
  Art").......................................30-40   57
RCA (2332 thru 2808)..................5-10   77-78
RCA (3032 "Cowboy
  Classics").................................30-50   52
  (10–inch LP.)
RCA (3095 "Cowboy Hymns and
  Spirituals") 30-50   52
  (10–inch LP.)
RCA (3162 "Western
  Classics").................................30-50   53
  (10–inch LP.)
RCA (3351 thru 4119)...............10-20   65-68
  (With "LPM" or "LSP" prefix.)
RCA (3468 "Best of the Sons of the
  Pioneers").................................5-10   79
RCA (4000 series) 4-8   81
VOCALION 8-12   64

Members: Roy Rogers; Tim Spencer; Bob Nolan; Ken Curtis; Hugh Farr; Karl Farr; Lloyd Perrymen; Shug Fisher; Tommy Doss.
  Also see ALLEN, Rex, Jr., & Sons of the Pioneers
  Also see CURTIS, Ken / Rex Allen & Arizona
   Wranglers
  Also see ROGERS, Roy

SOSEBEE, Tommy
C&W '53

Singles: 78rpm

CORAL..4-8   53

Singles: 7–inch

CORAL..5-10   53

SOUTH, Joe   *P&R '58/C&W '61*
(With the Believers)
Singles: 7–inch

A&M	4-8	68
ALL WOOD	8-12	62
APT	5-10	65
CAPITOL	3-8	67-75
COLUMBIA	8-12	67
FAIRLANE	8-12	61-62
ISLAND	3-5	75
MGM	5-10	63-64
NRC (Except 002)	10-15	58-60
NRC (002 "I'm Snowed")	30-40	58

LPs: 10/12–inch 33rpm

ACCORD	5-10	81
CAPITOL	8-15	68-72
ISLAND	8-12	70
MINE	8-12	70

SOUTH, Joe / Dells
LPs: 10/12–inch 33rpm

APPLE	15-25	71

SOUTH, Joe / Billy Joe Royal
LPs: 10/12–inch 33rpm

NASHVILLE	5-10	70s

Also see ROYAL, Billy Joe
Also see SOUTH, Joe

SOUTHER, J.D.   *LP '76/C&W '79*
(John David Souther)
Singles: 7–inch

ASYLUM	3-5	74-76
COLUMBIA	3-5	79
W.B.	3-4	85

LPs: 10/12–inch 33rpm

ASYLUM	8-10	72-76
COLUMBIA	5-10	79
W.B.	5-8	85

Also see LONGBRANCH PENNYWHISTLE
Also see RONSTADT, Linda, & J.D. Souther
Also see TAYLOR, James, & J.D. Souther
Also see TILLOTSON, Johnny, & J.D. Souther

SOUTHER - HILLMAN - FURAY BAND   *P&R/LP '74*
Singles: 7–inch

ASYLUM	3-5	74-75

LPs: 10/12–inch 33rpm

ASYLUM	8-10	74-75

Members: J. D. Souther; Chris Hillman; Richie Furay.
Also see FURAY, Richie
Also see HILLMAN, Chris
Also see SOUTHER, J.D.

SOUTHERN ASHE   *C&W '81*
Singles: 7–inch

SOUNDWAVES	3-4	81

SOUTHERN PACIFIC   *C&W '85*
Singles: 7–inch

W.B.	3-4	85-90

Picture Sleeves

W.B.	3-4	88

Members: Tim Goodman; Stuart Cook; John McFee;
Keith Knudsen; Kurt Howell; David Jenkins. Session:
Emmylou Harris.
Also see HARRIS, Emmylou

SOUTHERN PACIFIC & Carlene Carter   *C&W '89*
Singles: 7–inch

W.B.	3-4	89

Also see CARTER, Carlene
Also see SOUTHERN PACIFIC

SOUTHERN REIGN   *C&W '86*
Singles: 7–inch

REGAL	3-4	86-87
STEP ONE	3-4	87-88

Members: Jeff Crocker; Patsy McKeehan.

SOVINE, Red   *C&W '55*
(With the Girls)
Singles: 78rpm

DECCA (Except 30239)	5-10	54-57
DECCA (30239 "Juke Joint Johnny")	10-15	57
MGM	5-10	50-53

Singles: 7–inch

CHART	3-5	71-75
DECCA (Except 30239)	5-10	54-66
DECCA (30239 "Juke Joint Johnny")	20-30	57
GUSTO	3-5	77-80
MGM	8-15	50-53
RCA	4-8	62
RIC	4-6	64-65
STARDAY (Except 500 thru 800 series)	3-5	70-78
STARDAY (500 thru 800 series)	4-8	60-70

EPs: 7–inch 33/45rpm

MGM	10-20	57

LPs: 10/12–inch 33rpm

CMI	5-10	77
CHART	5-10	72-74
DECCA (4400 series)	15-25	64
DECCA (4700 series)	10-20	66
GUSTO/STARDAY	5-10	78

LAKE SHORE 8-12

MGM (3465 "Red Sovine")........ 30-40   57

METRO 10-15   67

NASHVILLE 6-12   70

POWER PAK 5-10   80s

RIC 10-15   65

SOMERSET 8-12   63

STARDAY (Except 100
series) 10-20   65-76

STARDAY (100 series) 15-25   61-62

STEREO FIDELITY..................... 8-12   63

VOCALION................................ 8-12   68

  Also see BEAVERS, Clyde, & Red Sovine
  Also see FELTS, Narvel / Red Sovine / Mel Tillis
  Also see MULLICAN, Moon / Cowboy Copas / Red
  Sovine
  Also see REEVES, Del / Red Sovine
  Also see SHEPARD, Jean

SOVINE, Red, & Goldie Hill   *C&W '55*

Singles: 78rpm

DECCA........................... 4-8   55

Singles: 7–inch

DECCA........................... 5-10   55

  Also see HILL, Goldie

SOVINE, Red, & Webb Pierce   *C&W '56*

Singles: 78rpm

DECCA........................... 4-8   56

Singles: 7–inch

DECCA........................... 8-12   56

  Also see PIERCE, Webb
  Also see SOVINE, Red

SOVINE, Roger   *C&W '68*

Singles: 7–inch

IMPERIAL 4-6   68-69

SPACEK, Sissy   *C&W '80*

Singles: 7–inch

ATLANTIC AMERICA 3-4   83-84

MCA 3-5   80

Picture Sleeves

MCA 3-5   80

LPs: 10/12–inch 33rpm

ATLANTIC AMERICA 5-8   83

SPACEK, Sissy, & Beverly D'Angelo

Singles: 7–inch

MCA 3-5   80

  Also see SPACEK, Sissy

SPEARS, Billie Jo   *C&W '68*

Singles: 7–inch

CAPITOL...............................3-5   68-71

LIBERTY...............................3-4   81

PARLIAMENT..........................3-4   84

U.A. (Except 50000 series)............3-5   74-80

U.A. (50000 series).......................3-6   66-67

LPs: 10/12–inch 33rpm

CAPITOL...............................5-15   68-79

KOALA.................................5-10   80s

LIBERTY...............................5-8   81

PICKWICK/HILLTOP 5-8   70s

U.A. 5-10   75-80

  Also see BUTLER, Larry, & Friends
  Also see REEVES, Del, & Billie Jo Spears

SPEARS, Bobby

Singles: 7–inch

MANCO................................4-8   63

  Also see CASSADY, Linda

SPEEGLE, David   *C&W '89*

(With Lonerider)

Singles: 7–inch

BITTER CREED............................3-4   89

SPEEKS, Ronnie   *C&W '81*

(With His Elrods)

Singles: 7–inch

DIMENSION...............................3-5   81

KING (5548 "What Is Your
Technique").............................75-100   61

PALETTE (5094 "Mister Glenn")....4-8   63

SPENCER, Teddy   *C&W '88*

Singles: 7–inch

OAK 3-4   88

SPENCER, Tracie   *P&R/LP '88*

Singles: 7–inch

CAPITOL......................................3-4   88-91

Picture Sleeves

CAPITOL......................................3-4   88-89

LPs: 10/12–inch 33rpm

CAPITOL......................................5-8   88-91

SPITZ, Michele   *C&W '81*

Singles: 7–inch

50 STATES.................................3-4   81

SPRINGER BROTHERS   *C&W '80*

Singles: 7–inch

ELEKTRA....................................3-4   80

SPRINGFIELD, Bobby Lee *C&W '83*
Singles: 7–inch

EPIC	3-4	87
KAT FAMILY	3-4	83

SPRINGFIELDS *C&W/P&R '62*
Singles: 7–inch

PHILIPS	4-6	62-63

LPs: 10/12–inch 33rpm

PHILIPS	15-25	62-63

Members: Dusty Springfield; Tom Springfield; Tim Field.

SPURZZ *C&W '80*
Singles: 7–inch

EPIC	3-5	80

Member: Tony Ingram.
Also see ATLANTA
Also see WELLER, Freddy

STACK, Billy *C&W '78*
Singles: 7–inch

CAPRICE	3-5	78-79

STAFF, Bobbi *C&W '66*
Singles: 7–inch

RCA	4-6	66

STAFFORD, Jim *P&R '73/C&W '74*
Singles: 7–inch

COLUMBIA	3-4	84
ELEKTRA	3-5	80-81
ISLAND	3-5	74
MGM	3-5	73-75
POLYDOR	3-5	75-78
TOWN HOUSE	3-5	82
W.B.	3-5	76-80

LPs: 10/12–inch 33rpm

MGM	8-10	74-75
POLYDOR	5-10	76

Also see LOBO

STAFFORD, Jo *P&R '44/C&W '47*
Singles: 78rpm

CAPITOL	3-8	43-50
COLUMBIA	3-5	50-57
COLUMBIA/SNOWY BLEACH (22270 "St. Louis Blues")	10-15	50s

(Promotional issue for Snowy Bleach and Glass Wax. No actual label name shown. Seven-inch 78rpm.)

Singles: 7–inch

COLPIX	4-6	62
COLUMBIA	5-10	50-60
DECCA	4-6	68

DOT	4-6	65
REPRISE	4-6	63

EPs: 7–inch 33/45rpm

CAPITOL	5-15	50-57
COLUMBIA	5-15	50-59

LPs: 10/12–inch 33rpm

BAINBRIDGE	5-8	82
CAPITOL (H-75 thru H-435) (10–inch LPs.)	20-40	50-53
CAPITOL (T-197 thru T-435)	15-25	55
CAPITOL (T-1653 thru T-2166) (Monaural.)	10-20	62-64
CAPITOL (ST-1653 thru ST-2166) (Stereo.)	12-25	62-64
CAPITOL (9014 "Songs of Faith") (10–inch LP.)	20-30	54
CAPITOL (11000 series)	5-8	79
COLUMBIA (584 thru 1339) (Monaural.)	15-25	54-59
COLUMBIA (1561 "Jo Plus Jazz") (Monaural.)	30-50	60
COLUMBIA (2500 series) (10–inch LPs.)	15-30	55
COLUMBIA (6000 series) (10–inch LPs.)	20-35	50-54
COLUMBIA (8080 "I'll Be Seeing You") (Stereo.)	20-30	59
COLUMBIA (8139 "Ballad of the Blues") (Stereo.)	20-30	59
COLUMBIA (8361 "Jo Plus Jazz") (Stereo.)	40-60	60
COLUMBIA/SNOWY BLEACH (22500 "I Only Have Eyes for You")	15-25	50s

(Promotional issue for Snowy Bleach. No actual label name shown.)

DECCA	10-15	68
DOT	10-15	66
TRIBUTE	5-10	71
VOCALION	8-12	68-69

Also see EDWARDS, Jonathan & Darlene
Also see INGLE, Red, & Natural Seven
Also see MacRAE, Gordon, & Jo Stafford
Also see MERCER, Johnny, Jo Stafford & Pied Pipers
Also see PIED PIPERS

STAFFORD, Jo, & Frankie Laine

P&R '51

Singles: 78rpm

COLUMBIA 4-8   51-53

Singles: 7–inch

COLUMBIA 5-10   51-53

EPs: 7–inch 33/45rpm

COLUMBIA 5-15   54

LPs: 10/12–inch 33rpm

COLUMBIA 20-30   54

STAFFORD, Jo, & Gordon MacRae

P&R '48

Singles: 78rpm

CAPITOL............................. 4-8   48-50

Singles: 7–inch

CAPITOL............................. 4-8   62

LPs: 10/12–inch 33rpm

CAPITOL (1600 & 1900
  series) 10-20   62-63
CAPITOL (11000 series)............... 4-8   79
Also see STAFFORD, Jo

STAFFORD, Terry

P&R/LP '64/C&W '73

Singles: 7–inch

ATLANTIC...................................... 3-5   73-74
CASINO 3-5   77
COLLECTABLES 3-4   80s
CRUSADER 4-8   64
ERIC.. 3-5   70s
FIRSTLINE..................................... 3-5   81
LANA 3-6   60s
MGM 3-5   71
MELODYLAND 3-5   75
MERCURY 4-8   66
PLAYER 3-4   89
SIDEWALK..................................... 4-8   66-67
TERRIFIC....................................... 3-5
W.B. 3-6   69

LPs: 10/12–inch 33rpm

ATLANTIC.................................... 8-12   73
CRUSADER (1001
  "Suspicion!")........................... 20-25   64
  (Monaural)
CRUSADER (1001
  "Suspicion!")........................... 25-35   64
  (Stereo)
Session: Davie Allan.

STALEY, Karen

C&W '88

Singles: 7–inch

MCA.. 3-4   88-89

STAMPLEY, Joe

C&W '71

Singles: 7–inch

ABC... 3-5   77
ABC/DOT....................................... 3-5   75-76
CHESS (1798 "Creation of
  Love")..................................... 10-20   63
DOT 3-6   70-74
EPIC.. 3-5   75-86
EVERGREEN 3-4   88-89
IMPERIAL 10-15   59
PARAMOUNT 3-6   70
PAULA 3-5   74

LPs: 10/12–inch 33rpm

ABC.. 5-10   77
ABC/DOT..................................... 8-12   74-76
ACCORD 5-10   82
DOT 8-12   73
EPIC.. 5-10   75-85
PHONORAMA 5-8   83
Also see BANDY, Moe, & Joe Stampley
Also see UNIQUES

STANLEY BROTHERS

C&W '60

Singles: 78rpm

COLUMBIA 4-8   51-52
KING 4-8   58
MERCURY....................................... 4-8   53-55
RICH-R-TONE 5-10   47

Singles: 7–inch

COLUMBIA 5-10   52
KING 4-8   58-65
MERCURY..................................... 5-10   53-55

EPs: 7–inch 33/45rpm

COLUMBIA 10-15   58
KING 5-10   61-62
STARDAY....................................... 8-12   59

LP: 10/12–inch 33rpm

CABIN CREEK (1 "Stanley Series,
  Vol. 1") 30-40
  (Four individual LPs.)
CABIN CREEK (2 "Stanley Series,
  Vol. 2") 5-10
  (Single LP.)
CABIN CREEK (203 "Bluegrass Gospel
  Favorites") 40-60   66
COLLECTOR'S CLASSICS 5-10
COOPER CREEK...................... 5-10
COUNTY 6-12   73

GTO (103-108).......................... 50-75   83
(Six individual LPs, pakaged as a set.)
GUSTO 5-10   80
GUSTO/KING............................. 6-12 75-76
HARMONY............................... 12-25 61-66
KING (645 thru 1013)................ 15-30 59-67
MELODEON................................ 5-10
MERCURY (20349 "Country Pickin' and
Singin").......................... 30-50   58
MERCURY (20384 "Hard
Times").................................. 25-35   63
(Monaural.)
MERCURY (60384 "Hard
Times").................................. 30-40   63
(Stereo.)
NASHVILLE 8-12   70
OLD HOMESTEAD 5-10
POWER PAK 5-10   80s
REBEL 5-10
RIMROCK 5-10
ROUNDER.................................. 5-10
STARDAY (106 "Mountain
Song") 25-35   59
STARDAY (122 "Sacred
Songs") 25-35   60
STARDAY (201 "Mountain
Music")................................... 20-30   62
STARDAY (384 "Jacob's
Vision")................................... 15-25   66
STARDAY (834 "Folk Concert").. 6-12   76
STARDAY (3003 "16 Hits") 5-10
STARDAY/KING 5-10
VINTAGE COLLECTOR'S CLUB (002 "Live at
Antioch College") 50-75   61
WANGO 6-12   76
WING 15-20   66
Members: Ralph Stanley; Carter Stanley.

STARCHER, Buddy   *C&W '49*
Singles: 78rpm
4 STAR.. 4-8 49-50s
Singles: 7–inch
BOONE 3-6   66
DECCA.. 3-6   66
4 STAR...................................... 5-10   50s
HEARTWARMING 3-5   67
STARDAY 4-8 59-66
EPs: 7–inch 33/45rpm
4 STAR...................................... 5-10   50s
STARDAY 5-10   61
LPs: 10/12–inch 33rpm
BLUEBONNET.......................... 10-20

DECCA 10-20   66
HEARTWARMING 5-10   68
STARDAY 10-20 62-66

STARK, Donna   *C&W '80*
Singles: 7–inch
RCI..3-5   80

STARLAND VOCAL BAND   *P&R/C&W/LP '76*
Singles: 7–inch
WINDSONG....................................3-5 76-80
LPs: 10/12–inch 33rpm
WINDSONG....................................8-10 76-80
Members: Bill Danoff; Taffy Danoff.
Also see BILL & TAFFY
Also see FAT CITY

STARR, Kay   *P&R '48/C&W '50*
(With the Crystalette All Stars)
Singles: 78rpm
CAPITOL......................................5-10 48-57
CRYSTALETTE 8-12   50
JEWEL (1000 "I Ain't Gonna
Cry")...20-30   45
MODERN 10-20   49
RCA 3-5 55-57
Singles: 7–inch
ABC...3-5 67-68
CAPITOL (811 thru 2887)............8-15 50-54
CAPITOL (4000 & 5000 series) ...4-10 58-64
CRYSTALETTE (632 "Where Or
When")....................................10-15   50
(Black vinyl.)
CRYSTALETTE (632 "Where Or
When")....................................15-25   50
(Colored vinyl.)
DOT 3-6   68
GNP...3-5 74-75
HAPPY TIGER..............................3-5   70
RCA (0100 series) 3-5   73
RCA (6000 & 7000 series).............4-8 55-59
Picture Sleeves
CAPITOL.......................................4-8   62
EPs: 7–inch 33/45rpm
CAPITOL.....................................5-15 50-61
RCA 5-10 55-58
LPs: 10/12–inch 33rpm
ABC...5-15   68
CAMDEN 10-20 60-61
CAPITOL (H-211 "Songs by Kay
Starr").....................................40-60   50
(10–inch LP.)

CAPITOL (T-211 "Songs by Kay Starr")...................... 20-40   55

CAPITOL (H-415 "The Hits of Kay Starr")...................... 20-35   53
(10–inch LP.)

CAPITOL (211 thru 1200) 15-25   53-59

CAPITOL (400 thru 900 series)... 5-15   63-75
(With "DT" or "SM" prefix.)

CAPITOL (1300 series)............. 15-25   60

CAPITOL (T-1438 "Kay Starr, Jazz Singer").................................. 20-30   60
(Monaural.)

CAPITOL (ST-1438 "Kay Starr, Jazz Singer").................................. 25-35   60
(Stereo.)

CAPITOL (1468 thru 2100 series) 10-20   61-64

CAPITOL (11000 series)............. 5-10   74-79

CORONET 10-20   63

CRYSTALETTE (4500 "Kay Starr Sings").................................. 50-100   52
(10–inch LP.)

GNP 5-10   74-75

LIBERTY (3280 "Swingin' with the Starr")..................................... 15-25   63

LIBERTY (9001 "Swingin' with the Starr")..................................... 35-45   56

RCA (1100 thru 1700 series) 15-25   55-57

RONDO-LETTE 20-30   58
Also see WILLIAMS, Tex

STARR, Kay, & Count Basie
LPs: 10/12–inch 33rpm

MCA 5-8   83

PARAMOUNT 10-15   69

STARR, Kay, & Tennessee Ernie Ford
Singles: 78rpm

CAPITOL..................................... 3-5   50-56
Singles: 7–inch

CAPITOL..................................... 5-10   50-56
EPs: 7–inch 33/45rpm

CAPITOL..................................... 5-15   56
Also see FORD, Tennessee Ernie

STARR, Kay / Erroll Garner
LPs: 10/12–inch 33rpm

CROWN 15-30   57

MODERN 25-35   56
Also see STARR, Kay

STARR, Kenny   *C&W '73*
Singles: 7–inch

MCA...3-5   73-78

SRO 3-5   82

S.S. TITANIC 3-4   81
LPs: 10/12–inch 33rpm

MCA...5-10   75

SRO 5-10   82
Also see LYNN, Loretta

STARR, Lucille   *P&R '64*
Singles: 7–inch

A&M 4-8   66

ALMO...4-8   64-65

EPIC...4-6   67-69
LPs: 10/12–inch 33rpm

A&M 20-30   66

EPIC...20-30   69
Also see BOB & LUCILLE
Also see CANADIAN SWEETHEARTS

STARR, Penny   *C&W '67*
(Penny DeHaven)
Singles: 7–inch

BAND BOX 4-8   66-67
Also see DeHAVEN, Penny

STARR, Ringo   *P&R/LP '70*
Singles: 12–inch 33/45rpm

ATLANTIC (93 "Drowning in the Sea of Love")..15-20   77
(Promotional issue only.)
Singles: 7–inch

APPLE (1831 "It Don't Come Easy")......................................4-8   71

APPLE (1849 "Back Off Boogaloo") 40-60   72
(With a blue apple on the label.)

APPLE (1849 "Back Off Boogaloo") 4-6   73
(With a green apple on the label.)

APPLE (1865 "Photograph")...........3-5   73

APPLE (1870 "You're Sixteen") 5-8   73
(With standard apple label.)

APPLE (1870 "You're Sixteen") 4-6   73
(With 5-point star label.)

APPLE (1872 "Oh My My")............4-6   74

APPLE (1876 "Only You")..............4-6   74

APPLE (1880 "No No Song").........4-6   75

APPLE (1882 "It's All Down to Goodnight Vienna")....................................4-6   75

APPLE (2969 "Beaucoups of Blues") 4-8   70

ATLANTIC (3361 "Dose of Rock 'N'
Roll") 10-20   76

ATLANTIC (3371 "Hey Baby") .. 10-20   76

ATLANTIC (3412 "Drowning in the Sea of
Love")................................... 75-100   77

ATLANTIC (3429 "Wings").......... 8-12   77

BOARDWALK (130 "Wrack My
Brain") 3-5   81

BOARDWALK (134 "Private
Property").................................. 3-5   82

CAPITOL (Orange label)............... 4-8   75

CAPITOL (Purple label) 3-5   78

CAPITOL (Black label) 3-4   83

PORTRAIT (70015 "Lipstick
Traces").................................... 5-10   78

PORTRAIT (70018 "Heart on My
Sleeve") 4-8   78

Picture Sleeves

APPLE (1826 "Beaucoups of
Blues")................................... 25-35   70
(Selection number 2969 mistakenly shown
as Apple 1826.)

APPLE (1831 "It Don't Come
Easy") 10-15   71

APPLE (1849 "Back Off
Boogaloo") 10-15   72

APPLE (1865 "Photograph") 8-12   73

APPLE (1870 "You're Sixteen") .. 8-12   73

APPLE (1876 "Only You")........... 5-10   74

APPLE (1882 "It's All Down to Goodnight
Vienna") 8-10   75

APPLE (2969 "Beaucoups of
Blues")................................... 12-18   70
(Selection number correctly shown.)

BOARDWALK (130 "Wrack My
Brain")....................................... 3-5   81

Promotional Singles

APPLE (1831 "It Don't Come
Easy")..................................... 15-20   71

APPLE (1849 "Back Off
Boogaloo") 35-45   72
(White label.)

APPLE (1865 "Photograph") 20-30   73

APPLE (1870 "You're
Sixteen").................................. 20-30   73

APPLE (1872 "Oh My My") 20-30   74

APPLE (1876 "Only You")......... 20-30   74

APPLE (1880 "No No Song") 20-30   75

APPLE (1882 "It's All Down to Goodnight
Vienna") 20-30   75

APPLE (1882 "Oo-Wee") 25-30   75

ATLANTIC (3361 "Dose of Rock 'N'
Roll") 20-30   76
(White label.)

ATLANTIC (3361 "Dose of Rock 'N'
Roll") 10-15   76
(Blue label.)

ATLANTIC (3371 "Hey Baby") ...20-30   76
(White label.)

ATLANTIC (3371 "Hey Baby") ...10-15   76
(Red-white and blue labels.)

ATLANTIC (3371 "Hey Baby") ...25-35   76
(Single-sided disc.)

ATLANTIC (3412 "Drowning in the Sea of
Love")....................................10-20   77

ATLANTIC (3429 "Wings").........20-25   77
(White label.)

ATLANTIC (3429 "Wings").........10-12   77
(Red-white and blue labels.)

BOARDWALK (130 "Wrack My
Brain")..8-12   81

BOARDWALK (134 "Private
Property")...................................8-12   82

PORTRAIT (70015 "Lipstick
Traces") 8-12   78

PORTRAIT (70018 "Heart on My
Sleeve") 8-12   78

LPs: 10/12–inch 33rpm

APPLE (3365 "Sentimental
Journey") 10-15   70

APPLE (3368 "Beaucoups of
Blues") 10-15   70

APPLE (3417 "Goodnight
Vienna") 10-15   75

APPLE (3422 "Blast from Your
Past")..10-15   75

APPLE (3413 "Ringo") 15-20   73
(Includes a 20-page booklet.)

APPLE (3413 "Ringo") 10-15   73
(With 4:05 version of *Six O'Clock.*)

ATLANTIC (18193 "Ringo's
Rotogravure") 8-12   76

ATLANTIC (19108 "Ringo the
4th") 8-12   77

BOARDWALK (33246 "Stop and Smell the
Roses") 8-10   81

CAPITOL.....................................5-12   80-81

PORTRAIT (35378 "Bad Boy") 8-10   78

Promotional LPs

APPLE (3413 "Ringo") 100-125   73
(With 5:26 version of *Six O'Clock.* Some
copies list the track at 5:26 though it actually
runs only 4:05.)

ATLANTIC (18193 "Ringo's
Rotogravure")............................ 10-20   76
(With programming sticker on front cover.)

ATLANTIC (19108 "Ringo
the 4th").................................... 10-20   77
(With programming sticker on front cover.)

PORTRAIT (35378 "Bad Boy") 25-30   78
(Labels reads "Advance Promotion.")

PORTRAIT (35378 "Bad Boy") 15-20   78
(Labels reads "Demonstration, Not For
Sale.")

Also see OWENS, Buck, & Ringo Starr

STATLER, Darrell   *C&W '69*
Singles: 7–inch
DOT.. 3-6   69

STATLER BROTHERS *C&W/P&R '65*
Singles: 7–inch
COLUMBIA 4-6   64-69
MERCURY 3-6   70-90

LPs: 10/12–inch 33rpm
CBS.. 5-10   82-85
COLUMBIA (CL-2000 series).... 15-25   66-67
(Monaural.)
COLUMBIA (CS-9000 series) ... 12-25   66-69
(Stereo.)
COLUMBIA (PC-9000 series) 5-8   80s
COLUMBIA (31000 series) 8-10   70s
51 WEST..................................... 5-8   80s
HARMONY................................. 6-12   71-73
MERCURY 5-10   71-90
PRIORITY 5-8   82
REALM....................................... 5-10
TIME-LIFE.................................... 5-8   81

Members: Harold Reid; Don Reid; Lew DeWitt; Phil
Balsley; Jimmy Fortune. Session: Carl Perkins; Ernest
Tubb.
Also see CASH, Johnny
Also see DeWITT, Lew
Also see PERKINS, Carl
Also see TUBB, Ernest

STEAGALL, Red   *C&W '72*
(With the Coleman County Cowboys; Red
Stegall)
Singles: 7–inch
ABC.. 3-5   78
ABC/DOT 3-5   76-77
CAPITOL..................................... 3-5   72-75
ELEKTRA..................................... 3-4   79-80

LP: 10/12–inch 33rpm
ABC.. 5-10   78
ABC/DOT 6-12   76
CAPITOL.................................... 10-20   72-74

HESSTON.................................5-8   83
MCA...5-10
Also see PRICE, David

STEARNS, June   *C&W '68*
Singles: 7–inch
COLUMBIA 3-6   68-69
DECCA 3-5   70-71

LP: 10/12–inch 33rpm
COLUMBIA 10-15   69
Also see AGNES & ORVILLE
Also see DUNCAN, Johnny, & June Stearns

STEEL, Ric   *C&W '87*
Singles: 7–inch
PANACHE....................................3-4   87-88

STEELE, Larry   *C&W '66*
(With the Wranglers)
Singles: 7–inch
ASSULT.......................................4-8   63
K-ARK..4-8   65-66

STEFFIN SISTERS   *C&W '89*
Singles: 7–inch
WINWARD 3-4   89

STEGALL, Keith   *C&W '80*
Singles: 7–inch
CAPITOL......................................3-5   80-81
EMI AMERICA 3-4   82
EPIC..3-4   84-86

STEGALL, Red: see STEAGALL, Red

STENMARK - MUELLER   *C&W '87*
Singles: 7–inch
ENVELOPE....................................3-4   87

STEPHENS, Ott   *C&W '63*
Singles: 7–inch
CHANCELLOR 4-8   63
CHART...4-6   65
REPRISE 4-6   64

STEVENS, Even   *C&W '75*
Singles: 7–inch
ELEKTRA......................................3-5   75

LP: 10/12–inch 33rpm
ELEKTRA......................................5-10   77
Also see OAK RIDGE BOYS

STEVENS, Even, & Sammi Smith   *C&W '75*

Singles: 7–inch

ELEKTRA........................... 3-5   75
Also see SMITH, Sammi

STEVENS, Even, & Sherry Grooms   *C&W '77*

Singles: 7–inch

ELEKTRA........................... 3-5   77
Also see GROOMS, Sherry
Also see STEVENS, Even

STEVENS, Geraldine   *C&W '69*

Singles: 7–inch

WORLD PACIFIC........................ 3-6   69

STEVENS, Jeff, & Bullets   *C&W '86*

Singles: 7–inch

ATLANTIC AMERICA 3-4   86-89

STEVENS, Lee J.   *C&W '89*

Singles: 7–inch

REGAL.......................... 3-4   88-89

STEVENS, Ray   *P&R '61/C&W '69*

(With the Merry Melody Singers)

Singles: 7–inch

BARNABY.....................................	3-5	70-76
CAPITOL.....................................	8-12	58-59
MCA (Except 53661).....................	3-4	85-89
MCA (53661 "I Saw Elvis in a UFO").....................................	5-10	89
MERCURY (66 "Butch Barbarian")................................	5-10	64
(Promotional issue only.)		
MERCURY (71000 & 72000 series)	4-8	61-68
MERCURY (810000 series)..........	3-5	83
MONUMENT	4-8	65-69
NRC	5-10	59-60
PREP	10-15	57
PRIORITY	3-4	80s
RCA..	3-5	81-82
W.B./AHAB....................................	3-5	76-79

Picture Sleeves

BARNABY	4-6	70
MCA	3-5	86
MERCURY	10-15	61-64
W.B./AHAB....................................	3-5	79

EPs: 7–inch 33/45rpm

MERCURY (85 "Ray Stevens") .10-15   62
(Promotional issue only. Not issued with cover.)

LPs: 10/12–inch 33rpm

BARNABY.....................................8-10		70-78
MCA..5-8		85-89
MERCURY (20732 "1,837 Seconds of Humor").................................50-75		62
MERCURY (20732 "Ahab the Arab")..20-25		62
(Reissue of *1,837 Seconds of Humor*.)		
MERCURY (20828 "This Is Ray Stevens") 20-30		63
MERCURY (60732 "1,837 Seconds of Humor")..................................60-80		62
MERCURY (60732 "Ahab the Arab")..25-35		62
(Reissue of *1,837 Seconds of Humor*.)		
MERCURY (60828 "This Is Ray Stevens") 25-35		63
MERCURY (61272 "The Best of Ray Stevens") 10-15		70
MERCURY (810000 series)...........5-8		83
MONUMENT..............................10-15		66-69
PICKWICK 5-10		
PRIORITY.....................................5-8		82
RCA 5-10		80-82
W.B. 5-10		76-79
WING 10-15		68

Session: Minnie Pearl; Jerry Clower.
Also see HENHOUSE FIVE PLUS TOO
Also see MINNIE PEARL

STEVENS, Ray / 4 Seasons

Singles: 7–inch

OLDIES 45....................................5-10   63

STEVENS, Ray / Tommy Roe / Bobby Rydell

LPs: 10/12–inch 33rpm

DESIGN (178 "Young Lovers")..15-20   63
Also see STEVENS, Ray

STEVENS, Ray / Hal Winters

LPs: 10/12–inch 33rpm

CROWN......................................12-18   63
Also see STEVENS, Ray

STEWART, Gary   *C&W '73*

(With the Nashville Edition; with Dean Dillon)

Singles: 7–inch

CORY (101 "Walk On Boy").......10-20		64
DECCA 3-5		71
HIGHTONE...................................3-4		88-89

KAPP	3-6	68-70
MCA	3-5	75
RCA	3-5	73-83
RED ASH	3-4	84

Picture Sleeves

| RCA | 3-5 | 82 |

LPs: 10/12-inch 33rpm

| MCA | 4-8 | 75 |
| RCA | 5-10 | 75-83 |

Also see CROWELL, Rodney
Also see HARRIS, Emmylou

STEWART, Vernon   *C&W '63*
Singles: 7-inch

| CHART | 4-8 | 63 |
| PEACH (751 "Mean Mean Baby") | 40-60 | 61 |

STEWART, Wynn   *C&W '56*
(With the Tourists; Win Stewart)
Singles: 78rpm

| CAPITOL | 5-10 | 56-57 |
| INTRO (6088 "I've Waited a Lifetime") | 15-20 | 54 |

Singles: 7-inch

ATLANTIC	3-4	74
CAPITOL (2000 series)	3-5	67-71
CAPITOL (3000 series)	8-15	56-57
CAPITOL (5000 series)	4-8	62-67
CHALLENGE	5-10	59-64
4 STAR	3-4	80
JACKPOT	10-15	59
PLAYBOY	3-5	75-76
PRETTY WORLD	3-4	85
RCA	3-5	72-73
WINS	3-5	78-79

Picture Sleeves

| CAPITOL | 4-8 | 67-69 |

LPs: 10/12-inch 33rpm

CAPITOL	10-20	67-75
PICKWICK/HILLTOP	5-12	67
PLAYBOY	5-10	76
STARDAY	8-12	68
WRANGLER (1006 "Wynn Stewart")	15-25	62

Member: Bobby Austin
Also see AUSTIN, Bobby
Also see PIERCE, Webb / Wynn Stewart

STEWART, Wynn, & Jan Howard   *C&W '60*
Singles: 7-inch

| CHALLENGE | 5-10 | 60 |

LP: 10/12-inch 33rpm

| CHALLENGE (611 "Sweethearts of Country Music") | 25-35 | 60 |
| STARDAY (421 "Their Hits") | 15-20 | 68 |

STONE, Cliffie, & His Orchestra   *C&W '47*
(With His Barn Dance Band; Cliffie Stone Singers; Cliffie Stone's Country Hombres)
Singles: 78rpm

| CAPITOL (Except 2910) | 3-6 | 47-57 |
| CAPITOL (2910 "Blue Moon of Kentucky") | 4-8 | 54 |

Singles: 7-inch

CAPITOL (Except 2910)	4-10	50-69
CAPITOL (2910 "Blue Moon of Kentucky")	10-20	54
TOWER	3-6	67

LPs: 10/12-inch 33rpm

CAPITOL (100 thru 300 series)	5-10	68-69
CAPITOL (1000 thru 1600 series)	20-40	58-62
CAPITOL (2100 series)	10-20	64
TOWER	10-15	67

Also see ADAMS, Kay
Also see CARSON, Cindy

STONE, Doug   *LP '90*
LPs: 10/12-inch 33rpm

| EPIC | 5-8 | 90 |

STONE PONEYS   *P&R/LP '67*
(Featuring Linda Ronstadt)
Singles: 7-inch

| CAPITOL | 5-10 | 67 |

Picture Sleeves

| CAPITOL | 5-10 | 67 |

LPs: 10/12-inch 33rpm

| CAPITOL (2600 & 2700 series) | 15-25 | 67 |

Also see RONSTADT, Linda

STONEMANS   *C&W '66*
(With the Tracy Schwartz Band; Stoneman Family)
Singles: 7-inch

| MGM | 4-6 | 66-68 |
| STARDAY | 4-8 | 62 |

LP: 10/12-inch 33rpm

CMH	5-12	76-82
FOLKWAYS	10-20	
MGM	10-20	66-70
NASHVILLE	8-12	68
RCA	6-12	70-71

STARDAY (393 "White
Lightning")............................. 15-25   65
SUNSET..................................... 10-15   68
WORLD PACIFIC...................... 15-20   64
Members: Pop Stoneman; Donna Stoneman; Scott
Stoneman; Van Stoneman; Roni Stoneman.
Also see DEAN, Jimmy / Stoneman Family

STOREY, Lewis   *C&W '86*
Singles: 7–inch

EPIC... 3-4   86

STOREY SISTERS   *P&R '58*
Singles: 7–inch

BATON.. 10-20   58
CAMEO 10-20   58
MERCURY 10-15   59
Members: Lillian Storey; Ann Storey.

STORIE, James   *C&W '88*
Singles: 7–inch

GMC.. 3-4   88

STOVALL, Vern   *C&W '67*
(With Janet McBride)
Singles: 7–inch

LONGHORN 4-6   67
LPs: 10/12–inch 33rpm
LONGHORN 15-25   67

STRAIT, George   *C&W '81*
Singles: 7–inch

MCA 3-5   81-91
LPs: 10/12–inch 33rpm
MCA 5-10   81-91
Also see ACE in the HOLE BAND

STREET, Mel   *C&W '72*
(With Sandy Powell)
Singles: 7–inch

GRT... 3-5   74-77
MERCURY 3-5   78
METROMEDIA COUNTRY 3-5   72-73
POLYDOR 3-5   77-78
ROYAL AMERICAN 3-5   72
SUNBIRD 3-5   80-81
SUNSET.. 3-5   79
LP: 10/12–inch 33rpm
GRT... 10-15   74-77
LAKESHORE 8-12
MERCURY 10-15   78
METROMEDIA COUNTRY 10-15   72-73
PHONORAMA............................. 5-10   82
POLYDOR................................. 10-15   77-78

SUNBIRD.................................... 10-15   80

STREETFEET   *C&W '83*
Singles: 7–inch

TRIPLE T 3-4   83

STREETS   *P&R/LP '83*
(Nightstreets)
Singles: 7–inch

ATLANTIC...................................... 3-4   83-84
EPIC.. 3-5   79-80
LPs: 10/12–inch 33rpm
ATLANTIC...................................... 5-8   83-84
EPIC.. 5-10   79
Member: Steve Walsh; Rick Taylor; Rick Taylor; Joyce
Hawthorne.
Also see NIGHTSTREETS

STREISAND, Barbra   *LP '63*
Singles: 12–inch 33/45rpm

COLUMBIA (White labels) 12-25   79-85
(Promotional issues only.)
Singles: 7–inch
ARISTA (123 "More Than You
Know") 4-6   75
COLUMBIA (04000 & 05000
series).. 3-4   83-86
COLUMBIA (10000 & 11000
series).. 3-5   76-80
COLUMBIA (3-42648 "My Coloring
Book")....................................... 20-30   62
(Compact 33 Single.)
COLUMBIA (4-42648 "My Coloring
Book")....................................... 8-12   62
COLUMBIA (42631 "Happy Days Are Here
Again") 5-10   63
COLUMBIA (42965 thru 43469).....4-6   64-65
COLUMBIA (43518 thru 46024).....3-5   66-74
Promotional Singles
COLUMBIA (04000 & 05000
series).. 3-5   83-86
COLUMBIA (10000 & 11000
series).. 3-5   76-80
COLUMBIA (4-42648 "My Coloring
Book")....................................... 15-25   62
COLUMBIA (42631 "Happy Days Are Here
Again") 10-15   63
COLUMBIA (42965 thru 43469)...5-10   64-65
COLUMBIA (43518 thru 46024).....4-8   66-74
COLUMBIA (79581 "People—Special Open-
End Interview")........................15-25   64
(Promotional issue only. Compact 33.)

Picture Sleeves

COLUMBIA (Except 43000 series &
    79581).. 3-5   73-85

COLUMBIA (43000 series) 4-8   66

COLUMBIA (79581 "People—Special Open-
    End Interview")........................ 15-25   64
    (Promotional issue only.)

LPs: 10/12–inch 33rpm

ARISTA 8-10   75

CAPITOL (2059 "Funny Girl") ... 10-20   64

COLUMBIA (1779 "The Legend of Barbra
    Streisand") 35-45   83
    (Promotional, one-hour interview program.)

COLUMBIA (1791 "Makes Me
    Feel")..................................... 15-20   83
    (Picture disc. Promotional issue only.)

COLUMBIA (CL-2007 thru
    CL-2682)................................. 15-25   63-67
    (Monaural. Black vinyl.)

COLUMBIA (2054 "The Second Barbra
    Streisand Album") 100-200   63
    (Colored vinyl. Promotional issue only.)

COLUMBIA (2478 "Color Me
    Barbra")............................. 100-200   66
    (Colored vinyl. Promotional issue only.)

COLUMBIA (3220 "Funny
    Girl")..................................... 10-15   68

COLUMBIA (CS-8807 thru
    CS-9557)................................. 15-25   63-68
    (Stereo. Black vinyl.)

COLUMBIA (8854 "The Second Barbra
    Streisand Album") 100-200   63
    (Colored vinyl. Promotional issue only.)

COLUMBIA (9278 "Color Me
    Barbra")............................. 100-200   66
    (Colored vinyl. Promotional issue only.)

COLUMBIA (9710 thru 9968).... 10-15   68-70

COLUMBIA (PC-8000 & PC-9000
    series) 5-8

COLUMBIA (JC-9000 series)........ 5-8

COLUMBIA (30086 thru 39480).. 5-15   70-84
    With "FC," "JC," "KC," or "PC" prefix.)

COLUMBIA (30378 thru
    33815).................................... 10-20   71-75
    (Quadrophonic. With "PCQ" prefix.)

COLUMBIA (39909 "Emotion") . 10-15   85
    (Picture disc.)

COLUMBIA (40092 thru 45369).. 5-10   85-89

COLUMBIA (42801 thru
    47678).................................... 15-30   82
    (Half-speed mastered. With "HC" prefix.)

20TH FOX 10-15   69

STREISAND, Barbra, & Kim Carnes   *P&R '84*

Singles: 7–inch

COLUMBIA 3-4   84
Also see CARNES, Kim

STREISAND, Barbra/ Marilyn Cooper

Singles: 7–inch

COLUMBIA 5-10
    (Promotional issue only.)

STREISAND, Barbra / Doris Day / Jim Nabors / Andre Kostelanetz

LPs: 10/12–inch 33rpm

COLUMBIA (1075 "Season's Greetings from
    Barbra Streisand & Friends")...15-25
    (Special products issue for Maxwell House
    Coffee Co.)

STREISAND, Barbra, & Neil Diamond   *P&R/C&W '78*

Singles: 7–inch

COLUMBIA 3-5   78
Also see DIAMOND, Neil

STREISAND, Barbra, & Barry Gibb   *P&R '80*

Singles: 7–inch

COLUMBIA 3-4   80-81

STREISAND, Barbra, & Don Johnson   *P&R '88*

Singles: 7–inch

COLUMBIA 3-4   88

STREISAND, Barbra, & Donna Summer   *P&R '79*

Singles: 12–inch 33/45rpm

COLUMBIA/CASABLANCA.........8-10   79
    (Promotional issue only. With special cover.)

Singles: 7–inch

COLUMBIA 3-5   79

Picture Sleeves

COLUMBIA 3-5   79
Also see STREISAND, Barbra

STRODE, Lance   *C&W '89*

Singles: 7–inch

BOOTSTRAP...................................3-4   89

STROMAN, Gene   *C&W '87*

Singles: 7–inch

CAPITOL...3-4   87

STRUNK, Jud   *C&W/P&R/LP '73*
(With the Coplin Kitchen Band)
Singles: 7–inch

CAPITOL.. 3-5   74
COBURT.. 3-5   71
COLUMBIA 3-5   70
MCA 3-5   77
MGM 3-5   72-73
MELODYLAND 3-5   75-76
LPs: 10/12–inch 33rpm
COLUMBIA 6-12   70
HARMONY..................................... 5-10   73
MCA 5-10   77
MGM 5-10   71-73

STUART, Marty   *C&W '85*
Singles: 7–inch
COLUMBIA 3-4   85-88
MCA 3-4   89-92
LP: 10/12–inch 33rpm
SUGAR HILL 5-10   80s
Session: Johnny Cash; Michael Coleman; Jerry
Douglas; Lester Flatt; Carl Jackson; Earl Scruggs; Doc
Watson; Merle Watson.
Also see CASH, Johnny
Also see FLATT, Lester, & Earl Scruggs
Also see JACKSON, Carl, Marty Stuart & Vicki Cook
Also see TRITT, Travis, & Marty Stuart
Also see WATSON, Doc

STUBBY & BUCCANEERS   *C&W '49*
Singles: 78rpm
DECCA.. 4-8   49
Also see IVES, Burl, with Captain Stubby &
Buccaneers

STUCKEY, Nat   *C&W '66*
Singles: 7–inch
MCA 3-5   76-78
PAULA 4-6   66-68
RCA... 3-6   68-75
LP: 10/12–inch 33rpm
CAMDEN....................................... 5-10   74
MCA 5-10   76
PAULA 10-20   66-67
RCA (Except "APD" series)......... 8-12   69-74
RCA (APD1-0080 "Nat
Stuckey")................................ 15-25   73
(Quadraphonic.)
Also see SMITH, Connie, & Nat Stuckey

SUDDERTH, Anna   *C&W '80*
Singles: 7–inch
VERITE 3-5   80

SULLIVAN, Gene   *C&W '57*
Singles: 78rpm
COLUMBIA 5-10   57
Singles: 7–inch
COLUMBIA 5-10   57
Also see WILEY & GENE

SULLIVAN, Phil   *C&W '59*
Singles: 7–inch
STARDAY 5-10   59

SUMMER, Scott   *C&W '79*
Singles: 7–inch
CON BRIO 3-5   79

SUN, Joe   *C&W '78*
Singles: 7–inch
A.M.I... 3-4   84-85
ELEKTRA....................................... 3-4   82-83
OVATION....................................... 3-5   78-80
LPs: 10/12–inch 33rpm
ELEKTRA....................................... 5-8   82-83
OVATION....................................... 5-10   78-80
Also see ANDREWS, Sheila, & Joe Sun

SUNSHINE RUBY   *C&W '53*
Singles: 78rpm
RCA 4-8   53
Singles: 7–inch
RCA 5-10   53
Session: Sonny James.
Also see JAMES, Sonny

SUPER GRIT COWBOY
BAND   *C&W '81*
Singles: 7–inch
HOODSWAMP............................... 3-4   81-83
LP: 10/12–inch 33rpm
HOODSWAMP............................... 5-10   81-83
Members: Curtis Wright; Bill Ellis.
Also see WRIGHT, Curtis

SUTTON, Glenn   *C&W/P&R '79*
Singles: 7–inch
ABC... 3-5   73
EPIC.. 4-6   67
MGM 4-8   64-65
MERCURY...................................... 3-5   78-86
LPs: 10/12–inch 33rpm
MERCURY...................................... 5-10   79
Also see KELLUM, Murray / Glenn Sutton

SWAMPWATER   *C&W '71*
Singles: 7–inch
KING 3-5   70

RCA... 3-5   71

LPs: 10/12–inch 33rpm

KING 10-15   70

RCA... 10-12   71

Member: Gib Guilbeau.
Also see BURRITO BROTHERS

SWAN, Billy   *C&W/P&R/LP '74*

Singles: 7–inch

A&M 3-5   78-79

COLUMBIA 3-5   76-77

EPIC 3-4   81-83

MGM 5-10   68

MERCURY 3-4   86-87

MONUMENT................................... 4-6   66-76

RISING SONS................................. 4-6   67

LPs: 10/12–inch 33rpm

A&M 5-10   78

COLUMBIA/MONUMENT 5-10   77

EPIC... 5-10   81

MONUMENT................................... 5-10   74-78

Also see BLACK TIE

SWEAT, Isaac Payton   *C&W '78*

Singles: 7–inch

BELLAIRE..................................... 3-5   80

GUSTO 3-5   78

LP: 10/12–inch 33rpm

BELLAIRE..................................... 5-10   80

PAID... 5-8

SWEET, Rachel   *C&W '76*

Singles: 12–inch 33/45rpm

STIFF/COLUMBIA 10-15   79

(Promotional issue only.)

Singles: 7–inch

COLUMBIA 3-5   81-83

DERRICK...................................... 3-5   76-78

PREMIER...................................... 3-5   74

STIFF/COLUMBIA 3-5   79-80

LPs: 10/12–inch 33rpm

ARC... 5-10   81

COLUMBIA 5-10   81-82

STIFF/COLUMBIA 5-10   79-80

Also see SMITH, Rex, & Rachel Sweet

SWEETHEARTS of the RODEO   *C&W '86*

Singles: 7–inch

COLUMBIA 3-4   86-91

Members: Janis Oliver; Kristine Oliver.

SWEETWATER   *C&W '81*

Singles: 7–inch

FAUCET...3-4   81

Member: Willie Wynn.
Also see OAK RIDGE BOYS
Also see TENNESSEANS

SWING SHIFT BAND   *C&W '88*

Singles: 7–inch

STEP ONE......................................3-4   88

SYKES, Bobby

LP: 10/12–inch 33rpm

JMI 8-10

Also see BISHOP, Bob
Also see MARTIN, Benny, & Bobby Sykes

SYLVIA   *C&W '79*

(Sylvia Kirby Allen)

Singles: 7–inch

RCA 3-5   79-87

RCA GOLD STANDARD 3-4   81

Picture Sleeves

RCA 3-4   81-86

LPs: 10/12–inch 33rpm

RCA 5-10   81-86

Also see GALWAY, James, & Sylvia

SYLVIA & Michael Johnson   *C&W '85*

Singles: 7–inch

RCA 3-4   86

Also see JOHNSON, Michael
Also see SYLVIA

SYLVIE & HER SILVER DOLLAR BAND   *C&W '89*

Singles: 7–inch

PLAYBACK.....................................3-4   89

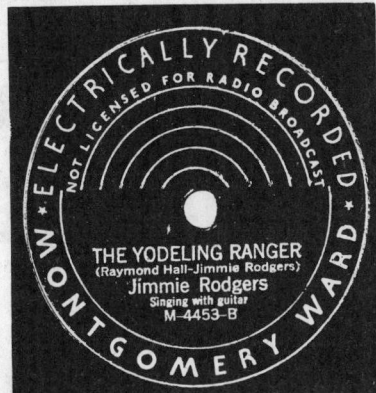

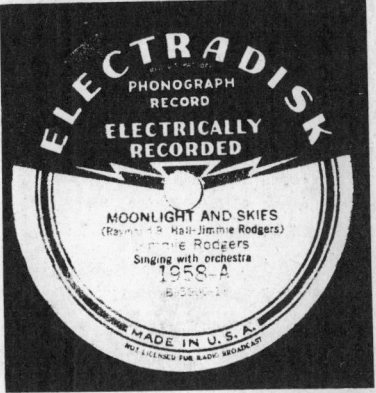

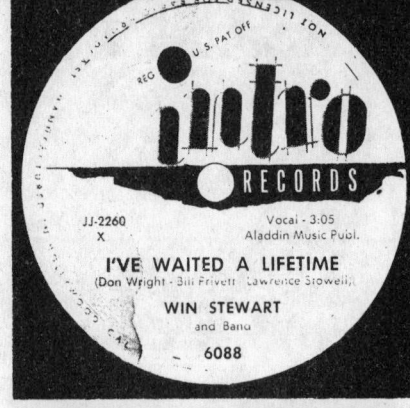

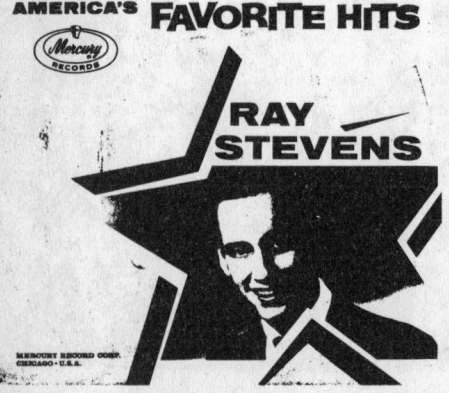

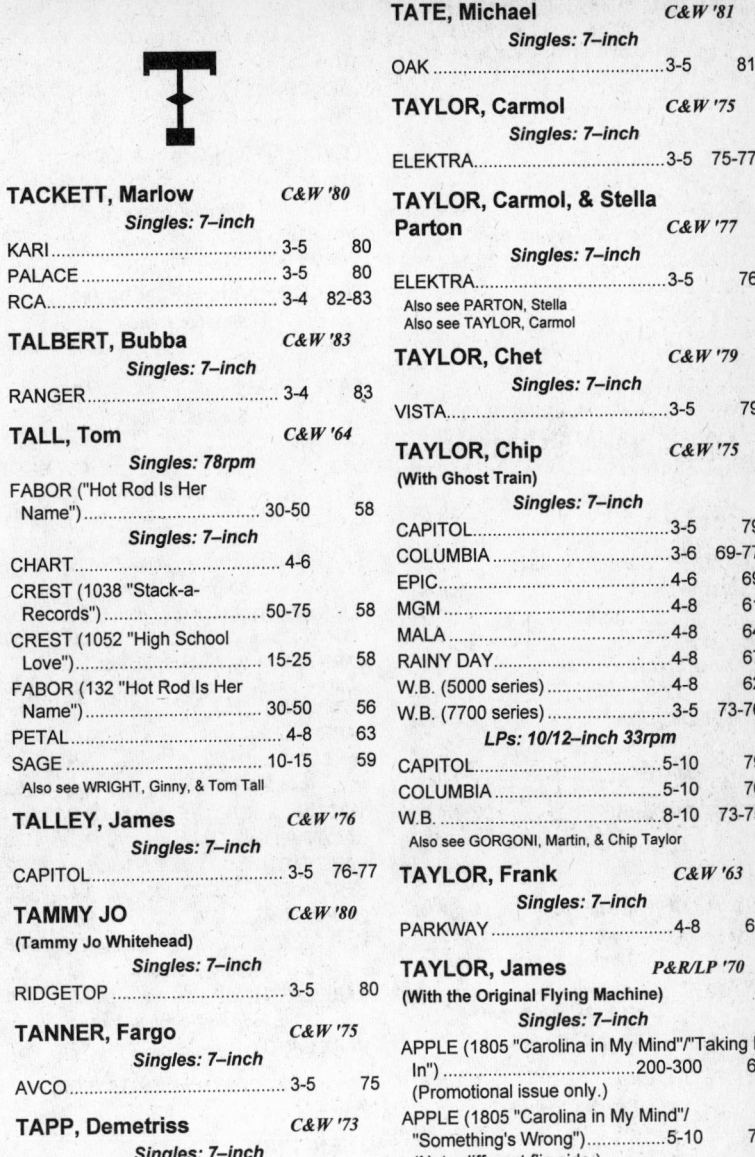

TACKETT, Marlow   *C&W '80*
Singles: 7–inch
KARI 3-5   80
PALACE 3-5   80
RCA... 3-4   82-83

TALBERT, Bubba   *C&W '83*
Singles: 7–inch
RANGER....................................... 3-4   83

TALL, Tom   *C&W '64*
Singles: 78rpm
FABOR ("Hot Rod Is Her
   Name")................................... 30-50   58
Singles: 7–inch
CHART... 4-6
CREST (1038 "Stack-a-
   Records")............................... 50-75   58
CREST (1052 "High School
   Love").................................... 15-25   58
FABOR (132 "Hot Rod Is Her
   Name")................................... 30-50   56
PETAL.. 4-8   63
SAGE 10-15   59
   Also see WRIGHT, Ginny, & Tom Tall

TALLEY, James   *C&W '76*
Singles: 7–inch
CAPITOL....................................... 3-5   76-77

TAMMY JO   *C&W '80*
(Tammy Jo Whitehead)
Singles: 7–inch
RIDGETOP 3-5   80

TANNER, Fargo   *C&W '75*
Singles: 7–inch
AVCO 3-5   75

TAPP, Demetriss   *C&W '73*
Singles: 7–inch
ABC.. 3-5   73
BRUNSWICK (55274 "Ring Dang
   Doo")...................................... 10-15   65

TATE, Michael   *C&W '81*
Singles: 7–inch
OAK 3-5   81

TAYLOR, Carmol   *C&W '75*
Singles: 7–inch
ELEKTRA....................................... 3-5   75-77

TAYLOR, Carmol, & Stella
Parton   *C&W '77*
Singles: 7–inch
ELEKTRA....................................... 3-5   76
   Also see PARTON, Stella
   Also see TAYLOR, Carmol

TAYLOR, Chet   *C&W '79*
Singles: 7–inch
VISTA... 3-5   79

TAYLOR, Chip   *C&W '75*
(With Ghost Train)
Singles: 7–inch
CAPITOL.. 3-5   79
COLUMBIA 3-6   69-77
EPIC.. 4-6   69
MGM 4-8   61
MALA 4-8   64
RAINY DAY 4-8   67
W.B. (5000 series) 4-8   62
W.B. (7700 series) 3-5   73-76
LPs: 10/12–inch 33rpm
CAPITOL.. 5-10   79
COLUMBIA 5-10   76
W.B. 8-10   73-75
   Also see GORGONI, Martin, & Chip Taylor

TAYLOR, Frank   *C&W '63*
Singles: 7–inch
PARKWAY 4-8   63

TAYLOR, James   *P&R/LP '70*
(With the Original Flying Machine)
Singles: 7–inch
APPLE (1805 "Carolina in My Mind"/"Taking It
   In") 200-300   69
   (Promotional issue only.)
APPLE (1805 "Carolina in My Mind"/
   "Something's Wrong").............. 5-10   70
   (Note different flip side.)
APPLE (PRO-1805 "Carolina on My
   Mind)...................................... 25-35   70
   (Note title variance. Promotional issue only.)

APPLE (4675 "More Apples, Radio Co-Op Ads") 125-175   69
(Single-sided disc. Promotional issue only.)
CAPITOL....................................... 3-5   76
COLUMBIA 3-5   77-88
EUPHORIA 3-5   71
W.B. 3-5   70-76

Picture Sleeves

COLUMBIA 3-4   81-88

LPs: 10/12–inch 33rpm

APPLE.. 10-15   69-70
COLUMBIA 5-10   77-88
EUPHORIA 12-15   71
TRIP 8-10   73
W.B. 8-10   70-77

Also see FLYING MACHINE
Also see SIMON, Carly, & James Taylor

TAYLOR, James, Art Garfunkel & Paul Simon   *P&R '78*

Singles: 7–inch

COLUMBIA 3-5   78

TAYLOR, James, & J.D. Souther   *P&R '81*

Singles: 7–inch

COLUMBIA 3-5   81

Also see SOUTHER, J.D.
Also see TAYLOR, James

TAYLOR, Jim   *C&W '78*

Singles: 7–inch

CHECKMATE................................. 3-5   78

TAYLOR, Judy   *C&W '82*

Singles: 7–inch

W.B. 3-4   82

TAYLOR, Karen   *C&W '82*
(Karen Taylor-Good)

Singles: 7–inch

MESA 3-4   82-84

LP: 10/12–inch 33rpm

MESA 5-10   84

TAYLOR, Les   *C&W '89*

Singles: 7–inch

EPIC... 3-4   89-91

Also see EXILE
Also see LYNNE, Shelby, & Les Taylor
Also see TOMORROW'S WORLD

TAYLOR, Livingston   *LP '70*

Singles: 7–inch

CAPRICORN................................. 3-5   70-73

EPIC.. 3-5   78-80

LPs: 10/12–inch 33rpm

ATCO.. 8-12   70
CAPRICORN 5-10   71-79
EPIC.. 5-10   78

TAYLOR, Livingston, & Leah Kunkel   *C&W '88*

Singles: 7–inch

CRITIQUE...................................... 3-4   88

Also see TAYLOR, Livingston

TAYLOR, Lynn, & Peachettes

Singles: 7–inch

CLOCK.. 8-12   60

TAYLOR, Mary   *C&W '67*

Singles: 7–inch

CAPITOL.. 4-6   66-67
DOT 4-6   68-69

LPs: 10/12–inch 33rpm

DOT 8-10   67

TAYLOR, R. Dean   *P&R '70/C&W '83*

Singles: 7–inch

AUDIO MASTER (1 "At the High School Dance")................................. 100-150   60
BARRY (3023 "At the High School Dance")..................................75-125   60
(Canadian.)
FARR 3-5   76
JANE.. 3-5   77
MALA (444 "I'll Remember") 25-50   62
MOTOWN 3-5
RAGAMUFFIN 3-5   79
RARE EARTH................................. 3-5   70-72
STRUMMER 3-4   83
20TH FOX...................................... 3-5   81
V.I.P. 10-20   65-68

Picture Sleeves

RARE EARTH................................. 3-5   71

LPs: 10/12–inch 33rpm

RARE EARTH............................. 10-15   70

TAYLOR-GOOD: Karen: see TAYLOR, Karen

TEEN KINGS

Singles: 78rpm

JE-WEL (101 "Ooby Dooby")..................................200-300   56

Singles: 7–inch

JE-WEL (101 "Ooby
Dooby") 500-600   56
(May read "Vocal Roy Oribson," instead of
"Orbison," on some labels. Beware since
some counterfeits exist that are difficult to
identify. Consult an expert if in doubt.)
Members: Roy Orbison; Johnny "Peanuts" Wilson; Billy
Par Ellis; James Monroe; Jack Kennelly.
Also see ORBISON, Roy

TENNESSEANS   *C&W '78*

Singles: 7–inch

CAPITOL 3-5   78
Members: Willie Wynn; Tony King.
Also see OAK RIDGE BOYS
Also see SWEETWATER

TENNESSEE ERNIE: see FORD, "Tennessee" Ernie

TENNESSEE EXPRESS   *C&W '81*

Singles: 7–inch

RCA 3-4   81-83

TENNESSEE PULLYBONE

                C&W '73

Singles: 7–inch

JMI 3-5   73
Also see BARE, Bobby

TERRY, Al   *C&W '54*

Singles: 78rpm

HICKORY 5-10   54-57

Singles: 7–inch

HICKORY 10-20   54-60

LP: 10/12–inch 33rpm

INDEX 5-10
LA LOUISIANNE 5-10

TERRY, Gordon   *C&W '70*

(With the Tennessee Guitars; with Tennessee
Fiddles)

Singles: 78rpm

CADENCE 5-10   57-58
COLUMBIA 4-8   55-56

Singles: 7–inch

CADENCE 5-10   57-58
CAPITOL 3-5   70
CHART 4-6   68
COLUMBIA 5-10   55-56
LIBERTY 4-8   62-63
RCA (Except 7632) 10-20   58-62
RCA (7632 "Lotta Lotta
Woman") 30-40   59

LPs: 10/12–inch 33rpm

CHART 10-15   68
LIBERTY 10-20   62
PLANTATION 5-10   77-81
RCA 10-20   62

TERRY, Tex

(With the Big Jim DeNoon Band; Ferlin Husky)

Singles: 78rpm

4 STAR ("Ozark Waltz") 15-25
(Selection number not known.)
Also see HUSKY, Ferlin

TEXAS PLAYBOYS   *C&W '77*

(Original Texas Playboys)

Singles: 7–inch

CAPITOL 3-5   77

LP: 10/12–inch 33rpm

CAPITOL 5-10   78-79
DELTA 6-12   80s
Member: Leon Rausch.
Also see ASLEEP at the WHEEL
Also see RAUSCH, Leon
Also see WILLS, Bob

TEXAS VOCAL COMPANY   *C&W '83*

Singles: 7–inch

RCA 3-4   83
Members: Sandy Skinner; Dave Roth; Dick Root.
Also see PRIDE, Charley

THOMAS, B.J.   *P&R '66*

(With the Triumphs)

Singles: 7–inch

ABC 3-5   75
BRAGG (103 "Billy & Sue") 10-20   66
CLEVELAND INT'L 3-4   83-84
COLLECTABLES 3-4   80s
COLUMBIA 3-4   83-86
HICKORY 4-8   66
LORI (9561 "For Your Precious
Love") 8-10   64
MCA 3-5   77-82
MYRRH 3-4   77-81
PACEMAKER (227 "I'm So Lonesome I Could
Cry") 10-15   64
PACEMAKER (231 "Mama") 5-10   65
PACEMAKER (234 "Bring Back the
Time") 5-10   65
PACEMAKER (239 "Tomorrow Never
Comes") 5-10   66
PACEMAKER (247 "Plain
Jane") 5-10   66

PACEMAKER (253 "Baby
Cried").. 5-10   66
PACEMAKER (256 "I Can't Help
It")... 5-10   65
PARAMOUNT 3-5   73-74
SCEPTER (12100 series) 4-8   66-67
SCEPTER (12200 thru 12364)...... 3-6   68-72
SCEPTER (21000 series) 3-5   73-74
VALERIE....................................... 4-8   60s
W.B. (5491 "Billy & Sue") 15-20   64
Picture Sleeves
MCA 3-5   79
LPs: 10/12–inch 33rpm
ABC.. 5-10   74-77
ACCORD.. 5-10   81-82
BUCKBOARD 5-10
CLEVELAND INT'L 5-10   83
COLUMBIA 5-8   86
DORAL.. 15-25   60s
   (Promotional mail-order issue, from Doral
   cigarettes.)
EXACT 5-10   80
EXCELSIOR.................................. 5-10   80
EVEREST 5-10   81
51 WEST....................................... 5-10   79
HICKORY (133 "Very Best") 20-30   66
MCA 5-10   77-82
MCA/SONGBIRD........................ 5-10   80
MYRRH 5-8   78-83
PACEMAKER (3001 "B.J. Thomas and the
   Triumphs")................................. 40-50   66
PARAMOUNT 5-10   73-74
PHOENIX 20 5-10   81
PICKWICK 5-8   78
PRIORITY 5-8   83
SCEPTER (535 thru 561).......... 10-20   66-67
SCEPTER (586 thru 597)............. 8-12   70-71
SCEPTER (5101 "Billy Joe
   Thomas").................................... 8-12   72
SCEPTER (5108 "Country")........ 8-12   72
SCEPTER (5112 "Greatest All-Time
   Hits") 10-15   73
SPRINGBOARD........................... 5-10   73-79
STARDAY 5-10   77
TRIP 5-10   76
U.A... 5-10   74
   Also see CHARLES, Ray, & B.J. Thomas
   Also see EDDY, Duane

THOMAS, Darrell   *C&W '79*
Singles: 7–inch
OZARK OPRY.............................. 3-5   79

THOMAS, Dick   *C&W '45*
(With His Nashville Ramblers)
Singles: 78rpm
DECCA 5-10   48-49
NATIONAL.....................................5-10   45-46
LPs: 10/12–inch 33rpm
VIKING...10-15

THOMAS, Jeff   *C&W '87*
Singles: 7–inch
REVOLVER 3-4   87

THOMPSON, Hank   *C&W '48*
(With the Brazos Valley Boys)
Singles: 78rpm
CAPITOL.......................................5-20   47-57
GLOBE (124 "Whoa
   Sailor") 100-200   46
Singles: 7–inch
ABC..3-5   75-79
ABC/DOT.......................................3-5   74-77
CAPITOL (1000 thru 3000
   series).......................................5-15   50-58
CAPITOL (4000 & 5000 series)....4-8   58-66
CHURCHILL 3-4   81-83
DOT 3-5   68-74
MCA 3-4   79-80
W.B. 4-6   66-67
Picture Sleeves
CAPITOL (4649 "Lost John").......5-10   61
EPs: 7–inch 33/45rpm
CAPITOL..10-20   53-59
LPs: 10/12–inch 33rpm
ABC..5-8   78
ABC/DOT.......................................5-10   74-77
CAPITOL (H-418 "Songs of the Brazos
   Valley")......................................60-80   53
   (10–inch LP.)
CAPITOL (T-418 "Songs of the Brazos
   Valley")......................................50-75   55
   (Green label.)
CAPITOL (T-618 "North of the Rio
   Grande") 40-60   55
   (Green label.)
CAPITOL (T-729 "New
   Recordings")............................30-50   55
CAPITOL (T-826 "Hank!")..........30-40   57
CAPITOL (T-975 "Dance
   Ranch")......................................30-40   58
CAPITOL (T-1111 thru
   T-2154).....................................15-25   59-64
   (Monaural.)

CAPITOL (ST-1111 through
ST-2154)................................. 15-30 59-64
(Stereo.)

CAPITOL (SM-2000 series) 5-8   75

CAPITOL (T-2274 thru
T-2800) 10-20 65-67
(Monaural.)

CAPITOL (ST-2274 through
ST-2826)................................. 10-25 65-67
(Stereo.)

CAPITOL (H-9111
"Favorites") 50-100   52
(10–inch LP.)

CAPITOL (11000 series)............... 5-8   79

CHURCHILL.................................. 5-8   84

DOT... 5-15 68-74

GUSTO 5-8   80

MCA/DOT...................................... 5-8

PICKWICK/HILLTOP 5-15 67-68

PROVINCIA 5-8

SEARS (135 "How Many Teardrops Will It
Take")...................................... 10-15   60s

STEP ONE 5-8   87

TOWER 8-15   68

WACO (101 "Hank Thompson Sings and
Plays Bob Wills")..................... 30-50

Session: Buddy Cagle.
Also see CAGLE, Buddy
Also see POTTER, Curtis

THOMPSON, Hank, & Merle Travis   *C&W '55*

(With the Brazos Valley Boys)
Singles: 78rpm

CAPITOL..................................... 5-10   55

Singles: 7–inch

CAPITOL..................................... 8-12   55

Also see THOMPSON, Hank
Also see TRAVIS, Merle

THOMPSON, J.W.   *C&W '79*

Singles: 7–inch

CENTURY 21............................... 3-4   84

NSD.. 3-5 80-81

SOUTHERN STAR 3-5   79

USA COUNTRY 3-4   83

THOMPSON, Sue   *P&R '61/C&W '72*

Singles: 78rpm

DECCA.. 5-10   55

MERCURY 5-10 51-54

Singles: 7–inch

DECCA.. 10-15   55

GUSTO 3-4   80s

HICKORY (Except 1100 & 1200
series)..3-6   66-76

HICKORY (1100 & 1200 series)....4-8   61-65

MERCURY 10-20   51-54

Picture Sleeves

HICKORY.......................................5-8   64

LPs: 10/12–inch 33rpm

HICKORY (Except 104 through
121)...8-15   69-74

HICKORY (104 thru 121)..........15-25   62-65

WING 10-15   66

Also see GIBSON, Don, & Sue Thompson
Also see LUMAN, Bob, & Sue Thompson

THORNTON, Marsha   *C&W '89*

Singles: 7–inch

MCA 3-4   89-90

THRASHER BROTHERS   *C&W '81*

Singles: 7–inch

MCA 3-4   81-83

LP: 10/12–inch 33rpm

MCA 5-10   82

PRESTIGE....................................6-12

Also see HALLMARK, Roger, & Thrasher Brothers

THREE SUNS   *P&R '44/C&W '50*

Singles: 78rpm

HIT 3-6   44

MAJESTIC 3-6   46

RCA 3-5   47-57

Singles: 7–inch

RCA 4-8   50-64

EPs: 7–inch 33/45rpm

RCA 5-10   50-61

ROYALE 5-10   50s

VARSITY......................................5-10   52

LPs: 10/12–inch 33rpm

CAMDEN 5-15   60-64

MUSICOR 5-10   66

RCA 5-20   50-76

RONDO..5-15   59

ROYALE 10-15   50s

VARSITY.....................................10-20   50-52

Members: Al Nevins; Marty Nevins; Art Dunn.

THREE SUNS, Rosalie Allen & Elton Britt   *C&W '50*

Singles: 78rpm

RCA 5-10   50

Also see ALLEN, Rosalie
Also see BRITT, Elton
Also see THREE SUNS

THROCKMORTON, Sonny   *C&W '76*
Singles: 7–inch

MCA	3-4	81
MERCURY	3-5	78-80
STARCREST	3-5	76

THUNDERKLOUD, Billy, & Chieftones   *C&W/P&R '75*
Singles: 7–inch

POLYDOR	3-5	76-77
20TH FOX	3-5	74-75

LPs: 10/12–inch 33rpm

SUPERIOR	8-12	74
20TH FOX	6-12	74-75

TIBOR BROTHERS   *C&W '76*
Singles: 7–inch

ARIOLA AMERICA	3-5	76
JOMAR	3-5	79

LP: 10/12–inch 33rpm

JOMAR	5-10	79

Members: Larry Tibor; Kurt Tibor; Harvey Tibor; Francis Tibor; Gerard Tibor.

TIERNY, Patti   *C&W '73*
Singles: 7–inch

MGM	3-5	73

TILLIS, Mel   *C&W '58*
(With the Statesiders; with Sue York)
Singles: 78rpm

COLUMBIA (40944 "Juke Box Man")	10-20	57
COLUMBIA (41000 series except 41026)	8-12	57
COLUMBIA (41026 "Hearts of Stone")	15-25	57

Singles: 7–inch

COLUMBIA (40944 "Juke Box Man")	10-20	57
COLUMBIA (41000 series except 41026)	8-12	57
COLUMBIA (41026 "Hearts of Stone")	15-25	57
COLUMBIA (41100 series except 41115 & 41986)	5-10	58-61
COLUMBIA (41115 "Teen Age Wedding")	15-25	58
COLUMBIA (3-41986 "Hearts of Stone") (Compact 33 Single.)	20-30	61
COLUMBIA (4-41986 "Hearts of Stone")	10-15	61
ELEKTRA	3-5	79-82

GUSTO	3-4	80s
KAPP	4-8	65-71
MCA	3-4	77-84
MGM	3-5	70-76
RCA	3-4	85-86
RADIO	3-4	89
RIC	5-10	65

LPs: 10/12–inch 33rpm

COLUMBIA (1724 "Heart Over Mind") (Monaural.)	15-25	62
COLUMBIA (1724 "Heart Over Mind") (Stereo.)	20-30	62
COLUMBIA (30253 "Heart Over Mind")	8-10	70
CORAL	5-10	73
ELEKTRA	5-10	79-83
GUSTO	5-8	80s
HARMONY	8-15	66-72
KAPP	8-15	66-71
MCA	5-12	73-84
MGM	5-12	70-78
PICKWICK	5-10	73
POWER PAK	5-8	
STARDAY	8-10	72
TEE VEE	8-10	70s
VOCALION	5-10	70-72

Also see EARWOOD, Mundo
Also see FELTS, Narvel / Red Sovine / Mel Tillis
Also see PIERCE, Webb, & Mel Tillis
Also see WILLS, Bob, & Mel Tillis

TILLIS, Mel, & Sherry Bryce   *C&W '71*
Singles: 7–inch

MGM	3-5	71-75

LP: 10/12–inch 33rpm

MGM	6-12	71-74

Also see BRYCE, Sherry

TILLIS, Mel, & Glen Campbell   *C&W '84*
Singles: 7–inch

MCA	3-4	84

Also see CAMPBELL, Glen

TILLIS, Mel, & Bill Phillips   *C&W '59*
Singles: 7–inch

COLUMBIA	5-10	59-60

Also see PHILLIPS, Bill

TILLIS, Mel, & Nancy Sinatra

C&W '81

Singles: 7–inch

ELEKTRA... 3-5   81

LPs: 10/12–inch 33rpm

ELEKTRA... 5-10   81

Also see SINATRA, Nancy
Also see TILLIS, Mel

TILLIS, Pam

C&W '84

Singles: 7–inch

ARISTA 3-4   90-91
W.B. 3-4   84-87

Also see TOMORROW'S WORLD

TILLMAN, Floyd

C&W '44

(With His Favorite Playboys)

Singles: 78rpm

COLUMBIA 4-8   46-49
DECCA... 4-8   44-45

Singles: 7–inch

CIMARRON..................................... 4-8   62
COLUMBIA 5-15   51-61
LIBERTY 5-10   60-61
SIMS 4-8   63

LP: 10/12–inch 33rpm

BAGATELLE 8-12   71
CIMARRON (2003 "Let's Make
   Memories")............................. 20-30   62
COLUMBIA 5-10   76
CRAZY CAJUN 5-10   75
51 WEST.. 5-9   79
GILLEY'S...................................... 10-15   81
HARMONY................................... 10-15   69
MUSICOR 10-20   67-68
PICKWICK/HILLTOP 8-10   65
RCA (1686 "Floyd Tillman's Greatest
   Hits") 30-40   58
STARDAY (310 "Let's Make
   Memories")............................. 15-20   65

TILLOTSON, Johnny

P&R '58

Singles: 7–inch

AMOS... 3-5   69-70
BARNABY 3-5   76
BUDDAH 3-5   71-73
CADENCE (1300 series)............. 5-10   58-61
CADENCE (1400 series)............... 4-8   61-63
COLUMBIA 3-5   73-75
ERIC... 3-4   70s
MGM 4-8   63-68
REWARD 3-4   82-84

U.A.. 3-5   76-77

Picture Sleeves

CADENCE 10-15   60
MGM 5-8   63-66

EPs: 7–inch 33/45rpm

CADENCE (114 "Dreamy
   Eyes") 25-35   60
CADENCE (33-1 "This Is Johnny
   Tillotson")............................... 15-25   61
("Cadence Little LP." With cardboard insert
in clear cover.)
CADENCE (33-2 "Music by Johnny
   Tillotson")............................... 15-25   61
("Cadence Little LP." With cardboard insert
in clear cover.)

LPs: 10/12–inch 33rpm

ACCORD 5-10   82
AMOS 10-15   69
BACK-TRAC 5-8   85
BARNABY...................................... 8-10   77
BUCKBOARD 5-10   80s
BUDDAH...................................... 10-15   72
CADENCE 25-40   61-63
EVEREST 5-8   82
METRO 10-15   66
MGM 12-20   64-71
ROWE/AMI 5-8   66
("Play Me" Sales Stimulator promotional
issue.)
U.A... 8-10   77

Session: Boots Randolph.
Also see GENEVIEVE
Also see RANDOLPH, Boots

TILLOTSON, Johnny / Ivan

Singles: 7–inch

OLDIES 45..................................... 5-8   64

Also see TILLOTSON, Johnny

TILLOTSON, Johnny / J.D. Souther

Singles: 7–inch

BUDDAH... 3-5   71

Also see SOUTHER, J.D.
Also see TILLOTSON, Johnny

TILTON, Sheila

C&W '76

Singles: 7–inch

CON BRIO 3-5   76

Also see TILTON SISTERS

TILTON SISTERS

Singles: 7–inch

BERTRAM 5-10   61
DOT (15939 "Why Why Why")....25-35   59

INTERNATIONAL 5-10 60

Members: Sheila Tilton; Gwen Tilton; Muriel Tilton.
Also see TILTON, Sheila

TINA & DADDY: see JONES, George

TINY TIM   *P&R/LP '68/C&W '88*

(Herbert Khaury)

Singles: 7–inch

BLUE CAT.................................... 5-10 65
CLOUDS 3-5 79
NLT 3-4 88
REPRISE 3-6 68-71
ROULETTE................................... 3-5 70s
SCEPTER 3-5 72
VIC TIM 3-5 71

LPs: 10/12–inch 33rpm

BOUQUET 10-12
REPRISE 10-20 68

TINY TIM & MISS VICKI

Singles: 7–inch

REPRISE 3-6 71

TINY TIM / Michelle Ramos / Bruce Haack

LPs: 10/12–inch 33rpm

RA-JO INT'L.................................. 5-8 86

Also see TINY TIM

TIPPIN, Aaron   *C&W '90*

Singles: 7–inch

RCA... 3-4 90-91

TODD, Dick, & Appalachian Wildcats   *C&W '67*

Singles: 7–inch

TOMMY & DONNA   *C&W '88*

Singles: 7–inch

OAK.. 3-4 88

TOMORROW'S WORLD   *C&W '90*

Singles: 7–inch

W.B. 3-4 90

Members: Lynn Anderson; Butch Baker; Shane Barmby; Billy Hill; Suzy Bogguss; Kix Brooks; T. Graham Brown; Burch Sisters; Holly Dunn; Foster & Lloyd; Vince Gill; Rusty Golden; William Lee Golden; Highway 101; Shelby Lynne; Johnny Rodriguez; Dan Seals; Les Taylor; Pam Tillis; Kevin Welch; Mac Wiseman.
Also see ANDERSON, Lynn
Also see BAKER, Butch
Also see BARMBY, Shane
Also see BILLY HILL
Also see BOGGUSS, Suzy
Also see BROOKS, Kix

Also see BROWN, T. Graham
Also see BURCH SISTERS
Also see DUNN, Holly
Also see FOSTER & LLOYD
Also see GILL, Vince
Also see GOLDEN, William Lee
Also see GOLDENS
Also see HIGHWAY 101
Also see LYNNE, Shelby
Also see RODRIGUEZ, Johnny
Also see SEALS, Dan
Also see TAYLOR, Les
Also see TILLIS, Pam
Also see WELCH, Kevin
Also see WISEMAN, Mac

TOMPALL & GLASER BROTHERS   *P&R '69*

(Tompall & Glasers; Tompall Glaser)

Singles: 7–inch

DECCA 5-10 59-65
ELEKTRA.......................................3-5 80-82
MGM 3-8 66-71
RICH 8-12 61
ROBBINS.......................................10-20 57

LPs: 10/12–inch 33rpm

DECCA (DL-4041 "This Land") 35-45 60
(Monaural.)
DECCA (DL7-4041 "This Land") 40-60 60
(Stereo.)
ELEKTRA.......................................5-10 81
MGM 10-20 67-75
U.A. (3540 "Ballad of *Namu the Killer Whale* and Others") 25-35 66
(Monaural.)
U.A. (6540 "Ballad of *Namu the Killer Whale* and Others") 30-40 66
(Stereo.)
VOCALION (3807 "Country Folk")..8-12 67

Members: Tompall Glaser; Jim Glaser; Chuck Glaser.
Also see GLASER, Chuck
Also see GLASER, Jim
Also see GLASER, Tompall

TOPEL & WARE   *C&W '87*

Singles: 7–inch

RCI...3-4 87

Members: Michael Topel; James Ware.

TOROK, Mitchell   *C&W/P&R '53*

(With the Louisiana Hayride Band; with Matches; with Ramona Redd)

Singles: 78rpm

ABBOTT.......................................10-20 53-54
DECCA 5-15 57-58

FBC (102 "Nacogdoches County
Line")...................................... 15-25   48
FBC (115 "Piney Woods
Boogie") 15-25   49

Singles: 7–inch

ABBOTT.................................... 12-25   53-54
CALICO....................................... 3-5
CAPITOL..................................... 4-8   62-63
DECCA.. 5-10 57-59
GUYDEN...................................... 5-10 59-60
INETTE 4-8   63
MERCURY 4-8   61
RCA.. 4-8   65
REPRISE 4-6   66-67

Picture Sleeves

GUYDEN.................................... 10-20 59-60

LPs: 10/12–inch 33rpm

CALICO....................................... 10-15
GUYDEN (502 "Caribbean") 25-35   60
(Monaural.)
GUYDEN (ST-502 "Caribbean") 35-50   60
(Stereo.)
REPRISE 10-15   66

Also see GREAT PRETENDER & Tennessee Two and
a Half

TOUCH of COUNTRY   *C&W '88*

Singles: 7–inch

OL 3-4   88-89

TRADER - PRICE   *C&W '89*

Singles: 7–inch

UNIVERSAL................................. 3-4   89

TRAITS   *P&R '66*

Singles: 7–inch

ASCOT....................................... 15-25   62
PACEMAKER............................. 10-15   67
RENNER (229 "Got My Mojo
Working") 10-15   62
(Black vinyl.)
RENNER (229 "Got My Mojo
Working") 20-30   62
(Colored vinyl. Promotional issue only.)
SCEPTER 3-5   66
TNT 10-15 59-60
UNIVERSAL............................... 10-15   66

LPs: 10/12–inch 33rpm

TNT (101 "Roy Head and the
Traits")................................. 100-150   65
Member: Roy Head.
Also see HEAD, Roy

TRAMMELL, Bobby Lee   *C&W '72*

Singles: 7–inch

ABC-PAR (9890 "Shirley Lee") ..50-75   58
ALLEY 15-25   62-63
ATLANTA................................... 15-25   62
ATLANTIC................................... 5-10   66
CAPITOL (3801 "You Mostest
Girl")... 5-8   73
CONFEDERATE (125 "Shake Me
Baby") 30-40
COUNTRY................................... 4-8   66
FABOR (127 "You Mostest
Girl").. 5-10   64
FABOR (4038 "Shirley Lee")....75-125   57
HOT (101 "Shimmy Lou") 20-30   59
HOT (102 "Betty Jean") 20-30   59
RADIO (102 "You Mostest
Girl")..30-40   58
RADIO (114 "My Susie Jane") ..30-40   58
SANTO....................................... 10-20
SIMS 5-10   63-65
SKYLA 8-12   62
SOUNCOT................................... 3-5   71-72
VANDEN (304 "Hi-O Silver")...... 15-25
WARRIOR (1554 "Woe Is
Me") 50-75   59

LPs: 10/12–inch 33rpm

ATLANTA (1503 "Arkansas
Twist")......................................50-75   62
SOUNCOT 10-20 71-72

Also see ROE, Tommy / Bobby Lee Trammell

TRAMMELL, Bobby Lee, & Jean Steakley

Singles: 7–inch

SOUNCOT.................................... 3-5   72

Also see TRAMMELL, Bobby Lee

TRASK, Diana   *C&W '68*

Singles: 7–inch

ABC/DOT..................................... 3-5   74-75
COLUMBIA 5-8   61-62
DIAL.. 4-8   68
DOT... 3-6   68-75
KARI.. 3-4   81
ROULETTE.................................. 5-10   59

LP: 10/12–inch 33rpm

ABC... 5-10 76-77
ABC/DOT..................................... 6-12 74-75
COLUMBIA 15-25   61
DOT 8-15   69-73

TRAVIS, Merle   *C&W/P&R '46*

Singles: 78rpm

CAPITOL	5-10	46-57

Singles: 7–inch

CAPITOL (1100 thru 3100 series)	5-15	50-55
CAPITOL (5600 series)	4-6	66

EPs: 7–inch 33/45rpm

CAPITOL	10-20	56-57

LP: 10/12–inch 33rpm

CMH	8-15	79-81
CAPITOL (T-650 "Guitar")	50-80	56
CAPITOL (SM-650 "Guitar")	5-10	75
CAPITOL (891 "Back Home")	50-60	57
CAPITOL (1391 "Walkin' the Strings")	50-60	60
CAPITOL (1664 "Travis")	30-40	62
CAPITOL (1956 "Songs of the Coal Mine")	50-60	57
CAPITOL (T/ST-2662 "Best of Merle Travis")	15-25	67
CAPITOL (SM-2662 "Best of Merle Travis")	5-10	75
CAPITOL (2938 "Strictly Guitar")	20-30	69
PICKWICK/HILLTOP	10-15	66
PREMIER	??	
SHASTA	10-15	
SPIN-O-RAMA	8-12	60s

Sessions: Renfro Valley Pioneers.
Also see THOMPSON, Hank, & Merle Travis

TRAVIS, Merle, & Johnny Bond

LP: 10/12–inch 33rpm

CAPITOL (249 "Great Songs of the Delmore Brothers")	25-50	69

Also see BOND, Johnny

TRAVIS, Merle, & Joe Maphis

LP: 10/12–inch 33rpm

CMH	8-12	
CAPITOL (T-2102 "Merle Travis & Joe Maphis, Two Great Guitars") (Monaural.)	40-50	64
CAPITOL (ST-2102 "Merle Travis & Joe Maphis, Two Great Guitars") (Stereo.)	50-60	64
CAPITOL (SM-2102 "Merle Travis & Joe Maphis, Two Great Guitars")	5-10	78

TRAVIS, Merle, & Mac Wiseman

LP: 10/12–inch 33rpm

CMH	8-12	82

Also see TRAVIS, Merle

Also see WISEMAN, Mac

TRAVIS, Randy   *C&W '85*

(Randy Traywick)

Singles: 7–inch

W.B.	3-4	85-91

LPs: 10/12–inch 33rpm

W.B.	5-8	85-91

Also see TRAYWICK, Randy
Also see WYNETTE, Tammy, & Randy Travis

TRAVIS, Randy, & George Jones   *C&W '90*

Singles: 7–inch

W.B.	3-4	90

TREVOR, Van   *C&W '66*

(With the Saturday Knights)

Singles: 7–inch

ATLANTIC	4-8	63
BAND BOX	8-15	66-67
CANADIAN AMERICAN	5-10	64
CORSICAN	10-15	61
DATE	4-8	67-68
VIVID (1004 "C'mon Now Baby")	15-20	63
(With the 4 Seasons.)		
ROYAL AMERICAN	4-6	69-71

LPs: 10/12–inch 33rpm

BAND BOX	10-15	67
DATE	10-15	67
ROYAL AMERICAN	8-12	70

Also see SATURDAY KNIGHTS

TRIBBLE, Mark   *C&W '89*

Singles: 7–inch

PALOMA	3-4	89

TRINITY, Bobby   *C&W '77*

Singles: 7–inch

GRT	3-5	77

TRINITY LANE   *C&W '88*

Singles: 7–inch

CURB	3-4	88

TRINITY RIVER BOYS

LPs: 10/12–inch 33rpm

PROSPECTOR (1 "Trinity River Boys")	30-40	64

Also see MURPHEY, Michael
Also see NESMITH, Michael

TRIO+ : see LEWIS, Jerry Lee, Carl Perkins & Charlie Rich

TRIPP, Allen   *C&W '82*

Singles: 7–inch

NASHVILLE 3-4   82

TRITT, Travis   *C&W '89*

Singles: 7–inch

W.B. 3-4   89-91

TRITT, Travis, & Marty Stuart   *C&W '91*

Singles: 7–inch

W.B. 3-4   91

Also see STUART, Marty
Also see TRITT, Travis

TUBB, Ernest   *P&R '41/C&W '44*

(With the Texas Troubadours; with "Friends")

Singles: 78rpm

BLUEBIRD (6693 "The Passing of Jimmie
   Rodgers") 200-400   30s
BLUEBIRD (7000 "T.B. Is Whipping
   Me") 100-200   30s
BLUEBIRD (8899 "Married Man
   Blues") 100-150   30s
BLUEBIRD (8966 "Right Train to
   Heaven") 100-150   30s
DECCA 10-20   40-57

Singles: 7–inch

CACHET 3-5   79
DECCA (28067 thru 30872) 5-10   52-59
DECCA (30952 thru 33014) 3-8   59-72
DECCA (46000 series) 5-15   50-52
1ST GENERATION 3-5   77
MCA 3-5   73
RHINO (74415 "Walking the Floor Over
   You") 3-5   91
   (Gold vinyl.)
RHINO (74415 "Walking the Floor Over
   You") 4-6   91
   (Blue vinyl.)
RHINO (74415 "Walking the Floor Over
   You") 8-12   91
   (Black vinyl.)

Picture Sleeves

RHINO (74415 "Walking the Floor Over
   You") 4-6   91

EPs: 7–inch 33/45rpm

DECCA 15-30   51-65

LP: 10/12–inch 33rpm

ACM 8-12
CACHET 8-12   79
CASTLE 5-10
CORAL 5-10   73

DECCA (159 "Ernest Tubb
   Story") 25-45   58
   (Monaural. Includes booklet.)
DECCA (7-159 "Ernest Tubb
   Story") 30-60   58
   (Stereo. Includes booklet.)
DECCA (5301 "Ernest Tubb
   Favorites") 75-100   51
   (10–inch LP.)
DECCA (5334 "Old Rugged Cross-Favorite
   Sacred Songs") 40-60   51
   (10–inch LP.)
DECCA (5497 "Sing a Song of
   Christmas") 40-60   54
   (10–inch LP.)
DECCA (8291 "Ernest Tubb
   Favorites") 40-60   56
DECCA (8553 "Daddy of 'Em
   All") 35-55   56
DECCA (8834 "The Importance of Being
   Ernest") 35-55   59
FIRST GENERATION (001 "Living
   Legend") 8-12   77
FIRST GENERATION (0002 "The Legend
   and the Legacy") 75-125   79
   (Back cover mentions "Ernest Tubb's
   Record Shop," "Gary Line Tours" and
   "Grand Ole Opry Tickets.")
FIRST GENERATION (0002 "The Legend
   and the Legacy") 60-80   79
   (No mention on back cover of "Ernest Tubb's
   Record Shop," "Gary Line Tours" or "Grand
   Ole Opry Tickets.")
FIRST GENERATION (0002 10-20   79
MCA 5-12   73-84
PICKWICK 5-10   70s
PICKWICK/HILLTOP 8-12
RADIOLA 5-10   83
RHINO (70902 "Live") 5-10   91
ROUNDER 5-10   82
TV (1033 "The Legend and the
   Legacy") 40-50   79
   (TV mail order offer.)

VOCALION.............................. 10-15   66-69

Session: Cal Smith; Jack Greene; Willie Nelson; Merle Haggard; Chet Atkins; Charlie Daniels; Jordanaires; Waylon Jennings; Vern Gosdin; Johnny Paycheck; Loretta Lynn; Marty Robbins; Wilburn Brothers; George Jones; Johnny Cash; Ferlin Husky/Simon Crum; Charlie Rich; Conway Twitty; Justin Tubb; Charlie McCoy; Jerry Kennedy; Grady Martin; Billy Grammer; Billy Byrd; Buddy Emmons; Pete Mitchell; Pete Drake; Kitty Wells; Webb Pierce; Patsy Cline.
Also see ANDREWS SISTERS & Ernest Tubb
Also see ATKINS, Chet
Also see CASH, Johnny
Also see CLINE, Patsy
Also see DANIELS, Charlie
Also see DRAKE, Pete
Also see FOLEY, Red, & Ernest Tubb
Also see GOSDIN, Vern
Also see GRAMMER, Billy
Also see GREENE, Jack
Also see HAGGARD, Merle
Also see HUSKY, Ferlin
Also see JENNINGS, Waylon
Also see JONES, George
Also see JORDANAIRES
Also see MARTIN, Grady, & His Slew Foot Five
Also see McCOY, Charlie
Also see NELSON, Willie
Also see PAYCHECK, Johnny
Also see RICH, Charlie
Also see ROBBINS, Marty
Also see SMITH, Cal
Also see STATLER BROTHERS
Also see TWITTY, Conway
Also see WELLS, Kitty

TUBB, Ernest, & Loretta Lynn   *C&W '69*
Singles: 7–inch
DECCA... 4-8   65-69
LP: 10/12–inch 33rpm
DECCA....................................... 15-25   65-69
MCA 8-12   73
Also see LYNN, Loretta

TUBB, Ernest / Justin Tubb
EPs: 7–inch 33/45rpm
DECCA (2422 "Jimmie Rodgers Favorites")............................... 20-30   57
Also see TUBB, Justin

TUBB, Ernest, & Wilburn Brothers   *C&W '58*
Singles: 7–inch
DECCA... 5-10   58
EPs: 7–inch 33/45rpm
DECCA....................................... 10-15   59
Also see TUBB, Ernest
Also see WILBURN BROTHERS

TUBB, Justin   *C&W '55*
(With Norma Gallant)
Singles: 78rpm
DECCA 5-15   53-57
Singles: 7–inch
CHALLENGE 5-10   60
CUTLASS 3-5   72-73
DECCA 5-15   53-59
DOT 3-6   69
FIRST GENERATION....................3-5   78-81
GROOVE 4-8   63-64
HILLTOP 3-5   75
RCA 4-8   65-67
2ND GENERATION......................3-5   77
STARDAY 5-10   60-62
EPs: 7–inch 33/45rpm
DECCA 10-20   57
LP: 10/12–inch 33rpm
CUTLASS (123 "Travelin' Singin' Man") 20-30   72
(Interestingly, reissued circa 1983 on cassette only, which credits Justin but pictures Ernest Tubb.)
DECCA (8644 "Country Boy in Love")..30-50   57
DOT 15-20   69
MCA/DOT 5-8
FIRST GENERATION (01 "Justin Tubb") 8-10   81
HILLTOP (102 "Hilltop Country Presents Justin Tubb")..........................5-8
(Mail order repackage of Hilltop 209.)
HILLTOP (209 "A New Country Heard From")......................................8-12   74
PHONORAMA (5565 "What's Wrong with the Way We're Doung It Now")..........5-8   83
(Repackage of First Generation 01.)
RCA 15-25   65
STARDAY (160 "Star of the Grand Ole Opry") 20-30   62
STARDAY (198 "Modern Country Music Sound")....................................20-30   62
STARDAY (334 "Best of Justin Tubb") 20-30   65
VOCALION 10-15   65-67
Also see HILL, Goldie, & Justin Tubb
Also see TUBB, Ernest, & Justin Tubb

TUBB, Justin, & Lorene Mann   *C&W '65*
Singles: 7–inch
RCA 4-6   65-66

LP: 10/12–inch 33rpm

RCA (3591 "Together and
Alone") 20-30   66
Also see MANN, Lorene

TUBB, Justin / Roger Miller
Singles: 7–inch

DECCA........................... 5-10   58
Also see MILLER, Roger
Also see TUBB, Justin

TUCKER, Jerry Lee   *C&W '88*
Singles: 7–inch

OAK... 3-4   88-89

TUCKER, Jimmy   *C&W '79*
Singles: 7–inch

GAR-PAX.................................. 3-5   79
NSD... 3-5   79-80

TUCKER, La Costa: see LA COSTA

TUCKER, Rick   *C&W '89*
Singles: 78rpm

COLUMBIA (41041 "Patty
Baby") 50-75   57
Singles: 7–inch

COLUMBIA (41041 "Patty
Baby") 50-75   57
HITSVILLE 3-5   76
OAK.. 3-4   89
VEEDA (4005 "I'll Be There").... 30-50   60
LPs: 10/12–inch 33rpm

HITSVILLE 5-10   76

TUCKER, Tanya   *C&W/P&R '72*
Singles: 7–inch

ARISTA 3-5   82-84
CAPITOL..................................... 3-4   85-88
COLUMBIA 3-5   72-77
MCA 3-5   75-81
Picture Sleeves

COLUMBIA 3-6   72-75
MCA 3-5   75-81
LPs: 10/12–inch 33rpm

ARISTA 5-8   82-84
CAPITOL..................................... 5-8   86
COLUMBIA ("KC" series)............ 5-10   72-75
COLUMBIA ("PC" series)............. 5-8   77
MCA 5-10   75-81
Sessions: John Prine; Jimmy Seals; Dash Crofts.
Also see AXTON, Hoyt
Also see CAMPBELL, Glen, & Tanya Tucker
Also see HARRIS, Emmylou
Also see SEALS & CROFTS

TUCKER, Tanya, & T. Graham Brown   *C&W '90*
Singles: 7–inch

CAPITOL...3-4   90
Also see BROWN, T. Graham

TUCKER, Tanya, & Glen Campbell   *C&W '80*
(Glen Campbell & Tanya Tucker)
Singles: 7–inch

CAPITOL...3-4   81
Also see CAMPBELL, Glen

TUCKER, Tanya, Paul Davis & Paul Overstreet   *C&W '87*
Singles: 7–inch

CAPITOL...3-4   87
Also see DAVIS, Paul
Also see OVERSTREET, Paul
Also see TUCKER, Tanya

TURNER, Grant   *C&W '64*
Singles: 7–inch

CHART....................................4-6   64

TURNER, Mary Lou   *C&W '74*
Singles: 7–inch

CHURCHILL 3-4   79-80
MCA... 3-5   74-78
Also see ANDERSON, Bill, & Mary Lou Turner

TURNER, Zeb   *C&W '49*
Singles: 78rpm

KING 5-8   49-50
LP: 10/12–inch 33rpm

AUDIO LAB (1537 "Country Music in the Zeb
Turner Style")...........................30-40   59

TUTTLE, Wesley, & His Texas Stars   *C&W '45*
(With Marilyn Tuttle)
Singles: 78rpm

CAPITOL...4-8   45-54
Singles: 7–inch

CAPITOL......................................6-12   52-54
SACRED 10-20

TWITTY, Conway   *P&R '57/C&W '66*
Singles: 78rpm

MERCURY..................................25-75   57
Singles: 7–inch

ABC-PAR (10507 "Go On and
Cry")..10-15   63
ABC-PAR (10550 "My Baby
Left Me") 15-25   64

CONWAY TWITTY FAN CLUB ("It's Only
Make Believe")........................ 10-15
(Promotional, fan club issue only.)

DECCA...	3-8	65-72
ELEKTRA.......................................	3-4	82-83
MCA..	3-5	73-82
MGM (500 series)	3-5	78
MGM (12000 & 13000 series).....	5-15	58-62
MGM (14000 series)	3-5	71-72
MGM (50000 series)	20-40	58-59
(Stereo.)		
MERCURY	20-40	57-58
MUSIGRAM	3-6	
(Flexi-disc.)		
POLYDOR......................................	3-4	80s
W.B.	3-4	83-86

Picture Sleeves

ELEKTRA.......................................	3-5	82
MGM	10-20	58-62

EPs: 7–inch 33/45rpm

MGM	20-30	58-59

LPs: 10/12–inch 33rpm

ACCORD..	5-10	82
ALLEGIANCE.................................	5-8	84
CT (1001 "Solid Gold")................	8-12	
CANDLELITE ("Living Legend")...................................	30-50	70s
(No selection number used.)		
CONWAY TWITTY/MCA (1002 "Conway Twitty")	8-10	
CORAL..	5-8	73
DECCA..	8-18	66-72
DEMAND.......................................	8-12	72
ELEKTRA.......................................	5-8	82-83
MCA	5-15	73-85
MGM (110 "Conway Twitty").....	15-20	70

MGM (3744 "Conway Twitty
Sings")................................... 50-100   59

MGM (E-3786 "Saturday Night with Conway
Twitty") 50-75   59
(Monaural.)

MGM (SE-3786 "Saturday Night with Conway
Twitty") 75-100   59
(Stereo.)

MGM (E-3818 "Lonely Blue
Boy") 50-75   60
(Monaural.)

MGM (SE-3818 "Lonely Blue
Boy") 75-100   60
(Stereo.)

MGM (E-3849 "Conway Twitty's Greatest
Hits") 50-75   60
(Monaural. Black label. With gatefold cover
and poster.)

MGM (SE-3849 "Conway Twitty's Greatest
Hits")......................................75-100   60
(Stereo. With gatefold cover and poster.)

MGM (3849 "Conway Twitty's Greatest
Hits")......................................15-20   68
(Blue and yellow label. With standard cover.)

MGM (E-3907 "The Rock and Roll
Story")....................................50-75   61
(Monaural.)

MGM (SE-3907 "The Rock and Roll
Story")....................................75-100   61
(Stereo.)

MGM (E-3943 "The Conway Twitty
Touch") 30-40   61
(Monaural.)

MGM (SE-3943 "The Conway Twitty
Touch") 35-50   61
(Stereo.)

MGM (E-4019 thru E-4217) 20-40   62-64
(Monaural.)

MGM (SE-4019 thru SE-4217)...25-50   62-64
(Stereo.)

MGM (4650 thru 4884)...............	10-20	69-73
METRO..	15-25	65

OPRYLAND (12636 "Conway Twitty, Then
and Now") 75-100
(Six-LP set. Promotional issue only.)

PICKWICK	10-15	72
SUNRISE MEDIA..........................	5-10	81
TEE VEE....................................	5-10	78
TROLLY CAR	5-10	

TWITTY BIRD (1001 "Solid
Gold").....................................10-12   82
(Two-LP.)

W.B.	5-10	83-86

Session: Fred Carter Jr.; Anthony Armstrong Jones;
Joni Lee.
Also see CARTER, Fred, Jr.
Also see JONES, Anthony Armstrong
Also see LEE, Joni
Also see LYNN, Loretta, & Conway Twitty
Also see MARTIN, Dean
Also see McDOWELL, Ronnie
Also see TUBB, Ernest

TWITTY, Kathy   *C&W '85*

Singles: 7–inch

PERMIAN....................................3-4   85
Also see JAMES, Jesseca

TWO HEARTS   *C&W '85*

Singles: 7–inch

MDJ...3-4   85-86
Members: Jama Bowen; Cathy Bowen.

TYLER, Bonnie   *P&R/C&W/LP '78*

Singles: 7–inch

CHRYSALIS	3-5	77
COLUMBIA	3-4	83-86
RCA	3-5	78-79

Picture Sleeves

COLUMBIA	3-4	83-86
RCA	3-5	78

LPs: 10/12–inch 33rpm

CHRYSALIS	8-12	77
COLUMBIA	5-8	83-86
RCA	5-10	78-81

TYLER, T. Texas   *C&W '46*

(With His Oklahoma Melody Boys)

Singles: 78rpm

DECCA	4-8	53-54
4 STAR	5-10	46-54

Singles: 7–inch

DECCA	5-10	53-54
4 STAR	10-20	53-54
KING	5-10	59-60
RCA	5-10	53-54

LP: 10/12–inch 33rpm

CAPITOL	15-25	62-65
DESIGN	10-20	62
INTERNATIONAL AWARD	8-12	60s
KING (664 "T. Texas Tyler")	30-50	59
KING (689 "The Great Texan")	25-40	60
KING (721 "T. Texas Tyler")	15-25	61
KING (734 "Songs Along the Way")	20-30	61
NASHVILLE	5-10	72
PICKWICK/HILLTOP	10-15	67
SOUND (607 "Deck of Cards")	35-55	58
STARDAY (379 "The Man with a Million Friends")	20-30	66
WRANGLER (1002 "T. Texas Tyler")	10-20	62

Also see CLINE, Patsy / T. Texas Tyler / Bill Taylor / Eddie Marvin
Also see PIERCE, Webb / Patsy Cline / T. Texas Tyler

TYNDALL, Lynne   *C&W '87*

Singles: 7–inch

EVERGREEN	3-4	87-89

USA for AFRICA / Quincy Jones   *P&R/R&B/D&D/C&W/LP '85*

(United Support of Artists for Africa)

Singles: 12–inch 33/45rpm

COLUMBIA	4-6	85

Singles: 7–inch

COLUMBIA	3-4	85

Picture Sleeves

COLUMBIA	3-4	85

LPs: 10/12–inch 33rpm

COLUMBIA	5-8	85

Members: Dan Aykroyd; Kim Carnes; Ray Charles; Bob Dylan; Daryl Hall; James Ingram; Michael Jackson; Jean-Michael Jarre; Al Jarreau; Waylon Jennings; Billy Joel; Quincy Jones; Cyndi Lauper; Huey Lewis; Kenny Loggins; Bette Midler; Steve Perry; Lionel Richie; Smokey Robinson; Kenny Rogers; Diana Ross; Paul Simon; Bruce Springsteen; Tina Turner; Dionne Warwick; Stevie Wonder.
Also see CARNES, Kim
Also see CHARLES, Ray
Also see JENNINGS, Waylon
Also see RICHIE, Lionel
Also see ROGERS, Kenny
Also see ROSS, Diana
Also see VOICES of AMERICA / U.S.A. for AFRICA

UNIQUES   *P&R '65*

Singles: 7–inch

DEMAND	3-5	
PARAMOUNT	3-5	70-72
PAULA	4-8	65-70

LPs: 10/12–inch 33rpm

PAULA	12-25	66-70

Members: Joe Stampley; Bobby Stampley; Jim Woodfield; Mike Love; Ray Mills; Bobby Sims; Ronnie Weiss.
Also see RIO GRANDE
Also see STAMPLEY, Joe

VALENTINO   *C&W '81*

(Valentino Enrique Hernandez)

Singles: 7–inch

GAIEE	3-5	75

RCA...3-4   81

VAN DYKE, Bruce   *C&W '89*
Singles: 7–inch
ARIA...3-4   89

VAN DYKE, Leroy   *P&R '56/C&W '57*
Singles: 78rpm
DOT (Except 15698) 4-8   56-57
DOT (15698 "Leather Jacket").. 20-40   57
Singles: 7–inch
ABC.. 3-5   74-75
ABC/DOT 3-5   75-77
DECCA 3-5   70-72
DOT (Except 15698) 5-15   56-57
DOT (15698 "Leather Jacket").. 50-75   57
KAPP.. 4-6   68-70
MCA 3-5   73
MERCURY 4-8   61-64
MOUNTAIN DEW....................... 5-10
PLANTATION.............................. 3-5   78
SUN.. 3-5   79
W.B... 4-6   65-67
Picture Sleeves
MERCURY 5-8   64
LPs: 10/12–inch 33rpm
DECCA.. 8-10   72
DOT 20-30   60s
HARMONY 8-12   69
KAPP 8-15   68-69
MCA 5-10   72-73
MERCURY 12-25   62-64
PLANTATION.............................. 5-10   77-79
SUN.. 5-8   74
W.B. 10-15   65-66
WING 8-15   65-66

VANWARMER, Randy
C&W/P&R/LP '79
Singles: 7–inch
BEARSVILLE 3-5   79
16TH AVE. 3-4   88
LPs: 10/12–inch 33rpm
BEARSVILLE 5-10   79-83

VASSY, Kin   *C&W '79*
Singles: 7–inch
EPIC.. 4-8   67
IA... 3-5   79-80
LIBERTY 3-4   81-83
UNI.. 3-6   69

Also see EDDY, Duane
Also see ROGERS, Kenny, & First Edition

VAUGHN, Sammy   *C&W '78*
Singles: 7–inch
ALPINE 3-5   78
OAK 3-5   79

VAUGHN, Sharon   *C&W '74*
Singles: 7–inch
ABC/DOT...................................... 3-5   75
CINNAMON 3-5   74
Also see FELTS, Narvel, & Sharon Vaughn

VEACH, Gail   *C&W '87*
Singles: 7–inch
CHOICE...................................... 3-4   88
PRAIRIE DUST............................ 3-4   87

VEGA BROTHERS   *C&W '86*
Singles: 7–inch
MCA.. 3-4   86
Members: Robert Vega; Ray Vega.

VERA, Billy   *P&R '67*
(With the Contrasts; with Beaters; with Blue Eyed Soul)
Singles: 7–inch
ATLANTIC..................................... 4-6   68-69
FLAVOR...................................... 10-15   64
MACOLA 3-4   87
MIDSONG 3-5   75-76
ORANGE 4-8   73
RHINO 3-4   86-87
RUST 10-20   62
LPs: 10/12–inch 33rpm
ATLANTIC................................... 10-15   68
MACOLA 5-8   87
MIDSONG INT'L 8-12   77
RHINO 5-8   86
Also see BILLY & BEATERS

VERA, Billy & Judy Clay   *P&R/R&B '67*
Singles: 7–inch
ATLANTIC..................................... 4-8   67-68
LPs: 10/12–inch 33rpm
ATLANTIC................................... 10-15   68

VERNON, Kenny   *C&W '66*
Singles: 7–inch
CAPITOL...................................... 3-5   72-74
CARAVAN 4-8   66
CHART... 4-8   68-71

EPIC 4-8 66-67
LP: 10/12–inch 33rpm
CAPITOL 5-10 73
CHART 8-12 71
Also see LINDSEY, LaWanda, & Kenny Vernon

VICKERY, Mack *C&W '77*
(Mac Vickery)
Singles: 7–inch
AFCO 4-8 66
GONE 8-12 59
PLAYBOY 3-5 77
PRINCETON (101 "High School
Blues") 50-100 60
LPs: 10/12–inch 33rpm
MEGA 10-15 70
Also see ATLANTA JAMES

VINCENT, Gene
(With His Blue Caps)

P&R/R&B/C&W/LP '56
Singles: 78rpm
CAPITOL 25-75 56-57
Promotional Singles: 78rpm
CAPITOL 50-100 56-57
(White or yellow labels.)
Singles: 7–inch
CAPITOL (3450 thru 3617) 20-30 56-57
CAPITOL (3678 "B-I-Bickey
Bi-Bo-Bo-Go") 20-30 57
CAPITOL (3763 thru 4665) 15-25 57-61
CAPITOL STAR LINE 3-6
CHALLENGE 15-20 66-67
FOREVER 10-20 69-70
KAMA SUTRA 8-12 70-73
PLAYGROUND (100 "Story of the
Rockers") 150-175 68
Picture Sleeves
CAPITOL (4237 "Right
Now") 800-1000 60
Promotional Singles: 7–inch
CAPITOL 50-100 56-61
(White or yellow labels.)
EPs: 7–inch 33/45rpm
CAPITOL (438 "Dance to the
Bop") 150-200 57
(Promotional issue only. Not issued with
cover.)
CAPITOL (764 "Bluejean
Bop") 75-125 57
(Price is for any of three volumes.)

CAPITOL (811 "Gene Vincent & His Blue
Caps") 75-125 57
(Price is for any of three volumes.)
CAPITOL (970 "Gene Vincent Rocks &
Bluecaps Roll") 75-125 58
(Price is for any of three volumes.)
CAPITOL (985 "Hot Rod
Gang") 350-400 58
(Green label. Soundtrack.)
CAPITOL (985 "Hot Rod
Gang") 400-450 58
(White label. Promotional issue.)
CAPITOL (1059 "Record
Date") 75-125 58
(Price is for any of three volumes.)
LPs: 10/12–inch 33rpm
CAPITOL (DKAO-380 "Gene Vincent's
Greatest") 15-25 69
CAPITOL (SM-380 "Gene Vincent's
Greatest") 5-10 78
CAPITOL (764 "Bluejean
Bop") 200-300 56
CAPITOL (811 "Gene Vincent & His Blue
Caps") 200-300 57
CAPITOL (970 "Gene Vincent
Rocks") 200-300 58
CAPITOL (1059 "Gene Vincent
Record Date") 200-300 58
CAPITOL (1207 "Sounds Like Gene
Vincent") 200-300 59
CAPITOL (1342 "Crazy
Times") 150-250 60
CAPITOL (11000 series) 8-12 74
CAPITOL (16000 series) 5-10 81
DANDELION 10-20 70
KAMA SUTRA 10-20 70-71
ROLLIN' ROCK 5-10 80-81
Also see MEYERS, Augie
Also see PRESLEY, Elvis

VINCENT, Gene / Tommy Sands / Sonny James / Ferlin Husky
LPs: 10/12–inch 33rpm
CAPITOL (1009 "Teen Age
Rock") 50-100 58
Also see HUSKY, Ferlin
Also see SANDS, Tommy

VINCENT, Gene / Frank Sinatra / Sonny James / Ron Goodwin
EPs: 7–inch 33/45rpm
CAPITOL (437 "Special Hit
Pressing") 75-100 57
(Promotional issue only. Not issued with
cover.)

Also see JAMES, Sonny

VINTON, Bobby   *P&R/R&B/LP '62*
(Bobby Vinton Orchestra)
Singles: 7–inch

ABC	3-5	74-77
ALPINE	10-15	59
AURAVISION (6722 "Rain, Rain Go Away")	4-6	64
(Cardboard flexi-disc, one of six by six different artists. Columbia Record Club "Enrollment Premium." Set came in a special paper sleeve.)		
CURB	3-4	88-89
ELEKTRA	3-5	78
EPIC (9000 series)	4-8	60-66
(Black vinyl.)		
EPIC (9000 series)	8-10	64
(Colored vinyl.)		
EPIC (10000 series)	3-6	66-75
LARC	3-4	83
MELODY	10-15	59
TAPESTRY	3-5	79-82

Picture Sleeves

EPIC	3-8	62-72
TAPESTRY	3-5	80

EPs: 7–inch 33/45rpm

EPIC	6-12	63-65
(Jukebox issues.)		

LPs: 10/12–inch 33rpm

ABC	8-10	74-77
CSP	5-10	80s
COLUMBIA	8-10	73
EPIC (500 series)	20-25	60
EPIC (3000 series)	15-20	60
EPIC (20000 series)	8-15	62-70
(Black vinyl.)		
EPIC (20468 "Blue on Blue")	20-40	63
(Colored vinyl. Promotional issue only.)		
EPIC (30000 series)	5-10	72-79
HARMONY	5-10	70
TAPESTRY	5-10	80

VINTON, Bobby / Chuck & Johnny
Singles: 7–inch

DIAMOND (121 "I Love You the Way You Are")	5-8	62

VINTON, Bobby, & Village Stompers
LPs: 10/12–inch 33rpm

EPIC	10-20	66

Also see VINTON, Bobby

VON, Vicki Rae   *C&W '87*
Singles: 7–inch

ATLANTIC AMERICA	3-4	87

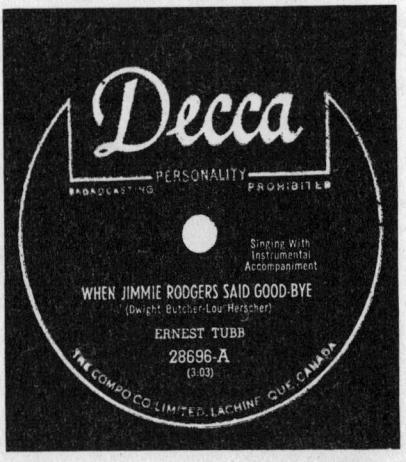

Also see SNOW, Hank / Hank Locklin / Porter Wagoner

WADE, Norman   *C&W '79*
Singles: 7–inch
ARTIC 4-8
CMI.. 4-8
NSD.. 3-5   79
LPs: 10/12–inch 33rpm
ARTIC 8-10

WAGONEERS   *C&W '88*
Singles: 7–inch
A&M 3-4   88-89

WAGONER, Porter   *C&W '54*
Singles: 78rpm
RCA.. 5-10   53-57
Singles: 7–inch
RCA (0013 thru 1007)................... 3-6   69-74
RCA (5086 thru 7638)................. 5-15   53-59
RCA (7708 thru 9979)................... 3-8   60-71
RCA (10124 thru 11998)............... 3-5   74-79
W.B. 3-4   82-83
EPs: 7–inch 33/45rpm
RCA.. 8-15   56
LPs: 10/12–inch 33rpm
ACCORD.. 5-8   82
CAMDEN 5-15   63-73
COUNTRY FIDELITY.................... 5-8   82
H.S.R.D. (782 "Natural
    Wonder") 15-25   81
MCA/DOT....................................... 5-8   86
MUSIC MASTERS 5-10
PICKWICK 5-10   75-77
RCA (Except 1300 through
    2900 series) 5-15   66-79
RCA (1358 "A Satisfied Mind").. 30-40   56
RCA (LPM-2447 thru
    LPM-2960) 10-20   62-65
    (Monaural.)
RCA (LSP-2447 thru
    LSP-2960)............................. 15-25   62-65
    (Stereo.)
TUDOR 5-8   84
W.B. 5-8   83
    Also see HUNLEY, Con
    Also see NORMA JEAN

WAGONER, Porter, & Skeeter Davis
LPs: 10/12–inch 33rpm
RCA 10-20   62
    Also see DAVIS, Skeeter

WAGONER, Porter, & Dolly
Parton   *C&W '67*
Singles: 7–inch
RCA 3-6   67-80
LPs: 10/12–inch 33rpm
RCA (Except 3926 thru 4841)......5-10   74-80
RCA (LPM-3926 "Just Between You and
    Me") 30-40   68
    (Monaural.)
RCA (LSP-3926 thru
    LSP-4841)................................10-20   68-73
    (Stereo.)
    Also see PARTON, Dolly
    Also see WAGONER, Porter

WAKELY, Jimmy   *P&R '43/C&W '44*
(With Les Baxter Chorus; with Velma Williams)
Singles: 78rpm
CAPITOL......................................3-6   48-52
CORAL..3-6   53-55
DECCA..4-8   43-57
JIMMY WAKELY SOUVENIR......5-10   50s
Singles: 7–inch
ARTCO 3-5   74
CAPITOL (1300 thru 2100
    series)......................................5-10   50-52
CORAL..4-8   53-55
DECCA 3-8   55-70
DOT 3-6   66
SHASTA (100 series)....................3-6   58-67
SHASTA (200 series)....................3-4   71
Picture Sleeves
SHASTA..5-10   58
EPs: 7–inch 33/45rpm
CAPITOL....................................10-20   50-53
CORAL.......................................10-15   54
DECCA 8-12   58
LPs: 10/12–inch 33rpm
ALBUM GLOBE 5-10   81
CAPITOL (4008 "Songs of the
    West") 25-50   50
    (10–inch LP.)
CAPITOL (9004 "Christmas on the
    Range")...................................20-40   53
    (10–inch LP.)
CORAL...4-8   73
DANNY 8-10

DECCA (8400 thru 8600
series) 20-35   56-57
DECCA (75000 thru 78000
series) 8-18   67-70
DOT 10-15   66
MCA 4-8   80s
MCR 10-15   74
SHASTA 5-15   58-75
TOPS 10-15
VOCALION 5-10   68-70

Also see CHANDLER, Karen, & Jimmy Wakely
Also see WHITING, Margaret, & Jimmy Wakely

WALKER, Billy   *C&W '54*

Singles: 78rpm

COLUMBIA 4-8   54-56

Singles: 7–inch

CAPRICE 3-4   79-80
CASINO 3-5   77
COLUMBIA (21000 series) 6-12   54-56
COLUMBIA (33000 series) 4-6   60s
COLUMBIA (40000 series) 5-10   56-60
COLUMBIA (42000 & 43000
series) 4-8   61-65
DIMENSION 3-4   83
MCA 3-5   77
MGM 3-5   70-74
MRC 3-4   77-78
MONUMENT 3-6   66-70
PAID 3-4   80
RCA 3-5   75-76
SCORPION 3-4   78
TALL TEXAN 3-4   85-88

Picture Sleeves

COLUMBIA 4-8   63-67

LPs: 10/12–inch 33rpm

COLUMBIA 10-20   63-69
FIRST GENERATION 5-10   81
GUSTO 5-8   78
H.S.R.D. 5-10   84
HARMONY 8-15   64-70
MGM 6-12   70-74
MONUMENT 8-18   66-72
RCA 5-10   75-76

WALKER, Billy, & Barbara
Fairchild   *C&W '80*

Singles: 7–inch

PAID 3-5   81

LPs: 10/12–inch 33rpm

PAID 5-10   81

Also see FAIRCHILD, Barbara

WALKER, Billy, & Brenda Kaye
Perry   *C&W '77*

Singles: 7–inch

MRC 3-5   77

Also see PERRY, Brenda Kaye
Also see WALKER, Billy

WALKER, Charlie   *C&W '56*

Singles: 78rpm

DECCA 4-8   54-56

Singles: 7–inch

CAPITOL 3-5   74
COLUMBIA 5-10   58-63
DECCA 5-15   54-56
EPIC 3-8   64-72
RCA 3-5   72-73

LP: 10/12–inch 33rpm

COLUMBIA 15-25   61
EPIC 8-15   ,65-71
HARMONY 10-15   67
PLANTATION 5-10   78-81
RCA 6-12   72-73
VOCALION 10-15   67

WALKER, Cindy   *C&W '44*

Singles: 78rpm

DECCA 4-8   42-44
COLUMBIA 5-10   56

Singles: 7–inch

COLUMBIA 8-12   56

LP: 10/12–inch 33rpm

MONUMENT 10-20   64

WALKER, Jerry Jeff   *P&R '68*

Singles: 7–inch

ATCO 3-6   68-70
MCA 3-5   73-80
SOUTH COAST 3-4   81
TRIED & TRUE 3-4   89

LPs: 10/12–inch 33rpm

ATCO (Except 297) 15-20   68-70
ATCO (297 "Five Years
Gone") 30-50   69
DECCA 10-12   72
ELEKTRA 8-10   70s
MCA 5-10   73-80
SOUTH COAST 5-10   81
VANGUARD 10-12   69

WALLACE, Jerry   *P&R '54*

(With the Jewels; with Jay Rand Orchestra & Chorus)

Singles: 78rpm

ALLIED	5-15	51-54
CHALLENGE	10-20	57
CLASS	5-10	53
MERCURY	5-10	55-56
TOPS	5-10	53
VOGUE	5-10	52
WING	5-10	56

Singles: 7–inch

ALLIED	10-15	54
BMA	3-5	77-78
CHALLENGE (1000 series)	10-15	57
CHALLENGE (9100 series)	4-8	61-63
CHALLENGE (59000 through 59098)	10-20	58-60
CHALLENGE (59200 series)	4-8	63-65
CLASS	8-12	53
DECCA	3-5	71-72
DOOR KNOB	3-5	79-80
ERIC	3-4	70s
4-STAR	3-5	78-79
GLENOLDEN	3-6	68
GUSTO	3-4	80s
LIBERTY	3-5	67-70
MCA	3-4	73-74
MGM	3-5	75-76
MERCURY (70000 series)	5-10	55-56
MERCURY (72000 series)	4-8	64-66
SUNSET	5-10	
TOPS	8-12	53
U.A.	3-5	72-75
VOGUE	10-15	52
WING	8-12	56

Picture Sleeves

CHALLENGE (59013 thru 59098)	8-12	58-60
CHALLENGE (59200 series)	4-8	63-65

EPs: 7–inch 33/45rpm

CHALLENGE	15-25	60

LPs: 10/12–inch 33rpm

BMA	8-10	77
CHALLENGE (606 "Just Jerry")	30-35	59
CHALLENGE (612 "There She Goes")	20-25	61
CHALLENGE (616 "Shutters and Boards")	15-20	63
CHALLENGE (619 "In the Misty Moonlight")	15-20	64
CHALLENGE (2002 "Greatest Hits")	10-15	69
DECCA	8-12	71-72
4-STAR	5-8	83
LIBERTY	10-12	68
MCA	8-10	73-74
MGM	8-10	75
MERCURY	10-15	66
PICKWICK	5-10	70s
U.A.	8-12	72-75
WING	10-12	68

Also see BARE, Bobby / Donna Fargo / Jerry Wallace

WALLACE, Jerry / Soul Surfers

Singles: 7–inch

CHALLENGE	4-8	64

Also see WALLACE, Jerry

WALSH, David   *C&W '85*

Singles: 7–inch

CHARTA	3-4	85-89

WARD, Dale   *P&R '63/C&W '68*

Singles: 7–inch

BIG WAY	4-8	60s
BOYD	4-8	62-65
DOT (16000 series)	4-8	63-65
DOT (17000 series)	3-5	71-72
MONUMENT	4-6	66-69
PARAMOUNT	4-6	69-70

Picture Sleeves

BOYD	10-20	62

WARD, Jacky   *C&W '72*

Singles: 7–inch

ASYLUM	3-4	82
ELECTRIC	3-4	87-88
MEGA	3-5	73
MERCURY	3-5	75-81
TARGET	3-5	72
W.B.	3-4	83

LP: 10/12–inch 33rpm

ASYLUM	5-10	82
MERCURY	6-12	77-80
SUNBIRD	5-10	80
TARGET	5-10	72

WARD, Jacky, & Reba McEntire   *C&W '79*

Singles: 7–inch

MERCURY	4-8	79

Also see McENTIRE, Reba
Also see WARD, Jacky

WARINER, Steve   *C&W '78*

Singles: 7–inch

ARISTA	3-4	91
MCA	3-4	84-90
RCA	3-5	78-84

LPs: 10/12–inch 33rpm

MCA	5-8	87-90
RCA	5-10	81-83

Also see CAMPBELL, Glen, & Steve Wariner
Also see LARSON, Nicolette

WARNER, Virgil   *C&W '67*

Singles: 7–inch

LHI	4-6	67-68

WARNER MACK: see MACK, Warner

WARNES, Jennifer   *P&R/C&W/LP '77*
(Jennifer Warren)

Singles: 12–inch 33/45rpm

20TH FOX ("It Goes Like It Goes")	4-8	79

(Shown as by Jennifer Warnes. No selection number used.)

20TH FOX (379 "It Goes Like It Goes")	8-10	79

(Shown as by Jennifer Warren.)

Singles: 7–inch

ARISTA	3-4	77-82
CYPRESS	3-4	87
PARROT	3-6	68
W.B.	3-5	83

LPs: 10/12–inch 33rpm

ARISTA	5-10	76-82
CYPRESS	5-8	87
REPRISE	5-10	72

Also see GILLETTE, Steve, & Jennifer Warnes
Also see JENNIFER
Also see MEDLEY, Bill, & Jennifer Warnes

WARNES, Jennifer, & Joe Cocker   *P&R '82*

Singles: 7–inch

ISLAND	3-4	82

Picture Sleeves

ISLAND	3-4	82

Also see WARNES, Jennifer

WARREN, Kelly   *C&W '79*
(Kelli Warren)

Singles: 7–inch

RCA	3-5	78-79

Also see NAYLOR, Jerry, & Kelli Warren

WASHINGTON, Jon   *C&W '88*

Singles: 7–inch

DOOR KNOB	3-4	88-89

WATERS, Chris   *C&W '80*

Singles: 7–inch

RIO	3-4	80-81

WATERS, Joe   *C&W '81*

Singles: 7–inch

NEW COLONY	3-4	81-84

WATSON, Clyde   *C&W '77*

Singles: 7–inch

GROOVY	3-5	77

WATSON, Doc   *C&W '73*
(With Merle Watson)

Singles: 7–inch

POPPY	3-5	72-74
U.A.	3-5	73-79

LPs: 10/12–inch 33rpm

FLYING FISH	5-8	81
FOLKWAYS	10-20	63-69
LIBERTY	5-8	83
POPPY	6-12	72
U.A.	8-15	75-76
VANGUARD	8-18	64-77
VERVE/FOLKWAYS	10-15	66

Also see ATKINS, Chet, & Doc Watson
Also see FLATT, Lester, Earl Scruggs & Doc Watson
Also see STUART, Marty

WATSON, Gene   *C&W '75*
(With the Farewell Party Band)

Singles: 7–inch

CAPITOL	3-5	75-80
CURB/MCA	3-4	85
DIXIE (2003 "I'll Always Love You")	20-30	58
EPIC	3-4	85-87
MCA	3-4	81-84
RESCO	4-6	75
TONKA	5-8	65
TRI DEC (8357 "My Rockin' Baby")	100-200	50s
W.B.	3-4	81-89

LP: 10/12–inch 33rpm

CAPITOL	5-12	75-84
MCA	5-10	81-84
STONEWAY	5-10	

Session: Tony Booth.
Also see BOOTH, Tony

WAYLON & WILLIE: see JENNINGS, Waylon, & Willie Nelson

WAYNE, Bobby   *C&W '71*

Singles: 7–inch

CAPITOL.................................. 3-5   71
Also see HAGGARD, Merle

WAYNE, Nancy   *C&W '74*

Singles: 7–inch

20TH CENTURY 3-5   74-75

WAYNE, Scotty

(Baldemar Huerta)

Singles: 7–inch

TALENT SCOUT (1008 "Only
   One").................................. 20-30   62
Also see FENDER, Freddy

WEATHERLY, Jim   *P&R/LP '74*

Singles: 7–inch

ABC..................................... 3-5   76-77
BUDDAH................................. 3-5   74-75
ELEKTRA................................ 3-5   79-80
ERIC.................................... 3-5   78
RCA..................................... 3-5   72-74
20TH FOX.............................. 4-8   65

Picture Sleeves

BUDDAH................................ 3-5   74

LPs: 10/12–inch 33rpm

ABC.................................... 5-10   77
BUDDAH................................ 5-10   74-75
RCA.................................... 8-12   72

WEAVERS   *P&R '50*

(With Gordon Jenkins' Orchestra)

Singles: 78rpm

DECCA.................................. 3-8   50-57

Singles: 7–inch

DECCA (27000 thru 29000
   series) 5-10   50-55
DECCA (31000 series)................. 4-8   62
NSD.................................... 3-5   82
VANGUARD.............................. 4-8   60-62

EPs: 7–inch 33/45rpm

DECCA................................. 5-15   51-52

LPs: 10/12–inch 33rpm

DECCA (173 "Best of the
   Weavers") 10-15   65
   (Monaural.)
DECCA (7173 "Best of the
   Weavers") 10-15   65
   (Stereo.)

DECCA (5285 "Folk Songs") 20-40   51
   (10–inch LP.)
DECCA (5373 "Merry
   Christmas") 20-40   52
   (10–inch LP.)
DECCA (74277 "Weavers
   Gold")............................. 10-15   70
VANGUARD (15-16 "Greatest
   Hits") 8-12   71
VANGUARD (2000 series) 10-20   59-63
VANGUARD (3000 thru 6000
   series)........................... 8-15   67-70
VANGUARD (9000 series) 12-25   56-63
VANGUARD (9100 series) 10-20   65
Members: Pete Seeger; Lee Hays; Fred Hellerman;
Ronnie Gilbert.
Also see JENKINS, Gordon, & His Orchestra
Also see SEEGER, Pete

WEAVERS & Terry
Gilkyson   *C&W '51*

Singles: 7–inch

DECCA 4-8   51

Singles: 7–inch

DECCA 8-10   51
Also see GILKYSON, Terry
Also see WEAVERS

WEBB, Jack: see WEBB, Jay Lee

WEBB, Jay Lee   *C&W '67*

(Jack Webb)

Singles: 7–inch

DECCA 3-6   67

LP: 10/12–inch 33rpm

DECCA 10-15   67-69
Also see LYNN, Loretta

WEBB, June   *C&W '58*

Singles: 7–inch

HICKORY.....................5-10   58

WEBBER, Rollie

Singles: 7–inch

COUNTRY ("Tired of Livin").......25-35
   (Selection number not known.)
Members: Rollie Webber; Buck Owens; Don Rich.
Also see OWENS, Buck

WEBSTER, Chase   *C&W '70*

Singles: 7–inch

DOT 4-8   61-63
CAMEO.............................4-8   63-64
SOUTHERN SOUND.................5-10   61
SHOW BIZ 3-5   70
SPUR 8-10

WEISSBERG, Eric   *P&R/C&W/LP '73*

(With Steve Mandell; with Deliverance; with Marshall Brickman)

Singles: 7–inch

EPIC	3-5	75
W.B.	3-5	72-73

LPs: 10/12–inch 33rpm

ELEKTRA	15-25	63
W.B.	5-10	73

Also see TARRIERS

WELCH, Ernie   *C&W '89*

Singles: 7–inch

DUCK TAPE	3-4	89

WELCH, Kevin   *C&W '89*

Singles: 7–inch

REPRISE	3-4	90
W.B.	3-4	89-90

Also see TOMORROW'S WORLD

WELK, Lawrence, & His Orchestra   *P&R '38/C&W '45*

Singles: 78rpm

CORAL	3-5	50-57
DECCA	3-6	42-45
MERCURY	3-5	50-55
OKEH	3-6	41
VOCALION	3-8	38-39

Singles: 7–inch

CORAL	3-8	50-66
DOT	3-8	59-67
MERCURY	3-8	50-55
RANWOOD	3-8	68-77

EPs: 7–inch 33/45rpm

CORAL	4-8	50-58
DOT	4-8	59-60
MERCURY	4-8	50-55

LPs: 10/12–inch 33rpm

CORAL	5-15	50-65
DECCA	5-10	72
DOT	5-15	59-67
HAMILTON	4-8	64-66
HARMONY	4-8	68-70
MCA	4-8	74-76
RANWOOD	4-8	68-85
SUNNYVALE	4-6	79
TRADITION	4-8	75
VOCALION	4-8	59-70
WING	4-8	60-62

Also see FOLEY, Red
Also see PRESLEY, Elvis / Lawrence Welk

WELLER, Freddy   *C&W/LP '69*

Singles: 7–inch

ABC/DOT	3-5	75
APT	4-8	65
COLUMBIA	3-6	69-80
DORE	5-10	61

LPs: 10/12–inch 33rpm

ABC/DOT	5-10	75
COLUMBIA	5-12	69-80
EPIC	8-12	74
51 WEST	5-8	80s

Also see SPURZZ

WELLMAN, Tiny   *C&W '88*

Singles: 7–inch

LEE ANN	3-4	88

WELLS, Kitty   *C&W/P&R '52*

Singles: 78rpm

DECCA	4-10	52-57
RCA	6-12	50

Singles: 7–inch

CAPRICORN	3-5	74-76
DECCA (28000 & 29000 series)	5-15	52-56
DECCA (30000 thru 32000 series)	3-10	56-71
MCA	3-4	73
RCA (0333 "Make Up Your Mind")	15-25	50
(Colored vinyl.)		
RUBOCA	3-5	79-80

Picture Sleeves

DECCA	4-6	69

EPs: 7–inch 33/45rpm

DECCA	5-15	55-65

LPs: 10/12–inch 33rpm

BULLDOG	5-10	
CAPRICORN	5-10	74
CORAL/MCA	5-8	84
DECCA (174 "Kitty Wells Story")	15-25	63
(Monaural. Includes booklet.)		
DECCA (7-174 "Kitty Wells Story")	20-30	63
(Stereo. Includes booklet.)		
DECCA (4075 thru 4929)	10-25	61-67
(Monaural.)		
DECCA (7-4075 thru 7-4929)	15-30	61-67
(Stereo.)		
DECCA (7-4961 thru 7-5350)	10-15	68-72
(Stereo.)		

DECCA (8293 "Country Hit
Parade") 35-45   56
(Monaural.)

DECCA (7-8293 "Country Hit
Parade") 15-25   68
(Stereo.)

DECCA (8552 "Winner of Your
Heart") 35-45   56

DECCA (7-8552 "Winner of Your
Heart") 10-15   65

DECCA (8732 "Lonely
Street") 30-40   58
(Monaural.)

DECCA (7-8732 "Lonely
Street") 10-15   65
(Stereo.)

DECCA (8858 "Dust on the
Bible") 25-35   59
(Monaural.)

DECCA (7-8858 "Dust on the
Bible") 10-15   68
(Stereo.)

DECCA (8888 "After Dark") 30-40   59
(Monaural.)

DECCA (7-8888 "After Dark") ... 10-15   68
(Stereo.)

DECCA (8979 "Kitty's Choice") . 25-35   59
(Monaural.)

DECCA (7-8979 "Kitty's
Choice") 30-40   59
(Stereo.)

EXACT 5-10   80
GOLDEN COUNTRY 5-10
IMPERIAL HOUSE...................... 5-10   80
KOALA 5-10   79
MCA 4-8   73-83
MISTLETOE................................. 5-8   80s
PICKWICK/HILLTOP 5-10   70s
ROUNDER 5-8   82
RUBOCA...................................... 8-12   79
SUFFOLK MARKETING 5-10   80
VOCALION.................................. 8-15   66-69

Also see ACUFF, Roy, & Kitty Wells
Also see ANTHONY, Rayburn, & Kitty
Wells
Also see JOHNNIE & JACK
Also see PARTON, Dolly / Kitty Wells
Also see PIERCE, Webb, & Kitty Wells
Also see TUBB, Ernest

WELLS, Kitty / Bill Anderson
LP: 10/12–inch 33rpm
MCA (734584 "Collector's
Album") 8-12
Also see ANDERSON, Bill

WELLS, Kitty, & Roy
Drusky   C&W '60
Singles: 7–inch
DECCA 4-8   60
LP: 10/12–inch 33rpm
PLAYBACK...................................5-10
Also see DRUSKY, Roy

WELLS, Kitty, & Red
Foley   C&W '54
Singles: 78rpm
DECCA 4-10   54-56
Singles: 7–inch
DECCA (29000 series) 5-15   54-56
DECCA (32000 series) 3-6   67-69
EPs: 7–inch 33/45rpm
DECCA 8-12   59
LPs: 10/12–inch 33rpm
DECCA 12-25   61-67
Also see FOLEY, Red

WELLS, Kitty, & Webb
Pierce   C&W '57
Singles: 78rpm
DECCA 5-10   57
Singles: 7–inch
DECCA 5-10   57-64
EPs: 7–inch 33/45rpm
DECCA 10-15   59
Also see PIERCE, Webb

WELLS, Kitty, & Johnny
Wright   C&W '68
Singles: 7–inch
DECCA 3-6   68-72
LP: 10/12–inch 33rpm
DECCA 10-20   68-72
Also see WELLS, Kitty
Also see WRIGHT, Johnny

WELLS, Mike   C&W '75
Singles: 7–inch
PLAYBOY 3-5   75-76

WENCE, Bill   C&W '79
Singles: 7–inch
RUSTIC...3-5   79-80

WEST, Dottie   C&W '63
(With Dale West)
Singles: 7–inch
ATLANTIC......................................4-8   62
LIBERTY 3-4   80-83
PERMIAN..3-4   84-85

RCA (Except 8000 series)	3-6	66-81
RCA (8000 series)	4-8	63-66
STARDAY (500 series)	4-8	60-61
STARDAY (700 series)	3-6	65
U.A.	3-4	76-80

Picture Sleeves

LIBERTY	3-5	80-81

LPs: 10/12–inch 33rpm

CAMDEN	5-10	71-73
COLUMBIA	5-10	80
GUSTO	5-8	82
LIBERTY	5-8	81-82
NASHVILLE	8-12	70s
PERMIAN	5-8	85
PICKWICK	5-10	75
POWER PAK	5-10	70s
RCA	8-18	65-75
STARDAY	10-20	64-65
U.A.	5-10	73-80

Session: Jordanaires.
Also see DEAN, Jimmy, & Dottie West
Also see JORDANAIRES
Also see REEVES, Jim, & Dottie West
Also see ROGERS, Kenny, & Dottie West

WEST, Dottie, & Don Gibson
C&W '70

Singles: 7–inch

RCA	3-5	69-70

LPs: 10/12–inch 33rpm

RCA	8-12	69

Also see GIBSON, Don

WEST, Dottie / Melba Montgomery

LPs: 10/12–inch 33rpm

STARDAY	10-20	65

Also see MONTGOMERY, Melba
Also see WEST, Dottie

WEST, Jim
C&W '79

(With Carol Chase; with Stephanie Winslow)

Singles: 7–inch

MACHO	3-5	79-81

LP: 10/12–inch 33rpm

HOME COMFORT	5-10	77

Also see CHASE, Carol

WEST, Shelly
C&W '83

Singles: 7–inch

VIVA	3-4	83-85
W.B.	3-4	83-86

LP: 10/12–inch 33rpm

VIVA	5-10	83
W.B.	5-10	83

Also see FRIZZELL, David, & Shelly West

WEST, Speedy
(Speedy West & Jimmy Bryant)

LP: 10/12–inch 33rpm

CAPITOL (H-520 "2 Guitars") (10–inch LP.)	45-55	55
CAPITOL (T-520 "2 Guitars")	30-50	55
CAPITOL (956 thru 1835)	15-25	58-62

WESTERN UNION BAND *C&W '88*

Singles: 7–inch

SHAWN-DEL	3-4	88

WHEELER, Billy Edd *C&W '64*
(With Rashell Richmond; with Joan Sommer; with Shelly Manne)

Singles: 7–inch

CAPITOL	3-5	75-76
KAPP	4-8	63-68
NSD	3-4	80-81
RCA	3-5	70-73
RADIO CINEMA	3-5	79
U.A.	3-6	69

Picture Sleeves

KAPP	4-8	67

LPs: 10/12–inch 33rpm

AVALANCHE	8-10	73
FLYING FISH	5-10	79
KAPP	10-20	64-68
MONITOR	15-25	61-62
RCA	8-10	71
U.A.	8-15	69

WHEELER, Karen *C&W '72*

Singles: 7–inch

CHART	3-5	72
RCA	3-5	74

Also see HARDEN TRIO

WHEELER, Onie *C&W '73*

Singles: 78rpm

COLUMBIA	10-30	55-57
OKEH	5-10	52-54
ORGANA	10-15	51

Singles: 7–inch

COLUMBIA	15-30	55-57
EPIC	4-8	62
OKEH	10-20	52-54
OLE WINDMILL	3-5	73
ROYAL AMERICAN	3-5	73
SUN (315 "Jump Right Out of This Juke Box")	15-25	59

Picture Sleeves

EPIC	4-8	62

LPs: 10/12–inch 33rpm

BRYLEN	5-10	
ONIE	8-12	73

WHIPPLE, Sterling   *C&W '78*
Singles: 7–inch

W.B.	3-5	78-79

WHISPERING WILL   *C&W '79*
Singles: 7–inch

VISTA	3-5	79

WHITE, Bill   *C&W '78*
Singles: 7–inch

PRAIRIE DUST	3-5	78

WHITE, Brian   *C&W '88*
Singles: 7–inch

OAK	3-4	88

WHITE, Charley   *C&W '79*
Singles: 7–inch

NSD	3-5	79

WHITE, Danny, & Linda Nail   *C&W '83*
Singles: 7–inch

GRAND PRIX	3-4	83

Also see NAIL, Linda

WHITE, L.E., & Lola Jean Dillon   *C&W '77*
Singles: 7–inch

EPIC	3-5	77

WHITE, Mack   *C&W '73*
Singles: 7–inch

COMMERCIAL	3-6	73-82
MICHELLE	4-8	64
PLAYBOY	3-5	74

LP: 10/12–inch 33rpm

COMMERCIAL	5-10	77-78

WHITE, Roger   *C&W '67*
Singles: 7–inch

BIG A	3-5	67
BLUE GIANT (001 "Somebody's Stealing My Baby")	40-60	

WHITE, Tony Joe   *P&R/LP '69*
(With the Mojos; with Waylon Jennings)
Singles: 7–inch

ARISTA	3-5	79
CASABLANCA	3-5	80
COLUMBIA	3-4	83-85
J-BECK	5-8	
MONUMENT	4-8	67-70
20TH FOX	3-5	76

LPs: 10/12–inch 33rpm

CASABLANCA	5-10	80
COLUMBIA	5-8	83
MONUMENT	8-15	69-70
20TH FOX	5-10	77
W.B.	8-10	71-73

Session: Waylon Jennings.
Also see JENNINGS, Waylon

WHITE WATER JUNCTION   *C&W '84*
Singles: 7–inch

JUNGLE ROGUE	3-4	84

WHITEHEAD, Benny   *C&W '73*
Singles: 7–inch

REPRISE	3-5	73

WHITES   *C&W '81*
Singles: 7–inch

CANAAN	3-4	89
CAPITOL	3-5	81
ELEKTRA	3-4	82
MCA/CURB	3-4	84-87
W.B.	3-4	83

LP: 10/12–inch 33rpm

MCA	5-10	84
W.B.	5-10	83

Members: Buck White; Patty White; Sharon White; Cheryl White.
Also see HARRIS, Emmylou

WHITING, Margaret   *P&R '46*
Singles: 78rpm

CAPITOL	3-8	46-56
DOT	3-8	57

Singles: 7–inch

CAPITOL	5-10	50-56
DOT	5-8	57-59
LONDON	3-6	66-70
VERVE	4-6	60

EPs: 7–inch 33/45rpm

CAPITOL	5-10	50-56

LPs: 10/12–inch 33rpm

CAPITOL	12-25	50-56
DOT	8-18	57-67
HAMILTON	5-15	59-65
LONDON	5-15	67-68
VERVE	10-20	60

Also see MARTIN, Dean, & Margaret Whiting

WHITING, Margaret, & Jimmy Wakely　　　*C&W '49*

Singles: 78rpm

CAPITOL	3-8	49-51

Singles: 7–inch

CAPITOL	5-10	49-51

EPs: 7–inch 33/45rpm

CAPITOL	8-15	53

LPs: 10/12–inch 33rpm

PICKWICK	8-12	67

Also see WHITING, Margaret
Also see WAKELY, Jimmy

WHITLEY, Keith　　　*C&W '84*

(With Patty Loveless)

Singles: 7–inch

RCA	3-4	84-89

LPs: 10/12–inch 33rpm

RCA	5-8	84-89

Also see LOVELESS, Patty
Also see McENTIRE, Reba
Also see SKAGGS, Ricky, & Keith Whitley

WHITLEY, Keith, & Lorrie Morgan　　　*C&W '90*

Singles: 7–inch

RCA	3-4	90

Also see MORGAN, Lorrie
Also see WHITLEY, Keith

WHITMAN, Slim　　　*C&W/P&R '52*

Singles: 78rpm

IMPERIAL	5-15	52-57

Singles: 7–inch

CLEVELAND INT'L	3-4	80-82
EPIC	3-4	84
IMPERIAL (5000 series)	5-10	61-63
IMPERIAL (8000 thru 8200 series)	10-25	52-58
IMPERIAL (8300 series)	8-12	59-60
IMPERIAL (50000 series)	3-5	70-71
IMPERIAL (65000 & 66000 series)	3-8	61-69
U.A.	3-8	70-77

EPs: 7–inch 33/45rpm

IMPERIAL	30-50	54-65

RCA (3217 "Slim Whitman Sings and Yodels")	100-150	54

LPs: 10/12–inch 33rpm

CAMDEN	8-12	66
CLEVELAND INT'L (Except AS-99875)	5-10	80-81
CLEVELAND INT'L (AS-99875 "Songs I Love to Sing")	25-35	80
(Picture disc. Promotional issue only. Reportedly 1,600 made.)		
EPIC	5-8	84
IMPERIAL (3004 "America's Favorite Folk Artist")	400-500	54
(10–inch LP.)		
IMPERIAL (9000 series)	35-50	56-60
(Maroon or black label with "Imperial" at top.)		
IMPERIAL (9000 series)	8-15	66
(Black label with "Imperial" on left side.)		
IMPERIAL (9100 series)	20-40	60-62
(Black label with "Imperial" at top.)		
IMPERIAL (9100 series)	8-15	66
(Black label with "Imperial" on left side.)		
IMPERIAL (9200 & 9300 series)	15-25	63-67
IMPERIAL (12100 series)	20-30	62
(Black label with "Imperial" at top.)		
IMPERIAL (12100 series)	8-15	66
(Black label with "Imperial" on left side.)		
IMPERIAL (12200 & 12300 series)	12-25	65-68
IMPERIAL (12400 series)	8-12	68-69
LIBERTY	5-10	80-82
PICKWICK	5-10	70s
RCA (3217 "Slim Whitman Sings and Yodels")	250-350	54
RCA (3700 series)	5-8	80
SUFFOLK MARKETING	8-12	79-82
SUNSET	8-12	66-70
U.A.	6-12	70-80

Also see WILLIAMS, Hank / Slim Whitman

WHITTAKER, Roger

P&R/LP '75/C&W '83

Singles: 7–inch

MAIN STREET	3-4	83-84
RCA	3-5	70-86

Picture Sleeves

RCA	3-5	80

LPs: 10/12–inch 33rpm

MAIN STREET	5-8	84
RCA	5-12	70-86

WICHITA LINEMEN C&W '77
(Featuring Greg Stevens)
Singles: 7–inch
LINEMEN 3-5 77-79

WICHITA TRAIN WHISTLE LP '68
Singles: 7–inch
DOT.. 5-8 68
LPs: 10/12–inch 33rpm
DOT.. 15-20 68
PACIFIC ARTS 8-10 78
Member: Michael Nesmith.
Also see NESMITH, Michael

WICKHAM, Lewie C&W '70
Singles: 7–inch
MCA 3-5 78
STARDAY 3-5 70

WICKLINE C&W '81
(Wickline Band Featuring Scott Gavin)
Singles: 7–inch
CASCADE MOUNTAIN................. 3-4 81-84

WIER, Rusty P&R/LP '75
Singles: 7–inch
ABC.. 3-5 74
BLACK HAT 3-4 87
COLUMBIA 3-5 76
COMPLEAT 3-4 83-84
LONGHORN 4-8 65
20TH FOX..................................... 3-5 75-76
LPs: 10/12–inch 33rpm
ABC.. 8-12 74
COLUMBIA 8-10 76
20TH FOX..................................... 8-10 75

WILBOURN, Bill, & Kathy Morrison C&W '68
(Bill Wilbourne & Kathy Morrison)
Singles: 7–inch
U.A. 3-6 68-70
LPs: 10/12–inch 33rpm
U.A. 8-10 69

WILBURN BROTHERS C&W '55
Singles: 78rpm
DECCA....................................... 5-15 54-57
Singles: 7–inch
DECCA (29190 thru 30428)........ 8-15 54-57
DECCA (30591 "Oo Bop Sha
  Boom") 15-25 58
DECCA (30686 thru 33027).......... 3-8 58-72

MCA.. 3-5 73
EPs: 7–inch 33/45rpm
DECCA 5-15 57-62
LPs: 10/12–inch 33rpm
CORAL.. 5-8 80s
DECCA (4142 thru 4645)........... 10-20 61-65
DECCA (4721 "Wilburn Brothers
  Show") 50-75 66
  (With Loretta Lynn, Ernest Tubb & Harold
  Morrison.)
DECCA (4817 thru 5291)............. 8-15 67-71
DECCA (8774 "Side By Side")...30-40 58
  (Monaural.)
DECCA (78774 "Side By
  Side") 50-75 58
  (Stereo.)
DECCA (8959 "Livin' in God's
  Country").................................20-30 59
  (Monaural.)
DECCA (78959 "Livin' in God's
  Country")..................................30-40 59
  (Stereo.)
DESIGN 8-12 60s
FIRST GENERATION.................5-10 81
KING (746 "The Wonderful Wilburn
  Brothers")...............................25-35 61
PHONORAMA 5-10
STETSON....................................5-10
VOCALION 5-15 62-70
WORD...5-8
Members: Teddy Wilburn; Doyle Wilburn. Session:
Anita Kerr Singers.
Also see KERR, Anita
Also see LYNN, Loretta
Also see PIERCE, Webb, & Wilburn Brothers
Also see TUBB, Ernest, & Wilburn Brothers

WILCOX, Harlow C&W/P&R '69
(With the Oakies)
Singles: 7–inch
IMPEL (002 "Groovy
  Grubworm") 15-25 68
PLANTATION 4-8 69-70
SSS INT'L 3-5 70s
Picture Sleeves
PLANTATION 4-6 69
LPs: 10/12–inch 33rpm
PLANTATION 5-10 70-71

WILD CHOIR C&W '86
Singles: 7–inch
RCA 3-4 86
Member: Gail Davies
Also see DAVIES, Gail

WILD COUNTRY

Singles: 7–inch

LSI (75-12-1 "Sweet Country
Woman") 25-35   70

LPs: 10/12–inch 33rpm

LSI (0275 "Wild Country") ... 500-1000   70
Members: Randy Owen; Jeff Cook; Teddy Gentry;
John B. Vartanian.
Also see ALABAMA

WILD ROSE   *C&W '89*

Singles: 7–inch

CAPITOL 3-4   90
UNIVERSAL 3-4   89

WILEY & GENE   *C&W '46*

Singles: 78rpm

COLUMBIA 4-8   45-46
Members: Wiley Walker; Gene Sullivan.
Also see SULLIVAN, Gene

WILKINS, David   *C&W '69*

(Little David Wilkins)

Singles: 7–inch

EPIC 3-5   78
JERE 3-4   86
MCA 3-5   73-77
PLANTATION 3-6   69
PLAYBOY 3-5   77-78

LP: 10/12–inch 33rpm

MCA 6-12   74-76
PLAYBOY 5-10   77
Also see RUSSELL, Johnny, & Little David Wilkins

WILLCOX, Pete   *C&W '82*

Singles: 7–inch

M&M (105 "The King") 5-10   82

WILLETT, Slim   *C&W '52*

(With the Brush Cutters; Slim Willet; Winston
Moore)

Singles: 78rpm

FOUR STAR 5-10   52-56
SLIM WILLET (133 "Four Hand
Blues") 20-40   53
STAR TALENT 10-20   50

Singles: 7–inch

EDMORAL (1010 "I've Been a
Wonderin") 15-25   50s
FOUR STAR 10-20   52-56

LPs: 10/12–inch 33rpm

AUDIO LAB (1542 "Slim
Willett") 30-40   60

WILLIAMS, Becky   *C&W '88*

Singles: 7–inch

COUNTRY PRIDE 3-4   88

WILLIAMS, Beth   *C&W '86*

Singles: 7–inch

BGM 3-4   86-87

WILLIAMS, Cootie   *R&B/C&W '44*

(With Eddie "Cleanhead" Vinson)

Singles: 78rpm

DERBY 15-30   51
HIT 15-30   44-45

Singles: 7–inch

DERBY (756 "Shotgun
Boogie") 50-100   51

LPs: 10/12–inch 33rpm

MOODSVILLE (27 "Solid
Trumpet") 20-30   62
(Monaural.)
MOODSVILLE (27-SD "Solid
Trumpet") 25-35   62
(Stereo.)
RCA (1718 "In Hi-Fi") 40-60   58
WARWICK (2027 "Do Nothing Till You Hear
from Me") 40-60   59

WILLIAMS, Cootie, & Wini Brown

LPs: 10/12–inch 33rpm

JARO (5001 "Around
Midnight") 40-60   60
Also see WILLIAMS, Cootie

WILLIAMS, Diana   *C&W/P&R '76*

Singles: 7–inch

CAPITOL 3-5   76
LITTLE GEM 3-5   77

WILLIAMS, Don   *C&W '72*

Singles: 7–inch

ABC 3-5   75-78
ABC/DOT 3-5   74-77
CAPITOL 3-4   86
DOT 3-5   74
JMI 3-5   72-74
MCA (Except 1763) 3-4   79-85
MCA (1763 "Special Message from Don
Williams for Your Radio
Station") 4-8   82
(Promotional issue only.)

LPs: 10/12–inch 33rpm

ABC (Except 28) 5-10   77-78
ABC (28 "Don Williams") 10-15   77
(Promotional issue only.)

ABC/DOT	8-10	74-77
CAPITOL	5-8	86
JMI	15-20	73-74
K-TEL	5-8	78
MCA (Except 44)	5-10	75-85
MCA (44 "Expressions")	15-20	78
(Picture disc.)		

Also see HARRIS, Emmylou, & Don Williams
Also see POZO SECO SINGERS

WILLIAMS, Hank   *C&W '47*

(With the Drifting Cowboys; Hank Williams as "Luke the Drifter;" with Audrey Williams)

Singles: 78rpm

MGM	20-30	47-55
STERLING (201 "Calling You")	300-400	47
STERLING (204 "Wealth Won't Save Your Soul")	250-300	47
STERLING (208 "I Don't Care")	200-250	47
STERLING (210 "Honky Tonkin")	200-250	47

Singles: 7–inch

MGM (100 series)	5-8	60s
MGM (10000 & 11000 series)	10-20	50-55
MGM (12000 series)	5-15	55-59
MGM (13000 series)	3-6	64-67

EPs: 7–inch 33/45rpm

ARHOOLIE	4-6	83
(Not issued with cover.)		
MGM (100 & 200 series)	25-50	52-54
MGM (1000 thru 1600 series)	15-30	55-60

LPs: 10/12–inch 33rpm

ACM	5-10	83
BLAINE HOUSE	15-20	72
BOLL WEEVIL	8-12	76
CMF	5-10	
CANDLELITE ("Golden Dream of Hank Williams")	15-20	70s
(Boxed 3-LP set.)		
CANDLELITE ("1951-52: Golden Dream of Hank Williams")	8-12	76
COLUMBIA (5616 "Hank Williams Treasury")	35-45	60s
(Four-LP set from the Columbia House record club.)		
GOLDEN COUNTRY	5-8	82
JAMBALAYA	5-10	
MGM (2 "36 of Hank Williams' Greatest Hits")	80-100	57
(Three LPs.)		

MGM (4 "36 More of Hank Williams' Greatest Hits")	80-100	58
(Three LPs.)		
MGM (107 "Hank Williams Sings")	50-100	51
(10–inch LP.)		
MGM (168 "Moanin' the Blues")	50-100	52
(10–inch LP.)		
MGM (202 "Memorial Album")	50-100	53
(10–inch LP.)		
MGM (203 "Hank Williams As Luke the Drifter")	50-100	53
(10–inch LP.)		
MGM (240-2 "24 Karat Hits, Hank Williams")	15-20	68
MGM (242 "Honky Tonkin")	50-100	54
(10–inch LP.)		
MGM (243 "I Saw the Light")	50-100	55
(10–inch LP.)		
MGM (291 "Ramblin' Man")	50-100	54
(10–inch LP.)		
MGM (912 "Hank Williams . . . Reflections by Those Who Loved Him")	100-200	75
(Boxed 3-LP set. Promotional issue only. Includes guest speakers: Roy Acuff, Little Jimmy Dickens, Lefty Frizzell, Pee Wee King, George Morgan, Bill Monroe, Minnie Pearl, Wesley Rose, Ernest Tubb, Grant Turner, Audrey Williams, Faron Young, and Hank Williams Jr.)		
MGM (1000 series)	8-10	76
(Special Products issue.)		
MGM (3219 "Ramblin' Man")	50-75	55
(Blue "sketch" cover.)		
MGM (3219 "Ramblin' Man")	25-45	
(Yellow "suit" cover.)		
MGM (3330 "Moanin' the Blues"	100-150	56
(Yellow label.)		
MGM (E-3200 thru 3900 series)	25-50	55-61
(Monaural. Through 3733, first issues have a yellow label.)		
MGM (SE-3200 thru 3900 series)	10-20	63-70
(Reprocessed stereo. Through 3733, first issues have a yellow label.)		
MGM (4000 thru 4700 series, except 4267)	10-20	63-71
MGM (4267 "The Hank Williams Story")	50-75	66
(Boxed 4-LP set.)		
MGM (4900 thru 5400 series)	5-10	75-77

METRO	10-15	65-67
POLYDOR..	5-15	83-84
SUNRISE MEDIA........................	8-10	81
TIME-LIFE (Except LCW-01)	5-8	81-82
TIME-LIFE (LCW-01 "Hank Williams")	10-15	81

(Boxed 3-LP set.)

Also see DRIFTING COWBOYS
Also see PRESLEY, Elvis / Hank Williams

WILLIAMS, Hank / Roy Acuff
LP: 10/12-inch 33rpm

LAMB & LION..............................	8-12

(Three LPs. Two by Hank Williams, one by Roy Acuff.)

Also see ACUFF, Roy

WILLIAMS, Hank / Slim Whitman
LPs: 10/12-inch 33rpm

SUNRISE MEDIA........................	8-10	81

Also see WHITMAN, Slim

WILLIAMS, Hank, & Hank Williams, Jr.   *LP '65*

(Hank Williams / Hank Williams Jr.; Hank Williams Jr. & Hank Williams Sr.)

Singles: 7-inch

W.B.	3-4	89

LPs: 10/12-inch 33rpm

COLUMBIA HOUSE ("Hank's Place").......................................	5-10	81

(One side by each artist. Bonus LP with boxed set below. Selection number not known.)

COLUMBIA HOUSE "Hank Williams / Hank Williams Jr.)	20-25	81

(Boxed 5-LP record club set. Selection number not known.)

MGM (4200 series)	15-25	65
MGM (4300 thru 4900 series) ...	10-15	66-74

Also see WILLIAMS, Hank
Also see WILLIAMS, Hank, Jr.

WILLIAMS, Hank, Jr.   *C&W/P&R '64*

(With the Cheatin' Hearts; with Mike Curb Congregation; Luke the Drifter Jr.)

Singles: 7-inch

CONSOL	10-20	

(Promotional issue from Consolidation Coal.)

ELEKTRA/CURB...........................	3-4	79-82
MGM (13000 series)	4-8	64-68
MGM (14000 series)	3-5	68-76
MGM GOLDEN CIRCLE..............	3-5	70s
W.B./CURB (Except 8000 series) .	3-4	82-88
W.B./CURB (8000 series)	3-4	77-78

Picture Sleeves

MGM (13000 series) 5-10		64-68

LPs: 10/12-inch 33rpm

CURB.......................................5-8		83-84
ELEKTRA....................................5-8		79-83
MGM (Except 5009)..................10-20		64-76
MGM (5009 "Hank Williams Jr. and Friends") 25-50		75
POLYDOR 5-8		
W.B. (Except 2092)....................5-10		77-87
W.B. (2092 "Interview")...............8-12		83

(Promotional issue only.)

W.B./CURB 5-8		85-91

Also see BOCEPHUS
Also see CASH, Johnny, & Hank Williams Jr.
Also see CHARLES, Ray, & Hank Williams Jr.
Also see FRANCIS, Connie, & Hank Williams Jr.
Also see JENNINGS, Waylon, & Hank Williams Jr.
Also see JONES, George
Also see KERSHAW, Doug, & Hank Williams Jr.
Also see KILGORE, Merle
Also see WILLIAMS, Hank, & Hank Williams Jr.

WILLIAMS, Hank, Jr., & Lois Johnson   *C&W '72*

Singles: 7-inch

MGM 3-5		70-72

LP: 10/12-inch 33rpm

MGM 6-12		70-72

Also see JOHNSON, Lois
Also see WILLIAMS, Hank, Jr.

WILLIAMS, Jason D.   *C&W '89*

Singles: 7-inch

RCA 3-4		89

WILLIAMS, Johnny   *R&B/C&W '72*

Singles: 7-inch

BASHIE..3-5		70
CUB 4-6		68
EPIC...3-5		72
PHILADELPHIA INT'L....................3-5		73

WILLIAMS, Lawton   *C&W '61*

(With the Anita Kerr Singers)

Singles: 7-inch

D 5-10		60
LE BILL 5-10		
MEGA 3-5		71
MERCURY.......................................4-8		61
RCA (7000 series) 5-10		58
RCA (8000 series) 4-6		64

LP: 10/12–inch 33rpm

MEGA	6-10	71

Also see KERR, Anita

WILLIAMS, Leona   *C&W '69*
Singles: 7–inch

ELEKTRA	3-4	81
HICKORY	3-6	69-73
MCA	3-5	78-79

LP: 10/12–inch 33rpm

HICKORY	10-20	70-72
MCA	5-10	76
MERCURY	5-10	84

Also see HAGGARD, Merle, & Leona Williams

WILLIAMS, Lois   *C&W '69*
Singles: 7–inch

STARDAY	3-6	69-70

LP: 10/12–inch 33rpm

STARDAY	8-12	70

WILLIAMS, Otis   *C&W '71*
(With the Midnight Cowboys)
Singles: 7–inch

DELUXE (6100 series)	5-10	59
KING	4-8	60-64
OKEH	4-6	66
STOP	3-5	71

LPs: 10/12–inch 33rpm

POWER PAK	8-10	74
STOP	8-12	71

Also see CHARMS

WILLIAMS, Paul   *LP '71/C&W '81*
Singles: 7–inch

A&M	3-4	72-77
PAID	3-4	81
PORTRAIT	3-4	79
REPRISE	3-4	70

LPs: 10/12–inch 33rpm

A&M	6-10	71-77
PAID	5-8	81
PORTRAIT	5-8	79
REPRISE	8-12	70

WILLIAMS, Tex   *C&W '46*
(With His Western Caravan; with Spade Cooley; with California Express)
Singles: 78rpm

CAPITOL	4-8	46-51
COLUMBIA	4-8	46
DECCA	4-8	53-55

Singles: 7–inch

BOONE	4-6	65-68
CAPITOL	5-10	51-60
DECCA	5-10	53-55
DOT	4-6	66
GRANITE	3-5	74
LIBERTY	4-8	63-65
MONUMENT	3-5	70-72
SHASTA	4-8	60-61

EPs: 7–inch 33/45rpm

CAMDEN	8-12	58
CAPITOL	10-15	56-57
DECCA	10-15	55

LP: 10/12–inch 33rpm

BOONE	10-15	66
CAMDEN (363 "Tex Williams' Best")	20-40	58
CAPITOL (1463 "Smoke! Smoke! Smoke!")	20-40	60
DECCA (4295 "Country Music Time")	15-25	62
DECCA (5565 "Dance-O-Rama") (10–inch LP.)	40-60	55
GARU	5-10	81
GRANITE	6-12	74
IMPERIAL	10-15	66
LIBERTY	15-25	63
MONUMENT	8-12	71
SHASTA	8-12	
SUNSET	10-15	66

Also see COOLEY, Spade, & His Orchestra
Also see STARR, Kay

WILLIAMS, Tucker   *C&W '80*
Singles: 7–inch

YATAHEY	3-4	80

WILLIAMS BROTHERS   *C&W '63*
Singles: 7–inch

DEL-MAR	4-8	63

Members: Jimmy Williams; Bobby Williams.

WILLING, Foy, & His Riders of the Purple Sage   *C&W '44*
Singles: 78rpm

CAPITOL	4-8	44-49
DECCA	4-8	45-46
MAJESTIC	4-8	46

LP: 10/12–inch 33rpm

ALLEGRO	5-8	
BIG BOSS	8-10	77
CROWN	8-10	60s

CUSTOM	8-10	60s
JUBILEE	15-25	62
ROULETTE (25035 "Cowboy")	25-35	58
ROYALE (6032) (10-inch LP.)	15-25	

Session: Red River Dave.

WILLING, Foy, Eddie Dean & His Riders of the Purple Sage
LPs: 10/12–inch 33rpm

ROYALE (6987 "Foy Willing & Eddie Dean")	25-50	

Also see DEAN, Eddie
Also see WILLING, Foy, & His Riders of the Purple Sage

WILLIS, Andra   *C&W '73*
Singles: 7–inch

CAPITOL	3-5	73

Also see FORD, Tennessee Ernie, & Andra Willis

WILLIS, Hal   *C&W '64*
Singles: 78rpm

ATLANTIC	150-200	57

Singles: 7–inch

ATHENS (704 "Crazy Little Mama")	75-125	58
ATLANTIC (1114 "Bop-A-Dee Bop-A-Doo")	150-200	57
DECCA	5-10	59
MERCURY	4-8	62
SIMS (Except 288)	4-8	64-66
SIMS (288 "Doggin' in the U.S. Mail")	5-10	66

LP: 10/12–inch 33rpm

ARC	10-15	
BONANZA	10-15	

WILLIS BROTHERS   *C&W '64*
Singles: 7–inch

STARDAY	3-8	62-70

LP: 10/12–inch 33rpm

CORONET (150 "Gunfighter Ballads of the Badmen")	10-20	
(The Willis Brothers are not credited on this LP, though they do one side.)		
MASTERPIECES	5-10	
NASHVILLE	10-15	60s
PICKWICK/HILLTOP	10-15	65
STARDAY (163 "In Action")	20-30	62
STARDAY (229 "Code of the West")	25-35	63
STARDAY (306 thru 466)	10-25	65-70

Members: Vic Willis; Guy Willis; Charles Willis.
Also see WILLIS, Vic, Trio

WILLIS, Vic, Trio
LP: 10/12–inch 33rpm

FIRST GENERATION	5-10	81

Also see WILLIS BROTHERS

WILLOUGHBY, Larry   *C&W '83*
Singles: 7–inch

ATLANTIC AMERICA	3-4	83-84

WILLS, Bob   *P&R '39/C&W '44*
(With His Texas Playboys; with Rusty McDonald; with Tommy Duncan)
Singles: 78rpm

ANTONES	15-25	
CAPITOL	3-5	76
COLUMBIA	5-10	43-48
DECCA	4-8	55-56
MGM	5-10	47-55
OKEH	5-10	40-45
VOCALION	10-20	33-39

Singles: 7–inch

DECCA	5-10	55-56
LIBERTY	4-8	60-64
LONGHORN	4-6	64
MGM	5-15	50-55

EPs: 7–inch 33/45rpm

COLUMBIA	10-20	57
DECCA	10-20	55
MGM	10-20	56

LP: 10/12–inch 33rpm

ANTONES (6000 "The Texas Playboys")	100-200	
(10–inch LP. Fan club issue.)		
ANTONES (6010 "The Texas Playboys")	100-200	
(10–inch LP. Fan club issue.)		
AUDIO/VIDEO	5-8	82
CAPITOL	10-20	76
COLUMBIA (Except 9003)	6-12	73-82
COLUMBIA (9003 "Round-Up")	50-75	50
(10–inch LP.)		
CORAL (20109 "Swing Along")	5-10	73
CORONET	8-12	60s
DECCA (5562 "Dance-O-Rama")	50-75	55
(10–inch LP.)		
DECCA (DL-8727 "Bob Wills & His Texas Playboys")	35-55	57
(Monaural.)		

DECCA (DL7-8727 "Bob Wills & His Texas
Playboys") 15-25   66
(Reprocessed stereo.)

DELTA 5-10   81-83

ENCORE .... ??   79

HARMONY (Except 7036) 10-20   63-69

HARMONY (7036 "Bob Wills
Special") 15-25   57

KAPP 8-12   66-71

KALEIDOSCOPE 5-10   82-83

LARIAT (1 "The Tiffany
Transcriptions") 50-75   77

LIBERTY 20-30   60-63

LONGHORN (001 "Bob Wills Keepsake
Album, #1") 50-75   65

LONGHORN (007 "Bob Wills Collector's
Series") 10-15

LONGHORN (011 "31st St.
Blues") 10-15

MCA 6-12   73-80s

MGM (91 "Ranch House
Favorites") 75-100   51
(10-inch LP.)

MGM (141 "Tribute to Bob
Wills") 8-12   71

MGM (3352 "Ranch House
Favorites") 50-75   56

MGM (4866 "History of Bob
Wills") 10-15   73

MGM (5303 "24 Great Hits") 8-12   77

METRO 10-15   67

PICKWICK 5-10   70s

RHINO (284 "Greatest Hits of
Texas") 8-12   85
(Texas-shaped, picture disc. Promotional
issue only.)

STARDAY (375 "San Antonio
Rose") 15-25   65

STARDAY (469 "Bob Wills
Story") 8-12   70

SUNSET 8-12   66-69

TEXAS ROSE 5-10

TIME-LIFE 5-10   81

TIME-LIFE ("Bob Wills") 10-15   82
(Boxed 3-LP set.)

TISHOMINGO (1 "The Tiffany Transcriptions,
1945-1948) 30-50   78

U.A. 8-15   71-74

VOCALION (3735 "Swing
Along") 10-20   65

VOCALION (3922 "San Antonio
Rose") 10-20   71

WESTERN HERITAGE 5-10   76

Also see DUNCAN, Tommy
Also see FORT WORTH DOUGHBOYS
Also see HAGGARD, Merle
Also see McAULIFFE, Leon
Also see TEXAS PLAYBOYS
Also see WILLS, Johnnie Lee, & His Boys

WILLS, Bob, & Mel Tillis
LP: 10/12-inch 33rpm
KAPP (3523 "King of Western
Swing") 15-25   67

KAPP (3639 "In Person") 15-25   68

MCA 5-10   80s

Also see TILLIS, Mel
Also see WILLS, Bob

WILLS, David   *C&W '74*
Singles: 7-inch
EPIC 3-5   74-88

RCA 3-4   83-84

U.A. 3-5   77-80

LP: 10/12-inch 33rpm
EPIC 5-10   75-88

RCA 5-10   84

Also see RICH, Charlie

WILLS, Johnnie Lee, & His
Boys   *C&W '50*
Singles: 78rpm
BULLET 4-8   49-50

LP: 10/12-inch 33rpm
CROWN 10-15   60s

DELTA 5-10   80s

FLYING FISH 5-10   80s

ROUNDER 5-10   80s

SIMS (101 "Where There's a Wills There's a
Way") 15-25   60s

SIMS (108 "Johnnie Lee Willis at the Tulsa
Stampede") 15-25   60s

Also see WILLS, Bob

WILLS, Tommy   *C&W '79*
(With His Twisting Tomcats; with Marti Maes)
Singles: 7-inch
AIR TOWN 4-8   66

CLUB MIAMI (501 "Let 'Em
Roll") 200-250

GOLDEN MOON 3-5   79

TERRY (110 "Aw Shucks") 5-10   62

EPs: 7-inch 33/45rpm
TERRY-GREGORY (1000 "Man with a
Horn") 8-12   62
(Jukebox issue.)

LP: 10/12-inch 33rpm
COUNTRY INT'L 5-10   75

GOLDEN MOON............................ 5-10   78

WILSON, Benny   *C&W '85*
Singles: 7–inch
COLUMBIA 3-4   85-86
Also see FRICKE, Janie

WILSON, Coleman   *C&W '61*
Singles: 7–inch
KING 5-8   61

WILSON, Hank   *LP '73*
(Leon Russell)
Singles: 7–inch
SHELTER...................................... 3-4   73-74
LPs: 10/12–inch 33rpm
SHELTER.. 8-10   73
Also see NELSON, Willie, & Hank Wilson
Also see RUSSELL, Leon

WILSON, Jim   *C&W '55*
(With June Wilson)
Singles: 78rpm
MERCURY 5-8   56
Singles: 7–inch
MERCURY 6-12   56
REED 5-10   59

WILSON, Larry Jon   *C&W '76*
Singles: 7–inch
MONUMENT................................... 3-5   76
LP: 10/12–inch 33rpm
MONUMENT................................... 5-10   76-78
Also see COE, David Allan

WILSON, Meri   *P&R/R&B/C&W '77*
Singles: 7–inch
BNA (8248 "Peter, the Meter
Reader")..................................... 5-10   81
GRT... 3-4   77
LPs: 10/12–inch 33rpm
GRT... 5-10   77

WILSON, Norro   *C&W '69*
(Norris Wilson)
Singles: 7–inch
CAPITOL....................................... 3-5   74
HICKORY...................................... 4-8   66
MGM 4-8   65-69
MERCURY 3-5   70
MONUMENT................................... 4-8   62
RCA... 3-5   72-73
SMASH 4-6   68-69

LP: 10/12–inch 33rpm
SMASH 8-12   69
Also see SMITH, Margo, & Norro Wilson

WINGS: see McCARTNEY, Paul

WINSLOW, Stephanie   *C&W '79*
Singles: 7–inch
CURB/MCA......................................3-4   83-84
OAK...3-4   83
PRIMERO 3-4   81-82
W.B./CURB......................................3-5   79-81

WINTERMUTE, Joann   *C&W '89*
Singles: 7–inch
CANYON CREEK 3-4   89
DOOR KNOB...............................3-4   89

WINTERS, Don   *C&W '61*
Singles: 78rpm
COIN (102 "Be My Baby")..........20-30   56
Singles: 7–inch
COIN (102 "Be My Baby")..........50-75   56
DECCA 5-10   60-62
HAMILTON 4-8   63

WISEMAN, Mac   *C&W '55*
(With Sonny Osborne; with Tommy Jackson;
with Shenandoah Cut-ups; with Johnny
Gimble; with Osborne Brothers; with "Friend")
Singles: 78rpm
DOT 5-10   55-57
Singles: 7–inch
CAPITOL.......................................4-8   62-63
CHURCHILL 3-5   78-79
DOT 5-10   55-59
MGM 4-6   68
RCA 3-6   69-73
EPs: 7–inch 33/45rpm
DOT 10-20   55
LP: 10/12–inch 33rpm
ABC..10-15   74-77
CMH...5-10   76-82
CAPITOL (1800 "Bluegrass
Favorites") 25-40   62
DOT (3084 "Tis Sweet to Be
Remembered").........................25-50   58
DOT (3135 thru 3697)................15-30   59-66
(Monaural.)
DOT (25135 thru 25896)............15-35   59-68
(Stereo.)
GILLEY'S 10-20
GUSTO 5-10

HAMILTON............................... 10-20   64-66
MCA 5-10
PICKWICK/HILLTOP 10-15   67
RCA... 6-12   70-75
RIDGE RUNNER 5-10
RURAL RHYTHM...................... 10-20
VETCO...................................... 10-20
  Also see OSBORNE BROTHERS & Mac Wiseman
  Also see TOMORROW'S WORLD

WOLF, Gary   *C&W '82*
Singles: 7–inch
COLUMBIA 3-4   82-83
MERCURY 3-4   84-85

WOLFPACK   *C&W '82*
Singles: 7–inch
LOBO 3-5   82
  Members: Narvel Felts; Lobo; Kenny Earl.
  Also see EARL, Kenny
  Also see FELTS, Narvel
  Also see LOBO

WOOD, Bobby   *P&R '64*
Singles: 7–inch
CHALLENGE 3-5   62
CINNAMON.................................. 3-4   74
JOY 3-5   63-65
LUCKY ELEVEN 3-4   73
MALA 3-5   66
MGM 3-4   67-69
SUN (369 "Everybody's
  Searchin") 50-100   61
LPs: 10/12–inch 33rpm
JOY (1001 "Bobby Wood")........ 15-20   64
  Also see PRESLEY, Elvis

WOOD, Danny   *C&W '76*
Singles: 7–inch
LONDON...................................... 3-5   76-77
RCA.. 3-4   80-81

WOOD, Del   *P&R/C&W '51*
Singles: 78rpm
DECCA.. 3-4   53-54
MERCURY 3-4   62-64
RCA.. 3-4   55-59
REPUBLIC 3-4   51-54
TENNESSEE 3-6   51
Singles: 7–inch
CHART.. 3-4   71-72
DECCA.. 3-5   53-54
MERCURY 3-4   62-64
PICKWICK 5-10   70s

RCA 3-5   55-59
REPUBLIC 3-8   51-54
TENNESSEE 5-10   51
EPs: 7–inch 33/45rpm
RCA 5-12   55-60
REPUBLIC....................................4-10   54-57
LPs: 10/12–inch 33rpm
AMBASSADOR..............................5-10
CAMDEN 5-12   62-64
CHART...5-8   71
COLUMBIA 8-12   66
LAMB & LION 5-8
MERCURY 5-12   62-64
PICKWICK 5-8   70s
RCA 5-15   55-60
REPUBLIC....................................5-15   54-57
VOCALION 5-10   60s
  Session: First Nashville Jesus Band.

WOOD, Nancy   *C&W '81*
Singles: 7–inch
MONTAGE..................................... 3-4   81

WOODS, Gene   *C&W '60*
Singles: 7–inch
HAP...5-10   60

WOODY, Bill   *C&W '79*
Singles: 7–inch
MCA..3-5   79

WOOLERY, Chuck   *C&W '77*
Singles: 7–inch
EPIC 3-4   80
W.B...3-5   77

WOOLEY, Amy   *C&W '82*
Singles: 7–inch
MCA..3-4   81-82
LP: 10/12–inch 33rpm
MCA..5-10   81

WOOLEY, Sheb   *P&R '55/C&W '62*
Singles: 78rpm
BLUEBONNET...........................20-30   54
BULLET (603 "I Can't Live Without
  You")..25-50   45
MGM 5-15   48-57
Singles: 7–inch
BLUEBONNET (125 "Peepin' Thru the
  Keyhole") 30-60   54
BLUEBONNET (130 "Too Long with the
  Wrong Woman") 30-50   54

MGM (11000 series) 10-20   52-55
MGM (12000 series) 5-15   55-61
MGM (13000 series) 4-8   61-68
MGM (14000 series) 3-6   68-75
POLYDOR.................................... 3-4

Picture Sleeves
MGM 4-8   59-62

EPs: 7–inch 33/45rpm
MGM 10-20   56-58

LPs: 10/12–inch 33rpm
LAKESHORE (621-2-3 "Ben Colder and Sheb
   Wooley") 10-20   70s
MGM (3299 "Blue Guitar") 30-50   56
MGM (3904 "Days of
   Rawhide").............................. 20-25   56
MGM (4136 thru 4026).............. 15-20   61-62
MGM (4275 thru 4615)................ 8-15   65-69
   Also see COLDER, Ben

WOPAT, Tom   *C&W '86*
Singles: 7–inch
CAPITOL 3-4   88
EMI AMERICA 3-4   86-87
EMI MANHATTAN 3-4   87-88

WORK, Jimmy   *C&W '55*
Singles: 78rpm
DOT... 4-8   55
Singles: 7–inch
ALL.. 4-8   61
DOT.. 5-10   55

WORTH, Marion   *C&W '59*
Singles: 7–inch
CHEROKEE 5-10   59
COLUMBIA 4-8   60-67
DECCA... 3-6   67-70
GUYDEN...................................... 5-10   59-60
Picture Sleeves
COLUMBIA 3-5   61-62
LPs: 10/12–inch 33rpm
COLUMBIA 10-20   63-64
DECCA.. 8-12   67
   Also see MORGAN, George, & Marion Worth

WRAYS, The   *C&W '83*
(Wray Brothers Band)
Singles: 7–inch
CIS 3-4   83
MERCURY 3-4   86-87
SASPARILLA 3-4   85
   Also see RAYE, Collin

WREN, Larry   *C&W '77*
Singles: 7–inch
50 STATES..................................3-5   77

WRIGHT, B.J.   *C&W '78*
Singles: 7–inch
SOUNDWAVES 3-5   78-80

WRIGHT, Bobby   *C&W '67*
Singles: 7–inch
ABC...3-5   73-75
DECCA 3-6   67-73
U.A. 3-5   77-79
LP: 10/12–inch 33rpm
ABC...5-10   74
DECCA 8-12   71

WRIGHT, Curtis   *C&W '89*
Singles: 7–inch
AIRBORNE 3-4   89
   Also see GOSDIN, Vern
   Also see SUPER GRIT COWBOY BAND

WRIGHT, Ginny   *C&W '54*
(With Jim Reeves)
Singles: 78rpm
FABOR (101 "I Love You") 10-15   53
FABOR (130 "Please Leave My Darlin'
   Alone") 8-12   55
Singles: 7–inch
FABOR (101 "I Love You") 15-20   53
FABOR (130 "Please Leave My Darlin'
   Alone") 10-15   55
   Also see REEVES, Jim

WRIGHT, Ginny, & Tom Tall   *C&W '55*
Singles: 78rpm
FABOR (117 "Are You Mine").........5-8   54
Singles: 7–inch
FABOR (117 "Are You Mine")....10-15   54
ZERO (106 "Are You Mine") 5-10   60
   Also see TALL, Tom
   Also see WRIGHT, Ginny

WRIGHT, Johnny   *C&W '64*
Singles: 7–inch
DECCA 4-6   64-68
LP: 10/12–inch 33rpm
DECCA 10-20   65-68
RUBOCA.......................................5-8
   Also see JOHNNY & JACK
   Also see WELLS, Kitty, & Johnny Wright

WRIGHT, Justin   *C&W '89*
Singles: 7–inch
BEAR 3-4   89

WRIGHT, Lee   *C&W '78*
Singles: 7–inch
POMPEII 4-8   68
PRAIRIE DUST 3-5   78-85

WRIGHT, Michelle   *C&W '90*
Singles: 7–inch
ARISTA 3-4   90

WRIGHT, Randy   *C&W '83*
Singles: 7–inch
MCA 3-4   83-84
SKIDMORE (1001 "Fifty-Fifty") . 15-25
  Also see MANDRELL, Barbara
  Also see NIXON, Nick

WRIGHT, Ruby   *C&W '64*
Singles: 7–inch
EPIC 4-6   66-67
KAPP.. 4-6   66
RIC 4-8   64
LP: 10/12–inch 33rpm
KAPP.. 10-15   66

WRIGHT, Sonny   *C&W '77*
Singles: 7–inch
ATLANTIC 5-10   60
DOOR KNOB 3-5   77-80
KAPP.. 3-6   69
LP: 10/12–inch 33rpm
KAPP.. 10-15   69
  Also see PEGGY SUE & Sonny Wright

WRIGHT BROTHERS   *C&W '81*
Singles: 7–inch
AIRBORNE 3-4   88
MERCURY 3-4   84-85
W.B. 3-4   81-83

WYATT, Gene   *C&W '68*
Singles: 7–inch
EBB (123 "Love Fever") 50-75   57
LUCKY SEVEN (101 "Prettiest Girl at the
  Dance") 40-60   59
MERCURY 4-6   68
PAULA 4-6   68

WYATT, Nina   *C&W '88*
Singles: 7–inch
CHARTA 3-4   88

WYATT BROTHERS   *C&W '86*
Singles: 7–inch
WYATT 3-4   86

WYNETTE, Tammy   *C&W '66*
(With Ricky Skaggs; with Emmylou Harris)
Singles: 7–inch
EPIC (Except 1) 3-8   66-86
EPIC (1 "Wonders You
  Perform")................................5-10   70
  (Colored vinyl. Promotional issue only.)
Picture Sleeves
EPIC...3-4   69-76
LPs: 10/12–inch 33rpm
CBS..5-10
COLUMBIA (Except "EQ"
  series)....................................5-10   72-73
COLUMBIA (EQ-30658 "We Sure Can
  Love Each Other") 10-15   71
  (Quadraphonic.)
COLUMBIA HOUSE (5856 "Tammy
  Wynette")...............................25-35   73
  (Boxed 6-LP set.)
COLUMBIA SPECIAL
  PRODUCTS...............................5-8   77-82
EPIC..5-15   68-86
HARMONY.....................................5-10   70-71
REALM...8-10   76
TIME-LIFE......................................5-8   81
  Also see CASH, Johnny / Tammy Wynette
  Also see GRAY, Mark, & Tammy Wynette
  Also see HOUSTON, David, & Tammy Wynette
  Also see JONES, George, & Tammy Wynette
  Also see LYNN, Loretta / Tammy Wynette
  Also see NEWTON, Wayne, & Tammy Wynette

WYNETTE, Tammy, & Randy Travis   *C&W '91*
Singles: 7–inch
EPIC...3-4   91
  Also see TRAVIS, Randy
  Also see WYNETTE, Tammy

YANKOVIC, Frankie, & His Yanks   *C&W '48*
(With the Marlin Sisters)
Singles: 78rpm
COLUMBIA 3-6   44-49

YANKEE.................................... 5-10   32

YARBROUGH, Bob   *C&W '71*
(Bob Yarborough)
Singles: 7–inch
MUSIC MILL................................... 3-5   76
SUGAR HILL.................................. 3-5   71

YATES, Jenny   *C&W '87*
Singles: 7–inch
MERCURY 3-4   87

YATES, Lori   *C&W '88*
Singles: 7–inch
COLUMBIA 3-4   88-89

YOAKAM, Dwight   *C&W/LP '86*
Singles: 7–inch
OAK... 15-25   86
REPRISE 3-4   86-90
LPs: 10/12–inch 33rpm
OAK (2356 "Guitars, Cadillacs,
   Etc.") 500-750   84
REPRISE 5-8   86-90

YOAKAM, Dwight, & Buck Owens   *C&W '88*
Singles: 7–inch
REPRISE 3-4   88
   Also see OWENS, Buck
   Also see YOAKAM, Dwight

YOUNG, Cole   *C&W '83*
Singles: 7–inch
EVERGREEN............................... 3-4   83

YOUNG, Donny
Singles: 7–inch
DECCA (Except 31077) 10-15   61
DECCA (31077 "Shakin' the
   Blues")...................................... 20-25   60
MERCURY 5-10   61-62
TODD... 4-8   64
   Also see PAYCHECK, Johnny

YOUNG, Donny, & Roger Miller
Singles: 7–inch
DECCA (30763 "On This Mountain
   Top") 15-25   58
   Also see MILLER, Roger
   Also see YOUNG, Donny

YOUNG, Faron   *C&W '53*
(With Margie Singleton; with Anita Kerr
Singers; with Jordanaires)
Singles: 78rpm
CAPITOL.....................................5-10   53-57
Singles: 7–inch
CAPITOL (2200 thru 3900
   series)..5-10   53-58
CAPITOL (4000 thru 4800
   series)..4-8   58-62
MCA...3-5   79-80
MERCURY...................................3-6   63-78
Picture Sleeves
CAPITOL.....................................5-10   61
MERCURY...................................4-8   62-68
EPs: 7–inch 33/45rpm
CAPITOL.....................................8-15   54-61
REPERTORY (1 "And Now").....10-15
LPs: 10/12–inch 33rpm
ALBUM GLOBE 5-8   81
ALLEGIANCE 5-8   84
BULLDOG 5-10
CBS...5-8   83
CAPITOL (778 "Sweethearts Or
   Strangers")...............................30-50   57
CAPITOL (1004 "Object of My
   Affection") 30-50   58
CAPITOL (1096 "This Is Faron
   Young")...................................30-50   58
CAPITOL (1185 "My Garden of
   Prayer")..................................30-50   59
CAPITOL (1245 "Talk About
   Hits") 30-40   59
CAPITOL (1450 thru 2536)........12-25   60-66
   (With "T," "DT" or "ST" prefix.)
CAPITOL (1500 series) 5-8   75
   (With "SM" prefix.)
CASTLE......................................5-8
EXACT.......................................5-8   80
FARON YOUNG (001 "20 Great
   Hits") 10-20
FARON YOUNG (003 "Family
   Favorites") 10-15
FARON YOUNG (004 "Faron Young Presents
   the Country Deputies") 10-15
FARON YOUNG (4-22-82 "Fortunes in
   Music")......................................8-15   82
IMPACT 5-10
K-TEL..5-10   77
MCA...4-8   79-83
MARY CARTER PAINTS (1000 "Faron Young
   Sings on Stage").....................20-30

Official Price Guide to Country Music Records

(Promotional issue only.)

MERCURY 5-15   63-77
MOUNTAIN DEW........................ 5-10
PHONORAMA.............................. 5-8   82
PICADILLY.................................... 5-10   80
PICKWICK/HILLTOP 8-12   66-68
REALM.. 5-8   81
SEARS 8-12
TOWER...................................... 12-15   66-68
WING 8-12   68

Session: Don Adams; Jordanaires.
 Also see ADAMS, Don
 Also see ATKINS, Chet / Faron Young
 Also see CLEMENTS, Vassar
 Also see FRANKS, Tillman
 Also see JORDANAIRES
 Also see KERR, Anita
 Also see MORRIS, Lamar
 Also see NELSON, Willie / Faron Young
 Also see OWENS, Buck / Faron Young / Ferlin Husky

YOUNG, Faron / Carl Perkins / Claude King

LPs: 10/12–inch 33rpm

PICKWICK/HILLTOP 8-15   65

 Also see KING, Claude
 Also see PERKINS, Carl

YOUNG, Faron, & Margie Singleton   *C&W '64*

Singles: 7–inch

MERCURY 4-6   64

 Also see SINGLETON, Margie
 Also see YOUNG, Faron

YOUNG, Neil   *LP '69/C&W '85*
(With Crazy Horse; with Shocking Pinks; with Bluenotes)

Singles: 12–inch 33/45rpm

GEFFEN.. 4-6   86

Singles: 7–inch

GEFFEN.. 3-4   83-86
REPRISE (0785 thru 0898)........... 3-5   68-70
REPRISE (0911 thru 1396)........... 3-5   70-79
REPRISE (49000 series, except
 49895)..................................... 3-5   79-81
REPRISE (49895 "Southern
 Pacific")................................. 15-25   81
 (Picture triangle-shaped disc. Promotional
 issue only.)

Picture Sleeves

GEFFEN.. 3-4   83
REPRISE 3-4   78-81

EPs: 7–inch 33/45rpm

REPRISE 10-15   72
 (Jukebox issue only.)

LPs: 10/12–inch 33rpm

GEFFEN 5-8   83-87
REPRISE (2000 series, except 2257 &
 2296)..5-8   72-90
REPRISE (2257 "Decade")........12-15   77
REPRISE (2296 "Live Rust") 10-12   79
REPRISE (6317 "Neil Young")...40-50   68
 (Front cover does NOT have Neil Young's
 name.)
REPRISE (6317 "Neil Young").....8-12   68
 (Front cover shows Neil Young's name.)
REPRISE (6349 "Everybody Knows This Is
 Nowhere") 10-12   69
REPRISE (6383 "After the Gold
 Rush")..10-12   70
REPRISE (6480 "Journey Through the
 Past")..12-15   72
W.B. 5-10   72-79

Session: Waylon Jennings.
 Also see CROSBY, STILLS, NASH & YOUNG
 Also see HARRIS, Emmylou
 Also see JENNINGS, Waylon
 Also see LARSON, Nicolette
 Also see STILLS - YOUNG BAND

YOUNG, Neil, & Jim Messina

Singles: 7–inch

REPRISE 3-5   70

 Also see MESSINA, Jim

YOUNG, Neil, & Graham Nash   *P&R '72*

Singles: 7–inch

REPRISE 3-4   72

 Also see NASH, Graham
 Also see YOUNG, Neil

YOUNG, Roger   *C&W '79*

Singles: 7–inch

DESSA..3-5   79

YOUNG, Steve   *C&W '77*

Singles: 7–inch

RCA 3-5   76-78

LPs: 10/12–inch 33rpm

A&M 10-15   69
RCA 10-15   68

YOUNGER, James & Michael: see YOUNGER BROTHERS

YOUNGER BROTHERS   *C&W '82*
(James & Michael Younger)

Singles: 7–inch

AIR...3-4   86
MCA...3-4   82-83

PERMIAN 3-4   85
Members: James Younger; Michael Younger.

YOUNGER BROTHERS
BAND   *C&W '84*
Singles: 7–inch
ERP 3-4   86
Member: Terry Gehman.

Z

ZACA CREEK   *C&W '89*
Singles: 7–inch
COLUMBIA 3-4   89-90

ZADORA, Pia   *C&W '79*
(With the London Symphony Orchestra)
Singles: 12–inch 33/45rpm
MCA 4-6   83
Singles: 7–inch
CURB 3-4   83
ELEKTRA 3-4   82-83
MCA 3-4   83-84
W.B./CURB 3-4   78-80
LPs: 10/12–inch 33rpm
CBS ASSOCIATED 5-8   86
ELEKTRA 5-8   82
Also see JACKSON, Jermaine, & Pia Zadora
Also see LITTLE PIA

ZADORA, Pia, & Lou Christie
Singles: 7–inch
MIDSONG (72013 "Don't Knock
My Love") 15-20
Also see ZADORA, Pia

ZEILER, Gayle   *C&W '82*
Singles: 7–inch
EQUA 3-5   80-81
Also see ETHEL & SHAMELESS HUSSIES

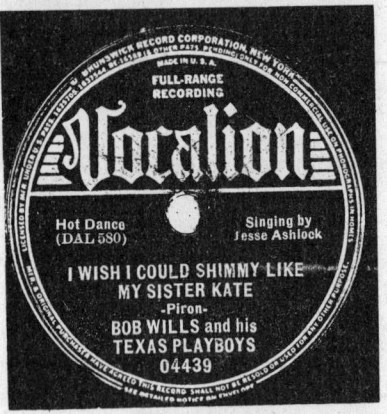

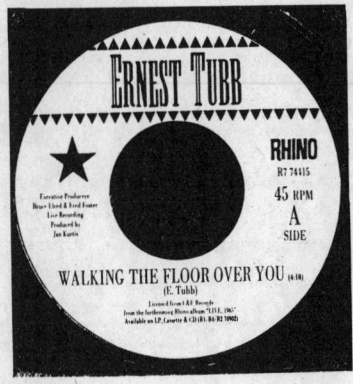

VARIOUS ARTISTS COMPILATIONS

6 Days on the Road - 6 Trucker Stars ....Hilltop (S) JS 6134   5-10   70s
    Dave Dudley; Johnny Dollar; Johnny Exit; Jim Nesbitt; Charlie Wiggs; Jimmy Gately.

10 Giant Country Hits - 10 Super Country Stars, Vol. 1.....MGM (S) SE-4920   5-10   73
    Hank Williams Jr.; Tompal and the Glaser Brothers; Billy Walker; Jeannie C. Riley; Mel
    Tillis & Sherry Bryce; Pat Boone and the First Nashville Jesus Band; Mel Tillis; Conway
    Twitty; Don Gibson; Sheb Wooley.

10 Great Country Hits, 10 Super Country Stars Vol. 1, ... MGM (M) SE-4920   5-10   72
    Hank Williams Jr.; Tompall and the Glaser Brothers; Billy Walker; Jeannie C. Riley; Mel
    Tillis & Sherry Bryce; Mel Tillis and the Statesiders; Pat Boone and the First Nashville
    Jesus Band; Conway Twitty; Don Gibson; Sheb Wooley.

10 Giant Country Hits - 10 Super Country Stars, Vol. 2.....MGM (S) SE-4921   5-10 . 72

10 Giant Country Hits - 10 Super Country Stars, Vol. 3.....MGM (S) SE-4922   5-10   72

10 Giant Country Hits - 10 Super Country Stars, Vol. 4.....MGM (S) SE-4923   5-10   72

12 Great Country Hits 12 Great Country Artists...... Showcase (S) CPR-9007   8-12
    Webb Pierce; Ferlin Husky; Patsy Cline; George Jones; Cowboy Copas; Carl Belew; Hank
    Locklin; Jimmy Dean; Justin Tubb; T. Texas Tyler; Red Sovine; Slim Willet.

12 Great Country Hits 12 Great Country Artists................ Hilltop (S) JS-6000   8-12   60s
    Patsy Cline; Carl Belew; Hank Locklin; Ferlin Husky; Justin Tubb; Webb Pierce; Slim
    Willet; George Jones; T. Texas Tyler; Cowboy Copas; Red Sovine; Jimmy Dean.

12 String Story ....Horizon (M) WP-1626   10-20   63

12 String Story .... Horizon (S) ST-1626   15-25   63
    Glen Campbell; Joe Maphis; Bob Gibson; others.

12 String Story, Vol. 2 ....Horizon (M) WP-1635   15-25   63

12 String Story, Vol. 2 .... Horizon (S) ST-1635   25-35   63
    James McGuinn; Glenn Campbell; Billy Strange; Frank Hamilton; Dick Rosmini; Tommy
    Tedesco; Joe Maphis; Mason Williams; Jim Helms; Howard Roberts; Fred Gerlack.

14 No. 1 Country Hits..RCA (S) AHL1-7004   5-10   85
    Dolly Parton; Sylvia; Earl Thomas Conley; Alabama; Waylon Jennings; Steve Wariner;
    Ronnie Milsap; Razzy Bailey; Jerry Reed; Eddy Raven; Charley Pride.

15 Country Greats............................ Columbia Musical Treasury (S) DS 556   5-10   60s
    Marty Robbins; Jimmy Dean; Tammy Wynette; Bob Luman; Van Trevor; Johnny Cash;
    Judy Lynn; George Morgan; David Houston; Terry White; Melba Montgomery; Hank
    Locklin; George Jones; Johnny Horton; Stonewall Jackson.

15 Country Hits & 15 Country Stars ....Hilltop (SE) JS-6064   5-10   60s
    Glen Campbell; Hank Locklin; Patsy Cline; Ferlin Husky; Wynn Stewart; Johnny Horton;
    Dave Dudley; Jerry Smith; Jimmy Dean; Charlie Ryan; Steweart Hambln; Hal Willis;
    Stewart Family; Webb Pierce; Floyd Cramer.

15 Great Country Artists, 15 Great Country
   Hits .... Pickwick Special Products (M) RMP 0101   10-20   68
    T. Texas Tyler; Stuart Hamblen; Patsy Cline; Floyd Tillman; Charli Ryan; Carl Belew; Hank
    Locklin; Slim Willet; Jimmy Dean; Johnny Cash; Sonny James; Ferlin Husky; Floyd
    Cramer; Dave Dudley; Maddox Bros & Rose.

15th Anniversary Country Music Awards............................. Ronco (S) 3220   5-10   80
    Mickey Gilley; Statler Brothers; Tanya Tucker; Cal Smith; Freddy Weller; Barbara Mandrell;
    Roger Miller; John Conlee; Charlie Rich; Linda Ronstadt; Ray Price; Donna Fargo; Freddy
    Fender; Tammy Wynette; Merle Haggard.

15th Annual Academy of Country Music Awards.......Columbia (ST) P-15419   5-10   80
    (Special products release for Ronco.) Mickey Gilley; Statler Brothers; Tanya Tucker; Cal
    Smith; Freddy Weller; Barbara Mandrell; Roger Miller; John Conlee; Charlie Rich; Linda
    Ronstadt; Johnny Paycheck; Ray Price; Donna Fargo; Freddy Fender; Tammy Wynette;
    Merle Haggard.

16 Country Gospel Hits... Everest (SE) CML 5   8-12   80
    Roy Acuff; T. Texas Tyler; Patsy Cline; Miller Family; Carl Story; Texas Jim Robertson;
    Maddox Brothers & Rose; Texas Jim Robertson.

16 Fiddler's Greatest Hits..Gusto (S) SD-3014   5-10   77
    Scotty Stoneman; Howdy Forrester; Chubby Wise; Buck Ryan; Buddy Spicher; Shorty
    Lavender; Ken Clark; Harry Choates; Mac Magaha; Benny Martin; Fiddlin' Arthur Smith;
    Curly Fox; Jerry Rivers; Fiddlin' Red Herron; Joe "Red" Hayes; Tommy Jackson.

16 Greatest Country Hits...Trip (S) TOP-16-26   5-10   76
   Sammi Smith; Ronnie Milsap; Buck Owens; Patsy Cline; George Jones; Orville Couch;
   Dave Dudley; Henson Cargill; Roger Miller; B.J. Thomas; Rex Allen; Melba Montgomery;
   Roy Drusky; Harold Dorman; Tex Ritter.
16 Greatest Truck Driver Hits ....Gusto (S) SD-3024   5-10   78
   Claude Gray; Willis Brothers; Red Sovine; Pete Drake; Jimmy Martin; Stanley Brothers;
   Charlie Moore; Hylo Brown; Del Reeves; Reno & Smiley; Slim Jacobs; Bobby Sykes;
   Moore & Napier; Coleman Wilson; Benny Martin; Tommy Hill Music Festival.
18 King-Size Country Hits .... Columbia (M) CL-2668   10-20   67
18 King-Size Country Hits... Columbia (S) CS-9468   10-20   67
   Cowboy Copas; Grandpa Jones; Stanley Brothers; others.
19 Hot Country Requests.. Epic (M) FE-39597   5-10   84
   Merle Haggard; Mickey Gilley; Willie Nelson; Ricky Skaggs; George Jones; B.J. Thomas;
   David Allan Coe; Merle Haggard & Willie Nelson; George Jones; Janie Fricke; Ronnie
   McDowell; B.J. Thomas; Mickey Gilley & Charly McClain; Larry Gatlin & the Gatlin
   Brothers.
19 Hot Country Requests, Vol. 2....................................... Epic (M) FE-40175   5-10   85
   Ricky Skaggs; Merle Haggard; Exile; George Jones; Willie Nelson; B.J. Thomas; Ronnie
   McDowell; Charly McClain; Crystal Gayle; Lacy J. Dalton; David Allan Cole; Johnny
   Rodriguez; Janie Fricke; Mickey Gilley; Rosanne Cash.
20 All Star Country Hits (2 LP) .... RCA (S) R 214225   8-12   77
   Ronnie Milsap; Dottsy; Floyd Cramer; Dickey Lee; Chet Atkins; Eddy Arnold; Bobby Bare;
   Dave & Sugar; Vernon Oxford; Willie Nelson; Jim Reeves; Billy Walker; Jim Brown & Helen
   Cornelius; Gary Stewart; Danny Davis; Charley Pride; Hank Snow; Jerry Reed; Dottie West;
   Charlie Rich.
20 Big Country Artists - 27 Hits (2 LP) ....GRT (S) 2103-704   8-12   74
   Johnny Cash; Charlie Rich; Jeannie C. Riley; Bill Justis; Carl Perkins; Roy Orbison; Jerry
   Lee Lewis; Donna Fargo; Johnny Tillotson; Mel Street; Ferlin Husky; Roy Clark; Jan
   Howard; Hagers; Lefty Frizzell; Bobby G. Rice; Johnny Carver; Stonewall Jackson; Ray
   Stevens; Billy Crash Craddock.
20 Famous Country Hits .... Crystal (S) CR 1400   5-10 ·
   Johnny Cash; George Jones; Henson Cargill; Patsy Cline; Conway Twitty; Ray Charles;
   Loretta Lynn; Bill Anderson; Lefty Frizzell; Hank Williams; Red Foley; Jack Greene; Kitty
   Wells; Jimmy Rodgers; Buck Owens; Ernest Tubb; Johnny Bond.
20 Famous Country Hits, Vol. 4 .... K-Tel (S) WV 320   5-10
   Johnny Cash; George Jones; Henson Cargill; Patsy Cline; Conway Twitty; Ray Charles;
   Loretta Lynn; Bill Anderson; Lefty Frizzell; Hank Williams; Red Foley; Johnny Bond; Jack
   Greene; Kitty Wells; Jimmy Rodgers; Buck Owens; Ernest Tubb.
20 Golden Souvenirs Of Music City USA, Vol. 2........Plantation (S) PLP-533   5-10   78
   (Green vinyl.) Johnny Cash; Jerry Lee Lewis; Rita Remington; Jeannie C. Riley; Leroy Van
   Dyke; Charlie Rich; Jimmy C. Newman; Hank Locklin; Charlie Walker; John Wesley Ryles;
   Willie Nelson; Dave Dudley; David Allan Coe; Jeannie C. Riley; James O'Gwynn; Murry
   Kellum; Gordon Terry; Paul Martin; Rufus Thibodeaux; Rex Allen Jr.; Jimmy Davis.
20 Great Hits - Country Sounds,
   Vol. 1 ....Ronco/Columbia Special Products (S) CS1-1001   5-10   72
   Sammi Smith; Tommy Overstreet; George Jones; Tammy Wynette; Henson Cargill; Lynn
   Anderson; Faron Young; Roy Drusky; Marty Robbins; Dave Dudley; David Houston;
   Johnny Cash; Roger Miller; Tom T. Hall; Statler Brothers; Jeannie Seely; Ray Price; Hank
   Thompson; Roy Clark.
20 Original Country Classics..................................... Mercury (S) MERC 301   5-10   73
   Tom T. Hall; Faron Young; Jerry Lee Lewis; Dave Dudley; Roger Miller; Roy Druskey;
   Statler Brothers.
20 Years of Hits.. Acuff-Rose (M) 102   15-25   68
   (Promotional issue only.) Jim Reeves; Carl Smith; Eddy Arnold; Pee Wee King; Don
   Gibson; Ernest Ashworth; Rusty & Doug; George Morgan; Marvin Rainwater; Marty
   Robbins.
20 Years of Hits.. Acuff-Rose (M) 106   15-25   68
   (Promotional issue only.)
21 Great Stars Sing the All Time Gospel
   Hits ....RCA Special Products (S) DVL-1-0421   5-10   79
   Dolly Parton; Jim Reeves; Webb Pierce; Tammy Wynette; Red Foley; Jimmy Davis; Charley
   Pride; Ray Price; Ernie Ford; Eddy Arnold; Carl Smith; Hank Snow; Connie Smith; Ernest
   Tubb; Kitty Wells; Porter Wagoner; George Jones; David Houston; Hank Williams; Johnny
   Cash.

22 Greatest Hit Folk
Songs ....Vanguard SPV-8/Columbia Musical Treasury (S) 1P 6015   8-12   73
Weavers; Joan Baez; Rooftop Singers; Buffy Sainte-Marie; Phil Ochs; Mimi & Richard
Farina; Ian & Sylvia; Country Gentlemen; Leon Bibb; Pete Seeger; Johnny Cash; Brothers
Four; Burl Ives; Leonard Cohen; Byrds; Mahalia Jackson; Carter Family; Flatt & Scruggs;
New Christy Minstrels.

22 High Ballin' Hits ....GRT (S) 2103-709   5-10   76
Red Sovine; Webb Pierce; Connie Eaton; Dave Peel; Johnny Dollar; Jim Gately; Roger
Miller; Dave Dudley; Conway Twitty; Roy Drusky; Bob Wills; Jimmy Dean; Jack Reno;
Michael Parks; Ray Pillow; Henson Cargill; Kitty Wells; Jim Nesbit; Hank Williams; Johnny
Exit; Tom T. Hall; Bobby Edwards; Clay Hart.

24 Country & Western Greats, Vol. 6...................................K-Tel (S) WU 321   5-10   72
Anne Murray; Glen Campbell; Sonny James; Ferlin Husky; Faron Young; Hank Thompson;
Roy Clark; Burl Ives; Loretta Lynn; Jeannie C. Riley; Hank Williams, Jr.; Patsy Cline;
Wanda Jackson; Kitty Wells; Bill Anderson; Bobby Helms; Red Foley; Mel Tillis; Johnny
Cash; Webb Pierce.

24 Great Truck Drivin' Songs..K-Tel (S) 3320   5-10   76
C.W. McCall; Dave Dudley; Hank Snow; Johnny Dollar; Willis Brothers; Bill Carlisle;
Connie Eaton & Dave Peel; Roy Drusky; Johnny Paycheck; Roger Miller; Porter Wagoner;
Johnny Horton; Carl Smith; Jim Nesbitt; Lavon Lyle; Jim & Jesse; Stoney Cooper & Wilma
Lee; Red Sovine.

24 Karat Gold From the Country (2 LP) ....MGM (S) SE-241-2   8-12   70s
Hank Williams; Arthur Smith; Conway Twitty; Johnny Tillotson; Marvin Rainwater; Roy
Acuff; Ben Colder; Jimmy Newman; Merle Kilgore; Osborne Brothers; Carson Robinson;
Tompall & the Glaser Brothers; Sheb Wooley.

25 Country Music Greats ....Starday (M) CMG-1   10-20   70s
Johnny Cash; Buck Owens; Cowboy Copas; George Jones; Moon Mullican; Hank Locklin;
Floyd Tillman; Dottie West; Patsy Cline; Webb Pierce; Tommy Hill; Blue Sky Boys; Justin
Tubb; Rex Allen; Jimmy Dean; Pee Wee King; Roger Miller; Willis Brothers; Smiley
Burnette; Joe Maphis; Johnny Bond; Roy Drusky; Pete Drake; Blue Boys; Lonzo & Oscar.

25 Country Music Greats, 2rd Anniversary Album......Homestead (S) AC 1-2   8-12
Johnny Cash; Buck Owens; Cowboy Copas; George Jones; Moon Mullican; Hank Locklin;
Floyd Tillman; Dottie West; Patsy Cline; Webb Pierce; Tommy Hill; Blue Sky Boys; Justin
Tubb; Rex Allen; Jimmy Dean; Pee Wee King; Roger Miller; Willis Brothers; Smiley
Burnette; Joe Maphis; Johnny Bond; Roy Drusky; Pete Drake; Blue Boys; Lonzo & Oscar.

25 Country Music Greats, 3rd Anniversary Album......Homestead (S) AC 1-2   8-12
Archie Campbell; Moon Mullican; Cowboy Copas; Roger Miller; Justin Tubb; Guy Mitchell;
Patsy Cline; Charley Walker; Webb Pierce; Pee Wee King; Jimmy Dean; Buck Owens;
George Morgan; Willis Brothers; Johnny Bond; Minnie Pearl; Carl Story; George Jones;
Sonny James; Dave Dudley; Stoneman Family; Stanley Brothers; Dottie West; Leon
McAuliffe; Red Sovine.

25 Golden Years - 25 Golden
Hits (2 LP) ....Lowery Group (S) No Number Used   25-35   71
(Promotional issue only.) Beatles; Lynn Anderson; Friend & Lover; Billy Joe Royal; Deep
Purple; Dennis Yost and the Classics IV; others.

25 Golden Years in Lowrey Country (2 LP) ....Lowery Group (S) LG-1   50-60   80
(Promotional issue only.) Elvis Presley; Sonny James; Hank Snow; Gene Vincent; Red
Foley & Kitty Wells; Wilburn Brothers; Jimmy Dean; Bill Lowery and the Smith Brothers;
Leroy Van Dyke; Ray Stevens; Brenda Lee; Johnny Cash; Porter Wagoner; Joe South;
Freddy Weller; Billy Joe Royal; Lynn Anderson; Sandy Posey; Roy Drusky; Dickey Lee.

25 Great Country Artists...Artistic (M) 711   8-12
Patsy Cline; Jimmy Dean; Wynn Stewart; Hank Locklin; Cowboy Copas & Johnny Bond;
Moon Mullican; George Jones; Arthur "Guitar" Smith; Eddie Dean; Webb Pierce; Jerry
Wallace; Archie Campbell; Hylo Brown; Red Sovine; Jan Howard; Sunshine Boys;
Stringbean; Carl Story; Willis Brothers; Justin Tubb; Lonesome Pine Fiddlers; Tommy Hill;
Leon Payne; Bobby Austin.

25 Great Country Artists.................Country Music Association (S) CMA 712   8-12   77
Roy Acuff; Bill Anderson; Eddy Arnold; Bobby Bare; Johnny Bond; Johnny Cash; Patsy
Cline; Dave Dudley; Red Foley; Lefty Frizzell; Don Gibson; Pee Wee King; Roger Miller;
George Morgan; Buck Owens; Ray Price; Jim Reeves; Tex Ritter; Marty Robbins; Hank
Snow; Hank Thompson; Merle Travis; Ernest Tubb; Kitty Wells; Hank Williams.

25 Great Country Stars and Hits..................................Pickwick (S) PTP-2085   8-12

George Jones; Patsy Cline; Johnny Cash; Carl Belew; Dave Dudley; Merle Kilgore; Jimmy Dean; Roy Drusky; Del Wood; Bobby Bare; Anita Carter; T. Texas Tyler; Sue Thompson; Maddox Brothers & Rose; Roger Miller; Rusty Draper; Faron Young; Leroy Van Dyke; Conway Twitty; Webb Pierce; Charlie Rich; Ferlin Husky; Hank Locklin; Rex Allen; Jan Howard.

25 Great Country Music Artists ....Country Hall of Fame (S) CMA 712   8-12

Roy Acuff; Bill Anderson; Eddy Arnold; Bobby Bare; Johnny Bond; Johnny Cash; Patsy Cline; Dave Dudley; Red Foley; Lefty Frizzell; Don Gibson; Pee Wee King; Roger Miller; George Morgan; Buck Owens; Ray Price; Jim Reeves; Tex Ritter; Marty Robbins; Hank Snow; Hank Thompson; Merle Travis; Ernest Tubb; Kitty Wells; Hank Williams.

25 Years of Country and Western Sacred Songs ....King (M) 807   20-30   63

25 Years of Country and Western Sacred Songs ....King (S) 807   20-30   63

Don Reno & Red Smiley; Cowboy Copas; T. Texas Tyler; Parker Family; others.

30 Golden Country Hits (2 LP)............RCA Special Products (S) DVL2-0447   8-12   80

(Mail order offer.) Hank Locklin; Connie Smith; George Jones; Hank Thompson; Jimmie Rodgers; Dave Dudley; Bobby Bare; Hank Williams; Bobby Helms; Jim Reeves; Kitty Wells; Porter Wagoner; Stuart Hamblen; Carl Butler; Don Gibson; Hank Snow; Webb Pierce; Ernest Ashworth; Skeeter Davis; Johnny Cash; Faron Young; Bill Anderson; Roger Miller; George Hamilton IV; Ray Price; Wanda Jackson; Pee Wee King; Carl Smith; Browns.

30 Grand Ole Country & Western Favorites .... Syndicate (S) SCW-30   10-20   64

Patsy Cline; Wilburn Brothers; Faron Young; Hank Locklin; George Jones; Floyd Tillman; Jan Howard; Ferlin Husky; Charlie Ryan; Stuart Hamblen; Sonny James; Maddox Brothers & Rose; Dave Dudley; Wally Fowler; Floyd Cramer; Johnny Horton; Webb Pierce; Rex Allen; Carl Belew; Billy Grammer; Bobby Austin; Wynn Stewart; Del Reeves; Johnny Sea; Champ Butler; David Houston; Claude King; Johnny Cash; Melba Montgomery; T. Texas Tyler.

30 Great Hits By 30 Great Country

Artists: 30 X 30...........................Columbia Musical Treasury (S) DS 342   10-15   68

David Houston; Statler Brothers; Jimmy Dean; Claude King; Stonewall Jackson; Carl Smith; Mel Tillis; Don Gibson; Marty Robbins; Little Jimmy Dickens; Carl Butler & Pearl;. Tammy Wynette; Billy Walker; Johnny Bond; George Morgan; Jordanaires; Johnny Cash; Ray Price; Carter Family; Harden Trio; Johnny Horton; Lefty Frizzell; Norma Jean; Lester Flatt & Earl Scruggs; Marion Worth; Bobby Lord; Carl Perkins; Skeets McDonald; Roy Drusky; Hawkshaw Hawkins.

30 Great Hits by 30 Great Country

Artists, 30 X 30, Vol. 2................ Columbia Musical Treasury (S) DS 365   10-15   68

David Houston; Marty Robbins; Van Trevor; Ray Price; Patsy Cline; Johnny & June Carter; George Morgan; Johnny Dollar; Johnny Horton; Faron Young; Stonewall Jackson; George Jones; Sonny James; T. Texas Tyler; Gene Autry; Tammy Wynette; Carl Smith; Claude King; Charlie Walker; Ferlin Husky; Statler Brothers; Jimmy Dean; Floyd Tillman; Carter Family; Melba Montgomery; Merle Kilgore; Hank Locklin; Wynn Stewart; Webb Pierce; Lucille Starr.

30 Great Hits by 30 Great Country Artists (2 LP).......Columbia (S) P2S 5218   10-20   68

(Columbia Record Club issue.) David Houston; Statler Brothers; Jimmy Dean; Claude King; Stonewall Jackson; Carl Smith; Mel Tillis; Don Gibson; Marty Robbins; Little Jimmy Dickens; Carl Butler & Pearl;. Tammy Wynette; Billy Walker; Johny Bond; George Morgan; Jordanaires; Johnny Cash; Ray Price; Carter Family; Harden Trio; Johnny Horton; Lefty Frizzell; Norma Jean; Lester Flatt & Earl Scruggs; Marion Worth; Bobby Lord; Carl Perkins; Skeets McDonald; Roy Drusky; Hawkshaw Hawkins.

30 Great Hits by 30 Great Country

Artists, Vol. 2 .... Columbia Musical Treasury (S) P2S 5220   8-12   68

(Columbia Record Club issue.) David Houston; Marty Robbins; Van Trevor; Ray Price; Patsy Cline; Johnny Cash & June Carter; George Morgan; Johnny Dollar; Johnny Horton; Faron Young; Stonewall Jackson; George Jones; Sonny James; T. Texas Tyler; Gene Autry; Tammy Wynette; Carl Smith; Claude King; Charlie Walker; Ferlin Husky; Statler Brothers; Jimmy Dean; Floyd Tillman; Carter Family; Melba Montgomery; Merle Kilgore; Hank Locklin; Wynn Stewart; Webb Pierce; Lucille Starr.

30 Great Hits by 30 Great Country Artists,

Vol. 3 (2 LP) .... Columbia Musical Treasuries (M) D 408   8-12   68

Marty Robbins; Jimmy Dean; Tammy Wynette; Bob Luman; Van Trevor; Flatt & Scruggs; Patsy Cline; Johnny Cash; Charlie Walker; George Jones; Stonewall Jackson; Judy Lynn; George Morgan; Johnny Horton; Charlie Rich; David Houston; Terry White; Mel Tillis; Wynn Stewart; Carl Smith; Jan Howard; Ray Price; Hank Locklin; Melba Montgomery; Chuck Wagon Gang; T. Texas Tyler; Faron Young; Lew DeWitt; Ferlin Husky; Webb Pierce.

30 Years of Bluegrass (2 LP) .... Gusto/Lake Shore (M) GT-101   10-15   77
Stanley Brothers; Flatt & Scruggs; Reno & Smiley; Country Gentlemen; Hylo Brown; Tommy Jackson; Jim & Jesse; Bill Clifton; Mac Wiseman; Bill Emerson; Allen Shelton; Red Allen; New Grass; Revival; Kentucky Travelers; Grandpa Jones; Bill Harell; Jim Eanes; Stringbean; Stoneman Family; Charles Moore; Moore & Napier; Buzz Busby; Carl Story.

30 Years of No. 1 Country Hits (7 LP) .... Reader's Digest (S) RBA-215-A   40-50   86
(Boxed set. Mail order offer.) Elvis Presley; George Hamilton IV; Jack Greene; B.J. Thomas; John Conlee; Everly Brothers; Eddy Arnold; Red Foley; Merle Haggard; Loretta Lynn; Roy Clark; Faron Young; Roger Miller; Jean Shepard & Ferlin Husky; Statler Brothers; Crystal Gayle; Hank Williams, Jr.; Bill Anderson & Jan Howard; Donna Fargo; Glen Campbell; Red Sovine; Del Reeves; Ferlin Husky; Waylon Jennings & Willie Nelson; Jerry Lee Lewis; Johnny Cash; Kendalls; Jim Reeves; Conway Twitty; Sammi Smith; Dolly Parton; Bobby Goldsboro; Hank Snow; Patsy Cline; Waylon Jennings; Webb Pierce; Don Williams; Kitty Wells; Hank Williams; Charley Pride; Hawkshaw Hawkins; Ronnie Milsap; Don Gibson; Tom T. Hall; Connie Smith; Hank Locklin; Tennessee Ernie Ford; George Jones; Pee Wee King; Bill Anderson; Sonny James; Browns; Leroy Van Dyke; Linda Ronstadt; Jerry Reed; Red Sovine & Webb Pierce; Hank Thompson.

40 Great Folk Songs (4 LP) .... Vanguard/Radio Shack (S) RS 50-2031   15-25   74
Weavers; Lester Flatt & Earl Scruggs with the Foggy Mountain Boys; Odetta; Ian & Sylvia; John Hammond; Joan Baez; Jack Elliott; Ed McCurdy; Jose Feliciano; Patrick Sky; Cisco Houston; Jim Kweskin; Leon Bibb; Bob Gibson; Mike Seeger; Greenbriar Boys; Paul Robeson; Doc Watson; Arbors; Mississippi John Hurt; Sonny Terry & Brownie McGhee; Clara Ward; Ronnie Gilbert; Pete Seeger; Rooftop Singers; Reverend Gary Davis; John Lee Hooker; Staple Singers; Hedy West; Buffy Sainte-Marie; Babysitters. (Made for Radio Shack store sales.)

50 Beloved Songs of Faith (Album No. 1) ...... Reader's Digest (S) BMR3-100   5-8   89
Elvis Presley; Loretta Lynn; Porter Wagoner; Scott Singers; Guy & Ralna; Red Foley; Kate Smith; Pat Boone; Jim Reeves; Statler Brothers; Cristy Lane; Jack Halloran Male Chorus; Charley Pride; Norma Zimmer & Jim Roberts; Perry Como.

50 Beloved Songs of Faith (Album No. 2) ...... Reader's Digest (S) BMR3-100   5-8   89
Dolly Parton; Jimmy Dean; Doris Ackers; Hank Williams Jr.; Browns; Jimmy Davis; Johnson Family; George Beverly Shea; Eddy Arnold; Three Suns; Floyd Cramer; Don Hustad Chorale; Bill Gaither Trio; Oak Ridge Boys; Tennessee Ernie Ford.

50 Beloved Songs of Faith (Album No. 3) ...... Reader's Digest (S) BMR3-100   5-8   89
(Mail order offer.) Johnny Cash; Tammy Wynette & George Jones; Willie Nelson; Roy Rogers & Dale Evans; Carter Family; Roy Acuff; Marty Robbins; Jim Roberts; Burl Ives; Mike Curb Congregation; David Houston; Anita Kerr; Ray Price; Larry Gatlin; Wayne Newton; B.J. Thomas; George Jones; Anita Bryant; Jim Nabors; Mormon Tabernacle Choir. (Three individual LPs but sold as a set. We value the set at $15 to $25.)

50 Country Greats (3 LP) .... Starday (S) P3S-5292   10-20
(Boxed set.) Glen Campbell; George Jones; Dolly Parton; Guy Mitchell; Webb Pierce; June Stearns; Gene Martin; Clyde Moody; Lonzo & Oscar; Red Sovine; Bobby Sykes; Melba Montgomery; Dave Dudley; Pee Wee King; Red Stewart; Patsy Cline; Jimmie Skinner; Minnie Pearl; Willis Brothers; Justin Tubb; T. Texas Tyler; Johnny Horton; Lulu Belle & Scotty; Grandpa Jones; Roy Wiggins; George Morgan; Flatt & Scruggs; Archie Campbell; Boots Randolf; Jimmy Richardson; Wilf Carter; Stonemans; Hawkshaw Hawkins; Arthur "Guitar" Smith; Stanley Brothers; Leon McAuliffe; Johnny Bond; Dottie West; Wynn Stewart; Sonny James; Roger Miller; Jimmy Dean; Carl Story; Johnny Cash; Snooky Lanson; Charlie Walker; Buck Owens; Pete Drake; Pop Stoneman; Kenny Roberts; Cowboy Copas.

50 Stars! 50 Hits (2 LP) .... Homestead (SE) 0008   8-12
Glen Campbell; Dolly Parton; Guy Mitchell; Wynn Stewart; Snooky Lanson; Melba Montgomery; Moon Mullican; Homesteaders; Grandpa Jones; Stonemans; Ray King; Kenny Roberts; Red Sovine; Pee Wee King; Justin Tubb; Clyde Moody; George Riddle; Texas Ruby; Pop Stoneman; Jim & Jesse; Dottie West; Webb Pierce; Dave Dudley; Johnny Cash; Bobby Sykes; Carl Story; Jim Glaser; Hylo Brown; Warren Robb; Patsy Cline; Stanley Brothers; Merle Kilgore; Minnie Pearl; Buck Owens; George Jones; Willis Brothers; Arthur Smith; Tommy Hill; Flatt & Scruggs; Jimmie Skinner; Cowboy Copas; Jan Howard; T. Texas Tyler; Boots Randolf; Jimmy Richardson; Lulu Belle & Scotty; Archie Campbell; Jackie Phelps; Roger Miller; Johnny Bond; George Morgan.

50 Stars! 50 Hits of Country Music (2 LP)..................... Starday (M) CMS-1/4   10-15 60s
    Justin Tubb; Benny Martin; George Riddle; Pete Drake; Red Hayes; Stanley Brothers; Carl
    Story; Texas Ruby; Tommy Hill; Sunshine Boys; Frankie Miller; Sonny James; T. Texas
    Tyler; Red Sovine; Cowboy Copas; David Houston; Johnny Horton; Minnie Pearl; Pee Wee
    King; Redd Stewart; Betty Amos; Archie Campbell; Melba Montgomery; Del Reeves; Denny
    Roberts; Moon Mullican; Arthur (Guitar Boogie) Smith; Homesteaders; Buddy Starcher;
    Willis Brothers; Jimmy Dean; Roger Miller; Dottie West; Johnny Bond; Hylo Brown; Rose
    Lee Maphis; Howard Vokes; Clyde Moody; Jim & Jesse; Lulu Belle & Scotty; Duke of
    Paducah; Jackie Phelps.

50 Years of Country Music (2 LP)............................Camden (S) ADL2-0782   8-12   74
    Chet Atkins; Carter Family; Waylon Jennings; Skeeter Davis; Porter Wagoner; Don Gibson;
    Dottie West; Sons of the Pioneers; others.

50 Years of Hit Songs (2 LP) ....Camden (S) ADL2-0779   8-12   74
    Ames Brothers; Paul Anka; Allan Jones; Helen Morgan; Kay Starr; others.

55 Original Country Classics (4 LP).......................... RCA/Sessions (S) ????   10-20
    (Mail order offer.) Don Gibson; Johnny Cash; Jim Reeves; Eddy Arnold; Kitty Wells; Rex
    Allen; George Jones; Patsy Cline; Roy Clark; Red Foley; Ernest Ashworth; Ray Price;
    Sonny James; Jimmie Rodgers; Carl Perkins; Hank Williams; Loretta Lynn; Red Sovine &
    Webb Pierce; others. (Special products. Made for Sessions.)

60 Top of the Chart Hits, #1 Country (6 LP).................. Columbia (S) P 6682   20-30 77
    (Mail order offer.) Al Dexter; George Morgan; Hank Williams; Margaret Whiting & Jimmy
    Wakely; Lefty Frizzell; Ray Price; Everly Brothers; Sonny James; Carl Smith; Marty
    Robbins; George Jones; Johnny Horton; Faron Young; Stonewall Jackson; Leroy Van
    Dyke; Billy Walker; Carl Butler & Pearl; Claude King; Johnny Cash; Flatt & Scruggs; Jimmy
    Dean; David Houston; Tammy Wynette; Little Jimmy Dickens; Glen Campbell; Lynn
    Anderson; Hank Williams, Jr.; Donna Fargo; Barbara Fairchild; Mel Tillis; Tom T. Hall;
    George Jones & Tammy Wynette; Charlie Rich; Tanya Tucker; George Jones; Willie
    Nelson; Johnny Rodriguez; Freddy Fender; Johnny Duncan; B.J. Thomas.

60 Years of Country Music (2 LP)................................RCA (S) CPL2-4351   10-20 82
    Elvis Presley; Henry C. Gilliland & A.C. (Eck) Robertson; Vernon Dalhart; Jimmie Rodgers;
    Carter Family; Wilf Carter; Milton Brown and His Musical Brownies; Bill Boyd and His
    Cowboy Ramblers; Blue Sky Boys; Hackberry Ramblers; Bill Monroe and His Bluegrass
    Boys; Elton Britt; Sons of the Pioneers; Hank Snow; Don Gibson; Jim Reeves; Chet
    Atkins; Eddy Arnold; Jerry Reed; Charley Pride; Waylon Jennings; Dolly Parton; Ronnie
    Milsap; Alabama.

60 Years of Grand Ole Opry (2 LP) ....RCA (S) CPL2-9507   10-20 86
    Uncle Dave Macon; Crook Brothers; DeFord Bailey; Paul Warmack & Gully Jumpers;
    Theron Hale & Daughters; Vagabonds; Asher Sizemore & Little Jimmie; Bradley Kincaid;
    Delmore Brothers with Fiddlin' Arthur Smith; Bill Monroe; Ernest Tubb; Eddy Arnold; Pee
    Wee King; Willis Brothers; Johnnie & Jack with Kitty Wells; Del Wood; Minnie Pearl &
    Grandpa Jones; Chet Atkins & Hank Snow; Jordanaires; Don Gibson; Hank Locklin; Jim
    Reeves & Dottie West; Porter Wagoner; Browns; Billy Walker; Connie Smith; Justin Tubb;
    George Hamilton IV; Bobby Bare & Skeeter Davis; Archie Campbell; Lester Flatt; Willie
    Nelson; Dolly Parton; Ronnie Milsap; Osborne Brothers.

100 All Time Country Hall of Fame Hits, Vol. 1 (2 LP) ...... TVP (S) TVP-1017   10-15 77
    Patsy Cline; Bobby Helms; Jan Howard; Jack Greene; Burl Ives; Conway Twitty; Johnny
    Wright; Bill Anderson; Kitty Wells; Red Sovine; Henson Cargill; B.J. Thomas; Sammi
    Smith; Ronnie Milsap; Orville Couch; Dave Dudley; Roger Miller; George Jones; Rex Allen;
    George Jones & Melsba Montgomery; Roy Drusky; Tex Ritter; Frankie Laine; Tex Williams;
    Jeanne Pruitt; Wilma Burgess; Bill Monroe; Ernest Tubb; Red Foley; Webb Pierce; Sons of
    the Pioneers; Brenda Lee; Billy Grammer; Hoosier Hot Shots; Buck Owens; Mac Davis.

100 All Time Country Hall of Fame Hits, Vol. 2 (2 LP) ...... TVP (S) TVP-1017   10-15 77
    Carl Belew; Sammi Smith; George Jones; Ronnie Milsap; B.J. Thomas; Henson Cargill;
    Jimmy Dean; Anita Bryant; Don Gibson; Tommy Cash; Tex Ritter; Mac Davis; Patsy Cline;
    Dave Dudley; Buck Owens; Nashville Singers; Roy Drusky; Jerry Wallace; Johnny Bond;
    Dorsey Burnette; Lonnie Mack; George Jones & Gene Pitney.

100 Proof Country .... Hilltop (S) JS-6176   8-12 60s
    George Jones; Statler Brothers; Tom T. Hall; Roger Miller; Flatt & Scruggs; Leroy Van
    Dyke; Roy Drusky.

All American Country (5 LP)..Sessions (S) OP 5506   20-25   84
    (Mail order offer. Boxed set.) Charly McClain; Willie Nelson; Merle Haggard; Janie Fricke;
    George Jones; Lacy J. Dalton; Gatlin Brothers; David Allen Coe; B.J. Thomas; Roseanne
    Cash; Waylon Jennings; Deborah Allen; Eieran Kane; Rex Allen Jr. & Margo Smith; Earl
    Thomas Conley; Judds; Razzy Bailey; Debby Boone; Jerry Lee Lewis; Johnny Lee; Whites;
    Vern Gosdin; Con Hunley; Bobby Goldsboro; Gail Davies; Conway Twitty; Eddie Rabbitt;
    Tompall & the Glaser Bros.; Mel Tillis; Sylvia; John Anderson; Ronnie Milsap; Donna
    Fargo; T.G. Sheppard; Emmylou Harris; Wright Brothers; Diana; Hank Williams Jr.; Crystal
    Gayle; Gary Morris; Eddy Raven; Statler Brothers; Reba McEntire; Bellamy Brothers; Karen
    Brooks; Susie Allanson; Steve Wariner.

All Night Sing.. Camden (M) CAL-767   5-10
    Blackwood Brothers; Speer Family; Original Carter Family; Statesmen Quartet; Porter
    Wagoner; Stuart Hamblen..

All Star All Time Folk Festival .... Camden (S) CAS-817   10-20   64
    Browns; Elton Britt; Limeliters; Browns; Buchanan Brothers; Jimmie Driftwood; Walter
    Forbes; Homer & Jethro; Raftsmen; Wayfarers; Windjammers.

All Star Country ....MGM (S) SE-4690   8-12   70
    Hank Williams; Hank Williams Jr.; Mel Tillis; Billy Walker; Sheb Wooley; Luke the Drifter;
    Luke the Drifter Jr.; Ben Colder; Tompall and the Glaser Brothers.

All Star Country .... Harmony (S) 11296   6-12   69
    Roy Acuff; Norma Jean; Johnny Cash; Marty Robbins; Carl Butler & Pearl; Lefty Frizzell;
    Stonewall Jackson; Ray Price.

All Star Country Christmas...Capitol (S) STBB-348   6-12   69
    Buck Owens; Glen Campbell; Tennessee Ernie Ford; Faron Young; Ferlin Husky; Sonny
    James; Tex Ritter; Roy Rogers & Dale Evans; Louvin Brothers.

All Star Country Hits ....MGM (S) SE-4787   6-12   71
    Conway Twitty; Billy Walker; Hank Williams; others.

All Star Country Music (8 LP).....................................Columbia (S) GSM-391   10-20   76

All Star Hootenanny ....Columbia (M) CL-2122   25-35   63

All Star Hootenanny ....Columbia (S) CS-8922   30-40   63
    Bob Dylan; Johnny Cash; New Christy Minstrels; Pete Seeger; Carolyn Hester; Flatt &
    Scruggs with Mother Maybelle Carter; Clancy Brothers & Tommy Makem; Leon Bibb; Oriel
    Smith; Brothers Four.

All Time Country and Western .... Decca (M) DL-4010   20-30   60

All Time Country and Western .... Decca (SE) DL7-4010   20-30   60
    Jimmie Davis; Ernest Tubb; Sons of the Pioneers; Red Foley; Bill Monroe; Webb Pierce;
    Kitty Wells; Goldie Hill; Justin Tubb; Bobby Helms; Patsy Cline.

All Time Country and Western, Vol. 2 .... Decca (M) DL-4090   20-25   61

All Time Country and Western, Vol. 2 .... Decca (SE) DL7-4090   20-25   61
    Jimmie Davis; Ernest Tubb; Kitty Wells; Webb Pierce; Red Foley; Bill Monroe; Warner
    Mack; Goldie Hill & Justin Tubb; Carl Belew; Tex Williams; Wilburn Brothers.

All Time Country and Western, Vol. 3 .... Decca (M) DL-4134   20-25   62

All Time Country and Western, Vol. 3 .... Decca (SE) DL7-4134   20-25   62
    Ernest Tubb; Kitty Wells; Webb Pierce; Red & Betty Foley; Bill Monroe; Bob Wills; T. Texas
    Tyler; Roy Acuff & Kitty Wells; Jimmie Davis; Jenny Lou Carson; Wilburn Brothers.

All Time Country and Western, Vol. 4 .... Decca (M) DL-4359   15-25   63

All Time Country and Western, Vol. 4 .... Decca (SE) DL7-4359   15-25   63
    Red Foley; Ernest Tubb; Kitty Wells; Webb Pierce; Loretta Lynn; Bill Monroe; Jimmy
    Martin; Patsy Cline; Jimmie Davis; Bill Anderson; Roy Drusky; Wilburn Brothers; Sons of
    the Pioneers.

All Time Country and Western, Vol. 5 .... Decca (M) DL-4549   15-25   64

All Time Country and Western, Vol. 5 .... Decca (SE) DL7-4549   15-25   64
    Rex Allen; Johnnie & Jack; Red Foley; Patsy Cline; Webb Pierce; Bobby Helms; Ernest
    Tubb; Bill Anderson; Jimmie Davis; Bill Monroe; Roy Drusky; Kitty Wells.

All Time Country and Western, Vol. 6 .... Decca (M) DL-4657   15-20   65

All Time Country and Western, Vol. 6 .... Decca (SE) DL7-4657   15-20   65
    Webb Pierce; Kitty Wells; Red Sovine; Goldie Hill; Loretta Lynn; Bill Anderson; Jimmie
    Davis; Patsy Cline; Kitty Wells & Red Foley; Bill Monroe; Wilburn Brothers; Red Foley;
    Ernest Tubb.

All Time Country and Western, Vol. 7 .... Decca (M) DL-4775   10-20   66

All Time Country and Western, Vol. 7 .... Decca (SE) DL7-4775   10-20   66
    Ernest Tubb; Kitty Wells; Webb Pierce; Roy Drusky; Loretta Lynn; Red & Betty Foley; Bill
    Monroe; Bob Wills; Patsy Cline; Jimmy Martin; Billy Grammer; Red Foley.

All Time Country and Western, Vol. 8 .... Decca (M) DL-????   10-20   67

All Time Country and Western, Vol. 8 .... Decca (S) DL7-????   10-20   67

All Time Country and Western, Vol. 9 .... Decca (S) DL-75025   10-20   68
     Loretta Lynn; Webb Pierce; Patsy Cline; Red Foley; Wilburn Brothers; Bill Monroe; Kitty
     Wells; Johnny Wright; Bill Anderson; Jimmy Martin; Jimmy Newman.

All Time Country and Western Hits .... King (M) 395-537   50-75   57

All Time Country and Western Hits .... King (M) 710   30-40   60
     Stanley Brothers; Webb Pierce; Hawkshaw Hawkins; others.

All Time Great Country and Western Songs .... Guest Star (M) G 1415   8-12
     Benny Martin; George Jones; Benny Barnes; Leon Payne; Red Sovine; Willis Brothers; Jim
     Glaser; Cowboy Copas; Moon Mullican; Frankie Miller; Benny Martin.

All Time Greatest Hits of Country
     Music (3 LP) .... RCA Special Products (S) DVL4-0629   15-20   83
     Johnny Cash; Sons of the Pioneers; Elton Britt; Roy Acuff; Hank Williams; Eddy Arnold;
     Jimmy Rodgers; Davis Sisters; Tex Ritter; Vaughn Monroe & the Quartet; Stuart Hamblen;
     Homer & Jethro; Chet Atkins; Pee Wee King & His Band featuring Redd Stewart; Porter
     Wagoner; Hank Snow; Don Gibson; Jim Reeves; Slim Whitman; Connie Smoth; Ernest
     Ashworth; Hank Locklin; Ferlin Husky; Red Sovine; Tennessee Ernie Ford; Jerry Reed;
     Hankshaw Hawkins; Bobby Bare; Sheb Wooley; Carlisles; Skeeter Davis; Browns; George
     Hamilton IV; Dottie West & the Jordanaires; Hank Thompson; George Jones; Barry Sadler;
     Sonny James; Moon Mullican.

All Time Hootenanny .... Decca (M) DL-4469   10-20   63

All Time Hootenanny .... Decca (S) DL 74469   15-25   63
     Weavers; Josh White; Bob Gibson; Tarriers; Oscar Brand; Bill Monroe; Tompall and the
     Glaser Brothers; Gateway Singers; Wilburn Brothers; Ivy League Trio; Sam Hinton;
     Richard Dyer-Bennett.

All Time Hootenanny Folk Favorites, Vol. 2 .... Decca (M) DL-4485   10-20   64

All Time Hootenanny Folk Favorites, Vol. 2 .... Decca (S) DL 74485   15-25   64
     Weavers; Josh White with Sonny Terry & Brownie McGhee; Bob Gibson; Oscar Brand;
     Gateway Singers; Bob Gibson; Tampall & the Glaser Brothers; Sam Hinton; Ivy League
     Trio; Bill Monroe & His Blue Grass Boys; Osborne Brothers; Tarriers; Wilburn Brothers.

Almost Persuaded .... Nashville (SE) NLP-2099   5-10   71
     Rose Maddox; Lois Williams; Dolly Parton; others.

America's Favorite Country and Western Stars .... Design (M) DLP-635   10-15   60s

America's Favorite Country and Western Stars .... Design (S) DLP-635   10-15   60s
     Johnny Horton; Frankie Miller; Jimmy Dean; Webb Pierce; Wilburn Brothers.

America's Greatest Country Stars Live and in Person ...... Harmony (M) 7414   8-15   67

America's Greatest Country Stars Live and in Person ..... Harmony (S) 11214   8-15   67
     Stonewall Jackson; Carl Smith; Johnny Cash; Billy Walker; Lefty Frizzell; Harold Bradley;
     Carl Butler & Pearl; Statler Brothers; June Carter.

American Banjo - Scruggs Style .... Folkways (M) FA 2314   10-20   60s
     Junie Scruggs; Joe Stewart; Snuffy Jenkins; Oren Jenkins; Eugene Cox; Veronica Cox;
     J.C. Sutphin; Larry Richardson; Don Bryant; Smiley Hobbs; Tom Morgan; Pete Roberts;
     Bob Baker & the Pike County Ramblers; Kenny Miller; Mike Seeger; Eric Weissberg; Ralph
     Rinzler.

American Christmas (From the Archives of Saturday Evening
     Post) (12 LP) .... Otis Conner Prod. (SP) 1A-12B   125-200   84
     (Boxed set. Includes programming inserts. Promotional issue only.) Elvis Presley; others.

American Country .... Capitol Creative Products (SP) SE-6900   8-12
     Tex Ritter; Sonny James; Glen Campbell; Anne Murray; Roy Rogers; Bobbie Gentry; Roy
     Acuff; Roy Clark; Ferlin Husky. (Made for American Motors Dealers.)

American Country Gold: see Country Music Cavalcade, American Country Gold

American Folk Singers and Balladeers (4 LP) .... Vanguard (SP) RL-5644   20-30   64
     (Boxed set. Mail order offer.) Joan Baez; Maybelle Carter; Lester Flatt & Earl Scruggs; Jack
     Elliott; Doc Watson; Sonny Terry & Brownie McGhee; others.

American - French Music of the Bayous of
     Louisiana .... Goldband (M) GR-7738   15-25   63
     Le Roy Broussard; Iry Le June; Linus Touchet; others.

Anthology of the 12 String Guitar .... Tradition/Everest (S) TR-2071   10-15   60s
     James McGuinn; Glen Campbell; Mason Williams; Bob Gibson; Howard Roberts; Joe
     Maphis; Billy Strange.

Army ROTC Presents "Country Line" .... No Label/Number Used   15-30   78
  Vernon Presley; Col. Tom Parker; Drifting Cowboys; Olivia Newton-John; Asleep at the
  Wheel; Bill Anderson; Jim Glaser; Merle Haggard; Johnny Paycheck; Ray Price Alumni;
  Vern Gosdin.
Around the Christmas Tree .... Decca (M) DL 38170   5-10   63
  Four Aces; Own Bradley Quintet; Dick Haymes; Columbus Boys Choir; Axel Stordahl & His
  Orchestra; Vincent Lopez & His Orchestra; Shulmerich Carillon Bells.
Award Winners .... RCA (S) APL1-2262   5-10   77
  Charley Pride; Chet Atkins; Dolly Parton; Dickey Lee; others.
Award Winners of the Country Music Association
  1968-1977 .... RCA (S) DPL 0305   5-10   78
  Glen Campbell; Johnny Cash; Merle Haggard; Sammi Smith; Charley Pride; Danny Davis;
  Ronnie Milsap; Freddy Fender; Dolly Parton; Crystal Gayle.
Backstage at the Grand Old Opry .... RCA (S) AHL1-4350   5-10   83
  Po' Folks; Roy Acuff; John Conlee; Dottie West; Osborne Brothers; Jimmy C. Newman;
  Connie Smith; Hank Snow; Boxcar Willie; B.J. Thomas; Bill Anderson. (From Nashville
  Network TV.)
Ballads and Songs .... Old Timey (M) LP-102   5-10
Banded Together .... Epic (S) JE 36177   5-10
  Johnny Cash; Willie Nelson; David Allan Coe; Johnny Paycheck; Charlie Daniels Band;
  Bobby Bare; George Jones.
Banded Together .... Columbia (S) ????   5-10
  Johnny Cash & Waylon Jennings; Willie Nelson; David Allan Coe; Johnny Paycheck;
  Charlie Daniels Band; Bobby Bare; George Jones & James Taylor.
Banjo (3 LP) .... Murray Hill (S) S-5395 X/3   12-20
  (Boxed set.) Jim McGuinn; Flatts & Scruggs; Eric Weissberg & Marshall Brickman; Dick
  Rossini; Mike Seeger; Pete Seeger; Joe Maphis; David Lindley; Erik Darling; Billy
  Cheatwood.
Banjo Bonanza (2 LP) .... Columbia Special Products (S) P-11890   8-12   74
Banjo Man .... Sire (S) SA-7527   12-18   77
  (Soundtrack.) Earl Scruggs; Jimmy Driftwood; Nitty Gritty Dirt Band; Doc & Merle Watson;
  Jack Elliot; Bob Dylan.
Banjo Story .... Horizon (M) WP-1623   10-20   64
Banjo Story .... Horizon (S) ST-1623   10-20   64
  Mason Williams; Joe Maphis; Mike Seeger; others.
Best of a Great Year, Vol. 1 .... RCA (M) LM 6074   5-10   72
  Jerry Reed; Eddy Arnold; Charley Pride; Porter Wagoner; others.
Best of a Great Year, Vol. 2 (2 LP) .... RCA (S) LSP-6088   8-12   72
  Charley Pride; Jim Ed Brown; Pat Daisy; Eddy Arnold; Hank Snow; Dolly Parton; Porter
  Wagoner; Chet Atkins; Dickey Lee; Skeeter Davis; Jerry Reed; Lester Flatt & Mac
  Wiseman; Dallas Frazier; Waylon Jennings; Nat Stuckey; Floyd Cramer; Dottie West;
  Kenny Price; Jim Reeves; Danny Davis & the Nashville Brass; George Hamilton IV; Connie
  Smith; George Jones.
Best of a Great Year, Vol. 3 (2 LP) .... RCA (S) CPL-2-0449   8-12   74
  Eddy Arnold; Chet Atkins; Dolly Parton; Connie Smith; Dottie West; Hank Snow; Charlie
  Rich; others.
Best of Bakersfield .... Capitol (S) ST-1111   5-10   72
  Buck Owens; Susan Raye; Freddie Hart; others.
Best of Bluegrass .... Wing (M) MGM-12267   10-15   60s
Best of Bluegrass .... Wing (S) SRW-16267   10-15   60s
  Jeffery Null & Denver Duke; Lew Childre; Benny Martin; Stanley Brothers; Carl Story & the
  Rambling Mountaineers; Flatt & Scruggs; Jimmie Skinner.
Best of Christmas .... RCA (S) CPL1-7013   5-10   85
  Elvis Presley; Dolly Parton; Willie Nelson; Alabama; Earl Thomas Conley; Waylon
  Jennings; Ronnie Milsap; Judds.
Best of Country .... MCP (S) 8009   5-10
  Sonny James; Roy Acuff; Jimmy Newman; Hawshaw Hawkins; Cowboy Copas; Don
  Gibson; Jimmy Dean.

Best of Country (4 LP)... Columbia (M) P4M-5061   15-20
Best of Country (4 LP)..Columbia (S) P4S-5062   15-20
(Boxed set.) Marty Robbins; Carl Smith; Ray Price; Johnny Bond; Al Dexter; Johnny Cash;
George Morgan; Claude King; Carl Perkins; Charlie Walker; Molly O'Day; David Houston;
Marion Worth; Floyd Tillman; Stonewall Jackson; Carl & Pearl Butler; Don Gibson; Statler
Brothers; Bob Atcher; Norma Jean; Carter Family; Billy Walker; Bob Wills; Bill Monroe;
Gene Autry; Bob Lord; Rose Maddox, Jimmy Dean; "Little" Jimmy Dickens; Flatt &
Scruggs; Johnny Norton; Hawkshaw Hawkins; Skeets McDonald; Chuck Wagon Gang.
Best of Country Comedy .... RCA (S) LSP-4126   10-20 68
Archie Campbell; Bob Corley; Don Bowman; Junior Samples; Dave Gardner; Homer &
Jethro; Fannie Flagg; Junior Samples & Archie Campbell.
Best of Country Crossovers, Vol. 1 .... Excelsior (S) XLP-88000   5-10 79
Kenny Rogers; Anne Murray; Bobby Goldsboro; Billie Jo Spears; Glen Campbell; Jessi
Colter; Crystal Gayle; Willie Nelson; Bobbie Gentry; Joe South; Linda Ronstadt; Asleep at
the Wheel.
Best of Country Music (2 LP) .... Capitol (S) SQB-91184   8-12
Buck Owens; Sonny James; Roy Clark; Jean Shepard; Hank Thompson; Ferlin Husky; Tex
Ritter; Wynn Stewart; Wanda Jackson; Charlie Louvin; Rose Maddox; Tommy Collins;
Leon McAuliffe; Glen Campbell; Faron Young; Bobby Durham; Mary Taylor; Ira Louvin;
Merle Travis; Neal Merritt; Ray Pillow; Mac Wiseman; Walter Hensley.
Best of Country Music .... Columbia Special Products (M) CS-243   8-12 66
Best of Country Music .... Columbia Special Products (S) CSP-243   10-15 66
Jimmy Dean; Ray Price; Collins Kids; Marion Worth; Stonewall Jackson; Carl Smith; Marty
Robbins; Johnny Cash; Lefty Frizzell; Bob Atcher; Little Jimmy Dickens; Carl Butler.
Best of Country Music, Vol. 7... K-Tel (S) WU 325   8-12 73
Susan Raye; Roy Clark; Leroy Van Dyke; Sonny James; Ned Miller; Patsy Cline; Kitty
Wells; Donna Fargo; Commander Cody; George Jones; Marvin Rainwater; Buck Owens;
Hank Williams; Webb Pierce; Johnny Paycheck; Wanda Jackson; Wynn Stewart; Johnny
Cash; Freddie Hart; Hank Thompson; LaWanda Lindsey.
Best of Grand Ole Opry................ Columbia Special Products (M) CSM 1047   8-12 60s
Marty Robbins; George Morgan; Lester Flatt & Earl Scruggs; Marion Worth; Jimmy Dean.
(Made for Shurfine Foods. Advertised in Life magazine.)
Best of the '50s.. RCA (S) AEL1-5800   8-12 86
Elvis Presley; Jim Reeves; Eddy Arnold; Hank Snow; Don Gibson; Porter Wagoner;
Browns; Pee Wee King; Hank Locklin.
Best of the '60s.. RCA (S) AEL1-5802   8-12 86
Elvis Presley; Jim Reeves; Eddy Arnold; Hank Snow; Jim Ed Brown; Hank Locklin; Charley
Pride; Skeeter Davis; Barry Sadler; George Hamilton IV.
Best of the '70s.. RCA (S) AEL1-5837   8-12 86
Elvis Presley; John Denver; Dolly Parton; Ronnie Milsap; Waylon & Willie; Jerry Reed;
Waylon Jennings; Charley Pride; Gary Stewart; Dave & Sugar.
Best of the '50s, '60s and '70s .... RCA (S) AEL1-5838   8-12 86
Elvis Presley; Eddy Arnold; Hank Snow; Don Gibson; Dolly Parton; Ronnie Milsap; Charley
Pride; Jerry Reed; Skeeter Davis.
Best of the Best.. Capitol (M) T-1654   15-25 62
Best of the Best...Capitol (S) ST-1654   20-30 62
Wanda Jackson; Hank Thompson; Faron Young; others.
Best of the Great Songs with a Folk-Country Accent: see Zenith Presents the Best of the Great
Songs with a Folk-Country Accent
Best of the Great Songs with a Folk-Country
Accent, Vol. 3 .... Capitol Creative Products (S) SL 6599   8-12
Glen Campbell; Ella Fitzgerald; Kingston Trio; Peggy Lee; Al Martino; Rod McKuen; Andy
Russell; Seekers; Jo Stafford; Kay Starr.
Best of Today's Country Hits (2 LP)................................. RCA (S) UPS-6017   8-12
Jim Reeves; Porter Wagoner; Dolly Parton; Don Gibson; Lynn Anderson; John Hartford;
Chet Atkins; Skeeter Davis; Hank Snow; Jim Ed Brown; George Hamilton IV; Jerry Reed;
Charley Pride; Connie Smith; Bobby Bare; Norma Jean; Jimmy Dean; Floyd Cramer; Dottie
West; Waylon Jennings; Hank Locklin; Liz Anderson; Leon Ashley.

Big Country (13 LP)...................................No Label Used (S) SH-3307   40-60
(Boxed set.) Glen Campbell; Bobbie Gentry; Sonny James; Merle Haggard & Bonnie
Owens; Jean Shepard; Tennessee Ernie Ford; Buck Owens; Wanda Jackson; Hank
Thompson; Tex Ritter; Roger Miller; Carlisles; George Jones; Johnny Horton; Benny
Barnes; Rusty Draper; Roy Drusky; Leroy Van Dyke; Jimmie Skinner; Faron Young Merle
Kilgore; Flatt & Scruggs; Country Road; Patsy Cline; Ferlin Husky; Dave Dudley; Stuart
Hamblen; T. Texas Tyler; Slim Willet; Jimmy Dean; Carl Belew; Texas Jim Robertson;
Floyd Tillman; Jan Howard; Hank Locklin.

Big Country (2 LP)..Mercury (S) SRP-2-605   10-20 60s
Roger Miller; Roy Drusky; Pete Drake; Anita Carter; Faron Young; Rex Allen; Dave Dudley;
Margie Singleton; George Jones; Mother Maybelle Carter; James O'Gwynn; Claude Gray;
Pricella Mitchell; Leroy Van Dyke; Johnny Sea; Lester Flatt & Earl Scruggs; Jimmie
Skinner; Tom T. Hall.

Big Country Hits, Vol. 1 ....RCA (M) LPM-3603   10-15 66
Big Country Hits, Vol. 1 ....RCA (S) LSP-3603   15-20 66
Jim Reeves; Don Gibson; Norma Jean; Connie Smith; Bobby Bare; Hank Snow; Chet
Atkins; Dottie West; Waylon Jennings; Bobby Bare & Skeeter Davis; Porter Wagoner;
Bobbi Staff.

Big Country Hits ....Pickwick (S) JS-6166   10-20 75
Elvis Presley; others.

Big Hit Country Songs..Alshire (S) 5169   5-10 70
Big Hits...Columbia (EP) B-13152   10-15 59
Big Hits...Columbia (EP) B-13531   10-15 59
Johnny Horton; Lefty Frizzell; Carl Perkins; Johnny Cash.

Big Hits...Columbia (M) CL-1353   20-30 59
Big Hits...Columbia (S) CS-8161   30-40 59
Johnny Horton; Lefty Frizzell; Carl Perkins; Johnny Cash; Ray Price; Charlie Walker;
Stonewall Jackson; George Morgan; Carl Smith; Freddie Hart.

Big Hits...Columbia (EP) B-2108   10-15 56
Big Hits...Columbia (M) CL-2574   25-35 56
Big John ....RCA Special Products (S) DPL1-0089   5-10 74
Eddie Bruce; Danny Davis; Eddy Arnold; Marilyn Maye; Kenny Price; Ragtimers; Don
Gibson; Dottie West; Floyd Cramer; Dickey Lee. (Made for John Deere Snowmobile.)

Big Sixteen Country and Western Favorites ....Musicor (M) MM-2076   10-20 66
Big Sixteen Country and Western Favorites ....Musicor (S) MS-3076   15-20 66
George Jones; Roger Miller; Melba Montgomery; Gene Pitney; others.

Big Train Express Railroad Songs—Country Style... Nashville (M) NLP 2019   10-15
Jim Glaser; Curly Fox; Rainbow Ranch Boys; Jimmy Williams; Red Ellis; Benny Martin;
Phipps Family; Stanley Brothers; Clinch Mountain Boys; Bill Clifton & Dixie Mountain
Boys; Country Gentlemen; Lew Childre; Howard Yokes; Moon Mullican; Lonesome Pine
Fiddlers.

Blue Ribbon Country (2 LP) ....Capitol (S) STBB-2969   10-15 69
Buck Owens; Sonny James; Bobbie Gentry; Johnny and Jonie Mosby; Wynn Stewart;
Merle Haggard; Glen Campbell; Jean Shepard; Dick Miles; Ferlin Husky; Tex Ritter; Bonnie
Owens; Wanda Jackson; Charlie Louvin; Chaparral Brothers.

Blue Ribbon Country, Vol. 2 (2 LP) ....Capitol (S) STBB-217   10-15 69
Glen Campbell; Merle Haggard; Wanda Jackson; others.

Blue Ribbon Country, Vol. 3 ....Capitol (S) SJA 7912   5-10 82
Jimmy C. Newman; Bobby Helms; Roy Drusky; Price Mitchell; Pee Wee King; Claude Grey;
Johnny Dollar; Kirk Hansard.

Blue Ridge Mountain Music ....Atlantic (M) 1347   25-35 60
Blue Ridge Mountain Music ....Atlantic (S) SD-1347   30-40 60
Bluegrass! ....Hilltop (S) PTP 2069-2   8-12
Flatt & Scruggs; Denver Duke; Jeffery Null; John Duffy & the Country Gentlemen; Jimmie
Skinner; Lew Childre; Benny Martin.

Bluegrass & Country By These Famous Artists.....Rural Rhythm (M) RR 155   8-12 60s
Wear Family; Ray Godfrey; Ernie Cook; Boys from Shioio; Autry Inman; Billy Carter;
Johnny Tyler.

Bluegrass for Collectors ....RCA (M) APM1-0568   8-12 74
J.E. Mainer and His Mountaineers; Bill Monroe's Bluegrass Boys; Charlie Monroe and the
Kentucky Pardners; Riley Puckett; Gid Tanner and His Skillet Lickers.

Bluegrass Hall of Fame.. Starday (M) S-181   15-25   62
Bluegrass Hall of Fame.. Starday (M) S-296   10-20   64
    Lester Flatt & Earl Scruggs; Hylo Brown; Stanley Brothers; others.
Bluegrass Oldies But Goodies .... Smash (M) MGS-27028   10-20   63
Bluegrass Oldies But Goodies .... Smash (S) SRS-67028   10-20   63
    Stanley Brothers; Carl Story; Hylo Brown; Red Allen; Stringbean; others.
Bluegrass Oldies But Goodies .... Cumberland (M) 29520   10-15   65
Bluegrass Oldies But Goodies .... Cumberland (S) 69520   10-15   65
    Stanley Brothers; Carl Story; Hylo Brown; Red Allen; Stringbean; others.
Bluegrass Sampler..Starday (M) SLP-183   15-25   62
Bluegrass Special .... Starday (M) S-115   15-25   60
Bluegrass Special .... Starday (S) SLP-115   15-25   60
Bluegrass Special ....World Pacific (S) 21898   8-12   69
    Folkswingers; Kentucky Colonels; Tut Taylor; others.
Bluegrass Spectactular .... Starday (M) S-232   15-20   63
Bluegrass Spectactular.. Starday (S) SLP-232   15-20   63
    Lester Flatt & Earl Scruggs; Carl Story; Stanley Brothers; others.
Bonanza of Country .... Hilltop (S) JS-6107   5-10
    George Jones; Leroy Van Dyke; Carlisles; Faron Young; Johnny Horton; Benny Barnes;
    Merle Kilgore; Rusty Draper; Jimmie Skinner.
Boogie Woogie Greatest Hits.. BW (M) 1000   5-10
    Pinetop Smith; Cripple Clarenc Lofton; Joe Sullivan; Meade Lux Lewis; Art Hodes; Louis
    Jordan; Red Nelson; Honey Hill; Pete Johnson; Albert Ammons; Bob Zurke; Freddie Slack.
Born to Be Country Boys...Share (S) JS-6104   5-10
Bright Lights & Country Music, Nashville
    Sound, Vol. 7......................... Columbia Musical Treasury (SE) 1P 6086   5-10   74
    Ray Price; Barbara Mandrell; Charlie Rich; Tanya Tucker; Freddy Weller; George Jones;
    Tammy Wynette; Mac Davis; Lynn Anderson; Johnny Cash. (Columbia House Record Club
    issue.)
Bright Lights and Honky Tonks .... Starday (M) S-239   15-20   63
Bright Lights and Honky Tonks .... Starday (S) SLP-239   15-20   63
Broken Heart for Every Guitar in Nashville ....????   5-10
    (Label and number not known.) Willie Nelson; Freddy Fender; Wilma Burgess; Jack Scott;
    B.J. Thomas; George Jones; Barbara Mandrell; Johnny "Piano" Wilson; Statler Brothers;
    Jack Greene.
Bronco Billy ....Elektra (ST) 5E-512   5-10   80
    (Soundtrack.) Ronnie Milsap; Penny DeHaven; Merle Haggard; Clint Eastwood; Reinsmen.
Bushel of Five String Banjos ....Pickwick (M) 6111   8-12
    Flatt & Scruggs; Stanley Brothers; Carl Story; Denver Duke; Jeffery Null.
Bushel of Top Country Hits! ....Design (M) DLP 642   10-15   60s
Bushel of Top Country Hits! ....Design (SE) SDLP 642   10-15   60s
    Ferlin Husky; Hank Locklin; Jan Howard; Del Reeves; Stewart Family; Larry Steele; Floyd
    Tillman; T. Texas Tyler; Hal Willis; Wilburn Brothers.
Bushel of Top Country Hits! ....Design (SE) GNPS-2152   10-15   60s
    Ferlin Husky; Hank Locklin; Jan Howard; Del Reeves; Stewart Family; Larry Steele; Floyd
    Tillman; T. Texas Tyler; Hal Willis; Wilburn Brothers.
Cajun Music - The Early '50s ....Arhoolie (M) 5008   8-12   69
    Shuk Richard and His Louisiana Aces; Texas Melody Boys; Floyd LeBlanc and His French
    Fiddle; Nathan Abshire; Lawrence Walker and His Wandering Aces; Elsie Deshotel and His
    Louisiana Rhythmaires; Amar DeVillier and His Louisiana Jambaleers; Wallace LaFleur;
    Sandy Austin; Harry Choates.
California Christmas..Capitol (S) ST-11226   5-10   73
    Buck Owens; Lawanda Lindsey; Buddy Alan; Susan Raye; Freddie Hart; others.
Capitol's Country Faith.. Capitol (S) SQ-91655   10-15   69
    Buck Owens; Sonny James; Ferlin Husky; Houle Lister & the Statemen Quartet; T. Texas
    Tyler; Louvin Brothers; Roy Acuff; Dale Evans; Jordanaires; Rose Maddox; Tennessee
    Ernie Ford. (Capitol Record Club issue.)
Capitol's Country Jamboree... Capitol (S) SQ-91654   10-15   69
    Sonny James; Glen Campbell; Wanda Jackson; Buck Owens; Merle Haggard; Charlie
    Louvin; Wynn Stewart; Ned Miller; Jody Miller; Ray Pillow; Bobby Austin; Jean Shepard;
    Ferlin Husky; Tex Ritter. (Capitol Record Club issue.)

CBS Salutes Country Music Month.............................Columbia (S) AS2535   5-10   86
    (Promotional issue only. Issued without cover.) George Jones; Ricky Skaggs; Exile; Charly
    McClain; Willie Nelson; John Conlee; Rosanne Cash; Willie Nelson, Johnny Cash, Waylon
    Jennings & Kris Kristofferson; Sweethearts of the Rodeo; Marty Stuart.
Christmas Country Style .... Capitol Creative Products (S) SL 6581   5-10
    Roy Rogers & Dale Evans; Ferlin Husky; Glen Campbell; Sonny James; Buck Owens;
    Louvin Brothers.
Christmas Greetings from Nashville........................Camden (S) ACL1-0256   5-10   73
    Eddy Arnold; Floyd Cramer; Porter Wagoner; others.
Christmas Greetings from Nashville..............................RCA (S) ANL1-1953   5-10   76
    Eddy Arnold; Chet Atkins; Dottie West; Floyd Cramer; Jim Reeves; Skeeter Davis; Hank
    Snow; others.
Christmas in the Country...Camden (S) ACL1-0256   5-10   73
    Blackwood Brothers Quartet; Anita Kerr Singers; Jim Reeves; others.
Christmas "The Johnny Cash Family".......................Columbia (S) KC 31754   8-12   72
    Johnny Cash; June Carter; Statler Brothers; Carter Family; Tommy Cash; Carl Perkins;
    Tennessee Three; Larry Butler.
Christmas Time...Vocalion (M) VL-3812   8-10   67
Christmas Time .... Vocalion (S) VL7-3812   8-10   67
    Loretta Lynn; Webb Pierce; Red Foley; Jimmie Davis; Kitty Wells; Ernest Tubb; Bobby
    Helms; Elton Britt; Maddox Brothers & Rose; Lonzo & Oscar.
Church in the Wildwood, Vol. 1 ....Capitol (EP) EPA-1-1113   5-10   59
Church in the Wildwood, Vol. 2 ....Capitol (EP) EPA-2-1113   5-10   59
Church in the Wildwood, Vol. 3 ....Capitol (EP) EPA-3-1113   5-10   59
Church in the Wildwood .... Capitol (M) T-1113   20-25   59
    Sonny James; Jordanaires; Tex Ritter; Tommy Collins; Statesmen; others.
Classic Country.. 4 Star (S) 4S-SP-105   5-10   77
    Jan Howard; Wynn Stewart; Johnny & Jonie; Carl Belew; George Morgan; Jimmy Elledge;
    Mary Ford; Billy Don Burns; Jeannie Seely; Betty Jean Robinson.
Classic Country Duets...MCA (S) 5599   5-10   85
    Don Williams & Emmylou Harris; Barbara Mandrell & Steve Wariner; Bill Anderson & Jan
    Howard; Jack Greene & Jeannie Seely; Loretta Lynn & Ernest Tubb; Barbara Mandrell &
    Lee Greenwood; Loretta Lynn & Conway Twitty; Kitty Wells & Roy Acuff; Kendalls; Merle
    Haggard & Leona Williams.
Classic Country Music (6 LP).......Smithsonian Institute/RCA (S) DML6-0914   35-50   90
    (Boxed set. Includes 85 page book. Made for BMG Direct Marketing record club.) Elvis
    Presley; Gid Tanner & His Skillet Lickers; Uncle Dave Macon & His Fruit Jar Drinkers;
    Bradley Kincaid; Vernon Dalhart; Carter Family; Jimmie Rodgers; Riley Puckett; Gene
    Autry & Jimmy Long; Shelton Brothers; Milton Brown & His Brownie; W. Lee O'Daniel &
    His Light Crust Doughboys with Leon Huff; Roy Acuff & His Crazy Tennesseeans; Bill
    Boyd & His Cowboy Ramblers; Patsy Montana & the Prairie Ramblers; Gene Autry; Sons of
    the Pioneers; Tex Ritter; Bob Wills & His Texas Playboys; Ernest Tubb; Ted Daffan's
    Texans; Jimmy Davis; Al Dexter & His Troopers; Elton Britt; Eddy Arnold; Roy Acuff & His
    Smoky Mountain Boys; Blue Sky Boys; Moon Mullican & His Showboys; Maddox Brothers
    & Rose; Merle Travis; Bill Monroe & His Blue Grass Boys; Lester Flatt & Earl Scruggs & the
    Foggy Mountain Boys; Floyd Tillman; Molly O'Day with the Cumberland Mountain Folks;
    Hank Snow & His Rainbow Ranch Boys; Jimmy Dickens; Pee Wee King & His Golden West
    Cowboys; Red Foley; Hank Williams; Lefty Frizzell; Hank Thompson & His Brazos Valley
    Boys; Kitty Wells; Webb Pierce; Chet Atkins; Eddy Arnold; Tennessee Ernie Ford; Everly
    Brothers; Jerry Lee Lewis; Sonny James; Johnny Cash; Ray Price Jim Reeves; Patsy
    Cline; Johnny Horton; Marty Robbins; Jimmy Dean; Louvin Brothers; Bobby Bare; George
    Jones & Melba Montgomery; Buck Owens; Faron Young; Bobbie Gentry; Roger Miller;
    Porter Wagoner; Willie Nelson; Glen Campbell; Osborne Brothers; Loretta Lynn; Dolly
    Parton; Johnny Cash; Tammy Wynette; Tom T. Hall; Charley Pride; Ray Price; Flying
    Burrito Brothers; Loretta Lynn & Conway Twitty; Kris Kristofferson; George Jones; Gram
    Parsons & Emmylou Harris; Waylon Jennings; Ronnie Milsap; Willie Nelson & Waylon
    Jennings; Rodney Crowell; Emmylou Harris; Charlie Daniels; Alabama; Hank Williams, Jr.;
    Ricky Skaggs; Dwight Yoakam; Bellamy Brothers; Dolly Parton; Judds.

Classic Country Music (8 LP)...................Smithsonian Institute (S) PB 15640   35-50   81
    (Boxed set. Includes 56 page booklet.) Eck Robertson; Fiddlin John Carson; Grayson &
    Whitter; Uncle Dave Macon; Vernon Dalhart; Charlie Poole; Gid Tanner & His Skillet
    Lickers; Smith's Sacred Singers; East Texas Serenaders; Darby & Tarlton; Buell Kazee;
    Bradley Kincaid; Carl Sprague; Ernest V. Stoneman; Carter Family Jimmy Rodgers; Arthur
    Smith; Riley Puckett; Cliff Carlisle; Coon Creek Girls; Mac and Bob; Callahan Brothers;
    Blue Sky Boys; Delmore Brothers; Monroe Brothers; Rouse Brothers; Red Foley; Karl &
    Harty; Lulu Belle & Scotty; J.E. Mainer's Mountaineers; Rex Griffin; Roy Acuff; Carter
    Family; Gene Autry & Jimmy Longs; Sons of the Pioneers; Patsy Montana; Montana Slim;
    Stuart Hamblen; Light Crust Doughboys with Leon Huff; Shelton Brothers; Jimmie Davis;
    Bill Boyd; Milton Brown & His Brownies; Bob Wills & His Texas Playboys; Leo Soileau;
    Woody Guthrie; Chuck Wagon Gang; Cliff Bruner's Texas Wanderers; Bob Wills & His
    Texas Playboys; Gene Autry; Ernest Tubb; Wiley Walker & Gene Sullivan; Ted Daffan's
    Texans; Elton Britt; Al Dexter; Tex Ritter; Molly O'Day; Jack Guthrie; Bailes Brothers; Roy
    Acuff; Merle Travis; Tex Ritter; Eddy Arnold; Tex Williams; Johnny & Jack; Jimmy
    Dickens; Maddox Brothers & Rose; Red Foley; Grandpa Jones; Cowboy Copas; Blue Sky
    Boys; Moon Mullican; Slim Whitman; Hank Snow; Leon Payne; Pee Wee King; Martha
    Carson; Floyd Tillman; Lefty Frizzell; Carl Smith; Hank Thompson; Kitty Wells; Wilma Lee
    & Stoney Cooper; Hank Williams; Webb Pierce; Johnny Cash; Tennessee Ernie Ford;
    Everly Brothers; Chet Atkins; Jim Reeves; Ray Price; Bobby Helms; Louvin Brothers;
    Johnny Horton; Marty Robbins; Rusty & Doug; Patsy Cline; Buck Owens; George Jones &
    Melba Montgomery; Bill Monroe & His Blue Grass Boys; Flatt & Scruggs; Stanley Brothers;
    Mac Wiseman; Jim & Jesse & the Virginia Boys; Osborne Brothers; Bill Clifton; Reno &
    Smiley; Lilly Brothers; Hylo Brown; Jimmy Martin; Kenny Baker; Doc Watson; Charlie
    Moore; Cliff Waldron & the New Shades of Grass; Country Gentlemen; Seldom Scene;
    Dave Dudley; Bobby Bare; Porter Wagoner; Roger Miller; Charley Pride; Tom T. Hall; Dolly
    Parton; Merle Haggard; Loretta Lynn; Tammy Wynette; Moe Bandy Flying Burrito Brothers;
    Willie Nelson.

Coming Home (2 LP) ....RCA (S) DVL2-0869   10-20   88
    (Mail order offer.) Elvis Presley; Dolly Parton; Hank Williams; Charley Pride; Wink
    Martindale; Jim Reeves; Johnny Cash; Kris Kristofferson; Original Carter Family; Porter
    Wagoner; Tom T. Hall; Cristy Lane; Red Foley; Willie Nelson; Walter Brennan; Ferlin
    Husky; Kitty Wells & Carol Sue; Roy Acuff; Marty Robbins; Molly O'Day; Merle Haggard;
    George Jones; Melba Montgomery; Tennessee Ernie Ford. (LPs packaged individaully but
    sold as a set.)

Cookin' with Country ....Hilltop (S) PTP 2074   8-12
    Glen Campbell; Bobbie Gentry; Sonny James; Tennessee Ernie Ford; Jean Shepard; Buck
    Owens; Roy Clark; Wanda Jackson; Hank Thompson; Tex Ritter; Patsy Cline; Hank
    Locklin; Wynn Stewart; Ferlin Husky; Johnny Horton; Dave Dudley; Jerry Smith; Jimmy
    Dean; Charlie Ryan; Stuart Hamblen; Hal Willis; Stewart Family; Webb Pierce; Floyd
    Cramer.

Country All Star Festival...................Capitol Creative Products (S) SLB-6721   8-12
    Roy Rogers; Susan Raye; Ferlin Husky; Buddy Alan; Jean Shepard; Dick Curless; Tex
    Ritter; Rose Maddox; Buck Owen's Buckaroos; Anne Murray; Wynn Stewart; Wanda
    Jackson; Hagers; Charlie Louvin; Melba Montgomery; Roy Clark; Billie Jo Spears; Johnny
    & Jonie Mosby; Merle Haggard's Strangers; Linda Ronstadt.

Country and Western .... Wrangler (M) 1001   10-20   62
Country and Western .... Wrangler (S) 1001   10-20   62
    Patsy Cline; Hank Locklin; others.

Country and Western All Star Instrumentals.............Guest Star (S) GS-1497   10-20   60s
    Moon Mullican; Arthur Smith; Roy Wiggins; Jackie Phelps; Tommy Hill; Benny Martin;
    Crook Brothers; Dean Manuel; Ken Clark.

Country and Western All Stars...........................Modern Sound (SE) MS-579   5-10
    Moon Mullican; Carl Story; Jack Rogers; Kathy Taylor; Chase Webster; Bill Pursell; Jimmy
    Wilkerson; Tommy Downs; Jack Bond; Katy Richards.

Country and Western Award Winners.............................Decca (M) DL-4837   10-20   67
Country and Western Award Winners............................Decca (S) DL7-4837   10-20   67
    Loretta Lynn; Jimmy C. Newman; Kitty Wells; others.

Country and Western Award Winners '64 ....Decca (M) DL-4622   10-20   65
Country and Western Award Winners '64 ....Decca (S) DL7-4622   10-20   65
    Loretta Lynn; Kitty Wells; Webb Pierce; Wilburn Brothers; Bill Anderson; Ernest Tubb;
    Patsy Cline; Jimmy Martin; Jimmy C. Newman; Ernest Tubb; Loretta Lynn.

Country and Western Bonanza...................................... Camay (M) CA-3001   8-12
    Don Gibson; Roy Acuff; Jimmy Newman; Bob Luman; Bill Haley & the Comets; Billy Byrd;
    Tennessee Ernie Ford; Bob Wills; Wesley Tuttle; Merle Travis; Tex Williams; Weavers;
    Brad Randy; Cass County Boys.

Country and Western Bonanza......................................Design (S) SDLP-638   8-12   60s

Country and Western Bonanza .... Nouveau (SE) SDLP-638   8-12
Faron Young; Wilburn Brothers; Bobby Austin; Hank Locklin; Del Reeves; Bobby Bare.

Country and Western Caravan .... RCA (EP) EPB-3220   15-25   54

Country and Western Caravan .... RCA (M) LPM-3220   35-50   54
(10–inch LP.)

Country and Western Classics (1955) .... Economic Consultants (M) 1955   20-40   73
(Mail order offer.) Elvis Presley; others.

Country and Western Classics (1956) .... Economic Consultants (M) 1956   20-40   73
(Mail order offer.) Elvis Presley; others.

Country and Western Classics (1957) .... Economic Consultants (M) 1957   20-40   73
(Mail order offer.) Elvis Presley; others.

Country and Western Classics (1958) .... Economic Consultants (M) 1958   20-40   73
(Mail order offer.) Elvis Presley; others.

Country and Western Favorites .... Capitol Creative Products (S) SL 6555   8-12
Buck Owens; Sonny James; Glen Campbell; Tex Ritter.

Country and Western Favorites .... Metro (M) M-530   10-20   65

Country and Western Favorites .... Metro (S) MS-530   10-20   65
Hank Williams; Marvin Rainwater; others.

Country and Western Favorites, Vol. 2 .... Metro (M) M-572   10-20   66

Country and Western Favorites, Vol. 2 .... Metro (S) MS-572   10-20   66
Hank Williams; Floyd Cramer; Jimmy Newman; others.

Country and Western Golden Goodies .... Custom (S) CS 1095   8-12
Bud Titus; Goldie Fields; Doye O'Dell; Lonnie Barron; Tom T. Hall; Ray Lunsford; Kelleys;
Larry Thornton; Rovers; Casey Clark; Evelyn Harlene; Whitey Knight.

Country and Western Golden Hit Parade .... Starday (S) SLP 245   10-15   62
Red Sovine; Willis Brothers; Leon Payne; George Jones; Archie Campbell; Justin Tubb;
Benny Martin; Bobby Sykes; Arthur "Guitar Boogie" Smith; Glenda Raye; Tom O'Neal;
others.

Country and Western Golden Hits .... Mercury (M) MG-21034   15-20   65

Country and Western Golden Hits .... Mercury (S) SR-61034   15-25   65
Claude Gray; Patti Page; George Jones; others.

Country and Western Golden Hits .... Wing (S) 16368   8-12   68
George Jones; Claude Gray; Rex Allen; others.

Country and Western Greats .... Rondo (M) R-2024   10-15   50s

Country and Western Greats .... Rondo (S) RS-2024   10-15   50s
Patsy Cline; Webb Pierce; Eddie Dean; others.

Country and Western Guitars, Vol. 1 .... Time (S) S-303   5-10

Country and Western Guitars, Vol. 2 .... Time (S) S-303   5-10
Kelso Herston & His Guitar Kings; Bobby Bond; Rick Hardin; Lloyd Green; Hargus
Robbins; Hugo Montenegro; Billy Hutch & His Harmonica & Band; Faye Tucker. (Vol. 2 has
same record number as Vol. 1.)

Country and Western Hall of Fame .... Design (S) SDLP-605   10-15   60s
Patsy Cline; Jimmy Dean; Ferlin Husky; Johnny & Jonie Mosby; Maddox Brothers & Rose;
Marvin Rainwater; Bobby Austin.

Country and Western Hits, Vol. 1 .... Bud-Jet (S) 301   8-12   65

Country and Western Hits, Vol. 2 .... Bud-Jet (S) 302   8-12   65

Country and Western Hits, Vol. 3 .... Bud-Jet (S) 303   8-12   65

Country and Western Hits, Vol. 14 .... Mountain Dew (S) S7060   10-15
Elvis Presley; Donna Fargo; Tom T. Hall; Billy "Crash" Craddock; Freddie Hart; Sonny
James; Faron Young; Charley Pride; Sonny James; Johnny Cash.

Country and Western Hits Made Famous by America's Greatest
Singers .... Somerset/Stereo Fidelity (S) SF-18400   10-20
Jerry Shook; Red Sovine; others.

Country and Western Jamboree .... Design (M) DLP-619   10-15   60s

Country and Western Jamboree .... Design (S) SDLP-619   10-15   60s
Floyd Cramer; Carl Belew; Stewart Family; Wynn Stewart; Jan Howard; T. Texas Tyler;
Johnny Sea; David Houston; Ferlin Husky; Johnny Horton.

Country and Western Jamboree .... Palace (M) M-718   8-12   60s
Lonzo & Oscar; Red Sovine; Gene Pierce; Woody & Sam Jones; Jack Todd & the
Hometowners; Red Henderson; Leon Jackson; Stanley Alpine; Morgan Woodward; Ned
Miles; Hank Payne.

Country and Western Jamboree .... King (M) 697   40-50   60
Hank Locklin; T. Texas Tyler; others.

Country and Western Jamboree (2 LP) .... Camden (S) ADL2-0579   8-12   74
    Rosalie Allen; Gene Autry; Bill Boyd; Dale Evans; Roy Rogers; Sons of the Pioneers; Three
    Suns; others

Country and Western Jamboree .... Custom Records (S) CS-1092   5-10   72

Country and Western Jubilee .... Guest Star (SE) GS 1478   10-15   60s
    Willie Nelson; David Houston; Jim Reeves; Ginny Wright; Warner Mack; Zeke Clements.

Country and Western Kings .... Pentagon (M) A-114   5-10

Country and Western Kings .... Pentagon (S) AS-114   5-10
    Sonny James; Roy Acuff; Jimmy Newman; others.

Country and Western Music, Vol. 5 .... Design (M) DLP-609   10-20   60s
    Charlie Ryan; Frankie Miller; T. Texas Tyler; Maddox Brothers & Rose; Stuart Hamblen;
    Slim Willet; Ferlin Husky; Carl Belew.

Country & Western Original Recordings .... Camay (M) CA-3001   15-25

Country & Western Original Recordings .... Camay (S) CA-3001-S   15-25
    Don Gibson; Roy Acuff; Bob Luman; Bill Haley; Billy Bryd; Jimmy Newman.

Country and Western Sacred Song Greats .... Rondo (M) R-2025   10-15   50s

Country and Western Sacred Song Greats .... Rondo (S) RS-2025   10-15   50s
    T. Texas Tyler; Stewart Family; others.

Country and Western Star Jamboree, Vol. 2 .... Hurrah (M) H-1040

Country and Western Star Jamboree, Vol. 2 .... Hurrah (S) HS-1040
    Patsy Cline; Ferlin Husky; Wynn Stewart; Jimmy Dean; Marvin Rainwater; Webb Pierce;
    Carl Belew; Hank Locklin; T. Texas Tyler; Bobby Austin.

Country and Western Stars .... Design (M) DLP-601   10-20   62

Country and Western Stars .... Design (S) SDLP-601   10-20   62
    Patsy Cline; Jimmy Dean; Carl Belew; Ferlin Husky; Maddox Brothers & Rose.

Country and Western Stars .... Pickwick (S) SDLP-601   5-10   75
    Ferlin Husky; Patsy Cline; Bobby Austin; Johnny & Jonie; Jimmy Dean; Maddox Brothers
    and Rose; Marvin Rainwater.

Country and Western Stars .... Design (M) DLP-605   10-20   62

Country and Western Stars .... Design (S) SDLP-605   10-20   62
    Jimmy Dean; Maddox Brothers & Rose; Bobby Austin; Patsy Cline; Ferliln Husky; Johnny
    & Jonie; Marvin Rainwater.

Country and Western Stars .... Pickwick (S) SDLP-605   5-10   75
    Ferlin Husky; Patsy Cline; Bobby Austin; Johnny & Jonie; Jimmy Dean; Maddox Brothers
    and Rose; Marvin Rainwater.

Country and Western Stars .... Design (M) DLP-606   10-20   64

Country and Western Stars .... Design (S) SDLP-606   10-20   64
    Wynn Stewart; Billy Brown; Johnny & Jonie; Jan Howard; Marvin Rainwater; Ferlin Husky;
    Jimmy Dean; Patsy Cline.

Country and Western Stars [Vol. 2?] .... Design (M) DLP-608   10-20   64

Country and Western Stars [Vol. 2?] .... Design (S) SDLP-608   10-20   64
    Slim Willet; Rocky Bill Ford; Charlie Ryan; T. Texas Tyler; Maddox Brothers & Rose; Ferlin
    Husky; Frankie Miller; Carl Belew; Stuart Hamblen.

Country and Western Stars .... Pickwick (M) SDLP-606   5-10   75
    Wynn Stewart; Billy Brown; Johnny & Jonie; Jan Howard; Marvin Rainwater; Ferlin Husky;
    Jimmy Dean; Patsy Cline.

Country Artists Int'l Presents .... Country Artists (S) 1003   5-10   71
    Jim Foster; Lorita Barlow; Bill Floyd; others.

Country Blues Classics .... Blues Classics (M) BC-5   10-20   65
    Willie Baker; Elmore James; others.

Country Bound .... Columbia Special Products (M) WU 3580   5-10   81
    Don Williams; Willie Nelson; Lacy J. Dalton; Statler Brothers; Tanya Tucker; Tammy
    Wynette & George Jones; Moe Bandy; Kendalls; Barbara Mandrell; Merle Haggard; Johnny
    Duncan; Crystal Gayle; John Conlee; Jennifer Warnes; Moe Bandy & Joe Stampley;
    Conway Twitty.

Country Boy - Country Girl .... Decca (M) DL-4201   15-25   62

Country Boy - Country Girl .... Decca (S) DL7-4201   20-30   62
    Kitty Wells; Webb Pierce; Goldie Hill; Red Sovine; Red Foley; Betty Foley; Billy Gray; Mimi
    Roman; Justin Tubb; others.

Country Boy - Country Girl...RCA (S) APL1-1244   5-10   76
  Jim Reeves & Dottie West; Bobby Bare & Skeeter Davis; Waylon Jennings & Anita Carter;
  other duets.
Country Boys - Country Girls ....Wing (M) MGW-12275   10-20   64
Country Boys - Country Girls ....Wing (S) SRW-16275   10-20   64
  George Jones; James O'Gwynn; Connie Hall; Jeanette Hicks; Virginia Spurlock; Margie
  Bowes; Betty Amos; Jimmy Skinner.
Country Cavalcade, Vol .1 .... Longines Symphonette (M) SQ 93087   5-10   60s
  Buck Owens; Bonnie Owens; Merle Haggard; Buddy Alan; Jody Miller; Wynn Stewart;
  Bobbie Gentry; Jean Shepard; Ferlin Husky; Linda Ronstadt; Sonny James; Jody Miller;
  Wanda Jackson.
Country Cavalcade, Vol .2 .... Longines Symphonette (M) SQ 93088   5-10   60s
  Tennessee Ernie Ford; Dale Evans; T. Texas Tyler; Dick Curless; Buck Owens; Rose
  Maddox; Ferlin Husky; Louvin Brothers; Jordanaires; Houie Lister.
Country Chart Busters..Columbia (S) 1P 6683   5-10   77
  (Columbia Record Club issue.) Marty Robbins; Tammy Wynette; Carl Smith; Tanya Tucker;
  Ray Price; Lynn Anderson; Stonewall Jackson; Johnny Cash.
Country Chart Busters Vol. 1 ....Columbia (S) KC-32720   5-10   73
  Freddy Weller; Lynn Anderson; Bob Luman; Sonny James; others.
Country Chart Busters Vol. 2 ....Columbia (S) KC-32718   5-10   73
  Marty Robbins; Tammy Wynette; Carl Smith; Tanya Tucker; Ray Price; Lynn Anderson;
  Stonewall Jackson; Johnny Cash; Jody Miller; Earl Scruggs.
Country Chart Busters Vol. 3 ....Columbia (S) KC-32721   5-10   73
  Lynn Anderson; Sonny James; Ray Price; Tammy Wynette; others.
Country Chart Busters Vol. 4 ....Columbia (S) KC-32723   5-10   73
  Charlie McCoy; George Jones; Jody Miller; Tommy Cash; others.
Country Chart Busters Vol. 5 ....Columbia (S) KC-32724   5-10   73
  Freddy Weller; Johnny Cash; Lynn Anderson; Connie Smith; others.
Country Christmas...Decca (S) DL 74343   10-20   60s
  Jimmie Davis; Roy Drusky; Red Foley; Bobby Helms; Jimmy Martin; Bill Monroe; Jimmy
  Newman; Webb Pierce; Ernest Tubb; Kitty Wells; Wilburn Brothers.
Country Christmas ....Epic (S) PE-36823   5-10   80
  Charlie Rich; Johnny Cash & Tommy Cash; Tanya Tucker; Ray Price; Bobby Vinton;
  Tammy Wynette; Connie Smith; George Jones; Marty Robbins; George Jones & Tammy
  Wynette.
Country Christmas ....King (M) 811   20-25   62
Country Christmas ....Monument (S) 18125   5-10   69
  Billy Walker; Linda Webb; Harold Bradley; Leamon Sisters; Ray Penninton; Grandpa
  Jones; others.
Country Christmas ....Columbia (S) CS-9888   5-10   69
  Johnny Cash; Tammy Wynette; Marty Robbins; Carl Smith; Gene Autry; others.
Country Christmas (3 LP)...Time-Life (S) STL-109   15-20   88
  (Boxed set. Mail order offer.) Elvis Presley; Loretta Lynn; George Strait; Gene Autry; Willie
  Nelson; Buck Owens; Merle Haggard; Roy Orbison; Marty Robbins; George Jones &
  Tammy Wynette; Bill Monroe; Statler Brothers; Reba McEntire; Alabama; Roger Miller;
  Jerry Lee Lewis; Jim Reeves; Davis Sisters; Chet Atkins; Charley Pride; Tammy Wynette;
  Ernest Tubb; Freddy Fender; Louvin Brothers; Dwight Yoakam; Red Simpson; Homer &
  Jethro; Hank Snow; Ronnnie Milsap; George Jones; Johnny Cash; Eddy Arnold; Mickey
  Gilley; Dolly Parton.
Country Christmas, Vol. 2 ....RCA (S) AYL1-4809   8-10   83
  Elvis Presley; Earl Thomas Conley; Dolly Parton; Jerry Reed; Eddy Arnold; Sylvia; Louise
  Mandrell; Alabama.
Country Christmas with Loretta Lynn and
  Friends ....MCA Special Products (S) 34979   8-12   70s
  Loretta Lynn; Burl Ives; Brenda Lee; Ernest Tubb; Bill Anderson; Voices of Christmas.
Country Classics, 40 Original Hits by Original
  Artists (3 LP) ....Adam VIII Ltd A-8024   10-20   70s
  Jeannie C. Riley; Eddy Arnold; Johnny Cash; Moon Mullican; Hank Snow; George Jones;
  Leroy Van Dyke; Everly Brothers; Hank Locklin; Jerry Lee Lewis; Red Foley; Red Sovine &
  Webb Pierce; Don Gibson; Roy Drusky & Priscilla Mitchell; Pee See King; Del Reeves;
  Cowboy Copas; Bobby Helms; Roger Miller; Jim Reeves; Davis Sisters; Connie Smith;
  Jimmie Rodgers; Porter Wagoner; Jerry Reed; George Hamilton IV; Kitty Wells; Hawkshaw
  Hawkins; George Jones; Red Foley; Tom T. Hall.

Country Classics .... Columbia Special Products (S) P 13612   5-10   76
Johnny Cash; Bill Anderson; Tammy Wynette; Red Foley; Lynn Anderson; George Jones;
Jeannie C. Riley; Jack Greene; Kitty Wells; David Houston; Tanya Tucker; Conway Twitty;
Loretta Lynn; Charlie Rich; Patsy Cline; Ray Price; Barbara Mandrell; Johnny Paycheck.

Country Classics .... Longines Symphonette (S) SYS-5445   5-10   76
(Mail order offer.) Tex Williams; T. Texas Tyler; Al Dexter; Harlan Howard; Tex Ritter;
Wanda Jackson; Geezinslaw Brothers; Jean Shepard; Ferlin Husky; Ned Miller.

Country Classics .... RCA (M) LPM-2313   15-25   61

Country Classics .... RCA (S) LSP-2313   20-30   61
Eddy Arnold; Jim Reeves; Hank Snow; Porter Wagoner; Elton Britt; Skeeter Davis; Don
Gibson; Three Suns; Johnnie and Jack; Browns; Hank Locklin; Sons of the Pioneers;
Rosalie Allen & Elton Britt.

Country Classics (90 Minutes of) (2 LP) .... Fleetwood (S) FMS 1022   10-15
Skeeter Davis; Jeannie C. Riley; Willis Brothers; Kendalls; Henson Cargill; Johnny
Paycheck; Sammi Smith; Jerry Lee Lewis; Bob Luman; Jack & Misty; Red Sovine; Don
Gibson; Tommy Cash; Justin Tubb; "Little" Jimmy Dickens; Kenny Price; Claude King;
Charlie Walker; Dave Dudley; Stoney Cooper & Wilma Lee; Roy Orbison; Ferlin Husky;
Marvin Rainwater; Johnny Cash; Ned Miller; Ernie Ashworth; Carl Perkins; Roy Drusky;
Bob Gallon; Claude Gray; Jan Howard; Bobby Helms.

Country Comes to Carnegie Hall .... ABC/Dot (S) 20879   8-10   77
Hank Thompson; Freddy Fender; Roy Clark; Don Williams; others.

Country Cousins .... Musicor (S) MS-3053   10-20   65
George Jones; Gene Piney; Connie Hall; others

Country Cream .... Columbia (S) C-10422   5-10
Lynn Anderson; Jerry Lee Lewis; Hank Thompson; Roger Miller; Faron Young; Leroy Van
Dyke; Anita Kerr Sisters; Dave Dudley; Ray Price; Tammy Wynette; Tommy Overstreet;
Roy Drusky; Roy Clark; Marty Robbins.

Country Cream .... Ford (M) 723   5-10   74
Dolly Long; Shorty Long; Dickson Hall; Lila Lou; Paul Tannen; others.

Country Delight .... Epic (S) KE-33165   5-10   74
Charlie McCoy; Kris Kristofferson; George Jones; Tammy Wynette; David Houston &
Barbara Mandrell; Tina & Mommy; Jody Miller & Johnny Paycheck; Charlie Rich; Bob
Luman; Tina & Daddy.

Country Duets .... RCA (S) LSP-4082   10-15   68
Jim Reeves & Dottie West; Hank Snow & Anita Carter; Hank Snow & Chet Atkins; Porter
Wagoner & Dolly Parton; others

Country Duos .... K-TEL (S) WU-3540   5-10   81
Willie Nelson & Leon Russell; Johnny Duncan & Janie Fricke; Jim Ed Brown & Helen
Cornelius; Bellamy Brothers; Rita Coolidge & Glen Campbell; Moe Bandy & Joe Stampley;
George Jones & Johnny Paycheck; Moe Bandy & Tammy Wynette; Dave & Sugar; Johnny
Rodriguez & Charly McClain; Louise Mandrell & R.C. Bannon; Johnny Cash & George
Jones; Loretta Lynn & Conway Twitty; Porter Wagoner & Dolly Parton.

Country Dynamite .... Columbia (EP) AS-5   5-15
(7 inch EP.) Freddy Weller; Tommy Cash; David Rogers; Bob Luman; Claude King; Arlene
Hardin; Charlie Rich.

Country Dynamite from Nashville .... Nashville (SE) NLP-2101   5-10   71
Dottie West; Rose Maddox; Red Sovine; others.

Country Express .... Starday (M) SLP-109   20-30   59
Wayne Raney; Stanley Brothers; Bill Wimberly; Bill Clifton; Jim & Jesse; Tommy Jackson;
Country Gentlemen; Herbie Remington; Wally Traugutt; Buzz Busby; Ken Clark.

Country Express .... Nashville (M) NLP-2006   10-15   64
Wayne Raney; Stanley Brothers; Bill Wimberly; Bill Clifton; Jim & Jesse; Tommy Jackson;
Country Gentlemen; Herbie Remington; Wally Traugutt; Buzz Busby; Ken Clark.

Country Express .... Commonwealth (S) WU-3380   5-10   77
Sammi Smith; Kenny Price; Claude Gray; Roy Drusky; Jan Howard; Bob Gillion; Jimmy C
Newman; Merle Kilgore; Claude King; Warner Mack; Ferlin Husky; Marvin Rainwater;
Bobby Helms; Skeeter Davis; Ned Miller; Henson Cargill; Tommy Collins; Margie Bowes;
Mitchell Torok; Pee Wee King.

Country Fair .... Capitol (S) SWBB-562   8-10   70
Glen Campbell; Joe South; Jean Shepard; Sonny James; Ferlin Husky; Buck Owens.

Country Favorites .... Somerset (S) 34300   5-10   70

Country Favorites .... Buckboard (S) 1038   5-10   76
George Jones; Roger Miller; Rex Allen; Don Gibson; Wanda Jackson; Merle Haggard;
Bobbie Gentry; Johnny & Jonie Mosby; Charlie Louvin.

Country Favorites .... Musico (S) MDS-1017   10-15   70s
George Jones; Roger Miller; Gene Pitney; Melba Montgomery; Rex Allen; Don Gibson.

Country Favorites .... Wyncote (M) W-9016   10-20   64

Country Favorites...Wyncote (S) SW-9016   10-20   64
    George Jones; Bill Mack; Claude Gray; others.
Country Gals - Country Hits (2 LP) ....Camden (S) ALD2-0177   8-12   73
    Liz Anderson; Martha Carson; Davis Sisters; Skeeter Davis; Norma Jean; Dolly Parton;
    Dottie West; others.
Country Get-Together .... Sunset (S) 5283   5-10   70
Country Giants (2 LP) .... Mercury (S) SRM-2-606   10-15   70
    Jerry Lee Lewis; Faron Young; Roger Miller; others.
Country Girl Hall of Fame..Starday (M) SLP 313   10-20   60s
    Dottie West; Texas Ruby; Jonie Mosby; Sue Thompson; Margie Singleton; Rose Maddox;
    June Stearns with Pete Drake's Talking Steel Guitar; Rose Lee Maphis; Helen Carter with
    Bobby Sykes; Patsy Cline; Cathy Copas; Lulu Belle Wiseman; Betty Amos; Connie Hall.
Country Girl Sing Me A Song .... Nashville (M) NLP-2029   5-10   70s
Country Girl Sing Me A Song .... Nashville (S) NLP-2029   5-10   70s
    Lulu Belle Wiseman; Betty Amos; Patsy Cline; Molly O'Day; Glenda Raye; Jeanette Hicks;
    Dottie West; Rose Lee Maphis; June Stearns; Margie Singleton; Texas Ruby; Cousin
    Minnie Pearl.
Country Girls .... Camden (S) CAS-2403   5-10   70
    Dottie West; Connie Smith; Norma Jean; Dolly Parton; Bonnie Guitar; Martha Carson;
    Lorene Mann; Skeeter Davis; Wendy Dawn.
Country Girls .... Commonwealth (S) BU-4800   5-10   78
    Faron Young; David Houston; Tommy Overstreet; Billy "Crash" Craddock; Bobby Helms;
    Bob Luman; Bobby Lewis; Del Reeves; Johnny Darrell; Joe Stampley; Compton Brothers;
    Justin Tubb; Charlie Walker; Jimy Skinner.
Country Girls Sing Country Songs .... Camden (M) CAL-959   10-15   66
Country Girls Sing Country Songs .... Camden (S) CAS-959   10-15   66
    Kitty Wells; Dottie West; Connie Smith; Norma Jean; Skeeter Davis; Liz Anderson.
Country Gold (2 LP) .... Columbia (M) P2M-5176   10-15   67
Country Gold (2 LP) ....Columbia (S) P2S-5176   10-15   67
    (Columbia Record Club issue.) David Houston; Tammy Wynette; Jimmy Dean; Claude
    King; Johnny Horton; George Morgan; Roy Drusky; Jim & Jesse; "Little" Jimmy Dickens;
    Ray Price; Norma Jean; Statler Brothers; Bobby Lord; Freddie Hart; Marty Robbins; Carl
    Smith; Johnny Cash; Lester Flatt & Earl Scruggs; Harden Trio; Johnny Bond; Lefty
    Frizzell; Charlie Walker; Stonewall Jackson; Jordanaires; Carl Perkins; Hawkshaw
    Hawkins; Billy Walker.
Country Gold (2 LP) ....Columbia (S) DS 491   10-15   69
    Tammy Wynette; David Houston; Johnny Cash; Leon Ashley; Glen Campbell; Charlie
    Walker; Margie Singleton; Marty Robbins; Boots Randolph & Jimmy Richardson; Claude
    King; George Jones; Jimmy Dean; Cowboy Copas; David Rogers; Johnny Horton; Leon
    Ashley; Jeannie C. Riley; Carl Smith; Autry Inman; Billy Walker; Flatt & Scruggs & the
    Foggy Mountain Boys; Bobby Barnett; Lucille Starr; Johnny Seay; Johnny Duncan; Red
    Sovine; Lefty Frizzell; Ray Price; Stonewall Jackson; Bob Wills.
Country Gold .... Sunset (S) 5259   5-10   69
    Buddy Cagle; Johnny Carver; Slim Whitman; Larry Butler; others.
Country Gold .... Harmony (SE) HS-11378   5-10   70
    Carl Smith; Johnny Cash; Johnny Horton; Tammy Wynette; Lynn Anderson; Jimmy Dean;
    Claude King; Leroy Van Dyke; David Houston.
Country Gold (2 LP) ....RCA (S) R-233899(e)   8-12   77
    Hank Snow; Uncle Dave Macon; Jimmie Rodgers; Minnie Pearl; Pee Wee King; Jim
    Reeves; Carter Family; Eddy Arnold; Grampa Jones; Bobby Bare; Don Gibson; Browns;
    Bill Monroe; Porter Wagoner; Chet Atkins; Charley Pride; Willie Nelson; Charlie Rich; Gary
    Stewart; Dottie West. (RCA Record Club issue. Mail order.)
Country Gold .... RCA (S) DPL1-0561   20-25   82
    Elvis Presley; Dolly Parton; Razzy Bailey; Earl Thomas Conley; Waylon Jennings; Ronnie
    Milsap; Alabama; Juice Newton & Silver Spur; Charley Pride & the Cherry Singers; Sylvia.
Country Gold, Vol. 1 .... Plantation (S) 5   8-10   69
    Jeannie C. Riley; Becki Bluefield; David Wilkins; Teresa Brewer; Marcie Dickerson; George
    Kent; others.

Country Gold, Vol. 1 .... United Artists (S) UA-LA412-E .... 5-10 ... 75
   Johnny Cash; Cowboy Copas; Hank Cochran; Jan Howard; Dave Dudley; others.

Country Gold, Vol. 1 .... Buckboard (SE) BBS 1005 .... 5-10 ... 70s
   Patsy Cline; Dave Dudley; Johnny Tillitson; Jerry Wallace; Orville Couch; Jack Scott; Anita
   Bryant.

Country Gold, Vol. 2 .... Harmony (S) H-30018 .... 5-10 ... 70
   Johnny Cash and the Carter Family; Marty Robbins; others.

Country Gold, Vol. 2 .... Buckboard (SE) BBS 1006 .... 5-10 ... 70s
   Patsy Cline; Jack Scott; Anita Bryant; Orville Couch; Johnny Tillotson; Jerry Wallace;
   Johnny Bond.

Country Gold, Vol. 5 .... Buckboard (SE) BBS 1018 .... 5-10 ... 70s
   Johnny Cash; Charlie Rich; Sammi Smith; Jeannie C. Riley; Jerry Lee Lewis; Carl Belew;
   Bill Black's Combo.

Country Gospel .... Gusto (S) GT-0069 .... 5-10 ... 70s
   Wanda Jackson; Claude Gray; Mac Wiseman; George Jones; Carl Smith; Tex Ritter; T.
   Texas Tyler; Ferlin Husky; "Little" Jimmy Dickens.

Country Gospel Favorites .... Rural Rhythm (M) RR 149 .... 8-12 ... 60s
   G.M. Farley; Gospeletts; Martin; Bill Carter & the Cooper Brothers; Billy & Gordon
   Hemrick; Owen & Mack; Charlie & Lee Cline; Happy Four; Masters Quartet.

Country Gospel Greats .... Rural Rhythm (M) RR 138 .... 8-12 ... 60s
   Onie Wheeler; Ray Baker; Jackie & Arlin Vaden; others.

Country Gospel Meeting .... Somerset (S) 34100 .... 5-10 ... 69

Country Gospel Songs .... Folkways (M) RBF-19 .... 5-10 ... 71

Country Greats .... Rural Rhythm (M) RR 155 .... 8-12 ... 60s
   Hall Wallis; Vandergrift Brothers; Salty Dog; Tony Douglas; Swaney Caldwell; Boys from
   Shilo; De Wayne Wear; James Worley; Doug La Vall; Dub Dickerson; others.

Country Greats .... Harmony (S) KH-30346 .... 5-10 ... 70
   Johnny Cash; Tammy Wynette; Marty Robbins; others.

Country Guitar .... Nashville (M) NLP-2021 .... 10-15 ... 66
   Billy Byrd & Jimmy Capps; Hardrock Gunter; Eddie Eddings; Thumbs Carlisle; Arthur
   "Guitar Boogie" Smith.

Country Guys & Gals .... Hilltop/Pickwick (SE) JS-6096 .... 8-12 ... 60s
   Buck Owens; Glen Clampbell; Roy Clark; Bobbie Gentry; Tex Ritter; Hank Thompson;
   Sonny James; Tennessee Ernie Ford; Wanda Jackson; Jean Shepard.

Country Hall of Fame .... Musico (S) MDS-1027 .... 10-15 ... 70s
   George Jones; Tommy Cash; Don Gibson; Marvin Rainwater, Jimmy Dean.

Country Hall of Fame, Vol. 1 .... Country Music Association (S) CMA 712 .... 5-10 ... 60s
   Roy Acuff; Bill Anderson; Eddy Arnold; Bobby Bare; Johnny Bond; Johnny Cash; Patsy
   Cline; Dave Dudley; Red Foley; Lefty Frizzell; Don Gibson; Pee Wee King; Roger Miller;
   George Morgan; Buck Owens; Ray Price; Jim Reeves; Tex Ritter; Marty Robbins; Hank
   Snow; Hank Thompson; Merle Travis; Ernest Tubb; Kitty Wells; Hank Williams.

Country Hall of Fame, Vol. 2 .... Country Music Association (S) CMA-800 .... 5-10 ... 60s
   Roger Miller; Patsy Cline; Leroy Van Dyke; Johnny Horton; Ferlin Husky; Sonny James;
   Floyd Cramer; Johnny Cash; Tex Williams; Del Wood; Jimmy Wakely; Chet Atkins; Faron
   Young; Buck Owens; Hank Williams; Webb Pierce; Loretta Lynn; Lefty Frizzell; Ray Price;
   George Jones; Rex Allen; Jimmie Rodgers; Flatt & Scruggs; Grandpa Jones; Kitty Wells.

Country Hall of Fame, Vol. 2 .... Telerad (S) CMA-800 .... 5-10 ... 60s
   (Mail order offer.) Roger Miller; Patsy Cline; Leroy Van Dyke; Johnny Horton; Ferlin Husky;
   Sonny James; Floyd Cramer; Johnny Cash; Tex Williams; Del Wood; Jimmy Wakely; Chet
   Atkins; Faron Young; Buck Owens; Hank Williams; Webb Pierce; Loretta Lynn; Lefty
   Frizzell; Ray Price; George Jones; Rex Allen; Jimmie Rodgers; Flatt & Scruggs; Grandpa
   Jones; Kitty Wells. (Special products. Made for Telerad Inc., Hollywood Album Center.)

Country Harvest .... K-Tel (S) BU 4160 .... 5-10 ... 81
   Billy Crash Craddock; Crystal Gayle; Willie Nelson; Jessi Colter; Melba Montgomery; Gene
   Watson; Mel Tillis; Barbara Mandrell; Ray Price; Ed Bruce; David Houston; Loretta Lynn;
   John Conlee.

Country Heaven (3 LP) .... RCA Special Prod./Telediscx (M) TD19/DVL3-0888 .... 10-20 ... 89
   Ernest Tubb; Hank Williams; Patsy Cline; Leon Payne; Lefty Frizzell; Bob Wills; George
   Morgan; Johnny Bond; Stuart Hamblen; Bob Luman; Jack Guthrie; Kenny Price; Skeets
   McDonald; Merle Travis; Vernon Hal Hart; Jimmy Wakely; T. Texas Tyler; Red Foley;
   Jimmie Rodgers; Red Sovine; Texas Jim Robertson; Johnny Horton; Wynn Stewart; Tex
   Williams; Al Dexter; Homer & Jethro; Lester Flatt; Nat Stuckey; Hawkshaw Hawkins;
   Delmore Brothers; Sons of the Pioneers; Carter Family; Elton Britt; Marty Robbins; Tex
   Ritter.

Country Hit Parade .... Chart (S) 3000 .... 5-10 ... 69
   Lynn Anderson; Kenny Vernon; Johnny Dollar; Gene Hood; Vince Bulla; Joe Gibson.

Country Hit Parade.. Starday (S) SLP-110   20-30   59
    Lois Williams; Willis Brothers; Red Sovine; others.
Country Hit Parade.. Nashville (SE) NLP-2089   5-10   70
    Lois Williams; Willis Brothers; Red Sovine; others.
Country Hits .... Columbia Special Products (S) CSS 1519   5-10
    Marty Robbins; Ray Price; David Houston; Carter Family; Flatt & Scruggs; Johnny Cash;
    Tammy Wynette.
Country Hits .... Design (M) DLP 609   10-15   60s
    Ferlin Husky; Carl Belew; Stuart Hamblen; Maddox Brothers & Rose; Frankie Miller; Slim
    Willet; Charlie Ryan; T. Texas Tyler.
Country Hits .... Petal (M) 2000   5-10
Country Hits By Country Stars .... Capitol (M) T-1912   15-20   63
Country Hits By Country Stars .... Capitol (S) ST-1912   15-25   63
    Ferlin Husky; Faron Young; Rose Maddox; Sonny James; others.
Country Hits for Highway and Home.. Mega (S) 1022   5-10   73
    Jack Reno; Alice Creech; Jackie Ward; Linda Gayle; Shoji Tabuchi.
Country Hits of the '40s... Capitol (S) ST-884   5-10   72
    Tennessee Ernie Ford; Tex Ritter; Jimmy Wakely; Jimmie Davis; Tex Williams; Margaret
    Whiting & Jimmy Wakely; Merle Travis; Al Dexter; Leon Payne; Jack Guthrie.
Country Hits of the '50s... Capitol (S) ST-885   8-12   72
Country Hits of the '50s... Capitol (S) SM-885   5-10   72
    Tennessee Ernie Ford; Ferlin Husky; Sonny James; Jean Shepard; Hank Thompson;
    Freddie Hart; Faron Young; Tommy Collins; Skeets McDonald.
Country Hits of the '60s... Capitol (S) ST-886   8-10   72
    Glen Campbell; Wanda Jackson; Buck Owens; Merle Haggard; Wynn Stewart; Faron
    Young; Tex Ritter; Roy Clark; Sonny James; Ferlin Husky.
Country Hits Parade.. RCA (M) LPM-3452   10-20   66
Country Hits Parade.. RCA (S) LSP-3452   15-20   66
    Hank Snow; Eddy Arnold; Connie Smith; Roger Miller; Norma Jean; Hank Locklin; George
    Hamilton IV; Bobby Bare; Jim Reeves; Skeeter Davis; Porter Wagoner.
Country Hits with Vocals .... Alshire (S) 2-119   5-10
Country Hits, Vol. 2 .... United Artists (M) UAL-3185   15-20   62
Country Hits, Vol. 2 .... United Artists (S) UAS-6185   20-25   62
    George Jones; Claude Gray; Jape Richardson; Bill Mack; Carl Sauceman; Leon Payne;
    Johnny Mathis; Herby Remington; Benny Barnes; James O'Gwynn; Jimmy Blakely; Tony
    Douglas.
Country Holiday........................... Columbia Musical Treasuries (SE) DS-467   5-10   68
    Jimmy Dean; Johnny Cash; Marty Robbins; Gene Autry; Chuck Wagon Gang; Anita Bryant;
    Stuart Hamblen; David Houston; "Little" Jimmy Dickens; Patti Page.
Country Humble Pie .... Koala (S) AW 14110   8-10   79
    Jerry Lee Lewis; Platters; Carl Perkins; Etta James; Merrill E. Moore; Roy Orbison;
    Jordanaires; Richard Berry & the Pharaohs; Bill Haley & the Comets.
Country Hymns .... Columbia (S) C30324   8-12
    Johnny Cash; Marty Robbins; Ray Price; Chuck Wagon Gang; Carl Smith; Jimmy Dean;
    Anita Bryant; Lester Flatt & Earl Scruggs; Statler Brothers; Carl Butler & Pearl; Stonewall
    Jackson.
Country Inspirations .... Lotus (M) BU-5780   5-10   83
    Tom T. Hall; Stuart Hamblen; Hank Williams; Danny Davis and the Nashville Brass; Statler
    Brothers; Cristy Lane; Larry Gatlin; Anne Muray; B.J. Thomas; Mahalia Jackson;
    Tennessee Ernie Ford; Don Gibson; Kris Kristofferson; Johnny Cash; Roy Acuff; Oak
    Ridge Boys.
Country Instrumentals .... Starday (EP) S-45-440   5-10   59
    Stanley Brothers; Wayne Raney; others.
Country Instrumentals, Vol. 1 .... RCA (S) LSP-4380   8-10   70
    Boots Randolph; Chet Atkins; Floyd Cramer; others.
Country Instrumentals, Vol. 2 .... RCA (S) LSP-4494   8-10   71
    Jerry Reed; Lester Flatt; Chet Atkins; others
Country Instrumentals, Vol. 3 .... RCA (S) LSP-4728   8-10   72
    Chet Atkins; Floyd Cramer; Boots Randolph; Jerry Reed; others.

Country Jamboree..Capitol (S) 91654   8-10
(Capitol Record Club issue.) Merle Haggard; Buck Owens; Sonny James; Glen Campbell; Wanda Jackson; Charlie Louvin; Wynn Stewart; Ned Miller; Jody Miller; Ray Pillow; Bobby Austin; Jean Shepard; Ferlin Husky; Tex Ritter.

Country Jubilee .... Decca (M) DL-4172   20-30   61

Country Jubilee .... Decca (M) 38237   20-30   61
Red Foley; Bill Monroe; Grady Martin; Mervin Shiner & the Jordanaires; Milton Brown & the Brownies; Jimmy Wakely; Red Sovine & the Gadabouts; Jimmy Wakely; Clayton McMichen's Georgia Wildcats; Webb Pierce; Shelton Brothers; Tompall & the Glaser Brothers; Rex Allen.

Country Jubilee of Stars..Guest Stars (M) G-1444   10-20   63

Country Jubilee of Stars..Guest Stars (S) GS-1444   10-20   63
Link Wray; others.

Country Jukebox... Pickwick (S) JS-6183   5-10   70s
Roger Miller; Tom T. Hall; Roy Drusky; George Kent; Norro Wilson.

Country Kings... Hass (S) 14074   5-10   78
Joe South; Buddy Mize; others.

Country Line.. K-Tel (S) WU 3450   5-10   79
Don Williams; Mel Tillis; Conway Twitty; Jim Ed Brown; Helen Cornelius; John Conlee; Larry Gatlin; Tany Tucker; Kendalls; Oak Ridge Boys; Crystal Gayle; Kenny Rogers; Barbara Mandrell; Anne Murray; Statler Brothers; Eddie Rabbitt.

Country Love...Harmony (S) KH-30608   5-10   71
Tammy Wynette; Johnny Cash; Marty Robbins; others.

Country Love, Vol. 1 & 2 (2 LP) .... RCA (SE) PRS-392   8-12   72
Don Gibson; Norma Jean; Jim Ed Brown; Floyd Cramer; Dickey Lee; Dottie West; Connie Smith; Danny Davis; Hank Snow; Skeeter Davis; John Hartford; Roger Miller; Browns; George Hamilton IV; Liz Anderson; Waylon Jennings; Porter Wagoner; Dolly Parton; Hank Locklin; Jim Reeves; Bobby Bare; Sonny James; Chet Atkins; Jerry Reed; Charley Pride.

Country Love, Vol. 1...Columbia (S) KG-30326   5-10   70
Charlie Rich; Johnny Cash; Lynn Anderson; Johnny Horton; others.

Country Love, Vol. 2...Columbia (S) KG-32010   5-10   73
Ray Price; Patti Page; Tommy Cash; Tammy Wynette; others.

Country Love, Vol. 3...Columbia (S) KG-32725   5-10   73
Arlene Harden; Lynn Anderson; Marty Robbins; George Jones; Charlie Rich; Ray Price; Freddy Weller; others.

Country Memories...?????   5-10
(Label and number not known.) Louvin Brothers; Tex Ritter; Jean Shepard & Ferlin Husky; Skeeter Davis; Pee Wee King; Wayne Raney; Moon Mullican; Red Sovine; Hawkshaw Hawkins; Cowboy Copas.

Country Memories (7 LP)....................... Reader's Digest/BMG (S) RBA-037   40-55   89
(Boxed set. Mail order offer. Includes booklet.) Elvis Presley; others.

Country Music All Time Favorites ....RCA (S) ????   5-10
Charley Pride; Ronnie Milsap; Dave & Sugar; Willie Nelson; Jim Ed Brown & Helen Cornelius; Razzy Bailey; Zella Lehr; Jerry Reed; Dickey Lee; others.

Country Music by the Wayside...Wayside (M) 1013   5-10   68

Country Music Cannonball..Starday (M) S-276   10-20   64

Country Music Cavalcade - American Country
Gold (3 LP)...................................... Candlelite (S) CU-161   10-20   80
(Boxed set.) Buddy Holly & the Crickets; Don Williams; Jimmie Rodgers; Red Foley & Betty Foley; Brenda Lee; Freddy Fender; Wilma Burgess; Narvel Felts; Jack Greene; Webb Pierce; Carl Dobkins, Jr.; Patsy Cline; Billy "Crash" Craddock; Ernest Tubb & the Texas Troubadors; Barbara Mandrell; Tanya Tucker; Conway Twitty; Kitty Wells; B.J. Thomas; Bill Anderson & Jan Howard.

Country Music Cavalcade - Midnight in Memphis (3 LP)..Candlelite (S) 1/2/3   10-20   75
(Mail order offer.) Conway Twitty; Jimmy Clanton; Patti Page; Rusty Draper; Tommy Edwards; Ray Peterson; Nightriders; Marvin Rainwater; Champs; Hank Williams; Jerry Lee Lewis; Mark Dinning; Pete Drake; Leroy Van Dyke; Joey Heatherton; Statler Brothers; Frank Slades & Cahpparell; Dicky Lee; Roger Miller.

Country Music Cavalcade - Nashville
Graffiti, Vol. 1 (3 LP).. Candlelite (S) P3 13235   10-20   76
Johnny Cash; Bobby Helms; Link Wray; Frank Slader & Chaperal; Statler Brothers; Marty Robbins; Buzz Clifford; Billy Grammer; Patti Page; Bobby Vinton; Johnny Ray; Ersel Hickey; Stonewall Jackson; Claude Kings; Guy Mitchell; Mindy Carson; Johnny Carson; Ray Price; Tennessee Saxes Plus Two; Carl Perkins; Jimmy Dean.

Country Music Cavalcade - Nashville
Graffiti (3 LP) .... Candlelite (S) CU-750   10-20   85
    Johnny Cash; Timi Yuro; Duane Eddy; Wink Martindale; Guy Mitchell; Jerry Lee Lewis;
    Patti Page; Carl McCoy; Sandy Posey; Johnny Ray; Margo Smith; Jimmy Dean; Bobby
    Helms; Roy Orbison; Frankie Laine; Dickey Lee; Claude King; Stonewall Jackson; Pat
    Boone; Jivin' Gene & the Jokers; Carl Mann; Jim Ed Brown; Carl Perkins; Jody Miller; Del
    Reeves.
Country Music Express .... Unart (S) S 21016   8-12   60s
    George Jones; Melba Montgomery; Judy Lynn; Al Caiola; Leroy Holmes; Bill Harell.
Country Music Festival .... Starday (M) S-274   10-20   64
Country Music Festival, Vol. 2 .... Starday (M) S-362   10-20   66
    Willis Brothers; Joe & Rose Maphis; Johnny Bond; others.
Country Music Goes to War .... Starday (M) S-374   10-20   66
    Willis Brothers; Jimmy Blakely; Dottie West; others.
Country Music Hall of Fame .... Design (S) SDLP-620   10-15   60s
    Roger Miller; Johnny Cash; Webb Pierce; Carl Belew; Jimmy Dean; Dave Dudley; Buck
    Owens; Del Reeves; George Jones; Sonny James.
Country Music Hall of Fame .... Starday (S) 9-468   10-20   70
    Buck Owens; Dolly Parton; George Jones; others.
Country Music Hall of Fame, Vol. 1 (2 LP) .... Starday (M) S-164   20-30   62
Country Music Hall of Fame, Vol. 1 (2 LP) ..... Starday (S) SLP-164   20-30   62
    Cowboy Copas; George Jones; Hank Locklin; others.
Country Music Hall of Fame, Vol. 2 .... Starday (M) S-190   15-25   62
Country Music Hall of Fame, Vol. 2 .... Starday (S) SLP-190   15-25   62
    Johnny Cash; Jimmy Dean; Red Sovine; George Jones Johnny Horton; Sue Thompson;
    Cowboy Copas; Rod Brasfield; Lester Flatt & Earl Scruggs; Buck Owens; A.P. Carter & the
    Carter Family; Jimmie Skinner; Roy Drusky; Roger Miller; Leon McAuliffe; Lulu Belle &
    Scotty; Blue Sky Boys; Arthur "Guitar Boogie" Smith; Johnny Bond; Moon Mullican;
    Smiley Burnette; Lew Childre; others.
Country Music Hall of Fame, Vol. 3 (2 LP) .... Starday (M) S-256   15-25   63
Country Music Hall of Fame, Vol. 3 (2 LP) ..... Starday (S) SLP-256   15-25   63
    Buck Owens; Jimmy Dean; Rex Allen; Minnie Pearl; Roger Miller; Jimmie Skinner; Red
    Sovine; Blue Sky Boys; Arthur "Guitar Boogie" Smith; T. Texas Tyler; Maddox Brothers &
    Rose; Johnny Horton; Hank Locklin; Flatt & Scruggs; Cowboy Copas; Patsy Cline;
    Hawshaw Hawkins; George Jones; Webb Pierce; Patsy Cline; others.
Country Music Hall of Fame, Vol. 4 (2 LP) .... Starday (M) S-295   15-25   64
    Patsy Cline; Lester Flatt & Earl Scruggs; Bob Wills; others.
Country Music Hall of Fame, Vol. 5 .... Starday (M) 360   10-20   66
    Floyd Tillman; Dottie West; Charlie Walker; others.
Country Music Hall of Fame, Vol. 6 .... Starday (M) 390   10-15   67
Country Music Hall of Fame, Vol. 6 .... Starday (S) 390   10-15   67
    George Morgan; Roger Miller; Melba Montgomery; others.
Country Music Hall of Fame, Vol. 7 .... Starday (S) 409   10-15   69
Country Music Hall of Fame, Vol. 8 .... Starday (S) 430   10-15   69
    Glen Campbell; Wynn Stewart; Jan Howard; others.
Country Music Hall of Fame, Vol. 9 .... Starday (S) 9-449   10-15   70
    Buck Owens; Minnie Pearl; Jimmy Dean; Red Sovine; Dolly Parton; others.
Country Music Hits .... Camden (M) CAL-686   10-20   62
Country Music Hits .... Camden (S) CAS-686   10-20   62
    Eddy Arnold; Jim Reeves; Don Gibson; Hank Snow; others.
Country Music Hits By Country Music Stars, Vol. 2, ... Camden (M) CAL-689   10-20   63
Country Music Hits By Country Music Stars, Vol. 2 ... Camden (SE) CAS-689   10-20   63
    Jim Reeves; Eddy Arnold; Davis Sisters; Hank Locklin; Don Gibson; Pee Wee King; Slim
    Whitman; Hal "Lone" Pine; Grandpa Jones; Elton Britt; Hank Snow; Gid Tanner.
Country Music Hootenanny .... Capitol (M) T-2009   20-25   63
Country Music Hootenenany .... Capitol (S) ST-2009   25-30   63
    Buck Owens; Merle Travis; Rose Maddox; others.
Country Music in the Modern Era (1940s - 1970s) .... New World (S) NW-207   50-70   76
    (Indended for library use only.) Elvis Presley; Eddy Arnold; Jim Reeves; Lefty Frizzell; Ray
    Price; Patsy Cline; Hank Snow; Kitty Wells; Ernest Tubb; Marty Robbins; Loretta Lynn;
    Johnny Cash; Buck Owens; Roger Miller; Merle Haggard; Dolly Parton; Kris Kristofferson.

Country Music Jamboree .... Mercury (M) MG-20350   30-40   58
Country Music Just for You .... Capitol ????   10-15
(Made for Coca-Cola.) Faron Young; Ferlin Husky; others.
Country Music Laugh-Out .... Starday (S) 452   5-10   70
Buck Owens; Junior Samples; Grandpa Jones; Archie Campbell; others.
Country Music Like You Want to Hear it .... Somerset (S) 34700   5-10   70
Country Music Memorial (2 LP) .... Starday (S) 9-451   8-12   70
Cowboy Copas; Stanly Bros.; Johnny Horton; Patsy Cline; Jimmy Osborne; Delmore
Brothers; Phil Sullivan; Texas Ruby; Lonzo & Oscar; Moon Mullican; Dean Manuel & the
Blue Boys; Smiley Burnette; Pop Stoneman; Tommy Duncan with Bob Wills; Eddie
McDuff; A.L. Phipps Family; Robert Lunn; Rod Brasfield; Lonnie Irving; Adrian Roland;
Hawkshaw Hawkins; Jimmy Osborne; Lew Childre; Leon Payne.
Country Music Memorial Album .... Starday (M) SLP 291   15-20   64
Cowboy Copas; Patsy Cline; Demore Brothers; Johnny Horton; Lew Childre; Texas Ruby;
Lonnie Irving; Phil Sullivan; Phipps Family; Hawshaw Hawkins; Rod Brasfield.
Country Music on the Go, Vol. 1 .... Sage & Sand (M) C-18   10-20   61
Eddie Dean; Charlie Williams; Les York; others.
Country Music on the Go, Vol. 2 .... Sage & Sand (M) C-20   10-20   61
Goldie Fields; Bud Titus; Casey Clark; others.
Country Music on the Go, Vol. 3 .... Sage & Sand (M) C-22   10-20   61
Tex Carman; Jimmy Patton; Wayne West; others.
Country Music on the Go, Vol. 4 .... Sage & Sand (M) C-24   10-20   61
Bud Titus; Goldie Fields; Rovers; Casey Clark; others.
Country Music Spectacular .... Starday (M) S-117   25-35   61
George Jones; Cowboy Copas; James O'Gwynn; Frankie Miller; others.
Country Music Spectacular (4 LP) .... Starday (M) SYM-6401   15-25   67
Country Music Spectacular (4 LP) .... Starday (S) SYS-6401   15-25   67
Cowboy Copas; George Jones; Dave Dudley; Maddox Brothers & Rose; Jimmie Skinner;
Red Sovine; Johnny Bond; Roger Miller; Merle Kilgore; Flatt & Scruggs; Boots Randolf;
Jimmy Richardson; Minnie Pearl; Willis Brothers; Webb Pierce; Sonny James; Roy
Drusky; Hawkshaw Hawkins; Patsy Cline; George Morgan; Buck Owens; Johnny Horton;
Ferlin Husky; Stoneman Family; Faron Young; Texas Ruby; Moon Mullican; Stringbean;
Wayne Raney; Frankie Miller; Margie Singleton; Joe & Rose Lee Maphis; Mac Wiseman;
Stanley Brothers; Carl Story; Grandpa Jones; Melba Montgomery; Carter Family; Leon
Payne; Bill Carlisle; Wilf Carter; Lonzo & Oscar.
Country Music Star Spectacular .... Hickory (M) 116   10-20   64
Country Music Story [Narrated] By Minnie Pearl .... Starday (M) SLP-397   10-15   60s
Minnie Pearl; Carter Family; George Jones; Leon McAuliffe; Dottie West; Flatt & Scruggs;
Cowboy Copas; Willis Brothers; Johnny Cash; Buck Owens; others.
Country Music Time .... Decca (M) DL 34057   10-20   60s
Jimmie Davis; Bill Monroe; Webb Pierce; Tommy Jackson; Montana Slim; Rex Allen; Red
Foley; Red Sovine; Billy Grammer; Roy Drusky; Bill Anderson; Ernest Tubb.
Country Music USA .... Candelite (S) CM 1/3   10-20   80
(Boxed set.) Troy Shondell; Jack Scott; Donnie Brooks; Sanford Clark; Buddy Knox;
Duane Eddy; Robin Luke; Ray Smith; J. Frank Wilson; Wanda Jackson; Kenny Price;
Jimmy Clanton; Patti Page; Henson Cargill; Jeannie Seely; Lonnie Mack; Kingston Trio;
Memphis Blue; Ned Miller; Johnny & the Hurricanes; Wynn Stewart; Jan Howard; Jimmy
Gilmer; Dorsey Burnette; Sue Thompson; Gene Simmons; Faron Young; Harden Trio.
Country Music USA .... Readers Digest/RCA (S) RD4-193   10-20   77
(Boxed set.) Glen Campbell; Bobbie Gentry; Buck Owens; Anne Murray; Freddie Hart;
Tennessee Ernie Ford; Roy Clark; Jody Miller; Sonny James; Jimmy Wakely & Margaret
Whiting; Hank Thompson; Tex Ritter; Roy Acuff; Jean Shepard; Faron Young; Louvin
Brothers; Ferlin Husky; Merle Travis; Hank Thompson; Tex Williams; Charlie Louvin &
Melba Montgomery; Wanda Jackson; Billie Jo Spears; Johnny & Jonie Mosby; Ned Miller;
Susan Raye; Buddy Alan; Merle Haggard; Roy Clark; Harlan Howard; Dick Curless; Red
Simpson; Roy Drusky; Buck Owens & Susan Raye; Jan Howard; Linda Ronstadt; Tony
Booth; LaWanda Lindsey; Melba Montgomery; Roy Rogers & Dale Evans; Jordanaires.
Country Music Who's Who .... Starday (M) SLP-304   15-20   64
Willis Brothers; Jimmy Dean; Joe Maphis; Johnny Cash; Roger Miller; Cowboy Copas;
George Jones; Dottie West; Jimmie Skinner; Dean Manuel; Duke of Paducah; Buck Owens;
Pee Wee King; Pete Drake.
Country Music Who's Who .... Starday (M) SLP-304   20-25   64
(Issued with 52 page booklet, also "premium certificate" coupon.) Willis Brothers; Jimmy
Dean; Joe Maphis; Johnny Cash; Roger Miller; Cowboy Copas; George Jones; Dottie West;
Jimmie Skinner; Dean Manuel; Duke of Paducah; Buck Owens; Pee Wee King; Pete Drake.

Country Music's Greatest Stars .... Nashville (M) NLP 2028   5-10
George Jones; Dottie West; Dave Dudley; Johnny Bond; Roy Drusky; Pete Drake & Talking Steel Guitar; Willis Brothers; Buck Owens; Charlie Walker; Roger Miller; Archie Campbell; Jimmy Dean.

Country Music's Top 14 ....CBS (S) CSP P 15829   5-10
Charlie Rich; Ray Price; Willie Nelson; Tammy Wynette; etc.

Country My Way (4 LP)................. Columbia Musical Treasury (SE) 4P 6212   15-20   75
(Boxed set. Record club issue.) Charlie Rich; David Houston; Lynn Anderson; Johnny Cash; Tanya Tucker; Tammy Wynette; Roy Clark.

Country Oldies But Goodies...................................... Smash (M) MGS-27016   10-20   62
Country Oldies But Goodies..Smash (S) SRS-67016   10-20   62
Cowboy Copas; Justin Tubb; Stanley Brothers; others.

Country Oldies You Know and Love .... Somerset (S) 33700   5-10   69

Country-Politan Hits ....Crystal (S) LP-1100   5-10
(Mail order offer.) Johnny Darrell; Jeannie C. Riley; Jack Greene; George Jones; Kitty Wells; Bobby Lewis; Red Foley; Linda Manning; Bobby Helms; Jimmie Rodgers; Glen Campbell; Henson Cargill; Jeannie Seely; Red Sovine; Burl Ives; Patsy Cline; Robert Mitchum; Buck Owens; Webb Pierce; Del Reeves; Loretta Lynn.

Country Pop (2 LP) ....Capitol (S) SLB-6872   8-12   73
Glen Campbell; Johnny Cash; Sonny James; Jeannie C. Riley; Roy Clark; Anne Murray; Ferlin Husky; Wanda Jackson; Faron Young; Tex Ritter; Bobbie Gentry; Wynn Stewart; Freddie Hart; Susan Raye; Tennessee Ernie Ford; Dick Curless; Dorsey Burnett; Anne Murray; Charlie Louvin & Melba Montgomery; Billie Jo Spears; Joe South; Linda Ronstadt.

Country Proud ....K-Tel WU 3670   5-10   84
Gary Morris; Crystal Gayle; John Conlee; Earl Thomas Conley; Deborah Allen; Janie Fricke; Willie Nelson; Lee Greenwood; Sylvia; Ronnie Milsap; Alabama; George Strait; Lynn Anderson; Jim Glaser; Ricky Scaggs; Don Williams.

Country Road ....K-Tel WU 3270   5-10   75
Charlie Rich; Mel Tillis; George Jones; Tammy Wynette; Sonny James; Barbara Mandrell; Ray Price; Lynn Anderson; David Houston; Billy Walker; Sheb Wooley; Carl Smith; Jody Miller; Stonewall Jackson; Johnny Horton; Carl Butler; Jud Strunk.

Country Roundup ....Epic (S) EGP-504   5-10   70
Tammy Wynette; Bob Luman; David Houston; Goldie Hill; Autry Inman; Jim and Jesse and the Virginia Boys; others.

Country Salute to Hank Williams.................................Harmony (M) HL-7265   15-20   60
Carl Perkins; Roy Acuff; Rose Maddox; others.

Country Side of Christmas .... Capitol Creative Products (S) SL 6586   5-10
Sonny James; Glen Campbell; Roy Rogers; Buck Owens; Hollywood Pops Orchestra; Al Martino; Roger Wagner Chorale; Korean Orphan Choir.

Country Sides (2 LP)..MCA (S) 1929   8-12   70s
Osborne Brothers; Tennessee Hound Dog; others.

Country Soft and Mellow (7 LP) .... Reader's Digest/BMG (SP) RB4-200   40-55   89
(Boxed set. Mail order offer. Includes booklet.) Elvis Presley; others.

Country Songs .... Camden (S) CAS-2333   8-10   69
Eddy Arnold; Bobby Bare; Don Gibson; Hank Snow; Porter Wagoner.

Country Sounds, Vol. 1 ...... Ronco/Columbia Special Products (S) CS 10847   5-10   72
Sammi Smith; Tommy Overstreet; George Jones & Tammy Wynette; Henson Cargill; Lynn Anderson; Faron Young; Roy Drusky; Marty Robbins; Dave Dudley; David Houston; Johnny Cash; Roger Miller; Tammy Wynette; Tom T. Hall; George Jones; Statler Brothers; Jeannie Seely; Ray Price; Hank Thompson; Roy Clark.

Country Special..Capitol (S) STBB-402   8-12   69
Glen Campbell; Ferlin Husky; Faron Young; Johnny & Jonie Mosby; Charlie Louvin; Buck Owens; Jody Miller; Sonny James; Wynn Stewart; Wanda Jackson; Louvin Brothers; Roy Acuff; Merle Haggard; Jean Shepard; Tennessee Ernie Ford; Jeannie Black; Hank Thompson.

Country Special...Columbia House (SP) DS-994   5-10   72
(TV offer.) Sammi Smith; Dave Dudley; George Jones; Jerry Lee Lewis; Tammy Wynette; Johnny Paycheck; Lynn Anderson; Mel Tillis & Sherry Bryce; Freddy Weller; Hank Williams Jr.

Country Spectactular...Columbia (M) CL-894   30-50   56
Rosemary Clooney; Gene Autry; Carl Smith; Don Cherry; Tunesmiths; Collins Kids.

Country Star Parade, Vol. 1 ....Vocalion (M) VL-3768   10-15   66
Country Star Parade, Vol. 1 ....Vocalion (S) VL 73768   10-15   66
Roger Miller; Roy Acuff; Wanda Jackson; Red Sovine; Louvin Brothers.

Country Star Parade, Vol. 2 .... Vocalion (M) VL-3804   10-15   67
Country Star Parade, Vol. 2 .... Vocalion (S) VL73804   10-15   67
    Roger Miller; Ernest Ashworth; Jenny Lou Carson; Justin Tubb; Mitchell Torok; Jason
    Fleming; Roger Miller.
Country Star Parade, Vol. 3 .... Vocalion (S) VL 73836   10-15   69
Country Stars, Country Hits .... Camden (M) CAL-793   10-20   64
Country Stars, Country Hits .... Camden (S) CAS-793   10-20   65
    Eddy Arnold; Hank Snow; Don Gibson; Chet Atkins; Homer & Jethro; Elton Britt; Jim
    Reeves; Pee Wee King; Red Stewart; Gid Tanner; Porter Wagoner; Montana Slim; Bill
    Boyd.
Country Stars of Today .... Power Pak (S) PO-287   5-10   75
    Freddy Fender; Jean Shepard; Johnny Paycheck; Mike Lunsford; Barbara Fairchild; Billy
    "Crash" Craddock; Narvel Felts; Buck Owens; Pozo Seco Singers; Stella Parton.
Country Stars Sing Sacred Songs .... Camden (M) CAL-2136   10-15   67
Country Stars Sing Sacred Songs .... Camden (S) CAS-2136   10-15   67
    Bobby Bare; Connie Smith; Hank Snow; Martha Carson; Browns; Kitty Wells; George
    Hamilton IV; Don Gibson; Sons of the Pioneers; Porter Wagoner.
Country Spectacular.. Columbia (M) CL-894   40-60   56
Country Spectacular (EP) .... Columbia B-8941/8942/8943   10-20   56
    Rosemary Clooney; Gene Autry; Carl Smith & Tunesmiths; Don Cherry; Collins Kids.
    (Price is for any of the three volumes.)
Country Standards from House of Bryant, Vol. 1 .... HB (S) 1001   10-15
    (Promotional issue only.) Glen Campbell & Bobbie Gentry; Bob Moore; Jim Reeves; Everly
    Brothers; Osborne Brothers; Eddy Arnold; Lynn Anderson; Chet Atkins; Ray Price.
Country Style.. Design (SE) SDLP-641   10-15
    Patsy Cline; Maddox Brothers & Rose; Jimmy Dean; Ferlin Husky; Melba Montgomery;
    Lonzo & Oscar.
Country Style (2 LP).. RCA (S) PRS-439   8-12   73
    Jim Reeves; Chet Atkins; Hank Locklin; Don Gibson; Skeeter Davis; Porter Wagoner;
    Norma Jean; Floyd Cramer; Bobby Bare; Liz Anderson; Jim Ed Brown; Danny Davis and
    the Nashville Brass; Hank Snow; Dickie Lee; Connie Smith; Bobby Bare; Skeeter Davis;
    Waylon Jennings; Leon Ashley; Dolly Parton; Jerry Reed; Dottie West; Jimmy Dean;
    Browns.
Country Sunshine (2 LP)................................... Adam VIII Ltd. (S) A8R-8011   8-10   74
    (Mail order offer.) Dottie West; Bobby Bare; Donna Fargo; Tommy Overstreet; Brenda Lee;
    Johnny Rodriguez; Tom T. Hall; Marty Robbins; Kenny Price; Porter Wagoner; Charlie
    Rich; Olivia Newton-John; Eddy Arnold; Dolly Parton; Jerry Reed; Faron Young; Roy
    Clark; Waylon Jennings; Johnny Bush; Jim Ed Brown.
Country Super Sounds (1956) .... Omega Sales (M) O-6-1956   20-40   73
    (Mail order offer.) Elvis Presley; others.
Country Super Sounds (1957) .... Omega Sales (M) O-6-1957   20-40   73
    (Mail order offer.) Elvis Presley; others.
Country Super Sounds (1958) .... Omega Sales (M) O-6-1958   20-40   73
    (Mail order offer.) Elvis Presley; others.
Country Time.. ????   5-10
    (Label and number not known.) Jody Miller; Willie Nelson; George Jones; Boots Randolf;
    David Wills; Mac Davis; Moe Bandy; Charlie McCoy; Tammy Wynette; Charlie Rich.
Country Time.. Columbia (S) ????   5-10   73
    (TV offer.) Ray Price; Faron Young; Jim Rodgers; Hank Thompson; Jimmy Wakely;
    Stonewall Jackson; Roger Miller; Johnny Cash; Arthur Smith; George Morgan; David
    Houston and Tammy Wynette; Lynn Anderson.
Country Times (2 LP).................... Columbia/Dynamic House (S) P-11797-A   8-12   73
    (Mail order offer.) Ray Price; Faron Young; Jimmie Rodgers; Hank Thompson; Jimmy
    Wakely; Stonewall Jackson; Roger Miller; Johnny Cash; Arthur Smith; George Morgan;
    David Houston & Tammy Wynette; Lynn Anderson.
Country Time Music .... Maverick (S) 1002   10-20
    Danny Darren; Skip & Gail; Billy B. and the Impressions; Kenny Christensen.
Country USA 1968 (2 LP) .... Time-Life (S) STL-11/CTR-06   8-12   89
    Waylon Jennings; Jerry Lee Lewis; Conway Twitty; George Jones; Osborne Brothers;
    Tammy Wynette; Merle Haggard; Buck Owens & His Buckaroos; Porter Wagoner & Dolly
    Parton; Charley Pride; Jeannie C. Riley; Glen Campbell; Johnny Cash; Loretta Lynn; Porter
    Wagoner; Flatt & Scruggs; Del Reeves; Henson Cargill.

Country Wine—100 Proof Country Hard Drinkin'

Hits (2 LP) ....Polystar (S) ????   8-12

Mel Tillis; Hank Williams, Jr.; Ben Colder; C.W. McCall; Billy Walker; Del Reeves; Doc &
Merle Watson; Wanda Jackson; Freddy Weller; David Wills; Johnny Cash; George Jones;
Roger Miller; Tom T. Hall; Roy Drusky; Faron Young; Johnny Rodriguez; Patti Page;
Cledus Maggard & the Citizens Band.

Country Winners '73...Columbia (S) IP-6067   5-10   73

Tanya Tucker; David Houston; Mac Davis; Tammy Wynette; Freddy Weller; Charlie Rich;
Lynn Anderson; Johnny Cash; Barbara Mandrell; Johnny Duncan.

Country's Best, Vol. 1..Capitol (EP) EAP 1-1179   5-10   59

Skeets McDonald; Jean Shepard; Tommy Collins; Hank Thompson.

Country's Best, Vol. 2..Capitol (EP) EAP 2-1179   5-10   59

Country's Best, Vol. 3..Capitol (EP) EAP 3-1179   5-10   59

Country's Best.. Capitol (M) T-1179   20-30   59

Faron Young; Skeets McDonald; Louvin Brothers; Jean Shepard & Ferlin Husky; Tex
Ritter; Tommy Collins; Freddie Hart; Hank Thompson; Wynn Stewart.

Country's Gospel (2 LP)...............................Word/Capitol (S) SL 6894/5   10-15   70s

Johnny Cash; Loretta Lynn; Jimmie Davis; Inspirations; Redd Harper; Marty Robbins; Cliff
Barrows; Ray Price; Pat Boone; Patsy Cline; Ernest Tubb; Joe Maphis; Bob Daniels;
Wilburn Brothers; Anita Bryant; Red Foley; Glen Campbell; Norma Zimmer; Jim Roberts;
Alan McGill; Happy Goodman Family; Roy Acuff; Burl Ives; Mary Jayne; Wayne Newton;
J.T. Adams; Wanda Jackson; Sonny James; Blue Ridge Quartet; Ferlin Husky; Roy
Rogers; Dale Evans & Tennessee Ernie Ford.

Country's Greatest Hits...Columbia (S) 465   5-10   69

(Columbia Record Club issue.) Johnny Cash; Johnny Horton; others.

Country's Greatest Hits, Vol. 1...Columbia (S) GP-9   5-10   69

Johnny Cash; George Morgan; Johnny Horton; "Little" Jimmy Dickens; Lonzo and Oscar;
Roy Acuff; Billy Walker; Jimmy Dean; Carl Smith; Flatt & Scruggs; Charlie Walker; Tommy
Collins; Statler Brothers; Marty Robbins; Ray Price.

Country's Greatest Hits, Vol. 2 (2 LP)............. Columbia (S) GP-19/CS 9930   8-12   69

Johnny Cash; Marty Robbins; Ray Price; Carl Smith; Stonewall Jackson; Carl Butler; Flatt
& Scruggs; Johnny Horton; Freddie Weller; Carl Perkins; Lefty Frizzell; Jimmy Dean; Little
Jimmy Dickens; Johnny Bond; Harden Trio; Claude King; Gene Autry; George Morgan;
Floyd Tillman; Bob Wills.

Country's Greatest Love Songs, 10 Years of Country

Gold (2 LP)... Columbia (SE) P2S 5644   8-12   70s

(Mail order. Columbia House Record Club issue.) Ray Price; Johnny Cash & June Carter;
David Houston & Tammy Wynette; Dave Dudley; Leon Ashley; Marty Robbins; Charlie
Rich; George Morgan; Roy Drusky; Jimmy Dean; Carl Smith; Johnny Cash; Lynn
Anderson; Claude King; Johnny Horton; Leroy Van Dyke; Tammy Wynette.

County Bound .... Columbia/Imperial House WU 3580   5-10   81

(Mail order offer.) Don Williams; Wille Nelson; Lacy J. Dalton; Statler Brothers; Tanya
Tucker; Tammy Wynette & George Jones; Moe Bandy & Joe Stampley; Kendalls; Barbara
Mandrell; Merle Haggard; Johnny Duncan; Crystal Gayle; John Conlee; Jennifer Warnes;
Conway Twitty.

Cowboy! ....Design (M) DLP-189   10-15

Gene Autry; Smiley Burnette; Eddie Dean; Foy Willing; Bradley Kincaid.

Cowboy Songs for Children ....Harmony (M) HL-9512   10-20   60

Fess Parker; Jerry Blaine; others.

Cowpoke .... Camay (S) CA 3040   5-10   60s

Tex Ritter; Tennessee Ernie Ford; Merle Travis; Wesley Tuttle; Tex Williams; Elton Britt;
Hank Fort; others.

Cream of the Country Crop.. Starday (M) S-394   10-15   67

Buck Owens; Johnny Cash; Sonny James; Dottie West; others.

Current Country Hits ....Harmony (EP) 16   10-20   56

Current Country Hits, Vol. 1 ....Harmony (M) HL-9008   30-50   56

Current Country Hits, Vol. 2 ....Harmony (M) HL-9011   30-50   56

Current Country Hits, Vol. 3 ....Harmony (M) HL-9016   30-50   56

Current Country Hits, Vol. 4 ....Harmony (M) HL-9020   30-50   56

Diesel Smoke, Dangerous Curves (And Other Truck Driver

Favorites) .... Starday (M) S-250   15-20   60s

Diesel Smoke, Dangerous Curves (And Other Truck Driver

Favorites) .... Starday (S) SLP-250   15-20   60s

Down a Country Road.................. Columbia Musical Treasury (SE) 1P 6112   5-10   75
> (Columbia House Record Club issue.) Tanya Tucker; Mac Davis; Tammy Wynette; Jody Miller; Charlie Rich; Roger Miller; Lynn Anderson; Ray Price; Flatt & Scruggs; Freddy Weller.

Dueling Banjos .... Pickwick (S) SPC 3340   8-12   73
> Bob & Sam Springer; Flatt & Scruggs; Stanley Brothers; John Duffy & the Country Gentlemen; Bill Emerson & His Country Banjo.

Duet Country ....Chart (S) 1014   5-10   69
> Lynn Anderson & Jerry Lane; Gordon Terry & Maxine Brown; Kenny Vernon & Lawanda Lindsey; others.

Dukes of Hazard ....Scotti Bros. (S) FZ-37712   15-25   81
> (Soundtrack.) Catherine Bach; James Best; Johnny Cash; Sorrell Booke; Doug Kershaw; others.

Dynamite Country Duets (Nashville's Best Songs and
    Performances).. Harmony (SP) KH-32479   5-10   73
> Johnny Cash & June Carter; Tammy Wynette & George Jones; Carl Butler & Pearl; Agnes & Orville; Lynn Anderson & Glenn Sutton; Johnny Duncan & June Stearns; Arlene Harden & Frank Jones; George Morgan & Marion Worth; Jody Miller & Johnny Paycheck; David Houston & Barbara Mandrell.

E-Z Country Programming, No. 2..RCA (M) No. 2   250-300   55
> (10–inch LP. Promotional issue only. Not issued with special cover.) Elvis Presley; Eddy Arnold; Nita, Rita & Ruby; Chet Atkins; Hank Snow; Sons of the Pioneers; Anita Carter; Skeeter Brown; Homer & Jethro; Hank Locklin; Stuart Hamblen.

E-Z Country Programming, No. 3..RCA (M) No. 3   250-300   55
> (10–inch LP. Promotional issue only. Not issued with special cover.) Elvis Presley; Eddy Arnold; Chet Atkins; Hank Snow; Hawkshaw Hawkins; Johnnie, & Jack and Ruby Wells; Jim Reeves; Dorothy Olsen; Porter Wagoner.

Early Country Music..Historical (S) 2   8-10   67
> Joe Evans; John Dilleshaw; Hap Hayes; others.

Echoes of the Ozarks, Vol. 1..County (M) 518   8-12   70s
> Pope's Arkansas Mountaineers; Morrison Twin Brothers String Band; Ashley's Melody Men; Carter Brothers & Son; Arkansas Barefoot Boys; Dutch Coleman & Red Whitehead.

Echoes of the Ozarks, Vol. 2..County (M) 519   8-12   70s
Echoes of the Ozarks, Vol. 3..County (M) 520   8-12   70s

Elected Performers of the Country Music Hall of
    Fame (2 LP) .... Columbia Special Products (S) P 12824   10-15   75
> Jimmie Rodgers; Eddy Arnold; Jim Reeves; Original Carter Family; Chet Atkins; Pee Wee King; Hank Williams; Fred Rose; Roy Acuff; Tex Ritter; Ernest Tubb; Uncle Dave Macon; Red Foley; Bob Wills; Gene Autry; Bill Monroe; Jimmie Davis; Patsy Cline; Owen Bradley.

Every Which Way But Loose.. Elektra (ST) SE-503   8-12   76
> (Soundtrack.) Eddie Rabbitt; Mel Tillis; Sondra Locke; Cliff Crofford; Charlie Rich; Larry Collins; Carol Chase; Sondra Locke & Phil Everly; Hank Thompson.

Everything Is Beautiful ....Columbia (S) ????   5-10
> Lynn Anderson; Marty Robbins; Johnny Cash & June Carter Cash; Mac Davis; Jim Nabors; Patti Page; Statler Brothers; Tammy Wynette; Lester Flatt & Earl Scruggs; Ray Price.

Fantastic Country, Vol. 1 .... RCA Special Products (S) PRS-387   8-12   72
> Michael Nesmith; Duane Eddy; Liz Anderson; Chet Atkins; Bobby Bare; Skeeter Davis; Jimmy Dean; Norman Luboff; Lorne Greene; George Hamilton IV; John Hartford; Pat McKinney; Roger Miller; Jerry Reed; Connie Smith; Sammi Smith; Hank Snow; Porter Wagoner. (Made for Salem-Select Distribution.)

Favorite Western Songs....................................... Rural Rhythm (M) FW 2114   8-12   60s
> Patsy Montana; De Wayne Wear; Roy Scott; Kenny Roberts; Jimmy Payton; Hall Wallis.

Favorites from Nashville.. Camden (S) X-9019   5-10   72
> Eddy Arnold; Sonny James; Norma Jean; Dottie West; Chet Atkins; Floyd Cramer; Jim Ed Brown; Skeeter Davis; Waylon Jennings; Roger Miller; Dolly Parton; Boots Randolph; Charlie Rich; Connie Smith; Hank Snow; Porter Wagoner.

Festival of RCA Victor Artists Gospel Sing .... RCA (M) LPM-2330   15-20   61
Festival of RCA Victor Artists Gospel Sing .... RCA (S) LSP-2330   15-25   61
> Jim Reeves; Blackwood Brothers; Statesmen; Don Gibson; others.

Fiddler's Hall of Fame .... Starday (M) S-209   15-20   63
Fiddler's Hall of Fame .... Starday (S) SLP-209   15-20   63
Fiddlin' Country Style ....Wyncote (S) SW-9077   8-12   64
> Stanley Brothers; Tommy Hill; Lonesome Pine Fiddlers; Ken Clark; Benny Martin; Chubby Wise; Herbie Remington; Wayne Raney; Eddie Eddings; Tommy Hill.

Fiddlin' Country Style .... Starday (M) S-114   15-25   60
Fiddlin' Country Style .... Starday (S) SLP-114   15-25   60

Fiddlin' Country Style .... Nashville (M) NLP-2015   10-15   65

Fire on the Strings.. Starday (M) M-221   10-20   67

Fire on the Strings... Starday (M) S-221   10-20   67
> Bob Wills; Boots Randolph with Jimmy Richardson; Lester Flatt & Earl Scruggs; Leon McAuliffe and His Cimarron Boys; Arthur Smith; Tommy Hill; Reno & Smiley; Tommy Jackson; Pete Drake.

Fire on the Strings...Starday (M) SYM-0127   10-20   67

Fire on the Strings...Starday (S) SYS-0127   10-20   67
> (RCA Record Club issue.) Bob Wills; Boots Randolph with Jimmy Richardson; Lester Flatt & Earl Scruggs; Leon McAuliffe and His Cimarron Boys; Arthur Smith; Tommy Hill; Reno & Smiley; Tommy Jackson; Pete Drake.

First of the Famous .... Capitol (M) T-2275   15-25   65
> Hank Thompson; Sonny James; Tex Ritter; Faron Young; Wanda Jackson; Ferlin Husky; Buck Owens; Jean Shepard; Tennessee Ernie Ford; Jimmy Wakely; Tex Williams; Merle Travis.

Five Kings of the Country World ....Harmony (S) KH-31561   6-12   72
> Johnny Cash; Ray Price; Marty Robbins; Jerry Reed; David Houston.

Five Queens of Country Music...................................Nashville (S) NLP 2057   8-12
> Patsy Cline; Dottie West; Jan Howard; Melba Montgomery; Margie Singleton.

Five Queens of the Country World............................Harmony (S) KH-31535   6-12   72
> Lynn Anderson; Tammy Wynette; Arlene Harden; Barbara Mandrell; Sammi Smith.

Five String Banjo Jamboree...................................Mercury (M) MGW-12299   10-20   65

Five String Banjo Jamboree...................................Mercury (S) SRW-16299   15-20   65
> Flatt and Scruggs; Stanley Brothers; Carl Story; others.

Folk Jamboree ....Columbia Special Products (S) CSP-205   10-20   60s
> Bob Dylan; Village Stompers; Johnny Cash; New Christy Minstrels; Les & Larry Elgart; Flatt & Scruggs; Clancy Brother; Tommy Makem; Pete Seeger; Brothers Four; Banjo Barons. (Made for Philco.)

Folk Sound ....Columbia Special Products (S) CSP-299   10-15   67
> New Christy Minstrels; Johnny Cash; Brothers Four; Statler Brothers; Simon & Garfunkel; Flatt & Scruggs; Marty Robbins; Bob Dylan; Jimmy Dean; Banjo Barons.

Folked Again - Best of Mountain Railroad,
   Vol. 1 ....Mountain Railroad (S) MR 52671   8-12   87
> Tom Paxton; Bob Gibson; Josh White Jr.; Gamble Rogers; Rod MacDonald; Free Hot Lunch; Dick Pinney; Steve Young; Betsy Kaske; Jim Post; Gibson & Camp; Dave Snaker Ray.

Folsom Prison Blues .... Nashville (SE) NLP-2059   5-10   68
> Johnny Cash; Lester Flatt & Earl Scruggs; Joe Maphis; Billie Morgan; Carl Story; Bill Dudley; Hylo Brown; Pee Wee King.

Folsom Prison Blues and Other Country Hits ...... Modern Sound (S) MS-599   5-10   69

For the Good Times ....Columbia (S) ????   5-10
> David Houston; Lynn Anderson; Lary Gatlin; Connie Smith; Joe Stampley; Sonny James; Johnny Cash; Charlie Rich; David Allen Coe; Tammy Wynette.

Forever Country .... Columbia Special Products (S) 13613   5-10   76
> Lynn Anderson; Ray Price; Loretta Lynn; David Houston; Johnny Cash; June Carter; Barbara Mandrell; Webb Pierce; Barbara Fairchild; George Jones; Tanya Tucker; Sonny James; Tammy Wynette; Henson Cargill; Jody Miller; Kitty Wells; Bill Anderson; George Morgan; Patsy Cline.

Forever Country Original Hits, Vol. I ....Forever (SE) 105   8-10   70
> Rex Allen; Rusty Draper; George Jones; Johnny Preston; Ned Miller; Jerry Wallace; Leroy Van Dyke; Claude Gray; Faron Young; Patsy Cline; others.

Four Big Hits: see PRICE, Ray / Johnny Horton / Carl Smith / George Morgan

Four Kings of Country Music: see JONES, George / Buck Owens / David Houston / Tommy Hill.

From Nashville with Love (3 LP) ....RCA (S) R 213764-1-2-3   10-20   72
> (RCA Record Club issue.) Jim Reeves; Dottie West; George Hamilton IV; Archie Campbell & Lorene Mann; Jimmy Dean; Floyd Cramer; Porter Wagoner & Skeeter Davis; Browns; Sonny James; Homer & Jethro; Willie Nelson; Anita Kerr Singers; Eddy Arnold; Liz Anderson; Nat Stuckey; Wendy Dawn; Justin Tubb; Roger Miller; John D. Loudermilk; Norma Jean; Jim Ed Brown; Chet Atkins; Connie Smith; Hank Snow; Don Bowman; Stuf Phillips; Don Gibson; Waylon Jennings; Hank Locklin; Bobby Bare.

Galaxy of Country & Western Golden Hits ....Mercury (S) SRD-12   15-25   60s
> George Jones; Claude Gray; Leroy Van Dyke; James O'Gwynn; Jimmy Skinner; Margie Bowes; George Jones & Margie Singleton; Margie Singleton; Benny Barnes; Merle Kilgore; Lawton Williams; Rex Allen.

Gentlemen's Choice (Country Hits By Nashville's Top Male
   Vocalists)..Harmony (S) KH-32480   5-10   73
     Ray Price; Marty Robbins; Claude King; Sonny James; others.
George Jones and His Country Cousins - Salute to the Grand Ole
   Opry .... United Artists (M) UAL-3309   15-20   63
George Jones and His Country Cousins - Salute to the Grand Ole
   Opry ....United Artists (S) UAS-6309   20-25   63
     George Jones; Sonny Burns; Kathy Dee; others.
Giant Country...United Artists (S) UAS-6745   5-10   70
     Del Reeves; George Jones; Johnny Darrell; Bobby Lewis.
Giants of Country Music...Design (S) SDLP-643   8-12   60s
     Carl Belew; Patsy Cline; Ferlin Husky; Hank Locklin; Webb Pierce; Rocky Bill Ford; Claude
     King; T. Texas Tyler; Slim Willet; Hal Willis.
Gold Guitar Awards 1957-1963....................................... Columbia (M) D2J-1   15-30   63
     (Promotional issue only. Special commemorative album, WSM Grand Ole Opry's 38th
     Birthday Celebration.) Ray Price; Marty Robbins; Johnny Cash; Johnny Horton; Stonewall
     Jackson; Jimmy Dean; Claude King; Bill Pursell.
Golden Age of Country
   Music (6 LP) .... Columbia Musical Treasury (S) P6S 5614   15-25   70s
     Johnny Cash; David Houston & Barbara Mandrell; Charlie Rich; Lynne Anderson; Bob
     Luman; Ray Price; Stonewall Jackson; Roy Clark; Johnny Horton; Jeannie C. Riley; John
     Wesley Ryles; Tammy Wynette; Johnny Cash; David Houston; Lefty Frizzell; Sandy Posey;
     George Jones; Statler Brothers; Conway Twitty; Tom T. Hall; Harden Trio; Claude King;
     Billy Walker; Dave Dudley; Hank Williams, Sr.; Bonnie Guitar; Roger Miller; Marty Robbins;
     George Morgan; Johnny Cash & June Carter; Jim Nabors; Leroy Van Dyke; Roy Acuff;
     Jerry Lee Lewis; Flatt & Scruggs; Arlene Harden; Roy Drusky; Jimmy Dickens; George
     Jones; Lynn Anderson; Carl Butler; Patti Page; Merle Kilgore.
Golden Age of Country Music,
   1940-1970 (7 LP) ....Readers Digest (S) RB4-005   20-30   87
     Jimmie Davis; Bob Wills & His Texas Playboys; Roy Acuff & His Smoky Mountain Boys;
     Elton Britt; Arthur Guitar Boogie Smith; Ernest Tubb; Merle Travis; Eddy Arnold; Zeke
     Manners & His Band; Red Foley; Hank Thompson; Hank Williams; Jimmy Wakely &
     Margaret Whiting; Wayne Raney; Patti Page; Hank Snow; Moon Mullican; Tennessee Ernie
     Ford; Webb Pierce; Slim Whitman; Red Foley; Davis Sisters; Kitty Wells; Johnny Cash;
     Faron Young; Everly Brothers; Ferlin Husky; Patsy Cline; Jim Reeves; Don Gobson; Bobby
     Helms; Hank Locklin; Tex Ritter; George Jones; Roy Drusky; Sheb Wooley; Roy Clark;
     Porter Wagoner; George Jones & Melba Montgomery; Roger Miller; Del Reeves; Charley
     Pride; Glen Campbell; Eddy Arnold; Bill Andrews with the Po' Boys; Hank Williams, Sr.;
     Sonny James.
Golden Classics, Vol. 1 ....Golden Classics (S) 103   5-10   70
Golden Classics, Vol. 2 ....Golden Classics (S) 104   5-10   70
Golden Classics, Vol. 3 ....Golden Classics (S) 105   5-10   70
Golden Classics, Vol. 4 ....Golden Classics (S) 106   5-10   70
Golden Classics, Vol. 5 ....Golden Classics (S) 107   5-10   70
Golden Classics, Vol. 6 ....Golden Classics (S) 108   5-10   70
Golden Classics, Vol. 7 ....Golden Classics (S) 109   5-10   70
Golden Classics, Vol. 8 ....Golden Classics (S) 110   5-10   70
Golden Classics, Vol. 9 ....Golden Classics (S) 111   5-10   70
Golden Classics, Vol. 10 ....Golden Classics (S) 112   5-10   70
     George Morgan; Dottie West; Buck Owens; Flatt & Scruggs; George Jones; others.
Golden Country .... Wyncote (M) W-9159   8-12   60s
Golden Country ....Wyncote (S) SW-9159   8-12   60s
     Jimmy Dean; George Jones; Country Johnny Mathis; Stoneman Family; Deputies.
Golden Country and Western Hits .... RCA (M) CPM-500   10-15   65
Golden Country and Western Hits .... RCA (S) CSP-500   10-15   65
     Hank Snow; Jim Reeves; Don Gibson; Floyd Cramer; Porter Wagoner; Eddy Arnold; Gene
     Autry; Skeeter Davis; Hank Locklin; Chet Atkins; George Hamilton IV; Bobby Bare.

Golden Country Hits.. United Artists (M) UAL-3327	10-15	64
Golden Country Hits...United Artists (S) UAS-6327	15-20	64
George Jones; Burl Ives; Judy Lynn; others.		
Golden Country Hits...Harmony (M) HL-7362	10-15	66
Golden Country Hits... Harmony (S) HS-11162	10-15	66
Ray Price; Flatt & Scruggs; Stonewall Jackson; Billy Walker; Bobby Helms; Freddie Hart; "Little" Jimmy Dickens; Mel Tillis; Carl Butler; Lefty Frizzell.		
Golden Country Hits (On Artistic): see Original Country Hits		
Golden Country Hits, Vol. 2..Harmony (M) HL-7391	10-15	66
Golden Country Hits, Vol. 2..Harmony (S) HS-11191	10-15	66
Johnny Horton; Jimmy Dean; Marion Worth.		
Golden Instrumentals Country Style .... Wing (M) MGW-12261	10-20	64
Golden Instrumentals Country Style ....Wing (S) SRW-16261	10-20	64
Golden Moments of Country and Western		
Music (2 LP).. Capitol (S) QB-90985	8-12	
Hank Thompson; Jean Shepard; Sonny James; Merle Haggard; Red Simpson; Buck Owens; Wanda Jackson; Ned Miller; Tex Ritter; Ferlin Husky; Tennessee Ernie Ford.		
Golden Sounds of Country Music ....Harmony (M) HL-7449	8-10	68
Golden Sounds of Country Music ....Harmony (S) HS-11249	8-10	68
Ray Price; Johnny Cash; Carl Smith; Johnny Horton; George Morgan; others.		
Golden Years of Gospel Greats........................... Modern Sound (S) MS-815	5-10	
J.T. Adams; Wally Fowler; John Daniels Quartet; Speer Family; Florida Boys; Sons of Song; Sego Brothers & Naomi; Wendy Bagwell; Jake Hess; Oak Ridge Quartet.		
Good Old Boys..Columbia (S) CSP P 14583	8-12	78
(Country Music Magazine.) David Wills; Freddy Fender; Johnny Paycheck; Freddy Weller; David Allen Coe; Tommy Cash; Sonny James; Joe Stampley; Ray Price; David Houston; Billy "Crash" Craddock; George Jones; Narvel Felts; Johnny Cash; Charlie Rich; Billy Swan.		
Good Old Country Boys (5 LP) ....Mercury/Columbia House (S) 5P 6000	20-30	73
(Boxed set. Record club issue.) Faron Young; Tom T. Hall; Roger Miller; Jerry Lee Lewis; others.		
Good Old Country Gospel.................................. Country Music (S) CM-1036	5-10	75
Loretta Lynn; Jimmie Davis; Red Foley; Bill Monroe; Ernest Tubb; Bill Anderson; Webb Pierce; Kitty Wells; Wilburn Brothers; Jimmy Martin.		
Good Old Country Gospel................................ Green Valley (S) MSM-35008	8-12	
Bill Anderson; Jimmie Davis; Red Foley; Bill Monroe; Loretta Lynn; Ernest Tubb; Kitty Wells; Webb Pierce; Wilburn Brothers; Jimmy Martin.		
Good Old Country Gospel... RCA (S) LSP-4778	5-10	72
Chet Atkins; Floyd Cramer; Dolly Parton; Dottie West; Charley Pride; Porter Wagoner; Connie Smith; Hank Snow; Skeeter Davis; Jim Reeves.		
Good Times in Country Music (2 LP).......... Columbia/Tampa (SE) C2-10419	8-12	70s
Ray Price; Faron Young; Jim Rodgers; Hank Thompson; Jimmy Wakely; Stonewall Jackson; Arthur Smith; Roger Miller; Lynn Anderson; Johnny Cash; Cowboy Copas; George Morgan; Kenny Roberts; Andy Wilson; David Houston & Tammy Wynette; Johnny Cash & June Carter; Grandpa Jones; Bill Clifton; Jim Nabors; Carl Story; Carl Smith; Roy Clark; Buck Owens; Johnny Bond; Dottie West; Jimmy Dean.		
Gospel Special 20 Great Songs by 20 Great Artists... Power Pak (S) PO-292	5-10	76
Wilma Lee & Stoney Cooper; Archie Campbell; Masters Family; Oak Ridge Quartet; Carl Story; Sunshine Boys; Stamps Quartet; Red Sovine; Reno & Smiley; Sego Brothers & Naomi; George Jones; Statesmen Quartet; Blue Ridge Quartet; T. Texas Tyler; Blackwood Singers; Speer Family; Prophets Quartet.		
Gospel's Top 20 All Time		
Favorites .... Columbia Special Products (S) P 13429	5-10	76
(Mail order.) Charlie Rich; Johnny Cash; Tammy Wynette; Statler Brothers; Kitty Wells; Jim Reeves; David Houston; Loretta Lynn; Roy Rogers; Chuck Wagon Gang; Marilyn Sellars; Roy Acuff; Hank Williams; Billy Walker; Carter Family.		

Grand Ole Country (8 LP) ....Columbia/Readers Digest RDA-122   25-40   74
Lynn Anderson; Johnny Cash; Tammy Wynette; David Houston; Marty Robbins; Johnny Horton; Charlie Rich; Tanya Tucker; Ray Price; Statler Brothers; Mac Davis; Flatt & Scruggs; June Carter; Mother Maybelle Carter; Tommy Cash; Carter Family; George Jones; Roger Miller; Jim & Jesse; George Hamilton IV; Stonewall Jackson; Statler Brothers; Terri Lane; Charlie Walker; Carl & Pearl Butler; Lefty Frizzell; Barbara Mandrell; Charlie McCoy; Charlie Rich; Jeannie Seely; Bob Luman; Carl Smith; Billy Walker; Boots Randolph; Bonnie Lou; Mel Tillis; Flatt & Scruggs; Arthur Smith; Lloyd Green; Jimmy Dean; Jack Cardwell; Claude King; Barbara Fairchild; Sonny James; Jody Miller; Johnny Paycheck; Connie Smith; Carl Perkins; Patti Page; Freddy Weller; "Little" Jimmy Dickens; Jody Miller; Anita Bryant; Faron Young; Johnny Bond; Dolly Parton; George Morgan; Floyd Tillman; Roy Acuff; Gene Autry; Moon Mullican.

Grand Ole Country .... Hilltop (S) JS-6157   5-10
Charlie Rich; Johnny Cash; T. Texas Tyler; Roy Orbison; Jerry Lee Lewis; Carl Belew; Conway Twitty; Patsy Cline; Webb Pierce; Jan Howard; Carl Perkins; Ferlin Husky; Jimmy Dean; Hank Locklin; Maddox Brothers & Rose.

Grand Ole Country Hits .... Camden (M) CAL-737   10-20   63
Grand Ole Country Hits .... Camden (SE) CAS-737   10-15   66
Hank Snow; Chet Atkins; Eddy Arnold; Pee Wee King; Lone Pine; Jimmie Rodgers; Don Gibson; Hank Locklin; Homer & Jethro; Jim Reeves; Gid Turner & the Skillets; Roy Rogers & the Sons of the Pioneers.

Grand Ole Country Hits .... Pickwick/Spectrum (S) ACL-7054   5-10   77
Hank Snow; Chet Atkins; Eddy Arnold; Pee Wee King; Redd Stewart; Jimmie Rodgers; Rainbow Ranch Boys; Don Gibson; Hank Locklin; Homer & Jethro; Jim Reeves; Roy Rogers; Sons of the Pioneers.

Grand Ole Opry Past and Present .... Hilltop (S) JS-6022   8-12   60s
Uncle Jimmy Thompson & Eva Thompson Jones; Webb Pierce; Faron Young; Carl Belew; Wilburn Brothers; Billy Grammer; Lonzo & Oscar.

Grand Ole Opry Spectacular (2 LP) .... Starday (M) S-242   15-20   63
Grand Ole Opry Spectacular (2 LP) .... Starday (S) SLP-242   15-20   63
George Jones; Grandpa Jones; Red Sovine; Margie Singleton; Jimmy Skinner; Dottie West; Leon Payne; Tommy Jackson; Archie Campbell; Hawshaw Hawkins; Texas Ruby; Jim & Jesse.

Great Country and Western Hits .... Hilltop/Pickwick (S) JS-6088   8-12   60s
Johnny Horton; Sue Thompson; Faron Young; Flatt & Scruggs; Jimmy Dean; Anita Carter; Leroy Van Dyke; Carlisles; Rex Allen; Del Wood; Margie Bowes.

Great Country and Western Hits (10 EP) .... RCA (EP) SPD-26   800-1000   56
(Boxed set. Includes insert/separator sheets.) Elvis Presley; Eddy Arnold; Chet Atkins; Johnnie & Jack; Homer & Jethro; Jim, Edward & Maxine Brown; Jim Reeves; Hank Snow; Sons of the Pioneers; Porter Wagoner; Del Wood.

Great Country and Western Stars .... MGM (M) 2E-12   15-25   64
Great Country and Western Stars .... MGM (S) S2E-12   20-30   64
Hank Williams; Sheb Wooley; Roy Acuff; others.

Great Country and Western Stars .... Wing (M) MGW-12268   10-20   64
Great Country and Western Stars .... Wing (S) SRW-16268   10-20   64
Johnny Horton; Jimmy Dean; Sue Thompson; Rex Allen; Carlisles.

Great Country Duets .... Columbia (S) C-30896   5-10   71
Johnny Cash & June Carter; Carl & Pearl Butler; others.

Great Country Favorites .... MGM (M) E-4211   10-20   64
Great Country Favorites .... MGM (S) SE-4211   15-20   64
Sheb Wooley; Hank Williams; Ben Colder; others.

Great Country Favorites (4 LP) .... Columbia (S) DS-393   10-20   73
Great Country Folk .... Harmony (S) KH-31109   5-10   72
Sammi Smith; Tommy Cash; Johnny Cash; others.

Great Country Folk, Vol. 2 .... Harmony (S) KH-31389   5-10   72
Carl Smith; Carl Butler; Johnny Cash; Lynn Anderson; others.

Great Country Gospel Groups .... Wing (M) MGW-12262   8-12   64
Great Country Gospel Groups .... Wing (S) SRW-16262   8-12   64
Flatt & Scruggs; Stanley Brothers; Masters Family; Carl Story & the Rambling Mountaineers; Tammy & Jim Wilson with the Chanters; Stamps Quartet.

Great Country Hits .... United Artists (M) UAL-3159   15-25   61
Bill Mack; Jim Blakley; others.

Great Country Hits ....Epic (S) BN 26550   5-10 70
  Tammy Wynette; David Houston; Jim and Jesse and the Virginia Boys; Charlie Walker;
  Stan Hitchcock; Tommy Cash; Mac Curtis; David Houston & Tammy Wynette; Bob Luman;
  Charlie Rich; Autry Inman.
Great Country Hits of the Year (3 LP)...................RCA Victor (S) CPL3-0697 10-20 74
  Eddy Arnold; Chet Atkins; George Jones; Dottie West; Karen Wheeler; Skeeter Davis;
  Floyd Cramer; Dolly Parton; Charlie Rich; Bobby Bare; Jim Ed Brown; Josie Brown;
  Johnny Bush; Danny Davis; Willie Nelson; George Hamilton IV; Waylon Jennings; George
  Jones; Dickey Lee; Ronnie Milsap; Kenny Price; Jerry Reed; Jim Reeves; Johnny Russell;
  Brian Shaw; Connie Smith; Hank Snow; Nat Stuckey; Porter Wagoner; Charlie Walker.
Great Country Love
  Songs (4 LP) ....Columbia Musical Treasury (SE) P4S 5400 15-20
  (Boxed set. Record club issue.) Roger Miller; Ray Conniff Singers; Tammy Wynette;Marty
  Robbins; Johnny Cash; Dave Dudley; David Houston; Freddie Weller; Patti Page; Ray
  Price; Leon Ashley; Bobby Vinton; John Wesley Ryles; Jerry Lee Lewis; Jimmy Dean; O.C.
  Smith; Roy Drusky; Frankie Laine; Bonnie Guitar; Jim Nabors; Stonewall Jackson; Roy
  Clark; Johnny Horton; Johnny Cash & June Carter; Carl Smith; Jerry Vale; Lefty Frizzell;
  Flatt & Scruggs.
Great Country Music .... Dot (M) DLP-3732 10-20 66
Great Country Music ....Dot (S) DLP-25732 10-20 66
  Cowboy Copas; Hank Garland; others.
Great Country Singers .... Columbia Special Products (S) CSS 1503 5-10
  Johnny Cash; Tammy Wynette; Anita Bryant; Marty Robbins; Chuck Wagon Gang; David
  Houston; Carl Smith; Roy Acuff; Ray Price; Stonewall Jackson.
Great Country Stars Singing Their Biggest
  Hits (4 LP) .... Capitol/Tampa (S) SLD-6870 20-25
  Buck Owens; Wanda Jackson; Hobby Helms; Sonny James; Patsy Cline; Tex Ritter; Red
  Foley; Wayne Rancy; Moon Mulligan; Merle Travis; Jimmy Wakely; T. Texas Tyler; Pete
  Seeger; Tennessee Ernie Ford; Hank Thompson; Ferflin Husky; Faron Young; Sonny
  James; Bill Anderson; Ernest Ashworth; Wynn Stewart; Conway Twitty; Jody Miller; Roy
  Clark; Leroy Van Dyke; Jeannie C. Riley; Billie Jo Spears; Glen Campbell; Bobbie Gentry;
  Susan Raye; Freddie Hart; Buddy Alan; Anne Murray; Joe South.
Great Country Stars Sing Their Great Country Hits.......... Capitol (M) T-2739 10-20 67
Great Country Stars Sing Their Great Country Hits.........Capitol (S) ST-2739 10-20 67
  Buck Owens; Jean Shepard; Wanda Jackson; others.
Great Folk Country Hits...................... Capitol Creative Products (S) SL 6647 8-12 60s
  Lettermen; Hedge & Donna; Al De Lory; Nancy Wilson; Glen Campbell; Ella Fitzgerald;
  Tennessee Ernie Ford; Kingston Trio.
Great Gospel Quartets.................... Columbia Special Products (S) P-13967 5-10 77
  (Produced by Country Music Magazine.) Imperials; Sego Brothers & Naomi; Floriday Boys;
  LeFevres; Stamps; Foggy River Boys; Blackwood Brothers; Oak Ridge; Wendy Bagwell &
  the Sunliters; Statesmen; Sons of Song; Jordanaires; Pine Ridge Boys; Trav'lers;
  Plainsmen; Rebels; Blue Ridge; Swanee River Boys; Gospel Singing Caravan; J.T. Adams
  & the Men of Texas; Speer Family; Dee White Chorale; Jerry & the Singing Goffs.
Great Gospel Songs.. Word (S) 8698 5-10 76
  Anita Kerr; Walt Mills; Norma Zimmer; Ray Price; Roy Clark; Carol Lawrence; Mary Jayne;
  Dale Evans; others.
Great Gospel Songs Encore! (2 LP) ....Word (S) WST-8645 8-12 76
  Danny Thomas; Wanda Jackson; Anita Bryant; Roy Rogers & Dale Evans; Dino; Happy
  Goodman Family; Kurt Kaiser; Gene Gaither & Mary Jane; Thrasher Brothers; Cliff
  Barrows; Love Song; Norma Zimmer; Evie; Ray Price; Ken Medema; Marijohn; Andrae
  Crouch; Pat Boone Family; 2nd Chapter of Acts; Dave Boyer; Ralph Carmichael;
  Inspirations; Barry McGuire; Jimmie Davis.
Great Moments at the Grand Ole Opry (2 LP)...............RCA (S) CPL2-1904 8-12 77
  Minnie Pearl; Connie Smith; Sonny James; Chet Atkins; Don Gibson; Dottie West; Ronnie
  Milsap; Billy Walker; Jim Ed Brown; Bobby Bare; Hank Snow; Dolly Parton; Porter
  Wagoner; Jim Reeves; Archie Campbell.
Great Ones...Capitol (M) T-1718 20-25 62
Great Ones..Capitol (S) ST-1718 25-30 62
  Buck Owens; Faron Young; Jeanne Black; Louvin Brothers; Tennessee Ernie Ford; Rose
  Maddox; Ferlin Husky; Tex Ritter; Wanda Jackson; Hank Thompson.

Great Songs of Faith and Inspiration (4 LP)...................... RCA (S) R 213812   15-20   72
(Boxed set.) Charley Pride; Blackwood Brothers Quartet featuring J.D. Sumner; Jimmy
Dean with the Imperials Quartet and the Jordanaires; Floyd Cramer; Dolly Parton; Porter
Wagoner; Billy Graham Crusade Choir; George Beverly Shea; Chet Atkins; Pat Boone; Jim
Reeves; Tony Fontaine; Rex Hubbard Singers; Bobby Bare; Nat Stuckey & Connie Smith;
Hank Snow; Statesmen Quartet; Don Gibson; Dottie West; Eddy Arnold; Sons of the
Pioneers; Skeeter Davis; Hank Locklin; Danny Davis & the Nashville Brass; Doris Akers;
Jack Holcomb; Speer Family; Wendy Bagwell & the Sunliters; Jerome Hines; Anita Kerr
Quartet; Cliff Barrows; Roy Rogers & Dale Evans; Archie Campbell; Norma Jean; Browns;
Jake Hess.

Great Stars of Country & Western, Vol. 2 ....Diplomat (S) DS 2408   8-12   60s
Dave Dudley; David Houston; Johnny Sea; Sonny James; Warner Mack; Willie Nelson;
Cowboy Copas.

Great Stars of Country & Western, Vol. 3 .... Diplomat (M) D 2416   8-12   60s
Cowboy Copas; Johnny Sea; Dave Dudley; Sonny James; Bill Carlisle.

Country and Western Golden Hit Parade...................... Starday (S) SLP 245   10-20   60s
Cowboy Copas; Red Sovine; Texas Ruby; Archie Campbell; Curly Fox; Justin Tubb;
Johnny Bond; Benny Martin; Willis Brothers; Dottie West; Dean Manuel; Buck Owens;
Bobby Sykes; Arthur Smith; Hylo Brown; Leon Payne; George Jones; Jimmie Skinner;
Cathy Copas; Glenda Raye; Tom O'Neal; others.

Greatest Comedy Stars of the Grand Old Opry .... Guest Star (S) GS-1475   10-20
Homer & Jethro; Cousin Jody; Lonzo & Oscar; Brother Oswald; Unkle Willie Potts.

Greatest Country and Western Hits,
No. 3...Columbia Limited Edition (S) LE 10035   5-10
Ray Price; Billy Walker; George Morgan; Mel Tillis; Carl Butler; Stonewall Jackson.

Greatest Country and Western Hits, No. 3 .... Columbia (M) CL-1816   15-25   62

Greatest Country and Western Hits, No. 3 .... Columbia (S) CS-8616   15-25   62
Ray Price; Mel Tillis; Carl Butler; Billy Walker; George Morgan; Stonewall Jackson.

Greatest Country and Western Hits, Vol. 4 .... Columbia (M) CL-2081   15-25   63

Greatest Country and Western Hits, Vol. 4 .... Columbia (S) CS-8881   15-25   63
Jimmy Dean; Marion Worth; Marty Robbins; Ray Price; Carl Smith; Lester Flatt & Earl
Scruggs; Johnny Cash; Claude King; Lefty Frizzell; Stonewall Jackson; "Little" Jimmy
Dickens; Carl Butler.

Greatest Country and Western Hits of the '70s..........Columbia (S) JC-36549   5-10   80
Larry Gatlin; Willie Nelson; Johnny Cash; David Allen Coe; Moe Bandy; Johnny Paycheck;
Charlie Rich; Joe Stampley; Marty Robbins; Mickey Gilley.

Greatest Country and Western Instrumentals............. Diplomat (S) DS-2600   10-15   60s
Cowboy Copas; Moon Mullican; Bill Boyd; Herb Remington; Lonnie Glosson; Hardrock
Gunter; Lonesome Pine; Riddlers; Chubby Wise; Eddie Eddings.

Greatest Country and Western Stars (5 LP) ....Showcase (S) SH-1503   15-25
(Boxed set.) Patsy Cline; Ferlin Husky; Carl Belew; T. Texas Tyler; Stuart Hamblen; Charlie
Ryan; David Houston; Johnny Horton; others.

Greatest Country and Western Stars & Hits (5 LP) ...Showcase (S) SH-1503   15-25
Patsy Cline; Ferlin Husky; Carl Belew; T. Texas Tyler; Stuart Hamblen; Slim Willet; Charlie
Ryan; Frankie Miller; Johnny Sea; David Houston; Johnny Horton; Jan Howard; Rose
Maddox; Wynn Stewart; Jimmy Dean; Maddox Brothers & Rose; Hank Locklin; Webb
Pierce; Rex Allen, others.

Greatest Country Fiddlers of Our Time......................... Starday (S) SLP 294   10-15   60s
Benny Martin; Tommy Hill; Curly Fox; Lonesome Pine Fiddlers; Scotty Stoneman; Jerry
Rivers; Howdy Forrester; Chubby Wise; Tommy Jackson; others.

Greatest Country Hits of the '70s.............................. Columbia (S) JC 36549   5-10   80
Larry Gatlin & the Gatlin Brothers; Willie Nelson; Johnny Cash; David Allen Coe; Moe
Bandy; Johnny Paycheck; Charlie Rich; Joe Stampley; Marty Robbins; Mickey Gilley.

Greatest Western Hits: see PRICE, Ray / Lefty Frizzell / Carl Smith

Greatest Western Hits...Columbia (M) CL-1976   20-30   59

Greatest Western Hits..Columbia (SE) CS-8776   10-20   63
Ray Price Carl Smith; Lefty Frizzell; Marty Robbins; others.

Greatest Western Hits, Vol. 2.....................................Columbia (M) CL-1408   20-30   60

Greatest Western Hits, Vol. 2...................................Columbia (SE) CS-8777   10-20   63
Ray Price; Carl Smith; George Morgan; "Little" Jimmy Dickens; Marty Robbins; Lefty
Frizzell.

Greatest Western Hits, Vol. 3.....................................Columbia (M) CL-????   15-25   63

Greatest Western Hits, Vol. 3..................................... Columbia (S) CS-????   15-25   63

Greatest Western Hits, Vol. 4..................................... Columbia (M) CL-2081   15-25   64

Greatest Western Hits, Vol. 4..................................... Columbia (S) CS-8881   15-25   64

Greatest Years of Country Music: see History of Country Music, Vol. 5

Guest Stars of the Hee-Haw Show ....Pickwick (SE) SS 6083   8-12
    Sonny James; Ferlin Husky; Faron Young; Buck Owens; Wynn Stewart; George Jones.

Harper Valley P.T.A. ....Plantation (S) PLP-700   10-15   78
    (Soundtrack. Colored vinyl.) Jeannie C. Riley; Nelson Riddle; Jerry Lee Lewis; Johnny
    Cash; Carol Channing & Rita Remmington.

Harper Valley P.T.A. .... Nashville (SE) NLP-2109   5-10   73
    Jeanne C. Riley; Dottie West; Rose Maddox; Sue Thompson; others.

Hats Off to Country ....Columbia Special Products (ST) P 15639   5-10   81
    (Promotional issue only.) Byrds; Willie Nelson; Johnny Cash; Johnny Paycheck; Charlie
    Rich; Tammy Wynette; New Riders of the Purple Sage; Earl Scruggs Revue; Lynn
    Anderson; Tanya Tucker. (Made for the Stetson Hat Company.)

Haul Off and Love Me .... Nashville (SE) NLP-2084   5-10   70
    Johnny Bond; Frankie Miller; Hank Penny; Willis Brothers; Wayne Raney; George Jones;
    others.

Hayride Medley ....Osborne Enterprises (EP) OE-819   5-10   84
    (Promotional issue only.) Johnny Horton; George Jones; Loretta Lynn; Ray Price; Marty
    Robbins; Jim Reeves; Hank Snow; Bob Luman; Ferlin Husky. (Issued without cover, as a
    bonus to buyers of Jerry Osborne's *Country Music* price guide.)

Hee Haw: see Stars of Hee-Haw

Hell Broke Loose in Georgia: North Georgia Fiddle Bands.....County (M) 514   8-12   70s

High Steppin' Country ....Columbia Special Products (S) P-12979   5-10   75
    Charlie Rich; Tammy Wynette; Johnny Cash; Barbara Mandrell; Marty Robbins; Statler
    Brothers; Ray Price; Tanya Tucker; Johnny Horton; Flatt & Scruggs; Jimmy Dean. (Made
    for Jarman Shoes for Men.)

Hillbilly Heaven.. Capitol Special Market (S) SL-8118   8-12   79
    Tex Ritter; Johnny Horton; Hank Williams; Red Foley; Patsy Cline; Cowboy Copas; George
    Morgan; Bob Wills & Tommy Duncan; Johnny Bond; Elton Britt; Jim Reeves; Lefty Frizzell;
    Moon Mullican; Ira Louvin with the Louvin Brothers; Carter Family; T. Texas Tyler; Skeets
    McDonald; Leon Payne; Jack Guthrie; Hawkshaw Hawkins.

Hillbilly Hit Parade ....Mercury (M) MG-20282   25-40   57

Hillbilly Hit Parade ....Starday (M) S-102   50-75   56

Hillbilly Hit Parade .... Starday (S) SLP-102   15-25   62
    George Jones; Leon Payne; Jeanette Hicks; George Jones & Jeanette Hicks; Benny
    Barnes; Eddie Blank; Red Hayes; Thumper Jones.

Hillbilly House Party .... Imperial (M) 9124   15-20   63
    Charlie Walker; Billy Briggs; others.

Hills and Home (30 Years of Bluegrass)..........................New World (S) 225   5-10   77
    Bill Monroe's Bluegrass Boys; Osborne Brothers; Country Gentlemen; others.

History of Country Music, Vol. 1................................ Radiant (S) RRC 1011   8-12   73
    Jimmie Rodgers; Ernest Tubb; Gene Autry; Carter Family; Pee Wee King; Sons of the
    Pioneers; Homer & Jethro; Elton Britt; Vaughn Monroe; Hank Snow; Chet Atkins; Del
    Wood; Slim Whitman; Davis Sisters; Stuart Hamblen.

History of Country Music (2 LP) .... UMI (S) 1600/1601   10-15   73
    Jimmie Rodgers; Ernest Tubb; Gene Autry; Carter Family; Pee Wee King; Sons of the
    Pioneers; Homer & Jethro; Elton Britt; Vaughn Monroe; Hank Snow; Chet Atkins; Del
    Wood; Slim Whitman; Davis Sisters; Stuart Hamblen; Roy Acuff; Cowboy Copas; Moon
    Mullican; Hank Williams; Tennessee Ernie Ford; Patti Page; Carlisles; Hank Thompson;
    Tex Ritter; Johnny Cash; George Jones.

History of Country Music, Vol. 2................................ Radiant (S) RRC 1012   8-12   73
    Roy Acuff; Cowboy Copas; Moon Mullican; Hank Williams; Tennessee Ernie Ford; Patti
    Page; Carlisles; Hank Thompson; Tex Ritter; Johnny Cash; George Jones.

History of Country Music, Vol. 2 (2 LP)....................................... UMI (S) 1650   10-15   73
    Porter Wagoner; Don Gibson; Browns; Jim Reeves; Jimmy Dean; Bobby Bare; Skeeter
    Davis; Norma Jean; Connie Smith; Roger Miller; Dottie West; Dolly Parton; Dickie Lee;
    Jerry Reed; Faron Young; Leroy Van Dyke; Ferlin Husky; Sonny James; Everly Brothers;
    George Jones; E. Ashworth; Red Sovine; Tom T. Hall; Jerry Lee Lewis; Johnny Cash.

History of Country Music, Vol. 3 (2 LP)...................... Radiant (S) RRC 1013   10-15   73
    Eddie Arnold; Hank Snow; Porter Wagoner; Jim Reeves; Hank Locklin; Bobby Bare;
    Waylon Jennings; Nat Stuckey; George Morgan; Dorsey Burnett; Gogi Grant; Patsy Cline;
    Marvin Rainwater; Jerry Wallace; Sheb Wooley; Hankshaw Hawkins; Roy Clark; Sammi
    Smith; Jacky Ward; Donna Fargo; Hank Thompson.

History of Country Music, Vol. 4 .... Radiant (S) RRC 1014   8-12 73
   Faron Young; Leroy Van Dyke; Ferlin Husky; Sonny James; Everly Brothers; George
   Jones; E. Ashworth; Roger Miller; Red Sovine; Tom T. Hall; Jerry Lee Lewis; Johnny Cash.

History of Country Music, Vol. 5, Lee Cash Presents . Radiant (S) RRC 1015   8-12 73
   (Single LP. Same as disc #1 of Vol. 3—including the same cover.) Eddy Arnold; Hank
   Snow; Porter Wagoner; Jim Reeves; Hank Locklin; Bobby Bare; Waylon Jennings; Nat
   Stuckey.

History of Country Music, Vol. 6 .... Radiant (S) RRC 1016   8-12 73
   George Morgan; Dorsey Burnett; Gogi Grant; Patsy Cline; Marvin Rainwater; Jerry Wallace;
   Sheb Wooley; Hawkshaw Hawkins; Bonny Guitar; Roy Clark; Sammi Smith; Jacky Ward;
   Hank Thompson; Donna Fargo.

History of Country Music, Vol. 7 .... Radiant (S) RRC 1019   8-12 81
   Johnny Cash; Everly Brothers; Jimmie Rodgers; Ernest Tubb; Ray Price; George Jones;
   Ferlin Husky; Johnny Horton; Patsy Cline; Bill Anderson.

History of Country Music, Vol. 8 .... Radiant (S) RRC 1020   8-12 81
   Burl Ives; Marty Robbins; Jim Reeves; Roger Miller; Webb Pierce; Slim Whitman; Kitty
   Wells; Faron Young.

History of Country Music, Vol. 9 .... Radiant (S) RRC 1021   8-12 81
   Buck Owens; Eddy Arnold; Dave Dudley; Sonny James; Merle Haggard; Tammy Wynette;
   George Jones; Bill Anderson.

History of Country Music, Vol. 10 .... Radiant (S) RRC 1022   8-12 81
   Billie Jo Spears; Charley Pride; Tompall & the Glaser Brothers; Bob Wills; Eddy Arnold;
   Jim Reeves; Browns; Sons of the Pioneers; George Hamilton IV.

History of Country Music, Vol. 11 .... Radiant (S) RRC 1023   8-12 81
   Lonzo & Oscar; Justin Tubb; Jim Reeves; Porter Wagoner; Skeeter Davis; Jim Ed Brown;
   Maxine Brown; Eddy Arnold; Hank Snow; Johnny & Jack.

History of Country Music, Vol. 12 .... Radiant (S) RRC 1024   8-12 81
   Eddy Arnold; Jim Reeves; Johnny & Jack; Hank Locklin; Faron Young; Tex Williams;
   Homer & Jethro; Porter Wagoner; George Hamilton IV.

Hit Parade of American Country Music (2 LP) .... Starday (M) S-184   15-25 62
Hit Parade of American Country Music (2 LP) .... Starday (S) SLP-184   15-25 62
   Buck Owens; George Jones; Cowboy Copas; Moon Mullican; Red Sovine; Frankie Miller;
   Justin Tubb; Archie Campbell; others.

Hit Parade of Bluegrass Stars .... Starday (M) S-343   15-20 65
Hit Parade of Bluegrass Stars .... Starday (S) SLP-343   15-20 65
   Don Reno & Red Smiley; Hylo Brown; Flatt & Scruggs; others.

Hit Parade of Country Music .... Starday (M) S-184   15-25 62
Hit Parade of Country Music .... Starday (S) SLP-184   15-25 62
Hit Sounds of Music City-West .... Tower (M) T-5070   10-15 67
Hit Sounds of Music City-West .... Tower (SE) DT-5070   10-15 67
   Dick Curless; Jan Howard; others.

Honest to Goodness Country Music Hits .... RCA (M) LPM-2564   15-20 ·62
Honest to Goodness Country Music Hits .... RCA (S) LSP-2564   20-25 62
   Hank Snow; Jim Reeves; Eddy Arnold; Porter Wagoner; Skeeter Davis; Jimmie Rodgers;
   Don Gibson; Browns; Hank Locklin; Pee Wee King; Elton Britt; Homer & Jethro.

Honest to Goodness Country Music Hits, Vol. 2 .... RCA (M) LPM-2633   15-20 63
Honest to Goodness Country Music Hits, Vol. 2 .... RCA (S) LSP-2633   20-25 63
   Jim Reeves; Hank Snow; Don Gibson; Pee Wee King; Browns; Porter Wagoner; Chet
   Atkins; Hank Locklin; Wade Ray; Eddy Arnold; Johnnie & Jack.

Honeysuckle Rose (2 LP) .... Columbia (ST) S2-36752   10-15 80
   (Soundtrack.) Willie Nelson; Johnny Gimble; Hank Cochran; Emmylou Harris; Jeannie
   Seely; Dyan Cannon; Amy Irving; Jody Payne; Kenneth Threadgill.

Honky Tonk Angels .... Nashville (SE) NLP-2081   5-10 70
   Dolly Parton; June Stearns; Dottie West; Melba Montgomery; Patsy Cline; Jan Howard;
   others.

Honky Tonk Favorites .... Mercury (M) MGW-12297   10-20 65
Honky Tonk Favorites .... Mercury (S) SRW-16297   15-20 65
   Johnny Horton; George Jones; Rex Allen; Betty Amos James O'Gwynn; Sue Thompson;
   Jimmie Skinner; Claude Gray; Benny Barnes; Jennie Lou Carson.

Honky Tonk Saturday Night .... Warner Special Products (S) OP 1511   5-10 81
   Emmylou Harris; Willy Nelson; Conway Twitty; Hank Williams; Gail Davis; Mickey Gilley;
   Tanya Tucker; Jerry Lee Lewis; John Conlee; Commander C & His Orchestra:

Honkytonk Man .... Warner Bros. (S) 1-23739   8-10   82
   (Soundtrack.) Clint Eastwood; Porter Wagoner; Ray Price; Marty Robbins; John Anderson;
   Linda Hopkins; Johnny Gimble and the Texas Swing Band; David Frizzell & Dottie West.
Hootenanny Bluegrass Style .... Mercury (M) MG-20857   10-20   63
Hootenanny Bluegrass Style .... Mercury (S) SR-60857   10-20   63
   Lester Flatt & Earl Scruggs; Stanley Brothers; Anita Carter; others.
Hootenanny Country Style .... Spin-O-Rama (M) M-126   8-12   60s
   Wetherly Brothers; Bayou Boys; Sons of the Soil; Virginia Mountaineers.
Hootenanny Hoe Down .... Camay (SE) CA 3036   8-12   60s
   Burl Ives; Connie Haines; Weavers; Mitchell Choirboys; Dinning Sisters; Florian Zabach;
   Robin Roberts; Jordanaires; Mary Mayo.
Hymns of Gold .... Columbia Special Products (S) CSP 10779   5-10   72
   (TV offer only.) Jerry Lee Lewis; Johnny Cash; Anita Kerr Singers; Roy Clark; Lynn
   Anderson; Jimmie Rodgers; David Houston; Jim Nabors; Marty Robbins; Pat Boone; Bob
   Daniels; Ray Price; George Morgan; Jimmy Dean; Patsy Cline; Patti Page; Charlie Walker;
   Tammy Wynette; Statler Brothers;
Hymns of Gold, Vol. 2 .... Columbia Special Products (S) CSP 12620   5-10   74
   (TV offer only.) Lynn Anderson; Anita Bryant; Wayne Newton; Pat Boone; Johnny Cash;
   Jordanaires; Jimmy Dean; Jim Nabors; Jo Stafford; Stuart Hamblen; George Jones; Bob
   Daniels; Roy Clark; Suzy Hamblen; Rosemary Clooney; Wanda Jackson; Tammy Wynette;
   Statler Bros.; Carter Family.
I Will Sing .... Columbia Musical Treasury (SE) 1P 6213   5-10   76
   Lynn Anderson; George Jones; Barbara Mandrell; Johnny Cash; Rosey Nix; Charlie Rich;
   Ray Price; Tammy Wynette; David Houston; Tanya Tucker; Roy Clark. (Columbia House
   Record Club issue.)
I'll Still Write Your Name in the Sand .... Nashville (SE) NLP-2067   5-10   69
   Mac Wiseman; Jim and Jesse; Stanley Brothers; Flatt and Scruggs.
In Concert (2 LP) ....RCA (S) CPL2-1014   5-10   75
   Charley Pride; Dolly Parton; Gary Stewart; Ronnie Milsap; Jerry Reed; Chet Atkins.
In Memory .... King (M) 835   15-25   63
In Memory ....King (S) 835   15-25   63
   Hawkshaw Hawkins; Cowboy Copas; others.
In Memory of these Great Artists .... King (M) 887   15-25   64
In Memory of these Great Artists ....King (S) KS-835   15-25   64
   Hawkshaw Hawkins; Cowboy Copas; others.
Instrumental Music of Southern Appalachians................. Tradition (M) 1007   25-35   50s
   Hobart Smith; Etta Baker; Boone Reid; Edd Presnell; Richard Chase; Lacey Phillips.
Jim Reeves and Some Friends... RCA (S) LSP-4112   5-10   69
   Jim Reeves; Dottie West; Leo Jackson; others.
Joy of Christmas ....Columbia Special Products (S) C-11087   5-10'   70s
   Marty Robbins; Lynn Anderson; Ray Price; Tammy Wynette; Chuck Wagon Gang; Johnny
   Cash.
Kooky Country... Era (S) PBU 4190   8-12   82
   Claude King; Johnny Preston; Jack & Misty; Dick Feller; Guy Drake; "Little" Jimmy
   Dickens; Ray Stevens; Hank Thompson; Charlie Walker; Tommy Collins; Billy Edd
   Wheeler; Larry Verne.
Ladies' Choice (Country Hits of Nashville's Top Female
  Vocalists).. Harmony (S) KH-32487   5-10   73
   Lynn Anderson; Jody Miller; Tammy Wynette; Tanya Tucker; others.
Let's Go to Church, Vol. 1 .... Capitol (EP) EPA-1-1042   5-8   59
Let's Go to Church, Vol. 2 .... Capitol (EP) EPA-2-1042   5-8   59
Let's Go to Church, Vol. 3 .... Capitol (EP) EPA-3-1042   5-8   59
Let's Go to Church .... Capitol (M) T-1042   15-25   59
   Faron Young; Tennessee Ernie Ford; Margaret Whiting; Jane Froman; Gordon MacRae;
   Jimmy Wakely.
Lonesome Valley.. Guest Star (M) G 1490   8-12
Lonesome Valley......................................:............. Guest Star (S) GS 1490   8-12
   Carl Story; Lonzo & Oscar; Frankie Miller; Stanley Brothers; Cowboy Copas; Jimmie
   Williams & Red Ellis; Phipps Family; Lewis Family; Sam & Kirk McGee.
Louisiana Cajun Music, Vol. 1 ....Old Timey (M) LP-108   5-10
Louisiana Cajun Music, Vol. 2......................................Old Timey (M) LP-109   5-10
Louisiana Cajun Music, Vol. 3......................................Old Timey (M) LP-110   5-10
Louisiana Cajun Music, Vol. 4......................................Old Timey (M) LP-111   5-10
Louisiana Cajun Music, Vol. 5......................................Old Timey (M) LP-114   5-10

Midnight Jamboree..Decca (M) DL-4045   15-25 61
Midnight Jamboree..Decca (M) DL7-4045   20-30 61
    Ernest Tubb & His Texas Troubadours; Patsy Cline; Webb Pierce; Kitty Wells; Wilburn
    Brothers; Buddy Emmons; Linda Flanagan; Jerry Hanlon.
More Bluegrass...Starday (S) SLP 296   10-20 60s
    Jim & Jesse; Bill Clifton; Bluegrass Champs; Hylo Brown; New River Boys; Carl Story; Red
    Allen; Stanley Brothers; Country Gentlemen; Benny Martin; Lonesome Pine Fiddlers; Jim
    Eanes; Jimmie Skinner; Jimmy Martin; Bob Osborne.
More Country & Western Favorites!................................Design (M) DLP-637   8-12 60s
More Country & Western Favorites!........................... Design (SE) SDLP-637   8-12 60s
    Ferlin Husky; Carl Belew; Patsy Cline; Hank Locklin; Rocky Bill Ford.
More Country Classics...RCA (M) LPM-2467   15-20 61
    Hank Snow; Eddy Arnold; Browns; Jim Reeves; Hank Locklin; Skeeter Davis; Del Wood;
    Don Gibson; Homer & Jethro; Porter Wagoner; Jimmie Driftwood; Johnnie & Jack.
More Country Gold...Sunset (S) 5290   5-10 70
    Bobby Goldsboro; Jerry Wallace; Del Reeves; Johnny Darrell; Willie Nelson.
More Country Music Festival...Starday (M) S-327   10-20 65
More Country Music Samplers.....................................Starday (M) SLP-178   10-20
    Justin Tubb; Archie Campbell; Willis Brothers; Pete Drake; "Little" Roy Wiggins; Cowboy
    Copas; Lew Childre; Sunshine Boys; Cathy Copas; Arthur "Guitar Boogie" Smith; Bill
    Clifton & His Dixie Mountain Boys; George Jones; Chubby Wise; Jim Glaser.
More Country Music Spectacular.....................................Starday (M) S-140   15-25 61
More! Wonderful World of Country Music, Vol. 2..........Starday (M) SLP-320   8-12
    Joe & Rose Lee Maphis; Wayne Raney; Benny Martin; Jackie Phelps; Dick Flood; Jimmie
    Skinner; Clyde Moody; Dean Manuel; Cowboy Copas; Pee Wee King; Redd Stewart; June
    Stearns; Gene Martin; George Jones; Gene Martin; Arthur "Guitar Boogie" Smith.
Movin' On ....Harold Mayer Productions (S) HMP-69   15-20 69
    (TV soundtrack. Documentary about AFL-CIO, United Transportation Union.) Arthur
    Kennedy (narration); Hank Snow; New Lost City Ramblers; Bonnie Dobson.
Music City USA ....Columbia (M) CL-2590   10-15 66
Music City USA (6 LP) ....Columbia House (S) 6P 6626   10-20 78
    C.W. McCall; Tammy Wynette & George Jones; Freddy Fender; Lynn Anderson; Mickey
    Gilley; Linda Ronstadt; Sonny James; Ray Price; Donna Fargo; Faron Young; Lynn
    Anderson & Glenn Sutton; Tammy Wynette & David Houston; Johnny Cash & June Carter
    Cash; David Houston & Barbara Mandrell; Roy Rogers & Dale Evans; Michael Murphy;
    Charlie Daniels Band; David Allan Coe; Marshall Chapman; Moe Bandy; Glen Campbell &
    Bobby Gentry; Lynn Anderson; Marty Robbins; Tex Ritter; Billie Jo Speers; Red Simpson;
    Dick Curless; Charlie Rich; Jody Miller; Roy Drusky; Jean Shepard; Mac Davis; Tanya
    Tucker; Johnny Cash; Statler Brothers; Roy Clark; Charlie McCoy; Wanda Jackson; Melba
    Montgomery; Wanda Jackson; Roy Acuff; David Houston; Hank Thompson;
    Ned Miller; Johnny Horton; Bob Wills; Stonewall Jackson.
Music Hall (Country Gold Award Album) (3 LP)..Plaza House (s) 6719/20/21   10-15
    Merle Haggard; Sonny James; Buck Owens; Tennessee Ernie Ford; others.
Music Lover's Album (3 LP) ....Columbia (S) 3P-6299   10-15
    (Boxed set.) Tammy Wynette; Mac Davis; Ray Price; Charlie McCoy; Lynn Anderson;
    Johnny Cash; Sonny James; Tanya Tucker; Jerry Vale; Johnny Mathis; Ray Conniff; John
    Davidson; Andre Kostelanetz; Ronnie Dyson; Bobby Vinton; Jim Nabors; Tony Bennett;
    Percy Faith; Robert Goulet; Steve Lawrence.
Music Row Greats... 4 Star (S) 4S-SP-111   5-10 77
    George Morgan; Carl Belew; Wynn Stewart; Jerry Fuller; Jan Howard; Mary Ford; Jimmy
    Elledge; Travis Brothers; Johnny & Jonie; Betty Jean Robinson.
Nashville.. Columbia/Magnavox (S) CSS-1341   8-15 60s
    Johnny Cash & June Carter; Flatt & Scruggs; Tammy Wynette; Marty Robbins; Ray Price;
    Johnny Cash. (Special products. Made for Magnavox.)
Nashville Bandstand ....King (M) 813   15-25 63
Nashville Bandstand ....King (S) S-813   15-25 63
    Hank Locklin; Cowboy Copas; Reno & Smiley; others.
Nashville Bandstand, Vol. 2 ....King (M) 847   15-25 63

Nashville Christmas Party .... RCA (M) LPM-2579   10-15   62
Nashville Christmas Party .... RCA (S) LSP-2579   10-15   62
    Skeeter Davis; Eddy Arnold; Porter Wagoner; John D. Loudermilk; Hank Snow; Anita Kerr
    Singers; Hank Locklin; Floyd Cramer; Jimy Elledge; Jim Edward Brown; Chet Atkins.
Nashville City Limits .... Columbia Musical Treasury (S) 1P-6627   5-10   77
    (Columbia Record Club issue.) Bobbie Gentry; Charlie Rich; Jody Miller; Sonny James;
    Ned Miller; Joe Stampley; Billie Jo Spears; Roy Clark; Melba Montgomery; Faron Young.
Nashville Gold (2 LP) .... RCA R 213295-1-2   8-12   70s
    Dolly Parton; Bobby Bare; Chet Atkins; Waylon Jennings; Connie Smith; Nat Stuckey;
    Jerry Reed; Willie Nelson; Nashville String Band; Jim Reeves; Norma Jean; John Denver;
    Dottie West; Kenny Price; Danny Davis; George Hamilton IV; Dallas Frazier; Eddy Arnold;
    Skeeter Davis; Floyd Cramer; Red Lane; Johnny Russell; Porter Wagoner.
Nashville Graffiti (2 LP) ..Candelite/Columbia Special Products (S) P2-12702   10-20   75
    Link Wray; Johnny Horton; Bobby Vinton; Ray Price; Buzz Clifford; Johnny Cash; Marty
    Robbins; Guy Mitchell; Patti Page; Ersel Hickey; Statler Brothers; Carl Perkins; Bobby
    Helms; Jimmy Dean; Mindy Carson; Claude King; Stonewall Jackson; Johnny Ray; Billy
    Grammer.
Nashville on My Mind ....????   5-10
    (Label and number not known.) Lynn Anderson; Mel Tillis; Jerry Wallace; Jody Miller;
    Johnny Paycheck; Mac Davis; Barbara Fairchild; David Allen Coe; Roger Miller; George
    Jones.
Nashville Package of Original Country Hits .... Mercury (S) SR-61375   5-10   72
    Jerry Lee Lewis; Roger Miller; George Jones; Statler Brothers; Leroy Van Dyke; Flatt &
    Scruggs; Faron Young; Roger Miller; Dave Dudley; Tom T. Hall; Bobby Bare; Roy Drusky &
    Priscilla Mitchell.
Nashville Saturday Night .... Columbia House (SE) 1P 6215   5-10   75
    (Record club issue.) Sonny James; Johnny Cash; Marion Worth; Ferlin Husky; Charlie
    Walker; Judy Lynn; Floyd Tillman; Marty Robbins; Patsy Cline; Johnny Bond.
Nashville Saturday Night .... Starday (M) S-128   20-30   61
    Cowboy Copas; George Jones; String Bean; Frankie Miller; Carl Story; Merle Kilgore;
    Benny Martin; Jim Eanes; Red Sovine; Cousin Jody; Margie Singleton; Lonzo & Oscar;
    Wally Fowler & the Oak Ridge Quartet; Wayne Raney.
Nashville Saturday Night .... Nashville (M) NLP-2009   10-15   64
Nashville Sound: Bright Lights & Country
    Music (6 LP) .... Columbia Musical Treasury (SE) 6P 6054   20-30   74
    (Boxed set. Columbia House Record Club issue.) John Wesley Ryles; Kitty Wells; David
    Hoiston; Barbara Fairchild; Johnny Paycheck; Bill Anderson; Freddy Weller; Mac Davis;
    Bonnie Guitar; Bob Luman; Tanya Tucker; Roger Miller; Donna Fargo; Hank Thompson;
    Lynn Anderson; Stonewall Jackson; Jerry Lee Lewis; Charlie Rich; Tammy Wynette;
    Jimmy Dean; Statler Brothers; Johnny Cash & June Carter; Jack Greene; Dave Dudley;
    Conway Twitty; Lefty Frizzell; Webb Pierce; Johnny Cash; Sonny James; Marty Robbins;
    Carl Smith; Mel Tillis; Jerry Wallace; Kris Kristofferson; Pat Boone; Roy Clark; Johnny
    Horton; Flatt & Scruggs; Jody Miller; Johnny Duncan; George Jones; Judy Lynn; Tom T.
    Hall; Barbara Mandrell; O.C. Smith; Ray Price; Joan Weber; Pete Drake; Jeannie C. Riley;
    Carter Family; Earl Scruggs.
Nashville Sound .... Design (S) DLP-634   8-12   66
    Patsy Cline; Carl Belew; Rocky Bill Ford; Hank Locklin; Ferlin Husky.
Nashville Sound, Vol. 7: see Bright Lights & Country Music Vol. 7
Nashville Sounds of Country Music .... Rural Rhythm (M) RR 150   8-12   60s
    Bob Jennings; Autry Inman; Swanny Caldwell; Kenny Smith; Johnny Tyler; Johnny
    Skilles; Jo Casey; Skiles-Akins-Cipoll; Bill Carter; Jerrie Walker; Hal Willis; Bobby Barnett;
Nashville Stars .... Crane/Norris (S) CN-100   5-10   70s
    (Mail order offer.) Johnny Rodriguez; Billy Crash Craddock; Donna Fargo; Gene Watson;
    Eddie Rabbitt; Don Williams; Conway Twitty; Barbara Mandrell; Willie Nelson; Joe
    Stampley; Linda Ronstadt; Waylon Jennings; Freddy Fender; Emmylou Harris; Ronnie
    Milsap; Glen Campbell; Tom T. Hall; Statler Brothers; Bill Anderson.
Nashville Steel Guitar ....Starday (M) SLP-138   15-20   61
    Pete Drake; Little Roy Wiggins; Don Helms; Jimmy Day; Herbie Remington; Dick Stubbs;
    Al Petty.
Nashville Steel Guitar .... Nashville (M) NLP-2017   10-15   65
    Pete Drake; Little Roy Wiggins; Don Helms; Jimmy Day; Herbie Remington; Dick Stubbs;
    Al Petty.
Nashville Wives .... Nashville (S) NLP-2104   8-12
    Judy West; Dolly Parton; Jan Howard; Melba Montgomery; Dottie West; Rose Maddox.

Nashville's Greatest Instrumentalists .... RCA (S) APL1-0167   5-10   73
    Chet Atkins; Floyd Cramer; Lester Flatt; Homer & Jethro; others.
Nashville's Greatest Instrumentalists, Vol. 2 .... RCA (S) APL1-0536   5-10   74
    Chet Atkins; Floyd Cramer; Jerry Reed; Kossi Gardner; others.
Nashville's Greatest Instrumentalists (With Their Great
   Hits) .... RCA (S) ANL1-2181   5-10   77
    Floyd Cramer; Roddy Bristol; Buck Trent; Jerry Reed; Chet Atkins; others.
New and Old Time Country & Folk Songs .... Rural Rhythm (M) RR 153   8-12   60s
    Ernie Cook; Boys From Shiola; Swanny Caldwell; Bill Carter; Johnny Skiles & Bob Hill;
    Bob Jennings; Autry Inman; Bobby Barnet; Kentucky Boys; Dewayne Wear; Johnny Tyler.
New Breed .... RCA (ST) CPL1-5491   5-10   85
    Juice Newton; Earl Thomas Conley; Gus Hardin; Vince Gill; Restless Heart; Eddy Raven;
    Judds.
New Country & Western Round-Up (5 LP) .... Capitol (S) SLER 6582   20-30   80s
    (Boxed set.) Buck Owens; Merle Haggard; Glen Campbell; Sonny James; Wynn Stewart;
    Tex Ritter; Geezinslaw Brothers; Buckaroos; Jean Shepard; Wanda Jackson; others.
Night at the Grand Old Opry, Vol. 1 .... Harmony (S) HS-11169   5-10
    Lester Flatt & Earl Scruggs; Carter Family; George Morgan & Marion Worth; Billy Walker.
Night at the Louisiana Hayride .... Wing (M) MGW-12200   20-25   60
    Johnny Horton; George Jones; Benny Barnes; Margie Singleton; Gray Bryant, Johnny
    Mathis; James O'Gwynn; Tibby Edwards; Jeanette Hicks; Eddie Bond.
Nitty Gritty Guitar .... Pickwick (S) SPC-3148   10-15
    Glen Campbell; Howard Roberts; Mason Williams; Billy Strange; 12 String Guitar Band.
No. 1 Country - 60 Top of the Chart Hits: see 60 Top of the Chart Hits, #1 Country
No. 1 Country 60 Top of the Chart Hits (6 LP) .... Columbia 6P 6682   20-30   77
    (Columbia Record Club issue.) Al Dexter; George Morgan; Hank Williams, Sr.; Margaret
    Whiting & Jimmy Wakely; Lefty Frizzell; Ray Price; Everly Brothers; Sonny James; Carl
    Smith; Marty Robbins; George Jones; Johnny Horton; Faron Young; Stonewall Jackson;
    Leroy Van Dyke; Billy Walker; Carl Butler & Pearl; Claude King; Johnny Cash; Flatt &
    Scruggs; Jimmy Dean; David Houston; Tammy Wynette; "Little" Jimmy Dickens; Glen
    Campbell; Lynn Anderson; Hank Williams, Jr.; Donna Fargo; Barbara Fairchild; Mel Tillis;
    Tom T. Hall; Charlie Rich; Tanya Tucker; Willie Nelson; Johnny Rodriguez; Freddy Fender;
    Johnny Duncan; B.J. Thomas.
Oklahoma Country .... ARI (S) 1025   8-12   82
    Sammi Smith; Bob Wills; Jody Miller; Sons of the Pioneers; Wanda Jackson; Kay Starr;
    Hoyt Axton; Conway Twitty; Carl Belew; Tommy Collins; Merle Travis; Jack Guthrie; Hank
    Thompson; Cal Smith.
Old and Good Country Hits .... Cumberland (M) 29521   10-15   65
Old and Good Country Hits .... Cumberland (S) 69521   10-15   65
    Leon Payne; Leon McAuliffe; Red Sovine; others.
Old and Heavy Gold (1956) .... Economic Consultants (M) 1956   20-40   73
Old and Heavy Gold (1957) .... Economic Consultants (M) 1957   20-40   73
Old and Heavy Gold (1958) .... Economic Consultants (M) 1958   20-40   73
Old and Heavy Gold (1959) .... Economic Consultants (M) 1959   10-15   73
Old and Heavy Gold (1960) .... Economic Consultants (M) 1960   20-40   73
Old and Heavy Gold (1961) .... Economic Consultants (M) 1961   20-40   73
Old and Heavy Gold (1962) .... Economic Consultants (M) 1962   20-40   73
Old Country Church .... Rural Rhythm (M) RR 148   8-12   60s
    Jackie & Arlin Vaden; Bill Carter; Cooper Crothers; Owen & Mack; George Frace; Johnny
    Tyler; James Baum.
Old Time Classics: Collection of Mountain Banjo Songs and
   Tunes .... County (M) 515   8-12   75
    Uncle Dave Macon; Lano Norris; Marion Underwood; Riley Puckett; R.B. Smith & S.J.
    Allgood; Red Headed Fiddlers; Bascom Lamar Lunsford; Frank Jenkins; Buell Kazee;
    Fisher Hendley & J. Small.
Old Time Classics: Collection of Mountain Blues .... County (M) 511   8-12   75
    Sam McGee; Lowe Stokes & His North Georgians; Jimmie Tarlton; Leake County Revelers;
    Carolina Tar Heels; Dock Boggs; Frank Hutchison; Narmour & Smith; Dick Justice; Burnett
    & Rutherford; Doc Roberts; Clarence Green.
Old Time Religion .... Power Pak (M) PO-254   5-10   75
    Charlie Rich; Johnny Cash; Jerry Lee Lewis; Sleepy LeBeef; Dave Rich; Jeannie C. Riley;
    Eddie Bond; Dee Mullins.

Old Time String Band Classics: Recorded 1927-1933...........County (M) 531   8-12   75
Luke Highnight & His Ozark Strutters; Alex Hood & His Railroad Boys; Dr. Humphrey Bate & His Possum Hunters; Roanoke Jug Band; Earl Johnson & His Clodhoppers; Fox Chasers; Sharp, Hinman & Sharp; Caplinger's Cumberland Mountain Entertainers' Allen County String Band; Ted Gossett's Band; Booker Orchestra; Floyd County Ramblers.

Oldies and Goodies (Country & Western #3)............... Crown (M) CLP-5241   20-25   60s
Gabbard & Holt; Jimmy Patten; Whitey Pullen; Wally & Don; others.

On Stage at the Grand Ole Opry.....................................Decca (M) DL-4393   20-25   64
On Stage at the Grand Ole Opry.....................................Decca (S) DL7-4393   25-30   64
Patsy Cline; Wilburn Brothers; Roy Drusky; others.

On the Road... RCA (M) LPM-3509   10-20   66
On the Road... RCA (S) LSP-3509   15-20   66
Porter Wagoner; Norma Jean; Speck Rhodes; others.

One Big Family.. Compleat (45) 679001-7   5-10   85
Roy Acuff; Rex Allen, Jr.; Lynn Anderson; Eddy Arnold; Chet Atkins; Bobby Bare; Lane Brody; T. Graham Brown; Little Jimmy Dickens; Karen Taylor-Good; Dobie Gray; Sonny James; George Jones; Kendalls; Dave Kirby; Neal Matthews; Kathy Mattea; O.B. McClinton; Ronnie McDowell; Colleen Peterson; Boots Randolf; Jerry Reed; Jeannie C. Riley; Ronny Robbins; Ray Sawyer; Troy Seals; Jeannie Seely; Rick Schulman; Gordon Stoker; Tanya Tucker; Mack Vickery; Porter Wagoner; Duane West; Leona Williams; Bergen White; Faron Young.

Opry Album .... Columbia Special Products (M) XTV 86113   10-20   50s
Flatts & Scruggs; Marty Robbins; Stonewall Jackson; Bobby Lord; Billy Walker; Ray Price; George Morgan; Hawshaw Hawkins; Carl Butler; Bill Carlisle.

Opry Old Timers.. Starday (S) SLP-182   15-25   62
Opry Time in Tennessee.. Starday (M) S-177   15-25   62
Opry Time in Tennessee... Starday (S) SLP-177   15-25   62
George Jones; Lester Flatt & Earl Scruggs; Cowboy Copas; others.

Original Country Hits, Vol. 1... Artistic (EP) 223   15-25   65
(7-inch, 33rpm. Also issued as Golden Country Hits and Western, Vol. 1.) Eddie Dean; Chuck Hawkins; Rex Trailer; Johnny Williams; Foy Willing & the Riders of the Purple Sage; Don Hughes; Sterling Blythe; Doye O'Dell.

Original Country Hits, Vol. 1... Liberty (M) LRP-3305   15-20   63
Johnny Cash; Joe Carson; Cowboy Copas; George Jones; Bobby Edwards; Walter Brennan; Wynn Steweart; Warren Smith; Jan Howard; Bob Wills; Johnny & Jonie; others.

Original Country Hits, Vol. 2... Artistic (EP) 224   15-25   65
(7-inch, 33rpm. Also issued as Western, Vol. 2 and also as Golden Country Hits.) Webb Pierce; Slim Willet; Ferlin Husky; T. Texas Tyler; Jimmy Dean; Rose Maddox; Hank Locklin; Pete Pike.

Original Country Hits, Vol. 2... Liberty (M) LRP-3345   15-20   64
Original Country Hits, No. 3 .... Liberty (M) LRP-3382   15-20   64
George Jones; Patsy Cline; Johnny Cash; Dave Dudley; Slim Whitman; Cowboy Copas; Johnny & Jonie Mosby; Wynn Stewart; Bob Wills & Tommy Duncan; Joe Carson; Pete Drake; Jan Howard.

Original Country Hits of the '50s (8 LP).. Reader's Digest (M) 446-RM-26040   25-40   78
(Boxed set.) Don Gibson; Red Foley; Hank Williams, Sr.; Kitty Wells; Eddy Arnold; Pee Wee King; Webb Pierce; Everly Brothers; Hank Snow; Jerry Lee Lewis; Elton Britt & Rosalie Allen; Ernest Tubb; Patti Page; Pine Toppers; Carlisles; Davis Sisters; Jim Reeves; Justin Tubb & Goldie Hill; Johnnie & Jack; Stuart Hamblen; Johnny Cash; Jimmie Rodgers; George Jones; Porter Wagoner; Browns; Carl Perkins; Hank Locklin; Bobby Helms; Patsy Cline; Don Gibson; Wilma Lee & Stoney Cooper; Skeeter Davis; Wilburn Brothers.

Original Golden Country Greats, Vol. 1...................... Liberty (S) LST-7569   10-15   68
Johnny Cash; Bobby Edwards; Walter Brennan; Cowboy Copas; Wynn Stewart; Jan Howard; George Jones; Warren Smith; Bob Wills & Tommy Duncan; Frankie Miller; Johnny & Jonie.

Original Golden Country Greats, Vol. 2...................... Liberty (S) LST-7570   10-15   68
Dave Dudley; Johnny Cash; Slim Whitman; Cowboy Copas; Hank Cochran; Joe Carson; Walter Brennan; Moon Mullican; Fendermen; Warren Smith; Willie Nelson; Bob Wills & Tommy Duncan.

Original Golden Country Greats, Vol. 3...................... Liberty (S) LST-7571   10-15   68
Dave Dudley; Patsy Cline; George Jones; Slim Whitman; Cowboy Copas; Jerry Wallace; Bob Wills & Tommy Duncan; Pete Drake; Jan Howard; Wynn Stewart; Joe Carson; Johnny & Jonie.

Original Golden Hits of the Great C&W Stars .... Mercury (M) MG-20825   15-20   63
Original Golden Hits of the Great C&W Stars .... Mercury (S) SR-60825   20-25   63
Faron Young; Rex Allen; Claude Gray; George Jones; Leroy Van Dyke; others.

Original Golden Town and Country Hits, Vol. 1 ...... Mercury (M) MGH-25008   15-25   64
    Brook Benton; Faron Young; Jerry Wallace; Patti Page; Claude Gray; Jerry Fuller; Rex
    Allen; Tom & Jerry; Patsy Cline; Rusty Draper; Ned Miller; Leroy Van Dyke.

Original Hit Performances–All Time Country and Western: see All Time Country and Western

Pick of the Country .... RCA (EP) EPA-5155   5-10   60
    Browns; Don Gibson; Porter Wagoner; Davis Sisters.

Pick of the Country .... RCA (M) LPM-2094   15-25   60

Pick of the Country .... RCA (S) LSP-2094   20-30   60
    Jim Reeves; Stuart Hamblen; Maxine & Bonnie Brown; Don Gibson; Porter Wagoner; Davis
    Sisters; Hank Snow; Browns; Eddy Arnold; Hank Locklin; Pee Wee King; Johnnie & Jack;
    Jimmie Rodgers.

Pick of the Country, Vol. 2 .... RCA (M) LPM-2956   10-20   65

Pick of the Country, Vol. 2 .... RCA (S) LSP-2956   15-20   65
    Eddy Arnold; Jim Reeves; George Hamilton IV; Porter Wagoner; Darrell Glenn; Johnnie &
    Jack; Skeeter Davis; Hank Snow; Homer & Jethro; Don Gibson; Hank Locklin; Kitty Wells.

Pink Cadillac .... Warner Bros. (S) 1-25922   5-10   89
    (Soundtrack.) Michael Martin Murphey; Hank Williams Jr.; Hank Williams Sr.; Jill Hollier;
    Randy Travis; Southern Pacific; J.C. Crowley; Billy Hill; Dion; Robben Ford.

Places in the Heart .... Varese Sarabande (S) 81229   8-10   84
    (Soundtrack.) Doc & Merle Watson; Texas Playboys.

Playboy Country .... Playboy (S) PB 129   8-12
    Mickey Gilley; Barbi Benton; Mike Wells; Wynn Stewart; Brenda Pepper; Boby Borchers;
    Chuck Price.

Pop Country Hits .... RCA (M) LPM-2949   10-20   64

Pop Country Hits .... RCA (S) LSP-2949   15-20   64
    Jim Reeves; Hank Locklin; Hank Snow; Don Gibson; George Hamilton IV; John D.
    Loudermilk; Bobby Bare; Skeeter Davis; Dottie West; Floyd Cramer; Porter Wagoner; Eddy
    Arnold.

Pop Hits Country Flavored .... RCA (S) PRS-417   5-10   72
    Danny Davis; Skeeter Davis; Willie Nelson; Chet Atkins; Dottie West; John Hartford;
    Nashville String Band; Liz Anderson; Waylon Jennings & Jessi Colter; Floyd Cramer.

Popular Hits from Nashville (9 LP) .... RCA (S) RDA-140   20-30   72

Praise the Lord .... Design (S) SDLP-615   5-10
    Maddox Brothers & Rose; T. Texas Tyler; Wally Fowler; Eddie Dean; Texas Jim Robertson.

Precious Memories .... Camden (S) CXS-9020   5-10   72
    Blackwood Brothers; Skeeter Davis; George Beverly Shea; Porter Wagoner; others.

Precious Memories of Sacred Hymns .... Modern Sound (S) MS-802   5-10
    Sons of Song; J.T. Adams; Dixie Echoes; Wendy Bagwell & the Sunlighters; Wally Fowler
    & the Oak Ridge Quartet; Jake Hess & the Jordanaires; Georgians; Plainsmen; Florida
    Boys; Sego Brothers & Naomi.

Prisoners Songs .... Starday (M) S-207   15-20   63
    Johnny Cash; James O'Gwynn; Hylo Brown; others.

Radar Blues .... King (S) KLP 1050   8-12   70s
    Coleman Wilson; Moore & Napier; Reno & Smiley; Stanley Brothers; Grand Pa Jones; Hylo
    Brown; Willis Brothers; Red Sovine; Red Sovine & Johnny Bond; Cowboy Copas;
    Hawkshaw Hawkins.

Railroad in Folksong .... RCA (M) LPV-532   10-15   66
    Carter Family; Jimmie Davis; Monroe Brothers; others.

Railroad Songs .... King (M) 869   20-30   63

Railroad Songs .... King (S) KS-869   20-30   63
    Grandpa Jones; Reno & Smiley; Stanley Brothers; others.

Red Foley Story .... Decca (M) DL-4341   25-35   63

Red Foley Story .... Decca (S) DL7-4341   30-40   63
    Red Foley; Patsy Cline; Kitty Wells; Ernest Tubb; Wilburn Brothers; others.

Redneck Mothers .... RCA (S) APL1-2438   5-10   77
    Johnny Russell; Gary Stewart; Willie Nelson; Bobby Bare; others.

Redneck Mothers .... RCA (S) AYL1-3674   5-8   80s
    Steve Young; Jerry Reed; Tennessee Pulleybone; Vernon Oxford; others.

Rip Roarin' Country .... K-Tel (S) WU 3760   5-10   83
     Alabama; Willie Nelson; Hank Williams, Jr.; Conway Twitty; Eddie Rabbitt; Moe Bandy;
     Bellamy Brothers; Mel Tillis; Waylon Jennings; George Jones; George Strait; Mel
     McDaniel; Johnny Cash; T.G. Sheppard; Delbert McClinton; Bobby Bare.

River Rat .... RCA (S) CBL1-5310   5-10   84
     (Soundtrack.) Alabama; Earl Thomas Conley; Deborah Allen; Bill Medley; Autograph; Joey
     Scarbury.

Road Music .... Gusto (S) GTV-107   5-10
     Red Sovine; Dave Dudley; Del Reeves; Coleman Wilson; T.H. Music Festival; Willis
     Brothers; Minnie Pearl; Moore & Napier; Tiny Harris; Rod Hart; Jimmy Martin; Jimmy
     Griggs; Lonnie Irving; Claude Gray.

Roadie (2 LP) .... Warner Bros. (ST) 2HS-3441   8-12   80
     (Soundtrack.) Cheap Trick; Pat Benetar; Teddy Pendergrass; Jay Ferguson; Blondie; Styx;
     Joe Ely Band; Alice Cooper; Eddie Rabbitt; Stephen Bishop; Yvonne Elliman; Sue Sadd &
     the Next; Asleep at the Wheel; Jerry Lee Lewis; Roy Orbison; Emmy Lou Harris; Hank
     Williams, Jr.

Roadie .... Warner Bros. (ST) PRO-A-885   10-20   80
     (Soundtrack. Promotional only issue.) Jerry Lee Lewis; Hank Williams, Jr.; Blondie; Roy
     Orbison, Emy Lou Harris; Eddie Rabbitt; Asleep at the Wheel.

Rockabilly: Roots of Rock and Roll .... Imperial House (S) WU 3590   5-10   82
     Carl Perkins; Gene Vincent; Buddy Holly & the Crickets; George Jones; Jerry Lee Lewis;
     Roy Orbison; Conway Twitty; Charlie Rick; Johnny Burnette; Big Bipper; Johnny Cash &
     the Tennessee Two; Chuck Miller; Billy Lee Riley; Guy Mitchell; Ray Campi & His
     Rockabilly Rebels.

Rockabilly Stars, Vol. 1 (2 LP) .... Epic (S) EG 37618   10-15   81
     Carl Smith; Scotty Moore; Bob Luman; Mac Curtis; Carl Perkins; Johnny Cash; Allan Rich;
     Mickey Gilley; Charlie Rich; Town Hall Party; Everly Brothers; "Little" Jimmy Dickens;
     Marty Robbins; Johnny Horton; Collins Kids.

Rockabilly Stars, Vol. 2 (2 LP) .... Epic (S) EG 37621   10-15   81
     Collins Kids; Everly Brothers; Sid King & the Five Strings; "Little" Jimmy Dickens; Jive
     After Five; Lorrie Collins; Ronnie Self; Link Wray; Sleepy LaBeef; Carl Perkins; Rick
     Nelson; Billy Lee Riley; Mickey Gilley; Johnny Cash.

Rockabilly Stars, Vol. 3 (2 LP) .... Epic (S) EG 37984   10-15   82
     Little Jimmy Dickens; Everly Brothers; Collins Kids; Joe Maphis & Larry Collins; Ronnie
     Self; John D. Loudermilk; Johnny Cash; Jimmy Murphy; Cliff Johnson; Onie Wheeler;
     Johnny Horton; Rose Maddox; Jaycee Hill; Carl Perkins; Werly Fairburn; Sid King & the
     Five Strings; Bobby Lord; Lorrie Collins; Leon Smith.

Roots of Rock and Roll and Rockabilly .... Imperial House (M) 3590   15-20   82
     Carl Perkins; Gene Vincent; Buddy Holly and the Crickets; George Jones; Charlie Rich;
     Johnny Cash; Johnny Burnette; Big Bopper; Ray Campi; Guy Mitchell; Billy Lee Riley;
     Chuck Miller; Jerry Lee Lewis; Roy Orbison; Conway Twitty.

Round-Up .... Capitol (S) SL-6641   8-10
     Glen Campbell; Bobbie Gentry; Al Martino; Lettermen; Tennessee Ernie Ford; Glen
     Campbell & Bobbie Gentry.

Roxy London W.C. 2 .... Harvest (S) SHSP-406   5-10   77
     (Live at Roxy Club in 1977.) Slaughter and the Dogs; Wire; Unwanted; Adverts; Johnny
     Moped; Eaters; X-Ray Specs; Buzzcocks.

Rustler's Rhapsody .... Warner Bros. (S) 1-25284   5-10   85
     (Soundtrack.) Gary Morris; Nitty Gritty Dirt Band; John Anderson; Pinkard & Bowden;
     Charlie McCoy; Pam Tillis; Randy Travis; Karen Brooks; Rex Allen Jr.; Rex Allen Sr.; Roy
     Rogers.

Sacred Songs .... Diplomat (M) 2603   8-12
     Carl Story; Lonzo & Oscar; Stanley Brothers; Cowboy Copas; Frankie Miller; Phipps
     Family; Lewis Family; Jimmie William & Red Ellis; Sam & Kirk McGee.

Sacred Songs .... Guest Star (S) GS-1498   8-12
     Carl Story; Stanley Brothers; Phipps Family; String Bean; Sam & Kirk McGee; Lonesome
     Pine Fiddlers; Stoneman Family; Hylo Brown; Frankie Miller.

Sacred Songs .... King (M) 395-556   20-30   57

San Antonio Rose Steel Guitar Rag .... Starday (M) 375   10-15   66

San Antonio Rose Steel Guitar Rag .... Starday (S) 375   10-15   66
     Leon McAuliffe; Bob Wills with Tommy Duncan; others.

Saturday Night at the Old Barn Dance .... Kapp (M) KL-1442   8-12   60s
     Bob Atcher; Arkie "The Arkansas Woodchopper"; Johnson Sisters; Ruth & Edith; Bob &
     Bobbie Thomas; Mary Jane Johnson; Red Blanchard; Sage Riders; Dolph Hewitt.

Saturday Night Grand Ole Opry .... Decca (M) DL-4303   15-25   62
Saturday Night Grand Ole Opry .... Decca (S) DL-74303   20-30   62
    Kitty Wells; Roy Drusky; Tommy Jackson; Bill Anderson; Tompall & the Glaser Brothers;
    Jimmy Newman; Ernest Tubb; Patsy Cline; Bill Monroe; Johnny & Jack; Billy Grammer;
    Wilburn Brothers; Roy Acuff & the Smoky Mountain Boys..

Saturday Night Grand Ole Opry (Vol. 2) .... Decca (M) DL-4539   10-20   64
Saturday Night Grand Ole Opry (Vol. 2) .... Decca (S) DL-74539   15-25   64
    Bill Anderson; Loretta Lynn; Bill Monroe; Tommy Jackson; Billy Grammer; Johnny Wright;
    Margie Bowes; Jimmy "C" Newman; Kitty Wells; Ernest Tubb; Tompall & the Glaser
    Brothers; Bill Phillips; Wilburn Brothers.

Saturday Night Jamboree .... Longines Symphonette Society (S) SYS-5182   8-12
    Glen Campbell; Roy Clark; Buckaroos; James Burton & Ralph Mooney; Les Paul; Merle
    Travis; Buck Owens; Strangers; Walter Hensley; Hank Thompson.

Saturday Night Shindig .... Mercury (M) MG-21036   10-20   65
Saturday Night Shindig .... Mercury (S) SR-61036   10-20   65
    Roy Drusky; Margie Singleton; Faron Young; others.

Schlitz Country .... RCA/Schlitz (S) DPL1-0472   8-10   80
    Willie Nelson; Charley Pride; Dottie West; Bobby Bare; Dave & Sugar; Gary Stewart; Dean
    Dillon; Ronnie Milsap; Tom T. Hall; Sylvia; Razzy Bailey; Jim Ed Brown & Helen Cornelius.
    (Made for the Schlitz Beer Co.)

Showcase of Country Stars...................................... Guest Star (S) GS-1426   5-10
    Sunshine Boys; Curly Gribbs; Moon Mullican; Red Sovine; Willis Brothers; Brother
    Oswald; George Jones; Dean Manuel; Sam & Kirk McGee; Cowboy Copas.

Sing A Song For Heaven's Sake (2 LP)............................ Tame (S) LP-1001   8-12   78
    Chuck Wagon Gang; Oak Ridge Boys; J.D. Sumner & the Stamps; Imperials; Klaudt Indian
    Family; Sewanee River Boys; Blackwood Brothers; Hovie Lister & the Statesmen; Billy
    Grammer; Rangers; Blue Ridge Quartet; Red Foley.

Sing Me A Country Song (6 LP).... Columbia Musical Treasury (SE) 6P 6111   20-30   74
    Tom T. Hall; Jody Miller; Johnny Duncan; Tammy Wynette; George Jones; Barbara
    Fairchild; Johnny Paycheck; Connie Smith; Bob Luman; Freddy Weller; Tanya Tucker; Mac
    Davis; Carl Smith; Marty Robbins; Roy Clark; Ray Price; Johnny Cash & June Carter; Mel
    Tillis; Charlie Rich; Tommy Cash; Lynn Anderson; Jud Strunk; Donna Fargo; Dave Dudley;
    David Houston; Jerry Reed; Jerry Lee Lewis; Barbara Mandrell & David Houston; Ray
    Stevens; Flatts & Scruggs; Lefty Frizzell; Johnny Cash; Sonny James; Roy Drusky;
    Priscilla Mitchell; Jimmy Dean; Charlie McCoy; Johnny Rodriguez; Boots Randolf; Roger
    Miller. (Boxed set. Columbia Record Club issue. Mail order.)

Sing Out America! (8 LP) .... RCA Custom/Readers Digest (S) RDA-037   35-45   80
    (Boxed set. With 16 page booket.) Dottie West; Asleep at the Wheel; Red Foley; Glen
    Campbell; Kate Smith; Ambrosian Singers; Fireside Singers; Robert Shaw Chorale; Arthur
    Fiedler & the Boston Pops; Tenessee Ernie Ford; Fred Waring; Roland Shaw Orchestra &
    the Spirit of Freedom Singers; Patti Page; Les Brown; Guy Lombardo; Buddy Bregman &
    His Orchestra; Perry Como; Margaret Whiting; Johnny Gibbs and His Orchestra; Andrews
    Sisters; John Gary; Louis Armstrong; Voices of Robert MacDonald; Pete Fountain; Jimmy
    Brown; Alan Braden & His Orchestra; Wally Scott Orchestra; Johnny Lawrence & His
    Orchestra; Lamplighters; Johnny Arthey Orchestra; Bing Crosby & the Jesters with Bob
    Haggart & His Orchestra; Frankie Carle; Eddy Arnold; Rosemary Squires; Judy Garland
    with Georgie Stoll & His Orchestra; Vic Flick & His Orchestra; Bobby Bare; Robert Q. Lewis
    & Betty Clooney with the Circle Five Orchestra; Alfred Drake & Joan Roberts; Cattlemen;
    Woody Herman; Mills Brothers; Al Capps Orchestra; Country Folk; Johnny Mercer; Dukes
    of Dixieland; Eddy Jones & His Orchestra; Louis Nunley; Golden Saxophone & the
    Romantic Strings; Pete King Chorale; Mike Sammes Singers; Judy Garland; Nick Ingman &
    His Orchestra; Al Vino Rey Orchestra; Yvonne King; Al Caiola Orchestra; Buddy Cole Trio;
    John McCarthy Male Chorus; Burl Ives; Hill Bowen & the Royal Philharmonic Orchestra;
    Merrymacs; Buddy Bregmann & His Orchestra; Danny Davis & the Nashville Brass;
    Weavers; University of Michigan Band.

Sing Popular Country Songs: see Country Songs

Six Pak, Vol. 1 .... Lone Star (S) L-4600   8-10   78
    Willie Nelson; Cooder Browne; Ray Wylie Hubbard; Don Bowman; Steve Fromholz;
    Geezinslaw Brothers.

Smokey and the Bandit.. MCA (ST) 2099   8-10   77
    Jerry Reed; Burt Reynolds; Bill Justis; Jackie Gleason.

Smokey and the Bandit... MCA (EP) S33-1961   10-15   77
    (Promotional issue only.) Jerry Reed; Bill Justis.

Smokey Mountain Ballads........................... Camden/Pickwick (M) ACL-7022   5-10   76
     Uncle Dave Macon; Wade Mainer, Zeke Morris & Steve Ledford; Dixon Brothers; Arthur
     Smith Trio; Monroe Brothers; Carter Family; J.E. Mainer's Mountaineers; Gid Tanner and
     His Skillet Lickers.

Smooth Country Greats .... RCA Special Products (S) DPL1 0092   5-10   74
     Jeannie C. Riley; Charlie Rich; Johnny Cash; Dottie West; Don Gibson; Eddy Arnold;
     Skeeter Davis; Jerry Reed; Porter Wagoner; Hank Snow. (Made for Kessler Whiskey.)

Snowfall...CBS (S) P-18879   5-10   86
     Willie Nelson; Johnny Mathis; Mitch Miller; Doris Day; Gene Autry; Andy Williams; Lynn
     Anderson; Tony Bennett; Percy Faith; Robert Goulet.

Solid Gold Country .... RCA (S) CPL1-4841   5-10   83
     Waylon Jennings; Jerry Reed; Gus Hardin; Earl Thomas Conlin; Troy Seals; Ronnie
     Milsap; Louise Mandrell; Sylvia; Charley Pride.

Songs of Faith and Inspiration (3 LP)........................Time-Life (S) STL-127   20-25   89
     (Boxed set. Mail order offer.) Elvis Presley; Buck Owens; Don Gibson; George Jones;
     Johnny Cash; Bill Monroe; Red Foley; Jim Reeves; Webb Pierce; Rex Allen; Ferlin Husky;
     Hank Williams; Patsy Cline; Roy Acuss; Kitty Wells; Eddy Arnold; Grandpa Jones; Merle
     Haggard; Porter Wagoner; Tammy Wynette; Stanley Brothers; Dolly Parton; Ray Price;
     Ricky Skaggs & Tony Rice; Louvin Brothers; Oak Ridge Boys; Loretta Lynn; Wilburn
     Brothers; Claude Gray; Ernest Tubb; Nitty Gritty Dirt Band.

Songs of Family Faith, Vol. 2 .... Word/Tee Vee WTV-506   5-10   78
     Carol Lawrence; Roy Clark; Wanda Jackson; George Beverly Shea; Anita Bryant; Ray
     Price; Anita Kerr Singers; Danny Thomas; B.J. Thomas; Roy Rogers & Dale Evans.

Songs of the Cowboy ....Design/Pickwick (SE) SDLP 189   8-12   62
     Gene Autry; Foy Willing; Smiley Burnette; Eddie Dean; Bradley Kincaid.

Songs of the Golden West .... Grand Award (M) GA-33-330   10-20
Songs of the Hills ....Audio Lab (M) AL 1515   10-20
     Jimmie Osborne; Shorty Long; Clyde Moody; Jack Cardwell; Redd Stewart; Luke
     McDaniel; Charlie Gore; Ann Jones; Jimmy Martin; Bob Osborne; Pop Eckler; Red Perkins;
     Harvie June Van.

Songs of the Great Hank Williams ....Alshire (S) 5136   8-10   69
Songs of the Rivers (The Oceans and the Seas) ....King (M) 871   15-25   63
     Moon Mullican; Cowboy Copas; Delmore Brothers; others.

Songs of the Singing Cowboys .... Bruno-Dean Ent. (S) RBS-119   5-10   80
     (Mail order offer. Some songs are rerecordings by original artists.) Gene Autry; Foy
     Willing; Ray Whitley; Bill Boyd's Cowboy Ramblers; Sons of the Pioneers; Walter Brennan;
     Tex Ritter; Eddie Dean; Roy Rogers & Dale Evans; Jimmy Wakely & Margaret Whiting; Rex
     Allen; Tex Williams; Jimmy Wakely; Johnn Bond.

Souled Out Country... Triune (S) 0001   5-10   73
     Linda K. Lance; Nashville Brass; Jordanaires; others.

Souled Out Country... Triune (S) 0004   5-10   74
     Lynda K. Lance; Dee Mullins; Bob Langston; Jimmy Dallas; others.

Sound of Bluegrass....................................Camden/Pickwick (S) ACLI-0535   5-10   74
     Wade Ray; Bluegrass Banjo Pickers; Country Fiddlers; Living Guitars; Country Pardners &
     Bill Price; Morris Brothers; Monroe Brothers; Blue Sky Boys; Lonesome Pine Fiddlers;
     Charlie Monroe.

Sounds of America..........................Columbia Special Products (S) CSP-144   10-15   60s
     Flatt & Scruggs; Halifax Three; Les & Larry Elgart; Village Stompers; New Christy
     Minstrels. (Made for Zenith.)

Souvenir of Arizona..LJR-114   100-200   63
     Waylon Jennings; Donnie Owens; others.

Souvenirs of Music City U.S.A. ....Plantation (S) PLP-506   5-10   78
     Jeannie C. Riley; Charlie Rich; Jimmy C. Newman; George Jones; Hank Locklin; Leroy Van
     Dyke; Gordon Terry; James O'Gwynn; Rita Remmington; Roy Orbison; David Allan Coe;
     Willie Nelson; Carl Perkins; Johnny Cash; Ray Pillow; Rex Allen Jr.; Sleepy LaBeef; David
     Wilkins; Carl Belew; David Houston.

Souvenirs of Music City U.S.A., Vol. 2 ....Plantation (S) PLP-533   5-10   78
     Johnny Cash; Jerry Lee Lewis; Charlie Rich; LeRoy Van Dyke; Jimmy C. Newman; Hank
     Locklin; Charlie Walker; John Wesley Ryles; Willie Nelson; Dave Dudley; Jeannie C. Riley;
     James O'Gwynn; Murray Kellum; Gordon Terry; Paul Martin; Rex Allen Jr.; Rufus
     Thibodeaux; Jimmie Davis; Rita Remington.

Square Dance Music...King (M) 395-562   20-30   57
     Red Herron; Curly Fox; others.

Starday - Dixie Rockabillys, Vol. 1 ....Starday/Gusto (M) GD 5017   8-12   79
     Link Davis; "Groovey" Joe Poovey; Rudy "Tutti" Grayzell; Sonny Fisher; Bill Mack; Fred
     Crawford; Cliff Blakely; Benny Joy.

Starday - Dixie Rockabillys, Vol. 2 ....Starday/Gusto (M) GD 5031   8-12   79
    Link Davis; Bill Mack; Sonny Fisher; Bob Doss; "Groovy" Joe Poovey; Thumper Jones;
    Rudy "Tutt" Grayzell; Cliff Blakely; Benny Joy.

Stars and Guests of the Louisiana Hayride................Guest Star (M) G 1492   8-12
    Margie Singleton; Country Johnny Mathis; Red Sovine; Sleepy LaBeef; Benny Barnes;
    Sonny Burns; Tibby Edwards; Hoot & Curly; Merle Kilgore; Eddie Bond.

Stars and Hits of Country Music............................... Nashville (M) NLP-2012   10-15   64
    George Jones; Cowboy Copas; Merle Kilgore; others.

Stars of Hee-Haw, Vol. 1...Capitol (S) ST-437   8-12   70
    Buck Owens; Buddy Alan & Don Rich; Susan Raye; Roy Clark; Hagers; Buck Owens &
    Susan Raye.

Stars of Hee-Haw, Vol. 2...Capitol (S) ST-670   8-12   71
    Buck Owens; Buddy Alan & Don Rich; Susan Raye; Roy Clark; Hagers; Buck Owens &
    Susan Raye.

Stars of the Grand Ole Opry (2 LP) ....RCA (M) LPM-6015   10-20   67
Stars of the Grand Ole Opry (2 LP) ....RCA (S) LSP-6015   10-20   67
    (Boxed set with booklet.) Hank Snow; Dottie West; Skeeter Davis; Kitty Wells; Porter
    Wagoner; Chet Atkins; Bobby Bare; Don Bowman; Browns; Archie Campbell; Martha
    Carson; Carter Family; Delmore Brothers; Jimmie Driftwood; Don Gibson; George
    Hamilton IV; Sonny James; Johnnie & Jack; Grandpa Jones; Bradley Kincaid; Pee Wee
    King; Hank Locklin; Lonzo & Oscar; John D. Loudermilk; Uncle Dave Macon; Roger Miller;
    Willie Nelson; Norma Jean; Leon Payne; Minnie Pearl; Boots Randolph; Wade Ray; Jim
    Reeves; Connie Smith; Ernest Stoneman; Justin Tubb; Slim Whitman; Willis Brothers; Del
    Wood.

Stars of the Grand Ole Opry 1926-1974 (2 LP) ....RCA (S) CPL 2-0466   10-15   74
    Grandpa Jones; Eddy Arnold; Jim Ed Brown; Chet Atkins; Don Gibson; Kitty Wells; Dotty
    Parton; Dottie West; Sonny James; Porter Wagoner; Uncle Dave Macon; Pee Wee King; Bill
    Monroe; Minnie Pearl; Lester Flatt; Lonzo & Oscar; Hank Snow; Carter Family; Del Wood;
    Martha Carson; Johnnie & Jack; Kitty Wells; Jim Reeves; Archie Campbell; George
    Hamilton IV; Hank Locklin; Browns; Bobby Bare; Connie Smith; Jeanne Pruett.

Stars of the Steel Guitar...Starday (M) S-350   10-20   65
    Pete Drake; Walter Haynes; Leon McAuliffe; others.

Steel Guitar and Dobro Spectacular! ....Starday (S) SLP 293   10-15 60s
    Buddy Emmons; Jerry Byrd; Cecil Campbell; Leon McAuliffe; others.

Steel Guitar Classics...Old Timey (M) LP-113   5-10   73
    Jimmy Tarlton; Sol Hoopii's Trio; Lemuel Turner; Kanui & Lula; Jenks "Tex" Carman; Cliff
    Carlisle; Jimmie Davis; Roy Acuff.

Steel Guitar Hall of Fame..Starday (S) SLP 233   8-12
    Jerry Byrd; Leon McAuliffe; "Little" Roy Wiggins; Shot Jackson; Buddy Emmons; Don
    Helms; Jimmy Day; Herbie Remington; Speedy Western; others.

Steel Guitar Hall of Fame...Nashville (S) NLP-2055   5-10
    Pete Drake; Leon McAuliffe; Herbie Remington; Jimmy Day; Shot Jackson; "Little" Roy
    Wiggins; Buddy Emmons; Jerry Byrd; Don Helms; Bashful Brother Oswald.

Suite Steel (Pedal Steel Guitar) ....Electra (S) 74072   8-12   70
    Buddy Emmons; Sneaky Pete; Rusty Young; J.D. Maness; Red Rhodes.

Sunday After Church...Hilltop (S) JS-6102   8-12
    Johnny Cash; Jeannie C. Riley; Jerry Lee Lewis.

Sunday Morning at Our House.....................................Design (S) SDLP-644   8-12
    Patsy Cline; Hank Locklin; Stewart Family; Maddox Brothers & Rose; Wally Fowler.

Sundown ....K-Tel (S) WU 3530   5-10   80
    Willie Nelson; Eddie Rabbitt; Moe Bandy & Joe Stampley; Barbara Mandrell; Don Williams;
    John Conlee; Gene Watson; Charlie Daniels Band; Larry Gatlin; Crystal Gayle; Jennifer
    Warnes; Conway Twitty; Jim Ed Brown & Helen Cornelius; Dave & Sugar; Kendalls; Statler
    Brothers.

Super Stars in Country Music ....K-TEL (M) WU-3430   5-10   78
    Kendalls; Johnny Duncan; Crystal Gayle; Larry Gatlin; Marty Robbins; Joe Stampley;
    George Jones & Tammy Wynette; Mel Tillis; Oak Ridge Boys; Loretta Lynn; Charlie Rich;
    Eddie Rabbitt; Roy Clark; Gene Watson; Don Williams; Freddy Fender; Dave & Sugar;
    Linda Ronstadt.

Swingin' Country, the Big Instrumental Hits From
Nashville..Nashville (S) NLP-2051   8-12
    Phil Baugh; Tommy Hill; Leon McAuliffe; Shot Jackson; Thumbs Carlisle; Joe Maphis;
    Pete Drake; Red Hayes; Jackie Phelps; "Little" Roy Wiggins.
TV Country Jamboree.. Camden (M) CAL-925   10-15   65
TV Country Jamboree.. Camden (S) CAS-925   10-15   65
    Eddy Arnold; Connie Smith; Hank Snow; others.
Take Me Home Country Roads (8 LP)..............Readers Digest (S) RD4-142   35-45   73
    (Boxed set. Mail order offer.) Jim Reeves; Johnny Cash; Loretta Lynn; Charley Pride;
    Sammi Smith; Hank Snow; Roger Miller; Eddy Arnold; Chet Atkins; Skeeter Davis; Don
    Gibson; Kitty Wells & Red Foley; Dolly Parton; Jimmy Dean; Bobby Bare; Owen Bradley;
    Wilma Burgess; Webb Pierce; Patsy Cline; George Hamilton IV; Danny Davis & the
    Nashville Brass; Warner Mack; Mel Tillis; Browns; Minnie Pearl; Ernest Tubb & Red Foley;
    Roy Rogers; Pee Wee King; Johnnie & Jack; Ernest Tubb; Bob Wills; Homer & Jethro;
    Porter Wagoner; Willie Nelson; Tom T. Hall; Lester Flatt & Mac Wiseman; Waylon
    Jennings; George Jones; Bobby Helms; Webb Pierce & Red Sovine; Connie Smith; Marty
    Robbins; Lynn & Liz Anderson; Jack Greene; Conway Twitty; Skeeter Davis & Bobby Bare;
    Wanda Jackson & Billy Gray; Norma Jean; Jerry Lee Lewis; Dave Dudley; Del Wood;
    Loretta Lynn & Conway Twitty; Duane Eddy; Elton Britt; Boots Randolf; Faron Young; Roy
    Orbison; Chet Atkins & Jerry Reed; Chet Atkins & the Anita Kerr Singers; Osborne
    Brothers; Sonny James; Anita Kerr Singers; Rex Allen; Porter Wagoner & Dolly Parton;
    Brenda Lee; Kitty Wells; Bill Monroe; Dottie West; Statler Brothers.
Tall Twelve .... Starday (M) S-337   10-20   65
    George Jones; Sonny James; Johnny Bond; Jim Reeves Blue Boys; Roger Miller; Willis
    Brothers; Johnny Cash; Faron Young; Buck Owens; Bobby Bare; Floyd Cramer; Jimmy
    Dean.
Tender Lovin' Country ....Warner Special Products (M) OP-1540   5-10   84
    Bellamy Brothers; Gail Davies; Johnny Lee; Don Williams; T.G. Sheppard with Karen
    Brooks; Con Hunley; Cary Morris; Emmylou Harris; Conway Twitty; John Anderson; John
    Conlee; Mel Tillis; Barbara Mandrell.
Tennessee Christmas ....MCA (EP) S45-17046   5-8   85
    (Colored vinyl. Paper sleeve.) Steve Wariner; Jimmy Buffett; Nicolette Larson; John
    Schneider.
Tennessee C & W Series...Design (S) SDLP-611   8-12   60s
    Carl Perkins; Hevelyn Duvall; Frank Simon; Carl Belew.
Tennessee Jamboree .... RCA (EP) EPB-3192   15-25   54
Tennessee Jamboree .... RCA (EP) EPB-3192   35-50   54
    (10–inch LP.)
Tex-Arkana-Louisiana Country: 1927-1932 ....Yazoo (M) ????   8-10
    Buddy Boy Hawkins; Henry Thomas; Blind Lemon Jefferson; Little Hat James; Six Cylinder
    Smith; Sammy Hill; King Solomon Hill; Willie Reed; Texas Alexander.
Texas Farewell - Texas Fiddlers 1922-30.............................County (M) 517   8-12   70s
Texas Sand .... Rambler (M) 101   10-15
    Tune Wranglers; Roy Newman & His Boys; Milton Brown & His Brownies; Cliff Bruner;
    Prairie Ramblers; Jimmie Revard & His Oklahoma Playboys; Johnny Tyler & His Riders of
    the Rio Grande; Curley Williams & His Georgia Peach Pickers; Sunshine Boys; Jesse
    Ashlock; T. Texas Tyler & His Oklahoma Melody Boys.
That Dobro Sound's Goin' 'Round......................Starday/Gusto (M) SLP-340   8-10   76
    Uncle Josh; Hoss Linneman; Bashful Brother Oswald; Shot Jackson; Deacon Brumfield.
That's Truck Drivin'... Starday (S) 357   10-20   65
    Red Sovine; Johnny Bond; Willis Brothers; others.
Them Old Country Songs (2 LP)....................................Tampa (S) PRS-404   8-12   72
    Jim Ed Brown; Davis Sisters; Jim Reeves; Del Wood; Stuart Hamblen; Porter Wagoner &
    Dolly Parton; Hank Snow; Skeeter Davis; Chet Atkins; Hank Locklin; Jimmy Dean & Dottie
    West; Homer & Jethro; Connie Smith; Bobby Bare; Waylon Jennings; Porter Wagoner;
    Hank Snow; Dottie West; Roger Miller; Dolly Parton; Leon Ashely; Nat Stuckey; Jerry
    Reed.
This Country's Gospel (2 LP)...Word (S) SL 6894/5   8-12
    Johnny Cash; Loretta Lynn; Jimmie Davis; Inspirations; Redd Harper; Marty Robbins; Cliff
    Barrows; Ray Price; Pat Boone; Patsy Cline; Ernest Tubb; Joe Maphis; Bob Daniels;
    Wilburn Brothers; Anita Bryant; Red Foley; Glen Campbell; Norma Zimmer & Jim Roberts;
    Alan McGill; Happy Goodman Family; Roy Acuff; Burl Ives; Mary Jayne; Wayne Newton;
    J.T. Adams; Wanda Jackson; Sonny James; Blue Ridge Quartet; Ferlin Husky; Roy
    Rogers; Dale Evans; Tennessee Ernie Ford.

This Is Music Country..Columbia (S) CSPS-401   8-12
   Johnny Cash; Flatt & Scruggs; June Stearns; Ray Price; Marion Worth; Jordanaires;
   Jimmy Dean; Carl Smith; Johnny Horton; Marty Robbins.

This Is Music from Nashville ....Columbia Special Products (S) C-10265   5-10

This is the Nashville Sound (2 LP) ....RCA (S) VPS-6037   8-12   71
   Charley Pride; Chet Atkins; Waylon Jennings; Connie Smith; Nat Stuckey; Dottie West;
   Kenny Price; Danny Davis and the Nashville Brass; George Hamilton IV; Porter Wagoner &
   Dolly Parton; Dallas Frazier; Eddy Arnold; Skeeter Davis; Floyd Cramer; Hank Snow; Hank
   Locklin; Jimmy Dean & Dottie West; Jerry Reed; Willie Nelson; Nashville String Band; Jim
   Reeves; Norma Jean; Jim Ed Brown.

This Land Is Your Land .... Columbia Musical Treasury (S) P4M-5061   8-12
   Johnny Horton; Jimmy Dean; Ray Price; Roy Acuff; Marty Robbins; Jordanaires; Johnny
   Cash; "Little" Jimmy Dickens; Norma Jean; Lefty Frizzell; Carl Smith.

Those Beverly Hill Billies...Rar-Art's (M) WLP-1000   35-55   62
   (Multi-color vinyl.) Ezra Paulette; Elton Britt; Zeke Manners; Hank Skillit; Tom Murray; Glen
   Rice; Lem Giles; Chuck Cook; Jad Dees.

Three Country Gentlemen: see SNOW, Hank / Hank Locklin / Porter Wagoner

Today's Country (5 LP) .... RCA (S) DML5-0486   20-25   82
   (Mail order. Special products. Boxed set.) Willie Nelson; Helen Cornelius; Razzy Bailey;
   Zella Lehr; Billy Walker; Porter Wagoner; Dottsy; Jim Ed Brown; Dickey Lee; Charley
   Pride; Dave & Sugar; Dottie West; Don Gibson; Connie Smith; Nat Stuckey; Jimmy Dean;
   Skeeter Davis; George Hamilton IV; Jim Reeves; Hank Snow; Tom T. Hall; Johnny Russell;
   Charlie Rich; Chet Atkins; Ray Stevens; Jerry Reed; Danny Davis & the Nashville Brass;
   Johnny Bush; Gary Stewart; Bobby Bare.

Top Country (3 LP)..Showcase (S) SH-3302   10-20
   (Boxed set.) Jerry Lee Lewis; Glen Campbell; Roy Clark; Buck Owens; Roy Acuff;
   Tennesssee Ernie Ford; Dave Dudley; Rusty Draper; Del Wood; Roy Drusky; Roger Miller;
   Flatt & Scruggs; Patsy Cline; Jimmy Dean; Bobby Bare; Stuart Hamblen; Tex Ritter; Hank
   Locklin; T. Texas Tyler; Texas Jim Robertson; Floyd Cramer; Cowboy Copas; Slim Willet;
   Justin Tubb; Jerry Smith; Ferlin Husky; Wanda Jackson; Sonny James; Johnny Horton;
   Rex Allen; Jean Shepard; Hank Thompson; George Jones; Patti Page; Sue Thompson;
   Charlie Louvin.

Touch of Country Love... K-Tel (S) WU 3490   5-10   80
   Eddie Rabbitt; Moe Bandy; Crystal Gayle; Lynn Anderson; Don Williams; Charlie Rich;
   Mickey Gilley; Willie Nelson; Barbara Mandrell; Tammy Wynette; Johnny Duncan; Tom
   Jones; Gene Watson; Conway Twitty; Billy "Crash" Craddock; John Conlee.

Traditional Country Classics 1927-1929 ....Historical (S) 8003   10-15   68

Traditional Fiddle Music of Mississippi, Vol. 1........................County (M) 528   8-12   70s

Traditional Fiddle Music of Mississippi, Vol. 2........................County (M) 529   8-12   70s

Truck and Country.. Nashville (SE) NLP-2066   5-10   69
   Ray King; Red Sovine; Merle Kilgore; others.

Truck Driver Songs ....King (M) 866   20-25   63

Truck Driver Songs ....King (S) KS-866   20-25   63
   Tommy Downs; Bob Newman; Swanee Caldwell; Coleman Wilson; Cowboy Jack Derrick;
   Charlie Moore; Bill Napier; Jimmy Logsdon.

Truck Driver's Queen .... Nashville (SE) NLP-2075   5-10   70
   Moore and Napier; Jimmy Logsdon; Reno and Smiley.

Truck Drivin' Man .... Nashville (M) NLP 2034   5-10
   Hylo Brown; Joe & Rose Lee Maphis; Willis Brothers; Tommy Hill's String Band; Johnny
   Bond; Red Sovine; Betty Amos; Benny Martin; Frankie Miller.

Truck Drivin' Son of a Gun .... Nashville (SE) NLP-2082   5-10   70
   Red Sovine; Willis Bros.; George Morgan; others.

Truck Driving Hits...Exact (S) EX211   5-10   80
   Dave Dudley; Kenny Price; Del Reeves; Red Simpson; Willis Brothers.

Truck Stop.. Nashville (SE) NLP-2052   8-12
   Tom O'Neal; Frankie Miller; Joe Maphis; Benny Martin; Lonnie Irving; Willis Brothers; Red
   Sovine; Johnny Bond; George Morgan.

Truck Stop Favorites.....................................Starday/Power Pak (S) PO 298   5-10   77
   Dave Dudley; Johnny Bond; Dollly Parton; Cowboy Copas; Slim Jacobs; Willis Brothers;
   Red Sovine; Dottie West; Johnny Paycheck; George Morgan.

Truck Stop Favorites... Nashville (SE) NLP-2096   8-12   71
   Dave Dudley; Johnny Bond; Cowboy Copas; others.

Truckin' On, Speed Limit 55 (2 LP) .... Capitol (S) SLB-8016   5-10   76
     Merle Haggard; Dick Curless; Dave Dudley; Red Simpson; Glen Campbell; C.W. McCall;
     Kenny Price; Roy Drusky; George Hamilton IV; Red Sovine; Freddie Hart; Willis Brothers;
     Cledus Maggard and the Citizens Band.

Tumbling Tumbleweeds (7 LP) .... RCA (S) RDA-229   10-20   82

Urban Cowboy (2 LP).. Asylum (S) DP-90002   10-15   80
     (Soundtrack.) Jimmy Buffett; Joe Walsh; Dan Fogelberg; Bob Seger and the Silver Bullet
     Band; Mickey Gilley; Johnny Lee; Anne Murray; Eagles; Bonnie Raitt; Charlie Daniels
     Band; Gilley's Urban Cowboy Band; Kenny Rogers; Boz Scaggs; Linda Ronstadt; John
     David Souther.

Urban Cowboy 2 .... Full Moon/Epic (ST) SE-36921   8-10   80
     (Soundtrack.) Bayou City Beats; Charlie Daniels Band; Mickey Gilley & Johnny Lee; J.D.
     Souther; Mickey Gilley.

Variety of Country Sacred Songs...................................... Audio Lab (M) 1557   15-25   60
     Brother Claude Ely; Trace Family Trio; others.

Various Country Artists, Vol. 1 .... Dot (S) 3700   10-15   66
     Johnny Bond; Cowboy Copas; Hank Garland; others.

Various Country Artists, Vol. 2 .... Dot (M) 3701   10-15   66
     Lonzo & Oscar; Bob Lamm; Big Jeff; others.

Various Country Artists, Vol. 3 .... Dot (M) 3702   10-15   66
     Mac Wiseman; Tommy Jackson; Roy Wiggins; others.

Various Country Artists, Vol. 4 .... Dot (M) 3703   10-15   66
     Joe Allison; Tennessee Drifters; Joe Claire; others.

Very Best of Country (2 LP) .... Columbia House (S) DS 907-6   8-12   72
     (Same contents as item below, P2S 5706.)

Very Best of Country (2 LP) .... Columbia House (S) P2S 5706   8-12   72
     (Columbia House Record Club issue.) Roger Miller; Lynn Anderson; Freddy Weller;
     Stonewall Jackson; David Houston; Ray Price; Jeannie C. Riley; Barbara Mandrell; Statler
     Brothers; Billy Walker; Claude King; Johnny Horton; Lefty Frizzell; Tom T. Hall; Johnny
     Cash; Marty Robbins; George Jones & Tammy Wynette.

Very Best of Country (2 LP) .... Columbia House (S) P2S 5643   8-12   72
     (Columbia House Record Club issue.) Roger Miller; Lynn Anderson; Dave Dudley; Freddy
     Weller; Stonewall Jackson; David Houston; Jimmy Dean; Ray Price; Jeannie C. Riley;
     David Houston & Barbara Mandrell; Statler Brothers; Flatt & Scruggs; Ian & Sylvia; Billy
     Walker; Harden Trio; George Jones & Tammy Wynette; Claude King; Johnny Horton; Lefty
     Frizzell; Tom T. Hall; Johnny Cash; Marty Robbins; Carl Butler; Shel Silverstein.

Very Best of Country Banjo... United Artists LA 411   10-15   75
     Jim McGuinn; Cheatwood; Mike Seeger; Dick Rosmini; Billy Faier; Joe Maphis; Dick
     Weisman; David Lindley; Mason Williams.

Very Best of Country Gold .... United Artists (S) UA-LA413-E   5-10   75
     Willie Nelson; Johnny Cash; Jerry Wallace; Slim Whitman; others.

Very Special Love Songs (3 LP) .... ????   10-15
     (Label and number not known.) Charlie Rich; Jody Miller; Jud Strunk; Tom T. Hall; Donna
     Fargo; Sonny James; Johnny Cash & June Carter; Jerry Reed; Jerry Lee Lewis; Barbara
     Fairchild; David Houston; Lynn Anderson; Roy Clark; Mac Davis; Earl Scruggs; Marty
     Robbins; Jim Nabors; Tammy Wynette; George Jones; Johnny Paycheck; Tanya Tucker;
     Jimmy Dean; Roger Miller; Marty Robbins; Johnny Cash; Anita Bryant.

Volunteer Jam.. Capricorn (S) CP-0172   5-10   76
     Charlie Daniels Band; Marshall Tucker Band; Dicky Betts; others.

Volunteer Jam 6 .... Epic (S) 36438   5-10   80
     Ted Nugent; Wet Willie; Crystal Gayle; others.

Volunteer Jam 7 .... Epic (S) 37178   5-10   81

Wanted! The Outlaws: see JENNINGS, Waylon, Willie Nelson, Jessi Colter, and Tompall
     Glaser

Welcome to Columbia Country .... Columbia (S) CWS-2   10-15   60s
     Johnny Cash; Arlene Harden; Stonewall Jackson; Statler Brothers; Carl Smith; Johnny
     Duncan; Judy Lynn; Marty Robbins; Harden Trio; Tommy Hunter; Ray Price; June Stearns;
     Lester Flatt & Earl Scruggs; Claude King; Billy Mize; Tommy Collins; Johnny Seay; Carl
     Butler & Pearl; Sammi Smith; Lefty Frizzell.

Welcome to Music City U.S.A. .... Columbia (M) CL-2590   10-15   66

Welcome to Music City U.S.A. .... Columbia (S) CS-9390   10-15   66
     Carl Smith; "Little" Jimmy Dickens; Billy Mize; Lester Flatt & Earl Scruggs; Del Wood;
     George Morgan & Marion Worth; Marty Robbins; Stonewall Jackson; Harden Trio; Claude
     King; Tommy Collins; Carl Butler & Pearl; Carter Family & Johnny Cash; Ray Price.

Western Gentlemen Brand, the Golden Country Hits ....Columbia (S) RS 1   8-12 60s
Flatt & Scruggs; Marty Robbins; Lefty Frizzell; Carl Butler & Pearl; Carm Smith; Marion Worth; Billy Walker; Ray Price; Claude King; "Little" Jimmy Dickens; George Morgan; Stonewall Jackson; Bob Atcher.

Western: see Original Country Hits

Western Hits..Sutton (SE) SSU 300   5-10
Martha Tilton; Ann Southern; Dave Denny; Riley Shepard; Santa Fe Rangers.

Western Star Parade..Vocalion (M) VL-3805   8-10 67

Western Star Parade.. Vocalion (S) VL7-3805   8-10 67
Sons of the Pioneers; Bob Wills; others.

Western Swing .... King (M) 876   20-30 64
Al Dexter; Spade Cooley; Red Stewart; Paul Howard; Leon Rusk; Curt Barret; Charlie Linville; Carolina Cotton; Luke Wills; Tex Atchison; Jimmy Widener; Jimmy Thompson.

Western Swing .... Old Timey (M) LP-105   5-10

Western Swing in Hi-Fi...Decca (M) DL-8730   25-35 58

Westward Ho... Camay (M) CA-3029   10-20

Westward Ho.. Camay (S) CA-3029-S   10-20
Tex Ritter; Bob Wills; Tex Williams; Wesley Tuttle; Hank Fort; Cass County Boys; Elton Britt; Katie Lee & Barbara Allen. (Cocredits Tennessee Ernie Ford and Merle Travis instead of Wesley Tuttle and Katie Lee & Barbara Allen.)

When Evening Shadows Fall .... RCA (S) LSP-4073   15-25 68
(Jimmie Rodgers tribute LP.) Elton Britt; Ernest Tubb; Jim Reeves; Hank Snow; Bradley Kincaid; Gene Autry; Jimmie Rodgers; Mrs. Jimmie Rodgers.

White Mansions...A&M (S) SP-6004   5-10 78
Waylon Jennings; Jessi Colter; others.

Who's Who of Country and Western Music .... Capitol (M) T-2538   10-20 66

Who's Who of Country and Western Music ....Capitol (S) ST-2538   10-20 66
Buck Owens; Ferlin Husky; Jean Shepard; Sonny James; Wanda Jackson; Tennessee Ernie Ford; Bonnie Owens; Tex Ritter; Charlie Louvin; Ned Miller; Merle Haggard; Hank Thompson.

Will the Circle Be Unbroken (3 LP) ....United Artists (S) UAS-9801   10-20 72
Maybelle Carter; Earl Scruggs; Doc Watson; Roy Acuff; Merle Travis; Jimmy Martin; Vassar Clements; Junior Huskey; Norman Blake; Nitty Gritty Dirt Band; Pete Oswald Kirby.

Winnin' Country .... 51 West/CBS (S) QR-16060   5-10 79
Johnny Cash; Johnny Duncan; Tammy Wynette; David Houston; Lynn Anderson.

Wishing You a Merry Christmas.................................RCA (S) LSP-4793   8-10 72

Wishing You a Merry Christmas...................................RCA (S) ANLI-1952   5-8 76
Chet Atkins; Floyd Cramer: Willie Nelson; Jim Reeves; Dottie West; Hank Snow; Charley Pride; others.

Wonderful Waltzes of Country Music............................ Starday (S) SLP-297   8-12
Cowboy Copas; Dean Manual; Blue Sky Boys; Red Sovine; Curly Fox; Johnny Bond; Pee Wee King & Red Stewart; Tommy Hill's String Band; Clyde Moody; Archie Campbell; Benny Martin; Lonesome Pine Fiddles; Shot Jackson & Buddy Emmons.

Wonderful World of Country Music .... Camden (S) CAS-9032   5-10 72
Chet Atkins; Floyd Cramer; Skeeter Davis; Don Gibson; Dottie West; Dolly Parton; Jim Reeves; others.

Wonderful World of Country Music ....Starday (M) SLP 270   8-12

Wonderful World of Country Music .... Starday (S) SLP 270   8-12
Cowboy Copas; Jimmie Skinner; Willis Brothers; Red Sovine; Bobby Sykes; Leon Payne; Blue Sky Boys; Benny Martin; Lulu Belle & Scotty; George Jones; Curly Fox & Texas Ruby; Al Phipps Family; Lonzo & Oscar; Johnny Bond; Howard Vokes; Merle Kilgore.

Wonderful World of Gospel and Sacred Music .... Starday (S) SLP-255   15-20 63

World of Country Giants... Columbia (S) G-30893   5-10 71
Marty Robbins; David Houston; Lynn Anderson; Carl Perkins; others.

World of Country Music (2 LP).. Capitol (S) NPB-5   10-20 65
Buck Owens; Sonny James; Roy Clark; Jean Shepard; Hank Thompson; Ferlin Husky; Leon McAuliffe; Glen Campbell; Faron Young; Bobby Durham; Mary Taylor; Red Johnson; Tex Ritter; Wynn Stewart; Wanda Jackson; Charlie Louvin; Rose Maddox; Tommy Collins; Ira Louvin; Merle Travis; Neal Merritt; Ray Pillow; Mac Wiseman; Walter Hensley.

World of Country Music...Design (S) SDLP-640   8-12 60s
Hal Willis; Larry Steele; Stuart Hamblen; Maddox Brothers & Rose; Johnny & Jonie Mosby; T. Texas Tyler; Del Reeves; Glen Campbell; Wynn Stewart; Jimmy Newman.

World's Greatest Bluegrass Bands .... CMH (S) 5900   5-10   77
    Osborne Brothers; Joe Maphis; Carl Story; Mac Wiseman.
World's Greatest Bluegrass Bands (2 LP) .... CMH (S) 5901   8-12   79
    Osborne Brothers; Merle Travis; Joe Maphis; Pinnacle Boys; Lester Flatt; Nashville Grass;
    Benny Martin; Josh Graves; Grandpa Jones; Jim Silvers; Mac Wiseman; Paul Warren;
    Bluegrass Cardinals; Don Reno; Arthur Smith; Bobby Smith; Boys From Shilott; Chubby
    Wise; Eddie Adcock & Martha; Carl Story; Tennessee Cut-ups.
World's Greatest Country Fiddlers (2 LP) .... CMH (S) 5904   8-12   82
    Johnny Gimble; Buddy Spicher; Red Herron; Paul Warren; Ramona Jones; Benny Martin;
    Clarence Tate; Kenny Baker & Bobby Osborne; Chubby Wise; Cliff Bruner; Joe Maphis;
    Randall Collins & Jerry Moore; Ronnie Stewart; Paul Warren; Vassar Clements; Josh
    Graves; Chubby Anthony.
World Wide Top 20 (2 LP) .... Columbia Special Products (S) P-14326   8-12   77
World Wide Top 20 (2 LP) .... Columbia Special Products (S) P-2-13749   8-12   76
    Glen Campbell; Charlie Rich; Jessi Colter; Kenny Rogers & the First Editon; Anne Murray;
    Linda Ronstadt; Mac Davis; Freddy Dender; Janis Joplin; B.J. Thomas; Emmylou Harris;
    Cal Smith; Merle Haggard; Ronnie Milsap; Crystal Gayle; Tanya Tucker; Freddie Hart;
    Willie Nelson; Tom T. Hall; Billy Crash Craddock.
Wyatt Earp, Cheyenne and Other TV Favorites .... RCA (M) LBY-1027   10-20
    Shorty Long & the Happy Fellows; Prairie Chiefs; Sons of the Pioneers; Roy Rogers & Dale
    Evans.
Y'all Come, Let's Have a Country Christmas .... Starday (M) SLP-123   20-25   60
You Must Have That Pure Religion .... Design (M) DLP-616   10-15   62
You Must Have That Pure Religion .... Design (S) SDLP-616   10-15   62
    Wally Flowers; Texas Jim Robertson; T. Texas Tyler; Maddox Brothers & Rose.
Your Cheatin' Heart .... Columbia DS 683   5-10   76
    (Columbia Record Club issue.) Stonewall Jackson; Billy Walker; Anita Bryant; Johnny
    Cash; Carl Smith; Marty Robbins; Charlie Walker; George Morgan; Johnny Horton; Frankie
    Laine.

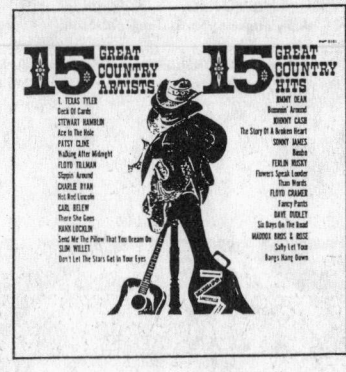

BUYERS & SELLERS DIRECTORY

After learning the current value of their collectibles, some collectors will decide it's time to offer them for sale. Others may choose to purchase additional items and continue building their collection. Still others will simply want to keep track of some of the latest products, supplies and services available to music collectors.

Regardless of whether you are moving in or out of the hobby, or just curious as to what's going on, let our Buyers and Sellers Directory point you in the right direction. There's something for everyone here — from dealers who want to buy as well as sell records, compact discs, and other music memorabilia, to sources for disc care and storage products, to publications vital to the music marketplace.

For infomation about how you can promote your products and services in the Buyers and Sellers Directory section of future price guides, contact: Osborne Enterprises, Box 255, Port Townsend, WA 98368. Phone (360) 385-1200. Fax (360) 385-6572

Your Hit Parade & American Top 10 Hits is 655 pages — five full pounds of music history — all under one cover.

Covers Your Hit Parade: 1935 - 1958.

Billboard Singles & Albums charts: 1958 - 1994.

For the first time, computer generated corrections to Billboard's year-end Country charts. Plus, the 1964 & '65 Country Singles charts and the 1964 R&B charts — finally!

Covers Popular, Easy Listening, Country, Jazz, Classical, Gospel, Rap, Alternative, Metal, Novelty, Beach, Instrumental, Christmas, R&B, New Age.

Has hundreds of photos and trivia questions, an artist-song index, and R.I.A.A. gold awards.

Order from:

Popular Culture Ink

1·800 678-8828

Most major credit cards accepted

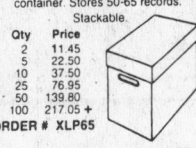

463

The Soundtrack Collector

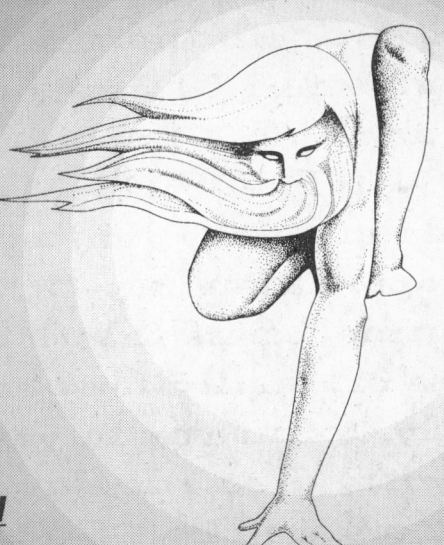

The Music Exchange

Largest Record Store in Kansas City!
Hard to Find and One of A Kind Recordings!
Looking for that unique or rare recording and can't find it?
Why don't you give us a try?

We accept want lists and will do our best to fill them! Call or send a SASE for more information, or just drop by the store. Let us help you with all your music needs! We provide a wide range of services including appraisals. We also buy records, tapes, CD's and other music related items. Our business hours are Mon.-Sat. 10am-9pm and Noon-6pm on Sun.

Please let us try and help you!

STILL A RECORD STORE!

The Music Exchange
207 Westport Road
Kansas City, MO 64111
(816) 931-7560

474

475

476

ABOUT THE AUTHOR

An avid collector of records for over 35 years, Jerry Osborne (pictured above in the mid-'70s with Marty Robbins) has also worked full-time as an author of record price guides and reference books since 1975.

In the 21 years since work began on his first *Record Collector's Price Guide*, the number of Jerry's published works on music now exceeds 200 — including 53 books and 152 periodicals. As busy as ever, he continues to produce several books per year.

Among other music-related ventures, Jerry has, since 1986, written the popular, weekly newspaper feature, *Mr. Music.* This entertaining and informative column, distributed nationally by World Features Syndicate, answers readers' questions about music and records.

The rest of Osborne's past is also saturated with music. Upon graduation from high school, he began a 14-year career in radio and television (1962–1976) as an announcer, or dee jay.

Over the years, Jerry founded and published three collectors news and marketplace magazines: *Record Digest* and *Music World* and the still-popular *DISCoveries*. In the mid-'80s, he began publication of *The Osborne Report*, a monthly newsletter covering new releases.

Osborne's influence and involvement in record collecting has been chronicled in virtually every major magazine and newspaper in the country: *Reader's Digest, The Wall Street Journal, USA Today, People Magazine, Esquire, Oui, National Enquirer, Money, Changing Times, Photoplay, High Fidelity, Billboard, Cash Box, Music City News, Collectibles, Kiplinger's, Woman's Day* and *Rolling Stone* —just to name a few.

Jerry has been a frequent guest on many major radio and TV talk shows, discussing the record collecting hobby. Among these are: "Good Morning America," The "Today Show" "The Nashville Network," and far too many local and regional shows to enumerate.

He worked in the mid-'80s as a technical advisor and consultant for the critically acclaimed ABC-TV nostalgic news-magazine program, "Our World," and has served as a consultant for HBO, and CBS-TV's "West 57th Street."

Clearly, no one person has been more responsible—directly or indirectly—for the amazing growth of the music collecting hobby.